HOCKEY GUIDE

2000-2001 EDITION

Editor/Hockey Guide
CRAIG CARTER

Editorial Director, Books
Steve Meyerhoff

Contributors
Christen Sager, Terry Shea

CONTENTS

ON THE COVER: Stanley Cup MVP Scott Stevens (Cover designed by Michael Behrens. Photos by Dilip Vishwanat/THE SPORTING NEWS.).

Spine photo: Brett Hull (File photo).

ISBN: 0-89204-637-6   10 9 8 7 6 5 4 3 2 1

2000-2001 NHL SEASON

NHL directory

Team information

Schedule

NATIONAL HOCKEY LEAGUE
DIRECTORY

LEAGUE OFFICES

OFFICERS

Commissioner
Gary B. Bettman
Director, administration & executive assistant to the commissioner
Debbie Jordan
Exec. vice president & chief legal officer
William Daly
Exec. v.p. and dir. of hockey operations
Colin Campbell
Exec. v.p. and chief operating officer
Jon Litner
Exec. v.p. and chief financial officer
Craig Hartnett
Senior vice president, hockey operations
Jim Gregory
Senior vice president, general counsel
David Zimmerman
Senior vice president, finance
Joseph DeSousa

NHL ENTERPRISES

President, NHL Enterprises
Ed Horne
Sr. vice president & general counsel
Richard Zahnd
Group vice president, communications
Bernadette Mansur
Group v.p., consumer products marketing
Brian Jennings
Group v.p., media ventures & strategic dev.
Doug Perlman
Group v.p., special events & entertainment
Frank Supovitz
Group vice president & managing dir., NHL International
Ken Yaffe

NHL COMMUNICATIONS STAFF

Group vice president, communications
Bernadette Mansur
Vice president, media relations
Frank Brown
V.p., public relations & media services
Gary Meagher (Toronto)
Chief statistician
Benny Ercolani (Toronto)
Director, communications
Jamey Horan
Director, corporate communications
John Krisiukenas
Director, media relations
Amy Early
Manager, community relations
Adrienne Brautigan
Manager, corporate communications & player publicity
Sandra Carreon
Manager, diversity task force
Nirva Milord
Manager, news services
Greg Inglis
Publicist, corporate communications
Joy Kalfus
Coordinator, public relations
David Keon (Toronto)
Associate, community relations
Ann Marie Lynch
Associate, news services
Adam Schwartz
Associate, public relations
Chris Tredree (Toronto)
Assistant, diversity task force
Jessica Murray
Assistant, public relations
Julie Young (Toronto)

NEW YORK OFFICE

Address
1251 Avenue of the Americas
47th Floor
New York, NY 10020
Phone
212-789-2000
FAX
212-789-2020

TAPPAN OFFICE (NHL PRODUCTIONS)

Address
183 Oak Tree Road
Tappan, NY 10983
Phone
914-365-6701
FAX
914-365-6010

TORONTO OFFICE

Address
50 Bay Street, 11th Floor
Toronto, Ont. M5J 2X8
Phone
416-981-2777
FAX
416-981-2779

MONTREAL OFFICE

Address
1800 McGill College Avenue
Suite 2600
Montreal, Que., Canada H3A 3J6
Phone
514-841-9220
FAX
514-284-0300

DIVISIONAL ALIGNMENT

EASTERN CONFERENCE

ATLANTIC DIVISION
New Jersey Devils
New York Islanders
New York Rangers
Philadelphia Flyers
Pittsburgh Penguins

NORTHEAST DIVISION
Boston Bruins
Buffalo Sabres
Montreal Canadiens
Ottawa Senators
Toronto Maple Leafs

SOUTHEAST DIVISION
Atlanta Thrashers
Carolina Hurricanes
Florida Panthers
Tampa Bay Lightning
Washington Capitals

WESTERN CONFERENCE

CENTRAL DIVISION
Chicago Blackhawks
Columbus Blue Jackets
Detroit Red Wings
Nashville Predators
St. Louis Blues

NORTHWEST DIVISION
Calgary Flames
Colorado Avalanche
Edmonton Oilers
Minnesota Wild
Vancouver Canucks

PACIFIC DIVISION
Mighty Ducks of Anaheim
Dallas Stars
Los Angeles Kings
Phoenix Coyotes
San Jose Sharks

MIGHTY DUCKS OF ANAHEIM
WESTERN CONFERENCE/PACIFIC DIVISION

MIGHTY DUCKS OF ANAHEIM

Anaheim Schedule
Home games shaded; D—Day game; *—All-Star Game at Denver.

October
SUN	MON	TUE	WED	THU	FRI	SAT
1	2	3	4	5	6 MIN	7
8 D STL	9	10	11 BOS	12	13	14 NJ
15	16 NYR	17 NYI	18	19	20 BUF	21 PHI
22	23 LA	24	25 LA	26	27 EDM	28
29 D CAL	30 EDM	31				

November
SUN	MON	TUE	WED	THU	FRI	SAT
			1 PHO	2	3	4 NSH
5 CHI	6	7	8 VAN	9	10	11 COL
12 DET	13	14	15 COL	16	17	18 PHO
19 NYI	20	21	22 NJ	23	24 CAL	25 EDM
26	27	28 VAN	29	30 SJ		

December
SUN	MON	TUE	WED	THU	FRI	SAT
					1	2
3 LA	4	5 STL	6 CBJ	7	8 MIN	9
10 DAL	11	12	13 CBJ	14	15 NYR	16
17 TB	18	19	20 ATL	21	22 DET	23 STL
24	25	26	27 DAL	28 NSH	29	30
31 MIN						

January
SUN	MON	TUE	WED	THU	FRI	SAT
	1	2	3 FLA	4	5 CAL	6
7	8	9	10 STL	11	12 BUF	13
14 D CAR	15 D PIT	16	17 ATL	18	19 PHO	20
21 COL	22	23	24 MIN	25	26 DET	27 CBJ
28	29	30	31 NSH			

February
SUN	MON	TUE	WED	THU	FRI	SAT
				1 PHO	2	3
4	* 5	6	7 CHI	8	9 WAS	10
11 CAR	12	13	14 EDM	15	16 DAL	17
18	19 CAL	20	21 SJ	22	23 SJ	24
25 CBJ	26	27	28 DET			

March
SUN	MON	TUE	WED	THU	FRI	SAT
				1	2 DAL	3
4 LA	5	6	7 MON	8	9 CHI	10
11 NSH	12	13 WAS	14 TOR	15	16 OTT	17
18 D CHI	19	20	21 DAL	22	23	24 D LA
25	26	27	28	29 SJ	30 VAN	31

April
SUN	MON	TUE	WED	THU	FRI	SAT
1 VAN	2	3	4 COL	5	6 PHO	7
8 SJ						

2000-2001 SEASON
CLUB DIRECTORY

Chairman and governor
Tony Tavares
President and general manager
Pierre Gauthier
Vice president of hockey operations
Jack Ferreira
Assistant general manager
David McNab
Chief amateur scout
Alain Chainey
Pro scout
Lucien DeBlois
Head coach
Craig Hartsburg _GUY CHARRON_
Assistant coach
Newell Brown

Mgr. of communications/team services
Alex Gilchrist
Media relations coordinator
Merit Tully
Media relations assistant
Mark Janko
Head athletic trainer
Chris Phillips
Assistant athletic trainer
Greg Thayer
Equipment manager
Mark O'Neill
Assistant equipment manager
John Allaway

DRAFT CHOICES
Rd.— Player	Ht./Wt.	Overall	Pos.	Last team
1— Alexei Smirnov	6-3/211	12	LW	Dynamo, Russia
2— Ilja Bryzgalov	6-3/196	44	G	Togliatti, Russia
4— Jonas Ronnqvist	6-1/200	98	W	Lulea, Sweden
5— Peter Podhradsky	6-1/185	134	D	Bratislava, Slovakia
5— Bill Cass	5-11/217	153	D	Boston College (ECAC)

MISCELLANEOUS DATA

Home ice (capacity)
The Arrowhead Pond of Anaheim
(17,174)
Address
2695 E. Katella Avenue
P.O. Box 61077
Anaheim, CA 92803-6177
Business phone
714-940-2900
Ticket information
714-940-2143

Website
www.mightyducks.com
Training site
Anaheim
Club colors
Purple, jade, silver and white
Radio affiliation
XTRA Sports (690 AM)
TV affiliation
KCAL (Channel 9), FOX Sports West 2
(Cable)

– 5 –

TRAINING CAMP ROSTER

No.	FORWARDS	Ht./Wt.	Place	Date (BORN)	NHL exp.	1999-2000 clubs
14	Antti Aalto (C)	6-2/210	Lappeenranta, Finland	3-4-75	0	Anaheim
	Maxim Balmochnykh	6-1/200	Lipetsk, U.S.S.R.	3-7-79	1	Cincinnati (AHL), Anaheim
42	Dan Bylsma (RW)	6-2/212	Grand Haven, Mich.	9-19-70	5	Los Angeles, Long Beach (IHL), Lowell (AHL)
	Marc Chouinard (C)	6-5/204	Charlesbourg, Ont.	5-5-77	0	Cincinnati (AHL)
17	Matt Cullen (C)	6-0/195	Virginia, Minn.	11-2-76	3	Anaheim
	Jim Cummins (RW)	6-2/219	Dearborn, Mich.	5-17-70	9	Montreal
15	Tony Hrkac (C)	5-11/170	Thunder Bay, Ont.	7-7-66	10	New York Islanders, Anaheim
	Jorgen Jonsson (LW)	6-0/195	Angelholm, Sweden	9-29-72	1	New York Islanders, Anaheim
9	Paul Kariya (LW)	5-10/180	Vancouver	10-16-74	6	Anaheim
29	Ladislav Kohn (RW)	5-10/172	Uherske Hrada, Czech.	3-4-75	4	Anaheim
12	Mike LeClerc (LW)	6-1/205	Winnipeg	11-10-76	4	Anaheim
	Jay Legault (LW)	6-4/217	Peterborough, Ont.	5-15-79	0	Cincinnati (AHL), Dayton (ECHL)
	Andy McDonald (C)	5-10/192		8-25-77	0	Colgate University (ECAC)
16	Marty McInnis (LW)	5-11/190	Weymouth, Mass.	6-2-70	9	Anaheim
	Jonas Ronnqvist (LW)	6-1/200	Sweden	8-22-73	0	Lulea (Sweden)
20	Steve Rucchin (C)	6-2/212	Thunder Bay, Ont.	7-4-71	6	Anaheim
	Kevin Sawyer (LW)	6-2/205	Christina Lake, B.C.	2-18-74	3	Phoenix, Springfield (AHL)
8	Teemu Selanne (RW)	6-0/200	Helsinki, Finland	7-3-70	8	Anaheim
	Alexei Smirnov (LW)	6-3/211	Tver, U.S.S.R.	1-28-82	0	Dynamo Moscow (Russian), Tver (Russian)
	Petr Tenkrat (RW)	6-1/185	Kladno, Czechoslovakia	5-31-77	0	Ilves Tampere (Finland)
13	German Titov (C)	6-1/201	Moscow, U.S.S.R.	10-15-65	7	Pittsburgh, Edmonton
	DEFENSEMEN					
	Bill Cass	5-11/217	Boston	9-30-80	0	Boston College (Hockey East)
28	Niclas Havelid	5-11/200	Enkoping, Sweden	4-12-73	1	Anaheim, Cincinnati (AHL)
23	Jason Marshall	6-2/200	Cranbrook, B.C.	2-22-71	7	Anaheim
	Antti-Jussi Niemi	6-1/183	Vantaa, Finland	9-22-77	0	Jokerit Helsinki (Finland)
	Peter Podhradsky	6-1/185	Bratislava, Czechoslovakia	12-10-79	0	Bratislava (Slovakia)
24	Ruslan Salei	6-1/206	Minsk, U.S.S.R.	11-2-74	4	Anaheim
3	Patrick Traverse	6-4/200	Montreal	3-14-74	3	Ottawa
27	Pascal Trepanier	6-0/210	Gaspe, Que.	4-9-73	3	Anaheim
7	Pavel Trnka	6-3/200	Plzen, Czechoslovakia	7-27-76	3	Anaheim
10	Oleg Tverdovsky	6-0/200	Donetsk, U.S.S.R.	5-18-76	6	Anaheim
6	Vitali Vishnevski	6-2/190	Kharkov, U.S.S.R.	3-18-80	1	Cincinnati (AHL), Anaheim
	GOALTENDERS					
	Ilja Bryzgalov	6-3/196	Togliatti, U.S.S.R.	6-22-80	0	Lada Togliatti (Russian)
47	Jean-Sebastien Giguere	6-0/185	Montreal	6-16-77	3	Saint John (AHL), Calgary
31	Guy Hebert	5-11/185	Troy, N.Y.	1-7-67	9	Anaheim
	Gregg Naumenko	6-1/201		3-30-77	0	Cincinnati (AHL)
30	Dominic Roussel	6-1/191	Hull, Que.	2-22-70	7	Anaheim

1999-2000 REVIEW
INDIVIDUAL STATISTICS

SCORING

	Games	G	A	Pts.	PIM	+/-	PPG	SHG	Shots	Shooting Pct.
Paul Kariya	74	42	44	86	24	22	11	3	324	13.0
Teemu Selanne	79	33	52	85	12	6	8	0	236	14.0
Steve Rucchin	71	19	38	57	16	9	10	0	131	14.5
Oleg Tverdovsky	82	15	36	51	30	5	5	0	153	9.8
Matt Cullen	80	13	26	39	24	5	1	0	137	9.5
Fredrik Olausson	70	15	19	34	28	-13	8	0	120	12.5
Ted Donato	81	11	19	30	26	-3	2	0	138	8.0
Marty McInnis	62	10	18	28	26	-4	2	1	129	7.8
Kip Miller*	30	6	17	23	4	1	2	0	32	18.8
Ladislav Kohn	77	5	16	21	27	-17	1	0	123	4.1
Mike LeClerc	69	8	11	19	70	-15	0	0	105	7.6
Jeff Nielsen	79	8	10	18	14	4	1	0	113	7.1
Antti Aalto	63	7	11	18	26	-13	1	0	102	6.9
Pavel Trnka	57	2	15	17	34	12	0	0	54	3.7
Tony Hrkac*	60	4	7	11	8	-2	1	0	37	10.8
Ruslan Salei	71	5	5	10	94	3	1	0	116	4.3
Niclas Havelid	50	2	7	9	20	0	0	0	70	2.9
Kevin Haller	67	3	5	8	61	-8	0	0	50	6.0
Jim McKenzie*	31	3	3	6	48	-5	0	0	22	13.6
Pascal Trepanier	37	0	4	4	54	2	0	0	33	0.0
Jorgen Jonsson*	13	1	2	3	0	-2	0	0	21	4.8

		Games	G	A	Pts.	PIM	+/-	PPG	SHG	Shots	Shooting Pct.
Stu Grimson	*NASHVILLE*	50	1	2	3	116	0	0	0	14	7.1
Jason Marshall		55	0	3	3	88	-10	0	0	41	0.0
Ted Drury*		11	1	1	2	6	-1	0	0	9	11.1
Vitaly Vishnevski		31	1	1	2	26	0	1	0	17	5.9
Guy Hebert (goalie)		68	0	2	2	2	0	0	0	0	0.0
Johan Davidsson*		5	1	0	1	2	0	0	0	8	12.5
Ed Ward*		8	1	0	1	15	-2	0	0	5	20.0
Maxim Balmochnykh		6	0	1	1	2	2	0	0	6	0.0
Frank Banham		3	0	0	0	2	0	0	0	4	0.0
Jeremy Stevenson		3	0	0	0	7	-1	0	0	2	0.0
Dominic Roussel (goalie)		20	0	0	0	6	0	0	0	0	0.0

GOALTENDING

	Games	Min.	Goals	SO	Avg.	W	L	T	ENG	Shots	Sv. Pct.
Guy Hebert	68	3976	166	4	2.51	28	31	9	8	1805	.908
Dominic Roussel	20	988	52	1	3.16	6	5	3	1	445	.883

*Played with two or more NHL teams.

RESULTS

OCTOBER

2— At Dallas ....L.....0-2
5— At Phoenix ....L.....0-4
8— Dallas ....W.....3-0
11—San Jose ....W.....5-3
13—At New Jersey ....L.....2-3
15—At Tampa Bay ....W.....3-2
16—At Florida ....L...*2-3
19—At Washington ....W.....7-1
21—At Chicago ....T...*5-5
24—Boston ....L.....2-3
27—Pittsburgh ....W...*2-1
29—Washington ....W.....5-2
31—Phoenix ....L.....0-3

NOVEMBER

3— Philadelphia ....T....*3-3
7— Edmonton ....W.....3-1
9— At Toronto ....W.....2-0
11—At Montreal ....L.....1-2
13—At Ottawa ....L.....2-4
15—At Detroit ....L.....3-6
17—Calgary ....W.....2-1
19—Chicago ....W.....4-2
22—Montreal ....L.....1-2
24—New Jersey ....L.....1-2
26—At Dallas ....W.....4-2
27—At Nashville ....W.....4-3

DECEMBER

1— Tampa Bay ....L.....2-4
3— Los Angeles ....T....*1-1

4— At Phoenix ....W.....2-1
8— Vancouver ....T....*2-2
10—Colorado ....L.....1-2
12—Atlanta ....W.....4-1
15—At Colorado ....W.....4-2
17—Chicago ....W.....2-0
19—Detroit ....W.....3-1
22—Phoenix ....L.....2-8
26—At San Jose ....W.....1-0
27—At Edmonton ....L.....1-4
29—At Calgary ....L.....1-3
31—At Dallas ....L.....4-5

JANUARY

5— Florida ....L.....1-5
7— At Carolina ....T....*4-4
8— At Detroit ....L.....3-5
12—Ottawa ....L.....0-2
14—St. Louis ....W.....3-1
15—At Phoenix ....L.....2-4
17—Buffalo ....L.....0-5
19—Dallas ....W.....3-1
21—Colorado ....T....*3-3
22—At San Jose ....L.....3-4
26—N.Y. Islanders ....L.....2-4
29—At Pittsburgh ....W.....7-1
31—At Boston ....W.....4-2

FEBRUARY

1— At Buffalo ....T....*2-2
3— At Philadelphia ....T....*3-3
8— At Los Angeles ....W.....5-3

9— Dallas ....L.....3-5
12—At St. Louis ....L.....3-6
14—At Chicago ....W.....4-3
16—Calgary ....W...*6-5
18—San Jose ....T....*4-4
21—St. Louis ....L.....2-4
23—Vancouver ....T....*4-4
27—Edmonton ....W.....3-2
29—At San Jose ....W.....4-2

MARCH

2— At Vancouver ....L.....1-3
3— At Calgary ....L.....1-4
5— Nashville ....W.....1-0
8— N.Y. Rangers ....L...*3-4
11—At St. Louis ....T...*1-1
14—At Colorado ....L.....2-4
15—Los Angeles ....T...*2-2
17—San Jose ....W.....4-2
19—Detroit ....W.....3-1
21—At Los Angeles ....W.....5-2
22—At Edmonton ....L.....1-2
24—At Vancouver ....L.....1-8
26—Phoenix ....W...*4-3

APRIL

1— At Los Angeles ....L.....1-2
3— Nashville ....W.....3-1
5— At Chicago ....L.....2-5
7— At Nashville ....W.....5-1
9— Los Angeles ....L...*3-4

*Denotes overtime game.

– 7 –

ATLANTA THRASHERS
EASTERN CONFERENCE/SOUTHEAST DIVISION

ATLANTA THRASHERS

Atlanta Schedule
Home games shaded; D—Day game; *—All-Star Game at Denver.

October

SUN	MON	TUE	WED	THU	FRI	SAT
1	2	3	4	5	6	7 NYR
8	9	10	11 WAS	12	13	14
15 TB	16	17 NJ	18	19	20 NYI	21 OTT
22	23	24	25 EDM	26	27 VAN	28 SJ
29	30	31				

November

SUN	MON	TUE	WED	THU	FRI	SAT
			1	2 LA	3	4 BOS
5	6 OTT	7	8	9	10	11
12 D WAS	13 FLA	14	15 NSH	16	17 PHI	18 PIT
19	20	21	22 TB	23 MON	24	25 WAS
26 MON	27	28	29 DET	30		

December

SUN	MON	TUE	WED	THU	FRI	SAT
					1 TB	2 CBJ
3	4 BOS	5	6 CAR	7	8 FLA	9 NYI
10	11 NJ	12	13 CHI	14	15 STL	16
17	18	19 LA	20 ANA	21	22 PHO	23
24	25	26 TOR	27	28 NYR	29 NYI	30
31						

January

SUN	MON	TUE	WED	THU	FRI	SAT
1 D WAS	2	3 MIN	4	5 PHI	6 PHI	
7	8	9	10 DAL	11	12 MON	13 WAS
14	15	16	17 ANA	18	19	20 D NJ
21 D NYI	22	23 NSH	24	25 TOR	26	27 PIT
28	29 NYR	30 PIT	31			

February

SUN	MON	TUE	WED	THU	FRI	SAT
				1 CAR	2	3
4	* 5	6	7 TOR	8	9 BOS	10 FLA
11	12	13 BUF	14	15 BUF	16	17 PHI
18	19	20	21 CAR	22	23 CHI	24
25 D COL	26	27 CAR	28			

March

SUN	MON	TUE	WED	THU	FRI	SAT
				1	2 FLA	3 FLA
4	5	6 COL	7	8 PIT	9	10 D BOS
11 CAL	12	13	14 OTT	15	16 CBJ	17
18 D VAN	19	20	21 TB	22 TB	23	24 MON
25	26 BUF	27	28 NJ	29	30 BUF	31

April

SUN	MON	TUE	WED	THU	FRI	SAT
1 NYR	D 2	3 OTT	4	5 DET	6 CAR	7
8						

2000-2001 SEASON
CLUB DIRECTORY

President and governor
Stan Kasten
Vice president and general manager
Dave Waddell
Vice president of sales and marketing
Derek Schiller
Vice president of public relations
Greg Hughes
Assistant general manager
Les Jackson
Dir. of player evaluation and dev.
Bob Owen
Director of marketing
Jim Pfeifer
Director of media relations
Tom Hughes
Multimedia specialist
John Heid
Junior publicist
Susan Sanderman
Director of team services
Michele Zarzaca
Director of ticket sales
Dan Froehlich
Manager of hockey operations
Jordy Bowman
Manager of hockey administration
Larry Simmons

Manager of community relations
Terry Hickman
Manager of fan development
David Cole
Manager of marketing
Rob Preiditsch
Manager of media relations
Rob Koch
Manager of ticket sales
Keith Brennan
Manager of ticket operations
Wendell Byrne
Head coach
Curt Fraser
Assistant coaches
Jay Leach
George Kingston
Head trainer
Scott Green
Equipment manager
Bobby Stewart
Strength & conditioning coach
Chris Reichert
Massage therapist
Inar Treiguts

DRAFT CHOICES

Rd.— Player	Ht./Wt.	Overall	Pos.	Last team
1— Dany Heatley	6-1/200	2	LW	Wisconsin (WCHA)
2— Ilja Nikulin	6-3/211	31	D	Tver, Russia
2— Libor Ustrnul	6-5/228	42	D	Plymouth (OHL)
4— Carl Mallette	6-1/188	107	C	Victoriaville (QMJHL)
4— Blake Robson	6-0/190	108	C	Portland (WHL)
5— Matt McRae	6-0/180	147	C	Cornell (ECAC)
6— Zdenek Smid	5-9/172	168	G	Karlovy Vary, Czech
6— Jef Dwyer	6-2/205	178	D	Choate, USHSE
6— Darcy Hordichuk	6-1/200	180	LW	Saskatoon (WHL)
8— Samu Isosalo	6-3/205	230	RW	North Bay (OHL)
8— Evan Nielsen	6-2/195	242	D	Notre Dame (CCHA)
8— Eric Bowen	6-2/225	244	RW	Portland (WHL)
9— Mark McRae	6-0/175	288	D	Cornell (ECAC)
9— Simon Gamache	5-10/182	290	C	Val-d'Or (QMJHL)

MISCELLANEOUS DATA

Home ice (capacity)
Philips Arena (18,545)
Address
1 CNN Center, Box 105583
Atlanta, GA 30348-5583
Business phone
404-827-5300
Ticket information
404-584-7825
Website
www.atlantathrashers.com

Training site
Duluth, GA
Club colors
Navy, blue, copper, bronze and gold
Radio affiliation
WQXI (790 AM)
TV affiliation
Turner South, WUPA/WPN (Channel 69)

TRAINING CAMP ROSTER

No.	FORWARDS	Ht./Wt.	BORN Place	Date	NHL exp.	1999-2000 clubs
	Bryan Adams (LW)	6-0/185	Fort St. James, B.C.	3-20-77	1	Orlando (IHL), Atlanta
28	Donald Audette (RW) DAL 5-8/184		Laval, Que.	9-23-69	11	Los Angeles, Atlanta
	Zdenek Blatny (C/LW)....	6-1/187	Brno, Czechoslovakia	1-14-81	0	Seattle (WHL), Kootenay (WHL)
	Hugo Boisvert (C).........	6-0/200	St. Eustache, Que.	2-11-76	0	Canadian nat'l team (Int'l)
15	Andrew Brunette (LW)...	6-1/210	Sudbury, Ont.	8-24-73	5	Atlanta
9	Hnat Domenichelli (LW).	6-0/194	Edmonton	2-17-76	4	Saint John (AHL), Calgary, Atlanta
22	Shean Donovan (RW)....	6-3/210	Timmins, Ont.	1-22-75	6	Colorado, Atlanta
21	Ray Ferraro (C).............	5-9/200	Trail, B.C.	8-23-64	16	Atlanta
12	Steve Guolla (C)	6-0/191	Scarborough, Ont.	3-15-73	4	Tampa Bay, Atlanta
	Dany Heatley (LW)........	6-1/200	Freiburg, Germany	1-21-81	0	Univ. of Wisconsin (WCHA)
	Darcy Hordichuk (LW)...	6-1/200	Kamsack, Sask.	8-10-80	0	Saskatoon (WHL)
17	Matt Johnson (LW)........	6-5/235	Welland, Ont.	11-23-75	6	Atlanta
	Tomi Kallio (LW)..........	6-1/180	Turku, Finland	1-27-77	0	TPS Turku (Finland)
24	Andreas Karlsson (C)	6-3/195	Leksand, Sweden	8-19-75	1	Orlando (IHL), Atlanta
27	Denny Lambert (LW)......	5-10/215	Wawa, Ont.	1-7-70	6	Atlanta
	Carl Mallette (C)	6-1/188	Pointe-Claire, Que.	11-17-81	0	Victoriaville (QMJHL)
	Wes Mason (LW)..........	6-2/190	Windsor, Ont.	12-12-77	0	Augusta (ECHL), Orlando (IHL), Louisville (AHL)
	Matt McRae (C)............	6-0/180	Toronto	4-29-81	0	Cornell University (ECAC)
	Martin Prochazka (LW)..	5-11/180	Slany, Czechoslovakia	3-3-72	2	Atlanta, Vsetin (Czech Republic)
	Blake Robson (C)	6-0/190	Calgary	3-31-82	0	Portland (WHL)
	Dan Snyder (C)	6-0/185	Elmira, Ont.	2-23-78	0	Orlando (IHL)
25	Steve Staios (RW/D)......	6-1/200	Hamilton, Ont.	7-28-73	5	Atlanta
13	Patrik Stefan (C)...........	6-3/200	Pribram, Czechoslovakia	9-16-80	1	Atlanta
	Per Svartvadet (LW)	6-1/190	Solleftea, Sweden	5-17-75	1	Atlanta, Orlando (IHL)
11	Dean Sylvester (RW)	6-2/210	Hanson, Mass.	12-30-72	2	Orlando (IHL), Atlanta
	Brad Tapper (RW).........				0	Rensselaer Poly. Inst. (ECAC)
37	Herbert Vasiljevs (C)......	5-11/180	Rigo, U.S.S.R.	5-27-76	2	Orlando (IHL), Atlanta
79	Vladimir Vujtek (LW).....	6-1/190	Ostrava, Czechoslovakia	2-17-72	5	Atlanta, Sparta Praha (Czech Republic)
	Brian Wesenberg (RW)..	6-3/173	Peterborough, Ont.	5-9-77	1	Philadelphia (AHL), Orlando (IHL)

DEFENSEMEN

No.		Ht./Wt.	Place	Date	exp.	1999-2000 clubs
2	Adam Burt	6-2/205	Detroit	1-15-69	12	Philadelphia
2	Petr Buzek	6-0/215	Jihlava, Czechoslovakia	4-26-77	3	Atlanta
29	Brett Clark....................	6-1/185	Wapella, Sask.	12-23-76	3	Orlando (IHL), Atlanta
	Jeff Dwyer	6-2/205	Wallingford, Conn.	11-22-80	0	Choate Rosemary Hall (Conn. H.S.)
6	David Harlock	6-2/220	Toronto	3-16-71	6	Atlanta
8	Frantisek Kaberle	6-0/185	Kladno, Czechoslovakia	11-8-73	1	Los Angeles, Long Beach (IHL), Lowell (AHL), Atlanta
	Geordie Kinnear............	6-1/195	Simcoe, Ont.	7-9-73	1	Orlando (IHL), Atlanta
5	Gord Murphy	6-3/195	Willowdale, Ont.	3-23-67	12	Atlanta
36	Rumun Ndur.................	6-2/222	Zaria, Nigeria	7-7-75	4	Hartford (AHL), Atlanta
	Ilya Nikulin..................	6-3/211	Moscow, U.S.S.R.	3-12-82	0	Tver (Russian)
4	Chris Tamer	6-2/208	Dearborn, Mich.	11-17-70	7	Atlanta
38	Yannick Tremblay	6-2/200	Pointe-aux-Trembles, Que.	11-15-75	4	Atlanta
	Libor Ustrnul	6-5/228	Olomouc, Czechoslovakia	2-20-82	0	Plymouth (OHL)
3	Sergei Vyshedkevich......	6-0/195	Moscow, U.S.S.R.	1-3-75	1	Orlando (IHL), Atlanta
	Mike Weaver.................	5-9/185	Bramalea, Ont.	5-2-78	0	Michigan State (CCHA)

GOALTENDERS

No.		Ht./Wt.	Place	Date	exp.	1999-2000 clubs
	Scott Fankhouser..........	6-2/206	Bismark, N.D.	7-1-75	1	Greenville (ECHL), Orlando (IHL), Atlanta, Louisville (AHL)
31	Scott Langkow...............	5-11/190	Sherwood Park, Alta.	4-21-75	4	Orlando (IHL), Atlanta
34	Norm Maracle................	5-9/195	Belleville, Ont.	10-2-74	3	Atlanta
1	Damian Rhodes	6-0/180	St. Paul, Minn.	5-28-69	8	Atlanta
	Zdenek Smid.................	5-9/172	Plzen, Czechoslovakia	2-3-80	0	HC Karlovy Vary (Czech Republic)

1999-2000 REVIEW

INDIVIDUAL STATISTICS

SCORING

	Games	G	A	Pts.	PIM	+/-	PPG	SHG	Shots	Shooting Pct.
Andrew Brunette............	81	23	27	50	30	-32	9	0	107	21.5
Ray Ferraro..................	81	19	25	44	88	-33	10	0	170	11.2
Nelson Emerson*...........	58	14	19	33	47	-24	4	0	183	7.7
Yannick Tremblay...........	75	10	21	31	22	-42	4	1	139	7.2
Dean Sylvester..............	52	16	10	26	24	-14	1	0	98	16.3
Patrik Stefan................	72	5	20	25	30	-20	1	0	117	4.3
Mike Stapleton..............	62	10	12	22	30	-29	4	0	146	6.8
Petr Buzek....................	63	5	14	19	41	-22	3	0	90	5.6
Darryl Shannon*............	49	5	13	18	65	-14	1	0	66	7.6
Kelly Buchberger*..........	68	5	12	17	139	-34	0	0	56	8.9
Johan Garpenlov............	73	2	14	16	31	-30	0	0	79	2.5
Hnat Domenichelli*........	27	6	9	15	4	-21	0	0	68	8.8
Andreas Karlsson	51	5	9	14	14	-17	1	0	74	6.8

	Games	G	A	Pts.	PIM	+/-	PPG	SHG	Shots	Shooting Pct.
Stephen Guolla*	20	4	9	13	4	-13	2	0	34	11.8
Donald Audette*	14	7	4	11	12	-4	0	1	50	14.0
Denny Lambert	73	5	6	11	219	-17	2	0	83	6.0
Shean Donovan*	33	4	7	11	18	-13	1	0	53	7.5
Gord Murphy	58	1	10	11	38	-26	0	0	74	1.4
Chris Tamer	69	2	8	10	91	-32	0	0	61	3.3
Maxim Galanov	40	4	3	7	20	-12	0	0	47	8.5
Per Svartvadet	38	3	4	7	6	-8	0	0	36	8.3
Matt Johnson	64	2	5	7	144	-11	0	0	54	3.7
Frantisek Kaberle*	14	1	6	7	6	-13	0	1	35	2.9
Ed Ward*	44	5	1	6	44	-5	0	2	51	9.8
David Harlock	44	0	6	6	36	-8	0	0	29	0.0
Steve Staios	27	2	3	5	66	-5	0	0	38	5.3
Jason Botterill*	25	1	4	5	17	-7	0	0	17	5.9
Sergei Vyshedkevich	7	1	3	4	2	-3	1	0	5	20.0
Herbert Vasiljevs	7	1	0	1	4	-3	0	0	2	50.0
Kevin Dean*	23	1	0	1	14	-5	0	1	9	11.1
Rumun Ndur	27	1	0	1	71	-17	0	0	6	16.7
Martin Prochazka	3	0	1	1	0	-1	0	0	5	0.0
Brett Clark	14	0	1	1	4	-12	0	0	13	0.0
Rick Tabaracci (goalie)*	1	0	0	0	0	0	0	0	0	0.0
Bryan Adams	2	0	0	0	0	-1	0	0	1	0.0
Vladimir Vujtek	3	0	0	0	0	0	0	0	2	0.0
Chris McAlpine*	3	0	0	0	2	-4	0	0	4	0.0
Geordie Kinnear	4	0	0	0	13	-1	0	0	2	0.0
Eric Bertrand*	8	0	0	0	4	-5	0	0	11	0.0
Scott Langkow (goalie)	15	0	0	0	0	0	0	0	0	0.0
Scott Fankhouser (goalie)	16	0	0	0	4	0	0	0	0	0.0
Damian Rhodes (goalie)	28	0	0	0	2	0	0	0	0	0.0
Norm Maracle (goalie)	32	0	0	0	0	0	0	0	0	0.0

GOALTENDING

	Games	Min.	Goals	SO	Avg.	W	L	T	ENG	Shots	Sv. Pct.
Scott Fankhouser	16	920	49	0	3.20	2	11	2	1	451	.891
Norm Maracle	32	1618	94	1	3.49	4	19	2	5	852	.890
Damian Rhodes	28	1561	101	1	3.88	5	19	3	3	803	.874
Rick Tabaracci*	1	59	4	0	4.07	0	1	0	0	32	.875
Scott Langkow	15	765	55	0	4.31	3	11	0	1	395	.861

*Played with two or more NHL teams.

RESULTS

OCTOBER
2— New Jersey ....L......1-4
7— Detroit ....L......1-7
9— Buffalo ....T....*5-5
14—At N.Y. Islanders..........W......2-0
16—At Tampa Bay ....T....*4-4
17—At N.Y. Rangers ....L......1-4
23—Colorado ....L.....*2-3
26—Calgary ....W......2-1
27—At Toronto ....L......0-4
31—Ottawa ....L......4-6

NOVEMBER
3— Tampa Bay ....W......4-1
6— At Boston ....L......2-4
10—At Florida ....L......1-4
12—At New Jersey ....L......1-5
13—At Montreal ....L......2-4
17—Tampa Bay ....W......5-4
19—Buffalo ....L......0-4
20—At Buffalo ....L......3-4
22—Vancouver ....W......6-3
25—Ottawa ....L......3-6
27—At Florida ....L......0-3
28—Dallas ....L......2-4

DECEMBER
3— Florida ....W......2-1
4— At N.Y. Islanders.............W......4-3
6— Nashville ....L....*3-4
8— At Los Angeles ....L......0-4
10—At San Jose ....L......1-4

12—At Anaheim....................L......1-4
15—Washington ....L......0-4
17—Boston ....L......1-3
18—At Carolina ....L......2-4
22—At Florida ....T....*3-3
23—At Philadelphia ....T....*4-4
26—Tampa Bay ....W......6-3
27—At Detroit ....L....*2-3
30—At Nashville ....L......0-6

JANUARY
1— Carolina ....L......2-4
4— At Buffalo ....W......5-4
6— Washington ....W......3-1
8— At Washington ....L......0-3
12—At Washington ....L......2-5
14—Philadelphia....................W......1-0
16—At N.Y. Rangers ....L......3-6
17—At Boston ....T....*3-3
19—Boston ....L......3-4
21—Florida ....T....*3-3
24—N.Y. Rangers ....L......3-6
27—At Pittsburgh ....L......1-4
29—At Tampa Bay ....L......1-2
31—Pittsburgh......................L....*1-2

FEBRUARY
2— At Dallas ....L......1-2
3— N.Y. Rangers ....L......3-6
9— At Pittsburgh ....L......2-5
11—San Jose ....L......0-3
12—Chicago ....L......3-4

15—At St. Louis....................L......1-4
16—Montreal ....L......1-5
20—At Phoenix ....L......2-4
22—At Colorado ....W......4-3
25—At Edmonton ....L......4-5
26—At Calgary ....L......2-5
29—Toronto ....L......0-4

MARCH
2— St. Louis ....L......2-5
4— At Ottawa ....L......2-3
6— At Montreal ....L......2-3
10—New Jersey ....L......0-9
12—At Carolina ....L......1-5
13—Edmonton ....L......0-3
16—N.Y. Islanders ....L......2-4
18—At Toronto ....W......4-1
21—At Ottawa ....L......1-7
22—Montreal ....T....*1-1
24—Pittsburgh ....L......3-5
26—Los Angeles ....L......1-4
28—At Washington ....L......2-5
29—Phoenix ....L......2-3
31—At New Jersey ....L......0-6

APRIL
2— N.Y. Islanders ....W......5-4
4— Philadelphia ....L......3-5
6— At Philadelphia ....L......1-3
8— Carolina ....L......3-4
9— At Carolina ....L......1-2
*Denotes overtime game.

BOSTON BRUINS
EASTERN CONFERENCE/NORTHEAST DIVISION

BOSTON BRUINS

Boston Schedule
Home games shaded; D—Day game; *—All-Star Game at Denver.

October
SUN	MON	TUE	WED	THU	FRI	SAT
1	2	3	4	5 OTT	6	7 PHI
8	9 FLA	D 10	11 ANA	12	13 LA	14 SJ
15	16	17 EDM	18	19	20 CAL	21
22	23	24	25	26 WAS	27	28 TOR
29 NYR	30	31 NYI				

November
SUN	MON	TUE	WED	THU	FRI	SAT
			1	2 CHI	3	4 ATL
5 TOR	6	7	8	9 OTT	10	11 NSH
12	13	14	15	16 NJ	17	18 MIN
19	20	21 OTT	22 DET	23	24 CAR D 25	
26 LA	27	28 PIT	29	30		

December
SUN	MON	TUE	WED	THU	FRI	SAT
					1 WAS	2 WAS
3	4 ATL	5	6 PIT	7	8 CBJ	9 NYR
10	11	12 BUF	13	14	15	16 CAR
17	18	19 PHI	20	21 TOR	22	23 DET
24	25	26	27 NYI	28	29 FLA	30 TB
31						

January
SUN	MON	TUE	WED	THU	FRI	SAT
	1 BUF	D 2	3	4	5 WAS	6 DAL
7	8	9 PIT	10 MON	11	12	13 NYR D
14	15	16 NJ	17	18 CAR	19 NSH	20
21	22 FLA	23	24 TOR	25	26 BUF	27 NJ
28	29	30 STL	31			

February
SUN	MON	TUE	WED	THU	FRI	SAT
				1 MON	2	3
4	* 5	6 PHI	7	8	9 ATL	10 TB
11	12	13	14	15 TB	16 FLA	17
18 CAR D	19	20	21 COL	22	23 DAL	24 STL
25	26	27 PHO	28			

March
SUN	MON	TUE	WED	THU	FRI	SAT
				1 TB	2	3 SJ D
4	5 PHI	6 BUF	7	8 OTT	9	10 ATL D
11	12	13	14	15 VAN	16	17 MON
18	19	20 PIT	21	22 MON	23	24 COL D
25 NYR	26	27	28 TOR	29	30 OTT	31 NYI

April
SUN	MON	TUE	WED	THU	FRI	SAT
1	2 MON	3	4 BUF	5	6 NJ	7 NYI
8						

2000-2001 SEASON
CLUB DIRECTORY

Owner and governor
Jeremy M. Jacobs
Alternative governor
Louis Jacobs
President, g.m. and alternate governor
Harry Sinden
V.p. of hockey operations, asst. general manager and alternate govorner
Mike O'Connell
Executive vice president
Richard Krezwick
Senior assistant to the president
Nate Greenberg
Asst. to the v.p. of hockey operations
Jeff Gorton
General counsel
Michael Wall
Director of administration
Dale Hamilton
Assistant to the president
Joe Curnane
Team travel coordinator/admin. asst.
Carol Gould
Coach
Pat Burns
Assistant coaches
Jacques Laperriere
Peter Laviolette

Director of scouting
Scott Bradley
Director of development
Bob Tindall
Coordinator of scouting information
Nickolai Bobrov
Scouting staff
Gerry Cheevers, Daniel Dore, Ernie Gare, Yuri Karmanov, Don Matheson, David McNamara, Tom McVie, Jim Morrison, Jean Ratelle, Don Saatzer, Tom Songin, Svenake Svensson
Director of media relations
Heidi Holland
Media relations assistant
Mark Awdycki
Dir. of marketing and community rel.
Sue Byrne
Athletic trainer
Don Del Negro
Physical therapist
Scott Waugh
Equipment manager
Peter Henderson
Assistant equipment managers
Chris "Muggsy" Aldrich
Keith Robinson

DRAFT CHOICES

Rd.— Player	Ht./Wt.	Overall	Pos.	Last team
1—Lars Jonsson	6-1/198	7	D	Leksand, Sweden
1—Martin Samuelsson	6-2/189	27	D	MoDo, Sweden
2—Andy Hilbert	5-11/190	37	C	Michigan (CCHA)
2—Ivan Huml	6-2/183	59	LW	Langley, BCHL
3—Tuukka Makela	6-3/202	66	LW	IFK Helsinki, Finland
3—Sergei Zinovjev	5-11/176	73	RW	Novokuznetsk, Russia
4—Brett Nowak	6-2/192	103	C/LW	Harvard (ECAC)
6—Jarno Kultanen	6-2/198	174	D	IFK Helsinki, Finland
7—Chris Berti	6-5/206	204	C/LW	Sarnia (OHL)
8—Zdenek Kutlak	6-3/207	237	D	Budejovice, Czech Rep.
9—Pavel Kolaruk	6-1/207	268	D	Slavia Praha, Czech
9—Andreas Lindstrom	6-5/210	279	LW	Lulea, Sweden

MISCELLANEOUS DATA

Home ice (capacity)
FleetCenter (17,565)
Address
One FleetCenter, Suite 250
Boston, MA 02114-1303
Business phone
617-624-1900
Ticket information
617-931-2222
Website
www.bostonbruins.com

Training site
Wilmington, MA
Club colors
Gold, black and white
Radio affiliation
WBZ (1030 AM) & Bruins Radio Network
TV affiliation
UPN38 (Channel 38) & NESN (New England Sports Network)

TRAINING CAMP ROSTER

No.	FORWARDS	Ht./Wt.	Place	BORN Date	NHL exp.	1999-2000 clubs
41	Jason Allison (C)	6-4/205	North York, Ont.	5-29-75	7	Boston
11	P.J. Axelsson (RW)	6-1/174	Kungalv, Sweden	2-26-75	3	Boston
17	Shawn Bates (C)	5-11/190	Melrose, Mass.	4-3-75	3	Boston
16	Ken Belanger (LW)	6-4/225	Sault Ste. Marie, Ont.	5-14-74	6	Boston
33	Anson Carter (C)	6-1/175	Toronto	6-6-74	4	Boston
22	Mikko Eloranta (C/LW)	6-0/185	Turku, Finland	8-24-72	1	Boston
42	Peter Ferraro (C)	5-10/180	Port Jefferson, N.Y.	1-24-73	5	Providence (AHL), Boston
	Lee Goren (RW)	6-3/190	Winnipeg	12-26-77	0	Univ. of North Dakota (WCHA)
51	Jay Henderson (LW)	5-11/188	Edmonton	9-17-78	2	Providence (AHL), Boston
	Andy Hilbert (C)	5-11/190	Howell, Mich.	2-6-81	0	Univ. of Michigan (CCHA)
	Ivan Huml (LW)	6-2/183	Kladno, Czechoslovakia	9-6-81	0	Langley (BCHL)
26	Mike Knuble (LW)	6-3/222	Toronto	7-4-72	4	New York Rangers, Boston
10	Cameron Mann (RW)	6-0/194	Thompson, Man.	4-20-77	3	Boston, Providence (AHL)
21	Eric Nickulas (RW)	5-11/190	Cape Cod, Mass.	3-25-75	2	Providence (AHL), Boston
	Brett Nowak (C/LW)	6-2/192	New Haven, Connecticut	5-20-81	0	Harvard University (ECAC)
	Samual Pahlsson (C)	5-11/190	Ornskoldsvik, Sweden	12-17-77	0	MoDo Ornskoldsvik (Sweden)
46	Sean Pronger (C)	6-3/210	Dryden, Ont.	11-30-72	5	Providence (AHL), Boston, Manitoba (IHL)
12	Brian Rolston (C/LW)	6-2/205	Flint, Mich.	2-21-73	6	New Jersey, Colorado, Boston
14	Sergei Samsonov (LW)	5-8/184	Moscow, U.S.S.R.	10-27-78	3	Boston
	Martin Samuelsson	6-2/189	Upperlands Vasby, Sweden	1-25-82	0	MoDo Ornskoldsvik Jrs. (Sweden Jr.)
28	Andre Savage	6-0/195	Ottawa	5-27-75	2	Providence (AHL), Boston
6	Joe Thornton (C)	6-4/225	London, Ont.	7-2-79	3	Boston
	Kyle Wanvig (RW)	6-2/197	Calgary	1-29-81	0	Kootenay (WHL), Red Deer (WHL)
54	Jeff Zehr (LW)	6-3/195	Woodstock, Ont.	12-10-78	1	Providence (AHL), Boston
	Sergei Zinovjev (RW)	5-11/176	Prokopjeusk, U.S.S.R.	3-4-80	0	Metallurg Novokuznetsk (Russian)
	DEFENSEMEN					
63	Elias Abrahamsson	6-3/227	Uppsala, Sweden	6-15-77	0	Providence (AHL), Hamilton (AHL)
49	Johnathan Aitken	6-4/210	Edmonton, Alta.	5-24-78	1	Providence (AHL), Boston
44	Nick Boynton	6-2/210	Etobicoke, Ont.	1-14-79	1	Providence (AHL), Boston
62	Vratislav Cech	6-3/196	Tabor, Czechoslovakia	1-28-79	0	Providence (AHL), Greenville (ECHL)
77	Paul Coffey	6-0/200	Weston, Ont.	6-1-61	20	Carolina
25	Hal Gill	6-7/240	Concord, Mass.	4-6-75	3	Boston
55	Jonathan Girard	5-11/192	Joliette, Que.	5-27-80	2	Boston, Providence (AHL), Moncton (QMJHL)
	Martin Grenier	6-5/230	Laval, Que.	11-2-80	0	Quebec (QMJHL)
	Lars Jonsson	6-1/198	Borlange, Sweden	1-2-82	0	Leksand (Sweden Jr.), Leksand (Sweden)
	Pavel Kolarik	6-1/207	Czechoslovakia	10-24-72	0	Slavia Praha (Czech Republic)
	Jamo Kultanen	6-2/198	Finland	1-8-73	0	HIFK Helsinki (Finland)
	Tuukka Makela	6-3/202	Helsinki, Finland	5-24-82	0	HIFK Helsinki (Finland)
18	Kyle McLaren	6-4/219	Humboldt, Sask.	6-18-77	5	Boston
34	Peter Popovic	6-6/239	Koping, Sweden	2-10-68	7	Pittsburgh
53	Brandon Smith	6-1/196	Hazelton, B.C.	2-25-73	2	Providence (AHL), Boston
32	Don Sweeney	5-10/184	St. Stephen, N.B.	8-17-66	12	Boston
66	Eric Van Acker	6-5/220	St. Jean, Que.	3-1-79	0	Providence (AHL), Greenville (ECHL)
20	Darren Van Impe	6-1/205	Saskatoon, Sask.	5-18-73	6	Boston
	GOALTENDERS					
34	Byron Dafoe	5-11/190	Sussex, England	2-25-71	8	Boston
47	John Grahame	6-2/210	Denver	8-31-75	1	Boston, Providence (AHL)
	Andrew Raycroft	6-0/150	Belleville, Ont.	5-4-80	0	Kingston (OHL)

1999-2000 REVIEW

INDIVIDUAL STATISTICS

SCORING

	Games	G	A	Pts.	PIM	+/-	PPG	SHG	Shots	Shooting Pct.
Joe Thornton	81	23	37	60	82	-5	5	0	171	13.5
Anson Carter	59	22	25	47	14	8	4	0	144	15.3
Sergei Samsonov	77	19	26	45	4	-6	6	0	145	13.1
Ray Bourque*	65	10	28	38	20	-11	6	0	217	4.6
Dave Andreychuk*	63	19	14	33	28	-11	7	0	192	9.9
Jason Allison	37	10	18	28	20	5	3	0	66	15.2
Darren Van Impe	79	5	23	28	73	-19	4	0	97	5.2
P.J. Axelsson	81	10	16	26	24	1	0	0	186	5.4
Steve Heinze	75	12	13	25	36	-8	2	0	145	8.3
Rob DiMaio*	50	5	16	21	42	-1	0	0	93	5.4
Andre Savage	43	7	13	20	10	-8	2	0	70	10.0
Kyle McLaren	71	8	11	19	67	-4	2	0	142	5.6

	Games	G	A	Pts.	PIM	+/-	PPG	SHG	Shots	Shooting Pct.
Mikko Eloranta	50	6	12	18	36	-10	1	0	59	10.2
Joe Murphy*	26	7	7	14	41	-7	3	0	68	10.3
Don Sweeney	81	1	13	14	48	-14	0	0	82	1.2
Cameron Mann	32	8	4	12	13	-6	1	0	48	16.7
Shawn Bates	44	5	7	12	14	-17	0	0	65	7.7
Hal Gill	81	3	9	12	51	0	0	0	120	2.5
Eric Nickulas	20	5	6	11	12	-1	1	0	28	17.9
Antti Laaksonen	27	6	3	9	2	3	0	0	23	26.1
Brian Rolston*	16	5	4	9	6	-4	3	0	66	7.6
Mattias Timander	60	0	8	8	22	-11	0	0	39	0.0
Mike Knuble*	14	3	3	6	8	-2	1	0	28	10.7
Brandon Smith	22	2	4	6	10	-4	0	0	24	8.3
Marty McSorley	27	2	3	5	62	2	0	0	24	8.3
Joe Hulbig	24	2	2	4	8	-8	0	0	15	13.3
Ken Belanger	37	2	2	4	44	-4	0	0	20	10.0
Jay Henderson	16	1	3	4	9	1	0	0	18	5.6
Landon Wilson	40	1	3	4	18	-6	0	0	67	1.5
Jonathan Girard	23	1	2	3	2	-1	0	0	17	5.9
Joel Prpic	14	0	3	3	0	-6	0	0	13	0.0
Marquis Mathieu	6	0	2	2	4	-2	0	0	3	0.0
Peter Ferraro	5	0	1	1	0	-1	0	0	3	0.0
Sean Pronger	11	0	1	1	13	-4	0	0	7	0.0
John Grahame (goalie)	24	0	1	1	8	0	0	0	0	0.0
Aaron Downey	1	0	0	0	0	0	0	0	0	0.0
Johnathan Aitken	3	0	0	0	0	-3	0	0	2	0.0
Jeff Zehr	4	0	0	0	2	-1	0	0	3	0.0
Nicholas Boynton	5	0	0	0	0	-5	0	0	6	0.0
Robbie Tallas (goalie)	27	0	0	0	6	0	0	0	0	0.0
Byron Dafoe (goalie)	41	0	0	0	0	0	0	0	0	0.0

GOALTENDING

	Games	Min.	Goals	SO	Avg.	W	L	T	ENG	Shots	Sv. Pct.
John Grahame	24	1344	55	2	2.46	7	10	5	1	609	.910
Byron Dafoe	41	2307	114	3	2.96	13	16	10	2	1030	.889
Robbie Tallas	27	1363	72	0	3.17	4	13	4	4	628	.885

Combination shutout: Tallas and Grahame.
*Played with two or more NHL teams.

RESULTS

OCTOBER

2—	Carolina	L	1-3
4—	At Toronto	L	0-4
7—	At Ottawa	L	3-4
9—	Philadelphia	T	*1-1
11—	Colorado	T	*3-3
13—	At Colorado	L	1-2
15—	At Dallas	T	*2-2
16—	At Phoenix	L	1-2
20—	At Los Angeles	T	*2-2
23—	At San Jose	W	3-1
24—	At Anaheim	W	3-2
28—	Tampa Bay	W	7-3
30—	Buffalo	W	3-0

NOVEMBER

4—	New Jersey	W	3-1
6—	Atlanta	W	4-2
10—	At Buffalo	L	2-6
11—	Toronto	W	*4-3
13—	At N.Y. Rangers	W	5-2
17—	At New Jersey	T	*2-2
18—	N.Y. Rangers	W	5-3
20—	Washington	L	0-3
22—	At Carolina	W	2-1
24—	At Nashville	W	5-2
26—	Vancouver	T	*2-2
28—	N.Y. Islanders	L	1-2

DECEMBER

2—	At Washington	T	*2-2
4—	Chicago	L	3-9
9—	Edmonton	T	*2-2
11—	Detroit	L	4-5
13—	Phoenix	W	2-0
14—	At Pittsburgh	L	2-4
17—	At Atlanta	W	3-1
18—	At St. Louis	L	0-4
21—	Nashville	L	1-3
23—	Montreal	T	*3-3
27—	At N.Y. Islanders	L	0-3
29—	At New Jersey	L	*4-5
30—	At Ottawa	L	*4-5

JANUARY

1—	New Jersey	T	*2-2
4—	At N.Y. Islanders	W	7-3
6—	Carolina	L	3-7
8—	N.Y. Islanders	L	2-5
11—	Toronto	L	2-3
13—	Buffalo	T	*0-0
15—	At Montreal	T	*2-2
17—	Atlanta	T	*3-3
19—	At Atlanta	W	4-3
20—	At Tampa Bay	W	4-2
22—	At Florida	L	*3-4
24—	Calgary	L	*3-4
29—	Buffalo	W	1-0
31—	Anaheim	L	2-4

FEBRUARY

1—	At Ottawa	T	*4-4
3—	Toronto	W	4-2
8—	Washington	T	*2-2
11—	At N.Y. Rangers	L	2-5
12—	Florida	L	1-5
16—	At Toronto	T	*3-3
21—	At Vancouver	L	2-5
23—	At Edmonton	L	2-4
25—	At Washington	W	3-0
26—	At Pittsburgh	T	*2-2
29—	Ottawa	L	3-5

MARCH

2—	Montreal	L	2-5
4—	Philadelphia	L	0-3
6—	Ottawa	L	1-5
8—	At Buffalo	L	*1-2
10—	At Carolina	W	5-3
11—	At Montreal	W	5-3
16—	At Chicago	L	*4-5
18—	Pittsburgh	W	3-2
19—	At Philadelphia	L	2-6
21—	Tampa Bay	W	4-0
23—	Florida	L	1-3
25—	Los Angeles	T	*4-4
29—	At Montreal	L	3-4
30—	St. Louis	L	2-3

APRIL

1—	N.Y. Rangers	T	*2-2
4—	At Tampa Bay	L	4-5
5—	At Florida	L	3-6
8—	At Philadelphia	L	0-3
9—	Pittsburgh	W	3-1

*Denotes overtime game.

BUFFALO SABRES
EASTERN CONFERENCE/NORTHEAST DIVISION

Buffalo Schedule

Home games shaded; D—Day game; *—All-Star Game at Denver.

October

SUN	MON	TUE	WED	THU	FRI	SAT
1	2	3	4	5 CHI	6	7 LA
8	9	10	11	12	13 EDM	14 VAN
15	16	17 MON	18	19	20 ANA	21 DET
22	23	24	25 CAR	26	27 TOR	28 CHI
29	30	31				

November

SUN	MON	TUE	WED	THU	FRI	SAT
			1	2	3 MON	4 PHI
5	6	7	8	9 NYI	10	11 NJ
12	13 CAL	14	15 DAL	16	17 MIN	18 STL
19	20	21	22 PHI	23	24 NYR	25 MON
26	27	28 OTT	29	30		

December

SUN	MON	TUE	WED	THU	FRI	SAT
					1 PIT	2 PIT
3	4	5 MON	6 NJ	7	8 NYR	9
10	11	12 BOS	13	14	15 CAR	16 FLA
17	18	19	20 WAS	21 WAS	22	23 SJ
24	25	26 PIT	27	28	29 OTT	30 NYI
31						

January

SUN	MON	TUE	WED	THU	FRI	SAT
	1 D BOS	2	3 TOR	4	5 TOR	6 NSH
7	8	9 SJ	10	11 LA	12 ANA	13
14	15	16 TB	17	18	19 FLA	20 TOR
21	22	23 CBJ	24	25	26 BOS	27 NYI
28	29	30	31 FLA			

February

SUN	MON	TUE	WED	THU	FRI	SAT
				1 TB	2	3
4	*5	6	7 NYR	8	9	10 OTT
11 MON	12	13 ATL	14	15 ATL	16	17 NJ
18	19 OTT	20	21	22	23 NJ	24 PHO
25 D TB	26	27 OTT	28			

March

SUN	MON	TUE	WED	THU	FRI	SAT
				1 PHI	2	3 D COL
4 D DAL	5	6 BOS	7	8	9 EDM	10
11	12	13	14 NYR	15	16 VAN	17 WAS
18	19	20 TOR	21 CAR	22	23	24 CAR
25	26 ATL	27 PIT	28	29	30 ATL	31

April

SUN	MON	TUE	WED	THU	FRI	SAT
1 TB	2 FLA	3	4 BOS	5	6 WAS	7
8 D PHI						

2000-2001 SEASON
CLUB DIRECTORY

Chairman of the board
John J. Rigas
Vice chairman of the board and counsel
Robert O. Swados
Vice chairman of the board
Robert E. Rich Jr.
Chief executive officer
Timothy J. Rigas
Executive vice president/administration
Ron Bertovich
Exec. v.p./finance & bus. development
Ed Hartman
Exec. v.p./integrated marketing
John Cimperman
Senior v.p./corporate sales
Kerry Atkinson
Senior v.p./legal and business affairs
Kevin Billet
Senior vice president/marketing
Christye Peterson
Vice president/communications
Michael Gilbert
Vice president/corporate relations
Seymour H. Knox IV
V.p./ticket sales and operations
John Sinclair
General manager
Darcy Regier
Assistant general manager
Larry Carriere
Director of communications
Gil Chorbajian
Communications coordinator
Gregg Huller

Director of player personnel
Don Luce
Professional scouts
Kevin Devine, Terry Martin
Scouting staff
Don Barrie, Jim Benning, Bo Berglund, Paul Merritt, Darryl Plandowski, Mike Racicot, Rudy Migay, David Volek
Head coach
Lindy Ruff
Associate coach
Don Lever
Assistant coach
To be announced
Strength and conditioning coach
Doug McKenney
Assistant strength coach
Dennis Cole
Goaltender coach
Jim Corsi
Administrative assistant coach
Jeff Holbrook
Head trainer/massage therapist
Jim Pizzutelli
Head equipment manager
Rip Simonick
Assistant equipment manager
George Babcock
On-site travel coordinator
Kim Christiano
Club doctor
Dr. John Marzo

DRAFT CHOICES

Rd.— Player	Ht./Wt.	Overall	Pos.	Last team
1— Artem Kriukov	6-3/180	15	F	Yaroslavl, Russia
2— Gerard Dicaire	6-2/190	48	D	Seattle (WHL)
4— Ghyslain Rousseau	6-0/161	111	G	Baie-Comeau (QMJHL)
5— Denis Denisov	6-0/183	149	LW	HC Moscow, Russia
7— Vasily Bizyayev		213		CSKA, Russia
7— Paul Gaustad	6-3/180	220	C/LW	Portland (WHL)
8— Sean McMorrow	6-4/199	258	D	Kitchener (OHL)
9— Ryan Courtney	6-2/195	277	LW	Windsor (OHL)

MISCELLANEOUS DATA

Home ice (capacity)
HSBC Arena (18,690)
Address
HSBC Arena
One Seymour H. Knox III Plaza
Buffalo, NY 14203
Business phone
716-855-4100
Ticket information
888-223-6000

Website
www.sabres.com
Training site
Buffalo, NY
Club colors
Black, white, red, gray and silver
Radio affiliation
WNUC (107.7 FM)
TV affiliation
Empire Sports Network

BUFFALO SABRES

TRAINING CAMP ROSTER

No.	FORWARDS	Ht./Wt.	Place	BORN Date	NHL exp.	1999-2000 clubs
	Jeremy Adduono (RW)..	6-0/182	Thunder Bay, Ont.	8-4-79	0	Rochester (AHL)
61	Maxim Afinogenov (RW)	5-11/176	Moscow, U.S.S.R.	9-4-79	1	Rochester (AHL), Buffalo
38	Dave Andreychuk (LW)..	6-4/220	Hamilton, Ont.	9-29-63	18	Boston, Colorado
41	Stu Barnes (C)	5-11/186	Spruce Grove, Alta.	12-25-70	9	Buffalo
	Milan Bartovic (LW)	5-11/183	Trencin, Czechoslovakia	4-20-81	0	Tri-City (WHL), Brandon (WHL)
	Eric Boulton (LW)	6-0/201	Halifax, Nova Scotia	8-17-76	0	Rochester (AHL)
37	Curtis Brown (C/LW)	6-0/190	Unity, Sask.	2-12-76	6	Buffalo
	Denis Denisov (LW)	6-0/183	Moscow, U.S.S.R.	12-31-81	0	HC CSKA Moscow (Russian)
17	Jean-Pierre Dumont	6-1/187	Montreal	5-1-78	2	Chicago, Cleveland (IHL), Rochester (AHL)
93	Doug Gilmour (LW/C)....	5-11/185	Kingston, Ont.	6-25-63	17	Chicago, Buffalo
77	Chris Gratton (C)	6-4/219	Brantford, Ont.	7-5-75	7	Tampa Bay, Buffalo
55	Denis Hamel (RW)	6-2/200	Lachute, Que.	5-10-77	1	Rochester (AHL), Buffalo
	Jaroslav Kristek (RW) ...	6-0/183	Zlin, Czechoslovakia	3-16-80	0	Tri-City (WHL)
	Artem Kriukov (C)	6-3/180	U.S.S.R.	3-5-82	0	Torpedo Yaroslavl (Russian)
	Norm Milley (RW)	5-11/175	Toronto	2-14-80	0	Sudbury (OHL)
	David Moravec (RW)	6-0/180	Czech Republic	3-24-73	1	Buffalo, HC Vitkovice (Czech Republic)
27	Michael Peca (C)	5-11/181	Toronto	3-26-74	7	Buffalo
26	Andrew Peters (LW)	6-4/195	St. Catharines, Ont.	5-5-80	0	Kitchener (OHL)
9	Erik Rasmussen (LW/C).	6-2/205	Minneapolis	3-28-77	3	Buffalo
32	Rob Ray (RW)	6-0/215	Stirling, Ont.	6-8-68	11	Buffalo
81	Miroslav Satan (RW)	6-1/195	Topolcany, Czechoslovakia	10-22-74	5	Dukla Trencin (Slovakia), Buffalo
23	Darren Van Oene (LW)..	6-3/207	Edmonton	1-18-78	0	Rochester (AHL)
25	Vaclav Varada (RW)	6-0/200	Vsetin, Czechoslovakia	4-26-76	5	HC Vitkovice (Czech Republic), Buffalo

DEFENSEMEN

No.	DEFENSEMEN	Ht./Wt.	Place	Date	exp.	1999-2000 clubs
51	Brian Campbell	5-11/185	Strathroy, Ont.	5-23-79	1	Buffalo, Rochester (AHL)
	Gerard Dicaire	6-2/190	Faro, Yukon	9-14-82	0	
29	Jason Holland	6-2/193	Morinville, Alta.	4-30-76	4	Buffalo, Rochester (AHL)
10	Doug Houda	6-2/190	Blairmore, Alta.	6-3-66	14	Rochester (AHL), Buffalo
21	Mike Hurlbut	6-2/200	Massena, N.Y.	7-10-66	5	Rochester (AHL), Buffalo
45	Dmitri Kalinin	6-2/198	Chelyabinsk, U.S.S.R.	7-22-80	1	Rochester (AHL), Buffalo
	Matt Kinch	5-11/189	Red Deer, Alta.	2-17-80	0	Calgary (WHL)
74	Jay McKee	6-3/205	Kingston, Ont.	9-8-77	5	Buffalo
42	Richard Smehlik	6-3/222	Ostrava, Czechoslovakia	1-23-70	8	Buffalo
	Henrik Tallinder	6-3/194	Stockholm, Sweden	1-10-79	0	AIK Solna (Sweden)
4	Rhett Warrener	6-1/210	Shaunavon, Sask.	1-27-76	5	Buffalo
5	Jason Woolley	6-1/207	Toronto	7-27-69	9	Buffalo
44	Alexei Zhitnik	5-11/215	Kiev, U.S.S.R.	10-10-72	8	Buffalo

GOALTENDERS

No.	GOALTENDERS	Ht./Wt.	Place	Date	exp.	1999-2000 clubs
43	Martin Biron	6-1/154	Lac St. Charles, Que.	8-15-77	3	Rochester (AHL), Buffalo
39	Dominik Hasek	5-11/168	Pardubice, Czechoslovakia	1-29-65	10	Buffalo
35	Mika Noronen	6-1/191	Tampere, Finland	6-17-79	0	Rochester (AHL)
	Ghyslain Rousseau	6-0/161	Black Lake, Que.	2-6-82	0	Baie-Comeau (QMJHL)

1999-2000 REVIEW

INDIVIDUAL STATISTICS

SCORING

	Games	G	A	Pts.	PIM	+/-	PPG	SHG	Shots	Shooting Pct.
Miroslav Satan	81	33	34	67	32	16	5	3	265	12.5
Curtis Brown	74	22	29	51	42	19	5	0	149	14.8
Stu Barnes	82	20	25	45	16	-3	8	2	137	14.6
Michael Peca	73	20	21	41	67	6	2	0	144	13.9
Vaclav Varada	76	10	27	37	62	12	0	0	140	7.1
Maxim Afinogenov	65	16	18	34	41	-4	2	0	128	12.5
Michal Grosek*	61	11	23	34	35	12	2	0	96	11.5
Jason Woolley	74	8	25	33	52	14	2	0	113	7.1
Geoff Sanderson	67	13	13	26	22	4	4	0	136	9.6
Brian Holzinger*	59	7	17	24	30	4	0	1	81	8.6
Dixon Ward	71	11	9	20	41	1	1	2	101	10.9
Vladimir Tsyplakov*	34	6	13	19	10	17	0	0	46	13.0
Jay McKee	78	5	12	17	50	5	1	0	84	6.0
Doug Gilmour*	11	3	14	17	12	3	2	0	13	23.1
Erik Rasmussen	67	8	6	14	43	1	0	0	76	10.5
James Patrick	66	5	8	13	22	8	0	0	40	12.5
Alexei Zhitnik	74	2	11	13	95	-6	1	0	139	1.4
Wayne Primeau*	41	5	7	12	38	-8	2	0	40	12.5
Richard Smehlik	64	2	9	11	50	13	0	0	67	3.0

	Games	G	A	Pts.	PIM	+/-	PPG	SHG	Shots	Shooting Pct.
Chris Gratton*	14	1	7	8	15	1	0	0	34	2.9
Brian Campbell	12	1	4	5	4	-2	0	0	10	10.0
Rob Ray	69	1	3	4	158	0	0	0	17	5.9
Cory Sarich*	42	0	4	4	35	2	0	0	49	0.0
Rhett Warrener	61	0	3	3	89	18	0	0	68	0.0
Chris Taylor	11	1	1	2	2	-2	0	0	15	6.7
Denis Hamel	3	1	0	1	0	-1	0	0	3	33.3
Domenic Pittis	7	1	0	1	6	1	0	0	6	16.7
Jason Holland	9	0	1	1	0	0	0	0	8	0.0
Dominik Hasek (goalie)	35	0	1	1	12	0	0	0	0	0.0
Doug Houda	1	0	0	0	12	0	0	0	0	0.0
Mike Hurlbut	1	0	0	0	2	1	0	0	1	0.0
David Moravec	1	0	0	0	0	-1	0	0	2	0.0
Dimitri Kalinin	4	0	0	0	4	0	0	0	3	0.0
Jean-Luc Grand-Pierre	11	0	0	0	15	-1	0	0	10	0.0
Paul Kruse	11	0	0	0	43	-2	0	0	7	0.0
Dwayne Roloson (goalie)	14	0	0	0	0	0	0	0	0	0.0
Martin Biron (goalie)	41	0	0	0	6	0	0	0	0	0.0

GOALTENDING

	Games	Min.	Goals	SO	Avg.	W	L	T	ENG	Shots	Sv. Pct.
Dominik Hasek	35	2066	76	3	2.21	15	11	6	2	937	.919
Martin Biron	41	2229	90	5	2.42	19	18	2	2	988	.909
Dwayne Roloson	14	677	32	0	2.84	1	7	3	2	277	.884

*Played with two or more NHL teams.

RESULTS

OCTOBER

2— At Detroit ....L......0-2
8— Washington ....L......2-3
9— At Atlanta ....T.....*5-5
11— Phoenix ....T.....*2-2
16— At Montreal.............................L......1-2
17— At Philadelphia........................L......2-5
20— Nashville ....L......3-4
22— Carolina ....W......7-3
23— At Ottawa ....L......0-4
27— Tampa Bay ....W......4-3
29— Florida ....W....*3-2
30— At Boston...............................L......0-3

NOVEMBER

3— At Dallas................................W....3-1
4— At Chicago ....W....*5-4
6— N.Y. Islanders.........................W......2-1
10— Boston ....W......6-2
12— At Tampa Bay ....L......2-4
13— At Florida ....L......1-3
16— At Pittsburgh ....L......2-3
19— At Atlanta ....W......4-0
20— Atlanta ....W......4-3
24— Washington ....W......5-2
26— St. Louis ....L......0-2
28— At Tampa Bay ....W....*3-2
30— Pittsburgh...............................L......1-4

DECEMBER

2— Philadelphia............................L......2-4
4— N.Y. Rangers...........................T....*1-1

6— At Toronto ....L.....*2-3
8— Ottawa ....T.....*0-0
10— Chicago ....W......2-1
14— Philadelphia ....W......3-1
17— Florida ....L......2-4
18— At N.Y. Islanders ....T.....*2-2
21— At N.Y. Rangers ....W......3-1
23— Colorado ....W......2-1
27— At New Jersey ....L......1-4
28— Detroit ....L......2-7

JANUARY

1— Toronto..............................W......8-1
3— At Toronto ....L......2-6
4— Atlanta ....L......4-5
6— New Jersey ....L......3-6
8— At Ottawa ....W......7-4
13— At Boston............................T.....*0-0
14— Montreal ....L......1-2
17— At Anaheim ....W......5-0
18— At Los Angeles ....L......3-5
20— At Phoenix ....L......1-2
22— At Carolina ....L......1-4
25— Tampa Bay ....W......2-1
28— Ottawa ....W......1-0
29— At Boston............................L......0-1

FEBRUARY

1— Anaheim ....T....*2-2
3— Ottawa ....W......4-2
8— At Colorado ....W......2-0
10— At Nashville ....W....*2-1

12— At Philadelphia...................L.....*2-3
13— Edmonton ....T.....*2-2
16— At Pittsburgh ....T.....*1-1
17— Vancouver ....L......1-2
19— Los Angeles ....W......4-1
21— New Jersey.........................W......3-2
25— N.Y. Rangers ....L......3-6
26— At Toronto ....L......2-5
28— At Florida ....W......5-2

MARCH

1— At N.Y. Rangers ....T.....*3-3
4— At N.Y. Islanders ....L......2-4
5— At Washington ....L......1-2
8— Boston ....W....*2-1
10— Montreal ....L......2-3
12— N.Y. Islanders ....W......4-2
15— At San Jose ....L....*5-6
16— At Vancouver ....L......3-6
18— At Calgary ....W......5-1
20— Montreal ....W......4-1
23— Calgary ....W......4-2
27— At Carolina ....W......5-1
31— Carolina ....L......1-3

APRIL

1— At Montreal ....W......2-0
3— Toronto..............................W......3-2
6— At New Jersey ....W......5-0
7— Pittsburgh...........................L.....*1-2
9— At Washington ....T....*1-1
*Denotes overtime game.

CALGARY FLAMES
WESTERN CONFERENCE/NORTHWEST DIVISION

Calgary Schedule

Home games shaded; D—Day game; *—All-Star Game at Denver.

October

SUN	MON	TUE	WED	THU	FRI	SAT
1	2	3	4	5 DET	6	7
8	9	10 COL	11	12 CBJ	13	14 NYI
15 DET	16	17	18 VAN	19	20 BOS	21 TOR
22	23 PHO	24	25	26 STL	27 MIN	28
29 D ANA	30	31				

November

SUN	MON	TUE	WED	THU	FRI	SAT
			1 EDM	2	3	4 PIT
5 MIN	6	7	8 MIN	9	10 FLA	11 TB
12 BUF	13	14	15	16 CHI	17	18 NYR
19 EDM	20	21	22 MIN	23	24 ANA	25 COL
26	27	28 NSH	29 DAL	30		

December

SUN	MON	TUE	WED	THU	FRI	SAT
					1	2 MON
3	4 SJ	5	6	7 NSH	8	9 CAR
10	11	12	13 MON	14 OTT	15	16 TOR
17	18	19 COL	20 PHO	21	22 EDM	23
24	25	26	27	28	29 VAN	30
31 MON						

January

SUN	MON	TUE	WED	THU	FRI	SAT
1	2	3 SJ	4	5 ANA	6 LA	
7	8	9	10	11 NSH	12	13 OTT
14 VAN	15	16	17 SJ	18	19	20
21 DET	22	23 PHO	24	25 LA	26	27 VAN
28	29	30 EDM	31			

February

SUN	MON	TUE	WED	THU	FRI	SAT
				1 CHI	2	3
4	*5 SJ	6	7	8	9 COL	10 VAN
11	12	13 WAS	14	15 STL	16	17
18 PHO	19 ANA	20	21	22 LA	23	24 EDM
25	26 DAL	27	28			

March

SUN	MON	TUE	WED	THU	FRI	SAT
				1 MIN	2	3 STL
4	5	6 TOR	7	8 PHI	9	10 PIT
11 ATL	12	13	14 CBJ	15 DET	16	17 STL
18	19 NJ	20	21	22 PHI	23	24 D CBJ
25 CHI	26 D	27 CBJ	28	29 COL	30	31 DAL

April

SUN	MON	TUE	WED	THU	FRI	SAT
1	2 DAL	3	4 CHI	5 NSH	6	7 LA
8						

2000-2001 SEASON
CLUB DIRECTORY

Co-owners
Grant A. Bartlett, N. Murray Edwards, Harley N. Hotchkiss, Ronald V. Joyce, Alvin G. Libin, Allan P. Markin, J.R. (Bud) McCaig, Byron J. Seaman, Daryl K. Seaman

President & chief executive officer
Ron Bremner

V.p., finance & administration
Michael Holditch

Vice president, marketing & sales
Garry McKenzie

Director, hockey operations
Al MacNeil

Head coach
Don Hay

Assistant coach
Brad McCrimmon

Director, hockey administration
Mike Burke

Sr. scout & special assignment scout
Ian McKenzie

Pro scout
Tod Button

Scouts
Mike Polano
Jeff Crisp

Scouting staff
Larry Johnston, Lars Norrman, Nikolai Ladigan, Jarmo Torvanen, Tomas Jelinek, Bill Berglund

Video coordinator
Gary Taylor

Director, communications
Peter Hanlon

Manager, media relations
Sean O'Brien

Controller
Len Burren

Director of marketing
John Vidalin

Director, retail operations
Dean Borle

Director, advertising and publishing
Pat Halls

Director, executive suites
Bob White

Business development manager
Al Molnar

Director, game presentation
Dave Imbach

Director, ticket operations
Jack Maloney

Director, ticket sales
Dave Sclanders

Physcal therapist
Terry Kane

Athletic therapist
Morris Boyer

Equipment manager
Gus Thorson

Strength & conditioning
Rich Hesketh

DRAFT CHOICES

Rd.— Player	Ht./Wt.	Overall	Pos.	Last team
1— Brent Krahn	6-4/200	9	G	Calgary (WHL)
2— Kurtis Foster	6-5/205	40	D	Peterborough (OHL)
2— Jarret Stoll	6-1/199	46	C	Kootenay (WHL)
4— Levente Szuper	5-11/178	116	G	Ottawa (OHL)
5— Wade Davis	6-4/185	141	D	Calgary (WHL)
5— Travis Moen	6-2/198	155	LW	Kelowna (WHL)
6— Jukka Hentunen	5-10/187	176	W	HPK Hameenlinna, Fin.
8— David Hajek	6-3/194	239	D	Chomutov, Czech Rep.
9— Micki Dupont	5-9/178	270	D	Kamloops (WHL)

MISCELLANEOUS DATA

Home ice (capacity)
Pengrowth Saddledome (17,139)

Address
P.O. Box 1540
Station M
Calgary, Alta. T2P 3B9

Business phone
403-777-2177

Ticket information
403-777-0000

Website
www.calgaryflames.com

Training site
Calgary

Club colors
Red, white, gold and black

Radio affiliation
66 CFR (660 AM)

TV affiliation
CTV Sportsnet, CBC-TV

CALGARY FLAMES

No.	FORWARDS	Ht./Wt.	Place	BORN Date	NHL exp.	1999-2000 clubs
26	Steve Begin (LW)	5-11/190	Trois-Rivieres, Que.	6-14-78	2	Calgary, Saint John (AHL)
28	Jason Botterill (LW)	6-4/220	Edmonton	5-19-76	3	Orlando (IHL), Atlanta, Calgary, Saint John (AHL)
8	Valeri Bure (RW) FLA	5-10/185	Moscow, U.S.S.R.	6-13-74	6	Calgary
7	Marc Bureau (C/RW)	6-1/203	Trois-Rivieres, Que.	5-19-66	11	Philadelphia, Calgary
17	Chris Clark (RW)	6-0/202	South Windsor, Conn.	3-8-76	1	Saint John (AHL), Calgary
38	Jeff Cowan (LW)	6-2/192	Scarborough, Ont.	9-27-76	1	Saint John (AHL), Calgary
23	Miikka Elomo (LW)	6-0/198	Turku, Finland	4-21-77	1	Portland (AHL), Washington
44	Rico Fata (RW)	5-11/197	Sault Ste. Marie, Ont.	2-12-80	2	Calgary, Saint John (AHL)
39	Benoit Gratton (LW)	5-11/194	Montreal	12-28-76	3	Saint John (AHL), Calgary
	Jukka Hentunen (LW)	5-10/187	Finland	5-3-74	0	HPK Hameenlinna (Finland)
12	Jarome Iginla (RW)	6-1/202	Edmonton	7-1-77	5	Calgary
21	Andreas Johansson (C)	6-2/202	Hofors, Sweden	5-19-73	5	Tampa Bay, Calgary
22	Bill Lindsay (LW) S.J.	6-0/195	Big Fork, Mont.	5-17-71	9	Calgary
	Dave Lowry (LW)	6-1/200	Sudbury, Ont.	2-14-65	15	San Jose
	Jesper Mattsson (C)	6-0/185	Malmo, Sweden	5-13-75	0	Malmo (Sweden)
	Travis Moen (LW)	6-2/198	Swift Current, Sask.	4-6-82	0	Kelowna (WHL)
62	Andrei Nazarov (LW)	6-5/234	Chelyabinsk, U.S.S.R.	4-22-74	7	Calgary
25	Dave Roche (LW)	6-4/230	Lindsay, Ont.	6-13-75	4	Saint John (AHL), Calgary
	Oleg Saprykin (C/LW)	6-0/187	Moscow, U.S.S.R.	2-12-81	1	Calgary, Seattle (WHL)
27	Marc Savard (C)	5-10/184	Ottawa	7-17-77	3	Calgary
11	Jeff Shantz (C)	6-0/195	Edmonton	10-10-73	7	Calgary
15	Martin St. Louis (RW)	5-9/185	Laval, Que.	9-8-71	2	Saint John (AHL), Calgary
16	Cory Stillman (LW) STL	6-0/194	Peterborough, Ont.	12-20-73	6	Calgary
	Jarrett Stoll (C)	6-1/199	Melville, Sask.	6-24-82	0	Kootenay (WHL)
	Shaun Sutter (C)	5-11/160	Red Deer, Alta.	6-2-80	0	Medicine Hat (WHL), Calgary (WHL)
	Daniel Tkaczuk (C) STL	6-1/197	Toronto	6-10-79	0	Saint John (AHL)
37	Sergei Varlamov (RW)	5-11/195	Kiev, U.S.S.R.	7-21-78	2	Saint John (AHL), Calgary
24	Jason Wiemer (C) FLA	6-1/220	Kimberley, B.C.	4-14-76	6	Calgary
23	Clarke Wilm (C)	6-0/202	Central Butte, Sask.	10-24-76	2	Calgary
	DEFENSEMEN					
5	Tommy Albelin	6-1/194	Stockholm, Sweden	5-21-64	13	Calgary
29	Wade Belak	6-4/222	Saskatoon, Sask.	3-7-76	4	Calgary (WHL)
	Wade Davis	6-4/185	Kamloops, B.C.	4-13-82	0	Calgary (WHL)
	Dallas Eakins	6-2/200	Dade City, Fla.	1-20-67	8	New York Islanders, Chicago (IHL)
	Kurtis Foster	6-5/205	Carp, Ont.	11-24-81	0	Peterborough (OHL)
3	Denis Gauthier	6-2/210	Montreal	10-1-76	3	Calgary
6	Phil Housley	5-10/185	St. Paul, Minn.	3-9-64	18	Calgary
	Toni Lydman	6-1/183	Lahti, Finland	9-25-77	0	HIFK Helsinki (Finland)
3	Stewart Malgunas	6-0/211	Prince George, B.C.	4-21-70	7	Utah (IHL), Calgary
53	Derek Morris	5-11/200	Edmonton	8-24-78	3	Calgary
28	Robyn Regehr	6-2/225	Recife, Brazil.	4-19-80	1	Saint John (AHL), Calgary
	Darryl Scoville	6-3/215	Regina, Sask.	10-13-75	1	Saint John (AHL), Calgary
55	Steve Smith	6-4/215	Glasgow, Scotland	4-30-63	16	Calgary
33	Brad Werenka	6-1/218	Two Hills, Alta.	2-12-69	6	Pittsburgh, Calgary
	GOALTENDERS					
40	Fred Brathwaite STL	5-7/175	Ottawa	11-24-72	5	Calgary, Saint John (AHL)
1	Tyrone Garner	6-1/200	Stoney Creek, Ont.	7-27-78	1	Saint John (AHL), Dayton (ECHL), Johnstown (ECHL)
	Brent Krahn	6-4/200	Winnipeg	4-2-82	0	Calgary (WHL)
	Lavente Szuper	5-11/178	Budapest, Hungary	6-11-80	0	Ottawa (OHL)
29	Mike Vernon	5-9/180	Calgary	2-24-63	17	San Jose, Florida

1999-2000 REVIEW
INDIVIDUAL STATISTICS

SCORING

	Games	G	A	Pts.	PIM	+/-	PPG	SHG	Shots	Shooting Pct.
Valeri Bure	82	35	40	75	50	-7	13	0	308	11.4
Jarome Iginla	77	29	34	63	26	0	12	0	256	11.3
Phil Housley	78	11	44	55	24	-12	5	0	176	6.3
Marc Savard	78	22	31	53	56	-2	4	0	184	12.0
Derek Morris	78	9	29	38	80	2	3	0	193	4.7
Andrei Nazarov	76	10	22	32	78	3	1	0	110	9.1
Jeff Shantz	74	13	18	31	30	-13	6	0	112	11.6
Jason Wiemer	64	11	11	22	120	-10	2	0	104	10.6
Clarke Wilm	78	10	12	22	67	-6	1	3	81	12.3
Cory Stillman	37	12	9	21	12	-9	6	0	59	20.3
Bill Lindsay S.J.	80	8	12	20	86	-7	0	0	147	5.4
Martin St. Louis	56	3	15	18	22	-5	0	0	73	4.1
Hnat Domenichelli*	32	5	9	14	12	0	1	0	57	8.8
Rene Corbet*	48	4	10	14	60	-7	0	0	100	4.0

	Games	G	A	Pts.	PIM	+/-	PPG	SHG	Shots	Shooting Pct.
Robyn Regehr	57	5	7	12	46	-2	2	0	64	7.8
Sergei Krivokrasov*	12	1	10	11	4	2	0	0	27	3.7
Tommy Albelin	41	4	6	10	12	-3	1	1	37	10.8
Andreas Johansson*	28	3	7	10	14	-3	1	0	47	6.4
Bobby Dollas*	49	3	7	10	28	4	1	0	36	8.3
Darryl Shannon*	27	1	8	9	22	-13	0	0	46	2.2
Cale Hulse	47	1	6	7	47	-11	0	0	41	2.4
Jeff Cowan	13	4	1	5	16	2	0	0	26	15.4
Marc Bureau*	9	1	3	4	2	-3	0	0	5	20.0
Steve Smith	20	0	4	4	42	-13	0	0	10	0.0
Sergei Varlamov	7	3	0	3	0	0	0	0	11	27.3
Brad Werenka*	12	1	1	2	21	-2	0	0	20	5.0
Steve Begin	13	1	1	2	18	-3	0	0	3	33.3
Denis Gauthier	39	1	1	2	50	-4	0	0	29	3.4
Pavel Torgaev*	9	0	2	2	4	0	0	0	12	0.0
Benoit Gratton	10	0	2	2	10	1	0	0	4	0.0
Travis Brigley	17	0	2	2	4	-6	0	0	17	0.0
Wade Belak	40	0	2	2	122	-4	0	0	11	0.0
Stewart Malgunas	4	0	1	1	2	1	0	0	0	0.0
Oleg Saprykin	4	0	1	1	2	-4	0	0	2	0.0
Chris Clark	22	0	1	1	14	-3	0	0	17	0.0
Steve Dubinsky	23	0	1	1	4	-12	0	0	29	0.0
Lee Sorochan	1	0	0	0	0	0	0	0	0	0.0
Rico Fata	2	0	0	0	0	-1	0	0	0	0.0
Dave Roche	2	0	0	0	5	-1	0	0	3	0.0
Jason Botterill*	2	0	0	0	0	-4	0	0	2	0.0
Darrel Scoville	6	0	0	0	2	1	0	0	1	0.0
Jean-Sebastien Giguere (goalie)	7	0	0	0	2	0	0	0	0	0.0
Eric Charron	21	0	0	0	37	-3	0	0	8	0.0
Grant Fuhr (goalie)	23	0	0	0	2	0	0	0	0	0.0
Fred Brathwaite (goalie)	61	0	0	0	4	0	0	0	0	0.0

GOALTENDING

	Games	Min.	Goals	SO	Avg.	W	L	T	ENG	Shots	Sv. Pct.
Jean-Sebastien Giguere	7	330	15	0	2.73	1	3	1	1	175	.914
Fred Brathwaite	61	3448	158	5	2.75	25	25	7	3	1664	.905
Grant Fuhr	23	1205	77	0	3.83	5	13	2	2	536	.856

*Played with two or more NHL teams.

RESULTS

OCTOBER
2— At San Jose .... L 3-5
6— St. Louis .... L 1-4
8— Montreal .... L 1-4
11— Carolina .... T *3-3
13— At Vancouver .... W ...*4-3
15— Los Angeles .... L 1-4
16— Vancouver .... T *4-4
19— At St. Louis .... L 1-7
22— At Florida .... W ...*3-2
23— At Tampa Bay .... L 1-2
26— At Atlanta .... L 1-2
28— At Ottawa .... W ...*4-3
30— At Toronto .... L 1-2

NOVEMBER
3— Nashville .... W ...*5-4
6— Florida .... L 3-6
10— San Jose .... W ...*4-3
13— Colorado .... L 2-5
16— At Phoenix .... L 1-2
17— At Anaheim .... L 1-2
19— Detroit .... W 3-1
23— N.Y. Islanders .... W 3-2
25— Chicago .... W ...*2-1
27— At Colorado .... L 1-7
30— At Carolina .... L 3-4

DECEMBER
2— At N.Y. Islanders .... W 5-0
4— At New Jersey .... W 4-2
6— At N.Y. Rangers .... L *2-3

7— At Montreal .... T *3-3
10— Vancouver .... W 3-2
12— At Chicago .... W 2-1
14— At St. Louis .... T *1-1
15— At Dallas .... L 1-5
18— Ottawa .... W 2-1
21— Dallas .... T *0-0
23— Edmonton .... W 2-1
26— At Vancouver .... W 2-0
27— At Philadelphia .... L 1-5
29— Anaheim .... W 3-1

JANUARY
2— Vancouver .... W 4-2
5— At Colorado .... L 0-4
6— At Chicago .... L 2-5
8— Tampa Bay .... W ...*3-2
12— Dallas .... W ...*2-1
15— Toronto .... W 4-0
18— Detroit .... W 6-1
19— At Edmonton .... L 0-7
21— Nashville .... W ...*5-4
24— At Boston .... W ...*4-3
26— At Washington .... L 1-2
28— At Detroit .... L 1-4
29— At Nashville .... L 1-3

FEBRUARY
1— St. Louis .... L *4-5
3— Chicago .... T *5-5
9— At Vancouver .... L *3-4
10— At Colorado .... L 2-3

12— At Phoenix .... L 3-4
14— At Los Angeles .... L *3-4
16— At Anaheim .... L *5-6
18— Edmonton .... W 4-2
19— At Edmonton .... W ...*3-2
23— Los Angeles .... L 2-7
25— Phoenix .... T *3-3
26— Atlanta .... W 5-2

MARCH
1— Pittsburgh .... W 8-2
3— Anaheim .... W 4-1
5— New Jersey .... T *2-2
7— Colorado .... L 3-8
9— Toronto .... L 2-6
11— At Los Angeles .... L 1-3
13— At San Jose .... L 3-5
15— Ottawa .... L 1-3
18— Buffalo .... L 1-5
19— At Edmonton .... W 3-2
22— At Detroit .... T *2-2
23— At Buffalo .... L 2-4
25— At Nashville .... W 2-1
31— Phoenix .... L 1-3

APRIL
1— San Jose .... W 3-0
3— At Dallas .... T *2-2
5— At St. Louis .... L 5-6
7— Colorado .... L 1-3
8— Edmonton .... L 3-6
*Denotes overtime game.

CAROLINA HURRICANES
EASTERN CONFERENCE/SOUTHEAST DIVISION

CAROLINA HURRICANES

Carolina Schedule
Home games shaded; D—Day game; *—All-Star Game at Denver.

October

SUN	MON	TUE	WED	THU	FRI	SAT
1	2	3	4	5	6	7 WAS
8	9	10 DAL	11	12	13 FLA	14 NSH
15	16	17	18 PIT	19	20	21 MON
22	23	24 SJ	25 BUF	26	27 NJ	28
29 STL	30	31 TB				

November

SUN	MON	TUE	WED	THU	FRI	SAT
			1	2	3 COL	4 SJ
5	6	7	8 TOR	9	10 TOR	11
12 D OTT	13	14	15 FLA	16 OTT	17	18 D NJ
19	20	21	22 PIT	23	24 D BOS	25
26 D NSH	27	28	29 FLA	30 PHI		

December

SUN	MON	TUE	WED	THU	FRI	SAT
					1	2
3 OTT	4	5	6 ATL	7	8	9 CAL
10	11	12	13 MIN	14	15 BUF	16 BOS
17	18	19 NYI	20	21	22	23 D PHI
24	25	26 TB	27 NYR	28	29 CBJ	30
31 CHI						

January

SUN	MON	TUE	WED	THU	FRI	SAT
	1	2	3 TB	4	5	6 COL
7 NYI	8	9 FLA	10	11	12 FLA	13
14 D ANA	15	16 MON	17	18 BOS	19	20 D LA
21	22 NYR	23	24 NYR	25	26	27 D PHI
28	29 TB	30	31 TOR			

February

SUN	MON	TUE	WED	THU	FRI	SAT
			1 ATL	2	3	
4 *	5	6	7 PHO	8 LA	9	10
11 ANA	12	13	14 DET	15	16 PHO	17
18 D BOS	19 PHI	20	21 ATL	22	23 NJ	24 WAS
25	26	27 ATL	28			

March

SUN	MON	TUE	WED	THU	FRI	SAT
				1 NYI	2 NJ	3
4 D CHI	5	6	7 CBJ	8 TB	9	10
11 EDM	12	13	14 MON	15 WAS	16	17
18 NYI	19	20	21 BUF	22	23 PIT	24 BUF
25	26 MON	27	28 WAS	29	30 WAS	31

April

SUN	MON	TUE	WED	THU	FRI	SAT
1 D OTT	2	3 STL	4 NYR	5	6 ATL	7
8 D PIT						

2000-2001 SEASON
CLUB DIRECTORY

Owner/governor
Peter Karmanos Jr.
General partner
Thomas Thewes
Chief executive officer/general manager
Jim Rutherford
President/chief operating officer
Jim Cain
Vice president/asst. general manager
Jason Karmanos
Chief financial officer
Mike Amendola
Head coach
Paul Maurice
Assistant coaches
Randy Ladouceur
Kevin McCarthy
Director of amateur scouting
Sheldon Ferguson
Amateur scouts
Laurence Ferguson
Willy Langer
Willy Lindstrom
Tony MacDonald
Bert Marshall
Terry E. McDonnell

Pro scout
Claude Larose
Goaltender coach/pro scout
Steve Weeks
Video coordinator
Chris Huffine
Head athletic therapist/strength and conditioning coach
Peter Friesen
Assistant athletic therapist
Stu Lempke
Equipment managers
Skip Cunningham
Wally Tatomir
Assistant equipment managers
Bob Gorman
Rick Szuber
Executive assistants, hockey operations
Tracey Moose
Kristina Owens
V.p. of public relations/communications
Chris Brown
Media relations director
Jerry Peters
Media relations assistant
Mike Sundheim

DRAFT CHOICES

Rd.— Player	Ht./Wt.	Overall	Pos.	Last team
2— Tomas Kurka	6-0/190	32	LW	Plymouth (OHL)
3— Ryan Bayda	5-11/185	80	LW	North Dakota (WCHA)
4— Niclas Wallin	6-2/207	97	D	Brynas, Sweden
4— Jared Newman	6-2/201	110	D	Plymouth (OHL)
6— Justin Forrest	5-8/167	181	D	U.S. Nat. Under 18 Exhib.
7— Magnus Kahnberg	6-1/174	212	F	Frolunda, Sweden
8— Craig Kowalski	5-9/190	235	G	Compuware, NAHL
9— Troy Ferguson	5-9/165	276	F	Michigan State (CCHA)

MISCELLANEOUS DATA

Home ice (capacity)
Entertainment & Sports Arena (18,730)
Address
1400 Edwards Mill Road
Raleigh, NC 27607
Business phone
919-467-7825
Ticket information
1-888-645-8491
Website
www.carolinahurricanes.com

Training site
Fort Myers, FL & Raleigh
Club colors
Red, black and silver
Radio affiliation
WRBZ (850 AM)
TV affiliation
FOX Sports South, HTS (Cable)

TRAINING CAMP ROSTER

No.	FORWARDS	Ht./Wt.	BORN Place	Date	NHL exp.	1999-2000 clubs
13	Bates Battaglia (LW)	6-2/205	Chicago	12-13-75	3	Carolina
	Ryan Bayda (LW)	5-11/185	Saskatoon, Sask.	12-9-80	0	Univ. of North Dakota (WCHA)
27	Rod Brind'Amour (C)	6-1/200	Ottawa	8-9-70	12	Philadelphia, Carolina
	Erik Cole (LW)	6-0/185	Oswego, N.Y.	11-6-78	0	Clarkson (ECAC), Cincinnati (IHL)
	Brad DeFauw (LW)	6-2/210	Edina, Minn.	11-10-77	0	Univ. of North Dakota (WCHA)
45	Gilbert Dionne (LW)	6-0/194	Drummondville, Que.	9-19-70	6	Cincinnati (IHL)
21	Ron Francis (C)	6-3/200	Sault Ste. Marie, Ont.	3-1-63	19	Carolina
23	Martin Gelinas (LW)	5-11/195	Shawinigan, Que.	6-5-70	12	Carolina
	Jeff Heerema (RW)	6-1/184	Thunder Bay, Ont.	1-17-80	0	Sarnia (OHL)
24	Sami Kapanen (RW)	5-10/175	Helsinki, Finland	6-14-73	5	Carolina
	Tomas Kurka (LW)	5-11/190	Litvinov, Czechoslovakia	12-14-81	0	Plymouth (OHL)
12	Craig MacDonald (C)	6-2/185	Antigonish, Nova Scotia	4-7-77	1	Cincinnati (IHL)
	Ian MacNeil (C)	6-2/178	Halifax, Nova Scotia	4-27-77	0	Cincinnati (IHL)
20	Sandy McCarthy (RW)	6-3/225	Toronto	6-15-72	7	Philadelphia, Carolina
61	Brent McDonald (C)	5-11/170	Olds, Alta.	10-7-79	0	Prince Albert (WHL), Spokane (WHL)
92	Jeff O'Neill (C)	6-0/195	King City, Ont.	2-23-76	5	Carolina
15	Byron Ritchie (C)	5-10/185	Burnaby, B.C.	4-24-77	2	Carolina, Cincinnati (IHL)
	Damian Surma (C)	6-3/189	Lincoln Park, Mich.	3-17-79	0	Plymouth (OHL)
	Jarslav Svoboda (RW)	6-1/174	Cervenka, Czechoslovakia	6-1-80	0	Kootenay (WHL)
	Josef Vasicek (C)	6-4/196	Havlickuv Brod, Czech.	9-12-80	0	Sault Ste. Marie (OHL)
16	Tommy Westlund (RW)	6-0/202	Fors, Sweden	12-29-74	1	Carolina
25	Shane Willis (RW)	6-0/176	Edmonton	6-13-77	2	Cincinnati (IHL), Carolina
	DEFENSEMEN					
	Justin Forrest	5-8/167	Westchester, N.Y.	4-15-81	0	
14	Steve Halko	6-1/190	Etobicoke, Ont.	3-8-74	3	Carolina
33	Dave Karpa ..N.Y.R.	6-1/210	Regina, Sask.	5-7-71	9	Cincinnati (IHL), Carolina
5	Marek Malik	6-5/210	Ostrava, Czechoslovakia	6-24-75	5	Carolina
	Jared Newman	6-2/201	Detroit	3-7-82	0	Plymouth (OHL)
8	Sandis Ozolinsh	6-3/205	Riga, U.S.S.R.	8-3-72	8	Colorado
45	David Tanabe	6-1/195	Minneapolis	7-19-80	1	Carolina, Cincinnati (IHL)
	Nikos Tselios	6-4/187	Oak Park, Ill.	1-20-79	0	Cincinnati (IHL)
	Niclas Wallin	6-2/207	Sweden	2-20-75	0	Brynas Gavle (Sweden)
2	Glen Wesley	6-1/201	Red Deer, Alta.	10-2-68	13	Carolina
	GOALTENDERS					
1	Arturs Irbe	5-8/190	Riga, U.S.S.R.	2-2-67	9	Carolina
	Jean-Marc Pelletier	6-3/195	Atlanta	3-4-78	1	Philadelphia (AHL), Cincinnati (IHL)
	Randy Petruk	5-10/185	Cranbrook, B.C.	4-23-78	0	Cincinnati (IHL), Florida (ECHL)

1999-2000 REVIEW

INDIVIDUAL STATISTICS

SCORING

	Games	G	A	Pts.	PIM	+/-	PPG	SHG	Shots	Shooting Pct.
Ron Francis	78	23	50	73	18	10	7	0	150	15.3
Jeff O'Neill	80	25	38	63	72	-9	4	0	189	13.2
Gary Roberts	69	23	30	53	62	-10	12	0	150	15.3
Sami Kapanen	76	24	24	48	12	10	7	0	229	10.5
Sean Hill	62	13	31	44	59	3	8	0	150	8.7
Robert Kron	81	13	27	40	8	-4	2	1	134	9.7
Paul Coffey	69	11	29	40	40	-6	6	0	155	7.1
Andrei Kovalenko	76	15	24	39	38	-13	2	0	114	13.2
Bates Battaglia	77	16	18	34	39	20	3	0	86	18.6
Martin Gelinas	81	14	16	30	40	-10	3	0	139	10.1
Paul Ranheim	79	9	13	22	6	-14	0	0	98	9.2
Glen Wesley	78	7	15	22	38	-4	1	0	99	7.1
Rod Brind'Amour*	33	4	10	14	22	-12	0	1	61	6.6
Marek Malik	57	4	10	14	63	13	0	0	57	7.0
Tommy Westlund	81	4	8	12	19	-10	0	1	67	6.0
Steven Halko	58	0	8	8	25	0	0	0	54	0.0
Jeff Daniels	69	3	4	7	10	-8	0	0	28	10.7
Dave Karpa	27	1	4	5	52	9	0	0	24	4.2
Kent Manderville*	56	1	4	5	12	-8	0	0	45	2.2
David Tanabe	31	4	0	4	14	-4	3	0	28	14.3
Nolan Pratt	64	3	1	4	90	-22	0	0	47	6.4
Byron Ritchie	26	0	2	2	17	-10	0	0	13	0.0
Curtis Leschyshyn	53	0	2	2	14	-19	0	0	31	0.0
Arturs Irbe (goalie)	75	0	1	1	14	0	0	0	0	0.0
Shane Willis	2	0	0	0	0	-1	0	0	1	0.0

	Games	G	A	Pts.	PIM	+/-	PPG	SHG	Shots	Shooting Pct.
Mark Fitzpatrick (goalie)	3	0	0	0	0	0	0	0	0	0.0
Eric Fichaud (goalie)*	9	0	0	0	2	0	0	0	0	0.0
Sandy McCarthy*	13	0	0	0	9	2	0	0	12	0.0

GOALTENDING

	Games	Min.	Goals	SO	Avg.	W	L	T	ENG	Shots	Sv. Pct.
Arturs Irbe	75	4345	175	5	2.42	34	28	9	8	1858	.906
Eric Fichaud	9	490	24	1	2.94	3	5	1	0	206	.883
Mark Fitzpatrick	3	107	8	0	4.49	0	2	0	1	68	.882

*Played with two or more NHL teams.

RESULTS

OCTOBER
2— At Boston ....W.....3-1
7— At Philadelphia ....W.....2-0
8— At N.Y. Rangers ....L.....1-3
11— At Calgary ....T...*3-3
13— At Edmonton ....T...*3-3
15— At Vancouver ....W.....4-1
20— At Toronto ....T...*3-3
22— At Buffalo ....L.....3-7
23— At Pittsburgh ....W.....3-2
29— New Jersey ....L.....2-4
30— At N.Y. Islanders.............W.....4-0

NOVEMBER
3— Toronto ....L.....0-6
5— At Detroit...........................L.....2-3
7— Washington ....W.....3-2
10— N.Y. Islanders ....L.....0-2
11— At Philadelphia................L.....1-4
13— Tampa Bay ....W.....4-2
17— Ottawa ....W.....2-1
19— At Washington ....T...*3-3
20— Dallas ....W.....1-0
22— Boston ....L.....1-2
24— Vancouver ....T...*1-1
26— At Tampa Bay ....T...*3-3
27— Pittsburgh ....W.....5-3
30— Calgary ....W.....4-3

DECEMBER
2— Toronto ....T...*2-2
4— At Colorado ....L.....1-3
7— At St. Louis ....W.....4-2
8— At Dallas ....L.....1-2
10— At Tampa Bay ....L.....2-3
15— Pittsburgh ....L.....3-6
18— Atlanta ....W.....4-2
20— Colorado ....L.....2-4
22— Detroit ....L.....1-4
23— At Ottawa ....L.....3-4
26— Florida ....W...*4-3
28— At Nashville ....L.....2-3

JANUARY
1— At Atlanta ....W.....4-2
4— Ottawa ....L.....1-2
6— At Boston ....W.....7-3
7— Anaheim ....T...*4-4
9— N.Y. Rangers ....W.....1-0
11— Philadelphia ....L.....3-4
14— At Florida ....L.....1-5
17— At New Jersey ....L.....2-5
18— At N.Y. Rangers ....L.....2-3
20— N.Y. Rangers ....L.....1-4
22— Buffalo ....W.....4-1
24— Montreal ....W...*3-2
27— Phoenix ....L.....2-4
28— New Jersey.........................W...*4-3
30— At Montreal.........................L.....0-3

FEBRUARY
1— Florida ....W.....4-2
3— At Washington ....L.....1-2
8— At N.Y. Islanders...............W.....4-3

12—At Tampa Bay ....W.....5-2
14—At Toronto ....W.....5-2
15—At Ottawa ....L.....1-5
17—Montreal ....L.....0-3
19—Tampa Bay ....W.....4-2
21—Washington ....T...*1-1
24—Florida ....L.....2-4
26—At Florida.............................W...*2-1

MARCH
1— At Phoenix ....L.....5-7
2— At Los Angeles ....W.....5-2
4— At San Jose ....W.....5-2
8— Chicago ....W.....4-1
10— Boston ....L.....3-5
12— Atlanta ....W.....5-1
15— Edmonton ....T...*2-2
17— At Washington ....L.....2-4
18— At Montreal.........................L.....2-3
21— At New Jersey ....W.....5-0
22— St. Louis ....L.....1-2
26— N.Y. Islanders ....W.....4-1
27— Buffalo ....L.....1-5
29— Nashville ....W.....3-1
31— At Buffalo ....W.....3-1

APRIL
2— Philadelphia.........................W.....1-0
3— At Pittsburgh ....L.....2-3
8— At Atlanta ....W.....4-3
9— Atlanta.................................W.....2-1
*Denotes overtime game.

CHICAGO BLACKHAWKS
WESTERN CONFERENCE/CENTRAL DIVISION

Chicago Schedule
Home games shaded; D—Day game; *—All-Star Game at Denver.

October

SUN	MON	TUE	WED	THU	FRI	SAT
1	2	3	4	5 BUF	6	7 CBJ
8	9	10	11	12 DET	13	14 MON
15 CBJ	16	17	18 NYR	19	20 DAL	21 STL
22	23	24	25	26 COL	27	28 BUF
29 MIN	30	31				

November

SUN	MON	TUE	WED	THU	FRI	SAT
			1	2 BOS	3 DET	4
5 ANA	6	7	8 SJ	9	10 MIN	11 TOR
12	13	14 VAN	15	16 CAL	17 EDM	18
19	20	21 PHO	22 SJ	23	24 MIN	D 25
26	27 DET	28	29	30 NSH		

December

SUN	MON	TUE	WED	THU	FRI	SAT
					1 NSH	2
3 CBJ	4	5	6	7 MIN	8	9 STL
10 STL	11	12	13 ATL	14	15 DAL	16 NSH
17	18	19	20	21 VAN	22	23 OTT D
24	25	26	27 PHO	28	29 DET	30
31 CAR						

January

SUN	MON	TUE	WED	THU	FRI	SAT
	1	2	3 VAN	4	5 EDM	6
7 TB	8	9 NYI	10 NJ	11	12 CBJ	13
14 COL	15	16	17 FLA	18	19 WAS	20
21 PIT	22	23	24	25 PHI	26 COL	27
28 VAN	29	30	31 EDM			

February

SUN	MON	TUE	WED	THU	FRI	SAT
				1 CAL	2	3
4	* 5	6 LA	7 ANA	8	9	10 SJ
11 PHO	12	13	14 SJ	15	16 STL	17
18 D LA	19 NYR	D 20	21 DET	22	23 ATL	24
25 TOR	26	27 WAS	28			

March

SUN	MON	TUE	WED	THU	FRI	SAT
				1 LA	2	3
4 D CAR	5	6	7 DAL	8	9 ANA	10 LA
11	12	13 DAL	14	15 NSH	16	17
18 D ANA	19	20	21	22 NSH	23	24 D STL
25 D CAL	26	27	28 OTT	29 PIT	30	31

April

SUN	MON	TUE	WED	THU	FRI	SAT
1 EDM	2	3	4 CAL	5	6 TOR	7
8 D CBJ						

2000-2001 SEASON
CLUB DIRECTORY

President
William W. Wirtz

Senior vice president/general manager
Robert J. Pulford

Vice president
Jack Davison

Manager of hockey operations
Mike Smith

Assistant general manager
Nick Beverley

Director of player personnel
Dale Tallon

Head coach
Alpo Suhonen

Assistant coaches
Denis Savard
Don Jackson

Goaltending consultant
Vladislav Tretiak

Scouts
Ron Anderson, Michel Dumas, Bruce
Franklin, Tim Higgins, Sakari Pietela

Manager of team services
David Stensby

Head trainers
Michael Gapski

Equipment manager
Troy Parchman

Assistant equipment manager
Lou Varga

Massage therapist
Pawel Prylinski

Vice president of marketing
Peter R. Wirtz

Exec. director of communications
Jim De Maria

Dir. of community relations/p.r. asst.
Barbara Davidson

Manager of public relations
Tony Ommen

Exec. dir. of marketing/merchandising
Jim Sofranko

Manager, special events
To be announced

Manager, game operations
To be announced

Director of ticket operations
James K. Bare

Sales manager
Doug Ryan

DRAFT CHOICES

Rd.— Player	Ht./Wt.	Overall	Pos.	Last team
1— Mikhail Yakubov	6-3/185	10	C	Togliatta, Russia
1— Pavel Vorobiev	6-0/183	11	RW	Yaroslavl, Russia
2— Jonas Nordqvist	6-2/191	49	C	Leksand, Sweden
3— Igor Radulov	6-0/176	74	LW	Yaroslavl, Russia
4— Scott Balan	6-2/194	106	D	Regina (WHL)
4— Olli Malmivaara	6-4/205	117	D	Jokerit, Finland
5— Alexander Barkunov	6-0/180	151	D	Yaroslavl, Russia
6— Michael Ayers	5-11/186	177	G	Dubuque, USHL
6— Joey Martin	6-3/198	193	D	Omaha, USHL
7— Cliff Loya	6-2/200	207	D	Maina (H. East)
7— Vladislav Luchkin	6-1/185	225	C	Cherepovets, Russia
8— Adam Berkhoel	5-11/165	240	G	Twin Cities, USHL
9— Peter Flache	6-5/190	262	C	Guelph (OHL)
9— Reto Von Arx	5-10/176	271	F	Davos, Switzerland
9— Arne Ramholt	6-3/215	291	D	Kloten, Switzerland

MISCELLANEOUS DATA

Home ice (capacity)
United Center (20,500)

Address
1901 W. Madison Street
Chicago, IL 60612

Business phone
312-455-7000

Ticket information
312-943-7000

Website
www.chicagoblackhawks.com

Training site
Chicago, IL

Club colors
Red, black and white

Radio affiliation
WMAQ (670 AM)

TV affiliation
FOX Sports Chicago

TRAINING CAMP ROSTER

No.	FORWARDS	Ht./Wt.	Place	BORN Date	NHL exp.	1999-2000 clubs
10	Tony Amonte (RW)	6-0/190	Hingham, Mass.	8-2-70	10	Chicago
34	Blair Atcheynum (RW)	6-2/198	Estevan, Sask.	4-20-69	4	Chicago
	Mark Bell (C/LW)	6-3/198	St. Paul's, Ont.	8-5-80	0	Ottawa (OHL)
	Kyle Calder (C)	5-11/180	Mannville, Alta.	1-5-79	1	Cleveland (IHL), Chicago
55	Eric Daze (RW)	6-6/234	Montreal	7-2-75	6	Chicago
17	Michal Grosek (LW)	6-2/216	Vyskov, Czechoslovakia	6-1-75	7	Buffalo, Chicago
	Chris Herperger (LW)	6-0/190	Esterhazy, Sask.	2-24-74	1	Chicago, Cleveland (IHL)
20	Mark Janssens (C)	6-3/216	Surrey, B.C.	5-19-68	13	Chicago
27	Ty Jones (RW)	6-3/218	Richland, Wash.	2-22-79	1	Cleveland (IHL), Florida (ECHL)
23	Jean-Yves Leroux (LW)	6-2/211	Montreal	6-24-76	4	Chicago
	Dmitri Levinsky (LW)	6-1/183	Ust-Kamenogorsk, U.S.S.R.	6-23-81	0	SKA St. Petersburg (Russian)
11	Josef Marha (C)	6-0/176	Havlickov Brod, Czech.	6-2-76	5	Chicago
X 19	Dean McAmmond (LW)	5-11/195	Grand Cache, Alta.	6-15-73	8	Chicago
	Jonas Nordqvist (C)	6-2/191	Leksand, Sweden	4-26-82	0	Leksand (Sweden Jr.), Leksand (Sweden)
92	Michael Nylander (C)	6-1/195	Stockholm, Sweden	10-3-72	7	Tampa Bay, Chicago
24	Bob Probert (LW)	6-3/225	Windsor, Ont.	6-5-65	15	Chicago
	Igor Radulov (LW)	6-0/176	U.S.S.R.	8-23-82	0	Yaroslavl (CIS)
26	Steve Sullivan (RW)	5-9/160	Timmins, Ont.	7-6-74	5	Toronto, Chicago
14	Ryan VandenBussche	6-0/200	Simcoe, Ont.	2-28-73	4	Chicago
	Pavel Vorobiev (RW)	6-0/183	Karaganda, U.S.S.R.	5-5-82	0	Torpedo Yaroslavl (Russian)
	Mikhail Yakubov (C)	6-3/185	Barnaul, U.S.S.R.	2-16-82	0	
26	Valeri Zelepukin (LW)	6-1/200	Voskresensk, U.S.S.R.	9-17-68	9	Philadelphia
13	Alexei Zhamnov (C)	6-1/200	Moscow, U.S.S.R.	10-1-70	8	Chicago
	DEFENSEMEN					
	Nolan Baumgartner	6-1/195	Calgary	3-23-76	4	Washington
33	Jamie Allison	6-1/195	Lindsay, Ont.	5-13-75	5	Chicago
	Scott Balan	6-2/194	Medicine Hat, Alta.	5-29-82	0	Regina (WHL)
	Alexander Barkunov	6-0/180	U.S.S.R.	5-13-81	0	Yaroslavl 2 (CIS.2)
3	Brad Brown	6-4/218	Baie Verte, Ont.	12-27-75	3	Chicago
6	Kevin Dean	6-3/210	Madison, Wis.	4-1-69	6	Atlanta, Dallas, Chicago
8	Anders Eriksson	6-2/220	Bollnas, Sweden	1-9-75	5	Chicago
	Olli Malmivaara	6-4/205	Kajaani, Finland	3-13-82	0	Jokerit Helsinki (Finland Jr.)
	Joey Martin	6-3/198	Fridley, Minn.	7-17-81	0	Omaha (USHL)
44	Bryan McCabe	6-1/210	Toronto	6-8-75	5	Chicago
	Steve McCarthy	6-0/197	Trail, B.C.	2-3-81	1	Chicago, Kootenay (WHL)
2	Boris Mironov	6-3/223	Moscow, U.S.S.R.	3-21-72	7	Chicago
	Jeff Paul	6-3/203	London, Ont.	3-1-78	0	Cleveland (IHL)
4	Doug Zmolek	6-2/220	Rochester, Minn.	11-3-70	8	Chicago
	GOALTENDERS					
	Michael Ayers	5-10/186	Weymouth, Mass.	1-16-80	0	Dubuque (USHL)
	Erasmo Saltarelli	5-11/185	Montreal	2-20-74	0	UHL (UHL), Springfield (AHL)
41	Jocelyn Thibault	5-11/170	Montreal	1-12-75	7	Chicago

1999-2000 REVIEW
INDIVIDUAL STATISTICS

SCORING

	Games	G	A	Pts.	PIM	+/-	PPG	SHG	Shots	Shooting Pct.
Tony Amonte	82	43	41	84	48	10	11	5	260	16.5
Steve Sullivan*	73	22	42	64	52	20	2	1	169	13.0
Alexei Zhamnov	71	23	37	60	61	7	5	0	175	13.1
Doug Gilmour*	63	22	34	56	51	-12	8	0	100	22.0
Michael Nylander*	66	23	28	51	26	9	4	0	112	20.5
Boris Mironov	58	9	28	37	72	-3	4	2	144	6.3
Eric Daze	59	23	13	36	28	-16	6	0	143	16.1
Dean McAmmond	76	14	18	32	72	11	1	0	118	11.9
Anders Eriksson	73	3	25	28	20	4	0	0	86	3.5
Bryan McCabe	79	6	19	25	139	-8	2	0	119	5.0
Sylvain Cote*	45	6	18	24	14	-4	5	0	78	7.7
Josef Marha	81	10	12	22	18	-10	2	1	91	11.0
Jean-Pierre Dumont	47	10	8	18	18	-6	0	0	86	11.6
Bob Probert	69	4	11	15	114	10	0	0	38	10.5
Blair Atcheynum	47	5	7	12	6	-8	0	0	48	10.4
Kevin Dean*	27	2	8	10	12	9	0	0	32	6.3
Doug Zmolek	43	2	7	9	60	6	0	0	24	8.3
Brad Brown	57	0	9	9	134	-1	0	0	15	0.0
Jean-Yves Leroux	54	3	5	8	43	-10	0	0	36	8.3
Dave Manson*	37	0	7	7	40	2	0	0	45	0.0

	Games	G	A	Pts.	PIM	+/-	PPG	SHG	Shots	Shooting Pct.
Michal Grosek*	14	2	4	6	12	-1	1	0	18	11.1
Mark Janssens	36	0	6	6	73	-2	0	0	14	0.0
Bryan Muir*	11	2	3	5	13	-1	0	1	19	10.5
Ed Olczyk	33	2	2	4	12	-8	0	0	33	6.1
Jamie Allison	59	1	3	4	102	-5	0	0	24	4.2
Radim Bicanek	11	0	3	3	4	7	0	0	8	0.0
Wendel Clark*	13	2	0	2	13	-2	0	0	27	7.4
Steve McCarthy	5	1	1	2	4	0	1	0	4	25.0
Kyle Calder	8	1	1	2	2	-3	0	0	5	20.0
Derek Plante*	17	1	1	2	2	-1	0	0	14	7.1
Ryan Vandenbussche	52	0	1	1	143	-3	0	0	19	0.0
Todd White*	1	0	0	0	0	0	0	0	0	0.0
Marc Lamothe (goalie)	2	0	0	0	0	0	0	0	0	0.0
Chris Herperger	9	0	0	0	5	-2	0	0	2	0.0
Steve Passmore (goalie)	24	0	0	0	9	0	0	0	0	0.0
Jocelyn Thibault (goalie)	60	0	0	0	2	0	0	0	0	0.0

GOALTENDING

	Games	Min.	Goals	SO	Avg.	W	L	T	ENG	Shots	Sv. Pct.
Steve Passmore	24	1388	63	1	2.72	7	12	3	4	654	.904
Jocelyn Thibault	60	3438	158	3	2.76	25	26	7	10	1679	.906
Marc Lamothe	2	116	10	0	5.17	1	1	0	0	50	.800

*Played with two or more NHL teams.

RESULTS

OCTOBER

4— At San Jose .... L 1-7
6— At Vancouver .... L 4-5
8— Phoenix .... T ... *3-3
10— Nashville .... T ... *3-3
15— Toronto .... L 1-2
16— At Pittsburgh .... T ... *3-3
21— Anaheim .... T ... *5-5
23— Detroit .... L 0-1
27— At Montreal .... W 1-0
29— At Detroit .... W 4-2
30— Los Angeles .... L 1-3

NOVEMBER

4— Buffalo .... L ... *4-5
5— At Nashville .... W 3-1
7— N.Y. Rangers .... L 1-3
10— Nashville .... L 2-4
12— N.Y. Islanders .... W 5-0
14— Edmonton .... L 3-6
16— At Los Angeles .... L 2-3
19— At Anaheim .... L 2-4
20— At Phoenix .... L 1-3
24— At Edmonton .... W 3-2
25— At Calgary .... L ... *1-2
27— At St. Louis .... L 3-8
30— At Ottawa .... L 1-2

DECEMBER

3— Detroit .... L 4-7
4— At Boston .... W 9-3
6— Edmonton .... W 5-1

9— New Jersey .... L 0-4
10— At Buffalo .... L 1-2
12— Calgary .... L 1-2
14— At San Jose .... W 5-2
17— At Anaheim .... L 0-2
18— At Los Angeles .... W 8-4
23— Dallas .... W 5-2
26— Pittsburgh .... L 2-4
27— At Washington .... T ... *2-2
30— Florida .... W 2-1
31— At Detroit .... T ... *4-4

JANUARY

2— San Jose .... L 1-4
6— Calgary .... W 5-2
8— At Nashville .... L 3-6
9— Colorado .... W 5-3
12— Vancouver .... W ... *3-2
13— At Detroit .... W 5-3
15— At Colorado .... L 1-3
17— San Jose .... W ... *5-4
19— At New Jersey .... L 1-4
21— St. Louis .... L 0-3
23— Dallas .... L 2-3
27— Colorado .... W 6-4
30— At Vancouver .... W 3-1

FEBRUARY

2— At Edmonton .... L 1-4
3— At Calgary .... T ... *5-5
12— At Atlanta .... W 4-3
14— Anaheim .... L 3-4

16— Los Angeles .... L 1-4
18— Washington .... L 4-5
20— Detroit .... W 6-4
22— At Philadelphia .... L 1-3
23— Nashville .... L 2-4
25— At Dallas .... W ... *4-3
27— At St. Louis .... W 4-1

MARCH

1— Montreal .... L 1-4
3— Tampa Bay .... W 5-1
5— Phoenix .... W 7-3
7— At Nashville .... L 1-3
8— At Carolina .... L 1-4
11— At Florida .... W 5-2
12— At Tampa Bay .... W 4-1
15— At Toronto .... W 5-2
16— Boston .... W ... *5-4
18— Dallas .... T ... *2-2
21— At Phoenix .... W 3-0
24— At Dallas .... L 1-5
26— St. Louis .... T ... *1-1
27— At Colorado .... L 1-3
30— Toronto .... W 4-0

APRIL

1— At N.Y. Islanders .... T ... *2-2
2— Vancouver .... L 2-3
5— Anaheim .... W 5-2
7— At St. Louis .... W ... *4-3
9— St. Louis .... W 3-1
*Denotes overtime game.

COLORADO AVALANCHE
WESTERN CONFERENCE/NORTHWEST DIVISION

COLORADO AVALANCHE

Colorado Schedule
Home games shaded; D—Day game; *—All-Star Game at Denver.

October
SUN	MON	TUE	WED	THU	FRI	SAT
1	2	3	4 DAL	5	6	7 EDM
8	9	10 CAL	11	12 VAN	13	14 CBJ
15	16	17 WAS	18 CBJ	19	20 FLA	21
22	23	24	25 NSH	26 CHI	27	28 EDM
29	30 PHO	31				

November
SUN	MON	TUE	WED	THU	FRI	SAT
			1 VAN	2	3 CAR	4
5	6	7 MIN	8	9 STL	10	11 ANA
12 PIT	13	14	15 ANA	16 PHO	17	18 LA D
19	20	21	22 CBJ	23	24	25 CAL
26	27	28	29 PHO	30		

December
SUN	MON	TUE	WED	THU	FRI	SAT
					1 DAL	2
3 NYR	4	5 NJ	6	7	8 TB	9 FLA
10 TB	11	12	13 PHI	14	15 DET	16
17	18	19 CAL	20	21 LA	22	23 VAN
24	25	26 NSH	27 EDM	28	29 NSH	30
31						

January
SUN	MON	TUE	WED	THU	FRI	SAT
	1	2 LA	3	4 SJ	5	6 CAR
7 DET	8	9	10 CBJ	11	12 MIN	13
14 CHI	15	16 NYI	17	18 VAN	19	20 SJ D
21 ANA	22	23	24	25	26 CHI	27 NSH
28	29	30 SJ	31			

February
SUN	MON	TUE	WED	THU	FRI	SAT
				1 VAN	2	3
4	*5	6	7 WAS	8	9 CAL	10 STL
11	12	13 MON	14	15 OTT	16	17 TOR
18	19 PIT	20	21 BOS	22	23 MIN	24
25 ATL	D 26	27	28			

March
SUN	MON	TUE	WED	THU	FRI	SAT
				1	2	3 BUF D
4 PHO	5	6 ATL	7	8 STL	9	10 DAL D
11 DAL	12	13 NJ	14	15	16	17 DET D
18 MIN	D 19	20 SJ	21	22 STL	23	24 BOS D
25	26	27	28 EDM	29 CAL	30	31 LA D

April
SUN	MON	TUE	WED	THU	FRI	SAT
1	2 EDM	3	4 ANA	5	6	7 DET D
8 MIN	D					

2000-2001 SEASON
CLUB DIRECTORY

Owner
E. Stanley Kroenke
President and general manager
Pierre Lacroix
V.p. and assistant general manager
Francois Giguere
Head coach
Bob Hartley
Assistant coaches
Jacques Cloutier
Bryan Trottier
Video coach
Paul Fixter
Vice president, player personnel
Michel Goulet
Director of hockey administration
Charlotte Grahame
Team services assistant
Ronnie Jameson
Consultant to the president
Dave Draper
Chief scout
Brian MacDonald
Pro scout
Brad Smith

Scouts
Yvon Gendron, Jim Hammett, Garth Joy, Steve Lyons, Don Paarup, Orval Tessier
Computer research consultant
John Donohue
Strength & conditioning coach
Paul Goldberg
Head athletic trainer
Pat Karns
Kinesiologist
Matt Sokolowski
Massage Therapist
Gregorio Pradera
Equipment managers
Wayne Flemming
Mark Miller
V.p., communications & team services
Jean Martineau
Dir. of special projects & new media
Hayne Ellis
Assistant director of media relations
Damen Zier

DRAFT CHOICES

Rd.— Player	Ht./Wt.	Overall	Pos.	Last team
1— Vaclav Nedorost	6-1/187	14	C	Budejovice, Czech Rep.
2— Jared Aulin	6-0/175	47	C	Kamloops (WHL)
2— Sergei Soin	6-0/176	50	C	Krylja Sovetov, Russia
2— Argis Saviels	6-1/192	63	D	Owen Sound (OHL)
3— Kurt Sauer	6-4/220	88	D	Spokane (WHL)
3— Sergei Kliazmine	6-3/194	92	LW	Tver, Russia
4— Brian Fahey	6-0/200	119	D	Wisconsin (WCHA)
5— John-Michael Liles	5-10/183	159	D	Michigan State (CCHA)
6— Chris Bahen	6-0/180	189	D	Clarkson (ECAC)
7— Aaron Molnar	6-1/165	221	G	London (OHL)
8— Darryl Bootland	6-2/183	252	RW	Toronto (OHL)
9— Sean Kotary	6-1/181	266	C	Northwood Prep, USHSE
9— Blake Ward	6-2/190	285	G	Tri-City (WHL)

MISCELLANEOUS DATA

Home ice (capacity)
Pepsi Center (18,007)
Address
1000 Chopper Cr.
Denver, CO 80204
Business phone
303-405-1100
Ticket information
303-405-1111
Website
www.coloradoavalanche.com

Training site
Denver
Club colors
Burgundy, steel blue, black, white and silver
Radio affiliation
KKFN (950 AM)
TV affiliation
FOX Sports Net (Cable)

TRAINING CAMP ROSTER

No.	FORWARDS	Ht./Wt.	Place	BORN Date	NHL exp.	1999-2000 clubs
	Jared Aulin (C)	5-11/175	Calgary	3-15-82	0	Kamloops (WHL)
	Yuri Babenko (C)	6-0/185	Penza, U.S.S.R.	1-2-78	0	Hershey (AHL)
18	Adam Deadmarsh (RW) LA	6-0/195	Trail, B.C.	5-10-75	6	Colorado
11	Chris Dingman (LW) CARD	6-4/245	Edmonton	7-6-76	3	Colorado
37	Chris Drury (C)	5-10/180	Trumbull, Conn.	8-20-76	2	Colorado
21	Peter Forsberg (C)	6-0/190	Ornskoldsvik, Sweden	7-20-73	6	Colorado
23	Milan Hejduk (RW)	5-11/185	Sstnad-Laberm, Czech.	2-14-76	2	Colorado
	Dan Hinote (RW)	6-0/190	Leesburg, Fla.	1-30-77	1	Colorado, Hershey (AHL)
	Sergei Kliazmine (LW) ...	6-3/194	Moscow, U.S.S.R.	3-1-82	0	Tver (Russian)
	Brad Larsen (LW)	6-0/210	Nakusp, B.C.	6-28-77	1	Hershey (AHL)
	Vaclav Nedorost (C)	6-1/187	Budejovice, Czechoslovakia	3-16-82	0	Budejovice (Czech Republic), Budejovice (Czech. Jrs.)
	Ville Nieminen (LW)	5-11/205	Tampere, Finland	4-6-77	1	Hershey (AHL), Colorado
27	Scott Parker (RW)	6-4/220	Hanford, Calif.	1-29-78	1	Hershey (AHL)
25	Shjon Podein (LW)	6-2/200	Eden Prairie, Minn.	3-5-68	8	Colorado
14	Dave Reid (LW)	6-1/217	Toronto	5-15-64	17	Colorado
19	Joe Sakic (C)	5-11/190	Burnaby, B.C.	7-7-69	12	Colorado
	Sergei Soin (C/LW)	6-0/176	Moscow, U.S.S.R.	3-31-82	0	Kryla Sov. Moscow (Russian)
40	Alex Tanguay (LW)	6-0/190	Ste.-Justine, Que.	11-21-79	1	Colorado
	Brian Willsie (RW)	6-0/190	London, Ont.	3-16-78	1	Hershey (AHL), Colorado
26	Stephane Yelle (C)	6-1/190	Ottawa	5-9-74	5	Colorado
	DEFENSEMEN					
	Chris Bahen	6-0/180	Montreal	11-16-80	0	Clarkson (ECAC)
77	Ray Bourque RET	5-11/215	Montreal	12-28-60	21	Boston, Colorado
7	Greg de Vries	6-3/215	Sundridge, Ont.	1-4-73	5	Colorado
	Brian Fahey	6-0/200	Des Plaines, Ill.	3-2-81	0	Univ. of Wisconsin (WCHA)
52	Adam Foote	6-1/202	Toronto	7-10-71	9	Colorado
5	Alexei Gusarov	6-3/185	Leningrad, U.S.S.R.	7-8-64	10	Colorado
24	Jon Klemm CHb	6-3/200	Cranbrook, B.C.	1-8-70	8	Colorado
	John-Michael Liles	5-9/183	Zionsville, Ind.	11-25-80	0	Michigan State (CCHA)
29	Eric Messier	6-2/200	Drummondville, Que.	10-29-73	4	Colorado
3	Aaron Miller LA	6-3/205	Buffalo	8-11-71	7	Colorado
4	Nolan Pratt TB	6-2/208	Fort McMurray, Alta.	8-14-75	4	Carolina
	Alexander Ryazantsev....	5-11/200	Moscow, U.S.S.R.	3-15-80	0	Victoriaville (QMJHL), Hershey (AHL)
	Kurt Sauer	6-3/220	St. Cloud, Minn.	1-16-81	0	Spokane (WHL)
	Argis Saviels	6-1/192	Riga, U.S.S.R.	1-15-82	0	Owen Sound (OHL)
55	Martin Skoula	6-3/218	Litvinov, Czechoslovakia	10-28-79	1	Colorado
43	Dan Smith	6-2/195	Fernie, B.C.	10-19-76	2	Hershey (AHL), Colorado
59	Brian White	6-1/180	Winchester, Mass.	2-7-76	1	Hershey (AHL)
	GOALTENDERS					
1	David Aebischer............	6-1/185	Fribourg, Switzerland	2-7-78	0	Hershey (AHL)
33	Patrick Roy	6-0/192	Quebec City	10-5-65	16	Colorado
	Philippe Sauve	6-0/175	Buffalo	2-27-80	0	Drummondville (QMJHL), Hull (QMJHL)

1999-2000 REVIEW
INDIVIDUAL STATISTICS

SCORING

	Games	G	A	Pts.	PIM	+/-	PPG	SHG	Shots	Shooting Pct.
Joe Sakic	60	28	53	81	28	30	5	1	242	11.6
Milan Hejduk	82	36	36	72	16	14	13	0	228	15.8
Chris Drury	82	20	47	67	42	8	7	0	213	9.4
Sandis Ozolinsh	82	16	36	52	46	17	6	0	210	7.6
Alex Tanguay	76	17	34	51	22	6	5	0	74	23.0
Peter Forsberg	49	14	37	51	52	9	3	0	105	13.3
Adam Deadmarsh LA	71	18	27	45	106	-10	5	0	153	11.8
Stephane Yelle	79	8	14	22	28	9	0	1	90	8.9
Shjon Podein	75	11	8	19	29	12	0	1	104	10.6
Dave Reid	65	11	7	18	28	12	0	0	86	12.8
Brian Rolston*	50	8	10	18	12	-6	1	0	107	7.5
Adam Foote	59	5	13	18	98	5	1	0	63	7.9
Martin Skoula	80	3	13	16	20	5	2	0	66	4.5
Ray Bourque*	14	8	6	14	6	9	7	0	43	18.6
Jon Klemm	73	5	7	12	34	26	0	0	64	7.8
Chris Dingman CAROLINA	68	8	3	11	132	-2	2	0	54	14.8
Claude Lemieux*	13	3	6	9	4	0	0	0	36	8.3
Eric Messier	61	3	6	9	24	0	1	0	28	10.7
Greg de Vries	69	2	7	9	73	-7	0	0	40	5.0

	Games	G	A	Pts.	PIM	+/-	PPG	SHG	Shots	Shooting Pct.
Aaron Miller .... LA	53	1	7	8	36	3	0	0	44	2.3
Alexei Gusarov	34	2	2	4	10	-8	0	0	16	12.5
Dan Hinote	27	1	3	4	10	0	0	0	14	7.1
Serge Aubin	15	2	1	3	6	1	0	0	14	14.3
Dave Andreychuk*	14	1	2	3	2	-9	1	0	41	2.4
Jeff Odgers	62	1	2	3	162	-7	0	0	29	3.4
Patrick Roy (goalie)	63	0	3	3	10	0	0	0	1	0.0
Marc Denis (goalie)	23	0	2	2	6	0	0	0	0	0.0
Shean Donovan*	18	1	0	1	8	-4	0	0	13	7.7
Christian Matte	5	0	1	1	4	-2	0	0	1	0.0
Ville Nieminen	1	0	0	0	0	0	0	0	2	0.0
Brian Willsie	1	0	0	0	0	0	0	0	1	0.0
Rick Tabaracci (goalie)*	2	0	0	0	0	0	0	0	0	0.0
Dan Smith	3	0	0	0	0	2	0	0	0	0.0
Sami Helenius	33	0	0	0	46	-5	0	0	6	0.0

GOALTENDING

	Games	Min.	Goals	SO	Avg.	W	L	T	ENG	Shots	Sv. Pct.
Rick Tabaracci*	2	60	2	0	2.00	1	0	0	0	18	.889
Patrick Roy	63	3704	141	2	2.28	32	21	8	5	1640	.914
Marc Denis	23	1203	51	3	2.54	9	8	3	2	618	.917

*Played with two or more NHL teams.

RESULTS

OCTOBER

5— At Nashville ....W.....3-2
6— At Toronto ....L.....1-2
8— At Pittsburgh ....T....*3-3
10— At N.Y. Islanders.............L.....2-4
11— At Boston.....................T....*3-3
13— Boston........................W.....2-1
16— Ottawa........................W.....3-1
20— At Montreal ....W.....2-1
21— At Ottawa ....L.....1-4
23— At Atlanta ....W....*3-2
27— At Detroit ....L.....3-5
28— At Philadelphia...............L....*4-5
30— Phoenix.......................L.....3-5

NOVEMBER

3— St. Louis.......................W.....5-0
5— N.Y. Rangers ....W.....4-1
11— At Los Angeles ....L.....2-5
13— At Calgary ....W.....5-2
15— At Vancouver ....T....*2-2
17— Florida........................L.....1-2
19— N.Y. Islanders ....L.....2-3
22— At Dallas......................W....*3-2
23— Los Angeles..................L.....2-6
26— At Phoenix....................L.....0-7
27— Calgary.......................W.....7-1
30— At Vancouver.................W.....4-2

DECEMBER

1— At Edmonton ....L.....1-3
4— Carolina.......................W.....3-1
6— Vancouver ....W.....5-2
8— At San Jose ....L.....2-4
10— At Anaheim ....W.....2-1
12— At Vancouver ....W....*3-2
15— Anaheim......................L.....2-4
17— At Detroit ....L.....2-5
18— At Nashville ....T....*2-2
20— At Carolina ....W.....4-2
23— At Buffalo.....................L.....1-2
27— St. Louis ....W.....5-1
29— Los Angeles ....W.....4-2

JANUARY

3— Edmonton.....................T....*2-2
5— Calgary........................W.....4-0
7— Montreal......................W.....4-1
9— At Chicago ....L.....3-5
11—Nashville......................W.....4-2
13—Pittsburgh.....................W.....4-3
15—Chicago ....W.....3-1
17—Phoenix ....W.....2-0
19—San Jose......................T....*0-0
21—At Anaheim ....T....*3-3
23—At Los Angeles ....L.....2-3
25—At San Jose ....W.....4-3
27—At Chicago ....L.....4-6
29—At St. Louis...................L.....0-4

FEBRUARY

1— Vancouver ....W.....2-1
3— San Jose ....T....*3-3
8— Buffalo.........................L.....0-2

10— Calgary.......................W.....3-2
13— Detroit ....L.....3-4
15— At Washington...............L.....1-2
17— At New Jersey ....T....*5-5
18— At N.Y. Rangers ....W.....4-2
20— Dallas.........................L.....1-2
22— Atlanta ....L.....3-4
25— At St. Louis...................L.....2-4
27— At Dallas......................T....*1-1
29— Edmonton....................L.....1-3

MARCH

2— New Jersey....................W.....5-0
4— Tampa Bay ....W.....4-1
7— At Calgary ....W.....8-3
10— At Edmonton ....W.....4-2
12— Philadelphia..................W.....3-1
14— Anaheim......................W.....4-2
16— Nashville ....T....*2-2
18— Detroit ....L.....3-4
20— Vancouver....................L.....2-3
23— At Phoenix ....W.....*2-1
26— At Dallas ....W....*2-1
27— Chicago ....W.....3-1
29— Edmonton....................W.....3-2

APRIL

2— Dallas..........................W....*3-2
5— At Edmonton ....W.....3-2
7— At Calgary ....W.....3-1
9— Detroit ....W.....3-2

*Denotes overtime game.

COLUMBUS BLUE JACKETS
WESTERN CONFERENCE/CENTRAL DIVISION

Columbus Schedule

Home games shaded; D—Day game; *—All-Star Game at Denver.

October

SUN	MON	TUE	WED	THU	FRI	SAT
1	2	3	4	5	6	7 CHI
8	9 LA	10	11	12 CAL	13	14 COL
15 CHI	16	17	18 COL	19	20	21 PIT
22 DET	23	24	25 SJ	26	27 WAS	28 DET
29	30	31 LA				

November

SUN	MON	TUE	WED	THU	FRI	SAT
			1 DAL	2	3	4 OTT
5 EDM	6	7	8	9 SJ	10	11 PHO
12	13	14 DAL	15	16 NSH	17 FLA	18
19 VAN	20	21	22 COL	23	24 DAL	25 DAL
26	27	28	29 PHI	30		

December

SUN	MON	TUE	WED	THU	FRI	SAT
					1	2 ATL
3 CHI	4	5	6 ANA	7	8 BOS	9
10 PHO	11	12	13 ANA	14 ANA	15	16 VAN
17	18 MON	19	20	21 OTT	22	23 NYI
24	25	26 STL	27 NJ	28	29 CAR	30
31 NJ						

January

SUN	MON	TUE	WED	THU	FRI	SAT
	1	2	3 EDM	4	5	6 VAN
7 EDM	8	9	10 COL	11	12 CHI	13
14 MIN	15 MIN	16	17 MIN	18	19	20
21 TB	22	23 BUF	24	25	26	27 ANA
28	29	30	31 DET			

February

SUN	MON	TUE	WED	THU	FRI	SAT
				1 STL	2	3
4	*5	6 STL	7	8 NSH	9	10 NSH
11 NYR	12 NYR	13	14 TOR	15	16 DET	17 PIT
18	19	20 SJ	21 PHO	22	23	24 LA D
25 ANA	26	27	28 PHO			

March

SUN	MON	TUE	WED	THU	FRI	SAT
			1 NSH	2	3	
4	5	6	7 CAR	8	9 FLA	10 TB
11	12	13	14 CAL	15	16 ATL	17 NYI
18 NSH	19 NSH	20	21 VAN	22	23	24 CAL D
25	26 EDM	27 CAL	28	29 LA	30	31

April

SUN	MON	TUE	WED	THU	FRI	SAT
1 STL	2	3 DET	4	5 STL	6 MIN	7
8 CHI	D					

2000-2001 SEASON
CLUB DIRECTORY

Owner/governor
John H. McConnell
Alternate governor
John P. McConnell
President/g.m./alternate governor
Doug MacLean
Assistant general manager
Jim Clark
Head coach
Dave King
Associate coach
Newell Brown
Assistant coach
To be announced
Director of amateur scouting
Don Boyd

Hockey operations coordinator
Chris MacFarland
Strength and conditioning coach
To be announced
Athletic trainer
To be announced
Equipment manager
Tim LeRoy
Assistant equipment manager
Jamie Healy
Director of communications
Todd Sharrock
Assistant director of communications
Dan Jones
Manager, multimedia and publications
Gary Kohn

DRAFT CHOICES

Rd.— Player	Ht./Wt.	Overall	Pos.	Last team
1— Rostislav Klesla	6-2/198	4	D	Brampton (OHL)
3— Ben Knopp	6-1/185	69	RW	Moose Jaw (WHL)
5— Petteri Nummelin	5-10/183	133	D	Davos, Switzerland
5— Scott Heffernan	6-5/187	138	D	Sarnia (OHL)
5— Tyler Kolarik	5-10/190	150	C	Deerfield, USHSE
6— Shane Bendera	5-11/170	169	G	Red Deer (WHL)
7— Janne Jokila	5-9/169	200	LW	TPS Jr., Finland
8— Peter Zingoni	5-11/180	231	C	New England, EJHL
9— Martin Paroulek		278	F	Slovnaft Vsetin, Czech
9— Andrej Nedorost	6-0/187	286	C	Trencin, Slovakia
9— Louis Mandeville	6-2/193	292	D	R.-Noranda (QMJHL)

MISCELLANEOUS DATA

Home ice (capacity)
Nationwide Arena (18,524)
Office address
Nationwide Arena
200 W. Nationwide Blvd.
Columbus, OH 43215
Business phone
614-246-4625
Ticket information
1-800-645-2657

Website
www.bluejackets.com
Training site
Columbus
Club colors
Red, white, blue and lime green
Radio affiliation
WBNS (1460 AM), WWCD (101.1 FM)
TV affiliation
Fox Sports Ohio

COLUMBUS BLUE JACKETS

No.	FORWARDS	Ht./Wt.	Place (BORN)	Date (BORN)	NHL exp.	1999-2000 clubs
42	Kevyn Adams (C)	6-1/195	Washington, D.C.	10-8-74	3	St. John's (AHL), Toronto
49	Serge Aubin (C)	6-0/190	Val d'Or, Que.	2-15-75	2	Hershey (AHL), Colorado
	Blake Bellefeuille (C)	5-10/208	Framingham, Mass.	12-27-77	0	Boston College (Hockey East)
	Jan Caloun (RW)	5-10/190	Usti-nad-Labem, Czech.	12-20-72	2	HIFK Helsinki (Finland)
	Mathieu Darche (LW)	6-1/225	St. Laurent, Que.	11-26-76	0	McGill University (CIAU)
49	Matt Davidson (RW)	6-2/190	Flin Flon, Man.	8-9-77	0	Rochester (AHL)
19	Kevin Dineen (RW)	5-11/189	Quebec City	10-28-63	16	Ottawa
17	Ted Drury (C/LW)	6-0/204	Boston	9-13-71	7	Anaheim, New York Islanders
25	Bruce Gardiner (C)	6-1/193	North York, Ont.	2-11-72	4	Ottawa, Tampa Bay
23	Steve Heinze (RW)	5-11/193	Lawrence, Mass.	1-30-70	9	Boston
	Ben Knopp (RW)	6-0/185	Calgary	4-8-82	0	Moose Jaw (WHL)
21	Espen Knutsen (C)	5-11/180	Oslo, Norway	1-12-72	1	Djurgarden Stockholm (Sweden)
	Tyler Kolarik (C)	5-10/190	Philadelphia	1-26-81	0	Deerfield Academy (USHS (East))
18	Robert Kron (C)	5-11/182	Brno, Czechoslovakia	2-27-67	10	Carolina
	Sergei Luchinkin (RW)	5-11/172	Dmitrov, U.S.S.R.	10-16-76	1	
	Brad Moran (C)	5-11/180	Abbotsford, B.C.	3-20-79	0	Calgary (WHL)
	Chris Nielsen (RW)	6-1/190	Moshi, Tanzania	2-16-80	0	Calgary (WHL)
29	Krzysztof Oliwa (RW)	6-5/235	Tychy, Poland	4-12-73	4	New Jersey
8	Geoff Sanderson (LW)	6-0/190	Hay River, Northwest Ter.	2-1-72	10	Buffalo
15	Reggie Savage (RW)	5-10/197	Montreal	5-1-70	3	Syracuse (AHL)
	Jonathan Schill (LW)	6-1/201	Kitchener, Ont.	6-28-79	0	Kingston (OHL)
	Martin Spanhel (LW)	6-2/202	Gottwaldov, Czechoslovakia	7-1-77	0	HC Keramika Plzen (Czech Republic)
	David Vyborny (C)	5-10/183	Jihlava, Czechoslovakia	1-22-75	0	Sparta Praha (Czech Republic)
	Jeff Williams (LW)	6-1/200	Pointe-Claire, Que.	2-11-76	0	Orlando (IHL), Albany (AHL)
29	Tyler Wright (C)	5-11/187	Canora, Sask.	4-6-73	8	Wilkes-Barre/Scranton (AHL), Pittsburgh

DEFENSEMEN

No.	DEFENSEMEN	Ht./Wt.	Place	Date	NHL exp.	1999-2000 clubs
	Jonas Andersson-Junkka	6-2/165	Kiruna, Sweden	5-4-75	0	HPK Hameenlinna (Finland)
32	Radim Bicanek	6-1/195	Uherske Hradiste, Czech.	1-18-75	5	Cleveland (IHL), Chicago
34	Jean-Luc Grand-Pierre	6-3/207	Montreal	2-2-77	2	Buffalo, Rochester (AHL)
	Scott Heffernan	6-5/187	Montreal	3-9-82	0	Sarnia (OHL)
6	Jamie Heward	6-2/207	Regina, Sask.	3-30-71	4	New York Islanders
	Rostislav Klesla	6-2/198	Novy Jicin, Czechoslovakia	3-21-82	0	Brampton (OHL)
	Petteri Nummelin	5-10/183	Turku, Finland	11-25-72	0	Davos (Switzerland)
4	Lyle Odelein	6-0/210	Quill Lake, Sask.	7-21-68	11	New Jersey, Phoenix
4	Jamie Pushor	6-3/220	Lethbridge, Alta.	2-11-73	5	Dallas
5	Deron Quint	6-2/209	Durham, N.H.	3-12-76	5	Phoenix, New Jersey
	Tommi Rajamaki	6-2/180	Pori, Finland	2-29-76	0	TPS Turku (Finland)
14	Bert Robertsson	6-3/210	Sodertalje, Sweden	6-30-74	3	Hamilton (AHL), Edmonton
37	Mattias Timander	6-3/215	Solleftea, Sweden	4-16-74	4	Boston, Hershey (AHL)
	Dan Watson	6-2/221	Glencoe, Ont.	10-5-79	0	Sarnia (OHL)

GOALTENDERS

No.	GOALTENDERS	Ht./Wt.	Place	Date	NHL exp.	1999-2000 clubs
	Shane Bendera	5-10/170	St. Albert, Alta.	7-13-82	0	Red Deer (WHL)
39	Frederic Chabot	5-11/187	Hebertville, Que.	2-12-68	5	Houston (IHL)
30	Marc Denis	6-0/190	Montreal	8-1-77	3	Colorado
	Greg Gardner	6-0/190	Mississauga, Ont.	11-21-75	0	Niagara (Indep.)
31	Ron Tugnutt	5-11/160	Scarborough, Ont.	10-22-67	12	Ottawa, Pittsburgh

RW 29 ALEX SELIANUV
RW 15 MIKE MANELUK

DALLAS STARS
WESTERN CONFERENCE/PACIFIC DIVISION

Dallas Schedule

Home games shaded; D—Day game; *—All-Star Game at Denver.

October

SUN	MON	TUE	WED	THU	FRI	SAT
1	2	3	4 COL	5	6	7 OTT
8	9 TOR	10 CAR	11	12 PHI	13	14 WAS
15	16	17	18 SJ	19	20 CHI	21 LA
22	23	24	25 VAN	26	27 PHO	28 STL
29	30	31				

November

SUN	MON	TUE	WED	THU	FRI	SAT
			1 CBJ	2	3 PHO	4
5	6	7	8	9	10	11 MON
12	13	14 CBJ	15 BUF	16	17 DET	18
19	20 TB	21	22 NSH	23	24 CBJ	25 CBJ
26	27	28	29 CAL	30		

December

SUN	MON	TUE	WED	THU	FRI	SAT
					1 COL	2 PHO
3	4	5	6 SJ	7 LA	8	9
10 ANA	11	12	13 EDM	14	15 CHI	16
17 D MIN	18	19	20 NJ	21 NYI	22	23 PIT
24	25	26	27 ANA	28	29 LA	30
31 NYR						

January

SUN	MON	TUE	WED	THU	FRI	SAT
	1	2	3	4 DET	5	6 BOS
7	8 NYR	9	10 ATL	11	12 DET	13
14 TB	15 FLA	16	17 NSH	18	19 PIT	20
21 PHO	22 VAN	23	24 NJ	25	26 SJ	27
28	29	30 LA	31			

February

SUN	MON	TUE	WED	THU	FRI	SAT
				1 SJ	2	3
4	*5	6	7 EDM	8	9 MIN	10
11 STL	12	13 NSH	14 LA	15	16 ANA	17
18 DET	19	20	21 MIN	22	23 BOS	24
25 EDM	26 CAL	27	28 VAN			

March

SUN	MON	TUE	WED	THU	FRI	SAT
				1	2 ANA	3
4 D BUF	5	6	7 CHI	8	9	10 D COL
11 COL	12	13 CHI	14	15	16 PHO	17
18 D OTT	19 MIN	20	21 ANA	22	23 NYI	24
25 STL	26	27	28 VAN	29	30 EDM	31 CAL

April

SUN	MON	TUE	WED	THU	FRI	SAT
1	2 CAL	3	4 NSH	5	6	7 D SJ
8						

2000-2001 SEASON
CLUB DIRECTORY

Owner and governor
Thomas O. Hicks

President and alternate governor
James R. Lites

General manager
Bob Gainey

Assistant general manager
Doug Armstrong

Director of hockey operations
Les Jackson

Director of hockey administration
Dan Stuchal

Director of team travel
Brian Poile

Chief amateur scout
Tim Bernhardt

Head coach
Ken Hitchcock

Assistant coaches
Doug Jarvis
Rick Wilson

Strength and conditioning coach
J.J. McQueen

Coaching assistant/video coordinator
Leon Friedrich

Head athletic trainer
Dave Surprenant

Head equipment manager
Dave Smith

Equipment manager
Rich Matthews

Equipment assistant
Mike Wroblewski

Director of media relations
Larry Kelly

Media relations assistant
Mark Janko

DRAFT CHOICES

Rd.— Player	Ht./Wt.	Overall	Pos.	Last team
1— Steve Ott	6-0/160	25	C	Windsor (OHL)
2— Dan Ellis	6-0/180	60	G	Omaha, USHL
3— Joel Lundqvist	6-0/183	68	C	Frolunda, Sweden
3— Alexei Tereschenko	5-11/176	91	C	Dynamo, Russia
4— Vadim Khomitski	6-1/185	123	D	HC Moscow, Russia
5— Ruslan Bernikov	6-3/198	139	RW	Amur Khabarovsk, Rus.
5— Artem Chernov	5-10/176	162	C	Novokuznetsk, Russia
6— Ladislav Vlcek	5-11/172	192	F	Kladno Jr., Czech Rep.
7— Marco Tuokko	5-11/172	219	C	TPS Jr., Finland
7— Antti Miettinen	5-11/176	224	C	Hameenlinna, Finland

MISCELLANEOUS DATA

Home ice (capacity)
Reunion Arena (17,001)

Address
211 Cowboys Parkway
Irving, TX 75063

Business phone
972-831-2401

Ticket information
214-467-8277

Website
www.dallasstars.com

Training site
Vail, CO & Irving, TX

Club colors
Green, black, gold and white

Radio affiliation
WBAP (820 AM)

TV affiliation
FOX Sports Southwest (Cable), KDFI
(Channel 27), KDFW (Channel 4)

DALLAS STARS

No.	FORWARDS	Ht./Wt.	Place	BORN Date	NHL exp.	1999-2000 clubs
	Ruslan Bernikov (RW)...	6-3/198	U.S.S.R.	12-4-77	0	SKA-Amur Khabarovsk (Russian)
	Tyler Bouck (RW)	6-0/185	Camrose, Alta.	1-13-80	0	Prince George (WHL)
	Artem Chernov (C)	5-10/176	Novokuznetsk, U.S.S.R.	4-28-82	0	Metallurg Novokuznetsk (Russian)
	Ryan Christie (LW)	6-3/200	Beamsville, Ont.	7-3-78	1	Michigan (IHL), Dallas
	Steve Gainey (LW)	6-0/180	Montreal	1-26-79	0	Michigan (IHL), Fort Wayne (UHL)
16	Brett Hull (RW).............	5-11/203	Belleville, Ont.	8-9-64	15	Dallas
	Niko Kapanen (C)	5-9/180	Hameenlinna, Finland	4-29-78	0	HPK Hameenlinna (Finland)
12	Mike Keane (RW)	6-0/185	Winnipeg	5-29-67	12	Dallas
	Marcus Kristofferson (C)	6-3/200	Ostersund, Sweden	1-22-79	0	HV 71 Jonkoping (Sweden), Blues Espoo (Finland)
15	Jamie Langenbrunner....	6-1/200	Duluth, Minn.	7-24-75	6	Dallas
	Greg Leeb (C)	5-9/160	Red Deer, Alta.	5-31-77	0	Michigan (IHL)
26	Jere Lehtinen (LW)	6-0/192	Espoo, Finland	6-24-73	5	Dallas
48	Warren Luhning (RW) ...	6-2/205	Edmonton	7-3-75	3	Dallas, Michigan (IHL)
	Joel Lundqvist (C)	6-0/183	Are, Sweden	3-2-82	0	V. Frolunda Goteborg (Sweden Jr.)
36	Roman Lyashenko (C)...	6-0/188	Murmansk, U.S.S.R.	5-2-79	1	Michigan (IHL), Dallas
29	Grant Marshall (RW)	6-1/193	Mississauga, Ont.	6-9-73	6	Dallas
9	Mike Modano (C)..........	6-3/205	Livonia, Mich.	6-7-70	12	Dallas
45	Brenden Morrow (LW)...	5-11/200	Carlisle, Sask.	1-16-79	1	Michigan (IHL), Dallas
22	Kirk Muller (C)...............	6-0/205	Kingston, Ont.	2-8-66	16	Dallas
15	Chris Murray (RW)	6-2/209	Port Hardy, B.C.	10-25-74	6	Dallas, Michigan (IHL)
25	Joe Nieuwendyk (C)	6-1/205	Oshawa, Ont.	9-10-66	14	Dallas
	Steve Ott (C/LW)...........	5-11/160	Stoney Point, Ont.	8-19-82	0	Windsor (OHL)
49	Jon Sim (LW)	5-10/184	New Glasgow, Nova Scotia	9-29-77	2	Michigan (IHL), Dallas
11	Blake Sloan (RW)	5-10/196	Park Ridge, Ill.	7-27-75	2	Dallas
	Alexei Tereschenko (C)..	5-11/176	Moznajsk, U.S.S.R.	12-16-80	0	Dynamo Moscow (Russian)
	Mathias Tjarnqvist (C) ..	6-1/183	Umea, Sweden	4-15-79	0	Djurgarden Stockholm (Sweden)
22	Shaun Van Allen (C)	6-1/204	Calgary	8-29-67	9	Ottawa
	Ladislav Vlcek (LW/RW) .	5-11/172	Czechoslovakia	9-26-81	0	Kladno (Czech. Jrs.)
46	Jamie Wright (LW)	6-0/195	Kitchener, Ont.	5-13-76	3	Michigan (IHL), Dallas
	DEFENSEMEN					
	Keith Aldridge...............	5-11/185	Detroit	7-20-73	1	Michigan (IHL), Dallas
18	Joel Bouchard...............	6-0/200	Montreal	1-23-74	6	Nashville, Dallas
2	Derian Hatcher.............	6-5/230	Sterling Heights, Mich.	6-4-72	9	Dallas
44	Sami Helenius...............	6-5/225	Helsinki, Finland	1-22-74	3	Colorado, Hershey (AHL)
	Richard Jackman 805..	6-2/192	Toronto	6-28-78	1	Michigan (IHL), Dallas
	Vadim Khomitski	6-1/185	Voskresensk, U.S.S.R.	7-21-82	0	HC CSKA Moscow (Russian)
	Alan Letang	6-0/205	Renfrew, Ont.	9-4-75	1	Dallas, Michigan (IHL)
37	Brad Lukowich...	6-1/200	Cranbrook, B.C.	8-12-76	3	Dallas
24	Richard Matvichuk	6-2/215	Edmonton	2-5-73	8	Dallas
5	Darryl Sydor	6-1/205	Edmonton	5-13-72	9	Dallas
	Evgueni Tsybuk.............	6-0/196	Chebarkul, U.S.S.R.	2-2-78	0	Michigan (IHL), Fort Wayne (UHL)
56	Sergei Zubov	6-1/200	Moscow, U.S.S.R.	7-22-70	8	Dallas
	GOALTENDERS					
30	Mike Bales	6-1/200	Prince Albert, Sask.	8-6-71	4	Michigan (IHL)
20	Ed Belfour....................	5-11/192	Carman, Man.	4-21-65	12	Dallas
	Dan Ellis	6-0/180	Saskatoon, Sask.	6-19-80	0	Omaha (USHL)
31	Rick Tabaracci	5-11/181	Toronto	1-2-69	11	Atlanta, Orlando (IHL), Colorado, Cleveland (IHL), Utah (IHL)
	Marty Turco	5-11/183	Sault Ste. Marie, Ont.	8-13-75	0	Michigan (IHL)

1999-2000 REVIEW
INDIVIDUAL STATISTICS

SCORING

	Games	G	A	Pts.	PIM	+/-	PPG	SHG	Shots	Shooting Pct.
Mike Modano..	77	38	43	81	48	0	11	1	188	20.2
Brett Hull	79	24	35	59	43	-21	11	0	223	10.8
Sergei Zubov..	77	9	33	42	18	-2	3	1	179	5.0
Jamie Langenbrunner......................................	65	18	21	39	68	16	4	2	153	11.8
Joe Nieuwendyk...	48	15	19	34	26	-1	7	0	110	13.6
Mike Keane..	81	13	21	34	41	9	0	4	85	15.3
Darryl Sydor..	74	8	26	34	32	6	5	0	132	6.1
Brenden Morrow...	64	14	19	33	81	8	3	0	113	12.4
Richard Matvichuk..	70	4	21	25	42	7	0	0	73	5.5
Derian Hatcher...	57	2	22	24	68	6	0	0	90	2.2
Kirk Muller..	47	7	15	22	24	-3	3	0	57	12.3
Blake Sloan...	67	4	13	17	50	11	0	0	78	5.1
Guy Carbonneau...	69	10	6	16	36	10	0	1	70	14.3

	Games	G	A	Pts.	PIM	+/-	PPG	SHG	Shots	Shooting Pct.
Aaron Gavey	41	7	6	13	44	0	1	0	39	17.9
Roman Lyashenko	58	6	6	12	10	-2	0	0	51	11.8
Sylvain Cote*	28	2	8	10	14	6	0	0	47	4.3
Scott Thornton*	30	6	3	9	38	-5	1	0	47	12.8
Jonathan Sim	25	5	3	8	10	4	2	0	44	11.4
Jere Lehtinen	17	3	5	8	0	1	0	0	29	10.3
Grant Marshall	45	2	6	8	38	-5	1	0	43	4.7
Jamie Pushor	62	0	8	8	53	0	0	0	27	0.0
Juha Lind*	34	3	4	7	6	-1	0	0	36	8.3
Pavel Patera	12	1	4	5	4	-1	0	0	18	5.6
Jamie Wright	23	1	4	5	16	4	0	0	15	6.7
Brad Lukowich	60	3	1	4	50	-14	0	0	33	9.1
Chris Murray	32	2	1	3	62	-7	0	0	25	8.0
Richard Jackman	22	1	2	3	6	-1	1	0	16	6.3
Brian Skrudland	22	1	2	3	22	0	0	0	16	6.3
Dave Manson*	26	1	2	3	22	10	0	0	21	4.8
Ed Belfour (goalie)	62	0	3	3	10	0	0	0	0	0.0
Derek Plante*	16	1	1	2	2	-4	1	0	17	5.9
Manny Fernandez (goalie)	24	0	2	2	2	0	0	0	0	0.0
Warren Luhning	10	0	1	1	13	-2	0	0	7	0.0
Joel Bouchard*	2	0	0	0	2	1	0	0	1	0.0
Keith Aldridge	4	0	0	0	0	1	0	0	6	0.0
Shawn Chambers	4	0	0	0	4	-2	0	0	2	0.0
Ryan Christie	5	0	0	0	0	-1	0	0	1	0.0
Alan Letang	8	0	0	0	2	-5	0	0	1	0.0
Kevin Dean*	14	0	0	0	10	-1	0	0	6	0.0

GOALTENDING

	Games	Min.	Goals	SO	Avg.	W	L	T	ENG	Shots	Sv. Pct.
Ed Belfour	62	3620	127	4	2.10	32	21	7	6	1571	.919
Manny Fernandez	24	1353	48	1	2.13	11	8	3	3	603	.920

*Played with two or more NHL teams.

RESULTS

OCTOBER
1— Pittsburgh ....W.....6-4
2— Anaheim........................W.....2-0
5— At Detroit......................W.....3-2
8— At Anaheim....................L.....0-3
9— At San Jose...................W.....3-2
13—San Jose........................L.....0-2
15—Boston...........................T....*2-2
16—At Nashville....................L.....2-3
20—Edmonton......................W.....2-1
22—New Jersey....................W...*2-1
25—At Toronto......................L.....0-4
30—Tampa Bay.....................L.....1-2

NOVEMBER
3— Buffalo............................L.....1-3
5— At Phoenix......................W.....6-4
6— At San Jose....................L.....1-2
9— At St. Louis.....................W.....5-2
10—Detroit...........................L.....2-4
17—At Washington................T....*2-2
18—At Philadelphia...............T....*1-1
20—At Carolina.....................L.....0-1
22—Colorado........................L....*2-3
24—Los Angeles ....W...*3-2
26—Anaheim........................L.....2-4
28—At Atlanta.......................W.....4-2
30—At N.Y. Islanders............W.....2-1

DECEMBER
1— At Montreal ....W.....3-2
4— At Ottawa ....W.....3-1

6— Phoenix ....L.....2-3
8— Carolina..........................W.....2-1
10—Florida............................W.....4-3
11—At St. Louis.....................L.....2-4
15—Calgary...........................W.....5-1
17—At Edmonton ....T....*2-2
18—At Vancouver..................W.....4-2
21—At Calgary ....T....*0-0
23—At Chicago......................L.....2-5
27—San Jose.........................L.....1-3
29—N.Y. Rangers ....W...*4-3
31—Anaheim.........................W.....5-4

JANUARY
3— Los Angeles ....W.....4-1
5— Nashville.........................W.....3-1
7— Vancouver ....L.....1-3
11—At Edmonton ....W.....3-2
12—At Calgary.......................L....*1-2
15—At Vancouver..................W.....2-1
19—At Anaheim.....................L.....1-3
20—At Los Angeles ....W.....5-2
23—At Chicago......................W.....3-2
26—Los Angeles ....W.....3-1
28—St. Louis.........................L.....1-3
31—Edmonton.......................W.....2-1

FEBRUARY
2— Atlanta.............................W.....2-1
3— At Phoenix.......................W.....2-0
9— At Anaheim......................W.....5-3
11—At Los Angeles ....L.....2-3

13—Washington ....W.....2-1
16—Nashville..........................W.....3-0
18—Phoenix ....L.....3-4
20—At Colorado......................W.....2-1
21—At Nashville......................L.....2-5
23—At Detroit..........................W.....5-2
25—Chicago ....L...*3-4
27—Colorado...........................T...*1-1

MARCH
1— Philadelphia.....................W.....2-0
3— At Phoenix.......................W.....4-1
5— Detroit..............................L.....3-5
8— Vancouver ....T....*3-3
10—N.Y. Islanders ....L...*3-4
12—St. Louis..........................W.....4-2
13—At N.Y. Rangers ....W.....4-3
15—At New Jersey ....W.....3-2
18—At Chicago.......................T...*2-2
19—San Jose..........................W.....5-3
24—Chicago ....W.....5-1
26—Colorado...........................L...*1-2
28—At Tampa Bay...................W.....4-2
29—At Florida..........................W.....4-1

APRIL
2— At Colorado ....L...*2-3
3— Calgary ....T...*2-2
5— At San Jose......................L.....2-5
7— At Los Angeles ....L.....2-3
9— Phoenix ....T...*2-2
*Denotes overtime game.

DETROIT RED WINGS
WESTERN CONFERENCE/CENTRAL DIVISION

Detroit Schedule
Home games shaded; D—Day game; *—All-Star Game at Denver.

October

SUN	MON	TUE	WED	THU	FRI	SAT
1	2	3	4	5 CAL	6 EDM	7
8	9	10	11 EDM	12 CHI	13	14
15 CAL	16	17 STL	18	19 NSH	20	21 BUF
22 CBJ	23	24	25 TB	26	27	28 CBJ
29	30	31 WAS				

November

SUN	MON	TUE	WED	THU	FRI	SAT
			1 MON	2	3 CHI	4
5	6	7	8 PHO	9	10	11 LA
12 ANA	13	14	15 SJ	16	17 DAL	18 NSH
19	20 NSH	21	22 BOS	23	24 VAN	25 NYI
26	27 CHI	28	29 ATL	30		

December

SUN	MON	TUE	WED	THU	FRI	SAT
					1 FLA	2 TB
3	4	5	6 TOR	7	8 PHI	9
10 PIT	11	12	13 FLA	14	15 COL	16 STL
17	18 EDM	19	20 SJ	21	22 ANA	23 BOS
24	25	26	27 MIN	28	29 CHI	30
31 LA						

January

SUN	MON	TUE	WED	THU	FRI	SAT
	1	2	3	4 DAL	5 MIN	6
7 COL	8	9 PHO	10	11	12 DAL	13
14 SJ	15 VAN	16	17	18	19	20 EDM
21 CAL	22	23	24 NSH	25	26 ANA	27
28	29	30 NJ	31 CBJ			

February

SUN	MON	TUE	WED	THU	FRI	SAT
				1	2	3
4 *	5	6 OTT	7	8 TOR	9	10 TOR
11	12	13	14 CAR	15	16 CBJ	17
18 DAL	19	20 NSH	21 CHI	22	23 STL	24
25 PHO	D 26	27	28 ANA			

March

SUN	MON	TUE	WED	THU	FRI	SAT
				1	2 PHO	3 LA
4	5	6 VAN	7	8	9	10 D STL
11 D MIN	12	13 VAN	14	15 CAL	16	17 D COL
18 SJ	19	20	21	22 MIN	23	24 D NYR
25	26	27	28 STL	29	30	31 D PHI

April

SUN	MON	TUE	WED	THU	FRI	SAT
1 WAS	2	3 CBJ	4	5 ATL	6	7 D COL
8						

2000-2001 SEASON
CLUB DIRECTORY

Owner/governor
Mike Ilitch
Owner/secretary-treasurer
Marian Ilitch
Vice president/alternate governor
Christopher Ilitch
Sr. vice president/alternate governor
Jim Devellano
General manager
Ken Holland
Assistant general manager
Jim Nill
Head coach
Scotty Bowman
Associate coaches
Dave Lewis
Barry Smith
Goaltending consultant
Jim Bedard
NHL scout
Dan Belisle
Pro scouts
Mark Howe
Glenn Merkosky

Scouts
Hakan Andersson, Bruce Haralson,
Vladimir Havluj, Mark Leach, Joe
McDonnell, Bruce Southern, Marty
Stein
Athletic trainer
John Wharton
Equipment manager
Paul Boyer
Assistant equipment managers
Tim Abbott
Rob Gagne
Assistant athletic trainer
Piet Van Zant
Masseurs
Daryl Pittman
Sergei Tchekmarev
Team physicians
Dr. John Finley
Dr. David Collon
Team dentist
C.J. Regula

DRAFT CHOICES

Rd.— Player	Ht./Wt.	Overall	Pos.	Last team
1— Niklas Kronvall	5-11/165	29	D	Djurgarden, Sweden
2— Tomas Kopecky	6-3/187	38	C	Trencin, Slovakia
4— Stefan Liv	6-0/172	102	G	HV-71 Jr., Sweden
4— Dmitri Semyenov	5-10/178	127	W	Dynamo, Russia
4— Alexander Seluyanov	6-1/172	128	D	UFA, Russia
4— Aaron Van Leusen	6-0/196	130	C/RW	Brampton (OHL)
6— Per Backer		187	F	Grums, Sweden
6— Paul Ballantyne	6-3/200	196	D	Sault Ste. Marie (OHL)
7— Jimmie Svensson		228	F	Vasteras IK Jr., Swe.
8— Todd Jackson	5-11/170	251	RW	U.S. Nat. Under 18 Ex.
8— Evgeni Bumagin		260		HC Moscow, Russia

MISCELLANEOUS DATA

Home ice (capacity)
Joe Louis Arena (19,983)
Address
600 Civic Center Drive
Detroit, MI 48226
Business phone
313-396-7544
Ticket information
248-645-6666
Website
www.detroitredwings.com

Training site
Traverse City, Mich.
Club colors
Red and white
Radio affiliation
WJR (760 AM)
TV affiliation
WKBD (Channel 50), FOX Sports
Detroit (Cable)

TRAINING CAMP ROSTER

No.	FORWARDS	Ht./Wt.	Place	BORN Date	NHL exp.	1999-2000 clubs
	Sean Avery (C/LW)	5-10/188		4-10-80	0	Kingston (OHL)
	Per Backer (RW/LW)		Sweden	1-4-82	0	Grums (Sweden)
	Ryan Barnes (LW)	6-1/201	Dunnville, Ont.	1-30-80	0	Barrie (OHL)
17	Doug Brown (RW)	5-11/185	New Haven, Conn.	6-12-64	14	Detroit
	Yuri Butsayev (C)..........	6-1/183	Togliatti, U.S.S.R.	10-11-78	1	Detroit, Cincinnati (AHL)
11	Mathieu Dandenault......	6-1/196	Magog, Que.	2-3-76	5	Detroit
	Adam DeLeeuw (LW).....	6-0/206	Brampton, Ont.	2-29-80	0	Toronto St. Michael's (OHL), Dayton (ECHL)
33	Kris Draper (C)	5-10/190	Toronto	5-24-71	10	Detroit
91	Sergei Fedorov (C)	6-2/200	Pskov, U.S.S.R.	12-13-69	10	Detroit
	Gilchrist, Brent (LW).....	5-11/180	Moose Jaw, Sask.	4-3-67	12	Detroit
96	Tomas Holmstrom (LW) .	6-0/198	Pieta, Sweden	1-23-73	4	Detroit
	Tomas Kopecky (C/LW) .	6-3/187		2-2-82	0	Dukla Trencin (Slovakia), Dukla Trencin Jrs. (Slovakia Jrs.)
13	Slava Kozlov (LW)	5-10/195	Voskresensk, U.S.S.R.	5-3-72	9	Detroit
20	Martin Lapointe (RW).....	5-11/215	Lachine, Que.	9-12-73	9	Detroit
18	Kirk Maltby (RW)..........	6-0/190	Guelph, Ont.	12-22-72	7	Detroit
25	Darren McCarty (RW).....	6-1/215	Burnaby, B.C.	4-1-72	7	Detroit
	Kent McDonell (RW)......	6-2/198	Cornwall, Ont.	3-1-79	0	Guelph (OHL)
37	Marc Rodgers (RW)	5-9/185	Shawville, Que.	3-16-72	1	Detroit, Manitoba (IHL)
	Dmitri Semyenov (LW) ..	5-10/178	U.S.S.R.	4-19-82	0	Dynamo Moscow (Russian)
14	Brendan Shanahan (LW)	6-3/215	Mimico, Ont.	1-23-69	13	Detroit
	Tomek Valtonen (LW)	6-1/198	Piotrkow Trybunalski, Pol.	1-8-80	0	Jokerit (Finland)
	Aaron Van Leusen (C) ...	6-0/196	Barrie, Ont.	10-28-81	0	Brampton (OHL)
15	Pat Verbeek (RW).........	5-9/192	Sarnia, Ont.	5-24-64	18	Detroit
36	B.J. Young (RW)...........	5-10/178	Anchorage, Alaska	7-23-77	1	Cincinnati (AHL), Detroit
19	Steve Yzerman (C).........	5-10/185	Cranbrook, B.C.	5-9-65	17	Detroit
	Henrik Zetterberg (C).....	5-11/180	Timra, Sweden	10-9-80	0	
	DEFENSEMEN					
	Paul Ballantyne.............	6-3/200	Waterloo, Ont.	7-16-82	0	Sault Ste. Marie (OHL)
24	Chris Chelios	6-1/190	Chicago	1-25-62	17	Detroit
28	Steve Duchesne	5-11/195	Sept-Iles, Que.	6-30-65	14	Detroit
2	Jiri Fischer	6-5/210	Horovice, Czechoslovakia	7-31-80	1	Detroit, Cincinnati (AHL)
23	Todd Gill	6-2/179	Brockville, Ont.	11-9-65	16	Phoenix, Detroit
44	Yan Golubovsky	6-3/183	Novosibirsk, U.S.S.R.	3-9-76	3	Detroit
	Niklas Kronvall..............	5-11/165	Stockholm, Sweden	1-12-81	0	Djurgarden Stockholm (Sweden)
5	Nicklas Lidstrom	6-2/190	Vasteras, Sweden	4-28-70	9	Detroit
55	Larry Murphy................	6-2/215	Scarborough, Ont.	3-8-61	20	Detroit
	Alexander Seluyanov	6-1/172	Ufa, U.S.S.R.	2-24-82	0	Ufa (Russian Div. II)
3	Jesse Wallin	6-2/190	Saskatoon, Sask.	3-10-78	1	Cincinnati (AHL), Detroit
27	Aaron Ward	6-2/225	Windsor, Ont.	1-17-73	6	Detroit
	GOALTENDERS					
	Jason Elliott..................	6-2/183	Chapman, Australia	10-11-75	0	Manitoba (IHL)
34	Manny Legace	5-9/165	Toronto	2-4-73	2	Manitoba (IHL), Detroit
	Stefan Liv....................	6-0/172	Sweden	12-21-80	0	HV 71 Jonkoping (Sweden Jr.)
30	Chris Osgood................	5-10/181	Peace River, Alta.	11-26-72	7	Detroit
31	Ken Wregget.................	6-1/210	Brandon, Man.	3-25-64	17	Detroit

1999-2000 REVIEW
INDIVIDUAL STATISTICS

SCORING

	Games	G	A	Pts.	PIM	+/-	PPG	SHG	Shots	Shooting Pct.
Steve Yzerman......................	78	35	44	79	34	28	15	2	234	15.0
Brendan Shanahan	78	41	37	78	105	24	13	1	283	14.5
Nicklas Lidstrom	81	20	53	73	18	19	9	4	218	9.2
Sergei Fedorov	68	27	35	62	22	8	4	4	263	10.3
Pat Verbeek	68	22	26	48	95	22	7	0	138	15.9
Igor Larionov	79	9	38	47	28	13	3	0	69	13.0
Martin Lapointe	82	16	25	41	121	17	1	1	127	12.6
Steve Duchesne	79	10	31	41	42	12	1	0	154	6.5
Larry Murphy	81	10	30	40	45	4	7	0	146	6.8
Vyacheslav Kozlov	72	18	18	36	28	11	4	0	165	10.9
Tomas Holmstrom	72	13	22	35	43	4	4	0	71	18.3
Chris Chelios	81	3	31	34	103	48	0	0	135	2.2
Doug Brown	51	10	8	18	12	8	0	1	67	14.9
Mathieu Dandenault	81	6	12	18	20	-12	0	0	98	6.1
Stacy Roest	49	7	9	16	12	-1	1	0	56	12.5
Kirk Maltby	41	6	8	14	24	1	0	2	71	8.5

	Games	G	A	Pts.	PIM	+/-	PPG	SHG	Shots	Shooting Pct.
Darren McCarty	24	6	6	12	48	1	0	0	40	15.0
Kris Draper	51	5	7	12	28	3	0	0	76	6.6
Yuri Butsayev	57	5	3	8	12	-6	0	0	46	10.9
Jiri Fischer	52	0	8	8	45	1	0	0	41	0.0
Brent Gilchrist	24	4	2	6	24	1	0	0	33	12.1
Darryl LaPlante	30	0	6	6	10	-2	0	0	19	0.0
Aaron Ward	36	1	3	4	24	-4	0	0	25	4.0
Yan Golubovsky	21	1	2	3	8	3	0	0	7	14.3
Todd Gill*	13	2	0	2	15	2	0	0	20	10.0
Marc Rodgers	21	1	1	2	10	-3	0	0	17	5.9
Ken Wregget (goalie)	29	0	1	1	0	0	0	0	0	0.0
Chris Osgood (goalie)	53	0	1	1	18	0	0	0	0	0.0
Jesse Wallin	1	0	0	0	0	-2	0	0	0	0.0
B.J. Young	1	0	0	0	0	0	0	0	1	0.0
Manny Legace (goalie)*	4	0	0	0	0	0	0	0	0	0.0

GOALTENDING

	Games	Min.	Goals	SO	Avg.	W	L	T	ENG	Shots	Sv. Pct.
Chris Osgood	53	3148	126	6	2.40	30	14	8	2	1349	.907
Ken Wregget	29	1579	70	0	2.66	14	10	2	1	700	.900
Manny Legace	4	240	11	0	2.75	4	0	0	0	117	.906

*Played with two or more NHL teams.

RESULTS

OCTOBER

2— Buffalo .... W 2-0
5— Dallas .... L 2-3
7— At Atlanta .... W 7-1
9— At Florida .... T *2-2
13— St. Louis .... W 4-2
16— Philadelphia .... W 3-2
20— San Jose .... W 6-3
23— At Chicago .... W 1-0
27— Colorado .... W 5-3
29— Chicago .... L 2-4
30— At St. Louis .... L *4-5

NOVEMBER

3— Los Angeles .... T *1-1
5— Carolina .... W 3-2
7— At Tampa Bay .... L 2-3
10— At Dallas .... W 4-2
12— Pittsburgh .... W *3-2
13— At Toronto .... T *1-1
15— Anaheim .... W 6-3
17— At Vancouver .... W 7-2
19— At Calgary .... L 1-3
20— At Edmonton .... L 1-2
24— St. Louis .... W 4-2
26— Edmonton .... W 4-2
28— Phoenix .... L 3-4

DECEMBER

1— San Jose .... W 4-2
3— At Chicago .... W 7-4
4— At Nashville .... L 1-4

8— Nashville .... W 6-3
10— Los Angeles .... W 3-1
11— At Boston .... W 5-4
15— Edmonton .... W 5-1
17— Colorado .... W 5-2
19— At Anaheim .... L 1-3
20— At San Jose .... W 4-3
22— At Carolina .... W 4-1
27— Atlanta .... W *3-2
28— At Buffalo .... W 7-2
31— Chicago .... T *4-4

JANUARY

2— At Pittsburgh .... L 3-4
4— Phoenix .... L 2-5
6— Nashville .... W 5-2
8— Anaheim .... W 5-3
11— At Montreal .... L 0-3
13— Chicago .... L 3-5
16— At Edmonton .... T *3-3
18— At Calgary .... L 1-6
19— At Vancouver .... T *3-3
22— At Ottawa .... W 3-2
26— Toronto .... W 4-2
28— Calgary .... W 4-1
29— New Jersey .... W 3-1
31— At Phoenix .... L 3-5

FEBRUARY

3— At Los Angeles .... L 3-6
8— St. Louis .... L 1-4
10— At St. Louis .... W 2-0

13— At Colorado .... W 4-3
14— At Phoenix .... W 3-1
16— Vancouver .... W 5-2
18— Los Angeles .... L 2-3
20— At Chicago .... L 4-6
21— At N.Y. Islanders .... W 2-0
23— Dallas .... L 2-5
25— N.Y. Islanders .... W 5-2
27— Tampa Bay .... W 3-1

MARCH

3— At Washington .... T *2-2
5— At Dallas .... W 5-3
7— At Los Angeles .... W 3-1
8— At San Jose .... T *1-1
10— At Nashville .... W 3-1
14— Nashville .... W *3-2
16— Toronto .... L *3-4
18— At Colorado .... W 4-3
19— At Anaheim .... L 1-3
22— Calgary .... T *2-2
23— At Nashville .... W 6-3
26— N.Y. Rangers .... W 8-2
27— At N.Y. Rangers ...... W 6-0
29— Vancouver .... W 6-3

APRIL

1— At St. Louis .... T *0-0
2— Montreal .... W *6-5
7— Washington .... L 2-4
9— At Colorado .... L 2-3

*Denotes overtime game.

EDMONTON OILERS
WESTERN CONFERENCE/NORTHWEST DIVISION

Edmonton Schedule

Home games shaded; D—Day game; *—All-Star Game at Denver.

October

SUN	MON	TUE	WED	THU	FRI	SAT
1	2	3	4	5	6 DET	7 COL
8	9	10 MON	11 DET	12	13 BUF	14
15 D MIN	16	17 BOS	18	19 TOR	20	21
22 PHO	23	24	25 ATL	26	27 ANA	28 COL
29	30 ANA	31				

November

SUN	MON	TUE	WED	THU	FRI	SAT
			1 CAL	2	3 MIN	4
5 CBJ	6	7 NYR	8	9 PHI	10	11 PIT
12 MIN	13	14 STL	15	16	17 CHI	18
19 CAL	20	21	22 TOR	23 OTT	24	25 ANA
26	27	28	29 MON	30		

December

SUN	MON	TUE	WED	THU	FRI	SAT
					1	2 VAN
3 SJ	4	5	6 NSH	7	8	9 LA
10	11	12	13 DAL	14 NSH	15	16 WAS
17	18 DET	19	20 VAN	21	22 CAL	23
24	25	26	27 COL	28 SJ	29	30 MON
31						

January

SUN	MON	TUE	WED	THU	FRI	SAT
	1 STL	2	3 CBJ	4	5 CHI	6
7 CBJ	8	9	10 NSH	11	12 VAN	13
14 OTT	15	16 NSH	17	18 STL	19	20 DET
21	22 SJ	23	24 SJ	25	26 PHO	27
28	29	30 CAL	31 CHI			

February

SUN	MON	TUE	WED	THU	FRI	SAT
				1	2	3
4	*5	6	7 DAL	8	9 PHO	10
11	12 LA	13	14 ANA	15	16 NYI	17 VAN
18	19	20 LA	21	22	23	24 CAL
25 DAL	26	27	28 STL			

March

SUN	MON	TUE	WED	THU	FRI	SAT
				1	2 MIN	3
4	5	6	7 TOR	8	9 BUF	10
11 D CAR	12	13 TB	14 FLA	15	16	17 NJ
18	19 PHI	20	21 LA	22	23	24 PHO
25	26 CBJ	27	28 COL	29	30 DAL	31

April

SUN	MON	TUE	WED	THU	FRI	SAT
1 CHI	D 2 COL	3	4 MIN	5	6	7 VAN
8						

2000-2001 SEASON
CLUB DIRECTORY

Owner
Edmonton Investors Group, Ltd.
Governor
Cal Nichols
Alternate governors
Kevin Lowe, Gordon Buchanan
President & chief executive officer
Patrick LaForge
General manager
Kevin Lowe
Exec. v.p./assistant general manager
Bruce MacGregor
Dir. of player personnel/hockey ops.
Kevin Prendergast
Assistant to the general manager
Scott Howson
Head coach
Craig MacTavish
Assistant coaches
Charlie Huddy
Bill Moores
Video coordinator
Brian Ross
Scouting staff
Ed Chadwick, Brad Davis, Lorne Davis, Harry Howell, Gilles Leger, Chris McCarthy, Kent Nilsson, Dave Semenko
Athletic trainer/therapist
Ken Lowe

Equipment manager
Barrie Stafford
Assistant equipment manager
Lyle Kulchisky
Massage therapist
Stewart Poirier
Team physicians
Dr. David C. Reid, Dr. Boris Boyko
Vice president, public relations
Bill Tuele
Information coordinator
Steve Knowles
Public relations manager
Bryn Griffiths
Public & community rel. coordinator
Fiona Liew
Executive vice president, business operations
Doug Piper
Vice president, finance
Doug Thomson
Vice president, sponsorships, sales & services
Allan Watt
Vice president, properties
Darrell Holowaychuk
Director of ticketing
John Yeomans
Director of broadcast
Don Metz

DRAFT CHOICES

Rd.— Player	Ht./Wt.	Overall	Pos.	Last team
1—Alexei Mikhnov	6-5/194	17	LW	Yaroslavl, Russia
2—Brad Winchester	6-5/208	35	LW	Wisconsin (WCHA)
3—Alexander Ljubimov	6-3/196	83	D	Samara, Russia
4—Lou Dickenson	6-1/192	113	C/LW	Mississauga (OHL)
5—Paul Flache	6-5/195	152	D	Brampton (OHL)
6—Shaun Norrie	6-2/180	184	RW	Calgary (WHL)
7—Joe Cullen	6-1/190	211	C/LW	Colorado (WCHA)
7—Matthew Lombardi	5-11/191	215	C	Victoriaville, AMJHL
8—Jason Platt	6-1/210	247	D	Omaha, USHL
9—Evgeny Muratov	5-10/178	274	LW	Neftechimik, Russia

MISCELLANEOUS DATA

Home ice (capacity)
Skyreach Centre (17,100)
Address
11230 110 Street
Edmonton, Alta. T5G 3H7
Business phone
780-414-4000
Ticket information
780-414-4000
Website
www.edmontonoilers.com

Training site
Sherwood Park, Alberta
Club colors
White, midnight blue, metallic copper and red
Radio affiliation
CHED (630 AM)
TV affiliation
The A Channel, CBXT TV & CTV SportsNet

EDMONTON OILERS

No.	FORWARDS	Ht./Wt.	Place	Born Date	NHL exp.	1999-2000 clubs
	Jason Chimera (C)	6-0/180	Edmonton	5-2-79	0	Hamilton (AHL)
37	Dan Cleary (LW)	6-0/203	Carbonear, Nfld.	12-18-78	3	Hamilton (AHL), Edmonton
	Paul Comrie (C)	5-11/192	Edmonton	2-7-77	1	Hamilton (AHL), Edmonton
17	Patrick Cote (LW)	6-3/218	Lasalle, Que.	1-24-75	5	Nashville
	Lou Dickenson (C/LW)	6-1/192	Ottawa	8-15-82	0	Mississauga Icedogs (OHL)
25	Josh Green (LW)	6-4/213	Camrose, Alta.	11-16-77	2	Lowell (AHL), New York Islanders
25	Mike Grier (RW)	6-1/227	Detroit	1-5-75	4	Edmonton
9	Bill Guerin (RW)	6-2/210	Wilbraham, Mass.	11-9-70	9	Edmonton
	Michael Henrich (RW)	6-2/206	Thornhill, Ont.	3-3-80	0	Barrie (OHL)
	Shawn Horcoff (C)	6-1/194	Trail, B.C.	9-17-78	0	Michigan State (CCHA)
15	Chad Kilger (C)	6-4/215	Cornwall, Ont.	11-27-76	5	Edmonton, Hamilton (AHL)
33	Dan LaCouture (LW)	6-1/201	Hyannis, Mass.	4-13-77	2	Hamilton (AHL), Edmonton
27	Georges Laraque (RW)	6-3/240	Montreal	12-7-76	3	Edmonton
26	Todd Marchant (LW)	5-10/178	Buffalo	8-12-73	7	Edmonton
	Alexei Mikhnov (LW)	6-5/194		8-31-82	0	Torpedo-2 Yaroslavl (Russian Div. II)
18	Ethan Moreau (LW)	6-2/205	Orillia, Ont.	9-22-75	5	Edmonton
17	Rem Murray (LW)	6-2/195	Stratford, Ont.	10-9-72	4	Edmonton
	Shaun Norrie (RW)	6-2/180	Calgary	9-15-82	0	Calgary (WHL)
	Michel Riesen (LW)	6-2/190	Oberbalm, Switzerland	4-11-79	0	Hamilton (AHL)
	Jani Rita (LW/RW)	6-1/206	Helsinki, Finland	7-25-81	0	Jokerit Helsinki (Finland)
	Tony Salmelainen (LW)	5-9/176	Espoo, Finland	8-8-81	0	HIFK Helsinki (Finland Jr.)
94	Ryan Smyth (LW)	6-1/195	Banff, Alta.	2-21-76	6	Edmonton
	Brian Swanson (C)	5-10/185	Eagle River, Alaska	3-24-76	0	Hamilton (AHL)
	Alexandre Volchkov	6-2/205	Moscow, U.S.S.R.	9-15-77	1	Portland (AHL), Washington, Hamilton (AHL)
39	Doug Weight (C)	5-11/200	Warren, Mich.	1-21-71	10	Edmonton
	Brad Winchester (LW)	6-5/208	Madison, Wis.	3-1-81	0	Univ. of Wisconsin (WCHA)

DEFENSEMEN

No.	DEFENSEMEN	Ht./Wt.	Place	Born Date	NHL exp.	1999-2000 clubs
34	Eric Brewer	6-3/220	Verona, B.C.	4-17-79	2	New York Islanders, Lowell (AHL)
23	Sean Brown	6-3/205	Oshawa, Ont.	11-5-76	4	Edmonton
	Paul Flache	6-5/195	Toronto	3-4-82	0	Brampton (OHL)
	Chris Hajt	6-3/206	Amherst, N.Y.	7-5-78	0	Hamilton (AHL)
	Alex Henry	6-5/220	Elliot Lake, Ont.	10-18-79	0	Hamilton (AHL)
	Alexander Ljubimov	6-3/196	Togliatti, U.S.S.R.	2-15-80	0	Samara (Russian)
44	Janne Niinimaa	6-2/220	Raahe, Finland	5-22-75	4	Edmonton
	Brad Norton	6-4/225	Cambridge, Mass.	2-13-75	0	Hamilton (AHL)
5	Tom Poti	6-3/215	Worcester, Mass.	3-22-77	2	Edmonton
	Alexei Semenov	6-6/210	Murmansk, U.S.S.R.	4-10-81	0	Sudbury (OHL), Hamilton (AHL)
21	Jason Smith	6-3/208	Calgary	11-2-73	7	Edmonton
55	Igor Ulanov	6-3/211	Kraskokamsk, U.S.S.R.	10-1-69	9	Montreal, Edmonton

GOALTENDERS

No.	GOALTENDERS	Ht./Wt.	Place	Born Date	NHL exp.	1999-2000 clubs
	Alex Fomitchev	5-10/180	Moscow, U.S.S.R.	2-19-79	0	Calgary (WHL), Seattle (WHL)
	Eric Heffler	6-3/190	Williamsville, N.Y.	2-29-76	0	Hamilton (AHL)
35	Tommy Salo	5-11/173	Surahammar, Sweden	2-1-71	6	Edmonton

1999-2000 REVIEW
INDIVIDUAL STATISTICS

SCORING

	Games	G	A	Pts.	PIM	+/-	PPG	SHG	Shots	Shooting Pct.
Doug Weight	77	21	51	72	54	6	3	1	167	12.6
Ryan Smyth	82	28	26	54	58	-2	11	0	238	11.8
Alex Selivanov	67	27	20	47	46	2	10	0	122	22.1
Bill Guerin	70	24	22	46	123	4	11	0	188	12.8
Roman Hamrlik	80	8	37	45	68	1	5	0	180	4.4
Todd Marchant	82	17	23	40	70	7	0	1	170	10.0
Tom Poti	76	9	26	35	65	8	2	1	125	7.2
Janne Niinimaa	81	8	25	33	89	14	2	2	133	6.0
Mike Grier	65	9	22	31	68	9	0	3	115	7.8
Ethan Moreau	73	17	10	27	62	8	1	0	106	16.0
Boyd Devereaux	76	8	19	27	20	7	0	1	108	7.4
Jim Dowd	69	5	18	23	45	10	2	0	103	4.9
Pat Falloon*	33	5	13	18	4	6	1	0	51	9.8
Josef Beranek*	58	9	8	17	39	-6	3	0	107	8.4
Georges Laraque	76	8	8	16	123	5	0	0	56	14.3
Rem Murray	44	9	5	14	8	-2	2	0	65	13.8
Jason Smith	80	3	11	14	60	16	0	0	96	3.1
Sean Brown	72	4	8	12	192	1	0	0	36	11.1

	Games	G	A	Pts.	PIM	+/-	PPG	SHG	Shots	Shooting Pct.
Daniel Cleary	17	3	2	5	8	-1	0	0	18	16.7
Chad Kilger	40	3	2	5	18	-6	0	0	32	9.4
Christian Laflamme*	50	0	5	5	32	-4	0	0	18	0.0
German Titov*	7	0	4	4	4	2	0	0	11	0.0
Bert Robertsson	52	0	4	4	34	-3	0	0	31	0.0
Paul Comrie	15	1	2	3	4	-2	0	0	11	9.1
Igor Ulanov*	14	0	3	3	10	-3	0	0	6	0.0
Brett Hauer	5	0	2	2	2	-2	0	0	8	0.0
Tommy Salo (goalie)	70	0	1	1	8	0	0	0	0	0.0
Mike Minard (goalie)	1	0	0	0	0	0	0	0	0	0.0
Michel Picard	2	0	0	0	2	0	0	0	2	0.0
Dan Lacouture	5	0	0	0	10	0	0	0	2	0.0
Kevin Brown	7	0	0	0	0	0	0	0	5	0.0
Bill Ranford (goalie)	16	0	0	0	2	0	0	0	0	0.0

GOALTENDING

	Games	Min.	Goals	SO	Avg.	W	L	T	ENG	Shots	Sv. Pct.
Tommy Salo	70	4164	162	2	2.33	27	28	13	0	1875	.914
Mike Minard	1	60	3	0	3.00	1	0	0	0	36	.917
Bill Ranford	16	785	47	0	3.59	4	6	3	0	407	.885

*Played with two or more NHL teams.

RESULTS

OCTOBER
1— N.Y. Rangers ....T....*1-1
6— Montreal.............................W.....2-1
7— At San Jose ....L....*2-3
9— St. Louis...........................L.....2-4
13—Carolina ....T....*3-3
16—Los Angeles ....W.....5-4
20—At Dallas...........................L.....1-2
21—At St. Louis....................L....*2-3
23—At Nashville ....L.....3-4
26—Phoenix ....W.....3-1
31—Nashville...........................W.....4-2

NOVEMBER
3— Florida ....T....*2-2
5— St. Louis...........................L.....1-2
7— At Anaheim.......................L.....1-3
9— At Los Angeles ....T....*1-1
10—At Phoenix......................L....*4-5
12—At St. Louis....................T....*2-2
14—At Chicago......................W.....6-3
20—Detroit ....W.....2-1
21—N.Y. Islanders ....T....*4-4
24—Chicago ....L.....2-3
26—At Detroit ....L.....2-4
27—At Toronto ....L.....2-5

DECEMBER
1— Colorado...........................W.....3-1
2— At Vancouver ....L....*2-3
4— Vancouver ....W.....3-2
6— At Chicago.........................L.....1-5

8— At N.Y. Rangers ....L....*1-2
9— At Boston...........................T....*2-2
11—At New Jersey ....W.....3-1
14—At N.Y. Islanders..............W.....4-2
15—At Detroit ....L.....1-5
17—Dallas................................T....*2-2
19—Ottawa...............................T....*3-3
21—Washington ....W.....6-2
23—At Calgary ....L.....1-2
27—Anaheim ....W.....4-1
30—At Los Angeles ....L.....2-8

JANUARY
1— At Phoenix.........................W.....5-4
3— At Colorado ....T....*2-2
5— San Jose............................T....*1-1
7— Tampa Bay ....W.....5-1
11—Dallas................................L.....2-3
14—Toronto..............................L....*2-3
16—Detroit ....T....*3-3
19—Calgary ....W.....7-0
22—Vancouver ....T....*3-3
24—Nashville ....L....*2-3
25—At Vancouver ....W....*5-4
28—At Tampa Bay ....W.....7-3
29—At Florida ....L.....1-2
31—At Dallas ....L.....1-2

FEBRUARY
2— Chicago ....W.....4-1
8— At Montreal ....W....*5-4
10—At Philadelphia ....W.....3-2

11—At Pittsburgh ....T....*2-2
13—At Buffalo............................T....*2-2
15—At Nashville ....W.....2-1
18—At Calgary ....L.....2-4
19—Calgary ....L....*2-3
21—Los Angeles ....W.....6-3
23—Boston ....W.....4-2
25—Atlanta ....W.....5-4
27—At Anaheim ....L.....2-3
29—At Colorado ....W.....3-1

MARCH
4— Pittsburgh...........................L.....2-3
7— Toronto ....L.....0-2
10—Colorado............................L.....2-4
12—At Nashville ....L.....3-4
13—At Atlanta ....W.....3-0
15—At Carolina ....T....*2-2
17—Ottawa...............................W.....4-2
19—Calgary ....L.....2-3
22—Anaheim ....W.....2-1
25—Vancouver ....L.....2-3
27—At San Jose ....W.....2-1
29—At Colorado ....L.....2-3

APRIL
1— Phoenix ....W....*4-3
3— San Jose............................L.....0-1
5— Colorado.............................L.....2-3
7— At Vancouver ....W....*5-4
8— At Calgary ....W.....6-3
*Denotes overtime game.

FLORIDA PANTHERS
EASTERN CONFERENCE/SOUTHEAST DIVISION

Florida Schedule
Home games shaded; D—Day game; *—All-Star Game at Denver.

October

SUN	MON	TUE	WED	THU	FRI	SAT
1	2	3	4	5	6 VAN	7
8	9 D BOS	10	11 NJ	12	13 CAR	14
15	16	17	18 PHO	19	20 COL	21
22 D MIN	23	24	25 NJ	26	27 NSH	28 OTT
29	30	31				

November

SUN	MON	TUE	WED	THU	FRI	SAT
			1 NYI	2	3	4 WAS
5	6	7	8 MON	9	10 CAL	11
12 ATL	13	14	15 CAR	16	17 CBJ	18 OTT
19	20	21 MON	22	23	24 TB	25 TB
26	27	28	29 CAR	30		

December

SUN	MON	TUE	WED	THU	FRI	SAT
					1 DET	2 STL
3	4 TOR	5	6 NYI	7	8 ATL	9 COL
10	11	12	13 DET	14	15 PIT	16 BUF
17	18 NYR	19	20 PIT	21	22 NJ	23 WAS
24	25	26	27 PHI	28	29 BOS	30 TOR
31						

January

SUN	MON	TUE	WED	THU	FRI	SAT
	1	2	3 ANA	4 LA	5	6 SJ
7	8	9 CAR	10	11	12 CAR	13 PHI
14	15 DAL	16	17 CHI	18	19 BUF	20 PHI
21	22 BOS	23	24 WAS	25	26 OTT	27 TB
28	29	30 TB	31 BUF			

February

SUN	MON	TUE	WED	THU	FRI	SAT
				1	2	3
4	*5	6	7 MIN	8	9 NYR	10 ATL
11	12	13	14 PHO	15	16 BOS	17
18	19 STL	20	21 PIT	22	23 OTT	24 D NYI
25	26 NJ	27	28 NYR			

March

SUN	MON	TUE	WED	THU	FRI	SAT
				1	2 ATL	3 ATL
4	5	6	7 SJ	8	9 CBJ	10
11 D NYI	12	13	14 EDM	15	16 PIT	17 TOR
18	19	20 MON	21 TOR	22	23 WAS	24
25	26	27	28 MON	29	30 TB	31

April

SUN	MON	TUE	WED	THU	FRI	SAT
1	2 BUF	3 PHI	4	5 WAS	6	7 D NYR
8						

2000-2001 SEASON
CLUB DIRECTORY

Chairman & chief executive officer
H. Wayne Huizenga
President & governor
William A. Torrey
V.p. and general manager
Bryan Murray
Assistant general manager
Chuck Fletcher
Head coach
Terry Murray
Assistant coaches
Slavomir Lener
Bill Smith
Pro scouts
Michael Abbamont
Duane Sutter
Director of amateur scouting
Tim Murray
Amateur scouts
Ron Harris, Wayne Meier, Billy Dea,
Todd Hearty, Marty Nanne, Sean
O'Brien

European scout
Pavel Routa
Head medical trainer
Stan Wong
Strength & conditioning coach
Ian Pyka
Equipment manager
Mark Brennan
Senior vice president
Steve Dangerfield
V.p., corporate sales and client services
Kimberly Terranova Sciarretta
Director of communications
Mike Hanson
Publications/communications coord.
Michael Citro
Director of finance/controller
Evelyn Lopez

DRAFT CHOICES

Rd.— Player	Ht./Wt.	Overall	Pos.	Last team
2— Vladimir Sapozhnikov	6-3/205	58	D	Novokuznetsk, Russia
3— Robert Fried	6-4/210	77	RW	Deerfield, USHSE
3— Sean O'Connor	6-3/211	82	RW	Moose Jaw (WHL)
4— Chris Eade	6-2/191	115	D	North Bay (OHL)
4— Davis Parley	6-2/164	120	G	Kamloops (WHL)
6— Josh Olson	6-5/220	190	LW	Omaha, USHL
8— Janis Sprukts	6-3/224	234	C	Lukko Rauma Jr., Fin.
8— Matthew Sommerfeld	6-2/192	253	LW	Swift Current (WHL)

MISCELLANEOUS DATA

Home ice (capacity)
National Car Rental Center (19,250)
Address
One Panther Parkway
Sunrise, FL 33323
Business phone
954-835-7000
Ticket information
954-835-7000
Website
www.flpanthers.com

Training site
Hull, Quebec
Club colors
Red, navy blue, yellow and gold
Radio affiliation
WQAM (560 AM)
TV affiliation
FOX SportsNet

TRAINING CAMP ROSTER

No.	FORWARDS	Ht./Wt.	Place	Date (BORN)	NHL exp.	1999-2000 clubs
9	Len Barrie (C)	6-0/200	Kimberley, B.C.	6-4-69	0	Long Beach (IHL), Los Angeles, Florida
40	Eric Boguniecki (C)	5-8/192	New Haven, Conn.	5-6-75	1	Louisville (AHL), Florida
10	Pavel Bure (RW)	5-10/189	Moscow, U.S.S.R.	3-31-71	9	Florida
	Jiri Dopita (C)	6-3/209	Sumperk, Czechoslovakia	12-2-68	0	Vsetin (Czech Republic)
	Dave Duerden (LW)	6-2/200	Oshawa, Ont.	4-11-77	1	Louisville (AHL), Florida
	Robert Fried (RW)	6-3/210	Philadelphia	3-8-81	0	Deerfield Academy (USHS (East))
	Kristian Huselius (LW)	6-1/183	Stockholm, Sweden	11-10-78	0	Vastra Frolunda HC Goteborg (Sweden)
62	Olli Jokinen (C)	6-3/218	Kuopio, Finland	12-5-78	3	New York Islanders
25	Viktor Kozlov (C)	6-5/232	Togliatti, U.S.S.R.	2-14-75	6	Florida
8	Igor Larionov (C)	5-10/170	Voskresensk, U.S.S.R.	12-3-60	10	Detroit
3	Paul Laus (RW)	6-1/212	Beamsville, Ont.	9-26-70	7	Florida
27	Scott Mellanby (RW) STL	6-1/205	Montreal	6-11-66	15	Florida
44	Rob Niedermayer (C) CAL	6-2/204	Cassiar, B.C.	12-28-74	7	Florida
48	Marcus Nilson (C)	6-2/193	Balsta, Sweden	3-1-78	2	Louisville (AHL), Florida
39	Ivan Novoseltsev (C)	6-1/183	Golitsino, U.S.S.R.	1-23-79	1	Louisville (AHL), Florida
	Sean O'Connor (RW)	6-2/211	Victoria, B.C.	10-19-81	0	Moose Jaw (WHL)
	Josh Olson (LW)	6-5/220	Grand Forks, N.D.	7-13-81	0	Omaha (USHL)
	Denis Shvidki (RW)	6-0/205	Kharkov, U.S.S.R.	11-21-80	0	Barrie (OHL)
16	Mike Sillinger (C)	5-11/191	Regina, Sask.	6-29-71	10	Tampa Bay, Florida
14	Ray Whitney (LW)	5-10/175	Fort Saskatchewan, Alta.	5-8-72	9	Florida
8	Peter Worrell (LW)	6-6/235	Pierrefonds, Que.	8-18-77	3	Florida
	DEFENSEMEN					
6	Dan Boyle SJ	5-11/190	Ottawa	7-12-76	2	Louisville (AHL), Florida
	Chris Eade	6-1/191	Etobicoke, Ont.	4-20-82	0	North Bay (OHL)
45	Brad Ference	6-3/196	Calgary	4-2-79	1	Louisville (AHL), Florida
4	Bret Hedican	6-2/205	St. Paul, Minn.	8-10-70	9	Florida
15	John Jakopin	6-5/239	Toronto	5-16-75	3	Florida, Louisville (AHL)
2	Lance Pitlick	5-11/211	Fridley, Minn.	11-5-67	6	Florida
6	Peter Ratchuk	6-1/185	Buffalo	9-10-77	1	Louisville (AHL)
	Vladimir Sapozhnikov	6-3/205	Seversk, U.S.S.R.	8-2-82	0	Novokuznetsk (Russian Div. II)
22	Todd Simpson	6-3/215	Edmonton	5-28-73	5	Florida
28	Jaroslav Spacek	5-11/198	Rokycany, Czechoslovakia	2-11-74	2	Florida
24	Robert Svehla	6-1/210	Martin, Czechoslovakia	1-2-69	6	Florida
7	Mike Wilson	6-6/212	Brampton, Ont.	2-26-75	5	Florida
	GOALTENDERS					
37	Trevor Kidd	6-2/190	Dugald, Man.	3-29-72	8	Florida, Louisville (AHL)
1	Roberto Luongo	6-3/175	St. Leonard, Que.	4-4-79	1	Lowell (AHL), New York Islanders
	Davis Parley	6-1/164	Grenfell, Sask.	9-4-82	0	Kamloops (WHL)
	Rich Shulmistra	6-2/185	Sudbury, Ont.	4-1-71	2	Louisville (AHL), Florida, Orlando (IHL)

1999-2000 REVIEW
INDIVIDUAL STATISTICS

SCORING

	Games	G	A	Pts.	PIM	+/-	PPG	SHG	Shots	Shooting Pct.
Pavel Bure	74	58	36	94	16	25	11	2	360	16.1
Ray Whitney	81	29	42	71	35	16	5	0	198	14.6
Viktor Kozlov	80	17	53	70	16	24	6	0	223	7.6
Robert Svehla	82	9	40	49	64	23	3	0	143	6.3
Scott Mellanby	77	18	28	46	126	14	6	0	134	13.4
Mark Parrish	81	26	18	44	39	1	6	0	152	17.1
Jaroslav Spacek	82	10	26	36	53	7	4	0	111	9.0
Rob Niedermayer	81	10	23	33	46	-5	1	0	135	7.4
Bret Hedican	76	6	19	25	68	4	2	0	58	10.3
Oleg Kvasha	78	5	20	25	34	3	2	0	110	4.5
Ray Sheppard	47	10	10	20	4	-4	5	0	74	13.5
Mike Wilson	60	4	16	20	35	10	0	0	65	6.2
Radek Dvorak*	35	7	10	17	6	5	0	0	67	10.4
Cameron Stewart	65	9	7	16	30	-2	0	0	52	17.3
Ryan Johnson*	66	4	12	16	14	1	0	0	44	9.1
Paul Laus	77	3	8	11	172	-1	0	0	44	6.8
Len Barrie*	14	4	6	10	6	4	0	0	15	26.7
Peter Worrell	48	3	6	9	169	-7	2	0	45	6.7
Mike Sillinger*	13	4	4	8	16	-1	2	0	20	20.0
Lance Pitlick	62	3	5	8	44	7	0	0	26	11.5
Todd Simpson	82	1	6	7	202	5	0	0	50	2.0
Filip Kuba	13	1	5	6	2	-3	1	0	16	6.3

	Games	G	A	Pts.	PIM	+/-	PPG	SHG	Shots	Shooting Pct.
Ivan Novoseltsev	14	2	1	3	8	-3	2	0	8	25.0
Alex Hicks	8	1	2	3	4	3	0	0	6	16.7
Dan Boyle	13	0	3	3	4	-2	0	0	9	0.0
Mike Vernon (goalie)*	34	0	3	3	2	0	0	0	0	0.0
Marcus Nilson	9	0	2	2	2	2	0	0	6	0.0
Brad Ference	13	0	2	2	46	2	0	0	10	0.0
Rich Shulmistra (goalie)	1	0	0	0	0	0	0	0	0	0.0
Dave Duerden	2	0	0	0	0	0	0	0	1	0.0
Craig Ferguson	3	0	0	0	0	-2	0	0	2	0.0
Eric Boguniecki	4	0	0	0	2	-1	0	0	5	0.0
Dwayne Hay*	6	0	0	0	2	-2	0	0	3	0.0
Sean Burke (goalie)*	7	0	0	0	2	0	0	0	0	0.0
Chris Wells	13	0	0	0	14	-5	0	0	5	0.0
Mikhail Shtalenkov (goalie)*	15	0	0	0	2	0	0	0	0	0.0
John Jakopin	17	0	0	0	26	-2	0	0	1	0.0
Trevor Kidd (goalie)	28	0	0	0	0	0	0	0	0	0.0

GOALTENDING

	Games	Min.	Goals	SO	Avg.	W	L	T	ENG	Shots	Sv. Pct.
Rich Shulmistra	1	60	1	0	1.00	1	0	0	0	21	.952
Mikhail Shtalenko*	15	882	34	0	2.31	8	4	2	0	369	.908
Mike Vernon*	34	2019	83	1	2.47	18	13	2	2	1020	.919
Sean Burke*	7	418	18	0	2.58	2	5	0	2	208	.913
Trevor Kidd	28	1574	69	1	2.63	14	11	2	0	809	.915

*Played with two or more NHL teams.

RESULTS

OCTOBER
2— Washington .... W 4-3
6— Los Angeles .... W 4-2
9— Detroit .... T *2-2
12— At Montreal .... W 2-1
13— At Toronto .... L 2-3
16— Anaheim .... W *3-2
20— Vancouver .... W 5-2
22— Calgary .... L *2-3
24— At Philadelphia .... L 0-2
27— N.Y. Islanders .... W 6-3
29— At Buffalo .... L *2-3
30— At Ottawa .... L 0-5

NOVEMBER
3— At Edmonton .... T *2-2
5— At Vancouver .... L 2-3
6— At Calgary .... W 6-3
10— Atlanta .... W 4-1
13— Buffalo .... W 3-1
17— At Colorado .... W 2-1
18— At St. Louis .... L 0-3
20— Pittsburgh .... W *2-1
24— Philadelphia .... L 1-6
26— N.Y. Rangers .... W 6-2
27— Atlanta .... W 3-0

DECEMBER
3— At Atlanta .... L 1-2
4— Washington .... W 2-1
8— At Phoenix .... W 6-1
10— At Dallas .... L 3-4

11— At Nashville .... W 4-2
15— Nashville .... W 3-2
17— At Buffalo .... W 4-2
18— At Pittsburgh .... W 5-2
20— Toronto .... L 4-6
22— Atlanta .... T *3-3
26— At Carolina .... L *3-4
27— At Tampa Bay .... W 6-1
30— At Chicago .... L 1-2

JANUARY
1— Tampa Bay .... W 7-5
5— At Anaheim .... W 5-1
6— At Los Angeles .... L 2-4
8— At San Jose .... W 4-2
12— N.Y. Islanders .... W 4-3
14— Carolina .... W 5-1
15— At Tampa Bay .... W 5-2
17— Philadelphia .... W 3-1
19— Washington .... L 1-3
21— At Atlanta .... T *3-3
22— Boston .... W *4-3
26— New Jersey .... L 2-3
27— At Philadelphia .... L 2-4
29— Edmonton .... W 2-1

FEBRUARY
1— At Carolina .... L 2-4
2— Montreal .... W 3-1
9— San Jose .... W 4-1
11— At Ottawa .... L 3-5
12— At Boston .... W 5-1

14— At Montreal .... L 1-4
16— N.Y. Rangers .... W 3-0
19— Pittsburgh .... L 1-2
21— Ottawa .... L 2-4
23— At Washington .... L *2-3
24— At Carolina .... W 4-2
26— Carolina .... L *1-2
28— Buffalo .... L 2-5

MARCH
1— Toronto .... W 3-1
3— At N.Y. Rangers .... L 2-4
4— St. Louis .... T *1-1
7— At Washington .... L 2-4
10— At Tampa Bay .... W 4-3
11— Chicago .... L 2-5
16— At Pittsburgh .... L 2-4
18— At N.Y. Islanders .... W 4-2
19— At New Jersey .... L 2-5
21— At N.Y. Rangers .... W 4-3
23— At Boston .... W 3-1
25— Montreal .... W 4-2
29— Dallas .... L 1-4
31— Ottawa .... W 3-1

APRIL
1— Tampa Bay .... T *3-3
3— New Jersey .... W 5-2
5— Boston .... W 6-3
8— At New Jersey .... L *1-2
9— At N.Y. Islanders .... L 2-3

*Denotes overtime game.

LOS ANGELES KINGS
WESTERN CONFERENCE/PACIFIC DIVISION

Los Angeles Schedule

Home games shaded; D—Day game; *—All-Star Game at Denver.

October

SUN	MON	TUE	WED	THU	FRI	SAT
1	2	3	4	5	6 WAS	7 BUF
8	9 CBJ	10	11 STL	12	13 BOS	14
15 PHO	16	17 NSH	18	19 STL	20	21 DAL
22	23 ANA	24	25 ANA	26	27	28 PHO
29	30	31 CBJ				

November

SUN	MON	TUE	WED	THU	FRI	SAT
			1	2 ATL	3	4 D NJ
5 D NYI	6	7 PHO	8	9 VAN	10	11 DET
12	13	14	15	16 NYI	17	18 D COL
19	20	21	22	23 NJ	24	25 PIT
26 BOS	27	28 NYR	29	30		

December

SUN	MON	TUE	WED	THU	FRI	SAT
					1	2 MIN
3 ANA	4	5	6	7 DAL	8	9 EDM
10 VAN	11	12	13	14 NYR	15	16 TB
17	18	19 ATL	20	21 COL	22 MIN	23
24	25	26 SJ	27	28 STL	29 DAL	30
31 DET						

January

SUN	MON	TUE	WED	THU	FRI	SAT
	1	2 COL	3	4 FLA	5	6 CAL
7	8	9	10	11 BUF	12	13 STL
14	15	16 OTT	17	18	19	20 D CAR
21	22 PHI	23	24	25 CAL	26	27 D MIN
28	29	30 DAL	31			

February

SUN	MON	TUE	WED	THU	FRI	SAT
				1 NSH	2	3
4	* 5	6 CHI	7	8 CAR	9	10 WAS
11	12 EDM	13	14 DAL	15	16 MIN	17
18 D CHI	19	20 EDM	21	22 CAL	23	24 D CBJ
25	26	27 NSH	28			

March

SUN	MON	TUE	WED	THU	FRI	SAT
				1 CHI	2	3 DET
4 ANA	5	6 MON	7	8 NSH	9	10 CHI
11	12	13	14 SJ	15	16	17 D SJ
18	19 PHO	20	21 EDM	22	23	24 D ANA
25	26 SJ	27 SJ	28	29 CBJ	30	31 D COL

April

SUN	MON	TUE	WED	THU	FRI	SAT
1	2 VAN	3 PHO	4	5 VAN	6	7 CAL
8						

2000-2001 SEASON
CLUB DIRECTORY

Owners
Philip F. Anschutz
Edward P. Roski, Jr.
Governor
Robert Sanderman
President
Tim Leiweke
Sr. vice president, general manager
Dave Taylor
Coach
Andy Murray
Assistant coaches
Ray Bennett
Mark Hardy
Dave Tippett
Assistant general manager
Kevin Gilmore
Assistant to general manager
John Wolf
Director of amateur scouting
Al Murray

Director of pro scouting
Ace Bailey
Scouting staff
Serge Aubry, Greg Drechsel, Gary
Harker, Rob Laird, Vaclav
Nedomansky, Parry Shockey, John
Stanton, Victor Tjumenev, Ari Vuori
V.p. of marketing and community dev.
Kurt Schwartzkopf
Dir., media relations and team services
Mike Altieri
Mgr., media relations and team services
Jeff Moeller
Media relations assistant
Lee Callans
Trainers
Rick Burrill, Grady Clark, Pete Demers,
Rick Garcia, Dave Good, Joe
Horrigan, Peter Millar, Robert Zolg

DRAFT CHOICES

Rd.— Player	Ht./Wt.	Overall	Pos.	Last team
1— Alexander Frolov	6-3/191	20	LW	Yaroslavl, Russia
2— Andreas Lilja	6-3/220	54	D	Malmo, Sweden
3— Yanick Lehoux	6-0/170	86	C	Baie Comeau (QMJHL)
4— Lubomir Visnovsky	5-10/172	118	D	Bratislava, Slovakia
5— Nathan Marsters	6-4/190	165	G	Chilliwack, BCJHL
7— Evgeny Federov	5-9/172	201	C	Molot Perm, Russia
7— Tim Eriksson	5-9/161	206	C	Frolunda, Sweden
7— Craig Olynick	6-1/185	218	D	Seattle (WHL)
8— Dan Welch	5-10/199	245	RW	Minnesota (WCHA)
8— Flavien Conne	5-10/176	250	C	Freibourg, Switzerland
9— Carl Grahn	6-0/169	282	G	Kalpa Jr., Finland

MISCELLANEOUS DATA

Home ice (capacity)
STAPLES Center (18,118)
Address
555 N. Nash Street
El Segundo, CA 90245
Business phone
213-742-7100
Ticket information
888-546-4752
Website
www.lakings.com

Training site
El Segundo, CA
Club colors
Purple, silver, black and white
Radio affiliation
KRLA (1110 AM)
TV affiliation
FOX Sports Net

LOS ANGELES KINGS

TRAINING CAMP ROSTER

No.	FORWARDS	Ht./Wt.	Place	Date	NHL exp.	1999-2000 clubs
			BORN			
11	Jason Blake (C)	5-10/180	Moorhead, Minn.	9-2-73	2	Los Angeles, Long Beach (IHL)
9	Kelly Buchberger (RW)	6-2/210	Langenburg, Sask.	12-2-66	14	Atlanta, Los Angeles
	Craig Charron (C)	5-10/175	North Easton, Mass.	11-15-67	1	St. John's (AHL), Lowell (AHL)
29	Brad Chartrand (RW)	5-11/191	Winnipeg	12-14-74	1	Los Angeles, Long Beach (IHL), Lowell (AHL)
19	Bob Corkum (C)	6-0/222	Salisbury, Mass.	12-18-67	10	Los Angeles
17	Nelson Emerson (RW)	5-10/180	Hamilton, Ont.	8-17-67	10	Atlanta, Los Angeles
	Alexander Frolov (LW)	6-3/191	Moscow, U.S.S.R.	6-19-82	0	Torpedo-2 Yaroslavl (Russian Div. II)
32	Stu Grimson (LW)	6-5/239	Kamloops, B.C.	5-20-65	12	Anaheim
23	Craig Johnson (LW)	6-2/197	St. Paul, Minn.	3-8-72	6	Los Angeles
22	Ian Laperriere (C/RW)	6-1/197	Montreal	1-19-74	7	Los Angeles
	Yanick Lehoux (C)	5-11/170	Montreal	4-8-82	0	Baie-Comeau (QMJHL)
27	Glen Murray (RW)	6-3/222	Halifax, Nova Scotia	11-1-72	9	Los Angeles
33	Zigmund Palffy (RW)	5-10/180	Skalica, Czechoslovakia	5-5-72	7	Los Angeles
	Greg Phillips (RW)	6-2/205	Winnipeg	3-27-78	0	Lowell (AHL)
37	Jason Podollan (RW/C)	6-1/202	Vernon, B.C.	2-18-76	3	Lowell (AHL), Los Angeles
20	Luc Robitaille (LW)	6-1/205	Montreal	2-17-66	14	Los Angeles
55	Pavel Rosa (RW/LW)	5-11/188	Most, Czechoslovakia	6-7-77	2	Long Beach (IHL), Los Angeles
	Andrei Shefer (LW)	6-1/180	Sverdlovsk, U.S.S.R.	7-26-81	0	Halifax (QMJHL)
21	Bryan Smolinski (C)	6-1/208	Toledo, Ohio	12-27-71	8	Los Angeles
15	Jozef Stumpel (C)	6-3/216	Nitra, Czechoslovakia	7-20-72	9	Los Angeles
21	Scott Thomas (LW)	6-2/200	Buffalo	1-18-70	2	Long Beach (IHL)
	Tomas Vlasak (C)	5-10/161	Prague, Czechoslovakia	2-1-75	0	HPK Hameenlinna (Finland)
	DEFENSEMEN					
5	Aki Berg	6-3/220	Turku, Finland	7-28-77	4	Los Angeles
4	Rob Blake	6-4/220	Simcoe, Ont.	12-10-69	11	Los Angeles
43	Philippe Boucher	6-3/221	St. Apollnaire, Que.	3-24-73	8	Long Beach (IHL), Los Angeles
8	Jere Karalahti	6-2/210	Helsinki, Finland	3-25-75	1	HIFK Helsinki (Finland), Long Beach (IHL), Los Angeles
	Andreas Lilja	6-3/220	Sweden	7-13-75	0	Malmo (Sweden)
44	Jaroslav Modry	6-2/219	Ceske-Budejovice, Czech.	2-27-71	6	Los Angeles, Long Beach (IHL)
54	Jan Nemecek	6-1/215	Pisek, Czechoslovakia	2-14-76	2	Long Beach (IHL), Los Angeles
14	Mattias Norstrom	6-2/201	Stockholm, Sweden	1-2-72	7	Los Angeles
	Joe Rullier	6-3/198	Montreal	1-28-80	0	Rimouski (QMJHL)
	Richard Seeley	6-2/199	Powell River, B.C.	4-30-79	0	Lowell (AHL)
	Lubomir Visnovsky	5-10/172	Czechoslovakia	8-11-76	0	Bratislava (Slovakia)
	GOALTENDERS					
34	Marcel Cousineau	5-9/180	Delson, Que.	4-30-73	4	Long Beach (IHL), Los Angeles
35	Stephane Fiset	6-1/198	Montreal	6-17-70	11	Los Angeles
	Nathan Marsters	6-4/190		1-28-80	0	Chilliwack (BCJHL)
29	Steve Passmore	5-9/165	Thunder Bay, Ont.	1-29-73	2	Chicago, Cleveland (IHL)
1	Jamie Storr	6-2/198	Brampton, Ont.	12-28-75	6	Los Angeles

1999-2000 REVIEW
INDIVIDUAL STATISTICS
SCORING

	Games	G	A	Pts.	PIM	+/-	PPG	SHG	Shots	Shooting Pct.
Luc Robitaille	71	36	38	74	68	11	13	0	221	16.3
Zigmund Palffy	64	27	39	66	32	18	4	0	186	14.5
Glen Murray	78	29	33	62	60	13	10	1	202	14.4
Jozef Stumpel	57	17	41	58	10	23	3	0	126	13.5
Rob Blake	77	18	39	57	112	10	12	0	327	5.5
Bryan Smolinski	79	20	36	56	48	2	2	0	160	12.5
Donald Audette*	49	12	20	32	45	6	1	0	112	10.7
Garry Galley	70	9	21	30	52	9	2	0	96	9.4
Craig Johnson	76	9	14	23	28	-10	1	0	106	8.5
Jason Blake	64	5	18	23	26	4	0	0	131	3.8
Ian Laperriere	79	9	13	22	185	-14	0	0	87	10.3
Marko Tuomainen	63	9	8	17	80	-12	2	1	74	12.2
Jere Karalahti	48	6	10	16	18	3	4	0	69	8.7
Aki Berg	70	3	13	16	45	-1	0	0	70	4.3
Sean O'Donnell	80	2	12	14	114	4	0	0	51	3.9
Mattias Norstrom	82	1	13	14	66	22	0	0	62	1.6
Vladimir Tsyplakov*	29	6	7	13	4	6	1	0	30	20.0
Len Barrie*	46	5	8	13	56	5	0	0	46	10.9
Brad Chartrand	50	6	6	12	17	4	0	1	51	11.8
Bob Corkum	45	5	6	11	14	0	0	0	45	11.1

– 44 –

	Games	G	A	Pts.	PIM	+/-	PPG	SHG	Shots	Shooting Pct.
Jaroslav Modry	26	5	4	9	18	-2	5	0	32	15.6
Dan Bylsma	64	3	6	9	55	-2	0	1	43	7.0
Frantisek Kaberle*	37	0	9	9	4	3	0	0	41	0.0
Steve McKenna	46	0	5	5	125	3	0	0	14	0.0
Kelly Buchberger*	13	2	1	3	13	-2	0	0	20	10.0
Nelson Emerson*	5	1	1	2	0	1	0	0	13	7.7
Stephane Fiset (goalie)	47	0	2	2	4	0	0	0	0	0.0
Jason Podollan	1	0	1	1	2	0	0	0	2	0.0
Jamie Storr (goalie)	42	0	1	1	4	0	0	0	0	0.0
Philippe Boucher	1	0	0	0	0	0	0	0	3	0.0
Bill Huard	1	0	0	0	2	0	0	0	0	0.0
Jan Nemecek	1	0	0	0	0	0	0	0	0	0.0
Steven Reinprecht	1	0	0	0	2	0	0	0	0	0.0
Pavel Rosa	3	0	0	0	0	-1	0	0	1	0.0
Marcel Cousineau (goalie)	5	0	0	0	0	0	0	0	0	0.0

GOALTENDING

	Games	Min.	Goals	SO	Avg.	W	L	T	ENG	Shots	Sv. Pct.
Marcel Cousineau	5	171	6	0	2.11	1	1	0	0	64	.906
Jamie Storr	42	2206	93	1	2.53	18	15	5	5	1008	.908
Stephane Fiset	47	2592	119	1	2.75	20	15	7	5	1208	.901

*Played with two or more NHL teams.

RESULTS

OCTOBER

2— At Nashville ....W 2-0
4— At St. Louis ....W 3-2
6— At Florida ....L 2-4
7— At Tampa Bay ....W 5-2
9— At Washington ....T...*2-2
15— At Calgary ....W 4-1
16— At Edmonton ....L 4-5
20— Boston ....T...*2-2
22— Phoenix ....L 3-6
24— San Jose ....W 4-3
26— Washington ....W 5-2
28— Pittsburgh ....W 5-3
30— At Chicago ....W 3-1

NOVEMBER

2— At Pittsburgh ....W 5-4
3— At Detroit ....T...*1-1
6— Philadelphia ....L 3-5
9— Edmonton ....T...*1-1
11— Colorado ....W 5-2
14— At Phoenix ....W 3-2
16— Chicago ....W 3-2
18— Phoenix ....L 2-3
20— Montreal ....L 3-5
23— At Colorado ....W 6-2
24— At Dallas ....W...*2-3
27— San Jose ....W 4-1

DECEMBER

3— At Anaheim ....T...*1-1
4— Tampa Bay ....T...*3-3

8— Atlanta ....W 4-0
10— At Detroit ....L 1-3
11— At Montreal ....W 4-2
14— At New Jersey ....L 1-7
15— At N.Y. Rangers ....L 3-8
18— Chicago ....L 4-8
22— At San Jose ....L 1-2
26— Phoenix ....L...*2-3
29— At Colorado ....L 2-4
30— Edmonton ....W 8-2

JANUARY

3— At Dallas ....L 1-4
4— At St. Louis ....T...*2-2
6— Florida ....W 4-2
11— Ottawa ....L 3-4
13— St. Louis ....L 2-3
15— At San Jose ....L...*2-3
18— Buffalo ....W 5-3
20— Dallas ....L 2-5
23— Colorado ....W 3-2
26— At Dallas ....L 1-3
27— At Nashville ....W 6-2
29— At Toronto ....L 2-3
31— N.Y. Islanders ....W 5-2

FEBRUARY

3— Detroit ....W 6-3
8— Anaheim ....L 3-5
9— At Phoenix ....W 5-2
11— Dallas ....W 3-2
14— Calgary ....W...*4-3

16— At Chicago ....W 4-1
18— At Detroit ....W 3-2
19— At Buffalo ....L 1-4
21— At Edmonton ....L 3-6
23— At Calgary ....W 7-2
25— At Vancouver ....W 5-2
26— At San Jose ....L 3-6
29— Vancouver ....T...*1-1

MARCH

2— Carolina ....L 2-5
4— Nashville ....W...*3-2
7— Detroit ....L 1-3
9— N.Y. Rangers ....W 3-1
11— Calgary ....W 3-1
13— Vancouver ....W...*3-2
15— At Anaheim ....T...*2-2
17— St. Louis ....L 0-4
19— Nashville ....L...*1-2
21— Anaheim ....L 2-5
23— At Philadelphia ....W...*3-2
25— At Boston ....T...*4-4
26— At Atlanta ....W 4-1
29— San Jose ....T...*1-1

APRIL

1— Anaheim ....W 2-1
3— At Phoenix ....L 1-2
5— At Vancouver ....T...*1-1
7— Dallas ....W 3-2
9— At Anaheim ....W...*4-3

*Denotes overtime game.

MINNESOTA WILD
WESTERN CONFERENCE/NORTHWEST DIVISION

MINNESOTA WILD

Minnesota Schedule
Home games shaded; D—Day game; *—All-Star Game at Denver.

October

SUN	MON	TUE	WED	THU	FRI	SAT
1	2	3	4	5	6 ANA	7 PHO
8	9	10	11 PHI	12	13 STL	14
15 D EDM	16	17	18 TB	19	20 SJ	21
22 D FLA	23	24 MON	25 TOR	26	27 CAL	28
29 CHI	30	31				

November

SUN	MON	TUE	WED	THU	FRI	SAT
			1	2	3 EDM	4
5 CAL	6	7 COL	8 CAL	9	10 CHI	11
12 EDM	13	14	15 NYR	16	17 BUF	18 BOS
19	20	21	22 CAL	23	24 D CHI	25
26 VAN	27	28 SJ	29	30 PHO		

December

SUN	MON	TUE	WED	THU	FRI	SAT
					1	2 LA
3	4	5	6	7 CHI	8 ANA	9
10 NSH	D 11	12	13 CAR	14 WAS	15	16
17 DAL	D 18	19	20 OTT	21	22 LA	23
24	25	26	27 DET	28	29 PHO	30
31 ANA						

January

SUN	MON	TUE	WED	THU	FRI	SAT
	1	2	3 ATL	4	5 DET	6 STL
7	8	9	10 WAS	11	12 COL	13
14 NYR	15 CBJ	16	17 CBJ	18	19 NYI	20
21 D NJ	22	23	24 ANA	25	26	27 D LA
28	29	30 VAN	31			

February

SUN	MON	TUE	WED	THU	FRI	SAT
				1	2	3
4	* 5	6	7 TB	8	9 DAL	10
11 D PIT	12	13	14 PIT	15	16 LA	17
18 D SJ	19	20	21 DAL	22	23 COL	24 NSH
25	26 VAN	27	28			

March

SUN	MON	TUE	WED	THU	FRI	SAT
				1 CAL	2 EDM	3
4 VAN	5	6 STL	7	8 NJ	9 NYI	10
11 D DET	12	13	14 STL	15 PHI	16	17
18 D COL	19 DAL	20	21 NSH	22 DET	23	24
25 D VAN	26	27	28 PHO	29	30	31 NSH

April

SUN	MON	TUE	WED	THU	FRI	SAT
1	2 SJ	3	4 EDM	5	6 CBJ	7
8 D COL						

2000-2001 SEASON
CLUB DIRECTORY

Owner
Bob Naegele Jr.
Chief executive officer
Jac Sperling
President
Tod Leiweke
Exec. vice president/general manager
Doug Risebrough
Chief amateur scout
Tom Thompson
Head coach
Jacques Lemaire

Assistant coach
To be announced
Dir. of hockey operations and legal affairs
Tom Lynn
V.p. of communications and broadcasting
Bill Robertson
Mgr. of media relations/team services
Chris Kelleher
Head athletic trainer
To be announced

DRAFT CHOICES

Rd.— Player	Ht./Wt.	Overall	Pos.	Last team
1— Marian Gaborik	6-1/183	3	LW	Trencin, Slovakia
2— Nick Schultz	6-0/187	33	D	Prince Albert (WHL)
4— Marc Cavosie	6-0/173	99	C/LW	Rensselaer (ECAC)
5— Maxim Suchinsky	5-8/158	132	W	Avangard OMSK, Rus.
6— Erik Reitz	6-0/192	170	D	Barrie (OHL)
7— Brian Passmore	5-11/180	199	C	Oshawa (OHL)
7— Peter Bartos	6-0/185	214	W	Budejovice, Czech Rep.
8— Lubomir Sekeras	6-0/176	232	D	Trinec, Czech Rep.
8— Eric Johansson	6-0/190	255	C	Tri-City (WHL)

MISCELLANEOUS DATA

Home ice (capacity)
Xcel Energy Center (18,600)
Office address
317 Washington Street
St. Paul, MN 55102
Business phone
651-222-9453
Ticket information
651-222-9453
Website
www.wild.com

Training site
Minneapolis
Club colors
Red, green, gold and wheat
Radio affiliation
WCCO (830 AM)
TV affiliation
FOX Sports Net (Cable), KMSP UPN
(Channel 9)

No.	FORWARDS	Ht./Wt.	BORN Place	Date	NHL exp.	1999-2000 clubs
	Steve Aronson (RW)......	6-1/205	Minnetonka, Minn.	7-15-78	0	University of St. Thomas (MIAC)
	Peter Bartos (LW).........	6-0/185	Martin, Czechoslovakia	9-15-73	0	HC Ceske Budejovice (Czech Republic)
	Brian Bonin (C).............	5-9/187	St. Paul, Minn.	11-28-73	1	Syracuse (AHL)
	Michal Bros (C).............	6-1/195	Olomouc, Czechoslovakia	1-25-76	0	Sparta Praha (Czech Republic)
	Dan Cavanaugh (C/RW).	6-1/190	Springfield, Mass.	3-3-80	0	Boston University (Hockey East)
	Marc Cavosie (C/LW).....	6-0/173	Albany, N.Y.	8-6-81	0	Rensselaer Poly. Inst. (ECAC)
	Jeff Daw (C)	6-3/190	Carlisle, Ont.	2-28-72	0	Cleveland (IHL), Houston (IHL), Lowell (AHL)
34	Jim Dowd (C)	6-1/190	Brick, N.J.	12-25-68	9	Edmonton
	Randy Fitzgerald (LW) ...	5-11/174	Toronto	9-5-79	0	Plymouth (OHL)
	Marian Gaborik (LW)	6-1/183	Trencin, Czechoslovakia	2-14-82	0	Dukla Trencin (Slovakia)
	Pete Gardiner (RW)	6-5/220	Toronto	9-29-77	0	Rensselaer Poly. Inst. (ECAC)
44	Aaron Gavey (LW)	6-2/200	Sudbury, Ont.	2-22-74	5	Michigan (IHL), Dallas
14	Darby Hendrickson (LW)	6-1/195	Richfield, Minn.	8-28-72	7	Vancouver, Syracuse (AHL)
25	Sergei Krivokrasov (RW)	5-11/185	Angarsk, U.S.S.R.	4-15-74	8	Nashville, Calgary
21	Darryl Laplante (LW)	6-0/198	Calgary	3-28-77	3	Cincinnati (AHL), Detroit
	Cory Larose (C).............	6-0/188	Campellton, N.B.	5-14-75	0	Univ. of Maine (Hockey East)
	Christian Matte (RW).....	5-11/170	Hull, Que.	1-20-75	4	Hershey (AHL), Colorado
7	Steve McKenna (LW).....	6-8/255	Toronto	8-21-73	4	Los Angeles
	Brett McLean (LW)	5-11/175		8-14-78	0	Saint John (AHL), Johnstown (ECHL)
19	Jeff Nielsen (RW)	6-0/200	Grand Rapids, Minn.	9-20-71	4	Anaheim
21	Kai Nurminen (LW)........	6-1/198	Turku, Finland	3-29-69	1	TPS Turku (Finland)
36	Jeff Odgers (RW)	6-0/200	Spy Hill, Sask.	5-31-69	9	Colorado
	Richard Park (C)............	5-11/190	Seoul, South Korea	5-27-76	5	Utah (IHL)
22	Pavel Patera (C)............	6-1/172	Kladno, Czechoslovakia	9-6-71	1	Dallas, Vsetin (Czech Republic)
33	Scott Pellerin (LW)	5-11/190	Shediac, N.B.	1-9-70	7	St. Louis
39	Stacy Roest (C)	5-9/185	Lethbridge, Alta.	3-15-74	2	Detroit
	Cam Stewart (LW).........	5-11/196	Kitchener, Ont.	9-18-71	5	Florida
	Maxim Suchinsky (LW) .	5-8/158	U.S.S.R.	7-1-74	0	Avangard Omsk (Russian)
	Rickard Wallin (C)	6-2/183	Stockholm, Sweden	4-9-80	0	
	Brendan Walsh (C)	5-9/181	Dorchester, Mass.	10-22-74	0	University of Maine (ECAC)
17	Wes Walz (C)................	5-10/185	Calgary	5-15-70	6	Long Beach (IHL), Lugano (Switz.)
	DEFENSEMEN					
	Artem Anisimov............	6-1/187	Kazan, U.S.S.R.	7-27-76	0	Ak Bars Kazan (Russian)
	Chris Armstrong..........	6-0/205	Regina, Sask.	6-26-75	0	Kentucky (AHL)
	Ladislav Benysek	6-2/190	Olomouc, Czechoslavakia	3-24-75	1	Sparta Praha (Czech Republic)
6	Brad Bombardir............	6-1/205	Powell River, B.C.	5-5-72	3	New Jersey
56	Ian Herbers..................	6-4/225	Jasper, Alta.	7-18-67	2	Detroit (IHL), Tampa Bay, New York Islanders
33	Filip Kuba....................	6-3/205	Ostrava, Czechoslovakia	12-29-76	2	Florida, Houston (IHL)
7	Curtis Leschyshyn	6-1/205	Thompson, Man.	9-21-69	12	Carolina
	Nick Naumenko ...~......	5-11/185	Chicago	7-7-74	0	Kansas City (IHL)
6	Sean O'Donnell ... ₿₨.	6-3/230	Ottawa	9-13-71	6	Los Angeles
	Oleg Orekhovsky...........	6-0/183	Krasnoyarsk, U.S.S.R.	11-3-77	0	Dynamo Moscow (Russian)
	Erik Reitz	6-0/192	Detroit	8-29-82	0	Barrie (OHL)
	Nick Schultz.................	6-0/187	Strasbourg, Sask.	8-25-82	0	Prince Albert (WHL)
	GOALTENDERS					
1	Zac Bierk	6-4/205	Peterborough, Ont.	9-17-76	3	Detroit (IHL), Tampa Bay
	David Brumby...............	6-1/190	Victoria, B.C.	5-21-75	0	Jackson (ECHL), Providence (AHL)
30	Manny Fernandez	6-0/185	Etobicoke, Ont.	8-27-74	5	Dallas
	Derek Gustafson	5-11/210	Gresham, Ore.	6-21-79	0	St. Lawrence Univ. (ECAC)
29	Jamie McLennan	6-0/190	Edmonton	6-30-71	6	St. Louis

MINNESOTA WILD

MONTREAL CANADIENS
EASTERN CONFERENCE/NORTHEAST DIVISION

Montreal Schedule

Home games shaded; D—Day game; *—All-Star Game at Denver.

October

SUN	MON	TUE	WED	THU	FRI	SAT
1	2	3	4	5	6 NJ	7 TOR
8	9	10 EDM	11 NYR	12	13	14 CHI
15	16	17 BUF	18	19 PHI	20	21 CAR
22	23	24 MIN	25	26	27 NYI	28 NYI
29	30	31				

November

SUN	MON	TUE	WED	THU	FRI	SAT
			1 DET	2	3 BUF	4 NYR
5	6	7	8 FLA	9	10 TB	11 DAL
12	13	14 TB	15	16	17 WAS	18 TOR
19	20	21 FLA	22	23 ATL	24	25 BUF
26	27 ATL	28	29 EDM	30 VAN		

December

SUN	MON	TUE	WED	THU	FRI	SAT
					1	2 CAL
3	4	5 BUF	6	7	8 OTT	9 OTT
10	11	12	13 CAL	14	15 NJ	16 PIT
17	18 CBJ	19	20	21 NSH	22	23 TOR
24	25	26	27 VAN	28	29	30 EDM
31 CAL						

January

SUN	MON	TUE	WED	THU	FRI	SAT
	1	2 NYI	3	4	5 PIT	6 OTT
7	8	9	10 BOS	11	12 ATL	13 PHO
14	15	16 CAR	17	18 TB	19	20 NYR
21	22	23 STL	24 PIT	25	26	27 D WAS
28 D OTT	29	30	31 NYR			

February

SUN	MON	TUE	WED	THU	FRI	SAT
				1 BOS	2	3
4	*5	6 NJ	7	8	9	10 NYI
11 BUF	12	13 COL	14	15	16	17 WAS
18 OTT	19	20	21 VAN	22	23 WAS	24 TOR
25	26	27 PHI	28 PIT			

March

SUN	MON	TUE	WED	THU	FRI	SAT
				1	2	3 PHI
4	5	6 LA	7 ANA	8	9	10 PHO
11 SJ	12	13	14 CAR	15	16	17 BOS
18	19	20 FLA	21	22 BOS	23	24 ATL
25	26 CAR	27	28 FLA	29 TB	30	31 TOR

April

SUN	MON	TUE	WED	THU	FRI	SAT
1	2 BOS	3	4	5 PHI	6	7 NJ
8						

2000-2001 SEASON
CLUB DIRECTORY

President
Pierre Boivin
General manager
Rejean Houle
Vice president, finance and admin.
Fred Steer
Exec. vice president & g.m. events
Aldo Giampaolo
V.p., marketing and sales
Pierre Ladouceur
Advertising, sponsorship & publications
Francois-Xavier Seigneur
Coach
Alain Vigneault
Assistant coaches
Clement Jodoin
Roland Melanson
Dir. of player development and scout
Claude Ruel
Pro scouts
Pierre Mondou
Mario Tremblay
Chief scout
Pierre Dorion

Scouts
Neil Armstrong, Bred Bandel, Elmer Benning, Frederick Corey, Hannu Laine, Mats Naslund, Gerry O'Flaherty, Doug Robinson, Antonio Routa, Richard Scammell, Nikolai Vakourov
Director of team services
Michele Lapointe
Club physician
Dr. Vincent Lacroix
Athletic trainer
Gaetan Lefebvre
Assistant to the athletic trainer
Graham Rynbend
Strength and conditioning coach
Stephane Dube
Equipment manager
Pierre Gervais
Assistants to the equipment manager
Robert Boulanger
Pierre Ouellette
Video supervisor
Mario Leblanc

DRAFT CHOICES

Rd.— Player	Ht./Wt.	Overall	Pos.	Last team
1— Ron Hainsey	6-3/187	13	D	Mass.-Lowell (H. East)
1— Marcel Hossa	6-1/200	16	C	Portland (WHL)
3— Jozef Balej	5-11/170	78	RW	Portland (WHL)
3— Tyler Hanchuck	6-3/210	79	D	Brampton (OHL)
4— Johan Eneqvist	6-0/183	109	LW	Leksand, Sweden
4— Christian Larrivee	6-3/185	114	C	Chicoutimi (QMJHL)
5— Ryan Glenn	6-2/210	145	D	Walpole, EJHL
6— Scott Selig	6-3/178	172	C/RW	Thayer Acad., USHSE
6— Petr Chvojka	6-0/189	182	D	Plzen Jr., Czech Rep.
8— Joni Puurula	5-11/180	243	G	Hermes Div. 1, Fin.
9— Jonathan Gauthier	6-1/187	275	D	R.-Noranda (QMJHL)

MISCELLANEOUS DATA

Home ice (capacity)
Molson Centre (21,273)
Address
1260 rue de la Gauchetiere Ouest
Montreal, Que. H3B 5E8
Business phone
514-932-2582
Ticket information
514-790-1245 & 1-800-361-4595
Website
www.canadiens.com

Training site
Montreal
Club colors
Red, white and blue
Radio affiliation
CJAD (800 AM), CBF (690 AM)
TV affiliation
CFJP-TV (TQS Cable 5)

TRAINING CAMP ROSTER

No.	FORWARDS	Ht./Wt.	Place	BORN Date	NHL exp.	1999-2000 clubs
	Aaron Asham (RW/C)....	5-11/195	Portage-La-Prairie, Man.	4-13-78	2	Montreal, Quebec (AHL)
	Jozef Balej (RW).............	5-11/170	Ilava, Czechoslovakia	2-22-82	0	Portland (WHL)
35	Andrei Bashkirov (LW)...	6-0/215	Shelekhov, U.S.S.R.	6-22-70	2	Quebec (AHL), Montreal
	Eric Bertrand (LW).........	6-1/205	St. Ephrem, Que.	4-16-75	1	Milwaukee (IHL), New Jersey, Philadelphia (AHL), Atlanta
	Sylvain Blouin (RW)	6-2/222	Montreal	5-21-74	3	Worcester (AHL)
17	Benoit Brunet (LW)	5-11/198	Montreal	8-24-68	11	Montreal
63	Craig Darby (C).............	6-3/200	Oneida, N.Y.	9-26-72	5	Montreal
	Johan Eneqvist (LW)	6-0/183	Nacka, Sweden	1-21-82	0	Leksand (Sweden Jr.)
46	Matt Higgins (C)	6-2/190	Vernon, B.C.	10-29-77	3	Montreal, Quebec (AHL)
	Marcel Hossa (C)..........	6-1/200	Ilava, Czechoslovakia	10-12-81	0	Portland (WHL)
11	Saku Koivu (C)	5-10/181	Turku, Finland	11-23-74	5	Montreal
	Christian Larrivee (C)	6-2/185	Gaspe, Que.	8-25-82	0	Chicoutimi (QMJHL)
47	Juha Lind (C/LW)	5-11/185	Helsinki, Finland	1-2-74	2	Dallas, Montreal
14	Trevor Linden (C) .w.R.sIt	6-4/211	Medicine Hat, Alta.	4-11-70	12	Montreal
6	Trent McCleary (RW)	6-0/180	Swift Current, Sask.	9-8-72	4	Montreal, Quebec (AHL)
32	Oleg Petrov (RW)	5-8/175	Moscow, U.S.S.R.	4-18-71	5	Quebec (AHL), Montreal
37	Patrick Poulin (C)	6-1/216	Vanier, Que.	4-23-73	9	Montreal
	Mike Ribeiro (C)	5-11/150	Montreal	2-10-80	1	Montreal, Quebec (AHL), R.-Noranda (QMJHL), Quebec (QMJHL)
26	Martin Rucinsky (LW)....	6-1/205	Most, Czechoslovakia	3-11-71	9	Montreal
	Michael Ryder (C).........	6-0/187	St. Jean, Nfld.	3-31-80	0	Hull (QMJHL)
49	Brian Savage (RW)	6-2/192	Sudbury, Ont.	2-24-71	7	Montreal
	Scott Selig (C/RW)	6-2/178	Philadelphia	3-2-81	0	Thayer Academy (Mass. H.S.)
28	P.J. Stock (C)..............	5-10/190	Victoriaville, Que.	5-26-75	3	Hartford (AHL), New York Rangers
	Jason Ward (RW/C)	6-2/193	Chapleau, Ont.	1-16-79	1	Quebec (AHL), Montreal
34	Sergei Zholtok (C) .MunN'	6-1/191	Riga, U.S.S.R.	12-2-72	6	Quebec (AHL), Montreal
15	Dainius Zubrus (RW).....	6-4/224	Elektrenai, U.S.S.R.	6-16-78	4	Montreal
	DEFENSEMEN					
51	Francis Bouillon	5-8/189	New York	10-17-75	1	Montreal
43	Patrice Brisebois...........	6-1/203	Montreal	1-27-71	10	Montreal
	Petr Chvojka	6-0/189	Slany, Czechoslovakia	5-27-82	0	Plzen Jrs. (Czech Republic)
39	Enrico Ciccone..............	6-5/220	Montreal	4-10-70	8	Essen (Germany)
28	Karl Dykhuis	6-3/214	Sept-Iles, Que.	7-8-72	8	Philadelphia, Montreal
	Ryan Glenn	6-2/210	New Westminster, B.C.	6-7-80	0	Walpole (EJHL)
	Miroslav Guren	6-2/213	Uherske Hradiste, Czech.	9-24-76	2	Montreal, Quebec (AHL)
	Ron Hainsey	6-2/187	Bolton, Conn.	3-24-81	0	Mass.-Lowell (Hockey East)
	Tyler Hanchuck	6-2/210	Sault Ste. Marie, Ont.	2-7-82	0	Brampton (OHL)
24	Christian Laflamme.......	6-1/210	St. Charles, Que.	11-24-76	4	Edmonton, Montreal
	Andrei Markov	6-0/185	Voskresensk, U.S.S.R.	12-20-78	0	Dynamo Moscow (Russian)
21	Barry Richter	6-2/200	Madison, Wis.	9-11-70	4	Montreal, Quebec (AHL), Manitoba (IHL)
52	Craig Rivet..................	6-2/207	North Bay, Ont.	9-13-74	6	Montreal
	Stephane Robidas..........	5-11/180	Sherbrooke, Que.	3-3-73	1	Quebec (AHL), Montreal
44	Sheldon Souray	6-4/230	Elk Point, Alta.	7-13-76	3	New Jersey, Montreal
22	Eric Weinrich	6-1/213	Roanoke, Va.	12-19-66	12	Montreal
	GOALTENDERS					
1	Eric Fichaud................	5-11/171	Anjou, Que.	11-4-75	5	Carolina, Quebec (AHL)
	Mathieu Garon..............	6-2/182	Chandler, Que.	1-9-78	0	Quebec (AHL)
31	Jeff Hackett.................	6-1/198	London, Ont.	6-1-68	11	Montreal
35	Kevin Hodson	6-0/182	Winnipeg	3-27-72	5	Tampa Bay, Detroit (IHL)
60	Jose Theodore..............	5-11/185	Laval, Que.	9-13-76	5	Montreal

1999-2000 REVIEW
INDIVIDUAL STATISTICS

SCORING

	Games	G	A	Pts.	PIM	+/-	PPG	SHG	Shots	Shooting Pct.
Martin Rucinsky	80	25	24	49	70	1	7	1	242	10.3
Dainius Zubrus	73	14	28	42	54	-1	3	0	139	10.1
Sergei Zholtok....................................	68	26	12	38	28	2	9	0	163	16.0
Patrice Brisebois..................................	54	10	25	35	18	-1	5	0	88	11.4
Trevor Linden......................................	50	13	17	30	34	-3	4	0	87	14.9
Brian Savage	38	17	12	29	19	-4	6	1	107	15.9
Benoit Brunet	50	14	15	29	13	3	6	1	103	13.6
Eric Weinrich	77	4	25	29	39	4	2	0	120	3.3
Shayne Corson....................................	70	8	20	28	115	-2	2	0	121	6.6
Oleg Petrov	44	2	24	26	8	10	1	0	96	2.1
Turner Stevenson..................................	64	8	13	21	61	-1	0	0	94	8.5
Saku Koivu	24	3	18	21	14	7	1	0	53	5.7

MONTREAL CANADIENS

	Games	G	A	Pts.	PIM	+/-	PPG	SHG	Shots	Shooting Pct.
Karl Dykhuis*	67	7	12	19	40	-3	3	1	64	10.9
Craig Darby	76	7	10	17	14	-14	0	1	90	7.8
Craig Rivet	61	3	14	17	76	11	0	0	71	4.2
Francis Bouillon	74	3	13	16	38	-7	2	0	76	3.9
Patrick Poulin	82	10	5	15	17	-15	0	1	82	12.2
Jesse Belanger	16	3	6	9	2	2	0	0	21	14.3
Jim Cummins	47	3	5	8	92	-5	0	0	33	9.1
Arron Asham	33	4	2	6	24	-7	0	1	29	13.8
Igor Ulanov*	43	1	5	6	76	-11	0	0	33	3.0
Scott Lachance	57	0	6	6	22	-4	0	0	41	0.0
Scott Thornton*	35	2	3	5	70	-7	0	0	36	5.6
Sheldon Souray*	19	3	0	3	44	7	0	0	39	7.7
Jason Ward	32	2	1	3	10	-1	1	0	24	8.3
Juha Lind*	13	1	2	3	4	-2	0	0	6	16.7
Miloslav Guren	24	1	2	3	12	-5	1	0	20	5.0
Mike Ribeiro	19	1	1	2	2	-6	1	0	18	5.6
Christian Laflamme*	15	0	2	2	8	-5	0	0	6	0.0
Barry Richter	23	0	2	2	8	-5	0	0	13	0.0
Matt Higgins	25	0	2	2	4	-6	0	0	9	0.0
Trent McCleary	12	1	0	1	4	2	0	0	4	25.0
Dave Morissette	1	0	0	0	5	0	0	0	0	0.0
Stephane Robidas	1	0	0	0	0	0	0	0	0	0.0
Andrei Bashkirov	2	0	0	0	0	0	0	0	0	0.0
Vladimir Malakhov*	7	0	0	0	4	0	0	0	7	0.0
Jose Theodore (goalie)	30	0	0	0	0	0	0	0	0	0.0
Jeff Hackett (goalie)	56	0	0	0	4	0	0	0	0	0.0

GOALTENDING

	Games	Min.	Goals	SO	Avg.	W	L	T	ENG	Shots	Sv. Pct.
Jose Theodore	30	1655	58	5	2.10	12	13	2	2	717	.919
Jeff Hackett	56	3301	132	3	2.40	23	25	7	2	1543	.914

*Played with two or more NHL teams.

RESULTS

OCTOBER

2— Toronto .... L 1-4
6— At Edmonton .... L 1-2
8— At Calgary .... W ... 4-1
9— At Vancouver .... L 1-4
12—Florida .... L 1-3
14— At Philadelphia .... W ...*5-4
16—Buffalo .... W ... 2-1
18—N.Y. Islanders .... L 2-4
20—Colorado .... L 1-2
23— At Toronto .... L 2-3
27—Chicago .... L 0-1
30—N.Y. Rangers .... T ...*2-2

NOVEMBER

3— At New Jersey .... L 2-3
4— At N.Y. Islanders ...... L ...*1-2
6— At Ottawa .... L 1-2
10— At Pittsburgh .... L 4-5
11—Anaheim .... W ... 2-1
13—Atlanta .... W ... 4-2
16—San Jose .... L 1-4
18— At Nashville .... L 1-6
20— At Los Angeles .... W ... 5-3
22— At Anaheim .... W ... 2-1
23— At San Jose .... W ...*3-2
27—Vancouver .... W ... 2-1

DECEMBER

1— Dallas .... L 2-3
3— At N.Y. Rangers .... L 2-3
4— Philadelphia .... L 2-3

7— Calgary .... T ...*3-3
9— At N.Y. Islanders ...... W ... 4-2
11—Los Angeles .... L 2-4
13— At Washington .... W ... 1-0
16—New Jersey .... L 1-2
18— At Toronto .... L 1-2
20—Pittsburgh .... W ... 5-1
23— At Boston .... T ...*3-3
27— At Ottawa .... T ...*4-4
29—Ottawa .... L 2-3

JANUARY

2— N.Y. Rangers .... T ...*2-2
4— At Washington .... L 1-6
6— At St. Louis .... L 3-4
7— At Colorado .... L 1-4
11—Detroit .... W ... 3-0
14— At Buffalo .... W ... 2-1
15—Boston .... T ...*2-2
19—N.Y. Islanders .... W ... 3-0
22—Pittsburgh .... W ... 4-2
24— At Carolina .... W ...*2-3
29—Philadelphia .... T ...*2-2
30—Carolina .... W ... 3-0

FEBRUARY

2— At Florida .... L 1-3
3— At Tampa Bay .... W ...*2-1
8— Edmonton .... L ...*4-5
10—Washington .... L 0-1
12—Ottawa .... W ... 5-4
14—Florida .... W ... 4-1

16— At Atlanta .... W ... 5-1
17— At Carolina .... W ... 3-0
19—Toronto .... W ... 2-1
22—Phoenix .... W ... 1-0
24—New Jersey .... W ...*3-2
26—Washington .... L 0-3
27— At New Jersey .... L 0-3

MARCH

1— At Chicago .... W ... 4-1
2— At Boston .... W ... 5-2
4— At Toronto .... L 3-4
6— Atlanta .... W ... 3-2
8— At Pittsburgh .... W ... 3-0
10— At Buffalo .... W ... 3-2
11—Boston .... L 3-5
14—Tampa Bay .... L 3-4
16— At Philadelphia .... T ...*1-1
18—Carolina .... W ... 3-2
20— At Buffalo .... L 1-4
22— At Atlanta .... T ...*1-1
25— At Florida .... L 2-4
26— At Tampa Bay .... W ... 3-1
29—Boston .... W ... 4-3

APRIL

1— Buffalo .... L 0-2
2— At Detroit .... L ...*5-6
5— At N.Y. Rangers .... W ... 3-0
6— Tampa Bay .... W ... 5-1
8— Ottawa .... L 1-3

*Denotes overtime game.

NASHVILLE PREDATORS
WESTERN CONFERENCE/CENTRAL DIVISION

Nashville Schedule
Home games shaded; D—Day game;
*—All-Star Game at Denver. †—Game played in Japan

October

SUN	MON	TUE	WED	THU	FRI	SAT
1	2	3	4	5	6 † PIT	7 † PIT
8	9	10	11	12	13 WAS	14 CAR
15	16	17 LA	18	19 DET	20	21 SJ
22	23	24 VAN	25 COL	26	27 FLA	28
29	30	31 STL				

November

SUN	MON	TUE	WED	THU	FRI	SAT
			1	2 PHI	3	4 ANA
5	6	7 NYI	8 NJ	9	10	11 BOS
12	13	14	15 ATL	16 CBJ	17	18 DET
19	20 DET	21	22 DAL	23	24 STL	25
26 D CAR	27	28 CAL	29	30 CHI		

December

SUN	MON	TUE	WED	THU	FRI	SAT
					1 CHI	2
3	4 VAN	5	6 EDM	7 CAL	8	9
10 D MIN	11	12 PHI	13	14 EDM	15	16 CHI
17	18	19	20 TOR	21 MON	22	23 D NYR
24	25	26 COL	27	28 ANA	29 COL	30
31						

January

SUN	MON	TUE	WED	THU	FRI	SAT
	1 D VAN	2	3	4 STL	5	6 BUF
7	8 VAN	9	10 EDM	11 CAL	12	13 SJ
14	15	16 EDM	17 DAL	18	19 BOS	20
21 STL	22	23 ATL	24 DET	25	26	27 COL
28	29 PHO	30	31 ANA			

February

SUN	MON	TUE	WED	THU	FRI	SAT
				1 LA	2	3
4	* 5	6	7	8 CBJ	9	10 CBJ
11	12	13 DAL	14	15	16 SJ	17
18 TB	19	20 DET	21 WAS	22	23	24 MIN
25	26	27 LA	28			

March

SUN	MON	TUE	WED	THU	FRI	SAT
				1 CBJ	2	3
4 D NYR	5	6 PHO	7	8 LA	9	10 SJ
11 ANA	12	13	14	15 CHI	16	17 PHO
18	19 CBJ	20	21 MIN	22 CHI	23	24 OTT
25	26	27	28	29 PHO	30	31 MIN

April

SUN	MON	TUE	WED	THU	FRI	SAT
1	2	3	4 DAL	5 CAL	6	7 STL
8						

2000-2001 SEASON
CLUB DIRECTORY

Owner, chairman and governor
Craig Leipold
Alternate governor
Terry London
President, COO and alternate governor
Jack Diller
Exec. v.p./g.m. and alternate governor
David Poile
Assistant general manager
Ray Shero
Dir. of media relations/team services
Frank Buonomo
Communications manager
Ken Anderson
Communications coordinator
Greg Harvey
Head coach
Barry Trotz
Assistant coaches
Paul Gardner
Brent Peterson

Chief amateur scout
Craig Channell
Director of player personnel
Paul Fenton
Strength and conditioning coach
Mark Nemish
Goaltending coach
Mitch Korn
Head athletic trainer
Dan Redmond
Equipment manager
Pete Rogers
Assistant equipment manager
Chris Scoppetto
Massage therapist
Anthony Garrett
Video coach
Robert Bouchard

DRAFT CHOICES

Rd.— Player	Ht./Wt.	Overall	Pos.	Last team
1— Scott Hartnell	6-2/192	6	RW	Prince Albert (WHL)
2— Daniel Widing	6-0/185	36	RW	Leksand, Sweden
3— Mattias Nilsson	6-3/189	72	D	MoDo, Sweden
3— Libor Pivko	6-3/192	89	LW	Havirov, Czech Rep.
5— Matt Hendricks	5-11/190	131	C	Blaine H.S., Minn.
5— Mike Stuart	6-1/193	137	D	Colorado (WCHA)
5— Matt Koalska	6-0/188	154	C	Twin Cities, USHL
6— Tomas Harant	6-3/180	173	D	Zilina, Slovakia
6— Zbynek Irgl	5-11/178	197	W	HC Vitkovice, Czech
7— Jure Penko		203	G	Green Bay, USHL
8— Mats Christeen	6-1/183	236	D	Sodertalje Jr., Sweden
9— Martin Hohener	6-1/172	284	D	Kloten, Switzerland

MISCELLANEOUS DATA

Home ice (capacity)
Nashville Arena (17,298)
Address
501 Broadway
Nashville, TN 37203
Business phone
615-770-2300
Ticket information
615-770-7825
Website
www.nashvillepredators.com

Training site
Nashville
Club colors
Blue, gold, silver, steel and orange
Radio affiliation
WTN (99.7 FM)
TV affiliation
FOX Sports South

TRAINING CAMP ROSTER

No.	FORWARDS	Ht./Wt.	Place	BORN Date	NHL exp.	1999-2000 clubs
	Denis Arkhipov (RW).....	6-3/195	Kazan, U.S.S.R.	5-19-79	0	Ak Bars Kazan (Russian)
	Martin Bartek (LW).......	6-0/197	Kindgssed Jill, Czech.	7-17-80	0	Moncton (QMJHL)
71	Sebastien Bordeleau (C) .	5-11/185	Vancouver	2-15-75	5	Nashville
	Marian Cisar (RW)........	6-0/192	Bratislava, Czechoslovakia	2-25-78	1	Milwaukee (IHL), Nashville
21	Tom Fitzgerald (RW)......	6-0/196	Billerica, Mass.	8-28-68	12	Nashville
40	David Gosselin (C)........	6-1/197	Levis, Que.	6-22-77	1	Milwaukee (IHL), Nashville
39	Sean Haggerty (LW)......	6-1/186	Rye, N.Y.	2-11-76	3	Kansas City (IHL), New York Islanders
	Scott Hartnell (RW)......	6-2/192	Regina, Sask.	4-18-82	0	Prince Albert (WHL)
	Matt Hendricks (C)	5-11/190	Minneapolis	6-19-81	0	Blaine (USHS (West))
	Zbynek Irgl (LW/RW).....	5-11/178	Ostrava, Czechoslovakia	11-29-80	0	HC Vitkovice (Czech Republic)
22	Greg Johnson (C)..........	5-10/202	Thunder Bay, Ont.	3-16-71	7	Nashville
10	Patric Kjellberg (LW).....	6-2/208	Trelleborg, Sweden	6-17-69	3	Nashville
	Matt Koalska (C)...........	5-11/188	St. Paul, Minn.	5-16-80	0	Twin Cities (USHL)
11	David Legwand (C)	6-2/185	Detroit	8-17-80	2	Nashville
18	Mark Mowers (C)	5-11/184	Whitesboro, N.Y.	2-16-74	2	Milwaukee (IHL), Nashville
16	Ville Peltonen (LW).......	5-10/181	Vantaa, Finland	5-24-73	4	Nashville
	Libor Pivko (LW)	6-3/192	Novy Vicin, Czechoslovakia	3-29-80	0	Havirov (Czech Republic)
27	Randy Robitaille (C)	5-11/198	Ottawa	10-12-75	4	Nashville
7	Cliff Ronning (C)...........	5-8/165	Vancouver	10-1-65	14	Nashville
	Ryan Tobler (LW)..........	6-3/192	Calgary	5-13-76	0	Milwaukee (IHL)
12	Rob Valicevic (C)..........	6-2/192	Detroit	1-6-71	2	Nashville
24	Scott Walker (RW)	5-10/190	Cambridge, Ont.	7-19-73	6	Nashville
12	Mike Watt (LW/C)	6-2/208	Seaforth, Ont.	3-31-76	3	New York Islanders, Lowell (AHL)
	Daniel Widing (RW)......	6-0/185	Gavle, Sweden	4-13-82	0	Leksand (Sweden Jr.), Leksand (Sweden)
43	Vitali Yachmenev (RW)..	5-9/190	Chelyabinsk, U.S.S.R.	1-8-75	5	Nashville
	DEFENSEMEN					
15	Drake Berehowsky.........	6-2/212	Toronto	1-3-72	9	Nashville
26	Bubba Berenzweig	6-2/218	Arlington Heights, Ill.	8-8-77	1	Milwaukee (IHL), Nashville
38	Alexandre Boikov	6-0/198	Chelyabinsk, U.S.S.R.	2-7-75	1	Milwaukee (IHL), Nashville
	Jayme Filipowicz...........	6-2/222	Arlington Heights, Ill.	6-15-76	0	Milwaukee (IHL)
42	Rory Fitzpatrick	6-2/205	Rochester, N.Y.	1-11-75	3	Worcester (AHL), Milwaukee (IHL)
	Tomas Harant	6-3/180	Slovakia	4-28-80	0	Zilina (Slovakia Jrs.)
23	Bill Houlder.................	6-2/211	Thunder Bay, Ont.	3-11-67	13	Tampa Bay, Nashville
32	Cale Hulse...................	6-3/215	Edmonton	11-10-73	5	Calgary
41	Richard Lintner.............	6-3/214	Trencin, Czechoslovakia	11-15-77	1	Nashville, Milwaukee (IHL)
8	Craig Millar	6-2/206	Winnipeg	7-12-76	4	Nashville, Milwaukee (IHL)
	Marc Moro	6-1/215	Toronto	7-17-77	2	Milwaukee (IHL), Nashville
20	John Namestnikov	5-11/190	Norvgrood, U.S.S.R.	10-9-71	6	Hartford (AHL), Milwaukee (IHL), Nashville
	Mattias Nilsson.............	6-3/189	Ornskoldsvik, Sweden	2-6-82	0	MoDo Ornskoldsvik Jrs. (Sweden Jr.)
3	Karlis Skrastins.............	6-1/205	Riga, U.S.S.R.	7-9-74	2	Milwaukee (IHL), Nashville
46	Pavel Skrbek................	6-3/213	Kladno, Czechoslovakia	8-9-78	1	Wilkes-Barre/Scranton (AHL), Milwaukee (IHL)
	Mike Stuart..................	6-0/193	Chicago	8-31-80	0	Colorado College (WCHA)
44	Kimmo Timonen	5-10/196	Kuopio, Finland	3-18-75	2	Nashville
5	Jan Vopat	6-0/210	Most, Czechoslovakia	3-22-73	5	Nashville, Milwaukee (IHL)
	GOALTENDERS					
1	Mike Dunham	6-3/200	Johnson City, N.Y.	6-1-72	4	Milwaukee (IHL), Nashville
	Brian Finley.................	6-2/180	Sault Ste. Marie, Ont.	7-3-81	0	Barrie (OHL)
	Jan Lasak	6-0/204	Zvolen, Czechoslovakia	4-10-79	0	Hampton Roads (ECHL)
30	Chris Mason	6-0/189	Red Deer, Alta.	4-20-76	1	Milwaukee (IHL)
29	Tomas Vokoun..............	6-3/183	Karlovy Vary, Czech.	7-2-76	3	Nashville, Milwaukee (IHL)

1999-2000 REVIEW

INDIVIDUAL STATISTICS

SCORING

	Games	G	A	Pts.	PIM	+/-	PPG	SHG	Shots	Shooting Pct.
Cliff Ronning	82	26	36	62	34	-13	7	0	248	10.5
Patric Kjellberg	82	23	23	46	14	-11	9	0	129	17.8
Greg Johnson	82	11	33	44	40	-15	2	0	133	8.3
Kimmo Timonen	51	8	25	33	26	-5	2	1	97	8.2
Vitali Yachmenev	68	16	16	32	12	5	1	1	120	13.3
Drake Berehowsky	79	12	20	32	87	-4	5	0	102	11.8
David Legwand	71	13	15	28	30	-6	4	0	111	11.7
Scott Walker	69	7	21	28	90	-16	0	1	98	7.1
Ville Peltonen	79	6	22	28	22	-1	2	0	125	4.8
Sergei Krivokrasov*	63	9	17	26	40	-7	3	0	132	6.8

	Games	G	A	Pts.	PIM	+/-	PPG	SHG	Shots	Shooting Pct.
Robert Valicevic	80	14	11	25	21	-11	2	1	113	12.4
Randy Robitaille	69	11	14	25	10	-13	2	0	113	9.7
Sebastien Bordeleau	60	10	13	23	30	-12	0	2	127	7.9
Tom Fitzgerald	82	13	9	22	66	-18	0	3	119	10.9
Craig Millar	57	3	11	14	28	-6	0	0	50	6.0
Bill Houlder*	57	2	12	14	24	-6	1	0	68	2.9
Karlis Skrastins	59	5	6	11	20	-7	1	0	51	9.8
Mark Mowers	41	4	5	9	10	0	0	0	50	8.0
Bob Boughner*	62	2	4	6	97	-13	0	0	32	6.3
Richard Lintner	33	1	5	6	22	-6	0	0	58	1.7
Joel Bouchard*	52	1	4	5	23	-11	0	0	60	1.7
Dan Keczmer	24	0	5	5	28	-2	0	0	21	0.0
David Gosselin	10	2	1	3	6	-4	0	0	14	14.3
Niklas Andersson*	7	0	1	1	0	0	0	0	7	0.0
Darren Turcotte	9	0	1	1	4	0	0	0	13	0.0
Tomas Vokoun (goalie)	33	0	1	1	8	0	0	0	0	0.0
Andy Berenzweig	2	0	0	0	0	-1	0	0	3	0.0
Alexandre Boikov	2	0	0	0	2	0	0	0	1	0.0
Yevgeny Namestnikov	2	0	0	0	2	0	0	0	3	0.0
Marian Cisar	3	0	0	0	4	-2	0	0	2	0.0
Philip Crowe	4	0	0	0	10	0	0	0	1	0.0
Jan Vopat	6	0	0	0	6	1	0	0	3	0.0
Marc Moro	8	0	0	0	40	-3	0	0	3	0.0
Patrick Cote	21	0	0	0	70	-7	0	0	8	0.0
Mike Dunham (goalie)	52	0	0	0	6	0	0	0	0	0.0

GOALTENDING

	Games	Min.	Goals	SO	Avg.	W	L	T	ENG	Shots	Sv. Pct.
Tomas Vokoun	33	1879	87	1	2.78	9	20	1	4	908	.904
Mike Dunham	52	3077	146	0	2.85	19	27	6	3	1584	.908

*Played with two or more NHL teams.

RESULTS

OCTOBER
2— Los Angeles .... L...0-2
5— Colorado .... L...2-3
10— At Chicago .... T....*3-3
11— At Toronto .... W...4-2
14— San Jose .... L...1-5
16— Dallas .... W...3-2
20— At Buffalo .... W...4-3
23— Edmonton .... W...4-3
28— At San Jose .... L...2-3
30— At Vancouver .... L...1-4
31— At Edmonton .... L...2-4

NOVEMBER
3— At Calgary .... L...*4-5
5— Chicago .... L...1-3
10— At Chicago .... W...4-2
11— At Ottawa .... W...2-1
13— At Pittsburgh .... L...2-6
18— Montreal .... W...6-1
20— Vancouver .... L...1-3
22— At St. Louis .... L...*2-3
24— Boston .... L...2-5
26— At Washington .... L...0-1
27— Anaheim .... L...3-4
30— Phoenix .... L...3-6

DECEMBER
2— At St. Louis .... L...1-3
4— Detroit .... W...4-1
6— At Atlanta .... W...*4-3
8— At Detroit .... L...3-6

10— St. Louis .... L...2-4
11— Florida .... L...2-4
14— At Tampa Bay .... T...*4-4
15— At Florida .... L...2-3
18— Colorado .... T...*2-2
19— At Philadelphia .... T...*1-1
21— At Boston .... W...3-1
23— St. Louis .... T...*2-2
26— At St. Louis .... W...3-2
28— Carolina .... W...3-2
30— Atlanta .... W...6-0

JANUARY
1— San Jose .... W...3-2
5— At Dallas .... L...1-3
6— At Detroit .... L...2-5
8— Chicago .... W...6-3
11— At Colorado .... L...2-4
13— Vancouver .... L...*3-4
15— Pittsburgh .... W...4-2
18— Phoenix .... T...*4-4
21— At Calgary .... L...*4-5
23— At Vancouver .... W...2-1
24— At Edmonton .... W...*3-2
27— Los Angeles .... L...2-6
29— Calgary .... W...3-1
31— At N.Y. Rangers .... L...1-5

FEBRUARY
2— At N.Y. Islanders .... W...6-4
3— At New Jersey .... L...1-4
10— Buffalo .... L...*1-2

12— Washington .... L...2-4
15— Edmonton .... L...1-2
16— At Dallas .... L...0-3
18— St. Louis .... L...1-2
21— Dallas .... W...5-2
23— At Chicago .... W...4-2
26— Tampa Bay .... L...2-3
29— New Jersey .... L...1-2

MARCH
2— At San Jose .... L...3-4
4— At Los Angeles .... L...*2-3
5— At Anaheim .... L...0-1
7— Chicago .... W...3-1
10— Detroit .... L...1-3
12— Edmonton .... W...4-3
14— At Detroit .... L...*2-3
16— At Colorado .... T...*2-2
17— At Phoenix .... W...*4-3
19— At Los Angeles .... W...*2-1
21— Philadelphia .... L...0-2
23— Detroit .... L...3-6
25— Calgary .... L...1-2
28— N.Y. Islanders .... W...3-2
29— At Carolina .... L...1-3
31— Vancouver .... W...2-1

APRIL
3— At Anaheim .... L...1-3
5— At Phoenix .... L...2-3
7— Anaheim .... L...1-5
*Denotes overtime game.

NEW JERSEY DEVILS
EASTERN CONFERENCE/ATLANTIC DIVISION

New Jersey Schedule

Home games shaded; D—Day game; *—All-Star Game at Denver.

October

SUN	MON	TUE	WED	THU	FRI	SAT
1	2	3	4	5	6 MON	7
8	9	10	11 FLA	12	13 OTT	14 ANA
15	16	17 ATL	18	19 WAS	20	21 TB
22	23	24	25 FLA	26	27 CAR	28 PIT
29	30	31				

November

SUN	MON	TUE	WED	THU	FRI	SAT
			1 PHI	2 TOR	3	4 D LA
5	6	7	8 NSH	9	10 PIT	11 BUF
12	13	14 SJ	15	16 BOS	17	18 D CAR
19	20	21	22 ANA	23 LA	24	25 SJ
26	27	28	29 NYR	30		

December

SUN	MON	TUE	WED	THU	FRI	SAT
					1 NYI	2
3 D NYI	4	5 COL	6 BUF	7	8	9 D WAS
10 ATL	11	12	13	14	15 MON	16 PHI
17	18	19	20 DAL	21	22 FLA	23 TB
24	25	26	27 CBJ	28	29 WAS	30
31 CBJ						

January

SUN	MON	TUE	WED	THU	FRI	SAT
	1	2 PHI	3	4 NYI	5	6 D NYR
7 PHO	8	9	10 CHI	11	12	13 TOR
14	15	16 BOS	17	18 PHI	19	20 D ATL
21 D MIN	22	23	24 DAL	25 STL	26	27 BOS
28	29	30 DET	31 NYI			

February

SUN	MON	TUE	WED	THU	FRI	SAT
				1	2	3
4 *	5	6 MON	7	8 OTT	9	10 D PIT
11 D NYR	12	13	14 OTT	15	16 PIT	17 BUF
18	19 TOR	20	21	22 BUF	23 CAR	24
25	26 FLA	27 NYI	28			

March

SUN	MON	TUE	WED	THU	FRI	SAT
				1	2 CAR	3
4 TB	5	6 OTT	7	8 MIN	9	10 D PHI
11	12	13 COL	14 PHO	15	16	17 EDM
18	19 CAL	20	21 NYR	22	23 VAN	24
25 PIT	26	27 TB	28 ATL	29	30	31 D NYR

April

SUN	MON	TUE	WED	THU	FRI	SAT
1	2	3 WAS	4	5	6 BOS	7 MON
8						

2000-2001 SEASON
CLUB DIRECTORY

President and general manager
Louis A. Lamoriello
Head coach
Larry Robinson
Assistant coaches
Vyacheslav Fetisov
Bobby Carpenter
Goaltending coach
Jacques Caron
Medical trainer
Bill Murray
Strength & conditioning coordinator
Michael Vasalani

Equipment manager
Dana McGuane
Assistant equipment managers
Lou Centanni
Harry Bricker
V.p., communications and broadcasting
Rick Minch
Director, public relations
Kevin Dessart
Director, information & publications
Mike Levine

DRAFT CHOICES

Rd.— Player	Ht./Wt.	Overall	Pos.	Last team
1— David Hale	6-2/204	22	D	Sioux City, USHL
2— Teemu Laine	6-1/194	39	RW	Jokerit, Finland
2— Aleksander Suglobov	6-0/176	56	C	Yaroslavl, Russia
2— Matt DeMarchi	6-3/180	57	D	Minnesota (WCHA)
2— Paul Martin	6-1/170	62	D	Elk River H.S., USHSW
3— Max Birbraer	6-2/185	67	LW	New Market, OPJHL
3— Michael Rupp	6-5/228	76	LW	Erie (OHL)
4— Phil Cole	6-4/190	125	D	Lethbridge (WHL)
5— Mike Jefferson	5-9/150	135	C	Barrie (OHL)
5— Matus Kostur	6-2/183	164	G	Banska Bystrica, Slov.
6— Deryk Engelland	6-2/202	194	D	Moose Jaw (WHL)
7— Ken Magowan	6-2/207	198	LW	Vernon, BCJHL
8— Warren McCutcheon	6-4/188	257	C	Lethbridge (WHL)

MISCELLANEOUS DATA

Home ice (capacity)
Continental Airlines Arena (19,040)
Address
P.O. Box 504
50 Route 120 North
East Rutherford, N.J. 07073
Business phone
201-935-6050
Ticket information
201-935-3900

Website
www.newjerseydevils.com
Training site
West Orange, NJ
Club colors
Red, black and white
Radio affiliation
WABC (770 AM)
TV affiliation
FOX Sports Net New York

TRAINING CAMP ROSTER

No.	FORWARDS	Ht./Wt.	Place	BORN — Date	NHL exp.	1999-2000 clubs
25	Jason Arnott (C)............	6-4/225	Collingworth, Ont.	10-11-74	7	New Jersey
	Jiri Bicek (LW)..............	5-10/195	Kosice, Czechoslovakia	12-3-78	0	Albany (AHL)
	Max Birbraer (LW).........	6-2/185	Ust-Kamenogorsk, U.S.S.R.	12-15-80	0	Newmarket (OPJA)
18	Sergei Brylin (C)...........	5-10/190	Moscow, U.S.S.R.	1-13-74	6	New Jersey
	Pierre Dagenais (LW)....	6-4/210	Blainville, Que.	3-4-78	0	Albany (AHL)
26	Patrik Elias (LW)...........	6-1/200	Trebic, Czechoslovakia	4-13-76	5	HC Pardubice (Czech Republic), New Jersey
23	Scott Gomez (C)............	5-11/200	Anchorage, Alaska	12-23-79	1	New Jersey
16	Bobby Holik (C).............	6-4/230	Jihlava, Czechoslovakia	1-1-71	10	New Jersey
	Mike Jefferson (C).........	5-9/190	Brampton, Ont.	10-21-80	0	Barrie (COJHL)
11	Steve Kelly (C).............	6-2/211	Vancouver	10-26-76	4	Detroit (IHL), Albany (AHL), New Jersey
	Teemu Laine (RW).........	6-0/194	Helsinki, Finland	8-9-82	0	Jokerit Helsinki (Finland), Jokerit Helsinki (Finland Jr.)
11	John Madden (C)............	5-11/195	Barrie, Ont.	5-4-73	2	New Jersey
21	Randy McKay (RW).......	6-2/210	Montreal	1-25-67	12	New Jersey
33	Jim McKenzie (RW).......	6-4/227	Gull Lake, Sask.	11-3-69	11	Anaheim, Washington
89	Alexander Mogilny (RW)	5-11/200	Khabarovsk, U.S.S.R.	2-18-69	11	Vancouver, New Jersey
20	Jay Pandolfo (LW).........	6-1/190	Winchester, Mass.	12-27-74	4	New Jersey
	Michael Rupp (LW)........	6-5/228	Cleveland	1-13-80	0	Erie (OHL)
23	Turner Stevenson (RW) .	6-3/226	Port Alberni, B.C.	5-18-72	8	Montreal
	Aleksander Suglobov.....	6-0/176	U.S.S.R.	1-15-82	0	Torpedo-2 Yaroslavl (Russian Div. II)
17	Petr Sykora (RW)..........	6-0/190	Plzen, Czechoslovakia	11-19-76	5	New Jersey
42	Ed Ward (RW)	6-3/220	Edmonton	11-10-69	7	Atlanta, Anaheim
	DEFENSEMEN					
	Josef Boumedienne ....TB	6-1/190	Stockholm, Sweden	1-12-78	0	Tappara Tampere (Finland)
	Phil Cole	6-3/190	Winnipeg	8-6-82	0	Lethbridge (WHL)
3	Ken Daneyko.................	6-1/215	Windsor, Ont.	4-17-64	17	New Jersey
	Matt DeMarchi..............	6-3/180	Bemidji, Minn.	5-4-81	0	Univ. of Minnesota (WCHA)
	Deryk Engelland............	6-1/202	Edmonton	4-3-82	0	Moose Jaw (WHL)
	Sascha Goc ....TB	6-2/220	Schwenningen, W. Germany	4-17-79	0	Albany (AHL)
	David Hale	6-2/204	Colorado Springs, Colo.	6-18-81	0	Sioux City (USHL)
	Andre Lakos	6-6/230	Vienna, Austria	7-29-79	0	Albany (AHL)
	Josh MacNevin	6-2/185	Calgary	7-14-77	0	Providence College (Hockey East), Albany (AHL)
	Paul Martin	6-1/170	Minneapolis	3-5-81	0	Elk River (USHS (West))
	Willie Mitchell	6-3/205	Port McNeill, B.C.	4-23-77	1	Albany (AHL), New Jersey
27	Scott Niedermayer........	6-1/200	Edmonton	8-31-73	9	New Jersey
28	Brian Rafalski	5-9/200	Dearborn, Mich.	9-28-73	1	New Jersey
4	Scott Stevens	6-1/215	Kitchener, Ont.	4-1-64	18	New Jersey
2	Ken Sutton	6-1/205	Edmonton	11-5-69	9	New Jersey, Albany (AHL)
5	Colin White	6-4/210	New Glasgow, Nova Scotia	12-12-77	1	Albany (AHL), New Jersey
	GOALTENDERS					
30	Martin Brodeur	6-2/205	Montreal	5-6-72	8	New Jersey
	J.F. Damphousse	6-0/175	St. Alexis-des-Monts, Que.	7-21-79	0	Albany (AHL), Augusta (ECHL)
	Frederic Henry	5-11/180	Cap Rouge, Que.	8-9-77	0	Albany (AHL)
	Matus Kostur................	6-2/183	Czechoslovakia	3-28-80	0	Banska Bystrica (Slovakia)
31	Chris Terreri..................	5-9/170	Providence, R.I.	11-15-64	13	New Jersey

NEW JERSEY DEVILS

1999-2000 REVIEW

INDIVIDUAL STATISTICS

SCORING

	Games	G	A	Pts.	PIM	+/-	PPG	SHG	Shots	Shooting Pct.
Patrik Elias................................	72	35	37	72	58	16	9	0	183	19.1
Scott Gomez................................	82	19	51	70	78	14	7	0	204	9.3
Petr Sykora................................	79	25	43	68	26	24	5	1	222	11.3
Jason Arnott................................	76	22	34	56	51	22	7	0	244	9.0
Bobby Holik................................	79	23	23	46	106	7	7	0	257	8.9
Randy McKay................................	67	16	23	39	80	8	3	0	116	13.8
Claude Lemieux*............................	70	17	21	38	86	-3	7	0	221	7.7
Scott Niedermayer........................	71	7	31	38	48	19	1	0	109	6.4
Brian Rafalski................................	75	5	27	32	28	21	1	0	128	3.9
Scott Stevens................................	78	8	21	29	103	30	0	1	133	6.0
Sergei Nemchinov........................	53	10	16	26	18	1	0	1	55	18.2
Brendan Morrison*........................	44	5	21	26	8	8	2	0	79	6.3
John Madden................................	74	16	9	25	6	7	0	6	115	13.9
Sergei Brylin................................	64	9	11	20	20	0	1	0	84	10.7

	Games	G	A	Pts.	PIM	+/-	PPG	SHG	Shots	Shooting Pct.
Krzysztof Oliwa	69	6	10	16	184	-2	1	0	61	9.8
Lyle Odelein*	57	1	15	16	104	-10	0	0	59	1.7
Jay Pandolfo	71	7	8	15	4	0	0	0	86	8.1
Sheldon Souray*	52	0	8	8	70	-6	0	0	74	0.0
Vadim Sharifijanov*	20	3	4	7	8	-6	0	0	20	15.0
Alexander Mogilny*	12	3	3	6	4	-4	2	0	35	8.6
Denis Pederson*	35	3	3	6	16	-7	0	0	41	7.3
Ken Daneyko	78	0	6	6	98	13	0	0	74	0.0
Vladimir Malakhov*	17	1	4	5	19	1	1	0	11	9.1
Martin Brodeur (goalie)	72	1	4	5	16	0	0	0	1	100.0
Brian Rolston*	11	3	1	4	0	-2	1	0	33	9.1
Brad Bombardir	32	3	1	4	6	-6	0	0	24	12.5
Colin White	21	2	1	3	40	3	0	0	29	6.9
Ken Sutton	6	0	2	2	2	2	0	0	10	0.0
Deron Quint*	4	1	0	1	2	-2	0	0	6	16.7
Steve Kelly	1	0	0	0	0	0	0	0	0	0.0
Willie Mitchell	2	0	0	0	0	1	0	0	2	0.0
Eric Bertrand*	4	0	0	0	0	-1	0	0	1	0.0
Chris Terreri (goalie)	12	0	0	0	2	0	0	0	0	0.0

GOALTENDING

	Games	Min.	Goals	SO	Avg.	W	L	T	ENG	Shots	Sv. Pct.
Martin Brodeur	72	4312	161	6	2.24	43	20	8	3	1797	.910
Chris Terreri	12	649	37	0	3.42	2	9	0	2	299	.876

*Played with two or more NHL teams.

RESULTS

OCTOBER

2— At Atlanta ....W.....4-1
7— Pittsburgh........................L.....5-7
9— Tampa Bay ....W.....1-0
11— At Ottawa ....T....*2-2
13—Anaheim............................W.....3-2
16—N.Y. Islanders ....W.....4-1
22— At Dallas............................L.....*1-2
23— At St. Louis.......................L.....1-3
27—St. Louis...........................W.....2-1
29— At Carolina ....W.....4-2
30— At Philadelphia.................L.....3-5

NOVEMBER

3— Montreal...........................W.....3-2
4— At Boston...........................L.....1-3
6— Toronto............................T....*3-3
9— Philadelphia.....................W.....2-1
12—Atlanta.............................W.....5-1
13— At Washington..................L.....2-4
17—Boston..............................T....*2-2
20—Ottawa.............................W.....3-1
24— At Anaheim ....W.....2-1
25— At Phoenix ....L.....2-4
28— At San Jose ....L.....*3-4

DECEMBER

1— N.Y. Rangers ....W.....3-2
3— Ottawa.............................W.....7-4
4— Calgary.............................L.....2-4
7— Pittsburgh ....W.....2-1
9— At Chicago.........................W.....4-0

11—Edmonton ....L.....1-3
14—Los Angeles ....W.....7-1
16— At Montreal ....W.....2-1
18—Washington ....W.....5-4
19— At N.Y. Islanders ....L.....3-5
22—Philadelphia ....W.....3-2
23— At Toronto.........................L.....1-4
26— At N.Y. Rangers ....T....*3-3
27—Buffalo..............................W.....4-1
29—Boston ....W....*5-4

JANUARY

1— At Boston...........................T....*2-2
3— At Ottawa ....W....*4-3
5— At Pittsburgh ....W.....3-1
6— At Buffalo...........................W.....6-3
8— Phoenix ....W.....4-3
11— At Tampa Bay ....W.....6-5
14—Washington ....L.....*2-3
15— At Philadelphia ....W.....4-1
17—Carolina ....W.....5-2
19—Chicago ....W.....4-1
21—N.Y. Islanders ....W.....4-0
26— At Florida..........................W.....3-2
28— At Carolina........................L.....*3-4
29— At Detroit...........................L.....1-3

FEBRUARY

2— At N.Y. Rangers ....W.....3-1
3— Nashville...........................W.....4-1
8— At N.Y. Rangers ....T....*2-2
9— N.Y. Rangers ....W.....4-1

13—San Jose ....W......3-1
15—Philadelphia ....W.....4-2
17—Colorado ....T.....*5-5
19—N.Y. Islanders ....L.....2-4
21— At Buffalo...........................L.....2-3
24— At Montreal ....L.....*2-3
25—Toronto ....L.....1-3
27—Montreal ....W.....3-0
29— At Nashville ....W.....2-1

MARCH

2— At Colorado ....L.....0-5
4— At Vancouver ....L.....2-4
5— At Calgary..........................T.....*2-2
10— At Atlanta ....W.....9-0
11— At Washington ....L.....2-4
13— At Pittsburgh ....W.....3-2
15—Dallas ....L.....2-3
17—Tampa Bay ....L.....1-3
19—Florida...............................W.....5-2
21—Carolina ....L.....0-5
24— At N.Y. Islanders...............W.....8-2
25— At Toronto..........................L.....3-5
28— At Pittsburgh ....L.....2-3
31—Atlanta...............................W.....6-0

APRIL

2— At Tampa Bay ....W......4-1
3— At Florida...........................L.....2-5
6— Buffalo...............................L.....0-5
8— Florida ....W....*2-1

*Denotes overtime game.

New York Islanders Schedule

Home games shaded; D—Day game; *—All-Star Game at Denver.

October

SUN	MON	TUE	WED	THU	FRI	SAT
1	2	3	4	5	6 TB	7
8	9	10	11 TOR	12	13	14 CAL
15	16	17 ANA	18	19	20 ATL	21 WAS
22	23	24	25	26	27 MON	28 MON
29	30	31 BOS				

November

SUN	MON	TUE	WED	THU	FRI	SAT
			1 FLA	2	3 TB	4
5 LA	D 6	7 NSH	8	9 BUF	10	11 SJ
12	13	14	15	16 LA	17	18 SJ
19 ANA	20	21	22 NYR	23	24 WAS	25 DET
26	27 TB	28	29	30 TOR		

December

SUN	MON	TUE	WED	THU	FRI	SAT
					1 NJ	2
3 NJ	D 4	5	6 FLA	7	8	9 ATL
10 PHI	11	12 WAS	13	14	15 TOR	16 OTT
17	18	19 CAR	20	21 DAL	22	23 CBJ
24	25	26	27 BOS	28	29 ATL	30 BUF
31						

January

SUN	MON	TUE	WED	THU	FRI	SAT
	1	2 MON	3	4 NJ	5	6 PHO
7 CAR	8	9 CHI	10	11	12 PIT	13 PIT
14	15	16 COL	17	18	19 MIN	20
21 ATL	D 22	23 OTT	24	25	26 NYR	27 BUF
28	29	30	31 NJ			

February

SUN	MON	TUE	WED	THU	FRI	SAT
				1 PHI	2	3
4	* 5	6	7 BUF	8	9 PHI	10 MON
11	12 OTT	13	14 PHI	15	16 EDM	17
18 VAN	19	20	21	22 PHI	23	24 FLA D
25 PIT	26	27 NJ	28			

March

SUN	MON	TUE	WED	THU	FRI	SAT
			1 CAR	2	3 TB	
4	5 NYR	6 WAS	7	8	9 MIN	10
11 FLA	D 12	13	14 PIT	15	16	17 CBJ
18 CAR	19	20 STL	21	22	23 DAL	24
25 PHO	26	27	28 NYR	29 NYR	30	31 BOS

April

SUN	MON	TUE	WED	THU	FRI	SAT
1	2 PIT	3	4 TOR	5	6 OTT	7 BOS
8						

Co-owners
Charles Wang
Sanjay Kumar
President
John Sanders
General manager
Mike Milbury
Assistant g.m./dir. of player personnel
Gordie Clark
Asst. to the g.m./mgr., player contracts
Mike Santos
Head coach
Butch Goring
Associate coach
Lorne Henning
Assistant coach
Greg Cronin

Head certified athletic trainer
Rich Campbell
Strength & conditioning coach
Sean Donellan
Head equipment manager
Joe McMahon
Assistant equipment managers
Rick Harper
Eric Miklich
Vice president, communications
Chris Botta
Manager of media relations
Jason Lagnese
Publications coordinator
Kerry Gwydir

DRAFT CHOICES

Rd.— Player	Ht./Wt.	Overall	Pos.	Last team
1— Rick DiPietro	6-0/185	1	G	Boston Univ. (H. East)
1— Raffi Torres	6-0/207	5	LW	Brampton (OHL)
4— Arto Tukio	6-0/189	101	D	Ilves-Tampere, Finland
4— Vladimir Gorbunov	6-0/176	105	W	HC Moscow, Russia
5— Dimitri Upper	6-0/176	136	C	Nizhny Novgorod, Kaz.
5— Kristofer Ottoson	5-10/187	148	W	Djurgarden, Sweden
7— Ryan Caldwell	6-2/174	202	D	Thunder Bay, USHL
9— Dimitri Altarev	6-3/191	264	F	Penza, Russia
9— Tomi Pettinen	6-3/211	267	D	Ilves-Tampere, Finland

MISCELLANEOUS DATA

Home ice (capacity)
Nassau Veterans Memorial Coliseum
(16,297)
Address
Uniondale, NY 11553
Business phone
516-794-4100
Ticket information
1-800-882-4753
Website
www.newyorkislanders.com

Training site
Syosset, NY
Club colors
Blue and orange
Radio affiliation
WJWR (620 AM), WLUX (530 AM)
TV affiliation
FOX Sports New York

TRAINING CAMP ROSTER

NEW YORK ISLANDERS

No.	FORWARDS	Ht./Wt.	Place	Date	NHL exp.	1999-2000 clubs
43	Mikael Andersson (LW) .	5-11/184	Malmo, Sweden	5-10-66	15	Philadelphia, New York Islanders
36	Niklas Andersson (LW) ..	5-9/175	Kunglav, Sweden	5-20-71	5	Chicago (IHL), N.Y.I., Nashville
18	Tim Connolly (C)	6-0/186	Baldwinsville, N.Y.	5-7-81	1	New York Islanders
21	Mariusz Czerkawski	6-0/199	Radomski, Poland	4-13-72	7	New York Islanders
14	Chris Ferraro (RW/C).....	5-10/185	Port Jefferson, N.Y.	1-24-73	5	New York Islanders, Providence (AHL)
	Vladimir Gorbunov (LW).	6-0/176	U.S.S.R.	4-22-82	0	HC CSKA Moscow (Russian)
15	Brad Isbister (RW)	6-4/228	Edmonton	5-7-77	3	New York Islanders
	Juraj Kolnik (RW)	5-10/182	Nitra, Czechoslovakia	11-13-80	0	Rimouski (QMJHL)
28	Jason Krog (C)	5-11/191	Fernie, B.C.	10-9-75	1	Lowell (AHL), N.Y.I., Providence (AHL)
13	Oleg Kvasha (C)	6-5/216	Moscow, U.S.S.R.	7-26-78	2	Florida
16	Dan Lacroix (C)	6-2/205	Montreal	3-11-69	7	Chicago (IHL), New York Islanders
13	Claude Lapointe (C)	5-9/183	Lachine, Que.	10-11-68	10	New York Islanders
44	Mark Lawrence (RW)	6-4/219	Burlington, Ont.	1-27-72	5	N.Y.I., Lowell (AHL), Chicago (IHL)
10	Mats Lindgren (C)	6-2/202	Skelleftea, Sweden	10-1-74	4	New York Islanders
	Justin Mapletoft (C).......	6-1/180	Lloydminster, Sask.	6-11-81	0	Red Deer (WHL)
32	Petr Mika (C)	6-4/195	Prague, Czechoslovakia	2-12-79	1	Lowell (AHL), New York Islanders
11	Bill Muckalt (RW)	6-1/200	Surrey, B.C.	7-15-74	2	Vancouver, New York Islanders
37	Dimitri Nabokov (C/LW) ..	6-2/209	Novosibirsk, U.S.S.R.	1-4-77	3	Lowell (AHL), New York Islanders
16	Vladimir Orszagh (RW)..	5-11/173	Banska Bystrica, Czech.	5-24-77	3	Lowell (AHL), New York Islanders
	Kristofer Ottoson (RW)..	5-10/187	Sweden	1-9-76	0	Djurgarden Stockholm (Sweden)
21	Mark Parrish (RW)	5-11/191	Edina, Minn.	2-2-77	2	Florida
24	Scott Pearson (LW)........	6-2/205	Cornwall, Ont.	12-19-69	10	Chicago (IHL), New York Islanders
	Taylor Pyatt (LW)	6-4/220	Thunder Bay, Ont.	8-19-81	0	Sudbury (OHL)
38	Dave Scatchard (C).......	6-2/220	Hinton, Alta.	2-20-76	3	Vancouver, New York Islanders
14	Mike Stapleton (C)........	5-10/185	Sarnia, Ont.	5-5-66	13	Atlanta
	Raffi Torres (LW)	6-0/207	Toronto	10-8-81	0	Brampton (OHL)
	Dimitri Upper (C)	6-0/176	U.S.S.R.	8-27-78	0	Tor. Nichny Nov. (Russian)
8	Steve Webb (RW)..........	6-0/208	Peterborough, Ont.	4-30-75	4	New York Islanders
	Mattias Weinhandl (RW).	6-0/183	Ljungby, Sweden	6-1-80	0	MoDo Ornskoldsvik (Sweden)

DEFENSEMEN

No.		Ht./Wt.	Place	Date	NHL exp.	1999-2000 clubs
34	Mathieu Biron	6-6/212	Lac St. Charles, Que.	4-29-80	1	New York Islanders
58	Aris Brimanis.................	6-3/195	Cleveland	3-14-72	4	Kansas City (IHL), New York Islanders
33	Eric Cairns	6-6/235	Oakville, Ont.	6-27-74	4	Providence (AHL), New York Islanders
3	Zdeno Chara	6-9/246	Trencin, Czechoslovakia	3-18-77	3	New York Islanders
41	Ray Giroux	5-11/185	North Bay, Ont.	7-20-76	1	Lowell (AHL), New York Islanders
5	Kevin Haller	6-2/199	Trochu, Alta.	12-5-70	11	Anaheim
22	Roman Hamrlik..............	6-2/215	Gottwaldov, Czechoslovakia	4-12-74	8	Edmonton
29	Kenny Jonsson	6-3/211	Angelholm, Sweden	10-6-74	6	New York Islanders
36	Evgeny Korolev.............	6-1/186	Moscow, U.S.S.R.	7-24-78	1	Lowell (AHL), New York Islanders
	Branislav Mezei.............	6-5/221	Nitra, Czechoslovakia	10-8-80	0	Belleville (OHL)
7	Ray Schultz...................	6-2/200	Red Deer, Alta.	11-14-76	3	Kansas City (IHL), New York Islanders
	Arto Tukio	6-0/189	Tampere, Finland	4-4-81	0	Ilves Tampere (Finland)

GOALTENDERS

No.		Ht./Wt.	Place	Date	NHL exp.	1999-2000 clubs
	Rick DiPietro.................	6-0/185	Lewiston, Maine	9-19-81	0	Boston University (Hockey East)
30	Wade Flaherty...............	6-0/187	Terrace, B.C.	1-11-68	8	New York Islanders
35	Stephen Valiquette.........	6-5/205	Etobicoke, Ont.	8-20-77	1	Providence (AHL), Trenton (ECHL), Lowell (AHL), New York Islanders
34	John Vanbiesbrouck	5-8/176	Detroit	9-4-63	18	Philadelphia

1999-2000 REVIEW

INDIVIDUAL STATISTICS

SCORING

	Games	G	A	Pts.	PIM	+/-	PPG	SHG	Shots	Shooting Pct.
Mariusz Czerkawski	79	35	35	70	34	-16	16	0	276	12.7
Brad Isbister............................	64	22	20	42	100	-18	9	0	135	16.3
Tim Connolly	81	14	20	34	44	-25	2	1	114	12.3
Claude Lapointe	76	15	16	31	60	-22	2	1	129	11.6
Jorgen Jonsson*	68	11	17	28	16	-6	1	2	95	11.6
Dave Scatchard*	44	12	14	26	93	0	0	1	103	11.7
Josh Green	49	12	14	26	41	-7	2	0	109	11.0
Kenny Jonsson	65	1	24	25	32	-15	1	0	84	1.2
Olli Jokinen	82	11	10	21	80	0	1	2	138	8.0
Jamie Heward	54	6	11	17	26	-9	2	0	92	6.5
Jamie Rivers............................	75	1	16	17	84	-4	1	0	95	1.1
Mats Lindgren	43	9	7	16	24	0	0	0	68	13.2
Gino Odjick*	46	5	10	15	90	-7	0	0	91	5.5
Mike Watt	45	5	6	11	17	-8	0	1	49	10.2
Dmitri Nabokov	26	4	7	11	16	-8	0	0	40	10.0
Zdeno Chara	65	2	9	11	57	-27	0	0	47	4.3
Niklas Andersson*	17	3	7	10	8	-3	1	0	24	12.5
Eric Cairns	67	2	7	9	196	-5	0	0	55	3.6

	Games	G	A	Pts.	PIM	+/-	PPG	SHG	Shots	Shooting Pct.
Raymond Giroux	14	0	9	9	10	0	0	0	24	0.0
Mathieu Biron	60	4	4	8	38	-13	2	0	70	5.7
Bill Muckalt*	12	4	3	7	4	5	0	0	26	15.4
Johan Davidsson*	14	2	4	6	0	0	0	0	21	9.5
Jason Krog	17	2	4	6	6	-1	1	0	22	9.1
Mark Lawrence	29	1	5	6	26	-13	0	0	33	3.0
Chris Ferraro	11	1	3	4	8	1	0	0	15	6.7
Steve Webb	65	1	3	4	103	-4	0	0	27	3.7
Vladimir Orszagh	11	2	1	3	4	1	0	0	16	12.5
Aris Brimanis	18	2	1	3	6	-5	2	0	16	12.5
Ted Drury*	55	2	1	3	31	-8	1	0	48	4.2
Evgeny Korolev	17	1	2	3	8	-10	0	0	7	14.3
Ian Herbers*	6	0	3	3	2	6	0	0	3	0.0
Mikael Andersson*	19	0	3	3	4	-1	0	0	19	0.0
Sean Haggerty	5	1	1	2	4	3	0	0	2	50.0
Vlad Chebaturkin	17	1	1	2	8	-3	0	0	9	11.1
Tony Hrkac*	7	0	2	2	0	-1	0	0	2	0.0
Richard Pilon*	9	0	2	2	34	-2	0	0	0	0.0
Eric Brewer	26	0	2	2	20	-11	0	0	30	0.0
Dallas Eakins	2	0	1	1	2	3	0	0	4	0.0
Scott Pearson	2	0	1	1	0	1	0	0	5	0.0
Ray Schultz	9	0	1	1	30	1	0	0	2	0.0
Kevin Weekes (goalie)*	36	0	1	1	0	0	0	0	1	0.0
Daniel Lacroix	1	0	0	0	0	-1	0	0	0	0.0
Petr Mika	3	0	0	0	0	-1	0	0	1	0.0
Wade Flaherty (goalie)	4	0	0	0	0	0	0	0	0	0.0
Stephen Valiquette (goalie)	6	0	0	0	0	0	0	0	0	0.0
Felix Potvin (goalie)*	22	0	0	0	2	0	0	0	0	0.0
Roberto Luongo (goalie)	24	0	0	0	0	0	0	0	0	0.0

GOALTENDING

	Games	Min.	Goals	SO	Avg.	W	L	T	ENG	Shots	Sv. Pct.
Stephen Valiquett	6	193	6	0	1.87	2	0	0	0	117	.949
Wade Flaherty	4	182	7	0	2.31	0	1	1	1	81	.914
Felix Potvin*	22	1273	68	1	3.21	5	14	3	3	632	.892
Roberto Luongo	24	1292	70	1	3.25	7	14	1	2	730	.904
Kevin Weekes*	36	2026	115	1	3.41	10	20	4	3	1173	.902

*Played with two or more NHL teams.

RESULTS

OCTOBER
2— At Tampa Bay ....L...2-4
10— Colorado.........................W.....4-2
11— N.Y. Rangers.................L.....2-4
14— Atlanta..........................L.....0-2
16— At New Jersey ....L.....1-4
18— At Montreal ....W.....4-2
23— Vancouver ....T...*2-2
27— At Florida ....L.....3-6
30— Carolina ....L.....0-4

NOVEMBER
3— At N.Y. Rangers ....T....*3-3
4— Montreal.......................W...*2-1
6— At Buffalo.....................L.....1-2
10— At Carolina ....W.....2-0
12— At Chicago ....L.....0-5
13— St. Louis ....L.....3-5
19— At Colorado ....W.....3-2
21— At Edmonton ....T....*4-4
23— At Calgary ....L.....2-3
27— Washington ....L.....3-4
28— At Boston ....W.....2-1
30— Dallas...........................L.....1-2

DECEMBER
2— Calgary ....L.....0-5
4— Atlanta..........................L.....3-4
7— At Washington ....L.....2-4
9— Montreal ....L.....2-4
11— At Ottawa.....................T....*1-1
14— Edmonton ....L.....2-4

JANUARY
15— At Toronto ....L.....1-5
18— Buffalo ....T...*2-2
19— New Jersey..................W.....5-3
21— Pittsburgh ....L.....0-4
23— N.Y. Rangers ....W.....4-2
27— Boston ....W.....3-0
29— Toronto ....L.....1-2
30— At Pittsburgh ....L.....3-9

2— Philadelphia ....L.....1-4
4— Boston ....L.....3-7
6— At Philadelphia.............L.....2-3
8— At Boston ....W.....5-2
10— Phoenix ....T...*2-2
12— At Florida ....L.....3-4
13— At Tampa Bay ....L.....2-4
15— N.Y. Rangers................L.....2-5
17— Ottawa..........................L...*3-4
19— At Montreal ....L.....0-3
21— At New Jersey ....L.....0-4
22— Tampa Bay ....W.....2-0
26— At Anaheim...................W.....4-2
29— At San Jose ....W...*3-2
31— At Los Angeles ....L.....2-5

FEBRUARY
2— Nashville ....L.....4-6
3— At Pittsburgh ....L.....2-4
8— Carolina ....L.....3-4
10— Tampa Bay ....W...*5-4
12— Pittsburgh ....W.....5-1

13— At N.Y. Rangers ....W.....4-2
15— San Jose.......................L.....1-4
17— At Philadelphia.............T...*2-2
19— At New Jersey ....W.....4-2
21— Detroit ....L.....0-2
25— At Detroit ....L.....2-5
26— Philadelphia ....L.....1-5
28— Washington ....L.....2-3

MARCH
2— Ottawa...........................T...*5-5
4— Buffalo ....W.....4-2
5— At Philadelphia ....W...*4-3
9— At Phoenix ....L.....0-5
10— At Dallas ....W...*4-3
12— At Buffalo......................L.....2-4
15— At Washington ....L.....3-4
16— At Atlanta ....W.....4-2
18— Florida ....L.....2-4
21— Pittsburgh ....L.....2-8
22— At Toronto ....W.....5-2
24— New Jersey....................L.....2-8
26— At Carolina ....L.....1-4
28— At Nashville ....L.....2-3

APRIL
1— Chicago ....T...*2-2
2— At Atlanta.......................L.....4-5
6— At Ottawa ....W.....2-1
7— Toronto ....L.....1-2
9— Florida ....W.....3-2

*Denotes overtime game.

NEW YORK RANGERS
EASTERN CONFERENCE/ATLANTIC DIVISION

New York Rangers Schedule

Home games shaded; D—Day game; *—All-Star Game at Denver.

October

SUN	MON	TUE	WED	THU	FRI	SAT
1	2	3	4	5	6	7 ATL
8	9	10	11 MON	12	13	14 PIT
15	16 ANA	17	18 CHI	19	20	21
22 TB	23	24 PHI	25	26 PHI	27 PIT	28
29 BOS	30	31				

November

SUN	MON	TUE	WED	THU	FRI	SAT
			1 TB	2 OTT	3	4 MON
5	6	7 EDM	8	9 WAS	10	11
12 PHO	13	14	15 MIN	16	17 VAN	18 CAL
19	20	21 TOR	22 NYI	23	24 BUF	25
26 OTT	27	28 LA	29 NJ	30		

December

SUN	MON	TUE	WED	THU	FRI	SAT
					1	2 TOR
3 COL	4	5	6 WAS	7	8 BUF	9 BOS
10	11	12 SJ	13	14 LA	15 ANA	16
17	18 FLA	19	20 STL	21	22	23 D NSH
24	25	26	27 CAR	28 ATL	29	30
31 DAL						

January

SUN	MON	TUE	WED	THU	FRI	SAT
	1	2	3	4 PHO	5	6 D NJ
7	8 DAL	9	10	11	12	13 D BOS
14 MIN	15	16 PHI	17	18 TOR	19	20 MON
21	22 CAR	23	24 CAR	25	26 NYI	27 TOR
28	29 ATL	30	31 MON			

February

SUN	MON	TUE	WED	THU	FRI	SAT
				1	2	3
4	*5	6 BUF	7	8	9 FLA	10
11 D NJ	12 CBJ	13 D	14	15	16	17 TB
18	19 D CHI	20	21	22	23 PIT	24
25 PHI	26 OTT	27	28 FLA			

March

SUN	MON	TUE	WED	THU	FRI	SAT
				1	2 PIT	3
4 NSH	D 5 NYI	6	7	8	9 WAS	10 OTT
11	12 PIT	13	14 BUF	15	16	17 D PHI
18	19 WAS	20	21 NJ	22	23	24 D DET
25 BOS	26	27	28 NYI	29 NYI	30	31 D NJ

April

SUN	MON	TUE	WED	THU	FRI	SAT
1 ATL	D 2	3	4 CAR	5 TB	6	7 D FLA
8						

2000-2001 SEASON
CLUB DIRECTORY

Chief executive officer/governor
David W. Checketts
President and g.m./alternate governor
Glen Sather
Executive v.p. and general counsel
Kenneth W. Munoz
Vice president and business manager
Francis P. Murphy
V.p., legal and business affairs
Marc Schoenfeld
Vice president, controller
John Cudmore
Alternate governor
Kenneth W. Munoz
Assistant general manager
Don Maloney
Head coach
Ron Low
Assistant coaches
Ted Green
Walt Kyle
Development coach
John Paddock
Assistant development coach
Mike Busniuk
Scouting staff
Darwin Bennett, Dave Brown, Ray Clearwater, Martin Madden, Martin Madden Jr., Kevin McDonald, Christer Rockstom, Dick Todd

Scouting manager
Bill Short
Video assistant
Jerry Dineen
Vice president of business operations
Mark Piazza
Vice president of marketing
Jeanie Baumgartner
Vice president of public relations
John Rosasco
Manager of public relations
Jason Vogel
Community relations assistant
Jennifer Schoenfeld
Team physician and orthopedic surgeon
Dr. Barton Nisonson
Assistant team physician
Dr. Anthony Maddalo
Medical trainer
Jim Ramsay
Equipment trainer
Acacio Marques

DRAFT CHOICES

Rd.— Player	Ht./Wt.	Overall	Pos.	Last team
2— Filip Novak	6-0/174	64	D	Regina (WHL)
3— Dominic Moore	6-0/180	95	C	Harvard (ECAC)
4— Jon Disalvatore	6-1/180	104	RW	Providence (H. East)
4— Premsyl Duben	6-3/200	112	D	Jihlava, Czech Rep.
5— Nathan Martz	6-3/169	140	C	Chilliwack, BCJHL
5— Brandon Snee	6-1/195	143	G	Union (ECAC)
6— Sven Helfenstein	5-11/176	175	C/RW	Kloten, Switzerland
7— Henrik Lundqvist	5-11/167	205	G	Frolunda, Sweden
8— Dan Eberly	6-0/180	238	D	Rensselaer (ECAC)
9— Martin Richter		269	D	Saipa, Czech Republic

MISCELLANEOUS DATA

Home ice (capacity)
Madison Square Garden (18,200)
Address
2 Pennsylvania Plaza
New York, NY 10121
Business phone
212-465-6486
Ticket information
212-307-7171
Website
www.newyorkrangers.com

Training site
Burlington, VT
Club colors
Blue, red and white
Radio affiliation
WFAN (660 AM)
TV affiliation
MSG Network

TRAINING CAMP ROSTER

No.	FORWARDS	Ht./Wt.	Place (BORN)	Date	NHL exp.	1999-2000 clubs
38	Derek Armstrong (C)	6-0/193	Ottawa	4-23-73	0	Hartford (AHL), New York Rangers
8	Pavel Brendl (RW) PHIL	6-1/197	Opocno, Czechoslovakia	3-23-81	0	Calgary (WHL), Hartford (AHL)
	Stefan Cherneski (RW)	6-0/195	Winnipeg	9-19-78	0	Hartford (AHL)
10	Jason Dawe (LW)	5-10/190	North York, Ont.	5-29-73	7	Milwaukee (IHL), Hartford (AHL), New York Rangers
19	Rob DiMaio (RW) DAL	5-10/190	Calgary	2-19-68	12	Boston, New York Rangers
20	Radek Dvorak (RW)	6-1/194	Tabor, Czechoslovakia	3-9-77	5	Florida, New York Rangers
14	Theo Fleury (RW)	5-6/180	Oxbow, Sask.	6-29-68	12	New York Rangers
36	Daniel Goneau (RW)	6-0/195	Lachine, Que.	1-16-76	3	Hartford (AHL), New York Rangers
9	Adam Graves (LW) S.J	6-0/200	Tecumseh, Ont.	4-12-68	13	New York Rangers
	Sven Helfenstein (C/RW)	5-11/190	Winterthur, Switzerland	7-30-82	0	Kloten (Switzerland)
27	Jan Hlavac (LW) PHIL	6-0/183	Prague, Czechoslovakia	9-20-76	1	New York Rangers, Hartford (AHL)
13	Valeri Kamensky (LW) DAL	6-2/202	Voskresensk, U.S.S.R.	4-18-66	9	New York Rangers
28	Eric Lacroix (LW)	6-1/207	Montreal	7-15-71	7	New York Rangers
19	Darren Langdon (LW)	6-1/210	Deer Lake, Nfld.	1-8-71	6	New York Rangers
16	Jamie Lundmark (C)	6-0/174	Edmonton	1-16-81	0	Moose Jaw (WHL)
15	John MacLean (RW) DAL	6-0/205	Oshawa, Ont.	11-20-64	17	New York Rangers
6	Manny Malhotra (C)	6-2/210	Mississauga, Ont.	5-18-80	2	New York Rangers, Hartford (AHL), Guelph (OHL)
	Nathan Martz (C)	6-3/169	Chilliwack, B.C.	3-4-81	0	Chilliwack (BCJHL)
11	Mark Messier (C)	6-1/205	Edmonton	1-18-61	21	Vancouver
	Dominic Moore (C)	6-0/180	Ontario	8-3-80	0	Harvard University (ECAC)
93	Petr Nedved (C)	6-3/195	Liberec, Czechoslovakia	12-9-71	9	New York Rangers
	Brad Smyth (RW)	6-0/195	Ottawa	3-13-73	4	Hartford (AHL)
26	Tim Taylor (C)	6-1/188	Stratford, Ont.	2-6-69	7	New York Rangers
14	Johan Witehall (RW)	6-1/198	Goteborg, Sweden	1-7-72	2	Hartford (AHL), New York Rangers
18	Mike York (C)	5-10/185	Pontiac, Mich.	1-3-78	1	New York Rangers

DEFENSEMEN

No.	DEFENSEMEN	Ht./Wt.	Place	Date	NHL exp.	1999-2000 clubs
25	Jason Doig O.T.T	6-3/228	Montreal	1-29-77	4	New York Rangers, Hartford (AHL)
	Premsyl Duben	6-3/200	Jihlava, Czechoslovakia	10-5-81	0	Jihlava (Slovakia)
3	Kim Johnsson PHIL	6-2/189	Malmo, Sweden	3-16-76	1	New York Rangers
	Tomas Kloucek	6-3/203	Prague, Czechoslovakia	3-7-80	0	Hartford (AHL)
2	Brian Leetch	6-0/185	Corpus Christi, Tex.	3-3-68	13	New York Rangers
24	Sylvain Lefebvre	6-3/205	Richmond, Que.	10-14-67	11	New York Rangers
7	Vladimir Malakhov	6-4/230	Sverdlovsk, U.S.S.R.	8-30-68	8	Montreal, New Jersey
	Mike Mottau	6-0/192	Quincy, Mass.	3-19-78	0	Boston College (Hockey East)
	Filip Novak	6-0/174	Ceske Budejovice, Czech.	5-7-82	0	Regina (WHL)
47	Rich Pilon S.C.L.L	6-2/220	Saskatoon, Sask.	4-30-68	12	N.Y. Islanders, N.Y. Rangers
	Dale Purinton	6-3/214	Fort Wayne, Ind.	10-11-76	1	Hartford (AHL), New York Rangers
5	Stephane Quintal	6-3/234	Boucherville, Que.	10-22-68	12	New York Rangers
	Alexei Vasiliev	6-1/192	Yaroslavl, U.S.S.R.	9-1-77	1	Hartford (AHL), New York Rangers
	Terry Virtue	6-0/197	Scarborough, Ont.	8-8-70	2	Hartford (AHL), New York Rangers

GOALTENDERS

No.	GOALTENDERS	Ht./Wt.	Place	Date	NHL exp.	1999-2000 clubs
	Jean-Francois Labbe	5-10/172	Sherbrooke, Que.	6-15-72	1	Hartford (AHL), New York Rangers
30	Kirk McLean	6-1/180	Willowdale, Ont.	6-26-66	15	New York Rangers
35	Mike Richter	5-11/185	Philadelphia	9-22-66	12	New York Rangers
	Brandon Snee	6-1/195	Philadelphia	6-10-80	0	Union College (ECAC)

1999-2000 REVIEW
INDIVIDUAL STATISTICS
SCORING

	Games	G	A	Pts.	PIM	+/-	PPG	SHG	Shots	Shooting Pct.
Petr Nedved	76	24	44	68	40	2	6	2	201	11.9
Theoren Fleury	80	15	49	64	68	-4	1	0	246	6.1
Michael York	82	26	24	50	18	-17	8	0	177	14.7
Jan Hlavac	67	19	23	42	16	3	6	0	134	14.2
John MacLean DALLAS S.J	77	18	24	42	52	-2	6	2	158	11.4
Adam Graves	77	23	17	40	14	-15	11	0	194	11.9
Radek Dvorak* DAL	46	11	22	33	10	0	2	1	90	12.2
Valeri Kamensky	58	13	19	32	24	-13	3	0	88	14.8
Mathieu Schneider	80	10	20	30	78	-6	3	0	228	4.4
Alexandre Daigle	58	8	18	26	23	-5	1	0	52	15.4
Brian Leetch	50	7	19	26	20	-16	3	0	124	5.6
Kevin Hatcher	74	4	19	23	38	-10	2	0	112	3.6
Kim Johnson	76	6	15	21	46	-13	1	0	101	5.9
Tim Taylor	76	9	11	20	72	-4	0	0	79	11.4
Stephane Quintal M.ON.	75	2	14	16	77	-10	0	0	102	2.0

	Games	G	A	Pts.	PIM	+/-	PPG	SHG	Shots	Shooting Pct.
Mike Knuble*	59	9	5	14	18	-5	1	0	50	18.0
Eric Lacroix	70	4	8	12	24	-12	0	0	46	8.7
Sylvain Lefebvre	82	2	10	12	43	-13	0	0	67	3.0
Kevin Stevens	38	3	5	8	43	-7	1	0	44	6.8
Todd Harvey*	31	3	3	6	62	-9	0	0	31	9.7
Rob DiMaio*	12	1	3	4	8	-8	0	0	18	5.6
Richard Pilon*	45	0	4	4	36	0	0	0	16	0.0
Johan Witehall	9	1	1	2	2	0	0	0	6	16.7
Jason Dawe	3	0	1	1	2	0	0	0	8	0.0
Jason Doig	7	0	1	1	22	-2	0	0	3	0.0
P.J. Stock	11	0	1	1	11	1	0	0	2	0.0
Darren Langdon	21	0	1	1	26	-2	0	0	13	0.0
Kirk McLean (goalie)	22	0	1	1	2	0	0	0	0	0.0
Derek Armstrong	1	0	0	0	0	0	0	0	1	0.0
Daniel Goneau	1	0	0	0	0	-1	0	0	3	0.0
Jean Labbe (goalie)	1	0	0	0	0	0	0	0	0	0.0
Dale Purinton	1	0	0	0	7	-1	0	0	1	0.0
Alexei Vasiljev	1	0	0	0	2	-1	0	0	0	0.0
Terry Virtue	1	0	0	0	0	-2	0	0	2	0.0
Milan Hnilicka (goalie)	2	0	0	0	0	0	0	0	0	0.0
Christopher Kenady	2	0	0	0	0	-1	0	0	1	0.0
Manny Malhotra	27	0	0	0	4	-6	0	0	18	0.0
Mike Richter (goalie)	61	0	0	0	4	0	0	0	0	0.0

GOALTENDING

	Games	Min.	Goals	SO	Avg.	W	L	T	ENG	Shots	Sv. Pct.
Mike Richter	61	3622	173	0	2.87	22	31	8	4	1815	.905
Kirk McLean	22	1206	58	0	2.89	7	8	4	2	558	.896
Jean Labbe	1	60	3	0	3.00	0	1	0	0	22	.864
Milan Hnilicka	2	86	5	0	3.49	0	1	0	1	44	.886

*Played with two or more NHL teams.

RESULTS

OCTOBER
1— At Edmonton .... T ... *1-1
2— At Vancouver .... L 1-2
5— Ottawa .... L 1-2
8— Carolina .... W 3-1
10— Phoenix .... W 4-2
11— At N.Y. Islanders .... W 4-2
14— Pittsburgh .... L 2-5
17— Atlanta .... W 4-1
19— San Jose .... L 1-2
20— At Philadelphia .... L 0-5
22— Philadelphia .... L 0-2
24— Vancouver .... L 0-3
30— At Montreal .... T ... *2-2

NOVEMBER
3— N.Y. Islanders .... T ... *3-3
5— At Colorado .... L 1-4
7— At Chicago .... W 3-1
10— Ottawa .... W 3-1
11— At Washington .... W ... *5-4
13— Boston .... L 2-5
18— At Boston .... L 3-5
20— At Toronto .... T ... *3-4
24— At Tampa Bay .... W 6-3
26— At Florida .... L 2-6

DECEMBER
1— At New Jersey .... L 2-3
3— Montreal .... W 3-2
4— At Buffalo .... T ... *1-1
6— Calgary .... W ... *3-2

8— Edmonton .... W ... *2-1
15— Los Angeles .... W 8-3
17— Washington .... L ... *2-3
19— Tampa Bay .... W ... *5-4
21— Buffalo .... L 1-3
23— At N.Y. Islanders .... L 2-4
26— New Jersey .... T ... *3-3
28— At Phoenix .... T ... *2-2
29— At Dallas .... L ... *3-4

JANUARY
2— At Montreal .... T ... *2-2
3— St. Louis .... L 2-5
5— Toronto .... W ... *3-2
8— At Toronto .... W 5-3
9— At Carolina .... L 0-1
15— At N.Y. Islanders .... W 5-2
16— Atlanta .... W 6-3
18— Carolina .... W 3-2
20— At Carolina .... W 4-1
22— At St. Louis .... W 4-1
24— At Atlanta .... W 6-3
25— At Pittsburgh .... W 4-3
27— Toronto .... L 3-4
29— At Ottawa .... L 2-3
31— Nashville .... W 5-1

FEBRUARY
2— New Jersey .... L 1-3
3— At Atlanta .... W 6-3
8— New Jersey .... T ... *2-2
9— At New Jersey .... L 1-4

11— Boston .... W 5-2
13— N.Y. Islanders .... L 2-4
15— At Tampa Bay .... T ... *2-2
16— At Florida .... L 0-3
18— Colorado .... L 2-4
20— Philadelphia .... L 2-3
22— Pittsburgh .... W 4-3
25— At Buffalo .... W 6-3
26— At Ottawa .... L 2-4

MARCH
1— Buffalo .... T ... *3-3
3— Florida .... W 4-2
6— At San Jose .... L 1-2
8— At Anaheim .... W ... *4-3
9— At Los Angeles .... L 1-3
11— At Pittsburgh .... L 1-3
13— Dallas .... L 3-4
15— Tampa Bay .... T ... *4-4
18— At Philadelphia .... W 3-2
19— At Pittsburgh .... L 4-5
21— Florida .... L 3-4
23— Washington .... L 1-4
26— At Detroit .... L 2-8
27— Detroit .... L 0-6

APRIL
1— At Boston .... T ... *2-2
3— At Washington .... L 1-4
5— Montreal .... L 0-3
9— Philadelphia .... L 1-4
*Denotes overtime game.

OTTAWA SENATORS
EASTERN CONFERENCE/NORTHEAST DIVISION

Ottawa Schedule

Home games shaded; D—Day game; *—All-Star Game at Denver.

October

SUN	MON	TUE	WED	THU	FRI	SAT
1	2	3	4	5 BOS	6	7 DAL
8	9	10	11	12	13 NJ	14 TOR
15	16	17 PHI	18	19 PIT	20	21 ATL
22	23	24	25 PIT	26	27 TB	28 FLA
29	30	31 TOR				

November

SUN	MON	TUE	WED	THU	FRI	SAT
			1	2 NYR	3	4 CBJ
5	6 ATL	7	8	9 BOS	10	11 D PHI
12 D CAR	13	14	15	16 CAR	17	18 FLA
19	20	21 BOS	22	23 EDM	24	25 TOR
26 NYR	27	28 BUF	29	30		

December

SUN	MON	TUE	WED	THU	FRI	SAT
					1	2 PHI
3 CAR	4	5 PIT	6	7	8 MON	9 MON
10	11	12	13	14 CAL	15	16 NYI
17	18	19	20 MIN	21 CBJ	22	23 D CHI
24	25	26	27 WAS	28	29 BUF	30 PIT
31						

January

SUN	MON	TUE	WED	THU	FRI	SAT
	1	2 STL	3	4 TB	5	6 MON
7	8	9	10 VAN	11	12	13 CAL
14 EDM	15	16 LA	17	18 WAS	19	20 TB
21	22	23 NYI	24	25 TB	26 FLA	27
28 D MON	29	30 WAS	31			

February

SUN	MON	TUE	WED	THU	FRI	SAT
				1	2	3
4	*5	6 DET	7	8 NJ	9	10 BUF
11	12 NYI	13	14 NJ	15 COL	16	17
18 MON	19 BUF	20	21	22 FLA	23	24 D VAN
25	26 NYR	27 BUF	28			

March

SUN	MON	TUE	WED	THU	FRI	SAT
				1 SJ	2	3 TOR
4	5	6 NJ	7	8 BOS	9	10 NYR
11 WAS	12	13	14 ATL	15	16 ANA	17
18 D DAL	19	20	21 PHO	22 SJ	23	24 NSH
25	26 PHI	27	28 CHI	29	30 BOS	31

April

SUN	MON	TUE	WED	THU	FRI	SAT
1 D CAR	2	3 ATL	4	5	6 NYI	7 TOR
8						

2000-2001 SEASON
CLUB DIRECTORY

Chairman, governor
Rod Bryden
President and CEO & alt. governor
Roy Mlakar
General manager
Marshall Johnston
Executive vice president
Steve Violetta
COO & alternate governor
Cyril Leeder
Head coach
Jacques Martin
Assistant coaches
Perry Pearn
Mike Murphy
Director of hockey operations
Trevor Timmins
Vice president, broadcast
Jim Steel
Vice president, communications
Phil Legault
Director, media relations
Morgan Quarry

Director, media relations
Steve Keogh
Manager, media relations
Ian Mendes
Media relations assistant
Jen Eves
Video coordinator & conditioning coach
Randy Lee
Head equipment manager
Ed Georgica
Assistant equipment manager
John Gervais
Head athletic trainer
Kevin Wagner
Massage therapist
Brad Joyal
Team doctor
Jamie Kissick, M.D.
Scouts
Paul Castron, Dale Engel, George Fargher, Gary Harker, Jarmo Kekalainen, Phil Myre, John Phelan, Andre Savard, Boris Shagus

DRAFT CHOICES

Rd.— Player	Ht./Wt.	Overall	Pos.	Last team
1— Anton Volchenkov	6-0/209	21	D	CSKA, Russia
2— Mathieu Chouinard	6-1/211	45	D	Shawinigan (QMJHL)
2— Antoine Vermette	6-0/184	55	C	Victoriaville (QMJHL)
3— Jan Bohac	6-2/189	87	C	Slavia Praha, Czech
4— Derrick Byfuglien	6-1/202	122	D	Fargo-Moorhead, USHL
5— Greg Zanon	5-11/200	156	D	Neb.-Omaha (CCHA)
5— Grant Potulny	6-2/194	157	C/LW	Lincoln, USHL
5— Sean Connolly	6-1/187	158	D	N. Michigan (CCHA)
6— Jason Maleyko	6-3/211	188	D	Brampton (OHL)
9— James Demone	6-5/220	283	D	Portland (WHL)

MISCELLANEOUS DATA

Home ice (capacity)
Corel Centre (18,500)
Address
1000 Palladium Drive
Kanata, Ont. K2VIA5
Business phone
613-599-0250
Ticket information
613-755-1166
Website
www.ottawasenators.com

Training site
Kanata, Ontario
Club colors
Black, red and gold
Radio affiliation
Team 1200 (1200 AM)
TV affiliation
CHRO TV, CTV Sportsnet

RWt -JEFF ULMER

TRAINING CAMP ROSTER

No.	FORWARDS	Ht./Wt.	Place	BORN Date	NHL exp.	1999-2000 clubs
11	Daniel Alfredsson (RW).	5-11/195	Partille, Sweden	12-11-72	5	Ottawa
20	Magnus Arvedson (LW).	6-2/198	Karlstad, Sweden	11-25-71	3	Ottawa
	Jan Bohac (C)	6-2/189	Tabor, Czechoslovakia	2-3-82	0	Slavia Praha (Czech Republic)
14	Radek Bonk (C)	6-3/210	Koprivnice, Czechoslovakia	1-9-76	6	HC Pardubice (Czech Rep.), Ottawa
25	Slava Butsayev (C)	6-2/220	Togliatti, U.S.S.R.	6-13-70	6	Tampa Bay, Grand Rapids (IHL), Ottawa
	Ivan Ciernik (RW)	6-1/234	Levice, Czechoslovakia	10-30-77	1	Grand Rapids (IHL)
10	Andreas Dackell (RW)	5-10/195	Gavle, Sweden	12-29-72	4	Ottawa
38	John Emmons (C)	6-0/185	San Jose, Calif.	8-17-74	1	Grand Rapids (IHL), Ottawa
12	Mike Fisher (C)	6-1/193	Peterborough, Ont.	6-5-80	1	Ottawa
17	Colin Forbes (LW)	6-3/205	New Westminister, B.C.	2-16-76	4	Tampa Bay, Ottawa
	Martin Havlat (C/LW)	6-1/178	Brno, Czechoslovakia	4-19-81	0	Zelezarny Trinec (Czech Republic)
18	Marian Hossa (LW)	6-1/199	Stara Lubovna, Czech.	1-12-79	3	Ottawa
15	Shawn McEachern (LW)	5-11/193	Waltham, Mass.	2-28-69	9	Ottawa
	Chris Neil (RW)	6-0/210	Markdale, Ont.	6-18-79	0	Grand Rapids (IHL), Mobile (ECHL)
	Rastislav Pavlikovsky	5-10/195	Dubnica, Czechoslovakia	3-2-77	0	G. Rapids (IHL), Philadelphia (AHL), Cincinnati (AHL)
	Grant Potulny (C/LW)	6-2/194	Grand Forks, N.D.	3-4-80	0	Lincoln (USHL)
13	Vaclav Prospal (C)	6-2/195	Ceske-Budejovice, Czech.	2-17-75	4	Ottawa
26	Andre Roy (RW)	6-4/213	Port Chester, N.Y.	2-8-75	3	Ottawa
56	Petr Schastlivy (LW)	6-1/204	Angarsk, U.S.S.R.	4-18-79	1	Grand Rapids (IHL), Ottawa
	Chris Szysky (RW)	5-11/205	White City, Sask.	6-8-76	0	Grand Rapids (IHL)
	Sergei Verenikin (RW)	5-11/187	Yaroslavl, U.S.S.R.	9-8-79	0	Torpedo Yaroslavl (Russian)
	Antoine Vermette (C)	6-0/184	St-Agapit, Que.	7-20-82	0	Victoriaville (QMJHL)
	Buddy Wallace (C)	6-1/195	Palantine, Ill.	12-18-75	0	Pee Dee (ECHL), Manitoba (IHL), Grand Rapids (IHL)
26	Todd White (C)	5-10/180	Kanata, Ont.	5-21-75	3	Cleveland (IHL), Chicago, Philadelphia (AHL), Philadelphia
19	Alexei Yashin (C)	6-3/225	Sverdlovsk, U.S.S.R.	11-5-73	6	
7	Rob Zamuner (LW)	6-3/203	Oakville, Ont.	9-17-69	9	Ottawa

DEFENSEMEN

No.	DEFENSEMEN	Ht./Wt.	Place	BORN Date	NHL exp.	1999-2000 clubs
	Derrick Byfuglien	6-1/202	Roseau, Minn.	12-23-80	0	Fargo (USHL)
	Sean Connolly	6-0/187	Dearborn, Mich.	10-8-80	0	Northern Michigan Univ. (CCHA)
	Kevin Grimes	6-3/218	Ottawa	8-19-79	0	Grand Rapids (IHL)
24	John Gruden	6-0/203	Virginia, Minn.	6-4-70	5	Grand Rapids (IHL), Ottawa
	Shane Hnidy	6-1/200	Brandon, Man.	11-8-75	0	Cincinnati (AHL)
29	Igor Kravchuk	6-1/218	Ufa, U.S.S.R.	9-13-66	9	Ottawa
	Joel Kwiatkowski	6-2/201	Kendersley, Saskatchewan	3-22-77	0	Cincinnati (AHL)
	Jason Maleyko	6-2/211	Windsor, Ont.	5-24-80	0	Brampton (OHL)
	Gavin McLeod	6-4/196	Fort Saskatchewan, Alta.	1-1-80	0	Kelowna (WHL)
7	Ricard Persson	6-1/201	Ostersund, Sweden.	8-24-69	5	St. Louis, Worcester (AHL)
4	Chris Phillips	6-3/215	Fort McMurray, Alta.	3-9-78	3	Ottawa
	Karel Rachunek	6-1/191	Gottwaldov, Czechoslovakia	8-27-79	1	Grand Rapids (IHL), Ottawa
6	Wade Redden	6-2/205	Lloydminster, Sask.	6-12-77	4	Ottawa
5	Sami Salo	6-3/192	Turku, Finland	9-2-74	2	Ottawa
	Anton Volchenkov	6-0/209	Moscow, U.S.S.R.	2-25-82	0	CSKA (Russian Div. II)
33	Jason York	6-1/200	Nepean, Ont.	5-20-70	8	Ottawa
	Greg Zanon	5-11/200	Burnaby, B.C.	6-5-80	0	University of Nebraska-Omaha (CCHA)

GOALTENDERS

No.	GOALTENDERS	Ht./Wt.	Place	BORN Date	NHL exp.	1999-2000 clubs
	Mathieu Chouinard	6-1/209	Laval, Que.	4-11-80	0	Shawinigan (QMJHL)
1	Jani Hurme	6-0/187	Turku, Finland	1-7-75	1	Grand Rapids (IHL), Ottawa
	Simon Lajeunesse	6-0/170	Quebec City	1-22-81	0	Moncton (QMJHL)
40	Patrick Lalime	6-3/185	St. Bonaventure, Que.	7-7-74	2	Ottawa
31	Rich Parent	6-3/215	Montreal	1-12-73	3	Utah (IHL), Tampa Bay, Detroit (IHL)

1999-2000 REVIEW
INDIVIDUAL STATISTICS

SCORING

	Games	G	A	Pts.	PIM	+/-	PPG	SHG	Shots	Shooting Pct.
Radek Bonk	80	23	37	60	53	-2	10	0	167	13.8
Daniel Alfredsson	57	21	38	59	28	11	4	2	164	12.8
Marian Hossa	78	29	27	56	32	5	5	0	240	12.1
Vaclav Prospal	79	22	33	55	40	-2	5	0	204	10.8
Shawn McEachern	69	29	22	51	24	2	10	0	219	13.2
Joe Juneau	65	13	24	37	22	3	2	0	126	10.3
Wade Redden	81	10	26	36	49	-1	3	0	163	6.1
Andreas Dackell	82	10	25	35	18	5	0	0	99	10.1
Jason York	79	8	22	30	60	-3	1	0	159	5.0
Magnus Arvedson	47	15	13	28	36	4	1	1	91	16.5
Shaun Van Allen	75	9	19	28	37	20	0	2	75	12.0

	Games	G	A	Pts.	PIM	+/-	PPG	SHG	Shots	Shooting Pct.
Patrick Traverse	66	6	17	23	21	17	1	0	73	8.2
Rob Zamuner	57	9	12	21	32	-6	0	1	103	8.7
Chris Phillips	65	5	14	19	39	12	0	0	96	5.2
Igor Kravchuk	64	6	12	18	20	-5	5	0	126	4.8
Sami Salo	37	6	8	14	2	6	3	0	85	7.1
Kevin Dineen	67	4	8	12	57	2	0	0	71	5.6
Janne Laukkanen*	60	1	11	12	55	14	0	0	62	1.6
Mike Fisher	32	4	5	9	15	-6	0	0	49	8.2
Andre Roy	73	4	3	7	145	3	0	0	39	10.3
Petr Schastlivy	13	2	5	7	2	4	1	0	22	9.1
Colin Forbes*	45	2	5	7	12	-1	0	0	54	3.7
Grant Ledyard	40	2	4	6	8	-3	0	0	42	4.8
Kevin Miller	9	3	2	5	2	1	1	0	11	27.3
Bruce Gardiner*	10	0	3	3	4	1	0	0	18	0.0
Yves Sarault*	11	0	2	2	7	-3	0	0	13	0.0
Steve Martins*	2	1	0	1	0	-1	0	0	3	33.3
Bobby Dollas*	1	0	0	0	0	2	0	0	0	0.0
Michael Fountain (goalie)	1	0	0	0	0	0	0	0	0	0.0
Erich Goldmann	1	0	0	0	0	0	0	0	0	0.0
Jani Hurme (goalie)	1	0	0	0	0	0	0	0	0	0.0
David Van Drunen	1	0	0	0	0	0	0	0	0	0.0
Viacheslav Butsayev*	3	0	0	0	0	-2	0	0	1	0.0
Karel Rachunek	6	0	0	0	2	0	0	0	3	0.0
Tom Barrasso (goalie)*	7	0	0	0	0	0	0	0	0	0.0
John Gruden	9	0	0	0	4	0	0	0	3	0.0
John Emmons	10	0	0	0	6	-2	0	0	3	0.0
Patrick Lalime (goalie)	38	0	0	0	4	0	0	0	0	0.0
Ron Tugnutt (goalie)*	44	0	0	0	0	0	0	0	0	0.0

GOALTENDING

	Games	Min.	Goals	SO	Avg.	W	L	T	ENG	Shots	Sv. Pct.
Jani Hurme	1	60	2	0	2.00	1	0	0	0	19	.895
Patrick Lalime	38	2038	79	3	2.33	19	14	3	1	834	.905
Ron Tugnutt*	44	2435	103	4	2.54	18	12	8	2	1020	.899
Tom Barrasso*	7	418	22	0	3.16	3	4	0	0	182	.879
Michael Fountain	1	16	1	0	3.75	0	0	0	0	6	.833

*Played with two or more NHL teams.

RESULTS

OCTOBER
2— At Philadelphia ....W....3-0
5— At N.Y. Rangers ....W....2-1
7— Boston....................W....4-3
9— Toronto...................W....4-3
11— New Jersey ....T....*2-2
14— At Phoenix...............L....3-4
16— At Colorado..............L....1-3
21— Colorado.................W....4-1
23— Buffalo..................W....4-0
28— Calgary..................L....*3-4
30— Florida..................W....5-0
31— At Atlanta...............W....6-4

NOVEMBER
3— At Washington.............L....1-3
4— Pittsburgh................W....2-1
6— Montreal..................W....2-1
10— At N.Y. Rangers..........W....4-3
11— Nashville................L....1-2
13— Anaheim..................W....4-2
17— At Carolina..............L....1-2
18— San Jose.................L....1-4
20— At New Jersey............L....1-3
25— At Atlanta...............W....6-3
26— At Pittsburgh............L....0-5
28— Philadelphia.............T....*3-3
30— Chicago..................W....2-1

DECEMBER
3— At New Jersey ....L....4-7
4— Dallas....................L....1-3

8— At Buffalo................T....*0-0
11— N.Y. Islanders ....T....*1-1
13— At Toronto...............W....3-1
16— At Vancouver.............W....2-1
18— At Calgary...............L....1-2
19— At Edmonton..............T....*3-3
23— Carolina.................W....4-3
27— Montreal.................T....*4-4
29— At Montreal..............W....3-2
30— Boston...................W....*5-4

JANUARY
3— New Jersey ....L....*3-4
4— At Carolina ....W....2-1
6— Phoenix...................W....5-2
8— Buffalo...................L....4-7
11— At Los Angeles ....W....4-3
12— At Anaheim...............W....2-0
16— At Washington............L....1-2
17— At N.Y. Islanders........W....*4-3
20— At Philadelphia..........T....*1-1
22— Detroit..................L....2-3
24— At Toronto ....T....*3-3
26— St. Louis................L....1-4
28— At Buffalo...............L....0-1
29— N.Y. Rangers ....W....3-2

FEBRUARY
1— Boston....................T....*4-4
3— At Buffalo................L....2-4
11— Florida ....W....5-3
12— At Montreal..............L....4-5

15—Carolina..................W....5-1
17—Tampa Bay.................W....6-2
19—Vancouver.................L....1-3
21— At Florida...............W....4-2
24— At Tampa Bay.............L....4-5
26—N.Y. Rangers..............W....4-2
28— At Pittsburgh............T....*1-1
29— At Boston................W....5-3

MARCH
2— At N.Y. Islanders.........T....*5-5
4— Atlanta...................W....3-2
6— At Boston.................W....5-1
9— Pittsburgh................W....7-0
11— Toronto..................L....2-4
15— At Calgary...............W....3-1
17— At Edmonton..............L....2-4
18— At Vancouver.............L....1-6
21—Atlanta...................W....7-1
23—Toronto...................W....3-2
25—Washington................L....3-4
28—Philadelphia..............W....5-2
30— At Tampa Bay.............L....3-6
31— At Florida...............L....1-3

APRIL
2— At St. Louis..............L....1-4
4—Washington.................W....4-0
6—N.Y. Islanders.............L....1-2
8— At Montreal...............W....3-1
9— Tampa Bay ....W....5-2
*Denotes overtime game.

PHILADELPHIA FLYERS
EASTERN CONFERENCE/ATLANTIC DIVISION

PHILADELPHIA FLYERS *(side margin)*

Philadelphia Schedule

Home games shaded; D—Day game; *—All-Star Game at Denver.

October

SUN	MON	TUE	WED	THU	FRI	SAT
1	2	3	4	5 VAN	6	7 BOS
8	9	10	11 MIN	12 DAL	13	14 PHO
15	16	17 OTT	18	19 MON	20	21 ANA
22	23	24 NYR	25	26 NYR	27	28
29 WAS	30	31				

November

SUN	MON	TUE	WED	THU	FRI	SAT
			1 NJ	2 NSH	3	4 BUF
5	6	7	8 PIT	9 EDM	10	11 D OTT
12	13	14	15 TOR	16	17 ATL	18 WAS
19	20	21	22 BUF	23	24 D PIT	25
26 PHO	27	28	29 CBJ	30 CAR		

December

SUN	MON	TUE	WED	THU	FRI	SAT
					1	2 OTT
3	4	5	6 TB	7	8 DET	9
10 NYI	11	12 NSH	13 COL	14	15	16 NJ
17	18	19 BOS	20	21 SJ	22	23 D CAR
24	25	26	27 FLA	28 TB	29	30 WAS
31						

January

SUN	MON	TUE	WED	THU	FRI	SAT
	1	2 NJ	3	4	5 ATL	6 ATL
7	8 STL	9	10	11	12 TB	13 FLA
14	15	16 NYR	17	18 NJ	19	20 FLA
21	22 LA	23	24	25 CHI	26	27 D CAR
28 D WAS	29	30	31 PIT			

February

SUN	MON	TUE	WED	THU	FRI	SAT
				1 NYI	2	3
4 *	5	6 BOS	7 PIT	8	9 NYI	10
11	12	13	14 NYI	15 TOR	16	17 ATL
18	19 CAR	20	21	22 NYI	23	24 D TB
25 NYR	26	27 MON	28			

March

SUN	MON	TUE	WED	THU	FRI	SAT
			1 BUF	2	3 MON
4	5 BOS	6	7	8 CAL	9	10 D NJ
11	12	13 STL	14	15 MIN	16	17 D NYR
18	19 EDM	20	21	22 CAL	23	24 TOR
25	26 OTT	27	28	29 TOR	30	31 D DET

April

SUN	MON	TUE	WED	THU	FRI	SAT
1	2	3 D FLA	4	5 MON	6	7 D PIT
8 D BUF						

2000-2001 SEASON
CLUB DIRECTORY

Chairman
Edward M. Snider
President and general manager
Bob Clarke
Chairman of the board emeritus
Joseph C. Scott
Executive vice president
Keith Allen
Exec. v.p. and chief operating officer
Ron Ryan
Assistant general manager
Paul Holmgren
Head coach
Craig Ramsay
Assistant coaches
Bill Barber
Mike Stothers
Goaltending coach
Rejean Lemelin
Pro scouts
Al Hill
Ron Hextall
Chief scout
Dennis Patterson
Scouts
Inge Hammarstrom
Vaclav Slansky
Simon Nolet
Evgeny Zimin
John Chapman
Blair Reid
Ticket manager
Cecilia Baker
Vice president, sales
Jack Betson

Vice president, sales
Kathi Gillin
Manager, sales and services
Nicole Allison
Assistant manager, sales and services
Diane Smith
Marketing assistant
Kevin Morley
Administration
Debbie Brown
Director of public relations
Zack Hill
Director of publications
Steve Majewski
Manager of game presentation and special events
Linda Held
Assistant director, public relations
Jill Lipson
Director, community relations
Linda Panasci
Director, fan services
Joe Kadlec
Public relations assistant
Kristin Lewandowski
Medical trainer
John Worley
Head equipment manager
Jim Evers
Equipment manager
Anthony Oratorio
Orthopedic surgeon
Arthur Bartolozzi

DRAFT CHOICES

Rd.— Player	Ht./Wt.	Overall	Pos.	Last team
1— Justin Williams	6-1/176	28	RW	Plymouth (OHL)
3— Alexander Drozdetsky ..	6-0/174	94	F	St. Petersburg, Russia
6— Roman Cechmanek	6-3/187	171	G	Slovnaft Vsetin, Czech
6— Colin Shields		195	RW	Cleveland, NAHL
7— John Eichelberger	6-2/182	210	C	Green Bay, USHL
7— Guillaume Lefebvre	6-1/195	227	C	R.-Noranda (QMJHL)
8— Regan Kelly	6-1/185	259	D	Nipawin, SJHL
9— Milan Kopecky	5-11/176	287	LW	Slavia Praha, Czech

MISCELLANEOUS DATA

Home ice (capacity)
First Union Center (19,519)
Address
First Union Center
3601 South Broad Street
Philadelphia, PA 19148
Business phone
215-465-4500
Ticket information
215-336-2000
Website
www.philadelphiaflyers.com

Training site
Voorhees, NJ
Club colors
Orange, white and black
Radio affiliation
WIP (610 AM)
TV affiliation
Comcast SportsNet (cable); UPN 57
WPSG-TV

TRAINING CAMP ROSTER

No.	FORWARDS	Ht./Wt.	Place	BORN Date	NHL exp.	1999-2000 clubs
	Tomas Divisek (C)	6-2/194	Most, Czechoslovakia	7-17-79	0	Philadelphia (AHL)
	Alexander Drozdetsky	6-0/174	Moscow, U.S.S.R.	11-10-81	0	SKA St. Petersburg (Russian)
	Ruslan Fedotenko (RW)	6-2/190	Kiev, U.S.S.R.	1-18-79	0	Philadelphia (AHL), Trenton (ECHL)
12	Simon Gagne (C)	6-0/175	Ste. Foy, Que.	2-29-80	1	Philadelphia
	Mark Greig (RW)	5-11/190	High River, Alta.	1-25-70	7	Philadelphia (AHL), Philadelphia
11	Jody Hull (RW)	6-2/195	Cambridge, Ont.	2-2-69	12	Orlando (IHL), Philadelphia
20	Keith Jones (RW)	6-2/200	Brantford, Ont.	11-8-68	8	Philadelphia
18	Daymond Langkow (C) PH	5-11/180 ɾ Edmonton		9-27-76	5	Philadelphia
10	John LeClair (LW)...........	6-3/226	St. Albans, Vt.	7-5-69	10	Philadelphia
88	Eric Lindros (C) RANGER	6-4/236 S	London, Ont.	2-28-73	8	Philadelphia
28	Kent Manderville (C)......	6-3/200	Edmonton	4-12-71	9	Carolina, Philadelphia
29	Gino Odjick (LW)	6-3/227	Maniwaki, Que.	9-7-70	10	New York Islanders, Philadelphia
25	Keith Primeau (C)...........	6-5/220	Toronto	11-24-71	10	Philadelphia
	Paul Ranheim (LW)	6-1/210	St. Louis	1-25-66	12	Carolina
8	Mark Recchi (RW)	5-10/185	Kamloops, B.C.	2-1-68	12	Philadelphia
	Colin Shields (RW)		Glasgow, Scotland	1-27-80	0	Cleveland (NAHL)
17	Kevin Stevens (LW)	6-3/230	Brockton, Mass.	4-15-65	13	New York Rangers
92	Rick Tocchet (RW).........	6-0/210	Scarborough, Ont.	4-9-64	16	Phoenix, Philadelphia
17	Steve Washburn (C)	6-2/198	Ottawa	4-10-75	5	Milwaukee (IHL), Philadelphia (AHL), Philadelphia
15	Peter White (C).............	5-11/200	Montreal	3-15-69	5	Philadelphia (AHL), Philadelphia
	Justin Williams (RW)	6-1/176	Cobourg, Ont.	10-4-81	0	Plymouth (OHL)
	DEFENSEMEN					
	Mikhail Chernov.............	6-2/196	Prokopjevsk, U.S.S.R.	11-11-78	0	Philadelphia (AHL)
43	Andy Delmore.................	6-1/192	Windsor, Ont.	12-26-76	2	Philadelphia (AHL), Philadelphia
37	Eric Desjardins	6-1/205	Rouyn, Que.	6-14-69	12	Philadelphia
44	Mark Eaton	6-2/205	Washington, Del.	5-6-77	1	Philadelphia, Philadelphia (AHL)
	Francis Lessard	6-2/184	Montreal	5-30-79	0	
3	Dan McGillis	6-2/225	Hawkesbury, Ont.	7-1-72	4	Philadelphia
	Dean Melanson	5-11/211	Antigonish, Nova Scotia	11-19-73	1	Philadelphia (AHL)
22	Luke Richardson.............	6-3/210	Kanata, Ont.	3-26-69	13	Philadelphia
55	Ulf Samuelsson	6-1/205	Fagersta, Sweden	3-26-64	16	Philadelphia
6	Chris Therien	6-4/230	Ottawa	12-14-71	6	Philadelphia
	Jeff Tory	5-11/190	Burnaby, B.C.	5-9-73	0	Philadelphia (AHL)
3	Zarley Zalapski..............	6-1/215	Edmonton	4-22-68	12	Long Beach (IHL), Utah (IHL), Philadelphia
	GOALTENDERS S.J.					
33	Brian Boucher............	6-1/190	Woonsocket, R.I.	8-1-77	1	Philadelphia, Philadelphia (AHL)
	Roman Cechmanek........	6-3/187	Czechoslovakia	3-2-71	0	Vsetin (Czech Republic)
35	Neil Little	6-1/193	Medicine Hat, Alta.	12-18-71	0	Philadelphia (AHL)
	Maxime Ouellet..............	6-0/180	Beauport, Que.	6-17-81	0	Quebec (QMJHL)

1999-2000 REVIEW
INDIVIDUAL STATISTICS

SCORING

	Games	G	A	Pts.	PIM	+/-	PPG	SHG	Shots	Shooting Pct.
Mark Recchi	82	28	63	91	50	20	7	1	223	12.6
John LeClair	82	40	37	77	36	8	13	0	249	16.1
Eric Lindros	55	27	32	59	83	11	10	1	187	14.4
Eric Desjardins	81	14	41	55	32	20	8	0	207	6.8
Daymond Langkow..	82	18	32	50	56	1	5	0	222	8.1
Simon Gagne..	80	20	28	48	22	11	8	1	159	12.6
Valeri Zelepukin...	77	11	21	32	55	-3	2	0	125	8.8
Mikael Renberg*...	62	8	21	29	30	-1	3	0	106	7.5
Keith Jones..	57	9	16	25	82	8	1	0	92	9.8
Daniel McGillis...	68	4	14	18	55	16	3	0	128	3.1
Keith Primeau..	23	7	10	17	31	10	1	0	51	13.7
Jody Hull	67	10	3	13	4	8	0	2	63	15.9
Chris Therien	80	4	9	13	66	11	1	0	126	3.2
Craig Berube..	77	4	8	12	162	3	0	0	63	6.3
Sandy McCarthy*...	58	6	5	11	111	-5	1	0	68	8.8
Rod Brind'Amour*...	12	5	3	8	4	-1	4	0	26	19.2
Andy Delmore...	27	2	5	7	8	-1	0	0	55	3.6
Luke Richardson..	74	2	5	7	140	14	0	0	50	4.0
Adam Burt..	67	1	6	7	45	-2	0	0	49	2.0
Rick Tocchet*...	16	3	3	6	23	4	2	0	23	13.0
Peter White..	21	1	5	6	6	1	0	0	24	4.2

	Games	G	A	Pts.	PIM	+/-	PPG	SHG	Shots	Shooting Pct.
Mark Greig	11	3	2	5	6	0	0	0	14	21.4
Mikael Andersson*	36	2	3	5	0	-2	0	1	38	5.3
Gino Odjick*	13	3	1	4	10	2	0	0	24	12.5
Marc Bureau*	54	2	2	4	10	-1	0	1	46	4.3
Ulf Samuelsson	49	1	2	3	58	8	0	0	17	5.9
Kent Manderville*	13	0	3	3	4	2	0	0	17	0.0
Mark Eaton	27	1	1	2	8	1	0	0	25	4.0
Zarley Zalapski	12	0	2	2	6	0	0	0	6	0.0
Todd White*	3	1	0	1	0	-1	0	0	4	25.0
Karl Dykhuis*	5	0	1	1	6	-2	0	0	5	0.0
Brian Boucher (goalie)	35	0	1	1	4	0	0	0	0	0.0
John Vanbiesbrouck (goalie)	50	0	1	1	6	0	0	0	0	0.0
Mike Maneluk	1	0	0	0	4	0	0	0	2	0.0
Steve Washburn	1	0	0	0	0	0	0	0	1	0.0
Jeff Lank	2	0	0	0	2	0	0	0	0	0.0

GOALTENDING

	Games	Min.	Goals	SO	Avg.	W	L	T	ENG	Shots	Sv. Pct.
Brian Boucher	35	2038	65	4	1.91	20	10	3	3	790	.918
John Vanbiesbrouck	50	2950	108	3	2.20	25	15	9	3	1143	.906

*Played with two or more NHL teams.

RESULTS

OCTOBER

2— Ottawa	L	0-3
7— Carolina	L	0-2
9— At Boston	T	*1-1
12— At Washington	L	4-5
14— Montreal	L	*4-5
16— At Detroit	L	2-3
17— Buffalo	W	5-2
20— N.Y. Rangers	W	5-0
22— At N.Y. Rangers	W	2-0
24— Florida	W	2-0
26— Vancouver	L	2-5
28— Colorado	W	*5-4
30— New Jersey	W	5-3

NOVEMBER

3— At Anaheim	T	*3-3
5— At San Jose	W	3-1
6— At Los Angeles	W	5-3
9— At New Jersey	L	1-2
11— Carolina	W	4-1
13— San Jose	W	3-2
18— Dallas	T	*1-1
20— Tampa Bay	W	4-1
22— At Tampa Bay	L	1-4
24— At Florida	W	6-1
26— Toronto	W	*3-2
28— At Ottawa	T	*3-3

DECEMBER

| 2— At Buffalo | W | 4-2 |
| 4— At Montreal | W | 3-2 |

(continued)

5— St. Louis	W	3-2
9— Toronto	W	4-2
11— At Toronto	L	4-6
14— At Buffalo	L	1-3
16— Phoenix	W	5-3
18— Tampa Bay	W	4-0
19— Nashville	T	*1-1
22— At New Jersey	L	2-3
23— Atlanta	T	*4-4
27— At Calgary	W	5-1
29— At Vancouver	W	*3-2

JANUARY

2— At N.Y. Islanders	W	4-1
6— N.Y. Islanders	W	3-2
8— Pittsburgh	W	6-2
11— At Carolina	W	4-3
14— At Atlanta	L	0-1
15— New Jersey	L	1-4
17— At Florida	L	1-3
20— Ottawa	T	*1-1
23— At Pittsburgh	T	*4-4
27— Florida	W	4-2
29— At Montreal	T	*2-2
30— At Washington	L	0-2

FEBRUARY

3— Anaheim	T	*3-3
9— At Toronto	W	4-2
10— Edmonton	L	2-3
12— Buffalo	W	*3-2
15— At New Jersey	L	2-4

(continued)

17— N.Y. Islanders	T	*2-2
19— Washington	W	4-2
20— At N.Y. Rangers	W	3-2
22— Chicago	W	3-1
24— Pittsburgh	W	*4-3
26— At N.Y. Islanders	W	5-1
29— At St. Louis	L	2-3

MARCH

1— At Dallas	L	0-2
4— At Boston	W	3-0
5— N.Y. Islanders	L	*3-4
8— At Tampa Bay	W	*3-2
9— Washington	W	3-1
12— At Colorado	L	1-3
13— At Phoenix	W	4-1
16— Montreal	T	*1-1
18— N.Y. Rangers	L	2-3
19— Boston	W	6-2
21— At Nashville	W	2-0
23— Los Angeles	L	*2-3
26— Pittsburgh	W	3-1
28— At Ottawa	L	2-5

APRIL

1— At Pittsburgh	W	3-2
2— At Carolina	L	0-1
4— At Atlanta	W	5-3
6— Atlanta	W	3-1
8— Boston	W	3-0
9— At N.Y. Rangers	W	4-1

*Denotes overtime game.

PHOENIX COYOTES
WESTERN CONFERENCE/PACIFIC DIVISION

Phoenix Schedule
Home games shaded; D—Day game; *—All-Star Game at Denver.

October

SUN	MON	TUE	WED	THU	FRI	SAT
1	2	3	4	5 STL	6	7 MIN
8	9	10	11	12 SJ	13	14 PHI
15 LA	16	17	18 FLA	19	20	21 VAN
22 EDM	23	24 CAL	25	26	27 DAL	28 LA
29	30 COL	31				

November

SUN	MON	TUE	WED	THU	FRI	SAT
			1 ANA	2	3 DAL	4
5	6	7 LA	8 DET	9	10	11 CBJ
12 NYR	13	14 WAS	15	16 COL	17	18 ANA
19	20	21 CHI	22	23	24	25 STL
26 PHI	27	28	29 COL	30 MIN		

December

SUN	MON	TUE	WED	THU	FRI	SAT
					1	2 DAL
3	4	5	6 VAN	7	8	9
10 CBJ	11	12	13	14 TB	15	16 SJ
17	18	19	20 CAL	21	22 ATL	23
24	25	26	27 CHI	28	29 MIN	30 STL
31						

January

SUN	MON	TUE	WED	THU	FRI	SAT
	1 SJ	2	3	4 NYR	5	6 NYI
7 NJ	8	9 DET	10	11	12 TOR	13 MON
14	15 STL	16	17 PIT	18	19 ANA	20
21 DAL	22	23 CAL	24 VAN	25	26 EDM	27
28	29 NSH	30	31			

February

SUN	MON	TUE	WED	THU	FRI	SAT
				1 ANA	2	3
4	* 5	6	7 CAR	8	9 EDM	10
11 CHI	12	13 TB	14 FLA	15	16 CAR	17
18 CAL	19	20	21 CBJ	22	23 BUF	24
25 DET	D 26	27 BOS	28 CBJ			

March

SUN	MON	TUE	WED	THU	FRI	SAT
				1	2 DET	3
4 COL	5	6 NSH	7	8 VAN	9	10 MON
11	12	13	14 NJ	15	16 DAL	17 NSH
18 LA	19	20	21 OTT	22	23	24 EDM
25 NYI	26	27	28 MIN	29 NSH	30	31 SJ

April

SUN	MON	TUE	WED	THU	FRI	SAT
1	2	3 LA	4	5 SJ	6 ANA	7
8						

2000-2001 SEASON
CLUB DIRECTORY

Owners
Steve Ellman
Wayne Gretzky
General manager
~~Bobby Smith~~ CLIFF FLETCHER
Assistant general manager
Taylor Burke
Director of hockey operations
Laurence Gilman
Head coach
Bob Francis
Assistant coaches
Rick Bowness
Wayne Fleming
Goaltending coach
Benoit Allaire

Strength & conditioning coach
Stieg Theander
Athletic therapist
Gord Hart
Massage therapist
Jukka Nieminen
Equipment managers
Stan Wilson
Tony DaCosta
Assistant equipment manager
Tony Silva
V.p. of media and player relations
Richard Nairn
Manager of media relations
Rick Braunstein

DRAFT CHOICES

Rd.— Player	Ht./Wt.	Overall	Pos.	Last team
1— Krystofer Kolanos	6-2/196	19	C	Boston Col. (H. East)
2— Alexander Tatarinov	5-11/176	53	RW	Yaroslavl, Russia
3— Ramzi Abid	6-2/205	85	LW	Halifax (QMJHL)
5— Nate Kiser	6-1/190	160	D	Plymouth (OHL)
6— Brent Gauvreau	6-3/194	186	C	Oshawa (OHL)
7— Igor Samoilov	5-11/189	217	D	Yaroslavl, Russia
8— Sami Venalainen	5-11/183	249	RW	Tappara Jr., Finland
9— Peter Fabus	6-1/191	281	F	Trencin, Slovakia

MISCELLANEOUS DATA

Home ice (capacity)
America West Arena (16,210)
Address
Alltel Ice Den
9375 E. Bell Road
Scottsdale, AZ 85260
Business phone
480-473-5600
Ticket information
480-473-7825
Website
www.phoenixcoyotes.com

Training site
Scottsdale, AZ
Club colors
Red, green, sand, sienna and purple
Radio affiliation
KDUS (1060 AM) and KDKB (93.3 FM)
TV affiliation
FOX Sports Net Arizona, WB 61, KTVK
(Channel 3)

TRAINING CAMP ROSTER

PHOENIX COYOTES

No.	FORWARDS	Ht./Wt.	Place	Date	NHL exp.	1999-2000 clubs
	Ramzi Abid (LW)	6-2/195	Montreal	3-24-80	0	Acadie-Bathurst (QMJHL), Halifax (QMJHL)
18	Mika Alatalo (LW)	6-0/202	Oulu, Finland	6-11-71	1	Phoenix
8	Daniel Briere (C)	5-10/181	Gatineau, Que.	10-6-77	3	Springfield (AHL), Phoenix
29	Louie DeBrusk (LW)	6-2/238	Cambridge, Ont.	3-19-71	9	Phoenix
19	Shane Doan (RW).........	6-2/218	Halkirk, Alta.	10-10-76	5	Phoenix
39	Travis Green (C) T.O.T.	6-2/200	Castlegar, B.C.	12-20-70	8	Phoenix
47	Tavis Hansen (C/RW).....	6-1/180	Prince Albert, Sask.	6-17-75	4	Springfield (AHL), Phoenix
	Jason Jaspers (C/LW) ...	6-0/185	Thunder Bay, Ont.	4-8-81	0	Sudbury (OHL)
39	Joe Juneau (LW) MONT .	6-0/199	Pont-Rouge, Que.	1-5-68	9	Ottawa
	Scott Kelman (C)	6-2/185	Winnipeg	5-7-81	0	Seattle (WHL)
	Krys Kolanos (C)	6-2/196	Calgary	7-27-81	0	Boston College (Hockey East)
10	Trevor Letowski (C)	5-10/176	Thunder Bay, Ont.	4-5-77	2	Phoenix
9	Brad May (LW)	6-1/210	Toronto	11-29-71	9	Vancouver
	Brad Ralph (LW)...........	6-2/198	Ottawa	10-17-80	0	Oshawa (OHL)
16	Robert Reichel (C) T.O.T.	5-10/186	Litvinov, Czechoslovakia	6-25-71	8	Litvinov (Czech Republic)
97	Jeremy Roenick (C) PHIL	6-0/207	Boston	1-17-70	12	Phoenix
	Wyatt Smith (C)	5-11/200	Thief River Falls, Minn.	2-13-77	1	Springfield (AHL), Phoenix
26	Mike Sullivan (C)	6-2/201	Marshfield, Mass.	2-28-68	9	Phoenix
	Alexander Tatarinov	5-11/176	Yekaterinburg, U.S.S.R.	4-14-82	1	Torpedo-2 Yaroslavl (Russian Div. II)
7	Keith Tkachuk (LW) St.L	6-2/225	Melrose, Mass.	3-28-72	9	Phoenix
27	Landon Wilson (RW).....	6-2/216	St. Louis	3-15-75	5	Boston, Providence (AHL)
36	Juha Ylonen (C)............	6-1/189	Helsinki, Finland	2-13-72	4	Phoenix
	DEFENSEMEN					
3	Keith Carney	6-2/211	Providence, R.I.	2-3-70	9	Phoenix
33	J.J. Daigneault..............	5-11/192	Montreal	10-12-65	15	Phoenix
	Dan Focht	6-6/226	Regina, Sask.	12-31-77	0	Jokerit (Finland), Springfield (AHL), Mississippi (ECHL)
23	Chris Joseph.................	6-3/212	Burnaby, B.C.	9-10-69	13	Vancouver, Phoenix
	Nate Kiser	6-1/190	Riverview, Mich.	5-4-82	0	Plymouth (OHL)
21	Jyrki Lumme..................	6-1/209	Tampere, Finland	7-16-66	12	Phoenix
24	Stan Neckar	6-1/207	Ceske-Budejovice, Czech.	12-22-75	6	Phoenix
27	Teppo Numminen	6-2/199	Tampere, Finland	7-3-68	12	Phoenix
	Kirill Safronov..............	6-2/196	Leningrad, U.S.S.R.	2-26-81	0	Quebec (QMJHL)
57	Robert Schnabel............	6-6/216	Prague, Czechoslovakia	11-10-78	0	
15	Radoslav Suchy............	6-1/191	Poprad, Czechoslovakia	4-7-76	1	Springfield (AHL), Phoenix
	Ossi Vaananen..............	6-3/200	Vantaa, Finland	8-18-80	0	Jokerit Helsinki (Finland)
	GOALTENDERS					
	Sylvain Daigle...............	5-8/185	St. Hyacinthe, Que.	10-20-76	0	Springfield (AHL), Mississippi (ECHL)
42	Robert Esche	6-0/188	Utica, N.Y.	1-22-78	2	Houston (IHL), Phoenix, Springfield (AHL)
35	Nikolai Khabibulin T.B.	6-1/195	Sverdlovsk, U.S.S.R.	1-13-73	5	Long Beach (IHL)

1999-2000 REVIEW
INDIVIDUAL STATISTICS

SCORING

	Games	G	A	Pts.	PIM	+/-	PPG	SHG	Shots	Shooting Pct.
Jeremy Roenick...	75	34	44	78	102	11	6	3	192	17.7
Shane Doan	81	26	25	51	66	6	1	1	221	11.8
Travis Green..	78	25	21	46	45	-4	6	0	157	15.9
Greg Adams	69	19	27	46	14	-1	5	0	129	14.7
Dallas Drake..	79	15	30	45	62	11	0	2	127	11.8
Keith Tkachuk	50	22	21	43	82	7	5	1	183	12.0
Teppo Numminen	79	8	34	42	16	21	2	0	126	6.3
Jyrki Lumme	74	8	32	40	44	9	4	0	142	5.6
Trevor Letowski	82	19	20	39	20	2	3	4	125	15.2
Rick Tocchet*	64	12	17	29	67	-5	2	0	107	11.2
Juha Ylonen..	76	6	23	29	12	-6	0	1	82	7.3
Mika Alatalo..	82	10	17	27	36	-3	1	0	107	9.3
Keith Carney	82	4	20	24	87	11	0	0	73	5.5
Mike Sullivan	79	5	10	15	10	-4	0	2	59	8.5
Benoit Hogue	27	3	10	13	10	-1	0	0	39	7.7
Deron Quint*	50	3	7	10	22	0	0	0	88	3.4
Stan Neckar..	66	2	8	10	36	1	0	0	34	5.9
Lyle Odelein*	16	1	7	8	19	1	1	0	30	3.3
Louie DeBrusk	61	4	3	7	78	1	0	0	24	16.7
Todd Gill*	41	1	6	7	30	-10	0	0	41	2.4

	Games	G	A	Pts.	PIM	+/-	PPG	SHG	Shots	Shooting Pct.
J.J. Daigneault	53	1	6	7	22	-16	0	0	44	2.3
Mikael Renberg*	10	2	4	6	2	0	0	0	16	12.5
Radoslav Suchy	60	0	6	6	16	2	0	0	36	0.0
Mikhail Shtalenkov (goalie)*	15	0	3	3	2	0	0	0	0	0.0
Daniel Briere	13	1	1	2	0	0	0	0	9	11.1
David Oliver	9	1	0	1	2	0	1	0	6	16.7
Jean-Guy Trudel	1	0	0	0	0	-1	0	0	0	0.0
Wyatt Smith	2	0	0	0	0	-2	0	0	0	0.0
Kevin Sawyer	3	0	0	0	12	1	0	0	0	0.0
Tavis Hansen	5	0	0	0	0	0	0	0	2	0.0
Robert Esche (goalie)	8	0	0	0	4	0	0	0	1	0.0
Chris Joseph*	9	0	0	0	0	-5	0	0	13	0.0
Bob Essensa (goalie)	30	0	0	0	0	0	0	0	0	0.0
Sean Burke (goalie)*	35	0	0	0	10	0	0	0	0	0.0

GOALTENDING

	Games	Min.	Goals	SO	Avg.	W	L	T	ENG	Shots	Sv. Pct.
Mikhail Shtalenkov*	15	904	36	2	2.39	7	6	2	3	370	.903
Sean Burke*	35	2074	88	3	2.55	17	14	3	1	1022	.914
Bob Essensa	30	1573	73	1	2.78	13	10	3	3	719	.898
Robert Esche	8	408	23	0	3.38	2	5	0	1	215	.893

*Played with two or more NHL teams.

RESULTS

OCTOBER
2— At St. Louis .... W 2-1
5— Anaheim .... W 4-0
8— At Chicago .... T ...*3-3
10— At N.Y. Rangers .... L 2-4
11— At Buffalo.................. T ...*2-2
14— Ottawa .... W 4-3
16— Boston....................... W 2-1
22— At Los Angeles .... W 6-3
23— Washington .... T ...*2-2
26— At Edmonton .... L 1-3
28— At Vancouver .... W 4-1
30— At Colorado .... W 5-3
31— At Anaheim .... W 3-0

NOVEMBER
3— At San Jose .... L 3-6
5— Dallas......................... L 4-6
10— Edmonton.................. W ..*5-4
12— Vancouver .... L 2-3
14— Los Angeles .... L 2-3
16— Calgary .... W 2-1
18— At Los Angeles .... W 3-2
20— Chicago .... W 3-1
25— New Jersey .... W 4-2
26— Colorado .... W 7-0
28— At Detroit................... W 4-3
30— At Nashville .... W 6-3

DECEMBER
2— Tampa Bay .... W 3-1
4— Anaheim .... L 1-2

6— At Dallas...................... W 3-2
8— Florida .... L 1-6
11— At Pittsburgh .... L 2-4
13— At Boston................... L 0-2
16— At Philadelphia........... L 3-5
19— San Jose .... W 4-3
21— St. Louis .... L 0-6
22— At Anaheim .... W 8-2
26— At Los Angeles .... W ..*3-2
28— N.Y. Rangers.............. T ...*2-2

JANUARY
1— Edmonton.................. L 4-5
4— At Detroit................... W 5-2
6— At Ottawa .... L 2-5
8— At New Jersey .... L 3-4
10— At N.Y. Islanders .... T ...*2-2
12— Pittsburgh .... W 3-1
15— Anaheim .... W 4-2
17— At Colorado .... L 0-2
18— At Nashville .... T ...*4-4
20— Buffalo....................... W 2-1
23— San Jose .... W ..*3-2
27— At Carolina .... W 4-2
28— At Washington .... L ...*2-3
31— Detroit....................... W 5-3

FEBRUARY
1— At San Jose .... W ..*1-0
3— Dallas......................... L 0-2
9— Los Angeles .... L 2-5
12— Calgary .... W 4-3

14— Detroit .... L 1-3
18— At Dallas.................... W 4-3
20— Atlanta .... W 4-2
22— At Montreal................ L 0-1
23— At Toronto .... L 3-5
25— At Calgary .... T ...*3-3
27— At Vancouver .... L 1-2

MARCH
1— Carolina..................... W 7-5
3— Dallas......................... L 1-4
5— At Chicago .... L 3-7
7— At St. Louis .... L 0-4
9— N.Y. Islanders .... W 5-0
11— Vancouver .... W 5-0
13— Philadelphia............... L 1-4
15— St. Louis .... L 3-5
17— Nashville .... L ...*3-4
21— Chicago .... L 0-3
23— Colorado .... L 2-4
24— At San Jose .... L 1-5
26— At Anaheim .... L ...*3-4
29— At Atlanta .... W 3-2
31— At Calgary .... W 3-1

APRIL
1— At Edmonton .... L ...*3-4
3— Los Angeles .... W 2-1
5— Nashville..................... W 3-2
7— San Jose.................... L 1-3
9— At Dallas.................... T ...*2-2
*Denotes overtime game.

PITTSBURGH PENGUINS
EASTERN CONFERENCE/ATLANTIC DIVISION

Pittsburgh Schedule
Home games shaded; D—Day game;
*—All-Star Game at Denver. †—Game played in Japan

October

SUN	MON	TUE	WED	THU	FRI	SAT
1	2	3	4	5	6 NSH	7 † NSH
8	9	10	11	12	13 TB	14 NYR
15	16	17	18 CAR	19 OTT	20	21 CBJ
22	23	24	25 OTT	26	27 NYR	28 NJ
29	30	31				

November

SUN	MON	TUE	WED	THU	FRI	SAT
			1 SJ	2	3 VAN	4 CAL
5	6	7	8 PHI	9	10 NJ	11 EDM
12	13 COL	14	15	16 STL	17	18 ATL
19	20	21	22 CAR	23	24 D PHI	25 LA
26	27	28 BOS	29	30		

December

SUN	MON	TUE	WED	THU	FRI	SAT
					1 BUF	2 BUF
3	4	5 OTT	6 BOS	7	8	9 TOR
10 DET	11	12	13 TOR	14	15 FLA	16 MON
17	18	19	20 FLA	21 TB	22	23 DAL
24	25	26 BUF	27 TOR	28	29	30 OTT
31						

January

SUN	MON	TUE	WED	THU	FRI	SAT
	1	2	3 WAS	4	5 MON	6
7	8 WAS	9 BOS	10	11	12 NYI	13 NYI
14	15 D ANA	16	17 PHO	18	19 DAL	20
21 CHI	22	23	24 MON	25	26	27 ATL
28	29	30 ATL	31 PHI			

February

SUN	MON	TUE	WED	THU	FRI	SAT
				1	2	3
4	*5	6	7 PHI	8	9	10 D NJ
11 D MIN	12	13	14 MIN	15	16 NJ	17 CBJ
18	19 D COL	20	21 FLA	22	23 NYR	24
25 NYI	26	27	28 MON			

March

SUN	MON	TUE	WED	THU	FRI	SAT
				1	2 NYR	3 WAS
4	5	6	7 WAS	8 ATL	9	10 CAL
11	12 NYR	13	14 NYI	15	16 FLA	17 TB
18	19	20 BOS	21	22	23 CAR	24
25 NJ	26	27 BUF	28	29 CHI	30	31 D STL

April

SUN	MON	TUE	WED	THU	FRI	SAT
1	2 NYI	3	4 TB	5	6	7 D PHI
8 D CAR						

2000-2001 SEASON
CLUB DIRECTORY

Ownership
Mario Lemieux and the Lemieux Group
Executive v.p./general manager
Craig Patrick
Executive vice president/COO
Tom Rooney
Executive vice president/CFO
Ken Sawyer
Assistant general manager
Ed Johnston
Head coach
Ivan Hlinka
Assistant coaches
Rick Kehoe
Joe Mullen
Goaltending coach and scout
Gilles Meloche
Head scout
Greg Malone
Scouts
Herb Brooks
Wayne Daniels
Charlie Hodge
Mark Kelley
Neil Shea

Vice president, general counsel
Ted Black
Vice president, corporate sales
David Soltesz
Vice president/controller
Kevin Hart
V.p./communications/marketing
Tom McMillan
Director of media relations
Steve Bovino
Manager, media relations
Keith Wehner
Vice president, ticket sales
Mark Anderson
Strength and conditioning coach
John Welday
Equipment manager
Steve Latin
Assistant equipment manager
Paul Flati
Trainers
Mark Mortland
Scott Johnson
Team physician
Dr. Charles Burke

DRAFT CHOICES

Rd.— Player	Ht./Wt.	Overall	Pos.	Last team
1— Brooks Orpik	6-3/217	18	D	Boston Col. (H. East)
2— Shane Endicott	6-4/200	52	C	Seattle (WHL)
3— Peter Hamerlik	6-1/187	84	G	Skalica, Slovakia
4— Michel Ouellet	6-1/182	124	RW	Rimouski (QMJHL)
5— David Koci	6-6/216	146	D	Sparta Praha Jr., Czech
6— Patrick Foley	6-0/216	185	LW	New Hamp. (H. East)
7— Jim Abbott	6-1/185	216	LW	New Hamp. (H. East)
8— Steven Crampton	6-2/197	248	RW	Moose Jaw (WHL)
9— Roman Simicek	6-1/190	273	C	HPK Hameenlinna, Fin.
9— Nick Boucher	5-11/175	280	G	Dartmouth (ECAC)

MISCELLANEOUS DATA

Home ice (capacity)
Mellon Arena (16,958)
Address
Mellon Arena
66 Mario Lemieux Place
Pittsburgh, PA 15219
Business phone
412-642-1300
Ticket information
412-642-7367 and 1-800-642-7367

Website
www.pittsburghpenguins.com
Training site
Canonsburg, PA
Club colors
Black, gold and white
Radio affiliation
3WS (94.5 FM and 970 AM)
TV affiliation
Fox Sports Net Pittsburgh

TRAINING CAMP ROSTER

No.	FORWARDS	Ht./Wt.	Place	Date	NHL exp.	1999-2000 clubs
36	Matthew Barnaby (LW)	6-0/189	Ottawa	5-4-73	8	Pittsburgh
18	Josef Beranek (LW)	6-2/195	Litvinov, Czechoslovakia	10-25-69	8	Edmonton, Pittsburgh
9	Rene Corbet (LW)	6-0/195	St. Hyacinthe, Que.	6-25-73	7	Calgary, Pittsburgh
	Greg Crozier (LW)	6-3/199	Williamsville, N.Y.	7-6-76	0	Wilkes-Barre/Scranton (AHL)
59	Robert Dome (C/LW)	6-0/210	Skalica, Czechoslovakia	1-29-79	2	W.-Barre/Scranton (AHL), Pittsburgh
	Shane Endicott (C)	6-4/200	Saskatoon, Sask.	12-21-81	0	Seattle (WHL)
	Patrick Foley (LW)	6-0/216	Boston	1-24-81	0	Univ. of New Hamp. (Hockey East)
38	Jan Hrdina (C)	6-0/200	Hradec Kralove, Czech.	2-5-76	2	Pittsburgh
68	Jaromir Jagr (RW)	6-2/235	Kladno, Czechoslovakia	2-15-72	10	Pittsburgh
	Alexei Kolkunov (C)	6-0/201	Belgorod, U.S.S.R.	2-3-77	0	Wilkes-Barre/Scranton (AHL)
	Tom Kostopoulos (RW)	6-0/205	Mississauga, Ont.	1-24-79	0	Wilkes-Barre/Scranton (AHL)
27	Alexei Kovalev (C)	6-1/215	Moscow, U.S.S.R.	2-24-73	8	Pittsburgh
	Milan Kraft (C)	6-3/191	Plzen, Czechoslovakia	1-17-80	0	Prince Albert (WHL)
20	Robert Lang (C)	6-2/216	Teplice, Czechoslovakia	12-19-70	7	Pittsburgh
	Alexandre Mathieu (C)	6-2/177	Repentigny, Que.	2-12-79	0	Wilkes-Barre/Scranton (AHL)
24	Ian Moran (RW/D)	6-0/206	Cleveland	8-24-72	6	Pittsburgh
95	Alexei Morozov (RW)	6-1/196	Moscow, U.S.S.R.	2-16-77	3	Pittsburgh
	Michel Ouellet (RW)	6-1/182	Rimouski, Que.	3-5-82	0	Rimouski (QMJHL)
32	Boris Protsenko (RW)	5-11/192	Kiev, U.S.S.R.	8-21-78	0	Wilkes-Barre/Scranton (AHL)
12	Martin Sonnenberg (LW)	6-0/184	Wetaskiwin, Alta.	1-23-78	2	Pittsburgh, W.-Barre/Scranton (AHL)
82	Martin Straka (C)	5-9/176	Plzen, Czechoslovakia	9-3-72	8	Pittsburgh
	Alexander Zevakhin (C)	6-0/187	Perm, U.S.S.R.	6-4-80	0	CSKA Moscow (Russian)
	DEFENSEMEN					
6	Bob Boughner	6-0/203	Windsor, Ont.	3-8-71	5	Nashville, Pittsburgh
22	Sven Butenschon	6-4/215	Itzehoe, West Germany	3-22-76	3	W.-Barre/Scranton (AHL), Pittsburgh
7	Andrew Ference	5-10/190	Edmonton	3-17-79	1	Pittsburgh, W.-Barre/Scranton (AHL)
8	Hans Jonsson	6-1/202	Jarved, Sweden	8-2-73	1	Pittsburgh
11	Darius Kasparaitis	5-11/212	Elektrenai, U.S.S.R.	10-16-72	8	Pittsburgh
3	Chris Kelleher	6-1/210	Cambridge, Mass.	3-23-75	0	Wilkes-Barre/Scranton (AHL)
	David Koci	6-6/216	Prague, Czechoslovakia	5-12-81	0	Sparta Praha Jrs. (Czech. Jrs.)
5	Janne Laukkanen	6-1/194	Lahti, Finland	3-19-70	6	Ottawa, Pittsburgh
	Josef Melichar	6-2/214	Ceske Budejovice, Czech.	1-20-79	0	Wilkes-Barre/Scranton (AHL)
	Brooks Orpik	6-3/217	Amherst, N.Y.	9-26-80	0	Boston College (Hockey East)
28	Michal Rozsival	6-1/208	Vlasim, Czechoslovakia	9-3-78	1	Pittsburgh
32	John Slaney	6-0/185	St. John's, Nfld.	2-7-72	7	Pittsburgh, W.-Barre/Scranton (AHL)
71	Jiri Slegr	6-0/206	Jihlava, Czechoslovakia	5-30-71	7	Pittsburgh
	Jeremy Van Hoof	6-3/200	Lindsay, Ont.	8-12-81	0	Ottawa (OHL)
	GOALTENDERS					
30	Jean-Sebastien Aubin	5-11/176	Montreal	7-19-77	2	W.-Barre/Scranton (AHL), Pittsburgh
	Sebastien Caron	6-1/150	Amqui, Que.	6-25-80	0	Rimouski (QMJHL)
	Peter Hamerlik	6-1/187	Myjava, Czechoslovakia	1-2-82	0	Skalica (Slovakia)
	Craig Hillier	6-1/183	Cole Harbour, Nova Scotia	2-28-78	0	W.-B./Scran. (AHL), Johnstown (ECHL), Toledo (ECHL), Charlotte (ECHL)
	Scott Myers	5-11/172	Winnipeg	6-11-79	0	Prince George (WHL)

1999-2000 REVIEW

INDIVIDUAL STATISTICS

SCORING

	Games	G	A	Pts.	PIM	+/-	PPG	SHG	Shots	Shooting Pct.
Jaromir Jagr	63	42	54	96	50	25	10	0	290	14.5
Alexei Kovalev	82	26	40	66	94	-3	9	2	254	10.2
Robert Lang	78	23	42	65	14	-9	13	0	142	16.2
Martin Straka	71	20	39	59	26	24	3	1	146	13.7
Jan Hrdina	70	13	33	46	43	13	3	0	84	15.5
German Titov*	63	17	25	42	34	-3	4	2	111	15.3
Alexei Morozov	68	12	19	31	14	12	0	1	101	11.9
Jiri Slegr	74	11	20	31	82	20	0	0	144	7.6
Matthew Barnaby	64	12	12	24	197	3	0	0	80	15.0
Rob Brown	50	10	13	23	10	-13	4	0	73	13.7
Tyler Wright	50	12	10	22	45	4	0	0	68	17.6
Michal Rozsival	75	4	17	21	48	11	1	0	73	5.5
Kip Miller*	44	4	15	19	10	-1	0	0	50	8.0
Darius Kasparaitis	73	3	12	15	146	-12	1	0	76	3.9
Hans Jonsson	68	3	11	14	12	-5	0	1	49	6.1
Pat Falloon*	30	4	9	13	10	-2	0	0	41	9.8
Ian Moran	73	4	8	12	28	-10	0	0	58	6.9

	Games	G	A	Pts.	PIM	+/-	PPG	SHG	Shots	Shooting Pct.
Brad Werenka*	61	3	8	11	69	15	0	0	42	7.1
Josef Beranek*	13	4	4	8	18	-6	1	0	32	12.5
Janne Laukkanen*	11	1	7	8	12	3	1	0	19	5.3
Robert Dome	22	2	5	7	0	1	0	0	27	7.4
Andrew Ference	30	2	4	6	20	3	0	0	26	7.7
Tom Chorske	33	1	5	6	2	-2	0	0	14	7.1
Peter Popovic	54	1	5	6	30	-8	0	0	23	4.3
Stephen Leach	56	2	3	5	24	-11	0	0	41	4.9
John Slaney	29	1	4	5	10	-10	1	0	27	3.7
Martin Sonnenberg	14	1	2	3	0	0	1	0	19	5.3
Daniel Trebil	3	1	0	1	0	2	0	0	2	50.0
Rene Corbet*	4	1	0	1	0	-4	1	0	9	11.1
Bob Boughner*	11	1	0	1	69	2	1	0	8	12.5
Jean-Sebastien Aubin (goalie)	51	0	1	1	2	0	0	0	0	0.0
Sven Butenschon	3	0	0	0	0	3	0	0	2	0.0
Ron Tugnutt (goalie)*	7	0	0	0	0	0	0	0	0	0.0
Tom Barrasso (goalie)*	18	0	0	0	6	0	0	0	0	0.0
Peter Skudra (goalie)	20	0	0	0	0	0	0	0	0	0.0
Dennis Bonvie	28	0	0	0	80	-2	0	0	6	0.0

GOALTENDING

	Games	Min.	Goals	SO	Avg.	W	L	T	ENG	Shots	Sv. Pct.
Ron Tugnutt*	7	374	15	0	2.41	4	2	0	0	197	.924
Jean-Sebastien Aubin	51	2789	120	2	2.58	23	21	3	3	1392	.914
Peter Skudra	20	922	48	1	3.12	5	7	3	2	374	.872
Tom Barrasso*	18	870	46	1	3.17	5	7	2	2	386	.881

*Played with two or more NHL teams.

RESULTS

OCTOBER
1— At Dallas ....L 4-6
7— At New Jersey ....W 7-5
8— Colorado ....T....*3-3
14— At N.Y. Rangers ....W 5-2
16— Chicago ....T....*3-3
23— Carolina ....L 2-3
27— At Anaheim ....L....*1-2
28— At Los Angeles ....L 3-5
30— At San Jose ....T....*1-1

NOVEMBER
2— Los Angeles ....L 4-5
4— At Ottawa ....L 1-2
6— Tampa Bay ....L 4-7
10— Montreal ....W 5-4
12— At Detroit ....L....*2-3
13— Nashville ....W 6-2
16— Buffalo ....W 3-2
18— At Tampa Bay ....L....*1-2
20— At Florida ....L....*1-2
23— Toronto ....W 3-1
26— Ottawa ....W 5-0
27— At Carolina ....L 3-5
30— At Buffalo ....W 4-1

DECEMBER
2— San Jose ....L 2-5
4— At Toronto ....L....*2-3
7— At New Jersey ....L 1-2
9— Washington ....W 3-0
11— Phoenix ....W 4-2

14— Boston ....W 4-2
15— At Carolina ....W 6-3
18— Florida ....L 2-5
20— At Montreal ....L 1-5
21— At N.Y. Islanders ....W 4-0
23— Tampa Bay ....W 4-3
26— At Chicago ....W 4-2
29— At Washington ....L....*2-3
30— N.Y. Islanders ....W 9-3

JANUARY
2— Detroit ....W 4-3
5— New Jersey ....L 1-3
7— Toronto ....W 5-2
8— At Philadelphia ....L 2-6
12— At Phoenix ....L 1-3
13— At Colorado ....L 3-4
15— At Nashville ....L 2-4
19— St. Louis ....W 3-1
22— At Montreal ....L 2-4
23— Philadelphia ....T....*4-4
25— N.Y. Rangers ....L 3-4
27— Atlanta ....W 4-1
29— Anaheim ....L 1-7
31— At Atlanta ....W....*2-1

FEBRUARY
1— Washington ....W 3-2
3— N.Y. Islanders ....W 4-2
9— Atlanta ....W 5-2
11— Edmonton ....T....*2-2
12— At N.Y. Islanders ....L 1-5

14— Vancouver ....W 3-0
16— Buffalo ....T....*1-1
19— At Florida ....W 2-1
21— At Tampa Bay ....L 1-2
22— At N.Y. Rangers ....L 3-4
24— At Philadelphia ....L....*3-4
26— Boston ....T....*2-2
28— Ottawa ....T....*1-1

MARCH
1— At Calgary ....L 2-8
4— At Edmonton ....W 3-2
8— Montreal ....L 0-3
9— At Ottawa ....L 0-7
11— N.Y. Rangers ....W 3-1
13— New Jersey ....L 2-3
16— Florida ....W 4-2
18— At Boston ....L 2-3
19— N.Y. Rangers ....W 5-4
21— At N.Y. Islanders ....W 8-2
24— At Atlanta ....W 5-3
26— At Philadelphia ....L 1-3
28— New Jersey ....W 3-2
30— At Washington ....W...*4-3

APRIL
1— Philadelphia ....L 2-3
3— Carolina ....W 3-2
5— At Toronto ....W 4-2
7— At Buffalo ....W...*2-1
9— At Boston ....L 1-3

*Denotes overtime game.

ST. LOUIS BLUES
WESTERN CONFERENCE/CENTRAL DIVISION

ST. LOUIS BLUES

St. Louis Schedule

Home games shaded; D—Day game; *—All-Star Game at Denver.

October

SUN	MON	TUE	WED	THU	FRI	SAT
1	2	3	4	5 PHO	6 SJ	7
8 ANA	D 9	10	11 LA	12	13 MIN	14
15	16	17 DET	18	19 LA	20	21 CHI
22	23	24	25	26 CAL	27	28 DAL
29 CAR	30	31 NSH				

November

SUN	MON	TUE	WED	THU	FRI	SAT
			1	2 WAS	3	4 TOR
5	6	7	8	9 COL	10	11 VAN
12	13	14 EDM	15	16 PIT	17	18 BUF
19	20	21 VAN	22	23	24 NSH	25 PHO
26	27	28	29 TOR	30		

December

SUN	MON	TUE	WED	THU	FRI	SAT
					1	2 FLA
3	4	5 ANA	6	7	8	9 CHI
10 CHI	11	12	13	14	15 ATL	16 DET
17	18	19	20 NYR	21	22	23 ANA
24	25	26 CBJ	27	28 LA	29	30 PHO
31						

January

SUN	MON	TUE	WED	THU	FRI	SAT
	1 EDM	2 OTT	3	4 NSH	5	6 MIN
7	8 PHI	9	10 ANA	11 SJ	12	13 LA
14	15 PHO	16	17	18 EDM	19	20 VAN
21 NSH	22	23 MON	24	25 NJ	26	27 SJ
28	29 TOR	30 BOS	31			

February

SUN	MON	TUE	WED	THU	FRI	SAT
				1 CBJ	2	3
4	* 5	6 CBJ	7	8 TB	9	10 COL
11 DAL	12	13	14	15 CAL	16 CHI	17
18	19 FLA	20 TB	21	22	23 DET	24 BOS
25	26 SJ	27	28 EDM			

March

SUN	MON	TUE	WED	THU	FRI	SAT
				1	2 VAN	3 CAL
4	5	6 MIN	7	8 COL	9	10 D DET
11	12	13 PHI	14 MIN	15	16	17 CAL
18	19	20 NYI	21	22 COL	23	24 D CHI
25 DAL	26	27	28 DET	29	30	31 D PIT

April

SUN	MON	TUE	WED	THU	FRI	SAT
1 CBJ	2	3 CAR	4	5 CBJ	6	7 NSH
8						

2000-2001 SEASON
CLUB DIRECTORY

Chairman of the board and owner
Bill Laurie
President & chief executive officer
Mark Sauer
Sr. vice president and general manager
Larry Pleau
Assistant general manager
John Ferguson Jr.
Head coach
Joel Quenneville
Assistant coaches
Jim Roberts
Mike Kitchen
Goaltending coach
Keith Allain
Athletic trainer
Ray Barile

Strength and conditioning coach
Aaron Komarek
Video coach
Jamie Kompon
Equipment manager
Bert Godin
Assistant equipment manager
Eric Bechtol
Director of communications
Jeff Trammel
Assistant director of communications
To be announced
Communications manager
Stan Richardson

DRAFT CHOICES

Rd.— Player	Ht./Wt.	Overall	Pos.	Last team
1— Jeff Taffe	6-2/180	30	C	Minnesota (WCHA)
2— David Morisset	6-2/195	65	RW	Seattle (WHL)
3— Justin Papineau	5-11/180	75	C	Belleville (OHL)
3— Antoine Bergeron	6-2/202	96	D	Val-d'Or (QMJHL)
4— Troy Riddle	5-10/172	129	C/RW	Des Moines, USHL
5— Craig Weller	6-3/195	167	D	Calgary Canucks, AJHL
7— Brett Lutes	6-0/182	229	LW	Montreal (QMJHL)
8— Reinhard Divis	5-11/187	261	G	Leksand, Sweden
9— Lauri Kinios	6-3/195	293	D	Montreal (QMJHL)

MISCELLANEOUS DATA

Home ice (capacity)
Kiel Center (To be announced)
Address
1401 Clark
St. Louis, MO 63103
Business phone
314-622-2500
Ticket information
314-241-1888
Website
www.stlouisblues.com

Training site
Chesterfield, MO
Club colors
Blue, gold, navy and white
Radio affiliation
KTRS (550 AM)
TV affiliation
KPLR (Channel 11) & FOX Sports
Midwest

ST. LOUIS BLUES

No.	FORWARDS	Ht./Wt.	Place	BORN Date	NHL exp.	1998-99 clubs
23	Lubos Bartecko (LW)	6-1/195	Kezmarok, Czechoslovakia	7-14-76	0	Worcester (AHL), St. Louis
	Derek Bekar (LW/C)	6-3/194	Burnaby, B.C.	9-15-75	1	Worcester (AHL), St. Louis
22	Craig Conroy (C)	6-2/193	Potsdam, N.Y.	9-4-71	6	St. Louis
18	Daniel Corso (C)	5-10/184	St. Hubert, Que.	4-3-78	0	Worcester (AHL)
38	Pavol Demitra (RW)	6-0/190	Dubnica, Czechoslovakia	11-29-74	7	St. Louis
10	Dallas Drake (RW)	6-1/190	Trail, B.C.	2-4-69	8	Phoenix
32	Mike Eastwood (C)	6-3/209	Cornwall, Ont.	7-1-67	9	St. Louis
26	Michal Handzus (C)	6-5/210	Banska Bystrica, Czech.	3-11-77	2	St. Louis
17	Jochen Hecht (C)	6-3/196	Mannheim, West Germany	6-21-77	2	St. Louis
	Reed Low (RW)	6-5/228	Moose Jaw, Sask.	6-26-76	0	Worcester (AHL)
21	Jamal Mayers (RW)	6-2/212	Toronto	10-24-74	3	St. Louis
	David Morisset (RW)	6-2/195	Langley, B.C.	4-6-81	0	Seattle (WHL)
47	Ladislav Nagy (C)	5-11/183	Presov, Yugoslavia	6-1-79	1	Worcester (AHL), St. Louis
9	Tyson Nash (LW)	5-11/195	Edmonton	3-11-75	2	St. Louis
	Justin Papineau (C)	5-10/160	Ottawa	1-15-80	0	Belleville (OHL)
	Andrei Podkonicky (C)	6-2/195	Zvolen, Czechoslovakia	5-9-78	0	Worcester (AHL)
15	Marty Reasoner (C)	6-0/203	Rochester, N.Y.	2-26-77	2	Worcester (AHL), St. Louis
25	Pascal Rheaume (LW)	6-1/209	Quebec City	6-21-73	4	St. Louis, Worcester (AHL)
	Troy Riddle (C/RW)	5-9/172	Minneapolis	8-24-81	0	Des Moines (USHL)
	Mark Rycroft (RW)	6-0/197			0	Univ. of Denver (WCHA)
	Jeff Taffe (C)	6-1/180	Hastings, Minn.	2-19-81	0	Univ. of Minnesota (WCHA)
	Andrei Troschinsky (C)	6-5/187	Ust-Kamenogorsk, U.S.S.R.	2-14-78	0	
77	Pierre Turgeon (C)	6-1/199	Rouyn, Que.	8-28-69	13	St. Louis
48	Scott Young (RW)	6-1/200	Clinton, Mass.	10-1-67	12	St. Louis
	DEFENSEMEN					
	Antoine Bergeron	6-2/202	Valcourt, Que.	12-14-81	0	Val-d'Or (QMJHL)
4	Marc Bergevin	6-1/214	Montreal	8-11-65	16	St. Louis
55	Vladimir Chebaturkin	6-2/212	Tyumen, U.S.S.R.	4-23-75	3	Lowell (AHL), New York Islanders
37	Jeff Finley	6-2/205	Edmonton	4-14-67	11	St. Louis
6	Sean Hill	6-0/203	Duluth, Minn.	2-14-70	10	Carolina
	Jan Horacek	6-4/206	Benesov, Czechoslovakia	5-22-79	0	Worcester (AHL)
	Barret Jackman	6-1/200	Trail, B.C.	3-5-81	0	Regina (WHL), Worcester (AHL)
2	Alexander Khavanov	6-2/190	Dynamo, U.S.S.R.	1-30-72	0	Dynamo (Russian)
	Al MacInnis	6-2/208	Inverness, Nova Scotia	7-11-63	19	St. Louis
	Jaroslav Obsut	6-1/185	Presov, Czechoslovakia	9-3-76	0	Worcester (AHL)
44	Chris Pronger	6-6/220	Dryden, Ont.	10-10-74	7	St. Louis
28	Todd Reirden	6-5/220	Deerfield, Ill.	6-25-71	2	St. Louis
	Bryce Salvador	6-1/194	Brandon, Man.	2-11-76	0	Worcester (AHL)
	Peter Smrek	6-1/194	Martin, Czechoslovakia	2-16-79	0	Worcester (AHL), Peoria (ECHL)
	Craig Weller	6-3/195	Calgary	3-17-81	0	Calgary Canucks (AJHL)
	GOALTENDERS					
35	Brent Johnson	6-2/200	Farmington, Mich.	3-12-77	1	Worcester (AHL)
30	Dwayne Roloson	6-1/190	Simcoe, Ont.	10-12-69	4	Buffalo
	Cody Rudkowsky	6-1/200	Willingdon, Alta.	7-21-78	0	Worcester (AHL), Peoria (ECHL)
1	Roman Turek	6-3/200	Pisek, Czechoslovakia	5-21-70	4	St. Louis

(handwritten annotations: "ATL", "FLA", "PHOE", "EDM", "BLUE", "DAL", "PHX.DE", "PHX.DE", "EDM", "DAL", "EDM", "NYR", "CAL", "D #7 DARREN RUMBLE", "RW 19 SCOTT MELANBY")

1999-2000 REVIEW
INDIVIDUAL STATISTICS

SCORING

	Games	G	A	Pts.	PIM	+/-	PPG	SHG	Shots	Shooting Pct.
Pavol Demitra	71	28	47	75	8	34	8	0	241	11.6
Pierre Turgeon	52	26	40	66	8	30	8	0	139	18.7
Chris Pronger	79	14	48	62	92	52	8	0	192	7.3
Michal Handzus	81	25	28	53	44	19	3	4	166	15.1
Scott Young	75	24	15	39	18	12	6	1	244	9.8
Lubos Bartecko	67	16	23	39	51	24	3	0	75	21.3
Al MacInnis	61	11	28	39	34	20	6	0	245	4.5
Mike Eastwood	79	19	15	34	32	5	1	3	83	22.9
Jochen Hecht	63	13	21	34	28	20	5	0	140	9.3
Craig Conroy	79	12	15	27	36	5	1	2	98	12.2
Stephane Richer*	36	8	17	25	14	7	4	0	63	12.7
Todd Reirden	56	4	21	25	32	18	0	0	77	5.2
Marty Reasoner	32	10	14	24	20	9	3	0	51	19.6
Scott Pellerin	80	8	15	23	48	6	0	2	120	6.7
Jamal Mayers	79	7	10	17	90	0	0	0	99	7.1
Terry Yake*	26	4	9	13	22	2	2	0	26	15.4
Tyson Nash	66	4	9	13	150	6	0	1	68	5.9

	Games	G	A	Pts.	PIM	+/-	PPG	SHG	Shots	Shooting Pct.
Dave Ellett	52	2	8	10	12	-4	0	0	41	4.9
Jeff Finley	74	2	8	10	38	26	0	0	31	6.5
Derek King*	19	2	7	9	6	0	1	0	29	6.9
Marc Bergevin	81	1	8	9	75	27	0	0	54	1.9
Ricard Persson	41	0	8	8	38	-2	0	0	30	0.0
Ladislav Nagy	11	2	4	6	2	2	1	0	15	13.3
Geoff Courtnall	6	2	2	4	6	3	0	0	15	13.3
Bob Bassen	27	1	3	4	26	-3	0	0	26	3.8
Pascal Rheaume	7	1	1	2	6	-2	0	0	5	20.0
Bryan Helmer	15	1	1	2	10	-3	1	0	19	5.3
Chris McAlpine*	21	1	1	2	14	1	0	0	25	4.0
Kelly Chase	25	0	1	1	118	-5	0	0	14	0.0
Roman Turek (goalie)	67	0	1	1	4	0	0	0	0	0.0
Derek Bekar	1	0	0	0	0	0	0	0	0	0.0
Jim Campbell	2	0	0	0	9	0	0	0	6	0.0
Rudy Poeschek	12	0	0	0	24	-3	0	0	8	0.0
Jamie McLennan (goalie)	19	0	0	0	2	0	0	0	0	0.0

GOALTENDING

	Games	Min.	Goals	SO	Avg.	W	L	T	ENG	Shots	Sv. Pct.
Roman Turek	67	3960	129	7	1.95	42	15	9	3	1470	.912
Jamie McLennan	19	1009	33	2	1.96	9	5	2	0	341	.903

*Played with two or more NHL teams.

RESULTS

OCTOBER

2—	Phoenix	L	1-2
4—	Los Angeles	L	2-3
6—	At Calgary	W	4-1
9—	At Edmonton	W	4-2
13—	At Detroit	L	2-4
16—	Toronto	W	4-2
19—	Calgary	W	7-1
21—	Edmonton	W	*3-2
23—	New Jersey	W	3-1
27—	At New Jersey	L	1-2
30—	Detroit	W	*5-4

NOVEMBER

3—	At Colorado	L	0-5
5—	At Edmonton	W	2-1
7—	At Vancouver	W	6-1
9—	Dallas	L	2-5
12—	Edmonton	T	*2-2
13—	At N.Y. Islanders	W	5-3
17—	At Toronto	W	3-2
18—	Florida	W	3-0
20—	San Jose	T	*1-1
22—	Nashville	W	*3-2
24—	At Detroit	L	2-4
26—	At Buffalo	W	2-0
27—	Chicago	W	8-3

DECEMBER

2—	Nashville	W	3-1
4—	San Jose	W	4-2
5—	At Philadelphia	L	2-3
7—	Carolina	L	2-4
10—	At Nashville	W	4-2
11—	Dallas	W	4-2
14—	Calgary	T	*1-1
18—	Boston	W	4-0
21—	At Phoenix	W	6-0
23—	At Nashville	T	*2-2
26—	Nashville	L	2-3
27—	At Colorado	L	1-5
30—	San Jose	W	*2-1

JANUARY

1—	At Washington	T	*1-1
3—	At N.Y. Rangers	W	5-2
4—	Los Angeles	T	*2-2
6—	Montreal	W	4-3
8—	Vancouver	W	4-2
11—	At San Jose	W	5-2
13—	At Los Angeles	W	3-2
14—	At Anaheim	L	1-3
19—	At Pittsburgh	L	1-3
21—	At Chicago	W	3-0
22—	N.Y. Rangers	L	1-4
26—	At Ottawa	W	4-1
28—	At Dallas	W	3-1
29—	Colorado	W	4-0

FEBRUARY

1—	At Calgary	W	*5-4
3—	At Vancouver	W	5-2
8—	At Detroit	W	4-1
10—	Detroit	L	0-2
12—	Anaheim	W	6-3
15—	Atlanta	W	4-1
18—	At Nashville	W	2-1
21—	At Anaheim	W	4-2
23—	At San Jose	W	4-1
25—	Colorado	W	4-2
27—	Chicago	L	1-4
29—	Philadelphia	W	3-2

MARCH

2—	At Atlanta	W	5-2
4—	At Florida	T	*1-1
7—	Phoenix	W	4-0
9—	Vancouver	T	*2-2
11—	Anaheim	T	*1-1
12—	At Dallas	L	2-4
15—	At Phoenix	W	5-3
17—	At Los Angeles	W	4-0
20—	Washington	W	2-1
22—	At Carolina	W	5-1
24—	At Tampa Bay	W	5-1
26—	At Chicago	T	*1-1
29—	Toronto	L	2-3
30—	At Boston	W	3-2

APRIL

1—	Detroit	T	*0-0
2—	Ottawa	W	4-1
5—	Calgary	W	6-5
7—	Chicago	L	*3-4
9—	At Chicago	L	1-3

*Denotes overtime game.

SAN JOSE SHARKS
WESTERN CONFERENCE/PACIFIC DIVISION

San Jose Schedule
Home games shaded; D—Day game; *—All-Star Game at Denver.

October

SUN	MON	TUE	WED	THU	FRI	SAT
1	2	3	4	5	6 STL	7
8	9	10	11	12 PHO	13	14 BOS
15	16	17	18 DAL	19	20 MIN	21 NSH
22	23	24 CAR	25 CBJ	26	27	28 ATL
29	30	31				

November

SUN	MON	TUE	WED	THU	FRI	SAT
			1 PIT	2	3	4 CAR
5 VAN	6	7	8 CHI	9 CBJ	10	11 NYI
12	13	14 NJ	15 DET	16	17	18 NYI
19	20	21	22 CHI	23	24	25 NJ
26	27	28 MIN	29	30 ANA		

December

SUN	MON	TUE	WED	THU	FRI	SAT
					1	2
3 EDM	4 CAL	5	6 DAL	7	8 VAN	9
10	11	12 NYR	13	14 CBJ	15	16 PHO
17	18 WAS	19	20 DET	21 PHI	22	23 BUF
24	25	26 LA	27	28 EDM	29	30 VAN
31						

January

SUN	MON	TUE	WED	THU	FRI	SAT
1 PHO	2	3 CAL	4 COL	5	6 FLA	
7	8	9 BUF	10	11 STL	12	13 NSH
14	15 DET	16	17 CAL	18	19	20 D COL
21	22 EDM	23	24 EDM	25	26 DAL	27 STL
28	29	30 COL	31			

February

SUN	MON	TUE	WED	THU	FRI	SAT
				1 DAL	2	3
4	*5	6 CAL	7	8 VAN	9	10 CHI
11	12	13	14 CHI	15	16 NSH	17
18 D MIN	19	20 CBJ	21 ANA	22	23 ANA	24
25	26 STL	27	28 TOR			

March

SUN	MON	TUE	WED	THU	FRI	SAT
				1 OTT	2	3 D BOS
4	5	6 TB	7 FLA	8	9	10 NSH
11	12 MON	13	14 LA	15	16	17 D LA
18 DET	19	20 COL	21	22 OTT	23	24
25	26 LA	27 LA	28	29 ANA	30	31 PHO

April

SUN	MON	TUE	WED	THU	FRI	SAT
1	2 MIN	3	4	5 PHO	6	7 D DAL
8 ANA						

2000-2001 SEASON
CLUB DIRECTORY

Owner & chairman
George Gund III
Co-owner
Gordon Gund
President & chief executive officer
Greg Jamison
Exec. v.p. and general manager
Dean Lombardi
Vice president & chief financial officer
Gregg Olson
VVice president & assistant g.m.
Wayne Thomas
Head coach
Darryl Sutter
Assistant coaches
Rich Preston
Cap Raeder
Strength & conditioning coach
Mac Read
Assistant to the general manager
Joe Will

Executive assistant
Brenda Will
Director of media relations
Ken Arnold
Media relations manager
Scott Emmert
Media relations coordinator
Ben Stephenson
Director of pro development
Doug Wilson
Head trainer
Tom Woodcock
Equipment manager
Mike Aldrich
Assistant equipment manager
Kurt Harvey
Team physician
Dr. Arthur J. Ting
Director of marketing and publicity
Beth Brigino

DRAFT CHOICES

Rd.— Player	Ht./Wt.	Overall	Pos.	Last team
2— Tero Maatta	6-1/205	41	D	Jokerit, Finland
5— Michael Pinc	5-11/180	142	C/LW	R.-Noranda (QMJHL)
5— Nolan Schaefer	6-1/175	166	G	Providence (H. East)
6— Michael Macho	6-1/169	183	C	Martin, Slovakia
8— Chad Wiseman	6-0/190	246	LW	Mississauga (OHL)
8— Pasi Saarinen	6-0/189	256	D	Ilves-Tampere, Finland

MISCELLANEOUS DATA

Home ice (capacity)
San Jose Arena (17,496)
Address
525 West Santa Clara Street
San Jose, CA 95113
Business phone
408-287-7070
Ticket information
408-287-7070
Website
www.sjsharks.com

Training site
San Jose
Club colors
Deep pacific teal, shimmering gray,
burnt orange and black
Radio affiliation
KARA (105.7 FM)
TV affiliation
FOX Sports Net

No.	FORWARDS	Ht./Wt.	Place	Born Date	NHL exp.	1999-2000 clubs
	Matt Bradley (RW).........	6-2/195	Stittsville, Ont.	6-13-78	0	Kentucky (AHL)
	Jonathan Cheechoo (RW)	6-0/205	Moose Factory, Ont.	7-15-80	0	Belleville (OHL)
25	Vincent Damphousse (C)	6-1/200	Montreal	12-17-67	14	San Jose
	Jon Disalvatore (RW)	6-1/180	Bangor, Me.	3-30-81	0	Providence College (Hockey East)
39	Jeff Friesen (LW)	6-0/205	Meadow Lake, Sask.	8-5-76	6	San Jose
21	Tony Granato (RW)	5-10/185	Downers Grove, Ill.	6-25-64	12	San Jose
9	Todd Harvey (RW).........	6-0/205	Hamilton, Ont.	2-17-75	6	New York Rangers, San Jose
15	Alex Korolyuk (RW).......	5-9/195	Moscow, U.S.S.R.	1-15-76	3	San Jose
	Michal Macho (C)	6-1/169	Martin, Czechoslovakia	1-17-82	0	Martimex Martin Jrs. (Slov. Jr.)
14	Patrick Marleau (C)........	6-2/210	Swift Current, Sask.	9-15-79	3	San Jose
37	Stephane Matteau (LW)	6-4/220	Rouyn-Noranda, Que.	9-2-69	10	San Jose
11	Owen Nolan (RW)	6-1/210	Belfast, Northern Ireland	2-12-72	10	San Jose
	Michael Pinc (C/LW)......	5-11/180	Most, Czechoslovakia	12-2-81	0	Rouyn-Noranda (QMJHL)
18	Mike Ricci (C)...............	6-0/190	Scarborough, Ont.	10-27-71	10	San Jose
	Mark Smith (C)..............	5-10/200	Eyebrow, Sask.	10-24-77	0	Kentucky (AHL)
22	Ronnie Stern (RW)	6-0/205	Ste. Agatha Des Mont, Que.	1-11-67	13	San Jose
19	Marco Sturm (LW)........	6-0/195	Dingolfing, West Germany	9-8-78	3	San Jose
24	Niklas Sundstrom (LW)	6-0/195	Ornskoldsvik, Sweden	1-6-75	5	San Jose
17	Scott Thornton (LW)......	6-3/216	London, Ont.	1-9-71	10	Montreal, Dallas
	Miroslav Zalesak (RW) ..	6-0/185	Skalica, Czechoslovakia	1-2-80	0	Drummondville (QMJHL)
DEFENSEMEN						
43	Scott Hannan...............	6-2/220	Richmond, B.C.	1-23-79	2	Kentucky (AHL), San Jose
23	Shawn Heins	6-4/210	Eganville, Ont.	12-24-73	2	Kentucky (AHL), San Jose
	Jeff Jillson	6-3/219	North Smithfield, R.I.	7-24-80	0	Univ. of Michigan (CCHA)
	Robert Jindrich............	5-11/190	Plezn, Czechoslovakia	11-14-76	0	Kentucky (AHL)
	Tero Maatta	6-1/205	Vantaa, Finland	1-2-82	0	Jokerit Helsinki (Finland Jr.)
27	Bryan Marchment	6-1/185	Scarborough, Ont.	5-1-69	12	San Jose
10	Marcus Ragnarsson	6-1/215	Ostervala, Sweden	8-13-71	5	San Jose
40	Mike Rathje................	6-5/235	Mannville, Alta.	5-11-74	7	San Jose
7	Brad Stuart	6-2/210	Rocky Mountain House, Alta.	11-6-79	1	San Jose
20	Gary Suter	6-0/215	Madison, Wis.	6-24-64	15	San Jose
42	Andy Sutton	6-6/245	Kingston, Ont.	3-10-75	2	San Jose, Kentucky (AHL)
GOALTENDERS						
	Johan Hedberg	5-11/185	Leksand, Sweden	5-5-73	0	Kentucky (AHL)
	Miikka Kiprusoff	6-2/190	Turku, Finland	10-26-76	0	Kentucky (AHL)
35	Evgeni Nabokov	6-0/200	Ust-Kamenogorsk, U.S.S.R.	7-25-75	1	Cleveland (IHL), San Jose, Kentucky (AHL)
	Nolan Schaefer............	6-1/175	Regina, Sask.	1-15-80	0	Providence College (Hockey East)
31	Steve Shields	6-3/215	Toronto	7-19-72	5	San Jose

1999-2000 REVIEW
INDIVIDUAL STATISTICS

SCORING

	Games	G	A	Pts.	PIM	+/-	PPG	SHG	Shots	Shooting Pct.
Owen Nolan	78	44	40	84	110	-1	18	4	261	16.9
Vincent Damphousse............	82	21	49	70	58	4	3	1	204	10.3
Jeff Friesen.....................	82	26	35	61	47	-2	11	3	191	13.6
Mike Ricci..........................	82	20	24	44	60	14	10	0	134	14.9
Patrick Marleau..................	81	17	23	40	36	-9	3	0	161	10.6
Niklas Sundstrom................	79	12	25	37	22	9	2	1	90	13.3
Brad Stuart.......................	82	10	26	36	32	3	5	1	133	7.5
Alexander Korolyuk.............	57	14	21	35	35	4	3	0	124	11.3
Gary Suter........................	76	6	28	34	52	7	2	1	175	3.4
Marco Sturm.....................	74	12	15	27	22	4	2	4	120	10.0
Stephane Matteau...............	69	12	12	24	61	-3	0	0	73	16.4
Jeff Norton	62	0	20	20	49	-2	0	0	45	0.0
Marcus Ragnarsson..............	63	3	13	16	38	13	0	0	60	5.0
Mike Rathje.......................	66	2	14	16	31	-2	0	0	46	4.3
Tony Granato	48	6	7	13	39	2	1	0	67	9.0
Todd Harvey*	40	8	4	12	78	-2	2	0	59	13.6
Ron Sutter	78	5	6	11	34	-3	0	1	68	7.4
Ronnie Stern.....................	67	4	5	9	151	-9	0	0	63	6.3
Dave Lowry	32	1	4	5	18	1	0	0	25	4.0
Bryan Marchment	49	0	4	4	72	3	0	0	51	0.0
Scott Hannan	30	1	2	3	10	7	0	0	28	3.6
Andy Sutton......................	40	1	1	2	80	-5	0	0	29	3.4
Murray Craven	19	0	2	2	4	-2	0	0	18	0.0

	Games	G	A	Pts.	PIM	+/-	PPG	SHG	Shots	Shooting Pct.
Brantt Myhres	13	0	1	1	97	0	0	0	2	0.0
Bob Rouse	26	0	1	1	19	-3	0	0	20	0.0
Steve Shields (goalie) *ANAHEIM*	67	0	1	1	29	0	0	0	0	0.0
Shawn Heins	1	0	0	0	2	-1	0	0	1	0.0
Evgeni Nabokov (goalie)	11	0	0	0	0	0	0	0	0	0.0
Mike Vernon (goalie)* *CALGARY*	15	0	0	0	0	0	0	0	0	0.0

GOALTENDING

	Games	Min.	Goals	SO	Avg.	W	L	T	ENG	Shots	Sv. Pct.
Evgeni Nabokov	11	414	15	1	2.17	2	2	1	2	166	.910
Mike Vernon* *CALGARY*	15	772	32	0	2.49	6	5	1	0	360	.911
Steve Shields *ANAHEIM*	67	3797	162	4	2.56	27	30	8	3	1826	.911

*Played with two or more NHL teams.

RESULTS

OCTOBER
2— Calgary ....W.....5-3
4— Chicago ....W.....7-1
7— Edmonton...................W....*3-2
9— Dallas ....L.....2-3
11—At Anaheim................L.....3-5
13—At Dallas ....W.....2-0
14—At Nashville ....W.....5-1
16—At Washington ....W.....3-2
19—At N.Y. Rangers.........W.....2-1
20—At Detroit.....................L.....3-6
23—Boston ....L.....1-3
24—At Los Angeles ....L.....3-4
28—Nashville......................W.....3-2
30—Pittsburgh....................T....*1-1
31—Washington ....W.....2-1

NOVEMBER
3— Phoenix ....W.....6-3
5— Philadelphia................L.....1-3
6— Dallas ....W.....2-1
9— At Vancouver ....T....*4-4
10—At Calgary....................L....*3-4
13—At Philadelphia............L.....2-3
15—At Toronto....................L.....2-4
16—At Montreal ....W.....4-1
18—At Ottawa ....W.....4-1
20—At St. Louis..................T....*1-1
23—Montreal ....L....*2-3
27—At Los Angeles ....L.....1-4
28—New Jersey...................W....*4-3

DECEMBER
1— At Detroit......................L.....2-4
2— At Pittsburgh................W.....5-2
4— At St. Louis..................L.....2-4
6— Tampa Bay ....T....*3-3
8— Colorado.......................W.....4-2
10—Atlanta..........................W.....4-1
14—Chicago ....L.....2-5
19—At Phoenix ....L.....3-4
20—Detroit...........................L.....3-4
22—Los Angeles ....W.....2-1
26—Anaheim ....L.....0-1
27—At Dallas ....W.....3-1
30—At St. Louis..................L....*1-2

JANUARY
1— At Nashville ....L.....2-3
2— At Chicago....................W.....4-1
5— At Edmonton ....T....*1-1
8— Florida ....L.....2-4
11—St. Louis.......................L.....2-5
15—Los Angeles ....W....*3-2
17—At Chicago....................L....*4-5
19—At Colorado...................T....*0-0
22—Anaheim ....W.....4-3
23—At Phoenix ....L....*2-3
25—Colorado........................L.....3-4
28—At Vancouver ....L.....1-4
29—N.Y. Islanders...............L....*2-3

FEBRUARY
1— Phoenix ....L....*0-1

3— At Colorado ....T....*3-3
8— At Tampa Bay ....W.....8-0
9— At Florida ....L.....1-4
11—At Atlanta ....W.....3-0
13—At New Jersey...............L.....1-3
15—At N.Y. Islanders..........W.....4-1
18—At Anaheim...................T....*4-4
23—St. Louis ....L.....1-4
26—Los Angeles ....W.....6-3
29—Anaheim ....L.....2-4

MARCH
2— Nashville.......................W.....4-3
4— Carolina ....L.....2-5
6— N.Y. Rangers ....W.....2-1
8— Detroit ....T....*1-1
13—Calgary ....W.....5-3
15—Buffalo ....W....*6-5
17—At Anaheim...................L.....2-4
19—At Dallas ....L.....3-5
22—Vancouver ....W.....4-3
24—Phoenix ....W.....5-1
27—Edmonton.......................L.....1-2
29—At Los Angeles ....T....*1-1

APRIL
1— At Calgary......................L.....0-3
3— At Edmonton ....W.....1-0
5— Dallas ....W.....5-2
7— At Phoenix......................W.....3-1
9— Vancouver ....L.....2-5

*Denotes overtime game.

TAMPA BAY LIGHTNING
EASTERN CONFERENCE/SOUTHEAST DIVISION

Tampa Bay Schedule
Home games shaded; D—Day game; *—All-Star Game at Denver.

October

SUN	MON	TUE	WED	THU	FRI	SAT
1	2	3	4	5	6 NYI	7
8 VAN	9	10	11	12	13 PIT	14
15 ATL	16	17	18 MIN	19	20	21 NJ
22 NYR	23	24	25 DET	26	27 OTT	28
29	30	31 CAR				

November

SUN	MON	TUE	WED	THU	FRI	SAT
			1 NYR	2	3 NYI	4
5 WAS	6	7	8	9	10 MON	11 CAL
12	13	14 MON	15	16	17 TOR	18
19	20 DAL	21	22 ATL	23	24 FLA	25 FLA
26 NYI	27	28	29 WAS	30		

December

SUN	MON	TUE	WED	THU	FRI	SAT
					1 ATL	2 DET
3	4	5	6 PHI	7	8 COL	9
10	11 COL	12	13	14 PHO	15	16 LA
17 ANA	18	19	20	21 PIT	22	23 NJ
24	25	26 CAR	27	28 PHI	29	30 BOS
31 TOR						

January

SUN	MON	TUE	WED	THU	FRI	SAT
	1	2	3 CAR	4 OTT	5	6
7 CHI	8	9	10 TOR	11	12 PHI	13
14 DAL	15	16 BUF	17	18 MON	19	20 OTT
21 CBJ	22	23 WAS	24	25 OTT	26	27 FLA
28	29 CAR	30 FLA	31			

February

SUN	MON	TUE	WED	THU	FRI	SAT
				1 BUF	2	3
4	*5	6 MIN	7	8 STL	9	10 BOS
11	12	13 PHO	14	15 BOS	16	17 NYR
18 NSH	19	20 STL	21	22	23	24 D PHI
25 D BUF	26	27	28			

March

SUN	MON	TUE	WED	THU	FRI	SAT
				1 BOS	2	3 NYI
4 NJ	5	6 SJ	7	8 CAR	9	10 CBJ
11	12	13 EDM	14	15 TOR	16	17 PIT
18	19	20	21 ATL	22 ATL	23	24 WAS
25	26	27 NJ	28	29 MON	30 FLA	31

April

SUN	MON	TUE	WED	THU	FRI	SAT
1 BUF	2	3	4 PIT	5 NYR	6	7
8 D WAS						

2000-2001 SEASON
CLUB DIRECTORY

Chief executive officer & governor
Tom Wilson
President
Ron Campbell
Senior v.p. & general manager
Rick Dudley
Assistant general manager
Jay Feaster
Senior advisor to the general manager
Cliff Fletcher *PHOENIX*
Head coach
Steve Ludzik

Assistant coach *HEAD*
John Torchetti
Goaltending consultant
Jeff Reese
Vice president of public relations
Bill Wickett
Director of public relations
Jay Preble
Media relations manager
Brian Potter

DRAFT CHOICES

Rd.— Player	Ht./Wt.	Overall	Pos.	Last team
1— Nikita Alexeev	6-5/215	8	RW	Erie (OHL)
2— Ruslan Zainullin	6-2/202	34	RW	Ak-Bars Kazan, Russia
3— Alexandre Kharitonov...	5-8/150	81	RW	Dynamo, Russia
4— Johan Hagglund	6-2/194	126	C	MoDo, Sweden
5— Pavel Sedov		161	RW	Voskresensk, Russia
6— Aaron Gionet	6-1/191	191	D	Kamloops (WHL)
7— Marek Priechodsky	6-2/194	222	D	Bratislava, Slovakia
7— Brian Eklund	6-5/200	226	G	Brown (ECAC)
8— Alexander Polukeyev....		233		
9— Thomas Ziegler	5-11/176	263	F	Ambri Piotta, Switz.

MISCELLANEOUS DATA

Home ice (capacity)
Ice Palace (19,758)
Address
401 Channelside Drive
Tampa, Fla. 33602
Business phone
716-301-6500
Ticket information
813-301-6600
Website
www.tampabaylightning.com

Training site
Brandon, FL
Club colors
Black, blue, silver and white
Radio affiliation
WDAE (1250 AM)
TV affiliation
Sunshine Network (Cable)

F- -ANTONBUT

TAMPA BAY LIGHTNING

No.	FORWARDS	Ht./Wt.	Place	BORN Date	NHL exp.	1999-2000 clubs
	Dmitri Afanasenkov (LW)	6-2/200	Arkhangelsk, U.S.S.R.	5-12-80	0	Sherbrooke (QMJHL)
	Nikita Alexeev (RW)	6-5/215	Murmansk, U.S.S.R.	12-27-81	0	Erie (OHL)
11	Shawn Burr (LW/C)	6-1/205	Sarnia, Ont.	7-1-66	16	Tampa Bay, Det. (IHL), Manitoba (IHL)
20	Stan Drulia (RW)	5-11/190	Elmira, N.Y.	1-5-68	2	Tampa Bay
34	Gordie Dwyer (LW)	6-2/216	Dalhousie, N.B.	1-25-78	1	Que. (AHL), Detroit (IHL), Tampa Bay
28	Nils Ekman (LW)	5-11/182	Stockholm, Sweden	3-11-76	1	Tampa Bay, Det. (IHL), L. Beach (IHL)
	Matt Elich (RW)	6-3/196	Detroit	9-22-79	1	Detroit (IHL), Tampa Bay
43	Kyle Freadrich (LW)	6-5/231	Edmonton	12-28-78	1	Det. (IHL), Louisiana (ECHL), T. Bay
	Johan Hagglund (C)	6-2/194	Ornskoldsvik, Sweden	6-9-82	0	MoDo Ornskoldsvik Jrs. (Sweden Jr.)
25	Dwayne Hay (LW)	6-1/183	London, Ont.	2-11-77	3	Louisville (AHL), Florida, Tampa Bay
9	Brian Holzinger (C/RW)	5-11/190	Parma, Ohio	10-10-72	6	Buffalo, Tampa Bay
10	Mike Johnson (RW)	6-2/200	Scarborough, Ont.	10-3-74	4	Toronto, Tampa Bay
17	Ryan Johnson (C)	6-1/200	Thunder Bay, Ont.	6-14-76	3	Florida, Tampa Bay
	Sheldon Keefe (RW)	5-11/185	Brampton, Ont.	9-17-80	0	Barrie (OHL)
25	Dan Kesa (RW)	6-1/200	Vancouver	11-23-71	4	Tampa Bay, Det. (IHL), Manitoba (IHL)
	Alexandre Kharitonov NY	5-8/150	U.S.S.R.	3-30-76	0	Dynamo Moscow (Russian)
4	Vincent Lecavalier (C)	6-4/205	Ile-Bizard, Que.	4-21-80	2	Tampa Bay
19	Steve Martins (C)	5-9/175	Gatineau, Que.	4-13-72	5	Ottawa, Tampa Bay
33	Fredrik Modin (LW)	6-4/220	Sundsvall, Sweden	10-8-74	4	Tampa Bay
22	Wayne Primeau (C)	6-3/225	Scarborough, Ont.	6-4-76	6	Buffalo, Tampa Bay
	Brad Richards (LW)	6-1/187	Montague, P.E.I.	5-2-80	0	Rimouski (QMJHL)
	Dale Rominiski (RW)	6-2/200	Farmington Hills, Mich.	10-1-75	1	Detroit (IHL), Tampa Bay
15	Jaroslav Svejkovsky	6-1/193	Plzen, Czechoslovakia	10-1-76	4	Washington, Tampa Bay
8	Todd Warriner (LW)	6-1/200	Blenheim, Ont.	1-3-74	6	Toronto, Tampa Bay
	Ruslan Zainullin (RW)	6-2/202	Kazan, U.S.S.R.	2-14-82	0	Ak Bars Kazan (Russian)

PHOE

No.	DEFENSEMEN	Ht./Wt.	Place	Date	exp.	1999-2000 clubs
49	Kaspars Astashenko	6-2/183	Riga, U.S.S.R.	2-7-75	1	Det. (IHL), L. Beach (IHL), Tam. Bay
7	Ben Clymer	6-1/195	Edina, Minn.	4-11-78	1	Detroit (IHL), Tampa Bay
27	Jassen Cullimore	6-5/220	Simcoe, Ont.	12-4-72	6	Providence (AHL), Tampa Bay
	Aaron Gionet	6-1/191	Campbell River, B.C.	6-28-82	0	Kamloops (WHL)
3	Sergey Gusev	6-1/205	Nizhny Tagil, U.S.S.R.	7-31-75	3	Tampa Bay
13	Pavel Kubina	6-4/230	Caledna, Czechoslovakia	4-15-77	3	Tampa Bay
	Kristian Kudroc	6-6/229	Michalovce, Czechoslovakia	5-21-81	0	Quebec (QMJHL)
	Mikko Kuparinen	6-4/218	Hameenlinna, Finland	3-29-77	0	Detroit (IHL), Long Beach (IHL), HIFK Helsinki (Finland)
71	Mario Larocque	6-4/195	Montreal	4-24-78	1	Detroit (IHL)
2	Paul Mara	6-4/210	Ridgewood, N.J.	9-7-79	2	Detroit (IHL), Tampa Bay
6	Bryan Muir	6-4/220	Winnipeg	6-8-73	5	Chicago, Tampa Bay
18	Marek Posmyk	6-5/209	Jihlava, Czechoslovakia	9-15-78	1	St. John's (AHL), Det. (IHL), Tam. Bay
21	Cory Sarich	6-3/193	Saskatoon, Sask.	8-16-78	2	Buffalo, Rochester (AHL), Tampa Bay
23	Petr Svoboda	6-2/198	Most, Czechoslovakia	2-14-66	16	Tampa Bay
30	Andrei Zyuzin	6-1/210	Ufa, U.S.S.R.	1-21-78	3	Tampa Bay

No.	GOALTENDERS	Ht./Wt.	Place	Date	exp.	1999-2000 clubs
39	Dan Cloutier	6-1/182	Mont-Laurier, Que.	4-22-76	3	Tampa Bay
35	Dieter Kochan	6-1/165	Saskatoon, Sask.	11-5-74	1	B.C. (UHL), Orl. (IHL), G. Rapids (IHL), Springfield (AHL), Tampa Bay
	Yevgeny Konstantinov	6-0/167	Kazan, U.S.S.R.	3-29-81	0	Ak Bars Kazan (Russian)
80	Kevin Weekes	6-0/195	Toronto	4-4-75	3	Vancouver, New York Islanders

1999-2000 REVIEW
INDIVIDUAL STATISTICS

SCORING

	Games	G	A	Pts.	PIM	+/-	PPG	SHG	Shots	Shooting Pct.
Vincent Lecavalier	80	25	42	67	43	-25	6	0	166	15.1
Fredrik Modin	80	22	26	48	18	-26	3	0	167	13.2
Mike Sillinger*	67	19	25	44	86	-29	6	3	126	15.1
Chris Gratton*	58	14	27	41	121	-24	4	0	168	8.3
Darcy Tucker*	50	14	20	34	108	-15	1	0	98	14.3
Stan Drulia	68	11	22	33	24	-18	1	2	94	11.7
Pavel Kubina	69	8	18	26	93	-19	6	0	128	6.3
Petr Svoboda	70	2	23	25	170	-11	2	0	93	2.2
Todd Warriner*	55	11	13	24	34	-14	3	1	100	11.0
Mike Johnson*	28	10	12	22	4	-2	4	0	43	23.3
Paul Mara	54	7	11	18	73	-27	4	0	78	9.0
Robert Petrovicky	43	7	10	17	14	2	1	0	50	14.0
Stephen Guolla*	46	6	10	16	11	2	2	0	52	11.5
Dan Kesa	50	4	10	14	21	-11	0	1	55	7.3
Stephane Richer*	20	7	5	12	4	2	1	0	47	14.9
Steve Martins*	57	5	7	12	37	-11	0	1	62	8.1
Andrei Zyuzin	34	2	9	11	33	-11	0	0	47	4.3
Jaroslav Svejkovsky*	29	5	5	10	28	-7	0	0	42	11.9
Bruce Gardiner*	41	3	6	9	37	-21	0	0	30	10.0
Ben Clymer	60	2	6	8	87	-26	2	0	98	2.0

	Games	G	A	Pts.	PIM	+/-	PPG	SHG	Shots	Shooting Pct.
Brian Holzinger*	14	3	3	6	21	-7	1	1	23	13.0
Andreas Johansson*	12	2	3	5	8	1	0	0	11	18.2
Wayne Primeau*	17	2	3	5	25	-4	0	0	35	5.7
Sergey Gusev	28	2	3	5	6	-9	1	0	23	8.7
Nils Ekman	28	2	2	4	36	-8	1	0	42	4.8
Michael Nylander*	11	1	2	3	4	-3	1	0	10	10.0
Bill Houlder*	14	1	2	3	2	-3	1	0	21	4.8
Marek Posmyk	18	1	2	3	20	1	0	0	22	4.5
Matt Elich	8	1	1	2	0	-1	0	0	5	20.0
Chris McAlpine*	10	1	1	2	10	-5	0	0	5	20.0
Dwayne Hay*	13	1	1	2	2	0	0	0	11	9.1
Bryan Muir*	30	1	1	2	32	-8	0	0	32	3.1
Jassen Cullimore	46	1	1	2	66	-12	0	0	23	4.3
Shawn Burr	4	0	2	2	0	2	0	0	6	0.0
Pavel Torgaev*	5	0	2	2	2	1	0	0	6	0.0
Ryan Johnson*	14	0	2	2	2	-9	0	0	5	0.0
Cory Sarich*	17	0	2	2	42	-8	0	0	20	0.0
Reid Simpson	26	1	0	1	103	-3	0	0	13	7.7
Dale Rominski	3	0	1	1	2	1	0	0	0	0.0
Kaspars Astashenko	8	0	1	1	4	-2	0	0	3	0.0
Zac Bierk (goalie)	12	0	1	1	0	0	0	0	0	0.0
Gordie Dwyer	24	0	1	1	135	-6	0	0	7	0.0
Viacheslav Butsayev*	2	0	0	0	0	-2	0	0	1	0.0
Andrei Skopintsev	4	0	0	0	6	-4	0	0	0	0.0
Dieter Kochan (goalie)	5	0	0	0	0	0	0	0	0	0.0
Daren Puppa (goalie)	5	0	0	0	2	0	0	0	0	0.0
Jeff Shevalier	5	0	0	0	2	-1	0	0	2	0.0
Colin Forbes*	8	0	0	0	18	-4	0	0	3	0.0
Kyle Freadrich	10	0	0	0	39	-1	0	0	0	0.0
Rich Parent (goalie)	14	0	0	0	2	0	0	0	0	0.0
Kevin Hodson (goalie)	24	0	0	0	2	0	0	0	0	0.0
Ian Herbers*	37	0	0	0	45	-12	0	0	11	0.0
Dan Cloutier (goalie)	52	0	0	0	29	0	0	0	0	0.0

GOALTENDING

	Games	Min.	Goals	SO	Avg.	W	L	T	ENG	Shots	Sv. Pct.
Dan Cloutier	52	2492	145	0	3.49	9	30	3	3	1258	.885
Zac Bierk	12	509	31	0	3.65	4	4	1	0	308	.899
Kevin Hodson	24	769	47	0	3.67	2	7	4	3	327	.856
Rich Parent	14	698	43	0	3.70	2	7	1	1	353	.878
Dieter Kochan	5	238	17	0	4.29	1	4	0	1	111	.847
Daren Puppa	5	249	19	0	4.58	1	2	0	0	129	.853

*Played with two or more NHL teams.

RESULTS

OCTOBER
2— N.Y. Islanders .... W 4-2
7— Los Angeles .... L 2-5
9— At New Jersey .... L 0-1
15—Anaheim .... L 2-3
16—Atlanta .... T .. *4-4
19—Vancouver .... L .. *5-6
23—Calgary .... W 2-1
27—At Buffalo .... L 3-4
28—At Boston .... L 3-7
30—At Dallas .... W 2-1

NOVEMBER
3— At Atlanta .... L 1-4
6— At Pittsburgh .... W 7-4
7— Detroit .... W 3-2
9— At Washington .... L 1-2
12—Buffalo .... W 4-2
13—At Carolina .... L 2-4
17—At Atlanta .... L 4-5
18—Pittsburgh .... W 2-1
20—At Philadelphia .... L 1-4
22—Philadelphia .... W 4-1
24—N.Y. Rangers .... L 3-6
26—Carolina .... T .. *3-3
28—Buffalo .... L .. *2-3

DECEMBER
1— At Anaheim .... W 4-2
2— At Phoenix .... L 1-3
4— At Los Angeles .... T .. *3-3
6— At San Jose .... T .. *3-3

10—Carolina .... W 3-2
14—Nashville .... T .. *4-4
18—At Philadelphia .... L 0-4
19—At N.Y. Rangers .... L .. *4-5
21—Toronto .... L 2-4
23—At Pittsburgh .... L 3-4
26—At Atlanta .... L 3-6
27—Florida .... L 1-6

JANUARY
1— At Florida .... L 5-7
5— At Vancouver .... T .. *3-3
7— At Edmonton .... L 1-5
8— At Calgary .... L .. *2-3
11—New Jersey .... L 5-6
13—N.Y. Islanders .... W 4-2
15—Florida .... L 2-5
17—Washington .... L 3-6
20—Boston .... L 2-4
22—At N.Y. Islanders .... L 0-2
24—At Washington .... L 2-8
25—At Buffalo .... L 1-2
28—Edmonton .... L 3-7
29—Atlanta .... W 2-1

FEBRUARY
1— Toronto .... L 3-5
3— Montreal .... L .. *1-2
8— San Jose .... L 0-8
10—At N.Y. Islanders .... L .. *4-5
12—Carolina .... L 2-5
15—N.Y. Rangers .... T .. *2-2

17—At Ottawa .... L 2-6
19—At Carolina .... L 2-4
21—Pittsburgh .... W 2-1
24—Ottawa .... W 5-4
26—At Nashville .... W 3-2
27—At Detroit .... L 1-3

MARCH
1— Washington .... L 2-4
3— At Chicago .... L 1-5
4— At Colorado .... L 1-4
8— Philadelphia .... L .. *2-3
10—Florida .... L 3-4
12—Chicago .... L 1-4
14—At Montreal .... W 4-3
15—At N.Y. Rangers .... T .. *4-4
17—At New Jersey .... W 3-1
19—At Washington .... L 2-5
21—At Boston .... L 0-4
24—St. Louis .... L 1-5
26—Montreal .... L 1-3
28—Dallas .... L 2-4
30—Ottawa .... W 6-3

APRIL
1— At Florida .... T .. *3-3
2— New Jersey .... L 1-4
4— Boston .... W 5-4
6— At Montreal .... L 1-5
8— At Toronto .... L 2-4
9— At Ottawa .... L 2-5
*Denotes overtime game.

TORONTO MAPLE LEAFS
EASTERN CONFERENCE/NORTHEAST DIVISION

Toronto Schedule
Home games shaded; D—Day game; *—All-Star Game at Denver.

October
SUN	MON	TUE	WED	THU	FRI	SAT
1	2	3	4	5	6	7 MON
8	9 DAL	10	11 NYI	12	13	14 OTT
15	16 VAN	17	18	19 EDM	20	21 CAL
22	23	24	25 MIN	26	27 BUF	28 BOS
29	30	31 OTT				

November
SUN	MON	TUE	WED	THU	FRI	SAT
			1	2 NJ	3	4 STL
5 BOS	6	7	8 CAR	9	10 CAR	11 CHI
12	13	14	15 PHI	16	17 TB	18 MON
19	20	21 NYR	22 EDM	23	24	25 OTT
26	27	28	29 STL	30 NYI		

December
SUN	MON	TUE	WED	THU	FRI	SAT
					1	2 NYR
3	4 FLA	5	6 DET	7	8	9 PIT
10	11	12	13 PIT	14	15 NYI	16 CAL
17	18	19	20 NSH	21 BOS	22	23 MON
24	25	26 ATL	27 PIT	28	29	30 FLA
31 TB						

January
SUN	MON	TUE	WED	THU	FRI	SAT
	1	2	3 BUF	4	5 BUF	6 WAS
7	8	9	10 TB	11	12 PHO	13 NJ
14	15	16	17 LA	18 NYR	19	20 BUF
21	22	23	24 BOS	25 ATL	26	27 NYR
28	29 STL	30	31 CAR			

February
SUN	MON	TUE	WED	THU	FRI	SAT
			1 WAS	2	3	
4	*5	6	7 ATL	8 DET	9	10 DET
11	12	13	14 CBJ	15 PHI	16	17 COL
18	19 NJ	20	21	22 VAN	23	24 MON
25 CHI	26	27	28 SJ			

March
SUN	MON	TUE	WED	THU	FRI	SAT
			1 WAS	2	3 OTT	
4	5	6 CAL	7 EDM	8	9	10 VAN
11	12	13	14 ANA	15 TB	16	17 FLA
18	19	20 BUF	21 FLA	22	23	24 PHI
25	26	27	28 BOS	29 PHI	30	31 MON

April
SUN	MON	TUE	WED	THU	FRI	SAT
1	2	3	4 NYI	5	6 CHI	7 OTT
8						

2000-2001 SEASON
CLUB DIRECTORY

Chairman of the board and governor
Steve A. Stavro
Alternate governor
Brian P. Bellmore
President and alternate governor
Ken Dryden
General manager and head coach
Pat Quinn
Assistant to the president
Bill Watters
Marketing/community representative
Darryl Sittler
Dir. of pro scouting and player personnel
Nick Beverley
Director of player evaluation
Joe Yannetti
Assistant coaches
Rick Ley
To be announced
Development coach
Paul Dennis
Director, hockey operations
Casey Vanden Heuvel

Vice president, sports communications & community development
John Lashway
Media relations director
Pat Park
Senior manager of ticket operations
Donna Henderson
Scouts
George Armstrong, Thommie Bergman, Mark Hillier, Larry Horning, Bob Johnson, Floyd Smith, Leonid Vaysfeld
Head athletic therapist
Chris Broadhurst
Athletic therapist
Brent Smith
Equipment manager
Brian Papineau
Assistant equipment manager
Dave Aleo
Trainer
Scott McKay

DRAFT CHOICES

Rd.— Player	Ht./Wt.	Overall	Pos.	Last team
1— Brad Boyes	6-0/181	24	C	Erie (OHL)
2— Kris Vernarsky	6-3/201	51	C	Plymouth (OHL)
3— Mikael Tellqvist	5-11/174	70	G	Djurgardens, Sweden
3— Jean-Francois Racine...	6-3/175	90	G	Drummondville (QMJHL)
4— Miguel Delisle	6-1/214	100	RW	Ottawa (OHL)
6— Vadim Sozinov	6-0/187	179	C	Novokuznetsk, Russia
7— Markus Seikola	6-1/194	209	D	TPS Jr., Finland
7— Lubos Velebny	6-1/189	223	D	Zvolen Jr., Slovakia
8— Alexander Shinkar		254		
9— Jean-Philippe Cote	6-1/195	265	D	Cape Breton (QMJHL)

MISCELLANEOUS DATA

Home ice (capacity)
Air Canada Centre (18,800)
Address
Air Canada Centre
40 Bay Street
Toronto, Ont. M5J 2X2
Business phone
416-815-5700
Ticket information
416-815-5700
Website
www.torontomapleleafs.com

Training site
Toronto
Club colors
Blue and white
Radio affiliation
TALK 640 (AM)
TV affiliation
CBC, CTVSportsnet, ON TV, Global TV, TSN, CFTO

TRAINING CAMP ROSTER

No.	FORWARDS	Ht./Wt.	Place	BORN Date	NHL exp.	1999-2000 clubs
	Nikolai Antropov (C)	6-5/203	Vost, Kazakhstan	2-18-80	1	St. John's (AHL), Toronto
94	Sergei Berezin (LW)	5-10/200	Voskresensk, U.S.S.R.	11-5-71	4	Toronto
16	Lonny Bohonos (RW)	5-11/192	Winnipeg	5-20-73	4	Manitoba (IHL)
	Brad Boyes (C)	6-0/181	Mississauga, Ont.	4-17-82	0	Erie (OHL)
	Luca Cereda (C)	6-2/203	Lugano, Switzerland	9-7-81	0	Ambri-Piotta (Switzerland)
27	Shayne Corson (LW)	6-1/198	Barrie, Ont.	8-13-66	15	Montreal
	Miguel Delisle (RW)	6-1/214	Cornwall, Ont.	4-6-82	0	Ottawa (OHL)
28	Tie Domi (RW)	5-10/200	Windsor, Ont.	11-1-69	11	Toronto
	Jeff Farkas (C)	6-0/185	Amherst, Mass.	1-24-78	1	Boston College (Hockey East), Toronto
14	Jonas Hoglund (LW)	6-3/215	Karlstad, Sweden	8-29-72	4	Toronto
12	Dmitri Khristich (RW)	6-2/195	Kiev, U.S.S.R.	7-23-69	10	Toronto
22	Igor Korolev (C)	6-1/190	Moscow, U.S.S.R.	9-6-70	8	Toronto
	Donald MacLean (C)	6-2/199	Sydney, Nova Scotia	1-14-77	1	Lowell (AHL), St. John's (AHL)
21	Adam Mair (C)	6-2/194	Hamilton, Ont.	2-15-79	2	St. John's (AHL), Toronto
18	Alyn McCauley (C)	5-11/190	Brockville, Ont.	5-29-77	3	Toronto, St. John's (AHL)
51	David Nemirovsky (RW)	6-2/200	Toronto	8-1-76	4	St. John's (AHL)
44	Yanic Perreault (C)	5-10/185	Sherbrooke, Que.	4-4-71	7	Toronto
10	Gary Roberts (LW)	6-1/190	North York, Ont.	5-23-66	14	Carolina
	Vadim Sozinov (C)	6-0/187	Kazakhstan	6-17-81	0	Novokuznetsk (Russian Div. II)
13	Mats Sundin (C)	6-5/220	Bromma, Sweden	2-13-71	10	Toronto
32	Steve Thomas (RW)	5-10/185	Stockport, England	7-15-63	16	Toronto
	Shawn Thornton (RW)	6-2/210	Oshawa, Ontario	7-23-79	0	St. John's (AHL)
16	Darcy Tucker (C)	5-11/185	Castor, Alta.	3-15-75	5	Tampa Bay, Toronto
10	Garry Valk (LW)	6-1/200	Edmonton	11-27-67	10	Toronto
	Kris Vernarsky (C)	6-2/201	Warren, Mich.	4-5-82	0	Plymouth (OHL)
	DEFENSEMEN					
34	Bryan Berard	6-1/190	Woonsocket, R.I.	3-5-77	4	Toronto
4	Cory Cross	6-5/219	Lloydminster, Alta.	7-31-75	7	Toronto
	Nathan Dempsey	6-0/190	Spruce Grove, Alta.	7-14-74	2	St. John's (AHL), Toronto
4	Gerald Diduck	6-2/220	Edmonton	4-6-65	16	Toronto
15	Tomas Kaberle	6-2/200	Rakovnik, Czechoslovakia	3-2-78	2	Toronto
52	Alexander Karpovtsev	6-3/215	Moscow, U.S.S.R.	4-7-70	7	Toronto
55	Danny Markov	6-1/190	Moscow, U.S.S.R.	7-11-76	3	Toronto
33	Chris McAllister	6-8/225	Saskatoon, Sask.	6-16-75	3	Toronto
	D.J. Smith	6-2/205	Windsor, Ont.	5-13-77	2	St. John's (AHL), Toronto
	Dmitri Yakushin	6-0/200	Kharkov, Ukraine	1-21-78	1	St. John's (AHL), Toronto
36	Dmitry Yushkevich	5-11/208	Yaroslavl, U.S.S.R.	11-19-71	8	Toronto
	GOALTENDERS					
31	Curtis Joseph	5-11/190	Keswick, Ont.	4-29-67	11	Toronto
	Jean-Francois Racine	6-3/175	St-Hyacinthe, Que.	4-27-82	0	Drummondville (QMJHL)
	Mikael Tellqvist	5-11/174	Sweden	9-19-79	0	Djurgarden Stockholm (Sweden)
29	Jimmy Waite	6-1/190	Sherbrooke, Que.	4-15-69	11	St. John's (AHL)

1999-2000 REVIEW

INDIVIDUAL STATISTICS

SCORING

	Games	G	A	Pts.	PIM	+/-	PPG	SHG	Shots	Shooting Pct.
Mats Sundin	73	32	41	73	46	16	10	2	184	17.4
Steve Thomas	81	26	37	63	68	1	9	0	151	17.2
Jonas Hoglund	82	29	27	56	10	-2	9	1	215	13.5
Igor Korolev	80	20	26	46	22	12	5	3	101	19.8
Yanic Perreault	58	18	27	45	22	3	5	0	114	15.8
Tomas Kaberle	82	7	33	40	24	3	2	0	82	8.5
Sergei Berezin	61	26	13	39	2	8	5	0	241	10.8
Dmitri Khristich	53	12	18	30	24	8	3	0	79	15.2
Nik Antropov	66	12	18	30	41	0	0	0	89	13.5
Bryan Berard	64	3	27	30	42	11	1	0	98	3.1
Dimitri Yushkevich	77	3	24	27	55	2	2	1	103	2.9
Mike Johnson*	52	11	14	25	23	8	2	1	89	12.4
Garry Valk	73	10	14	24	44	-2	0	1	91	11.0
Darcy Tucker*	27	7	10	17	55	3	0	2	40	17.5
Alexander Karpovtsev	69	3	14	17	54	9	3	0	51	5.9
Cory Cross	71	4	11	15	64	3	0	0	60	6.7
Tie Domi	70	5	9	14	198	-5	0	0	64	7.8
Kevyn Adams	52	5	8	13	39	-7	0	0	70	7.1
Alyn McCauley	45	5	5	10	10	-6	1	0	41	12.2
Danny Markov	59	0	10	10	28	13	0	0	38	0.0

TORONTO MAPLE LEAFS

	Games	G	A	Pts.	PIM	+/-	PPG	SHG	Shots	Shooting Pct.
Kris King...	39	2	4	6	55	4	0	0	24	8.3
Todd Warriner*......................................	18	3	1	4	2	6	0	0	33	9.1
Wendel Clark*.......................................	20	2	2	4	21	-3	0	0	36	5.6
Gerald Diduck.......................................	26	0	3	3	33	2	0	0	18	0.0
Chris McAllister	36	0	3	3	68	-4	0	0	12	0.0
Nathan Dempsey	6	0	2	2	2	2	0	0	3	0.0
Adam Mair..	8	1	0	1	6	-1	0	0	7	14.3
Sylvain Cote*.......................................	3	0	1	1	0	1	0	0	3	0.0
Steve Sullivan*....................................	7	0	1	1	4	-1	0	0	11	0.0
Greg Andrusak	9	0	1	1	4	1	0	0	5	0.0
Glenn Healy (goalie)	20	0	1	1	2	0	0	0	0	0.0
Curtis Joseph (goalie)	63	0	1	1	14	0	0	0	1	0.0
Dmitriy Yakushin	2	0	0	0	2	0	0	0	1	0.0
Derek King*...	3	0	0	0	2	-2	0	0	4	0.0
D.J. Smith..	3	0	0	0	5	-1	0	0	2	0.0

GOALTENDING

	Games	Min.	Goals	SO	Avg.	W	L	T	ENG	Shots	Sv. Pct.
Curtis Joseph	63	3801	158	4	2.49	36	20	7	4	1854	.915
Glenn Healy	20	1164	59	2	3.04	9	10	0	1	527	.888

*Played with two or more NHL teams.

RESULTS

OCTOBER
2— At Montreal ....W......4-1
4— Boston.............................W......4-0
6— Colorado..........................W......2-1
9— At Ottawa.........................L......3-4
11— Nashville ....L......2-4
13— Florida ....W......3-2
15— At Chicago ....W......2-1
16— At St. Louis......................L......2-4
20— Carolina ....T....*3-3
23— Montreal ....W......3-2
25— Dallas ....W......4-0
27— Atlanta ....W......4-0
30— Calgary ....W......2-1

NOVEMBER
3— At Carolina ....W......6-0
5— At Washington ....L......3-5
6— At New Jersey ....T....*3-3
9— Anaheim ....L......0-2
11— At Boston...........................L....*3-4
13— Detroit ....T....*1-1
15— San Jose ....W......4-2
17— St. Louis ....L......2-3
20— N.Y. Rangers ....W....*4-3
23— At Pittsburgh ....L......1-3
26— At Philadelphia..................T....*2-3
27— Edmonton.........................W......5-2
29— Washington ....W......3-1

DECEMBER
2— At Carolina........................T....*2-2

4— Pittsburgh ....W....*3-2
6— Buffalo.............................W....*3-2
9— At Philadelphia..................L......2-4
11— Philadelphia.....................W......6-4
13— Ottawa ....L......1-3
15— N.Y. Islanders ....W......5-1
18— Montreal ....W......2-1
20— At Florida..........................W......6-4
21— At Tampa Bay ....W......4-2
23— New Jersey.......................W......4-1
29— At N.Y. Islanders...............W......2-1

JANUARY
1— At Buffalo..........................L......1-8
3— Buffalo.............................W......6-2
5— At N.Y. Rangers ....L....*2-3
7— At Pittsburgh ....L......2-5
8— N.Y. Rangers ....L......3-5
11— At Boston...........................W......3-2
14— At Edmonton ....W....*3-2
15— At Calgary ....L......0-4
17— At Vancouver.....................W....*5-4
22— Washington ....T....*5-5
24— Ottawa ....T....*3-3
26— At Detroit ....L......2-4
27— At N.Y. Rangers.................W......4-3
29— Los Angeles ....W......3-2

FEBRUARY
1— At Tampa Bay ....W......5-3
3— At Boston...........................L......2-4
9— Philadelphia......................L......2-4

12— Vancouver ....L......1-4
14— Carolina ....L......2-5
16— Boston ....T....*3-3
19— At Montreal ....L......1-2
23— Phoenix ....W......5-3
25— At New Jersey ....W......3-1
26— Buffalo ....W......5-2
29— At Atlanta ....W......4-0

MARCH
1— At Florida..........................L......1-3
4— Montreal ....W......4-3
6— At Vancouver....................W....*6-5
7— At Edmonton ....W......2-0
9— At Calgary ....W......6-2
11— At Ottawa ....W......4-2
15— Chicago ....L......2-5
16— At Detroit ....W....*4-3
18— Atlanta ....L......1-4
22— N.Y. Islanders ....L......2-5
23— At Ottawa ....L......2-3
25— New Jersey.......................W......5-3
29— At St. Louis ....W......3-2
30— At Chicago ....L......0-4

APRIL
1— At Washington ....W......4-3
3— At Buffalo...........................L......2-3
5— Pittsburgh ....L......2-4
7— At N.Y. Islanders...............W......2-1
8— Tampa Bay ....W......4-2
*Denotes overtime game.

VANCOUVER CANUCKS
WESTERN CONFERENCE/NORTHWEST DIVISION

Vancouver Schedule
Home games shaded; D—Day game; *—All-Star Game at Denver.

October
SUN	MON	TUE	WED	THU	FRI	SAT
1	2	3	4	5 PHI	6 FLA	7
8 TB	9	10	11	12 COL	13	14 BUF
15 TOR	16	17	18 CAL	19	20	21 PHO
22	23	24 NSH	25 DAL	26	27 ATL	28
29	30	31				

November
SUN	MON	TUE	WED	THU	FRI	SAT
			1 COL	2	3 PIT	4
5 SJ	6	7	8 ANA	9 LA	10	11 STL
12	13	14 CHI	15	16	17 NYR	18
19 CBJ	20	21 STL	22 WAS	23	24 DET	25
26 D MIN	27	28 ANA	29	30 MON		

December
SUN	MON	TUE	WED	THU	FRI	SAT
					1	2 EDM
3	4 NSH	5	6 PHO	7	8 SJ	9
10 LA	11	12	13	14	15	16 CBJ
17	18	19	20 EDM	21 CHI	22	23 COL
24	25	26	27 MON	28	29 CAL	30 SJ
31						

January
SUN	MON	TUE	WED	THU	FRI	SAT
	1 D NSH	2	3 CHI	4	5	6 CBJ
7	8 NSH	9	10 OTT	11	12 EDM	13
14 CAL	15	16 DET	17	18 COL	19	20 STL
21	22 DAL	23	24 PHO	25	26	27 CAL
28 CHI	29	30 MIN	31			

February
SUN	MON	TUE	WED	THU	FRI	SAT
				1 COL	2	3
4	*5	6	7	8 SJ	9	10 CAL
11	12	13	14 WAS	15	16	17 EDM
18 NYI	19	20	21 MON	22 TOR	23	24 D OTT
25	26 MIN	27	28 DAL			

March
SUN	MON	TUE	WED	THU	FRI	SAT
				1	2 STL	3
4 MIN	5	6 DET	7	8 PHO	9	10 TOR
11	12	13 DET	14	15 BOS	16 BUF	17
18 D ATL	19	20	21 CBJ	22	23 NJ	24
25 D MIN	26	27	28 DAL	29	30 ANA	31

April
SUN	MON	TUE	WED	THU	FRI	SAT
1 ANA	2 LA	3	4	5 LA	6	7 EDM
8						

2000-2001 SEASON
CLUB DIRECTORY

Chairman and governor
John E. McCaw Jr.
President and CEO, alternate governor
Stanley B. McCammon
President and g.m., alternate governor
Brian P. Burke
Chief operating officer
David Cobb
Vice president, finance and CFO
Victor de Bonis
V.p. and general manager, operations
Harvey Jones
Sr. v.p., director of hockey operations
David M. Nonis
Senior v.p., sales and marketing
John Rizzardini
Vice president, player personnel
Steve Tambellini
Vice president, amateur scouting
Mike Penny
Executive assistant
Patti Timms
Head coach
Marc Crawford
Assistant coaches
Jack McIlhargey
Mike Johnston

Strength & conditioning coach
Peter Twist
Scouting information coordinator
Jonathan Wall
Manager, media relations
Chris Brumwell
Coordinator, media relations
T.C. Carling
Assistant, media relations
Rob Viccars
Manager, community relations
Veronica Varhaug
Coordinator, community relations
Lisa Denton
Assistant, community relations
Alex Mitchell
Medical trainer
Mike Bernstein
Massage therapist
Dave Schima
Equipment manager
Pat O'Neill
Assistant equipment manager
Darren Granger

DRAFT CHOICES

Rd.— Player	Ht./Wt.	Overall	Pos.	Last team
1— Nathan Smith	6-2/192	23	C	Swift Current (WHL)
3— Thatcher Bell	6-0/172	71	C	Rimouski (QMJHL)
3— Tim Branham	6-2/185	93	D	Barrie (OHL)
5— Pavel Duma	6-1/183	144	C	Neftechimik, Russia
7— Brandon Reid	5-8/165	208	C	Halifax (QMJHL)
8— Nathan Barrett	5-11/192	241	C	Lethbridge (WHL)
9— Tim Smith	5-9/160	272	C	Spokane (WHL)

MISCELLANEOUS DATA

Home ice (capacity)
General Motors Place (18,422)
Address
800 Griffiths Way
Vancouver, B.C. V6B 6G1
Business phone
604-899-4600
Ticket information
604-280-4400
Website
www.canucks.com

Training site
Burnaby, B.C.
Club colors
Deep blue, sky blue, deep red, white and silver
Radio affiliation
CKNW (980 AM)
TV affiliation
VTV (Channel 9), CTV Sportsnet (Cable)

VANCOUVER CANUCKS

No.	FORWARDS	Ht./Wt.	Place	Date	NHL exp.	1999-2000 clubs
	Thatcher Bell (C)............	6-0/172	Charlottetown, P.E.I.	2-1-82	0	Rimouski (QMJHL)
44	Todd Bertuzzi (LW)	6-3/230	Sudbury, Ont.	2-2-75	5	Vancouver
8	Donald Brashear (LW) ...	6-2/230	Bedford, Ind.	1-7-72	7	Vancouver
25	Andrew Cassels (C).......	6-1/185	Bramalea, Ont.	7-23-69	11	Vancouver
	Artem Chubarov (C)	6-1/189	Gorky, U.S.S.R.	12-12-79	1	Vancouver, Syracuse (AHL)
24	Matt Cooke (C)	5-11/205	Belleville, Ont.	9-7-78	2	Syracuse (AHL), Vancouver
15	Harold Druken (C)	6-0/200	St. John's, Nfld.	1-26-79	1	Syracuse (AHL), Vancouver
	Pavel Duma (C)	6-1/183	Karaganda, U.S.S.R.	6-20-81	0	Neftekhimik Nizhnekamsk (Russian)
21	Josh Holden (C)	6-1/190	Calgary	1-18-78	2	Syracuse (AHL), Vancouver
	Steve Kariya (LW).........	5-7/170	Vancouver	12-22-77	1	Vancouver, Syracuse (AHL)
26	Trent Klatt (RW)	6-1/210	Minneapolis	1-30-71	9	Syracuse (AHL), Vancouver
7	Brendan Morrison (C)....	5-11/190	Pitt Meadows, B.C.	8-12-75	3	HC Pardubice (Czech Republic), New Jersey, Vancouver
	Justin Morrison (RW)....	6-3/200	Los Angeles	8-10-79	0	Colorado College (WCHA)
19	Markus Naslund (LW)....	6-0/186	Ornskoldsvik, Sweden	7-30-73	7	Vancouver
20	Denis Pederson (C)	6-2/205	Prince Albert, Sask.	9-10-75	5	New Jersey, Vancouver
	Jarkko Ruutu (RW)........	6-2/194	Vantaa, Finland	8-23-75	1	Syracuse (AHL), Vancouver
72	Peter Schaefer (LW)	5-11/195	Yellow Grass, Sask.	7-12-77	2	Vancouver, Syracuse (AHL)
	Jeff Scissons (C)	6-1/190	Saskatoon, Sask.	11-24-76	0	Minnesota-Duluth (WCHA)
	Daniel Sedin (LW).........	6-1/194	Ornskoldsvik, Sweden	9-26-80	0	MoDo Ornskoldsvik (Sweden)
	Henrik Sedin (C)	6-2/196	Ornskoldsvik, Sweden	9-26-80	0	MoDo Ornskoldsvik (Sweden)
17	Vadim Sharifijanov (RW)	6-0/205	Ufa, U.S.S.R.	12-23-75	3	New Jersey, Vancouver
	Nathan Smith (C)...........	6-1/192	Strathcona, Alta.	2-9-82	0	Swift Current (WHL)
	Lubomir Vaic (C)	5-9/165	Spisska Nova Ves, Czech.	3-6-77	2	Syracuse (AHL), Vancouver
	DEFENSEMEN					
7	Bryan Allen	6-4/210	Kingston, Ont.	8-21-80	0	Oshawa (OHL), Syracuse (AHL)
6	Adrian Aucoin	6-2/210	Ottawa	7-3-73	6	Vancouver
23	Murray Baron	6-3/225	Prince George, B.C.	6-1-67	11	Vancouver
	Ryan Bonni	6-4/190	Winnipeg	2-18-79	1	Syracuse (AHL), Vancouver
	Tim Branham	6-2/185	Minoqua, Wis.	5-10-81	0	Barrie (OHL)
4	Greg Hawgood...............	5-10/190	St. Albert, Alta.	8-10-68	10	Vancouver
	Darrell Hay...................	6-0/190	Kamloops, B.C.	4-2-80	0	
55	Ed Jovanovski...............	6-2/210	Windsor, Ont.	6-26-76	5	Vancouver
	Zenith Komarniski.........	6-0/200	Edmonton	8-13-78	1	Syracuse (AHL), Vancouver
	Brad Leeb				1	Syracuse (AHL), Vancouver
2	Mattias Ohlund	6-3/210	Pitea, Sweden	9-9-76	3	Vancouver
3	Brent Sopel	6-1/205	Saskatoon, Sask.	1-7-77	2	Syracuse (AHL), Vancouver
34	Jason Strudwick	6-3/220	Edmonton	7-17-75	4	Vancouver
	Rene Vydareny	6-1/198	Bratislava, Czechoslovakia	5-6-81	0	Rimouski (QMJHL)
	GOALTENDERS					
	Alfie Michaud...............	5-10/177	Selkirk, Man.	11-6-76	1	Syracuse (AHL), Vancouver
29	Felix Potvin	6-1/190	Anjou, Que.	6-23-71	9	New York Islanders, Vancouver
32	Corey Schwab..............	6-0/180	North Battleford, Sask.	11-4-70	5	Orlando (IHL), Vancouver, Syracuse (AHL)

1999-2000 REVIEW
INDIVIDUAL STATISTICS

SCORING

	Games	G	A	Pts.	PIM	+/-	PPG	SHG	Shots	Shooting Pct.
Markus Naslund	82	27	38	65	64	-5	6	2	271	10.0
Andrew Cassels	79	17	45	62	16	8	6	0	109	15.6
Mark Messier	66	17	37	54	30	-15	6	0	131	13.0
Todd Bertuzzi	80	25	25	50	126	-2	4	0	173	14.5
Alexander Mogilny*	47	21	17	38	16	7	3	1	126	16.7
Peter Schaefer...	71	16	15	31	20	0	2	2	101	15.8
Ed Jovanovski..	75	5	21	26	54	-3	1	0	109	4.6
Adrian Aucoin...	57	10	14	24	30	7	4	0	126	7.9
Greg Hawgood..	79	5	17	22	26	5	2	0	70	7.1
Trent Klatt..	47	10	10	20	26	-8	8	0	100	10.0
Mattias Ohlund	42	4	16	20	24	6	2	1	63	6.3
Steve Kariya	45	8	11	19	22	9	0	0	41	19.5
Harry York	54	4	13	17	20	-4	1	1	50	8.0
Brad May	59	9	7	16	90	-2	0	0	66	13.6
Harold Druken	33	7	9	16	10	14	2	0	69	10.1
Donald Brashear	60	11	2	13	136	-9	1	0	83	13.3
Matt Cooke	51	5	7	12	39	3	0	1	58	8.6
Bill Muckalt*	33	4	8	12	17	6	1	0	53	7.5

	Games	G	A	Pts.	PIM	+/-	PPG	SHG	Shots	Shooting Pct.
Murray Baron	81	2	10	12	67	8	0	0	48	4.2
Chris Joseph*	38	2	9	11	6	-4	1	0	73	2.7
Darby Hendrickson	40	5	4	9	14	-3	0	1	39	12.8
Brendan Morrison*	12	2	7	9	10	4	0	0	17	11.8
Artem Chubarov	49	1	8	9	10	-4	0	0	53	1.9
Brent Sopel	18	2	4	6	12	9	0	0	11	18.2
Josh Holden	6	1	5	6	2	2	0	0	5	20.0
Denis Pederson*	12	3	2	5	2	1	0	0	15	20.0
Chris O'Sullivan	11	0	5	5	2	2	0	0	16	0.0
Jason Strudwick	63	1	3	4	64	-13	0	0	18	5.6
Dave Scatchard*	21	0	4	4	24	-3	0	0	25	0.0
Vadim Sharifijanov*	17	2	1	3	14	-7	1	0	26	7.7
Zenith Komarniski	18	1	1	2	8	-1	0	0	21	4.8
Garth Snow (goalie)	32	0	2	2	8	0	0	0	0	0.0
Felix Potvin (goalie)*	34	0	2	2	2	0	0	0	0	0.0
Jarkko Ruutu	8	0	1	1	6	-1	0	0	4	0.0
Doug Bodger	13	0	1	1	4	-6	0	0	11	0.0
Brad Leeb	2	0	0	0	2	-2	0	0	3	0.0
Alfie Michaud (goalie)	2	0	0	0	0	0	0	0	0	0.0
Ryan Bonni	3	0	0	0	0	-1	0	0	1	0.0
Lubomir Vaic	4	0	0	0	0	0	0	0	2	0.0
Corey Schwab (goalie)	6	0	0	0	2	0	0	0	0	0.0
Kevin Weekes (goalie)*	20	0	0	0	0	0	0	0	0	0.0

GOALTENDING

	Games	Min.	Goals	SO	Avg.	W	L	T	ENG	Shots	Sv. Pct.
Felix Potvin*	34	1966	85	0	2.59	12	13	7	4	906	.906
Garth Snow	32	1712	76	0	2.66	10	15	3	1	775	.902
Kevin Weekes*	20	987	47	1	2.86	6	7	4	3	461	.898
Corey Schwab	6	269	16	0	3.57	2	1	1	0	115	.861
Alfie Michaud	2	69	5	0	4.35	0	1	0	0	27	.815

*Played with two or more NHL teams.

RESULTS

OCTOBER
2— N.Y. Rangers ....W......2-1
6— Chicago ....W......5-4
9— Montreal ....W......4-1
13—Calgary ....L....*3-4
15—Carolina ....L......1-4
16—At Calgary ....T...*4-4
19—At Tampa Bay ....W...*6-5
20—At Florida ....L......2-5
23—At N.Y. Islanders ....T...*2-2
24—At N.Y. Rangers ....W......3-0
26—At Philadelphia ....W......5-2
28—Phoenix ....L......1-4
30—Nashville ....W......4-1

NOVEMBER
5— Florida ....W......3-2
7— St. Louis ....L......1-6
9— San Jose ....T...*4-4
12—At Phoenix ....W......3-2
15—Colorado ....T...*2-2
17—Detroit ....L......2-7
20—At Nashville ....W......3-1
22—At Atlanta ....L......3-6
24—At Carolina ....T...*1-1
26—At Boston ....T...*2-2
27—At Montreal ....L......1-2
30—Colorado ....L......2-4

DECEMBER
2— Edmonton ....W....*3-2
4— At Edmonton ....L......2-3

6— At Colorado ....L......2-5
8— At Anaheim ....T...*2-2
10—At Calgary ....L......2-3
12—Colorado ....L...*2-3
16—Ottawa ....L......1-2
18—Dallas ....L......2-4
22—Washington ....W......6-3
26—Calgary ....L......0-2
29—Philadelphia ....L...*2-3

JANUARY
2— At Calgary ....L......2-4
5— Tampa Bay ....T...*3-3
7— At Dallas ....W......3-1
8— At St. Louis ....L......2-4
12—At Chicago ....L...*2-3
13—At Nashville ....W...*4-3
15—Dallas ....L......1-2
17—Toronto ....L...*4-5
19—Detroit ....T...*3-3
22—At Edmonton ....T...*3-3
23—Nashville ....L......1-2
25—Edmonton ....L...*4-5
28—San Jose ....W......4-1
30—Chicago ....L......1-3

FEBRUARY
1— At Colorado ....L......1-2
3— St. Louis ....L......2-5
9— Calgary ....W...*4-3
12—At Toronto ....W......4-1
14—At Pittsburgh ....L......0-3

16—At Detroit ....L......2-5
17—At Buffalo ....W......2-1
19—At Ottawa ....W......3-1
21—Boston ....W......5-2
23—At Anaheim ....T...*4-4
25—Los Angeles ....L......2-5
27—Phoenix ....W......2-1
29—At Los Angeles ....T...*1-1

MARCH
2— Anaheim ....W......3-1
4— New Jersey ....W......4-2
6— Toronto ....L...*5-6
8— At Dallas ....T...*3-3
9— At St. Louis ....T...*2-2
11—At Phoenix ....L......0-5
13—At Los Angeles ....L...*2-3
16—Buffalo ....W......6-3
18—Ottawa ....W......6-1
20—At Colorado ....L......3-2
22—At San Jose ....L......3-4
24—Anaheim ....W......8-1
25—At Edmonton ....W......3-2
29—At Detroit ....L......3-6
31—At Nashville ....L......1-2

APRIL
2— At Chicago ....W......3-2
5— Los Angeles ....T...*1-1
7— Edmonton ....L...*4-5
9— At San Jose ....W......5-2
*Denotes overtime game.

VANCOUVER CANUCKS

WASHINGTON CAPITALS
EASTERN CONFERENCE/SOUTHEAST DIVISION

WASHINGTON CAPITALS

Washington Schedule
Home games shaded; D—Day game; *—All-Star Game at Denver.

October

SUN	MON	TUE	WED	THU	FRI	SAT
1	2	3	4	5	6 LA	7 CAR
8	9	10	11 ATL	12	13 NSH	14 DAL
15	16	17 COL	18	19 NJ	20	21 NYI
22	23	24	25	26 BOS	27 CBJ	28
29 PHI	30	31 DET				

November

SUN	MON	TUE	WED	THU	FRI	SAT
			1	2 STL	3	4 FLA
5 TB	6	7	8	9 NYR	10	11
12 D ATL	13	14 PHO	15	16	17 MON	18 PHI
19	20	21	22 VAN	23	24 NYI	25 ATL
26	27	28	29 TB	30		

December

SUN	MON	TUE	WED	THU	FRI	SAT
					1 BOS	2 BOS
3	4	5	6 NYR	7	8	9 D NJ
10	11	12 NYI	13	14 MIN	15	16 EDM
17	18 SJ	19	20 BUF	21 BUF	22	23 FLA
24	25	26	27 OTT	28	29 NJ	30 PHI
31						

January

SUN	MON	TUE	WED	THU	FRI	SAT
	1 D ATL	2	3 PIT	4	5 BOS	6 TOR
7 PIT	8	9	10 MIN	11	12	13 ATL
14	15	16	17	18 OTT	19 CHI	20
21	22	23 TB	24 FLA	25	26	27 D MON
28 D PHI	29	30 OTT	31			

February

SUN	MON	TUE	WED	THU	FRI	SAT
			1 TOR	2	3	
4	*5	6	7 COL	8	9 ANA	10 LA
11	12	13 CAL	14 VAN	15	16	17 MON
18	19	20	21 NSH	22	23 MON	24 CAR
25	26	27 CHI	28			

March

SUN	MON	TUE	WED	THU	FRI	SAT
				1 TOR	2	3 PIT
4	5	6 NYI	7 PIT	8	9 NYR	10
11 OTT	12	13 ANA	14	15 CAR	16	17 BUF
18	19 NYR	20	21	22	23 FLA	24 TB
25	26	27	28 CAR	29	30 CAR	31

April

SUN	MON	TUE	WED	THU	FRI	SAT
1 DET	2	3 NJ	4	5 FLA	6 BUF	7
8 D TB						

2000-2001 SEASON

CLUB DIRECTORY

Owners
Ted Leonis
Jonathan Ledecky
Raul Fernandez
Michael Jordan
Dick Patrick
President and governor
Dick Patrick
Senior v.p. of business operations
Declan J. Bolger
Vice president/general manager
George McPhee
Director of hockey operations
Shawn Simpson
Assistant to the general manager
Frank Provenzano
Director of amateur scouting
Ross Mahoney
Head coach
Ron Wilson
Assistant coaches
Tim Army
Tim Hunter

Goaltender consultant
Dave Prior
Team physician
Dr. Ben Shaffer
Trainer
Greg Smith
Equipment manager
Doug Shearer
Assistant equipment manager
Craig Leydig
Equipment assistant
Brian Metzger
Strength and conditioning coach
Frank Costello
Massage therapist
Curt Millar
Vice president, communications
Andrew McGowan
Assistant director, public relations
Jesse Price

DRAFT CHOICES

Rd.— Player	Ht./Wt.	Overall	Pos.	Last team
1— Brian Sutherby	6-2/180	26	C	Moose Jaw (WHL)
2— Matt Pettinger	6-1/205	43	LW	Calgary (WHL)
2— Jakub Cutta	6-3/195	61	D	Swift Current (WHL)
4— Ryan Vanbuskirk	6-2/207	121	D	Sarnia (OHL)
5— Ivan Nepriayev		163		Yaroslavl, Russia
9— Bjorn Nord	6-0/198	289	D	Djurgarden, Sweden

MISCELLANEOUS DATA

Home ice (capacity)
MCI Center (18,672)
Address
MCI Center
601 F St., NW
Washington, DC 20004
Business phone
202-266-2200
Ticket information
202-266-2277

Website
www.washingtoncaps.com
Training site
Odenton, MD
Club colors
Bronze and blue
Radio affiliation
WTEM (980 AM)
TV affiliation
HTS, WBDC (Channel 50)

D- -FRANTSER KUCER

TRAINING CAMP ROSTER

No.	FORWARDS	Ht./Wt.	Place	BORN Date	NHL exp.	1999-2000 clubs
	Krys Barch (LW)	6-2/199	Guelph, Ont.	3-26-80	0	London (OHL), Portland (AHL)
	Kris Beech (C) ...P.,IIS	6-2/178	Salmon Arm, B.C.	2-5-81	0	Calgary (WHL)
32	Craig Berube (LW)	6-1/205	Calahoo, Alta.	12-17-65	14	Philadelphia
28	James Black (LW)	6-0/203	Regina, Sask.	8-15-69	10	Washington
12	Peter Bondra (LW)	6-1/205	Luck, Ukraine	2-7-68	10	Washington
8	Jan Bulis (C)	6-1/201	Pardubice, Czechoslovakia	3-18-78	3	Washington
10	Ulf Dahlen (RW)	6-3/191	Ostersund, Sweden	1-12-67	11	Washington
36	Mike Eagles (C)	5-10/195	Sussex, N.B.	3-7-63	16	Washington
11	Jeff Halpern (C)	5-11/198	Potomac, Md.	5-3-76	1	Washington
26	Matt Herr (LW)	6-2/203	Hackensack, N.J.	5-26-76	1	Portland (AHL)
22	Steve Konowalchuk	6-2/210	Salt Lake City	11-11-72	9	Washington
20	Glen Metropolit (C)	5-11/196	Toronto	6-25-74	1	Washington, Portland (AHL)
26	Ryan Mulhern (RW)	6-1/202	Philadelphia	1-11-73	1	Portland (AHL)
9	Joe Murphy (RW)	6-0/190	London, Ont.	10-17-67	14	Boston, Washington
13	Andrei Nikolishin (C)	6-0/214	Vorkuta, U.S.S.R.	3-25-73	6	Washington
77	Adam Oates (C)	5-10/180	Weston, Ont.	8-27-62	15	Washington
	Mike Peluso (C)	6-1/208	Denver	9-2-74	0	Portland (AHL)
	Matt Pettinger (LW)	6-0/205	Victoria, B.C.	10-22-80	0	Univ. of Denver (WCHA), Calgary (WHL)
14	Joe Sacco (RW)	6-1/190	Medford, Mass.	2-4-69	10	Washington
17	Chris Simon (LW)	6-4/231	Wawa, Ont.	1-30-72	8	Washington
	Michal Sivek (C) ...I.\916	6-3/209	Nachod, Czechoslovakia	1-21-81	0	Prince Albert (WHL)
	Charlie Stephens (C)	6-4/225	Nilestown, Ont.	4-5-81	0	Guelph (OHL)
	Brian Sutherby (C)	6-2/180	Edmonton	3-1-82	0	Moose Jaw (WHL)
	Trent Whitfield (C)	5-11/199	Estevan, Sask.	6-17-77	1	Portland (AHL), Washington
27	Terry Yake (C)	5-11/190	New Westminster, B.C.	10-22-68	10	St. Louis, Washington
44	Richard Zednik (RW)	6-0/199	Bystrica, Czechoslovakia	1-6-76	5	Washington
DEFENSEMEN						
3	Sylvain Cote	6-0/190	Quebec City	1-19-66	16	Toronto, Chicago, Dallas
	Jakub Cutta	6-3/195	Yablonec, Czechoslovakia	12-29-81	0	Swift Current (WHL)
55	Sergei Gonchar	6-2/208	Chelyabinsk, U.S.S.R.	4-13-74	6	Washington
3	Jamie Huscroft	6-3/206	Creston, B.C.	1-9-67	10	Portland (AHL), Washington
6	Calle Johansson	5-11/203	Goteborg, Sweden	2-14-67	13	Washington
2	Ken Klee	6-1/211	Indianapolis	4-24-71	6	Washington
15	Dmitri Mironov	6-4/229	Moscow, U.S.S.R.	12-25-65	9	Washington
29	Joe Reekie	6-3/225	Victoria, B.C.	2-22-65	15	Washington
4	Alexei Tezikov	6-1/198	Togliatti, U.S.S.R.	6-22-78	2	Portland (AHL), Washington
19	Brendan Witt	6-2/224	Humboldt, Sask.	2-20-75	6	Washington
GOALTENDERS						
1	Craig Billington	5-10/166	London, Ont.	9-11-66	12	Washington
37	Olaf Kolzig	6-3/226	Johannesburg, South Africa	4-6-70	9	Washington

1999-2000 REVIEW

INDIVIDUAL STATISTICS

SCORING

	Games	G	A	Pts.	PIM	+/-	PPG	SHG	Shots	Shooting Pct.
Adam Oates	82	15	56	71	14	13	5	0	93	16.1
Sergei Gonchar	73	18	36	54	52	26	5	0	181	9.9
Chris Simon	75	29	20	49	146	11	7	0	201	14.4
Steve Konowalchuk	82	16	27	43	80	19	3	0	146	11.0
Peter Bondra	62	21	17	38	30	5	5	3	187	11.2
Ulf Dahlen	75	15	23	38	8	11	5	0	106	14.2
Richard Zednik	69	19	16	35	54	6	1	0	179	10.6
Calle Johansson	82	7	25	32	24	13	1	0	138	5.1
Jan Bulis	56	9	22	31	30	7	0	0	92	9.8
Jeff Halpern	79	18	11	29	39	21	4	4	108	16.7
Andrei Nikolishin	76	11	14	25	28	6	0	2	98	11.2
Joe Sacco	79	7	16	23	50	7	0	0	117	6.0
Dmitri Mironov	73	3	19	22	28	7	1	0	99	3.0
Ken Klee	80	7	13	20	79	8	0	0	113	6.2
Glen Metropolit	30	6	13	19	4	5	1	0	57	10.5
James Black	49	8	9	17	6	-1	1	0	71	11.3
Joe Murphy*	29	5	8	13	53	8	1	0	50	10.0
Terry Yake*	35	6	5	11	12	2	1	0	29	20.7
Brendan Witt	77	1	7	8	114	5	0	0	64	1.6
Joe Reekie	59	0	7	7	50	21	0	0	32	0.0
Jeff Toms	20	1	2	3	4	-1	0	0	18	5.6

	Games	G	A	Pts.	PIM	+/-	PPG	SHG	Shots	Shooting Pct.
Jaroslav Svejkovsky*	23	1	2	3	2	-7	1	0	18	5.6
Jim McKenzie*	30	1	2	3	16	0	0	0	10	10.0
Mike Eagles	25	2	0	2	15	-7	0	0	13	15.4
Alexei Tezikov	23	1	1	2	2	-2	1	0	18	5.6
Rob Zettler	12	0	2	2	19	-1	0	0	15	0.0
Olaf Kolzig (goalie)	73	0	2	2	6	0	0	0	0	0.0
Miika Elomo	2	0	1	1	2	1	0	0	3	0.0
Nolan Baumgartner	8	0	1	1	2	1	0	0	6	0.0
Barrie Moore	1	0	0	0	0	0	0	0	2	0.0
Alexander Volchkov	3	0	0	0	0	-2	0	0	1	0.0
Jamie Huscroft	7	0	0	0	11	-5	0	0	4	0.0
Craig Billington (goalie)	13	0	0	0	0	0	0	0	0	0.0

GOALTENDING

	Games	Min.	Goals	SO	Avg.	W	L	T	ENG	Shots	Sv. Pct.
Olaf Kolzig	73	4371	163	5	2.24	41	20	11	1	1957	.917
Craig Billington	13	611	28	2	2.75	3	6	1	2	310	.910

*Played with two or more NHL teams.

RESULTS

OCTOBER
2— At Florida ....L......3-4
8— At Buffalo ....W......3-2
9— Los Angeles.....................T....*2-2
12— Philadelphia.....................W......5-4
16— San Jose...........................L......2-3
19— Anaheim............................L......1-7
23— At Phoenix ....T....*2-2
26— At Los Angeles ....L......2-5
29— At Anaheim ....L......2-5
31— At San Jose ....L......1-2

NOVEMBER
3— Ottawa.............................W......3-1
5— Toronto...........................W......5-3
7— At Carolina.......................L......2-3
9— Tampa Bay ....W......2-1
11— N.Y. Rangers....................L....*4-5
13— New Jersey......................W......4-2
17— Dallas.............................T....*2-2
19— Carolina..........................T....*3-3
20— At Boston ....W......3-0
24— At Buffalo.........................L......2-5
26— Nashville..........................W......1-0
27— At N.Y. Islanders...............W......4-3
29— At Toronto ....L......1-3

DECEMBER
2— Boston ....T....*2-2
4— At Florida ....L......1-2
7— N.Y. Islanders ....W......4-2
9— At Pittsburgh ....L......0-3

13— Montreal ....L......0-1
15— At Atlanta ....W......4-0
17— At N.Y. Rangers...............W....*3-2
18— At New Jersey ....L......4-5
21— At Edmonton ....L......2-6
22— At Vancouver ....L......3-6
27— Chicago ....T....*2-2
29— Pittsburgh ....W....*3-2

JANUARY
1— St. Louis ....T....*1-1
4— Montreal ....W......6-1
6— At Atlanta ....L......1-3
8— Atlanta ....W......3-0
12— At Atlanta ....W......5-2
14— At New Jersey ....W....*3-2
16— Ottawa ....W......2-1
17— At Tampa Bay ....W......6-3
19— At Florida ....W......3-1
22— At Toronto ....T....*5-5
24— Tampa Bay ....W......8-2
26— Calgary ....W......2-1
28— Phoenix ....W....*3-2
30— Philadelphia......................W......2-0

FEBRUARY
1— At Pittsburgh ....L......2-3
3— Carolina ....W......2-1
8— At Boston..........................T....*2-2
10— At Montreal ....W......1-0
12— At Nashville ....W......4-2
13— At Dallas ....L......1-2

15— Colorado...........................W......2-1
18— At Chicago ....W......5-4
19— At Philadelphia...................L......2-4
21— At Carolina.........................T....*1-1
23— Florida ....W....*3-2
25— Boston ....L......0-3
26— At Montreal ....W......3-0
28— At N.Y. Islanders................W......3-2

MARCH
1— At Tampa Bay ....W......4-2
3— Detroit ....T....*2-2
5— Buffalo ....W......2-1
7— Florida ....W......4-2
9— At Philadelphia...................L......1-3
11— New Jersey........................W......4-2
15— N.Y. Islanders ....W......4-3
17— Carolina.............................W......4-2
19— Tampa Bay ....W......5-2
20— At St. Louis........................L......1-2
23— At N.Y. Rangers ....W......4-1
25— At Ottawa ....W......4-3
28— Atlanta ....W......5-2
30— Pittsburgh..........................L....*3-4

APRIL
1— Toronto ....L......3-4
3— N.Y. Rangers ....W......4-1
4— At Ottawa ....L......0-4
7— At Detroit ....W......4-2
9— Buffalo ....T....*1-1
*Denotes overtime game.

SCHEDULE

*Denotes afternoon game.

WEDNESDAY, OCTOBER 4
Colorado at Dallas

THURSDAY, OCTOBER 5
Ottawa at Boston
Chicago at Buffalo
Vancouver at Philadelphia
Detroit at Calgary
St. Louis at Phoenix

FRIDAY, OCTOBER 6
Montreal at New Jersey
Los Angeles at Washington
N.Y. Islanders at Tampa Bay
Vancouver at Florida
Detroit at Edmonton
Minnesota at Anaheim
St. Louis at San Jose
Nashville vs. Pittsburgh at Japan

SATURDAY, OCTOBER 7
Los Angeles at Buffalo
Montreal at Toronto
Dallas at Ottawa
Boston at Philadelphia
Washington at Carolina
N.Y. Rangers at Atlanta
Chicago at Columbus
Colorado at Edmonton
Minnesota at Phoenix
Pittsburgh vs. Nashville at Japan

SUNDAY, OCTOBER 8
Vancouver at Tampa Bay
St. Louis at Anaheim*

MONDAY, OCTOBER 9
Florida at Boston*
Dallas at Toronto
Los Angeles at Columbus

TUESDAY, OCTOBER 10
Edmonton at Montreal
Dallas at Carolina
Colorado at Calgary

WEDNESDAY, OCTOBER 11
N.Y. Islanders at Toronto
Florida at New Jersey
Montreal at N.Y. Rangers
Washington at Atlanta
Edmonton at Detroit
Philadelphia at Minnesota
Boston at Anaheim
St. Louis at Los Angeles

THURSDAY, OCTOBER 12
Detroit at Chicago
Philadelphia at Dallas
Columbus at Calgary
Colorado at Vancouver
Phoenix at San Jose

FRIDAY, OCTOBER 13
New Jersey at Ottawa
Tampa Bay at Pittsburgh
Carolina at Florida
Minnesota at St. Louis
Washington at Nashville
Buffalo at Edmonton
Boston at Los Angeles

SATURDAY, OCTOBER 14
Ottawa at Toronto
Chicago at Montreal
Anaheim at New Jersey
Calgary at N.Y. Islanders
N.Y. Rangers at Pittsburgh
Washington at Dallas
Carolina at Nashville
Columbus at Colorado
Buffalo at Vancouver
Philadelphia at Phoenix
Boston at San Jose

SUNDAY, OCTOBER 15
Atlanta at Tampa Bay
Calgary at Detroit
Columbus at Chicago
Edmonton at Minnesota*
Phoenix at Los Angeles

MONDAY, OCTOBER 16
Anaheim at N.Y. Rangers
Toronto at Vancouver

TUESDAY, OCTOBER 17
Buffalo at Montreal
Anaheim at N.Y. Islanders
Ottawa at Philadelphia
Colorado at Washington
New Jersey at Atlanta
St. Louis at Detroit
Los Angeles at Nashville
Boston at Edmonton

WEDNESDAY, OCTOBER 18
Carolina at Pittsburgh
Colorado at Columbus
N.Y. Rangers at Chicago
San Jose at Dallas
Tampa Bay at Minnesota
Calgary at Vancouver
Florida at Phoenix

THURSDAY, OCTOBER 19
Pittsburgh at Ottawa
Montreal at Philadelphia
New Jersey at Washington
Nashville at Detroit
Los Angeles at St. Louis
Toronto at Edmonton

FRIDAY, OCTOBER 20
Anaheim at Buffalo
N.Y. Islanders at Atlanta
Dallas at Chicago
San Jose at Minnesota
Florida at Colorado
Boston at Calgary

SATURDAY, OCTOBER 21
Carolina at Montreal
Atlanta at Ottawa
Tampa Bay at New Jersey
Anaheim at Philadelphia
Columbus at Pittsburgh
N.Y. Islanders at Washington
Buffalo at Detroit
Chicago at St. Louis
Los Angeles at Dallas
San Jose at Nashville
Toronto at Calgary
Phoenix at Vancouver

SUNDAY, OCTOBER 22
Tampa Bay at N.Y. Rangers
Detroit at Columbus
Florida at Minnesota*
Phoenix at Edmonton

MONDAY, OCTOBER 23
Los Angeles at Anaheim

TUESDAY, OCTOBER 24
Minnesota at Montreal
Philadelphia at N.Y. Rangers
San Jose at Carolina
Vancouver at Nashville
Phoenix at Calgary

WEDNESDAY, OCTOBER 25
Carolina at Buffalo
Minnesota at Toronto
Ottawa at Pittsburgh
New Jersey at Florida
Tampa Bay at Detroit
San Jose at Columbus
Vancouver at Dallas
Nashville at Colorado
Atlanta at Edmonton
Anaheim at Los Angeles

THURSDAY, OCTOBER 26
Washington at Boston
N.Y. Rangers at Philadelphia
Colorado at Chicago
Calgary at St. Louis

FRIDAY, OCTOBER 27
Toronto at Buffalo
Montreal at N.Y. Islanders
Pittsburgh at N.Y. Rangers
New Jersey at Carolina
Ottawa at Tampa Bay
Washington at Columbus
Phoenix at Dallas
Florida at Nashville
Calgary at Minnesota
Atlanta at Vancouver
Edmonton at Anaheim

SATURDAY, OCTOBER 28
Toronto at Boston
N.Y. Islanders at Montreal
New Jersey at Pittsburgh
Ottawa at Florida
Columbus at Detroit
Buffalo at Chicago
Dallas at St. Louis
Edmonton at Colorado
Los Angeles at Phoenix
Atlanta at San Jose

SUNDAY, OCTOBER 29
Boston at N.Y. Rangers
Washington at Philadelphia
St. Louis at Carolina
Chicago at Minnesota
Anaheim at Calgary*

MONDAY, OCTOBER 30
Phoenix at Colorado
Anaheim at Edmonton

TUESDAY, OCTOBER 31
Toronto at Ottawa
Boston at N.Y. Islanders

2000-2001 NHL SEASON *Schedule*

Detroit at Washington
Tampa Bay at Carolina
Los Angeles at Columbus
St. Louis at Nashville

WEDNESDAY, NOVEMBER 1
Detroit at Montreal
Philadelphia at New Jersey
Tampa Bay at N.Y. Rangers
N.Y. Islanders at Florida
Columbus at Dallas
Calgary at Edmonton
Colorado at Vancouver
Phoenix at Anaheim
Pittsburgh at San Jose

THURSDAY, NOVEMBER 2
Chicago at Boston
New Jersey at Toronto
N.Y. Rangers at Ottawa
Nashville at Philadelphia
Los Angeles at Atlanta
Washington at St. Louis

FRIDAY, NOVEMBER 3
Montreal at Buffalo
N.Y. Islanders at Tampa Bay
Chicago at Detroit
Carolina at Colorado
Minnesota at Edmonton
Pittsburgh at Vancouver
Dallas at Phoenix

SATURDAY, NOVEMBER 4
Atlanta at Boston
N.Y. Rangers at Montreal
Columbus at Ottawa
Los Angeles at New Jersey*
Buffalo at Philadelphia
Washington at Florida
Toronto at St. Louis
Anaheim at Nashville
Pittsburgh at Calgary
Carolina at San Jose

SUNDAY, NOVEMBER 5
Boston at Toronto
Los Angeles at N.Y. Islanders*
Washington at Tampa Bay
Edmonton at Columbus
Anaheim at Chicago
Minnesota at Calgary
San Jose at Vancouver

MONDAY, NOVEMBER 6
Ottawa at Atlanta

TUESDAY, NOVEMBER 7
Nashville at N.Y. Islanders
Edmonton at N.Y. Rangers
Minnesota at Colorado
Phoenix at Los Angeles

WEDNESDAY, NOVEMBER 8
Carolina at Toronto
Nashville at New Jersey
Philadelphia at Pittsburgh
Montreal at Florida
San Jose at Chicago
Calgary at Minnesota
Detroit at Phoenix
Vancouver at Anaheim

THURSDAY, NOVEMBER 9
Ottawa at Boston
N.Y. Islanders at Buffalo
Edmonton at Philadelphia
N.Y. Rangers at Washington
San Jose at Columbus

St. Louis at Colorado
Vancouver at Los Angeles

FRIDAY, NOVEMBER 10
Pittsburgh at New Jersey
Toronto at Carolina
Montreal at Tampa Bay
Calgary at Florida
Minnesota at Chicago

SATURDAY, NOVEMBER 11
Nashville at Boston
Chicago at Toronto
Buffalo at New Jersey
San Jose at N.Y. Islanders
Ottawa at Philadelphia*
Edmonton at Pittsburgh
Calgary at Tampa Bay
Phoenix at Columbus
Montreal at Dallas
Anaheim at Colorado
St. Louis at Vancouver
Detroit at Los Angeles

SUNDAY, NOVEMBER 12
Phoenix at N.Y. Rangers
Atlanta at Washington*
Ottawa at Carolina*
Edmonton at Minnesota
Detroit at Anaheim

MONDAY, NOVEMBER 13
Calgary at Buffalo
Atlanta at Florida
Pittsburgh at Colorado

TUESDAY, NOVEMBER 14
Tampa Bay at Montreal
San Jose at New Jersey
Phoenix at Washington
Dallas at Columbus
St. Louis at Edmonton
Chicago at Vancouver

WEDNESDAY, NOVEMBER 15
Dallas at Buffalo
Philadelphia at Toronto
Florida at Carolina
Nashville at Atlanta
San Jose at Detroit
N.Y. Rangers at Minnesota
Colorado at Anaheim

THURSDAY, NOVEMBER 16
New Jersey at Boston
Carolina at Ottawa
Pittsburgh at St. Louis
Columbus at Nashville
Chicago at Calgary
Colorado at Phoenix
N.Y. Islanders at Los Angeles

FRIDAY, NOVEMBER 17
Minnesota at Buffalo
Tampa Bay at Toronto
Montreal at Washington
Philadelphia at Atlanta
Dallas at Detroit
Florida at Columbus
Chicago at Edmonton
N.Y. Rangers at Vancouver

SATURDAY, NOVEMBER 18
Minnesota at Boston
Toronto at Montreal
Florida at Ottawa
Carolina at New Jersey*
Washington at Philadelphia
Atlanta at Pittsburgh

Buffalo at St. Louis
Detroit at Nashville
N.Y. Rangers at Calgary
Anaheim at Phoenix
Colorado at Los Angeles*
N.Y. Islanders at San Jose

SUNDAY, NOVEMBER 19
Vancouver at Columbus
Calgary at Edmonton
N.Y. Islanders at Anaheim

MONDAY, NOVEMBER 20
Nashville at Detroit
Tampa Bay at Dallas

TUESDAY, NOVEMBER 21
Florida at Montreal
Boston at Ottawa
Toronto at N.Y. Rangers
Vancouver at St. Louis
Chicago at Phoenix

WEDNESDAY, NOVEMBER 22
Philadelphia at Buffalo
Edmonton at Toronto
N.Y. Rangers at N.Y. Islanders
Carolina at Pittsburgh
Vancouver at Washington
Atlanta at Tampa Bay
Boston at Detroit
Dallas at Nashville
Calgary at Minnesota
Columbus at Colorado
New Jersey at Anaheim
Chicago at San Jose

THURSDAY, NOVEMBER 23
Edmonton at Ottawa
Montreal at Atlanta
New Jersey at Los Angeles

FRIDAY, NOVEMBER 24
Carolina at Boston*
N.Y. Rangers at Buffalo
Pittsburgh at Philadelphia*
N.Y. Islanders at Washington
Florida at Tampa Bay
Vancouver at Detroit
Columbus at Dallas
St. Louis at Nashville
Chicago at Minnesota*
Anaheim at Calgary

SATURDAY, NOVEMBER 25
Ottawa at Toronto
Buffalo at Montreal
Detroit at N.Y. Islanders
Los Angeles at Pittsburgh
Washington at Atlanta
Tampa Bay at Florida
Dallas at Columbus
Phoenix at St. Louis
Calgary at Colorado
Anaheim at Edmonton
New Jersey at San Jose

SUNDAY, NOVEMBER 26
Los Angeles at Boston
Ottawa at N.Y. Rangers
Phoenix at Philadelphia
Nashville at Carolina*
Vancouver at Minnesota*

MONDAY, NOVEMBER 27
Atlanta at Montreal
Tampa Bay at N.Y. Islanders
Chicago at Detroit

TUESDAY, NOVEMBER 28
Pittsburgh at Boston
Buffalo at Ottawa
Los Angeles at N.Y. Rangers
Calgary at Nashville
Anaheim at Vancouver
Minnesota at San Jose

WEDNESDAY, NOVEMBER 29
St. Louis at Toronto
N.Y. Rangers at New Jersey
Tampa Bay at Washington
Detroit at Atlanta
Carolina at Florida
Philadelphia at Columbus
Calgary at Dallas
Phoenix at Colorado
Montreal at Edmonton

THURSDAY, NOVEMBER 30
Toronto at N.Y. Islanders
Philadelphia at Carolina
Nashville at Chicago
Montreal at Vancouver
Minnesota at Phoenix
Anaheim at San Jose

FRIDAY, DECEMBER 1
Pittsburgh at Buffalo
N.Y. Islanders at New Jersey
Boston at Washington
Tampa Bay at Atlanta
Detroit at Florida
Chicago at Nashville
Dallas at Colorado

SATURDAY, DECEMBER 2
Washington at Boston
N.Y. Rangers at Toronto
Philadelphia at Ottawa
Buffalo at Pittsburgh
Detroit at Tampa Bay
Atlanta at Columbus
Florida at St. Louis
Montreal at Calgary
Edmonton at Vancouver
Dallas at Phoenix
Minnesota at Los Angeles

SUNDAY, DECEMBER 3
New Jersey at N.Y. Islanders*
Colorado at N.Y. Rangers
Ottawa at Carolina
Columbus at Chicago
San Jose at Edmonton
Los Angeles at Anaheim

MONDAY, DECEMBER 4
Florida at Toronto
Boston at Atlanta
San Jose at Calgary
Nashville at Vancouver

TUESDAY, DECEMBER 5
Buffalo at Montreal
Pittsburgh at Ottawa
Colorado at New Jersey
Anaheim at St. Louis

WEDNESDAY, DECEMBER 6
New Jersey at Buffalo
Washington at N.Y. Rangers
Tampa Bay at Philadelphia
Boston at Pittsburgh
Carolina at Atlanta
N.Y. Islanders at Florida
Toronto at Detroit

Anaheim at Columbus
Nashville at Edmonton
Vancouver at Phoenix
Dallas at San Jose

THURSDAY, DECEMBER 7
Minnesota at Chicago
Nashville at Calgary
Dallas at Los Angeles

FRIDAY, DECEMBER 8
Montreal at Ottawa
Buffalo at N.Y. Rangers
Florida at Atlanta
Colorado at Tampa Bay
Philadelphia at Detroit
Boston at Columbus
Anaheim at Minnesota
Vancouver at San Jose

SATURDAY, DECEMBER 9
N.Y. Rangers at Boston
Pittsburgh at Toronto
Ottawa at Montreal
Washington at New Jersey*
Atlanta at N.Y. Islanders
Colorado at Florida
Chicago at St. Louis
Carolina at Calgary
Los Angeles at Edmonton

SUNDAY, DECEMBER 10
N.Y. Islanders at Philadelphia
Pittsburgh at Detroit
St. Louis at Chicago
Nashville at Minnesota*
Los Angeles at Vancouver
Columbus at Phoenix
Dallas at Anaheim

MONDAY, DECEMBER 11
Atlanta at New Jersey
Tampa Bay at Colorado

TUESDAY, DECEMBER 12
Buffalo at Boston
Washington at N.Y. Islanders
Philadelphia at Nashville
N.Y. Rangers at San Jose

WEDNESDAY, DECEMBER 13
Calgary at Montreal
Toronto at Pittsburgh
Chicago at Atlanta
Florida at Detroit
Edmonton at Dallas
Carolina at Minnesota
Philadelphia at Colorado
Columbus at Anaheim

THURSDAY, DECEMBER 14
Calgary at Ottawa
Minnesota at Washington
Edmonton at Nashville
Tampa Bay at Phoenix
N.Y. Rangers at Los Angeles
Columbus at San Jose

FRIDAY, DECEMBER 15
Montreal at New Jersey
Toronto at N.Y. Islanders
Florida at Pittsburgh
Buffalo at Carolina
St. Louis at Atlanta
Chicago at Dallas
Detroit at Colorado
N.Y. Rangers at Anaheim

SATURDAY, DECEMBER 16
Carolina at Boston
Florida at Buffalo
Calgary at Toronto
Pittsburgh at Montreal
N.Y. Islanders at Ottawa
New Jersey at Philadelphia
Edmonton at Washington
Detroit at St. Louis
Chicago at Nashville
Columbus at Vancouver
San Jose at Phoenix
Tampa Bay at Los Angeles

SUNDAY, DECEMBER 17
Dallas at Minnesota*
Tampa Bay at Anaheim

MONDAY, DECEMBER 18
Columbus at Montreal
Florida at N.Y. Rangers
San Jose at Washington
Edmonton at Detroit

TUESDAY, DECEMBER 19
Philadelphia at Boston
Carolina at N.Y. Islanders
Calgary at Colorado
Atlanta at Los Angeles

WEDNESDAY, DECEMBER 20
Nashville at Toronto
Dallas at New Jersey
St. Louis at N.Y. Rangers
Buffalo at Washington
Pittsburgh at Florida
San Jose at Detroit
Ottawa at Minnesota
Vancouver at Edmonton
Calgary at Phoenix
Atlanta at Anaheim

THURSDAY, DECEMBER 21
Toronto at Boston
Washington at Buffalo
Nashville at Montreal
Dallas at N.Y. Islanders
San Jose at Philadelphia
Pittsburgh at Tampa Bay
Ottawa at Columbus
Vancouver at Chicago
Los Angeles at Colorado

FRIDAY, DECEMBER 22
New Jersey at Florida
Anaheim at Detroit
Los Angeles at Minnesota
Edmonton at Calgary
Atlanta at Phoenix

SATURDAY, DECEMBER 23
Detroit at Boston
San Jose at Buffalo
Toronto at Montreal
Chicago at Ottawa*
Columbus at N.Y. Islanders
Nashville at N.Y. Rangers*
Carolina at Philadelphia*
Dallas at Pittsburgh
Florida at Washington
New Jersey at Tampa Bay
Anaheim at St. Louis
Vancouver at Colorado

TUESDAY, DECEMBER 26
Pittsburgh at Buffalo
Toronto at Atlanta
Carolina at Tampa Bay

Columbus at St. Louis
Colorado at Nashville
San Jose at Los Angeles

WEDNESDAY, DECEMBER 27
Washington at Ottawa
Columbus at New Jersey
Boston at N.Y. Islanders
Toronto at Pittsburgh
N.Y. Rangers at Carolina
Philadelphia at Florida
Minnesota at Detroit
Phoenix at Chicago
Anaheim at Dallas
Edmonton at Colorado
Montreal at Vancouver

THURSDAY, DECEMBER 28
Atlanta at N.Y. Rangers
Philadelphia at Tampa Bay
Los Angeles at St. Louis
Anaheim at Nashville
Edmonton at San Jose

FRIDAY, DECEMBER 29
Ottawa at Buffalo
Washington at New Jersey
Atlanta at N.Y. Islanders
Boston at Florida
Carolina at Columbus
Detroit at Chicago
Los Angeles at Dallas
Phoenix at Minnesota
Nashville at Colorado
Vancouver at Calgary

SATURDAY, DECEMBER 30
Buffalo at N.Y. Islanders
Ottawa at Pittsburgh
Philadelphia at Washington
Boston at Tampa Bay
Toronto at Florida
Phoenix at St. Louis
Montreal at Edmonton
Vancouver at San Jose

SUNDAY, DECEMBER 31
Chicago at Carolina
Toronto at Tampa Bay
Los Angeles at Detroit
New Jersey at Columbus
N.Y. Rangers at Dallas
Anaheim at Minnesota
Montreal at Calgary

MONDAY, JANUARY 1
Boston at Buffalo*
Atlanta at Washington*
Edmonton at St. Louis
Vancouver at Nashville*
San Jose at Phoenix

TUESDAY, JANUARY 2
St. Louis at Ottawa
Philadelphia at New Jersey
Montreal at N.Y. Islanders
Los Angeles at Colorado

WEDNESDAY, JANUARY 3
Buffalo at Toronto
Washington at Pittsburgh
Tampa Bay at Carolina
Edmonton at Columbus
Vancouver at Chicago
Atlanta at Minnesota
Florida at Anaheim
Calgary at San Jose

THURSDAY, JANUARY 4
Tampa Bay at Ottawa
N.Y. Islanders at New Jersey
Dallas at Detroit
Nashville at St. Louis
San Jose at Colorado
N.Y. Rangers at Phoenix
Florida at Los Angeles

FRIDAY, JANUARY 5
Toronto at Buffalo
Montreal at Pittsburgh
Boston at Washington
Philadelphia at Atlanta
Edmonton at Chicago
Detroit at Minnesota
Calgary at Anaheim

SATURDAY, JANUARY 6
Dallas at Boston
Washington at Toronto
Montreal at Ottawa
Phoenix at N.Y. Islanders
New Jersey at N.Y. Rangers*
Atlanta at Philadelphia
Colorado at Carolina
Minnesota at St. Louis
Buffalo at Nashville
Columbus at Vancouver
Calgary at Los Angeles
Florida at San Jose

SUNDAY, JANUARY 7
Phoenix at New Jersey
N.Y. Islanders at Carolina
Colorado at Detroit
Tampa Bay at Chicago
Columbus at Edmonton

MONDAY, JANUARY 8
Dallas at N.Y. Rangers
Pittsburgh at Washington
Philadelphia at St. Louis
Nashville at Vancouver

TUESDAY, JANUARY 9
Pittsburgh at Boston
Chicago at N.Y. Islanders
Florida at Carolina
Phoenix at Detroit
Buffalo at San Jose

WEDNESDAY, JANUARY 10
Tampa Bay at Toronto
Boston at Montreal
Chicago at New Jersey
Dallas at Atlanta
Colorado at Columbus
Washington at Minnesota
Nashville at Edmonton
Ottawa at Vancouver
St. Louis at Anaheim

THURSDAY, JANUARY 11
Nashville at Calgary
Buffalo at Los Angeles
St. Louis at San Jose

FRIDAY, JANUARY 12
Phoenix at Toronto
N.Y. Islanders at Pittsburgh
Montreal at Atlanta
Philadelphia at Tampa Bay
Carolina at Florida
Chicago at Columbus
Detroit at Dallas
Colorado at Minnesota
Vancouver at Edmonton
Buffalo at Anaheim

SATURDAY, JANUARY 13
N.Y. Rangers at Boston*
Phoenix at Montreal
Toronto at New Jersey
Pittsburgh at N.Y. Islanders
Atlanta at Washington
Philadelphia at Florida
Ottawa at Calgary
St. Louis at Los Angeles
Nashville at San Jose

SUNDAY, JANUARY 14
Minnesota at N.Y. Rangers
Anaheim at Carolina*
Dallas at Tampa Bay
Colorado at Chicago
Ottawa at Edmonton
Calgary at Vancouver

MONDAY, JANUARY 15
Anaheim at Pittsburgh*
Dallas at Florida
Minnesota at Columbus
St. Louis at Phoenix
Detroit at San Jose

TUESDAY, JANUARY 16
Tampa Bay at Buffalo
Carolina at Montreal
Los Angeles at Ottawa
Boston at New Jersey
Philadelphia at N.Y. Rangers
Edmonton at Nashville
N.Y. Islanders at Colorado
Detroit at Vancouver

WEDNESDAY, JANUARY 17
Los Angeles at Toronto
Anaheim at Atlanta
Florida at Chicago
Nashville at Dallas
Columbus at Minnesota
Pittsburgh at Phoenix
Calgary at San Jose

THURSDAY, JANUARY 18
Tampa Bay at Montreal
Washington at Ottawa
Toronto at N.Y. Rangers
New Jersey at Philadelphia
Boston at Carolina
Edmonton at St. Louis
Vancouver at Colorado

FRIDAY, JANUARY 19
Florida at Buffalo
Washington at Chicago
Pittsburgh at Dallas
Boston at Nashville
N.Y. Islanders at Minnesota
Phoenix at Anaheim

SATURDAY, JANUARY 20
Buffalo at Toronto
N.Y. Rangers at Montreal
Tampa Bay at Ottawa
Atlanta at New Jersey*
Florida at Philadelphia
Los Angeles at Carolina*
Vancouver at St. Louis
Detroit at Edmonton
Colorado at San Jose*

SUNDAY, JANUARY 21
N.Y. Islanders at Atlanta*
Tampa Bay at Columbus
Pittsburgh at Chicago
St. Louis at Nashville

New Jersey at Minnesota*
Detroit at Calgary
Dallas at Phoenix
Colorado at Anaheim

MONDAY, JANUARY 22
Florida at Boston
Los Angeles at Philadelphia
N.Y. Rangers at Carolina
Vancouver at Dallas
San Jose at Edmonton

TUESDAY, JANUARY 23
Columbus at Buffalo
St. Louis at Montreal
Ottawa at N.Y. Islanders
Washington at Tampa Bay
Atlanta at Nashville
Phoenix at Calgary

WEDNESDAY, JANUARY 24
Boston at Toronto
Carolina at N.Y. Rangers
Montreal at Pittsburgh
Florida at Washington
Nashville at Detroit
New Jersey at Dallas
Phoenix at Vancouver
Minnesota at Anaheim
Edmonton at San Jose

THURSDAY, JANUARY 25
Toronto at Atlanta
Ottawa at Tampa Bay
Philadelphia at Chicago
New Jersey at St. Louis
Calgary at Los Angeles

FRIDAY, JANUARY 26
Boston at Buffalo
N.Y. Islanders at N.Y. Rangers
Ottawa at Florida
Anaheim at Detroit
San Jose at Dallas
Chicago at Colorado
Phoenix at Edmonton

SATURDAY, JANUARY 27
New Jersey at Boston
N.Y. Rangers at Toronto
Washington at Montreal*
Buffalo at N.Y. Islanders
Atlanta at Pittsburgh
Philadelphia at Carolina*
Tampa Bay at Florida
Anaheim at Columbus
San Jose at St. Louis
Colorado at Nashville
Vancouver at Calgary
Minnesota at Los Angeles*

SUNDAY, JANUARY 28
Ottawa at Montreal*
Philadelphia at Washington*
Chicago at Vancouver

MONDAY, JANUARY 29
Atlanta at N.Y. Rangers
Tampa Bay at Carolina
Toronto at St. Louis
Nashville at Phoenix

TUESDAY, JANUARY 30
St. Louis at Boston
Detroit at New Jersey
Ottawa at Washington
Pittsburgh at Atlanta
Florida at Tampa Bay
Edmonton at Calgary

Minnesota at Vancouver
Dallas at Los Angeles
Colorado at San Jose

WEDNESDAY, JANUARY 31
New Jersey at N.Y. Islanders
Montreal at N.Y. Rangers
Philadelphia at Pittsburgh
Toronto at Carolina
Buffalo at Florida
Detroit at Columbus
Chicago at Edmonton
Nashville at Anaheim

THURSDAY, FEBRUARY 1
Montreal at Boston
N.Y. Islanders at Philadelphia
Toronto at Washington
Carolina at Atlanta
Buffalo at Tampa Bay
Columbus at St. Louis
Chicago at Calgary
Colorado at Vancouver
Anaheim at Phoenix
Nashville at Los Angeles
Dallas at San Jose

SUNDAY, FEBRUARY 4
All-Star Game at Denver*

TUESDAY, FEBRUARY 6
Philadelphia at Boston
New Jersey at Montreal
Buffalo at N.Y. Rangers
Minnesota at Tampa Bay
Ottawa at Detroit
St. Louis at Columbus
San Jose at Calgary
Chicago at Los Angeles

WEDNESDAY, FEBRUARY 7
N.Y. Islanders at Buffalo
Atlanta at Toronto
Philadelphia at Pittsburgh
Minnesota at Florida
Edmonton at Dallas
Washington at Colorado
Carolina at Phoenix
Chicago at Anaheim

THURSDAY, FEBRUARY 8
New Jersey at Ottawa
Toronto at Detroit
Tampa Bay at St. Louis
Columbus at Nashville
San Jose at Vancouver
Carolina at Los Angeles

FRIDAY, FEBRUARY 9
Philadelphia at N.Y. Islanders
Boston at Atlanta
N.Y. Rangers at Florida
Minnesota at Dallas
Calgary at Colorado
Edmonton at Phoenix
Washington at Anaheim

SATURDAY, FEBRUARY 10
Tampa Bay at Boston
Detroit at Toronto
N.Y. Islanders at Montreal
Buffalo at Ottawa
New Jersey at Pittsburgh*
Florida at Atlanta
Nashville at Columbus
St. Louis at Colorado
Calgary at Vancouver
Washington at Los Angeles
Chicago at San Jose

SUNDAY, FEBRUARY 11
Montreal at Buffalo
New Jersey at N.Y. Rangers*
St. Louis at Dallas
Pittsburgh at Minnesota*
Chicago at Phoenix
Carolina at Anaheim

MONDAY, FEBRUARY 12
N.Y. Islanders at Ottawa
N.Y. Rangers at Columbus
Edmonton at Los Angeles

TUESDAY, FEBRUARY 13
Colorado at Montreal
Buffalo at Atlanta
Phoenix at Tampa Bay
Dallas at Nashville
Washington at Calgary

WEDNESDAY, FEBRUARY 14
Columbus at Toronto
Ottawa at New Jersey
Philadelphia at N.Y. Islanders
Minnesota at Pittsburgh
Phoenix at Florida
Carolina at Detroit
San Jose at Chicago
Los Angeles at Dallas
Washington at Vancouver
Edmonton at Anaheim

THURSDAY, FEBRUARY 15
Atlanta at Buffalo
Colorado at Ottawa
Toronto at Philadelphia
Boston at Tampa Bay
Calgary at St. Louis

FRIDAY, FEBRUARY 16
Pittsburgh at New Jersey
Phoenix at Carolina
Boston at Florida
Columbus at Detroit
St. Louis at Chicago
Anaheim at Dallas
San Jose at Nashville
Los Angeles at Minnesota
N.Y. Islanders at Edmonton

SATURDAY, FEBRUARY 17
New Jersey at Buffalo
Colorado at Toronto
Washington at Montreal
Atlanta at Philadelphia
N.Y. Rangers at Tampa Bay
Pittsburgh at Columbus
Vancouver at Edmonton

SUNDAY, FEBRUARY 18
Montreal at Ottawa
Boston at Carolina*
Los Angeles at Chicago*
Detroit at Dallas
Tampa Bay at Nashville
San Jose at Minnesota*
N.Y. Islanders at Vancouver
Calgary at Phoenix

MONDAY, FEBRUARY 19
Ottawa at Buffalo
New Jersey at Toronto
Chicago at N.Y. Rangers*
Carolina at Philadelphia
Colorado at Pittsburgh*
St. Louis at Florida
Calgary at Anaheim

TUESDAY, FEBRUARY 20
St. Louis at Tampa Bay
Detroit at Nashville
Los Angeles at Edmonton
Columbus at San Jose

WEDNESDAY, FEBRUARY 21
Vancouver at Montreal
Florida at Pittsburgh
Nashville at Washington
Atlanta at Carolina
Detroit at Chicago
Minnesota at Dallas
Boston at Colorado
Columbus at Phoenix
San Jose at Anaheim

THURSDAY, FEBRUARY 22
Vancouver at Toronto
Florida at Ottawa
Buffalo at New Jersey
Philadelphia at N.Y. Islanders
Los Angeles at Calgary

FRIDAY, FEBRUARY 23
Phoenix at Buffalo
N.Y. Rangers at Pittsburgh
Montreal at Washington
New Jersey at Carolina
St. Louis at Detroit
Atlanta at Chicago
Boston at Dallas
Minnesota at Colorado
Anaheim at San Jose

SATURDAY, FEBRUARY 24
Montreal at Toronto
Vancouver at Ottawa*
Florida at N.Y. Islanders*
Tampa Bay at Philadelphia*
Washington at Carolina
Boston at St. Louis
Minnesota at Nashville
Edmonton at Calgary
Columbus at Los Angeles*

SUNDAY, FEBRUARY 25
Tampa Bay at Buffalo*
N.Y. Rangers at Philadelphia
N.Y. Islanders at Pittsburgh
Phoenix at Detroit*
Toronto at Chicago
Atlanta at Colorado*
Dallas at Edmonton
Columbus at Anaheim

MONDAY, FEBRUARY 26
Florida at New Jersey
Ottawa at N.Y. Rangers
San Jose at St. Louis
Vancouver at Minnesota
Dallas at Calgary

TUESDAY, FEBRUARY 27
Phoenix at Boston
Buffalo at Ottawa
New Jersey at N.Y. Islanders
Montreal at Philadelphia
Chicago at Washington
Carolina at Atlanta
Los Angeles at Nashville

WEDNESDAY, FEBRUARY 28
San Jose at Toronto
Pittsburgh at Montreal
Florida at N.Y. Rangers
Phoenix at Columbus
St. Louis at Edmonton

Dallas at Vancouver
Detroit at Anaheim

THURSDAY, MARCH 1
Tampa Bay at Boston
San Jose at Ottawa
Carolina at N.Y. Islanders
Buffalo at Philadelphia
Toronto at Washington
Los Angeles at Chicago
Columbus at Nashville
Minnesota at Calgary

FRIDAY, MARCH 2
Carolina at New Jersey
Pittsburgh at N.Y. Rangers
Atlanta at Florida
Minnesota at Edmonton
St. Louis at Vancouver
Detroit at Phoenix
Dallas at Anaheim

SATURDAY, MARCH 3
San Jose at Boston*
Ottawa at Toronto
Philadelphia at Montreal
Tampa Bay at N.Y. Islanders
Pittsburgh at Washington
Florida at Atlanta
Buffalo at Colorado*
St. Louis at Calgary
Detroit at Los Angeles

SUNDAY, MARCH 4
Tampa Bay at New Jersey
Carolina at Chicago*
Buffalo at Dallas*
N.Y. Rangers at Nashville*
Minnesota at Vancouver
Colorado at Phoenix
Los Angeles at Anaheim

MONDAY, MARCH 5
N.Y. Islanders at N.Y. Rangers
Boston at Philadelphia

TUESDAY, MARCH 6
Buffalo at Boston
Ottawa at New Jersey
Washington at N.Y. Islanders
Colorado at Atlanta
San Jose at Tampa Bay
St. Louis at Minnesota
Toronto at Calgary
Detroit at Vancouver
Nashville at Phoenix
Montreal at Los Angeles

WEDNESDAY, MARCH 7
Washington at Pittsburgh
Columbus at Carolina
San Jose at Florida
Chicago at Dallas
Toronto at Edmonton
Montreal at Anaheim

THURSDAY, MARCH 8
Ottawa at Boston
Minnesota at New Jersey
Calgary at Philadelphia
Pittsburgh at Atlanta
Carolina at Tampa Bay
Colorado at St. Louis
Vancouver at Phoenix
Nashville at Los Angeles

FRIDAY, MARCH 9
Edmonton at Buffalo
Minnesota at N.Y. Islanders

N.Y. Rangers at Washington
Columbus at Florida
Chicago at Anaheim

SATURDAY, MARCH 10
Atlanta at Boston*
N.Y. Rangers at Ottawa
New Jersey at Philadelphia*
Calgary at Pittsburgh
Columbus at Tampa Bay
Detroit at St. Louis*
Colorado at Dallas*
Toronto at Vancouver
Montreal at Phoenix
Chicago at Los Angeles
Nashville at San Jose

SUNDAY, MARCH 11
Florida at N.Y. Islanders*
Ottawa at Washington
Edmonton at Carolina*
Calgary at Atlanta
Detroit at Minnesota*
Dallas at Colorado
Nashville at Anaheim

MONDAY, MARCH 12
Pittsburgh at N.Y. Rangers
Montreal at San Jose

TUESDAY, MARCH 13
St. Louis at Philadelphia
Anaheim at Washington
Edmonton at Tampa Bay
Vancouver at Detroit
Dallas at Chicago
New Jersey at Colorado

WEDNESDAY, MARCH 14
N.Y. Rangers at Buffalo
Anaheim at Toronto
Atlanta at Ottawa
N.Y. Islanders at Pittsburgh
Montreal at Carolina
Edmonton at Florida
Calgary at Columbus
St. Louis at Minnesota
New Jersey at Phoenix
Los Angeles at San Jose

THURSDAY, MARCH 15
Vancouver at Boston
Minnesota at Philadelphia
Carolina at Washington
Toronto at Tampa Bay
Calgary at Detroit
Nashville at Chicago

FRIDAY, MARCH 16
Vancouver at Buffalo
Anaheim at Ottawa
Columbus at Atlanta
Pittsburgh at Florida
Phoenix at Dallas

SATURDAY, MARCH 17
Boston at Montreal
N.Y. Rangers at Philadelphia*
Buffalo at Washington
Pittsburgh at Tampa Bay
Toronto at Florida
N.Y. Islanders at Columbus
Phoenix at Nashville
Detroit at Colorado*
St. Louis at Calgary
New Jersey at Edmonton
San Jose at Los Angeles*

SUNDAY, MARCH 18
N.Y. Islanders at Carolina
Vancouver at Atlanta*
Anaheim at Chicago*
Ottawa at Dallas*
Minnesota at Colorado*
Detroit at San Jose

MONDAY, MARCH 19
Washington at N.Y. Rangers
Nashville at Columbus
Dallas at Minnesota
New Jersey at Calgary
Philadelphia at Edmonton
Phoenix at Los Angeles

TUESDAY, MARCH 20
Toronto at Buffalo
Florida at Montreal
Boston at Pittsburgh
N.Y. Islanders at St. Louis
San Jose at Colorado

WEDNESDAY, MARCH 21
Florida at Toronto
N.Y. Rangers at New Jersey
Buffalo at Carolina
Tampa Bay at Atlanta
Vancouver at Columbus
Anaheim at Dallas
Nashville at Minnesota
Ottawa at Phoenix
Edmonton at Los Angeles

THURSDAY, MARCH 22
Montreal at Boston
Atlanta at Tampa Bay
Minnesota at Detroit
Nashville at Chicago
Colorado at St. Louis
Philadelphia at Calgary
Ottawa at San Jose

FRIDAY, MARCH 23
Vancouver at New Jersey
Pittsburgh at Carolina
Washington at Florida
N.Y. Islanders at Dallas

SATURDAY, MARCH 24
Colorado at Boston*
Carolina at Buffalo
Philadelphia at Toronto
Atlanta at Montreal
Detroit at N.Y. Rangers*
Washington at Tampa Bay
Calgary at Columbus*
Chicago at St. Louis*
Ottawa at Nashville
Edmonton at Phoenix
Anaheim at Los Angeles*

SUNDAY, MARCH 25
Pittsburgh at New Jersey
Boston at N.Y. Rangers
Calgary at Chicago*

St. Louis at Dallas
Vancouver at Minnesota*
N.Y. Islanders at Phoenix

MONDAY, MARCH 26
Philadelphia at Ottawa
Montreal at Carolina
Buffalo at Atlanta
Columbus at Edmonton
San Jose at Los Angeles

TUESDAY, MARCH 27
Buffalo at Pittsburgh
New Jersey at Tampa Bay
Columbus at Calgary
Los Angeles at San Jose

WEDNESDAY, MARCH 28
Boston at Toronto
N.Y. Islanders at N.Y. Rangers
Carolina at Washington
New Jersey at Atlanta
Montreal at Florida
St. Louis at Detroit
Ottawa at Chicago
Phoenix at Minnesota
Colorado at Edmonton
Dallas at Vancouver

THURSDAY, MARCH 29
N.Y. Rangers at N.Y. Islanders
Toronto at Philadelphia
Chicago at Pittsburgh
Montreal at Tampa Bay
Phoenix at Nashville
Colorado at Calgary
Columbus at Los Angeles
Anaheim at San Jose

FRIDAY, MARCH 30
Atlanta at Buffalo
Boston at Ottawa
Washington at Carolina
Tampa Bay at Florida
Dallas at Edmonton
Anaheim at Vancouver

SATURDAY, MARCH 31
N.Y. Islanders at Boston
Toronto at Montreal
N.Y. Rangers at New Jersey*
Detroit at Philadelphia*
St. Louis at Pittsburgh*
Minnesota at Nashville
Dallas at Calgary
San Jose at Phoenix
Colorado at Los Angeles*

SUNDAY, APRIL 1
Carolina at Ottawa*
N.Y. Rangers at Atlanta*
Buffalo at Tampa Bay
Washington at Detroit
St. Louis at Columbus
Edmonton at Chicago*
Vancouver at Anaheim

MONDAY, APRIL 2
Montreal at Boston
Pittsburgh at N.Y. Islanders
Buffalo at Florida
Calgary at Dallas
Edmonton at Colorado
Vancouver at Los Angeles
Minnesota at San Jose

TUESDAY, APRIL 3
Florida at Philadelphia
New Jersey at Washington
Ottawa at Atlanta
Detroit at Columbus
Carolina at St. Louis
Los Angeles at Phoenix

WEDNESDAY, APRIL 4
Boston at Buffalo
N.Y. Islanders at Toronto
Carolina at N.Y. Rangers
Tampa Bay at Pittsburgh
Calgary at Chicago
Nashville at Dallas
Anaheim at Colorado
Minnesota at Edmonton

THURSDAY, APRIL 5
Philadelphia at Montreal
Florida at Washington
N.Y. Rangers at Tampa Bay
Atlanta at Detroit
Columbus at St. Louis
Calgary at Nashville
Los Angeles at Vancouver
Phoenix at San Jose

FRIDAY, APRIL 6
Washington at Buffalo
Boston at New Jersey
Ottawa at N.Y. Islanders
Atlanta at Carolina
Toronto at Chicago
Columbus at Minnesota
Phoenix at Anaheim

SATURDAY, APRIL 7
N.Y. Islanders at Boston
New Jersey at Montreal
Toronto at Ottawa
Pittsburgh at Philadelphia*
N.Y. Rangers at Florida*
Colorado at Detroit*
Nashville at St. Louis
Los Angeles at Calgary
Edmonton at Vancouver
Dallas at San Jose*

SUNDAY, APRIL 8
Philadelphia at Buffalo*
Tampa Bay at Washington*
Pittsburgh at Carolina*
Chicago at Columbus*
Colorado at Minnesota*
San Jose at Anaheim

1999-2000 NHL REVIEW

Regular season

Stanley Cup playoffs

All-Star Game

Awards

Player draft

REGULAR SEASON

FINAL STANDINGS

EASTERN CONFERENCE

NORTHEAST DIVISION

	G	W	L	T	RT	Pts.	GF	GA	Home	Away	Div. Rec.
Toronto Maple Leafs	82	45	30	7	3	100	246	222	24-12-5-0	21-18-2-3	10-8-2-1
Ottawa Senators	82	41	30	11	2	95	244	210	24-12-5-2	17-18-6-0	11-5-4-0
Buffalo Sabres	82	35	36	11	4	85	213	204	21-15-5-1	14-21-6-3	9-9-2-1
Montreal Canadiens	82	35	38	9	4	83	196	194	18-18-5-1	17-20-4-3	7-10-3-0
Boston Bruins	82	24	39	19	6	73	210	248	12-18-11-1	12-21-8-5	5-10-5-2

ATLANTIC DIVISION

	G	W	L	T	RT	Pts.	GF	GA	Home	Away	Div. Rec.
Philadelphia Flyers	82	45	25	12	3	105	237	179	25-9-7-0	20-16-5-0	12-6-2-1
New Jersey Devils	82	45	29	8	5	103	251	203	28-10-3-1	17-19-5-4	13-5-2-0
Pittsburgh Penguins	82	37	37	8	6	88	241	236	23-11-7-0	14-26-1-6	9-10-1-1
New York Rangers	82	29	41	12	3	73	218	246	15-21-5-1	14-20-7-2	5-12-3-0
New York Islanders	82	24	49	9	1	58	194	275	10-26-5-1	14-23-4-0	6-12-2-0

SOUTHEAST DIVISION

	G	W	L	T	RT	Pts.	GF	GA	Home	Away	Div. Rec.
Washington Capitals	82	44	26	12	2	102	227	194	26-7-8-2	18-19-4-0	14-4-2-0
Florida Panthers	82	43	33	6	6	98	244	209	26-11-4-2	17-22-2-4	10-7-3-3
Carolina Hurricanes	82	37	35	10	0	84	217	216	20-16-5-0	17-19-5-0	12-5-3-0
Tampa Bay Lightning	82	19	54	9	7	54	204	310	13-24-4-4	6-30-5-3	2-15-3-0
Atlanta Thrashers	82	14	61	7	4	39	170	313	9-29-3-3	5-32-4-1	5-12-3-0

WESTERN CONFERENCE

CENTRAL DIVISION

	G	W	L	T	RT	Pts.	GF	GA	Home	Away	Div. Rec.
St. Louis Blues	82	51	20	11	1	114	248	165	24-10-7-1	27-10-4-0	8-7-3-1
Detroit Red Wings	82	48	24	10	2	108	278	210	28-10-3-1	20-14-7-1	10-6-2-1
Chicago Blackhawks	82	33	39	10	2	78	242	245	16-20-5-1	17-19-5-1	7-8-3-0
Nashville Predators	82	28	47	7	7	70	199	240	15-23-3-2	13-24-4-5	6-10-2-2

PACIFIC DIVISION

	G	W	L	T	RT	Pts.	GF	GA	Home	Away	Div. Rec.
Dallas Stars	82	43	29	10	6	102	211	184	21-15-5-4	22-14-5-2	12-11-1-0
Los Angeles Kings	82	39	31	12	4	94	245	228	21-15-5-2	18-16-7-2	8-13-3-3
Phoenix Coyotes	82	39	35	8	4	90	232	228	22-17-2-1	17-18-6-3	13-10-1-1
San Jose Sharks	82	35	37	10	7	87	225	214	21-17-3-3	14-20-7-4	11-11-2-2
Mighty Ducks of Anaheim	82	34	36	12	3	83	217	227	19-15-7-2	15-21-5-1	11-10-3-1

NORTHWEST DIVISION

	G	W	L	T	RT	Pts.	GF	GA	Home	Away	Div. Rec.
Colorado Avalanche	82	42	29	11	1	96	233	201	25-12-4-0	17-17-7-1	13-3-2-0
Edmonton Oilers	82	32	34	16	8	88	226	212	18-14-9-3	14-20-7-5	7-9-2-2
Vancouver Canucks	82	30	37	15	8	83	227	237	16-20-5-6	14-17-10-2	4-11-3-3
Calgary Flames	82	31	41	10	5	77	211	256	20-15-6-1	11-26-4-4	8-9-1-1

Note: RT denotes games in which the team is tied after regulation time, but loses in overtime; teams receive two points for each victory, one for each tie and one for each overtime loss.

INDIVIDUAL LEADERS

SCORING

TOP SCORERS

	Games	G	A	Pts.	PIM	+/-	PPG	SHG	Shots	Shooting Pct.
Jaromir Jagr, Pittsburgh	63	42	54	96	50	25	10	0	290	14.5
Pavel Bure, Florida	74	58	36	94	16	25	11	2	360	16.1
Mark Recchi, Philadelphia	82	28	63	91	50	20	7	1	223	12.6
Paul Kariya, Anaheim	74	42	44	86	24	22	11	3	324	13.0
Teemu Selanne, Anaheim	79	33	52	85	12	6	8	0	236	14.0
Owen Nolan, San Jose	78	44	40	84	110	-1	18	4	261	16.9
Tony Amonte, Chicago	82	43	41	84	48	10	11	5	260	16.5

	Games	G	A	Pts.	PIM	+/-	PPG	SHG	Shots	Shooting Pct.
Mike Modano, Dallas	77	38	43	81	48	0	11	1	188	20.2
Joe Sakic, Colorado	60	28	53	81	28	30	5	1	242	11.6
Steve Yzerman, Detroit	78	35	44	79	34	28	15	2	234	15.0
Brendan Shanahan, Detroit	78	41	37	78	105	24	13	1	283	14.5
Jeremy Roenick, Phoenix	75	34	44	78	102	11	6	3	192	17.7
John LeClair, Philadelphia	82	40	37	77	36	8	13	0	249	16.1
Valeri Bure, Calgary	82	35	40	75	50	-7	13	0	308	11.4
Pavol Demitra, St. Louis	71	28	47	75	8	34	8	0	241	11.6
Luc Robitaille, Los Angeles	71	36	38	74	68	11	13	0	221	16.3
Mats Sundin, Toronto	73	32	41	73	46	16	10	2	184	17.4
Doug Gilmour, Chicago-Buffalo	74	25	48	73	63	-9	10	0	113	22.1
Ron Francis, Carolina	78	23	50	73	18	10	7	0	150	15.3
Nicklas Lidstrom, Detroit	81	20	53	73	18	19	9	4	218	9.2

The scoring leader is awarded the Art Ross Memorial Trophy.
*Led league.
†Tied for league lead.

Games
Claude Lemieux, Col.-N.J. 83
41 players with...............................82

Points
Jaromir Jagr, Pittsburgh 96
Pavel Bure, Florida 94
Mark Recchi, Philadelphia 91
Paul Kariya, Anaheim 86
Teemu Selanne, Anaheim 85
Owen Nolan, San Jose 84
Tony Amonte, Chicago 84
Mike Modano, Dallas 81
Joe Sakic, Colorado 81
Steve Yzerman, Detroit 79

Points by a defenseman
Nicklas Lidstrom, Detroit 73
Chris Pronger, St. Louis 62
Rob Blake, Los Angeles 57
Eric Desjardins, Philadelphia.............55
Phil Housley, Calgary 55

Goals
Pavel Bure, Florida 58
Owen Nolan, San Jose 44
Tony Amonte, Chicago 43
Jaromir Jagr, Pittsburgh 42
Paul Kariya, Anaheim 42
Brendan Shanahan, Detroit 41
John LeClair, Philadelphia 40
Mike Modano, Dallas 38
Milan Hejduk, Colorado 36
Luc Robitaille, Los Angeles...............36

Assists
Mark Recchi, Philadelphia..................63
Adam Oates, Washington 56
Jaromir Jagr, Pittsburgh 54
Viktor Kozlov, Florida 53
Nicklas Lidstrom, Detroit 53
Joe Sakic, Colorado 53
Teemu Selanne, Anaheim 52
Scott Gomez, New Jersey 51
Doug Weight, Edmonton 51
Ron Francis, Carolina 50

Power-play goals
Owen Nolan, San Jose 18
Mariusz Czerkawski, N.Y. Islanders......16
Steve Yzerman, Detroit......................15
Ray Bourque, Bos.-Col. 13
Valeri Bure, Calgary 13
Milan Hejduk, Colorado 13
Robert Lang, Pittsburgh 13
John LeClair, Philadelphia 13
Luc Robitaille, Los Angeles................13
Brendan Shanahan, Detroit 13

Shorthanded goals
John Madden, New Jersey 6
Tony Amonte, Chicago 5
Sergei Fedorov, Detroit.........................4
Jeff Halpern, Washington 4
Michal Handzus, St. Louis......................4
Mike Keane, Dallas 4
Trevor Letowski, Phoenix.......................4
Nicklas Lidstrom, Detroit 4
Owen Nolan, San Jose 4
Marco Sturm, San Jose...........................4

Game-winning goals
Pavel Bure, Florida 14
Jeremy Roenick, Phoenix......................12
Patrik Elias, New Jersey.........................9
Milan Hejduk, Colorado 9
Brendan Shanahan, Detroit 9
Steve Thomas, Toronto...........................9

Game-tying goals
Mike Modano, Dallas..............................3
Niklas Sundstrom, San Jose 3
Richard Zednik, Washington 3
18 players with.....................................2

Shots
Pavel Bure, Florida 360
Rob Blake, Los Angeles 327
Paul Kariya, Anaheim 324
Valeri Bure, Calgary 308
Jaromir Jagr, Pittsburgh 290

Shooting percentage
(82 shots minimum)
Mike Eastwood, St. Louis................22.9
Doug Gilmour, Chi.-Buf. 22.1
Alex Selivanov, Edmonton 22.1
Andrew Brunette, Atlanta 21.5
Mike Modano, Dallas 20.2

Plus/minus
Chris Pronger, St. Louis 52
Chris Chelios, Detroit 48
Pavol Demitra, St. Louis 34
Pierre Turgeon, St. Louis 30
Scott Stevens, New Jersey 30
Joe Sakic, Colorado 30
Steve Yzerman, Detroit......................28
Marc Bergevin, St. Louis....................27
Sergei Gonchar, Washington 26
Jeff Finley, St. Louis 26
Jon Klemm, Colorado.........................26

Penalty minutes
Denny Lambert, Atlanta....................219
Todd Simpson, Florida 202
Tie Domi, Toronto 198
Matthew Barnaby, Pittsburgh 197

Eric Cairns, N.Y. Islanders................196
Sean Brown, Edmonton 192
Ian Laperriere, Los Angeles 185
Krzysztof Oliwa, New Jersey 184
Paul Laus, Florida............................172
Petr Svoboda, Tampa Bay 170

Consecutive-game point streaks
Jarome Iginla, Calgary 16
Patrick Elias, New Jersey 15
Jaromir Jagr, Pittsburgh 15
Luc Robitaille, Los Angeles................15
Pierre Turgeon, St. Louis 15

Consecutive-game goal streaks
Jaromir Jagr, Pittsburgh 7
Joe Sakic, Colorado 7
Tony Amonte, Chicago ....(twice) 6
Paul Kariya, Anaheim 6
Owen Nolan, San Jose 6

Consecutive-game assist streaks
Pierre Turgeon, St. Louis 12
Joe Sakic, Colorado 10
Theoren Fleury, N.Y. Rangers 8
Jeremy Roenick, Phoenix......................8
Pavel Bure, Florida 7
Pavel Demitra, St. Louis 7
Doug Gilmour, Chi.-Buf. 7
Cliff Ronning, Nash. 7

Most games scoring three or more goals
Pavel Bure, Florida 4
Petr Nedved, N.Y. Rangers 3
Jaromir Jagr, Pittsburgh 2
Jeremy Roenick, Phoenix......................2
Joe Sakic, Colorado 2
Brian Savage, Montreal 2
Alex Selivanov, Edmonton 2

Points by a rookie
Scott Gomez, New Jersey 70
Alex Tanguay, Colorado 51
Michael York, N.Y. Rangers 50
Simon Gagne, Philadelphia 48
Jan Hlavac, N.Y. Rangers 42

Goals by a rookie
Michael York, N.Y. Rangers 26
Simon Gagne, Philadelphia 20
Scott Gomez, New Jersey 19
Jan Hlavac, N.Y. Rangers 19
Trevor Letowski, Phoenix 19

Assists by a rookie
Scott Gomez, New Jersey 51
Alex Tanguay, Colorado 34
Simon Gagne, Philadelphia 28
Brian Rafalski, New Jersey.................27
Brad Stuart, San Jose 26

GOALTENDING

Games

Arturs Irbe, Carolina 75
Olaf Kolzig, Washington 73
Martin Brodeur, New Jersey 72
Tommy Salo, Edmonton 70
Guy Hebert, Anaheim 68

Minutes

Olaf Kolzig, Washington 4371
Arturs Irbe, Carolina 4345
Martin Brodeur, New Jersey 4312
Tommy Salo, Edmonton 4164
Guy Hebert, Anaheim 3976

Goals allowed

Arturs Irbe, Carolina 175
Mike Richter, N.Y. Rangers 173
Guy Hebert, Anaheim 166
Olaf Kolzig, Washington 163
Tommy Salo, Edmonton 162
Steve Shields, San Jose 162
Kevin Weekes, Van.-NYI 162

Shutouts

Roman Turek, St. Louis 7
Martin Brodeur, New Jersey 6
Chris Osgood, Detroit 6
Martin Biron, Buffalo 5
Fred Brathwaite, Calgary 5
Arturs Irbe, Carolina 5
Olaf Kolzig, Washington 5
Jose Theodore, Montreal 5

Lowest goals-against average
(25 games played minimum)

Brian Boucher, Philadelphia 1.91
Roman Turek, St. Louis 1.95
Jose Theodore, Montreal 2.10272
Ed Belfour, Dallas 2.10497
John Vanbiesbrouck, Philadelphia 2.20

Highest goals-against average
(25 games played minimum)

Damian Rhodes, Atlanta 3.88
Dan Cloutier, Tampa Bay 3.491
Norm Maracle, Atlanta 3.486
Kevin Weekes, Van.-NYI 3.23
Robbie Tallas, Boston 3.169
Tom Barrasso, Pit.-Ott. 3.168

Games won

Martin Brodeur, New Jersey 43
Roman Turek, St. Louis 42
Olaf Kolzig, Washington 41
Curtis Joseph, Toronto 36
Arturs Irbe, Carolina 34

Best winning percentage
(25 games played minimum)

Roman Turek, St. Louis (42-15-9) ... .705
Martin Brodeur, N.J. (43-20-8) .... .662
Chris Osgood, Detroit (30-14-8) ...... .654
Brian Boucher, Phi. (20-10-3) .... .652
Olaf Kolzig, Washington (41-20-11). .646

Worst winning percentage
(25 games played minimum)

Norm Maracle, Atlanta (4-19-2) .... .200
Damian Rhodes, Atlanta (5-19-3) .... .241
Dan Cloutier, Tampa Bay (9-30-3).... .250
Robbie Tallas, Boston (4-13-4) .... .286
Tomas Vokoun, Nashville (9-20-1)... .317

Games lost

Guy Hebert, Anaheim 31
Mike Richter, N.Y. Rangers 31
Dan Cloutier, Tampa Bay 30
Steve Shields, San Jose 30
Arturs Irbe, Carolina 28
Tommy Salo, Edmonton 28

Tie games

Tommy Salo, Edmonton 13
Olaf Kolzig, Washington 11
Byron Dafoe, Boston 10
Felix Potvin, NYI-Van. 10
Guy Hebert, Anaheim 9
Arturs Irbe, Carolina 9
Roman Turek, St. Louis 9
John Vanbiesbrouck, Philadelphia 9

Shots against

Olaf Kolzig, Washington 1957
Tommy Salo, Edmonton 1875
Arturs Irbe, Carolina 1858
Curtis Joseph, Toronto 1854
Steve Shields, San Jose 1826

Saves

Olaf Kolzig, Washington 1794
Tommy Salo, Edmonton 1713
Curtis Joseph, Toronto 1696
Arturs Irbe, Carolina 1683
Steve Shields, San Jose 1664

Highest save percentage
(25 games played minimum)

Ed Belfour, Dallas .... .9192
Jose Theodore, Montreal .... .9191
Dominik Hasek, Buffalo .... .9189
Brian Boucher, Philadelphia .... .9177
Olaf Kolzig, Washington .... .91671
Mike Vernon, S.J.-Fla. .... .91667

Lowest save percentage
(25 games played minimum)

Damian Rhodes, Atlanta .... .874
Tom Barrasso, Pit.-Ott. .... .880
Dan Cloutier, Tampa Bay .... .8847
Robbie Tallas, Boston .... .8854
Byron Dafoe, Boston .... .889

STATISTICS OF PLAYERS WITH TWO OR MORE TEAMS

SCORING

	Games	G	A	Pts.	PIM	+/-	PPG	SHG	Shots	Shooting Pct.
Mikael Andersson, Philadelphia	36	2	3	5	0	-2	0	1	38	5.3
Mikael Andersson, N.Y. Islanders	19	0	3	3	4	-1	0	0	19	0.0
Totals	55	2	6	8	4	-3	0	1	57	3.5
Niklas Andersson, N.Y. Islanders	17	3	7	10	8	-3	1	0	24	12.5
Niklas Andersson, Nashville	7	0	1	1	0	0	0	0	7	0.0
Totals	24	3	8	11	8	-3	1	0	31	9.7
Dave Andreychuk, Boston	63	19	14	33	28	-11	7	0	192	9.9
Dave Andreychuk, Colorado	14	1	2	3	2	-9	1	0	41	2.4
Totals	77	20	16	36	30	-20	8	0	233	8.6
Donald Audette, Los Angeles	49	12	20	32	45	6	1	0	112	10.7
Donald Audette, Atlanta	14	7	4	11	12	-4	0	1	50	14.0
Totals	63	19	24	43	57	2	1	1	162	11.7
Tom Barrasso, Pittsburgh (goalie)	18	0	0	0	6	0	0	0	0	0.0
Tom Barrasso, Ottawa (goalie)	7	0	0	0	0	0	0	0	0	0.0
Totals	25	0	0	0	6	0	0	0	0	0.0
Len Barrie, Los Angeles	46	5	8	13	56	5	0	0	46	10.9
Len Barrie, Florida	14	4	6	10	6	4	0	0	15	26.7
Totals	60	9	14	23	62	9	0	0	61	14.8
Josef Beranek, Edmonton	58	9	8	17	39	-6	3	0	107	8.4
Josef Beranek, Pittsburgh	13	4	4	8	18	-6	1	0	32	12.5
Totals	71	13	12	25	57	-12	4	0	139	9.4
Eric Bertrand, New Jersey	4	0	0	0	0	-1	0	0	1	0.0
Eric Bertrand, Atlanta	8	0	0	0	4	-5	0	0	11	0.0
Totals	12	0	0	0	4	-6	0	0	12	0.0
Jason Botterill, Atlanta	25	1	4	5	17	-7	0	0	17	5.9
Jason Botterill, Calgary	2	0	0	0	0	-4	0	0	2	0.0
Totals	27	1	4	5	17	-11	0	0	19	5.3

	Games	G	A	Pts.	PIM	+/–	PPG	SHG	Shots	Shooting Pct.
Joel Bouchard, Nashville	52	1	4	5	23	-11	0	0	60	1.7
Joel Bouchard, Dallas	2	0	0	0	2	1	0	0	1	0.0
Totals	54	1	4	5	25	-10	0	0	61	1.6
Bob Boughner, Nashville	62	2	4	6	97	-13	0	0	32	6.3
Bob Boughner, Pittsburgh	11	1	0	1	69	2	1	0	8	12.5
Totals	73	3	4	7	166	-11	1	0	40	7.5
Ray Bourque, Boston	65	10	28	38	20	-11	6	0	217	4.6
Ray Bourque, Colorado	14	8	6	14	6	9	7	0	43	18.6
Totals	79	18	34	52	26	-2	13	0	260	6.9
Rod Brind'Amour, Philadelphia	12	5	3	8	4	-1	4	0	26	19.2
Rod Brind'Amour, Carolina	33	4	10	14	22	-12	0	1	61	6.6
Totals	45	9	13	22	26	-13	4	1	87	10.3
Kelly Buchberger, Atlanta	68	5	12	17	139	-34	0	0	56	8.9
Kelly Buchberger, Los Angeles	13	2	1	3	13	-2	0	0	20	10.0
Totals	81	7	13	20	152	-36	0	0	76	9.2
Marc Bureau, Philadelphia	54	2	2	4	10	-1	0	1	46	4.3
Marc Bureau, Calgary	9	1	3	4	2	-3	0	0	5	20.0
Totals	63	3	5	8	12	-4	0	1	51	5.9
Sean Burke, Florida (goalie)	7	0	0	0	2	0	0	0	0	0.0
Sean Burke, Phoenix (goalie)	35	0	0	0	10	0	0	0	0	0.0
Totals	42	0	0	0	12	0	0	0	0	0.0
Viacheslav Butsayev, Tampa Bay	2	0	0	0	0	-2	0	0	1	0.0
Viacheslav Butsayev, Ottawa	3	0	0	0	0	-2	0	0	1	0.0
Totals	5	0	0	0	0	-4	0	0	2	0.0
Wendel Clark, Chicago	13	2	0	2	13	-2	0	0	27	7.4
Wendel Clark, Toronto	20	2	2	4	21	-3	0	0	36	5.6
Totals	33	4	2	6	34	-5	0	0	63	6.3
Rene Corbet, Calgary	48	4	10	14	60	-7	0	0	100	4.0
Rene Corbet, Pittsburgh	4	1	0	1	0	-4	1	0	9	11.1
Totals	52	5	10	15	60	-11	1	0	109	4.6
Sylvain Cote, Toronto	3	0	1	1	0	1	0	0	3	0.0
Sylvain Cote, Chicago	45	6	18	24	14	-4	5	0	78	7.7
Sylvain Cote, Dallas	28	2	8	10	14	6	0	0	47	4.3
Totals	76	8	27	35	28	3	5	0	128	6.3
Johan Davidsson, Anaheim	5	1	0	1	2	0	0	0	8	12.5
Johan Davidsson, N.Y. Islanders	14	2	4	6	0	0	0	0	21	9.5
Totals	19	3	4	7	2	0	0	0	29	10.3
Kevin Dean, Atlanta	23	1	0	1	14	-5	0	1	9	11.1
Kevin Dean, Dallas	14	0	0	0	10	-1	0	0	6	0.0
Kevin Dean, Chicago	27	2	8	10	12	9	0	0	32	6.3
Totals	64	3	8	11	36	3	0	1	47	6.4
Rob DiMaio, Boston	50	5	16	21	42	-1	0	0	93	5.4
Rob DiMaio, N.Y. Rangers	12	1	3	4	8	-8	0	0	18	5.6
Totals	62	6	19	25	50	-9	0	0	111	5.4
Bobby Dollas, Ottawa	1	0	0	0	0	2	0	0	0	0.0
Bobby Dollas, Calgary	49	3	7	10	28	4	1	0	36	8.3
Totals	50	3	7	10	28	6	1	0	36	8.3
Hnat Domenichelli, Calgary	32	5	9	14	12	0	1	0	57	8.8
Hnat Domenichelli, Atlanta	27	6	9	15	4	-21	0	0	68	8.8
Totals	59	11	18	29	16	-21	1	0	125	8.8
Shean Donovan, Colorado	18	1	0	1	8	-4	0	0	13	7.7
Shean Donovan, Atlanta	33	4	7	11	18	-13	1	0	53	7.5
Totals	51	5	7	12	26	-17	1	0	66	7.6
Ted Drury, Anaheim	11	1	1	2	6	-1	0	0	9	11.1
Ted Drury, N.Y. Islanders	55	2	1	3	31	-8	1	0	48	4.2
Totals	66	3	2	5	37	-9	1	0	57	5.3
Radek Dvorak, Florida	35	7	10	17	6	5	0	0	67	10.4
Radek Dvorak, N.Y. Rangers	46	11	22	33	10	0	2	1	90	12.2
Totals	81	18	32	50	16	5	2	1	157	11.5
Karl Dykhuis, Philadelphia	5	0	1	1	6	-2	0	0	5	0.0
Karl Dykhuis, Montreal	67	7	12	19	40	-3	3	1	64	10.9
Totals	72	7	13	20	46	-5	3	1	69	10.1
Nelson Emerson, Atlanta	58	14	19	33	47	-24	4	0	183	7.7
Nelson Emerson, Los Angeles	5	1	1	2	0	1	0	0	13	7.7
Totals	63	15	20	35	47	-23	4	0	196	7.7
Pat Falloon, Edmonton	33	5	13	18	4	6	1	0	51	9.8
Pat Falloon, Pittsburgh	30	4	9	13	10	-2	0	0	41	9.8
Totals	63	9	22	31	14	4	1	0	92	9.8
Colin Forbes, Tampa Bay	8	0	0	0	18	-4	0	0	3	0.0
Colin Forbes, Ottawa	45	2	5	7	12	-1	0	0	54	3.7
Totals	53	2	5	7	30	-5	0	0	57	3.5

	Games	G	A	Pts.	PIM	+/-	PPG	SHG	Shots	Shooting Pct.
Bruce Gardiner, Ottawa	10	0	3	3	4	1	0	0	18	0.0
Bruce Gardiner, Tampa Bay	41	3	6	9	37	-21	0	0	30	10.0
Totals	51	3	9	12	41	-20	0	0	48	6.3
Todd Gill, Phoenix	41	1	6	7	30	-10	0	0	41	2.4
Todd Gill, Detroit	13	2	0	2	15	2	0	0	20	10.0
Totals	54	3	6	9	45	-8	0	0	61	4.9
Doug Gilmour, Chicago	63	22	34	56	51	-12	8	0	100	22.0
Doug Gilmour, Buffalo	11	3	14	17	12	3	2	0	13	23.1
Totals	74	25	48	73	63	-9	10	0	113	22.1
Chris Gratton, Tampa Bay	58	14	27	41	121	-24	4	0	168	8.3
Chris Gratton, Buffalo	14	1	7	8	15	1	0	0	34	2.9
Totals	72	15	34	49	136	-23	4	0	202	7.4
Michal Grosek, Buffalo	61	11	23	34	35	12	2	0	96	11.5
Michal Grosek, Chicago	14	2	4	6	12	-1	1	0	18	11.1
Totals	75	13	27	40	47	11	3	0	114	11.4
Stephen Guolla, Tampa Bay	46	6	10	16	11	2	2	0	52	11.5
Stephen Guolla, Atlanta	20	4	9	13	4	-13	2	0	34	11.8
Totals	66	10	19	29	15	-11	4	0	86	11.6
Todd Harvey, N.Y. Rangers	31	3	3	6	62	-9	0	0	31	9.7
Todd Harvey, San Jose	40	8	4	12	78	-2	2	0	59	13.6
Totals	71	11	7	18	140	-11	2	0	90	12.2
Dwayne Hay, Florida	6	0	0	0	2	-2	0	0	3	0.0
Dwayne Hay, Tampa Bay	13	1	1	2	2	0	0	0	11	9.1
Totals	19	1	1	2	4	-2	0	0	14	7.1
Ian Herbers, Tampa Bay	37	0	0	0	45	-12	0	0	11	0.0
Ian Herbers, N.Y. Islanders	6	0	3	3	2	6	0	0	3	0.0
Totals	43	0	3	3	47	-6	0	0	14	0.0
Brian Holzinger, Buffalo	59	7	17	24	30	4	0	1	81	8.6
Brian Holzinger, Tampa Bay	14	3	3	6	21	-7	1	1	23	13.0
Totals	73	10	20	30	51	-3	1	2	104	9.6
Bill Houlder, Tampa Bay	14	1	2	3	2	-3	1	0	21	4.8
Bill Houlder, Nashville	57	2	12	14	24	-6	1	0	68	2.9
Totals	71	3	14	17	26	-9	2	0	89	3.4
Tony Hrkac, N.Y. Islanders	7	0	2	2	0	-1	0	0	2	0.0
Tony Hrkac, Anaheim	60	4	7	11	8	-2	1	0	37	10.8
Totals	67	4	9	13	8	-3	1	0	39	10.3
Andreas Johansson, Tampa Bay	12	2	3	5	8	1	0	0	11	18.2
Andreas Johansson, Calgary	28	3	7	10	14	-3	1	0	47	6.4
Totals	40	5	10	15	22	-2	1	0	58	8.6
Mike Johnson, Toronto	52	11	14	25	23	8	2	1	89	12.4
Mike Johnson, Tampa Bay	28	10	12	22	4	-2	4	0	43	23.3
Totals	80	21	26	47	27	6	6	1	132	15.9
Ryan Johnson, Florida	66	4	12	16	14	1	0	0	44	9.1
Ryan Johnson, Tampa Bay	14	0	2	2	2	-9	0	0	5	0.0
Totals	80	4	14	18	16	-8	0	0	49	8.2
Jorgen Jonsson, N.Y. Islanders	68	11	17	28	16	-6	1	2	95	11.6
Jorgen Jonsson, Anaheim	13	1	2	3	0	-2	0	0	21	4.8
Totals	81	12	19	31	16	-8	1	2	116	10.3
Chris Joseph, Vancouver	38	2	9	11	6	-4	1	0	73	2.7
Chris Joseph, Phoenix	9	0	0	0	0	-5	0	0	13	0.0
Totals	47	2	9	11	6	-9	1	0	86	2.3
Frantisek Kaberle, Los Angeles	37	0	9	9	4	3	0	0	41	0.0
Frantisek Kaberle, Atlanta	14	1	6	7	6	-13	0	1	35	2.9
Totals	51	1	15	16	10	-10	0	1	76	1.3
Derek King, Toronto	3	0	0	0	2	-2	0	0	4	0.0
Derek King, St. Louis	19	2	7	9	6	0	1	0	29	6.9
Totals	22	2	7	9	8	-2	1	0	33	6.1
Mike Knuble, N.Y. Rangers	59	9	5	14	18	-5	1	0	50	18.0
Mike Knuble, Boston	14	3	3	6	8	-2	1	0	28	10.7
Totals	73	12	8	20	26	-7	2	0	78	15.4
Sergei Krivokrasov, Nashville	63	9	17	26	40	-7	3	0	132	6.8
Sergei Krivokrasov, Calgary	12	1	10	11	4	2	0	0	27	3.7
Totals	75	10	27	37	44	-5	3	0	159	6.3
Christian Laflamme, Edmonton	50	0	5	5	32	-4	0	0	18	0.0
Christian Laflamme, Montreal	15	0	2	2	8	-5	0	0	6	0.0
Totals	65	0	7	7	40	-9	0	0	24	0.0
Janne Laukkanen, Ottawa	60	1	11	12	55	14	0	0	62	1.6
Janne Laukkanen, Pittsburgh	11	1	7	8	12	3	1	0	19	5.3
Totals	71	2	18	20	67	17	1	0	81	2.5
Claude Lemieux, Colorado	13	3	6	9	4	0	0	0	36	8.3
Claude Lemieux, New Jersey	70	17	21	38	86	-3	7	0	221	7.7
Totals	83	20	27	47	90	-3	7	0	257	7.8

	Games	G	A	Pts.	PIM	+/–	PPG	SHG	Shots	Shooting Pct.
Juha Lind, Dallas	34	3	4	7	6	-1	0	0	36	8.3
Juha Lind, Montreal	13	1	2	3	4	-2	0	0	6	16.7
Totals	47	4	6	10	10	-3	0	0	42	9.5
Vladimir Malakhov, Montreal	7	0	0	0	4	0	0	0	7	0.0
Vladimir Malakhov, New Jersey	17	1	4	5	19	1	1	0	11	9.1
Totals	24	1	4	5	23	1	1	0	18	5.6
Kent Manderville, Carolina	56	1	4	5	12	-8	0	0	45	2.2
Kent Manderville, Philadelphia	13	0	3	3	4	2	0	0	17	0.0
Totals	69	1	7	8	16	-6	0	0	62	1.6
Dave Manson, Chicago	37	0	7	7	40	2	0	0	45	0.0
Dave Manson, Dallas	26	1	2	3	22	10	0	0	21	4.8
Totals	63	1	9	10	62	12	0	0	66	1.5
Steve Martins, Ottawa	2	1	0	1	0	-1	0	0	3	33.3
Steve Martins, Tampa Bay	57	5	7	12	37	-11	0	1	62	8.1
Totals	59	6	7	13	37	-12	0	1	65	9.2
Chris McAlpine, St. Louis	21	1	1	2	14	1	0	0	25	4.0
Chris McAlpine, Tampa Bay	10	1	1	2	10	-5	0	0	5	20.0
Chris McAlpine, Atlanta	3	0	0	0	2	-4	0	0	4	0.0
Totals	34	2	2	4	26	-8	0	0	34	5.9
Sandy McCarthy, Philadelphia	58	6	5	11	111	-5	1	0	68	8.8
Sandy McCarthy, Carolina	13	0	0	0	9	2	0	0	12	0.0
Totals	71	6	5	11	120	-3	1	0	80	7.5
Jim McKenzie, Anaheim	31	3	3	6	48	-5	0	0	22	13.6
Jim McKenzie, Washington	30	1	2	3	16	0	0	0	10	10.0
Totals	61	4	5	9	64	-5	0	0	32	12.5
Kip Miller, Pittsburgh	44	4	15	19	10	-1	0	0	50	8.0
Kip Miller, Anaheim	30	6	17	23	4	1	2	0	32	18.8
Totals	74	10	32	42	14	0	2	0	82	12.2
Alexander Mogilny, Vancouver	47	21	17	38	16	7	3	1	126	16.7
Alexander Mogilny, New Jersey	12	3	3	6	4	-4	2	0	35	8.6
Totals	59	24	20	44	20	3	5	1	161	14.9
Brendan Morrison, New Jersey	44	5	21	26	8	8	2	0	79	6.3
Brendan Morrison, Vancouver	12	2	7	9	10	4	0	0	17	11.8
Totals	56	7	28	35	18	12	2	0	96	7.3
Bill Muckalt, Vancouver	33	4	8	12	17	6	1	0	53	7.5
Bill Muckalt, N.Y. Islanders	12	4	3	7	4	5	0	0	26	15.4
Totals	45	8	11	19	21	11	1	0	79	10.1
Bryan Muir, Chicago	11	2	3	5	13	-1	0	1	19	10.5
Bryan Muir, Tampa Bay	30	1	1	2	32	-8	0	0	32	3.1
Totals	41	3	4	7	45	-9	0	1	51	5.9
Joe Murphy, Boston	26	7	7	14	41	-7	3	0	68	10.3
Joe Murphy, Washington	29	5	8	13	53	8	1	0	50	10.0
Totals	55	12	15	27	94	1	4	0	118	10.2
Michael Nylander, Tampa Bay	11	1	2	3	4	-3	1	0	10	10.0
Michael Nylander, Chicago	66	23	28	51	26	9	4	0	112	20.5
Totals	77	24	30	54	30	6	5	0	122	19.7
Lyle Odelein, New Jersey	57	1	15	16	104	-10	0	0	59	1.7
Lyle Odelein, Phoenix	16	1	7	8	19	1	1	0	30	3.3
Totals	73	2	22	24	123	-9	1	0	89	2.2
Gino Odjick, N.Y. Islanders	46	5	10	15	90	-7	0	0	91	5.5
Gino Odjick, Philadelphia	13	3	1	4	10	2	0	0	24	12.5
Totals	59	8	11	19	100	-5	0	0	115	7.0
Denis Pederson, New Jersey	35	3	3	6	16	-7	0	0	41	7.3
Denis Pederson, Vancouver	12	3	2	5	2	1	0	0	15	20.0
Totals	47	6	5	11	18	-6	0	0	56	10.7
Richard Pilon, N.Y. Islanders	9	0	2	2	34	-2	0	0	0	0.0
Richard Pilon, N.Y. Rangers	45	0	4	4	36	0	0	0	16	0.0
Totals	54	0	6	6	70	-2	0	0	16	0.0
Derek Plante, Dallas	16	1	1	2	2	-4	1	0	17	5.9
Derek Plante, Chicago	17	1	1	2	2	-1	0	0	14	7.1
Totals	33	2	2	4	4	-5	1	0	31	6.5
Felix Potvin, N.Y. Islanders (goalie)	22	0	0	0	2	0	0	0	0	0.0
Felix Potvin, Vancouver (goalie)	34	0	2	2	2	0	0	0	0	0.0
Totals	56	0	2	2	4	0	0	0	0	0.0
Wayne Primeau, Buffalo	41	5	7	12	38	-8	2	0	40	12.5
Wayne Primeau, Tampa Bay	17	2	3	5	25	-4	0	0	35	5.7
Totals	58	7	10	17	63	-12	2	0	75	9.3
Deron Quint, Phoenix	50	3	7	10	22	0	0	0	88	3.4
Deron Quint, New Jersey	4	1	0	1	2	-2	0	0	6	16.7
Totals	54	4	7	11	24	-2	0	0	94	4.3
Mikael Renberg, Philadelphia	62	8	21	29	30	-1	3	0	106	7.5

	Games	G	A	Pts.	PIM	+/−	PPG	SHG	Shots	Shooting Pct.
Mikael Renberg, Phoenix	10	2	4	6	2	0	0	0	16	12.5
Totals	72	10	25	35	32	−1	3	0	122	8.2
Stephane Richer, Tampa Bay	20	7	5	12	4	2	1	0	47	14.9
Stephane Richer, St. Louis	36	8	17	25	14	7	4	0	63	12.7
Totals	56	15	22	37	18	9	5	0	110	13.6
Brian Rolston, New Jersey	11	3	1	4	0	−2	1	0	33	9.1
Brian Rolston, Colorado	50	8	10	18	12	−6	1	0	107	7.5
Brian Rolston, Boston	16	5	4	9	6	−4	3	0	66	7.6
Totals	77	16	15	31	18	−12	5	0	206	7.8
Cory Sarich, Buffalo	42	0	4	4	35	2	0	0	49	0.0
Cory Sarich, Tampa Bay	17	0	2	2	42	−8	0	0	20	0.0
Totals	59	0	6	6	77	−6	0	0	69	0.0
Dave Scatchard, Vancouver	21	0	4	4	24	−3	0	0	25	0.0
Dave Scatchard, N.Y. Islanders	44	12	14	26	93	0	0	1	103	11.7
Totals	65	12	18	30	117	−3	0	1	128	9.4
Darryl Shannon, Atlanta	49	5	13	18	65	−14	1	0	66	7.6
Darryl Shannon, Calgary	27	1	8	9	22	−13	0	0	46	2.2
Totals	76	6	21	27	87	−27	1	0	112	5.4
Vadim Sharifijanov, New Jersey	20	3	4	7	8	−6	0	0	20	15.0
Vadim Sharifijanov, Vancouver	17	2	1	3	14	−7	1	0	26	7.7
Totals	37	5	5	10	22	−13	1	0	46	10.9
Mikhail Shtalenkov, Phoenix (goalie)	15	0	3	3	2	0	0	0	0	0.0
Mikhail Shtalenkov, Florida (goalie)	15	0	0	0	2	0	0	0	0	0.0
Totals	30	0	3	3	4	0	0	0	0	0.0
Mike Sillinger, Tampa Bay	67	19	25	44	86	−29	6	3	126	15.1
Mike Sillinger, Florida	13	4	4	8	16	−1	2	0	20	20.0
Totals	80	23	29	52	102	−30	8	3	146	15.8
Sheldon Souray, New Jersey	52	0	8	8	70	−6	0	0	74	0.0
Sheldon Souray, Montreal	19	3	0	3	44	7	0	0	39	7.7
Totals	71	3	8	11	114	1	0	0	113	2.7
Steve Sullivan, Toronto	7	0	1	1	4	−1	0	0	11	0.0
Steve Sullivan, Chicago	73	22	42	64	52	20	2	1	169	13.0
Totals	80	22	43	65	56	19	2	1	180	12.2
Jaroslav Svejkovsky, Washington	23	1	2	3	2	−7	1	0	18	5.6
Jaroslav Svejkovsky, Tampa Bay	29	5	5	10	28	−7	0	0	42	11.9
Totals	52	6	7	13	30	−14	1	0	60	10.0
Rick Tabaracci, Atlanta (goalie)	1	0	0	0	0	0	0	0	0	0.0
Rick Tabaracci, Colorado (goalie)	2	0	0	0	0	0	0	0	0	0.0
Totals	3	0	0	0	0	0	0	0	0	0.0
Scott Thornton, Montreal	35	2	3	5	70	−7	0	0	36	5.6
Scott Thornton, Dallas	30	6	3	9	38	−5	1	0	47	12.8
Totals	65	8	6	14	108	−12	1	0	83	9.6
German Titov, Pittsburgh	63	17	25	42	34	−3	4	2	111	15.3
German Titov, Edmonton	7	0	4	4	4	2	0	0	11	0.0
Totals	70	17	29	46	38	−1	4	2	122	13.9
Rick Tocchet, Phoenix	64	12	17	29	67	−5	2	0	107	11.2
Rick Tocchet, Philadelphia	16	3	3	6	23	4	2	0	23	13.0
Totals	80	15	20	35	90	−1	4	0	130	11.5
Pavel Torgaev, Calgary	9	0	2	2	4	0	0	0	12	0.0
Pavel Torgaev, Tampa Bay	5	0	2	2	2	1	0	0	6	0.0
Totals	14	0	4	4	6	1	0	0	18	0.0
Vladimir Tsyplakov, Los Angeles	29	6	7	13	4	6	1	0	30	20.0
Vladimir Tsyplakov, Buffalo	34	6	13	19	10	17	0	0	46	13.0
Totals	63	12	20	32	14	23	1	0	76	15.8
Darcy Tucker, Tampa Bay	50	14	20	34	108	−15	1	0	98	14.3
Darcy Tucker, Toronto	27	7	10	17	55	3	0	2	40	17.5
Totals	77	21	30	51	163	−12	1	2	138	15.2
Ron Tugnutt, Ottawa (goalie)	44	0	0	0	0	0	0	0	0	0.0
Ron Tugnutt, Pittsburgh (goalie)	7	0	0	0	0	0	0	0	0	0.0
Totals	51	0	0	0	0	0	0	0	0	0.0
Igor Ulanov, Montreal	43	1	5	6	76	−11	0	0	33	3.0
Igor Ulanov, Edmonton	14	0	3	3	10	−3	0	0	6	0.0
Totals	57	1	8	9	86	−14	0	0	39	2.6
Mike Vernon, San Jose (goalie)	15	0	0	0	0	0	0	0	0	0.0
Mike Vernon, Florida (goalie)	34	0	3	3	2	0	0	0	0	0.0
Totals	49	0	3	3	2	0	0	0	0	0.0
Ed Ward, Atlanta	44	5	1	6	44	−5	0	2	51	9.8
Ed Ward, Anaheim	8	1	0	1	15	−2	0	0	5	20.0
Totals	52	6	1	7	59	−7	0	2	56	10.7
Todd Warriner, Toronto	18	3	1	4	2	6	0	0	33	9.1
Todd Warriner, Tampa Bay	55	11	13	24	34	−14	3	1	100	11.0
Totals	73	14	14	28	36	−8	3	1	133	10.5

	Games	G	A	Pts.	PIM	+/−	PPG	SHG	Shots	Shooting Pct.
Kevin Weekes, Vancouver (goalie)	20	0	0	0	0	0	0	0	0	0.0
Kevin Weekes, N.Y. Islanders (goalie)	36	0	1	1	0	0	0	0	1	0.0
Totals	56	0	1	1	0	0	0	0	1	0.0
Brad Werenka, Pittsburgh	61	3	8	11	69	15	0	0	42	7.1
Brad Werenka, Calgary	12	1	1	2	21	-2	0	0	20	5.0
Totals	73	4	9	13	90	13	0	0	62	6.5
Todd White, Chicago	1	0	0	0	0	0	0	0	0	0.0
Todd White, Philadelphia	3	1	0	1	0	-1	0	0	4	25.0
Totals	4	1	0	1	0	-1	0	0	4	25.0
Terry Yake, St. Louis	26	4	9	13	22	2	2	0	26	15.4
Terry Yake, Washington	35	6	5	11	12	2	1	0	29	20.7
Totals	61	10	14	24	34	4	3	0	55	18.2

GOALTENDING

	Games	Min.	Goals	SO	Avg.	W	L	T	ENG	Shots	Sv. Pct.
Tom Barrasso, Pittsburgh	18	870	46	1	3.17	5	7	2	2	386	.881
Tom Barrasso, Ottawa	7	418	22	0	3.16	3	4	0	0	182	.879
Totals	25	1288	68	1	3.17	8	11	2	2	568	.880
Sean Burke, Florida	7	418	18	0	2.58	2	5	0	2	208	.913
Sean Burke, Phoenix	35	2074	88	3	2.55	17	14	3	1	1022	.914
Totals	42	2492	106	3	2.55	19	19	3	3	1230	.914
Felix Potvin, N.Y. Islanders	22	1273	68	1	3.21	5	14	3	3	632	.892
Felix Potvin, Vancouver	34	1966	85	0	2.59	12	13	7	4	906	.906
Totals	56	3239	153	1	2.83	17	27	10	7	1538	.901
Mikhail Shtalenko, Phoenix	15	904	36	2	2.39	7	6	2	3	370	.903
Mikhail Shtalenko, Florida	15	882	34	0	2.31	8	4	2	0	369	.908
Totals	30	1786	70	2	2.35	15	10	4	3	739	.905
Rick Tabaracci, Atlanta	1	59	4	0	4.07	0	1	0	0	32	.875
Rick Tabaracci, Colorado	2	60	2	0	2.00	1	0	0	0	18	.889
Totals	3	119	6	0	3.03	1	1	0	0	50	.880
Ron Tugnutt, Ottawa	44	2435	103	4	2.54	18	12	8	2	1020	.899
Ron Tugnutt, Pittsburgh	7	374	15	0	2.41	4	2	0	0	197	.924
Totals	51	2809	118	4	2.52	22	14	8	2	1217	.903
Mike Vernon, San Jose	15	772	32	0	2.49	6	5	1	0	360	.911
Mike Vernon, Florida	34	2019	83	1	2.47	18	13	2	2	1020	.919
Totals	49	2791	115	1	2.47	24	18	3	2	1380	.917
Kevin Weekes, Vancouver	20	987	47	1	2.86	6	7	4	3	461	.898
Kevin Weekes, N.Y. Islanders	36	2026	115	1	3.41	10	20	4	3	1173	.902
Totals	56	3013	162	2	3.23	16	27	8	6	1634	.901

MISCELLANEOUS

HAT TRICKS

(Players scoring three or more goals in a game)

Date	Player, Team	Opp.	Goals	Date	Player, Team	Opp.	Goals
10-4-99—	Jeff Friesen, San Jose	Chi.	3	1-4-00—	Sergei Gonchar, Washington	Mon.	3
10-4-99—	Owen Nolan, San Jose	Chi.	3	1-5-00—	Adam Deadmarsh, Colorado	Cal.	3
10-7-99—	Alexei Morozov, Pittsburgh	N.J.	3	1-5-00—	Viktor Kozlov, Florida	Ana.	3
10-7-99—	Luc Robitaille, Los Angeles	T.B.	3	1-8-00—	Petr Nedved, N.Y. Rangers	Tor.	3
10-8-99—	Brian Savage, Montreal	Cal.	3	1-8-00—	Miroslav Satan, Buffalo	Ott.	3
10-12-99—	Peter Bondra, Washington	Phi.	3	1-24-00—	Petr Nedved, N.Y. Rangers	Atl.	3
10-14-99—	Brian Savage, Montreal	Phi.	3	1-31-00—	Radek Dvorak, N.Y. Rangers	Nash.	3
10-16-99—	Glen Murray, Los Angeles	Edm.	3	2-8-00—	Trevor Linden, Montreal	Edm.	3
10-28-99—	Dave Andreychuk, Boston	T.B.	4	2-11-00—	Jan Hlavac, N.Y. Rangers	Bos.	3
11-10-99—	Robert Valicevic, Nashville	Chi.	3	2-12-00—	Pavol Demitra, St. Louis	Ana.	3
11-14-99—	Alex Selivanov, Edmonton	Chi.	4	2-18-00—	Shjon Podein, Colorado	NYR	3
11-22-99—	Dean Sylvester, Atlanta	Van.	3	2-21-00—	Georges Laraque, Edmonton	L.A.	3
11-25-99—	Jeremy Roenick, Phoenix	N.J.	3	2-25-00—	Petr Nedved, N.Y. Rangers	Buf.	3
11-26-99—	Jaromir Jagr, Pittsburgh	Ott.	3	2-25-00—	Michael Peca, Buffalo	NYR	3
11-26-99—	Jeremy Roenick, Phoenix	Col.	3	2-25-00—	Stephane Richer, St. Louis	Col.	3
11-26-99—	Teemu Selanne, Anaheim	Dal.	3	3-7-00—	Joe Sakic, Colorado	Cal.	3
12-2-99—	Pierre Turgeon, St. Louis	Nash.	3	3-8-00—	Bates Battaglia, Carolina	Chi.	3
12-4-99—	Michael Nylander, Chicago	Bos.	4	3-12-00—	Tony Amonte, Chicago	T.B.	3
12-6-99—	Sandis Ozolinsh, Colorado	Van.	3	3-13-00—	Ryan Smyth, Edmonton	Atl.	3
12-8-99—	Pavel Bure, Florida	Pho.	3	3-17-00—	Boyd Devereaux, Edmonton	Ott.	3
12-9-99—	Eric Lindros, Philadelphia	Tor.	3	3-18-00—	Pavel Bure, Florida	NYI	3
12-17-99—	Pavel Bure, Florida	Buf.	3	3-23-00—	Joe Sakic, Colorado	Pho.	3
12-20-99—	Nik Antropov, Toronto	Fla.	3	3-26-00—	Martin Lapointe, Detroit	NYR	3
12-21-99—	Mike Eastwood, St. Louis	Pho.	3	4-5-00—	Marc Savard, Calgary	St.L.	4
12-26-99—	Scott Gomez, New Jersey	NYR	3	4-8-00—	Alex Selivanov, Edmonton	Cal.	3
12-30-99—	Jaromir Jagr, Pittsburgh	NYI	3	4-9-00—	Mariusz Czerkawski, N.Y. Islanders	Fla.	3
1-1-00—	Pavel Bure, Florida	T.B.	4				

1999-2000 NHL REVIEW *Regular season*

1999-2000 NHL REVIEW *Regular season*

Date	Player, Team	Opponent	Time	Final score
10-7-99	Mike Ricci, San Jose	Edmonton	3:44	San Jose 3, Edmonton 2
10-13-99	Valeri Bure, Calgary	Vancouver	3:05	Calgary 4, Vancouver 3
10-14-99	Brian Savage, Montreal	Philadelphia	3:22	Montreal 5, Philadelphia 4
10-16-99	Jaroslav Spacek, Florida	Anaheim	1:26	Florida 3, Anaheim 2
10-19-99	Mark Messier, Vancouver	Tampa Bay	0:43	Vancouver 6, Tampa Bay 5
10-21-99	Jeff Finley, St. Louis	Edmonton	0:19	St. Louis 3, Edmonton 2
10-22-99	Sergei Zubov, Dallas	New Jersey	0:32	Dallas 2, New Jersey 1
10-22-99	Derek Morris, Calgary	Florida	0:20	Calgary 3, Florida 2
10-23-99	Joe Sakic, Colorado	Atlanta	0:40	Colorado 3, Atlanta 2
10-27-99	Teemu Selanne, Anaheim	Pittsburgh	3:38	Anaheim 2, Pittsburgh 1
10-28-99	Jeff Shantz, Calgary	Ottawa	3:07	Calgary 4, Ottawa 3
10-28-99	Valeri Zelepukin, Philadelphia	Colorado	4:51	Philadelphia 5, Colorado 4
10-29-99	Geoff Sanderson, Buffalo	Florida	4:54	Buffalo 3, Florida 2
10-30-99	Pavol Demitra, St. Louis	Detroit	0:56	St. Louis 5, Detroit 4
11-3-99	Tommy Albelin, Calgary	Nashville	4:56	Calgary 5, Nashville 4
11-4-99	Curtis Brown, Buffalo	Chicago	1:14	Buffalo 5, Chicago 4
11-4-99	Jamie Heward, N.Y. Islanders	Montreal	0:47	N.Y. Islanders 2, Montreal 1
11-10-99	Cory Stillman, Calgary	San Jose	4:23	Calgary 4, San Jose 3
11-10-99	Jyrki Lumme, Phoenix	Edmonton	1:51	Phoenix 5, Edmonton 4
11-11-99	P.J. Axelsson, Boston	Toronto	3:58	Boston 4, Toronto 3
11-11-99	Tim Taylor, N.Y. Rangers	Washington	1:04	N.Y. Rangers 5, Washington 4
11-12-99	Sergei Fedorov, Detroit	Pittsburgh	0:36	Detroit 3, Pittsburgh 2
11-20-99	Mike Wilson, Florida	Pittsburgh	2:57	Florida 2, Pittsburgh 1
11-20-99	Igor Korolev, Toronto	N.Y. Rangers	1:16	Toronto 4, N.Y. Rangers 3
11-22-99	Adam Deadmarsh, Colorado	Dallas	0:34	Colorado 3, Dallas 2
11-22-99	Mike Eastwood, St. Louis	Nashville	2:39	St. Louis 3, Nashville 2
11-23-99	Craig Rivet, Montreal	San Jose	3:50	Montreal 3, San Jose 2
11-24-99	Richard Matvichuk, Dallas	Los Angeles	2:55	Dallas 3, Los Angeles 2
11-25-99	Cory Stillman, Calgary	Chicago	2:05	Calgary 2, Chicago 1
11-26-99	Mark Recchi, Philadelphia	Toronto	4:08	Philadelphia 3, Toronto 2
11-28-99	Patrick Marleau, San Jose	New Jersey	4:54	San Jose 4, New Jersey 3
11-28-99	Michal Grosek, Buffalo	Tampa Bay	2:26	Buffalo 3, Tampa Bay 2
12-2-99	Todd Bertuzzi, Vancouver	Edmonton	1:51	Vancouver 3, Edmonton 2
12-4-99	Mats Sundin, Toronto	Pittsburgh	0:27	Toronto 3, Pittsburgh 2
12-6-99	Randy Robitaille, Nashville	Atlanta	2:26	Nashville 4, Atlanta 3
12-6-99	Tim Taylor, N.Y. Rangers	Calgary	0:32	N.Y. Rangers 3, Calgary 2
12-6-99	Steve Thomas, Toronto	Buffalo	1:05	Toronto 3, Buffalo 2
12-8-99	Adam Graves, N.Y. Rangers	Edmonton	3:15	N.Y. Rangers 2, Edmonton 1
12-12-99	Milan Hejduk, Colorado	Vancouver	1:36	Colorado 3, Vancouver 2
12-17-99	Calle Johansson, Washington	N.Y. Rangers	0:31	Washington 3, N.Y. Rangers 2
12-19-99	Theoren Fleury, N.Y. Rangers	Tampa Bay	0:45	N.Y. Rangers 5, Tampa Bay 4
12-26-99	Nolan Pratt, Carolina	Florida	0:27	Carolina 4, Florida 3
12-26-99	Jeremy Roenick, Phoenix	Los Angeles	3:18	Phoenix 3, Los Angeles 2
12-27-99	Steve Duchesne, Detroit	Atlanta	3:21	Detroit 3, Atlanta 2
12-29-99	Jamie Langenbrunner, Dallas	N.Y. Rangers	3:17	Dallas 4, N.Y. Rangers 3
12-29-99	Patrik Elias, New Jersey	Boston	0:19	New Jersey 5, Boston 4
12-29-99	Adam Burt, Philadelphia	Vancouver	2:34	Philadelphia 3, Vancouver 2
12-29-99	Adam Oates, Washington	Pittsburgh	4:32	Washington 3, Pittsburgh 2
12-30-99	Jason York, Ottawa	Boston	1:23	Ottawa 5, Boston 4
12-30-99	Al MacInnis, St. Louis	San Jose	3:40	St. Louis 2, San Jose 1
1-3-00	Brendan Morrison, New Jersey	Ottawa	2:52	New Jersey 4, Ottawa 3
1-5-00	Adam Graves, N.Y. Rangers	Toronto	4:26	N.Y. Rangers 3, Toronto 2
1-8-00	Phil Housley, Calgary	Tampa Bay	4:28	Calgary 3, Tampa Bay 2
1-12-00	Jason Wiemer, Calgary	Dallas	2:03	Calgary 2, Dallas 1
1-12-00	Sylvain Cote, Chicago	Vancouver	3:16	Chicago 3, Vancouver 2
1-13-00	Mark Messier, Vancouver	Nashville	3:29	Vancouver 4, Nashville 3
1-14-00	Mats Sundin, Toronto	Edmonton	2:59	Toronto 3, Edmonton 2
1-14-00	Adam Oates, Washington	New Jersey	4:37	Washington 3, New Jersey 2
1-15-00	Jeff Friesen, San Jose	Los Angeles	1:05	San Jose 3, Los Angeles 2
1-17-00	Doug Gilmour, Chicago	San Jose	0:56	Chicago 5, San Jose 4
1-17-00	Marian Hossa, Ottawa	N.Y. Islanders	3:57	Ottawa 4, N.Y. Islanders 3
1-17-00	Steve Thomas, Toronto	Vancouver	4:55	Toronto 5, Vancouver 4
1-21-00	Valeri Bure, Calgary	Nashville	3:06	Calgary 5, Nashville 4
1-22-00	Pavel Bure, Florida	Boston	1:31	Florida 4, Boston 3
1-23-00	Jyrki Lumme, Phoenix	San Jose	4:16	Phoenix 3, San Jose 2
1-24-00	Marc Savard, Calgary	Boston	1:56	Calgary 4, Boston 3
1-24-00	Marek Malik, Carolina	Montreal	0:55	Carolina 3, Montreal 2
1-24-00	Sergei Krivokrasov, Nashville	Edmonton	1:19	Nashville 3, Edmonton 2
1-25-00	Ethan Moreau, Edmonton	Vancouver	4:00	Edmonton 5, Vancouver 4
1-28-00	Jeff O'Neill, Carolina	New Jersey	0:16	Carolina 4, New Jersey 3
1-28-00	Calle Johansson, Washington	Phoenix	4:59	Washington 3, Phoenix 2

Date	Player, Team	Opponent	Time	Final score
1-29-00	Mathieu Biron, N.Y. Islanders	San Jose	2:43	N.Y. Islanders 3, San Jose 2
1-31-00	Robert Lang, Pittsburgh	Atlanta	4:28	Pittsburgh 2, Atlanta 1
2-1-00	Pavol Demitra, St. Louis	Calgary	2:02	St. Louis 5, Calgary 4
2-1-00	Keith Carney, Phoenix	San Jose	1:32	Phoenix 1, San Jose 0
2-3-00	Martin Rucinsky, Montreal	Tampa Bay	0:31	Montreal 2, Tampa Bay 1
2-8-00	Jason Smith, Edmonton	Montreal	3:04	Edmonton 5, Montreal 4
2-9-00	Mattias Ohlund, Vancouver	Calgary	1:22	Vancouver 4, Calgary 3
2-10-00	Jason Woolley, Buffalo	Nashville	4:08	Buffalo 2, Nashville 1
2-10-00	Tim Connolly, N.Y. Islanders	Tampa Bay	3:49	N.Y. Islanders 5, Tampa Bay 4
2-12-00	John LeClair, Philadelphia	Buffalo	2:28	Philadelphia 3, Buffalo 2
2-14-00	Sean O'Donnell, Los Angeles	Calgary	1:42	Los Angeles 4, Calgary 3
2-16-00	Oleg Tverdovsky, Anaheim	Calgary	1:40	Anaheim 6, Calgary 5
2-19-00	Marc Savard, Calgary	Edmonton	0:35	Calgary 3, Edmonton 2
2-23-00	Chris Simon, Washington	Florida	0:55	Washington 3, Florida 2
2-24-00	Benoit Brunet, Montreal	New Jersey	0:58	Montreal 3, New Jersey 2
2-24-00	Luke Richardson, Philadelphia	Pittsburgh	4:51	Philadelphia 4, Pittsburgh 3
2-25-00	Doug Gilmour, Chicago	Dallas	1:11	Chicago 4, Dallas 3
2-26-00	Jeff O'Neill, Carolina	Florida	2:28	Carolina 2, Florida 1
3-4-00	Jozef Stumpel, Los Angeles	Nashville	0:28	Los Angeles 3, Nashville 2
3-5-00	Mariusz Czerkawski, N.Y. Islanders	Philadelphia	0:59	N.Y. Islanders 4, Philadelphia 3
3-6-00	Mats Sundin, Toronto	Vancouver	3:13	Toronto 6, Vancouver 5
3-8-00	Brian Leetch, N.Y. Rangers	Anaheim	0:29	N.Y. Rangers 4, Anaheim 3
3-8-00	Stu Barnes, Buffalo	Boston	1:54	Buffalo 2, Boston 1
3-8-00	Eric Desjardins, Philadelphia	Tampa Bay	3:49	Philadelphia 3, Tampa Bay 2
3-10-00	Olli Jokinen, N.Y. Islanders	Dallas	3:32	N.Y. Islanders 4, Dallas 3
3-13-00	Jozef Stumpel, Los Angeles	Vancouver	3:53	Los Angeles 3, Vancouver 2
3-14-00	Brendan Shanahan, Detroit	Nashville	4:10	Detroit 3, Nashville 2
3-15-00	Jeff Friesen, San Jose	Buffalo	2:56	San Jose 6, Buffalo 5
3-16-00	Steve Sullivan, Chicago	Boston	1:39	Chicago 5, Boston 4
3-16-00	Mats Sundin, Toronto	Detroit	1:38	Toronto 4, Detroit 3
3-17-00	Greg Johnson, Nashville	Phoenix	3:56	Nashville 4, Phoenix 3
3-19-00	Cliff Ronning, Nashville	Los Angeles	0:51	Nashville 2, Los Angeles 1
3-23-00	Jozef Stumpel, Los Angeles	Philadelphia	1:20	Los Angeles 3, Philadelphia 2
3-26-00	Oleg Tverdovsky, Anaheim	Phoenix	3:47	Anaheim 4, Phoenix 3
3-26-00	Milan Hejduk, Colorado	Dallas	3:17	Colorado 2, Dallas 1
3-30-00	Hans Jonsson, Pittsburgh	Washington	2:25	Pittsburgh 4, Washington 3
4-1-00	Tom Poti, Edmonton	Phoenix	3:07	Edmonton 4, Phoenix 3
4-2-00	Shjon Podein, Colorado	Dallas	4:13	Colorado 3, Dallas 2
4-2-00	Martin Lapointe, Detroit	Montreal	4:45	Detroit 6, Montreal 5
4-7-00	Jaromir Jagr, Pittsburgh	Buffalo	0:13	Pittsburgh 2, Buffalo 1
4-7-00	Alexei Zhamnov, Chicago	St. Louis	3:35	Chicago 4, St. Louis 3
4-7-00	Rem Murray, Edmonton	Vancouver	4:01	Edmonton 5, Vancouver 4
4-8-00	Jason Arnott, New Jersey	Florida	0:47	New Jersey 2, Florida 1
4-9-00	Glen Murray, Los Angeles	Anaheim	1:06	Los Angeles 4, Anaheim 3

PENALTY-SHOT INFORMATION

Date	Shooter, Team	Goaltender, Team	Scored	Final score
10-9-99	Miroslav Satan, Buffalo	Damian Rhodes, Atlanta	Yes	Buffalo 5, Atlanta 5
10-15-99	Stan Drulia, Tampa Bay	Dominic Roussel, Anaheim	No	Anaheim 3, Tampa Bay 2
10-16-99	Doug Gilmour, Chicago	Peter Skudra, Pittsburgh	No	Chicago 3, Pittsburgh 3
10-24-99	Mike Ricci, San Jose	Stephane Fiset, Los Angeles	No	Los Angeles 4, San Jose 3
10-27-99	Teemu Selanne, Anaheim	Jean-Sebastien Aubin, Pittsburgh	No	Anaheim 2, Pittsburgh 1
10-30-99	Valeri Zelepukin, Philadelphia	Martin Brodeur, New Jersey	No	Philadelphia 5, New Jersey 3
11-11-99	Richard Zednik, Washington	Mike Richter, N.Y. Rangers	No	N.Y. Rangers 5, Washington 4
11-18-99	Terry Yake, St. Louis	Sean Burke, Florida	No	St. Louis 5, Florida 0
11-18-99	Kimmo Timonen, Nashville	Jeff Hackett, Montreal	Yes	Nashville 6, Montreal 1
11-24-99	Fredrik Olausson, Anaheim	Martin Brodeur, New Jersey	Yes	New Jersey 2, Anaheim 1
11-30-99	Andrew Cassels, Vancouver	Patrick Roy, Colorado	No	Colorado 4, Vancouver 2
12-2-99	Jeremy Roenick, Phoenix	Dan Cloutier, Tampa Bay	Yes	Phoenix 3, Tampa Bay 1
12-11-99	Martin Rucinsky, Montreal	Jamie Storr, Los Angeles	No	Los Angeles 4, Montreal 2
12-28-99	Miroslav Satan, Buffalo	Ken Wregget, Detroit	No	Detroit 7, Buffalo 2
12-30-99	Jeff Friesen, San Jose	Roman Turek, St. Louis	No	St. Louis 2, San Jose 1
12-30-99	Pierre Turgeon, St. Louis	Steve Shields, San Jose	No	St. Louis 2, San Jose 1
1-6-00	Petr Sykora, New Jersey	Dwayne Roloson, Buffalo	Yes	New Jersey 6, Buffalo 3
1-7-00	Mike Sillinger, Tampa Bay	Tommy Salo, Edmonton	No	Edmonton 5, Tampa Bay 1
1-8-00	Daniel Alfredsson, Ottawa	Martin Biron, Buffalo	No	Buffalo 7, Ottawa 4
1-10-00	Brad Ibister, N.Y. Islanders	Sean Burke, Phoenix	Yes	N.Y. Islanders 2, Phoenix 2
1-11-00	Alexander Korolyuk, San Jose	Roman Turek, St. Louis	Yes	St. Louis 5, San Jose 2
1-12-00	Claude Lapointe, N.Y. Islanders	Mike Vernon, Florida	No	Florida 4, N.Y. Islanders 3
1-12-00	Keith Tkachuk, Phoenix	Jean-Sebastien Aubin, Pittsburgh	No	Phoenix 3, Pittsburgh 1
1-13-00	Dan Kesa, Tampa Bay	Roberto Luongo, N.Y. Islanders	No	Tampa Bay 4, N.Y. Islanders 2
1-19-00	Martin Straka, Pittsburgh	Roman Turek, St. Louis	Yes	Pittsburgh 3, St. Louis 1
1-31-00	Randy Robitaille, Nashville	Mike Richter, N.Y. Rangers	No	N.Y. Rangers 5, Nashville 1

Date	Shooter, Team	Goaltender, Team	Scored	Final score
2-14-00—	Kevyn Adams, Toronto	Arturs Irbe, Carolina	No	Carolina 5, Toronto 2
2-23-00—	Viktor Kozlov, Florida	Olaf Kolzig, Washington	Yes	Washington 3, Florida 2
2-29-00—	John Madden, New Jersey	Mike Dunham, Nashville	No	New Jersey 2, Nashville 1
3-4-00—	Daniel Alfredsson, Ottawa	Scott Langkow, Atlanta	Yes	Ottawa 3, Atlanta 2
3-4-00—	Miroslav Satan, Buffalo	Kevin Weekes, N.Y. Islanders	No	N.Y. Islanders 4, Buffalo 2
3-4-00—	Olli Jokinen, N.Y. Islanders	Dominik Hasek, Buffalo	Yes	N.Y. Islanders 4, Buffalo 2
3-10-00—	Patrik Elias, New Jersey	Damian Rhodes, Atlanta	Yes	New Jersey 9, Atlanta 0
3-11-00—	Sergei Nemchinov, New Jersey	Olaf Kolzig, Washington	No	Washington 4, New Jersey 2
3-13-00—	Radek Dvorak, N.Y. Rangers	Emmanuel Fernandez, Dallas	No	Dallas 4, N.Y. Rangers 3
3-16-00—	Brad Ibister, N.Y. Islanders	Damian Rhodes, Atlanta	No	N.Y. Islanders 4, Atlanta 2
3-17-00—	Jeremy Roenick, Phoenix	Tomas Vokoun, Nashville	Yes	Nashville 4, Phoenix 3
3-18-00—	Chris Drury, Colorado	Ken Wregget, Detroit	Yes	Detroit 4, Colorado 3
3-21-00—	Tim Connolly, N.Y. Islanders	Jean-Sebastien Aubin, Pittsburgh	Yes	Pittsburgh 8, N.Y. Islanders 2
4-1-00—	Ulf Dahlen, Washington	Curtis Joseph, Toronto	No	Toronto 4, Washington 3

TEAM STREAKS

Most consecutive games won
Phoenix, Nov. 16-Dec. 2	8
Colorado, Mar. 23-Apr. 9	8
N.Y. Rangers, Jan. 15-25	7
Montreal, Feb. 12-24	7
Seven streaks of	6

Most consecutive games undefeated
Washington, Jan. 8-30	11
New Jersey, Dec. 26-Jan. 11	9
Phoenix, Nov. 16-Dec. 2	8
Nashville, Dec. 18-Jan. 1	8
St. Louis, Dec. 30-Jan. 13	8
Detroit, Feb. 25-Mar. 14	8
Colorado, Mar. 23-Apr. 9	8

Most consecutive home games won
Washington, Jan. 4-Feb. 23	10
Buffalo, Oct. 22-Nov. 24	7
Calgary, Dec. 29-Jan. 21	7
New Jersey, Jan. 17-Feb. 15	7
Washington, Mar. 5-28	7

Most consecutive home games undefeated
Philadelphia, Oct. 28-Jan. 8	15
Washington, Dec. 27-Feb. 23	13
New Jersey, Oct. 9-Dec. 3	12
Colorado, Dec. 27-Feb. 3	12
Five streaks of	8

Most consecutive road games won
St. Louis, Jan. 21-Mar. 2	10
New Jersey, Jan. 3-26	6
Colorado, Mar. 7-Apr. 7	6
Anaheim, Nov. 26-Dec. 26	5
N.Y. Rangers, Jan. 15-25	5
Toronto, Mar. 6-16	5

Most consecutive road games undefeated
St. Louis, Jan. 21-Mar. 4	11
New Jersey, Dec. 26-Jan. 26	8
Detroit, Feb. 21-Mar. 18	7
Dallas, Feb. 23-Mar. 29	7
Colorado, Feb. 27-Apr. 7	7

TEAM OVERTIME GAMES

	OVERALL					HOME					AWAY				
Team	G	W	L	T	Pct.	G	W	L	T	Pct.	G	W	L	T	Pct.
Carolina	14	4	0	10	.643	8	3	0	5	.688	6	1	0	5	.583
N.Y. Islanders	15	5	1	9	.633	8	2	1	5	.563	7	3	0	4	.714
Toronto	17	7	3	7	.618	8	3	0	5	.688	9	4	3	2	.556
Colorado	17	5	1	11	.618	5	1	0	4	.600	12	4	1	7	.625
St. Louis	17	5	1	11	.618	12	4	1	7	.625	5	1	0	4	.600
Calgary	26	11	5	10	.615	13	6	1	6	.692	13	5	4	4	.538
Chicago	17	5	2	10	.588	9	3	1	5	.611	8	2	1	5	.563
Washington	19	5	2	12	.579	13	3	2	8	.538	6	2	0	4	.667
N.Y. Rangers	21	6	3	12	.571	10	4	1	5	.650	11	2	2	7	.500
Philadelphia	21	6	3	12	.571	14	4	3	7	.536	7	2	0	5	.643
Detroit	16	4	2	10	.563	8	4	1	3	.688	8	0	1	7	.438
Buffalo	20	5	4	11	.525	8	2	1	5	.563	12	3	3	6	.500
Los Angeles	21	5	4	12	.524	10	3	2	5	.550	11	2	2	7	.500
Anaheim	18	3	3	12	.500	12	3	2	7	.542	6	0	1	5	.417
Montreal	17	4	4	9	.500	7	1	1	5	.500	10	3	3	4	.500
Phoenix	16	4	4	8	.500	5	2	1	2	.600	11	2	3	6	.455
Ottawa	15	2	2	11	.500	8	1	2	5	.438	7	1	0	6	.571
New Jersey	16	3	5	8	.438	6	2	1	3	.583	10	1	4	5	.350
Edmonton	28	4	8	16	.429	13	1	3	9	.423	15	3	5	7	.433
San Jose	21	4	7	10	.429	10	4	3	3	.550	11	0	4	7	.318
Dallas	19	3	6	10	.421	12	3	4	5	.458	7	0	2	5	.357
Nashville	18	4	7	7	.417	5	0	2	3	.300	13	4	5	4	.462
Pittsburgh	17	3	6	8	.412	7	0	0	7	.500	10	3	6	1	.350
Vancouver	28	4	9	15	.411	14	2	7	5	.321	14	2	2	10	.500
Boston	26	1	6	19	.404	13	1	1	11	.500	13	0	5	8	.308
Florida	15	3	6	6	.400	9	3	2	4	.556	6	0	4	2	.167
Atlanta	11	0	4	7	.318	6	0	3	3	.250	5	0	1	4	.400
Tampa Bay	16	0	7	9	.281	8	0	4	4	.250	8	0	3	5	.313
Totals	261	115	115	146	—	261	65	50	146	.529	261	50	65	146	.471

STANLEY CUP PLAYOFFS

CONFERENCE QUARTERFINALS

EASTERN CONFERENCE

	W	L	Pts.	GF	GA
Philadelphia Flyers	4	1	8	14	8
Buffalo Sabres	1	4	2	8	14

(Philadelphia won Eastern Conference quarterfinals, 4-1)
Thur. April 13—Buffalo 2, at Philadelphia 3
Fri. April 14—Buffalo 1, at Philadelphia 2
Sun. April 16—Philadelphia 2, at Buffalo 0
Tue. April 18—Philadelphia 2, at Buffalo 3 (a)
Thur. April 20—Buffalo 2, at Philadelphia 5
(a)—Stu Barnes scored at 4:42 (OT) for Buffalo.

	W	L	Pts.	GF	GA
Pittsburgh Penguins	4	1	8	17	8
Washington Capitals	1	4	2	8	17

(Pittsburgh won Eastern Conference quarterfinals, 4-1)
Thur. April 13—Pittsburgh 7, at Washington 0
Sat. April 15—Washington 1, at Pittsburgh 2 (b)
Mon. April 17—Washington 3, at Pittsburgh 4
Wed. April 19—Pittsburgh 2, at Washington 3
Fri. April 21—Pittsburgh 2, at Washington 1
(b)—Jaromir Jagr scored at 5:49 (OT) for Pittsburgh.

	W	L	Pts.	GF	GA
Toronto Maple Leafs	4	2	8	17	10
Ottawa Senators	2	4	4	10	17

(Toronto won Eastern Conference quarterfinals, 4-2)
Wed. April 12—Ottawa 0, at Toronto 2
Sat. April 15—Ottawa 1, at Toronto 5
Mon. April 17—Toronto 3, at Ottawa 4
Wed. April 19—Toronto 1, at Ottawa 0
Sat. April 22—Ottawa 1, at Toronto 2 (c)
Mon. April 24—Toronto 4, at Ottawa 3
(c)—Steve Thomas scored at 14:47 (OT) for Toronto.

	W	L	Pts.	GF	GA
New Jersey Devils	4	0	8	12	6
Florida Panthers	0	4	0	6	12

(New Jersey won Eastern Conference quarterfinals, 4-0)
Thur. April 13—Florida 3, at New Jersey 4
Sun. April 16—Florida 1, at New Jersey 2
Tue. April 18—New Jersey 2, at Florida 1
Thur. April 20—New Jersey 4, at Florida 1

WESTERN CONFERENCE

	W	L	Pts.	GF	GA
San Jose Sharks	4	3	8	20	22
St. Louis Blues	3	4	7	22	20

(San Jose won Western Conference quarterfinals, 4-3)
Wed. April 12—San Jose 3, at St. Louis 5
Sat. April 15—San Jose 4, at St. Louis 2
Mon. April 17—St. Louis 1, at San Jose 2
Wed. April 19—St. Louis 2, at San Jose 2
Fri. April 21—San Jose 3, at St. Louis 5
Sun. April 23—St. Louis 6, at San Jose 2
Tue. April 25—San Jose 3, at St. Louis 1

	W	L	Pts.	GF	GA
Dallas Stars	4	1	8	14	11
Edmonton Oilers	1	4	2	11	14

(Dallas won Western Conference quarterfinals, 4-1)
Wed. April 12—Edmonton 1, at Dallas 2
Thur. April 13—Edmonton 0, at Dallas 3
Sun. April 16—Dallas 2, at Edmonton 5
Tue. April 18—Dallas 4, at Edmonton 3
Fri. April 21—Edmonton 2, at Dallas 3

	W	L	Pts.	GF	GA
Colorado Avalanche	4	1	8	17	10
Phoenix Coyotes	1	4	2	10	17

(Colorado won Western Conference quarterfinals, 4-1)
Thur. April 13—Phoenix 3, at Colorado 6
Sat. April 15—Phoenix 1, at Colorado 3
Mon. April 17—Colorado 4, at Phoenix 2
Wed. April 19—Colorado 2, at Phoenix 3
Fri. April 21—Phoenix 1, at Colorado 2

	W	L	Pts.	GF	GA
Detroit Red Wings	4	0	8	15	6
Los Angeles Kings	0	4	0	6	15

(Detroit won Western Conference quarterfinals, 4-0)
Thur. April 13—Los Angeles 0, at Detroit 2
Sat. April 15—Los Angeles 5, at Detroit 8
Mon. April 17—Detroit 2, at Los Angeles 1
Wed. April 19—Detroit 3, at Los Angeles 0

CONFERENCE SEMIFINALS

EASTERN CONFERENCE

	W	L	Pts.	GF	GA
Philadelphia Flyers	4	2	8	15	14
Pittsburgh Penguins	2	4	4	14	15

(Philadelphia won Eastern Conference semifinals, 4-2)
Thur. April 27—Pittsburgh 2, at Philadelphia 0
Sat. April 29—Pittsburgh 4, at Philadelphia 1
Tue. May 2—Philadelphia 4, at Pittsburgh 3 (d)
Thur. May 4—Philadelphia 2, at Pittsburgh 1 (e)
Sun. May 7—Pittsburgh 3, at Philadelphia 6
Tue. May 9—Philadelphia 2, at Pittsburgh 1
(d)—Andy Delmore scored at 11:01 (OT) for Philadelphia.
(e)—Keith Primeau scored at 12:01 (5OT) for Philadelphia.

	W	L	Pts.	GF	GA
New Jersey Devils	4	2	8	16	9
Toronto Maple Leafs	2	4	4	9	16

(New Jersey won Eastern Conference semifinals, 4-2)
Thur. April 27—New Jersey 1, at Toronto 2
Sat. April 29—New Jersey 1, at Toronto 0
Mon. May 1—Toronto 1, at New Jersey 5
Wed. May 3—Toronto 3, at New Jersey 2
Sat. May 6—New Jersey 4, at Toronto 3
Mon. May 8—Toronto 0, at New Jersey 3

WESTERN CONFERENCE

	W	L	Pts.	GF	GA
Dallas Stars	4	1	8	15	7
San Jose Sharks	1	4	2	7	15

(Dallas won Western Conference semifinals, 4-1)
Fri. April 28—San Jose 0, at Dallas 4
Sun. April 30—San Jose 0, at Dallas 1
Tue. May 2—Dallas 1, at San Jose 2
Fri. May 5—Dallas 5, at San Jose 4
Sun. May 7—San Jose 1, at Dallas 4

	W	L	Pts.	GF	GA
Colorado Avalanche	4	1	8	23	13
Detroit Red Wings	1	4	2	13	23

(Colorado won Western Conference semifinals, 4-1)
Thur. April 27—Detroit 0, at Colorado 2
Sat. April 29—Detroit 1, at Colorado 3
Mon. May 1—Colorado 1, at Detroit 3
Wed. May 3—Colorado 3, at Detroit 2 (f)
Fri. May 5—Detroit 2, at Colorado 4
(f)—Chris Drury scored at 10:21 (OT) for Colorado.

1999-2000 NHL REVIEW *Stanley Cup playoffs*

CONFERENCE FINALS

EASTERN CONFERENCE

	W	L	Pts.	GF	GA
New Jersey Devils	4	3	8	18	15
Philadelphia Flyers	3	4	6	15	18

(New Jersey won Eastern Conference finals, 4-3)
Sun. May 14—New Jersey 4, at Philadelphia 1
Tues. May 16—New Jersey 3, at Philadelphia 4
Thur. May 18—Philadelphia 4, at New Jersey 2
Sat. May 20—Philadelphia 3, at New Jersey 1
Mon. May 22—New Jersey 4, at Philadelphia 1
Wed. May 24—Philadelphia 1, at New Jersey 2
Fri. May 26—New Jersey 2, at Philadelphia 1

WESTERN CONFERENCE

	W	L	Pts.	GF	GA
Dallas Stars	4	3	8	14	13
Colorado Avalanche	3	4	6	13	14

(Dallas won Western Conference finals, 4-3)
Sat. May 13—Colorado 2, at Dallas 0
Mon. May 15—Colorado 2, at Dallas 3
Fri. May 19—Dallas 0, at Colorado 2
Sun. May 21—Dallas 4, at Colorado 1
Tue. May 23—Colorado 2, at Dallas 3 (g)
Thur. May 25—Dallas 1, at Colorado 2
Sat. May 27—Colorado 2, at Dallas 3
(g)—Joe Nieuwendyk scored at 12:10 (OT) for Dallas.

STANLEY CUP FINALS

	W	L	Pts.	GF	GA
New Jersey Devils	4	2	8	15	9
Dallas Stars	2	4	4	9	15

(New Jersey won Stanley Cup championship, 4-2)
Tue. May 30—Dallas 3, at New Jersey 7
Thur. June 1—Dallas 2, at New Jersey 1
Sat. June 3—New Jersey 2, at Dallas 1
Mon. June 5—New Jersey 3, at Dallas 1
Thur. June 8—Dallas 1, at New Jersey 0 (h)
Sat. June 10—New Jersey 2, at Dallas 1 (i)
(h)—Mike Modano scored at 6:21 (3OT) for Dallas.
(i)—Jason Arnott scored at 8:20 (2OT) for New Jersey.

GAME SUMMARIES, STANLEY CUP FINALS

GAME 1

AT NEW JERSEY, MAY 30
New Jersey 7, Dallas 3

Dallas	1	0	2	—	3
New Jersey	1	3	3	—	7

FIRST PERIOD—1. New Jersey, Arnott 5 (Sykora, Elias), 7:22. 2. Dallas, Sydor 1 (Lehtinen, Keane), 13:13. No penalties.

SECOND PERIOD—3. New Jersey, Daneyko 1 (Brylin, Madden), 2:52. 4. New Jersey, Sykora 7 (Elias, Arnott), 10:28. 5. New Jersey, Stevens 3 (Pandolfo, Rafalski), 16:04. Penalty—Hatcher, Dallas (slashing), 18:20.

THIRD PERIOD—6. New Jersey, Brylin 2 (McKay), 2:21. 7. New Jersey, Sykora 8 (Arnott, Elias), 3:02. 8. New Jersey, Arnott 6 (Holik, Sykora), 5:12 (pp). 9. Dallas, Sim 1 (Carbonneau), 7:43. 10. Dallas, Muller 2 (Carbonneau), 7:55. Penalties—Thornton, Dallas (roughing), 3:35; Manson, Dallas (slashing), 12:05; Manson, Dallas (elbowing), 19:55.

Shots on goal—Dallas 5-7-6-18; New Jersey 7-9-10-26. Power-play opportunities—Dallas 0 of 0; New Jersey 1 of 4. Goalies—Dallas, Belfour 12-6 (18 shots-12 saves), Fernandez (3:02 third, 8-7); New Jersey, Brodeur 13-5 (18-15). A—19,040. Referees—Don Koharski, Bill McCreary. Linesmen—Ray Scapinello, Jay Sharrers.

GAME 2

AT NEW JERSEY, JUNE 1
Dallas 2, New Jersey 1

Dallas	1	0	1	—	2
New Jersey	1	0	0	—	1

FIRST PERIOD—1. Dallas, Hull 10 (Modano, Matvichuk), 4:25. 2. New Jersey, Mogilny 4 (Gomez, Stevens), 12:42. Penalties—Lemieux, New Jersey (holding), 8:20; Sloan, Dallas (roughing), 10:56; Rafalski, New Jersey (roughing), 10:56; Matvichuk, Dallas (roughing), 13:52; Holik, New Jersey (roughing), 13:52; Matvichuk, Dallas (roughing), 18:27.

SECOND PERIOD—No scoring or penalties.

THIRD PERIOD—3. Dallas, Hull 11 (Lehtinen, Modano), 15:44. Penalty—Sim, Dallas (hooking), 10:48.

Shots on goal—Dallas 3-7-7-17; New Jersey 9-8-11-28. Power-play opportunities—Dallas 0 of 1; New Jersey 0 of 2. Goalies—Dallas, Belfour 13-6 (28 shots-27 saves); New Jersey, Brodeur 13-6 (17-15). A—19,040. Referees—Kerry Fraser, Dan Marouelli. Linesmen—Gord Broseker, Dan Schachte.

GAME 3

AT DALLAS, JUNE 3
New Jersey 2, Dallas 1

New Jersey	1	1	0	—	2
Dallas	1	0	0	—	1

FIRST PERIOD—1. Dallas, Cote 2 (unassisted), 13:08 (pp). 2. New Jersey, Arnott 7 (Rafalski, White), 18:06. Penalties—Nemchinov, New Jersey (slashing), 12:46; Malakhov, New Jersey (interference), 13:51; Lemieux, New Jersey (cross-checking), 15:02.

SECOND PERIOD—3. New Jersey, Sykora 9 (Arnott, Rafalski), 12:27 (pp). Penalties—Hull, Dallas (interference), 8:09; Cote, Dallas (elbowing), 11:03.

THIRD PERIOD—No scoring. Penalty—Brodeur, New Jersey, served by Arnott (delay of game), 15:45.

Shots on goal—New Jersey 10-16-5-31; Dallas 7-9-7-23. Power-play opportunities—New Jersey 1 of 2; Dallas 1 of 4. Goalies—New Jersey, Brodeur 14-6 (23 shots-22 saves); Dallas, Belfour 13-7 (31-29). A—17,000. Referees—Terry Gregson, Don Koharski. Linesmen—Ray Scapinello, Jay Sharrers.

GAME 4

AT DALLAS, JUNE 5
New Jersey 3, Dallas 1

New Jersey	0	0	3	—	3
Dallas	0	1	0	—	1

FIRST PERIOD—No scoring. Penalties—Morrow, Dallas (obstruction-tripping), 14:38; Manson, Dallas (slashing), 17:27; Niedermayer, New Jersey (obstruction-holding), 19:34.

SECOND PERIOD—1. Dallas, Nieuwendyk 7 (Sydor, Hull), 18:02 (pp). Penalties—Sykora, New Jersey (hooking), 5:45; Keane, Dallas (boarding), 8:45; McKay, New Jersey (hooking), 11:59; Malakhov, New Jersey (cross-checking), 16:38.

THIRD PERIOD—2. New Jersey, Brylin 3 (Mogilny, Malakhov), 2:27. 3. New Jersey, Madden 3 (Nemchinov, Daneyko), 4:51 (sh). 4. New Jersey, Rafalski 2 (Elias), 6:08. Penalties—White, New Jersey (interference), 3:17; Sim, Dallas (slashing), 11:43.

Shots on goal—New Jersey 8-8-15-31; Dallas 6-7-4-17. Power-play opportunities—New Jersey 0 of 4; Dallas 1 of 5. Goalies—New Jersey, Brodeur 15-6 (17 shots-16 saves); Dallas, Belfour 13-8 (31-28). A—17,001. Referees—Kerry Fraser, Bill McCreary. Linesmen—Gord Broseker, Dan Schachte.

AT NEW JERSEY, JUNE 8
Dallas 1, New Jersey 0 (3OT)

Dallas	0	0	0	0	0	0	— 1
New Jersey	0	0	0	0	0	0	— 0

FIRST PERIOD—No scoring. Penalties—Hatcher, Dallas (hooking), 11:01; Holik, New Jersey (interference), 11:43.

SECOND PERIOD—No scoring. Penalties—Sykora, New Jersey (high-sticking), 14:23; Lehtinen, Dallas (high-sticking), 17:01.

THIRD PERIOD—No scoring. Penalty—Morrow, Dallas (obstruction-tripping), 13:45.

FIRST OVERTIME—No scoring or penalties.

SECOND OVERTIME—No scoring or penalties.

THIRD OVERTIME—1. Dallas, Modano 10 (Hull, Lehtinen), 6:21. No penalties.

Shots on goal—Dallas 11-6-5-5-12-2-41; New Jersey 7-11-9-10-8-3-48. Power-play opportunities—Dallas 0 of 2; New Jersey 0 of 3. Goalies—Dallas, Belfour 14-8 (48 shots-48 saves); New Jersey, Brodeur 15-7 (41-40). A—19,040. Referees—Don Koharski, Dan Marouelli. Linesmen—Ray Scapinello, Jay Sharrers.

AT DALLAS, JUNE 10
New Jersey 2, Dallas 1 (2OT)

New Jersey	0	1	0	0	1	— 2
Dallas	0	1	0	0	0	— 1

FIRST PERIOD—No scoring. Penalties—Daneyko, New Jersey (slashing), 4:36; Sim, Dallas (elbowing), 6:54; Daneyko, New Jersey (high-sticking), 13:45.

SECOND PERIOD—1. New Jersey, Niedermayer 5 (Lemieux, Pandolfo), 5:18 (sh). 2. Dallas, Keane 2 (Thornton, Modano), 6:27. Penalties—Rafalski, New Jersey (holding), 3:30; Stevens, New Jersey (roughing), 13:48; Hatcher, Dallas (roughing), 13:48; White, New Jersey (roughing), 19:21; Thornton, Dallas (roughing), 19:21.

THIRD PERIOD—No scoring or penalties.

FIRST OVERTIME—No scoring. Penalty—Arnott, New Jersey (cross-checking), 18:43.

SECOND OVERTIME—3. New Jersey, Arnott (Elias, Stevens), 8:20. No penalties.

Shots on goal—New Jersey 11-13-7-11-3-45; Dallas 7-9-13-1-1-31. Power-play opportunities—New Jersey 0 of 1; Dallas 0 of 4. Goalies—New Jersey, Brodeur 16-7 (31 shots-30 saves); Dallas, Belfour 14-9 (45-43). A—17,001. Referees—Terry Gregson, Bill McCreary. Linesmen—Gord Broseker, Dan Schachte.

INDIVIDUAL LEADERS

Goals: Brett Hull, Dallas (11)
Assists: Patrik Elias, New Jersey (13)
Brett Hull, Dallas (13)
Mike Modano, Dallas (13)
Points: Brett Hull, Dallas (24)
Penalty minutes: Rick Tocchet, Philadelphia (49)
Goaltending average: Martin Brodeur, New Jersey (1.61)
Shutouts: Ed Belfour, Dallas (4)

TOP SCORERS

	Games	G	A	Pts.	PIM
Brett Hull, Dallas	23	11	13	24	4
Mike Modano, Dallas	23	10	13	23	10
Jason Arnott, New Jersey	23	8	12	20	18
Patrik Elias, New Jersey	23	7	13	20	9
Mark Recchi, Philadelphia	18	6	12	18	6
Petr Sykora, New Jersey	23	9	8	17	10
Jaromir Jagr, Pittsburgh	11	8	8	16	6
Peter Forsberg, Colorado	16	7	8	15	12
Adam Deadmarsh, Colorado	17	4	11	15	21
Chris Drury, Colorado	17	4	10	14	4

INDIVIDUAL STATISTICS

BUFFALO SABRES

(Lost Eastern Conference quarterfinals to Philadelphia, 4-1)

SCORING

	Games	G	A	Pts.	PIM
Miroslav Satan	5	3	2	5	0
Curtis Brown	5	1	3	4	6
Stu Barnes	5	3	0	3	2
Geoff Sanderson	5	0	2	2	8
Jason Woolley	5	0	2	2	2
Richard Smehlik	5	1	0	1	0
Maxim Afinogenov	5	0	1	1	2
Doug Gilmour	5	0	1	1	0
Chris Gratton	5	0	1	1	4
James Patrick	5	0	1	1	2
Michael Peca	5	0	1	1	4
Vladimir Tsyplakov	5	0	1	1	4
Dixon Ward	5	0	1	1	2
Jason Holland	1	0	0	0	0
Jay Mckee	1	0	0	0	0
Chris Taylor	2	0	0	0	2
Erik Rasmussen	3	0	0	0	4
Jean-Luc Grand-Pierre	4	0	0	0	4
Alexei Zhitnik	4	0	0	0	8
Dominik Hasek (goalie)	5	0	0	0	2
Vaclav Varada	5	0	0	0	8
Rhett Warrener	5	0	0	0	2

GOALTENDING

	Gms.	Min.	W	L	T	G	SO	Avg.
Dominik Hasek	5	301	1	4	0	12	0	2.39

COLORADO AVALANCHE

(Lost Western Conference finals to Dallas, 4-3)

SCORING

	Games	G	A	Pts.	PIM
Peter Forsberg	16	7	8	15	12
Adam Deadmarsh	17	4	11	15	21
Chris Drury	17	4	10	14	4
Sandis Ozolinsh	17	5	5	10	20
Milan Hejduk	17	5	4	9	6
Joe Sakic	17	2	7	9	8
Ray Bourque	13	1	8	9	8
Adam Foote	16	0	7	7	28
Shjon Podein	17	5	0	5	8
Dave Andreychuk	17	3	2	5	18
Dave Reid	17	1	3	4	0
Jon Klemm	17	2	1	3	9
Alex Tanguay	17	2	1	3	2
Stephane Yelle	17	1	2	3	4
Aaron Miller	17	1	1	2	6
Martin Skoula	17	0	2	2	4
Eric Messier	14	0	1	1	4
Serge Aubin	17	0	1	1	6

	Games	G	A	Pts.	PIM
Patrick Roy (goalie)	17	0	1	1	4
Jeff Odgers	4	0	0	0	0
Greg De Vries	5	0	0	0	4

GOALTENDING

	Gms.	Min.	W	L	T	G	SO	Avg.
Patrick Roy	17	1039	11	6	0	31	3	1.79

DALLAS STARS

(Lost Stanley Cup finals to New Jersey, 4-2)

SCORING

	Games	G	A	Pts.	PIM
Brett Hull	23	11	13	24	4
Mike Modano	23	10	13	23	10
Joe Nieuwendyk	23	7	3	10	18
Sergei Zubov	18	2	7	9	6
Scott Thornton	23	2	7	9	28
Jamie Langenbrunner	15	1	7	8	18
Richard Matvichuk	23	2	5	7	14
Darryl Sydor	23	1	6	7	6
Brenden Morrow	21	2	4	6	22
Guy Carbonneau	23	2	4	6	12
Mike Keane	23	2	4	6	14
Jere Lehtinen	13	1	5	6	2
Kirk Muller	23	2	3	5	18
Derian Hatcher	23	1	3	4	29
Roman Lyashenko	16	2	1	3	0
Sylvain Cote	23	2	1	3	8
Aaron Gavey	13	1	2	3	10
Jonathan Sim	7	1	0	1	6
Grant Marshall	14	0	1	1	4
Manny Fernandez (goalie)	1	0	0	0	0
Jamie Pushor	5	0	0	0	5
Blake Sloan	16	0	0	0	12
Ed Belfour (goalie)	23	0	0	0	8
Dave Manson	23	0	0	0	33

GOALTENDING

	Gms.	Min.	W	L	T	G	SO	Avg.
Ed Belfour	23	1443	14	9	0	45	4	1.87
Manny Fernandez	1	17	0	0	0	1	0	3.53

DETROIT RED WINGS

(Lost Western Conference semifinals to Colorado, 4-1)

SCORING

	Games	G	A	Pts.	PIM
Sergei Fedorov	9	4	4	8	4
Nicklas Lidstrom	9	2	4	6	4
Brendan Shanahan	9	3	2	5	10
Larry Murphy	9	2	3	5	2
Tomas Holmstrom	9	3	1	4	16
Martin Lapointe	9	3	1	4	20
Steve Yzerman	8	0	4	4	0
Steve Duchesne	9	0	4	4	10
Vyacheslav Kozlov	8	2	1	3	12
Igor Larionov	9	1	2	3	6
Kris Draper	9	2	0	2	6
Pat Verbeek	9	1	1	2	2
Doug Brown	3	0	1	1	0
Kirk Maltby	8	0	1	1	4
Chris Chelios	9	0	1	1	8
Todd Gill	9	0	1	1	4
Darren McCarty	9	0	1	1	12
Chris Osgood (goalie)	9	0	1	1	4
Stacy Roest	3	0	0	0	0
Aaron Ward	3	0	0	0	0
Mathieu Dandenault	6	0	0	0	2
Brent Gilchrist	6	0	0	0	6

GOALTENDING

	Gms.	Min.	W	L	T	G	SO	Avg.
Chris Osgood	9	547	5	4	0	18	2	1.97

EDMONTON OILERS

(Lost Western Conference quarterfinals to Dallas, 4-1)

SCORING

	Games	G	A	Pts.	PIM
Bill Guerin	5	3	2	5	9
Doug Weight	5	3	2	5	4
Jim Dowd	5	2	1	3	4
German Titov	5	1	1	2	0
Janne Niinimaa	5	0	2	2	2
Todd Marchant	3	1	0	1	2
Ryan Smyth	5	1	0	1	6
Daniel Cleary	4	0	1	1	2
Roman Hamrlik	5	0	1	1	4
Georges Laraque	5	0	1	1	6
Ethan Moreau	5	0	1	1	0
Rem Murray	5	0	1	1	2
Tom Poti	5	0	1	1	0
Jason Smith	5	0	1	1	4
Kevin Brown	1	0	0	0	0
Dan Lacouture	1	0	0	0	0
Sean Brown	3	0	0	0	23
Chad Kilger	3	0	0	0	0
Bert Robertsson	5	0	0	0	0
Tommy Salo (goalie)	5	0	0	0	2
Alex Selivanov	5	0	0	0	8
Igor Ulanov	5	0	0	0	6

GOALTENDING

	Gms.	Min.	W	L	T	G	SO	Avg.
Tommy Salo	5	297	1	4	0	14	0	2.83

FLORIDA PANTHERS

(Lost Eastern Conference quarterfinals to New Jersey, 4-0)

SCORING

	Games	G	A	Pts.	PIM
Pavel Bure	4	1	3	4	2
Mike Sillinger	4	2	1	3	2
Rob Niedermayer	4	1	0	1	6
Ray Whitney	4	1	0	1	4
Peter Worrell	4	1	0	1	8
Alex Hicks	4	0	1	1	4
Viktor Kozlov	4	0	1	1	0
Scott Mellanby	4	0	1	1	2
Mark Parrish	4	0	1	1	0
Lance Pitlick	4	0	1	1	0
Robert Svehla	4	0	1	1	4
Len Barrie	4	0	0	0	0
Bret Hedican	4	0	0	0	0
Oleg Kvasha	4	0	0	0	8
Paul Laus	4	0	0	0	0
Todd Simpson	4	0	0	0	0
Jaroslav Spacek	4	0	0	0	0
Mike Vernon (goalie)	4	0	0	0	10
Mike Wilson	4	0	0	0	0

GOALTENDING

	Gms.	Min.	W	L	T	G	SO	Avg.
Mike Vernon	4	237	0	4	0	12	0	3.04

LOS ANGELES KINGS

(Lost Western Conference quarterfinals to Detroit, 4-0)

SCORING

	Games	G	A	Pts.	PIM
Luc Robitaille	4	2	2	4	6
Jozef Stumpel	4	0	4	4	8

	Games	G	A	Pts.	PIM
Zigmund Palffy	4	2	0	2	0
Rob Blake	4	0	2	2	4
Craig Johnson	4	1	0	1	2
Sean O'Donnell	4	1	0	1	4
Jere Karalahti	4	0	1	1	2
Nelson Emerson	1	0	0	0	0
Jamie Storr (goalie)	1	0	0	0	0
Marko Tuomainen	1	0	0	0	0
Aki Berg	2	0	0	0	2
Jaroslav Modry	2	0	0	0	2
Jason Blake	3	0	0	0	0
Dan Bylsma	3	0	0	0	0
Kelly Buchberger	4	0	0	0	4
Brad Chartrand	4	0	0	0	6
Bob Corkum	4	0	0	0	0
Stephane Fiset (goalie)	4	0	0	0	0
Garry Galley	4	0	0	0	0
Ian Laperriere	4	0	0	0	2
Glen Murray	4	0	0	0	2
Mattias Norstrom	4	0	0	0	6
Bryan Smolinski	4	0	0	0	2

GOALTENDING

	Gms.	Min.	W	L	T	G	SO	Avg.
Stephane Fiset	4	200	0	3	0	10	0	3.00
Jamie Storr	1	36	0	1	0	2	0	3.33

NEW JERSEY DEVILS

(Winner of 2000 Stanley Cup)

SCORING

	Games	G	A	Pts.	PIM
Jason Arnott	23	8	12	20	18
Patrik Elias	23	7	13	20	9
Petr Sykora	23	9	8	17	10
Scott Stevens	23	3	8	11	6
Scott Gomez	23	4	6	10	4
Claude Lemieux	23	4	6	10	28
Bobby Holik	23	3	7	10	14
Sergei Brylin	17	3	5	8	0
Brian Rafalski	23	2	6	8	8
Scott Niedermayer	22	5	2	7	10
Alexander Mogilny	23	4	3	7	4
John Madden	20	3	4	7	0
Colin White	23	1	5	6	18
Randy Mckay	23	0	6	6	9
Sergei Nemchinov	21	3	2	5	2
Vladimir Malakhov	23	1	4	5	18
Jay Pandolfo	23	0	5	5	0
Ken Daneyko	23	1	2	3	14
Brad Bombardir	1	0	0	0	0
Steve Brule	1	0	0	0	0
Steve Kelly	10	0	0	0	4
Martin Brodeur (goalie)	23	0	0	0	10

GOALTENDING

	Gms.	Min.	W	L	T	G	SO	Avg.
Martin Brodeur	23	1450	16	7	0	39	2	1.61

OTTAWA SENATORS

(Lost Eastern Conference quarterfinals to Toronto, 4-2)

SCORING

	Games	G	A	Pts.	PIM
Daniel Alfredsson	6	1	3	4	2
Vaclav Prospal	6	0	4	4	4
Andreas Dackell	6	2	1	3	2
Joe Juneau	6	2	1	3	0
Shawn Mceachern	6	0	3	3	4
Rob Zamuner	6	2	0	2	2
Igor Kravchuk	6	1	1	2	0

	Games	G	A	Pts.	PIM
Sami Salo	6	1	1	2	0
Jason York	6	0	2	2	2
Colin Forbes	5	1	0	1	14
Chris Phillips	6	0	1	1	4
Shaun Van Allen	6	0	1	1	9
Kevin Miller	1	0	0	0	0
Petr Schastlivy	1	0	0	0	0
Andre Roy	5	0	0	0	2
Magnus Arvedson	6	0	0	0	6
Tom Barrasso (goalie)	6	0	0	0	2
Radek Bonk	6	0	0	0	8
Marian Hossa	6	0	0	0	2
Grant Ledyard	6	0	0	0	16
Patrick Traverse	6	0	0	0	2

GOALTENDING

	Gms.	Min.	W	L	T	G	SO	Avg.
Tom Barrasso	6	372	2	4	0	16	0	2.58

PHILADELPHIA FLYERS

(Lost Eastern Conference finals to New Jersey, 4-3)

SCORING

	Games	G	A	Pts.	PIM
Mark Recchi	18	6	12	18	6
John LeClair	18	6	7	13	6
Keith Primeau	18	2	11	13	13
Eric Desjardins	18	2	10	12	2
Rick Tocchet	18	5	6	11	49
Daymond Langkow	16	5	5	10	23
Simon Gagne	17	5	5	10	2
Daniel McGillis	18	2	6	8	12
Andy Delmore	18	5	2	7	14
Keith Jones	18	3	3	6	14
Valeri Zelepukin	18	1	2	3	12
Peter White	16	0	2	2	0
Eric Lindros	2	1	0	1	0
Craig Berube	18	1	0	1	23
Adam Burt	11	0	1	1	4
Jody Hull	18	0	1	1	0
Kent Manderville	18	0	1	1	22
Luke Richardson	18	0	1	1	41
Chris Therien	18	0	1	1	12
Mark Greig	3	0	0	0	0
Mark Eaton	7	0	0	0	0
Brian Boucher (goalie)	18	0	0	0	0

GOALTENDING

	Gms.	Min.	W	L	T	G	SO	Avg.
Brian Boucher	18	1183	11	7	0	40	1	2.03

PHOENIX COYOTES

(Lost Western Conference quarterfinals to Colorado, 4-1)

SCORING

	Games	G	A	Pts.	PIM
Jeremy Roenick	5	2	2	4	10
Travis Green	5	2	1	3	2
Shane Doan	4	1	2	3	8
Benoit Hogue	5	1	2	3	2
Mikael Renberg	5	1	2	3	4
Trevor Letowski	5	1	1	2	4
Teppo Numminen	5	1	1	2	0
Keith Tkachuk	5	1	1	2	4
Dallas Drake	5	0	1	1	4
Jyrki Lumme	5	0	1	1	2
Radoslav Suchy	5	0	1	1	0
Mike Sullivan	5	0	1	1	0
Daniel Briere	1	0	0	0	0
J.J. Daigneault	1	0	0	0	0
Juha Ylonen	1	0	0	0	0

	Games	G	A	Pts.	PIM
Louie DeBrusk	3	0	0	0	0
Greg Adams	5	0	0	0	0
Mika Alatalo	5	0	0	0	2
Sean Burke (goalie)	5	0	0	0	0
Keith Carney	5	0	0	0	17
Stan Neckar	5	0	0	0	0
Lyle Odelein	5	0	0	0	16

GOALTENDING

	Gms.	Min.	W	L	T	G	SO	Avg.
Sean Burke	5	296	1	4	0	16	0	3.24

PITTSBURGH PENGUINS

(Lost Eastern Conference semifinals to Philadelphia, 4-2)

SCORING

	Games	G	A	Pts.	PIM
Jaromir Jagr	11	8	8	16	6
Jan Hrdina	9	4	8	12	2
Martin Straka	11	3	9	12	10
Robert Lang	11	3	3	6	0
Janne Laukkanen	11	2	4	6	10
Alexei Kovalev	11	1	5	6	10
Jiri Slegr	10	2	3	5	19
Tyler Wright	11	3	1	4	17
Rob Brown	11	1	2	3	0
Josef Beranek	11	0	3	3	4
Rene Corbet	7	1	1	2	9
Darius Kasparaitis	11	1	1	2	10
Matthew Barnaby	11	0	2	2	29
Bob Boughner	11	0	2	2	15
John Slaney	2	1	0	1	2
Pat Falloon	10	1	0	1	2
Hans Jonsson	11	0	1	1	6
Ian Moran	11	0	1	1	2
Peter Skudra (goalie)	1	0	0	0	0
Michal Rozsival	2	0	0	0	4
Alexei Morozov	5	0	0	0	0
Peter Popovic	10	0	0	0	10
Ron Tugnutt (goalie)	11	0	0	0	2

GOALTENDING

	Gms.	Min.	W	L	T	G	SO	Avg.
Ron Tugnutt	11	746	6	5	0	22	2	1.77
Peter Skudra	1	20	0	0	0	1	0	3.00

ST. LOUIS BLUES

(Lost Western Conference quarterfinals to San Jose, 4-3)

SCORING

	Games	G	A	Pts.	PIM
Jochen Hecht	7	4	6	10	2
Scott Young	6	6	2	8	8
Chris Pronger	7	3	4	7	32
Pierre Turgeon	7	0	7	7	0
Al MacInnis	7	1	3	4	14
Jamal Mayers	7	0	4	4	2
Marty Reasoner	7	2	1	3	4
Michal Handzus	7	0	3	3	6
Ladislav Nagy	6	1	1	2	0
Lubos Bartecko	7	1	1	2	0
Mike Eastwood	7	1	1	2	6
Craig Conroy	7	0	2	2	2
Jeff Finley	7	0	2	2	4
Ricard Persson	3	1	0	1	0
Stephane Richer	3	1	0	1	0
Tyson Nash	6	1	0	1	24
Todd Reirden	4	0	1	1	0
Marc Bergevin	7	0	1	1	6
Dave Ellett	7	0	1	1	2
Scott Pellerin	7	0	0	0	2
Roman Turek (goalie)	7	0	0	0	0

GOALTENDING

	Gms.	Min.	W	L	T	G	SO	Avg.
Roman Turek	7	415	3	4	0	19	0	2.75

SAN JOSE SHARKS

(Lost Western Conference semifinals to Dallas, 4-1)

SCORING

	Games	G	A	Pts.	PIM
Owen Nolan	10	8	2	10	6
Vincent Damphousse	12	1	7	8	16
Gary Suter	12	2	5	7	12
Mike Ricci	12	5	1	6	2
Jeff Friesen	11	2	2	4	10
Mike Rathje	12	1	3	4	8
Marco Sturm	12	1	3	4	6
Bryan Marchment	11	2	1	3	12
Dave Lowry CALGARY	12	1	2	3	6
Alexander Korolyuk	9	0	3	3	6
Marcus Ragnarsson	12	0	3	3	10
Patrick Marleau	5	1	1	2	2
Stephane Matteau	10	0	2	2	8
Niklas Sundstrom	12	0	2	2	2
Ron Sutter	12	0	2	2	10
Ronnie Stern RET	3	1	0	1	11
Todd Harvey	12	0	1	1	8
Brad Stuart	12	1	0	1	6
Scott Hannan	1	0	1	1	0
Tony Granato	12	0	1	1	14
Jeff Norton PITS.	12	0	1	1	7
Evgeni Nabokov (goalie)	1	0	0	0	0
Steve Shields (goalie)	12	0	0	0	0

GOALTENDING

	Gms.	Min.	W	L	T	G	SO	Avg.
Evgeni Nabokov	1	20	0	0	0	0	0	0.00
Steve Shields	12	696	5	7	0	36	0	3.10

TORONTO MAPLE LEAFS

(Lost Eastern Conference semifinals to New Jersey, 4-2)

SCORING

	Games	G	A	Pts.	PIM
Steve Thomas	12	6	3	9	10
Sergei Berezin	12	4	4	8	0
Mats Sundin	12	3	5	8	10
Darcy Tucker	12	4	2	6	15
Jonas Hoglund	12	2	4	6	2
Tomas Kaberle	11	1	4	5	0
Igor Korolev	12	0	4	4	6
Dmitri Khristich	12	1	2	3	0
Garry Valk	12	1	2	3	14
Alexander Karpovtsev	11	0	3	3	4
Danny Markov	12	0	3	3	10
Wendel Clark	6	1	1	2	4
Dimitri Yushkevich	12	1	1	2	4
Cory Cross	12	0	2	2	2
Jeff Farkas	3	1	0	1	0
Kevyn Adams	12	1	0	1	7
Yanic Perreault	1	0	1	1	0
Gerald Diduck	10	0	1	1	14
Tie Domi	12	0	1	1	20
Kris King	1	0	0	0	2
Greg Andrusak	3	0	0	0	2
Nik Antropov	3	0	0	0	4
Adam Mair	5	0	0	0	8
Alyn McCauley	5	0	0	0	6
Curtis Joseph (goalie)	12	0	0	0	10

GOALTENDING

	Gms.	Min.	W	L	T	G	SO	Avg.
Curtis Joseph	12	729	6	6	0	25	1	2.06

WASHINGTON CAPITALS

(Lost Eastern Conference quarterfinals to Pittsburgh, 4-1)

SCORING

	Games	G	A	Pts.	PIM
Jeff Halpern	5	2	1	3	0
Calle Johansson	5	1	2	3	0
Adam Oates	5	0	3	3	4
Chris Simon	4	2	0	2	24
Peter Bondra	5	1	1	2	4
Andrei Nikolishin	5	0	2	2	4
Sergei Gonchar	5	1	0	1	6
Steve Konowalchuk	5	1	0	1	2
Ulf Dahlen	5	0	1	1	2
Ken Klee	5	0	1	1	10
Joe Reekie	5	0	1	1	2
Craig Billington	1	0	0	0	0
Jim McKenzie	1	0	0	0	0
Glen Metropolit	2	0	0	0	2
Trent Whitfield	3	0	0	0	0
Brendan Witt	3	0	0	0	0
Terry Yake	3	0	0	0	0
Dmitri Mironov	4	0	0	0	4
Olaf Kolzig	5	0	0	0	0
Joe Murphy	5	0	0	0	8
Joe Sacco	5	0	0	0	4
Richard Zednik	5	0	0	0	5
Rob Zettler	5	0	0	0	2

GOALTENDING

	Gms.	Min.	W	L	T	G	SO	Avg.
Craig Billington	1	20	0	0	0	1	0	3.00
Olaf Kolzig	5	284	1	4	0	16	0	3.38

MISCELLANEOUS

HAT TRICKS

(Players scoring three or more goals in a game)

Date	Player, Team	Opp.	Goals	Date	Player, Team	Opp.	Goals
4-15-00	Martin Lapointe, Detroit	L.A.	3	4-23-00	Scott Young, St. Louis	S.J.	3
4-16-00	Doug Weight, Edmonton	Dal.	3	5-7-00	Andy Delmore, Philadelphia	Pit.	3
4-18-00	Bill Guerin, Edmonton	Dal.	3				

OVERTIME GOALS

Date	Player, Team	Opponent	Time	Final score
4-15-00	Jaromir Jagr, Pittsburgh	Washington	5:49	Pittsburgh 2, Washington 1
4-18-00	Stu Barnes, Buffalo	Philadelphia	4:42	Buffalo 3, Philadelphia 2
4-22-00	Steve Thomas, Toronto	Ottawa	14:47	Toronto 2, Ottawa 1
5-2-00	Andy Delmore, Philadelphia	Pittsburgh	11:01	Philadelphia 4, Pittsburgh 3
5-3-00	Chris Drury, Colorado	Detroit	10:21	Colorado 3, Detroit 2
5-4-00	Keith Primeau, Philadelphia	Pittsburgh	‡12:01	Philadelphia 2, Pittsburgh 1
5-23-00	Joe Nieuwendyk, Dallas	Colorado	12:10	Dallas 3, Colorado 2
6-8-00	Mike Modano, Dallas	New Jersey	†6:21	Dallas 1, New Jersey 0
6-10-00	Jason Arnott, New Jersey	Dallas	*8:20	New Jersey 2, Dallas 1

*Goal scored in second overtime.
†Goal scored in third overtime.
‡Goal scored in fifth overtime.

PENALTY-SHOT INFORMATION

Date	Shooter	Goaltender	Scored	Final score
4-16-00	Eric Desjardins, Philadelphia	Dominik Hasek, Buffalo	No	Philadelphia 2, Buffalo 0

1999-2000 NHL REVIEW *Stanley Cup playoffs*

ALL-STAR GAME

AT AIR CANADA CENTRE, TORONTO, FEBRUARY 6, 2000

ROSTERS

WORLD

Coach: Scotty Bowman, Detroit Red Wings
Assistant coach: Joel Quenneville, St. Louis Blues

Forwards (Pos.)	Club	Country
Radek Bonk (C)	Ottawa Senators	Czech Rep.
Pavel Bure (LW)	Florida Panthers	Russia
Valeri Bure (RW)	Calgary Flames	Russia
Mariusz Czerkawski (C)	New York Islanders	Poland
Pavol Demitra (LW)	St. Louis Blues	Slovakia
Patrik Elias (LW)†	New Jersey Devils	Czech Rep.
Milan Hejduk (RW)	Colorado Avalanche	Czech Rep.
Jaromir Jagr (RW)*	Pittsburgh Penguins	Czech Rep.
Sami Kapanen (LW)	Carolina Hurricanes	Finland
Viktor Kozlov (C)	Florida Panthers	Russia
Martin Rucinsky (RW)	Montreal Canadiens	Czech Rep.
Miroslav Satan (LW)	Buffalo Sabres	Slovakia
Teemu Selanne (RW)*	Mighty Ducks of Anaheim	Finland
Mats Sundin (C)*	Toronto Maple Leafs	Sweden
Defensemen		
Petr Buzek	Atlanta Thrashers	Czech Rep.
Nicklas Lidstrom*	Detroit Red Wings	Sweden
Teppo Numminen	Phoenix Coyotes	Finland
Sandis Ozolinsh*	Colorado Avalanche	Latvia
Petr Svoboda	Tampa Bay Lightning	Czech Rep.
Kimmo Timonen	Nashville Predators	Finland
Dmitry Yushkevich	Toronto Maple Leafs	Russia
Sergei Zubov	Dallas Stars	Russia
Goaltenders		
Olaf Kolzig	Washington Capitals	Germany
Tommy Salo	Edmonton Oilers	Sweden
Roman Turek†*	St. Louis Blues	Czech Rep.

*In starting lineup.

†Elias replaced injured Peter Forsberg (Colorado), Turek replaced injured Dominik Hasek (Buffalo).

NOTE: Timonen injured and did not play; his roster spot was not filled.

NORTH AMERICA

Coach: Pat Quinn, Toronto Maple Leafs
Assistant coach: Roger Neilson, Philadelphia Flyers

Forwards (Pos.)	Club	Country
Tony Amonte (RW)	Chicago Blackhawks	U.S.A.
Scott Gomez (LW)	New Jersey Devils	U.S.A.
Paul Kariya (LW)*	Anaheim Mighty Ducks	Canada
John LeClair (LW)	Philadelphia Flyers	U.S.A.
Eric Lindros (C)	Philadelphia Flyers	Canada
Mark Messier (C)	Vancouver Canucks	Canada
Mike Modano (C)	Dallas Stars	U.S.A.
Owen Nolan (LW)	San Jose Sharks	Canada
Mark Recchi (RW)	Philadelphia Flyers	Canada
Jeremy Roenick (C)	Phoenix Coyotes	U.S.A.
Joe Sakic (RW)	Colorado Avalanche	Canada
Brendan Shanahan (LW)*	Detroit Red Wings	Canada
Steve Yzerman (C)*	Detroit Red Wings	Canada
Ray Whitney (LW)†	Florida Panthers	Canada
Defensemen		
Rob Blake*	Los Angeles Kings	Canada
Ray Bourque	Boston Bruins	Canada
Chris Chelios	Detroit Red Wings	U.S.A.
Eric Desjardins	Philadelphia Flyers	Canada
Phil Housley	Calgary Flames	U.S.A.
Al MacInnis	St. Louis Blues	Canada
Chris Pronger*	St. Louis Blues	Canada
Scott Stevens	New Jersey Devils	Canada
Goaltenders		
Martin Brodeur	New Jersey Devils	Canada
Curtis Joseph*	Toronto Maple Leafs	Canada
Mike Richter	New York Rangers	U.S.A.

*In starting lineup.

†Whitney replaced injured Pierre Turgeon (St. Louis).

GAME SUMMARY

World 9, North America 4

World	3	2	4	—	9
North America	2	2	0	—	4

FIRST PERIOD—1. World, Demitra 1 (Yushkevich, Elias), 3:12. 2. World, Jagr 1 (Rucinsky), 10:50. 3. North America, Sakic (Whitney, Recci), 13:56. 4. World, Yushkevich 1 (Kozlov, P. Bure), 14:35. 5. North America, Roenick 1 (Modano), 19:30.

SECOND PERIOD—6. World, P. Bure 1 (V. Bure), 0:33. 7. World, P. Bure 2 (V. Bure, Kozlov), 8:38. 8. North America, Amonte 1 (Modano, Bourque), 12:14. 9. North America, Whitney 1 (Desjardins, Messier), 17:08.

THIRD PERIOD—10. World, Demitra 2 (Hejduk, Elias), 8:52. 11. World, P. Bure 3 (Lidstrom, Kozlov), 9:31. 12. Satan 1 (Czerkawski, Bonk), 10:51. 13. Bonk 1 (Jagr, Rucinsky), 19:28. Penalty—World, Ozolinsh (hooking), 5:51.

Shots on goal—World 20-13-15-48; North America 13-11-8-32. Power-play opportunities—World 0 of 0; North America 0 of 1. Goalies—World, Turek (13 shots, 11 saves), Salo W (0:00 second, 11-9), Kolzig (0:00 third, 8-8); North America, Joseph (20-17), Brodeur L (0:00 second, 13-11), Richter (0:00 third, 14-11). A—19,300. Referees—Kerry Fraser, Don Koharski. Linesmen—Gerard Gauthier, Ray Scapinello.

AWARDS

ALL-STAR TEAM

Roman Turek, St. Louis..Goaltender
Chris Pronger, St. Louis..Defense
Nicklas Lidstrom, Detroit...Defense
Paul Kariya, Anaheim..Left wing
Steve Yzerman, Detroit...Center
Jaromir Jagr, Pittsburgh..Right wing

Note: THE SPORTING NEWS All-Star Team is selected by the NHL players.

AWARD WINNERS

Player of the Year: Jaromir Jagr, Pittsburgh
Coach of the Year: Joel Quenneville, St. Louis
Rookie of the Year: Scott Gomez, New Jersey
Executive of the Year: Larry Pleau, St. Louis

Note: THE SPORTING NEWS player and rookie awards are selected by the NHL players, the coaches award by the NHL coaches and the executive award by NHL executives.

NATIONAL HOCKEY LEAGUE
ALL-STAR TEAMS

First team	Position	Second team
Olaf Kolzig, Washington	Goaltender	Roman Turek, St. Louis
Nicklas Lidstrom, Detroit	Defense	Rob Blake, Los Angeles
Chris Pronger, St. Louis	Defense	Eric Desjardins, Philadelphia
Brendan Shanahan, Detroit	Left wing	Paul Kariya, Anaheim
Steve Yzerman, Detroit	Center	Mike Modano, Dallas
Jaromir Jagr, Pittsburgh	Right wing	Pavel Bure, Florida

AWARD WINNERS

Art Ross Trophy: Jaromir Jagr, Pittsburgh
Maurice Richard Trophy: Pavel Bure, Florida
Hart Memorial Trophy: Chris Pronger, St. Louis
James Norris Memorial Trophy: Chris Pronger, St. Louis
Vezina Trophy: Olaf Kolzig, Washington
Bill Jennings Trophy: Roman Turek, St. Louis
Calder Memorial Trophy: Scott Gomez, New Jersey

Lady Byng Memorial Trophy: Pavol Demitra, St. Louis
Conn Smythe Trophy: Scott Stevens, New Jersey
Bill Masterton Memorial Trophy: Ken Daneyko, New Jersey
Frank J. Selke Trophy: Steve Yzerman, Detroit
Jack Adams Award: Joel Quenneville, St. Louis
King Clancy Trophy: Curtis Joseph, Toronto

1999-2000 NHL REVIEW *Awards*

PLAYER DRAFT

ENTRY DRAFT—JUNE 24-25, 2000

FIRST ROUND

No.—Selecting club	Player	Pos.	Previous team (league)
1—N.Y. Islanders	Rick DiPietro	G	Boston University (H. East)
2—Atlanta	Dany Heatley	LW	Wisconsin (WCHA)
3—Minnesota	Marian Gaborik	LW	Trencin, Slovakia
4—Columbus	Rostislav Klesla	D	Brampton (OHL)
5—N.Y. Islanders (from Tampa Bay)	Raffi Torres	LW	Brampton (OHL)
6—Nashville	Scott Hartnell	RW	Prince Albert (WHL)
7—Boston	Lars Jonsson	D	Leksand, Sweden
8—Tampa Bay (from N.Y. Rangers)	Nikita Alexeev	RW	Erie (OHL)
9—Calgary	Brent Krahn	G	Calgary (WHL)
10—Chicago	Mikhail Yakubov	C	Togliatta, Russia
11—Chicago (from Vancouver)	Pavel Vorobiev	RW	Yaroslavl, Russia
12—Anaheim	Alexei Smirnov	LW	Dynamo, Russia
13—Montreal	Ron Hainsey	D	Mass.-Lowell (H. East)
14—Colorado (from Carolina)	Vaclav Nedorost	C	Budejovice, Czech Republic
15—Buffalo	Artem Kriukov	F	Yaroslavl, Russia
16—Montreal (from San Jose)	Marcel Hossa	C	Portland (WHL)
17—Edmonton	Alexei Mikhnov	LW	Yaroslavl, Russia
18—Pittsburgh	Brooks Orpik	D	Boston College (H. East)
19—Phoenix	Krystofer Kolanos	C	Boston College (H. East)
20—Los Angeles	Alexander Frolov	LW	Yaroslavl, Russia
21—Ottawa	Anton Volchenkov	D	CSKA, Russia
22—New Jersey (from Colorado)	David Hale	D	Sioux City, USHL
23—Vancouver (from Florida)	Nathan Smith	C	Swift Current (WHL)
24—Toronto	Brad Boyes	C	Erie (OHL)
25—Dallas	Steve Ott	C	Windsor (OHL)
26—Washington	Brian Sutherby	C	Moose Jaw (WHL)
27—Boston (from New Jersey)	Martin Samuelsson	D	MoDo, Sweden
28—Philadelphia (from Phi. through T.B.)	Justin Williams	RW	Plymouth (OHL)
29—Detroit	Niklas Kronvall	D	Djurgarden, Sweden
30—St. Louis	Jeff Taffe	C	Minnesota (WCHA)

SECOND ROUND

No.—Selecting club	Player	Pos.	Previous team (league)
31—Atlanta	Ilja Nikulin	D	Tver, Russia
32—Carolina (from C'bus through Colo.)	Tomas Kurka	LW	Plymouth (OHL)
33—Minnesota	Nick Schultz	D	Prince Albert (WHL)
34—Tampa Bay	Ruslan Zainullin	RW	Ak-Bars Kazan, Russia
35—Edmonton (from N.Y. Islanders)	Brad Winchester	LW	Wisconsin (WCHA)
36—Nashville	Daniel Widing	RW	Leksand, Sweden
37—Boston	Andy Hilbert	C	Michigan (CCHA)
38—Detroit (from N.Y. Rangers)	Tomas Kopecky	C	Trencin, Slovakia
39—New Jersey (from N.Y. Islanders)	Teemu Laine	RW	Jokerit, Finland
40—Calgary	Kurtis Foster	D	Peterborough (OHL)
41—San Jose (from Chicago)	Tero Maatta	D	Jokerit, Finland
42—Atlanta (from Vancouver)	Libor Ustrnul	D	Plymouth (OHL)
43—Washington (from Anaheim)	Matt Pettinger	LW	Calgary (WHL)
44—Anaheim (from Montreal)	Ilja Bryzgalov	G	Togliatti, Russia
45—Ottawa	Mathieu Chouinard	D	Shawinigan (QMJHL)
46—Calgary (from Colorado)	Jarret Stoll	C	Kootenay (WHL)
47—Colorado (from Carolina)	Jared Aulin	C	Kamloops (WHL)
48—Buffalo	Gerard Dicaire	D	Seattle (WHL)
49—Chicago (from San Jose)	Jonas Nordqvist	C	Leksand, Sweden
50—Colorado	Sergei Soin	C	Krylja Sovetov, Russia
51—Toronto (from Edmonton)	Kris Vernarsky	C	Plymouth (OHL)
52—Pittsburgh	Shane Endicott	C	Seattle (WHL)
53—Phoenix	Alexander Tatarinov	RW	Yaroslavl, Russia
54—Los Angeles	Andreas Lilja	D	Malmo, Sweden
55—Ottawa	Antoine Vermette	C	Victoriaville (QMJHL)
56—New Jersey	Aleksander Suglobov	C	Yaroslavl, Russia
57—New Jersey (from Colorado)	Matt DeMarchi	D	Minnesota (WCHA)
58—Florida	Vladimir Sapozhnikov	D	Novokuznetsk, Russia
59—Boston (from Toronto)	Ivan Huml	LW	Langley, BCHL
60—Dallas	Dan Ellis	G	Omaha, USHL

No.—Selecting club	Player	Pos.	Previous team (league)
61— Washington	Jakub Cutta	D	Swift Current (WHL)
62— New Jersey	Paul Martin	D	Elk River H.S., USHSW
63— Colorado (from Phi. through Car.)	Argis Saviels	D	Owen Sound (OHL)
64— N.Y. Rangers (from Detroit)	Filip Novak	D	Regina (WHL)
65— St. Louis	David Morisset	RW	Seattle (WHL)

THIRD ROUND

No.—Selecting club	Player	Pos.	Previous team (league)
66— Boston	Tuukka Makela	LW	IFK Helsinki, Finland
67— New Jersey (from Atl. through Van.)	Max Birbraer	LW	New Market, OPJHL
68— Dallas (from Minnesota)	Joel Lundqvist	C	Frolunda, Sweden
69— Columbus	Ben Knopp	RW	Moose Jaw (WHL)
70— Toronto (from Tampa Bay)	Mikael Tellqvist	G	Djurgardens, Sweden
71— Vancouver (from N.Y. Islanders)	Thatcher Bell	C	Rimouski (QMJHL)
72— Nashville	Mattias Nilsson	D	MoDo, Sweden
73— Boston	Sergei Zinovjev	RW	Novokuznetsk, Russia
74— Chi. (from N.Y.R. through T.B. and S.J.)	Igor Radulov	LW	Yaroslavl, Russia
75— St. Louis (from Calgary)	Justin Papineau	C	Belleville (OHL)
76— New Jersey (from Chicago)	Michael Rupp	LW	Erie (OHL)
77— Florida (from Vancouver)	Robert Fried	RW	Deerfield, USHSE
78— Montreal (from Anaheim)	Jozef Balej	RW	Portland (WHL)
79— Montreal	Tyler Hanchuck	D	Brampton (OHL)
80— Carolina	Ryan Bayda	LW	North Dakota (WCHA)
81— Tampa Bay (from Buffalo)	Alexandre Kharitonov	RW	Dynamo, Russia
82— Florida (from San Jose)	Sean O'Connor	RW	Moose Jaw (WHL)
83— Edmonton	Alexander Ljubimov	D	Samara, Russia
84— Pittsburgh	Peter Hamerlik	G	Skalica, Slovakia
85— Phoenix	Ramzi Abid	LW	Halifax (QMJHL)
86— Los Angeles	Yanick Lehoux	C	Baie Comeau (QMJHL)
87— Ottawa	Jan Bohac	C	Slavia Praha, Czech Republic
88— Colorado	Kurt Sauer	D	Spokane (WHL)
89— Nashville (from Florida)	Libor Pivko	LW	Havirov, Czech Republic
90— Toronto	Jean-Francois Racine	G	Drummondville (QMJHL)
91— Dallas	Alexei Tereschenko	C	Dynamo, Russia
92— Colorado (from Washington)	Sergei Kliazmine	LW	Tver, Russia
93— Vancouver (from New Jersey)	Tim Branham	D	Barrie (OHL)
94— Philadelphia	Alexander Drozdetsky	F	St. Petersburg, Russia
95— N.Y. Rangers (from Detroit)	Dominic Moore	C	Harvard (ECAC)
96— St. Louis	Antoine Bergeron	D	Val-d'Or (QMJHL)

FOURTH ROUND

No.—Selecting club	Player	Pos.	Previous team (league)
97— Carolina (from Atlanta)	Niclas Wallin	D	Brynas, Sweden
98— Ana. (from C'bus through N.Y.I. & C'bus)	Jonas Ronnqvist	W	Lulea, Sweden
99— Minnesota	Marc Cavosie	C/LW	Rensselaer (ECAC)
100— Toronto (from Tampa Bay)	Miguel Delisle	RW	Ottawa (OHL)
101— N.Y. Islanders	Arto Tukio	D	Ilves-Tampere, Finland
102— Detroit (from Nashville)	Stefan Liv	G	HV-71 Jr., Sweden
103— Boston	Brett Nowak	C/LW	Harvard (ECAC)
104— N.Y.R. (from N.Y.R. through S.J.)	Jon Disalvatore	RW	Providence (H. East)
105— N.Y.I. (from Cal. through T.B.)	Vladimir Gorbunov	W	HC Moscow, Russia
106— Chicago	Scott Balan	D	Regina (WHL)
107— Atlanta (from Vancouver)	Carl Mallette	C	Victoriaville (QMJHL)
108— Atlanta (from Ana. through Car.)	Blake Robson	C	Portland (WHL)
109— Montreal	Johan Eneqvist	LW	Leksand, Sweden
110— Carolina	Jared Newman	D	Plymouth (OHL)
111— Buffalo	Ghyslain Rousseau	G	Baie-Comeau (QMJHL)
112— N.Y. Rangers (from San Jose)	Premsyl Duben	D	Jihlava, Czech Republic
113— Edmonton	Lou Dickenson	C/LW	Mississauga (OHL)
114— Montreal (from Pittsburgh)	Christian Larrivee	C	Chicoutimi (QMJHL)
115— Florida (from Phoenix)	Chris Eade	D	North Bay (OHL)
116— Calgary (from Buf. through Wash.)	Levente Szuper	G	Ottawa (OHL)
117— Chicago (from Los Angeles)	Olli Malmivaara	D	Jokerit, Finland
118— Los Angeles (from Ottawa)	Lubomir Visnovsky	D	Bratislava, Slovakia
119— Colorado	Brian Fahey	D	Wisconsin (WCHA)
120— Florida	Davis Parley	G	Kamloops (WHL)
121— Wash. (from Tor. through Ana. & Chi.)	Ryan Vanbuskirk	D	Sarnia (OHL)
122— Ottawa	Derrick Byfuglien	D	Fargo-Moorhead, USHL
123— Dallas	Vadim Khomitski	D	HC Moscow, Russia
124— Pit. (from Wash. through Ana. & Mon.)	Michel Ouellet	RW	Rimouski (QMJHL)

No.—Selecting club	Player	Pos.	Previous team (league)
125—New Jersey	Phil Cole	D	Lethbridge (WHL)
126—Tampa Bay (from Philadelphia)	Johan Hagglund	C	MoDo, Sweden
127—Detroit	Dmitri Semyenov	W	Dynamo, Russia
128—Detroit	Alexander Seluyanov	D	UFA, Russia
129—St. Louis	Troy Riddle	C/RW	Des Moines, USHL
130—Detroit	Aaron Van Leusen	C/RW	Brampton (OHL)

FIFTH ROUND

No.—Selecting club	Player	Pos.	Previous team (league)
131—Nashville (from Atlanta)	Matt Hendricks	C	Blaine H.S., Minn.
132—Minnesota	Maxim Suchinsky	W	Avangard OMSK, Russia
133—Columbus	Petteri Nummelin	D	Davos, Switzerland
134—Anaheim (from Tampa Bay)	Peter Podhradsky	D	Bratislava, Slovakia
135—New Jersey	Mike Jefferson	C	Barrie (OHL)
136—N.Y. Islanders	Dimitri Upper	C	Nizhny Novgorod, Kazakstan
137—Nashville	Mike Stuart	D	Colorado (WCHA)
138—Columbus (from Boston)	Scott Heffernan	D	Sarnia (OHL)
139—Dallas	Ruslan Bernikov	RW	Amur Khabarovsk, Russia
140—N.Y. Rangers	Nathan Martz	C	Chilliwack, BCJHL
141—Calgary	Wade Davis	D	Calgary (WHL)
142—San Jose (from Chicago)	Michael Pinc	C/LW	Rouyn-Noranda (QMJHL)
143—N.Y. Rangers (from San Jose)	Brandon Snee	G	Union (ECAC)
144—Vancouver	Pavel Duma	C	Neftechimik, Russia
145—Montreal (from Anaheim)	Ryan Glenn	D	Walpole, EJHL
146—Pittsburgh (from Montreal)	David Koci	D	Sparta Praha Jr., Czech Republic
147—Atlanta (from Carolina)	Matt McRae	C	Cornell (ECAC)
148—N.Y. Islanders (from Car. through Phi.)	Kristofer Ottoson	W	Djurgarden, Sweden
149—Buffalo	Denis Denisov	LW	HC Moscow, Russia
150—Columbus (from S.J. through Buf.)	Tyler Kolarik	C	Deerfield, USHSE
151—Chicago (from L.A. through Wash.)	Alexander Barkunov	C	Yaroslavl, Russia
152—Edmonton	Paul Flache	D	Brampton (OHL)
153—Anaheim (from Pittsburgh)	Bill Cass	D	Boston College (ECAC)
154—Nashville (from Pho. through Edm.)	Matt Koalska	C	Twin Cities, USHL
155—Calgary	Travis Moen	LW	Kelowna (WHL)
156—Ottawa (from Los Angeles)	Greg Zanon	D	Nebraska-Omaha (CCHA)
157—Ottawa (from Los Angeles)	Grant Potulny	C/LW	Lincoln, USHL
158—Ottawa	Sean Connolly	D	Northern Michigan (CCHA)
159—Colorado	John-Michael Liles	D	Michigan State (CCHA)
160—Phoenix (from Florida)	Nate Kiser	D	Plymouth (OHL)
161—Tampa Bay (from Toronto)	Pavel Sedov		Voskresensk, Russia
162—Dallas	Artem Chernov	C	Novokuznetsk, Russia
163—Washington	Ivan Nepriayev		Yaroslavl, Russia
164—New Jersey	Matus Kostur	G	Banska Bystrica, Slovakia
165—Los Angeles (from Philadelphia)	Nathan Marsters	G	Chilliwack, BCJHL
166—San Jose (from Detroit)	Nolan Schaefer	G	Providence (H. East)
167—St. Louis	Craig Weller	D	Calgary Canucks, AJHL

SIXTH ROUND

No.—Selecting club	Player	Pos.	Previous team (league)
168—Atlanta	Zdenek Smid	G	Karlovy Vary, Czech Republic
169—Columbus	Shane Bendera	G	Red Deer (WHL)
170—Minnesota	Erik Reitz	D	Barrie (OHL)
171—Philadelphia (from Tampa Bay)	Roman Cechmanek	G	Slovnaft Vsetin, Czech Republic
172—Montreal (from N.Y.I. through Phi.)	Scott Selig	C/RW	Thayer Academy, USHSE
173—Nashville	Tomas Harant	D	Zilina, Slovakia
174—Boston	Jarno Kultanen	D	IFK Helsinki, Finland
175—N.Y. Rangers	Sven Helfenstein	C/RW	Kloten, Switzerland
176—Calgary	Jukka Hentunen	W	HPK Hameenlinna, Finland
177—Chicago	Michael Ayers	G	Dubuque, USHL
178—Atlanta (from Van. through Phi.)	Jef Dwyer	D	Choate, USHSE
179—Toronto (from Anaheim)	Vadim Sozinov	C	Novokuznetsk, Russia
180—Atlanta (from Montreal)	Darcy Hordichuk	LW	Saskatoon (WHL)
181—Carolina	Justin Forrest	D	U.S. National Under 18, Exhibition
182—Montreal (from Buffalo)	Petr Chvojka	D	Plzen Jr., Czech Republic
183—San Jose	Michael Macho	C	Martin, Slovakia
184—Edmonton	Shaun Norrie	RW	Calgary (WHL)
185—Pittsburgh	Patrick Foley	LW	New Hampshire (H. East)
186—Phoenix	Brent Gauvreau	C	Oshawa (OHL)
187—Detroit (from Los Angeles)	Per Backer	F	Grums, Sweden
188—Ottawa	Jason Maleyko	D	Brampton (OHL)

No.—Selecting club	Player	Pos.	Previous team (league)
189—Colorado	Chris Bahen	D	Clarkson (ECAC)
190—Florida	Josh Olson	LW	Omaha, USHL
191—Tampa Bay (from Toronto)	Aaron Gionet	D	Kamloops (WHL)
192—Dallas	Ladislav Vlcek	F	Kladno Jr., Czech Republic
193—Chicago (from Washington)	Joey Martin	D	Omaha, USHL
194—New Jersey	Deryk Engelland	D	Moose Jaw (WHL)
195—Philadelphia	Colin Shields	RW	Cleveland, NAHL
196—Detroit	Paul Ballantyne	D	Sault Ste. Marie (OHL)
197—Nashville (from St. Louis)	Zbynek Irgl	W	HC Vitkovice, Czech Republic

SEVENTH ROUND

No.—Selecting club	Player	Pos.	Previous team (league)
198—New Jersey (from Atlanta)	Ken Magowan	LW	Vernon, BCJHL
199—Minnesota	Brian Passmore	C	Oshawa (OHL)
200—Columbus	Janne Jokila	LW	TPS Jr., Finland
201—L.A. (from T.B. through Wash.)	Evgeny Federov	C	Molot Perm, Russia
202—N.Y.I. (from N.Y.I. through T.B.)	Ryan Caldwell	D	Thunder Bay, USHL
203—Nashville	Jure Penko	G	Green Bay, USHL
204—Boston	Chris Berti	C/LW	Sarnia (OHL)
205—N.Y. Rangers	Henrik Lundqvist	G	Frolunda, Sweden
206—L.A. (from Cal. through Wash.)	Tim Eriksson	D	Frolunda, Sweden
207—Chicago	Cliff Loya	D	Maina (H. East)
208—Vancouver	Brandon Reid	C	Halifax (QMJHL)
209—Toronto (from Anaheim)	Markus Seikola	D	TPS Jr., Finland
210—Philadelphia (from Mon. through T.B.)	John Eichelberger	C	Green Bay, USHL
211—Edmonton	Joe Cullen	C/LW	Colorado (WCHA)
212—Carolina	Magnus Kahnberg	F	Frolunda, Sweden
213—Buffalo	Vasily Bizyayev		CSKA, Russia
214—Minnesota (from San Jose)	Peter Bartos	W	Budejovice, Czech Republic
215—Edmonton	Matthew Lombardi	C	Victoriaville, AMJHL
216—Pittsburgh	Jim Abbott	LW	New Hampshire (H. East)
217—Phoenix	Igor Samoilov	D	Yaroslavl, Russia
218—Los Angeles	Craig Olynick	D	Seattle (WHL)
219—Dallas	Marco Tuokko	C	TPS Jr., Finland
220—Buffalo (from Ott. through T.B.)	Paul Gaustad	C/LW	Portland (WHL)
221—Colorado	Aaron Molnar	G	London (OHL)
222—Tampa Bay (from Florida)	Marek Priechodsky	D	Bratislava, Slovakia
223—Toronto	Lubos Velebny	D	Zvolen Jr., Slovakia
224—Dallas	Antti Miettinen	C	Hameenlinna, Finland
225—Chicago (from Washington)	Vladislav Luchkin	C	Cherepovets, Russia
226—Tampa Bay (from New Jersey)	Brian Eklund	G	Brown (ECAC)
227—Philadelphia	Guillaume Lefebvre	C	Rouyn-Noranda (QMJHL)
228—Detroit	Jimmie Svensson	F	Vasteras IK Jr., Sweden
229—St. Louis	Brett Lutes	LW	Montreal (QMJHL)

EIGHTH ROUND

No.—Selecting club	Player	Pos.	Previous team (league)
230—Atlanta	Samu Isosalo	RW	North Bay (OHL)
231—Columbus	Peter Zingoni	C	New England, EJHL
232—Minnesota	Lubomir Sekeras	D	Trinec, Czech Republic
233—Tampa Bay	Alexander Polukeyev		
234—Florida (from N.Y. Islanders)	Janis Sprukts	C	Lukko Rauma Jr., Finland
235—Carolina	Craig Kowalski	G	Compuware, NAHL
236—Nashville	Mats Christeen	D	Sodertalje Jr., Sweden
237—Boston	Zdenek Kutlak	D	Budejovice, Czech Republic
238—N.Y. Rangers	Dan Eberly	D	Rensselaer (ECAC)
239—Calgary	David Hajek	D	Chomutov, Czech Republic
240—Chicago	Adam Berkhoel	G	Twin Cities, USHL
241—Vancouver	Nathan Barrett	C	Lethbridge (WHL)
242—Atlanta (from Anaheim)	Evan Nielsen	D	Notre Dame (CCHA)
243—Montreal	Joni Puurula	G	Hermes Div. 1, Finland
244—Atlanta (from Carolina)	Eric Bowen	RW	Portland (WHL)
245—Los Angeles (from Buffalo)	Dan Welch	RW	Minnesota (WCHA)
246—San Jose	Chad Wiseman	LW	Mississauga (OHL)
247—Edmonton	Jason Platt	D	Omaha, USHL
248—Pittsburgh	Steven Crampton	RW	Moose Jaw (WHL)
249—Phoenix	Sami Venalainen	RW	Tappara Jr., Finland
250—Los Angeles	Flavien Conne	C	Freibourg, Switzerland
251—Detroit (from Ottawa)	Todd Jackson	RW	U.S. National Under 18, Exhibition
252—Colorado	Darryl Bootland	RW	Toronto (OHL)

No.—Selecting club	Player	Pos.	Previous team (league)
253—Florida	Matthew Sommerfeld	LW	Swift Current (WHL)
254—Toronto	Alexander Shinkar		
255—Minnesota (from Dallas)	Eric Johansson	C	Tri-City (WHL)
256—San Jose (from Washington)	Pasi Saarinen	D	Ilves-Tampere, Finland
257—New Jersey	Warren McCutcheon	C	Lethbridge (WHL)
258—Buffalo (from Calgary)	Sean McMorrow	D	Kitchener (OHL)
259—Philadelphia	Regan Kelly	D	Nipawin, SJHL
260—Detroit	Evgeni Bumagin		HC Moscow, Russia
261—St. Louis	Reinhard Divis	G	Leksand, Sweden

NINTH ROUND

No.—Selecting club	Player	Pos.	Previous team (league)
262—Chicago (from Atlanta)	Peter Flache	C	Guelph (OHL)
263—Tampa Bay (from Min. through N.J.)	Thomas Ziegler	F	Ambri Piotta, Switzerland
264—N.Y. Islanders (from Columbus)	Dimitri Altarev	F	Penza, Russia
265—Toronto (from Tampa Bay)	Jean-Philippe Cote	D	Cape Breton (QMJHL)
266—Colorado (from N.Y. Islanders)	Sean Kotary	C	Northwood Prep, USHSE
267—N.Y. Islanders (from Nashville)	Tomi Pettinen	D	Ilves-Tampere, Finland
268—Boston	Pavel Kolaruk	D	Slavia Praha, Czech Republic
269—N.Y. Rangers	Martin Richter	D	Saipa, Czech Republic
270—Calgary	Micki Dupont	D	Kamloops (WHL)
271—Chicago	Reto Von Arx	F	Davos, Switzerland
272—Vancouver	Tim Smith	C	Spokane (WHL)
273—Pittsburgh (from Anaheim)	Roman Simicek	C	HPK Hameenlinna, Finland
274—Edmonton	Evgeny Muratov	LW	Neftechimik, Russia
275—Montreal	Jonathan Gauthier	D	Rouyn-Noranda (QMJHL)
276—Carolina	Troy Ferguson	F	Michigan State (CCHA)
277—Buffalo	Ryan Courtney	LW	Windsor (OHL)
278—Columbus (from San Jose)	Martin Paroulek	F	Slovnaft Vsetin, Czech Republic
279—Boston (from Edmonton)	Andreas Lindstrom		Lulea, Sweden
280—Pittsburgh	Nick Boucher	G	Dartmouth (ECAC)
281—Phoenix	Peter Fabus	F	Trencin, Slovakia
282—Los Angeles	Carl Grahn	G	Kalpa Jr., Finland
283—Ottawa	James Demone	D	Portland (WHL)
284—Nashville	Martin Hohener	D	Kloten, Switzerland
285—Colorado	Blake Ward	G	Tri-City (WHL)
286—Columbus (from Florida)	Andrej Nedorost	C	Trencin, Slovakia
287—Philadelphia (from Tor. through T.B.)	Milan Kopecky	LW	Slavia Praha, Czech Republic
288—Atlanta (from Dallas)	Mark McRae	D	Cornell (ECAC)
289—Washington	Bjorn Nord	D	Djurgarden, Sweden
290—Atlanta (from New Jersey)	Simon Gamache	C	Val-d'Or (QMJHL)
291—Chicago (from Philadelphia)	Arne Ramholt	D	Kloten, Switzerland
292—Columbus (from Detroit)	Louis Mandeville	D	Rouyn-Noranda (QMJHL)
293—St. Louis	Lauri Kinios	D	Montreal (QMJHL)

EXPANSION DRAFT

JUNE 23, 2000

COLUMBUS BLUE JACKETS

Forwards	Previous team
Kevyn Adams (C)	Toronto Maple Leafs
Kevin Dineen (RW)	Ottawa Senators
Dallas Drake (RW)	Phoenix Coyotes
Ted Drury (C)	New York Islanders
Bruce Gardiner (C)	Tampa Bay Lightning
Steve Heinze (RW)	Boston Bruins
Robert Kron (LW)	Carolina Hurricanes
Sergei Luchinkin (LW)	Dallas Stars
Barrie Moore (C)	Washington Capitals
Geoff Sanderson (LW)	Buffalo Sabres
Turner Stevenson* (RW)	Montreal Canadiens
Martin Streit (LW)	Philadelphia Flyers
Dmitri Subbotin (LW)	New York Rangers
Jeff Williams (C)	New Jersey Devils
Tyler Wright (C)	Pittsburgh Penguins

Defensemen	
Jonas Andersson-Junkka	Pittsburgh Penguins
Radim Bicanek	Chicago Blackhawks
Lyle Odelein	Phoenix Coyotes
Jamie Pushor	Dallas Stars
Tommi Rajamaki	Toronto Maple Leafs
Bert Robertsson	Edmonton Oilers
Mathieu Schneider	New York Rangers
Mattias Timander	Boston Bruins

Goaltenders	
Frederic Chabot	Montreal Canadiens
Dwayne Roloson	Buffalo Sabres
Rick Tabaracci	Colorado Avalanche

*Columbus traded Stevenson to New Jersey to complete an earlier trade for RW Krzysztof Oliwa.

MINNESOTA WILD

Forwards	Previous team
Michael Bros (C)	San Jose Sharks
Jeff Daw (C)	Chicago Blackhawks
Jim Dowd (C)	Edmonton Oilers
Darby Hendrickson (C)	Vancouver Canucks
Joe Juneau† (C/LW)	Ottawa Senators
Sergei Krivokrasov (RW)	Calgary Flames
Darryl Laplante (C)	Detroit Red Wings
Steve McKenna (LW)	Los Angeles Kings
Jeff Nielsen (RW)	Mighty Ducks of Anaheim
Steffan Nilsson (RW)	Vancouver Canucks
Jeff Odgers (RW)	Colorado Avalanche
Scott Pellerin (LW)	St. Louis Blues
Stacy Roest (C)	Detroit Red Wings
Cam Stewart (LW)	Florida Panthers

Defensemen	
Artem Anisimov	Philadelphia Flyers
Chris Armstrong	San Jose Sharks
Ladislav Benysek	Mighty Ducks of Anaheim
Ian Herbers	New York Islanders
Filip Kuba	Calgary Flames
Curtis Leschyshyn	Carolina Hurricanes
Sean O'Donnell	Los Angeles Kings
Oleg Orekhovsky	Washington Capitals

Goaltenders	
Zac Bierk	Tampa Bay Lightning
Jamie McLennan	St. Louis Blues
Chris Terreri‡	New Jersey Devils
Mike Vernon§	Florida Panthers

†Minnesota traded Juneau to Phoenix for C Rickard Wallin.
‡Minnesota traded Terreri back to New Jersey, along with a 2001 ninth-round draft pick, for D Brad Bombardir.
§Minnesota traded Vernon to Calgary for the rights to C Dan Cavanaugh and a 2001 eighth-round draft pick.

1999-2000 NHL REVIEW Expansion draft

NHL HISTORY

Stanley Cup champions

All-Star Games

Year-by-year standings

Records

Statistical leaders

Award winners

The Sporting News awards

Hall of Fame

Milestones

Team by team

STANLEY CUP CHAMPIONS

LIST OF WINNERS

The Stanley Cup was donated in 1893 to be awarded to signify supremacy in Canadian amateur hockey. Eventually, other teams, including professional clubs and clubs outside of Canada, began vying for the trophy. Since 1926 only NHL clubs have competed for the Stanley Cup.

Season	Club	Coach	Season	Club	Coach
1892-93—Montreal Am. Ath. Assn.*			1948-49—Toronto Maple Leafs		Hap Day
1893-94—Montreal Am. Ath. Assn.*			1949-50—Detroit Red Wings		Tommy Ivan
1894-95—Montreal Victorias*		Mike Grant†	1950-51—Toronto Maple Leafs		Joe Primeau
1895-96—(Feb. '96) Winnipeg Victorias*		J. Armitage	1951-52—Detroit Red Wings		Tommy Ivan
1895-96—(Dec. '96) Montreal Victorias*		Mike Grant†	1952-53—Montreal Canadiens		Dick Irvin
1896-97—Montreal Victorias*		Mike Grant†	1953-54—Detroit Red Wings		Tommy Ivan
1897-98—Montreal Victorias*		F. Richardson	1954-55—Detroit Red Wings		Jimmy Skinner
1898-99—Montreal Shamrocks*		H.J. Trihey†	1955-56—Montreal Canadiens		Toe Blake
1899-1900—Montreal Shamrocks*		H.J. Trihey†	1956-57—Montreal Canadiens		Toe Blake
1900-01—Winnipeg Victorias*		D.H. Bain	1957-58—Montreal Canadiens		Toe Blake
1901-02—Montreal Am. Ath. Assn.*		C. McKerrow	1958-59—Montreal Canadiens		Toe Blake
1902-03—Ottawa Silver Seven*		A.T. Smith	1959-60—Montreal Canadiens		Toe Blake
1903-04—Ottawa Silver Seven*		A.T. Smith	1960-61—Chicago Black Hawks		Rudy Pilous
1904-05—Ottawa Silver Seven*		A.T. Smith†	1961-62—Toronto Maple Leafs		Punch Imlach
1905-06—Montreal Wanderers*		Cecil Blachford†	1962-63—Toronto Maple Leafs		Punch Imlach
1906-07—(Jan. '07) Kenora Thistles*		Tommy Phillips†	1963-64—Toronto Maple Leafs		Punch Imlach
1906-07—(Mar. '07) Montreal Wanderers*		Cecil Blachford	1964-65—Montreal Canadiens		Toe Blake
1907-08—Montreal Wanderers*		Cecil Blachford	1965-66—Montreal Canadiens		Toe Blake
1908-09—Ottawa Senators*		Bruce Stuart†	1966-67—Toronto Maple Leafs		Punch Imlach
1909-10—Montreal Wanderers*		Pud Glass†	1967-68—Montreal Canadiens		Toe Blake
1910-11—Ottawa Senators*		Bruce Stuart†	1968-69—Montreal Canadiens		Claude Ruel
1911-12—Quebec Bulldogs*		C. Nolan	1969-70—Boston Bruins		Harry Sinden
1912-13—Quebec Bulldogs*		Joe Malone†	1970-71—Montreal Canadiens		Al MacNeil
1913-14—Toronto Blueshirts*		Scotty Davidson†	1971-72—Boston Bruins		Tom Johnson
1914-15—Vancouver Millionaires*		Frank Patrick	1972-73—Montreal Canadiens		Scotty Bowman
1915-16—Montreal Canadiens*		George Kennedy	1973-74—Philadelphia Flyers		Fred Shero
1916-17—Seattle Metropolitans*		Pete Muldoon	1974-75—Philadelphia Flyers		Fred Shero
1917-18—Toronto Arenas		Dick Carroll	1975-76—Montreal Canadiens		Scotty Bowman
1919-20—Ottawa Senators		Pete Green	1976-77—Montreal Canadiens		Scotty Bowman
1920-21—Ottawa Senators		Pete Green	1977-78—Montreal Canadiens		Scotty Bowman
1921-22—Toronto St. Pats		Eddie Powers	1978-79—Montreal Canadiens		Scotty Bowman
1922-23—Ottawa Senators		Pete Green	1979-80—New York Islanders		Al Arbour
1923-24—Montreal Canadiens		Leo Dandurand	1980-81—New York Islanders		Al Arbour
1924-25—Victoria Cougars*		Lester Patrick	1981-82—New York Islanders		Al Arbour
1925-26—Montreal Maroons		Eddie Gerard	1982-83—New York Islanders		Al Arbour
1926-27—Ottawa Senators		Dave Gill	1983-84—Edmonton Oilers		Glen Sather
1927-28—New York Rangers		Lester Patrick	1984-85—Edmonton Oilers		Glen Sather
1928-29—Boston Bruins		Cy Denneny	1985-86—Montreal Canadiens		Jean Perron
1929-30—Montreal Canadiens		Cecil Hart	1986-87—Edmonton Oilers		Glen Sather
1930-31—Montreal Canadiens		Cecil Hart	1987-88—Edmonton Oilers		Glen Sather
1931-32—Toronto Maple Leafs		Dick Irvin	1988-89—Calgary Flames		Terry Crisp
1932-33—New York Rangers		Lester Patrick	1989-90—Edmonton Oilers		John Muckler
1933-34—Chicago Black Hawks		Tommy Gorman	1990-91—Pittsburgh Penguins		Bob Johnson
1934-35—Montreal Maroons		Tommy Gorman	1991-92—Pittsburgh Penguins		Scotty Bowman
1935-36—Detroit Red Wings		Jack Adams	1992-93—Montreal Canadiens		Jacques Demers
1936-37—Detroit Red Wings		Jack Adams	1993-94—New York Rangers		Mike Keenan
1937-38—Chicago Black Hawks		Bill Stewart	1994-95—New Jersey Devils		Jacques Lemaire
1938-39—Boston Bruins		Art Ross	1995-96—Colorado Avalanche		Marc Crawford
1939-40—New York Rangers		Frank Boucher	1996-97—Detroit Red Wings		Scotty Bowman
1940-41—Boston Bruins		Cooney Weiland	1997-98—Detroit Red Wings		Scotty Bowman
1941-42—Toronto Maple Leafs		Hap Day	1998-99—Dallas Stars		Ken Hitchcock
1942-43—Detroit Red Wings		Jack Adams	1999-00—New Jersey Devils		Larry Robinson
1943-44—Montreal Canadiens		Dick Irvin	NOTE: 1918-19 series between Montreal and Seattle cancelled		
1944-45—Toronto Maple Leafs		Hap Day	after five games because of influenza epidemic.		
1945-46—Montreal Canadiens		Dick Irvin	*Stanley Cups won by non-NHL clubs.		
1946-47—Toronto Maple Leafs		Hap Day	†Team captain.		
1947-48—Toronto Maple Leafs		Hap Day			

ALL-STAR GAMES

Date	Site	Winning team, score	Losing team, score	Att.
2-14-34†	Maple Leaf Gardens, Toronto	Toronto Maple Leafs, 7	NHL All-Stars, 3	*14,000
11-3-37‡	Montreal Forum	NHL All-Stars, 6	Montreal All-Stars§, 5	8,683
10-29-39∞	Montreal Forum	NHL All-Stars, 5	Montreal Canadiens, 2	*6,000
10-13-47	Maple Leaf Gardens, Toronto	NHL All-Stars, 4	Toronto Maple Leafs, 3	14,169
11-3-48	Chicago Stadium	NHL All-Stars, 3	Toronto Maple Leafs, 1	12,794
10-10-49	Maple Leaf Gardens, Toronto	NHL All-Stars, 3	Toronto Maple Leafs, 1	13,541
10-8-50	Olympia Stadium, Detroit	Detroit Red Wings, 7	NHL All-Stars, 1	9,166
10-9-51	Maple Leaf Gardens, Toronto	First Team▲, 2	Second Team▲, 2	11,469
10-5-52	Olympia Stadium, Detroit	First Team▲, 1	Second Team▲, 1	10,680
10-3-53	Montreal Forum	NHL All-Stars, 3	Montreal Canadiens, 1	14,153
10-2-54	Olympia Stadium, Detroit	NHL All-Stars, 2	Detroit Red Wings, 2	10,689
10-2-55	Olympia Stadium, Detroit	Detroit Red Wings, 3	NHL All-Stars, 1	10,111
10-9-56	Montreal Forum	NHL All-Stars, 1	Montreal Canadiens, 1	13,095
10-5-57	Montreal Forum	NHL All-Stars, 5	Montreal Canadiens, 3	13,095
10-4-58	Montreal Forum	Montreal Canadiens, 6	NHL All-Stars, 3	13,989
10-3-59	Montreal Forum	Montreal Canadiens, 6	NHL All-Stars, 1	13,818
10-1-60	Montreal Forum	NHL All-Stars, 2	Montreal Canadiens, 1	13,949
10-7-61	Chicago Stadium	NHL All-Stars, 3	Chicago Blackhawks, 1	14,534
10-6-62	Maple Leaf Gardens, Toronto	Toronto Maple Leafs, 4	NHL All-Stars, 1	14,236
10-5-63	Maple Leaf Gardens, Toronto	NHL All-Stars, 3	Toronto Maple Leafs, 3	14,034
10-10-64	Maple Leaf Gardens, Toronto	NHL All-Stars, 3	Toronto Maple Leafs, 2	14,232
10-20-65	Montreal Forum	NHL All-Stars, 5	Montreal Canadiens, 2	14,284
1-18-67	Montreal Forum	Montreal Canadiens, 3	NHL All-Stars, 0	14,284
1-16-68	Maple Leaf Gardens, Toronto	Toronto Maple Leafs, 4	NHL All-Stars, 3	15,753
1-21-69	Montreal Forum	West Division, 3	East Division, 3	16,260
1-20-70	St. Louis Arena	East Division, 4	West Division, 1	16,587
1-19-71	Boston Garden	West Division, 2	East Division, 1	14,790
1-25-72	Met Sports Center, Bloomington, Minn.	East Division, 3	West Division, 2	15,423
1-30-73	Madison Square Garden, New York	East Division, 5	West Division, 4	16,986
1-29-74	Chicago Stadium	West Division, 6	East Division, 4	16,426
1-21-75	Montreal Forum	Wales Conference, 7	Campbell Conference, 1	16,080
1-20-76	The Spectrum, Philadelphia	Wales Conference, 7	Campbell Conference, 5	16,436
1-25-77	Pacific Coliseum, Vancouver	Wales Conference, 4	Campbell Conference, 3	15,607
1-24-78	Buffalo Memorial Auditorium	Wales Conference, 3	Campbell Conference, 2 (OT)	16,433
	1979 All-Star Game replaced by Challenge Cup series between Team NHL and Soviet Union			
2-5-80	Joe Louis Arena, Detroit	Wales Conference, 6	Campbell Conference, 3	21,002
2-10-81	The Forum, Los Angeles	Campbell Conference, 4	Wales Conference, 1	15,761
2-9-82	Capital Centre, Landover, Md.	Wales Conference, 4	Campbell Conference, 2	18,130
2-8-83	Nassau Coliseum, Long Island, N.Y.	Campbell Conference, 9	Wales Conference, 3	15,230
1-31-84	Meadowlands Arena, East Rutherford, N.J.	Wales Conference, 7	Campbell Conference, 6	18,939
2-12-85	Olympic Saddledome, Calgary	Wales Conference, 6	Campbell Conference, 4	16,683
2-4-86	Hartford Civic Center	Wales Conference, 4	Campbell Conference, 3 (OT)	15,126
	1987 All-Star Game replaced by Rendez-Vous '87 between Team NHL and Soviet Union			
2-9-88	St. Louis Arena	Wales Conference, 6	Campbell Conference, 5 (OT)	17,878
2-7-89	Northlands Coliseum, Edmonton	Campbell Conference, 9	Wales Conference, 5	17,503
1-21-90	Pittsburgh Civic Arena	Wales Conference, 12	Campbell Conference, 7	17,503
1-19-91	Chicago Stadium	Campbell Conference, 11	Wales Conference, 5	18,472
1-18-92	The Spectrum, Philadelphia	Campbell Conference, 10	Wales Conference, 6	17,380
2-6-93	Montreal Forum	Wales Conference, 16	Campbell Conference, 6	17,137
1-22-94	Madison Square Garden, New York	Eastern Conference, 9	Western Conference, 8	18,200
	1995 All-Star Game canceled because of NHL lockout			
1-20-96	FleetCenter, Boston	Eastern Conference 5	Western Conference 4	17,565
1-18-97	San Jose Arena	Eastern Conference 11	Western Conference 7	17,442
1-18-98	General Motors Place, Vancouver	North America 8	World 7	18,422
1-24-99	Ice Palace, Tampa	North America 8	World 6	19,758
2-6-00	Air Canada Centre, Toronto	World 9	North America 4	19,300

*Estimated figure.

†Benefit game for Toronto Maple Leafs left wing Ace Bailey, who suffered a career-ending skull injury earlier in the season.

‡Benefit game for the family of Montreal Canadiens center Howie Morenz, who died of a heart attack earlier in the year.

§Montreal All-Star roster made up of players from Montreal Canadiens and Maroons.

∞Benefit game for the family of Montreal Canadiens defenseman Babe Siebert, who drowned earlier in the year.

▲First Team roster supplemented by players from the four American clubs and Second Team roster supplemented by players from the two Canadian clubs.

NHL HISTORY *All-Star Games*

MOST VALUABLE PLAYERS

Date	Player, All-Star Game team (regular-season team)	Date	Player, All-Star Game team (regular-season team)
10-6-62	Eddie Shack, Toronto Maple Leafs	2-9-82	Mike Bossy, Wales Conf. (New York Islanders)
10-5-63	Frank Mahovlich, Toronto Maple Leafs	2-8-83	Wayne Gretzky, Campbell Conf. (Edmonton Oilers)
10-10-64	Jean Beliveau, All-Stars (Montreal Canadiens)	1-31-84	Don Maloney, Wales Conf. (New York Rangers)
10-20-65	Gordie Howe, All-Stars (Detroit Red Wings)	2-12-85	Mario Lemieux, Wales Conf. (Pittsburgh Penguins)
1-18-67	Henri Richard, Montreal Canadiens	2-4-86	Grant Fuhr, Campbell Conf. (Edmonton Oilers)
1-16-68	Bruce Gamble, Toronto Maple Leafs	2-9-88	Mario Lemieux, Wales Conf. (Pittsburgh Penguins)
1-21-69	Frank Mahovlich, East Div. (Detroit Red Wings)	2-7-89	Wayne Gretzky, Campbell Conf. (Los Angeles Kings)
1-20-70	Bobby Hull, East Div. (Chicago Blackhawks)	1-21-90	Mario Lemieux, Wales Conf. (Pittsburgh Penguins)
1-19-71	Bobby Hull, West Div. (Chicago Blackhawks)	1-19-91	Vincent Damphousse, Camp. Conf. (Tor. Maple Leafs)
1-25-72	Bobby Orr, East Division (Boston Bruins)	1-18-92	Brett Hull, Campbell Conf. (St. Louis Blues)
1-30-73	Greg Polis, West Division (Pittsburgh Penguins)	2-6-93	Mike Gartner, Wales Conf. (New York Rangers)
1-29-74	Garry Unger, West Division (St. Louis Blues)	1-22-94	Mike Richter, Eastern Conf. (New York Rangers)
1-21-75	Syl Apps Jr., Wales Conf. (Pittsburgh Penguins)	1-20-96	Ray Bourque, Eastern Conf. (Boston Bruins)
1-20-76	Peter Mahovlich, Wales Conf. (Montreal Canadiens)	1-18-97	Mark Recchi, Eastern Conf. (Montreal Canadiens)
1-25-77	Rick Martin, Wales Conference (Buffalo Sabres)	1-18-98	Teemu Selanne, North America (Ana. Mighty Ducks)
1-24-78	Billy Smith, Campbell Conf. (New York Islanders)	1-24-99	Wayne Gretzky, North America (New York Rangers)
2-5-80	Reggie Leach, Campbell Conf. (Philadelphia Flyers)	2-6-00	Pavel Bure, World (Florida Panthers)
2-10-81	Mike Liut, Campbell Conf. (St. Louis Blues)		

YEAR-BY-YEAR STANDINGS

Note: Prior to 1926-27 season, clubs outside the NHL also competed for the Stanley Cup. Non-NHL clubs are denoted in parentheses. Sometimes playoff rounds were decided by total goals scored, rather than by games won.

1917-18

Team	W	L	T	Pts.	GF	GA
Montreal Canadiens	13	9	0	26	115	84
Toronto Arenas	13	9	0	26	108	109
Ottawa Senators	9	13	0	18	102	114
Montreal Wanderers	1	5	0	2	17	35

PLAYOFFS

Semifinals: Toronto 10 goals, Montreal Canadiens 7 goals (2-game series); Vancouver (PCHL) 3 goals, Seattle (PCHL) 2 goals (2-game series).
Stanley Cup finals: Toronto 3, Vancouver (PCHL) 2.

1918-19

Team	W	L	T	Pts.	GF	GA
Ottawa Senators	12	6	0	24	71	54
Montreal Canadiens	10	8	0	20	88	78
Toronto Arenas	5	13	0	10	65	92

PLAYOFFS

Semifinals: Seattle (PCHL) 7 goals, Vancouver 5 goals (2-game series); Montreal Canadiens 3, Ottawa 1.
Stanley Cup finals: Series between Montreal Canadiens and Seattle (PCHL) abandoned (with each team winning two games and one game tied) due to influenza epidemic.

1919-20

Team	W	L	T	Pts.	GF	GA
Ottawa Senators	19	5	0	38	121	64
Montreal Canadiens	13	11	0	26	129	113
Toronto St. Patricks	12	12	0	24	119	106
Quebec Bulldogs	4	20	0	8	91	177

PLAYOFFS

Semifinals: Seattle (PCHL) 7 goals, Vancouver (PCHL) 3 goals (2-game series).
Stanley Cup finals: Ottawa 3, Seattle (PCHL) 2.

1920-21

Team	W	L	T	Pts.	GF	GA
Toronto St. Patricks	15	9	0	30	105	100
Ottawa Senators	14	10	0	28	97	75
Montreal Canadiens	13	11	0	26	112	99
Hamilton Tigers	6	18	0	12	92	132

PLAYOFFS

Semifinals: Vancouver (PCHL) 2, Seattle (PCHL) 0; Ottawa 2, Toronto 0.
Stanley Cup finals: Ottawa 3, Vancouver (PCHL) 2.

1921-22

Team	W	L	T	Pts.	GF	GA
Ottawa Senators	14	8	2	30	106	84
Toronto St. Patricks	13	10	1	27	98	97
Montreal Canadiens	12	11	1	25	88	94
Hamilton Tigers	7	17	0	14	88	105

PLAYOFFS

Preliminaries: Regina (WCHL) 2 goals, Calgary (WCHL) 1 goal (2-game series); Regina (WCHL) 3, Edmonton (WCHL) 2; Vancouver (PCHL) 2, Seattle (PCHL) 0; Vancouver (PCHL) 5 goals, Regina (WCHL) 2 goals (2-game series); Toronto 5 goals, Ottawa 4 goals (2-game series).
Stanley Cup finals: Toronto 3, Vancouver (PCHL) 2.

1922-23

Team	W	L	T	Pts.	GF	GA
Ottawa Senators	14	9	1	29	77	54
Montreal Canadiens	13	9	2	28	73	61
Toronto St. Patricks	13	10	1	27	82	88
Hamilton Tigers	6	18	0	12	81	110

PLAYOFFS

Quarterfinals: Ottawa 3 goals, Montreal Canadiens 2 goals (2-game series); Vancouver (PCHL) 5 goals, Victoria (PCHL) 3 goals (2-game series). **Semifinals:** Ottawa 3, Vancouver (PCHL) 1; Edmonton (WCHL) 4 goals, Regina (WCHL) 3 goals (2-game series).
Stanley Cup finals: Ottawa 2, Edmonton (WCHL) 0.

1923-24

Team	W	L	T	Pts.	GF	GA
Ottawa Senators	16	8	0	32	74	54
Montreal Canadiens	13	11	0	26	59	48
Toronto St. Patricks	10	14	0	20	59	85
Hamilton Tigers	9	15	0	18	63	68

PLAYOFFS

First round: Vancouver (PCHL) 4 goals, Seattle (PCHL) 3 goals (2-game series); Calgary (WCHL) 4 goals, Regina (WCHL) 2 goals (2-game series). **Second round:** Montreal Canadiens 2, Ottawa 0; Calgary (WCHL) 2, Vancouver (PCHL) 1. **Third round:** Montreal Canadiens 2, Vancouver (PCHL) 0.
Stanley Cup finals: Montreal Canadiens 2, Calgary (WCHL) 0.

1924-25

Team	W	L	T	Pts.	GF	GA
Hamilton Tigers	19	10	1	39	90	60
Toronto St. Patricks	19	11	0	38	90	84
Montreal Canadiens	17	11	2	36	93	56
Ottawa Senators	17	12	1	35	83	66
Montreal Maroons	9	19	2	20	45	65
Boston Bruins	6	24	0	12	49	119

PLAYOFFS

Quarterfinals: Victoria (WCHL) 6 goals, Saskatoon (WCHL) 4 goals (2-game series). **Semifinals:** Montreal Canadiens 2, Toronto 0; Victoria (WCHL) 3 goals, Calgary (WCHL) 1 goal (2-game series).
Stanley Cup finals: Victoria (WCHL) 3, Montreal Canadiens 1.

1925-26

Team	W	L	T	Pts.	GF	GA
Ottawa Senators	24	8	4	52	77	42
Montreal Maroons	20	11	5	45	91	73
Pittsburgh Pirates	19	16	1	39	82	70
Boston Bruins	17	15	4	38	92	85
New York Americans	12	20	4	28	68	89
Toronto St. Patricks	12	21	3	27	92	114
Montreal Canadiens	11	24	1	23	79	108

PLAYOFFS

Quarterfinals: Victoria (WHL) 4 goals, Saskatoon (WHL) 3 goals (2-game series); Montreal Maroons 6 goals, Pittsburgh 4 goals (2-game series). **Semifinals:** Victoria (WHL) 5 goals, Edmonton (WHL) 3 goals (2-game series); Montreal Maroons 2 goals, Ottawa 1 goal (2-game series).
Stanley Cup finals: Montreal Maroons 3, Victoria (WHL) 1.

1926-27

AMERICAN DIVISION

Team	W	L	T	Pts.	GF	GA
New York Rangers	25	13	6	56	95	27
Boston Bruins	21	20	3	45	97	89
Chicago Blackhawks	19	22	3	41	115	116
Pittsburgh Pirates	15	26	3	33	79	108
Detroit Cougars	12	28	4	28	76	105

CANADIAN DIVISION

Team	W	L	T	Pts.	GF	GA
Ottawa Senators	30	10	4	64	89	69
Montreal Canadiens	28	14	2	58	99	67
Montreal Maroons	20	20	4	44	71	68
New York Americans	17	25	2	36	82	91
Toronto St. Patricks	15	24	5	35	79	94

PLAYOFFS

League quarterfinals: Montreal Canadiens 2 goals, Montreal Maroons 1 goal (2-game series); Boston 10 goals, Chicago 5 goals (2-game series). **Semifinals:** Ottawa 5 goals, Montreal Canadiens 1 goal (2-game series); Boston 3 goals, N.Y. Rangers 1 goal (2-game series).
Stanley Cup finals: Ottawa 2, Boston 0.

1927-28

AMERICAN DIVISION

Team	W	L	T	Pts.	GF	GA
Boston Bruins	20	13	11	51	77	70
New York Rangers	19	16	9	47	94	79
Pittsburgh Pirates	19	17	8	46	67	76
Detroit Cougars	19	19	6	44	88	79
Chicago Blackhawks	7	34	3	17	68	134

CANADIAN DIVISION

Team	W	L	T	Pts.	GF	GA
Montreal Canadiens	26	11	7	59	116	48
Montreal Maroons	24	14	6	54	96	77
Ottawa Senators	20	14	10	50	78	57
Toronto Maple Leafs	18	18	8	44	89	88
New York Americans	11	27	6	28	63	128

PLAYOFFS

League quarterfinals: Montreal Maroons 3 goals, Ottawa 1 goal (2-game series); N.Y. Rangers 6 goals, Pittsburgh 4 goals (2-game series). **Semifinals:** Montreal Maroons 3 goals, Montreal Canadiens 2 goals (2-game series); N.Y. Rangers 5 goals, Boston 2 goals (2-game series).
Stanley Cup finals: N.Y. Rangers 3, Montreal Maroons 2.

1928-29

AMERICAN DIVISION

Team	W	L	T	Pts.	GF	GA
Boston Bruins	26	13	5	57	89	52
New York Rangers	21	13	10	52	72	65
Detroit Cougars	19	16	9	47	72	63
Pittsburgh Pirates	9	27	8	26	46	80
Chicago Blackhawks	7	29	8	22	33	85

CANADIAN DIVISION

Team	W	L	T	Pts.	GF	GA
Montreal Canadiens	22	7	15	59	71	43
New York Americans	19	13	12	50	53	53
Toronto Maple Leafs	21	18	5	47	85	69
Ottawa Senators	14	17	13	41	54	67
Montreal Maroons	15	20	9	39	67	65

PLAYOFFS

League quarterfinals: N.Y. Rangers 1 goal, N.Y. Americans 0 goals (2-game series); Toronto 7 goals, Detroit 2 goals (2-game series). **Semifinals:** Boston 3, Montreal Canadiens 0; N.Y. Rangers 2, Toronto 0.
Stanley Cup finals: Boston 2, N.Y. Rangers 0.

1929-30

AMERICAN DIVISION

Team	W	L	T	Pts.	GF	GA
Boston Bruins	38	5	1	77	179	98
Chicago Blackhawks	21	18	5	47	117	111
New York Rangers	17	17	10	44	136	143
Detroit Cougars	14	24	6	34	117	133
Pittsburgh Pirates	5	36	3	13	102	185

CANADIAN DIVISION

Team	W	L	T	Pts.	GF	GA
Montreal Maroons	23	16	5	51	141	114
Montreal Canadiens	21	14	9	51	142	114
Ottawa Senators	21	15	8	50	138	118
Toronto Maple Leafs	17	21	6	40	116	124
New York Americans	14	25	5	33	113	161

PLAYOFFS

League quarterfinals: Montreal Canadiens 3 goals, Chicago 2 goals (2-game series); N.Y. Rangers 6 goals, Ottawa 3 goals (2-game series). **Semifinals:** Boston 3, Montreal Maroons 1; Montreal Canadiens 2, N.Y. Rangers 0.
Stanley Cup finals: Montreal Canadiens 2, Boston 0.

1930-31

AMERICAN DIVISION

Team	W	L	T	Pts.	GF	GA
Boston Bruins	28	10	6	62	143	90
Chicago Blackhawks	24	17	3	51	108	78
New York Rangers	19	16	9	47	106	87
Detroit Falcons	16	21	7	39	102	105
Philadelphia Quakers	4	36	4	12	76	184

CANADIAN DIVISION

Team	W	L	T	Pts.	GF	GA
Montreal Canadiens	26	10	8	60	89	60
Toronto Maple Leafs	22	13	9	53	99	53
Montreal Maroons	20	18	6	46	106	46
New York Americans	18	16	10	46	76	74
Ottawa Senators	10	30	4	24	91	142

PLAYOFFS

League quarterfinals: Chicago 4 goals, Toronto 3 goals (2-game series); N.Y. Rangers 8 goals, Montreal Maroons 1 goal (2-game series). **Semifinals:** Montreal Canadiens 3, Boston 2; Chicago 2, N.Y. Rangers 0.
Stanley Cup finals: Montreal Canadiens 3, Chicago 2.

1931-32

AMERICAN DIVISION

Team	W	L	T	Pts.	GF	GA
New York Rangers	23	17	8	54	134	112
Chicago Blackhawks	18	19	11	47	86	101
Detroit Falcons	18	20	10	46	95	108
Boston Bruins	15	21	12	42	122	117

CANADIAN DIVISION

Team	W	L	T	Pts.	GF	GA
Montreal Canadiens	25	16	7	57	128	111
Toronto Maple Leafs	23	18	7	53	155	127
Montreal Maroons	19	22	7	45	142	139
New York Americans	16	24	8	40	95	142

League quarterfinals: Toronto 6 goals, Chicago 2 goals (2-game series); Montreal Maroons 3 goals, Detroit 1 goal (2-game series). **Semifinals:** N.Y. Rangers 3, Montreal Canadiens 1; Toronto 4 goals, Montreal Maroons 3 (2-game series). **Stanley Cup finals:** Toronto 3, N.Y. Rangers 0.

1932-33

AMERICAN DIVISION

Team	W	L	T	Pts.	GF	GA
Boston Bruins	25	15	8	58	124	88
Detroit Red Wings	25	15	8	58	111	93
New York Rangers	23	17	8	54	135	107
Chicago Blackhawks	16	20	12	44	88	101

CANADIAN DIVISION

Team	W	L	T	Pts.	GF	GA
Toronto Maple Leafs	24	18	6	54	119	111
Montreal Maroons	22	20	6	50	135	119
Montreal Canadiens	18	25	5	41	92	115
New York Americans	15	22	11	41	91	118
Ottawa Senators	11	27	10	32	88	131

PLAYOFFS

League quarterfinals: Detroit 5 goals, Montreal Maroons 2 goals (2-game series); N.Y. Rangers 8 goals, Montreal Canadiens 5 goals (2-game series). **Semifinals:** Toronto 3, Boston 2; N.Y. Rangers 6 goals, Detroit 3 goals (2-game series). **Stanley Cup finals:** N.Y. Rangers 3, Toronto 1.

1933-34

AMERICAN DIVISION

Team	W	L	T	Pts.	GF	GA
Detroit Red Wings	24	14	10	58	113	98
Chicago Blackhawks	20	17	11	51	88	83
New York Rangers	21	19	8	50	120	113
Boston Bruins	18	25	5	41	111	130

CANADIAN DIVISION

Team	W	L	T	Pts.	GF	GA
Toronto Maple Leafs	26	13	9	61	174	119
Montreal Canadiens	22	20	6	50	99	101
Montreal Maroons	19	18	11	49	117	122
New York Americans	15	23	10	40	104	132
Ottawa Senators	13	29	6	32	115	143

PLAYOFFS

League quarterfinals: Chicago 4 goals, Montreal Canadiens 3 goals (2-game series); Montreal Maroons 2 goals, N.Y. Rangers 1 goal (2-game series). **Semifinals:** Detroit 3, Toronto 2; Chicago 6 goals, Montreal Maroons 2 goals (2-game series). **Stanley Cup finals:** Chicago 3, Detroit 1.

1934-35

AMERICAN DIVISION

Team	W	L	T	Pts.	GF	GA
Boston Bruins	26	16	6	58	129	112
Chicago Blackhawks	26	17	5	57	118	88
New York Rangers	22	20	6	50	137	139
Detroit Red Wings	19	22	7	45	127	114

CANADIAN DIVISION

Team	W	L	T	Pts.	GF	GA
Toronto Maple Leafs	30	14	4	64	157	111
Montreal Maroons	24	19	5	53	123	92
Montreal Canadiens	19	23	6	44	110	145
New York Americans	12	27	9	33	100	142
St. Louis Eagles	11	31	6	28	86	144

League quarterfinals: Montreal Maroons 1 goal, Chicago 0 goals (2-game series); N.Y. Rangers 6 goals, Montreal Canadiens 5 goals (2-game series). **Semifinals:** Toronto 3, Boston 1; Montreal Maroons 5 goals, N.Y. Rangers 4 (2-game series). **Stanley Cup finals:** Montreal Maroons 3, Toronto 0.

1935-36

AMERICAN DIVISION

Team	W	L	T	Pts.	GF	GA
Detroit Red Wings	24	16	8	56	124	103
Boston Bruins	22	20	6	50	92	83
Chicago Blackhawks	21	19	8	50	93	92
New York Rangers	19	17	12	50	96	50

CANADIAN DIVISION

Team	W	L	T	Pts.	GF	GA
Montreal Maroons	22	16	10	54	114	106
Toronto Maple Leafs	23	19	6	52	126	106
New York Americans	16	25	7	39	109	122
Montreal Canadiens	11	26	11	33	82	123

PLAYOFFS

League quarterfinals: Toronto 8 goals, Boston 6 goals (2-game series); N.Y. Americans 7 goals, Chicago 5 goals (2-game series). **Semifinals:** Detroit 3, Montreal Maroons 0; Toronto 2, N.Y. Americans 1. **Stanley Cup finals:** Detroit 3, Toronto 1.

1936-37

AMERICAN DIVISION

Team	W	L	T	Pts.	GF	GA
Detroit Red Wings	25	14	9	59	128	102
Boston Bruins	23	18	7	53	120	110
New York Rangers	19	20	9	47	117	106
Chicago Blackhawks	14	27	7	35	99	131

CANADIAN DIVISION

Team	W	L	T	Pts.	GF	GA
Montreal Canadiens	24	18	6	54	115	111
Montreal Maroons	22	17	9	53	126	110
Toronto Maple Leafs	22	21	5	49	119	115
New York Americans	15	29	4	34	122	161

PLAYOFFS

League quarterfinals: Montreal Maroons 2, Boston 1; N.Y. Rangers 2, Toronto 0. **Semifinals:** Detroit 3, Montreal Canadiens 2; N.Y. Rangers 2, Montreal Maroons 0. **Stanley Cup finals:** Detroit 3, N.Y. Rangers 2.

1937-38

AMERICAN DIVISION

Team	W	L	T	Pts.	GF	GA
Boston Bruins	30	11	7	67	142	89
New York Rangers	27	15	6	60	149	96
Chicago Blackhawks	14	25	9	37	97	139
Detroit Red Wings	12	25	11	35	99	133

CANADIAN DIVISION

Team	W	L	T	Pts.	GF	GA
Toronto Maple Leafs	24	15	9	57	151	127
New York Americans	19	18	11	49	110	111
Montreal Canadiens	18	17	13	49	123	128
Montreal Maroons	12	30	6	30	101	149

PLAYOFFS

League quarterfinals: N.Y. Americans 2, N.Y. Rangers 1; Chicago 2, Montreal Canadiens 1. **Semifinals:** Toronto 3, Boston 0; Chicago 2, N.Y. Americans 1. **Stanley Cup finals:** Chicago 3, Toronto 1.

NHL HISTORY *Year-by-year standings*

1938-39

Team	W	L	T	Pts.	GF	GA
Boston Bruins	36	10	2	74	156	76
New York Rangers	26	16	6	58	149	105
Toronto Maple Leafs	19	20	9	47	114	107
New York Americans	17	21	10	44	119	157
Detroit Red Wings	18	24	6	42	107	128
Montreal Canadiens	15	24	9	39	115	146
Chicago Blackhawks	12	28	8	32	91	132

PLAYOFFS

League quarterfinals: Toronto 2, N.Y. Americans 0; Detroit 2, Montreal 1. **Semifinals:** Boston 4, N.Y. Rangers 3; Toronto 2, Detroit 1.
Stanley Cup finals: Boston 4, Toronto 1.

1939-40

Team	W	L	T	Pts.	GF	GA
Boston Bruins	31	12	5	67	170	98
New York Rangers	27	11	10	64	136	77
Toronto Maple Leafs	25	17	6	56	134	110
Chicago Blackhawks	23	19	6	52	112	120
Detroit Red Wings	16	26	6	38	90	126
New York Americans	15	29	4	34	106	140
Montreal Canadiens	10	33	5	25	90	167

PLAYOFFS

League quarterfinals: Toronto 2, Chicago 0; Detroit 2, N.Y. Americans 1. **Semifinals:** N.Y. Rangers 4, Boston 2; Toronto 2, Detroit 0.
Stanley Cup finals: N.Y. Rangers 4, Toronto 2.

1940-41

Team	W	L	T	Pts.	GF	GA
Boston Bruins	27	8	13	67	168	102
Toronto Maple Leafs	28	14	6	62	145	99
Detroit Red Wings	21	16	11	53	112	102
New York Rangers	21	19	8	50	143	125
Chicago Blackhawks	16	25	7	39	112	139
Montreal Canadiens	16	26	6	38	121	147
New York Americans	8	29	11	27	99	186

PLAYOFFS

League quarterfinals: Detroit 2, N.Y. Rangers 1; Chicago 2, Montreal 1. **Semifinals:** Boston 4, Toronto 3; Detroit 2, Chicago 0.
Stanley Cup finals: Boston 4, Detroit 0.

1941-42

Team	W	L	T	Pts.	GF	GA
New York Rangers	29	17	2	60	177	143
Toronto Maple Leafs	27	18	3	57	158	136
Boston Bruins	25	17	6	56	160	118
Chicago Blackhawks	22	23	3	47	145	155
Detroit Red Wings	19	25	4	42	140	147
Montreal Canadiens	18	27	3	39	134	173
Brooklyn Americans	16	29	3	35	133	175

PLAYOFFS

League quarterfinals: Boston 2, Chicago 1; Detroit 2, Montreal 1. **Semifinals:** Toronto 4, New York 2; Detroit 2, Boston 0.
Stanley Cup finals: Toronto 4, Detroit 3.

1942-43

Team	W	L	T	Pts.	GF	GA
Detroit Red Wings	25	14	11	61	169	124
Boston Bruins	24	17	9	57	195	176
Toronto Maple Leafs	22	19	9	53	198	159
Montreal Canadiens	19	19	12	50	181	191
Chicago Blackhawks	17	18	15	49	179	180
New York Rangers	11	31	8	30	161	253

PLAYOFFS

League semifinals: Detroit 4, Toronto 2; Boston 4, Montreal 1.
Stanley Cup finals: Detroit 4, Boston 0.

1943-44

Team	W	L	T	Pts.	GF	GA
Montreal Canadiens	38	5	7	83	234	109
Detroit Red Wings	26	18	6	58	214	177
Toronto Maple Leafs	23	23	4	50	214	174
Chicago Blackhawks	22	23	5	49	178	187
Boston Bruins	19	26	5	43	223	268
New York Rangers	6	39	5	17	162	310

PLAYOFFS

League semifinals: Montreal 4, Toronto 1; Chicago 4, Detroit 1.
Stanley Cup finals: Montreal 4, Chicago 0.

1944-45

Team	W	L	T	Pts.	GF	GA
Montreal Canadiens	38	8	4	80	228	121
Detroit Red Wings	31	14	5	67	218	161
Toronto Maple Leafs	24	22	4	52	183	161
Boston Bruins	16	30	4	36	179	219
Chicago Blackhawks	13	30	7	33	141	194
New York Rangers	11	29	10	32	154	247

PLAYOFFS

League semifinals: Toronto 4, Montreal 2; Detroit 4, Boston 3.
Stanley Cup finals: Toronto 4, Detroit 3.

1945-46

Team	W	L	T	Pts.	GF	GA
Montreal Canadiens	28	17	5	61	172	134
Boston Bruins	24	18	8	56	167	156
Chicago Blackhawks	23	20	7	53	200	178
Detroit Red Wings	20	20	10	50	146	159
Toronto Maple Leafs	19	24	7	45	174	185
New York Rangers	13	28	9	35	144	191

PLAYOFFS

League semifinals: Montreal 4, Chicago 0; Boston 4, Detroit 1.
Stanley Cup finals: Montreal 4, Boston 1.

1946-47

Team	W	L	T	Pts.	GF	GA
Montreal Canadiens	34	16	10	78	189	138
Toronto Maple Leafs	31	19	10	72	209	172
Boston Bruins	26	23	11	63	190	175
Detroit Red Wings	22	27	11	55	190	193
New York Rangers	22	32	6	50	167	186
Chicago Blackhawks	19	37	4	42	193	274

PLAYOFFS

League semifinals: Montreal 4, Boston 1; Toronto 4, Detroit 1.
Stanley Cup finals: Toronto 4, Montreal 2.

1947-48

Team	W	L	T	Pts.	GF	GA
Toronto Maple Leafs	32	15	13	77	182	143
Detroit Red Wings	30	18	12	72	187	148
Boston Bruins	23	24	13	59	167	168
New York Rangers	21	26	13	55	176	201
Montreal Canadiens	20	29	11	51	147	169
Chicago Blackhawks	20	34	6	46	195	225

PLAYOFFS

League semifinals: Toronto 4, Boston 1; Detroit 4, New York 2.
Stanley Cup finals: Toronto 4, Detroit 0.

1948-49

Team	W	L	T	Pts.	GF	GA
Detroit Red Wings	34	19	7	75	195	145
Boston Bruins	29	23	8	66	178	163
Montreal Canadiens	28	23	9	65	152	126
Toronto Maple Leafs	22	25	13	57	147	161
Chicago Blackhawks	21	31	8	50	173	211
New York Rangers	18	31	11	47	133	172

PLAYOFFS
League semifinals: Detroit 4, Montreal 3; Toronto 4, Boston 1.
Stanley Cup finals: Toronto 4, Detroit 0.

1949-50

Team	W	L	T	Pts.	GF	GA
Detroit Red Wings	37	19	14	88	229	164
Montreal Canadiens	29	22	19	77	172	150
Toronto Maple Leafs	31	27	12	74	176	173
New York Rangers	28	31	11	67	170	189
Boston Bruins	22	32	16	60	198	228
Chicago Blackhawks	22	38	10	54	203	244

PLAYOFFS
League semifinals: Detroit 4, Toronto 3; New York 4, Montreal 1.
Stanley Cup finals: Detroit 4, New York 3.

1950-51

Team	W	L	T	Pts.	GF	GA
Detroit Red Wings	44	13	13	101	236	139
Toronto Maple Leafs	41	16	13	95	212	138
Montreal Canadiens	25	30	15	65	173	184
Boston Bruins	22	30	18	62	178	197
New York Rangers	20	29	21	61	169	201
Chicago Blackhawks	13	47	10	36	171	280

PLAYOFFS
League semifinals: Montreal 4, Detroit 2; Toronto 4, Boston 1.
Stanley Cup finals: Toronto 4, Montreal 1.

1951-52

Team	W	L	T	Pts.	GF	GA
Detroit Red Wings	44	14	12	100	215	133
Montreal Canadiens	34	26	10	78	195	164
Toronto Maple Leafs	29	25	16	74	168	157
Boston Bruins	25	29	16	66	162	176
New York Rangers	23	34	13	59	192	219
Chicago Blackhawks	17	4	9	43	158	241

PLAYOFFS
League semifinals: Detroit 4, Toronto 0; Montreal 4, Boston 3.
Stanley Cup finals: Detroit 4, Montreal 0.

1952-53

Team	W	L	T	Pts.	GF	GA
Detroit Red Wings	36	16	18	90	222	133
Montreal Canadiens	28	23	19	75	155	148
Boston Bruins	28	29	13	69	152	172
Chicago Blackhawks	27	28	15	69	169	175
Toronto Maple Leafs	27	30	13	67	156	167
New York Rangers	17	37	16	50	152	211

PLAYOFFS
League semifinals: Boston 4, Detroit 2; Montreal 4, Chicago 3.
Stanley Cup finals: Montreal 4, Boston 1.

1953-54

Team	W	L	T	Pts.	GF	GA
Detroit Red Wings	37	19	14	88	191	132
Montreal Canadiens	35	24	11	81	195	141
Toronto Maple Leafs	32	24	14	78	152	131
Boston Bruins	32	28	10	74	177	181
New York Rangers	29	31	10	68	161	182
Chicago Blackhawks	12	51	7	31	133	242

PLAYOFFS
League semifinals: Detroit 4, Toronto 1; Montreal 4, Boston 0.
Stanley Cup finals: Detroit 4, Montreal 3.

1954-55

Team	W	L	T	Pts.	GF	GA
Detroit Red Wings	42	17	11	95	204	134
Montreal Canadiens	41	18	11	93	228	157
Toronto Maple Leafs	24	24	22	70	147	135
Boston Bruins	23	26	21	67	169	188
New York Rangers	17	35	18	52	150	210
Chicago Blackhawks	13	40	17	43	161	235

PLAYOFFS
League semifinals: Detroit 4, Toronto 0; Montreal 4, Boston 1.
Stanley Cup finals: Detroit 4, Montreal 3.

1955-56

Team	W	L	T	Pts.	GF	GA
Montreal Canadiens	45	15	10	100	222	131
Detroit Red Wings	30	24	16	76	183	148
New York Rangers	32	28	10	74	204	203
Toronto Maple Leafs	24	33	13	61	153	181
Boston Bruins	23	34	13	59	147	185
Chicago Blackhawks	19	39	12	50	155	216

PLAYOFFS
League semifinals: Montreal 4, New York 1; Detroit 4, Toronto 1.
Stanley Cup finals: Montreal 4, Detroit 1.

1956-57

Team	W	L	T	Pts.	GF	GA
Detroit Red Wings	38	20	12	88	198	157
Montreal Canadiens	35	23	12	82	210	155
Boston Bruins	34	24	12	80	195	174
New York Rangers	26	30	14	66	184	227
Toronto Maple Leafs	21	34	15	57	174	192
Chicago Blackhawks	16	39	15	47	169	225

PLAYOFFS
League semifinals: Boston 4, Detroit 1; Montreal 4, New York 1.
Stanley Cup finals: Montreal 4, Boston 1.

1957-58

Team	W	L	T	Pts.	GF	GA
Montreal Canadiens	43	17	10	96	250	158
New York Rangers	32	25	13	77	195	188
Detroit Red Wings	29	29	12	70	176	207
Boston Bruins	27	28	15	69	199	194
Chicago Blackhawks	24	39	7	55	163	202
Toronto Maple Leafs	21	38	11	53	192	226

PLAYOFFS
League semifinals: Montreal 4, Detroit 0; Boston 4, New York 2.
Stanley Cup finals: Montreal 4, Boston 2.

1958-59

Team	W	L	T	Pts.	GF	GA
Montreal Canadiens	39	18	13	91	258	158
Boston Bruins	32	29	9	73	205	215
Chicago Blackhawks	28	29	13	69	197	208
Toronto Maple Leafs	27	32	11	65	189	201
New York Rangers	26	32	12	64	201	217
Detroit Red Wings	25	37	8	58	167	218

PLAYOFFS

League semifinals: Montreal 4, Chicago 2; Toronto 4, Boston 3.
Stanley Cup finals: Montreal 4, Toronto 1.

1959-60

Team	W	L	T	Pts.	GF	GA
Montreal Canadiens	40	18	12	92	255	178
Toronto Maple Leafs	35	26	9	79	199	195
Chicago Blackhawks	28	29	13	69	191	180
Detroit Red Wings	26	29	15	67	186	197
Boston Bruins	28	34	8	64	220	241
New York Rangers	17	38	15	49	187	247

PLAYOFFS

League semifinals: Montreal 4, Chicago 0; Toronto 4, Detroit 2.
Stanley Cup finals: Montreal 4, Toronto 0.

1960-61

Team	W	L	T	Pts.	GF	GA
Montreal Canadiens	41	19	10	92	254	188
Toronto Maple Leafs	39	19	12	90	234	176
Chicago Blackhawks	29	24	17	75	198	180
Detroit Red Wings	25	29	16	66	195	215
New York Rangers	22	38	10	54	204	248
Boston Bruins	15	42	13	43	176	254

PLAYOFFS

League semifinals: Chicago 4, Montreal 2; Detroit 4, Toronto 1.
Stanley Cup finals: Chicago 4, Detroit 2.

1961-62

Team	W	L	T	Pts.	GF	GA
Montreal Canadiens	42	14	14	98	259	166
Toronto Maple Leafs	37	22	11	85	232	180
Chicago Blackhawks	31	26	13	75	217	186
New York Rangers	26	32	12	64	195	207
Detroit Red Wings	23	33	14	60	184	219
Boston Bruins	15	47	8	38	177	306

PLAYOFFS

League semifinals: Chicago 4, Montreal 2; Toronto 4, New York 2.
Stanley Cup finals: Toronto 4, Chicago 2.

1962-63

Team	W	L	T	Pts.	GF	GA
Toronto Maple Leafs	35	23	12	82	221	180
Chicago Blackhawks	32	21	17	81	194	178
Montreal Canadiens	28	19	23	79	225	183
Detroit Red Wings	32	25	13	77	200	194
New York Rangers	22	36	12	56	211	233
Boston Bruins	14	39	17	45	198	281

PLAYOFFS

League semifinals: Toronto 4, Montreal 1; Detroit 4, Chicago 2.
Stanley Cup finals: Toronto 4, Detroit 1.

1963-64

Team	W	L	T	Pts.	GF	GA
Montreal Canadiens	36	21	13	85	209	167
Chicago Blackhawks	36	22	12	84	218	169
Toronto Maple Leafs	33	25	12	78	192	172
Detroit Red Wings	30	29	11	71	191	204
New York Rangers	22	38	10	54	186	242
Boston Bruins	18	40	12	48	170	212

PLAYOFFS

League semifinals: Toronto 4, Montreal 3; Detroit 4, Chicago 3.
Stanley Cup finals: Toronto 4, Detroit 3.

1964-65

Team	W	L	T	Pts.	GF	GA
Detroit Red Wings	40	23	7	87	224	175
Montreal Canadiens	36	23	11	83	211	185
Chicago Blackhawks	34	28	8	76	224	176
Toronto Maple Leafs	30	26	14	74	204	173
New York Rangers	20	38	12	52	179	246
Boston Bruins	21	43	6	48	166	253

PLAYOFFS

League semifinals: Chicago 4, Detroit 3; Montreal 4, Toronto 2.
Stanley Cup finals: Montreal 4, Chicago 3.

1965-66

Team	W	L	T	Pts.	GF	GA
Montreal Canadiens	41	21	8	90	239	173
Chicago Blackhawks	37	25	8	82	240	187
Toronto Maple Leafs	34	25	11	79	208	187
Detroit Red Wings	31	27	12	74	221	194
Boston Bruins	21	43	6	48	174	275
New York Rangers	18	41	11	47	195	261

PLAYOFFS

League semifinals: Montreal 4, Toronto 0; Detroit 4, Chicago 2.
Stanley Cup finals: Montreal 4, Detroit 2.

1966-67

Team	W	L	T	Pts.	GF	GA
Chicago Blackhawks	41	17	12	94	264	170
Montreal Canadiens	32	25	13	77	202	188
Toronto Maple Leafs	32	27	11	75	204	211
New York Rangers	30	28	12	72	188	189
Detroit Red Wings	27	39	4	58	212	241
Boston Bruins	17	43	10	44	182	253

PLAYOFFS

League semifinals: Toronto 4, Chicago 2; Montreal 4, New York 0.
Stanley Cup finals: Toronto 4, Montreal 2.

1967-68

EAST DIVISION

Team	W	L	T	Pts.	GF	GA
Montreal Canadiens	42	22	10	94	236	167
New York Rangers	39	23	12	90	226	183
Boston Bruins	37	27	10	84	259	216
Chicago Blackhawks	32	26	16	80	212	222
Toronto Maple Leafs	33	31	10	76	209	176
Detroit Red Wings	27	35	12	66	245	257

WEST DIVISION

Team	W	L	T	Pts.	GF	GA
Philadelphia Flyers	31	32	11	73	173	179
Los Angeles Kings	31	33	10	72	200	224

Team	W	L	T	Pts.	GF	GA
St. Louis Blues	27	31	16	70	177	191
Minnesota North Stars	27	32	15	69	191	226
Pittsburgh Penguins	27	34	13	67	195	219
Oakland Seals	15	42	17	42	153	219

PLAYOFFS

Division semifinals: Montreal 4, Boston 0; Chicago 4, New York 2; St. Louis 4, Philadelphia 3; Minnesota 4, Los Angeles 3. **Division finals:** Montreal 4, Chicago 1; St. Louis 4, Minnesota 3. **Stanley Cup finals:** Montreal 4, St. Louis 0.

1968-69

EAST DIVISION

Team	W	L	T	Pts.	GF	GA
Montreal Canadiens	46	19	11	103	271	202
Boston Bruins	42	18	16	100	303	221
New York Rangers	41	26	9	91	231	196
Toronto Maple Leafs	35	26	15	85	234	217
Detroit Red Wings	33	31	12	78	239	221
Chicago Blackhawks	34	33	9	77	280	246

WEST DIVISION

Team	W	L	T	Pts.	GF	GA
St. Louis Blues	37	25	14	88	204	157
Oakland Seals	29	36	11	69	219	251
Philadelphia Flyers	20	35	21	61	174	225
Los Angeles Kings	24	42	10	58	185	260
Pittsburgh Penguins	20	45	11	51	189	270
Minnesota North Stars	18	43	15	51	189	252

PLAYOFFS

Division semifinals: Montreal 4, New York 0; Boston 4, Toronto 0; St. Louis 4, Philadelphia 0; Los Angeles 4, Oakland 3. **Division finals:** Montreal 4, Boston 2; St. Louis 4, Los Angeles 0. **Stanley Cup finals:** Montreal 4, St. Louis 0.

1969-70

EAST DIVISION

Team	W	L	T	Pts.	GF	GA
Chicago Blackhawks	45	22	9	99	250	170
Boston Bruins	40	17	19	99	277	216
Detroit Red Wings	40	21	15	95	246	199
New York Rangers	38	22	16	92	246	189
Montreal Canadiens	38	22	16	92	244	201
Toronto Maple Leafs	29	34	13	71	222	242

WEST DIVISION

Team	W	L	T	Pts.	GF	GA
St. Louis Blues	37	27	12	86	224	179
Pittsburgh Penguins	26	38	12	64	182	238
Minnesota North Stars	19	35	22	60	224	257
Oakland Seals	22	40	14	58	169	243
Philadelphia Flyers	17	35	24	58	197	225
Los Angeles Kings	14	52	10	38	168	290

PLAYOFFS

Division semifinals: Chicago 4, Detroit 0; Boston 4, N.Y. Rangers 2; St. Louis 4, Minnesota 2; Pittsburgh 4, Oakland 0. **Division finals:** Boston 4, Chicago 0; St. Louis 4, Pittsburgh 2. **Stanley Cup finals:** Boston 4, St. Louis 0.

1970-71

EAST DIVISION

Team	W	L	T	Pts.	GF	GA
Boston Bruins	57	14	7	121	399	207
New York Rangers	49	18	11	109	259	177
Montreal Canadiens	42	23	13	97	291	216
Toronto Maple Leafs	37	33	8	82	248	211
Buffalo Sabres	24	39	15	63	217	291
Vancouver Canucks	24	46	8	56	229	296
Detroit Red Wings	22	45	11	55	209	308

WEST DIVISION

Team	W	L	T	Pts.	GF	GA
Chicago Blackhawks	49	20	9	107	277	184
St. Louis Blues	34	25	19	87	223	208
Philadelphia Flyers	28	33	17	73	207	225
Minnesota North Stars	28	34	16	72	191	223
Los Angeles Kings	25	40	13	63	239	303
Pittsburgh Penguins	21	37	20	62	221	240
California Golden Seals	20	53	5	45	199	320

PLAYOFFS

Division semifinals: Montreal 4, Boston 3; N.Y. Rangers 4, Toronto 2; Chicago 4, Philadelphia 0; Minnesota 4, St. Louis 2. **Division finals:** Montreal 4, Minnesota 2; Chicago 4, N.Y. Rangers 3. **Stanley Cup finals:** Montreal 4, Chicago 3.

1971-72

EAST DIVISION

Team	W	L	T	Pts.	GF	GA
Boston Bruins	54	13	11	119	330	204
New York Rangers	48	17	13	109	317	192
Montreal Canadiens	46	16	16	108	307	205
Toronto Maple Leafs	33	31	14	80	209	208
Detroit Red Wings	33	35	10	76	261	262
Buffalo Sabres	16	43	19	51	203	289
Vancouver Canucks	20	50	8	48	203	297

WEST DIVISION

Team	W	L	T	Pts.	GF	GA
Chicago Blackhawks	46	17	15	107	256	166
Minnesota North Stars	37	29	12	86	212	191
St. Louis Blues	28	39	11	67	208	247
Philadelphia Flyers	26	38	14	66	220	258
Pittsburgh Penguins	26	38	14	66	200	236
California Golden Seals	21	39	18	60	216	288
Los Angeles Kings	20	49	9	49	206	305

PLAYOFFS

Division semifinals: Boston 4, Toronto 1; N.Y. Rangers 4, Montreal 2; Chicago 4, Pittsburgh 0; St. Louis 4, Minnesota 3. **Division finals:** N.Y. Rangers 4, Chicago 0; Boston 4, St. Louis 0. **Stanley Cup finals:** Boston 4, N.Y. Rangers 2.

1972-73

EAST DIVISION

Team	W	L	T	Pts.	GF	GA
Montreal Canadiens	52	10	16	120	329	184
Boston Bruins	51	22	5	107	330	235
New York Rangers	47	23	8	102	297	208
Buffalo Sabres	37	27	14	88	257	219
Detroit Red Wings	37	29	12	86	265	243
Toronto Maple Leafs	27	41	10	64	247	279
Vancouver Canucks	22	47	9	53	233	339
New York Islanders	12	60	6	30	170	347

WEST DIVISION

Team	W	L	T	Pts.	GF	GA
Chicago Blackhawks	42	27	9	93	284	225
Philadelphia Flyers	37	30	11	85	296	256
Minnesota North Stars	37	30	11	85	254	230
St. Louis Blues	32	34	12	76	233	251
Pittsburgh Penguins	32	37	9	73	257	265

Team	W	L	T	Pts.	GF	GA
Los Angeles Kings	31	36	11	73	232	245
Atlanta Flames	25	38	15	65	191	239
California Golden Seals	16	46	16	48	213	323

PLAYOFFS

Division semifinals: Montreal 4, Buffalo 2; N.Y. Rangers 4, Boston 1; Chicago 4, St. Louis 1; Philadelphia 4, Minnesota 2. **Division finals:** Montreal 4, Philadelphia 1; Chicago 4, N.Y. Rangers 1.
Stanley Cup finals: Montreal 4, Chicago 2.

1973-74

EAST DIVISION

Team	W	L	T	Pts.	GF	GA
Boston Bruins	52	17	9	113	349	221
Montreal Canadiens	45	42	9	99	293	240
New York Rangers	40	24	14	94	300	251
Toronto Maple Leafs	35	27	16	86	274	230
Buffalo Sabres	32	34	12	76	242	250
Detroit Red Wings	29	39	10	68	255	319
Vancouver Canucks	24	43	11	59	224	296
New York Islanders	19	41	18	56	182	247

WEST DIVISION

Team	W	L	T	Pts.	GF	GA
Philadelphia Flyers	50	16	12	112	273	164
Chicago Blackhawks	41	14	23	105	272	164
Los Angeles Kings	33	33	12	78	233	231
Atlanta Flames	30	34	14	74	214	238
Pittsburgh Penguins	28	41	9	65	242	273
St. Louis Blues	26	40	12	64	206	248
Minnesota North Stars	23	38	17	63	235	275
California Golden Seals	13	55	10	36	195	342

PLAYOFFS

Division semifinals: Boston 4, Toronto 0; N.Y. Rangers 4, Montreal 2; Philadelphia 4, Atlanta 0; Chicago 4, Los Angeles 1. **Division finals:** Boston 4, Chicago 2; Philadelphia 4, N.Y. Rangers 3.
Stanley Cup finals: Philadelphia 4, Boston 2.

1974-75

PRINCE OF WALES CONFERENCE

ADAMS DIVISION

Team	W	L	T	Pts.	GF	GA
Buffalo Sabres	49	16	15	113	354	240
Boston Bruins	40	26	14	94	345	245
Toronto Maple Leafs	31	33	16	78	280	309
California Golden Seals	19	48	13	51	212	316

NORRIS DIVISION

Team	W	L	T	Pts.	GF	GA
Montreal Canadiens	47	14	19	113	374	225
Los Angeles Kings	42	17	21	105	269	185
Pittsburgh Penguins	37	28	15	89	326	289
Detroit Red Wings	23	45	12	58	259	335
Washington Capitals	8	67	5	21	181	446

CLARENCE CAMPBELL CONFERENCE

PATRICK DIVISION

Team	W	L	T	Pts.	GF	GA
Philadelphia Flyers	51	18	11	113	293	181
New York Rangers	37	29	14	88	319	276
New York Islanders	33	25	22	88	264	221
Atlanta Flames	34	31	15	83	243	233

SMYTHE DIVISION

Team	W	L	T	Pts.	GF	GA
Vancouver Canucks	38	32	10	86	271	254
St. Louis Blues	35	31	14	84	269	267
Chicago Blackhawks	37	35	8	82	268	241
Minnesota North Stars	23	50	7	53	221	341
Kansas City Scouts	15	54	11	41	184	328

PLAYOFFS

Preliminaries: Toronto 2, Los Angeles 1; Chicago 2, Boston 1; Pittsburgh 2, St. Louis 0; N.Y. Islanders 2, N.Y. Rangers 1. **Quarterfinals:** Philadelphia 4, Toronto 0; Buffalo 4, Chicago 1; Montreal 4, Vancouver 1; N.Y. Islanders 4, Pittsburgh 3. **Semifinals:** Philadelphia 4, N.Y. Islanders 3; Buffalo 4, Montreal 2.
Stanley Cup finals: Philadelphia 4, Buffalo 2.

1975-76

PRINCE OF WALES CONFERENCE

ADAMS DIVISION

Team	W	L	T	Pts.	GF	GA
Boston Bruins	48	15	17	113	313	237
Buffalo Sabres	46	21	13	105	339	240
Toronto Maple Leafs	34	31	15	83	294	276
California Golden Seals	27	42	11	65	250	278

NORRIS DIVISION

Team	W	L	T	Pts.	GF	GA
Montreal Canadiens	58	11	11	127	337	174
Los Angeles Kings	38	33	9	85	263	265
Pittsburgh Penguins	35	33	12	82	339	303
Detroit Red Wings	26	44	10	62	226	300
Washington Capitals	11	59	10	32	224	394

CLARENCE CAMPBELL CONFERENCE

PATRICK DIVISION

Team	W	L	T	Pts.	GF	GA
Philadelphia Flyers	51	13	16	118	348	209
New York Islanders	42	21	17	101	297	190
Atlanta Flames	35	33	12	82	262	237
New York Rangers	29	42	9	67	262	333

SMYTHE DIVISION

Team	W	L	T	Pts.	GF	GA
Chicago Blackhawks	32	30	18	82	254	261
Vancouver Canucks	33	32	15	81	271	272
St. Louis Blues	29	37	14	72	249	290
Minnesota North Stars	20	53	7	47	195	303
Kansas City Scouts	12	56	12	36	190	351

PLAYOFFS

Preliminaries: Buffalo 2, St. Louis 1; N.Y. Islanders 2, Vancouver 0; Los Angeles 2, Atlanta 0; Toronto 2, Pittsburgh 1. **Quarterfinals:** Montreal 4, Chicago 0; Philadelphia 4, Toronto 3; Boston 4, Los Angeles 3; N.Y. Islanders 4, Buffalo 2. **Semifinals:** Montreal 4, N.Y. Islanders 1; Philadelphia 4, Boston 1.
Stanley Cup finals: Montreal 4, Philadelphia 0.

1976-77

PRINCE OF WALES CONFERENCE

ADAMS DIVISION

Team	W	L	T	Pts.	GF	GA
Boston Bruins	49	23	8	106	312	240
Buffalo Sabres	48	24	8	104	301	220
Toronto Maple Leafs	33	32	15	81	301	285
Cleveland Barons	25	42	13	63	240	292

NORRIS DIVISION

Team	W	L	T	Pts.	GF	GA
Montreal Canadiens	60	8	12	132	387	171
Los Angeles Kings	34	31	15	83	271	241
Pittsburgh Penguins	34	33	13	81	240	252
Washington Capitals	24	42	14	62	221	307
Detroit Red Wings	16	55	9	41	183	309

CLARENCE CAMPBELL CONFERENCE

PATRICK DIVISION

Team	W	L	T	Pts.	GF	GA
Philadelphia Flyers	48	16	16	112	323	213
New York Islanders	47	21	12	106	288	193
Atlanta Flames	34	34	12	80	264	265
New York Rangers	29	37	14	72	272	310

SMYTHE DIVISION

Team	W	L	T	Pts.	GF	GA
St. Louis Blues	32	39	9	73	239	276
Minnesota North Stars	23	39	18	64	240	310
Chicago Blackhawks	26	43	11	63	240	298
Vancouver Canucks	25	42	13	63	235	294
Colorado Rockies	20	46	14	54	226	307

PLAYOFFS

Preliminaries: N.Y. Islanders 2, Chicago 0; Buffalo 2, Minnesota 0; Los Angeles 2, Atlanta 1; Toronto 2, Pittsburgh 1. **Quarterfinals:** Montreal 4, St. Louis 0; Philadelphia 4, Toronto 2; Boston 4, Los Angeles 2; N.Y. Islanders 4, Buffalo 0. **Semifinals:** Montreal 4, N.Y. Islanders 2; Boston 4, Philadelphia 0. **Stanley Cup finals:** Montreal 4, Boston 0.

1977-78

PRINCE OF WALES CONFERENCE

ADAMS DIVISION

Team	W	L	T	Pts.	GF	GA
Boston Bruins	51	18	11	113	333	218
Buffalo Sabres	44	19	17	105	288	215
Toronto Maple Leafs	41	29	10	92	271	237
Cleveland Barons	22	45	13	57	230	325

NORRIS DIVISION

Team	W	L	T	Pts.	GF	GA
Montreal Canadiens	59	10	11	129	359	183
Detroit Red Wings	32	34	14	78	252	266
Los Angeles Kings	31	34	15	77	243	245
Pittsburgh Penguins	25	37	18	68	254	321
Washington Capitals	17	49	14	48	195	321

CLARENCE CAMPBELL CONFERENCE

PATRICK DIVISION

Team	W	L	T	Pts.	GF	GA
New York Islanders	48	17	15	111	334	210
Philadelphia Flyers	45	20	15	105	296	200
Atlanta Flames	34	27	19	87	274	252
New York Rangers	30	37	13	73	279	280

SMYTHE DIVISION

Team	W	L	T	Pts.	GF	GA
Chicago Blackhawks	32	29	19	83	230	220
Colorado Rockies	19	40	21	59	257	305
Vancouver Canucks	20	43	17	57	239	320
St. Louis Blues	20	47	13	53	195	304
Minnesota North Stars	18	53	9	45	218	325

PLAYOFFS

Preliminaries: Philadelphia 2, Colorado 0; Buffalo 2, N.Y. Rangers 1; Toronto 2, Los Angeles 0; Detroit 2, Atlanta 0. **Quarterfinals:** Montreal 4, Detroit 1; Boston 4, Chicago 0; Toronto 4, N.Y. Islanders 3; Philadelphia 4, Buffalo 1. **Semifinals:** Montreal 4, Toronto 0; Boston 4, Philadelphia 1. **Stanley Cup finals:** Montreal 4, Boston 2.

1978-79

PRINCE OF WALES CONFERENCE

ADAMS DIVISION

Team	W	L	T	Pts.	GF	GA
Boston Bruins	43	23	14	100	316	270
Buffalo Sabres	36	28	16	88	280	263
Toronto Maple Leafs	34	33	13	81	267	252
Minnesota North Stars	28	40	12	68	257	289

NORRIS DIVISION

Team	W	L	T	Pts.	GF	GA
Montreal Canadiens	52	17	11	115	337	204
Pittsburgh Penguins	36	31	13	85	281	279
Los Angeles Kings	34	34	12	80	292	286
Washington Capitals	24	41	15	63	273	338
Detroit Red Wings	23	41	16	62	252	295

CLARENCE CAMPBELL CONFERENCE

PATRICK DIVISION

Team	W	L	T	Pts.	GF	GA
New York Islanders	51	15	14	116	358	214
Philadelphia Flyers	40	25	15	95	281	248
New York Rangers	40	29	11	91	316	292
Atlanta Flames	41	31	8	90	327	280

SMYTHE DIVISION

Team	W	L	T	Pts.	GF	GA
Chicago Blackhawks	29	36	15	73	244	277
Vancouver Canucks	25	42	13	63	217	291
St. Louis Blues	18	50	12	48	249	348
Colorado Rockies	15	53	12	42	210	331

PLAYOFFS

Preliminaries: Philadelphia 2, Vancouver 1; N.Y. Rangers 2, Los Angeles 0; Toronto 2, Atlanta 0; Pittsburgh 2, Buffalo 1. **Quarterfinals:** N.Y. Islanders 4, Chicago 0; Montreal 4, Toronto 0; Boston 4, Pittsburgh 0; N.Y. Rangers 4, Philadelphia 1. **Semifinals:** N.Y. Rangers 4, N.Y. Islanders 2; Montreal 4, Boston 3. **Stanley Cup finals:** Montreal 4, N.Y. Rangers 1.

1979-80

PRINCE OF WALES CONFERENCE

ADAMS DIVISION

Team	W	L	T	Pts.	GF	GA
Buffalo Sabres	47	17	16	110	318	201
Boston Bruins	46	21	13	105	310	234
Minnesota North Stars	36	28	16	88	311	253
Toronto Maple Leafs	35	40	5	75	304	327
Quebec Nordiques	25	44	11	61	248	313

NORRIS DIVISION

Team	W	L	T	Pts.	GF	GA
Montreal Canadiens	47	20	13	107	328	240
Los Angeles Kings	30	36	14	74	290	313
Pittsburgh Penguins	30	37	13	73	251	303
Hartford Whalers	27	34	19	73	303	312
Detroit Red Wings	26	43	11	63	268	306

CLARENCE CAMPBELL CONFERENCE

PATRICK DIVISION

Team	W	L	T	Pts.	GF	GA
Philadelphia Flyers	48	12	20	116	327	254
New York Islanders	39	28	13	91	281	247

NHL HISTORY Year-by-year standings

Team	W	L	T	Pts.	GF	GA
New York Rangers	38	32	10	86	308	284
Atlanta Flames	35	32	13	83	282	269
Washington Capitals	27	40	13	67	261	293

SMYTHE DIVISION

Team	W	L	T	Pts.	GF	GA
Chicago Blackhawks	34	27	19	87	241	250
St. Louis Blues	34	34	12	80	266	278
Vancouver Canucks	27	37	16	70	256	281
Edmonton Oilers	28	39	13	69	301	322
Winnipeg Jets	20	49	11	51	214	314
Colorado Rockies	19	48	13	51	234	308

PLAYOFFS

Preliminaries: Philadelphia 3, Edmonton 0; Buffalo 3, Vancouver 1; Montreal 3, Hartford 0; Boston 3, Pittsburgh 2; N.Y. Islanders 3, Los Angeles 1; Minnesota 3, Toronto 0; Chicago 3, St. Louis 0; N.Y. Rangers 3, Atlanta 1. **Quarterfinals:** Philadelphia 4, N.Y. Rangers 1; Buffalo 4, Chicago 0; Minnesota 4, Montreal 3; N.Y. Islanders 4, Boston 1. **Semifinals:** Philadelphia 4, Minnesota 1; N.Y. Islanders 4, Buffalo 2. **Stanley Cup finals:** N.Y. Islanders 4, Philadelphia 2.

1980-81

PRINCE OF WALES CONFERENCE

ADAMS DIVISION

Team	W	L	T	Pts.	GF	GA
Buffalo Sabres	39	20	21	99	327	250
Boston Bruins	37	30	13	87	316	272
Minnesota North Stars	35	28	17	87	291	263
Quebec Nordiques	30	32	18	78	314	318
Toronto Maple Leafs	28	37	15	71	322	367

NORRIS DIVISION

Team	W	L	T	Pts.	GF	GA
Montreal Canadiens	45	22	13	103	332	232
Los Angeles Kings	43	24	13	99	337	290
Pittsburgh Penguins	30	37	13	73	302	345
Hartford Whalers	21	41	18	60	292	372
Detroit Red Wings	19	43	18	56	252	339

CLARENCE CAMPBELL CONFERENCE

PATRICK DIVISION

Team	W	L	T	Pts.	GF	GA
New York Islanders	48	18	14	110	355	260
Philadelphia Flyers	41	24	15	97	313	249
Calgary Flames	39	27	14	92	329	298
New York Rangers	30	36	14	74	312	317
Washington Capitals	26	36	18	70	286	317

SMYTHE DIVISION

Team	W	L	T	Pts.	GF	GA
St. Louis Blues	45	18	17	107	352	281
Chicago Blackhawks	31	33	16	78	304	315
Vancouver Canucks	28	32	20	76	289	301
Edmonton Oilers	29	35	16	74	328	327
Colorado Rockies	22	45	13	57	258	344
Winnipeg Jets	9	57	14	32	246	400

PLAYOFFS

Preliminaries: N.Y. Islanders 3, Toronto 0; St. Louis 3, Pittsburgh 2; Edmonton 3, Montreal 0; N.Y. Rangers 3, Los Angeles 1; Buffalo 3, Vancouver 0; Philadelphia 3, Quebec 2; Calgary 3, Chicago 0; Minnesota 3, Boston 0. **Quarterfinals:** N.Y. Islanders 4, Edmonton 2; N.Y. Rangers 4, St. Louis 2; Minnesota 4, Buffalo 1; Calgary 4, Philadelphia 3. **Semifinals:** N.Y. Islanders 4, N.Y. Rangers 0; Minnesota 4, Calgary 2. **Stanley Cup finals:** N.Y. Islanders 4, Minnesota 1.

1981-82

PRINCE OF WALES CONFERENCE

ADAMS DIVISION

Team	W	L	T	Pts.	GF	GA
Montreal Canadiens	46	17	17	109	360	223
Boston Bruins	43	27	10	96	323	285
Buffalo Sabres	39	26	15	93	307	273
Quebec Nordiques	33	31	16	82	356	345
Hartford Whalers	21	41	18	60	264	351

PATRICK DIVISION

Team	W	L	T	Pts.	GF	GA
New York Islanders	54	16	10	118	385	250
New York Rangers	39	27	14	92	316	306
Philadelphia Flyers	38	31	11	87	325	313
Pittsburgh Penguins	31	36	13	75	310	337
Washington Capitals	26	41	13	65	319	338

CLARENCE CAMPBELL CONFERENCE

NORRIS DIVISION

Team	W	L	T	Pts.	GF	GA
Minnesota North Stars	37	23	20	94	346	288
Winnipeg Jets	33	33	14	80	319	332
St. Louis Blues	32	40	8	72	315	349
Chicago Blackhawks	30	38	12	72	332	363
Toronto Maple Leafs	20	44	16	56	298	380
Detroit Red Wings	21	47	12	54	270	351

SMYTHE DIVISION

Team	W	L	T	Pts.	GF	GA
Edmonton Oilers	48	17	15	111	417	295
Vancouver Canucks	30	33	17	77	290	286
Calgary Flames	29	34	17	75	334	345
Los Angeles Kings	24	41	15	63	314	369
Colorado Rockies	18	49	13	49	241	362

PLAYOFFS

Wales Conference division semifinals: Quebec 3, Montreal 2; Boston 3, Buffalo 1; N.Y. Islanders 3, Pittsburgh 2; N.Y. Rangers 3, Philadelphia 1. **Division finals:** Quebec 4, Boston 3; N.Y. Islanders 4, N.Y. Rangers 2. **Conference finals:** N.Y. Islanders 4, Quebec 0.

Campbell Conference division semifinals: Chicago 3, Minnesota 1; St. Louis 3, Winnipeg 1; Los Angeles 3, Edmonton 2; Vancouver 3, Calgary 0. **Division finals:** Chicago 4, St. Louis 2; Vancouver 4, Los Angeles 1. **Conference finals:** Vancouver 4, Chicago 1.

Stanley Cup finals: N.Y. Islanders 4, Vancouver 0.

1982-83

PRINCE OF WALES CONFERENCE

ADAMS DIVISION

Team	W	L	T	Pts.	GF	GA
Boston Bruins	50	20	10	110	327	228
Montreal Canadiens	42	24	14	98	350	286
Buffalo Sabres	38	29	13	89	318	285
Quebec Nordiques	34	34	12	80	343	336
Hartford Whalers	19	54	7	45	261	403

PATRICK DIVISION

Team	W	L	T	Pts.	GF	GA
Philadelphia Flyers	49	23	8	106	326	240
New York Islanders	42	26	12	96	302	226
Washington Capitals	39	25	16	94	306	283
New York Rangers	35	35	10	80	306	287
New Jersey Devils	17	49	14	48	230	338
Pittsburgh Penguins	18	53	9	45	257	394

CLARENCE CAMPBELL CONFERENCE

NORRIS DIVISION

Team	W	L	T	Pts.	GF	GA
Chicago Blackhawks	47	23	10	104	338	268
Minnesota North Stars	40	24	16	96	321	290
Toronto Maple Leafs	28	40	12	68	293	330
St. Louis Blues	25	40	15	65	285	316
Detroit Red Wings	21	44	15	57	263	344

SMYTHE DIVISION

Team	W	L	T	Pts.	GF	GA
Edmonton Oilers	47	21	12	106	424	315
Calgary Flames	32	34	14	78	321	317
Vancouver Canucks	30	35	15	75	303	309
Winnipeg Jets	33	39	8	74	311	333
Los Angeles Kings	27	41	12	66	308	365

PLAYOFFS

Wales Conference division semifinals: Boston 3, Quebec 1; Buffalo 3, Montreal 0; N.Y. Rangers 3, Philadelphia 0; N.Y. Islanders 3, Washington 1. **Division finals:** Boston 4, Buffalo 3; N.Y. Islanders 4, N.Y. Rangers 2. **Conference finals:** N.Y. Islanders 4, Boston 2.
Campbell Conference division semifinals: Chicago 3, St. Louis 1; Minnesota 3, Toronto 1; Edmonton 3, Winnipeg 0; Calgary 3, Vancouver 1. **Division finals:** Chicago 4, Minnesota 1; Edmonton 4, Calgary 0. **Conference finals:** Edmonton 4, Chicago 0.
Stanley Cup finals: N.Y. Islanders 4, Edmonton 0.

1983-84

PRINCE OF WALES CONFERENCE

ADAMS DIVISION

Team	W	L	T	Pts.	GF	GA
Boston Bruins	49	25	6	104	336	261
Buffalo Sabres	48	25	7	103	315	257
Quebec Nordiques	42	28	10	94	360	278
Montreal Canadiens	35	40	5	75	286	295
Hartford Whalers	28	42	10	66	288	320

PATRICK DIVISION

Team	W	L	T	Pts.	GF	GA
New York Islanders	50	26	4	104	357	269
Washington Capitals	48	27	5	101	308	226
Philadelphia Flyers	44	26	10	98	350	290
New York Rangers	42	29	9	93	314	304
New Jersey Devils	17	56	7	41	231	350
Pittsburgh Penguins	16	58	6	38	254	390

CLARENCE CAMPBELL CONFERENCE

NORRIS DIVISION

Team	W	L	T	Pts.	GF	GA
Minnesota North Stars	39	31	10	88	345	344
St. Louis Blues	32	41	7	71	293	316
Detroit Red Wings	31	42	7	69	298	323
Chicago Blackhawks	30	42	8	68	277	311
Toronto Maple Leafs	26	45	9	61	303	387

SMYTHE DIVISION

Team	W	L	T	Pts.	GF	GA
Edmonton Oilers	57	18	5	119	446	314
Calgary Flames	34	32	14	82	311	314
Vancouver Canucks	32	39	9	73	306	328
Winnipeg Jets	31	38	11	73	340	374
Los Angeles Kings	23	44	13	59	309	376

PLAYOFFS

Wales Conference division semifinals: Montreal 3, Boston 0; Quebec 3, Buffalo 0; N.Y. Islanders 3, N.Y. Rangers 2; Washington 3, Philadelphia 0. **Division finals:** Montreal 4,

Quebec 2; N.Y. Islanders 4, Washington 1. **Conference finals:** N.Y. Islanders 4, Montreal 2.
Campbell Conference division semifinals: Minnesota 3, Chicago 2; St. Louis 3, Detroit 1; Edmonton 3, Winnipeg 0; Calgary 3, Vancouver 1. **Division finals:** Minnesota 4, St. Louis 3; Edmonton 4, Calgary 3. **Conference finals:** Edmonton 4, Minnesota 0.
Stanley Cup finals: Edmonton 4, N.Y. Islanders 1.

1984-85

PRINCE OF WALES CONFERENCE

ADAMS DIVISION

Team	W	L	T	Pts.	GF	GA
Montreal Canadiens	41	27	12	94	309	262
Quebec Nordiques	41	30	9	91	323	275
Buffalo Sabres	38	28	14	90	290	237
Boston Bruins	36	34	10	82	303	287
Hartford Whalers	30	41	9	69	268	318

PATRICK DIVISION

Team	W	L	T	Pts.	GF	GA
Philadelphia Flyers	53	20	7	113	348	241
Washington Capitals	46	25	9	101	322	240
New York Islanders	40	34	6	86	345	312
New York Rangers	26	44	10	62	295	345
New Jersey Devils	22	48	10	54	264	346
Pittsburgh Penguins	24	51	5	53	276	385

CLARENCE CAMPBELL CONFERENCE

NORRIS DIVISION

Team	W	L	T	Pts.	GF	GA
St. Louis Blues	37	31	12	86	299	288
Chicago Blackhawks	38	35	7	83	309	299
Detroit Red Wings	27	41	12	66	313	357
Minnesota North Stars	25	43	12	62	268	321
Toronto Maple Leafs	20	52	8	48	253	358

SMYTHE DIVISION

Team	W	L	T	Pts.	GF	GA
Edmonton Oilers	49	20	11	109	401	298
Winnipeg Jets	43	27	10	96	358	332
Calgary Flames	41	27	12	94	363	302
Los Angeles Kings	34	32	14	82	339	326
Vancouver Canucks	25	46	9	59	284	401

PLAYOFFS

Wales Conference division semifinals: Montreal 3, Boston 2; Quebec 3, Buffalo 2; Philadelphia 3, N.Y. Rangers 0; N.Y. Islanders 3, Washington 2. **Division finals:** Quebec 4, Montreal 3; Philadelphia 4, N.Y. Islanders 1. **Conference finals:** Philadelphia 4, Quebec 2.
Campbell Conference division semifinals: Minnesota 3, St. Louis 0; Chicago 3, Detroit 0; Edmonton 3, Los Angeles 0; Winnipeg 3, Calgary 1. **Division finals:** Chicago 4, Minnesota 2; Edmonton 4, Winnipeg 0. **Conference finals:** Edmonton 4, Chicago 2.
Stanley Cup finals: Edmonton 4, Philadelphia 1.

1985-86

PRINCE OF WALES CONFERENCE

ADAMS DIVISION

Team	W	L	T	Pts.	GF	GA
Quebec Nordiques	43	31	6	92	330	289
Montreal Canadiens	40	33	7	87	330	280
Boston Bruins	37	31	12	86	311	288
Hartford Whalers	40	36	4	84	332	302
Buffalo Sabres	37	37	6	80	296	291

PATRICK DIVISION

Team	W	L	T	Pts.	GF	GA
Philadelphia Flyers	53	23	4	110	335	241
Washington Capitals	50	23	7	107	315	272
New York Islanders	39	29	12	90	327	284
New York Rangers	36	38	6	78	280	276
Pittsburgh Penguins	34	38	8	76	313	305
New Jersey Devils	28	49	3	59	300	374

CLARENCE CAMPBELL CONFERENCE

NORRIS DIVISION

Team	W	L	T	Pts.	GF	GA
Chicago Blackhawks	39	33	8	86	351	349
Minnesota North Stars	38	33	9	85	327	305
St. Louis Blues	37	34	9	83	302	291
Toronto Maple Leafs	25	48	7	57	311	386
Detroit Red Wings	17	57	6	40	266	415

SMYTHE DIVISION

Team	W	L	T	Pts.	GF	GA
Edmonton Oilers	56	17	7	119	426	310
Calgary Flames	40	31	9	89	354	315
Winnipeg Jets	26	47	7	59	295	372
Vancouver Canucks	23	44	13	59	282	333
Los Angeles Kings	23	49	8	54	284	389

PLAYOFFS

Wales Conference division semifinals: Hartford 3, Quebec 0; Montreal 3, Boston 0; N.Y. Rangers 3, Philadelphia 2; Washington 3, N.Y. Rangers 0. **Division finals:** Montreal 4, Hartford 3; N.Y. Rangers 4, Washington 2. **Conference finals:** Montreal 4, N.Y. Rangers 1.
Campbell Conference division semifinals: Toronto 3, Chicago 0; St. Louis 3, Minnesota 2; Edmonton 3, Vancouver 0; Calgary 3, Winnipeg 0. **Division finals:** St. Louis 4, Toronto 3; Calgary 4, Edmonton 3. **Conference finals:** Calgary 4, St. Louis 3. **Stanley Cup finals:** Montreal 4, Calgary 1.

1986-87

PRINCE OF WALES CONFERENCE

ADAMS DIVISION

Team	W	L	T	Pts.	GF	GA
Hartford Whalers	43	30	7	93	287	270
Montreal Canadiens	41	29	10	92	277	241
Boston Bruins	39	34	7	85	301	276
Quebec Nordiques	31	39	10	72	267	276
Buffalo Sabres	28	44	8	64	280	308

PATRICK DIVISION

Team	W	L	T	Pts.	GF	GA
Philadelphia Flyers	46	26	8	100	310	245
Washington Capitals	38	32	10	86	285	278
New York Islanders	35	33	12	82	279	281
New York Rangers	34	38	8	76	307	323
Pittsburgh Penguins	30	38	12	72	297	290
New Jersey Devils	29	45	6	64	293	368

CLARENCE CAMPBELL CONFERENCE

NORRIS DIVISION

Team	W	L	T	Pts.	GF	GA
St. Louis Blues	32	33	15	79	281	293
Detroit Red Wings	34	36	10	78	260	274
Chicago Blackhawks	29	37	14	72	290	310
Toronto Maple Leafs	32	42	6	70	286	319
Minnesota North Stars	30	40	10	70	296	314

SMYTHE DIVISION

Team	W	L	T	Pts.	GF	GA
Edmonton Oilers	50	24	6	106	372	284
Calgary Flames	46	31	3	95	318	289

Team	W	L	T	Pts.	GF	GA
Winnipeg Jets	40	32	8	88	279	271
Los Angeles Kings	31	41	8	70	318	341
Vancouver Canucks	29	43	8	66	282	314

PLAYOFFS

Wales Conference division semifinals: Quebec 4, Hartford 2; Montreal 4, Boston 0; Philadelphia 4, N.Y. Rangers 2; N.Y. Islanders 4, Washington 3. **Division finals:** Montreal 4, Quebec 3; Philadelphia 4, N.Y. Islanders 3. **Conference finals:** Philadelphia 4, N.Y. Islanders 3.
Campbell Conference division semifinals: Toronto 4, St. Louis 2; Detroit 4, Chicago 0; Edmonton 4, Los Angeles 1; Winnipeg 4, Calgary 2. **Division finals:** Detroit 4, Toronto 3; Edmonton 4, Winnipeg 0. **Conference finals:** Edmonton 4, Detroit 1. **Stanley Cup finals:** Edmonton 4, Philadelphia 3.

1987-88

PRINCE OF WALES CONFERENCE

ADAMS DIVISION

Team	W	L	T	Pts.	GF	GA
Montreal Canadiens	45	22	13	103	298	238
Boston Bruins	44	30	6	94	300	251
Buffalo Sabres	37	32	11	85	283	305
Hartford Whalers	35	38	7	77	249	267
Quebec Nordiques	32	43	5	69	271	306

PATRICK DIVISION

Team	W	L	T	Pts.	GF	GA
New York Islanders	39	31	10	88	308	267
Philadelphia Flyers	38	33	9	85	292	282
Washington Capitals	38	33	9	85	281	249
New Jersey Devils	38	36	6	82	295	296
New York Rangers	36	34	10	82	300	283
Pittsburgh Penguins	36	35	9	81	319	316

CLARENCE CAMPBELL CONFERENCE

NORRIS DIVISION

Team	W	L	T	Pts.	GF	GA
Detroit Red Wings	41	28	11	93	322	269
St. Louis Blues	34	38	8	76	278	294
Chicago Blackhawks	30	41	9	69	284	326
Toronto Maple Leafs	21	49	10	52	273	345
Minnesota North Stars	19	48	13	51	242	349

SMYTHE DIVISION

Team	W	L	T	Pts.	GF	GA
Calgary Flames	48	23	9	105	397	305
Edmonton Oilers	44	25	11	99	363	288
Winnipeg Jets	33	36	11	77	292	310
Los Angeles Kings	30	42	8	68	318	359
Vancouver Canucks	25	46	9	59	272	320

PLAYOFFS

Wales Conference division semifinals: Montreal 4, Hartford 2; Boston 4, Buffalo 2; New Jersey 4, N.Y. Islanders 2; Washington 4, Philadelphia 3. **Division finals:** Boston 4, Montreal 1; New Jersey 4, Washington 3. **Conference finals:** Boston 4, New Jersey 3.
Campbell Conference division semifinals: Detroit 4, Toronto 2; St. Louis 4, Chicago 1; Calgary 4, Los Angeles 1; Edmonton 4, Winnipeg 1. **Division finals:** Detroit 4, St. Louis 1; Edmonton 4, Calgary 0. **Conference finals:** Edmonton 4, Detroit 1. **Stanley Cup finals:** Edmonton 4, Boston 0.

NHL HISTORY *Year-by-year standings*

– 144 –

PRINCE OF WALES CONFERENCE

ADAMS DIVISION

Team	W	L	T	Pts.	GF	GA
Montreal Canadiens	53	18	9	115	315	218
Boston Bruins	37	29	14	88	289	256
Buffalo Sabres	38	35	7	83	291	299
Hartford Whalers	37	38	5	79	299	290
Quebec Nordiques	27	46	7	61	269	342

PATRICK DIVISION

Team	W	L	T	Pts.	GF	GA
Washington Capitals	41	29	10	92	305	259
Pittsburgh Penguins	40	33	7	87	347	349
New York Rangers	37	35	8	82	310	307
Philadelphia Flyers	36	36	8	80	307	285
New Jersey Devils	27	41	12	66	281	325
New York Islanders	28	47	5	61	265	325

CLARENCE CAMPBELL CONFERENCE

NORRIS DIVISION

Team	W	L	T	Pts.	GF	GA
Detroit Red Wings	34	34	12	80	313	316
St. Louis Blues	33	35	12	78	275	285
Minnesota North Stars	27	37	16	70	258	278
Chicago Blackhawks	27	41	12	66	297	335
Toronto Maple Leafs	28	46	6	62	259	342

SMYTHE DIVISION

Team	W	L	T	Pts.	GF	GA
Calgary Flames	54	17	9	117	354	226
Los Angeles Kings	42	31	7	91	376	335
Edmonton Oilers	38	34	8	84	325	306
Vancouver Canucks	33	39	8	74	251	253
Winnipeg Jets	26	42	12	64	300	355

PLAYOFFS

Wales Conference division semifinals: Montreal 4, Hartford 0; Boston 4, Buffalo 1; Philadelphia 4, Washington 2; Pittsburgh 4, N.Y. Rangers 0. **Division finals:** Montreal 4, Boston 1; Philadelphia 4, Pittsburgh 3. **Conference finals:** Montreal 4, Philadelphia 2.
Campbell Conference division semifinals: Chicago 4, Detroit 2; St. Louis 4, Minnesota 1; Calgary 4, Vancouver 3; Los Angeles 4, Edmonton 3. **Division finals:** Chicago 4, St. Louis 1; Calgary 4, Los Angeles 0. **Conference finals:** Calgary 4, Chicago 1.
Stanley Cup finals: Calgary 4, Montreal 2.

PRINCE OF WALES CONFERENCE

ADAMS DIVISION

Team	W	L	T	Pts.	GF	GA
Boston Bruins	46	25	9	101	289	232
Buffalo Sabres	45	27	8	98	286	248
Montreal Canadiens	41	28	11	93	288	234
Hartford Whalers	38	33	9	85	275	268
Quebec Nordiques	12	61	7	31	240	407

PATRICK DIVISION

Team	W	L	T	Pts.	GF	GA
New York Rangers	36	31	13	85	279	267
New Jersey Devils	37	34	9	83	295	288
Washington Capitals	36	38	6	78	284	275
New York Islanders	31	38	11	73	281	288
Pittsburgh Penguins	32	40	8	72	318	359
Philadelphia Flyers	30	39	11	71	290	297

CLARENCE CAMPBELL CONFERENCE

NORRIS DIVISION

Team	W	L	T	Pts.	GF	GA
Chicago Blackhawks	41	33	6	88	316	294
St. Louis Blues	37	34	9	83	295	279
Toronto Maple Leafs	38	38	4	80	337	358
Minnesota North Stars	36	40	4	76	284	291
Detroit Red Wings	28	38	14	70	288	323

SMYTHE DIVISION

Team	W	L	T	Pts.	GF	GA
Calgary Flames	42	23	15	99	348	265
Edmonton Oilers	38	28	14	90	315	283
Winnipeg Jets	37	32	11	85	298	290
Los Angeles Kings	34	39	7	75	338	337
Vancouver Canucks	25	41	14	64	245	306

PLAYOFFS

Wales Conference division semifinals: Boston 4, Hartford 3; Montreal 4, Buffalo 3; N.Y. Rangers 4, N.Y. Islanders 1; Washington 4, New Jersey 2. **Division finals:** Boston 4, Montreal 1; Washington 4, N.Y. Rangers 1. **Conference finals:** Boston 4, Washington 0.
Campbell Conference division semifinals: Chicago 4, Minnesota 3; St. Louis 4, Toronto 1; Los Angeles 4, Calgary 2; Edmonton 4, Winnipeg 3. **Division finals:** Chicago 4, St. Louis 3; Edmonton 4, Los Angeles 0. **Conference finals:** Edmonton 4, Chicago 2.
Stanley Cup finals: Edmonton 4, Boston 1.

PRINCE OF WALES CONFERENCE

ADAMS DIVISION

Team	W	L	T	Pts.	GF	GA
Boston Bruins	44	24	12	100	299	264
Montreal Canadiens	39	30	11	89	273	249
Buffalo Sabres	31	30	19	81	292	278
Hartford Whalers	31	38	11	73	238	276
Quebec Nordiques	16	50	14	46	236	354

PATRICK DIVISION

Team	W	L	T	Pts.	GF	GA
Pittsburgh Penguins	41	33	6	88	342	305
New York Rangers	36	31	13	85	297	265
Washington Capitals	37	36	7	81	258	258
New Jersey Devils	32	33	15	79	272	264
Philadelphia Flyers	33	37	10	76	252	267
New York Islanders	25	45	10	60	223	290

CLARENCE CAMPBELL CONFERENCE

NORRIS DIVISION

Team	W	L	T	Pts.	GF	GA
Chicago Blackhawks	49	23	8	106	284	211
St. Louis Blues	47	22	11	105	310	250
Detroit Red Wings	34	38	8	76	273	298
Minnesota North Stars	27	39	14	68	256	266
Toronto Maple Leafs	23	46	11	57	241	318

SMYTHE DIVISION

Team	W	L	T	Pts.	GF	GA
Los Angeles Kings	46	24	10	102	340	254
Calgary Flames	46	26	8	100	344	263
Edmonton Oilers	37	37	6	80	272	272
Vancouver Canucks	28	43	9	65	243	315
Winnipeg Jets	26	43	11	63	260	288

PLAYOFFS

Wales Conference division semifinals: Boston 4, Hartford 2; Montreal 4, Buffalo 2; Pittsburgh 4, New Jersey 3; Washington

4, N.Y. Rangers 2. **Division finals:** Boston 4, Montreal 3; Pittsburgh 4, Washington 1. **Conference finals:** Pittsburgh 4, Boston 2.
Campbell Conference division semifinals: Minnesota 4, Chicago 2; St. Louis 4, Detroit 3; Los Angeles 4, Vancouver 2; Edmonton 4, Calgary 3. **Division finals:** Minnesota 4, St. Louis 2; Edmonton 4, Los Angeles 2. **Conference finals:** Minnesota 4, Edmonton 1.
Stanley Cup finals: Pittsburgh 4, Minnesota 2.

1991-92

PRINCE OF WALES CONFERENCE

ADAMS DIVISION

Team	W	L	T	Pts.	GF	GA
Montreal Canadiens	41	28	11	93	267	207
Boston Bruins	36	32	12	84	270	275
Buffalo Sabres	31	37	12	74	289	299
Hartford Whalers	26	41	13	65	247	283
Quebec Nordiques	20	48	12	52	255	318

PATRICK DIVISION

Team	W	L	T	Pts.	GF	GA
New York Rangers	50	25	5	105	321	246
Washington Capitals	45	27	8	98	330	275
Pittsburgh Penguins	39	32	9	87	343	308
New Jersey Devils	38	31	11	87	289	259
New York Islanders	34	35	11	79	291	299
Philadelphia Flyers	32	37	11	75	252	273

CLARENCE CAMPBELL CONFERENCE

NORRIS DIVISION

Team	W	L	T	Pts.	GF	GA
Detroit Red Wings	43	25	12	98	320	256
Chicago Blackhawks	36	29	15	87	257	236
St. Louis Blues	36	33	11	83	279	266
Minnesota North Stars	32	42	6	70	246	278
Toronto Maple Leafs	30	43	7	67	234	294

SMYTHE DIVISION

Team	W	L	T	Pts.	GF	GA
Vancouver Canucks	42	26	12	96	285	250
Los Angeles Kings	35	31	14	84	287	296
Edmonton Oilers	36	34	10	82	295	297
Winnipeg Jets	33	32	15	81	251	244
Calgary Flames	31	37	12	74	296	305
San Jose Sharks	17	58	5	39	219	359

PLAYOFFS

Wales Conference division semifinals: Montreal 4, Hartford 3; Boston 4, Buffalo 3; N.Y. Rangers 4, New Jersey 3; Pittsburgh 4, Washington 3. **Division finals:** Boston 4, Montreal 0; Pittsburgh 4, N.Y. Rangers 2. **Conference finals:** Pittsburgh 4, Boston 0.
Campbell Conference division semifinals: Detroit 4, Minnesota 3; Chicago 4, St. Louis 2; Vancouver 4, Winnipeg 3; Edmonton 4, Los Angeles 2. **Division finals:** Chicago 4, Detroit 0; Edmonton 4, Vancouver 2. **Conference finals:** Chicago 4, Edmonton 0.
Stanley Cup finals: Pittsburgh 4, Chicago 0.

1992-93

PRINCE OF WALES CONFERENCE

ADAMS DIVISION

Team	W	L	T	Pts.	GF	GA
Boston Bruins	51	26	7	109	332	268
Quebec Nordiques	47	27	10	104	351	300
Montreal Canadiens	48	30	6	102	326	280
Buffalo Sabres	38	36	10	86	335	297
Hartford Whalers	26	52	6	58	284	369
Ottawa Senators	10	70	4	24	202	395

PATRICK DIVISION

Team	W	L	T	Pts.	GF	GA
Pittsburgh Penguins	56	21	7	119	367	268
Washington Capitals	43	34	7	93	325	286
New York Islanders	40	37	7	87	308	299
New Jersey Devils	40	37	7	87	335	297
Philadelphia Flyers	36	37	11	83	319	319
New York Rangers	34	39	11	79	304	308

CLARENCE CAMPBELL CONFERENCE

NORRIS DIVISION

Team	W	L	T	Pts.	GF	GA
Chicago Blackhawks	47	25	12	106	279	230
Detroit Red Wings	47	28	9	103	369	280
Toronto Maple Leafs	44	29	11	99	288	241
St. Louis Blues	37	36	11	85	282	278
Minnesota North Stars	36	38	10	82	272	293
Tampa Bay Lightning	23	54	7	53	245	332

SMYTHE DIVISION

Team	W	L	T	Pts.	GF	GA
Vancouver Canucks	46	29	9	101	346	278
Calgary Flames	43	30	11	97	322	282
Los Angeles Kings	39	35	10	88	338	340
Winnipeg Jets	40	37	7	87	322	320
Edmonton Oilers	26	50	8	60	242	337
San Jose Sharks	11	71	2	24	218	414

PLAYOFFS

Wales Conference division semifinals: Buffalo 4, Boston 0; Montreal 4, Quebec 2; Pittsburgh 4, New Jersey 1; N.Y. Islanders 4, Washington 2. **Division finals:** Montreal 4, Buffalo 0; N.Y. Islanders 4, Pittsburgh 3. **Conference finals:** Montreal 4, N.Y. Islanders 1.
Campbell Conference division semifinals: St. Louis 4, Chicago 0; Toronto 4, Detroit 3; Vancouver 4, Winnipeg 2; Los Angeles 4, Calgary 2. **Division finals:** Toronto 4, St. Louis 3; Los Angeles 4, Vancouver 2. **Conference finals:** Los Angeles 4, Toronto 3.
Stanley Cup finals: Montreal 4, Los Angeles 1.

1993-94

EASTERN CONFERENCE

ATLANTIC DIVISION

Team	W	L	T	Pts.	GF	GA
New York Rangers	52	24	8	112	299	231
New Jersey Devils	47	25	12	106	306	220
Washington Capitals	39	35	10	88	277	263
New York Islanders	36	36	12	84	282	264
Florida Panthers	33	34	17	83	233	233
Philadelphia Flyers	35	39	10	80	294	314
Tampa Bay Lightning	30	43	11	71	224	251

NORTHEAST DIVISION

Team	W	L	T	Pts.	GF	GA
Pittsburgh Penguins	44	27	13	101	299	285
Boston Bruins	42	29	13	97	289	252
Montreal Canadiens	41	29	14	96	283	248
Buffalo Sabres	43	32	9	95	282	218
Quebec Nordiques	34	42	8	76	277	292
Hartford Whalers	27	48	9	63	227	288
Ottawa Senators	14	61	9	37	201	397

WESTERN CONFERENCE

CENTRAL DIVISION

Team	W	L	T	Pts.	GF	GA
Detroit Red Wings	46	30	8	100	356	275
Toronto Maple Leafs	43	29	12	98	280	243
Dallas Stars	42	29	13	97	286	265
St. Louis Blues	40	33	11	91	270	283
Chicago Blackhawks	39	36	9	87	254	240
Winnipeg Jets	24	51	9	57	245	344

PACIFIC DIVISION

Team	W	L	T	Pts.	GF	GA
Calgary Flames	42	29	13	97	302	256
Vancouver Canucks	41	40	3	85	279	276
San Jose Sharks	33	35	16	82	252	265
Mighty Ducks of Anaheim	33	46	5	71	229	251
Los Angeles Kings	27	45	12	66	294	322
Edmonton Oilers	25	45	14	64	261	305

PLAYOFFS

Eastern Conference quarterfinals: N.Y. Rangers 4, N.Y. Islanders 0; Washington 4, Pittsburgh 2; New Jersey 4, Buffalo 3; Boston 4, Montreal 3. **Semifinals:** N.Y. Rangers 4, Washington 1; New Jersey 4, Boston 2. **Finals:** N.Y. Rangers 4, New Jersey 3.
Western Conference quarterfinals: San Jose 4, Detroit 3; Vancouver 4, Calgary 3; Toronto 4, Chicago 2; Dallas 4, St. Louis 0. **Semifinals:** Toronto 4, San Jose 3; Vancouver 4, Dallas 1. **Finals:** Vancouver 4, Toronto 1. **Stanley Cup finals:** N.Y. Rangers 4, Vancouver 3.

1994-95

EASTERN CONFERENCE

ATLANTIC DIVISION

Team	W	L	T	Pts.	GF	GA
Philadelphia Flyers	28	16	4	60	150	132
New Jersey Devils	22	18	8	52	136	121
Washington Capitals	22	18	8	52	136	120
New York Rangers	22	23	3	47	139	134
Florida Panthers	20	22	6	46	115	127
Tampa Bay Lightning	17	28	3	37	120	144
New York Islanders	15	28	5	35	126	158

NORTHEAST DIVISION

Team	W	L	T	Pts.	GF	GA
Quebec Nordiques	30	13	5	65	185	134
Pittsburgh Penguins	29	16	3	61	181	158
Boston Bruins	27	18	3	57	150	127
Buffalo Sabres	22	19	7	51	130	119
Hartford Whalers	19	24	5	43	127	141
Montreal Canadiens	18	23	7	43	125	148
Ottawa Senators	9	34	5	23	117	174

WESTERN CONFERENCE

CENTRAL DIVISION

Team	W	L	T	Pts.	GF	GA
Detroit Red Wings	33	11	4	70	180	117
St. Louis Blues	28	15	5	61	178	135
Chicago Blackhawks	24	19	5	53	156	115
Toronto Maple Leafs	21	19	8	50	135	146
Dallas Stars	17	23	8	42	136	135
Winnipeg Jets	16	25	7	39	157	177

PACIFIC DIVISION

Team	W	L	T	Pts.	GF	GA
Calgary Flames	24	17	7	55	163	135
Vancouver Canucks	18	18	12	48	153	148
San Jose Sharks	19	25	4	42	129	161
Los Angeles Kings	16	23	9	41	142	174
Edmonton Oilers	17	27	4	38	136	183
Mighty Ducks of Anaheim	16	27	5	37	125	164

PLAYOFFS

Eastern Conference quarterfinals: N.Y. Rangers 4, Quebec 2; Pittsburgh 4, Washington 3; Philadelphia 4, Buffalo 1; New Jersey 4, Boston 1. **Semifinals:** New Jersey 4, Pittsburgh 1; Philadelphia 4, N.Y. Rangers 0. **Finals:** New Jersey 4, Philadelphia 2.
Western Conference quarterfinals: Detroit 4, Dallas 1; Vancouver 4, St. Louis 3; Chicago 4, Toronto 3; San Jose 4, Calgary 3. **Semifinals:** Detroit 4, San Jose 0; Chicago 4, Vancouver 0. **Finals:** Detroit 4, Chicago 1. **Stanley Cup finals:** New Jersey 4, Detroit 0.

1995-96

EASTERN CONFERENCE

ATLANTIC DIVISION

Team	W	L	T	Pts.	GF	GA
Philadelphia Flyers	45	24	13	103	282	208
New York Rangers	41	27	14	96	272	237
Florida Panthers	41	31	10	92	254	234
Washington Capitals	39	32	11	89	234	204
Tampa Bay Lightning	38	32	12	88	238	248
New Jersey Devils	37	33	12	86	215	202
New York Islanders	22	50	10	54	229	315

NORTHEAST DIVISION

Team	W	L	T	Pts.	GF	GA
Pittsburgh Penguins	49	29	4	102	362	284
Boston Bruins	40	31	11	91	282	269
Montreal Canadiens	40	32	10	90	265	248
Hartford Whalers	34	39	9	77	237	259
Buffalo Sabres	33	42	7	73	247	262
Ottawa Senators	18	59	5	41	191	291

WESTERN CONFERENCE

CENTRAL DIVISION

Team	W	L	T	Pts.	GF	GA
Detroit Red Wings	62	13	7	131	325	181
Chicago Blackhawks	40	28	14	94	273	220
Toronto Maple Leafs	34	36	12	80	247	252
St. Louis Blues	32	34	16	80	219	248
Winnipeg Jets	36	40	6	78	275	291
Dallas Stars	26	42	14	66	227	280

PACIFIC DIVISION

Team	W	L	T	Pts.	GF	GA
Colorado Avalanche	47	25	10	104	326	240
Calgary Flames	34	37	11	79	241	240
Vancouver Canucks	32	35	15	79	278	278
Mighty Ducks of Anaheim	35	39	8	78	234	247
Edmonton Oilers	30	44	8	68	240	304
Los Angeles Kings	24	40	18	66	256	302
San Jose Sharks	20	55	7	47	252	357

PLAYOFFS

Eastern Conference quarterfinals: Philadelphia 4, Tampa Bay 2; Pittsburgh 4, Washington 2; N.Y. Rangers 4, Montreal 2; Florida 4, Boston 1. **Semifinals:** Florida 4, Philadelphia 2; Pittsburgh 4, N.Y. Rangers 1. **Finals:** Florida 4, Pittsburgh 3.
Western Conference quarterfinals: Detroit 4, Winnipeg 2; Colorado 4, Vancouver 2; Chicago 4, Calgary 0; St. Louis 4, Toronto 2. **Semifinals:** Detroit 4, St. Louis 3; Colorado 4, Chicago 2. **Finals:** Colorado 4, Detroit 2. **Stanley Cup finals:** Colorado 4, Florida 0.

1996-97

EASTERN CONFERENCE

ATLANTIC DIVISION

Team	W	L	T	Pts.	GF	GA
New Jersey Devils	45	23	14	104	231	182
Philadelphia Flyers	45	24	13	103	274	217
Florida Panthers	35	28	19	89	221	201
New York Rangers	38	34	10	86	258	231
Washington Capitals	33	40	9	75	214	231
Tampa Bay Lightning	32	40	10	74	217	247
New York Islanders	29	41	12	70	240	250

NORTHEAST DIVISION

Team	W	L	T	Pts.	GF	GA
Buffalo Sabres	40	30	12	92	237	208
Pittsburgh Penguins	38	36	8	84	285	280
Ottawa Senators	31	36	15	77	226	234
Montreal Canadiens	31	36	15	77	249	276
Hartford Whalers	32	39	11	75	226	256
Boston Bruins	26	47	9	61	234	300

WESTERN CONFERENCE

CENTRAL DIVISION

Team	W	L	T	Pts.	GF	GA
Dallas Stars	48	26	8	104	252	198
Detroit Red Wings	38	26	18	94	253	197
Phoenix Coyotes	38	37	7	83	240	243
St. Louis Blues	36	35	11	83	236	239
Chicago Blackhawks	34	35	13	81	223	210
Toronto Maple Leafs	30	44	8	68	230	273

PACIFIC DIVISION

Team	W	L	T	Pts.	GF	GA
Colorado Avalanche	49	24	9	107	277	205
Mighty Ducks of Anaheim	36	33	13	85	245	233
Edmonton Oilers	36	37	9	81	252	247
Vancouver Canucks	35	40	7	77	257	273
Calgary Flames	32	41	9	73	214	239
Los Angeles Kings	28	43	11	67	214	268
San Jose Sharks	27	47	8	62	211	278

PLAYOFFS

Eastern Conference quarterfinals: New Jersey 4, Montreal 1; Buffalo 4, Ottawa 3; Philadelphia 4, Pittsburgh 1; N.Y. Rangers 4, Florida 1. **Semifinals:** N.Y. Rangers 4, New Jersey 1; Philadelphia 4, Buffalo 1. **Finals:** Philadelphia 4, N.Y. Rangers 1.
Western Conference quarterfinals: Colorado 4, Chicago 2; Edmonton 4, Dallas 3; Detroit 4, St. Louis 2; Anaheim 4, Phoenix 3. **Semifinals:** Colorado 4, Edmonton 1; Detroit 4, Anaheim 0. **Finals:** Detroit 4, Colorado 2.
Stanley Cup finals: Detroit 4, Philadelphia 0.

1997-98

EASTERN CONFERENCE

ATLANTIC DIVISION

Team	W	L	T	Pts.	GF	GA
New Jersey Devils	48	23	11	107	225	166
Philadelphia Flyers	42	29	11	95	242	193
Washington Capitals	40	30	12	92	219	202
New York Islanders	30	41	11	71	212	225
New York Rangers	25	39	18	68	197	231
Florida Panthers	24	43	15	63	203	256
Tampa Bay Lightning	17	55	10	44	151	269

NORTHEAST DIVISION

Team	W	L	T	Pts.	GF	GA
Pittsburgh Penguins	40	24	18	98	228	188
Boston Bruins	39	30	13	91	221	194
Buffalo Sabres	36	29	17	89	211	187
Montreal Canadiens	37	32	13	87	235	208
Ottawa Senators	34	33	15	83	193	200
Carolina Hurricanes	33	41	8	74	200	219

WESTERN CONFERENCE

CENTRAL DIVISION

Team	W	L	T	Pts.	GF	GA
Dallas Stars	49	22	11	109	242	167
Detroit Red Wings	44	23	15	103	250	196
St. Louis Blues	45	29	8	98	256	204
Phoenix Coyotes	35	35	12	82	224	227
Chicago Blackhawks	30	39	13	73	192	199
Toronto Maple Leafs	30	43	9	69	194	237

PACIFIC DIVISION

Team	W	L	T	Pts.	GF	GA
Colorado Avalanche	39	26	17	95	231	205
Los Angeles Kings	38	33	11	87	227	225
Edmonton Oilers	35	37	10	80	215	224
San Jose Sharks	34	38	10	78	210	216
Calgary Flames	26	41	15	67	217	252
Mighty Ducks of Anaheim	26	43	13	65	205	261
Vancouver Canucks	25	43	14	64	224	273

PLAYOFFS

Eastern Conference quarterfinals: Ottawa 4, New Jersey 2; Washington 4, Boston 2; Buffalo 4, Philadelphia 1; Montreal 4, Pittsburgh 2. **Semifinals:** Washington 4, Ottawa 1; Buffalo 4, Montreal 0. **Finals:** Washington 4, Buffalo 2.
Western Conference quarterfinals: Edmonton 4, Colorado 3; Dallas 4, San Jose 2; Detroit 4, Phoenix 2; St. Louis 4, Los Angeles 0. **Semifinals:** Dallas 4, Edmonton 1; Detroit 4, St. Louis 2. **Finals:** Detroit 4, Dallas 2.
Stanley Cup finals: Detroit 4, Washington 0.

1998-99

EASTERN CONFERENCE

ATLANTIC DIVISION

Team	W	L	T	Pts.	GF	GA
New Jersey Devils	47	24	11	105	248	196
Philadelphia Flyers	37	26	19	93	231	196
Pittsburgh Penguins	38	30	14	90	242	225
New York Rangers	33	38	11	77	217	227
New York Islanders	24	48	10	58	194	244

NORTHEAST DIVISION

Team	W	L	T	Pts.	GF	GA
Ottawa Senators	44	23	15	103	239	179
Toronto Maple Leafs	45	30	7	97	268	231
Boston Bruins	39	30	13	91	214	181
Buffalo Sabres	37	28	17	91	207	175
Montreal Canadiens	32	39	11	75	184	209

SOUTHEAST DIVISION

Team	W	L	T	Pts.	GF	GA
Carolina Hurricanes	34	30	18	86	210	202
Florida Panthers	30	34	18	78	210	228
Washington Capitals	31	45	6	68	200	218
Tampa Bay Lightning	19	54	9	47	179	292

WESTERN CONFERENCE

CENTRAL DIVISION

Team	W	L	T	Pts.	GF	GA
Detroit Red Wings	43	32	7	93	245	202
St. Louis Blues	37	32	13	87	237	209
Chicago Blackhawks	29	41	12	70	202	248
Nashville Predators	28	47	7	63	190	261

PACIFIC DIVISION

Team	W	L	T	Pts.	GF	GA
Dallas Stars	51	19	12	114	236	168
Phoenix Coyotes	39	31	12	90	205	197
Anaheim Mighty Ducks	35	34	13	83	215	206
San Jose Sharks	31	33	18	80	196	191
Los Angeles Kings	32	45	5	69	189	222

NORTHWEST DIVISION

Team	W	L	T	Pts.	GF	GA
Colorado Avalanche	44	28	10	98	239	205
Edmonton Oilers	33	37	12	78	230	226
Calgary Flames	30	40	12	72	211	234
Vancouver Canucks	23	47	12	58	192	258

PLAYOFFS

Eastern Conference quarterfinals: Pittsburgh 4, New Jersey 3; Buffalo 4, Ottawa 0; Boston 4, Carolina 2; Toronto 4, Philadelphia 2. **Semifinals:** Toronto 4, Pittsburgh 2; Buffalo 4, Boston 2. **Finals:** Buffalo 4, Toronto 1.
Western Conference quarterfinals: Dallas 4, Edmonton 0; Colorado 4, San Jose 2; Detroit 4, Anaheim 0; St. Louis 4, Phoenix 3. **Semifinals:** Dallas 4, St. Louis 2; Colorado 4, Detroit 2. **Finals:** Dallas 4, Colorado 3.
Stanley Cup finals: Dallas 4, Buffalo 2.

RECORDS

INDIVIDUAL—CAREER

Most seasons
NHL: 26—Gordie Howe, Detroit Red Wings and Hartford Whalers, 1946-47 through 1970-71 and 1979-80.
CHL: 9—Richie Hansen, Fort Worth Texans, Salt Lake Golden Eagles, Wichita Wind, 1975-76 through 1983-84.
AHL: 20—Fred Glover, Indianapolis Caps, St. Louis Flyers, Cleveland Barons.
    Willie Marshall, Pittsburgh Hornets, Rochester Americans, Hershey Bears, Providence Reds, Baltimore Clippers.
IHL: 18—Glenn Ramsay, Cincinnati Mohawks, Fort Wayne Komets, Troy Bruins, Toledo Blades, St. Paul Saints, Omaha Knights, Des Moines Oak Leafs, Toledo Hornets, Port Huron Flags, 1956-57 through 1973-74.

Most games played
NHL: 1,767—Gordie Howe, Detroit Red Wings and Hartford Whalers (26 seasons).
AHL: 1,205—Willie Marshall, Pittsburgh Hornets, Rochester Americans, Hershey Bears, Providence Reds, Baltimore Clippers (20 seasons).
IHL: 1,054—Jock Callander, Toledo Goaldiggers, Muskegon Lumberjacks, Atlanta Knights and Cleveland Lumberjacks (17 seasons).
CHL: 575—Richie Hansen, Fort Worth Texans, Salt Lake Golden Eagles, Wichita Wind (9 seasons).
WHA: 551—Andre Lacroix, Philadelphia Blazers, New York Golden Blades, Jersey Knights, San Diego Mariners, Houston Aeros and New England Whalers (7 seasons).

Most goals
NHL: 894—Wayne Gretzky, Edmonton Oilers, Los Angeles Kings, St. Louis Blues, New York Rangers (20 seasons).
IHL: 547—Dave Michayluk, Kalamazoo Wings, Muskegon Lumberjacks, Cleveland Lumberjacks (13 seasons).
AHL: 523—Willie Marshall, Pittsburgh Hornets, Rochester Americans, Hershey Bears, Providence Reds, Baltimore Clippers (20 seasons).
WHA: 316—Marc Tardif, Quebec Nordiques (6 seasons).
CHL: 204—Richie Hansen, Fort Worth Texans, Salt Lake Golden Eagles, Wichita Wind (9 seasons).

Most assists
NHL: 1,963—Wayne Gretzky, Edmonton Oilers, Los Angeles Kings, St. Louis Blues, New York Rangers (20 seasons).
AHL: 852—Willie Marshall, Pittsburgh Hornets, Hershey Bears, Rochester Americans, Providence Reds, Baltimore Clippers (20 seasons).
IHL: 826—Len Thornson, Huntington Hornets, Indianapolis Chiefs, Fort Wayne Komets (13 seasons).
WHA: 547—Andre Lacroix, Philadelphia Blazers, Jersey Knights, San Diego Mariners, Houston Aeros, New England Whalers (7 seasons).
CHL: 374—Richie Hansen, Fort Worth Texans, Salt Lake Golden Eagles, Wichita Wind (9 seasons).

Most points
NHL: 2,857—Wayne Gretzky, Edmonton Oilers, Los Angeles Kings, St. Louis Blues, New York Rangers (20 seasons).
AHL: 1,375—Willie Marshall, Pittsburgh Hornets, Hershey Bears, Rochester Americans, Providence Reds, Baltimore Clippers (20 seasons).
IHL: 1,252—Len Thornson, Huntington Hornets, Indianapolis Chiefs, Fort Wayne Komets (13 seasons).
WHA: 798—Andre Lacroix, Philadelphia Blazers, Jersey Knights, San Diego Mariners, Houston Aeros, New England Whalers (7 seasons).
CHL: 578—Richie Hansen, Fort Worth Texans, Salt Lake Golden Eagles, Wichita Wind (9 seasons).

Most penalty minutes
NHL: 3,966—Dave "Tiger" Williams, Toronto Maple Leafs, Vancouver Canucks, Detroit Red Wings, Los Angeles Kings, Hartford Whalers (13 seasons).
AHL: 2,402—Fred Glover, Indianapolis Caps, St. Louis Flyers, Cleveland Barons (20 seasons).
IHL: 2,175—Gord Malinoski, Dayton Gems, Saginaw Gears (9 seasons).
WHA: 962—Paul Baxter, Cleveland Crusaders, Quebec Nordiques (5 seasons).
CHL: 899—Brad Gassoff, Tulsa Oilers, Dallas Black Hawks (5 seasons).

Most shutouts
NHL: 103—Terry Sawchuk, Detroit Red Wings, Boston Bruins, Los Angeles Kings, New York Rangers, Toronto Maple Leafs (20 seasons).
AHL: 45—Johnny Bower, Cleveland Barons, Providence Reds (11 seasons).
IHL: 45—Glenn Ramsay, Cincinnati Mohawks, Fort Wayne Komets, Troy Bruins, Toledo Blades, St. Paul Saints, Omaha Knights, Des Moines Oak Leafs, Toledo Hornets, Port Huron Flags (18 seasons).
WHA: 16—Ernie Wakely, Winnipeg Jets, San Diego Mariners, Houston Aeros (6 seasons).
CHL: 12—Michel Dumas, Dallas Black Hawks (4 seasons).
    Mike Veisor, Dallas Black Hawks (5 seasons).

INDIVIDUAL—SEASON

Most goals
NHL: 92—Wayne Gretzky, Edmonton Oilers, 1981-82 season.
WHA: 77—Bobby Hull, Winnipeg Jets, 1974-75 season.
CHL: 77—Alain Caron, St. Louis Braves, 1963-64 season.
IHL: 75—Dan Lecours, Milwaukee Admirals, 1982-83 season.
AHL: 70—Stephan Lebeau, Sherbrooke Canadiens, 1988-89 season.

Most goals by a defenseman
NHL: 48—Paul Coffey, Edmonton Oilers, 1985-86 season.
IHL: 34—Roly McLenahan, Cincinnati Mohawks, 1955-56 season.

CHL: 29—Dan Poulin, Nashville South Stars, 1981-82 season.
AHL: 28—Greg Tebbutt, Baltimore Skipjacks, 1982-83 season.
WHA: 24—Kevin Morrison, Jersey Knights, 1973-74 season.

Most assists
NHL: 163—Wayne Gretzky, Edmonton Oilers, 1985-86 season.
IHL: 109—John Cullen, Flint Spirits, 1987-88 season.
WHA: 106—Andre Lacroix, San Diego Mariners, 1974-75 season.
AHL: 89—George "Red" Sullivan, Hershey Bears, 1953-54 season.
CHL: 81—Richie Hansen, Salt Lake Golden Eagles, 1981-82 season.

Most assists by a defenseman
NHL: 102—Bobby Orr, Boston Bruins, 1970-71 season.
IHL: 86—Gerry Glaude, Muskegon Zephyrs, 1962-63 season.
WHA: 77—J. C. Tremblay, Quebec Nordiques, 1975-76 season.
AHL: 62—Craig Levie, Nova Scotia Voyageurs, 1980-81 season.
       Shawn Evans, Nova Scotia Oilers, 1987-88 season.
CHL: 61—Barclay Plager, Omaha Knights, 1963-64 season.

Most points
NHL: 215—Wayne Gretzky, Edmonton Oilers, 1985-86 season.
IHL: 157—John Cullen, Flint Spirits, 1987-88 season.
WHA: 154—Marc Tardif, Quebec Nordiques, 1977-78 season.
AHL: 138—Don Biggs, Binghamton Rangers, 1992-93 season.
CHL: 125—Alain Caron, St. Louis Braves, 1963-64 season.

Most points by a defenseman
NHL: 139—Bobby Orr, Boston Bruins, 1970-71 season.
IHL: 101—Gerry Glaude, Muskegon Zephyrs, 1962-63 season.
WHA: 89—J. C. Tremblay, Quebec Nordiques, 1972-73 and 1975-76 seasons.
CHL: 85—Dan Poulin, Nashville South Stars, 1981-82 season.
AHL: 84—Greg Tebbutt, Baltimore Skipjacks, 1982-83 season.

Most penalty minutes
IHL: 648—Kevin Evans, Kalamazoo, 1986-87 season.
NHL: 472—Dave Schultz, Philadelphia Flyers, 1974-75 season.
AHL: 446—Robert Ray, Rochester Americans, 1988-89 season.
CHL: 411—Randy Holt, Dallas Black Hawks, 1974-75 season.
WHA: 365—Curt Brackenbury, Minnesota Fighting Saints and Quebec Nordiques, 1975-76 season.

Most shutouts
NHL: 22—George Hainsworth, Montreal Canadiens, 1928-29 season.
NHL: 15—(modern era) Tony Esposito, Chicago Black Hawks, 1969-70 season.
IHL: 10—Charlie Hodge, Cincinnati Mohawks, 1953-54 season.
       Joe Daley, Winnipeg Jets, 1975-76 season.
CHL: 9—Marcel Pelletier, St. Paul Rangers, 1963-64 season.
AHL: 9—Gordie Bell, Buffalo Bisons, 1942-43 season.
WHA: 5—Gerry Cheevers, Cleveland Crusaders, 1972-73 season.

Lowest goals against average
NHL: 0.98—George Hainsworth, Montreal Canadiens, 1928-29 season.
AHL: 1.79—Frank Brimsek, Providence Reds, 1937-38 season.
IHL: 1.88—Glenn Ramsay, Cincinnati Mohawks, 1956-57 season.
CHL: 2.16—Russ Gillow, Oklahoma City Blazers, 1967-68 season.
WHA: 2.57—Don McLeod, Houston Aeros, 1973-74 season.

INDIVIDUAL—GAME

Most goals
NHL: 7—Joe Malone, Quebec Bulldogs vs. Toronto St. Pats, January 31, 1920.
NHL: 6—(modern era) Syd Howe, Detroit Red Wings vs. N.Y. Rangers, Feb. 3, 1944.
       Gordon "Red" Berenson, St. Louis Blues vs. Philadelphia, Nov. 7, 1968.
       Darryl Sittler, Toronto Maple Leafs vs. Boston, Feb. 7, 1976.
CHL: 6—Jim Mayer, Dallas Black Hawks, February 23, 1979.
AHL: 6—Bob Heron, Pittsburgh Hornets, 1941-42.
       Harry Pidhirny, Springfield Indians, 1953-54.
       Camille Henry, Providence Reds, 1955-56.
       Patrick Lebeau, Fredericton Canadiens, Feb. 1, 1991.
IHL: 6—Pierre Brillant, Indianapolis Chiefs, Feb. 18, 1959.
       Bryan McLay, Muskegon Zephyrs, Mar. 8, 1961.
       Elliott Chorley, St. Paul Saints, Jan. 17, 1962.
       Joe Kastelic, Muskegon Zephyrs, Mar. 1, 1962.
       Tom St. James, Flint Generals, Mar. 15, 1985.
WHA: 5—Ron Ward, New York Raiders vs. Ottawa, January 4, 1973.
       Ron Climie, Edmonton Oilers vs. N.Y. Golden Blades, November 6, 1973.
       Andre Hinse, Houston Aeros vs. Edmonton, Jan. 16, 1975.
       Vaclav Nedomansky, Toronto Toros vs. Denver Spurs, Nov. 13, 1975.
       Wayne Connelly, Minnesota Fighting Saints vs. Cincinnati Stingers, Nov. 27, 1975.
       Ron Ward, Cleveland Crusaders vs. Toronto Toros, Nov. 30, 1975.
       Real Cloutier, Quebec Nordiques fs. Phoenix Roadrunners, Oct. 26, 1976.

Most assists
  AHL: 9—Art Stratton, Buffalo Bisons vs. Pittsburgh, Mar. 17, 1963.
   IHL: 9—Jean-Paul Denis, St. Paul Saints, Jan. 17, 1962.
  NHL: 7—Billy Taylor, Detroit Red Wings vs. Chicago, Mar. 16, 1947.
      Wayne Gretzky, Edmonton Oilers vs. Washington, Feb. 15, 1980.
  WHA: 7—Jim Harrison, Alberta Oilers vs. New York, January 30, 1973.
      Jim Harrison, Cleveland Crusaders vs. Toronto, Nov. 30, 1975.
  CHL: 6—Art Stratton, St. Louis Braves, 1966-67.
      Ron Ward, Tulsa Oilers, 1967-68.
      Bill Hogaboam, Omaha Knights, January 15, 1972.
      Jim Wiley, Tulsa Oilers, 1974-75.
Most points
   IHL: 11—Elliott Chorley, St. Paul Saints, Jan. 17, 1962.
      Jean-Paul Denis, St. Paul Saints, Jan. 17, 1962.
  NHL: 10—Darryl Sittler, Toronto Maple Leafs vs. Boston, Feb. 7, 1976.
  WHA: 10—Jim Harrison, Alberta Oilers vs. New York, January 30, 1973.
  AHL: 9—Art Stratton, Buffalo Bisons vs Pittsburgh, Mar. 17, 1963.
  CHL: 8—Steve Vickers, Omaha Knights vs. Kansas City, Jan. 15, 1972.
Most penalty minutes
  NHL: 67—Randy Holt, Los Angeles Kings vs. Philadelphia, March 11, 1979.
   IHL: 63—Willie Trognitz, Dayton Gems, Oct. 29, 1977.
  AHL: 54—Wally Weir, Rochester Americans vs. New Brunswick, Jan. 16, 1981.
  CHL: 49—Gary Rissling, Birmingham Bulls vs. Salt Lake, Dec. 5, 1980.
  WHA: 46—Dave Hanson, Birmingham Bulls vs. Indianapolis, Feb. 5, 1978.

STANLEY CUP PLAYOFFS
INDIVIDUAL—CAREER

Most years in playoffs: 20—Gordie Howe, Detroit, Hartford.
                Larry Robinson, Montreal, Los Angeles.
Most consecutive years in playoffs: 20—Larry Robinson, Montreal, Los Angeles.
Most games: 236—Mark Messier, Edmonton, New York Rangers.
Most games by goaltender: 196—Patrick Roy, Montreal, Colorado.
Most goals: 122—Wayne Gretzky, Edmonton, Los Angeles, St. Louis, New York Rangers.
Most assists: 260—Wayne Gretzky, Edmonton, Los Angeles, St. Louis, New York Rangers.
Most points: 382—Wayne Gretzky, Edmonton, Los Angeles, St. Louis, New York Rangers.
Most penalty minutes: 729—Dale Hunter, Quebec, Washington, Colorado.
Most shutouts: 14—Jacques Plante, Montreal, St. Louis.

INDIVIDUAL—SEASON

Most goals: 19—Reggie Leach, Philadelphia (1975-76).
            Jari Kurri, Edmonton (1984-85).
Most goals by a defenseman: 12—Paul Coffey, Edmonton (1984-85).
Most assists: 31—Wayne Gretzky, Edmonton (1987-88).
Most assists by a defenseman: 25—Paul Coffey, Edmonton (1984-85).
Most points: 47—Wayne Gretzky, Edmonton (1984-85).
Most points by a defenseman: 37—Paul Coffey, Edmonton (1984-85).
Most penalty minutes: 141—Chris Nilan, Montreal (1985-86).
Most shutouts: 4—Clint Benedict, Montreal Maroons (1927-28); Dave Kerr, N.Y. Rangers (1936-37); Frank McCool, Toronto (1944-
    45); Terry Sawchuk, Detroit (1951-52); Bernie Parent, Philadelphia (1974-75); Ken Dryden, Montreal (1976-77); Ed Belfour, Dallas
    (1999-2000).
Most consecutive shutouts: 3—Frank McCool, Toronto (1944-45).

INDIVIDUAL—GAME

Most goals: 5—Maurice Richard, Montreal vs. Toronto, March 23, 1944.
            Darryl Sittler, Toronto vs. Philadelphia, April 22, 1976.
            Reggie Leach, Philadelphia vs. Boston, May 6, 1976.
            Mario Lemieux, Pittsburgh vs. Philadelphia, April 25, 1989.
Most assists: 6—Mikko Leinonen, N.Y. Rangers vs. Philadelphia, April 8, 1982.
            Wayne Gretzky, Edmonton vs. Los Angeles, April 9, 1987.
Most points: 8—Patrik Sundstrom, New Jersey vs. Washington, April 22, 1988.
            Mario Lemieux, Pittsburgh vs. Philadelphia, April 25, 1989.

CLUB

Most Stanley Cup championships: 24—Montreal Canadiens.
Most consecutive Stanley Cup championships: 5—Montreal Canadiens.
Most final series apperances: 32—Montreal Canadiens.
Most years in playoffs: 72—Montreal Canadiens.
Most consecutive playoff appearances: 29—Boston Bruins.
Most consecutive playoff game victories: 12—Edmonton Oilers.
Most goals, one team, one game: 13—Edmonton vs. Los Angeles, April 9, 1987.
Most goals, one team, one period: 7—Montreal Canadiens vs. Toronto, March 30, 1944, 3rd period.

STATISTICAL LEADERS

YEAR BY YEAR

1917-18

Goals

Joe Malone, Mon. Canadiens 44
Cy Denneny, Ottawa 36
Reg Noble, Toronto 28
Newsy Lalonde, Mon. Canadiens 23
Corbett Denneny, Toronto 20

**Lowest goals-against average
(Min. 15 games)**

Georges Vezina, Mon. Canadiens 3.82
Hap Holmes, Toronto 4.75
Clint Benedict, Ottawa 5.18

Shutouts

Clint Benedict, Ottawa 1
Georges Vezina, Mon. Canadiens 1

1918-19

Goals

Odie Cleghorn, Montreal 24
Newsy Lalonde, Montreal......................21
Cy Denneny, Ottawa 18
Frank Nighbor, Ottawa...........................17
Didier Pitre, Montreal 15

**Lowest goals-against average
(Min. 15 games)**

Clint Benedict, Ottawa 2.94
Georges Vezina, Montreal 4.33
Bert Lindsay, Toronto 5.19

Shutouts

Clint Benedict, Ottawa 2
Georges Vezina, Montreal 1

1919-20

Goals

Joe Malone, Quebec.............................39
Newsy Lalonde, Montreal......................36
Frank Nighbor, Ottawa..........................26
Corbett Denneny, Toronto 23
Reg Noble, Toronto 24

**Lowest goals-against average
(Min. 15 games)**

Clint Benedict, Ottawa 2.67
Georges Vezina, Montreal 4.71
Frank Brophy, Quebec 7.05

Shutouts

Clint Benedict, Ottawa 5

1920-21

Goals

Cecil Dye, Tor.-Ham..............................35
Cy Denneny, Ottawa 34
Newsy Lalonde, Montreal......................32
Joe Malone, Hamilton 28
Three players tied with..........................19

**Lowest goals-against average
(Min. 15 games)**

Clint Benedict, Ottawa 3.13
Jake Forbes, Toronto..........................3.90

Georges Vezina, Montreal 4.13
Howard Lockhart, Hamilton 5.50

Shutouts

Clint Benedict, Ottawa 2
Howard Lockhart, Hamilton 1
Georges Vezina, Montreal 1

1921-22

Goals

Harry Broadbent, Ottawa......................30
Cecil Dye, Toronto.................................30
Cy Denneny, Ottawa 28
Joe Malone, Hamilton 23
Odie Cleghorn, Montreal 21

**Lowest goals-against average
(Min. 15 games)**

Clint Benedict, Ottawa 3.50
Georges Vezina, Montreal 3.92
John Roach, Toronto............................4.14
Howard Lockhart, Hamilton 4.29

Shutouts

Clint Benedict, Ottawa 2

1922-23

Goals

Cecil Dye, Toronto.................................26
Billy Boucher, Montreal 25
Cy Denneny, Ottawa 23
Odie Cleghorn, Montreal 18
Jack Adams, Toronto 18

**Lowest goals-against average
(Min. 15 games)**

Clint Benedict, Ottawa 2.25
Georges Vezina, Montreal 2.54
John Roach, Toronto............................3.67
Jake Forbes, Hamilton.........................4.58

Shutouts

Clint Benedict, Ottawa 4
Georges Vezina, Montreal 2
John Roach, Toronto...............................1

1923-24

Goals

Cy Denneny, Ottawa 22
Billy Burch, Hamilton.............................16
Billy Boucher, Montreal 16
Cecil Dye, Toronto.................................16
Aurel Joliat, Montreal 15

**Lowest goals-against average
(Min. 15 games)**

Georges Vezina, Montreal 2.00
Clint Benedict, Ottawa 2.05
Jake Forbes, Hamilton.........................2.83
John Roach, Toronto............................3.48

Shutouts

Clint Benedict, Ottawa 3
Georges Vezina, Montreal 3
Jake Forbes, Hamilton...........................1
John Roach, Toronto...............................1

1924-25

Goals

Cecil Dye, Toronto.................................38
Howie Morenz, Mon. Canadiens...........30
Aurel Joliat, Mon. Canadiens................29
Cy Denneny, Ottawa 28
Jack Adams, Toronto 21
Billy Burch, Hamilton.............................21

Points

Cecil Dye, Toronto.................................44
Cy Denneny, Ottawa 42
Aurel Joliat, Mon. Canadiens................40
Howie Morenz, Mon. Canadiens...........34
Billy Boucher, Mon. Canadiens.............31

**Lowest goals-against average
(Min. 15 games)**

Georges Vezina, Mon. Canadiens 1.87
Jake Forbes, Hamilton........................2.00
Clint Benedict, Mon. Maroons.............2.17
Alex Connell, Ottawa 2.20
John Roach, Toronto............................2.80

Shutouts

Alex Connell, Ottawa 7
Jake Forbes, Hamilton............................6
Georges Vezina, Mon. Canadiens 5
Clint Benedict, Mon. Maroons 2
Charles Stewart, Boston..........................2

1925-26

Goals

Nels Stewart, Mon. Maroons.................34
Carson Cooper, Boston 28
Jimmy Herberts, Boston 26
Cy Denneny, Ottawa 24
Howie Morenz, Mon. Canadiens...........23

Points

Nels Stewart, Mon. Maroons.................42
Cy Denneny, Ottawa 36
Carson Cooper, Boston 31
Jimmy Heberts, Boston..........................31
Three players tied with...........................26

**Lowest goals-against average
(Min. 15 games)**

Alex Connell, Ottawa 1.17
Roy Worters, Pittsburgh 1.94
Clint Benedict, Mon. Maroons.............2.03
Charles Stewart, Boston......................2.29
Jake Forbes, New York........................2.39

Shutouts

Alex Connell, Ottawa 15
Roy Worters, Pittsburgh 7
Clint Benedict, Mon. Maroons 6
Charles Stewart, Boston..........................6
Jake Forbes, New York 2
John Roach, Toronto...............................2

1926-27

Goals

Bill Cook, N.Y. Rangers 33
Cecil Dye, Chicago 25

Howie Morenz, Mon. Canadiens..........25
Billy Burch, N.Y. Americans................19
Three players tied with.......................18

Assists
Dick Irvine, Chicago..........................18
Frank Boucher, N.Y. Rangers..............15
Irvine Bailey, Toronto 13
Frank Fredrickson, Bos.-Det...............13
Frank Clancy, Ottawa 10

Points
Bill Cook, N.Y. Rangers 37
Dick Irvin, Chicago.............................36
Howie Morenz, Mon. Canadiens........32
Frank Fredrickson, Det.-Bos...............31
Babe Dye, Chicago............................30

Penalty minutes
Nels Stewart, Mon. Maroons..............133
Eddie Shore, Boston..........................130
Reginald Smith, Ottawa.....................125
Albert Siebert, Mon. Maroons 116
George Boucher, Ottawa....................115

Lowest goals-against average
(Min. 25 games)
Clint Benedict, Mon. Maroons..........1.51
George Hainsworth, Mon. Canadiens..1.52
Lorne Chabot, N.Y. Rangers 1.56
Alex Connell, Ottawa 1.57
Hal Winkler, NYR-Bos. 1.81

Shutouts
George Hainsworth, Mon. Canadiens...14
Clint Benedict, Mon. Maroons.............13
Alex Connell, Ottawa 12
Lorne Chabot, N.Y. Rangers 10
Jake Forbes, N.Y. Americans 8

1927-28

Goals
Howie Morenz, Mon. Canadiens..........33
Aurel Joliat, Mon. Canadiens..............28
Nels Stewart, Mon. Maroons...............27
Frank Boucher, N.Y. Rangers..............23
George Hay, Detroit 22

Assists
Howie Morenz, Mon. Canadiens..........18
Fred Cook, N.Y. Rangers 14
George Hay, Detroit 13
Frank Boucher, N.Y. Rangers..............12
Aurel Joliat, Mon. Canadiens..............11
Sylvio Mantha, Mon. Canadiens 11

Points
Howie Morenz, Mon. Canadiens..........51
Aurel Joliat, Mon. Canadiens..............39
Frank Boucher, N.Y. Rangers..............35
George Hay, Detroit 35
Nels Stewart, Mon. Maroons...............34

Penalty minutes
Eddie Shore, Boston..........................165
Ivan Johnson, N.Y. Rangers 146
Clarence Boucher, N.Y. Americans....129
Albert Siebert, Mon. Maroons 109
Aurel Joliat, Mon. Canadiens.............105

Lowest goals-against average
(Min. 25 games)
George Hainsworth, Mon. Canadiens...1.09
Alex Connell, Ottawa 1.29
Hal Winkler, Boston...........................1.59
Roy Worters, Pittsburgh 1.73
Clint Benedict, Mon. Maroons...........1.75

Shutouts
Alex Connell, Ottawa 15
Hal Winkler, Boston............................15
George Hainsworth, Mon. Canadiens...13
Lorne Chabot, N.Y. Rangers 11
Harry Holmes, Detroit 11

1928-29

Goals
Irvine Bailey, Toronto 22
Nels Stewart, Mon. Maroons...............21
Carson Cooper, Detroit.......................18
Howie Morenz, Mon. Canadiens..........17
Harry Oliver, Boston 17

Assists
Frank Boucher, N.Y. Rangers..............16
Andy Blair, Toronto.............................15
Gerald Lowrey, Pit.-Tor.......................12
Irvine Bailey, Toronto 10
Howie Morenz, Mon. Canadiens..........10

Points
Irvine Bailey, Toronto 32
Nels Stewart, Mon. Maroons...............29
Carson Cooper, Detroit.......................27
Howie Morenz, Mon. Canadiens..........27
Andy Blair, Toronto.............................27

Penalty minutes
Mervyn Dutton, Mon. Maroons..........139
Lionel Conacher, N.Y. Americans.......132
Reginald Smith, Mon. Maroons 120
Eddie Shore, Boston............................96
Alex Smith, Ottawa..............................96

Lowest goals-against average
(Min. 25 games)
George Hainsworth, Mon. Canadiens..0.98
Tiny Thompson, Boston 1.18
Roy Worters, N.Y. Americans............1.21
Clarence Dolson, Detroit 1.43
John Roach, N.Y. Rangers 1.48

Shutouts
George Hainsworth, Mon. Canadiens...22
John Roach, N.Y. Rangers 13
Roy Worters, N.Y. Americans..............13
Lorne Chabot, Toronto 12
Tiny Thompson, Boston 12

1929-30

Goals
Ralph Weiland, Boston.........................43
Aubrey Clapper, Boston.......................41
Howie Morenz, Mon. Canadiens..........40
Nels Stewart, Mon. Maroons...............39
Hec Kilrea, Ottawa 36

Assists
Frank Boucher, N.Y. Rangers..............36
Norman Gainor, Boston.......................31
Bill Cook, N.Y. Rangers 30
Ralph Weiland, Boston.........................30
Frank Clancy, Ottawa..........................23

Points
Ralph Weiland, Boston.........................73
Frank Boucher, N.Y. Rangers..............62
Aubrey Clapper, Boston.......................61
Bill Cook, N.Y. Rangers 59
Hec Kilrea, Ottawa 58

Penalty minutes
Joe Lamb, Ottawa 119
Sylvio Mantha, Mon. Canadiens 108

Eddie Shore, Boston..........................105
Mervyn Dutton, Mon. Maroons...........98
Harvey Rockburn, Detroit....................97

Lowest goals-against average
(Min. 25 games)
Tiny Thompson, Boston 2.23
Charles Gardiner, Chicago.................2.52
James Walsh, Mon. Maroons.............2.55
George Hainsworth, Mon. Canadiens..2.57
Alex Connell, Ottawa 2.68

Shutouts
Lorne Chabot, Toronto 6
George Hainsworth, Mon. Canadiens....4
Alex Connell, Ottawa 3
Charles Gardiner, Chicago 3
Tiny Thompson, Boston 3

1930-31

Goals
Charlie Conacher, Toronto 31
Bill Cook, N.Y. Rangers 30
Howie Morenz, Mon. Canadiens..........28
Ebbie Goodfellow, Detroit....................25
Nels Stewart, Mon. Maroons...............25
Ralph Weiland, Boston.........................25

Assists
Joe Primeau, Toronto...........................32
Frank Boucher, N.Y. Rangers..............27
Ebbie Goodfellow, Detroit....................23
Howie Morenz, Mon. Canadiens..........23
Aurel Joliat, Mon. Canadiens..............22

Points
Howie Morenz, Mon. Canadiens..........51
Ebbie Goodfellow, Detroit....................48
Charlie Conacher, Toronto 43
Bill Cook, N.Y. Rangers 42
Ace Bailey, Toronto.............................42

Penalty minutes
Harvey Rockburn, Detroit....................118
Eddie Shore, Boston..........................105
Darcy Coulson, Philadelphia.............103
Allan Shields, Philadelphia 98
Marty Burke, Mon. Canadiens 91
Joe Lamb, Ottawa 91

Lowest goals-against average
(Min. 25 games)
Roy Worters, N.Y. Americans............1.68
Charles Gardiner, Chicago 1.77
John Roach, N.Y. Rangers 1.98
George Hainsworth, Mon. Canadiens..2.02
Tiny Thompson, Boston 2.05

Shutouts
Charles Gardiner, Chicago 12
George Hainsworth, Mon. Canadiens....8
Roy Worters, N.Y. Americans................8
John Roach, N.Y. Rangers 7
Lorne Chabot, Toronto 6
Clarence Dolson, Detroit 6

1931-32

Goals
Charles Conacher, Toronto 34
Bill Cook, N.Y. Rangers 34
Harvey Jackson, Toronto.....................28
Dave Trottier, Mon. Maroons...............26
Howie Morenz, Mon. Canadiens..........24

Assists
Joe Primeau, Toronto...........................37
Reginald Smith, Mon. Maroons 33

Harvey Jackson, Toronto......................25
Howie Morenz, Mon. Canadiens...........25
Aurel Joliat, Mon. Canadiens................24

Points

Harvey Jackson, Toronto......................53
Joe Primeau, Toronto...........................50
Howie Morenz, Mon. Canadiens...........49
Charlie Conacher, Toronto 48
Bill Cook, N.Y. Rangers 48

Penalty minutes

Georges Mantha, N.Y. Americans.......107
Nick Wasnie, N.Y. Rangers.................106
Reginald Horner, Toronto 97
Dave Trottier, Mon. Maroons................94
Alex Levinsky, N.Y. Rangers................88

Lowest goals-against average
(Min. 25 games)

Charles Gardiner, Chicago.................2.10
Alex Connell, Detroit...........................2.25
George Hainsworth, Mon. Canadiens..2.32
John Roach, N.Y. Rangers..................2.34
Tiny Thompson, Boston 2.42

Shutouts

John Roach, N.Y. Rangers 9
Tiny Thompson, Boston 9
Alex Connell, Detroit...............................6
George Hainsworth, Mon. Canadiens.....6
Roy Worters, N.Y. Americans.................5

1932-33

Goals

Bill Cook, N.Y. Rangers 28
Harvey Jackson, Toronto......................27
Martin Barry, Boston 24
Fred Cook, N.Y. Rangers 22
Lawrence Northcott, Mon. Maroons 22

Assists

Frank Boucher, N.Y. Rangers...............28
Eddie Shore, Boston............................27
Paul Haynes, Mon. Maroons 25
Norman Himes, N.Y. Americans 25
Johnny Gagnon, Mon. Canadiens 23

Points

Bill Cook, N.Y. Rangers 50
Harvey Jackson, Toronto......................44
Lawrence Northcott, Mon. Maroons 43
Reg Smith, Mon. Maroons....................41
Paul Haynes, Mon. Maroons.................41

Penalty minutes

Reginald Horner, Toronto 144
Ivan Johnson, N.Y. Rangers...............127
Allan Shields, Ottawa 119
Eddie Shore, Boston..........................102
Vern Ayres, N.Y. Americans.................97

Lowest goals-against average
(Min. 25 games)

Tiny Thompson, Boston 1.83
John Roach, Detroit.............................1.93
Charles Gardiner, Chicago.................2.10
Dave Kerr, Mon. Maroons 2.20
Andy Aitkenhead, N.Y. Rangers........2.23

Shutouts

Tiny Thompson, Boston 11
John Roach, Detroit 10
George Hainsworth, Mon. Canadiens.....8
Bill Beveridge, Ottawa 5
Lorne Chabot, Toronto 5
Charles Gardiner, Chicago 5
Roy Worters, N.Y. Americans.................5

1933-34

Goals

Charlie Conacher, Toronto 32
Marty Barry, Boston 27
Aurel Joliat, Mon. Canadiens................22
Nels Stewart, Boston............................22
Johnny Sorrell, Detroit 21

Assists

Joe Primeau, Toronto...........................32
Frank Boucher, N.Y. Rangers...............30
Cecil Dillon, N.Y. Rangers....................26
Elwyn Romnes, Chicago.......................21
Charlie Conacher, Toronto 20

Points

Charlie Conacher, Toronto 52
Joe Primeau, Toronto...........................46
Frank Boucher, N.Y. Rangers...............44
Marty Barry, Boston 39
Cecil Dillon, N.Y. Rangers....................39

Penalty minutes

Reginald Horner, Toronto 146
Lionel Conacher, Chicago.....................87
Ivan Johnson, N.Y. Rangers.................86
Nels Stewart, Boston............................68
Earl Seibert, N.Y. Rangers...................66

Lowest goals-against average
(Min. 25 games)

Charles Gardiner, Chicago.................1.73
Wilfred Cude, Det.-Mon. C. 1.57
Roy Worters, N.Y. Americans.............2.14
Lorne Chabot, Mon. Canadiens 2.15
Andy Aitkenhead, N.Y. Rangers........2.35

Shutouts

Charles Gardiner, Chicago 10
Lorne Chabot, Mtl Canadiens 8
Andy Aitkenhead, N.Y. Rangers.............7
Dave Kerr, Mon. Maroons 6
Wilfred Cude, Det.-Mon. C. 5
Tiny Thompson, Boston 5

1934-35

Goals

Charlie Conacher, Toronto 36
Cecil Dillon, N.Y. Rangers....................25
Syd Howe, St.L.-Det.............................22
Harvey Jackson, Toronto......................22
Three players tied with.........................21

Assists

Art Chapman, N.Y. Americans 34
Frank Boucher, N.Y. Rangers...............32
Larry Aurie, Detroit 29
Herb Lewis, Detroit 27
Howie Morenz, Chicago 26
Eddie Shore, Boston.............................26

Points

Charlie Conacher, Toronto 57
Syd Howe, St. Louis-Detroit.................47
Larry Aurie, Detroit 46
Frank Boucher, N.Y. Rangers...............44
Harvey Jackson, Toronto......................44

Penalty minutes

Reginald Horner, Toronto 125
Irvine Frew, St. Louis 89
Earl Seibert, N.Y. Rangers...................86
Albert Siebert, Boston...........................80
Ralph Bowman, St.L.-Det......................72

Lowest goals-against average
(Min. 25 games)

Lorne Chabot, Chicago.......................1.83
Alex Connell, Mon. Maroons 1.92
Norman Smith, Detroit.......................2.08
George Hainsworth, Toronto 2.28
Tiny Thompson, Boston 2.33

Shutouts

Alex Connell, Mon. Maroons 9
Lorne Chabot, Chicago...........................8
George Hainsworth, Toronto 8
Tiny Thompson, Boston 8
Dave Kerr, N.Y. Rangers 4
John Roach, Det.-Tor. 4

1935-36

Goals

Charlie Conacher, Toronto 23
Bill Thoms, Toronto..............................23
Marty Barry, Detroit..............................21
David Schriner, N.Y. Americans............19
Reginald Smith, Mon. Maroons 19

Assists

Art Chapman, N.Y. Americans 28
David Schriner, N.Y. Americans............26
Elwyn Romnes, Chicago.......................25
Herb Lewis, Detroit 23
Paul Thompson, Chicago 23

Points

David Schriner, N.Y. Americans............45
Marty Barry, Detroit..............................40
Paul Thompson, Chicago 40
Five players tied with............................38

Penalty minutes

Reginald Horner, Toronto 167
Allan Shields, Mon. Maroons 81
Reginald Smith, Mon. Maroons 75
Charlie Conacher, Toronto 74
Three players tied with 69

Lowest goals-against average
(Min. 25 games)

Tiny Thompson, Boston 1.73
Mike Karakas, Chicago.......................1.92
Dave Kerr, N.Y. Rangers 2.02
Norman Smith, Detroit........................2.14
Bill Beveridge, Mon. Maroons 2.22

Shutouts

Tiny Thompson, Boston 10
Mike Karakas, Chicago...........................9
George Hainsworth, Toronto 8
Dave Kerr, N.Y. Rangers 8
Wilfred Cude, Mon. Canadiens 6
Norman Smith, Detroit.............................6

1936-37

Goals

Larry Aurie, Detroit 23
Nels Stewart, Bos.-NYA.......................23
Mehlville Keeling, N.Y. Rangers...........22
Harvey Jackson, Toronto......................21
David Schriner, N.Y. Americans............21

Assists

Syl Apps, Toronto.................................29
Marty Barry, Detroit..............................27
Bob Gracie, Mon. Maroons 25
David Schriner, N.Y. Americans............25
Art Chapman, N.Y. Americans 23

Points

David Schriner, N.Y. Americans	46
Syl Apps, Toronto	45
Marty Barry, Detroit	44
Larry Aurie, Detroit	43
Harvey Jackson, Toronto	40

Penalty minutes

Reginald Horner, Toronto	124
Allan Shields, NYA-Bos.	94
Lionel Conacher, Mon. Maroons	64
Jack Portland, Boston	58
Joe Jerwa, Bos.-NYA	57

Lowest goals-against average
(Min. 25 games)

Norman Smith, Detroit	2.13
Dave Kerr, N.Y. Rangers	2.21
Wilfred Cude, Mon. Canadiens	2.24
Tiny Thompson, Boston	2.29
Turk Broda, Toronto	2.32

Shutouts

Norman Smith, Detroit	6
Tiny Thompson, Boston	6
Wilfred Cude, Mon. Canadiens	5
Mike Karakas, Chicago	5
Dave Kerr, N.Y. Rangers	4

1937-38

Goals

Gord Drillon, Toronto	26
Georges Mantha, Mon. Canadiens	23
Paul Thompson, Chicago	22
Syl Apps, Toronto	21
Cecil Dillon, N.Y. Rangers	21
David Schriner, N.Y. Americans	21

Assists

Syl Apps, Toronto	29
Art Chapman, N.Y. Americans	27
Gord Drillon, Toronto	26
Phil Watson, N.Y. Rangers	25
Bill Thoms, Toronto	24

Points

Gord Drillon, Toronto	52
Syl Apps, Toronto	50
Paul Thompson, Chicago	44
Georges Mantha, Mon. Canadiens	42
Cecil Dillon, N.Y. Rangers	39
Bill Cowley, Boston	39

Penalty minutes

Reginald Horner, Toronto	82
Art Coulter, N.Y. Rangers	80
Ott Heller, N.Y. Rangers	68
Stew Evans, Mon. Maroons	59
Four players tied with	56

Lowest goals-against average
(Min. 25 games)

Tiny Thompson, Boston	1.85
Dave Kerr, N.Y. Rangers	2.00
Earl Robertson, N.Y. Americans	2.31
Turk Broda, Toronto	2.64
Wilfred, Cude, Mon. Canadiens	2.68

Shutouts

Dave Kerr, N.Y. Rangers	8
Tiny Thompson, Boston	7
Turk Broda, Toronto	6
Earl Robertson, N.Y. Americans	6
Wilfred Cude, Mon. Canadiens	3
Norman Smith, Detroit	3

1938-39

Goals

Roy Conacher, Boston	26
Toe Blake, Montreal	24
Alex Shibicky, N.Y. Rangers	24
Clint Smith, N.Y. Rangers	21
Brian Hextall, N.Y. Rangers	20

Assists

Bill Cowley, Boston	34
Paul Haynes, Montreal	33
David Schriner, N.Y. Americans	31
Marty Barry, Detroit	28
Tom Anderson, N.Y. Americans	27

Points

Toe Blake, Montreal	47
David Schriner, N.Y. Americans	44
Bill Cowley, Boston	42
Clint Smith, N.Y. Rangers	41
Marty Barry, Detroit	41

Penalty minutes

Reginald Horner, Toronto	85
Murray Patrick, N.Y. Rangers	64
Art Coulter, N.Y. Rangers	58
Stew Evans, Montreal	58
Earl Seibert, Chicago	57

Lowest goals-against average
(Min. 25 games)

Frank Brimsek, Boston	1.59
Dave Kerr, N.Y. Rangers	2.18
Turk Broda, Toronto	2.23
Tiny Thompson, Bos.-Det.	2.49
Mike Karakas, Chicago	2.75

Shutouts

Frank Brimsek, Boston	10
Turk Broda, Toronto	8
Dave Kerr, N.Y. Rangers	6
Mike Karakas, Chicago	5
Tiny Thompson, Bos.-Det.	4

1939-40

Goals

Brian Hextall, N.Y. Rangers	24
Woody Dumart, Boston	22
Milt Schmidt, Boston	22
Herb Cain, Boston	21
Gord Drillon, Toronto	21

Assists

Milt Schmidt, Boston	30
Phil Watson, N.Y. Rangers	28
Bill Cowley, Boston	27
Bob Bauer, Boston	26
Syd Howe, Detroit	23

Points

Milt Schmidt, Boston	52
Woody Dumart, Boston	43
Bob Bauer, Boston	43
Gord Drillon, Toronto	40
Bill Cowley, Boston	40

Penalty minutes

Reginald Horner, Toronto	87
Art Coulter, N.Y. Rangers	68
Erwin Chamberlain, Toronto	63
Jack Church, Toronto	62
Walter Pratt, N.Y. Rangers	61

Lowest goals-against average
(Min. 25 games)

Dave Kerr, N.Y. Rangers	1.60
Paul Goodman, Chicago	2.00

(continued)

Frank Brimsek, Boston	2.04
Turk Broda, Toronto	2.30
Tiny Thompson, Detroit	2.61

Shutouts

Dave Kerr, N.Y. Rangers	8
Frank Brimsek, Boston	6
Earl Robertson, N.Y. Americans	6
Turk Broda, Toronto	4
Paul Goodman, Chicago	4

1940-41

Goals

Brian Hextall, N.Y. Rangers	26
Roy Conacher, Boston	24
David Schriner, Toronto	24
Gord Drillon, Toronto	23
Three players tied with	20

Assists

Bill Cowley, Boston	45
Neil Colville, N.Y. Rangers	28
Bill Taylor, Toronto	26
Milton Schmidt, Boston	25
Phil Watson, N.Y. Rangers	25

Points

Bill Cowley, Boston	62
Brian Hextall, N.Y. Rangers	44
Gord Drillon, Toronto	44
Syl Apps, Toronto	44
Lynn Patrick, N.Y. Rangers	44
Syd Howe, Detroit	44

Penalty minutes

Jimmy Orlando, Detroit	99
Clifford Goupille, Montreal	81
Erwin Chamberlain, Montreal	75
Joe Cooper, Chicago	66
Des Smith, Boston	61

Lowest goals-against average
(Min. 25 games)

Turk Broda, Toronto	2.06
Frank Brimsek, Boston	2.12
John Mowers, Detroit	2.12
Dave Kerr, N.Y. Rangers	2.60
Bert Gardiner, Montreal	2.84

Shutouts

Frank Brimsek, Boston	6
Turk Broda, Toronto	5
John Mowers, Detroit	4
Bert Gardiner, Montreal	2
Paul Goodman, Chicago	2
Dave Kerr, N.Y. Rangers	2

1941-42

Goals

Lynn Patrick, New York	32
Roy Conacher, Boston	24
Robert Hamill, Bos.-Chi.	24
Brian Hextall, New York	24
Gord Drillon, Toronto	23
Don Grosso, Detroit	23

Assists

Phil Watson, New York	37
Brian Hextall, New York	32
Syd Abel, Detroit	31
Don Grosso, Detroit	30
Bill Thoms, Chicago	30

Points

Brian Hextall, New York	56
Lynn Patrick, New York	54
Don Grosso, Detroit	53

Phil Watson, New York.........................52
Syd Abel, Detroit 49

Penalty minutes

Pat Egan, Brooklyn............................104
Jack Stewart, Detroit..........................93
Ken Reardon, Montreal 83
Jimmy Orlando, Detroit........................81
Bingo Kampman, Toronto 67

Lowest goals-against average
(Min. 25 games)

Frank Brimsek, Boston 2.44
Turk Broda, Toronto 2.83
Jim Henry, New York..........................2.98
John Mowers, Detroit..........................3.06
Sam LoPresti, Chicago 3.23

Shutouts

Turk Broda, Toronto 6
John Mowers, Detroit..............................5
Frank Brimsek, Boston 3
Sam LoPresti, Chicago 3
Three players tied with 3

1942-43

Goals

Doug Bentley, Chicago 33
Joseph Benoit, Montreal 30
Gord Drillon, Montreal 28
Lorne Carr, Toronto 27
Bill Cowley, Boston..............................27
Brian Hextall, New York........................27

Assists

Bill Cowley, Boston..............................45
Max Bentley, Chicago 44
Herbert O'Connor, Montreal 43
Billy Taylor, Toronto.............................42
Doug Bentley, Chicago 40
Elmer Lach, Montreal 40

Points

Doug Bentley, Chicago 73
Bill Cowley, Boston..............................72
Max Bentley, Chicago 70
Lynn Patrick, New York 61
Lorne Carr, Toronto 60
Billy Taylor, Toronto.............................60

Penalty minutes

James Orlando, Detroit.........................89
Reginald Hamilton, Toronto 68
Jack Stewart, Detroit...........................68
Erwin Chamberlain, Boston..................67
Victor Myles, New York........................57

Lowest goals-against average
(Min. 25 games)

John Mowers, Detroit...........................2.48
Turk Broda, Toronto 3.18
Frank Brimsek, Boston 3.52
Bert Gardiner, Chicago 3.60
Paul Bibeault, Montreal 3.82

Shutouts

John Mowers, Detroit..............................6
Bill Beveridge, New York 1
Paul Bibeault, Montreal 1
Frank Brimsek, Boston 1
Turk Broda, Toronto 1
Bert Gardiner, Chicago 1

1943-44

Goals

Doug Bentley, Chicago 38
Herb Cain, Boston 36

Lorne Carr, Toronto 36
Carl Liscombe, Detroit 36
Moderre Bruneteau, Detroit...................35

Assists

Clint Smith, Chicago............................49
Elmer Lach, Montreal 48
Herb Cain, Boston 46
Herbert O'Connor, Montreal 42
Bill Cowley, Boston..............................41
Art Jackson, Boston.............................41

Points

Herb Cain, Boston 82
Doug Bentley, Chicago 77
Lorne Carr, Toronto 74
Carl Liscombe, Detroit 73
Elmer Lach, Montreal 72
Clint Smith, Chicago............................72

Penalty minutes

Mike McMahon, Montreal 78
Harold Jackson, Detroit........................76
Pat Egan Det.-Bos..............................75
Bob Dill, New York 66
Erwin Chamberlain, Montreal 65

Lowest goals-against average
(Min. 25 games)

Bill Durnan, Montreal 2.18
Paul Bibeault, Toronto 3.00
Connie Dion, Detroit............................3.08
Mike Karakas, Chicago 3.04
Bert Gardiner, Boston..........................5.17

Shutouts

Paul Bibeault, Toronto 5
Mike Karakas, Chicago 3
Bill Durnan, Montreal 2
Connie Dion, Detroit................................1
Jim Franks, Bos.-Det...............................1
Bert Gardiner, Boston..............................1

1944-45

Goals

Maurice Richard, Montreal....................50
Herb Cain, Boston 32
Toe Blake, Montreal.............................29
Ted Kennedy, Toronto..........................29
Bill Mosienko, Chicago.........................28

Assists

Elmer Lach, Montreal 54
Bill Cowley, Boston..............................40
Toe Blake, Montreal.............................38
Gus Bodnar, Toronto 36
Syd Howe, Detroit 36

Points

Elmer Lach, Montreal 80
Maurice Richard, Montreal....................73
Toe Blake, Montreal.............................67
Bill Cowley, Boston..............................65
Five players tied with............................54

Penalty minutes

Bob Dill, New York 59
Joe Cooper, Chicago 50
Hal Jackson, Detroit.............................45
Pete Horeck, Chicago 44
Ted Lindsay, Detroit 43

Lowest goals-against average
(Min. 25 games)

Bill Durnan, Montreal 2.42
Harry Lumley, Detroit...........................3.22
Frank McCool, Toronto.........................3.22

Mike Karakas, Chicago 3.90
Paul Bibeault, Boston...........................4.46

Shutouts

Mike Karakas, Chicago 4
Frank McCool, Toronto............................4
Bill Durnan, Montreal 1
Harry Lumley, Detroit 1
Ken McAuley, New York 1

1945-46

Goals

Gaye Stewart, Toronto..........................37
Max Bentley, Chicago 31
Toe Blake, Montreal.............................29
Maurice Richard, Montreal....................27
Clint Smith, Chicago............................26

Assists

Elmer Lach, Montreal 34
Max Bentley, Chicago 30
Bill Mosienko, Chicago.........................30
Albert DeMarco, New York 27
Alex Kaleta, Chicago............................27

Points

Max Bentley, Chicago 61
Gaye Stewart, Toronto..........................52
Toe Blake, Montreal.............................50
Clint Smith, Chicago............................50
Maurice Richard, Montreal....................48
Bill Mosienko, Chicago.........................48

Penalty minutes

Jack Stewart, Detroit...........................73
Armand Guidolin, Boston 62
John Mariucci, Chicago........................58
Emile Bouchard, Montreal 52
Maurice Richard, Montreal....................50

Lowest goals-against average
(Min. 25 games)

Bill Durnan, Montreal 2.60
Paul Bibeault, Bos.-Mon......................2.88
Harry Lumley, Detroit...........................3.18
Frank Brimsek, Boston 3.26
Mike Karakas, Chicago 3.46

Shutouts

Bill Durnan, Montreal 4
Paul Bibeault, Bos.-Mon..........................2
Frank Brimsek, Boston 2
Harry Lumley, Detroit 2
Three players tied with 1

1946-47

Goals

Maurice Richard, Montreal....................45
Bobby Bauer, Boston 30
Roy Conacher, Detroit..........................30
Max Bentley, Chicago 29
Ted Kennedy, Toronto..........................28

Assists

Billy Taylor, Detroit 46
Max Bentley, Chicago 43
Milt Schmidt, Boston 35
Doug Bentley, Chicago 34
Ted Kennedy, Toronto..........................32

Points

Max Bentley, Chicago 72
Maurice Richard, Montreal....................71
Billy Taylor, Detroit 63
Milt Schmidt, Boston 62
Ted Kennedy, Toronto..........................60

Penalty minutes
Gus Mortson, Toronto 133
Johnny Mariucci, Chicago 110
Murph Chamberlain, Montreal 97
Jimmy Thomson, Toronto 97
Bill Ezinicki, Toronto 93

Lowest goals-against average
(Min. 25 games)
Bill Durnan, Montreal 2.30
Turk Broda, Toronto 2.86
Frank Brimsek, Boston 2.91
Charlie Rayner, New York................3.05
Harry Lumley, Detroit.......................3.05

Shutouts
Charlie Rayner, New York 5
Turk Broda, Toronto 4
Bill Durnan, Montreal 4
Frank Brimsek, Boston 3
Harry Lumley, Detroit 3

1947-48

Goals
Ted Lindsay, Detroit 33
Elmer Lach, Montreal 30
Maurice Richard, Montreal...................28
Gaye Stewart, Tor.-Chi..........................27
Syl Apps, Toronto..................................26
Max Bentley, Chi.-Tor. 26

Assists
Doug Bentley, Chicago 37
Buddy O'Connor, New York..................36
Edgar Laprade, New York.....................34
Elmer Lach, Montreal 31
Sid Abel, Detroit....................................30

Points
Elmer Lach, Montreal 61
Buddy O'Connor, New York...................60
Doug Bentley, Chicago 57
Gaye Stewart, Tor.-Chi..........................56
Max Bentley, Chi.-Tor. 54
Bud Poile, Tor.-Chi. 54

Penalty minutes
Bill Barilko, Toronto.............................147
Ken Reardon, Montreal 129
Gus Mortson, Toronto 118
Bill Ezinicki, Toronto 97
Ted Lindsay, Detroit 95

Lowest goals-against average
(Min. 25 games)
Turk Broda, Toronto 2.38
Harry Lumley, Detroit 2.45
Bill Durnan, Montreal 2.74
Frank Brimsek, Boston 2.82
Jim Henry, New York.........................3.19

Shutouts
Harry Lumley, Detroit 7
Turk Broda, Toronto 5
Bill Durnan, Montreal 5
Frank Brimsek, Boston 3
Jim Henry, New York...............................2

1948-49

Goals
Sid Abel, Detroit....................................28
Doug Bentley, Chicago 28
Jim Conacher, Det.-Chi. 26
Roy Conacher, Chicago 26
Ted Lindsay, Detroit 26
Harry Watson, Toronto 26

Assists
Doug Bentley, Chicago 43
Roy Conacher, Chicago 42
Paul Ronty, Boston................................29
Ted Lindsay, Detroit 28
Sid Abel, Detroit....................................26
Gus Bodnar, Chicago............................26

Points
Roy Conacher, Chicago 68
Doug Bentley, Chicago 66
Sid Abel, Detroit....................................54
Ted Lindsay, Detroit 54
Jim Conacher, Det.-Chi. 49
Paul Ronty, Boston................................49

Penalty minutes
Bill Ezinicki, Toronto...........................145
Bep Guidolin, Det.-Chi.......................116
Erwin Chamberlain, Montreal.............111
Maurice Richard, Montreal..................110
Ken Reardon, Montreal 103

Lowest goals-against average
(Min. 25 games)
Bill Durnan, Montreal 2.10
Harry Lumley, Detroit 2.42
Turk Broda, Toronto 2.68
Frank Brimsek, Boston 2.72
Claude Rayner, New York 2.90

Shutouts
Bill Durnan, Montreal 10
Claude Rayner, New York 7
Harry Lumley, Detroit 6
Turk Broda, Toronto 5
Frank Brimsek, Boston 1
Gordon Henry, Boston............................1

1949-50

Goals
Maurice Richard, Montreal...................43
Gordie Howe, Detroit.............................35
Sid Abel, Detroit....................................34
Gordie Howe, Detroit.............................35
Metro Prystai, Chicago..........................29
John Peirson, Boston.............................27

Assists
Ted Lindsay, Detroit 55
Paul Ronty, Boston................................36
Sid Abel, Detroit....................................35
Bep Guidolin, Chicago 34
Doug Bentley, Chicago 33
Gordie Howe, Detroit.............................33
Elmer Lach, Montreal 33

Points
Ted Lindsay, Detroit 78
Sid Abel, Detroit....................................69
Gordie Howe, Detroit.............................68
Maurice Richard, Montreal....................65
Paul Ronty, Boston................................59

Penalty minutes
Bill Ezinicki, Toronto...........................144
Gus Kyle, New York.............................143
Ted Lindsay, Detroit 141
Bill Gadsby, Chicago...........................138
Gus Mortson, Toronto 125

Lowest goals-against average
(Min. 25 games)
Bill Durnan, Montreal 2.20
Harry Lumley, Detroit........................2.35
Turk Broda, Toronto 2.45
Chuck Rayner, New York...................2.62
Jack Gelineau, Boston 3.28

Shutouts
Tuck Broda, Toronto 9
Bill Durnan, Montreal 8
Harry Lumley, Detroit 7
Chuck Rayner, New York.........................6
Frank Brimsek, Chicago 5

1950-51

Goals
Gordie Howe, Detroit.............................43
Maurice Richard, Montreal....................42
Tod Sloan, Toronto................................31
Sid Smith, Toronto.................................30
Roy Conacher, Chicago 26

Assists
Gordie Howe, Detroit.............................43
Ted Kennedy Toronto 43
Max Bentley, Toronto 41
Milton Schmidt, Boston 39
Sid Abel, Detroit....................................38

Points
Gordie Howe, Detroit.............................86
Maurice Richard, Montreal....................66
Max Bentley, Toronto 62
Sid Abel, Detroit....................................61
Milt Schmidt, Boston 61
Ted Kennedy, Toronto............................61

Penalty minutes
Gus Mortson, Toronto 142
Tom Johnson, Montreal 128
Bill Ezinicki, Boston 119
Tony Leswick, New York 112
Ted Lindsay, Detroit 110

Lowest goals-against average
(Min. 25 games)
Al Rollins, Toronto 1.75
Terry Sawchuk, Detroit......................1.98
Turk Broda, Toronto 2.19
Gerry McNeil, Montreal 2.63
Jack Gelineau, Boston.......................2.81

Shutouts
Terry Sawchuk, Detroit..........................11
Turk Broda, Toronto 6
Gerry McNeil, Montreal 6
Al Rollins, Toronto 5
Jack Gelineau, Boston............................4

1951-52

Goals
Gordie Howe, Detroit.............................47
Bill Mosienko, Chicago..........................31
Bernie Geoffrion, Montreal 30
Ted Lindsay, Detroit 30
Maurice Richard, Montreal....................27
Sid Smith, Toronto 27

Assists
Elmer Lach, Montreal 50
Don Raleigh, New York 42
Gordie Howe, Detroit.............................39
Ted Lindsay, Detroit 39
Sid Abel, Detroit....................................36

Points
Gordie Howe, Detroit.............................86
Ted Lindsay, Detroit 69
Elmer Lach, Montreal 65
Don Raleigh, New York 61
Sid Smith, Toronto 57

Penalty minutes

Gus Kyle, Boston...............................127
Ted Lindsay, Detroit...........................123
Fern Flaman, Toronto 110
Gus Mortson, Toronto 106
Al Dewsbury, Chicago 99

Lowest goals-against average
(Min. 25 games)

Terry Sawchuk, Detroit.......................1.90
Al Rollins, Toronto.............................2.20
Gerry McNeil, Montreal 2.34
Jim Henry, Boston...............................2.51
Claude Rayner, New York 3.00

Shutouts

Terry Sawchuk, Detroit...........................12
Jim Henry, Boston...................................7
Gerry McNeil, Montreal 5
Al Rollins, Toronto..................................5
Harry Lumley, Chicago 2
Claude Rayner, New York 2

1952-53

Goals

Gordie Howe, Detroit..............................49
Ted Lindsay, Detroit................................32
Wally Hergesheimer, New York 30
Maurice Richard, Montreal......................28
Fleming Mackell, Boston 27

Assists

Gordie Howe, Detroit..............................46
Alex Delvecchio, Detroit.........................43
Ted Lindsay, Detroit................................39
Paul Ronty, New York..............................38
Metro Prystai, Detroit..............................34

Points

Gordie Howe, Detroit..............................95
Ted Lindsay, Detroit................................71
Maurice Richard, Montreal......................61
Wally Hergesheimer, New York 59
Alex Delvecchio, Detroit.........................59

Penalty minutes

Maurice Richard, Montreal....................112
Ted Lindsay, Detroit..............................111
Fern Flaman, Toronto 110
George Gee, Chicago..............................99
Leo Boivin, Toronto................................97
Al Dewsbury, Chicago 97

Lowest goals-against average
(Min. 25 games)

Terry Sawchuk, Detroit.......................1.90
Gerry McNeil, Montreal 2.12
Harry Lumley, Toronto 2.38
Jim Henry, Boston...............................2.46
Al Rollins, Chicago 2.50

Shutouts

Harry Lumley, Toronto 10
Gerry McNeil, Montreal 10
Terry Sawchuk, Detroit.............................9
Jim Henry, Boston...................................7
Al Rollins, Chicago 6

1953-54

Goals

Maurice Richard, Montreal......................37
Gordie Howe, Detroit..............................33
Bernie Geoffrion, Montreal 29
Wally Hergesheimer, New York 27
Ted Lindsay, Detroit................................26

Assists

Gordie Howe, Detroit..............................48
Bert Olmstead, Montreal 37
Ted Lindsay, Detroit................................36
Four players tied with.............................33

Points

Gordie Howe, Detroit..............................81
Maurice Richard, Montreal......................67
Ted Lindsay, Detroit................................62
Bernie Geoffrion, Montreal 54
Bert Olmstead, Montreal 52

Penalty minutes

Gus Mortson, Chicago 132
Maurice Richard, Montreal....................112
Douglas Harvey, Montreal 110
Ted Lindsay, Detroit..............................110
Gordie Howe, Detroit............................109
Ivan Irwin, New York.............................109

Lowest goals-against average
(Min. 25 games)

Harry Lumley, Toronto 1.85
Terry Sawchuk, Detroit.......................1.92
Gerry McNeil, Montreal 2.15
Jim Henry, Boston...............................2.58
John Bower, New York 2.60

Shutouts

Harry Lumley, Toronto 13
Terry Sawchuk, Detroit...........................12
Jim Henry, Boston...................................8
Gerry McNeil, Montreal 6
John Bower, New York 5
Jacques Plante, Montreal 5

1954-55

Goals

Bernie Geoffrion, Montreal 38
Maurice Richard, Montreal......................38
Jean Beliveau, Montreal 37
Sid Smith, Toronto..................................33
Gordie Howe, Detrot...............................29
Danny Lewicki, New York........................29

Assists

Bert Olmstead, Montreal 48
Doug Harvey, Montreal 43
Ted Kennedy, Toronto.............................42
George Sullivan, Chicago 42
Earl Reibel, Detroit.................................41

Points

Bernie Geoffrion, Montreal 75
Maurice Richard, Montreal......................74
Jean Beliveau, Montreal 73
Earl Reibel, Detroit.................................66
Gordie Howe, Detroit..............................62

Penalty minutes

Fern Flaman, Boston 150
Tony Leswick, Detroit............................137
Bucky Hollingworth, Chicago 135
Gus Mortson, Chicago 133
Jean Beliveau, Montreal 125

Lowest goals-against average
(Min. 25 games)

Terry Sawchuk, Detroit.......................1.94
Harry Lumley, Toronto 1.94
Jacques Plante, Montreal 2.11
John Henderson, Boston......................2.40
Jim Henry, Boston...............................3.00

Shutouts

Terry Sawchuk, Detroit...........................12
Harry Lumley, Toronto 8

John Henderson, Boston............................5
Jacques Plante, Montreal 5
Gump Worsley, New York 4

1955-56

Goals

Jean Beliveau, Montreal 47
Gordie Howe, Detroit..............................38
Maurice Richard, Montreal......................38
Tod Sloan, Toronto..................................37
Bernie Goeffrion, Montreal 29

Assists

Bert Olmstead, Montreal 56
Andy Bathgate, New York........................47
Bill Gadsby, New York 42
Jean Beliveau, Montreal 41
Gordie Howe, Detroit..............................41

Points

Jean Beliveau, Montreal 88
Gordie Howe, Detroit..............................79
Maurice Richard, Montreal......................71
Bert Olmstead, Montreal 70
Tod Sloan, Toronto..................................66
Andy Bathgate, New York........................66

Penalty minutes

Lou Fontinato, New York........................202
Ted Lindsay, Detroit..............................161
Jean Beliveau, Montreal 143
Bob Armstrong, Boston 122
Vic Stasiuk, Boston 118

Lowest goals-against average
(Min. 25 games)

Jacques Plante, Montreal 1.86
Glenn Hall, Detroit...............................2.11
Terry Sawchuk, Boston........................2.66
Harry Lumley, Toronto 2.69
Gump Worsley, New York 2.90

Shutouts

Glenn Hall, Detroit..................................12
Terry Sawchuk, Boston..............................9
Jacques Plante, Montreal 7
Gump Worsley, New York 4
Harry Lumley, Toronto 3
Al Rollins, Chicago 3

1956-57

Goals

Gordie Howe, Detroit..............................44
Jean Beliveau, Montreal 33
Maurice Richard, Montreal......................33
Ed Litzenberger, Chicago........................32
Real Chevrefils, Boston 31

Assists

Ted Lindsay, Detroit................................55
Jean Beliveau, Montreal 51
Andy Bathgate, New York........................50
Gordie Howe, Detroit..............................45
Doug Harvey, Montreal 44

Points

Gordie Howe, Detroit..............................89
Ted Lindsay, Detroit................................85
Jean Beliveau, Montreal 84
Andy Bathgate, New York........................77
Ed Litzenberger, Chicago........................64

Penalty minutes

Gus Mortson, Chicago 147
Lou Fontinato, New York........................139

NHL HISTORY Statistical leaders

Leo LaBine, Boston 128
Pierre Pilote, Chicago 117
Jack Evans, New York 110

Lowest goals-against average
(Min. 25 games)
Jacques Plante, Montreal 2.02
Glenn Hall, Detroit 2.24
Terry Sawchuk, Boston 2.38
Don Simmons, Boston 2.42
Ed Chadwick, Toronto 2.74

Shutouts
Jacques Plante, Montreal 9
Ed Chadwick, Toronto 5
Glenn Hall, Detroit 4
Don Simmons, Boston 4
Al Rollins, Chicago 3
Gump Worsley, New York 3

1957-58

Goals
Dickie Moore, Montreal 36
Gordie Howe, Detroit 33
Camille Henry, New York 32
Fleming Mackell, Boston 32
Andy Bathgate, New York 30
Bronco Horvath, Boston 30

Assists
Henri Richard, Montreal 52
Andy Bathgate, New York 48
Dickie Moore, Montreal 48
Gordie Howe, Detroit 44
Fleming Mackell, Boston 40

Points
Dickie Moore, Montreal 84
Henri Richard, Montreal 80
Andy Bathgate, New York 78
Gordie Howe, Detroit 77
Bronco Horvath, Boston 66

Penalty minutes
Lou Fontinato, New York 152
Forbes Kennedy, Detroit 135
Doug Harvey, Montreal 131
Ted Lindsay, Chicago 110
Jack Evans, New York 108

Lowest goals-against average
(Min. 25 games)
Jacques Plante, Montreal 2.09
Gump Worsley, New York 2.32
Don Simmons, Boston 2.45
Harry Lumley, Boston 2.84
Glenn Hall, Chicago 2.88

Shutouts
Jacques Plante, Montreal 9
Glenn Hall, Chicago 7
Don Simmons, Boston 5
Gump Worsley, New York 4
Ed Chadwick, Toronto 4

1958-59

Goals
Jean Beliveau, Montreal 45
Dickie Moore, Montreal 41
Andy Bathgate, N.Y Rangers 40
Ed Litzenberger, Chicago 33
Andy Hebenton, New York 33

Assists
Dickie Moore, Montreal 55
Andy Bathgate, New York 48

Jean Beliveau, Montreal 46
Bill Gadsby, New York 46
Gordie Howe, Detroit 46

Points
Dickie Moore, Montreal 96
Jean Beliveau, Montreal 91
Andy Bathgate, New York 88
Gordie Howe, Detroit 78
Ed Litzenberger, Chicago 77

Penalty minutes
Ted Lindsay, Chicago 184
Lou Fontinato, New York 149
Carl Brewer, Toronto 125
Jim Bartlett, New York 118
Pete Goegan, Detroit 109
Eddie Shack, New York 109

Lowest goals-against average
(Min. 25 games)
Jacques Plante, Montreal 2.15
Johnny Bower, Toronto 2.74
Glenn Hall, Chicago 2.97
Eddie Chadwick, Toronto 3.00
Gump Worsley, New York 3.06

Shutouts
Jacques Plante, Montreal 9
Terry Sawchuk, Detroit 5
Johnny Bower, Toronto 3
Eddie Chadwick, Toronto 3
Don Simmons, Boston 3

1959-60

Goals
Bobby Hull, Chicago 39
Bronco Horvath, Boston 39
Jean Beliveau, Montreal 34
Dean Prentice, New York 32
Bernie Geoffrion, Montreal 30
Henri Richard, Montreal 30

Assists
Don McKenney, Boston 49
Andy Bathgate, New York 48
Gordie Howe, Detroit 45
Henri Richard, Montreal 43
Bobby Hull, Chicago 42

Points
Bobby Hull, Chicago 81
Bronco Horvath, Boston 80
Jean Beliveau, Montreal 74
Andy Bathgate, New York 74
Henri Richard, Montreal 73
Gordie Howe, Detroit 73

Penalty minutes
Carl Brewer, Toronto 150
Lou Fontinato, New York 137
Vic Stasiuk, Boston 121
Stan Mikita, Chicago 119
Fern Flamen, Boston 112

Lowest goals-against average
(Min. 25 games)
Jacques Plante, Montreal 2.54
Glenn Hall, Chicago 2.57
Terry Sawchuk, Detroit 2.69
Johnny Bower, Toronto 2.73
Don Simmons, Boston 3.36

Shutouts
Glenn Hall, Chicago 6
Johnny Bower, Toronto 5
Terry Sawchuk, Detroit 5
Jacques Plante, Montreal 3

Harry Lumley, Boston 2
Don Simmons, Boston 2

1960-61

Goals
Bernie Geoffrion, Montreal 50
Frank Mahovlich, Toronto 48
Dickie Moore, Montreal 35
Jean Beliveau, Montreal 32
Bobby Hull, Chicago 31

Assists
Jean Beliveau, Montreal 58
Red Kelly, Toronto 50
Gordie Howe, Detroit 49
Andy Bathgate, New York 48
Bill Hay, Chicago 48

Points
Bernie Geoffrion, Montreal 95
Jean Beliveau, Montreal 90
Frank Mahovlich, Toronto 84
Andy Bathgate, New York 77
Gordie Howe, Detroit 72

Penalty minutes
Pierre Pilote, Chicago 165
Reg Fleming, Chicago 145
Jean Guy Talbot, Montreal 143
Frank Mahovlich, Toronto 131
Eric Nesterenko, Chicago 125

Lowest goals-against average
(Min. 25 games)
Johnny Bower, Toronto 2.50
Charlie Hodge, Montreal 2.53
Jacques Plante, Montreal 2.80
Hank Bassen, Detroit 2.97
Terry Sawchuk, Detroit 3.17

Shutouts
Glenn Hall, Chicago 6
Charlie Hodge, Montreal 4
Johnny Bower, Toronto 2
Jacques Plante, Montreal 2
Terry Sawchuk, Detroit 2

1961-62

Goals
Bobby Hull, Chicago 50
Gordie Howe, Detroit 33
Frank Mahovlich, Toronto 33
Claude Provost, Montreal 33
Gilles Tremblay, Montreal 32

Assists
Andy Bathgate, New York 56
Bill Hay, Chicago 52
Stan Mikita, Chicago 52
Gordie Howe, Detroit 44
Alex Delvecchio, Detroit 43

Points
Bobby Hull, Chicago 84
Andy Bathgate, New York 84
Gordie Howe, Detroit 77
Stan Mikita, Chicago 77
Frank Mahovlich, Toronto 71

Penalty minutes
Lou Fontinato, Montreal 167
Ted Green, Boston 116
Bob Pulford, Toronto 98
Stan Mikita, Chicago 97
Eric Nesterenko, Chicago 97
Pierre Pilote, Chicago 97

Lowest goals-against average
(Min. 25 games)

Jacques Plante, Montreal 2.37
John Bower, Toronto 2.58
Glenn Hall, Chicago 2.66
Henry Bassen, Detroit 2.81
Gump Worsley, New York 2.90

Shutouts

Glenn Hall, Chicago 9
Terry Sawchuk, Detroit 5
Jacques Plante, Montreal 4
Henry Bassen, Detroit 3
Three players tied with 2

1962-63

Goals

Gordie Howe, Detroit 38
Camille Henry, New York 37
Frank Mahovlich, Toronto 36
Andy Bathgate, New York 35
Parker MacDonald, Detroit 33

Assists

Henri Richard, Montreal 50
Jean Beliveau, Montreal 49
Gordie Howe, Detroit 48
Andy Bathgate, New York 46
Stan Mikita, Chicago 45

Points

Gordie Howe, Detroit 86
Andy Bathgate, New York 81
Stan Mikita, Chicago 76
Frank Mahovlich, Toronto 73
Henri Richard, Montreal 73

Penalty minutes

Howie Young, Detroit 273
Carl Brewer, Toronto 168
Lou Fontinato, Montreal 141
Ted Green, Boston 117
Bill Gladsby, Detroit 116

Lowest goals-against average
(Min. 25 games)

Jacques Plante, Montreal 2.46
Terry Sawchuk, Detroit 2.48
Don Simmons, Toronto 2.50
Glenn Hall, Chicago 2.51
Johnny Bower, Toronto 2.62

Shutouts

Glenn Hall, Chicago 5
Jacques Plante, Montreal 5
Terry Sawchuk, Detroit 3
Gump Worsley, New York 2
Four players tied with 1

1963-64

Goals

Bobby Hull, Chicago 43
Stan Mikita, Chicago 39
Ken Wharram, Chicago 39
Camille Henry, New York 29
Jean Beliveau, Montreal 28

Assists

Andy Bathgate, N.Y.-Tor. 58
Jean Beliveau, Montreal 50
Stan Mikita, Chicago 50
Gordie Howe, Detroit 47
Pierre Pilote, Chicago 46

Points

Stan Mikita, Chicago 89
Bobby Hull, Chicago 87
Jean Beliveau, Montreal 78

Andy Bathgate, N.Y.-Tor. 77
Gordie Howe, Detroit 73

Penalty minutes

Vic Hadfield, New York 151
Terry Harper, Montreal 149
Stan Mikita, Chicago 146
Ted Green, Boston 145
Reg Fleming, Chicago 140

Lowest goals-against average
(Min. 25 games)

Johnny Bower, Toronto 2.12
Charlie Hodge, Montreal 2.26
Glenn Hall, Chicago 2.30
Terry Sawchuk, Detroit 2.70
Eddie Johnston, Boston 3.01

Shutouts

Charlie Hodge, Montreal 8
Glenn Hall, Chicago 7
Ed Johnston, Boston 6
Johnny Bower, Toronto 5
Terry Sawchuk, Detroit 5

1964-65

Goals

Norm Ullman, Detroit 42
Bobby Hull, Chicago 39
Gordie Howe, Detroit 29
Stan Mikita, Chicago 28
Claude Provost, Montreal 27

Assists

Stan Mikita, Chicago 59
Gordie Howe, Detroit 47
Pierre Pilote, Chicago 45
Alex Delvecchio, Detroit 42
Norm Ullman, Detroit 41

Points

Stan Mikita, Chicago 87
Norm Ullman, Detroit 83
Gordie Howe, Detroit 76
Bobby Hull, Chicago 71
Alex Delvecchio, Detroit 67

Penalty minutes

Carl Brewer, Toronto 177
Ted Lindsay, Detroit 173
Pierre Pilote, Chicago 162
Bob Baun, Toronto 160
John Ferguson, Montreal 156
Ted Green, Boston 156

Lowest goals-against average
(Min. 25 games)

Johnny Bower, Toronto 2.38
Roger Crozier, Detroit 2.42
Glenn Hall, Chicago 2.43
Denis DeJordy, Chicago 2.52
Terry Sawchuk, Toronto 2.56

Shutouts

Roger Crozier, Detroit 6
Glenn Hall, Chicago 4
Johnny Bower, Toronto 3
Denis DeJordy, Chicago 3
Charlie Hodge, Montreal 3
Ed Johnston, Boston 3

1965-66

Goals

Bobby Hull, Chicago 54
Frank Mahovlich, Toronto 32
Alex Delvecchio, Detroit 31
Norm Ullman, Detroit 31

Stan Mikita, Chicago 30
Bobby Rousseau, Montreal 30

Assists

Jean Beliveau, Montreal 48
Stan Mikita, Chicago 48
Bobby Rousseau, Montreal 48
Gordie Howe, Detroit 46
Bobby Hull, Chicago 43

Points

Bobby Hull, Chicago 97
Stan Mikita, Chicago 78
Bobby Rousseau, Montreal 78
Jean Beliveau, Montreal 77
Gordie Howe, Detroit 75

Penalty minutes

Reg Fleming, Bos.-N.Y. 166
John Ferguson, Montreal 153
Bryan Watson, Detroit 133
Ted Green, Boston 113
Vic Hadfield, New York 112

Lowest goals-against average
(Min. 25 games)

Johnny Bower, Toronto 2.25
Gump Worsley, Montreal 2.36
Charlie Hodge, Montreal 2.58
Glenn Hall, Chicago 2.63
Roger Crozier, Detroit 2.78

Shutouts

Roger Crozier, Detroit 7
Bruce Gamble, Toronto 4
Glenn Hall, Chicago 4
Johnny Bower, Toronto 3
Cesare Maniago, New York 2
Gump Worsley, Montreal 2

1966-67

Goals

Bobby Hull, Chicago 52
Stan Mikita, Chicago 35
Ken Wharram, Chicago 31
Rod Gilbert, New York 28
Bruce MacGregor, Detroit 28

Assists

Stan Mikita, Chicago 62
Phil Goyette, New York 49
Pierre Pilote, Chicago 46
Bobby Rousseau, Montreal 44
Norm Ullman, Detroit 44

Points

Stan Mikita, Chicago 97
Bobby Hull, Chicago 80
Norm Ullman, Detroit 70
Ken Wharram, Chicago 65
Gordie Howe, Detroit 65

Penalty minutes

John Ferguson, Montreal 177
Reg Fleming, New York 146
Gary Bergman, Detroit 129
Gilles Marotte, Boston 112
Ed Van Impe, Chicago 111

Lowest goals-against average
(Min. 25 games)

Glenn Hall, Chicago 2.38
Denis DeJordy, Chicago 2.46
Charlie Hodge, Montreal 2.60
Ed Giacomin, New York 2.61
Johnny Bower, Toronto 2.64

Shutouts

Ed Giacomin, New York 9
Roger Crozier, Detroit 4

Denis DeJordy, Chicago 4
Charlie Hodge, Montreal.......................3
Three players tied with 2

1967-68

Goals
Bobby Hull, Chicago 44
Stan Mikita, Chicago 40
Gordie Howe, Detroit...........................39
Phil Esposito, Boston 35
Wayne Connelly, Minnesota 35

Assists
Phil Esposito, Boston 49
Alex Delvecchio, Detroit 48
Rod Gilbert, New York..........................48
Stan Mikita, Chicago 47
Jean Ratelle, New York.........................46

Points
Stan Mikita, Chicago 87
Phil Esposito, Boston 84
Gordie Howe, Detroit...........................82
Jean Ratelle, New York.........................78
Rod Gilbert, New York..........................77

Penalty minutes
Gary Dornhoefer, Philadelphia............134
Ted Green, Boston.............................133
Reg Fleming, New York.......................132
Forbes Kennedy, Philadelphia............130
Kent Douglas, Oak.-Det.....................126

Lowest goals-against average
(Min. 25 games)
Gump Worsley, Montreal 1.98
Johnny Bower, Toronto 2.25
Boug Favell, Philadelphia 2.27
Bruce Gamble, Toronto 2.31
Ed Giacomin, New York......................2.44

Shutouts
Ed Giacomin, New York...........................8
Les Binkley, Pittburgh 6
Cesare Maniago, Minnesota 6
Lorn Worsley, Montreal 6
Bruce Gamble, Toronto 5
Glen Hall, St. Louis 5

1968-69

Goals
Bobby Hull, Chicago 58
Phil Esposito, Boston 49
Frank Mahovlich, Detroit 49
Ken Hodge, Boston 45
Gordie Howe, Detroit...........................44

Assists
Phil Esposito, Boston 77
Stan Mikita, Chicago 67
Gordie Howe, Detroit...........................59
Alex Delvecchio, Detroit 58
Four players tied with..........................49

Points
Phil Esposito, Boston 126
Bobby Hull, Chicago 107
Gordie Howe, Detroit.........................103
Stan Mikita, Chicago 97
Ken Hodge, Boston 90

Penalty minutes
Forbes Kennedy, Phi.-Tor. 219
Jim Dorey, Toronto.............................200
John Ferguson, Montreal 185
Carol Vadnais, Oakland 151
Don Awrey, Bosotn.............................149

Lowest goals-against average
(Min. 25 games)
Jacques Plante, St. Louis 1.96
Glenn Hall, St. Louis 2.17
Gump Worsley, Montreal 2.26
Ron Edwards, Detroit.......................2.54
Ed Giacomin, New York.....................2.55

Shutouts
Ed Giacomin, New York...........................7
Jaques Plante, St. Louis 5
Gump Worsley, Montreal 5
Roy Edwards, Detroit 4
Gary Smith, Oakland 4
Gerry Desjardins, Los Angeles...............4

1969-70

Goals
Phil Esposito, Boston 43
Garry Unger, Detroit 42
Stan Mikita, Chicago 39
Bobby Hull, Chicago 38
Frank Mahovlich, Detroit 38

Assists
Bobby Orr, Boston 87
Phil Esposito, Boston 56
Tommy Williams, Minnesota 52
Walt Tkaczuk, New York.......................50
Phil Goyette, St. Louis 49

Points
Bobby Orr, Boston 120
Phil Esposito, Boston 99
Stan Mikita, Chicago 86
Phil Goyette, St. Louis 78
Walt Tkaczuk, New York.......................77

Penalty minutes
Keith Magnuson, Chicago 213
Carol Vadnais, California 212
Bryan Watson, Pittsburgh 189
Barry Gibbs, Minnesota.......................182
Earl Heiskala, Philadelphia 171

Lowest goals-against average
(Min. 25 games)
Ernie Wakely, St. Louis......................2.11
Tony Esposito, Chicago 2.17
Jacques Plante St. Louis 2.19
Ed Giacomin, New York......................2.36
Roy Edwards, Detroit 2.59

Shutouts
Tony Esposito, Chicago 15
Ed Giacomin, New York...........................6
Bruce Gambel, Toronto 5
Jacques Plante, St. Louis 5
Gerry Cheevers, Boston 4
Rogie Vachon, Montreal 4
Ernie Wakely, St. Louis...........................4

Wins by goaltenders
Tony Esposito, Chicago 38
Ed Giacomin, New York.........................35
Rogie Vachon, Montreal 31
Gerry Cheevers, Boston 24
Roy Edwards, Detroit 24

1970-71

Goals
Phil Esposito, Boston 76
John Bucyk, Boston 51
Bobby Hull, Chicago 44
Ken Hodge, Boston 43
Dennis Hull, Chicago 40

Assists
Bobby Orr, Boston 102
Phil Esposito, Boston 76
John Bucyk, Boston 65
Ken Hodge, Boston 62
Wayne Cashman, Boston 58

Points
Phil Esposito, Boston 152
Bobby Orr, Boston 139
John Bucyk, Boston 116
Ken Hodge, Boston 105
Bobby Hull, Chicago 96

Penalty minutes
Keith Magnuson, Chicago 291
Dennis Hextall, California 217
Jim Dorey, Toronto.............................198
Pete Mahovlich, Montreal 181
Tracy Pratt, Buffalo.............................179

Lowest goals-against average
(Min. 25 games)
Jacques Plante, Toronto....................1.88
Ed Giacomin, New York......................2.15
Tony Esposito, Chicago 2.27
Gilles Villemure, New York 2.29
Glenn Hall, St. Louis 2.41

Shutouts
Ed Giacomin, New York...........................8
Tony Esposito, Chicago 6
Cesare Maniago, Minnesota 5
Jacques Plante, Toronto...........................4
Ed Johnston, Boston...............................4
Gilles Villemure, New York 4

Wins by goaltenders
Tony Esposito, Chicago 35
Ed Johnston, Boston.............................30
Gerry Cheevers, Boston 27
Ed Giacomin, New York.........................27
Jacques Plante, Toronto.........................24

1971-72

Goals
Phil Esposito, Boston 66
Vic Hadfield, New York.........................50
Bobby Hull, Chicago 50
Yvan Cournoyer, Montreal 47
Jean Ratelle, New York.........................46

Assists
Bobby Orr, Boston 80
Phil Esposito, Boston 67
Jean Ratelle, New York.........................63
Vic Hadfield, New York.........................56
Fred Stanfield, Boston..........................56

Points
Phil Esposito, Boston 133
Bobby Orr, Boston 117
Jean Ratelle, New York.......................109
Vic Hadfield, New York.......................106
Rod Gilbert, New York..........................97

Penalty minutes
Bryan Watson, Pittsburgh 212
Keith Magnuson, Chicago 199
Gary Dornhoefer, Philadelphia............183
Barclay Plager, St. Louis 176
Rick Floey, Philadelphia......................168

Lowest goals-against average
(Min. 25 games)
Tony Esposito, Chicago 1.76
Gilles Villemure, New York 2.08

Lorne Worsley, Minnesota	2.12
Ken Dryden, Montreal	2.34
Gary Smith, Chicago	2.41

Shutouts
Tony Esposito, Chicago	9
Ken Dryden, Montreal	8
Gary Smith, Chicago	5
Doug Favell, Philadelphia	5
Al Smith, Detroit	4
Gilles Meloche, California	4

Wins by goaltenders
Tony Esposito, Chicago	31
Gerry Cheevers, Boston	27
Ed Johnston, Boston	27
Ed Giacomin, New York	24
Gilles Villemure, New York	24

1972-73

Goals
Phil Esposito, Boston	55
Mickey Redmond, Detroit	52
Rick McLeish, Philadelphia	50
Jacques Lemaire, Montreal	44
Three players tied with	41

Assists
Phil Esposito, Boston	75
Bobby Orr, Boston	72
Bobby Clarke, Philadelphia	67
Pit Martin, Chicago	61
Gilbert Perreault, Buffalo	60

Points
Phil Esposito, Boston	130
Bobby Clarke, Philadelphia	104
Bobby Orr, Boston	101
Rick MacLeish, Philadelphia	100
Jacques Lemaire, Montreal	95

Penalty minutes
Dave Schultz, Philadelphia	259
Bob Kelly, Philadelphia	238
Steve Durbano, St. Louis	231
Andre Dupont, St.L.-Phi.	215
Don Saleski, Philadelphia	205

Lowest goals-against average
(Min. 25 games)
Ken Dryden, Montreal	2.26
Gilles Villemure, N.Y. Rangers	2.29
Tony Esposito, Chicago	2.51
Roy Edwards, Detroit	2.63
Dave Dryden, Buffalo	2.68

Shutouts
Ken Dryden, Montreal	6
Roy Edwards, Detroit	6
Tony Esposito, Chicago	4
Cesare Maniago, Minnesota	4
Rogie Vachon, Los Angeles	4

Wins by goaltenders
Ken Dryden, Montreal	33
Tony Esposito, Chicago	32
Roy Edwards, Detroit	27
Ed Giacomin, N.Y. Rangers	26
Ed Johnston, Boston	24

1973-74

Goals
Phil Esposito, Boston	61
Ken Hodge, Boston	50
Richard Martin, Buffalo	52
Mickey Redmond, Detroit	51
Bill Goldsworthy, Minnesota	48

Assists
Bobby Orr, Boston	90
Phil Esposito, Boston	77
Dennis Hextall, Minnesota	62
Syl Apps, Pittsburgh	61
Andre Boudrias, Vancouver	59
Wayne Cashman, Boston	59

Points
Phil Esposito, Boston	145
Bobby Orr, Boston	122
Ken Hodge, Boston	105
Wayne Cashman, Boston	89
Bobby Clarke, Philadelphia	87

Penalty minutes
Dave Schultz, Philadelphia	348
Steve Durbano, St.L.-Pit.	284
Bryan Watson, Pit.-St.L.-Det.	255
Andre Dupont, Philadelphia	216
Gary Howatt, N.Y. Islanders	204

Lowest goals-against average
(Min. 25 games)
Bernie Parent, Philadelphia	1.89
Tony Esposito, Chicago	2.04
Doug Favell, Toronto	2.71
Wayne Thomas, Montreal	2.76
Dan Bouchard, Atlanta	2.77

Shutouts
Bernie Parent, Philadelphia	12
Tony Esposito, Chicago	10
Gilles Gilbert, Boston	6
Dan Bouchard, Atlanta	5
Ed Giacomin, N.Y. Rangers	5
Rogie Vachon, Los Angeles	5

Wins by goaltenders
Bernie Parent, Philadelphia	47
Tony Esposito, Chicago	34
Gilles Gilbert, Boston	34
Ed Giacomin, N.Y. Rangers	30
Rogie Vachon, Los Angeles	28

1974-75

Goals
Phil Esposito, Boston	61
Guy Lafleur, Montreal	53
Rick Martin, Buffalo	52
Danny Grant, Detroit	50
Marcel Dionne, Detroit	47

Assists
Bobby Clarke, Philadelphia	89
Bobby Orr, Boston	89
Pete Mahovlich, Montreal	82
Marcel Dionne, Detroit	74
Phil Esposito, Boston	66
Guy Lafleur, Montreal	66

Points
Bobby Orr, Boston	135
Phil Esposito, Boston	127
Marcel Dionne, Detroit	121
Guy Lafleur, Montreal	119
Pete Mahovlich, Montreal	117

Penalty minutes
Dave Schultz, Philadelphia	472
Andre Dupont, Philadelphia	276
Phil Russell, Chicago	260
Bryan Watson, Detroit	238
Bob Gassoff, St. Louis	222

Lowest goals-against average
(Min. 25 games)
Bernie Parent, Philadelphia	2.03
Rogie Vachon, Los Angeles	2.24
Gary Edwards, Los Angeles	2.34
Chico Resch, N.Y. Islanders	2.47
Ken Dryden, Montreal	2.69

Shutouts
Bernie Parent, Philadelphia	12
Tony Esposito, Chicago	6
Gary Smith, Vancouver	6
Rogie Vachon, Los Angeles	6
Phil Myre, Atlanta	5

Wins by goaltenders
Bernie Parent, Philadelphia	44
Tony Esposito, Chicago	34
Gary Smith, Vancouver	32
Ken Dryden, Montreal	30
Rogie Vachon, Los Angeles	27

1975-76

Goals
Reggie Leach, Philadelphia	61
Guy Lafleur, Montreal	56
Pierre Larouche, Pittsburgh	53
Jean Pronovost, Pittsburgh	52
Bill Barber, Philadelphia	50
Danny Gare, Buffalo	50

Assists
Bobby Clarke, Philadelphia	89
Pete Mahovlich, Montreal	71
Guy Lafleur, Montreal	69
Gilbert Perreault, Buffalo	69
Jean Ratelle, NYR-Bos.	69

Points
Guy Lafleur, Montreal	125
Bobby Clarke, Philadelphia	119
Gilbert Perreault, Buffalo	113
Bill Barber, Philadelphia	112
Pierre Larouche, Pittsburgh	111

Penalty minutes
Steve Durbano, Pit.-K.C.	370
Bryan Watson, Detroit	322
Dave Schultz, Philadelphia	307
Bob Gassoff, St. Louis	306
Dave Williams, Toronto	306

Lowest goals-against average
(Min. 25 games)
Ken Dryden, Montreal	2.03
Chico Resch, N.Y. Islanders	2.07
Dan Bouchard, Atlanta	2.54
Wayne Stephenson, Philadelphia	2.58
Billy Smith, N.Y. Islanders	2.61

Shutouts
Ken Dryden, Montreal	8
Chico Resch, N.Y. Islanders	7
Rogie Vachon, Los Angeles	5
Tony Esposito, Chicago	4
Jim Rutherford, Detroit	4

Wins by goaltenders
Ken Dryden, Montreal	42
Wayne Stephenson, Philadelphia	40
Gilles Gilbert, Boston	33
Tony Esposito, Chicago	30
Gerry Desjardins, Buffalo	29

1976-77

Goals
Steve Shutt, Montreal	60
Guy Lafleur, Montreal	56

Marcel Dionne, Los Angeles................53
Rick MacLeish, Philadelphia................49
Wilf Paiement, Colorado......................41

Assists
Guy Lafleur, Montreal..........................80
Marcel Dionne, Los Angeles.................69
Larry Robinson, Montreal 66
Borje Salming, Toronto 66
Tim Young, Minnesota 66

Points
Guy Lafleur, Montreal........................136
Marcel Dionne, Los Angeles...............122
Steve Shutt, Montreal........................105
Rick MacLeish, Philadelphia................97
Gilbert Perreault, Buffalo 95
Tim Young, Minnesota 95

Penalty minutes
Dave Williams, Toronto 338
Dennis Polonich, Detroit 274
Bob Gassoff, St. Louis 254
Phil Russell, Chicago 233
Dave Schultz, Los Angeles 232

Lowest goals-against average
(Min. 25 games)
Michel Larocque, Montreal...............2.09
Ken Dryden, Montreal 2.14
Chico Resch, N.Y. Islanders 2.28
Billy Smith, N.Y. Islanders................2.50
Don Edwards, Buffalo.......................2.51

Shutouts
Ken Dryden, Montreal 10
Rogie Vachon, Los Angeles 8
Bernie Parent, Philadelphia 5
Dunc Wilson, Pittsburgh 5
Michel Larocque, Montreal...................4
Mike Palmateer, Toronto 4

Wins by goaltenders
Ken Dryden, Montreal 41
Bernie Parent, Philadelphia 35
Rogie Vachon, Los Angeles.................33
Gerry Desjardins, Buffalo 31
Gerry Cheevers, Boston 30

1977-78

Goals
Guy Lafleur, Montreal..........................60
Mike Bossy, N.Y. Islanders 53
Steve Shutt, Montreal..........................49
Lanny McDonald, Toronto 47
Bryan Trottier, N.Y. Islanders..............46

Assists
Bryan Trottier, N.Y. Islanders..............77
Guy Lafleur, Montreal..........................72
Darryl Sittler, Toronto 72
Bobby Clarke, Philadelphia..................68
Denis Potvin, N.Y. Islanders 64

Points
Guy Lafleur, Montreal........................132
Bryan Trottier, N.Y. Islanders............123
Darryl Sittler, Toronto 117
Jacques Lemaire, Montreal 97
Denis Potvin, N.Y. Islanders 94

Penalty minutes
Dave Schultz, L.A.-Pit........................405
Dave Williams, Toronto 351
Dennis Polonich, Detroit 254
Randy Holt, Chi.-Cle..........................249
Andre Dupont, Philadelphia................225

Lowest goals-against average
(Min. 25 games)
Ken Dryden, Montreal 2.05
Bernie Parent, Philadelphia 2.22
Gilles Gilbert, Boston 2.53
Chico Resch, N.Y. Islanders 2.55
Tony Esposito, Chicago 2.63

Shutouts
Bernie Parent, Philadelphia 7
Ken Dryden, Montreal 5
Don Edwards, Buffalo............................5
Tony Esposito, Chicago 5
Mike Palmateer, Toronto 5

Wins by goaltenders
Don Edwards, Buffalo..........................38
Ken Dryden, Montreal 37
Mike Palmateer, Toronto 34
Bernie Parent, Philadelphia 29
Rogie Vachon, Los Angeles.................29

1978-79

Goals
Mike Bossy, N.Y. Islanders 69
Marcel Dionne, Los Angeles.................59
Guy Lafleur, Montreal..........................52
Guy Chouinard, Atlanta.......................50
Bryan Trottier, N.Y. Islanders..............47

Assists
Bryan Trottier, N.Y. Islanders..............87
Guy Lafleur, Montreal..........................77
Marcel Dionne, Los Angeles.................71
Bob MacMillan, Atlanta 71
Denis Potvin, N.Y. Islanders 70

Points
Bryan Trottier, N.Y. Islanders............134
Marcel Dionne, Los Angeles...............130
Guy Lafleur, Montreal........................129
Mike Bossy, N.Y. Islanders 126
Bob MacMillan, Atlanta 108

Penalty minutes
Dave Williams, Toronto 298
Randy Holt, Van.-L.A..........................282
Dave Schultz, Pit.-Buf. 243
Dave Hutchison, Toronto....................235
Willi Plett, Atlanta 213

Lowest goals-against average
(Min. 25 games)
Ken Dryden, Montreal 2.30
Chico Resch, N.Y. Islanders 2.50
Bernie Parent, Philadelphia 2.70
Michel Larocque, Montreal...............2.84
Billy Smith, N.Y. Islanders................2.87

Shutouts
Ken Dryden, Montreal 5
Tony Esposito, Chicago 4
Mario Lessard, Los Angeles 4
Mike Palmateer, Toronto 4
Bernie Parent, Philadelphia 4

Wins by goaltenders
Dan Bouchard, Atlanta 32
Ken Dryden, Montreal 30
Don Edwards, Buffalo..........................26
Mike Palmateer, Toronto 26
Chico Resch, N.Y. Islanders 26

1979-80

Goals
Charlie Simmer, Los Angeles 56
Blaine Stoughton, Hartford..................56

Danny Gare, Buffalo 56
Marcel Dionne, Los Angeles.................53
Mike Bossy, N.Y. Islanders 51
Wayne Gretzky, Edmonton 51

Assists
Wayne Gretzky, Edmonton 86
Marcel Dionne, Los Angeles.................84
Guy Lafleur, Montreal..........................75
Gil Perreault, Buffalo 66
Bryan Trottier, N.Y. Islanders..............62

Points
Marcel Dionne, Los Angeles...............137
Wayne Gretzky, Edmonton 137
Guy Lafleur, Montreal........................125
Gil Perreault, Buffalo 106
Mike Rogers, Hartford.......................105

Penalty minutes
Jimmy Mann, Winnipeg 287
Paul Holmgren, Philadelphia 267
Terry O'Reilly, Boston........................265
Terry Ruskowski, Chicago 252
Paul Mulvey, Washington....................240

Lowest goals-against average
(Min. 25 games)
Bob Sauve, Buffalo............................2.36
Denis Herron, Montreal 2.51
Don Edwards, Buffalo........................2.57
Gilles Gilbert, Boston 2.73
Pete Peeters, Philadelphia................2.73

Shutouts
Tony Esposito, Chicago 6
Gerry Cheevers, Boston 4
Bob Sauve, Buffalo................................4
Rogie Vachon, Detroit 4
Michel Larocque, Montreal...................3
Chico Resch, N.Y. Islanders 3

Wins by goaltenders
Mike Liut, St. Louis 32
Tony Esposito, Chicago 31
Pete Peeters, Philadelphia..................29
Gilles Meloche, Minnesota 27
Denis Herron, Montreal 25

1980-81

Goals
Mike Bossy, N.Y. Islanders 68
Marcel Dionne, Los Angeles.................58
Charlie Simmer, Los Angeles 56
Wayne Gretzky, Edmonton 55
Rick Kehoe, Pittsburgh........................55

Assists
Wayne Gretzky, Edmonton 109
Kent Nilsson, Calgary 82
Marcel Dionne, Los Angeles.................77
Bernie Federko, St. Louis 73
Bryan Trottier, N.Y. Islanders..............72

Points
Wayne Gretzky, Edmonton 164
Marcel Dionne, Los Angeles...............135
Kent Nilsson, Calgary 131
Mike Bossy, N.Y. Islanders 119
Dave Taylor, Los Angeles 112

Penalty minutes
Dave Williams, Vancouver..................333
Paul Holmgren, Philadelphia 306
Chris Nilan, Montreal 262
Jim Korn, Detroit 246
Willi Plett, Calgary.............................237
Behn Wilson, Philadelphia.................237

Lowest goals-against average (Min. 25 games)
Richard Sevigny, Montreal 2.40
Rick St. Croix, Philadelphia.............2.49
Don Edwards, Buffalo.......................2.96
Pete Peeters, Philadelphia 2.96
Michel Larocque, Montreal...............3.03

Shutouts
Don Edwards, Buffalo.............................3
Chico Resch, N.Y. Islanders 3
11 goalies tied with 2

Wins by goaltenders
Mario Lessard, Los Angeles.................35
Mike Liut, St. Louis 33
Tony Esposito, Chicago 29
Greg Millen, Pittsburgh 25
Rogie Vachon, Boston..........................25

1981-82

Goals
Wayne Gretzky, Edmonton 92
Mike Bossy, N.Y. Islanders 64
Dennis Maruk, Washington 60
Dino Ciccarelli, Minnesota...................55
Rick Vaive, Toronto 54

Assists
Wayne Gretzky, Edmonton 120
Peter Stastny, Quebec 93
Denis Savard, Chicago 87
Mike Bossy, N.Y. Islanders 83
Bryan Trottier, N.Y. Islanders...............79

Points
Wayne Gretzky, Edmonton 212
Mike Bossy, N.Y. Islanders 147
Peter Stastny, Quebec 139
Dennis Maruk, Washington 136
Bryan Trottier, N.Y. Islanders.............129

Penalty minutes
Paul Baxter, Pittsburgh.......................407
Dave Williams, Toronto 341
Glen Cochrane, Philadelphia..............329
Pat Price, Pittsburgh 322
Al Secord, Chicago.............................303

Lowest goals-against average (Min. 25 games)
Denis Herron, Montreal 2.64
Rick Wamsley, Montreal.....................2.75
Bill Smith, N.Y.Islanders.....................2.97
Roland Melanson, N.Y. Islanders 3.23
Grant Fuhr, Edmonton 3.31

Shutouts
Denis Herron, Montreal 3
Richard Brodeur, Vancouver 2
Mario Lessard, Los Angeles....................2
Mike Liut, St. Louis..................................2
Pat Riggin, Calgary 2
Doug Soetaert, Winnipeg........................2
Rick Wamsley, Montreal..........................2

Wins by goaltenders
Billy Smith, N.Y. Islanders....................32
Grant Fuhr, Edmonton...........................28
Mike Liut, St. Louis 28
Dan Bouchard, Quebec.........................27
Don Edwards, Buffalo............................26
Gilles Meloche, Minnesota 26

1982-83

Goals
Wayne Gretzky, Edmonton 71
Lanny McDonald, Calgary 66
Mike Bossy, N.Y. Islanders 60
Michel Goulet, Quebec 57
Marcel Dionne, Los Angeles................56

Assists
Wayne Gretzky, Edmonton 125
Denis Savard, Chicago 85
Peter Stastny, Quebec 77
Paul Coffey, Edmonton.........................67
Bobby Clarke, Philadelphia 62

Points
Wayne Gretzky, Edmonton 196
Peter Stastny, Quebec 124
Denis Savard, Chicago 120
Mike Bossy, N.Y. Islanders 118
Marcel Dionne, Los Angeles...............107
Barry Pederson, Boston 107

Penalty minutes
Randy Holt, Washington 275
Dave Williams, Vancouver...................265
Brian Sutter, St. Louis 254
Paul Baxter, Pittsburgh........................238
Jim Korn, Toronto 238

Lowest goals-against average (Min. 25 games)
Pete Peeters, Boston 2.36
Roland Melanson, N.Y. Islanders 2.66
Billy Smith, N.Y. Islanders................2.87
Pelle Lindbergh, Philadelphia 2.98
Murray Bannerman, Chicago............3.10

Shutouts
Pete Peeters, Boston 8
Murray Bannerman, Chicago...................4
Bob Froese, Philadelphia........................4
Pelle Lindbergh, Philadelphia.................3
Corrado Micalef, Detroit 2
Ed Mio, N.Y. Rangers.............................2

Wins by goaltenders
Pete Peeters, Boston 40
Andy Moog, Edmonton 33
Rick Wamsley, Montreal.......................27
Bob Sauve, Buffalo................................25
Murray Bannerman, Chicago................24
Roland Melanson, N.Y. Islanders 24

1983-84

Goals
Wayne Gretzky, Edmonton 87
Michel Goulet, Quebec 56
Glenn Anderson, Edmonton 54
Tim Kerr, Philadelphia 54
Jari Kurri, Edmonton.............................52
Rick Vaive, Toronto 52

Assists
Wayne Gretzky, Edmonton 118
Paul Coffey, Edmonton.........................86
Barry Pederson, Boston 77
Peter Stastny, Quebec 73
Bryan Trottier, N.Y. Islanders...............71

Points
Wayne Gretzky, Edmonton 205
Paul Coffey, Edmonton.......................126
Michel Goulet, Quebec 121
Peter Stastny, Quebec 119
Mike Bossy, N.Y. Islanders 118

Penalty minutes
Chris Nilan, Montreal 338
Willie Plett, Minnesota 316
Gary Rissling, Pittsburgh 297

Lowest goals-against average (Min. 25 games)
Dave Williams, Vancouver..................294
Jim Korn, Toronto 257

Lowest goals-against average (Min. 25 games)
Pat Riggin, Washington 2.66
Tom Barrasso, Buffalo......................2.84
Al Jensen, Washington.....................2.91
Doug Keans, Boston.........................2.84
Bob Froese, Philadelphia..................3.14

Shutouts
Pat Riggin, Washington 4
Al Jensen, Washington...........................4
Mike Liut, St. Louis 3
Nine goalies tied with..............................2

Wins by goaltenders
Grant Fuhr, Edmonton 30
Peter Peeters, Boston..........................29
Dan Bouchard, Quebec........................29
Bob Froese, Philadelphia.....................28
Glen Hanlon, N.Y. Rangers..................28

1984-85

Goals
Wayne Gretzky, Edmonton 73
Jari Kurri, Edmonton..............................71
Mike Bossy, N.Y. Islanders 58
Michel Goulet, Quebec 55
John Ogrodnick, Detroit.......................55

Assists
Wayne Gretzky, Edmonton 135
Paul Coffey, Edmonton.........................84
Marcel Dionne, Los Angeles................80
Dale Hawerchuk, Winnipeg..................77
Bernie Federko, St. Louis.....................73

Points
Wayne Gretzky, Edmonton 208
Jari Kurri, Edmonton 135
Dale Hawerchuk, Winnipeg 130
Marcel Dionne, Los Angeles...............126
Paul Coffey, Edmonton.......................121

Penalty minutes
Chris Nilan, Montreal 358
Torrie Robertson, Hartford 337
John Blum, Boston...............................263
Tim Hunter, Calgary 259
Bob McGill, Toronto 250

Lowest goals-against average (Min. 25 games)
Tom Barrasso, Buffalo.......................2.66
Pat Riggin, Washington.....................2.98
Pelle Lindbergh, Philadelphia...........3.02
Steve Penney, Montreal....................3.08
Bob Sauve, Buffalo............................3.22
Warren Skorodenski, Chicago 3.22

Shutouts
Tom Barrasso, Buffalo............................5
Kelly Hrudey, N.Y. Islanders 2
Bob Janecyk, Los Angeles 2
Pelle Lindbergh, Philadelphia 2
Pat Riggin, Washington 2
Warren Skorodenski, Chicago 2
Steve Weeks, Hartford............................2

Wins by goaltenders
Pelle Lindbergh, Philadelphia 40
Brian Hayward, Winnipeg.....................33
Reggie Lemelin, Calgary 30
Pat Riggin, Washington 28
Murray Bannerman, Chicago................27

1985-86

Goals
Jari Kurri, Edmonton 68
Mike Bossy, N.Y. Islanders 61
Tim Kerr, Philadelphia 58
Glenn Anderson, Edmonton 54
Michel Goulet, Quebec 53

Assists
Wayne Gretzky, Edmonton 163
Mario Lemieux, Pittsburgh....................93
Paul Coffey, Edmonton..........................90
Peter Stastny, Quebec 81
Neal Broten, Minnesota........................76

Points
Wayne Gretzky, Edmonton 215
Mario Lemieux, Pittsburgh................141
Paul Coffey, Edmonton........................138
Jari Kurri, Edmonton 131
Mike Bossy, N.Y. Islanders 123

Penalty minutes
Joey Kocur, Detroit............................377
Torrie Robertson, Hartford 358
Dave Williams, Los Angeles 320
Tim Hunter, Calgary 291
Dave Brown, Philadelphia...................277

Lowest goals-against average
(Min. 25 games)
Bob Froese, Philadelphia 2.55
Al Jensen, Washington.........................3.18
Kelly Hrudey, N.Y. Islanders 3.21
Clint Malarchuk, Quebec 3.21
John Vanbiesbrouck, N.Y. Rangers ...3.32

Shutouts
Bob Froese, Philadelphia 5
Clint Malarchuk, Quebec 4
Doug Soetaert, Montreal 3
John Vanbiesbrouck, N.Y. Rangers 3

Wins by goaltenders
Bob Froese, Philadelphia 31
John Vanbiesbrouck, N.Y. Rangers 31
Tom Barrasso, Buffalo...........................29
Rejean Lemelin, Calgary 29
Grant Fuhr, Edmonton 29

1986-87

Goals
Wayne Gretzky, Edmonton 62
Tim Kerr, Philadelphia 58
Mario Lemieux, Pittsburgh....................54
Jari Kurri, Edmonton 54
Dino Ciccarelli, Minnesota...................52

Assists
Wayne Gretzky, Edmonton 121
Ray Bourque, Boston 72
Mark Messier, Edmonton 70
Kevin Dineen, Hartford.........................69
Bryan Trottier, N.Y. Islanders...............64

Points
Wayne Gretzky, Edmonton 183
Jari Kurri, Edmonton 108
Mario Lemieux, Pittsburgh................107
Mark Messier, Edmonton 107
Doug Gilmour, St. Louis 105

Penalty minutes
Dave Williams, Los Angeles 358
Tim Hunter, Calgary 357
Brian Curran, N.Y. Islanders 356

Basil McRae, Det.-Que. 342
Rick Tocchet, Philadelphia.................286

Lowest goals-against average
(Min. 25 games)
Brian Hayward, Montreal...................2.81
Patrick Roy, Montreal 2.93
Ron Hextall, Philadelphia 3.00
Daniel Berthiaume, Winnipeg...........3.17
Mario Gosselin, Quebec 3.18
Glen Hanlon, Detroit............................3.18

Shutouts
Mike Liut, Hartford 4
Bill Ranford, Boston 3
Rejean Lemelin, Calgary........................2
Allan Bester, Toronto 2
Tom Barrasso, Buffalo............................2

Wins by goaltenders
Ron Hextall, Philadelphia 37
Mike Liut, Hartford 31
Mike Vernon, Calgary 30
Andy Moog, Edmonton 28
Alain Chevrier, New Jersey.................24

1987-88

Goals
Mario Lemieux, Pittsburgh...................70
Craig Simpson, Pit.-Edm.....................56
Jimmy Carson, Los Angeles...............55
Luc Robitaille, Los Angeles 53
Joe Nieuwendyk, Calgary 51

Assists
Wayne Gretzky, Edmonton 109
Mario Lemieux, Pittsburgh...................98
Denis Savard, Chicago..........................87
Dale Hawerchuk, Winnipeg..................77
Mark Messier, Edmonton 74

Points
Mario Lemieux, Pittsburgh................168
Wayne Gretzky, Edmonton 149
Denis Savard, Chicago........................131
Dale Hawerchuk, Winnipeg...............121
Luc Robitaille, Los Angeles...............111
Peter Stastny, Quebec 111
Mark Messier, Edmonton 111

Penalty minutes
Bob Probert, Detroit............................398
Basil McRae, Minnesota.....................378
Tim Hunter, Calgary 337
Richard Zemlak, Minnesota...............307
Jay Miller, Boston................................304

Lowest goals-against average
(Min. 25 games)
Pete Peeters, Washington 2.78
Brian Hayward, Montreal...................2.86
Patrick Roy, Montreal 2.90
Rejean Lemelin, Boston 2.93
Greg Stefan, Detroit 3.11

Shutouts
Grant Fuhr, Edmonton 4
Glen Hanlon, Detroit..............................4
Clint Malarchuk, Washington 3
Kelly Hrudey, N.Y. Islanders 3
Rejean Lemelin, Boston 3
Patrick Roy, Montreal 3

Wins by goaltenders
Grant Fuhr, Edmonton 40
Mike Vernon, Calgary 39
Ron Hextall, Philadelphia 30

John Vanbiesbrouck, N.Y. Rangers 27
Tom Barrasso, Buffalo...........................25
Mike Liut, Hartford 25

1988-89

Goals
Mario Lemieux, Pittsburgh...................85
Bernie Nicholls, Los Angeles 70
Steve Yzerman, Detroit........................65
Wayne Gretzky, Los Angeles 54
Joe Nieuwendyk, Calgary 51
Joe Mullen, Calgary.............................51

Assists
Mario Lemieux, Pittsburgh................114
Wayne Gretzky, Los Angeles 114
Steve Yzerman, Detroit........................90
Paul Coffey, Pittsburgh.........................83
Bernie Nicholls, Los Angeles..............80

Points
Mario Lemieux, Pittsburgh................199
Wayne Gretzky, Los Angeles 168
Steve Yzerman, Detroit......................155
Bernie Nicholls, Los Angeles............150
Rob Brown, Pittsburgh.......................115

Penalty minutes
Tim Hunter, Calgary 375
Basil McRae, Minnesota.....................365
Dave Manson, Chicago.......................352
Marty McSorley, Los Angeles............350
Mike Hartman, Buffalo........................316

Lowest goals-against average
(Min. 25 games)
Patrick Roy, Montreal 2.47
Mike Vernon, Calgary 2.65
Pete Peeters, Washington 2.85
Brian Hayward, Montreal...................2.90
Rick Wamsley, Calgary.......................2.96

Shutouts
Greg Millen, St. Louis 6
Pete Peeters, Washington 4
Kirk McLean, Vancouver 4
Peter Sidorkiewicz, Hartford.................4
Patrick Roy, Montreal 4

Wins by goaltenders
Mike Vernon, Calgary 37
Patrick Roy, Montreal 33
Ron Hextall, Philadelphia 30
John Vanbiesbrouck, N.Y. Rangers 28
Kelly Hrudey, NYI-L.A..........................28

1989-90

Goals
Brett Hull, St. Louis.............................72
Steve Yzerman, Detroit........................62
Cam Neely, Boston..............................55
Brian Bellows, Minnesota....................55
Pat LaFontaine, N.Y. Islanders............54

Assists
Wayne Gretzky, Los Angeles 102
Mark Messier, Edmonton 84
Adam Oates, St. Louis.........................79
Mario Lemieux, Pittsburgh...................78
Paul Coffey, Pittsburgh........................74

Points
Wayne Gretzky, Los Angeles 142
Mark Messier, Edmonton 129
Steve Yzerman, Detroit......................127
Mario Lemieux, Pittsburgh................123
Brett Hull, St. Louis...........................113

Penalty minutes

Basil McRae, Minnesota 351
Alan May, Washington 339
Marty McSorley, Los Angeles.............322
Troy Mallette, N.Y. Rangers 305
Wayne Van Dorp, Chicago 303

Lowest goals-against average
(Min. 25 games)

Mike Liut, Har.-Was......................2.527
Patrick Roy, Montreal.....................2.534
Rejean Lemelin, Boston 2.805
Andy Moog, Boston 2.886
Daren Puppa, Buffalo 2.888

Shutouts

Mike Liut, Har.-Was..........................4
Andy Moog, Boston 3
Mike Fitzpatrick, N.Y. Islanders 3
Patrick Roy, Montreal 3
Jon Casey, Minnesota 3

Wins by goaltenders

Patrick Roy, Montreal.......................31
Daren Puppa, Buffalo 31
Jon Casey, Minnesota 31
Andy Moog, Boston 24
Bill Ranford, Edmonton 24

1990-91

Goals

Brett Hull, St. Louis............................86
Cam Neely, Boston 51
Theo Fleury, Calgary..........................51
Steve Yzerman, Detroit 51
Mike Gartner, N.Y. Rangers 49

Assists

Wayne Gretzky, Los Angeles 122
Adam Oates, St. Louis........................90
Al MacInnis, Calgary 75
Ray Bourque, Boston 73
Mark Recchi, Pittsburgh 73

Points

Wayne Gretzky, Los Angeles 163
Brett Hull, St. Louis..........................131
Adam Oates, St. Louis......................115
Mark Recchi, Pittsburgh 113
John Cullen, Pit.-Har. 110

Penalty minutes

Rob Ray, Buffalo 350
Mike Peluso, Chicago.......................320
Bob Probert, Detroit 315
Craig Berube, Philadelphia 293
Gino Odjick, Vancouver 296

Lowest goals-against average
(Min. 25 games)

Ed Belfour, Chicago 2.47
Don Beaupre, Washington 2.64
Patrick Roy, Montreal 2.71
Andy Moog, Boston 2.87
Pete Peters, Philadelphia..................2.88

Shutouts

Don Beaupre, Washington 5
Andy Moog, Boston 4
Bob Essesna, Winnipeg 4
Ed Belfour, Chicago 4
John Vanbiesbrouck, N.Y. Rangers 3
Jon Casey, Minnesota 3
Kelly Hrudey, Los Angeles...................3
Vincent Riendeau, St. Louis 3

Wins by goaltenders

Ed Belfour, Chicago 43
Mike Vernon, Calgary 31
Tim Cheveldae, Detroit 30
Vincent Riendeau, St. Louis 29
Tom Barrasso, Pittsburgh 27
Bill Ranford, Edmonton.....................27

1991-92

Goals

Brett Hull, St. Louis............................70
Kevin Stephens, Pittsburgh................54
Gary Roberts, Calgary 53
Jeremy Roenick, Chicago...................53
Pat LaFontaine, Buffalo 46

Assists

Wayne Gretzky, Los Angeles 90
Mario Lemieux, Pittsburgh 87
Brian Leech, N.Y. Rangers.................80
Adam Oates, St.L.-Bos.......................79
Dale Hawerchuck, Buffalo 75

Points

Mario Lemieux, Pittsburgh 131
Kevin Stephens, Pittsburgh 123
Wayne Gretzky, Los Angeles 121
Brett Hull, St. Louis..........................109
Luc Robitaille, Los Angeles...............107
Mark Messier, N.Y. Rangers 107

Penalty minutes

Mike Peluso, Chicago.......................408
Rob Ray, Buffalo 354
Gino Odjick, Vancouver 348
Ronnie Stern, Calgary 338
Link Gaetz, San Jose 326

Lowest goals-against average
(Min. 25 games)

Patrick Roy, Montreal 2.36
Ed Belfour, Chicago 2.70
Kirk McLean, Vancouver 2.74
John Vanbiesbrouck, N.Y Rangers....2.85
Bob Essensa, Winnipeg 2.88

Shutouts

Ed Belfour, Chicago 5
Bob Essesna, Winnipeg 5
Kirk McLean, Vancouver 5
Patrick Roy, Montreal 5
Ron Hextall, Philadelphia 3
Mike Richter, N.Y Rangers 3
Kay Whitmore, Hartford 3

Wins by goaltenders

Tim Cheveldae, Detroit 38
Kirk McLean, Vancouver 38
Patrick Roy, Montreal........................36
Don Beaupre, Washington 29
Andy Moog, Boston 28

1992-93

Goals

Alexander Mogilny, Buffalo................76
Teemu Selanne, Winnipeg 76
Mario Lemieux, Pittsburgh................69
Luc Robitaille, Los Angeles 63
Pavel Bure, Vancouver 60

Assists

Adam Oates, Boston 97
Doug Gilmour, Toronto......................95
Pat LaFontaine, Buffalo 95
Mario Lemieux, Pittsburgh................91
Craig Janney, St. Louis 82

Points

Mario Lemieux, Pittsburgh................160
Pat LaFontaine, Buffalo 148
Adam Oates, Boston.........................142
Steve Yzerman, Detroit.....................137
Teemu Selanne, Winnipeg 137

Penalty minutes

Marty McSorley, Los Angeles.............399
Gino Odjick, Vancouver 370
Tie Domi, NYR-Win. 344
Nick Kypreos, Hartford 325
Mike Peluso, Ottawa.........................318

Lowest goals-against average
(Min. 25 games)

Felix Potvin, Toronto 2.50
Ed Belfour, Chicago 2.59
Tom Barrasso, Pittsburgh 3.01
Curtis Joseph, St. Louis.....................3.02
Kay Whitmore, Vancouver.................3.10

Shutouts

Ed Belfour, Chicago 7
Tommy Soderstrom, Philadelphia 5
Tom Barrasso, Pittsburgh 4
Tim Cheveldae, Detroit 4
John Vanbiesbrouck, N.Y. Rangers 4

Wins by goaltenders

Tom Barrasso, Pittsburgh 43
Ed Belfour, Chicago 41
Andy Moog, Boston 37
Tim Cheveldae, Detroit 34
Bob Essensa, Winnipeg 33

1993-94

Goals

Pavel Bure, Vancouver 60
Brett Hull, St. Louis............................57
Sergei Federov, Detroit......................56
Dave Andreychuk, Toronto 53
Adam Graves, N.Y. Rangers 52
Brendan Shannahan, St. Louis 52
Ray Sheppard, Detroit.......................52

Assists

Wayne Gretzky, Los Angeles 92
Doug Gilmour, Toronto......................84
Adam Oates, Boston..........................80
Sergei Zubov, N.Y. Rangers 77
Ray Bourque, Boston 71

Points

Wayne Gretzky, Los Angeles 130
Segei Fedorov, Detroit......................120
Adam Oates, Boston.........................112
Doug Gilmour, Toronto.....................111
Pavel Bure, Vancouver 107
Mike Recchi, Philadelphia 107
Jeremy Roenick, Chicago..................107

Penalty minutes

Tie Domi, Winnipeg...........................347
Shane Churla, Dallas 333
Warren Rychel, Los Angeles 322
Craig Berube, Washington 305
Kelly Chase, St. Louis........................278

Lowest goals-against average
(Min. 27 games)

Dominik Hasek, Buffalo.....................1.95
Martin Brodeur, New Jersey..............2.40
Patrick Roy, Montreal 2.50
John Vanbiesbrouck, Florida 2.53
Mike Richter, N.Y. Rangers................2.57

Shutouts
Ed Belfour, Chicago 7
Dominik Hasek, Buffalo 7
Patrick Roy, Montreal 7
Ron Hextall, N.Y. Islanders 5
Mike Richter, N.Y. Rangers...................5

Wins by goaltenders
Mike Richter, N.Y. Rangers...................42
Ed Belfour, Chicago 37
Curtis Joseph, St. Louis 36
Patrick Roy, Montreal.............................35
Felix Potvin, Toronto...............................34

1994-95

Goals
Peter Bondra, Washington 34
Jaromir Jagr, Pittsburgh 32
Owen Nolan, Quebec............................30
Ray Sheppard, Detroit...........................30
Alexei Zhamnov, Winnipeg...................30

Assists
Ron Francis, Pittsburgh 48
Paul Coffey, Detroit 44
Joe Sakic, Quebec 43
Eric Lindros, Philadelphia......................41
Adam Oates, Boston...............................41

Points
Jaromir Jagr, Pittsburgh 70
Eric Lindros, Philadelphia......................70
Alexei Zhamnov, Winnipeg...................65
Joe Sakic, Quebec 62
Ron Francis, Pittsburgh 59

Penalty minutes
Enrico Ciccone, Tampa Bay 225
Shane Churla, Dallas 186
Bryan Marchment, Edmonton 184
Craig Berube, Washington 173
Rob Ray, Buffalo 173

Lowest goals-against average
(Min. 13 games)
Dominik Hasek, Buffalo 2.111
Rick Tabaracci, Was.-Cal. 2.114
Jim Carey, Washington 2.13
Chris Osgood, Detroit.........................2.26
Ed Belfour, Chicago 2.28

Shutouts
Ed Belfour, Chicago 5
Dominik Hasek, Buffalo 5
Jim Carey, Washington 4
Arturs Irbe, San Jose 4
Blaine Lacher, Boston.............................4
John Vanbiesbrouck, Florida.................4

Wins by goaltenders
Ken Wregget, Pittsburgh........................25
Ed Belfour, Chicago 22
Trevor Kidd, Calgary...............................22
Curtis Joseph, St. Louis 20
Martin Broduer, New Jersey 19
Dominik Hasek, Buffalo 19
Blaine Lacher, Boston.............................19
Mike Vernon, Detroit...............................19

1995-96

Goals
Mario Lemieux, Pittsburgh....................69
Jaromir Jagr, Pittsburgh 62
Alexander Mogilny, Vancouver 55
Peter Bondra, Washington 52
John LeClair, Philadelphia 51
Joe Sakic, Colorado 51

Assists
Ron Francis, Pittsburgh 92
Mario Lemieux, Pittsburgh...................92
Jaromir Jagr, Pittsburgh 87
Peter Forsberg, Colorado.....................86
Wayne Gretzky, L.A.-St.L. 79
Doug Weight, Edmonton 79

Points
Mario Lemieux, Pittsburgh...................161
Jaromir Jagr, Pittsburgh 149
Joe Sakic, Colorado 120
Ron Francis, Pittsburgh 119
Peter Forsberg, Colorado 116

Penalty minutes
Matthew Barnaby, Buffalo 335
Enrico Ciccone, T.B.-Chi. 306
Tie Domi, Toronto 297
Brad May, Buffalo 295
Rob Ray, Buffalo 287

Lowest goals-against average
(Min. 25 games)
Ron Hextall, Philadelphia 2.176
Chris Osgood, Detroit.........................2.178
Jim Carey, Washington 2.256
Mike Vernon, Detroit 2.264
Martin Brodeur, New Jersey..............2.34

Shutouts
Jim Carey, Washington 9
Martin Brodeur, New Jersey.................6
Chris Osgood, Detroit.............................5
Daren Puppa, Tampa Bay 5
Sean Burke, Hartford...............................4
Jeff Hackett, Chicago 4
Guy Hebert, Anaheim 4
Ron Hextall, Philadelphia 4

Wins by goaltenders
Chris Osgood, Detroit.............................39
Jim Carey, Washington 35
Martin Brodeur, New Jersey.................34
Bill Ranford, Edm.-Bos. 34
Patrick Roy, Mon.-Col. 34

1996-97

Goals
Keith Tkachuk, Phoenix 52
Teemu Selanne, Anaheim 51
John LeClair, Philadelphia 50
Mario Lemieux, Pittsburgh...................50
Zigmund Pfaffy, N.Y. Islanders............48

Assists
Wayne Gretzky, N.Y. Rangers 72
Mario Lemieux, Pittsburgh...................72
Ron Francis, Pittsburgh 63
Steve Yzerman, Detroit..........................63
Doug Weight, Edmonton 61

Points
Mario Lemieux, Pittsburgh...................122
Teemu Selanne, Anaheim 109
Paul Kariya, Anaheim 99
Wayne Gretzky, N.Y. Rangers 97
John LeClair, Philadelphia 97

Penalty minutes
Gino Odjick, Vancouver.........................371
Bob Probert, Chicago 326
Paul Laus, Florida....................................313
Rob Ray, Buffalo 286
Tie Domi, Toronto 275

Lowest goals-against average
(Min. 25 games)
Martin Brodeur, New Jersey..............1.88
Andy Moog, Dallas..............................2.15
Jeff Hackett, Chicago..........................2.16
Dominik Hasek, Buffalo......................2.27
John Vanbiesbrouck, Florida.............2.29

Shutouts
Martin Brodeur, New Jersey.................10
Nikolai Khabibulin, Phoenix..................7
Patrick Roy, Colorado.............................7
Curtis Joseph, Edmonton......................6
Chris Osgood, Detroit.............................6

Wins by goaltenders
Patrick Roy, Colorado.............................38
Martin Brodeur, New Jersey.................37
Dominik Hasek, Buffalo 37
Grant Fuhr, St. Louis...............................33
Mike Richter, N.Y. Rangers...................33

1997-98

Goals
Peter Bondra, Washington 52
Teemu Selanne, Anaheim 52
Pavel Bure, Vancouver...........................51
John LeClair, Philadelphia 51
Zigmund Palffy, N.Y. Islanders 45

Assists
Wayne Gretzky, N.Y. Rangers 67
Jaromir Jagr, Pittsburgh 67
Peter Forsberg, Colorado.....................66
Ron Francis, Pittsburgh 62
Adam Oates, Washington......................58
Jozef Stumpel, Los Angeles 58

Points
Jaromir Jagr, Pittsburgh 102
Peter Forsberg, Colorado.....................91
Pavel Bure, Vancouver...........................90
Wayne Gretzky, N.Y. Rangers 90
John LeClair, Philadelphia 87
Zigmund Palffy, N.Y. Islanders 87
Ron Francis, Pittsburgh 87

Penalty minutes
Donald Brashear, Vancouver 372
Tie Domi, Toronto 365
Krzysztof Oliwa, New Jersey 295
Paul Laus, Florida....................................293
Richard Pilon, N.Y. Islanders................291

Lowest goals-against average
(Min. 25 games)
Ed Belfour, Dallas................................1.88
Martin Brodeur, New Jersey..............1.89
Tom Barrasso, Pittsburgh 2.07
Dominik Hasek, Buffalo......................2.09
Ron Hextall, Philadelphia 2.165
Trevor Kidd, Carolina..........................2.168
Jamie McLennan, St. Louis.............2.171

Shutouts
Dominik Hasek, Buffalo 13
Martin Brodeur, New Jersey.................10
Ed Belfour, Dallas 9
Jeff Hackett, Chicago 8
Curtis Joseph, Edmonton......................8

Wins by goaltenders
Martin Brodeur, New Jersey.................41
Ed Belfour, Dallas 37
Dominik Hasek, Buffalo 33
Olaf Kolzig, Washington.........................33
Chris Osgood, Detroit.............................33

1998-99

Goals
Teemu Selanne, Anaheim 47
Tony Amonte, Chicago 44
Jaromir Jagr, Pittsburgh 44
Alexei Yashin, Ottawa 44
John LeClair, Philadelphia 43
Joe Sakic, Colorado 41
Theoren Fleury, Cal.-Col. 40
Eric Lindros, Philadelphia....................40
Miroslav Satan, Buffalo 40
Paul Kariya, Anaheim 39
Luc Robitaille, Los Angeles 39

Assists
Jaromir Jagr, Pittsburgh 83
Peter Forsberg, Colorado 67
Paul Kariya, Anaheim 62
Teemu Selanne, Anaheim 60
Joe Sakic, Colorado 55
Jason Allison, Boston............................53
Theoren Fleury, Cal.-Col. 53
Wayne Gretzky, N.Y. Rangers 53
Eric Lindros, Philadelphia....................53

Pavol Demitra, St. Louis 52
Mats Sundin, Toronto...........................52

Points
Jaromir Jagr, Pittsburgh 127
Teemu Selanne, Anaheim 107
Paul Kariya, Anaheim 101
Peter Forsberg, Colorado 97
Joe Sakic, Colorado 96
Alexei Yashin, Ottawa 94
Eric Lindros, Philadelphia....................93
Theoren Fleury, Cal.-Col. 93
John LeClair, Philadelphia 90
Pavol Demitra, St. Louis 89

Penalty minutes
Rob Ray, Buffalo 261
Jeff Odgers, Colorado 259
Peter Worrell, Florida 258
Patrick Cote, Nashville 242
Krzysztof Oliwa, New Jersey 240
Denny Lambert, Nashville 218
Paul Laus, Florida...............................218
Donald Brashear, Vancouver 209
Bob Probert, Chicago 206
Brad Brown, Mon.-Chi. 205

Lowest goals-against average (Min. 25 games)
Ron Tugnutt, Ottawa 1.79
Dominik Hasek, Buffalo...................1.87
Byron Dafoe, Boston 1.9845
Ed Belfour, Dallas 1.9953
Roman Turek, Dallas 2.08

Shutouts
Byron Dafoe, Boston 10
Dominik Hasek, Buffalo........................9
Nikolai Khabibulin, Phoenix..................8
Guy Hebert, Anaheim 6
Arturs Irbe, Carolina..............................6
Garth Snow, Vancouver........................6
John Vanbiesbrouck, Philadelphia..........6

Wins by goaltenders
Martin Brodeur, New Jersey.................39
Ed Belfour, Dallas 35
Curtis Joseph, Toronto........................35
Chris Osgood, Detroit..........................34
Byron Dafoe, Boston 32
Nikolai Khabibulin, Phoenix.................32
Patrick Roy, Colorado..........................32

AWARD WINNERS

LEAGUE AWARDS

ART ROSS TROPHY

(Leading scorer)

Season	Player, Team	Pts.
1917-18	Joe Malone, Montreal	44
1918-19	Newsy Lalonde, Montreal	32
1919-20	Joe Malone, Quebec Bulldogs	45
1920-21	Newsy Lalonde, Montreal	41
1921-22	Punch Broadbelt, Ottawa	46
1922-23	Babe Dye, Toronto	37
1923-24	Cy Denneny, Ottawa	23
1924-25	Babe Dye, Toronto	44
1925-26	Nels Stewart, Montreal Maroons	42
1926-27	Bill Cook, N.Y. Rangers	37
1927-28	Howie Morenz, Montreal	51
1928-29	Ace Bailey, Toronto	32
1929-30	Cooney Weiland, Boston	73
1930-31	Howie Morenz, Montreal	51
1931-32	Harvey Jackson, Toronto	53
1932-33	Bill Cook, N.Y. Rangers	50
1933-34	Charlie Conacher, Toronto	52
1934-35	Charlie Conacher, Toronto	57
1935-36	Dave Schriner, N.Y. Americans	45
1936-37	Dave Schriner, N.Y. Americans	46
1937-38	Gordie Drillion, Toronto	52
1938-39	Toe Blake, Montreal	47
1939-40	Milt Schmidt, Boston	52
1940-41	Bill Cowley, Boston	62
1941-42	Bryan Hextall, N.Y. Rangers	56
1942-43	Doug Bentley, Chicago	73
1943-44	Herbie Cain, Boston	82
1944-45	Elmer Lach, Montreal	80
1945-46	Max Bentley, Chicago	61
1946-47	Max Bentley, Chicago	72
1947-48	Elmer Lach, Montreal	61
1948-49	Roy Conacher, Chicago	68
1949-50	Ted Lindsay, Detroit	78
1950-51	Gordie Howe, Detroit	86
1951-52	Gordie Howe, Detroit	86
1952-53	Gordie Howe, Detroit	95
1953-54	Gordie Howe, Detroit	81
1954-55	Bernie Geoffrion, Montreal	75
1955-56	Jean Beliveau, Montreal	88
1956-57	Gordie Howe, Detroit	89
1957-58	Dickie Moore, Montreal	84
1958-59	Dickie Moore, Montreal	96
1959-60	Bobby Hull, Chicago	81
1960-61	Bernie Geoffrion, Montreal	95
1961-62	Bobby Hull, Chicago	84
1962-63	Gordie Howe, Detroit	86
1963-64	Stan Mikita, Chicago	89
1964-65	Stan Mikita, Chicago	87
1965-66	Bobby Hull, Chicago	97
1966-67	Stan Mikita, Chicago	97
1967-68	Stan Mikita, Chicago	87
1968-69	Phil Esposito, Boston	126
1969-70	Bobby Orr, Boston	120
1970-71	Phil Esposito, Boston	152
1971-72	Phil Esposito, Boston	133
1972-73	Phil Esposito, Boston	130
1973-74	Phil Esposito, Boston	145
1974-75	Bobby Orr, Boston	135
1975-76	Guy Lafleur, Montreal	125
1976-77	Guy Lafleur, Montreal	136
1977-78	Guy Lafleur, Montreal	132
1978-79	Bryan Trottier, N.Y. Islanders	134

Season	Player, Team	Pts.
1979-80	Marcel Dionne, Los Angeles	137
1980-81	Wayne Gretzky, Edmonton	164
1981-82	Wayne Gretzky, Edmonton	212
1982-83	Wayne Gretzky, Edmonton	196
1983-84	Wayne Gretzky, Edmonton	205
1984-85	Wayne Gretzky, Edmonton	208
1985-86	Wayne Gretzky, Edmonton	215
1986-87	Wayne Gretzky, Edmonton	183
1987-88	Mario Lemieux, Pittsburgh	168
1988-89	Mario Lemieux, Pittsburgh	199
1989-90	Wayne Gretzky, Los Angeles	142
1990-91	Wayne Gretzky, Los Angeles	163
1991-92	Mario Lemieux, Pittsburgh	131
1992-93	Mario Lemieux, Pittsburgh	160
1993-94	Wayne Gretzky, Los Angeles	130
1994-95	Jaromir Jagr, Pittsburgh	70
1995-96	Mario Lemieux, Pittsburgh	161
1996-97	Mario Lemieux, Pittsburgh	122
1997-98	Jaromir Jagr, Pittsburgh	102
1998-99	Jaromir Jagr, Pittsburgh	127
1999-00	Jaromir Jagr, Pittsburgh	96

The award was originally known as the Leading Scorer Trophy. The present trophy, first given in 1947, was presented to the NHL by Art Ross, former manager-coach of the Boston Bruins. In event of a tie, the player with the most goals receives the award.

MAURICE RICHARD TROPHY

(Leading goal scorer)

Season	Player, Team	Goals
1998-99	Teemu Selanne, Anaheim	47
1999-00	Pavel Bure, Florida	58

HART MEMORIAL TROPHY

(Most Valuable Player)

Season	Player, Team
1923-24	Frank Nighbor, Ottawa
1924-25	Billy Burch, Hamilton
1925-26	Nels Stewart, Montreal Maroons
1926-27	Herb Gardiner, Montreal
1927-28	Howie Morenz, Montreal
1928-29	Roy Worters, N.Y. Americans
1929-30	Nels Stewart, Montreal Maroons
1930-31	Howie Morenz, Montreal
1931-32	Howie Morenz, Montreal
1932-33	Eddie Shore, Boston
1933-34	Aurel Joliat, Montreal
1934-35	Eddie Shore, Boston
1935-36	Eddie Shore, Boston
1936-37	Babe Siebert, Montreal
1937-38	Eddie Shore, Boston
1938-39	Toe Blake, Montreal
1939-40	Ebbie Goodfellow, Detroit
1940-41	Bill Cowley, Boston
1941-42	Tom Anderson, N.Y. Americans
1942-43	Bill Cowley, Boston
1943-44	Babe Pratt, Toronto
1944-45	Elmer Lach, Montreal
1945-46	Max Bentley, Chicago
1946-47	Maurice Richard, Montreal
1947-48	Buddy O'Connor, N.Y. Rangers
1948-49	Sid Abel, Detroit
1949-50	Chuck Rayner, N.Y. Rangers
1950-51	Milt Schmidt, Boston
1951-52	Gordie Howe, Detroit

Season	Player, Team
1952-53	Gordie Howe, Detroit
1953-54	Al Rollins, Chicago
1954-55	Ted Kennedy, Toronto
1955-56	Jean Beliveau, Montreal
1956-57	Gordie Howe, Detroit
1957-58	Gordie Howe, Detroit
1958-59	Andy Bathgate, N.Y. Rangers
1959-60	Gordie Howe, Detroit
1960-61	Bernie Geoffrion, Montreal
1961-62	Jacques Plante, Montreal
1962-63	Gordie Howe, Detroit
1963-64	Jean Beliveau, Montreal
1964-65	Bobby Hull, Chicago
1965-66	Bobby Hull, Chicago
1966-67	Stan Mikita, Chicago
1967-68	Stan Mikita, Chicago
1968-69	Phil Esposito, Boston
1969-70	Bobby Orr, Boston
1970-71	Bobby Orr, Boston
1971-72	Bobby Orr, Boston
1972-73	Bobby Clarke, Philadelphia
1973-74	Phil Esposito, Boston
1974-75	Bobby Clarke, Philadelphia
1975-76	Bobby Clarke, Philadelphia
1976-77	Guy Lafleur, Montreal
1977-78	Guy Lafleur, Montreal
1978-79	Bryan Trottier, N.Y. Islanders
1979-80	Wayne Gretzky, Edmonton
1980-81	Wayne Gretzky, Edmonton
1981-82	Wayne Gretzky, Edmonton
1982-83	Wayne Gretzky, Edmonton
1983-84	Wayne Gretzky, Edmonton
1984-85	Wayne Gretzky, Edmonton
1985-86	Wayne Gretzky, Edmonton
1986-87	Wayne Gretzky, Edmonton
1987-88	Mario Lemieux, Pittsburgh
1988-89	Wayne Gretzky, Los Angeles
1989-90	Mark Messier, Edmonton
1990-91	Brett Hull, St. Louis
1991-92	Mark Messier, N.Y. Rangers
1992-93	Mario Lemieux, Pittsburgh
1993-94	Sergei Fedorov, Detroit
1994-95	Eric Lindros, Philadelphia
1995-96	Mario Lemieux, Pittsburgh
1996-97	Dominik Hasek, Buffalo
1997-98	Dominik Hasek, Buffalo
1998-99	Jaromir Jagr, Pittsburgh
1999-00	Chris Pronger, St. Louis

JAMES NORRIS MEMORIAL TROPHY

(Outstanding defenseman)

Season	Player, Team
1953-54	Red Kelly, Detroit
1954-55	Doug Harvey, Montreal
1955-56	Doug Harvey, Montreal
1956-57	Doug Harvey, Montreal
1957-58	Doug Harvey, Montreal
1958-59	Tom Johnson, Montreal
1959-60	Doug Harvey, Montreal
1960-61	Doug Harvey, Montreal
1961-62	Doug Harvey, N.Y. Rangers
1962-63	Pierre Pilote, Chicago
1963-64	Pierre Pilote, Chicago
1964-65	Pierre Pilote, Chicago
1965-66	Jacques Laperriere, Montreal
1966-67	Harry Howell, N.Y. Rangers
1967-68	Bobby Orr, Boston
1968-69	Bobby Orr, Boston
1969-70	Bobby Orr, Boston
1970-71	Bobby Orr, Boston
1971-72	Bobby Orr, Boston

Season	Player, Team
1972-73	Bobby Orr, Boston
1973-74	Bobby Orr, Boston
1974-75	Bobby Orr, Boston
1975-76	Denis Potvin, N.Y. Islanders
1976-77	Larry Robinson, Montreal
1977-78	Denis Potvin, N.Y. Islanders
1978-79	Denis Potvin, N.Y. Islanders
1979-80	Larry Robinson, Montreal
1980-81	Randy Carlyle, Pittsburgh
1981-82	Doug Wilson, Chicago
1982-83	Rod Langway, Washington
1983-84	Rod Langway, Washington
1984-85	Paul Coffey, Edmonton
1985-86	Paul Coffey, Edmonton
1986-87	Ray Bourque, Boston
1987-88	Ray Bourque, Boston
1988-89	Chris Chelios, Montreal
1989-90	Ray Bourque, Boston
1990-91	Ray Bourque, Boston
1991-92	Brian Leetch, N.Y. Rangers
1992-93	Chris Chelios, Chicago
1993-94	Ray Bourque, Boston
1994-95	Paul Coffey, Detroit
1995-96	Chris Chelios, Chicago
1996-97	Brian Leetch, N.Y. Rangers
1997-98	Rob Blake, Los Angeles
1998-99	Al MacInnis, St. Louis
1999-00	Chris Pronger, St. Louis

VEZINA TROPHY

(Outstanding goaltender)

Season	Player, Team	GAA
1926-27	George Hainsworth, Montreal	1.52
1927-28	George Hainsworth, Montreal	1.09
1928-29	George Hainsworth, Montreal	0.98
1929-30	Tiny Thompson, Boston	2.23
1930-31	Roy Worters, N.Y. Americans	1.68
1931-32	Charlie Gardiner, Chicago	2.10
1932-33	Tiny Thompson, Boston	1.83
1933-34	Charlie Gardiner, Chicago	1.73
1934-35	Lorne Chabot, Chicago	1.83
1935-36	Tiny Thompson, Boston	1.71
1936-37	Normie Smith, Detroit	2.13
1937-38	Tiny Thompson, Boston	1.85
1938-39	Frank Brimsek, Boston	1.60
1939-40	Dave Kerr, N.Y. Rangers	1.60
1940-41	Turk Broda, Toronto	2.60
1941-42	Frank Brimsek, Boston	2.38
1942-43	Johnny Mowers, Detroit	2.48
1943-44	Bill Durnan, Montreal	2.18
1944-45	Bill Durnan, Montreal	2.42
1945-46	Bill Durnan, Montreal	2.60
1946-47	Bill Durnan, Montreal	2.30
1947-48	Turk Broda, Toronto	2.38
1948-49	Bill Durnan, Montreal	2.10
1949-50	Bill Durnan, Montreal	2.20
1950-51	Al Rollins, Toronto	1.75
1951-52	Terry Sawchuk, Detroit	1.98
1952-53	Terry Sawchuk, Detroit	1.94
1953-54	Harry Lumley, Toronto	1.85
1954-55	Terry Sawchuk, Detroit	1.94
1955-56	Jacques Plante, Montreal	1.86
1956-57	Jacques Plante, Montreal	2.02
1957-58	Jacques Plante, Montreal	2.09
1958-59	Jacques Plante, Montreal	2.15
1959-60	Jacques Plante, Montreal	2.54
1960-61	Johnny Bower, Toronto	2.50
1961-62	Jacques Plante, Montreal	2.37
1962-63	Glenn Hall, Chicago	2.51
1963-64	Charlie Hodge, Montreal	2.26

Season	Player, Team	GAA
1964-65—	Terry Sawchuk, Toronto	2.56
	Johnny Bower, Toronto	2.38
1965-66—	Lorne Worsley, Montreal	2.36
	Charlie Hodge, Montreal	2.58
1966-67—	Glenn Hall, Chicago	2.38
	Denis DeJordy, Chicago	2.46
1967-68—	Lorne Worsley, Montreal	1.98
	Rogatien Vachon, Montreal	2.48
1968-69—	Glenn Hall, St. Louis	2.17
	Jacques Plante, St. Louis	1.96
1969-70—	Tony Esposito, Chicago	2.17
1970-71—	Ed Giacomin, N.Y. Rangers	2.15
	Gilles Villemure, N.Y. Rangers	2.29
1971-72—	Tony Esposito, Chicago	1.76
	Gary Smith, Chicago	2.41
1972-73—	Ken Dryden, Montreal	2.26
1973-74—	Bernie Parent, Philadelphia	1.89
	Tony Esposito, Chicago	2.04
1974-75—	Bernie Parent, Philadelphia	2.03
1975-76—	Ken Dryden, Montreal	2.03
1976-77—	Ken Dryden, Montreal	2.14
	Michel Larocque, Montreal	2.09
1977-78—	Ken Dryden, Montreal	2.05
	Michel Larocque, Montreal	2.67
1978-79—	Ken Dryden, Montreal	2.30
	Michel Larocque, Montreal	2.84
1979-80—	Bob Sauve, Buffalo	2.36
	Don Edwards, Buffalo	2.57
1980-81—	Richard Sevigny, Montreal	2.40
	Michel Larocque, Montreal	3.03
	Denis Herron, Montreal	3.50
1981-82—	Billy Smith, N.Y. Islanders	2.97
1982-83—	Pete Peeters, Boston	2.36
1983-84—	Tom Barrasso, Buffalo	2.84
1984-85—	Pelle Lindbergh, Philadelphia	3.02
1985-86—	John Vanbiesbrouck, N.Y. Rangers	3.32
1986-87—	Ron Hextall, Philadelphia	3.00
1987-88—	Grant Fuhr, Edmonton	3.43
1988-89—	Patrick Roy, Montreal	2.47
1989-90—	Patrick Roy, Montreal	2.53
1990-91—	Ed Belfour, Chicago	2.47
1991-92—	Patrick Roy, Montreal	2.36
1992-93—	Ed Belfour, Chicago	2.59
1993-94—	Dominik Hasek, Buffalo	1.95
1994-95—	Dominik Hasek, Buffalo	2.11
1995-96—	Jim Carey, Washington	2.26
1996-97—	Dominik Hasek, Buffalo	2.27
1997-98—	Dominik Hasek, Buffalo	2.09
1998-99—	Dominik Hasek, Buffalo	1.87
1999-00—	Olaf Kolzig, Washington	2.24

The award was formerly presented to the goaltender(s) having played a minimum of 25 games for the team with the fewest goals scored against. Beginning with the 1981-82 season, it was awarded to the outstanding goaltender.

BILL JENNINGS TROPHY

(Leading goaltender)

Season	Player, Team	GAA
1981-82—	Denis Herron, Montreal	2.64
	Rick Wamsley, Montreal	2.75
1982-83—	Roland Melanson, N.Y. Islanders	2.66
	Billy Smith, N.Y. Islanders	2.87
1983-84—	Pat Riggin, Washington	2.66
	Al Jensen, Washington	2.91
1984-85—	Tom Barrasso, Buffalo	2.66
	Bob Sauve, Buffalo	3.22
1985-86—	Bob Froese, Philadelphia	2.55
	Darren Jensen, Philadelphia	3.68
1986-87—	Brian Hayward, Montreal	2.81
	Patrick Roy, Montreal	2.93

Season	Player, Team	GAA
1987-88—	Brian Hayward, Montreal	2.86
	Patrick Roy, Montreal	2.90
1988-89—	Patrick Roy, Montreal	2.47
	Brian Hayward, Montreal	2.90
1989-90—	Rejean Lemelin, Boston	2.81
	Andy Moog, Boston	2.89
1990-91—	Ed Belfour, Chicago	2.47
1991-92—	Patrick Roy, Montreal	2.36
1992-93—	Ed Belfour, Chicago	2.59
1993-94—	Dominik Hasek, Buffalo	1.95
	Grant Fuhr, Buffalo	3.68
1994-95—	Ed Belfour, Chicago	2.28
1995-96—	Chris Osgood, Detroit	2.17
	Mike Vernon, Detroit	2.26
1996-97—	Martin Brodeur, New Jersey	1.88
	Mike Dunham, New Jersey	2.55
1997-98—	Martin Brodeur, New Jersey	1.89
1998-99—	Ed Belfour, Dallas	1.99
	Roman Turek, Dallas	2.08
1999-00—	Roman Turek, St. Louis	1.95

The award is presented to the goaltender(s) having played a minimum of 25 games for the team with the fewest goals scored against.

CALDER MEMORIAL TROPHY

(Rookie of the year)

Season	Player, Team
1932-33—	Carl Voss, Detroit
1933-34—	Russ Blinco, Montreal Maroons
1934-35—	Dave Schriner, N.Y. Americans
1935-36—	Mike Karakas, Chicago
1936-37—	Syl Apps, Toronto
1937-38—	Cully Dahlstrom, Chicago
1938-39—	Frank Brimsek, Boston
1939-40—	Kilby Macdonald, N.Y. Rangers
1940-41—	John Quilty, Montreal
1941-42—	Grant Warwick, N.Y. Rangers
1942-43—	Gaye Stewart, Toronto
1943-44—	Gus Bodnar, Toronto
1944-45—	Frank McCool, Toronto
1945-46—	Edgar Laprade, N.Y. Rangers
1946-47—	Howie Meeker, Toronto
1947-48—	Jim McFadden, Detroit
1948-49—	Pentti Lund, N.Y. Rangers
1949-50—	Jack Gelineau, Boston
1950-51—	Terry Sawchuk, Detroit
1951-52—	Bernie Geoffrion, Montreal
1952-53—	Lorne Worsley, N.Y. Rangers
1953-54—	Camille Henry, N.Y. Rangers
1954-55—	Ed Litzenberger, Chicago
1955-56—	Glenn Hall, Detroit
1956-57—	Larry Regan, Boston
1957-58—	Frank Mahovlich, Toronto
1958-59—	Ralph Backstrom, Montreal
1959-60—	Bill Hay, Chicago
1960-61—	Dave Keon, Toronto
1961-62—	Bobby Rousseau, Montreal
1962-63—	Kent Douglas, Toronto
1963-64—	Jacques Laperriere, Montreal
1964-65—	Roger Crozier, Detroit
1965-66—	Brit Selby, Toronto
1966-67—	Bobby Orr, Boston
1967-68—	Derek Sanderson, Boston
1968-69—	Danny Grant, Minnesota
1969-70—	Tony Esposito, Chicago
1970-71—	Gilbert Perreault, Buffalo
1971-72—	Ken Dryden, Montreal
1972-73—	Steve Vickers, N.Y. Rangers
1973-74—	Denis Potvin, N.Y. Islanders
1974-75—	Eric Vail, Atlanta
1975-76—	Bryan Trottier, N.Y. Islanders
1976-77—	Willi Plett, Atlanta

Season	Player, Team
1977-78	Mike Bossy, N.Y. Islanders
1978-79	Bobby Smith, Minnesota
1979-80	Ray Bourque, Boston
1980-81	Peter Stastny, Quebec
1981-82	Dale Hawerchuk, Winnipeg
1982-83	Steve Larmer, Chicago
1983-84	Tom Barrasso, Buffalo
1984-85	Mario Lemieux, Pittsburgh
1985-86	Gary Suter, Calgary
1986-87	Luc Robitaille, Los Angeles
1987-88	Joe Nieuwendyk, Calgary
1988-89	Brian Leetch, N.Y. Rangers
1989-90	Sergei Makarov, Calgary
1990-91	Ed Belfour, Chicago
1991-92	Pavel Bure, Vancouver
1992-93	Teemu Selanne, Winnipeg
1993-94	Martin Brodeur, New Jersey
1994-95	Peter Forsberg, Quebec
1995-96	Daniel Alfredsson, Ottawa
1996-97	Bryan Berard, N.Y. Islanders
1997-98	Sergei Samsonov, Boston
1998-99	Chris Drury, Colorado
1999-00	Scott Gomez, New Jersey

The award was originally known as the Leading Rookie Award. It was renamed the Calder Trophy in 1936-37 and became the Calder Memorial Trophy in 1942-43, following the death of NHL President Frank Calder.

LADY BYNG MEMORIAL TROPHY

(Most gentlemanly player)

Season	Player, Team
1924-25	Frank Nighbor, Ottawa
1925-26	Frank Nighbor, Ottawa
1926-27	Billy Burch, N.Y. Americans
1927-28	Frank Boucher, N.Y. Rangers
1928-29	Frank Boucher, N.Y. Rangers
1929-30	Frank Boucher, N.Y. Rangers
1930-31	Frank Boucher, N.Y. Rangers
1931-32	Joe Primeau, Toronto
1932-33	Frank Boucher, N.Y. Rangers
1933-34	Frank Boucher, N.Y. Rangers
1934-35	Frank Boucher, N.Y. Rangers
1935-36	Doc Romnes, Chicago
1936-37	Marty Barry, Detroit
1937-38	Gordie Drillon, Toronto
1938-39	Clint Smith, N.Y. Rangers
1939-40	Bobby Bauer, Boston
1940-41	Bobby Bauer, Boston
1941-42	Syl Apps, Toronto
1942-43	Max Bentley, Chicago
1943-44	Clint Smith, Chicago
1944-45	Bill Mosienko, Chicago
1945-46	Toe Blake, Montreal
1946-47	Bobby Bauer, Boston
1947-48	Buddy O'Connor, N.Y. Rangers
1948-49	Bill Quackenbush, Detroit
1949-50	Edgar Laprade, N.Y. Rangers
1950-51	Red Kelly, Detroit
1951-52	Sid Smith, Toronto
1952-53	Red Kelly, Detroit
1953-54	Red Kelly, Detroit
1954-55	Sid Smith, Toronto
1955-56	Earl Reibel, Detroit
1956-57	Andy Hebenton, N.Y. Rangers
1957-58	Camille Henry, N.Y. Rangers
1958-59	Alex Delvecchio, Detroit
1959-60	Don McKenney, Boston
1960-61	Red Kelly, Toronto
1961-62	Dave Keon, Toronto
1962-63	Dave Keon, Toronto
1963-64	Ken Wharram, Chicago

Season	Player, Team
1964-65	Bobby Hull, Chicago
1965-66	Alex Delvecchio, Detroit
1966-67	Stan Mikita, Chicago
1967-68	Stan Mikita, Chicago
1968-69	Alex Delvecchio, Detroit
1969-70	Phil Goyette, St. Louis
1970-71	John Bucyk, Boston
1971-72	Jean Ratelle, N.Y. Rangers
1972-73	Gilbert Perreault, Buffalo
1973-74	John Bucyk, Boston
1974-75	Marcel Dionne, Detroit
1975-76	Jean Ratelle, N.Y. R.-Boston
1976-77	Marcel Dionne, Los Angeles
1977-78	Butch Goring, Los Angeles
1978-79	Bob MacMillan, Atlanta
1979-80	Wayne Gretzky, Edmonton
1980-81	Rick Kehoe, Pittsburgh
1981-82	Rick Middleton, Boston
1982-83	Mike Bossy, N.Y. Islanders
1983-84	Mike Bossy, N.Y. Islanders
1984-85	Jari Kurri, Edmonton
1985-86	Mike Bossy, N.Y. Islanders
1986-87	Joe Mullen, Calgary
1987-88	Mats Naslund, Montreal
1988-89	Joe Mullen, Calgary
1989-90	Brett Hull, St. Louis
1990-91	Wayne Gretzky, Los Angeles
1991-92	Wayne Gretzky, Los Angeles
1992-93	Pierre Turgeon, N.Y. Islanders
1993-94	Wayne Gretzky, Los Angeles
1994-95	Ron Francis, Pittsburgh
1995-96	Paul Kariya, Anaheim
1996-97	Paul Kariya, Anaheim
1997-98	Ron Francis, Pittsburgh
1998-99	Wayne Gretzky, N.Y. Rangers
1999-00	Pavol Demitra, St. Louis

The award was originally known as the Lady Byng Trophy. After winning the award seven times, Frank Boucher received permanent possession and a new trophy was donated to the NHL in 1936. After Lady Byng's death in 1949, the NHL changed the name to Lady Byng Memorial Trophy.

CONN SMYTHE TROPHY

(Playoff MVP)

Season	Player, Team
1964-65	Jean Beliveau, Montreal
1965-66	Roger Crozier, Detroit
1966-67	Dave Keon, Toronto
1967-68	Glenn Hall, St. Louis
1968-69	Serge Savard, Montreal
1969-70	Bobby Orr, Boston
1970-71	Ken Dryden, Montreal
1971-72	Bobby Orr, Boston
1972-73	Yvan Cournoyer, Montreal
1973-74	Bernie Parent, Philadelphia
1974-75	Bernie Parent, Philadelphia
1975-76	Reggie Leach, Philadelphia
1976-77	Guy Lafleur, Montreal
1977-78	Larry Robinson, Montreal
1978-79	Bob Gainey, Montreal
1979-80	Bryan Trottier, N.Y. Islanders
1980-81	Butch Goring, N.Y. Islanders
1981-82	Mike Bossy, N.Y. Islanders
1982-83	Billy Smith, N.Y. Islanders
1983-84	Mark Messier, Edmonton
1984-85	Wayne Gretzky, Edmonton
1985-86	Patrick Roy, Montreal
1986-87	Ron Hextall, Philadelphia
1987-88	Wayne Gretzky, Edmonton
1988-89	Al MacInnis, Calgary
1989-90	Bill Ranford, Edmonton

Season	Player, Team
1990-91—Mario Lemieux, Pittsburgh
1991-92—Mario Lemieux, Pittsburgh
1992-93—Patrick Roy, Montreal
1993-94—Brian Leetch, N.Y. Rangers
1994-95—Claude Lemieux, New Jersey
1995-96—Joe Sakic, Colorado
1996-97—Mike Vernon, Detroit
1997-98—Steve Yzerman, Detroit
1998-99—Joe Nieuwendyk, Dallas
1999-00—Scott Stevens, New Jersey

BILL MASTERTON MEMORIAL TROPHY

(Sportsmanship—dedication to hockey)

Season   Player, Team
1967-68—Claude Provost, Montreal
1968-69—Ted Hampson, Oakland
1969-70—Pit Martin, Chicago
1970-71—Jean Ratelle, N.Y. Rangers
1971-72—Bobby Clarke, Philadelphia
1972-73—Lowell MacDonald, Pittsburgh
1973-74—Henri Richard, Montreal
1974-75—Don Luce, Buffalo
1975-76—Rod Gilbert, N.Y. Rangers
1976-77—Ed Westfall, N.Y. Islanders
1977-78—Butch Goring, Los Angeles
1978-79—Serge Savard, Montreal
1979-80—Al MacAdam, Minnesota
1980-81—Blake Dunlop, St. Louis
1981-82—Glenn Resch, Colorado
1982-83—Lanny McDonald, Calgary
1983-84—Brad Park, Detroit
1984-85—Anders Hedberg, N.Y. Rangers
1985-86—Charlie Simmer, Boston
1986-87—Doug Jarvis, Hartford
1987-88—Bob Bourne, Los Angeles
1988-89—Tim Kerr, Philadelphia
1989-90—Gord Kluzak, Boston
1990-91—Dave Taylor, Los Angeles
1991-92—Mark Fitzpatrick, N.Y. Islanders
1992-93—Mario Lemieux, Pittsburgh
1993-94—Cam Neely, Boston
1994-95—Pat LaFontaine, Buffalo
1995-96—Gary Roberts, Calgary
1996-97—Tony Granato, San Jose
1997-98—Jamie McLennan, St. Louis
1998-99—John Cullen, Tampa Bay
1999-00—Ken Daneyko, New Jersey

Presented by the Professional Hockey Writers' Association to the player who best exemplifies the qualities of perseverance, sportsmanship and dedication to hockey.

FRANK J. SELKE TROPHY

(Best defensive forward)

Season   Player, Team
1977-78—Bob Gainey, Montreal
1978-79—Bob Gainey, Montreal
1979-80—Bob Gainey, Montreal
1980-81—Bob Gainey, Montreal
1981-82—Steve Kasper, Boston
1982-83—Bobby Clarke, Philadelphia
1983-84—Doug Jarvis, Washington
1984-85—Craig Ramsay, Buffalo
1985-86—Troy Murray, Chicago
1986-87—Dave Poulin, Philadelphia
1987-88—Guy Carbonneau, Montreal
1988-89—Guy Carbonneau, Montreal
1989-90—Rick Meagher, St. Louis
1990-91—Dirk Graham, Chicago
1991-92—Guy Carbonneau, Montreal

Season	Player, Team
1992-93—Doug Gilmour, Toronto
1993-94—Sergei Fedorov, Detroit
1994-95—Ron Francis, Pittsburgh
1995-96—Sergei Fedorov, Detroit
1996-97—Michael Peca, Buffalo
1997-98—Jere Lehtinen, Dallas
1998-99—Jere Lehtinen, Dallas
1999-00—Steve Yzerman, Detroit

JACK ADAMS TROPHY

(Coach of the year)

Season   Coach, Team
1973-74—Fred Shero, Philadelphia
1974-75—Bob Pulford, Los Angeles
1975-76—Don Cherry, Boston
1976-77—Scotty Bowman, Montreal
1977-78—Bobby Kromm, Detroit
1978-79—Al Arbour, N.Y. Islanders
1979-80—Pat Quinn, Philadelphia
1980-81—Red Berenson, St. Louis
1981-82—Tom Watt, Winnipeg
1982-83—Orval Tessier, Chicago
1983-84—Bryan Murray, Washington
1984-85—Mike Keenan, Philadelphia
1985-86—Glen Sather, Edmonton
1986-87—Jacques Demers, Detroit
1987-88—Jacques Demers, Detroit
1988-89—Pat Burns, Montreal
1989-90—Bob Murdoch, Winnipeg
1990-91—Brian Sutter, St. Louis
1991-92—Pat Quinn, Vancouver
1992-93—Pat Burns, Toronto
1993-94—Jacques Lemaire, New Jersey
1994-95—Marc Crawford, Quebec
1995-96—Scotty Bowman, Detroit
1996-97—Ted Nolan, Buffalo
1997-98—Pat Burns, Boston
1998-99—Jacques Martin, Ottawa
1999-00—Joel Quenneville, St. Louis

KING CLANCY TROPHY

(Humanitarian contributions)

Season   Player, Team
1987-88—Lanny McDonald, Calgary
1988-89—Bryan Trottier, N.Y. Islanders
1989-90—Kevin Lowe, Edmonton
1990-91—Dave Taylor, Los Angeles
1991-92—Ray Bourque, Boston
1992-93—Dave Poulin, Boston
1993-94—Adam Graves, N.Y. Rangers
1994-95—Joe Nieuwendyk, Calgary
1995-96—Kris King, Winnipeg
1996-97—Trevor Linden, Vancouver
1997-98—Kelly Chase, St. Louis
1998-99—Rob Ray, Buffalo
1999-00—Curtis Joseph, Toronto

ALL-STAR TEAMS

(As selected by members of the Professional
Hockey Writers' Association at the end of each season)

1930-31

First team		Second team
Aurel Joliet, Mon. C.	LW	Bun Cook, N.Y.R.
Howie Morenz, Mon. C.	C	Frank Boucher, N.Y.R.
Bill Cook, N.Y.R.	RW	Dit Clapper, Bos.
Eddie Shore, Bos.	D	Sylvio Mantha, Mon.
King Clancy, Tor.	D	Ching Johnson, N.Y.R.
Charlie Gardiner, Chi.	G	Tiny Thompson, Bos.

1931-32

First team		Second team
Harvey Jackson, Tor.	LW	Aurel Joliat, Mon. C.
Howie Morenz, Mon. C.	C	Hooley Smith, Mon. M.
Bill Cook, N.Y.R.	RW	Charlie Conacher, Tor.
Eddie Shore, Bos.	D	Sylvio Mantha, Mon. C.
Ching Johnson, N.Y.R.	D	King Clancy, Tor.
Charlie Gardiner, Chi.	G	Roy Worters, N.Y.A.

1932-33

First team		Second team
Baldy Northcott, Mon. M.	LW	Harvey Jackson, Tor.
Frank Boucher, N.Y.R.	C	Howie Morenz, Mon.
Bill Cook, N.Y.R.	RW	Charlie Conacher, Tor.
Eddie Shore, Bos.	D	King Clancy, Tor.
Ching Johnson, N.Y.R.	D	Lionel Conacher, Mon. M.
John Ross Roach, Det.	G	Charlie Gardiner, Chi.

1933-34

First team		Second team
Harvey Jackson, Tor.	LW	Aurel Joliat, Mon. C.
Frank Boucher, N.Y.R.	C	Joe Primeau, Tor.
Charlie Conacher, Tor.	RW	Bill Cook, N.Y.R.
King Clancy, Tor.	D	Eddie Shore, Bos.
Lionel Conacher, Chi.	D	Ching Johnson, N.Y.R.
Charlie Gardiner, Chi.	G	Roy Worters, N.Y.A.

1934-35

First team		Second team
Harvey Jackson, Tor.	LW	Aurel Joliat, Mon. C.
Frank Boucher, N.Y.R.	C	Cooney Welland, Det.
Charlie Conacher, Tor.	RW	Dit Clapper, Bos.
Eddie Shore, Bos.	D	Cy Wentworth, Mon. M.
Earl Seibert, N.Y.R.	D	Art Coulter, Chi.
Lorne Chabot, Chi.	G	Tiny Thompson, Bos.

1935-36

First team		Second team
Dave Schriner, N.Y.A.	LW	Paul Thompson, Chi.
Hooley Smith, Mon. M.	C	Bill Thoms, Tor.
Charlie Conacher, Tor.	RW	Cecil Dillon, N.Y.R.
Eddie Shore, Bos.	D	Earl Seibert, Chi.
Babe Siebert, Bos.	D	Ebbie Goodfellow, Det.
Tiny Thompson, Bos.	G	Wilf Cude, Mon. C.

1936-37

First team		Second team
Harvey Jackson, Tor.	LW	Dave Schriner, N.Y.A.
Marty Barry, Det.	C	Art Chapman, N.Y.A.
Larry Aurie, Det.	RW	Cecil Dillon, N.Y.R.
Babe Siebert, Mon. C.	D	Earl Seibert, Chi.
Ebbie Goodfellow, Det.	D	Lionel Conacher, Mon. M.
Norm Smith, Det.	G	Wilf Cude, Mon. C.

1937-38

First team		Second team
Paul Thompson, Chi.	LW	Toe Blake, Mon. C.
Bill Cowley, Bos.	C	Syl Apps, Tor.
Cecil Dillon, N.Y.R.	RW	Cecil Dillon, N.Y.R.
Gord Drillon, Tor.	(tied)	Gord Drillon, Tor.
Eddie Shore, Bos.	D	Art Coulter, N.Y.R.
Babe Siebert, Mon. C.	D	Earl Seibert, Chi.
Tiny Thompson, Bos.	G	Dave Kerr, N.Y.R.

1938-39

First team		Second team
Toe Blake, Mon.	LW	Johnny Gottselig, Chi.
Syl Apps, Tor.	C	Neil Colville, N.Y.R.
Gord Drillon, Tor.	RW	Bobby Bauer, Bos.
Eddie Shore, Bos.	D	Earl Seibert, Chi.
Dit Clapper, Bos.	D	Art Coulter, N.Y.R.
Frank Brimsek, Bos.	G	Earl Robertson, N.Y.A.

1939-40

First team		Second team
Toe Blake, Mon.	LW	Woody Dumart, Bos.
Milt Schmidt, Bos.	C	Neil Colville, N.Y.R.
Bryan Hextall, N.Y.R.	RW	Bobby Bauer, Bos.
Dit Clapper, Bos.	D	Art Coulter, N.Y.R.
Ebbie Goodfellow, Det.	D	Earl Seibert, Chi.
Dave Kerr, N.Y.R.	G	Frank Brimsek, Bos.

1940-41

First team		Second team
Dave Schriner, Tor.	LW	Woody Dumart, Bos.
Bill Cowley, Bos.	C	Syl Apps, Tor.
Bryan Hextall, N.Y.R.	RW	Bobby Bauer, Bos.
Dit Clapper, Bos.	D	Earl Seibert, Chi.
Wally Stanowski, Tor.	D	Ott Heller, N.Y.R.
Turk Broda, Tor.	G	Frank Brimsek, Bos.

1941-42

First team		Second team
Lynn Patrick, N.Y.R.	LW	Sid Abel, Det.
Syl Apps, Tor.	C	Phil Watson, N.Y.R.
Bryan Hextall, N.Y.R.	RW	Gord Drillon, Tor.
Earl Seibert, Chi.	D	Pat Egan, Bkl.
Tommy Anderson, Bkl.	D	Bucko McDonald, Tor.
Frank Brimsek, Bos.	G	Turk Broda, Tor.

1942-43

First team		Second team
Doug Bentley, Chi.	LW	Lynn Patrick, N.Y.R.
Bill Cowley, Bos.	C	Syl Apps, Tor.
Lorne Carr, Tor.	RW	Bryan Hextall, N.Y.R.
Earl Seibert, Chi.	D	Jack Crawford, Bos.
Jack Stewart, Det.	D	Bill Hollett, Bos.
Johnny Mowers, Det.	G	Frank Brimsek, Bos.

1943-44

First team		Second team
Doug Bentley, Chi.	LW	Herb Cain, Bos.
Bill Cowley, Bos.	C	Elmer Lach, Mon.
Lorne Carr, Tor.	RW	Maurice Richard, Mon.
Earl Seibert, Chi.	D	Emile Bouchard, Mon.
Babe Pratt, Tor.	D	Dit Clapper, Bos.
Bill Durnan, Mon.	G	Paul Bibeault, Tor.

1944-45

First team		Second team
Toe Blake, Mon.	LW	Syd Howe, Det.
Elmer Lach, Mon.	C	Bill Cowley, Bos.
Maurice Richard, Mon.	RW	Bill Mosienko, Chi.
Emile Bouchard, Mon.	D	Glen Harmon, Mon.
Bill Hollett, Det.	D	Babe Pratt, Tor.
Bill Durnan, Mon.	G	Mike Karakas, Chi.

1945-46

First team		Second team
Gaye Stewart, Tor.	LW	Toe Blake, Mon.
Max Bentley, Chi.	C	Elmer Lach, Mon.
Maurice Richard, Mon.	RW	Bill Mosienko, Chi.
Jack Crawford, Bos.	D	Kenny Reardon, Mon.
Emile Bouchard, Mon.	D	Jack Stewart, Det.
Bill Durnan, Mon.	G	Frank Brimsek, Bos.

1946-47

First team		Second team
Doug Bentley, Chi.	LW	Woody Dumart, Bos.
Milt Schmidt, Bos.	C	Max Bentley, Chi.
Maurice Richard, Mon.	RW	Bobby Bauer, Bos.
Kenny Reardon, Mon.	D	Jack Stewart, Det.
Emile Bouchard, Mon.	D	Bill Quackenbush, Det.
Bill Durnan, Mon.	G	Frank Brimsek, Bos.

1947-48

First team		Second team
Ted Lindsay, Det.	LW	Gaye Stewart, Chi.
Elmer Lach, Mon.	C	Buddy O'Connor, N.Y.R.
Maurice Richard, Mon.	RW	Bud Poile, Chi.
Bill Quackenbush, Det.	D	Kenny Reardon, Mon.
Jack Stewart, Det.	D	Neil Colville, N.Y.R.
Turk Broda, Tor.	G	Frank Brimsek, Bos.

1948-49

First team		Second team
Roy Conacher, Chi.	LW	Ted Lindsay, Det.
Sid Abel, Det.	C	Doug Bentley, Chi.
Maurice Richard, Mon.	RW	Gordie Howe, Det.
Bill Quackenbush, Det.	D	Glen Harmon, Mon.
Jack Stewart, Det.	D	Kenny Reardon, Mon.
Bill Durnan, Mon.	G	Chuck Rayner, N.Y.R.

1949-50

First team		Second team
Ted Lindsay, Det.	LW	Tony Leswick, N.Y.R.
Sid Abel, Det.	C	Ted Kennedy, Tor.
Maurice Richard, Mon.	RW	Gordie Howe, Det.
Gus Mortson, Tor.	D	Leo Reise, Det.
Kenny Reardon, Mon.	D	Red Kelly, Det.
Bill Durnan, Mon.	G	Chuck Rayner, N.Y.R.

1950-51

First team		Second team
Ted Lindsay, Det.	LW	Sid Smith, Tor.
Milt Schmidt, Bos.	C	Sid Abel, Det.
	(tied)	Ted Kennedy, Tor.
Gordie Howe, Det.	RW	Maurice Richard, Mon.
Red Kelly, Det.	D	Jim Thomson, Tor.
Bill Quackenbush, Bos.	D	Leo Reise, Det.
Terry Sawchuk, Det.	G	Chuck Rayner, N.Y.R.

1951-52

First team		Second team
Ted Lindsay, Det.	LW	Sid Smith, Tor.
Elmer Lach, Mon.	C	Milt Schmidt, Bos.
Gordie Howe, Det.	RW	Maurice Richard, Mon.
Red Kelly, Det.	D	Hy Buller, N.Y.R.
Doug Harvey, Mon.	D	Jim Thomson, Tor.
Terry Sawchuk, Det.	G	Jim Henry, Bos.

1952-53

First team		Second team
Ted Lindsay, Det.	LW	Bert Olmstead, Mon.
Fleming Mackell, Bos.	C	Alex Delvecchio, Det.
Gordie Howe, Det.	RW	Maurice Richard, Mon.
Red Kelly, Det.	D	Bill Quackenbush, Bos.
Doug Harvey, Mon.	D	Bill Gadsby, Chi.
Terry Sawchuk, Det.	G	Gerry McNeil, Mon.

1953-54

First team		Second team
Ted Lindsay, Det.	LW	Ed Sandford, Bos.
Ken Mosdell, Mon.	C	Ted Kennedy, Tor.
Gordie Howe, Det.	RW	Maurice Richard, Mon.
Red Kelly, Det.	D	Bill Gadsby, Chi.
Doug Harvey, Mon.	D	Tim Horton, Tor.
Harry Lumley, Tor.	G	Terry Sawchuk, Det.

1954-55

First team		Second team
Sid Smith, Tor.	LW	Danny Lewicki, N.Y.R.
Jean Beliveau, Mon.	C	Ken Mosdell, Mon.
Maurice Richard, Mon.	RW	Bernie Geoffrion, Mon.
Doug Harvey, Mon.	D	Bob Goldham, Det.
Red Kelly, Det.	D	Fern Flaman, Bos.
Harry Lumley, Tor.	G	Terry Sawchuk, Det.

1955-56

First team		Second team
Ted Lindsay, Det.	LW	Bert Olmstead, Mon.
Jean Beliveau, Mon.	C	Tod Sloan, Tor.
Maurice Richard, Mon.	RW	Gordie Howe, Det.
Doug Harvey, Mon.	D	Red Kelly, Det.
Bill Gadsby, N.Y.R.	D	Tom Johnson, Mon.
Jacques Plante, Mon.	G	Glenn Hall, Det.

1956-57

First team		Second team
Ted Lindsay, Det.	LW	Real Chevrefils, Bos.
Jean Beliveau, Mon.	C	Eddie Litzenberger, Chi.
Gordie Howe, Det.	RW	Maurice Richard, Mon.
Doug Harvey, Mon.	D	Fern Flaman, Bos.
Red Kelly, Det.	D	Bill Gadsby, N.Y.R.
Glenn Hall, Det.	G	Jacques Plante, Mon.

1957-58

First team		Second team
Dickie Moore, Mon.	LW	Camille Henry, N.Y.R.
Henri Richard, Mon.	C	Jean Beliveau, Mon.
Gordie Howe, Det.	RW	Andy Bathgate, N.Y.R.
Doug Harvey, Mon.	D	Fern Flaman, Bos.
Bill Gadsby, N.Y.R.	D	Marcel Pronovost, Det.
Glenn Hall, Chi.	G	Jacques Plante, Mon.

1958-59

First team		Second team
Dickie Moore, Mon.	LW	Alex Delvecchio, Det.
Jean Beliveau, Mon.	C	Henri Richard, Mon.
Andy Bathgate, N.Y.R.	RW	Gordie Howe, Det.
Tom Johnson, Mon.	D	Marcel Pronovost, Det.
Bill Gadsby, N.Y.R.	D	Doug Harvey, Mon.
Jacques Plante, Mon.	G	Terry Sawchuk, Det.

1959-60

First team		Second team
Bobby Hull, Chi.	LW	Dean Prentice, N.Y.R.
Jean Beliveau, Mon.	C	Bronco Horvath, Bos.
Gordie Howe, Det.	RW	Bernie Geoffrion, Mon.
Doug Harvey, Mon.	D	Allan Stanley, Tor.
Marcel Pronovost, Det.	D	Pierre Pilote, Chi.
Glenn Hall, Chi.	G	Jacques Plante, Mon.

1960-61

First team		Second team
Frank Mahovlich, Mon.	LW	Dickie Moore, Mon.
Jean Beliveau, Mon.	C	Henri Richard, Mon.
Bernie Geoffrion, Mon.	RW	Gordie Howe, Det.
Doug Harvey, Mon.	D	Allan Stanley, Tor.
Marcel Pronovost, Det.	D	Pierre Pilote, Chi.
Johnny Bower, Tor.	G	Glenn Hall, Chi.

1961-62

First team		Second team
Bobby Hull, Chi.	LW	Frank Mahovlich, Tor.
Stan Mikita, Chi.	C	Dave Keon, Tor.
Andy Bathgate, N.Y.R.	RW	Gordie Howe, Det.
Doug Harvey, N.Y.R.	D	Carl Brewer, Tor.
Jean-Guy Talbot, Mon.	D	Pierre Pilote, Chi.
Jacques Plante, Mon.	G	Glenn Hall, Chi.

1962-63

First team		Second team
Frank Mahovlich, Tor.	LW	Bobby Hull, Chi.
Stan Mikita, Chi.	C	Henri Richard, Mon.
Gordie Howe, Det.	RW	Andy Bathgate, N.Y.R.
Pierre Pilote, Chi.	D	Tim Horton, Tor.
Carl Brewer, Tor.	D	Elmer Vasko, Chi.
Glenn Hall, Chi.	G	Terry Sawchuk, Det.

1963-64

First team		Second team
Bobby Hull, Chi.	LW	Frank Mahovlich, Tor.
Stan Mikita, Chi.	C	Jean Beliveau, Mon.
Ken Wharram, Chi.	RW	Gordie Howe, Det.
Pierre Pilote, Chi.	D	Elmer Vasko, Chi.
Tim Horton, Tor.	D	Jacques Laperriere, Mon.
Glenn Hall, Chi.	G	Charlie Hodge, Mon.

1964-65

First team		Second team
Bobby Hull, Chi.	LW	Frank Mahovlich, Tor.
Norm Ullman, Det.	C	Stan Mikita, Chi.
Claude Provost, Mon.	RW	Gordie Howe, Det.
Pierre Pilote, Chi.	D	Bill Gadsby, Det.
Jacques Laperriere, Mon.	D	Carl Brewer, Tor.
Roger Crozier, Det.	G	Charlie Hodge, Mon.

1965-66

First team		Second team
Bobby Hull, Chi.	LW	Frank Mahovlich, Tor.
Stan Mikita, Chi.	C	Jean Beliveau, Mon.
Gordie Howe, Det.	RW	Bobby Rousseau, Mon.
Jacques Laperriere, Mon.	D	Allan Stanley, Tor.
Pierre Pilote, Chi.	D	Pat Stapleton, Chi.
Glenn Hall, Chi.	G	Gump Worsley, Mon.

1966-67

First team		Second team
Bobby Hull, Chi.	LW	Don Marshall, N.Y.R.
Stan Mikita, Chi.	C	Norm Ullman, Det.
Ken Wharram, Chi.	RW	Gordie Howe, Det.
Pierre Pilote, Chi.	D	Tim Horton, Tor.
Harry Howell, N.Y.R.	D	Bobby Orr, Bos.
Ed Giacomin, N.Y.R.	G	Glenn Hall, Chi.

1967-68

First team		Second team
Bobby Hull, Chi.	LW	Johnny Bucyk, Bos.
Stan Mikita, Chi.	C	Phil Esposito, Bos.
Gordie Howe, Det.	RW	Rod Gilbert, N.Y.R.
Bobby Orr, Bos.	D	J.C. Tremblay, Mon.
Tim Horton, Tor.	D	Jim Neilson, N.Y.R.
Gump Worsley, Mon.	G	Ed Giacomin, N.Y.R.

1968-69

First team		Second team
Bobby Hull, Chi.	LW	Frank Mahovlich, Det.
Phil Esposito, Bos.	C	Jean Beliveau, Mon.
Gordie Howe, Det.	RW	Yvan Cournoyer, Mon.
Bobby Orr, Bos.	D	Ted Green, Bos.
Tim Horton, Tor.	D	Ted Harris, Mon.
Glenn Hall, St.L.	G	Ed Giacomin, N.Y.R.

1969-70

First team		Second team
Bobby Hull, Chi.	LW	Frank Mahovlich, Det.
Phil Esposito, Bos.	C	Stan Mikita, Chi.
Gordie Howe, Det.	RW	John McKenzie, Bos.
Bobby Orr, Bos.	D	Carl Brewer, Det.
Brad Park, N.Y.R.	D	Jacques Laperriere, Mon.
Tony Esposito, Chi.	G	Ed Giacomin, N.Y.R.

1970-71

First team		Second team
Johnny Bucyk, Bos.	LW	Bobby Hull, Chi.
Phil Esposito, Bos.	C	Dave Keon, Tor.
Ken Hodge, Bos.	RW	Yvan Cournoyer, Mon.
Bobby Orr, Bos.	D	Brad Park, N.Y.R.
J.C. Tremblay, Mon.	D	Pat Stapleton, Chi.
Ed Giacomin, N.Y.R.	G	Jacques Plante, Tor.

1971-72

First team		Second team
Bobby Hull, Chi.	LW	Vic Hadfield, N.Y.R.
Phil Esposito, Bos.	C	Jean Ratelle, N.Y.R.
Rod Gilbert, N.Y.R.	RW	Yvan Cournoyer, Mon.
Bobby Orr, Bos.	D	Bill White, Chi.
Brad Park, N.Y.R.	D	Pat Stapleton, Chi.
Tony Esposito, Chi.	G	Ken Dryden, Mon.

1972-73

First team		Second team
Frank Mahovlich, Mon.	LW	Dennis Hull, Chi.
Phil Esposito, Bos.	C	Bobby Clarke, Phi.
Mickey Redmond, Det.	RW	Yvan Cournoyer, Mon.
Bobby Orr, Bos.	D	Brad Park, N.Y.R.
Guy Lapointe, Mon.	D	Bill White, Chi.
Ken Dryden, Mon.	G	Tony Esposito, Chi.

1973-74

First team		Second team
Richard Martin, Buf.	LW	Wayne Cashman, Bos.
Phil Esposito, Bos.	C	Bobby Clarke, Phi.
Ken Hodge, Bos.	RW	Mickey Redmond, Det.
Bobby Orr, Bos.	D	Bill White, Chi.
Brad Park, N.Y.R.	D	Barry Ashbee, Phi.
Bernie Parent, Phi.	G	Tony Esposito, Chi.

1974-75

First team		Second team
Richard Martin, Buf.	LW	Steve Vickers, N.Y.R.
Bobby Clarke, Phi.	C	Phil Esposito, Bos.
Guy Lafleur, Mon.	RW	Rene Robert, Buf.
Bobby Orr, Bos.	D	Guy Lapointe, Mon.
Denis Potvin, N.Y.I.	D	Borje Salming, Tor.
Bernie Parent, Phi.	G	Rogie Vachon, L.A.

1975-76

First team		Second team
Bill Barber, Phi.	LW	Richard Martin, Buf.
Bobby Clarke, Phi.	C	Gilbert Perreault, Buf.
Guy Lafleur, Mon.	RW	Reggie Leach, Phi.
Denis Potvin, N.Y.I.	D	Borje Salming, Tor.
Brad Park, Bos.	D	Guy Lapointe, Mon.
Ken Dryden, Mon.	G	Glenn Resch, N.Y.I.

1976-77

First team		Second team
Steve Shutt, Mon.	LW	Richard Martin, Buf.
Marcel Dionne, L.A.	C	Gilbert Perreault, Buf.
Guy Lafleur, Mon.	RW	Lanny McDonald, Tor.
Larry Robinson, Mon.	D	Denis Potvin, N.Y.I.
Borje Salming, Tor.	D	Guy Lapointe, Mon.
Ken Dryden, Mon.	G	Rogie Vachon, L.A.

1977-78

First team		Second team
Clark Gillies, N.Y.I.	LW	Steve Shutt, Mon.
Bryan Trottier, N.Y.I.	C	Darryl Sittler, Tor.
Guy Lafleur, Mon.	RW	Mike Bossy, N.Y.I.
Denis Potvin, N.Y.I.	D	Larry Robinson, Mon.
Brad Park, Bos.	D	Borje Salming, Tor.
Ken Dryden, Mon.	G	Don Edwards, Buf.

1978-79

First team		Second team
Clark Gillies, N.Y.I.	LW	Bill Barber, Phi.
Bryan Trottier, N.Y.I.	C	Marcel Dionne, L.A.
Guy Lafleur, Mon.	RW	Mike Bossy, N.Y.I.
Denis Potvin, N.Y.I.	D	Borje Salming, Tor.
Larry Robinson, Mon.	D	Serge Savard, Mon.
Ken Dryden, Mon.	G	Glenn Resch, N.Y.I.

NHL HISTORY *Award winners*

1979-80

First team		Second team
Charlie Simmer, L.A.	LW	Steve Shutt, Mon.
Marcel Dionne, L.A.	C	Wayne Gretzky, Edm.
Guy Lafleur, Mon.	RW	Danny Gare, Buf.
Larry Robinson, Mon.	D	Borje Salming, Tor.
Ray Bourque, Bos.	D	Jim Schoenfeld, Buf.
Tony Esposito, Chi.	G	Don Edwards, Buf.

1980-81

First team		Second team
Charlie Simmer, L.A.	LW	Bill Barber, Phi.
Wayne Gretzky, Edm.	C	Marcel Dionne, L.A.
Mike Bossy, N.Y.I.	RW	Dave Taylor, L.A.
Denis Potvin, N.Y.I.	D	Larry Robinson, Mon.
Randy Carlyle, Pit.	D	Ray Bourque, Bos.
Mike Liut, St.L.	G	Mario Lessard, L.A.

1981-82

First team		Second team
Mark Messier, Edm.	LW	John Tonelli, N.Y.I.
Wayne Gretzky, Edm.	C	Bryan Trottier, N.Y.I.
Mike Bossy, N.Y.I.	RW	Rick Middleton, Bos.
Doug Wilson, Chi.	D	Paul Coffey, Edm.
Ray Bourque, Bos.	D	Brian Engblom, Mon.
Bill Smith, N.Y.I.	G	Grant Fuhr, Edm.

1982-83

First team		Second team
Mark Messier, Edm.	LW	Michel Goulet, Que.
Wayne Gretzky, Edm.	C	Denis Savard, Chi.
Mike Bossy, N.Y.I.	RW	Lanny McDonald, Cal.
Mark Howe, Phi.	D	Ray Bourque, Bos.
Rod Langway, Was.	D	Paul Coffey, Edm.
Pete Peeters, Bos.	G	Roland Melanson, N.Y.I.

1983-84

First team		Second team
Michel Goulet, Que.	LW	Mark Messier, Edm.
Wayne Gretzky, Edm.	C	Bryan Trottier, N.Y.I.
Mike Bossy, N.Y.I.	RW	Jari Kurri, Edm.
Rod Langway, Was.	D	Paul Coffey, Edm.
Ray Bourque, Bos.	D	Denis Potvin, N.Y.I.
Tom Barrasso, Buf.	G	Pat Riggin, Was.

1984-85

First team		Second team
John Ogrodnick, Det.	LW	John Tonelli, N.Y.I.
Wayne Gretzky, Edm.	C	Dale Hawerchuk, Win.
Jari Kurri, Edm.	RW	Mike Bossy, N.Y.I.
Paul Coffey, Edm.	D	Rod Langway, Was.
Ray Bourque, Bos.	D	Doug Wilson, Chi.
Pelle Lindbergh, Phi.	G	Tom Barrasso, Buf.

1985-86

First team		Second team
Michel Goulet, Que.	LW	Mats Naslund, Mon.
Wayne Gretzky, Edm.	C	Mario Lemieux, Pit.
Mike Bossy, N.Y.I.	RW	Jari Kurri, Edm.
Paul Coffey, Edm.	D	Larry Robinson, Mon.
Mark Howe, Phi.	D	Ray Bourque, Bos.
John Vanbiesbrouck, N.Y.R.	G	Bob Froese, Phi.

1986-87

First team		Second team
Michel Goulet, Que.	LW	Luc Robitaille, L.A.
Wayne Gretzky, Edm.	C	Mario Lemieux, Pit.
Jari Kurri, Edm.	RW	Tim Kerr, Phi.
Ray Bourque, Bos.	D	Larry Murphy, Was.
Mark Howe, Phi.	D	Al MacInnis, Cal.
Ron Hextall, Phi.	G	Mike Liut, Har.

1987-88

First team		Second team
Luc Robitaille, L.A.	LW	Michel Goulet, Que.
Mario Lemieux, Pit.	C	Wayne Gretzky, Edm.
Hakan Loob, Cal.	RW	Cam Neely, Bos.
Ray Bourque, Bos.	D	Gary Suter, Cal.
Scott Stevens, Was.	D	Brad McCrimmon, Cal.
Grant Fuhr, Edm.	G	Patrick Roy, Mon.

1988-89

First team		Second team
Luc Robitaille, L.A.	LW	Gerard Gallant, Det.
Mario Lemieux, Pit.	C	Wayne Gretzky, L.A.
Joe Mullen, Cal.	RW	Jari Kurri, Edm.
Chris Chelios, Mon.	D	Al MacInnis, Cal.
Paul Coffey, Pit.	D	Ray Bourque, Bos.
Patrick Roy, Mon.	G	Mike Vernon, Cal.

1989-90

First team		Second team
Luc Robitaille, L.A.	LW	Brian Bellows, Min.
Mark Messier, Edm.	C	Wayne Gretzky, L.A.
Brett Hull, St.L.	RW	Cam Neely, Bos.
Ray Bourque, Bos.	D	Paul Coffey, Pit.
Al MacInnis, Cal.	D	Doug Wilson, Chi.
Patrick Roy, Mon.	G	Daren Puppa, Buf.

1990-91

First team		Second team
Luc Robitaille, L.A.	LW	Kevin Stevens, Pit.
Wayne Gretzky, L.A.	C	Adam Oates, St.L.
Brett Hull, St.L.	RW	Cam Neely, Bos.
Ray Bourque, Bos.	D	Chris Chelios, Chi.
Al MacInnis, Cal.	D	Brian Leetch, N.Y.R.
Ed Belfour, Chi.	G	Patrick Roy, Mon.

1991-92

First team		Second team
Kevin Stevens, Pit.	LW	Luc Robitaille, L.A.
Mark Messier, N.Y.R.	C	Mario Lemieux, Pit.
Brett Hull, St.L.	RW	Mark Recchi, Pit., Phi.
Brian Leetch, N.Y.R.	D	Phil Housley, Win.
Ray Bourque, Bos.	D	Scott Stevens, N.J.
Patrick Roy, Mon.	G	Kirk McLean, Van.

1992-93

First team		Second team
Luc Robitaille, L.A.	LW	Kevin Stevens, Pit.
Mario Lemieux, Pit.	C	Pat LaFontaine, Buf.
Teemu Selanne, Win.	RW	Alexander Mogilny, Buf.
Chris Chelios, Chi.	D	Larry Murphy, Pit.
Ray Bourque, Bos.	D	Al Iafrate, Was.
Ed Belfour, Chi.	G	Tom Barrasso, Pit.

1993-94

First team		Second team
Brendan Shanahan, St.L.	LW	Adam Graves, N.Y.R.
Sergei Fedorov, Det.	C	Wayne Gretzky, L.A.
Pavel Bure, Van.	RW	Cam Neely, Bos.
Ray Bourque, Bos.	D	Al MacInnis, Cal.
Scott Stevens, N.J.	D	Brian Leetch, N.Y.R.
Dominik Hasek, Buf.	G	John Vanbiesbrouck, Fla.

1994-95

First team		Second team
John LeClair, Mon., Phi.	LW	Keith Tkachuk, Win.
Eric Lindros, Phi.	C	Alexei Zhamnov, Win.
Jaromir Jagr, Pit.	RW	Theoren Fleury, Cal.
Paul Coffey, Det.	D	Ray Bourque, Bos.
Chris Chelios, Chi.	D	Larry Murphy, Pit.
Dominik Hasek, Buf.	G	Ed Belfour, Chi.

	1995-96			1997-98	
First team		**Second team**	**First team**		**Second team**
Paul Kariya, Ana.	LW	John LeClair, Phi.	John LeClair, Phi.	LW	Keith Tkachuk, Pho.
Mario Lemieux, Pit.	C	Eric Lindros, Phi.	Peter Forsberg, Col.	C	Wayne Gretzky, N.Y.R.
Jaromir Jagr, Pit.	RW	Alexander Mogilny, Van.	Jaromir Jagr, Pit.	RW	Teemu Selanne, Ana.
Chris Chelios, Chi.	D	Vladimir Konstantinov, Det.	Nicklas Lidstrom, Det.	D	Chris Pronger, St.L.
Ray Bourque, Bos.	D	Brian Leetch, N.Y.R.	Rob Blake, L.A.	D	Scott Niedermayer, N.J.
Jim Carey, Was.	G	Chris Osgood, Det.	Dominik Hasek, Buf.	G	Martin Brodeur, N.J.

	1996-97			1998-99	
First team		**Second team**	**First team**		**Second team**
Paul Kariya, Ana.	LW	John LeClair, Phi.	Paul Kariya, Ana.	LW	John LeClair, Phi.
Mario Lemieux, Pit.	C	Wayne Gretzky, N.Y.R.	Peter Forsberg, Col.	C	Alexei Yashin, Ott.
Teemu Selanne, Ana.	RW	Jaromir Jagr, Pit.	Jaromir Jagr, Pit.	RW	Teemu Selanne, Ana.
Brian Leetch, N.Y.R.	D	Chris Chelios, Chi.	Nicklas Lidstrom, Det.	D	Ray Bourque, Bos.
Sandis Ozolinsh, Col.	D	Scott Stevens, N.J.	Al MacInnis, St.L.	D	Eric Desjardins, Phi.
Dominik Hasek, Buf.	G	Martin Brodeur, N.J.	Dominik Hasek, Buf.	G	Byron Dafoe, Bos.

THE SPORTING NEWS AWARDS

PLAYER OF THE YEAR

1967-68—E. Div.: Stan Mikita, Chicago
    W. Div.: Red Berenson, St. Louis
1968-69—E. Div.: Phil Esposito, Boston
    W. Div.: Red Berenson, St. Louis
1969-70—E. Div.: Bobby Orr, Boston
    W. Div.: Red Berenson, St. Louis
1970-71—E. Div.: Phil Esposito, Boston
    W. Div.: Bobby Hull, Chicago
1971-72—E. Div.: Jean Ratelle, N.Y. Rangers
    W. Div.: Bobby Hull, Chicago
1972-73—E. Div.: Phil Esposito, Boston
    W. Div.: Bobby Clarke, Philadelphia
1973-74—E. Div.: Phil Esposito, Boston
    W. Div.: Bernie Parent, Philadelphia
1974-75—Camp. Conf.: Bobby Clarke, Philadelphia
    Wales Conf.: Guy Lafleur, Montreal
1975-76—Bobby Clarke, Philadelphia
1976-77—Guy Lafleur, Montreal
1977-78—Guy Lafleur, Montreal
1978-79—Bryan Trottier, N.Y. Islanders
1979-80—Marcel Dionne, Los Angeles
1980-81—Wayne Gretzky, Edmonton
1981-82—Wayne Gretzky, Edmonton
1982-83—Wayne Gretzky, Edmonton
1983-84—Wayne Gretzky, Edmonton
1984-85—Wayne Gretzky, Edmonton
1985-86—Wayne Gretzky, Edmonton
1986-87—Wayne Gretzky, Edmonton
1987-88—Mario Lemieux, Pittsburgh
1988-89—Mario Lemieux, Pittsburgh
1989-90—Mark Messier, Edmonton
1990-91—Brett Hull, St. Louis
1991-92—Mark Messier, N.Y. Rangers
1992-93—Mario Lemieux, Pittsburgh
1993-94—Sergei Fedorov, Detroit
1994-95—Eric Lindros, Philadelphia
1995-96—Mario Lemieux, Pittsburgh
1996-97—Dominik Hasek, Buffalo
1997-98—Dominik Hasek, Buffalo
1998-99—Jaromir Jagr, Pittsburgh
1999-00—Jaromir Jagr, Pittsburgh

ROOKIE OF THE YEAR

1967-68—E. Div.: Derek Sanderson, Boston
    W. Div.: Bill Flett, Los Angeles
1968-69—E. Div.: Brad Park, N.Y. Rangers
    W. Div.: Norm Ferguson, Oakland

1969-70—E. Div.: Tony Esposito, Chicago
    W. Div.: Bobby Clarke, Philadelphia
1970-71—E. Div.: Gil Perreault, Buffalo
    W. Div.: Jude Drouin, Minnesota
1971-72—E. Div.: Richard Martin, Buffalo
    W. Div.: Gilles Meloche, California
1972-73—E. Div.: Steve Vickers, N.Y. Rangers
    W. Div.: Bill Barber, Philadelphia
1973-74—E. Div.: Denis Potvin, N.Y. Islanders
    W. Div.: Tom Lysiak, Atlanta
1974-75—Camp. Conf.: Eric Vail, Atlanta
    Wales Conf.: Pierre Larouche, Pittsburgh
1975-76—Bryan Trottier, N.Y. Islanders
1976-77—Willi Plett, Atlanta
1977-78—Mike Bossy, N.Y. Islanders
1978-79—Bobby Smith, Minnesota
1979-80—Ray Bourque, Boston
1980-81—Peter Stastny, Quebec
1981-82—Dale Hawerchuk, Winnipeg
1982-83—Steve Larmer, Chicago
1983-84—Steve Yzerman, Detroit
1984-85—Mario Lemieux, Pittsburgh
1985-86—Wendel Clark, Toronto
1986-87—Ron Hextall, Philadelphia
1987-88—Joe Nieuwendyk, Calgary
1988-89—Brian Leetch, N.Y. Rangers
1989-90—Jeremy Roenick, Chicago
1990-91—Ed Belfour, Chicago
1991-92—Tony Amonte, N.Y. Rangers
1992-93—Teemu Selanne, Winnipeg
1993-94—Jason Arnott, Edmonton
1994-95—Peter Forsberg, Quebec
1995-96—Eric Daze, Chicago
1996-97—Bryan Berard, N.Y. Islanders
1997-98—Sergei Samsonov, Boston
1998-99—Chris Drury, Colorado
1999-00—Scott Gomez, New Jersey

NHL COACH OF THE YEAR

1944-45—Dick Irvin, Montreal
1945-46—Johnny Gottselig, Chicago
1979-80—Pat Quinn, Philadelphia
1980-81—Red Berenson, St. Louis
1981-82—Herb Brooks, N.Y. Rangers
1982-83—Gerry Cheevers, Boston
1983-84—Bryan Murray, Washington
1984-85—Mike Keenan, Philadelphia
1985-86—Jacques Demers, St. Louis
1986-87—Jacques Demers, Detroit
1987-88—Terry Crisp, Calgary

1988-89—Pat Burns, Montreal
1989-90—Mike Milbury, Boston
1990-91—Tom Webster, Los Angeles
1991-92—Pat Quinn, Vancouver
1992-93—Pat Burns, Toronto
1993-94—Jacques Lemaire, New Jersey
1994-95—Marc Crawford, Quebec
1995-96—Scotty Bowman, Detroit
1996-97—Ken Hitchcock, Dallas
1997-98—Pat Burns, Boston
1998-99—Jacques Martin, Ottawa
1999-00—Joel Quenneville, St. Louis
NOTE: The Coach of the Year Award was not given from 1946-47 through 1978-79 seasons.

NHL EXECUTIVE OF THE YEAR

1972-73—Sam Pollock, Montreal
1973-74—Keith Allen, Philadelphia
1974-75—Bill Torrey, N.Y. Islanders
1975-76—Sam Pollock, Montreal
1976-77—Harry Sinden, Boston
1977-78—Ted Lindsay, Detroit
1978-79—Bill Torrey, N.Y. Islanders
1979-80—Scotty Bowman, Buffalo
1980-81—Emile Francis, St. Louis
1981-82—John Ferguson, Winnipeg
1982-83—David Poile, Washington
1983-84—David Poile, Washington
1984-85—John Ferguson, Winnipeg
1985-86—Emile Francis, Hartford
1986-87—John Ferguson, Winnipeg
1987-88—Cliff Fletcher, Calgary
1988-89—Bruce McNall, Los Angeles
1989-90—Harry Sinden, Boston
1990-91—Craig Patrick, Pittsburgh
1991-92—Neil Smith, N.Y. Rangers
1992-93—Cliff Fletcher, Toronto
1993-94—Bobby Clarke, Florida
1994-95—Bobby Clarke, Philadelphia
1995-96—Bryan Murray, Florida
1996-97—John Muckler, Buffalo
1997-98—Craig Patrick, Pittsburgh
1998-99—Craig Patrick, Pittsburgh
1999-00—Larry Pleau, St. Louis

THE SPORTING NEWS ALL-STAR TEAMS

(As selected by six hockey writers in 1944-45 and 1945-46
and by a vote of league players since 1967-68;
no teams selected from 1946-47 through 1966-67)

1944-45

First team		Second team
Maurice Richard, Mon.	W	Bill Mosienko, Chi.
Toe Blake, Mon.	W	Sweeney Schriner, Tor.
Elmer Lach, Mon.	C	Bill Cowley, Bos.
Emile Bouchard, Mon.	D	Earl Seibert, Det.
Bill Hollett, Det.	D	Babe Pratt, Tor.
Bill Durnan, Mon.	G	Frank McCool, Tor.

1945-46

First team		Second team
Gaye Stewart, Tor.	LW	Doug Bentley, Chi.
Max Bentley, Chi.	C	Elmer Lach, Mon.
Bill Mosienko, Chi.	RW	Maurice Richard, Mon.
Emile Bouchard, Mon.	D	Jack Crawford, Bos.
Jack Stewart, Det.	D	Babe Pratt, Tor.
Bill Durnan, Mon.	G	Harry Lumley, Det.

1967-68

EAST DIVISION First team		WEST DIVISION First team
Bobby Hull, Chi.	LW	Ab McDonald, Pit.
Stan Mikita, Chi.	C	Red Berenson, St.L.
Gordie Howe, Det.	RW	Wayne Connelly, Min.
Bobby Orr, Bos.	D	Bill White, L.A.
Tim Horton, Tor.	D	Mike McMahon, Min.
Ed Giacomin, N.Y.R.	G	Glenn Hall, St.L.

Second team		Second team
Johnny Bucyk, Bos.	LW	Bill Sutherland, Phi.
Phil Esposito, Bos.	C	Ray Cullen, Min.
Rod Gilbert, N.Y.R.	RW	Bill Flett, L.A.
J.C. Tremblay, Mon.	D	Ar Arbour, St.L.
Gary Bergman, Det.	D	Ed Van Impe, Phi.
Gump Worsley, Mon.	G	Doug Favell, Phi.

1968-69

EAST DIVISION First team		WEST DIVISION First team
Bobby Hull, Chi.	LW	Danny Grant, Min.
Phil Esposito, Bos.	C	Red Berenson, St.L.
Gordie Howe, Det.	RW	Norm Ferguson, Oak.
Bobby Orr, Bos.	D	Bill White, L.A.
Tim Horton, Tor.	D	Ar Arbour, St.L.
Ed Giacomin, N.Y.R.	G	Glenn Hall, St.L.

Second team		Second team
Frank Mahovlich, Det.	LW	Ab McDonald, St.L.
Stan Mikita, Chi.	C	Ted Hampson, Oak.
Yvan Cournoyer, Mon.	RW	Claude LaRose, Min.
J.C. Tremblay, Mon.	D	Carol Vadnais, Oak.
Jim Neilson, N.Y.R.	D	Ed Van Impe, Phi.
Bruce Gamble, Tor.	G	Bernie Parent, Phi.

1969-70

EAST DIVISION		WEST DIVISION
Bobby Hull, Chi.	LW	Dean Prentice, Pit.
Stan Mikita, Chi.	C	Red Berenson, St.L.
Ron Ellis, Tor.	RW	Bill Goldsworthy, Min.
Bobby Orr, Bos.	D	Al Arbour, St.L.
Brad Park, N.Y.R.	D	Bob Woytowich, Pit.
Tony Esposito, Chi.	G	Bernie Parent, Phi.

1970-71

EAST DIVISION		WEST DIVISION
Johnny Bucyk, Bos.	LW	Bobby Hull, Chi.
Phil Esposito, Bos.	C	Stan Mikita, Chi.
Ken Hodge, Bos.	RW	Bill Goldsworthy, Min.
Bobby Orr, Bos.	D	Pat Stapleton, Chi.
J.C. Tremblay, Mon.	D	Bill White, Chi.
Ed Giacomin, N.Y.R.	G	Tony Esposito, Chi.

1971-72

EAST DIVISION		WEST DIVISION
Vic Hadfield, N.Y.R.	LW	Bobby Hull, Chi.
Phil Esposito, Bos.	C	Bobby Clarke, Phi.
Rod Gilbert, N.Y.R.	RW	Bill Goldsworthy, Min.
Bobby Orr, Bos.	D	Pat Stapleton, Chi.
Brad Park, N.Y.R.	D	Bill White, Chi.
Ken Dryden, Mon.	G	Tony Esposito, Chi.

1972-73

EAST DIVISION		WEST DIVISION
Frank Mahovlich, Mon.	LW	Dennis Hull, Chi.
Phil Esposito, Bos.	C	Bobby Clarke, Phi.
Mickey Redmond, Det.	RW	Bill Flett, Phi.
Bobby Orr, Bos.	D	Bill White, Chi.
Guy Lapointe, Mon.	D	Barry Gibbs, Min.
Ken Dryden, Mon.	G	Tony Esposito, Chi.

1973-74

EAST DIVISION

First team

Richard Martin, Buf.	LW
Phil Esposito, Bos.	C
Ken Hodge, Bos.	RW
Bobby Orr, Bos.	D
Brad Park, N.Y.R.	D
Gilles Gilbert, Bos.	G

Second team

Frank Mahovlich, Mon.	LW
Darryl Sittler, Tor.	C
Mickey Redmond, Det.	RW
Guy Lapointe, Mon.	D
Borje Salming, Tor.	D
Ed Giacomin, N.Y.R.	D

WEST DIVISION

First team

Lowell MacDonald, Pit.	
Bobby Clarke, Phi.	
Bill Goldsworthy, Min.	
Bill White, Chi.	
Barry Ashbee, Phi.	
Bernie Parent, Phi.	

Second team

Dennis Hull, Chi.	
Stan Mikita, Chi.	
Jean Pronovost, Pit.	
Don Awrey, St.L.	
Dave Burrows, Pit.	
Tony Esposito, Chi.	

1974-75

CAMPBELL CONFERENCE

First team

Steve Vickers, N.Y.R.	LW
Bobby Clarke, Phi.	C
Rod Gilbert, N.Y.R.	RW
Denis Potvin, N.Y.I.	D
Brad Park, N.Y.R.	D
Bernie Parent, Phi.	G

Second team

Eric Vail, Atl.	LW
Stan Mikita, Chi.	C
Reggie Leach, Phi.	RW
Jim Watson, Phi.	D
Phil Russell, Chi.	D
Gary Smith, Van.	D

WALES CONFERENCE

First team

Richard Martin, Buf.	
Phil Esposito, Bos.	
Guy Lafleur, Mon.	
Bobby Orr, Bos.	
Guy Lapointe, Mon.	
Rogie Vachon, L.A.	

Second team

Danny Grant, Det.	
Gilbert Perreault, Buf.	
Rene Robert, Buf.	
Borje Salming, Tor.	
Terry Harper, L.A.	
Ken Dryden, Mon.	

1975-76

First team

Bill Barber, Phi.	LW
Bobby Clarke, Phi.	C
Guy Lafleur, Mon.	RW
Denis Potvin, N.Y.I.	D
Brad Park, Bos.	D
Ken Dryden, Mon.	G

Second team

Richard Martin, Buf.	
Pete Mahovlich, Mon.	
Reggie Leach, Phi.	
Guy Lapointe, Mon.	
Borje Salming, Tor.	
Glenn Resch, N.Y.I.	

1976-77

First team

Steve Shutt, Mon.	LW
Marcel Dionne, L.A.	C
Guy Lafleur, Mon.	RW
Larry Robinson, Mon.	D
Borje Salming, Tor.	D
	(tied)
Rogie Vachon, L.A.	G

Second team

Clark Gillies, N.Y.I.	
Gilbert Perreault, Buf.	
Lanny McDonald, Tor.	
Guy Lapointe, Mon.	
Serge Savard, Mon.	
Denis Potvin, N.Y.I.	
Ken Dryden, Mon.	

1977-78

First team

Clark Gillies, N.Y.I.	LW
Bryan Trottier, N.Y.I.	C
Guy Lafleur, Mon.	RW
Borje Salming, Tor.	D
Larry Robinson, Mon.	D
Ken Dryden, Mon.	G

Second team

Steve Shutt, Mon.	
Darryl Sittler, Tor.	
Terry O'Reilly, Bos.	
Denis Potvin, N.Y.I.	
Serge Savard, Mon.	
Don Edwards, Buf.	

1978-79

First team

Clark Gillies, N.Y.I.	LW
Bryan Trottier, N.Y.I.	C
Guy Lafleur, Mon.	RW
Denis Potvin, N.Y.I.	D
Larry Robinson, Mon.	D
Ken Dryden, Mon.	G

Second team

Bob Gainey, Mon.	
Marcel Dionne, L.A.	
Mike Bossy, N.Y.I.	
Borje Salming, Tor.	
Serge Savard, Mon.	
Glenn Resch, N.Y.I.	

1979-80

First team

Charlie Simmer, L.A.	LW
Marcel Dionne, L.A.	C
Guy Lafleur, Mon.	RW
Larry Robinson, Mon.	D
Borje Salming, Tor.	D
Tony Esposito, Chi.	G

Second team

Steve Shutt, Mon.	
Wayne Gretzky, Edm.	
Danny Gare, Buf.	
Barry Beck, Col., N.Y.R.	
Mark Howe, Har.	
Don Edwards, Buf.	

1980-81

First team

Charlie Simmer, L.A.	LW
Wayne Gretzky, Edm.	C
Mike Bossy, N.Y.I.	RW
Randy Carlyle, Pit.	D
Denis Potvin, N.Y.I.	D
Mike Liut, St.L.	G

Second team

Bill Barber, Phi.	
Marcel Dionne, L.A.	
Dave Taylor, L.A.	
Larry Robinson, Mon.	
Ray Bourque, Bos.	
Don Beaupre, Min.	

1981-82

First team

Mark Messier, Edm.	LW
Wayne Gretzky, Edm.	C
Mike Bossy, N.Y.I.	RW
Doug Wilson, Chi.	D
Ray Bourque, Bos.	D
Bill Smith, N.Y.I.	G

Second team

John Tonelli, N.Y.I.	
Bryan Trottier, N.Y.I.	
Rick Middleton, Bos.	
Paul Coffey, Edm.	
Larry Robinson, Mon.	
Grant Fuhr, Edm.	

1982-83

First team

Mark Messier, Edm.	LW
Wayne Gretzky, Edm.	C
Lanny McDonald, Cal.	RW
Mark Howe, Phi.	D
Rod Langway, Was.	D
Pete Peeters, Bos.	G

Second team

Michel Goulet, Que.	
Denis Savard, Chi.	
Mike Bossy, N.Y.I.	
Ray Bourque, Bos.	
Paul Coffey, Edm.	
Andy Moog, Edm.	

1983-84

First team

Michel Goulet, Que.	LW
Wayne Gretzky, Edm.	C
Rick Middleton, Bos.	RW
Ray Bourque, Bos.	D
Rod Langway, Was.	D
Pat Riggin, Was.	G

Second team

John Ogrodnick, Det.	
Bryan Trottier, N.Y.I.	
Mike Bossy, N.Y.I.	
Paul Coffey, Edm.	
Denis Potvin, N.Y.I.	
Tom Barrasso, Buf.	

1984-85

First team

Michel Goulet, Que.	LW
Wayne Gretzky, Edm.	C
Jari Kurri, Edm.	RW
Ray Bourque, Bos.	D
Paul Coffey, Edm.	D
Pelle Lindbergh, Phi.	G

Second team

John Ogrodnick, Det.	
Dale Hawerchuk, Win.	
Mike Bossy, N.Y.I.	
Rod Langway, Was.	
Doug Wilson, Chi.	
Tom Barrasso, Buf.	

1985-86

First team

Michel Goulet, Que.	LW
Wayne Gretzky, Edm.	C
Mike Bossy, N.Y.I.	RW
Paul Coffey, Edm.	D
Mark Howe, Phi.	D
John Vanbiesbrouck, N.Y.R.	G

Second team

Mats Naslund, Mon.	
Mario Lemieux, Pit.	
Jari Kurri, Edm.	
Ray Bourque, Bos.	
Larry Robinson, Mon.	
Grant Fuhr, Edm.	

1986-87

First team

Michel Goulet, Que.	LW
Wayne Gretzky, Edm.	C
Tim Kerr, Phi.	RW
Ray Bourque, Bos.	D
Mark Howe, Phi.	D
Mike Liut, Har.	G

Second team

Luc Robitaille, L.A.	
Mark Messier, Edm.	
Kevin Dineen, Har.	
Larry Murphy, Was.	
Paul Coffey, Edm.	
Ron Hextall, Phi.	

1987-88

First team		Second team
Luc Robitaille, L.A.	LW	Michel Goulet, Que.
Mario Lemieux, Pit.	C	Wayne Gretzky, Edm.
Cam Neely, Bos.	RW	Hakan Loob, Cal.
Ray Bourque, Bos.	D	Scott Stevens, Was.
Gary Suter, Cal.	D	Brad McCrimmon, Cal.
Grant Fuhr, Edm.	G	Tom Barrasso, Buf.

1988-89

First team		Second team
Luc Robitaille, L.A.	LW	Mats Naslund, Mon.
Mario Lemieux, Pit.	C	Wayne Gretzky, L.A.
Joe Mullen, Cal.	RW	Jari Kurri, Edm.
Paul Coffey, Pit.	D	Ray Bourque, Bos.
Chris Chelios, Mon.	D	Gary Suter, Cal.
Patrick Roy, Mon.	G	Mike Vernon, Cal.

1989-90

First team		Second team
Luc Robitaille, L.A.	LW	Brian Bellows, Min.
Mark Messier, Edm.	C	Pat LaFontaine, N.Y.I.
Brett Hull, St.L.	RW	Cam Neely, Bos.
Ray Bourque, Bos.	D	Doug Wilson, Chi.
Al MacInnis, Cal.	D	Paul Coffey, Pit.
Patrick Roy, Mon.	G	Daren Puppa, Buf.

1990-91

First team		Second team
Luc Robitaille, L.A.	LW	Kevin Stevens, Pit.
Wayne Gretzky, L.A.	C	Adam Oates, St.L.
Brett Hull, St.L.	RW	Cam Neely, Bos.
Ray Bourque, Bos.	D	Brian Leetch, N.Y.R.
Al MacInnis, Cal.	D	Chris Chelios, Chi.
Ed Belfour, Chi.	G	Patrick Roy, Mon.

1991-92

First team		Second team
Kevin Stevens, Pit.	LW	Luc Robitaille, L.A.
Mark Messier, N.Y.R.	C	Wayne Gretzky, L.A.
Brett Hull, St.L.	RW	Joe Mullen, Pit.
Brian Leetch, N.Y.R.	D	Phil Housley, Win.
Ray Bourque, Bos.	D	Chris Chelios, Chi.
Patrick Roy, Mon.	G	Kirk McLean, Van.

1992-93

First team		Second team
Luc Robitaille, L.A.	LW	Kevin Stevens, Pit.
Mario Lemieux, Pit.	C	Doug Gilmour, Tor.
Teemu Selanne, Win.	RW	Alexander Mogilny, Buf.
Chris Chelios, Chi.	D	Larry Murphy, Pit.
Ray Bourque, Bos.	D	Al Iafrate, Was.
Tom Barrasso, Pit.	G	Ed Belfour, Chi.

1993-94

First team		Second team
Adam Graves, N.Y.R.	LW	Dave Andreychuk, Tor.
Sergei Fedorov, Det.	C	Wayne Gretzky, L.A.
Cam Neely, Bos.	RW	Pavel Bure, Van.
Ray Bourque, Bos.	D	Brian Leetch, N.Y.R.
Scott Stevens, N.J.	D	Al MacInnis, Cal.
John Vanbiesbrouck, Fla.	G	Dominik Hasek, Buf.

1994-95

LW	John LeClair, Mon.-Phi.
C	Eric Lindros, Philadelphia
RW	Jaromir Jagr, Pittsburgh
D	Paul Coffey, Detroit
D	Ray Bourque, Boston
G	Dominik Hasek, Buffalo

1995-96

LW	Keith Tkachuk, Winnipeg
C	Mario Lemieux, Pittsburgh
RW	Jaromir Jagr, Pittsburgh
D	Chris Chelios, Chicago
D	Ray Bourque, Boston
G	Chris Osgood, Detroit

1996-97

LW	John LeClair, Philadelphia
C	Mario Lemieux, Pittsburgh
RW	Teemu Selanne, Anaheim
D	Chris Chelios, Chicago
D	Brian Leetch, N.Y. Rangers
G	Dominik Hasek, Buffalo

1997-98

LW	John LeClair, Philadelphia
C	Peter Forsberg, Colorado
RW	Teemu Selanne, Anaheim
D	Rob Blake, Los Angeles
D	Nicklas Lidstrom, Detroit
G	Dominik Hasek, Buffalo

1998-99

LW	Paul Kariya, Anaheim
C	Alexei Yashin, Ottawa
RW	Jaromir Jagr, Pittsburgh
D	Al MacInnis, St. Louis
D	Nicklas Lidstrom, Detroit
G	Dominik Hasek, Buffalo

HALL OF FAME

ROSTER OF MEMBERS

NOTE: Leagues other than the NHL with which Hall of Fame members are associated are denoted in parentheses. Abbreviations: **AAHA:** Alberta Amateur Hockey Association. **AHA:** Amateur Hockey Association of Canada. **CAHL:** Canadian Amateur Hockey League. **EAA:** Eaton Athletic Association. **ECAHA:** Eastern Canada Amateur Hockey Association. **ECHA:** Eastern Canada Hockey Association. **FAHL:** Federal Amateur Hockey League. **IHL:** International Professional Hockey League. **MHL:** Manitoba Hockey League. **MNSHL:** Manitoba and Northwestern Senior Hockey League. **MPHL:** Maritime Pro Hockey League. **MSHL:** Manitoba Senior Hockey League. **NHA:** National Hockey Association. **NOHA:** Northern Ontario Hockey Association. **OHA:** Ontario Hockey Association. **OPHL:** Ontario Professional Hockey League. **PCHA:** Pacific Coast Hockey Association. **WCHL:** Western Canada Hockey League. **WHA:** World Hockey Association. **WHL:** Western Hockey League. **WinHL:** Winnipeg Hockey League. **WOHA:** Western Ontario Hockey Association.

PLAYERS

Player	Elec. year/ how elected*	Pos.†	First season	Last season	Stanley Cup wins‡	Teams as player
Abel, Sid	1969/P	C	1938-39	1953-54	3	Detroit Red Wings, Chicago Blackhawks
Adams, Jack	1959/P	C	1917-18	1926-27	2	Toronto Arenas, Vancouver Millionaires (PCHA), Toronto St. Pats, Ottawa Senators
Apps, Syl	1961/P	C	1936-37	1947-48	3	Toronto Maple Leafs
Armstrong, George	1975/P	RW	1949-50	1970-71	4	Toronto Maple Leafs
Bailey, Ace	1975/P	RW	1926-27	1933-34	1	Toronto Maple Leafs
Bain, Dan	1945/P	C	1895-96	1901-02	3	Winnipeg Victorias (MHL)
Baker, Hobey	1945/P	Ro.	1910	1915	0	Princeton University, St. Nicholas
Barber, Bill	1990/P	LW	1972-73	1983-84	2	Philadelphia Flyers
Barry, Marty	1965/P	C	1927-28	1939-40	2	New York Americans, Boston Bruins, Detroit Red Wings, Montreal Canadiens
Bathgate, Andy	1978/P	RW	1952-53	1974-75	1	New York Rangers, Toronto Maple Leafs, Detroit Red Wings, Pittsburgh Penguins, Vancouver Blazers (WHA)
Bauer, Bobby	1996/V	LW	1935-36	1951-52	2	Boston Bruins
Beliveau, Jean	1972/P	C	1950-51	1970-71	10	Montreal Canadiens
Benedict, Clint	1965/P	G	1917-18	1929-30	4	Ottawa Senators, Montreal Maroons
Bentley, Doug	1964/P	LW	1939-40	1953-54	0	Chicago Blackhawks, New York Rangers
Bentley, Max	1966/P	C	1940-41	1953-54	3	Toronto Maple Leafs, New York Rangers
Blake, Toe	1966/P	LW	1932-33	1947-48	3	Montreal Maroons, Montreal Canadiens
Boivin, Leo	1986/P	D	1951-52	1969-70	0	Toronto Maple Leafs, Boston Bruins, Detroit Red Wings, Pittsburgh Penguins, Minnesota North Stars
Boon, Dickie	1952/P	D	1897	1905	2	Montreal Monarchs, Montreal AAA (CAHL), Montreal Wanderers (FAHL)
Bossy, Mike	1991/P	RW	1977-78	1986-87	4	New York Islanders
Bouchard, Butch	1966/P	D	1941-42	1955-56	4	Montreal Canadiens
Boucher, Frank	1958/P	C	1921-22	1943-44	2	Ottawa Senators, Vancouver Maroons, New York Rangers
Boucher, George	1960/P	F/D	1915-16	1931-32	4	Ottawa Senators, Montreal Maroons, Chicago Blackhawks
Bower, Johnny	1976/P	G	1953-54	1969-70	0	New York Rangers, Toronto Maple Leafs
Bowie, Russell	1945/P	C	1898-99	1907-08	1	Montreal Victorias
Brimsek, Frank	1966/P	G	1938-39	1951-52	0	Boston Bruins, Chicago Blackhawks
Broadbent, Punch	1962/P	RW	1912-13	1928-29	4	Ottawa Senators, Montreal Maroons, New York Americans
Broda, Turk	1967/P	G	1936-37	1928-29	0	Toronto Maple Leafs
Bucyk, John	1981/P	LW	1955-56	1977-78	2	Detroit Red Wings, Boston Bruins
Burch, Billy	1974/P	C	1922-23	1932-33	0	Hamilton Tigers, New York Americans, Chicago Blackhawks
Cameron, Harry	1962/P	D	1912-13	1925-26	3	Toronto Blueshirts, Toronto Arenas, Montreal Wanderers, Ottawa Senators, Toronto St. Pats, Montreal Canadiens, Saskatoon (WCHL)
Cheevers, Gary	1985/P	G	1961-62	1979-80	2	Toronto Maple Leafs, Boston Bruins, Cleveland Crusaders (WHA)
Clancy, King	1958/P	D	1921-22	1936-37	3	Ottawa Senators, Toronto Maple Leafs
Clapper, Dit	1947/P	RW	1927-28	1946-47	3	Boston Bruins
Clarke, Bobby	1987/P	C	1969-70	1983-84	2	Philadelphia Flyers
Cleghorn, Sprague	1958/P	D	1909-10	1927-28	3	New York Crescents, Renfrew Creamery Kings (NHA), Montreal Wanderers, Ottawa Senators, Toronto St. Pats, Toronto St. Pats, Montreal Canadiens, Boston Bruins
Colville, Neil	1967/P	C/D	1935-36	1948-49	1	New York Rangers
Conacher, Charlie	1961/P	RW	1929-30	1940-41	1	Toronto Maple Leafs, Detroit Red Wings, New York Americans
Conacher, Lionel	1994/V	D	1925-26	1936-37	2	Pittsburgh Pirates, New York Americans, Montreal Maroons, Chicago Blackhawks
Conacher, Roy	1998/V	LW	1938-39	1951-52	2	Boston Bruins, Detroit Red Wings, Chicago Blackhawks
Connell, Alex	1958/P	G	1924-25	1936-37	2	Ottawa Senators, Detroit Red Wings, New York Americans, Montreal Maroons

Player	Elec. year/ how elected*	Pos.†	First season	Last season	Stanley Cup wins‡	Teams as player
Cook, Bill	1952/P	RW	1921-22	1936-37	2	Saskatoon, New York Rangers
Cook, Bun	1995/V	LW	1926-27	1936-37	2	New York Rangers, Boston Bruins
Coulter, Art	1974/P	D	1931-32	1941-42	2	Chicago Blackhawks, New York Rangers
Cournoyer, Yvan	1982/P	RW	1963-64	1978-79	10	Montreal Canadiens
Cowley, Bill	1968/P	C	1934-35	1946-47	2	St. Louis Eagles, Boston Bruins
Crawford, Rusty	1962/P	LW	1912-13	1925-26	1	Quebec Bulldogs, Ottawa Senators, Toronto Arenas, Saskatoon (WCHL), Calgary (WCHL), Vancouver (WHL)
Darragh, Jack	1962/P	RW	1910-11	1923-24	4	Ottawa Senators
Davidson, Scotty	1950/P	RW	1912-13	1913-14	0	Toronto (NHA)
Day, Hap	1961/P	LW	1924-25	1937-38	1	Toronto St. Pats, Toronto Maple Leafs, New York Americans
Delvecchio, Alex	1977/P	C	1950-51	1973-74	3	Detroit Red Wings
Denneny, Cy	1959/P	LW	1914-15	1928-29	5	Toronto Shamrocks (NHA), Toronto Arenas (NHA), Ottawa Senators, Boston Bruins
Dionne, Marcel	1992/P	C	1971-72	1988-89	0	Detroit Red Wings, Los Angeles Kings, New York Rangers
Drillon, Gord	1975/P	LW	1936-37	1942-43	1	Toronto Maple Leafs, Montreal Canadiens
Drinkwater, Graham	1950/P	F/D	1892-93	1898-99	5	Montreal Victorias
Dryden, Ken	1983/P	G	1970-71	1978-79	6	Montreal Canadiens
Dumart, Woody	1992/V	LW	1935-36	1953-54	2	Boston Bruins
Dunderdale, Tommy	1974/P	C	1906-07	1923-24	0	Winnipeg Maple Leafs (MHL), Montreal Shamrocks (NHA), Quebec Bulldogs (NHA), Victoria (PCHA), Portland (PCHA), Saskatoon (WCHL), Edmonton (WCHL)
Durnan, Bill	1964/P	G	1943-44	1949-50	2	Montreal Canadiens
Dutton, Red	1958/P	D	1921-22	1935-36	0	Calgary Tigers (WCHL), Montreal Maroons, New York Americans
Dye, Babe	1970/P	RW	1919-20	1930-31	1	Toronto St. Pats, Hamilton Tigers, Chicago Blackhawks, New York Americans, Toronto Maple Leafs
Esposito, Phil	1984/P	C	1963-64	1980-81	2	Chicago Blackhawks, Boston Bruins, New York Rangers
Esposito, Tony	1988/P	G	1968-69	1983-84	1	Montreal Canadiens, Chicago Blackhawks
Farrell, Arthur	1965/P	F	1896-97	1900-01	2	Montreal Shamrocks (AHA/CAHL)
Flaman, Fern	1990/V	D	1944-45	1960-61	1	Boston Bruins, Toronto Maple Leafs
Foyston, Frank	1958/P	C	1912-13	1927-28	3	Toronto Blueshirts (NHA), Seattle Metropolitans (PCHA), Victoria Cougars (WCHL/WHL), Detroit Cougars
Fredrickson, Frank	1958/P	C	1920-21	1930-31	1	Victoria Aristocrats (PCHA), Victoria Cougars (PCHA/WCHL/WHL), Detroit Cougars, Boston Bruins, Pittsburgh Pirates, Detroit Falcons
Gadsby, Bill	1970/P	D	1946-47	1965-66	0	Chicago Blackhawks, New York Rangers, Detroit Red Wings
Gainey, Bob	1992/P	LW	1973-74	1988-89	5	Montreal Canadiens
Gardiner, Chuck	1945/P	G	1927-28	1933-34	1	Chicago Blackhawks
Gardiner, Herb	1958/P	D	1921-22	1928-29	0	Calgary Tigers (WCHL), Montreal Canadiens, Chicago Blackhawks
Gardner, Jimmy	1962/P	LW	1900-01	1914-15	3	Montreal Hockey Club (CAHL), Montreal Wanderers (FAHL/ECHA/NHA), Calumet (IHL), Pittsburgh (IHL), Montreal Shamrocks (ECAHA),New Westminster Royals (PCHA), Montreal Canadiens (NHA)
Geoffrion, Boom Boom	1972/P	RW	1950-51	1967-68	6	Montreal Canadiens, New York Rangers
Gerard, Eddie	1945/P	F/D	1913-14	1922-23	4	Ottawa Senators (NHA/NHL), Toronto St. Pats
Giacomin, Eddie	1987/P	G	1965-66	1977-78	0	New York Rangers, Detroit Red Wings
Gilbert, Rod	1982/P	RW	1960-61	1977-78	0	New York Rangers
Gilmour, Billy	1962/P	RW	1902-03	1915-16	5	Ottawa Silver Seven (CAHL/FAHL/ECAHA), Montreal Victorias (ECAHA), Ottawa Senators (ECHA/NHA)
Goheen, Moose	1952/P	D	1914	1918	0	St. Paul Athletic Club, 1920 U.S. Olympic Team
Goodfellow, Ebbie	1963/P	C	1929-30	1942-43	3	Detroit Cougars, Detroit Falcons, Detroit Red Wings
Goulet, Michel	1998/P	LW	1978-79	1993-94	0	Birmingham Bulls (WHA), Quebec Nordiques, Chicago Blackhawks
Grant, Mike	1950/P	D	1893-94	1901-02	5	Montreal Victorias (AHA/CAHL), Montreal Shamrocks (CAHL)
Green, Shorty	1962/P	RW	1923-24	1926-27	0	Hamilton Tigers, New York Americans
Gretzky, Wayne	1999/P	C	1978-79	1998-99	4	Indianapolis Racers (WHA), Edmonton (WHA/NHL), Los Angeles Kings, St. Louis Blues, New York Rangers
Griffis, Si	1950/P	Ro./D	1902-03	1918-19	2	Rat Portage Thistles (MNSHL), Kenora Thistles (MSHL), Vancouver Millionaires (PCHA)
Hainsworth, George	1961/P	G	1923-24	1936-37	2	Saskatoon Crescents (WCHL/WHL), Montreal Canadiens
Hall, Glenn	1975/P	G	1952-53	1970-71	1	Detroit Red Wings, Chicago Blackhawks, St. Louis Blues
Hall, Joe	1961/P	F/D	1903-04	1918-19	2	Winnipeg (MSHL), Quebec Bulldogs (ECAHA/NHA), Brandon (MHL), Montreal (ECAHA), Montreal Shamrocks (ECAHA/NHA), Montreal Wanderers (ECHA), Montreal Canadiens

Player	Elec. year/ how elected*	Pos.†	First season	Last season	Stanley Cup wins‡	Teams as player
Harvey, Doug	1973/P	D	1947-48	1968-69	6	Montreal Canadiens, New York Rangers, Detroit Red Wings, St. Louis Blues
Hay, George	1958/P	LW	1921-22	1933-34	0	Regina Capitals (WCHL), Portland Rosebuds (WHL), Chicago Blackhawks, Detroit Cougars, Detroit Falcons, Detroit Red Wings
Hern, Riley	1962/P	G	1906-07	1910-11	3	Montreal Wanderers (ECAHA/ECHA/NHA)
Hextall, Bryan	1969/P	RW	1936-37	1947-48	1	New York Rangers
Holmes, Hap	1972/P	G	1912-13	1927-28	0	Toronto Blueshirts (NHA), Seattle Metropolitans (PCHA), Toronto Arenas, Victoria Cougars, Detroit Cougars
Hooper, Tom	1962/P	F	1904-05	1907-08	2	Rat Portage Thistles (MNSHL), Kenora Thistles (SHL), Montreal Wanderers (ECAHA), Montreal (ECAHA)
Horner, Red	1965/P	D	1928-29	1939-40	1	Toronto Maple Leafs
Horton, Tim	1977/P	D	1949-50	1973-74	4	Toronto Maple Leafs, New York Rangers, Pittsburgh Penguins, Buffalo Sabres
Howe, Gordie	1972/P	RW	1946-47	1979-80	4	Detroit Red Wings, Houston Aeros (WHA), New England Whalers (WHA), Hartford Whalers
Howe, Syd	1965/P	F/D	1929-30	1945-46	3	Ottawa Senators, Philadelphia Quakers, Toronto Maple Leafs, St. Louis Eagles, Detroit Red Wings
Howell, Harry	1979/P	D	1952-53	1975-76	0	New York Rangers, Oakland Seals, California Golden Seals, New York Golden Blades/Jersey Knights (WHA), San Diego Mariners (WHA), Calgary Cowboys (WHA)
Hull, Bobby	1983/P	LW	1957-58	1979-80	1	Chicago Blackhawks, Winnipeg Jets (WHA/NHL), Hartford Whalers
Hutton, Bouse	1962/P	G	1898-99	1903-04	1	Ottawa Silver Seven (CAHL)
Hyland, Harry	1962/P	RW	1908-09	1917-18	1	Montreal Shamrocks (ECHA), Montreal Wanderers (NHA), New Westminster Royals (PCHA), Ottawa Senators
Irvin, Dick	1958/P	C	1916-17	1928-29	0	Portland Rosebuds (PCHA), Regina Capitals (WCHL), Chicago Blackhawks
Jackson, Busher	1971/P	LW	1929-30	1943-44	1	Toronto Maple Leafs, New York Americans, Boston Bruins
Johnson, Ching	1958/P	D	1926-27	1937-38	2	New York Rangers, New York Americans
Johnson, Moose	1952/P	LW/D	1903-04	1921-22	4	Montreal AAA (CAHL), Montreal Wanderers (ECAHA/ECHA/NHA), New Westminster Royals (PCHA), Portland Rosebuds (PCHA), Victoria Aristocrats (PCHA)
Johnson, Tom	1970/P	D	1947-48	1964-65	6	Montreal Canadiens, Boston Bruins
Joliat, Aurel	1947/P	LW	1922-23	1937-38	3	Montreal Canadiens
Keats, Duke	1958/P	C	1915-16	1928-29	0	Toronto Arenas (NHA), Edmonton Eskimos (WCHL/WHL), Detroit Cougars, Chicago Blackhawks
Kelly, Red	1969/P	C	1947-48	1966-67	8	Detroit Red Wings, Toronto Maple Leafs
Kennedy, Ted	1966/P	C	1942-43	1956-57	5	Toronto Maple Leafs
Keon, Dave	1986/P	C	1960-61	1981-82	4	Toronto Maple Leafs, Minnesota Fighting Saints (WHA), Indianapolis Racers (WHA), New England Whalers (WHA), Hartford Whalers
Lach, Elmer	1966/P	C	1940-41	1953-54	3	Montreal Canadiens
Lafleur, Guy	1988/P	RW	1971-72	1990-91	5	Montreal Canadiens, New York Rangers, Quebec Nordiques
Lalonde, Newsy	1950/P	C/Ro.	1904-05	1926-27	1	Cornwall (FAHL), Portage La Prairie (MHL), Toronto (OPHL), Montreal Canadiens (NHA/NHL), Renfrew Creamery Kings (NHA), Vancouver Millionaires (PCHA), Saskatoon Sheiks (WCHL), Saskatoon Crescents (WCHL/WHL), New York Americans
Laperriere, Jacques	1987/P	D	1962-63	1973-74	6	Montreal Canadiens
Lapointe, Guy	1993/P	D	1968-69	1983-84	6	Montreal Canadiens, St. Louis Blues, Boston Bruins
Laprade, Edgar	1993/V	C	1945-46	1954-55	0	New York Rangers
Laviolette, Jack	1962/P	D/LW	1903-04	1917-18	1	Montreal Nationals (FAHL), Montreal Shamrocks (ECAHA/ECHA), Montreal Canadiens (NHA/NHL)
Lehman, Hughie	1958/P	G	1908-09	1927-28	1	Berlin Dutchmen (OPHL), Galt (OPHL), New Westminster Royals (PCHA), Vancouver Millionaires, Vancouver Maroons, Chicago Blackhawks
Lemaire, Jacques	1984/P	C	1967-68	1978-79	8	Montreal Canadiens
Lemieux, Mario	1997/P	C	1984-85	1996-97	2	Pittsburgh Penguins
LeSueur, Percy	1961/P	G	1905-06	1915-16	3	Smith Falls (FAHL), Ottawa Senators (ECAHA/ECHA/NHA), Toronto Shamrocks (NHA), Toronto Blueshirts (NHA)
Lewis, Herbie	1989/V	LW	1928-29	1938-39	2	Detroit Cougars, Detroit Falcons, Detroit Red Wings
Lindsay, Ted	1966/P	LW	1944-45	1964-65	4	Detroit Red Wings, Chicago Blackhawks
Lumley, Harry	1980/P	G	1943-44	1959-60	1	Detroit Red Wings, New York Rangers, Chicago Blackhawks, Toronto Maple Leafs, Boston Bruins

Player	Elec. year/ how elected*	Pos.†	First season	Last season	Stanley Cup wins‡	Teams as player
MacKay, Mickey	1952/P	C/Ro.	1914-15	1929-30	1	Vancouver Millionaires (PCHA), Vancouver Maroons (PCHA/WCHL/WHL), Chicago Blackhawks, Pittsburgh Pirates, Boston Bruins
Mahovlich, Frank	1981/P	LW	1956-57	1977-78	6	Toronto Maple Leafs, Detroit Red Wings, Montreal Canadiens, Toronto Toros (WHA), Birmingham Bulls (WHA)
Malone, Joe	1950/P	C/LW	1908-09	1923-24	3	Quebec (ECHA), Waterloo (OPHL), Quebec Bulldogs (NHA/NHL), Montreal Canadiens, Hamilton Tigers
Mantha, Sylvio	1960/P	D	1923-24	1936-37	3	Montreal Canadiens, Boston Bruins
Marshall, Jack	1965/P	C/D	1900-01	1916-17	6	Winnipeg Victorias, Montreal AAA (CAHL), Montreal Wanderers (FAHL/ECAHA/NHA), Montreal Montagnards (FAHL), Montreal Shamrocks (ECAHA/ECHA), Toronto Blueshirts (NHA)
Maxwell, Fred	1962/P	Ro.	1914	1925	0	Winnipeg Monarchs (MSHL), Winnipeg Falcons (MSHL)
McDonald, Lanny	1992/P	RW	1973-74	1988-89	1	Toronto Maple Leafs, Colorado Rockies, Calgary Flames
McGee, Frank	1945/P	C/Ro.	1902-03	1905-06	4	Ottawa Silver Seven
McGimsie, Billy	1962/P	F	1902-03	1906-07	1	Rat Portage Thistles (MNSHL/MSHL), Kenora Thistles (MSHL)
McNamara, George	1958/P	D	1907-08	1916-17	1	Montreal Shamrocks (ECAHA/ECHA), Waterloo (OPHL), Toronto Tecumsehs (NHA), Toronto Ontarios (NHA), Toronto Blueshirts (NHA), Toronto Shamrocks (NHA), 228th Battalion (NHA)
Mikita, Stan	1983/P	C	1958-59	1979-80	1	Chicago Blackhawks
Moore, Dickie	1974/P	RW	1951-52	1967-68	6	Montreal Canadiens, Toronto Maple Leafs, St. Louis Blues
Moran, Paddy	1958/P	G	1901-02	1916-17	2	Quebec Bulldogs (CAHL/ECAHA/ECHA/NHA), Haileybury (NHA)
Morenz, Howie	1945/P	C	1923-24	1936-37	3	Montreal Canadiens, Chicago Blackhawks, New York Rangers
Mosienko, Bill	1965/P	RW	1941-42	1954-55	0	Chicago Blackhawks
Mullen, Joe	2000/P	RW	1979-80	1996-97	3	St. Louis Blues, Calgary Flames, Pittsburgh Penguins, Boston Bruins
Nighbor, Frank	1947/P	LW/C	1912-13	1929-30	5	Toronto Blueshirts (NHA), Vancouver Millionaires, (PCHA), Ottawa Senators, Toronto Maple Leafs
Noble, Reg	1962/P	LW/C/D	1916-17	1932-33	3	Toronto Blueshirts (NHA), Montreal Canadiens (NHA), Toronto Arenas, Toronto St. Pats, Montreal Maroons, Detroit Cougars, Detroit Falcons, Detroit Red Wings
O'Connor, Buddy	1988/V	C	1941-42	1950-51	2	Montreal Canadiens, New York Rangers
Oliver, Harry	1967/P	F	1921-22	1936-37	1	Calgary Tigers (WCHL/WHL), Boston Bruins, New York Americans
Olmstead, Bert	1985/P	LW	1948-49	1961-62	5	Chicago Blackhawks, Montreal Canadiens, Toronto Maple Leafs
Orr, Bobby	1979/P	D	1966-67	1978-79	2	Boston Bruins, Chicago Blackhawks
Parent, Bernie	1984/P	G	1965-66	1978-79	2	Boston Bruins, Philadelphia Flyers, Toronto Maple Leafs, Philadelphia Blazers (WHA)
Park, Brad	1988/P	D	1968-69	1984-85	0	New York Rangers, Boston Bruins, Detroit Red Wings
Patrick, Lester	1947/P	D/Ro./G	1903-04	1926-27	3	Brandon, Westmount (CAHL), Montreal Wanderers (ECAHA), Edmonton Eskimos (AAHA), Renfrew Millionaires (NHA), Victoria Aristocrats (PCHA), Spokane Canaries (PCHA), Seattle Metropolitans (PCHA), Seattle Metropolitans(PCHA), Victoria Cougars (WHA), New York Rangers
Patrick, Lynn	1980/P	LW	1934-35	1945-46	1	New York Rangers
Perreault, Gilbert	1990/P	C	1970-71	1986-87	0	Buffalo Sabres
Phillips, Tommy	1945/P	LW	1902-03	1911-12	1	Montreal AAA (CAHL), Toronto Marlboros (OHA), Rat Portage Thistles, Kenora Thistles (MHL), Ottawa Ottawa Senators (ECAHA), Edmonton Eskimos (AAHA), Vancouver Millionaires (PCHA)
Pilote, Pierre	1975/P	D	1955-56	1968-69	1	Chicago Blackhawks, Toronto Maple Leafs
Pitre, Didier	1962/P	D/Ro.	1903-04	1922-23	0	Montreal Nationals (FAHL/CAHL), Montreal Shamrocks (ECAHA), Edmonton Eskimos (AAHA), Montreal Canadiens (NHA/NHL), Vancouver Millionaires (PCHA)
Plante, Jacques	1978/P	G	1952-53	1974-75	6	Montreal Canadiens, New York Rangers, St. Louis Blues, Toronto Maple Leafs, Boston Bruins, Edmonton Oilers
Potvin, Denis	1991/P	D	1973-74	1987-88	4	New York Islanders
Pratt, Babe	1966/P	D	1935-36	1946-47	2	New York Rangers, Toronto Maple Leafs, Boston Bruins
Primeau, Joe	1963/P	C	1927-28	1935-36	1	Toronto Maple Leafs
Pronovost, Marcel	1978/P	D	1950-51	1966-67	5	Detroit Red Wings, Toronto Maple Leafs
Pulford, Bob	1991/P	LW	1956-57	1971-72	4	Toronto Maple Leafs, Los Angeles Kings
Pulford, Harvey	1945/P	D	1893-94	1907-08	4	Ottawa Silver Seven/Senators (AHA/CAHL/FAHL/ECAHA)

Player	Elec. year/ how elected*	Pos.†	First season	Last season	Stanley Cup wins‡	Teams as player
Quackenbush, Bill	1976/P	D	1942-43	1955-56	0	Detroit Red Wings, Boston Bruins
Rankin, Frank	1961/P	Ro.	1906	1914	0	Stratford (OHA), Eatons (EAA), Toronto St. Michaels (OHA)
Ratelle, Jean	1985/P	C	1960-61	1980-81	0	New York Rangers, Boston Bruins
Rayner, Chuck	1973/P	G	1940-41	1952-53	0	New York Americans, New York Rangers
Reardon, Ken	1966/P	D	1940-41	1949-50	1	Montreal Canadiens
Richard, Henri	1979/P	C	1955-56	1974-75	11	Montreal Canadiens
Richard, Rocket	1961/P	RW	1942-43	1959-60	8	Montreal Canadiens
Richardson, George	1950/P		1906	1912	0	14th Regiment, Queen's University
Roberts, Gordon	1971/P	LW	1909-10	1919-20	0	Ottawa Senators (NHA), Montreal Wanderers (NHA), Vancouver Millionaires (PCHA), Seattle Metropolitans (PCHA)
Robinson, Larry	1995/P	D	1972-73	1991-92	6	Montreal Canadiens, Los Angeles Kings
Ross, Art	1945/P	D	1904-05	1917-18	2	Westmount (CAHL), Brandon (MHL), Kenora Thistles (MHL), Montreal Wanderers (ECAHA/ECHA/NHA/NHL), Haileybury (NHA), Ottawa Senators (NHA)
Russell, Blair	1965/P	RW/C	1899-00	1907-08	0	Montreal Victorias (CAHL/ECAHA)
Russell, Ernie	1965/P	Ro./C	1904-05	1913-14	4	Montreal Winged Wheelers (CAHL), Montreal Wanderers (ECAHA/NHA)
Ruttan, Jack	1962/P		1905	1913	0	Armstrong's Point, Rustler, St. John's College, Manitoba Varsity (WSHL), Winnipeg (WinHL)
Salming, Borje	1996/P	D	1973-74	1989-90	0	Toronto Maple Leafs, Detroit Red Wings
Savard, Dennis	2000/P	C	1980-81	1996-97	1	Chicago Blackhawks, Montreal Canadiens, Tampa Bay Lightning
Savard, Serge	1986/P	D	1966-67	1982-83	7	Montreal Canadiens, Winnipeg Jets
Sawchuk, Terry	1971/P	G	1949-50	1969-70	4	Detroit Red Wings, Boston Bruins, Toronto Maple Leafs, Los Angeles Kings, New York Rangers
Scanlan, Fred	1965/P	F	1897-98	1902-03	3	Montreal Shamrocks (AHA/CAHL), Winnipeg Victorias (MSHL)
Schmidt, Milt	1961/P	C	1936-37	1954-55	2	Boston Bruins
Schriner, Sweeney	1962/P	LW	1934-35	1945-46	2	New York Americans, Toronto Maple Leafs
Seibert, Earl	1963/P	D	1931-32	1945-46	2	New York Rangers, Chicago Blackhawks, Detroit Red Wings
Seibert, Oliver	1961/P	D	1900	1906		Berlin Rangers (WOHA), Houghton (IHL), Guelph (OPHL), London (OPHL)
Shore, Eddie	1947/P	D	1924-25	1939-40	2	Regina Capitals (WCHL), Edmonton Eskimos (WHL), Boston Bruins, New York Americans
Shutt, Steve	1993/P	LW	1972-73	1984-85	5	Montreal Canadiens, Los Angeles Kings
Siebert, Babe	1964/P	LW/D	1925-26	1938-39	2	Montreal Maroons, New York Rangers, Boston Bruins, Montreal Canadiens
Simpson, Joe	1962/P	D	1921-22	1930-31	0	Edmonton Eskimos (WCHL), New York Americans
Sittler, Darryl	1989/P	C	1970-71	1984-85	0	Toronto Maple Leafs, Philadelphia Flyers, Detroit Red Wings
Smith, Alf	1962/P	RW	1894-95	1907-08	4	Ottawa Silver Seven/Senators (AHA/CAHL/FAHL/ECAHA), Kenora Thistles (MHL)
Smith, Billy	1993/P	G	1971-72	1988-89	4	Los Angeles Kings, New York Islanders
Smith, Clint	1991/V	C	1936-37	1946-47	1	New York Rangers, Chicago Blackhawks
Smith, Hooley	1972/P	RW	1924-25	1940-41	2	1924 Canadian Olympic Team, Ottawa Senators, Montreal Maroons, Boston Bruins, New York Americans
Smith, Tommy	1973/P	LW/C	1905-06	1919-20	1	Ottawa Vics (FAHL), Ottawa Senators (ECAHA), Brantford (OPHL), Moncton (MPHL), Quebec Bulldogs (NHA/NHL), Toronto Ontarios (NHA), Montreal Canadiens (NHA)
Stanley, Allan	1981/P	D	1948-49	1968-69	4	New York Rangers, Chicago Blackhawks, Boston Bruins, Toronto Maple Leafs, Philadelphia Flyers
Stanley, Barney	1962/P	RW/D	1914-15	1925-26	1	Vancouver Millionaires (PCHA), Calgary Tigers (WCHL), Regina Capitals (WCHL), Edmonton Eskimos (WCHL/WHL)
Stastny, Peter	1998/P	C	1980-81	1994-95	0	Quebec Nordiques, New Jersey Devils, St. Louis Blues
Stewart, Black Jack	1964/P	D	1938-39	1951-52	2	Detroit Red Wings, Chicago Blackhawks
Stewart, Nels	1962/P	C	1925-26	1939-40	1	Montreal Maroons, Boston Bruins, New York Americans, Boston Bruins
Stuart, Bruce	1961/P	F	1989-99	1910-11	3	Ottawa Senators (CAHL/ECHA/NHA), Quebec Bulldogs (CAHL), Pittsburgh (IHL), Houghton (IHL), Portage Lake (IHL), Montreal Wanderers (ECAHA)
Stuart, Hod	1945/P	D	1898-99	1906-07	1	Ottawa Senators, Quebec Bulldogs, Calumet (IHL), Pittsburgh (IHL), Montreal Wanderers
Taylor, Cyclone	1947/P	D/Ro./C	1907-08	1922-23	2	Ottawa Senators (ECAHA/ECHA), Renfrew Creamery Kings (NHA), Vancouver Millionaires (PCHA)
Thompson, Tiny	1959/P	G	1928-29	1939-40	1	Boston Bruins, Detroit Red Wings
Tretiak, Vladislav	1989/P	G	1969	1984	0	Central Red Army

Player	Elec. year/ how elected*	Pos.†	First season	Last season	Stanley Cup wins‡	Teams as player
Trihey, Harry	1950/P	C	1896-97	1900-01	2	Montreal Shamrocks (AHA/CAHL)
Trottier, Bryan	1997/P	C	1975-76	1993-94	6	New York Islanders, Pittsburgh Penguins
Ullman, Norm	1982/P	C	1955-56	1976-77	0	Detroit Red Wings, Toronto Maple Leafs, Edmonton Oilers (WHA)
Vezina, Georges	1945/P	G	1910-11	1925-26	2	Montreal Canadiens (NHA/NHL)
Walker, Jack	1960/P	LW/Ro.	1910-11	1927-28	3	Port Arthur, Toronto Blueshirts (NHA), Seattle Metropolitans (PCHA), Victoria Cougars (WCHL/WHL), Detroit Cougars
Walsh, Marty	1962/P	C	1905-06	1911-12	2	Queens University (OHA), Ottawa Senators (ECAHA/ECHA/NHA)
Watson, Harry E.	1962/P	C	1915	1931	0	St. Andrews (OHA), Aura Lee Juniors (OHA), Toronto Dentals (OHA), Toronto Granites (OHA), 1924 Canadian Olympic Team, Toronto National Sea Fleas (OHA)
Watson, Harry P.	1994/V	LW	1941-42	1956-57	5	Brooklyn Americans, Detroit Red Wings, Toronto Maple Leafs, Chicago Blackhawks
Weiland, Cooney	1971/P	C	1928-29	1938-39	0	Boston Bruins, Ottawa Senators, Detroit Red Wings
Westwick, Harry	1962/P	Ro.	1894-95	1907-08	4	Ottawa Senators/Silver Seven (AHA/CAHL/FAHL/ECAHA/), Kenora Thistles
Whitcroft, Frederick	1962/P	Ro.	1906-07	1909-10	0	Kenora Thistles (MSHL), Edmonton Eskimos (AAHA), Renfrew Millionaires (NHA)
Wilson, Gord	1962/P	D	1918	1933	0	Port Arthur War Veterans (OHA), Iroquois Falls (NOHA), Port Arthur Bearcats (OHA)
Worsley, Gump	1980/P	G	1952-53	1973-74	4	New York Rangers, Montreal Canadiens, Minnesota North Stars
Worters, Roy	1969/P	G	1925-26	1936-37	0	Pittsburgh Pirates, New York Americans, Montreal Canadiens

*Denotes whether enshrinee was elected by regular election (P) or veterans committee (V).
†Primary positions played during career: C—center; D—defense; G—goaltender; LW—left wing; Ro.—rover; RW—right wing.
‡Stanley Cup wins column refers to wins as a player in the players section and as a coach in the coaches section.

BUILDERS

Builder	Election year	Stanley Cup wins‡	Designation for induction
Adams, Charles F.	1960		Founder, Boston Bruins (1924)
Adams, Weston W.	1972		President and chairman, Boston Bruins (1936-69)
Aheam, Frank	1962		Owner, Ottawa Senators (1924-34)
Ahearne, Bunny	1977		President, International Hockey Federation (1957-75)
Allan, Sir Montagu	1945		Donator of Allan Cup, awarded anually to senior amateur champion of Canada (1908)
Allen, Keith	1992	0	Coach, Philadelphia Flyers (1967-68 and 1968-69); general manager and executive, Philadelphia Flyers (1966-present)
Arbour, Al	1996	4	Coach, St. Louis Blues, New York Islanders, 1970-71, 1971-72 to 1972-73, 1973-74 through 1985-86 and 1988-89 to 1993-94; vice president of hockey operations and consultant, New York Islanders (1994 to 1998)
Ballard, Harold	1977		Owner and chief executive, Toronto Maple Leafs (1961-90)
Bauer, Father David	1989		Developer and coach of first Canadian National Hockey Team
Bickell, J.P.	1978		First president and chairman of the board, Toronto Maple Leafs (1927-51)
Bowman, Scotty	1991	8	Coach, St. Louis Blues, Montreal Canadiens, Buffalo Sabres, Pittsburgh Penguins, Detroit Red Wings (1967-68 through 1979-80, 1981-82 through 1986-87 and 1991-92 through present); general manager, St. Louis Blues, Buffalo Sabres (1969-70, 1970-71 and 1979-80 through 1986-87)
Brown, George V.	1961		U.S. hockey pioneer; organizer, Boston Athletic Association hockey team (1910); general manager, Boston Arena and Boston Garden (1934-37)
Brown, Walter A.	1962		Co-owner and president, Boston Bruins (1951-64); general manager, Boston Gardens
Buckland, Frank	1975		Amateur hockey coach and manager; president and treasurer, Ontario Hockey Association
Bush, Walter L.	2000		President, Minnesota North Stars (1967-1978); president, USA Hockey; vice president, International Ice Hockey Federation
Butterfield, Jack	1980		President, American Hockey League
Calder, Frank	1947		First president, National Hockey League (1917-43)
Campbell, Angus	1964		First president, Northern Ontario Hockey Association (1919); executive, Ontario Hockey Association
Campbell, Clarence	1966		Referee (1929-40); president, National Hockey League (1946-77)
Cattarinich, Joseph	1977		General manager, Montreal Canadiens (1909-10); co-owner, Montreal Canadiens (1921-35)
Dandurand, Leo	1963	1	Co-owner, Montreal Canadiens (1921-35); coach, Montreal Canadiens (1920-21 through 1924-25 and 1934-35); general manager, Montreal Canadiens (1920-21 through 1934-35)

Builder	Election year	Stanley Cup wins‡	Designation for induction
Dilio, Frank	1964		Secretary and president, Junior Amateur Hockey Association; registrar and secretary, Quebec Amateur Hockey League (1943-62)
Dudley, George	1958		President, Canadian Amateur Hockey Association (1940-42); treasurer, Ontario Hockey Association; president, International Ice Hockey Federation
Dunn, Jimmy	1968		President, Manitoba Amateur Hockey Association (1945-51); president, Canadian Amateur Hockey Association
Francis, Emile	1982	0	General manager, New York Rangers,St. Louis Blues, Hartford Whalers (1964-65 through 1988-89); coach, New York Rangers, St. Louis Blues (1965-66 through 1974-75, 1976-77, 1981-82 and 1982-83); president, Hartford Whalers (1983-1993)
Gibson, Jack	1976		Organizer, International League (1903-07), world's first professional hockey league
Gorman, Tommy	1963	2	Co-founder, National Hockey League (1917); coach, Ottawa Senators, New York Americans, Chicago Blackhawks, Montreal Maroons (1917-1938); general manager, Montreal Canadiens (1941-42 through 1945-46)
Griffiths, Frank	1993		Chairman, Vancouver Canucks (1974 through 1994)
Hanley, Bill	1986		Secretary-manager, Ontario Hockey Association
Hay, Charles	1974		Coordinator, 1972 series between Canada and Soviet Union; president, Hockey Canada
Hendy, Jim	1968		President, United States Hockey League; general manager, Cleveland Barons (AHL); publisher, Hockey Guide (1933-51)
Hewitt, Foster	1965		Hockey broadcaster
Hewitt, William	1947		Sports editor, Toronto Star; secretary, Ontario Hockey Association (1903-61); registrar and treasurer, Canadian Amateur Hockey Association
Hume, Fred	1962		Co-developer, Western Hockey League, New Westminster Royals
Imlach, Punch	1984	4	Coach, Toronto Maple Leafs, Buffalo Sabres (1958-59 through 1968-69, 1970-71, 1971-72 and 1979-80); general manager, Toronto Maple Leafs, Buffalo Sabres (1958-59 through 1968-69, 1970-71 through 1977-78 and 1979-80 through 1981-82)
Ivan, Tommy	1974	3	Coach, Detroit Red Wings, Chicago Blackhawks (1947-48 through 1953-54, 1956-57 and 1957-58); general manager, Chicago Blackhawks (1954-55 through 1976-77)
Jennings, Bill	1975		President, New York Rangers
Johnson, Bob	1992	1	Coach, Calgary Flames, Pittsburgh Penguins (1982-83 through 1986-87, 1990-91 and 1991-92)
Juckes, Gordon	1979		President, Saskatchewan Amateur Hockey Association; director, Canadian Amateur Hockey Association (1960-78)
Kilpatrick,General J.R.	1960		President, New York Rangers, Madison Square Garden; director, NHL Players' Pension Society; NHL Governor
Knox III, Seymour	1993		Chairman and president, Buffalo Sabres (1970-71 through 1995-96)
Leader, Al	1969		President, Western Hockey League (1944-69)
LeBel, Bob	1970		Founder and president, Interprovincial Senior League (1944-47); president, Quebec Amateur Hockey League, Canadian Amateur Hockey Association, International Ice Hockey Federation (1955-63)
Lockhart, Tommy	1965		Organizer and president, Eastern Amateur Hockey League, Amateur Hockey Association of the United States; business manager, New York Rangers
Loicq, Paul	1961		President and referee, International Ice Hockey Federation (1922-47)
Mariucci, John	1985		Minnesota hockey pioneer; coach, 1956 U.S. Olympic Team
Mathers, Frank	1992		Coach, president and general manager, Hershey Bears (AHL)
McLaughlin, Major Frederic	1963		Owner and first president, Chicago Blackhawks; general manager, Chicago Blackhawks (1926-27 through 1941-42)
Milford, Jake	1984		Coach, New York Rangers organization; general manager, Los Angeles Kings, Vancouver Canucks (1973-74 through 1981-82)
Molson, Senator Hartland De Montarville	1973		President and chairman, Montreal Canadiens (1957-68)
Morrison, Scotty	1999		Referee-in-chief; chairman, Hall of Fame
Murray, Monsignor Athol	1998		Founded hockey programs in Saskatchewan; founded Notre Dame College in Wilcox
Nelson, Francis	1947		Sports editor, Toronto Globe; vice president, Ontario Hockey Association (1903-05); Governor, Amateur Athletic Union of Canada
Norris, Bruce	1969		Owner, Detroit Red Wings, Olympic Stadium (1955-82)
Norris, James Sr.	1958		Co-owner, Detroit Red Wings (1933-43)
Norris, James Dougan	1962		Co-owner, Detroit Red Wings (1933-43), Chicago Blackhawks (1946-66)
Northey, William	1947		President, Montreal Amateur Athletic Association; managing director, Montreal Forum; first trustee, Allan Cup (1908)
O'Brien, J. Ambrose	1962		Organizer, National Hockey Association (1909); co-founder, Montreal Canadiens
O'Neil, Brian	1994		Director of administration, NHL (1966); executive director, NHL (1971); executive vice-president, NHL (1977)
Page, Fred	1993		President, Canadian Amateur Hockey Association (1966-68); chairman of the board, British Columbia Junior Hockey League (1983 through present)
Patrick, Frank	1958		Co-organizer and president, Pacific Coast Hockey Association (1911); owner, manager, player/coach, Vancouver Millionaires (PCHA); managing director, National Hockey League; coach, Boston Bruins (1934-35 and 1935-36); manager, Montreal Canadiens

Builder	Election year	Stanley Cup wins‡	Designation for induction
Pickard, Allan	1958		President, Saskatchewan Amateur Hockey Association, Saskatchewan Senior League, Western Canada Senior League;governor, Saskatchewan Junior League, Western Canada Junior League; president, Canadian Amateur Hockey Association (1947-50)
Pilous, Rudy	1985	1	Coach, Chicago Blackhawks, Winnipeg Jets (1957-58 through 1962-63 and 1974-75); manager, Winnipeg Jets (WHA); scout, Detroit Red Wings, Los Angeles Kings
Poile, Bud	1990		General manager, Philadelphia Flyers, Vancouver Canucks (1967-68 through 1972-73); vice president, World Hockey Association; commissioner, Central Hockey League, International Hockey League
Pollock, Sam	1978		Director of personnel, Montreal Canadiens (1950-64); general manager, Montreal Canadiens (1964-65 through 1977-78)
Raymond, Sen. Donat	1958		President, Canadian Arena Company (Montreal Maroons, Montreal Canadiens) (1924-25 through 1955); chairman, Canadian Arena Company (1955-63)
Robertson, John Ross	1947		President, Ontario Hockey Association (1901-05)
Robinson, Claude	1947		First secretary, Canadian Amateur Hockey Association (1914); manager, 1932 Canadian Olympic Team
Ross, Philip	1976		Trustee, Stanley Cup (1893-1949)
Sabetzki, Gunther	1995		President, International Ice Hockey Federation (1975-1994)
Sather, Glen	1997	4	Coach, Edmonton Oilers (1976-89 and 1993-94); general manager, Edmonton Oilers (1979 to present)
Selke, Frank	1960		Assistant general manager, Toronto Maple Leafs; general manager, Montreal Canadiens (1946-47 through 1963-64)
Sinden, Harry	1983	1	Coach, Boston Bruins (1966-67 through 1969-70, 1979-80 and 1984-85); coach, 1972 Team Canada; general manager, Boston Bruins (1972-73 through present)
Smith, Frank	1962		Co-founder and secretary, Beaches Hockey League (later Metropolitan Toronto Hockey League (1911-62)
Smythe, Conn	1958	0	President, Toronto Maple Leafs, Maple Leaf Gardens, general manager, Toronto Maple Leafs (1927-28 through 1956-57); coach, Toronto Maple Leafs (1926-27 through 1930-31)
Snider, Ed	1988		Owner, Philadelphia Flyers (1967-68 through present)
Stanley of Preston, Lord	1945		Donator, Stanley Cup (1893)
Sutherland, Capt. James	1947		President, Ontario Hockey Association (1915-17); president, Canadian Amateur Hockey Association (1919-21)
Tarasov, Anatoli	1974		Coach, Soviet National Team
Torrey, Bill	1995		Executive vice president, California Seals; general manager, New York Islanders; president, Florida Panthers (1967-present)
Turner, Lloyd	1958		Co-organizer, Western Canadian Hockey League (1918); organizer, Calgary Tigers
Tutt, Thayer	1978		President, International Ice Hockey Federation (1966-69), Amateur Hockey Association of the United States
Voss, Carl	1974		President, U.S. Hockey League; first NHL referee-in-chief
Waghorne, Fred	1961		Pioneer and hockey official, Toronto Hockey League
Wirtz, Arthur	1971		Co-owner, Detroit Red Wings, Olympia Stadium, Chicago Stadium, St. Louis Arena, Madison Square Garden, Chicago Blackhawks
Wirtz, Bill	1976		President, Chicago Blackhawks (1966 through present); chairman, NHL Board of Governors
Ziegler, John	1987		President, National Hockey League (1977-92)

‡Stanley Cup wins column refers to wins as a player in the players section and as a coach in the builders section.

REFEREES/LINESMEN

Referee/linesman	Election year	First season	Last season	Position
Armstrong, Neil	1991	1957	1977	Linesman and referee
Ashley, John	1981	1959	1972	Referee
Chadwick, Bill	1964	1940	1955	Linesman and referee
D'Amico, John	1993	1964-65	1987-88	Linesman
Elliott, Chaucer	1961	1903	1913	Referee (OHA)
Hayes, George	1988	1946-47	1964-65	Linesman
Hewitson, Bobby	1963	1924	1934	Referee
Ion, Mickey	1961	1913	1943	Referee (PCHL/NHL)
Pavelich, Marty	1987	1956-57	1978-79	Linesman
Rodden, Mike	1962			Referee
Smeaton, Cooper	1961			Referee (NHA/NHL); referee-in-chief (NHL) (1931-37); trustee, Stanley Cup (1946-78)
Storey, Red	1967	1951	1959	Referee
Udvari, Frank	1973	1951-52	1965-66	Referee; supervisor of NHL officials
Van Hellemond, Andy	1999	1972-73	1995-96	Referee

MILESTONES

(Players and coaches active in the NHL in the 1999-2000 season are in boldface)

CAREER

FORWARDS/DEFENSEMEN

20 SEASONS

Rk. Player	No.
1. Gordie Howe	26
2. Alex Delvecchio	24
Tim Horton	24
4. John Bucyk	23
5. Stan Mikita	22
Doug Mohns	22
Dean Prentice	22
8. George Armstrong	21
Ray Bourque	**21**
Harry Howell	21
Mark Messier	**21**
Eric Nesterenko	21
Marcel Pronovost	21
Jean Ratelle	21
Allan Stanley	21
Ron Stewart	21
17. Jean Beliveau	20
Paul Coffey	**20**
Bill Gadsby	20
Wayne Gretzky	20
Red Kelly	20
Larry Murphy	**20**
Henri Richard	20
Larry Robinson	20
Norm Ullman	20

Total number of players: (25)

1,200 GAMES

Rk. Player	No.
1. Gordie Howe	1,767
2. Larry Murphy	**1,558**
3. Alex Delvecchio	1,549
4. John Bucyk	1,540
5. Ray Bourque	**1,532**
6. Wayne Gretzky	1,487
7. Mark Messier	**1,479**
8. Tim Horton	1,446
9. Mike Gartner	1,432
10. Harry Howell	1,411
11. Norm Ullman	1,410
12. Ron Francis	**1,407**
Dale Hunter	1,407
14. Stan Mikita	1,394
15. Paul Coffey	**1,391**
16. Doug Mohns	1,390
17. Larry Robinson	1,384
18. Dean Prentice	1,378
19. Scott Stevens	**1,353**
Ron Stewart	1,353
21. Marcel Dionne	1,348
22. Guy Carbonneau	**1,318**
23. Red Kelly	1,316
24. Dave Keon	1,296
25. Pat Verbeek	**1,293**
26. Phil Housley	**1,288**
27. Dave Andreychuk	**1,287**
28. Phil Esposito	1,282
29. Jean Ratelle	1,281
30. Bryan Trottier	1,279
31. Doug Gilmour	**1,271**
32. Craig Ludwig	1,256

Rk. Player	No.
Henri Richard	1,256
Steve Yzerman	**1,256**
35. Kevin Lowe	1,254
36. Jari Kurri	1,251
37. Bill Gadsby	1,248
38. Allan Stanley	1,244
39. Dino Ciccarelli	1,232
40. Eddie Westfall	1,227
41. Brad McCrimmon	1,222
42. Eric Nesterenko	1,219
43. Marcel Pronovost	1,206
44. Al MacInnis	**1,203**

Total number of players: (44)

500 GOALS

Rk. Player	No.
1. Wayne Gretzky	894
2. Gordie Howe	801
3. Marcel Dionne	731
4. Phil Esposito	717
5. Mike Gartner	708
6. Mark Messier	**627**
Steve Yzerman	**627**
8. Mario Lemieux	613
9. Bobby Hull	610
Brett Hull	**610**
11. Dino Ciccarelli	608
12. Jari Kurri	601
13. Mike Bossy	573
14. Guy Lafleur	560
15. John Bucyk	556
16. Luc Robitaille	**553**
17. Dave Andreychuk	**552**
18. Michel Goulet	548
19. Maurice Richard	544
20. Stan Mikita	541
21. Frank Mahovlich	533
22. Bryan Trottier	524
23. Dale Hawerchuk	518
24. Gilbert Perreault	512
25. Jean Beliveau	507
26. Joe Mullen	502
27. Lanny McDonald	500
Pat Verbeek	**500**

Total number of players: (28)

700 ASSISTS

Rk. Player	No.
1. Wayne Gretzky	1,963
2. Paul Coffey	**1,131**
3. Ray Bourque	**1,117**
4. Ron Francis	**1,087**
Mark Messier	**1,087**
6. Gordie Howe	1,049
7. Marcel Dionne	1,040
8. Steve Yzerman	**935**
9. Stan Mikita	926
10. Larry Murphy	**910**
11. Bryan Trottier	901
12. Adam Oates	**894**
13. Dale Hawerchuk	891
14. Doug Gilmour	**883**
15. Mario Lemieux	881
16. Phil Esposito	873

Rk. Player	No.
17. Denis Savard	865
18. Bobby Clarke	852
19. Alex Delvecchio	825
20. Phil Housley	**817**
21. Gilbert Perreault	814
22. John Bucyk	813
23. Al MacInnis	**803**
24. Jari Kurri	797
25. Guy Lafleur	793
26. Peter Stastny	789
27. Jean Ratelle	776
28. Bernie Federko	761
29. Larry Robinson	750
30. Denis Potvin	742
31. Norm Ullman	739
32. Bernie Nicholls	734
33. Jean Beliveau	712

Total number of players: (33)

1,000 POINTS

Rk. Player	No.
1. Wayne Gretzky	2,857
2. Gordie Howe	1,850
3. Marcel Dionne	1,771
4. Mark Messier	1,714
5. Phil Esposito	1,590
6. Steve Yzerman	**1,562**
7. Ron Francis	**1,559**
8. Paul Coffey	**1,527**
9. Ray Bourque	**1,520**
10. Mario Lemieux	1,494
11. Stan Mikita	1,467
12. Bryan Trottier	1,425
13. Dale Hawerchuk	1,409
14. Jari Kurri	1,398
15. John Bucyk	1,369
16. Guy Lafleur	1,353
17. Denis Savard	1,338
18. Mike Gartner	1,335
19. Gilbert Perreault	1,326
20. Doug Gilmour	**1,305**
21. Alex Delvecchio	1,281
22. Jean Ratelle	1,267
23. Peter Stastny	1,239
24. Norm Ullman	1,229
25. Jean Beliveau	1,219
26. Bobby Clarke	1,210
27. Bernie Nicholls	1,209
28. Dino Ciccarelli	1,200
29. Adam Oates	**1,197**
30. Larry Murphy	**1,195**
31. Dave Andreychuk	**1,176**
32. Bobby Hull	1,170
33. Michel Goulet	1,152
34. Luc Robitaille	**1,150**
35. Bernie Federko	1,130
Phil Housley	**1,130**
37. Mike Bossy	1,126
38. Darryl Sittler	1,121
39. Brett Hull	**1,104**
Al MacInnis	**1,104**
41. Frank Mahovlich	1,103
42. Glenn Anderson	1,099
43. Dave Taylor	1,069
44. Joe Mullen	1,063

Rk. Player	No.
Pierre Turgeon	1,063
46. Joe Sakic	1,060
47. Denis Potvin	1,052
48. Henri Richard	1,046
49. Bobby Smith	1,036
50. Brian Bellows	1,022
51. Rod Gilbert	1,021
52. Dale Hunter	1,020
53. Pat LaFontaine	1,013
Pat Verbeek	1,013
55. Steve Larmer	1,012
56. Lanny McDonald	1,006
57. Brian Propp	1,004

Total number of players: (57)

2,000 PENALTY MINUTES

Rk. Player	No.
1. Dave Williams	3,966
2. Dale Hunter	3,565
3. Marty McSorley	3,381
4. Tim Hunter	3,146
5. Chris Nilan	3,043
6. Bob Probert	3,021
7. Rick Tocchet	2,863
8. Craig Berube	2,813
9. Pat Verbeek	2,760
10. Rob Ray	2,687
11. Dave Manson	2,666
12. Tie Domi	2,656
13. Scott Stevens	2,607
14. Willie Plett	2,572
15. Joey Kocur	2,519
16. Basil McRae	2,457
17. Ulf Samuelsson	2,453
18. Gino Odjick	2,391
19. Chris Chelios	2,385
20. Jay Wells	2,359
21. Ken Daneyko	2,339
22. Garth Butcher	2,302
23. Shane Churla	2,301
24. Dave Schultz	2,294
25. Laurie Boschman	2,265
26. Ken Baumgartner	2,244
27. Rob Ramage	2,226
28. Bryan Watson	2,212
29. Steve Smith	2,122
30. Terry O'Reilly	2,095
31. Al Secord	2,093
32. Gary Roberts	2,079
33. Ronnie Stern	2,077
34. Mick Vukota	2,071
35. Gord Donnelly	2,069
36. Mike Foligno	2,049
37. Phil Russell	2,038
38. Kevin Dineen	2,029
39. Kris King	2,022
40. Kelly Chase	2,017
41. Harold Snepsts	2,009

Total number of players: (41)

GOALTENDERS

15 SEASONS

Rk. Goaltender	No.
1. Terry Sawchuk	21
Gump Worsley	21
3. Grant Fuhr	19
4. Glenn Hall	18
Gilles Meloche	18
Andy Moog	18
Jacques Plante	18
Billy Smith	18

Rk. Goaltender	No.
John Vanbiesbrouck	18
10. Tom Barrasso	17
Don Beaupre	17
Mike Vernon	17
Ken Wregget	17
14. Tony Esposito	16
Eddie Johnston	16
Harry Lumley	16
Patrick Roy	16
Rogie Vachon	16
19. Johnny Bower	15
Kelly Hrudey	15
Reggie Lemelin	15
Cesare Maniago	15
Kirk McLean	15
Bill Ranford	15

Total number of goaltenders: (24)

600 GAMES

Rk. Goaltender	No.
1. Terry Sawchuk	971
2. Glenn Hall	906
3. Tony Esposito	886
4. Grant Fuhr	868
5. Gump Worsley	862
6. Patrick Roy	841
7. Jacques Plante	837
8. John Vanbiesbrouck	829
9. Harry Lumley	804
10. Rogie Vachon	795
11. Gilles Meloche	788
12. Tom Barrasso	733
13. Mike Vernon	722
14. Andy Moog	713
15. Billy Smith	680
16. Kelly Hrudey	677
17. Don Beaupre	667
18. Mike Liut	663
19. Dan Bouchard	655
20. Bill Ranford	647
21. Turk Broda	629
22. Ed Belfour	612
23. Ed Giacomin	610
24. Ron Hextall	608
Bernie Parent	608
26. Greg Millen	604

Total number of goaltenders: (26)

30,000 MINUTES

Rk. Goaltender	No.
1. Terry Sawchuk	57,205
2. Glenn Hall	53,484
3. Tony Esposito	52,585
4. Gump Worsley	50,232
5. Jacques Plante	49,553
6. Patrick Roy	49,108
7. Grant Fuhr	48,945
8. Harry Lumley	48,107
9. John Vanbiesbrouck	47,545
10. Rogie Vachon	46,298
11. Gilles Meloche	45,401
12. Tom Barrasso	41,760
13. Mike Vernon	41,378
14. Andy Moog	40,151
15. Billy Smith	38,431
16. Turk Broda	38,173
17. Mike Liut	38,155
18. Kelly Hrudey	38,084
19. Dan Bouchard	37,919
20. Don Beaupre	37,396
21. Bill Ranford	35,937

Rk. Goaltender	No.
22. Ed Giacomin	35,693
23. Greg Millen	35,377
24. Ed Belfour	35,173
25. Bernie Parent	35,136
26. Ron Hextall	34,750
27. Eddie Johnston	34,209
28. Tiny Thompson	34,174
29. Curtis Joseph	33,957
30. Kirk McLean	33,870
31. Cesare Maniago	32,570
32. Glenn Resch	32,279
33. Johnny Bower	32,077
34. Ken Wregget	31,663
35. Mike Richter	31,659
36. Frank Brimsek	31,210
37. John Roach	30,423
38. Roy Worters	30,175

Total number of goaltenders: (38)

2.50 OR UNDER GOALS-AGAINST AVERAGE

(Goaltenders with 10,000 or more minutes)

Rk. Goaltender	Min.	GAA
1. Alex Connell	26,030	1.91
George Hainsworth	29,415	1.91
3. Chuck Gardiner	19,687	2.02
4. Lorne Chabot	25,309	2.04
5. Tiny Thompson	34,174	2.08
6. Dave Kerr	26,519	2.17
7. Martin Brodeur	25,939	2.20
8. Ken Dryden	23,352	2.24
9. Dominik Hasek	25,969	2.26
10. Roy Worters	30,175	2.27
11. Clint Benedict	22,321	2.32
Norman Smith	12,297	2.32
13. Bill Durnan	22,945	2.36
Gerry McNeil	16,535	2.36
15. Jacques Plante	49,553	2.38
16. John Roach	30,423	2.46
17. Ed Belfour	35,173	2.47

Total number of goaltenders: (17)

200 GAMES WON

Rk. Goaltender	No.
1. Terry Sawchuk	447
2. Patrick Roy	444
3. Jacques Plante	434
4. Tony Esposito	423
5. Glenn Hall	407
6. Grant Fuhr	403
7. Andy Moog	372
8. Mike Vernon	371
9. John Vanbiesbrouck	358
10. Rogie Vachon	355
11. Tom Barrasso	353
12. Gump Worsley	335
13. Harry Lumley	332
14. Ed Belfour	308
15. Billy Smith	305
16. Turk Broda	302
17. Ron Hextall	296
18. Mike Liut	293
19. Ed Giacomin	289
20. Dan Bouchard	286
21. Curtis Joseph	284
Tiny Thompson	284
23. Kelly Hrudey	271
24. Gilles Meloche	270
Bernie Parent	270
26. Don Beaupre	268
27. Ken Dryden	258

<table>
<tr><td colspan="6">

Rk.	Goaltender	No.
28.	**Frank Brimsek**	252
	Mike Richter	**252**
30.	Johnny Bower	251
31.	George Hainsworth	247
32.	Pete Peeters	246
33.	**Martin Brodeur**	**244**
34.	**Bill Ranford**	**240**
35.	**Kirk McLean**	**237**
36.	Eddie Johnston	236
	Reggie Lemelin	236
38.	Glenn Resch	231
39.	Gerry Cheevers	230
40.	**Ken Wregget**	**225**
41.	John Roach	218
42.	Greg Millen	215
43.	**Dominik Hasek**	**210**
44.	Bill Durnan	208
	Don Edwards	208
46.	Lorne Chabot	206
	Roger Crozier	206
48.	Rick Wamsley	204
49.	Dave Kerr	203

</td></tr>
</table>

Total number of goaltenders: (49)

200 GAMES LOST

Rk.	Goaltender	No.
1.	Gump Worsley	353
2.	Gilles Meloche	351
3.	Terry Sawchuk	337
4.	Glenn Hall	327
5.	Harry Lumley	324
6.	**John Vanbiesbrouck**	**318**
7.	Tony Esposito	307
8.	**Grant Fuhr**	**295**
9.	Rogie Vachon	291
10.	Greg Millen	284
11.	**Bill Ranford**	**279**
12.	Don Beaupre	277
13.	Mike Liut	271
14.	Kelly Hrudey	265
15.	**Patrick Roy**	**264**
16.	Cesare Maniago	261
17.	**Tom Barrasso**	**259**
18.	Eddie Johnston	256
19.	**Kirk McLean**	**252**
20.	**Ken Wregget**	**248**
21.	Jacques Plante	246
22.	**Mike Vernon**	**241**
23.	Gary Smith	237
24.	Billy Smith	233
	Roy Worters	233
26.	Dan Bouchard	232
27.	Jim Rutherford	227
28.	Turk Broda	224
	Glenn Resch	224
30.	**Curtis Joseph**	**216**
31.	Ron Hextall	214
32.	Andy Moog	209
	Chuck Rayner	209
34.	Ed Giacomin	206
35.	Al Rollins	205
36.	John Roach	204
37.	Denis Herron	203
	Ron Low	203
39.	Glen Hanlon	202

Total number of goaltenders: (39)

75 GAMES TIED

Rk.	Goaltender	No.
1.	Terry Sawchuk	188
2.	Glenn Hall	165

Rk.	Goaltender	No.
3.	Tony Esposito	151
4.	Gump Worsley	150
5.	Harry Lumley	143
6.	Jacques Plante	137
7.	Gilles Meloche	131
8.	Bernie Parent	121
9.	Rogie Vachon	115
10.	**Grant Fuhr**	**114**
	John Vanbiesbrouck	**114**
12.	Dan Bouchard	113
13.	Billy Smith	105
14.	**Patrick Roy**	**103**
15.	Turk Broda	101
16.	Ed Giacomin	97
17.	Cesare Maniago	96
18.	Johnny Bower	90
19.	Greg Millen	89
20.	Kelly Hrudey	88
	Andy Moog	88
22.	Eddie Johnston	87
23.	**Mike Vernon**	**86**
24.	Al Rollins	84
25.	**Ed Belfour**	**82**
	Glenn Resch	82
27.	**Tom Barrasso**	**81**
28.	Frank Brimsek	80
29.	Don Edwards	77
	Chuck Rayner	77
31.	Denis Herron	76
	Phil Myre	76
	Bill Ranford	**76**
34.	Don Beaupre	75
	Dave Kerr	75
	Tiny Thompson	75

Total number of goaltenders: (36)

25 SHUTOUTS

Rk.	Goaltender	No.
1.	Terry Sawchuk	103
2.	George Hainsworth	94
3.	Glenn Hall	84
4.	Jacques Plante	82
5.	Tiny Thompson	81
	Alex Connell	81
7.	Tony Esposito	76
8.	Lorne Chabot	73
9.	Harry Lumley	71
10.	Roy Worters	66
11.	Turk Broda	62
12.	John Roach	58
13.	Clint Benedict	57
14.	Bernie Parent	55
15.	Ed Giacomin	54
16.	Dave Kerr	51
	Rogie Vachon	51
18.	**Ed Belfour**	**49**
19.	**Patrick Roy**	**48**
20.	Ken Dryden	46
21.	**Dominik Hasek**	**45**
22.	Gump Worsley	43
23.	**Martin Brodeur**	**42**
	Charlie Gardiner	42
25.	Frank Brimsek	40
26.	**John Vanbiesbrouck**	**38**
27.	Johnny Bower	37
28.	**Tom Barrasso**	**35**
29.	Bill Durnan	34
30.	Eddie Johnston	32
31.	Roger Crozier	30
	Cesare Maniago	30
33.	Jim Henry	28

Rk.	Goaltender	No.
	Mike Karakas	28
	Gerry McNeil	28
	Andy Moog	28
	Al Rollins	28
38.	Dan Bouchard	27
39.	Gerry Cheevers	26
	Curtis Joseph	**26**
	Glenn Resch	26
	Gary Smith	26
43.	**Grant Fuhr**	**25**
	Mike Liut	25
	Chuck Rayner	25

Total number of goaltenders: (45)

COACHES

500 GAMES

Rk.	Coach	No.
1.	**Scotty Bowman**	**1,977**
2.	Al Arbour	1,606
3.	Dick Irvin	1,437
4.	Billy Reay	1,102
5.	Jacques Demers	1,006
6.	Mike Keenan	995
7.	Jack Adams	982
8.	Bryan Murray	975
9.	**Roger Neilson**	**973**
10.	Sid Abel	963
11.	Toe Blake	914
12.	**Pat Quinn**	**908**
13.	Punch Imlach	879
14.	Bob Berry	860
15.	**Pat Burns**	**847**
16.	Glen Sather	842
17.	Michel Bergeron	792
18.	**Brian Sutter**	**782**
19.	Emile Francis	778
20.	Bob Pulford	771
21.	Milt Schmidt	769
22.	Red Kelly	742
23.	Fred Shero	734
24.	Art Ross	728
25.	**Terry Murray**	**701**
26.	**John Muckler**	**648**
27.	Terry Crisp	631
28.	Jack Evans	614
29.	Tommy Ivan	610
30.	Lester Patrick	604
31.	Eddie Johnston	596
32.	Jim Schoenfeld	580
33.	Hap Day	546
34.	Frank Boucher	525
35.	Johnny Wilson	517
36.	Bob McCammon	511
37.	**Herb Brooks**	**506**

Total number of coaches: (37)

250 GAMES WON

Rk.	Coach	No.
1.	**Scotty Bowman**	**1,148**
2.	Al Arbour	781
3.	Dick Irvin	690
4.	Billy Reay	542
5.	Mike Keenan	506
6.	Toe Blake	500
7.	Bryan Murray	484
8.	Glen Sather	464
9.	**Pat Quinn**	**447**
10.	**Roger Neilson**	**443**
11.	Jack Adams	423

Rk. Coach	No.
12. Pat Burns	409
Jacques Demers	409
14. Punch Imlach	395
15. Emile Francis	393
16. Fred Shero	390
17. Bob Berry	384
18. Sid Abel	382
19. Art Ross	361
20. Brian Sutter	360
21. Terry Murray	354
22. Michel Bergeron	338
23. Bob Pulford	336
24. Tommy Ivan	302
25. Terry Crisp	286
26. Lester Patrick	281
27. Red Kelly	278
28. John Muckler	276
29. Eddie Johnston	266
30. Hap Day	259
31. Jim Schoenfeld	256
32. Don Cherry	250
Milt Schmidt	250

Total number of coaches: (33)

250 GAMES LOST

Rk. Coach	No.
1. Al Arbour	577
2. Scotty Bowman	539
3. Dick Irvin	521
4. Jacques Demers	467
5. Sid Abel	426
6. Jack Adams	397
7. Milt Schmidt	393
8. Billy Reay	385
9. Mike Keenan	372
Roger Neilson	372
11. Bryan Murray	368
12. Bob Berry	355
13. Michel Bergeron	350
14. Pat Quinn	345
15. Punch Imlach	336
16. Red Kelly	330
17. Brian Sutter	319
18. Pat Burns	310
19. Bob Pulford	305
20. Jack Evans	303
21. John Muckler	288
22. Art Ross	277

Rk. Coach	No.
23. Emile Francis	273
24. Glen Sather	268
25. Terry Crisp	267
26. Terry Murray	265
27. Frank Boucher	263
Tom McVie	263
29. Toe Blake	255
30. Tom Watt	252
31. Eddie Johnston	251

Total number of coaches: (31)

100 GAMES TIED

Rk. Coach	No.
1. Scotty Bowman	295
2. Al Arbour	248
3. Dick Irvin	226
4. Billy Reay	175
5. Jack Adams	162
6. Toe Blake	159
7. Roger Neilson	158
8. Sid Abel	155
9. Punch Imlach	148
10. Red Kelly	134
11. Jacques Demers	130
Bob Pulford	130
13. Pat Burns	128
14. Milt Schmidt	126
15. Bryan Murray	123
16. Bob Berry	121
17. Fred Shero	119
18. Mike Keenan	117
19. Pat Quinn	116
20. Emile Francis	112
Tommy Ivan	112
22. Glen Sather	110
23. Lester Patrick	107
24. Michel Bergeron	104
25. Brian Sutter	103

Total number of coaches: (25)

.525 WINNING PERCENTAGE
(Coaches with 300 or more games)

Rk. Coach	Games	Pct.
1. Scotty Bowman	1,982	.654
2. Claude Ruel	305	.648
3. Toe Blake	914	.634
4. Floyd Smith	309	.626
5. Ken Hitchcock	371	.625

Rk. Coach	Games	Pct.
6. Glen Sather	842	.616
7. Fred Shero	734	.612
8. Gerry Cheevers	376	.604
9. Don Cherry	480	.601
10. Tommy Ivan	610	.587
11. Jacques Lemaire	393	.580
12. Emile Francis	778	.577
13. Marc Crawford	413	.576
14. Billy Reay	1,102	.571
15. Terry Murray	701	.568
16. Mike Keenan	995	.567
17. Al Arbour	1,606	.564
18. Pat Burns	847	.562
19. Dick Irvin	1,437	.559
Bryan Murray	975	.559
21. Art Ross	728	.558
22. Lester Patrick	604	.554
23. Pat Quinn	908	.558
24. Hap Day	546	.549
25. Fred Creighton	421	.548
Bob Johnson	480	.548
27. Harry Sinden	330	.545
28. Roger Neilson	973	.536
29. Punch Imlach	879	.534
30. Darryl Sutter	462	.531
31. Brian Sutter	782	.529

Total number of coaches: (31)

STANLEY CUP CHAMPIONSHIPS
(Includes Stanley Cup championships as NHL coach only)

Rk. Coach	No.
1. Toe Blake	8
Scotty Bowman	8
3. Hap Day	5
4. Al Arbour	4
Dick Irvin	4
Punch Imlach	4
Glen Sather	4
8. Jack Adams	3
Pete Green	3
Tommy Ivan	3
11. Tommy Gorman	2
Cecil Hart	2
Lester Patrick	2
Fred Shero	2

Total number of coaches: (14)

SEASON

FORWARDS/DEFENSEMEN

60 GOALS

Season	Player, Team	No.
1981-82	Wayne Gretzky, Edm.	92
1983-84	Wayne Gretzky, Edm.	87
1990-91	Brett Hull, St.L.	86
1988-89	Mario Lemieux, Pit.	85
1971-72	Phil Esposito, Bos.	76
1992-93	Alexander Mogilny, Buf.	76
1992-93	Teemu Selanne, Win.	76
1984-85	Wayne Gretzky, Edm.	73
1989-90	Brett Hull, St.L.	72
1982-83	Wayne Gretzky, Edm.	71
1984-85	Jari Kurri, Edm.	71
1991-92	Brett Hull, St.L.	70
1987-88	Mario Lemieux, Pit.	70
1988-89	Bernie Nicholls, L.A.	70

Season	Player, Team	No.
1978-79	Mike Bossy, NYI	69
1992-93	Mario Lemieux, Pit.	69
1995-96	Mario Lemieux, Pit.	69
1980-81	Mike Bossy, NYI	68
1973-74	Phil Esposito, Bos.	68
1985-86	Jari Kurri, Edm.	68
1972-73	Phil Esposito, Bos.	66
1982-83	Lanny McDonald, Cal.	66
1988-89	Steve Yzerman, Det.	65
1981-82	Mike Bossy, NYI	64
1992-93	Luc Robitaille, L.A.	63
1986-87	Wayne Gretzky, Edm.	62
1995-96	Jaromir Jagr, Pit.	62
1989-90	Steve Yzerman, Det.	62
1985-86	Mike Bossy, NYI	61
1974-75	Phil Esposito, Bos.	61
1975-76	Reggie Leach, Phi.	61
1982-83	Mike Bossy, NYI	60

Season	Player, Team	No.
1992-93	Pavel Bure, Van.	60
1993-94	Pavel Bure, Van.	60
1977-78	Guy Lafleur, Mon.	60
1981-82	Dennis Maruk, Was.	60
1976-77	Steve Shutt, Mon.	60

Total number of occurrences: (37)

50-GOAL SEASONS

Rk. Player	No.	Cons.
1. Mike Bossy	9	9
Wayne Gretzky	9	8
3. Guy Lafleur	6	6
Marcel Dionne	6	5
Mario Lemieux	6	3
6. Phil Esposito	5	5
Brett Hull	5	5
Steve Yzerman	5	4
Bobby Hull	5	2

Rk.	Player	No.	Cons.
10.	Michel Goulet	4	4
	Tim Kerr	4	4
	Jari Kurri	4	4
	Pavel Bure	4	2
14.	John LeClair	3	3
	Rick Vaive	3	3
	Cam Neely	3	2
	Teemu Selanne	3	2
	Luc Robitaille	3	1
19.	Dave Andreychuk	2	2
	Rick Martin	2	2
	Dennis Maruk	2	2
	Joe Nieuwendyk	2	2
	Mickey Redmond	2	2
	Jeremy Roenick	2	2
	Brendan Shanahan	2	2
	Charlie Simmer	2	2
	Kevin Stevens	2	2
	Keith Tkachuk	2	2
	Glenn Anderson	2	1
	Peter Bondra	2	1
	Dino Ciccarelli	2	1
	Danny Gare	2	1
	Pat LaFontaine	2	1
	Pierre Larouche	2	1
	Reggie Leach	2	1
	Alexander Mogilny	2	1
	Stephane Richer	2	1
	Blaine Stoughton	2	1
39.	Wayne Babych	1	1
	Bill Barber	1	1
	Brian Bellows	1	1
	John Bucyk	1	1
	Mike Bullard	1	1
	Bob Carpenter	1	1
	Jimmy Carson	1	1
	Guy Chouinard	1	1
	Sergei Fedorov	1	1
	Theoren Fleury	1	1
	Mike Gartner	1	1
	Bernie Geoffrion	1	1
	Danny Grant	1	1
	Adam Graves	1	1
	Vic Hadfield	1	1
	Dale Hawerchuk	1	1
	Ken Hodge	1	1
	Jaromir Jagr	1	1
	Paul Kariya	1	1
	Rick Kehoe	1	1
	Gary Leeman	1	1
	Hakan Loob	1	1
	Rick MacLeish	1	1
	Lanny McDonald	1	1
	Mark Messier	1	1
	Rick Middleton	1	1
	Mike Modano	1	1
	Joe Mullen	1	1
	Bernie Nicholls	1	1
	John Ogrodnick	1	1
	Jean Pronovost	1	1
	Mark Recchi	1	1
	Jacques Richard	1	1
	Maurice Richard	1	1
	Gary Roberts	1	1
	Joe Sakic	1	1
	Al Secord	1	1
	Ray Sheppard	1	1
	Steve Shutt	1	1
	Craig Simpson	1	1
	Bryan Trottier	1	1
	Pierre Turgeon	1	1

Total number of players: (80)

40 GOALS BY ROOKIES

Season	Player, Team	No.
1992-93	Teemu Selanne, Win.	76
1977-78	Mike Bossy, NYI	53
1987-88	Joe Nieuwendyk, Cal.	51
1981-82	Dale Hawerchuk, Win.	45
1986-87	Luc Robitaille, L.A.	45
1971-72	Rick Martin, Buf.	44
1981-82	Barry Pederson, Bos.	44
1982-83	Steve Larmer, Chi.	43
1984-85	Mario Lemieux, Pit.	43
1992-93	Eric Lindros, Phi.	41
1980-81	Darryl Sutter, Chi.	40
1983-84	Sylvain Turgeon, Har.	40
1984-85	Warren Young, Pit.	40

Total number of players: (13)

125 POINTS

Season	Player	No.
1985-86	Wayne Gretzky, Edm.	215
1981-82	Wayne Gretzky, Edm.	212
1984-85	Wayne Gretzky, Edm.	208
1983-84	Wayne Gretzky, Edm.	205
1988-89	Mario Lemieux, Pit.	199
1982-83	Wayne Gretzky, Edm.	196
1986-87	Wayne Gretzky, Edm.	183
1988-89	Wayne Gretzky, L.A.	168
1987-88	Mario Lemieux, Pit.	168
1980-81	Wayne Gretzky, Edm.	164
1990-91	Wayne Gretzky, L.A.	163
1995-96	Mario Lemieux, Pit.	161
1992-93	Mario Lemieux, Pit.	160
1988-89	Steve Yzerman, Det.	155
1970-71	Phil Esposito, Bos.	152
1988-89	Bernie Nicholls, L.A.	150
1987-88	Wayne Gretzky, Edm.	149
1995-96	Jaromir Jagr, Pit.	149
1992-93	Pat LaFontaine, Buf.	148
1981-82	Mike Bossy, NYI	147
1973-74	Phil Esposito, Bos.	145
1989-90	Wayne Gretzky, L.A.	142
1992-93	Adam Oates, Bos.	142
1985-86	Mario Lemieux, Pit.	141
1970-71	Bobby Orr, Bos.	139
1981-82	Peter Stastny, Que.	139
1985-86	Paul Coffey, Edm.	138
1979-80	Wayne Gretzky, Edm.	137
1979-80	Marcel Dionne, L.A.	137
1992-93	Steve Yzerman, Det.	137
1976-77	Guy Lafleur, Mon.	136
1981-82	Dennis Maruk, Was.	136
1980-81	Marcel Dionne, L.A.	135
1984-85	Jari Kurri, Edm.	135
1974-75	Bobby Orr, Bos.	135
1978-79	Bryan Trottier, NYI	134
1971-72	Phil Esposito, Bos.	133
1977-78	Guy Lafleur, Mon.	132
1992-93	Pierre Turgeon, NYI	132
1992-93	Teemu Selanne, Win.	132
1990-91	Brett Hull, St.L.	131
1991-92	Mario Lemieux, Pit.	131
1985-86	Jari Kurri, Edm.	131
1980-81	Kent Nilsson, Cal.	131
1987-88	Denis Savard, Chi.	131
1972-73	Phil Esposito, Bos.	130
1978-79	Marcel Dionne, L.A.	130
1984-85	Dale Hawerchuk, Win.	130
1993-94	Wayne Gretzky, L.A.	130
1989-90	Mark Messier, Edm.	129
1978-79	Guy Lafleur, Mon.	129
1981-82	Bryan Trottier, NYI	129
1974-75	Phil Esposito, Bos.	127
1992-93	Doug Gilmour, Tor.	127
1992-93	Alexander Mogilny, Buf.	127
1989-90	Steve Yzerman, Det.	127
1998-99	Jaromir Jagr, Pit.	127
1968-69	Phil Esposito, Bos.	126
1978-79	Mike Bossy, NYI	126
1983-84	Paul Coffey, Edm.	126
1984-85	Marcel Dionne, L.A.	126
1975-76	Guy Lafleur, Mon.	125
1979-80	Guy Lafleur, Mon.	125

Total number of occurrences: (63)

100-POINT SEASONS

Rk.	Player	No.	Cons.
1.	Wayne Gretzky	15	13
2.	Mario Lemieux	10	6
3.	Marcel Dionne	8	5
4.	Mike Bossy	7	6
	Peter Stastny	7	6
6.	Guy Lafleur	6	6
	Bobby Orr	6	6
	Steve Yzerman	6	6
	Dale Hawerchuk	6	5
	Jari Kurri	6	5
	Bryan Trottier	6	5
	Mark Messier	6	2
13.	Denis Savard	5	2
14.	Brett Hull	4	4
	Paul Coffey	4	3
	Bernie Federko	4	3
	Michel Goulet	4	2
	Adam Oates	4	2
	Luc Robitaille	4	2
	Joe Sakic	4	2
21.	Mike Rogers	3	3
	Glenn Anderson	3	2
	Bobby Clarke	3	2
	Doug Gilmour	3	2
	Bernie Nicholls	3	2
	Mark Recchi	3	2
	Jaromir Jagr	3	1
27.	Pavel Bure	2	2
	Jimmy Carson	2	2
	Pete Mahovlich	2	2
	Barry Pederson	2	2
	Jeremy Roenick	2	2
	Charlie Simmer	2	2
	Kevin Stevens	2	2
	Dave Taylor	2	2
	Dino Ciccarelli	2	1
	Sergei Fedorov	2	1
	Theoren Fleury	2	1
	Ron Francis	3	1
	Pat LaFontaine	2	1
	Rick Middleton	2	1
	Alexander Mogilny	2	1
	Kent Nilsson	2	1
	Gilbert Perreault	2	1
	Jean Ratelle	2	1
	Darryl Sittler	2	1
	Teemu Selanne	2	1
	Pierre Turgeon	2	1

Total number of players: (48)

75 POINTS BY ROOKIES

Season	Player, Team	No.
1992-93	Teemu Selanne, Win.	132
1980-81	Peter Stastny, Que.	109
1981-82	Dale Hawerchuk, Win.	103
1992-93	Joe Juneau, Bos.	102
1984-85	Mario Lemieux, Pit.	100

NHL HISTORY *Milestones*

Season	Player, Team	No.
1981-82	Neal Broten, Min.	98
1975-76	Bryan Trottier, NYI	95
1987-88	**Joe Nieuwendyk, Cal.**	**92**
1981-82	Barry Pederson, Bos.	92
1977-78	Mike Bossy, NYI	91
1982-83	Steve Larmer, Chi.	90
1981-82	Marian Stastny, Que.	89
1983-84	**Steve Yzerman, Det.**	**87**
1989-90	Sergei Makarov, Cal.	86
1980-81	Anton Stastny, Que.	85
1986-87	**Luc Robitaille, L.A.**	**84**
1993-94	**Mikael Renberg, Phi.**	**82**
1986-87	Jimmy Carson, L.A.	79
1990-91	**Sergei Fedorov, Det.**	**79**
1993-94	**Alexei Yashin, Ott.**	**79**
1971-72	Marcel Dionne, L.A.	77
1980-81	**Larry Murphy, L.A.**	**76**
1981-82	Mark Pavelich, NYR	76
1983-84	Dave Poulin, Phi.	76
1992-93	**Eric Lindros, Phi.**	**75**
1980-81	Jari Kurri, Edm.	75
1989-90	**Mike Modano, Min.**	**75**
1979-80	Brian Propp, Phi.	75
1980-81	Denis Savard, Chi.	75

Total number of players: (29)

350 PENALTY MINUTES

Season	Player, Team	No.
1974-75	Dave Schultz, Phi.	472
1981-82	Paul Baxter, Pit.	409
1991-92	Mike Peluso, Chi.	408
1977-78	Dave Schultz, L.A.-Pit.	405
1992-93	**Marty McSorley, L.A.**	**399**
1987-88	**Bob Probert, Det.**	**398**
1987-88	Basil McRae, Min.	378

Season	Player, Team	No.
1985-86	**Joey Kocur, Det.**	**377**
1988-89	Tim Hunter, Cal.	375
1997-98	**Donald Brashear, Van.**	**372**
1996-97	**Gino Odjick, Van.**	**371**
1975-76	Steve Durbano, Pit.-K.C.	370
1992-93	**Gino Odjick, Van.**	**370**
1988-89	Basil McRae, Min.	365
1997-98	**Tie Domi, Tor.**	**365**
1986-87	Tim Hunter, Cal.	361
1984-85	Chris Nilan, Mon.	358
1985-86	Torrie Robertson, Har.	358
1986-87	Tiger Williams, L.A.	358
1986-87	Brian Curran, NYI	356
1991-92	**Rob Ray, Buf.**	**354**
1988-89	**Dave Manson, Chi.**	**352**
1977-78	Tiger Williams, Tor.	351
1989-90	Basil McRae, Min.	351
1988-89	**Marty McSorley, L.A.**	**350**
1990-91	**Rob Ray, Buf.**	**350**

Total number of occurrences: (26)

GOALTENDERS

10 SHUTOUTS

Season	Goaltender, Team	No.
1928-29	George Hainsworth, Mon. C.	22
1925-26	Alex Connell, Ott.	15
1927-28	Alex Connell, Ott.	15
1927-28	Hal Winkler, Bos.	15
1969-70	Tony Esposito, Chi.	15
1926-27	George Hainsworth, Mon. C.	14
1926-27	Clint Benedict, Mon. M.	13
1926-27	Alex Connell, Ott.	13
1927-28	George Hainsworth, Mon. C.	13

Season	Goaltender, Team	No.
1928-29	John Roach, NYR	13
1928-29	Roy Worters, NYA	13
1953-54	Harry Lumley, Tor.	13
1997-98	**Dominik Hasek, Buf.**	**13**
1928-29	Lorne Chabot, Tor.	12
1928-29	Tiny Thompson, Bos.	12
1930-31	Chuck Gardiner, Chi.	12
1951-52	Terry Sawchuk, Det.	12
1953-54	Terry Sawchuk, Det.	12
1954-55	Terry Sawchuk, Det.	12
1955-56	Glenn Hall, Det.	12
1973-74	Bernie Parent, Phi.	12
1974-75	Bernie Parent, Phi.	12
1927-28	Lorne Chabot, NYR	11
1927-28	Harry Holmes, Det.	11
1928-29	Clint Benedict, Mon. M.	11
1928-29	Joe Miller, Pit.	11
1932-33	Tiny Thompson, Bos.	11
1950-51	Terry Sawchuk, Det.	11
1926-27	Lorne Chabot, NYR	10
1927-28	Roy Worters, Pit.	10
1928-29	Clarence Dolson, Det.	10
1932-33	John Roach, Det.	10
1933-34	Chuck Gardiner, Chi.	10
1935-36	Tiny Thompson, Bos.	10
1938-39	Frank Brimsek, Bos.	10
1948-49	Bill Durnan, Mon.	10
1952-53	Harry Lumley, Tor.	10
1952-53	Gerry McNeil, Mon.	10
1973-74	Tony Esposito, Chi.	10
1976-77	Ken Dryden, Mon.	10
1996-97	**Martin Brodeur, N.J.**	**10**
1997-98	**Martin Brodeur, N.J.**	**10**
1998-99	**Byron Dafoe, Bos.**	**10**

Total number of occurrences: (43)

GAME
FORWARDS/DEFENSEMEN

FIVE GOALS

Date	Player	Team	Opponents	Goals
December 19, 1917	Joe Malone	Montreal	at Ottawa	5
December 19, 1917	Harry Hyland	Montreal Wanderers	vs. Toronto	5
January 12, 1918	Joe Malone	Montreal	vs. Toronto	5
February 2, 1918	Joe Malone	Montreal	vs. Toronto	5
January 10, 1920	Newsy Lalonde	Montreal	vs Toronto	6
January 31, 1920	Joe Malone	Quebec Bulldogs	vs. Toronto	7
March 6, 1920	Mickey Roach	Toronto St. Pats	vs. Quebec	5
March 10, 1920	Joe Malone	Quebec Bulldogs	vs. Ottawa	6
January 26, 1921	Corb Denneny	Toronto St. Pats	vs. Hamilton	6
February 16, 1921	Newsy Lalonde	Montreal	vs. Hamilton	5
March 7, 1921	Cy Denneny	Ottawa Senators	vs. Hamilton	6
December 16, 1922	Babe Dye	Toronto St. Pats	vs. Montreal	5
December 5, 1924	Redvers Green	Hamilton Tigers	at Toronto	5
December 22, 1924	Babe Dye	Toronto St. Pats	at Boston	5
January 7, 1925	Harry Broadbent	Montreal Maroons	at Hamilton	5
December 14, 1929	Pit Lepine	Montreal	vs. Ottawa	5
March 18, 1930	Howie Morenz	Montreal	vs. New York Americans	5
January 19, 1932	Charlie Conacher	Toronto	vs. New York Americans	5
February 6, 1943	Ray Getliffe	Montreal	vs. Boston	5
December 28, 1944	Maurice Richard	Montreal	vs. Detroit	5
February 3, 1944	Syd Howe	Detroit	vs. New York Rangers	6
January 8, 1947	Howie Meeker	Toronto	vs. Chicago	5
February 19, 1955	Bernie Geoffrion	Montreal	vs. New York Rangers	5
February 1, 1964	Bobby Rousseau	Montreal	vs. Detroit	5
November 7, 1968	Red Berenson	St. Louis	at Philadelphia	6
February 15, 1975	Yvan Cournoyer	Montreal	vs. Chicago	5
October 12, 1976	Don Murdoch	New York Rangers	at Minnesota	5
November 7, 1976	Darryl Sittler	Toronto	vs. Boston	6

Date	Player	Team	Opponents	Goals
February 2, 1977	Ian Turnbull	Toronto	vs. Detroit	5
December 23, 1978	Bryan Trottier	New York Islanders	vs. New York Rangers	5
January 15, 1979	Tim Young	Minnesota	at New York Rangers	5
January 6, 1981	John Tonelli	New York Islanders	vs. Toronto	5
February 18, 1981	Wayne Gretzky	Edmonton	vs. St. Louis	5
December 30, 1981	Wayne Gretzky	Edmonton	vs. Philadelphia	5
February 3, 1982	Grant Mulvey	Chicago	vs. St. Louis	5
February 13, 1982	Bryan Trottier	New York Islanders	vs. Philadelphia	5
March 2, 1982	Willie Lindstrom	Winnipeg	at Philadelphia	5
February 23, 1983	Mark Pavelich	New York Rangers	vs. Hartford	5
November 19, 1983	Jari Kurri	Edmonton	vs. New Jersey	5
January 8, 1984	Bengt Gustafsson	Washington	at Philadelphia	5
February 3, 1984	Pat Hughes	Edmonton	vs. Calgary	5
December 15, 1984	Wayne Gretzky	Edmonton	at St. Louis	5
February 6, 1986	**Dave Andreychuk**	**Buffalo**	**at Boston**	**5**
December 6, 1987	Wayne Gretzky	Edmonton	vs. Minnesota	5
December 31, 1988	Mario Lemieux	Pittsburgh	vs. New Jersey	5
January 11, 1989	**Joe Nieuwendyk**	**Calgary**	**vs. Winnipeg**	**5**
March 5, 1992	**Mats Sundin**	**Quebec**	**at Hartford**	**5**
April 9, 1993	Mario Lemieux	Pittsburgh	at New York Rangers	5
February 5, 1994	**Peter Bondra**	**Washington**	**vs. Tampa Bay**	**5**
February 17, 1994	**Mike Ricci**	**Quebec**	**vs. San Jose**	**5**
April 1, 1995	**Alexei Zhamnov**	**Winnipeg**	**at Los Angeles**	**5**
March 26, 1996	Mario Lemieux	Pittsburgh	vs. St. Louis	5
December 26, 1996	**Sergei Fedorov**	**Detroit**	**vs. Washington**	**5**

Total number of occurrences: (53)

TEAM BY TEAM

MIGHTY DUCKS OF ANAHEIM

YEAR-BY-YEAR RECORDS

Season	W	L	T	RT	Pts.	Finish	W	L	Highest round	Coach
1993-94	33	46	5	—	71	4th/Pacific	—	—		Ron Wilson
1994-95	16	27	5	—	37	6th/Pacific	—	—		Ron Wilson
1995-96	35	39	8	—	78	4th/Pacific	—	—		Ron Wilson
1996-97	36	33	13	—	85	2nd/Pacific	4	7	Conference semifinals	Ron Wilson
1997-98	26	43	13	—	65	6th/Pacific	—	—		Pierre Page
1998-99	35	34	13	—	83	3rd/Pacific	0	4	Conference quarterfinals	Craig Hartsburg
1999-00	34	36	12	3	83	5th/Pacific	—	—		Craig Hartsburg

FIRST-ROUND ENTRY DRAFT CHOICES

Year   Player, Overall, Last amateur team (league)
1993—Paul Kariya, 4, University of Maine
1994—Oleg Tverdovsky, 2, Krylja Sovetov, CIS
1995—Chad Kilger, 4, Kingston (OHL)
1996—Ruslan Salei, 9, Las Vegas (IHL)

Year   Player, Overall, Last amateur team (league)
1997—Mikael Holmqvist, 18, Djurgarden Stockholm (Sweden)
1998—Vitali Vishnevsky, 5, Torpedo Yaroslavl (Russia)
1999—No first-round selection
2000—Alexei Smirnov, 12, Dynamo (Russia)

SINGLE-SEASON INDIVIDUAL RECORDS

FORWARDS/DEFENSEMEN

Most goals
52—Teemu Selanne, 1997-98

Most assists
62—Paul Kariya, 1998-99

Most points
109—Teemu Selanne, 1996-97

Most penalty minutes
285—Todd Ewen, 1995-96

Most power play goals
25—Teemu Selanne, 1998-99

Most shorthanded goals
3—Bob Corkum, 1993-94
    Paul Kariya, 1995-96
    Paul Kariya, 1996-97
    Paul Kariya, 1999-00

Most games with three or more goals
3—Teemu Selanne, 1997-98

Most shots
429—Paul Kariya, 1998-99

GOALTENDERS

Most games
69—Guy Hebert, 1998-99

Most minutes
4,083—Guy Hebert, 1998-99

Most shots against
2,133—Guy Hebert, 1996-97

Most goals allowed
172—Guy Hebert, 1996-97

Lowest goals-against average
2.42—Guy Hebert, 1998-99

Most shutouts
6—Guy Hebert, 1998-99

Most wins
31—Guy Hebert, 1998-99

Most losses
29—Guy Hebert, 1998-99

Most ties
12—Guy Hebert, 1996-97

FRANCHISE LEADERS

Players in boldface played for club in 1999-2000

FORWARDS/DEFENSEMEN

Games
Steve Rucchin...........................398
Paul Kariya 376
Joe Sacco...................................333
Teemu Selanne 333
Bobby Dollas..............................305

Goals
Paul Kariya 210
Teemu Selanne 199
Steve Rucchin...........................103
Joe Sacco.....................................62
Garry Valk 40

Assists
Paul Kariya 254
Teemu Selanne 224
Steve Rucchin...........................197
Fredrik Olausson.........................84
Joe Sacco.....................................68

Points
Paul Kariya 464
Teemu Selanne 423
Steve Rucchin...........................300
Joe Sacco...................................130
Fredrik Olausson 119

Penalty minutes
David Karpa.................................788
Todd Ewen..................................650
Jason Marshall 601
Stu Grimson 583
Warren Rychel............................416

GOALTENDERS

Games
Guy Hebert 400
Mikhail Shtalenkov 122
Dominic Roussel.........................38
Ron Tugnutt 28
Tom Askey.....................................7

Shutouts
Guy Hebert....................................25
Mikhail Shtalenkov 3
Dominic Roussel 2
Ron Tugnutt 1

Goals-against average
(2400 minutes minimum)
Guy Hebert 2.71
Mikhail Shtalenkov 3.14

Wins
Guy Hebert 161
Mikhail Shtalenkov 34
Dominic Roussel.........................10
Ron Tugnutt 10

ATLANTA FLAMES (DEFUNCT)
YEAR-BY-YEAR RECORDS

	REGULAR SEASON					PLAYOFFS			
Season	W	L	T	Pts.	Finish	W	L	Highest round	Coach
1972-73	25	38	15	65	7th/West	—	—		Bernie Geoffrion
1973-74	30	34	14	74	4th/West	0	4	Division semifinals	Bernie Geoffrion
1974-75	34	31	15	83	4th/Patrick	—	—		Bernie Geoffrion, Fred Creighton
1975-76	35	33	12	82	3rd/Patrick	0	2	Preliminaries	Fred Creighton
1976-77	34	34	12	80	3rd/Patrick	1	2	Preliminaries	Fred Creighton
1977-78	34	27	19	87	3rd/Patrick	0	2	Preliminaries	Fred Creighton
1978-79	41	31	8	90	4th/Patrick	0	2	Preliminaries	Fred Creighton
1979-80	35	32	13	83	4th/Patrick	1	3	Preliminaries	Al MacNeil

Franchise relocated to Calgary following 1979-80 season.

FIRST-ROUND ENTRY DRAFT CHOICES

Year   Player, Overall, Last amateur team (league)
1972—Jacques Richard, 2, Quebec (QMJHL)
1973—Tom Lysiak, 2, Medicine Hat (WCHL)
        Vic Mercredi, 16, New Westminster (WCHL)
1974—No first-round selection
1975—Richard Mulhern, 8, Sherbrooke (QMJHL)

Year   Player, Overall, Last amateur team (league)
1976—Dave Shand, 8, Peterborough (OHL)
        Harold Phillipoff, 10, New Westminster (WCHL)
1977—No first-round selection
1978—Brad Marsh, 11, London (OHL)
1979—Paul Reinhart, 12, Kitchener (OHL)

SINGLE-SEASON INDIVIDUAL RECORDS

FORWARDS/DEFENSEMEN

Most goals
50—Guy Chouinard, 1978-79

Most assists
71—Bob MacMillan, 1978-79

Most points
108—Bob MacMillan, 1978-79

Most penalty minutes
231—Willi Plett, 1979-80

Most power play goals
14—Kent Nilsson, 1979-80

Most shorthanded goals
3—Bill Clement, 1976-77

Most games with three or more goals
3—Eric Vail, 1974-75

Most shots
277—Tom Lysiak, 1976-77

GOALTENDERS

Most games
64—Dan Bouchard, 1978-79

Most minutes
3,624—Dan Bouchard, 1978-79

Most goals allowed
201—Dan Bouchard, 1978-79

Lowest goals-against average
2.54—Dan Bouchard, 1975-76

Most shutouts
5—Dan Bouchard, 1973-74
   Phil Myre, 1974-75

Most wins
32—Dan Bouchard, 1978-79

Most losses
23—Phil Myre, 1972-73

Most ties
19—Dan Bouchard, 1977-78

FRANCHISE LEADERS

FORWARDS/DEFENSEMEN

Games
Eric Vail 469
Rey Comeau 468
Tom Lysiak 445
Curt Bennett 405
Randy Manery 377

Goals
Eric Vail 174
Tom Lysiak 155
Curt Bennett 126
Guy Chouinard 126
Ken Houston 91
Willi Plett..91

Assists
Tom Lysiak 276
Eric Vail 209
Guy Chouinard 168
Randy Manery 142
Curt Bennett 140

Points
Tom Lysiak 431
Eric Vail 383
Guy Chouinard 294
Curt Bennett 266
Bob MacMillan 221

Penalty minutes
Willi Plett 740
Ken Houston 332
Tom Lysiak 329
Ed Kea 283
Randy Manery 242

GOALTENDERS

Games
Dan Bouchard 384
Phil Myre 211
Pat Riggin 25
Yves Belanger 22
Reggie Lemelin 21

Shutouts
Dan Bouchard 20
Phil Myre..11
Pat Riggin 2
Yves Belanger 1

Goals-against average (2400 minutes minimum)
Dan Bouchard 3.00
Phil Myre..3.21

Wins
Dan Bouchard 166
Phil Myre..76
Pat Riggin 11
Yves Belanger 8
Reggie Lemelin 8

ATLANTA THRASHERS
YEAR-BY-YEAR RECORDS

		REGULAR SEASON						PLAYOFFS		
Season	W	L	T	RT	Pts.	Finish	W	L	Highest round	Coach
1999-00	14	61	7	4	39	5th/Southeast	—	—		Curt Fraser

FIRST-ROUND ENTRY DRAFT CHOICES

Year Player, Overall, Last amateur team (league)
1999—Patrik Stefan, 1, Long Beach (IHL)

Year Player, Overall, Last amateur team (league)
2000—Dany Heatley, 2, Wisconsin (WCHA)

SINGLE-SEASON INDIVIDUAL RECORDS

FORWARDS/DEFENSEMEN

Most goals
23—Andrew Brunette, 1999-2000

Most assists
27—Andrew Brunette, 1999-2000

Most points
50—Andrew Brunette, 1999-2000

Most penalty minutes
219—Denny Lambert, 1999-2000

Most power play goals
10—Ray Ferraro, 1999-2000

Most shorthanded goals
2—Ed Ward, 1999-2000

Most games with three or more goals
1—Dean Sylvester, 1999-2000

Most shots
183—Nelson Emerson, 1999-2000

GOALTENDERS

Most games
32—Norm Maracle, 1999-2000

Most minutes
1,618—Norm Maracle, 1999-2000

Most shots against
852—Norm Maracle, 1999-2000

Most goals allowed
101—Damian Rhodes, 1999-2000

Lowest goals-against average
3.49—Norm Maracle, 1999-2000

Most shutouts
1—Norm Maracle, 1999-2000
    Damian Rhodes, 1999-2000

Most wins
5—Damian Rhodes, 1999-2000

Most losses
19—Norm Maracle, 1999-2000
    Damian Rhodes, 1999-2000

Most ties
3—Damian Rhodes, 1999-2000

FRANCHISE LEADERS

FORWARDS/DEFENSEMEN

Games
Andrew Brunette 81
Ray Ferraro 81
Yannick Tremblay 75
Johan Garpenlov 73
Denny Lambert 73

Goals
Andrew Brunette 23
Ray Ferraro 19
Dean Sylvester 16
Nelson Emerson 14
Mike Stapleton 10
Yannick Tremblay 10

Assists
Andrew Brunette 27
Ray Ferraro 25
Yannick Tremblay 21
Patrik Stefan................................20
Nelson Emerson 19

Points
Andrew Brunette 50
Ray Ferraro 44
Nelson Emerson..........................33
Yannick Tremblay 31
Dean Sylvester 26

Penalty minutes
Denny Lambert 219
Matt Johnson............................144
Kelly Buchberger 139
Chris Tamer 91
Ray Ferraro 88

GOALTENDERS

Games
Norm Maracle 32
Damian Rhodes 28
Scott Fankhouser 16
Scott Langkow 15
Rick Tabaracci 1

Shutouts
Norm Maracle..............................1
Damian Rhodes............................1

Goals-against average
(1200 minutes minimum)
Norm Maracle........................3.49
Damian Rhodes......................3.88

Wins
Damian Rhodes..............................5
Norm Maracle 4
Scott Langkow 3
Scott Fankhouser 2

BOSTON BRUINS
YEAR-BY-YEAR RECORDS

		REGULAR SEASON						PLAYOFFS		
Season	W	L	T	RT	Pts.	Finish	W	L	Highest round	Coach
1924-25	6	24	0	—	12	6th	—	—		Art Ross
1925-26	17	15	4	—	38	4th	—	—		Art Ross
1926-27	21	20	3	—	45	2nd/American	*2	2	Stanley Cup finals	Art Ross
1927-28	20	13	11	—	51	1st/American	*0	1	Semifinals	Art Ross
1928-29	26	13	5	—	57	1st/American	5	0	Stanley Cup champ	Cy Denneny
1929-30	38	5	1	—	77	1st/American	3	3	Stanley Cup finals	Art Ross
1930-31	28	10	6	—	62	1st/American	2	3	Semifinals	Art Ross
1931-32	15	21	12	—	42	4th/American	—	—		Art Ross
1932-33	25	15	8	—	58	1st/American	2	3	Semifinals	Art Ross

		REGULAR SEASON					PLAYOFFS			
Season	W	L	T	RT	Pts.	Finish	W	L	Highest round	Coach
1933-34	18	25	5	—	41	4th/American	—	—		Art Ross
1934-35	26	16	6	—	58	1st/American	1	3	Semifinals	Frank Patrick
1935-36	22	20	6	—	50	2nd/American	1	1	Quarterfinals	Frank Patrick
1936-37	23	18	7	—	53	2nd/American	1	2	Quarterfinals	Art Ross
1937-38	30	11	7	—	67	1st/American	0	3	Semifinals	Art Ross
1938-39	36	10	2	—	74	1st	8	4	Stanley Cup champ	Art Ross
1939-40	31	12	5	—	67	1st	2	4	Semifinals	Ralph (Cooney) Weiland
1940-41	27	8	13	—	67	1st	8	3	Stanley Cup champ	Ralph (Cooney) Weiland
1941-42	25	17	6	—	56	3rd	2	3	Semifinals	Art Ross
1942-43	24	17	9	—	57	2nd	4	5	Stanley Cup finals	Art Ross
1943-44	19	26	5	—	43	5th	—	—		Art Ross
1944-45	16	30	4	—	36	4th	3	4	League semifinals	Art Ross
1945-46	24	18	8	—	56	2nd	5	5	Stanley Cup finals	Dit Clapper
1946-47	26	23	11	—	63	3rd	1	4	League semifinals	Dit Clapper
1947-48	23	24	13	—	59	3rd	1	4	League semifinals	Dit Clapper
1948-49	29	23	8	—	66	2nd	1	4	League semifinals	Dit Clapper
1949-50	22	32	16	—	60	5th	—	—		George Boucher
1950-51	22	30	18	—	62	4th	†1	4	League semifinals	Lynn Patrick
1951-52	25	29	16	—	66	4th	3	4	League semifinals	Lynn Patrick
1952-53	28	29	13	—	69	3rd	5	6	League semifinals	Lynn Patrick
1953-54	32	28	10	—	74	4th	0	4	League semifinals	Lynn Patrick
1954-55	23	26	21	—	67	4th	1	4	League semifinals	Lynn Patrick, Milt Schmidt
1955-56	23	34	13	—	59	5th	—	—		Milt Schmidt
1956-57	34	24	12	—	80	3rd	5	5	Stanley Cup finals	Milt Schmidt
1957-58	27	28	15	—	69	4th	6	6	Stanley Cup finals	Milt Schmidt
1958-59	32	29	9	—	73	2nd	3	4	League semifinals	Milt Schmidt
1959-60	28	34	8	—	64	5th	—	—		Milt Schmidt
1960-61	15	42	13	—	43	6th	—	—		Milt Schmidt
1961-62	15	47	8	—	38	6th	—	—		Phil Watson
1962-63	14	39	17	—	45	6th	—	—		Phil Watson, Milt Schmidt
1963-64	18	40	12	—	48	6th	—	—		Milt Schmidt
1964-65	21	43	6	—	48	6th	—	—		Milt Schmidt
1965-66	21	43	6	—	48	5th	—	—		Milt Schmidt
1966-67	17	43	10	—	44	6th	—	—		Harry Sinden
1967-68	37	27	10	—	84	3rd/East	0	4	Division semifinals	Harry Sinden
1968-69	42	18	16	—	100	2nd/East	6	4	Division finals	Harry Sinden
1969-70	40	17	19	—	99	2nd/East	12	2	Stanley Cup champ	Harry Sinden
1970-71	57	14	7	—	121	1st/East	3	4	Division semifinals	Tom Johnson
1971-72	54	13	11	—	119	1st/East	12	3	Stanley Cup champ	Tom Johnson
1972-73	51	22	5	—	107	2nd/East	1	4	Division semifinals	Tom Johnson, Bep Guidolin
1973-74	52	17	9	—	113	1st/East	10	6	Stanley Cup finals	Bep Guidolin
1974-75	40	26	14	—	94	2nd/Adams	1	2	Preliminaries	Don Cherry
1975-76	48	15	17	—	113	1st/Adams	5	7	Semifinals	Don Cherry
1976-77	49	23	8	—	106	1st/Adams	8	6	Stanley Cup finals	Don Cherry
1977-78	51	18	11	—	113	1st/Adams	10	5	Stanley Cup finals	Don Cherry
1978-79	43	23	14	—	100	1st/Adams	7	4	Semifinals	Don Cherry
1979-80	46	21	13	—	105	2nd/Adams	4	6	Quarterfinals	Fred Creighton, Harry Sinden
1980-81	37	30	13	—	87	2nd/Adams	0	3	Preliminaries	Gerry Cheevers
1981-82	43	27	10	—	96	2nd/Adams	6	5	Division finals	Gerry Cheevers
1982-83	50	20	10	—	110	1st/Adams	9	8	Conference finals	Gerry Cheevers
1983-84	49	25	6	—	104	1st/Adams	0	3	Division semifinals	Gerry Cheevers
1984-85	36	34	10	—	82	4th/Adams	2	3	Division semifinals	Gerry Cheevers, Harry Sinden
1985-86	37	31	12	—	86	3rd/Adams	0	3	Division semifinals	Butch Goring
1986-87	39	34	7	—	85	3rd/Adams	0	4	Division semifinals	Butch Goring, Terry O'Reilly
1987-88	44	30	6	—	94	2nd/Adams	12	6	Stanley Cup finals	Terry O'Reilly
1988-89	37	29	14	—	88	2nd/Adams	5	5	Division finals	Terry O'Reilly
1989-90	46	25	9	—	101	1st/Adams	13	8	Stanley Cup finals	Mike Milbury
1990-91	44	24	12	—	100	1st/Adams	10	9	Conference finals	Mike Milbury
1991-92	36	32	12	—	84	2nd/Adams	8	7	Conference finals	Rick Bowness
1992-93	51	26	7	—	109	1st/Adams	0	4	Division semifinals	Brian Sutter
1993-94	42	29	13	—	97	2nd/Northeast	6	7	Conference semifinals	Brian Sutter
1994-95	27	18	3	—	57	3rd/Northeast	1	4	Conference quarterfinals	Brian Sutter
1995-96	40	31	11	—	91	2nd/Northeast	1	4	Conference quarterfinals	Steve Kasper
1996-97	26	47	9	—	61	6th/Northeast	—	—		Steve Kasper
1997-98	39	30	13	—	91	2nd/Northeast	2	4	Conference quarterfinals	Pat Burns
1998-99	39	30	13	—	91	3th/Northeast	6	6	Conference semifinals	Pat Burns
1999-00	24	39	19	6	73	5th/Northeast	—	—		Pat Burns

*Won-lost record does not indicate tie(s) resulting from two-game, total-goals series that year (two-game, total-goals series were played from 1917-18 through 1935-36).

†Tied after one overtime (curfew law).

FIRST-ROUND ENTRY DRAFT CHOICES

Year	Player, Overall, Last amateur team (league)
1969	Don Tannahill, 3, Niagara Falls (OHL)
	Frank Spring, 4, Edmonton (WCHL)
	Ivan Boldirev, 11, Oshawa (OHL)
1970	Reggie Leach, 3, Flin Flon (WCHL)
	Rick MacLeish, 4, Peterborough (OHL)
	Ron Plumb, 9, Peterborough (OHL)
	Bob Stewart, 13, Oshawa (OHL)
1971	Ron Jones, 6, Edmonton (WCHL)
	Terry O'Reilly, 14, Oshawa (OHL)
1972	Mike Bloom, 16, St. Catharines (OHL)
1973	Andre Savard, 6, Quebec (QMJHL)
1974	Don Laraway, 18, Swift Current (WCHL)
1975	Doug Halward, 14, Peterborough (OHL)
1976	Clayton Pachal, 16, New Westminster (WCHL)
1977	Dwight Foster, 16, Kitchener (OHL)
1978	Al Secord, 16, Hamilton (OHL)
1979	Ray Bourque, 8, Verdun (QMJHL)
	Brad McCrimmon, 15, Brandon (WHL)
1980	Barry Pederson, 18, Victoria (WHL)
1981	Norm Leveille, 14, Chicoutimi (QMJHL)
1982	Gord Kluzak, 1, Billings (WHL)*
1983	Nevin Markwart, 21, Regina (WHL)

Year	Player, Overall, Last amateur team (league)
1984	Dave Pasin, 19, Prince Albert (WHL)
1985	No first-round selection
1986	Craig Janney, 13, Boston College
1987	Glen Wesley, 3, Portland (WHL)
	Stephane Quintal, 14, Granby (QMJHL)
1988	Robert Cimetta, 18, Toronto (OHL)
1989	Shayne Stevenson, 17, Kitchener (OHL)
1990	Bryan Smolinski, 21, Michigan State University
1991	Glen Murray, 18, Sudbury (OHL)
1992	Dmitri Kvartalnov, 16, San Diego (IHL)
1993	Kevyn Adams, 25, Miami of Ohio
1994	Evgeni Riabchikov, 21, Molot-Perm (Russia)
1995	Kyle McLaren, 9, Tacoma (WHL)
	Sean Brown, 21, Belleville (OHL)
1996	Johnathan Aitken, 8, Medicine Hat (WHL)
1997	Joe Thornton, 1, Sault Ste. Marie (OHL)*
	Sergei Samsonov, 8, Detroit (IHL)
1998	No first-round selection
1999	Nicholas Boynton, 21, Ottawa (OHL)
2000	Lars Jonsson, 7, Leksand, Sweden
	Martin Samuelsson, 27, MoDo, Sweden

*Designates first player chosen in draft.

SINGLE-SEASON INDIVIDUAL RECORDS

FORWARDS/DEFENSEMEN

Most goals
76—Phil Esposito, 1970-71

Most assists
102—Bobby Orr, 1970-71

Most points
152—Phil Esposito, 1970-71

Most penalty minutes
302—Jay Miller, 1987-88

Most power play goals
28—Phil Esposito, 1971-72

Most shorthanded goals
7—Jerry Toppazzini, 1957-58
   Ed Westfall, 1970-71
   Derek Sanderson, 1971-72

Most games with three or more goals
7—Phil Esposito, 1970-71

Most shots
550—Phil Esposito, 1970-71

GOALTENDERS

Most games
70—Frank Brimsek, 1949-50
   Jack Gelineau, 1950-51
   Eddie Johnston, 1964-64

Most minutes
4,200—Frank Brimsek, 1949-50
   Jack Gelineau, 1950-51
   Eddie Johnston, 1964-64

Most goals allowed
244—Frank Brimsek, 1949-50

Lowest goals-against average
1.18—Tiny Thompson, 1928-29

Most shutouts
15—Hal Winkler, 1927-28

Most wins
40—Pete Peeters, 1982-83

FRANCHISE LEADERS

Players in boldface played for club in 1999-2000

FORWARDS/DEFENSEMEN

Games

Ray Bourque	**1518**
John Bucyk	1436
Wayne Cashman	1027
Terry O'Reilly	891
Rick Middleton	881

Goals

John Bucyk	545
Phil Esposito	459
Rick Middleton	402
Ray Bourque	**395**
Cam Neely	344

Assists

Ray Bourque	**1111**
John Bucyk	794
Bobby Orr	624
Phil Esposito	553
Wayne Cashman	516

Points

Ray Bourque	**1506**
John Bucyk	1339
Phil Esposito	1012
Rick Middleton	898
Bobby Orr	888

Penalty minutes

Terry O'Reilly	2095
Mike Milbury	1552
Keith Crowder	1261
Wayne Cashman	1041
Ray Bourque	**1087**

GOALTENDERS

Games

Cecil Thompson	468
Frankie Brimsek	444
Eddie Johnston	443
Gerry Cheevers	416
Gilles Gilbert	277

Shutouts

Cecil Thompson	74
Frankie Brimsek	35
Eddie Johnston	27
Gerry Cheevers	26
Jim Henry	24

Goals-against average
(2400 minutes minimum)

Hal Winkler	1.56
Cecil Thompson	1.99
Byron Dafoe	**2.31**
Charles Stewart	2.46
John Henderson	2.52

Wins

Tiny Thompson	252
Frankie Brimsek	230
Gerry Cheevers	229
Eddie Johnston	182
Gilles Gilbert	155

NHL HISTORY Team by team

BUFFALO SABRES
YEAR-BY-YEAR RECORDS

Season	W	L	T	RT	Pts.	Finish	W	L	Highest round	Coach
						REGULAR SEASON			**PLAYOFFS**	
1970-71	24	39	15	—	63	5th/East	—	—		Punch Imlach
1971-72	16	43	19	—	51	6th/East	—	—		Punch Imlach, Joe Crozier
1972-73	37	27	14	—	88	4th/East	2	4	Division semifinals	Joe Crozier
1973-74	32	34	12	—	76	5th/East	—	—		Joe Crozier
1974-75	49	16	15	—	113	1st/Adams	10	7	Stanley Cup finals	Floyd Smith
1975-76	46	21	13	—	105	2nd/Adams	4	5	Quarterfinals	Floyd Smith
1976-77	48	24	8	—	104	2nd/Adams	2	4	Quarterfinals	Floyd Smith
1977-78	44	19	17	—	105	2nd/Adams	3	5	Quarterfinals	Marcel Pronovost
1978-79	36	28	16	—	88	2nd/Adams	1	2	Preliminaries	Marcel Pronovost, Bill Inglis
1979-80	47	17	16	—	110	1st/Adams	9	5	Semifinals	Scotty Bowman
1980-81	39	20	21	—	99	1st/Adams	4	4	Quarterfinals	Roger Neilson
1981-82	39	26	15	—	93	3rd/Adams	1	3	Division semifinals	Jim Roberts, Scotty Bowman
1982-83	38	29	13	—	89	3rd/Adams	6	4	Division finals	Scotty Bowman
1983-84	48	25	7	—	103	2nd/Adams	0	3	Division semifinals	Scotty Bowman
1984-85	38	28	14	—	90	3rd/Adams	2	3	Divison semifinals	Scotty Bowman
1985-86	37	37	6	—	80	5th/Adams	—	—		Jim Schoenfeld, Scotty Bowman
1986-87	28	44	8	—	64	5th/Adams	—	—		Scotty Bowman, Craig Ramsay
1987-88	37	32	11	—	85	3rd/Adams	2	4	Division semifinals	Ted Sator
1988-89	38	35	7	—	83	3rd/Adams	1	4	Division semifinals	Ted Sator
1989-90	45	27	8	—	98	2nd/Adams	2	4	Division semifinals	Rick Dudley
1990-91	31	30	19	—	81	3rd/Adams	2	4	Division semifinals	Rick Dudley
										Ted Sator
1991-92	31	37	12	—	74	3rd/Adams	3	4	Division semifinals	Rick Dudley, John Muckler
1992-93	38	36	10	—	86	4th/Adams	4	4	Division finals	John Muckler
1993-94	43	32	9	—	95	4th/Northeast	3	4	Conference quarterfinals	John Muckler
1994-95	22	19	7	—	51	4th/Northeast	1	4	Conference quarterfinals	John Muckler
1995-96	33	42	7	—	73	5th/Northeast	—	—		Ted Nolan
1996-97	40	30	12	—	92	1st/Northeast	5	7	Conference semifinals	Ted Nolan
1997-98	36	29	17	—	89	3rd/Northeast	10	5	Conference finals	Lindy Ruff
1998-99	37	28	17	—	91	4rd/Northeast	14	7	Stanley Cup finals	Lindy Ruff
1999-00	35	36	11	4	85	3rd/Northeast	1	4	Conference quarterfinals	Lindy Ruff

FIRST-ROUND ENTRY DRAFT CHOICES

Year   Player, Overall, Last amateur team (league)

1970—Gilbert Perreault, 1, Montreal (OHL)*
1971—Rick Martin, 5, Montreal (OHL)
1972—Jim Schoenfeld, 5, Niagara Falls (OHL)
1973—Morris Titanic, 12, Sudbury (OHL)
1974—Lee Fogolin, 11, Oshawa (OHL)
1975—Robert Sauve, 17, Laval (QMJHL)
1976—No first-round selection
1977—Ric Seiling, 14, St. Catharines (OHL)
1978—Larry Playfair, 13, Portland (WHL)
1979—Mike Ramsey, 11, University of Minnesota
1980—Steve Patrick, 20, Brandon (WHL)
1981—Jiri Dudacek, 17, Kladno (Czechoslovakia)
1982—Phil Housley, 6, South St. Paul H.S. (Minn.)
        Paul Cyr, 9, Victoria (WHL)
        Dave Andreychuk, 16, Oshawa (OHL)
1983—Tom Barrasso, 5, Acton Boxboro H.S. (Mass.)
        Norm Lacombe, 10, Univ. of New Hampshire
        Adam Creighton, 11, Ottawa (OHL)
1984—Bo Andersson, 18, Vastra Frolunda (Sweden)

1985—Carl Johansson, 14, Vastra Frolunda (Sweden)
1986—Shawn Anderson, 5, Team Canada
1987—Pierre Turgeon, 1, Granby (QMJHL)*
1988—Joel Savage, 13, Victoria (WHL)
1989—Kevin Haller, 14, Regina (WHL)
1990—Brad May, 14, Niagara Falls (OHL)
1991—Philippe Boucher, 13, Granby (QMJHL)
1992—David Cooper, 11, Medicine Hat (WHL)
1993—No first-round selection
1994—Wayne Primeau, 17, Owen Sound (OHL)
1995—Jay McKee, 14, Niagara Falls (OHL)
        Martin Biron, 16, Beauport (QMJHL)
1996—Erik Rasmussen, 7, University of Minnesota
1997—Mika Noronen, 21, Tappara Tampere (Finland)
1998—Dimitri Kalinin, 18, Traktor Chelyabinsk (Russia)
1999—Barrett Heisten, 20, Maine (H. East)
2000—Artem Kriukov, 15, Yaroslavl (Russia)
*Designates first player chosen in draft.

SINGLE-SEASON INDIVIDUAL RECORDS

FORWARDS/DEFENSEMEN

Most goals
76—Alexander Mogilny, 1992-93

Most assists
95—Pat LaFontaine, 1992-93

Most points
148—Pat LaFontaine, 1992-93

Most penalty minutes
354—Rob Ray, 1991-92

Most power play goals
28—Dave Andreychuk, 1991-92

Most shorthanded goals
8—Don Luce, 1994-95

Most games with three or more goals
7—Rick Martin, 1995-96
    Alexander Mogilny, 1992-93

Most shots
360—Alexander Mogilny, 1992-93

GOALTENDERS

Most games
72—Don Edwards, 1997-78
    Dominik Hasek, 1997-98

Most minutes
4,220—Dominik Hasek, 1997-98

Most shots against
2,190—Roger Crozier, 1971-72

NHL HISTORY Team by team

Most goals allowe
214—Roger Crozier, 1971-72
    Tom Barrasso, 1985-86

Lowest goals-against average
1.87—Dominik Hasek, 1998-99

Most shutouts
13—Dominik Hasek, 1997-98

Most wins
38—Don Edwards, 1977-78

Most losses
34—Roger Crozier, 1971-72

Most ties
17—Don Edwards, 1977-78

FRANCHISE LEADERS

Players in boldface played for club in 1999-2000

FORWARDS/DEFENSEMEN

Games
Gilbert Perreault 1191
Craig Ramsay 1070
Mike Ramsey 911
Bill Hajt 854
Don Luce 766

Goals
Gilbert Perreault 512
Rick Martin 382
Dave Andreychuk 348
Danny Gare 267
Craig Ramsay 252

Assists
Gilbert Perreault 814
Dave Andreychuk 423
Craig Ramsay 420
Phil Housley 380
Rene Robert 330

Points
Gilbert Perreault 1326
Dave Andreychuk 771
Rick Martin 695
Craig Ramsay 672
Phil Housley 558

Penalty minutes
Rob Ray 2687
Mike Foligno 1450
Larry Playfair 1390
Brad May 1323
Matthew Barnaby 1248

GOALTENDERS

Games
Dominik Hasek 424
Don Edwards 307
Tom Barrasso 266
Bob Sauve 246
Daren Puppa 215

Shutouts
Dominik Hasek 44
Don Edwards 14
Tom Barrasso 13
Roger Crozier 10
Bob Sauve 7

Goals-against average
(2400 minutes minimum)
Dominik Hasek 2.24
Gerry Desjardins 2.81
Don Edwards 2.90
Dave Dryden 3.06
Bob Sauve 3.20

Wins
Dominik Hasek 197
Don Edwards 156
Tom Barrasso 124
Bob Sauve 119
Daren Puppa 96

CALGARY FLAMES
YEAR-BY-YEAR RECORDS

Season	W	L	T	RT	Pts.	Finish	W	L	Highest round	Coach
1980-81	39	27	14	—	92	3rd/Patrick	9	7	Semifinals	Al MacNeil
1981-82	29	34	17	—	75	3rd/Smythe	0	3	Division semifinals	Al MacNeil
1982-83	32	34	14	—	78	2nd/Smythe	4	5	Division finals	Bob Johnson
1983-84	34	32	14	—	82	2nd/Smythe	6	5	Division finals	Bob Johnson
1984-85	41	27	12	—	94	3rd/Smythe	1	3	Division semifinals	Bob Johnson
1985-86	40	31	9	—	89	2nd/Smythe	12	10	Stanley Cup finals	Bob Johnson
1986-87	46	31	3	—	95	2nd/Smythe	2	4	Division semifinals	Bob Johnson
1987-88	48	23	9	—	105	1st/Smythe	4	5	Division finals	Terry Crisp
1988-89	54	17	9	—	117	1st/Smythe	16	6	Stanley Cup champ	Terry Crisp
1989-90	42	23	15	—	99	1st/Smythe	2	4	Division semifinals	Terry Crisp
1990-91	46	26	8	—	100	2nd/Smythe	3	4	Division semifinals	Doug Risebrough
1991-92	31	37	12	—	74	5th/Smythe	—	—		Doug Risebrough, Guy Charron
1992-93	43	30	11	—	97	2nd/Smythe	2	4	Division semifinals	Dave King
1993-94	42	29	13	—	97	1st/Pacific	3	4	Conference quarterfinals	Dave King
1994-95	24	17	7	—	55	1st/Pacific	3	4	Conference quarterfinals	Dave King
1995-96	34	37	11	—	79	T2nd/Pacific	0	4	Conference quarterfinals	Pierre Page
1996-97	32	41	9	—	73	5th/Pacific	—	—		Pierre Page
1997-98	26	41	15	—	67	5th/Pacific	—	—		Brian Sutter
1998-99	30	40	12	—	72	3rd/Pacific	—	—		Brian Sutter
1999-00	31	41	10	5	77	4th/Pacific	—	—		Brian Sutter

Franchise was formerly in Atlanta from 1972-73 through 1979-80 seasons.

FIRST-ROUND ENTRY DRAFT CHOICES

Year   Player, Overall, Last amateur team (league)
1980—Denis Cyr, 13, Montreal (OHL)
1981—Al MacInnis, 15, Kitchener (OHL)
1982—No first-round selection
1983—Dan Quinn, 13, Belleville (OHL)
1984—Gary Roberts, 12, Ottawa (OHL)
1985—Chris Biotti, 17, Belmont Hill H.S. (Mass.)
1986—George Pelawa, 16, Bemidji H.S. (Minn.)
1987—Bryan Deasley, 19, University of Michigan
1988—Jason Muzzatti, 21, Michigan State University
1989—No first-round selection
1990—Trevor Kidd, 11, Brandon (WHL)

Year   Player, Overall, Last amateur team (league)
1991—Niklas Sundblad, 19, AIK (Sweden)
1992—Cory Stillman, 6, Windsor (OHL)
1993—Jesper Mattsson, 18, Malmo (Sweden)
1994—Chris Dingman, 19, Brandon (WHL)
1995—Denis Gauthier, 20, Drummondville (QMJHL)
1996—Derek Morris, 13, Regina (WHL)
1997—Daniel Tkaczuk, 6, Barrie (OHL)
1998—Rico Fata, 6, London (OHL)
1999—Oleg Saprykin, 11, Seattle (WHL)
2000—Brent Krahn, 9, Calgary (WHL)

SINGLE-SEASON INDIVIDUAL RECORDS

FORWARDS/DEFENSEMEN

Most goals
66—Lanny McDonald, 1982-83

Most assists
82—Kent Nilsson, 1980-81

Most points
131—Kent Nilsson, 1980-81

Most penalty minutes
375—Tim Hunter, 1988-89

Most power play goals
31—Joe Nieuwendyk, 1987-88

Most shorthanded goals
9—Kent Nilsson, 1984-85

Most games with three or more goals
5—Hakan Loob, 1987-88
 Theo Fleury, 1990-91

Most shots
353—Theo Fleury, 1995-96

GOALTENDERS

Most games
64—Mike Vernon, 1987-88
 Mike Vernon, 1992-93

Most minutes
3,732—Mike Vernon, 1992-93

Most goals allowed
229—Rejean Lemelin, 1985-86

Lowest goals-against average
2.45—Fred Brathwaite, 1998-99

Most shutouts
5—Fred Brathwaite, 1999-2000

Most wins
39—Mike Vernon, 1987-88

Most losses
30—Mike Vernon, 1991-92

Most ties
11—Pat Riggin, 1981-82

FRANCHISE LEADERS

Players in boldface played for club in 1999-2000

FORWARDS/DEFENSEMEN

Games

Al MacInnis	803
Theo Fleury	791
Joel Otto	730
Jim Peplinski	711
Gary Suter	617

Goals

Theo Fleury	364
Joe Nieuwendyk	314
Gary Roberts	257
Kent Nilsson	229
Lanny McDonald	215

Assists

Al MacInnis	609
Theo Fleury	466
Gary Suter	437
Joe Nieuwendyk	302
Paul Reinhart	297

Points

Theo Fleury	830
Al MacInnis	822
Joe Nieuwendyk	616
Gary Suter	565
Gary Roberts	505

Penalty minutes

Tim Hunter	2405
Gary Roberts	1736
Joel Otto	1642
Jim Peplinski	1467
Ronnie Stern	1288

GOALTENDERS

Games

Mike Vernon	467
Reggie Lemelin	303
Trevor Kidd	178
Don Edwards	114
Rick Wamsley	111

Shutouts

Trevor Kidd	10
Mike Vernon	9
Fred Brathwaite	6
Reggie Lemelin	6
Rick Tabaracci	4
Rick Wamsley	4

Goals-against average
(2400 minutes minimum)

Fred Brathwaite	**2.65**
Rick Tabaracci	2.81
Trevor Kidd	2.83
Dwayne Roloson	2.95
Mike Vernon	3.28

Wins

Mike Vernon	248
Reggie Lemelin	136
Trevor Kidd	72
Rick Wamsley	53
Don Edwards	40

CALIFORNIA GOLDEN SEALS (DEFUNCT)
YEAR-BY-YEAR RECORDS

	REGULAR SEASON					PLAYOFFS			
Season	W	L	T	Pts.	Finish	W	L	Highest round	Coach
1967-68*	15	42	17	42	6th/West	—	—		Bert Olmstead, Gordie Fashoway
1968-69*	29	36	11	69	2nd/West	3	4	Division semifinals	Fred Glover
1969-70*	22	40	14	58	4th/West	0	4	Division semifinals	Fred Glover
1970-71	20	53	5	45	7th/West	—	—		Fred Glover
1971-72	21	39	18	60	6th/West	—	—		Fred Glover, Vic Stasiuk
1972-73	16	46	16	48	8th/West	—	—		Garry Young, Fred Glover
1973-74	13	55	10	36	8th/West	—	—		Fred Glover, Marsh Johnston
1974-75	19	48	13	51	4th/Adams	—	—		Marsh Johnston
1975-76	27	42	11	65	4th/Adams	—	—		Jack Evans

*Oakland Seals.
Franchise relocated and became Cleveland Barons following 1975-76 season.

FIRST-ROUND ENTRY DRAFT CHOICES

Year   Player, Overall, Last amateur team (league)
1969—Tony Featherstone, 7, Peterborough (OHA)
1970—Chris Oddleifson, 10 Winnipeg (WCHL)
1971—No first-round selection
1972—No first-round selection

Year   Player, Overall, Last amateur team (league)
1973—No first-round selection
1974—Rick Hampton, 3, St. Catharines (OHA)
 Ron Chipperfield, 17, Brandon (WCHL)
1975—Ralph Klassen, 3, Saskatoon (WCHL)

INDIVIDUAL SINGLE-SEASON RECORDS

FORWARDS/DEFENSEMEN

Most goals
34—Norm Ferguson, 1968-69

Most assists
49—Ted Hampson, 1968-69

Most points
75—Ted Hampson, 1968-69

Most penalty minutes
217—Dennis Hextall, 1970-71

Most power play goals
12—Bill Hicke, 1967-68

Most shorthanded goals
5—Dennis Maruk, 1975-76

Most games with three or more goals
2—Earl Ingarfield, 1969-70
Reggie Leach, 1973-74
Al MacAdam, 1975-76
Wayne Merrick, 1975-76

Most shots
274—Carol Vadnais, 1968-69

GOALTENDERS

Most games
71—Gary Smith, 1970-71

Most minutes
3,975—Gary Smith, 1970-71

Most goals allowed
256—Gary Smith, 1970-71

Lowest goals-against average
2.86—Charlie Hodge, 1967-68

Most shutouts
4—Gary Smith, 1968-69
Gilles Meloche, 1971-72

Most wins
19—Gary Smith, 1969-70
Gary Smith, 1970-71

Most losses
48—Gary Smith, 1970-71

Most ties
14—Gilles Meloche, 1972-73

FRANCHISE LEADERS

FORWARDS/DEFENSEMEN

Games
Bert Marshall.................................313
Gary Ehman 297
Joey Johnston...............................288
Norm Ferguson 279
Gary Croteau 270

Goals
Joey Johnston..................................84
Bill Hicke 79
Norm Ferguson 73
Gary Ehman 69
Carol Vadnais 63

Assists
Ted Hampson 123
Bill Hicke 101
Joey Johnston...............................101
Gary Ehman 86
Carol Vadnais 83

Points
Joey Johnston...................................185
Ted Hampson 184
Bill Hicke 180
Gary Ehman 155
Carol Vadnais 146

Penalty minutes
Carol Vadnais 560
Bob Stewart....................................499
Bert Marshall..................................395
Joey Johnston.................................308
Doug Roberts..................................280

GOALTENDERS

Games
Gilles Meloche................................250
Gary Smith 211
Charlie Hodge...................................86
Gary Simmons 74
Marv Edwards 35

Shutouts
Gary Smith 9
Gilles Meloche...................................8
Gary Simmons 4
Charlie Hodge....................................3
Marv Edwards 1

Goals-against average
(2400 minutes minimum)
Charlie Hodge................................3.09
Gary Smith 3.33
Gary Simmons 3.49
Gilles Meloche...............................3.83

Wins
Charlie Hodge................................3.09
Gary Smith 3.33
Gary Simmons 3.49
Gilles Meloche...............................3.83

CAROLINA HURRICANES

YEAR-BY-YEAR RECORDS

	REGULAR SEASON						PLAYOFFS			
Season	W	L	T	RT	Pts.	Finish	W	L	Highest round	Coach
1997-98	33	41	8	—	74	6th/Northeast	—	—		Paul Maurice
1998-99	34	30	18	—	86	1st/Southeast	2	4	Conference quarterfinals	Paul Maurice
1999-00	37	35	10	0	84	3rd/Southeast	—	—		Paul Maurice

Franchise was formerly known as Hartford Whalers and relocated to Carolina following 1996-97 season.

FIRST-ROUND ENTRY DRAFT CHOICES

Year   Player, Overall, Last amateur team (league)
1998—Jeff Heerema, 11, Sarnia (OHL)
1999—David Tanabe, 16, Wisconsin (WCHA)

Year   Player, Overall, Last amateur team (league)
2000—No first-round selection

SINGLE-SEASON INDIVIDUAL RECORDS

FORWARDS/DEFENSEMEN

Most goals
26—Keith Primeau, 1998-99

Most assists
50—Ron Francis, 1999-2000

Most points
73—Ron Francis, 1999-2000

Most penalty minutes
204—Stu Grimson, 1997-98

Most power play goals
12—Gary Roberts, 1999-2000

Most shorthanded goals
3—Keith Primeau, 1997-98

Most games with three or more goals
2—Sami Kapanen, 1997-98

Most shots
254—Sami Kapanen, 1998-99

GOALTENDERS

Most games
75—Arturs Irbe, 1999-2000

Most minutes	Lowest goals-against average	Most losses
4,345—Arturs Irbe, 1999-2000	2.17—Trevor Kidd, 1997-98	28—Arturs Irbe, 1999-2000

Most shots against
1,858—Arturs Irbe, 1999-2000

Most goals allowed
175—Arturs Irbe, 1999-2000

Most shutouts
6—Arturs Irbe, 1998-99

Most wins
34—Arturs Irbe, 1999-2000

Most ties
12—Arturs Irbe, 1998-99

FRANCHISE LEADERS

Players in boldface played for club in 1999-2000

FORWARDS/DEFENSEMEN

Games
Sami Kapanen 238
Robert Kron 237
Glen Wesley 234
Paul Ranheim..........................230
Jeff O'Neill 229

Goals
Sami Kapanen..........................74
Jeff O'Neill..........................60
Gary Roberts..........................57
Keith Primeau..........................56
Ron Francis..........................44

Assists
Sami Kapanen..........................96
Gary Roberts..........................87
Ron Francis..........................81
Jeff O'Neill..........................73
Keith Primeau..........................69

Points
Sami Kapanen 170
Gary Roberts 144
Jeff O'Neill 133
Ron Francis 125
Keith Primeau..........................125

Penalty minutes
Gary Roberts 343
Nolan Pratt..........................229
Jeff O'Neill 205
Stu Grimson..........................204
Kevin Dineen 202

GOALTENDERS

Games
Arturs Irbe 137
Trevor Kidd..........................72
Sean Burke..........................25
Eric Fichaud 9
Kirk McLean..........................8

Shutouts
Arturs Irbe..........................11
Trevor Kidd..........................5
Sean Burke..........................1
Eric Fichaud 1

Goals-against average
(2400 minutes minimum)
Arturs Irbe 2.33
Trevor Kidd..........................2.34

Wins
Arturs Irbe..........................61
Trevor Kidd..........................28
Sean Burke..........................7
Kirk McLean 4
Eric Fichaud 3

CHICAGO BLACKHAWKS
YEAR-BY-YEAR RECORDS

		REGULAR SEASON					PLAYOFFS			
Season	W	L	T	RT	Pts.	Finish	W	L	Highest round	Coach
1926-27	19	22	3	—	41	3rd/American	*0	1	Quarterfinals	Pete Muldoon
1927-28	7	34	3	—	17	5th/American	—	—		Barney Stanley, Hugh Lehman
1928-29	7	29	8	—	22	5th/American	—	—		Herb Gardiner
1929-30	21	18	5	—	47	2nd/American	*0	1	Quarterfinals	Tom Schaughnessy, Bill Tobin
1930-31	24	17	3	—	51	2nd/American	*5	3	Stanley Cup finals	Dick Irvin
1931-32	18	19	11	—	47	2nd/American	1	1	Quarterfinals	Dick Irvin, Bill Tobin
1932-33	16	20	12	—	44	4th/American	—	—		Godfrey Matheson, Emil Iverson
1933-34	20	17	11	—	51	2nd/American	6	2	Stanley Cup champ	Tom Gorman
1934-35	26	17	5	—	57	2nd/American	*0	1	Quarterfinals	Clem Loughlin
1935-36	21	19	8	—	50	3rd/American	1	1	Quarterfinals	Clem Loughlin
1936-37	14	27	7	—	35	4th/American	—	—		Clem Loughlin
1937-38	14	25	9	—	37	3rd/American	7	3	Stanley Cup champ	Bill Stewart
1938-39	12	28	8	—	32	7th	—	—		Bill Stewart, Paul Thompson
1939-40	23	19	6	—	52	4th	0	2	Quarterfinals	Paul Thompson
1940-41	16	25	7	—	39	5th	2	3	Semifinals	Paul Thompson
1941-42	22	23	3	—	47	4th	1	2	Quarterfinals	Paul Thompson
1942-43	17	18	15	—	49	5th	—	—		Paul Thompson
1943-44	22	23	5	—	49	4th	4	5	Stanley Cup finals	Paul Thompson
1944-45	13	30	7	—	33	5th	—	—		Paul Thompson, John Gottselig
1945-46	23	20	7	—	53	3rd	0	4	League semifinals	John Gottselig
1946-47	19	37	4	—	42	6th	—	—		John Gottselig
1947-48	20	34	6	—	46	6th	—	—		John Gottselig, Charlie Conacher
1948-49	21	31	8	—	50	5th	—	—		Charlie Conacher
1949-50	22	38	10	—	54	6th	—	—		Charlie Conacher
1950-51	13	47	10	—	36	6th	—	—		Ebbie Goodfellow
1951-52	17	44	9	—	43	6th	—	—		Ebbie Goodfellow
1952-53	27	28	15	—	69	4th	3	4	League semifinals	Sid Abel
1953-54	12	51	7	—	31	6th	—	—		Sid Abel
1954-55	13	40	17	—	43	6th	—	—		Frank Eddolls
1955-56	19	39	12	—	50	6th	—	—		Dick Irvin
1956-57	16	39	15	—	47	6th	—	—		Tommy Ivan
1957-58	24	39	7	—	55	5th	—	—		Tommy Ivan, Rudy Pilous

	REGULAR SEASON						PLAYOFFS			
Season	W	L	T	RT	Pts.	Finish	W	L	Highest round	Coach
1958-59	28	29	13	—	69	3rd	2	4	League semifinals	Rudy Pilous
1959-60	28	29	13	—	69	3rd	0	4	League semifinals	Rudy Pilous
1960-61	29	24	17	—	75	3rd	8	4	Stanley Cup champ	Rudy Pilous
1961-62	31	26	13	—	75	3rd	6	6	Stanley Cup finals	Rudy Pilous
1962-63	32	21	17	—	81	2nd	2	4	League semifinals	Rudy Pilous
1963-64	36	22	12	—	84	2nd	3	4	League semifinals	Billy Reay
1964-65	34	28	8	—	76	3rd	7	7	Stanley Cup finals	Billy Reay
1965-66	37	25	8	—	82	2nd	2	4	League semifinals	Billy Reay
1966-67	41	17	12	—	94	1st	2	4	League semifinals	Billy Reay
1967-68	32	26	16	—	80	4th/East	5	6	Division finals	Billy Reay
1968-69	34	33	9	—	77	6th/East	—	—		Billy Reay
1969-70	45	22	9	—	99	1st/East	4	4	Division finals	Billy Reay
1970-71	49	20	9	—	107	1st/West	11	7	Stanley Cup finals	Billy Reay
1971-72	46	17	15	—	107	1st/West	4	4	Division finals	Billy Reay
1972-73	42	27	9	—	93	1st/West	10	6	Stanley Cup finals	Billy Reay
1973-74	41	14	23	—	105	2nd/West	6	5	Division finals	Billy Reay
1974-75	37	35	8	—	82	3rd/Smythe	3	5	Quarterfinals	Billy Reay
1975-76	32	30	18	—	82	1st/Smythe	0	4	Quarterfinals	Billy Reay
1976-77	26	43	11	—	63	3rd/Smythe	0	2	Preliminaries	Billy Reay, Bill White
1977-78	32	29	19	—	83	1st/Smythe	0	4	Quarterfinals	Bob Pulford
1978-79	29	36	15	—	73	1st/Smythe	0	4	Quarterfinals	Bob Pulford
1979-80	34	27	19	—	87	1st/Smythe	3	4	Quarterfinals	Eddie Johnston
1980-81	31	33	16	—	78	2nd/Smythe	0	3	Preliminaries	Keith Magnuson
1981-82	30	38	12	—	72	4th/Norris	8	7	Conference finals	Keith Magnuson, Bob Pulford
1982-83	47	23	10	—	104	1st/Norris	7	6	Conference finals	Orval Tessier
1983-84	30	42	8	—	68	4th/Norris	2	3	Division semifinals	Orval Tessier
1984-85	38	35	7	—	83	2nd/Norris	9	6	Conference finals	Orval Tessier, Bob Pulford
1985-86	39	33	8	—	86	1st/Norris	0	3	Division semifinals	Bob Pulford
1986-87	29	37	14	—	72	3rd/Norris	0	4	Division semifinals	Bob Pulford
1987-88	30	41	9	—	69	3rd/Norris	1	4	Division semifinals	Bob Murdoch
1988-89	27	41	12	—	66	4th/Norris	9	7	Conference finals	Mike Keenan
1989-90	41	33	6	—	88	1st/Norris	10	10	Conference finals	Mike Keenan
1990-91	49	23	8	—	106	1st/Norris	2	4	Division semifinals	Mike Keenan
1991-92	36	29	15	—	87	2nd/Norris	12	6	Stanley Cup finals	Mike Keenan
1992-93	47	25	12	—	106	1st/Norris	0	4	Division semifinals	Darryl Sutter
1993-94	39	36	9	—	87	5th/Central	2	4	Conference quarterfinals	Darryl Sutter
1994-95	24	19	5	—	53	3rd/Central	9	7	Conference finals	Darryl Sutter
1995-96	40	28	14	—	94	2nd/Central	6	4	Conference semifinals	Craig Hartsburg
1996-97	34	35	13	—	81	5th/Central	2	4	Conference quarterfinals	Craig Hartsburg
1997-98	30	39	13	—	73	5th/Central	—	—		Craig Hartsburg
1998-99	29	41	12	—	70	3rd/Central	—	—		Dirk Graham, Lorne Molleken
1999-00	33	39	10	2	78	3rd/Central	—	—		Lorne Molleken, Bob Pulford

*Won-lost record does not indicate tie(s) resulting from two-game, total-goals series that year (two-game, total-goals series were played from 1917-18 through 1935-36).

FIRST-ROUND ENTRY DRAFT CHOICES

Year Player, Overall, Last amateur team (league)

1969—J.P. Bordeleau, 13, Montreal (OHL)
1970—Dan Maloney, 14, London (OHL)
1971—Dan Spring, 12, Edmonton (WCHL)
1972—Phil Russell, 13, Edmonton (WCHL)
1973—Darcy Rota, 13, Edmonton (WCHL)
1974—Grant Mulvey, 16, Calgary (WCHL)
1975—Greg Vaydik, 7, Medicine Hat (WCHL)
1976—Real Cloutier, 9, Quebec (WHA)
1977—Doug Wilson, 6, Ottawa (OHL)
1978—Tim Higgins, 10, Ottawa (OHL)
1979—Keith Brown, 7, Portland (WHL)
1980—Denis Savard, 3, Montreal (QMJHL)
　　　Jerome Dupont, 15, Toronto (OHL)
1981—Tony Tanti, 12, Oshawa (OHL)
1982—Ken Yaremchuk, 7, Portland (WHL)
1983—Bruce Cassidy, 18, Ottawa (OHL)
1984—Ed Olczyk, 3, U.S. Olympic Team
1985—Dave Manson, 11, Prince Albert (WHL)

1986—Everett Sanipass, 14, Verdun (QMJHL)
1987—Jimmy Waite, 8, Chicoutimi (QMJHL)
1988—Jeremy Roenick, 8, Thayer Academy (Mass.)
1989—Adam Bennett, 6, Sudbury (OHL)
1990—Karl Dykhuis, 16, Hull (QMJHL)
1991—Dean McAmmond, 22, Prince Albert (WHL)
1992—Sergei Krivokrasov, 12, Central Red Army, CIS
1993—Eric Lecompte, 24, Hull (QMJHL)
1994—Ethan Moreau, 14, Niagara Falls (OHL)
1995—Dimitri Nabokov, 19, Krylja Sovetov, CIS
1996—No first-round selection
1997—Daniel Cleary, 13, Belleville (OHL)
　　　Ty Jones, 16, Spokane (WHL)
1998—Mark Bell, 8, Ottawa (OHL)
1999—Steve McCarthy, 23, Kootenay (WHL)
2000—Mikhail Yakubov, 10, Togliatta, Russia
　　　Pavel Vorobiev, 11, Yaroslavl, Russia

NHL HISTORY *Team by team*

SINGLE-SEASON INDIVIDUAL RECORDS

FORWARDS/DEFENSEMEN

Most goals
58—Bobby Hull, 1968-69

Most assists
87—Denis Savard, 1981-82
Denis Savard, 1987-88

Most points
131—Denis Savard, 1987-88

Most penalty minutes
408—Mike Peluso, 1991-92

Most power play goals
24—Jeremy Roenick, 1993-94

Most shorthanded goals
10—Dirk Graham, 1988-89

Most games with three or more goals
4—Bobby Hull, 1959-60
Bobby Hull, 1965-66

Most shots
414—Bobby Hull, 1968-69

GOALTENDERS

Most games
74—Ed Belfour, 1990-91

Most minutes
4,219—Tony Esposito, 1974-75

Most goals allowed
246—Harry Lumley, 1950-51
Tony Esposito, 1980-81

Lowest goals-against average
1.73—Charles Gardiner, 1933-34

Most shutouts
15—Tony Esposito, 1969-70

Most wins
43—Ed Belfour, 1990-91

Most losses
47—Al Rollins, 1953-54

Most ties
21—Tony Esposito, 1973-74

FRANCHISE LEADERS

Players in boldface played for club in 1999-2000

FORWARDS/DEFENSEMEN

Games

Stan Mikita	1394
Bobby Hull	1036
Eric Nesterenko	1013
Bob Murray	1008
Doug Wilson	938

Goals

Bobby Hull	604
Stan Mikita	541
Steve Larmer	406
Denis Savard	377
Dennis Hull	298

Assists

Stan Mikita	926
Denis Savard	719
Doug Wilson	554
Bobby Hull	549
Steve Larmer	517

Points

Stan Mikita	1467
Bobby Hull	1153
Denis Savard	1096
Steve Larmer	923
Doug Wilson	779

GOALTENDERS

Games

Tony Esposito	873
Glenn Hall	618
Ed Belfour	415
Mike Karakas	331
Charlie Gardiner	316

Shutouts

Tony Esposito	74
Glenn Hall	51
Chuck Gardiner	42
Ed Belfour	30
Mike Karakas	28

**Goals-against average
(2400 minutes minimum)**

Lorne Chabot	1.83
Charlie Gardiner	2.02
Paul Goodman	2.17
Jeff Hackett	2.45
Dominik Hasek	2.58

Wins

Tony Esposito	418
Glenn Hall	275
Ed Belfour	201
Murray Bannerman	116
Mike Karakas	114

CLEVELAND BARONS (DEFUNCT)
YEAR-BY-YEAR RECORDS

	REGULAR SEASON					PLAYOFFS			
Season	W	L	T	Pts.	Finish	W	L	Highest round	Coach
1976-77	25	42	13	63	4th/Adams	—	—		Jack Evans
1977-78	22	45	13	57	4th/Adams	—	—		Jack Evans

Franchise was formerly known as California Golden Seals and relocated to Cleveland following 1995-96 season. Barons disbanded after 1977-78 season. Owners bought Minnesota franchise and a number of Cleveland players were awarded to North Stars; remaining players were dispersed to other clubs in draft.

FIRST-ROUND ENTRY DRAFT CHOICES

Year   Player, Overall, Last amateur team (league)
1976—Bjorn Johansson, 5, Orebro IK (Sweden)

Year   Player, Overall, Last amateur team (league)
1977—Mike Crombeen, 5, Kingston (OHA)

SINGLE-SEASON INDIVIDUAL RECORDS

FORWARDS/DEFENSEMEN

Most goals
36—Dennis Maruk, 1977-78

Most assists
50—Dennis Maruk, 1976-77

Most points
78—Dennis Maruk, 1976-77

Most penalty minutes
229—Randy Holt, 1977-78

Most power play goals
7—Mike Fidler, 1976-77
Kris Manery, 1977-78

Most shorthanded goals
2—Dennis Maruk, 1977-78

Most games with three or more goals
1—Bob Murdoch, 1976-77
   Dennis Maruk, 1977-78
   Chuck Arnason, 1977-78

Most shots
268—Dennis Maruk, 1976-77

GOALTENDERS

Most games
54—Gilles Meloche, 1977-78

Most minutes
3,100—Gilles Meloche, 1977-78

Most goals allowed
195—Gilles Meloche, 1977-78

Lowest goals-against average
3.47—Gilles Meloche, 1976-77

Most shutouts
2—Gary Edwards, 1976-77
   Gilles Meloche, 1976-77

Most wins
19—Gilles Meloche, 1976-77

Most losses
27—Gilles Meloche, 1977-78

Most ties
8—Gilles Meloche, 1977-78

FRANCHISE LEADERS

FORWARDS/DEFENSEMEN

Games
Al MacAdam 160
Dennis Maruk 156
Greg Smith 154
Dave Gardner 151
Bob Stewart 145

Goals
Dennis Maruk 64
Mike Fidler 40
Al MacAdam 38
Bob Murdoch 37
Dave Gardner 35

Assists
Dennis Maruk 85
Al MacAdam 73
Dave Gardner 47
Greg Smith 47
Bob Murdoch 45

Points
Dennis Maruk 149
Al MacAdam 111
Mike Fidler 84
Dave Gardner 82
Bob Murdoch 82

Penalty minutes
Randy Holt 229
Len Frig 213
Bob Stewart 192
Greg Smith 157
Mike Christie 128

GOALTENDERS

Games
Gilles Meloche 105
Gary Edwards 47
Gary Simmons 15

Shutouts
Gilles Meloche 3
Gary Edwards 2
Gary Simmons 1

Goals-against average
(2400 minutes minimum)
Gary Edwards 4.36
Gilles Meloche 3.62

Wins
Gilles Meloche 35
Gary Edwards 10
Gary Simmons 2

COLORADO AVALANCHE
YEAR-BY-YEAR RECORDS

| | REGULAR SEASON | | | | | | PLAYOFFS | | | |
Season	W	L	T	RT	Pts.	Finish	W	L	Highest round	Coach
1995-96	47	25	10	—	104	1st/Pacific	16	6	Stanley Cup champ	Marc Crawford
1996-97	49	24	9	—	107	1st/Pacific	10	7	Conference finals	Marc Crawford
1997-98	39	26	17	—	95	1st/Pacific	3	4	Conference quarterfinals	Marc Crawford
1998-99	44	28	10	—	98	1st/Northwest	11	8	Conference finals	Bob Hartley
1999-00	42	29	11	1	96	1st/Northwest	11	6	Conference finals	Bob Hartley

Franchise was formerly known as Quebec Nordiques and relocated to Colorado following 1994-95 season.

FIRST-ROUND ENTRY DRAFT CHOICES

Year Player, Overall, Last amateur team (league)
1996—Peter Ratchuk, 25, Shattuck-St. Mary's H.S. (Min.)
1997—Kevin Grimes, 26, Kingston (OHL)
1998—Alex Tanguay, 12, Halifax (QMJHL)
   Martin Skoula, 17, Barrie (OHL)

Year Player, Overall, Last amateur team (league)
   Robyn Regehr, 19, Kamloops (WHL)
   Scott Parker, 20, Kelowna (WHL)
1999—Mihail Kuleshov, 25, Cherepovec, Russia
2000—Vaclav Nedorost, 14, Budejovice, Czech Republic

SINGLE-SEASON INDIVIDUAL RECORDS

FORWARDS/DEFENSEMEN

Most goals
51—Joe Sakic, 1995-96

Most assists
86—Peter Forsberg, 1995-96

Most points
120—Joe Sakic, 1995-96

Most penalty minutes
259—Jeff Odgers, 1998-99

Most power play goals
18—Valeri Kamensky, 1995-96

Most shorthanded goals
6—Joe Sakic, 1995-96

Most games with three or more goals
2—Peter Forsberg, 1995-96
   Valeri Kamensky, 1995-96
   Claude Lemieux, 1995-96
   Joe Sakic, 1999-2000

Most shots
315—Claude Lemieux, 1995-96

GOALTENDERS

Most games
65—Patrick Roy, 1997-98

Most minutes
3,835—Patrick Roy, 1997-98

Most shots against
1,861—Patrick Roy, 1996-97

Most goals allowed	Most shutouts	Most losses
153—Patrick Roy, 1997-98	7—Patrick Roy, 1996-97	21—Patrick Roy, 1999-2000
Lowest goals-against average	**Most wins**	**Most ties**
2.28—Patrick Roy, 1999-2000	38—Patrick Roy, 1996-97	13—Patrick Roy, 1997-98

FRANCHISE LEADERS

Players in boldface played for club in 1999-2000

FORWARDS/DEFENSEMEN

Games
Stephane Yelle	382
Adam Deadmarsh	366
Adam Foote	351
Peter Forsberg	346
Joe Sakic	344

Goals
Joe Sakic	169
Peter Forsberg	127
Adam Deadmarsh	116
Valeri Kamensky	106
Claude Lemieux	106

Assists
Peter Forsberg	314
Joe Sakic	265
Sandis Ozolinsh	181
Valeri Kamensky	155
Adam Deadmarsh	129

Points
Peter Forsberg	441
Joe Sakic	434
Valeri Kamensky	261
Sandis Ozolinsh	253
Adam Deadmarsh	245

Penalty minutes
Adam Deadmarsh	608
Adam Foote	537
Jeff Odgers	472
Claude Lemieux	381
Peter Forsberg	374

GOALTENDERS

Games
Patrick Roy	290
Craig Billington	67
Stephane Fiset	37
Marc Denis	28
Jocelyn Thibault	10

Shutouts
Patrick Roy	19
Marc Denis	3
Craig Billington	2
Stephane Fiset	1

Goals-against average (2400 minutes minimum)
Patrick Roy	2.37
Craig Billington	2.61

Wins
Patrick Roy	155
Craig Billington	30
Stephane Fiset	22
Marc Denis	10
Jocelyn Thibault	3

COLORADO ROCKIES (DEFUNCT)
YEAR-BY-YEAR RECORDS

	REGULAR SEASON					PLAYOFFS			
Season	W	L	T	Pts.	Finish	W	L	Highest round	Coach
1976-77	20	46	14	54	5th/Smythe	—	—		John Wilson
1977-78	19	40	21	59	2nd/Smythe	0	2	Preliminaries	Pat Kelly
1978-79	15	53	12	42	4th/Smythe	—	—		Pat Kelly, Bep Guidolin
1979-80	19	48	13	51	6th/Smythe	—	—		Don Cherry
1980-81	22	45	13	57	5th/Smythe	—	—		Billy MacMillan
1981-82	18	49	13	49	5th/Smythe	—	—		Bert Marshall, Marshall Johnston

Franchise was formerly known as Kansas City Scouts and relocated to Colorado following 1975-76 season; franchise relocated and became New Jersey Devils following 1981-82 season.

FIRST-ROUND ENTRY DRAFT CHOICES

Year   Player, Overall, Last amateur team (league)
1976—Paul Gardner, 11, Oshawa (OHL)
1977—Barry Beck, 2, New Westminster (WCHL)
1978—Mike Gillis, 5, Kingston (OHL)
1979—Rob Ramage, 1, Birmingham (WHA)*

Year   Player, Overall, Last amateur team (league)
1980—Paul Gagne, 19, Windsor (OHL)
1981—Joe Cirella, 5, Oshawa (OHL)
*Designates first player chosen in draft.

SINGLE-SEASON INDIVIDUAL RECORDS

FORWARDS/DEFENSEMEN

Most goals
41—Wilf Paiement, 1976-77

Most assists
56—Wilf Paiement, 1977-78

Most points
87—Wilf Paiement, 1977-78

Most penalty minutes
201—Rob Ramage, 1981-82

Most power play goals
14—Paul Gardner, 1978-79

Most shorthanded goals
5—Wilf Paiement, 1976-77

Most games with three or more goals
1—Held by many players

Most shots
298—Lanny McDonald, 1980-81

GOALTENDERS

Most games
61—Chico Resch, 1981-82

Most minutes
3,424—Chico Resch, 1981-82

Most goals allowed
230—Chico Resch, 1981-82

Lowest goals-against average
3.49—Bill McKechnie, 1979-80

Most shutouts
1—Held by many goaltenders

Most wins
16—Chico Resch, 1981-82

Most losses
31—Chico Resch, 1981-82

Most ties
11—Chico Resch, 1981-82
 Doug Favell, 1977-78

NHL HISTORY Team by team

FRANCHISE LEADERS

FORWARDS/DEFENSEMEN

Games
Mike Kitchen 354
Ron Delorme 314
Wilf Paiement 257
Randy Pierce 240
Gary Croteau 234
Rob Ramage 234

Goals
Wilf Paiement 106
Paul Gardner 83
Ron Delorme 66
Lanny McDonald 66
Gary Croteau 65

Assists
Wilf Paiement 148
Rob Ramage 91
Merlin Malinowski 86
Paul Gardner 77
Lanny McDonald 75

Points
Wilf Paiement 254
Paul Gardner 160
Lanny McDonald 141
Gary Croteau 136
Merlin Malinowski 132
Rob Ramage 132

Penalty minutes
Rob Ramage 529
Wilf Paiement 336
Mike Kitchen 294
Ron Delorme 284
Randy Pierce 206

GOALTENDERS

Games
Michel Plasse 126
Doug Favell 84
Hardy Astrom 79
Chico Resch 69
Bill Oleschuk 54

Shutouts
Doug Favell 1
Bill McKenzie 1
Bill Oleschuk 1

Goals-against average
(2400 minutes minimum)
Hardy Astrom 3.77
Doug Favell 3.82
Michel Plasse 3.91
Chico Resch 3.97
Bill Oleschuk 4.00

Wins
Michel Plasse 24
Doug Favell 21
Chico Resch 18
Hardy Astrom 15
Bill McKenzie 12

DALLAS STARS
YEAR-BY-YEAR RECORDS

			REGULAR SEASON					PLAYOFFS		
Season	W	L	T	RT	Pts.	Finish	W	L	Highest round	Coach
1993-94	42	29	13	—	97	3rd/Central	5	4	Conference semifinals	Bob Gainey
1994-95	17	23	8	—	42	5th/Central	1	4	Conference quarterfinals	Bob Gainey
1995-96	26	42	14	—	66	6th/Central	—	—		Bob Gainey, Ken Hitchcock
1996-97	48	26	8	—	104	1st/Central	3	4	Conference quarterfinals	Ken Hitchcock
1997-98	49	22	11	—	109	1st/Central	10	7	Conference finals	Ken Hitchcock
1998-99	51	19	12	—	114	1st/Pacific	16	7	Stanley Cup champ	Ken Hitchcock
1999-00	43	29	10	6	102	1st/Pacific	14	9	Stanley Cup finals	Ken Hitchcock

Franchise was formerly known as Minnesota North Stars and relocated to Dallas following 1992-93 season.

FIRST-ROUND ENTRY DRAFT CHOICES

Year   Player, Overall, Last amateur team (league)
1993—Todd Harvey, 9, Detroit (OHL)
1994—Jason Botterill, 20, Michigan (CCHA)
1995—Jarome Iginla, 11, Kamloops (WHL)
1996—Richard Jackman, 5, Sault Ste. Marie (OHL)

Year   Player, Overall, Last amateur team (league)
1997—Brenden Morrow, 25, Portland (WHL)
1998—No first-round selection
1999—No first-round selection
2000—Steve Ott, 25, Windsor (OHL)

SINGLE-SEASON INDIVIDUAL RECORDS

FORWARDS/DEFENSEMEN

Most goals
50—Mike Modano, 1993-94

Most assists
57—Russ Courtnall, 1993-94

Most points
93—Mike Modano, 1993-94

Most penalty minutes
333—Shane Churla, 1993-94

Most power play goals
18—Mike Modano, 1993-94

Most shorthanded goals
5—Mike Modano, 1996-97
   Mike Modano, 1997-98

Most games with three or more goals
3—Mike Modano, 1998-99

Most shots
320—Mike Modano, 1995-96

GOALTENDERS

Most games
62—Ed Belfour, 1999-2000

Most minutes
3,620—Ed Belfour, 1999-2000

Most shots against
1,604—Andy Moog, 1993-94

Most goals allowed
170—Andy Moog, 1993-94

Lowest goals-against average
1.88—Ed Belfour, 1997-98

Most shutouts
9—Ed Belfour, 1997-98

Most wins
37—Ed Belfour, 1997-98

Most losses
21—Ed Belfour, 1999-2000

Most ties
10—Ed Belfour, 1997-98

NHL HISTORY Team by team

FRANCHISE LEADERS

Players in boldface played for club in 1999-2000

FORWARDS/DEFENSEMEN

Games

Derian Hatcher	**475**
Mike Modano	**470**
Craig Ludwig	433
Richard Matvichuk	**377**
Guy Carbonneau	364

Goals

Mike Modano	**226**
Joe Nieuwendyk	126
Jamie Langenbrunner	**68**
Jere Lehtinen	**68**
Pat Verbeek	65

Assists

Mike Modano	**281**
Joe Nieuwendyk	215
Sergei Zubov	**151**
Darryl Sydor	**141**
Derian Hatcher	**140**

Points

Mike Modano	**507**
Joe Nieuwendyk	241
Sergei Zubov	**193**
Derian Hatcher	**185**
Darryl Sydor	**184**

Penalty minutes

Derian Hatcher	**844**
Shane Churla	687
Craig Ludwig	534
Todd Harvey	449
Pat Verbeek	431

GOALTENDERS

Games

Ed Belfour	**184**
Andy Moog	175
Darcy Wakaluk	88
Roman Turek	55
Arturs Irbe	35

Shutouts

Ed Belfour	**18**
Andy Moog	8
Darcy Wakaluk	6
Arturs Irbe	3
Roman Turek	2

Goals-against average
(2400 minutes minimum)

Ed Belfour	**1.99**
Roman Turek	2.14
Andy Moog	2.75
Darcy Wakaluk	3.21

Wins

Ed Belfour	**104**
Andy Moog	75
Darcy Wakaluk	31
Roman Turek	30
Arturs Irbe	17

DETROIT RED WINGS
YEAR-BY-YEAR RECORDS

		REGULAR SEASON					PLAYOFFS			
Season	W	L	T	RT	Pts.	Finish	W	L	Highest round	Coach
1926-27†	12	28	4	—	28	5th/American	—	—		Art Duncan, Duke Keats
1927-28†	19	19	6	—	44	4th/American	—	—		Jack Adams
1928-29†	19	16	9	—	47	3rd/American	0	2	Quarterfinals	Jack Adams
1929-30†	14	24	6	—	34	4th/American	—	—		Jack Adams
1930-31‡	16	21	7	—	39	4th/American	—	—		Jack Adams
1931-32‡	18	20	10	—	46	3rd/American	*0	1	Quarterfinals	Jack Adams
1932-33	25	15	8	—	58	2nd/American	2	2	Semifinals	Jack Adams
1933-34	24	14	10	—	58	1st/American	4	5	Stanley Cup finals	Jack Adams
1934-35	19	22	7	—	45	4th/American	—	—		Jack Adams
1935-36	24	16	8	—	56	1st/American	6	1	Stanley Cup champ	Jack Adams
1936-37	25	14	9	—	59	1st/American	6	4	Stanley Cup champ	Jack Adams
1937-38	12	25	11	—	35	4th/American	—	—		Jack Adams
1938-39	18	24	6	—	42	5th	3	3	Semifinals	Jack Adams
1939-40	16	26	6	—	38	5th	2	3	Semifinals	Jack Adams
1940-41	21	16	11	—	53	3rd	4	5	Stanley Cup finals	Jack Adams
1941-42	19	25	4	—	42	5th	7	5	Stanley Cup finals	Jack Adams
1942-43	25	14	11	—	61	1st	8	2	Stanley Cup champ	Jack Adams
1943-44	26	18	6	—	58	2nd	1	4	League semifinals	Jack Adams
1944-45	31	14	5	—	67	2nd	7	7	Stanley Cup finals	Jack Adams
1945-46	20	20	10	—	50	4th	1	4	League semifinals	Jack Adams
1946-47	22	27	11	—	55	4th	1	4	League semifinals	Jack Adams
1947-48	30	18	12	—	72	2nd	4	6	Stanley Cup finals	Tommy Ivan
1948-49	34	19	7	—	75	1st	4	7	Stanley Cup finals	Tommy Ivan
1949-50	37	19	14	—	88	1st	8	6	Stanley Cup champ	Tommy Ivan
1950-51	44	13	13	—	101	1st	2	4	League semifinals	Tommy Ivan
1951-52	44	14	12	—	100	1st	8	0	Stanley Cup champ	Tommy Ivan
1952-53	36	16	18	—	90	1st	2	4	League semifinals	Tommy Ivan
1953-54	37	19	14	—	88	1st	8	4	Stanley Cup champ	Tommy Ivan
1954-55	42	17	11	—	95	1st	8	3	Stanley Cup champ	Jimmy Skinner
1955-56	30	24	16	—	76	2nd	5	5	Stanley Cup finals	Jimmy Skinner
1956-57	38	20	12	—	88	1st	1	4	League semifinals	Jimmy Skinner
1957-58	29	29	12	—	70	3rd	0	4	League semifinals	Jimmy Skinner, Sid Abel
1958-59	25	37	8	—	58	6th	—	—		Sid Abel
1959-60	26	29	15	—	67	4th	2	4	League semifinals	Sid Abel
1960-61	25	29	16	—	66	4th	6	5	Stanley Cup finals	Sid Abel
1961-62	23	33	14	—	60	5th	—	—		Sid Abel
1962-63	32	25	13	—	77	4th	5	6	Stanley Cup finals	Sid Abel
1963-64	30	29	11	—	71	4th	7	7	Stanley Cup finals	Sid Abel
1964-65	40	23	7	—	87	1st	3	4	League semifinals	Sid Abel
1965-66	31	27	12	—	74	4th	6	6	Stanley Cup finals	Sid Abel

Season	\u00A0	REGULAR SEASON					PLAYOFFS			
Season	W	L	T	RT	Pts.	Finish	W	L	Highest round	Coach
1966-67	27	39	4	—	58	5th	—	—		Sid Abel
1967-68	27	35	12	—	66	6th/East	—	—		Sid Abel
1968-69	33	31	12	—	78	5th/East	—	—		Bill Gadsby
1969-70	40	21	15	—	95	3rd/East	0	4	Division semifinals	Bill Gadsby, Sid Abel
1970-71	22	45	11	—	55	7th/East	—	—		Ned Harkness, Doug Barkley
1971-72	33	35	10	—	76	5th/East	—	—		Doug Barkley, Johnny Wilson
1972-73	37	29	12	—	86	5th/East	—	—		Johnny Wilson
1973-74	29	39	10	—	68	6th/East	—	—		Ted Garvin, Alex Delvecchio
1974-75	23	45	12	—	58	4th/Norris	—	—		Alex Delvecchio
1975-76	26	44	10	—	62	4th/Norris	—	—		Ted Garvin, Alex Delvecchio
1976-77	16	55	9	—	41	5th/Norris	—	—		Alex Delvecchio, Larry Wilson
1977-78	32	34	14	—	78	2nd/Norris	3	4	Quarterfinals	Bobby Kromm
1978-79	23	41	16	—	62	5th/Norris	—	—		Bobby Kromm
1979-80	26	43	11	—	63	5th/Norris	—	—		Bobby Kromm, Ted Lindsay
1980-81	19	43	18	—	56	5th/Norris	—	—		Ted Lindsay, Wayne Maxner
1981-82	21	47	12	—	54	6th/Norris	—	—		Wayne Maxner, Billy Dea
1982-83	21	44	15	—	57	5th/Norris	—	—		Nick Polano
1983-84	31	42	7	—	69	3rd/Norris	1	3	Division semifinals	Nick Polano
1984-85	27	41	12	—	66	3rd/Norris	0	3	Division semifinals	Nick Polano
1985-86	17	57	6	—	40	5th/Norris	—	—		Harry Neale, Brad Park, Dan Belisle
1986-87	34	36	10	—	78	2nd/Norris	9	7	Conference finals	Jacques Demers
1987-88	41	28	11	—	93	1st/Norris	9	7	Conference finals	Jacques Demers
1988-89	34	34	12	—	80	1st/Norris	2	4	Division semifinals	Jacques Demers
1989-90	28	38	14	—	70	5th/Norris	—	—		Jacques Demers
1990-91	34	38	8	—	76	3rd/Norris	3	4	Division semifinals	Bryan Murray
1991-92	43	25	12	—	98	1st/Norris	4	7	Division finals	Bryan Murray
1992-93	47	28	9	—	103	2nd/Norris	3	4	Division semifinals	Bryan Murray
1993-94	46	30	8	—	100	1st/Central	3	4	Division semifinals	Scotty Bowman
1994-95	33	11	4	—	70	1st/Central	12	6	Stanley Cup finals	Scotty Bowman
1995-96	62	13	7	—	131	1st/Central	10	9	Conference finals	Scotty Bowman
1996-97	38	26	18	—	94	2nd/Central	16	4	Stanley Cup champ	Scotty Bowman
1997-98	44	23	15	—	103	2nd/Central	16	6	Stanley Cup champ	Scotty Bowman
1998-99	43	32	7	—	93	1st/Central	6	4	Conference semifinals	Scotty Bowman
1999-00	48	24	10	2	108	2nd/Central	5	4	Conference semifinals	Scotty Bowman

*Won-lost record does not indicate tie(s) resulting from two-game, total goals series that year (two-game, total-goals series were played from 1917-18 through 1935-36).

†Detroit Cougars.

‡Detroit Falcons.

FIRST-ROUND ENTRY DRAFT CHOICES

Year   Player, Overall, Last amateur team (league)

1969—Jim Rutherford, 10, Hamilton (OHL)
1970—Serge Lajeunesse, 12, Montreal (OHL)
1971—Marcel Dionne, 2, St. Catharines (OHL)
1972—No first-round selection
1973—Terry Richardson, 11, New Westminster (WCHL)
1974—Bill Lochead, 9, Oshawa (OHL)
1975—Rick Lapointe, 5, Victoria (WCHL)
1976—Fred Williams, 4, Saskatoon (WCHL)
1977—Dale McCourt, 1, St. Catharines (OHL)*
1978—Willie Huber, 9, Hamilton (OHL)
         Brent Peterson, 12, Portland (WCHL)
1979—Mike Foligno, 3, Sudbury (OHL)
1980—Mike Blaisdell, 11, Regina (WHL)
1981—No first-round selection
1982—Murray Craven, 17, Medicine Hat (WHL)
1983—Steve Yzerman, 4, Peterborough (OHL)
1984—Shawn Burr, 7, Kitchener (OHL)

Year   Player, Overall, Last amateur team (league)

1985—Brent Fedyk, 8, Regina (WHL)
1986—Joe Murphy, 1, Michigan State University*
1987—Yves Racine, 11, Longueuil (QMJHL)
1988—Kory Kocur, 17, Saskatoon (WHL)
1989—Mike Sillinger, 11, Regina (WHL)
1990—Keith Primeau, 3, Niagara Falls (OHL)
1991—Martin Lapointe, 10, Laval (QMJHL)
1992—Curtis Bowen, 22, Ottawa (OHL)
1993—Anders Eriksson, 22, MoDo, Sweden
1994—Yan Golbvovsky, 23, Dynamo Moscow, CIS
1995—Maxim Kuznetsov, 26, Dynamo Moscow, CIS
1996—Jesse Wallin, 26, Red Deer (WHL)
1997—No first-round selection
1998—Jiri Fischer, 25, Hull (QMJHL)
1999—No first-round selection
2000—Niklas Kronvall, 29, Djurgarden, Sweden
*Designates first player chosen in draft.

SINGLE-SEASON INDIVIDUAL RECORDS

FORWARDS/DEFENSEMEN

Most goals
65—Steve Yzerman, 1988-89

Most assists
90—Steve Yzerman, 1988-89

Most points
155—Steve Yzerman, 1988-89

Most penalty minutes
398—Bob Probert, 1987-88

Most power play goals
21—Mickey Redmond, 1973-74
      Dino Ciccarelli, 1992-93

Most shorthanded goals
10—Marcel Dionne, 1974-75

Most games with three or more goals
4—Frank Mahovlich, 1968-69
      Steve Yzerman, 1990-91

Most shots
388—Steve Yzerman, 1988-89

GOALTENDERS

Most games
72—Tim Cheveldae, 1991-92

Most minutes
4,236—Tim Cheveldae, 1991-92

Most goals allowed
226—Tim Cheveldae, 1991-92

Lowest goals-against average
1.43—Dolly Dodson, 1928-29

Most shutouts
12—Terry Sawchuk, 1951-52
 Terry Sawchuk, 1953-54
 Terry Sawchuk, 1954-55
 Glenn Hall, 1955-56

Most wins
44—Terry Sawchuk, 1950-51
 Terry Sawchuk, 1951-52

FRANCHISE LEADERS

Players in boldface played for club in 1999-2000

FORWARDS/DEFENSEMEN

Games
Gordie Howe 1687
Alex Delvecchio..............................1549
Steve Yzerman 1256
Marcel Pronovost..............................983
Norm Ullman.......................................875

Goals
Gordie Howe 786
Steve Yzerman.......................627
Alex Delvecchio.................................456
Ted Lindsay..335
Norm Ullman.......................................324

Assists
Gordie Howe 1023
Steve Yzerman.......................935
Alex Delvecchio.................................825
Norm Ullman.......................................434
Sergei Fedorov 433

Points
Gordie Howe 1809
Steve Yzerman 1562
Alex Delvecchio..............................1281
Norm Ullman.......................................758
Sergei Fedorov 734

GOALTENDERS

Games
Terry Sawchuk....................................734
Harry Lumley 324
Jim Rutherford 314
Roger Crozier 310
Greg Stefan 299

Shutouts
Terry Sawchuk......................................85
Harry Lumley 26
Chris Osgood 23
Roger Crozier 20
Clarence Dolson 17
Glenn Hall..17

Harry Holmes 17
Norm Smith..17

Goals-against average
(2400 minutes minimum)
Clarence Dolson 2.06
Harry Holmes 2.11
Glenn Hall...2.14
Alex Connell 2.25
John Ross Roach 2.26

Wins
Terry Sawchuk....................................352
Chris Osgood 196
Harry Lumley 163
Roger Crozier 130
Tim Cheveldae 128

EDMONTON OILERS
YEAR-BY-YEAR RECORDS

			REGULAR SEASON					PLAYOFFS	
Season	W	L	T	RT	Pts.	Finish	W	L	Highest round	Coach
1972-73*	38	37	3	—	79	5th	—	—		Ray Kinasewich
1973-74†	38	37	3	—	79	3rd	1	4	League quarterfinals	Brian Shaw
1974-75†	36	38	4	—	76	5th	—	—		Brian Shaw, Bill Hunter
1975-76†	27	49	5	—	59	4th	0	4	League quarterfinals	Clare Drake, Bill Hunter
1976-77†	34	43	4	—	72	4th	1	4	League quarterfinals	Bep Guidolin, Glen Sather
1977-78†	38	39	3	—	79	5th	1	4	League quarterfinals	Glen Sather
1978-79†	48	30	2	—	98	1st	6	7	Avco World Cup finals	Glen Sather
1979-80	28	39	13	—	69	4th/Smythe	0	3	Preliminaries	Glen Sather
1980-81	29	35	16	—	74	4th/Smythe	5	4	Quarterfinals	Glen Sather
1981-82	48	17	15	—	111	1st/Smythe	2	3	Division semifinals	Glen Sather
1982-83	47	21	12	—	106	1st/Smythe	11	5	Stanley Cup finals	Glen Sather
1983-84	57	18	5	—	119	1st/Smythe	15	4	Stanley Cup champ	Glen Sather
1984-85	49	20	11	—	109	1st/Smythe	15	3	Stanley Cup champ	Glen Sather
1985-86	56	17	7	—	119	1st/Smythe	6	4	Division finals	Glen Sather
1986-87	50	24	6	—	106	1st/Smythe	16	5	Stanley Cup champ	Glen Sather
1987-88	44	25	11	—	99	2nd/Smythe	16	2	Stanley Cup champ	Glen Sather
1988-89	38	34	8	—	84	3rd/Smythe	3	4	Division semifinals	Glen Sather
1989-90	38	28	14	—	90	2nd/Smythe	16	6	Stanley Cup champ	John Muckler
1990-91	37	37	6	—	80	3rd/Smythe	9	9	Conference finals	John Muckler
1991-92	36	34	10	—	82	3rd/Smythe	8	8	Conference finals	Ted Green
1992-93	26	50	8	—	60	5th/Smythe	—	—		Ted Green
1993-94	25	45	14	—	64	6th/Pacific	—	—		Ted Green, Glen Sather
1994-95	17	27	4	—	38	5th/Pacific	—	—		George Burnett, Ron Low
1995-96	30	44	8	—	68	5th/Pacific	—	—		Ron Low
1996-97	36	37	9	—	81	3rd/Pacific	5	7	Conference semifinals	Ron Low
1997-98	35	37	10	—	80	3rd/Pacific	5	7	Conference semifinals	Ron Low
1998-99	33	37	12	—	78	2nd/Northwest	0	4	Conference quarterfinals	Ron Low
1999-00	32	34	16	8	82	2nd/Northwest	1	4	Conference quarterfinals	Kevin Lowe

*Alberta Oilers, members of World Hockey Association.
†Members of World Hockey Association.

FIRST-ROUND ENTRY DRAFT CHOICES

Year	Player, Overall, Last amateur team (league)
1979	Kevin Lowe, 21, Quebec (QMJHL)
1980	Paul Coffey, 6, Kitchener (OHL)
1981	Grant Fuhr, 8, Victoria (WHL)
1982	Jim Playfair, 20, Portland (WHL)
1983	Jeff Beukeboom, 19, Sault Ste. Marie (OHL)
1984	Selmar Odelein, 21, Regina (WHL)
1985	Scott Metcalfe, 20, Kingston (OHL)
1986	Kim Issel, 21, Prince Albert (WHL)
1987	Peter Soberlak, 21, Swift Current (WHL)
1988	Francois Leroux, 19, St. Jean (QMJHL)
1989	Jason Soules, 15, Niagara Falls (OHL)
1990	Scott Allison, 17, Prince Albert (WHL)
1991	Tyler Wright, 12, Swift Current (WHL)
	Martin Rucinsky, 20, Litvinov, Czechoslovakia

Year	Player, Overall, Last amateur team (league)
1992	Joe Hulbig, 13, St. Sebastian H.S. (Mass.)
1993	Jason Arnott, 7, Oshawa (OHL)
	Nick Stajduhar, 16, London (OHL)
1994	Jason Bonsignore, 4, Niagara Falls (OHL)
	Ryan Smyth, 6, Moose Jaw (WHL)
1995	Steve Kelly, 6, Prince Albert (WHL)
1996	Boyd Devereaux, 6, Kitchener (OHL)
	Matthieu Descoteaux, 19, Shawinigan (QMJHL)
1997	Michel Riessen, 14, HC Biel, Switzerland
1998	Michael Henrich, 13, Barrie (OHL)
1999	Jani Rita, 13, Jokerit Helsinki, Finland
2000	Alexei Mikhnov, 17, Yaroslavl, Russia

NOTE: Edmonton chose Dave Dryden, Bengt Gustafsson and Ed Mio as priority selections before the 1979 expansion draft.

SINGLE-SEASON INDIVIDUAL RECORDS

FORWARDS/DEFENSEMEN

Most goals
92—Wayne Gretzky, 1981-82

Most assists
163—Wayne Gretzky, 1985-86

Most points
215—Wayne Gretzky, 1985-86

Most penalty minutes
286—Steve Smith, 1987-88

Most power play goals
20—Wayne Gretzky, 1983-84
Ryan Smyth, 1996-97

Most shorthanded goals
12—Wayne Gretzky, 1983-84

Most games with three or more goals
10—Wayne Gretzky, 1981-82
Wayne Gretzky, 1983-84

Most shots
369—Wayne Gretzky, 1981-82

GOALTENDERS

Most games
75—Grant Fuhr, 1987-88

Most minutes
4,304—Grant Fuhr, 1987-88

Most goals allowed
246—Grant Fuhr, 1987-88

Lowest goals-against average
2.33—Tommy Salo, 1999-2000

Most shutouts
8—Curtis Joseph, 1997-98

Most wins
40—Grant Fuhr, 1987-88

Most losses
38—Bill Ranford, 1992-93

Most ties
14—Grant Fuhr, 1981-82

FRANCHISE LEADERS

Players in boldface played for club in 1999-2000

FORWARDS/DEFENSEMEN

Games

Kevin Lowe	1037
Mark Messier	851
Glenn Anderson	828
Kelly Buchberger	795
Jari Kurri	754

Goals

Wayne Gretzky	583
Jari Kurri	474
Glenn Anderson	413
Mark Messier	392
Paul Coffey	209

Assists

Wayne Gretzky	1086
Mark Messier	642
Jari Kurri	569
Glenn Anderson	483
Paul Coffey	460

Points

Wayne Gretzky	1669
Jari Kurri	1043
Mark Messier	1034
Glenn Anderson	896
Paul Coffey	669

Penalty minutes

Kelly Buchberger	1747
Kevin McClelland	1298
Kevin Lowe	1236
Mark Messier	1122
Steve Smith	1080

GOALTENDERS

Games

Bill Ranford	433
Grant Fuhr	423
Andy Moog	235
Curtis Joseph	177
Tommy Salo	**83**

Shutouts

Curtis Joseph	14
Grant Fuhr	9
Bill Ranford	8
Andy Moog	4
Mikhail Shtalenkov	3

Goals-against average
(2400 minutes minimum)

Tommy Salo	**2.33**
Bob Essensa	2.73
Curtis Joseph	2.90
Bill Ranford	3.51
Andy Moog	3.61

Wins

Grant Fuhr	226
Bill Ranford	163
Andy Moog	143
Curtis Joseph	76
Tommy Salo	**35**

FLORIDA PANTHERS
YEAR-BY-YEAR RECORDS

	REGULAR SEASON						PLAYOFFS			
Season	W	L	T	RT	Pts.	Finish	W	L	Highest round	Coach
1993-94	33	34	17	—	83	5th/Atlantic	—	—		Roger Neilson
1994-95	20	22	6	—	46	5th/Atlantic	—	—		Roger Neilson
1995-96	41	31	10	—	92	3rd/Atlantic	12	10	Stanley Cup finals	Doug MacLean

	REGULAR SEASON					PLAYOFFS			
Season	W	L	T	RT	Pts.	Finish	W	L	Highest round	Coach
1996-97	35	28	19	—	89	3rd/Atlantic	1	4	Conference quarterfinals	Doug MacLean
1997-98	24	43	15	—	63	6th/Atlantic	—	—		Doug MacLean, Bryan Murray
1998-99	30	34	18	—	78	2nd/Southeast	—	—		Terry Murray
1999-00	43	33	6	6	98	2nd/Southeast	0	4	Conference quarterfinals	Terry Murray

FIRST-ROUND ENTRY DRAFT CHOICES

Year   Player, Overall, Last amateur team (league)
1993—Rob Niedermayer, 5, Medicine Hat (WHL)
1994—Ed Jovanovski, 1, Windsor (OHL)*
1995—Radek Dvorak, 10, Budejovice, Czech Republic
1996—Marcus Nilson, 20, Djurgarden-Stockholm, Sweden
1997—Mike Brown, 20, Red Deer (WHL)

Year   Player, Overall, Last amateur team (league)
1998—No first-round selection
1999—Denis Shvidki, 12, Barrie (OHL)
2000—No first-round selection
*Designates first player chosen in draft.

SINGLE-SEASON INDIVIDUAL RECORDS

FORWARDS/DEFENSEMEN

Most goals
58—Pavel Bure, 1999-2000

Most assists
53—Viktor Kozlov, 1999-2000

Most points
94—Pavel Bure, 1999-2000

Most penalty minutes
313—Paul Laus, 1996-97

Most power play goals
19—Scott Mellanby, 1995-96

Most shorthanded goals
6—Tom Fitzgerald, 1995-96

Most games with three or more goals
4—Pavel Bure, 1999-2000

Most shots
360—Pavel Bure, 1999-2000

GOALTENDERS

Most games
60—John Vanbiesbrouck, 1996-97

Most minutes
3,451—John Vanbiesbrouck, 1997-98

Most shots against
1,912—John Vanbiesbrouck, 1993-94

Most goals allowed
165—John Vanbiesbrouck, 1997-98

Lowest goals-against average
2.29—John Vanbiesbrouck, 1996-97

Most shutouts
4—John Vanbiesbrouck, 1994-95
    John Vanbiesbrouck, 1997-98

Most wins
27—John Vanbiesbrouck, 1996-97

Most losses
29—John Vanbiesbrouck, 1997-98

Most ties
11—Sean Burke, 1998-99

FRANCHISE LEADERS

Players in boldface played for club in 1999-2000

FORWARDS/DEFENSEMEN

Games
Scott Mellanby...........................512
Paul Laus...................................460
Rob Niedermayer......................451
Bill Lindsay...............................443
Robert Svehla...........................409

Goals
Scott Mellanby...........................153
Rob Niedermayer........................89
Ray Whitney................................87
Radek Dvorak..............................69
Bill Lindsay..................................63

Assists
Scott Mellanby...........................188
Robert Svehla............................185
Rob Niedermayer......................145
Ray Whitney...............................109
Viktor Kozlov................................99

Points
Scott Mellanby...........................341
Rob Niedermayer......................234
Robert Svehla............................233
Ray Whitney...............................196
Radek Dvorak............................162

Penalty minutes
Paul Laus 1479
Scott Mellanby...........................907
Bill Lindsay................................492
Ed Jovanovski...........................467
Brian Skrudland.........................401

GOALTENDERS

Games
John Vanbiesbrouck....................268
Mark Fitzpatrick.........................119
Sean Burke..................................66
Kirk McLean.................................37
Mike Vernon 34

Shutouts
John Vanbiesbrouck.....................13
Mark Fitzpatrick............................4
Sean Burke 3
Kirk McLean 2
Trevor Kidd....................................1
Mike Vernon...................................1

Goals-against average
(2400 minutes minimum)
John Vanbiesbrouck....................2.58
Sean Burke 2.65
Mark Fitzpatrick.........................2.71

Wins
John Vanbiesbrouck....................106
Mark Fitzpatrick...........................43
Sean Burke 23
Mike Vernon 18
Trevor Kidd..................................14

HAMILTON TIGERS (DEFUNCT)
YEAR-BY-YEAR RECORDS

	REGULAR SEASON					PLAYOFFS			
Season	W	L	T	Pts.	Finish	W	L	Highest round	Coach
1920-21	6	18	0	12	4th	—	—		Percy Thompson
1921-22	7	17	0	14	4th	—	—		Percy Thompson
1922-23	6	18	0	12	4th	—	—		Art Ross

Season	W	L	T	Pts.	Finish		W	L	Highest round		Coach
				REGULAR SEASON					PLAYOFFS		
1923-24	9	15	0	18	4th		*—	—			Percy Lesueur
1924-25	19	10	1	39	1st		*—	—			Jimmy Gardner

*Refused to participate in playoffs—held out for more compensation.

Franchise was formerly known as Quebec Bulldogs and relocated to Hamilton following 1919-20 season; franchise relocated and became New York Americans following 1924-1925 season.

HARTFORD WHALERS (DEFUNCT)
YEAR-BY-YEAR RECORDS

Season	W	L	T	Pts.	Finish		W	L	Highest round	Coach
				REGULAR SEASON					PLAYOFFS	
1972-73*	46	30	2	94	1st		12	3	Avco World Cup champ	Jack Kelley
1973-74*	43	31	4	90	1st		3	4	League quarterfinals	Ron Ryan
1974-75*	43	30	5	91	1st		2	4	League quarterfinals	Ron Ryan, Jack Kelley
1975-76*	33	40	7	73	3rd		6	4	League semifinals	Jack Kelley, Don Blackburn, Harry Neale
1976-77*	35	40	6	76	4th		1	4	League quarterfinals	Harry Neale
1977-78*	44	31	5	93	2nd		8	6	Avco World Cup finals	Harry Neale
1978-79*	37	34	9	83	4th		5	5	League semifinals	Bill Dineen, Don Blackburn
1979-80	27	34	19	73	4th/Norris		0	3	Preliminaries	Don Blackburn
1980-81	21	41	18	60	4th/Norris		—	—		Don Blackburn, Larry Pleau
1981-82	21	41	18	60	5th/Adams		—	—		Larry Pleau
1982-83	19	54	7	45	5th/Adams		—	—		Larry Kish, Larry Pleau, John Cunniff
1983-84	28	42	10	66	5th/Adams		—	—		Jack Evans
1984-85	30	41	9	69	5th/Adams		—	—		Jack Evans
1985-86	40	36	4	84	4th/Adams		6	4	Division finals	Jack Evans
1986-87	43	30	7	93	1st/Adams		2	4	Division semifinals	Jack Evans
1987-88	35	38	7	77	4th/Adams		2	4	Division semifinals	Jack Evans, Larry Pleau
1988-89	37	38	5	79	4th/Adams		0	4	Division semifinals	Larry Pleau
1989-90	38	33	9	85	4th/Adams		3	4	Division semifinals	Rick Ley
1990-91	31	38	11	73	4th/Adams		2	4	Division semifinals	Rick Ley
1991-92	26	41	13	65	4th/Adams		3	4	Division semifinals	Jim Roberts
1992-93	26	52	6	58	5th/Adams		—	—		Paul Holmgren
1993-94	27	48	9	63	6th/Northeast		—	—		Paul Holmgren, Pierre McGuire
1994-95	19	24	5	43	5th/Northeast		—	—		Paul Holmgren
1995-96	34	39	9	77	4th/Northeast		—	—		Paul Holmgren, Paul Maurice
1996-97	32	39	11	75	5th/Northeast		—	—		Paul Maurice

*New England Whalers, members of World Hockey Association.

Franchise relocated and became Carolina Hurricanes following 1996-97 season.

FIRST-ROUND ENTRY DRAFT CHOICES

Year Player, Overall, Last amateur team (league)

1979—Ray Allison, 18, Brandon (WHL)
1980—Fred Arthur, 8, Cornwall (QMJHL)
1981—Ron Francis, 4, Sault Ste. Marie (OHL)
1982—Paul Lawless, 14, Windsor (OHL)
1983—Sylvain Turgeon, 2, Hull (QMJHL)
          David A. Jensen, 20, Lawrence Academy (Mass.)
1984—Sylvain Cote, 11, Quebec (QMJHL)
1985—Dana Murzyn, 5, Calgary (WHL)
1986—Scott Young, 11, Boston University
1987—Jody Hull, 18, Peterborough (OHL)
1988—Chris Govedaris, 11, Toronto (OHL)

Year Player, Overall, Last amateur team (league)

1989—Robert Holik, 10, Jihlava (Czechoslovakia)
1990—Mark Greig, 15, Lethbridge (WHL)
1991—Patrick Poulin, 9, St. Hyacinthe (QMJHL)
1992—Robert Petrovicky, 9, Dukla Trencin (Czech.)
1993—Chris Pronger, 2, Peterborough (OHL)
1994—Jeff O'Neill, 5, Guelph (OHL)
1995—Jean-Sebastien Giguere, 13, Halifax (QMJHL)
1996—No first-round selection
1997—Nikos Tselios, 22, Belleville (OHL)
NOTE: Hartford chose Jordy Douglas, John Garrett and Mark Howe as priority selections before the 1979 expansion draft.

SINGLE-SEASON INDIVIDUAL RECORDS

FORWARDS/DEFENSEMEN

Most goals
56—Blaine Stoughton, 1979-80

Most assists
69—Ron Francis, 1989-90

Most points
105—Mike Rogers, 1979-80
        Mike Rogers, 1980-81

Most penalty minutes
358—Torrie Robertson, 1985-86

Most power play goals
21—Geoff Sanderson, 1992-93

Most shorthanded goals
4—Mike Rogers, 1980-81
    Kevin Dineen, 1984-85

Most games with three or more goals
3—Mike Rogers, 1980-81
    Blaine Stoughton, 1981-82

GOALTENDERS

Most games
66—Sean Burke, 1995-96

Most minutes
3,669—Sean Burke, 1995-96

Most goals allowed
282—Greg Millen, 1982-83

Lowest goals-against average
2.64—Mike Liut, 1989-90

Most shutouts
4—Mike Liut, 1986-87
Peter Sidorkiewicz, 1988-89
Sean Burke, 1995-96
Sean Burke, 1996-97

Most wins
31—Mike Liut, 1986-87

Most losses
38—Greg Millen, 1982-83

Most ties
12—John Garrett, 1980-81
Greg Millen, 1982-83

FRANCHISE LEADERS

FORWARDS/DEFENSEMEN

Games
Ron Francis	714
Kevin Dineen	587
Adam Burt	499
Dave Tippett	483
Ulf Samuelsson	463

Goals
Ron Francis	264
Kevin Dineen	235
Blaine Stoughton	219
Pat Verbeek	192
Geoff Sanderson	189

Assists
Ron Francis	557
Kevin Dineen	268
Andrew Cassels	253
Pat Verbeek	211
Dave Babych	196

Points
Ron Francis	821
Kevin Dineen	503
Pat Verbeek	403
Blaine Stoughton	377
Geoff Sanderson	352

Penalty minutes
Torrie Robertson	1368
Kevin Dineen	1239
Pat Verbeek	1144
Ulf Samuelsson	1108
Adam Burt	723

GOALTENDERS

Games
Sean Burke	256
Mike Liut	252
Greg Millen	219
Peter Sidorkiewicz	178
John Garrett	122

Shutouts
Mike Liut	13
Sean Burke	10
Peter Sidorkiewicz	8
Greg Millen	4
Steve Weeks	4

Goals-against average
(2400 minutes minimum)
Sean Burke	3.12
Jason Muzzatti	3.23
Peter Sidorkiewicz	3.33
Mike Liut	3.36
Kay Whitmore	3.61

Wins
Mike Liut	115
Sean Burke	101
Peter Sidorkiewicz	71
Greg Millen	62
Steve Weeks	42

KANSAS CITY SCOUTS (DEFUNCT)
YEAR-BY-YEAR RECORDS

	REGULAR SEASON					PLAYOFFS			
Season	W	L	T	Pts.	Finish	W	L	Highest round	Coach
1974-75	15	54	11	41	5th/Smythe	—	—		Bep Guidolin
1975-76	12	56	12	36	5th/Smythe	—	—		Bep Guidolin, Sid Abel, Eddie Bush

Franchise relocated and became Colorado Rockies following 1975-76 season; franchise later relocated and became New Jersey Devils after 1981-82 season.

FIRST-ROUND ENTRY DRAFT CHOICES

Year Player, Overall, Last amateur team (league)
1974—Wilf Paiement, 2, St. Catharines (OHL)

Year Player, Overall, Last amateur team (league)
1975—Barry Dean, 2, Medicine Hat (WCHL)

SINGLE-SEASON INDIVIDUAL RECORDS

FORWARDS/DEFENSEMEN

Most goals
27—Guy Charron, 1975-76

Most assists
44—Guy Charron, 1975-76

Most points
71—Guy Charron, 1975-76

Most penalty minutes
209—Steve Durbano, 1975-76

Most power play goals
11—Simon Nolet, 1974-75

Most shorthanded goals
2—Ed Gilbert, 1974-75
Simon Nolet, 1974-75

Most games with three or more goals
1—Wilf Paiement, 1975-76

Most shots
226—Guy Charron, 1975-76

GOALTENDERS

Most games
64—Denis Herron, 1975-76

Most minutes
3,620—Denis Herron, 1975-76

Most goals allowed
243—Denis Herron, 1975-76

Lowest goals-against average
4.03—Denis Herron, 1975-76

Most shutouts
Never accomplished

Most wins
11—Denis Herron, 1975-76

Most losses
39—Denis Herron, 1975-76

Most ties
11—Denis Herron, 1975-76

FRANCHISE LEADERS

FORWARDS/DEFENSEMEN

Games
Gary Croteau 156
Randy Rota 151
Robin Burns 149
Dave Hudson....................................144
Wilf Paiement 135

Goals
Wilf Paiement 47
Guy Charron 40
Simon Nolet 36
Robin Burns 31
Gary Croteau 27
Randy Rota 27

Assists
Guy Charron 73
Dave Hudson......................................52
Simon Nolet 47
Wilf Paiement 35

Gary Bergman 33
Robin Burns 33

Points
Guy Charron 113
Simon Nolet 83
Wilf Paiement 82
Dave Hudson......................................72
Robin Burns 64

Penalty minutes
Wilf Paiement 222
Steve Durbano...................................209
Jean-Guy Lagace..............................130
Larry Johnston 122
Robin Burns 107

GOALTENDERS

Games
Denis Herron 86
Peter McDuffe 36
Michel Plasse 24
Bill McKenzie.......................................22
Bill Oleschuk 1

Shutouts
Never occurred

Goals-against average
(2400 minutes minimum)
Denis Herron 3.96

Wins
Denis Herron 15
Peter McDuffe 7
Michel Plasse 4
Bill McKenzie...1

LOS ANGELES KINGS
YEAR-BY-YEAR RECORDS

Season	W	L	T	RT	Pts.	Finish	W	L	Highest round	Coach
1967-68	31	33	10	—	72	2nd/West	3	4	Division semifinals	Red Kelly
1968-69	24	42	10	—	58	4th/West	4	7	Division finals	Red Kelly
1969-70	14	52	10	—	38	6th/West	—	—		Hal Laycoe, Johnny Wilson
1970-71	25	40	13	—	63	5th/West	—	—		Larry Regan
1971-72	20	49	9	—	49	7th/West	—	—		Larry Regan, Fred Glover
1972-73	31	36	11	—	73	6th/West	—	—		Bob Pulford
1973-74	33	33	12	—	78	3rd/West	1	4	Division semifinals	Bob Pulford
1974-75	42	17	21	—	105	2nd/Norris	1	2	Preliminaries	Bob Pulford
1975-76	38	33	9	—	85	2nd/Norris	5	4	Quarterfinals	Bob Pulford
1976-77	34	31	15	—	83	2nd/Norris	4	5	Quarterfinals	Bob Pulford
1977-78	31	34	15	—	77	3rd/Norris	0	2	Preliminaries	Ron Stewart
1978-79	34	34	12	—	80	3rd/Norris	0	2	Preliminaries	Bob Berry
1979-80	30	36	14	—	74	2nd/Norris	1	3	Preliminaries	Bob Berry
1980-81	43	24	13	—	99	2nd/Norris	1	3	Preliminaries	Bob Berry
1981-82	24	41	15	—	63	4th/Smythe	4	6	Division finals	Parker MacDonald, Don Perry,
1982-83	27	41	12	—	66	5th/Smythe	—	—		Don Perry
1983-84	23	44	13	—	59	5th/Smythe	—	—		Don Perry, Rogie Vachon,
										Roger Neilson
1984-85	34	32	14	—	82	4th/Smythe	0	3	Division semifinals	Pat Quinn
1985-86	23	49	8	—	54	5th/Smythe	—	—		Pat Quinn
1986-87	31	41	8	—	70	4th/Smythe	1	4	Division semifinals	Pat Quinn, Mike Murphy
1987-88	30	42	8	—	68	4th/Smythe	1	4	Division semifinals	Mike Murphy, Rogie Vachon,
										Robbie Ftorek
1988-89	42	31	7	—	91	2nd/Smythe	4	7	Division finals	Robbie Ftorek
1989-90	34	39	7	—	75	4th/Smythe	4	6	Division finals	Tom Webster
1990-91	46	24	10	—	102	1st/Smythe	6	6	Division finals	Tom Webster
1991-92	35	31	14	—	84	2nd/Smythe	2	4	Division semifinals	Tom Webster
1992-93	39	35	10	—	88	3rd/Smythe	13	11	Stanley Cup finals	Barry Melrose
1993-94	27	45	12	—	66	5th/Pacific	—	—		Barry Melrose
1994-95	16	23	9	—	41	4th/Pacific	—	—		Barry Melrose, Rogie Vachon
1995-96	24	40	18	—	66	6th/Pacific	—	—		Larry Robinson
1996-97	28	43	11	—	67	6th/Pacific	—	—		Larry Robinson
1997-98	38	33	11	—	87	2nd/Pacific	0	4	Conference quarterfinals	Larry Robinson
1998-99	32	45	5	—	69	5th/Pacific	—	—		Larry Robinson
1999-00	39	31	12	4	94	2nd/Pacific	0	4	Conference quarterfinals	Andy Murray

FIRST-ROUND ENTRY DRAFT CHOICES

Year   Player, Overall, Last amateur team (league)
1969—No first-round selection
1970—No first-round selection
1971—No first-round selection

Year   Player, Overall, Last amateur team (league)
1972—No first-round selection
1973—No first-round selection
1974—No first-round selection

Year	Player, Overall, Last amateur team (league)
1975	Tim Young, 16, Ottawa (OHL)
1976	No first-round selection
1977	No first-round selection
1978	No first-round selection
1979	Jay Wells, 16, Kingston (OHL)
1980	Larry Murphy, 4, Peterborough (OHL)
	Jim Fox, 10, Ottawa (OHL)
1981	Doug Smith, 2, Ottawa (OHL)
1982	No first-round selection
1983	No first-round selection
1984	Craig Redmond, 6, Canadian Olympic Team
1985	Craig Duncanson, 9, Sudbury (OHL)
	Dan Gratton, 10, Oshawa (OHL)
1986	Jimmy Carson, 2, Verdun (QMJHL)
1987	Wayne McBean, 4, Medicine Hat (WHL)

Year	Player, Overall, Last amateur team (league)
1988	Martin Gelinas, 7, Hull (QMJHL)
1989	No first-round selection
1990	Darryl Sydor, 7, Kamloops (WHL)
1991	No first-round selection
1992	No first-round selection
1993	No first-round selection
1994	Jamie Storr, 7, Owen Sound (OHL)
1995	Aki-Petteri Berg, 3, TPS Jrs., Finland
1996	No first-round selection
1997	Olli Jokinen, 3, IFK Helsinki, Finland
	Matt Zultek, 15, Ottawa (OHL)
1998	Mathieu Biron, 21, Shawinigan (QMJHL)
1999	No first-round selection
2000	Alexander Frolov, 20, Yaroslavl, Russia

SINGLE-SEASON INDIVIDUAL RECORDS

FORWARDS/DEFENSEMEN

Most goals
70—Bernie Nicholls, 1988-89

Most assists
122—Wayne Gretzky, 1990-91

Most points
168—Wayne Gretzky, 1988-89

Most penalty minutes
399—Marty McSorley, 1992-93

Most power play goals
26—Luc Robitaille, 1991-92

Most shorthanded goals
8—Bernie Nicholls, 1988-89

Most games with three or more goals
5—Jimmy Carson, 1987-88

Most shots
385—Bernie Nicholls, 1988-89

GOALTENDERS

Most games
70—Rogie Vachon, 1977-78

Most minutes
4,107—Rogie Vachon, 1977-78

Most shots against
2,219—Kelly Hrudey, 1993-94

Most goals allowed
228—Kelly Hrudey, 1993-94

Lowest goals-against average
2.24—Rogie Vachon, 1974-75

Most shutouts
8—Rogie Vachon, 1977-78

Most wins
35—Mario Lessard, 1980-81

Most losses
31—Kelly Hrudey, 1993-94

Most ties
13—Rogie Vachon, 1974-75
Rogie Vachon, 1977-78
Kelly Hrudey, 1991-92

FRANCHISE LEADERS

Players in boldface played for club in 1999-2000

FORWARDS/DEFENSEMEN

Games
Dave Taylor	1111
Marcel Dionne	921
Luc Robitaille	**850**
Butch Goring	736
Mike Murphy	673

Goals
Marcel Dionne	550
Luc Robitaille	**483**
Dave Taylor	431
Bernie Nicholls	327
Butch Goring	275

Assists
Marcel Dionne	757
Wayne Gretzky	672
Dave Taylor	638
Luc Robitaille	**508**
Bernie Nicholls	431

Points
Marcel Dionne	1307
Dave Taylor	1069
Luc Robitaille	**991**
Wayne Gretzky	918
Bernie Nicholls	758

Penalty minutes
Marty McSorley	1846
Dave Taylor	1589
Jay Wells	1446
Rob Blake	**982**
Mark Hardy	858

GOALTENDERS

Games
Rogie Vachon	389
Kelly Hrudey	360
Mario Lessard	240
Stephane Fiset	**193**
Gary Edwards	155

Shutouts
Rogie Vachon	32
Stephane Fiset	**10**
Kelly Hrudey	10
Mario Lessard	9
Gerry Desjardins	7
Gary Edwards	7
Jamie Storr	**7**

Goals-against average
(2400 minutes minimum)
Jamie Storr	**2.52**
Stephane Fiset	**2.80**
Rogie Vachon	2.86
Wayne Rutledge	3.34
Gary Edwards	3.39

Wins
Rogie Vachon	171
Kelly Hrudey	145
Mario Lessard	92
Stephane Fiset	**77**
Gary Edwards	54

NHL HISTORY Team by team

MINNESOTA NORTH STARS (DEFUNCT)

YEAR-BY-YEAR RECORDS

	REGULAR SEASON						PLAYOFFS			
Season	W	L	T	RT	Pts.	Finish	W	L	Highest round	Coach
1967-68	27	32	15	—	69	4th/West	7	7	Division finals	Wren Blair
1968-69	18	43	15	—	51	6th/West	—	—		Wren Blair, John Muckler
1969-70	19	35	22	—	60	3rd/West	2	4	Division semifinals	Wren Blair, Charlie Burns

		REGULAR SEASON					PLAYOFFS			
Season	W	L	T	RT	Pts.	Finish	W	L	Highest round	Coach
1970-71	28	34	16	—	72	4th/West	6	6	Division finals	Jack Gordon
1971-72	37	29	12	—	86	2nd/West	3	4	Division semifinals	Jack Gordon
1972-73	37	30	11	—	85	3rd/West	2	4	Division semifinals	Jack Gordon
1973-74	23	38	17	—	63	7th/West	—	—		Jack Gordon, Parker MacDonald
1974-75	23	50	7	—	53	4th/Smythe	—	—		Jack Gordon, Charlie Burns
1975-76	20	53	7	—	47	4th/Smythe	—	—		Ted Harris
1976-77	23	39	18	—	64	2nd/Smythe	0	2	Preliminaries	Ted Harris
1977-78	18	53	9	—	45	5th/Smythe	—	—		Ted Harris, Andre Beaulieu, Lou Nanne
1978-79	28	40	12	—	68	4th/Adams	—	—		Harry Howell, Glen Sonmor
1979-80	36	28	16	—	88	3rd/Adams	8	7	Semifinals	Glen Sonmor
1980-81	35	28	17	—	87	3rd/Adams	12	7	Stanley Cup finals	Glen Sonmor
1981-82	37	23	20	—	94	1st/Norris	1	3	Division semifinals	Glen Sonmor, Murray Oliver
1982-83	40	24	16	—	96	2nd/Norris	4	5	Division finals	Glen Sonmor, Murray Oliver
1983-84	39	31	10	—	88	1st/Norris	7	9	Conference finals	Bill Maloney
1984-85	25	43	12	—	62	4th/Norris	5	4	Division finals	Bill Maloney, Glen Sonmor
1985-86	38	33	9	—	85	2nd/Norris	2	3	Division semifinals	Lorne Henning
1986-87	30	40	10	—	70	5th/Norris	—	—		Lorne Henning, Glen Sonmor
1987-88	19	48	13	—	51	5th/Norris	—	—		Herb Brooks
1988-89	27	37	16	—	70	3rd/Norris	1	4	Division semifinals	Pierre Page
1989-90	36	40	4	—	76	4th/Norris	3	4	Division semifinals	Pierre Page
1990-91	27	39	14	—	68	4th/Norris	14	9	Stanley Cup finals	Bob Gainey
1991-92	32	42	6	—	70	4th/Norris	3	4	Division semifinals	Bob Gainey
1992-93	36	38	10	—	82	5th/Norris	—	—		Bob Gainey

Franchise relocated and became Dallas Stars following 1992-93 season.

FIRST-ROUND ENTRY DRAFT CHOICES

Year   Player, Overall, Last amateur team (league)
1969—Dick Redmond, 5, St. Catharines (OHL)
Dennis O'Brien, 14, St. Catharines (OHL)
1970—No first-round selection
1971—No first-round selection
1972—Jerry Byers, 12, Kitchener (OHL)
1973—No first-round selection
1974—Doug Hicks, 6, Flin Flon (WCHL)
1975—Brian Maxwell, 4, Medicine Hat (WCHL)
1976—Glen Sharpley, 3, Hull (QMJHL)
1977—Brad Maxwell, 7, New Westminster (WCHL)
1978—Bobby Smith, 1, Ottawa (OHL)*
1979—Craig Hartsburg, 6, Birmingham (WHA)
Tom McCarthy, 10, Oshawa (OHL)
1980—Brad Palmer, 16, Victoria (WHL)

Year   Player, Overall, Last amateur team (league)
1981—Ron Meighan, 13, Niagara Falls (OHL)
1982—Brian Bellows, 2, Kitchener (OHL)
1983—Brian Lawton, 1, Mount St. Charles H.S. (R.I.)*
1984—David Quinn, 13, Kent H.S. (Ct.)
1985—No first-round selection
1986—Warren Babe, 12, Lethbridge (WHL)
1987—Dave Archibald, 6, Portland (WHL)
1988—Mike Modano, 1, Prince Albert (WHL)*
1989—Doug Zmolek, 7, John Marshall H.S. (Minn.)
1990—Derian Hatcher, 8, North Bay (OHL)
1991—Richard Matvichuk, 8, Saskatoon (WHL)
1992—No first-round selection
*Designates first player chosen in draft.

SINGLE-SEASON INDIVIDUAL RECORDS

FORWARDS/DEFENSEMEN

Most goals
55—Dino Ciccarelli, 1981-82
Brian Bellows, 1989-90

Most assists
76—Neal Broten, 1985-86

Most points
114—Bobby Smith, 1981-82

Most penalty minutes
382—Basil McRae, 1987-88

Most power play goals
22—Dino Ciccarelli, 1986-87

Most shorthanded goals
6—Bill Collins, 1969-70

Most games with three or more goals
3—Bill Goldsworthy, 1973-74
Dino Ciccarelli, 1981-82
Dino Ciccarelli, 1983-84
Tom McCarthy, 1984-85
Scott Bjugstad, 1985-86
Dino Ciccarelli, 1985-86

Most shots
321—Bill Goldsworthy, 1973-74

GOALTENDERS

Most games
64—Cesare Maniago, 1968-69

Most minutes
3,599—Cesare Maniago, 1968-69

Most goals allowed
216—Pete LoPresti, 1977-78

Lowest goals-against average
2.12—Gump Worsley, 1971-72

Most shutouts
6—Cesare Maniago, 1967-68

Most wins
31—Jon Casey, 1989-90

Most losses
35—Pete LoPresti, 1977-78

Most ties
16—Cesare Maniago, 1969-70

FRANCHISE LEADERS

FORWARDS/DEFENSEMEN

Games

Neal Broten	876
Curt Giles	760
Brian Bellows	753
Fred Barrett	730
Bill Goldsworthy	670

Goals

Brian Bellows	342
Dino Ciccarelli	332
Bill Goldsworthy	267
Neal Broten	249
Steve Payne	228

Assists

Neal Broten	547
Brian Bellows	380
Bobby Smith	369
Dino Ciccarelli	319
Tim Young	316

Points

Neal Broten	796
Brian Bellows	722
Dino Ciccarelli	651
Bobby Smith	554
Bill Goldsworthy	506

Penalty minutes

Basil McRae	1567
Shane Churla	1194
Willi Plett	1137
Brad Maxwell	1031
Mark Tinordi	872

GOALTENDERS

Games

Cesare Maniago	420
Gilles Meloche	328
Jon Casey	325
Don Beaupre	316
Pete LoPresti	173

Shutouts

Cesare Maniago	29
Jon Casey	12
Gilles Meloche	9
Pete LoPresti	5
Don Beaupre	4
Brian Hayward	4

Goals-against average (2400 minutes minimum)

Gump Worsley	2.62
Cesare Maniago	3.17
Jon Casey	3.28
Gilles Gilbert	3.39
Gary Edwards	3.44
Darcy Wakaluk	3.44

Wins

Cesare Maniago	143
Gilles Meloche	141
Jon Casey	128
Don Beaupre	126
Pete LoPresti	43

MONTREAL CANADIENS
YEAR-BY-YEAR RECORDS

Season	W	L	T	RT	Pts.	Finish	W	L	Highest round	Coach
1917-18	13	9	0	—	26	1st/3rd	1	1	Semifinals	George Kennedy
1918-19	10	8	0	—	20	1st/2nd	†*6	3	Stanley Cup finals	George Kennedy
1919-20	13	11	0	—	26	2nd/3rd	—	—		George Kennedy
1920-21	13	11	0	—	26	3rd/2nd	—	—		George Kennedy
1921-22	12	11	1	—	25	3rd	—	—		Leo Dandurand
1922-23	13	9	2	—	28	2nd	1	1	Quarterfinals	Leo Dandurand
1923-24	13	11	0	—	26	2nd	6	0	Stanley Cup champ	Leo Dandurand
1924-25	17	11	2	—	36	3rd	3	3	Stanley Cup finals	Leo Dandurand
1925-26	11	24	1	—	23	7th	—	—		Cecil Hart
1926-27	28	14	2	—	58	2nd/Canadian	*1	1	Semifinals	Cecil Hart
1927-28	26	11	7	—	59	1st/Canadian	*0	1	Semifinals	Cecil Hart
1928-29	22	7	15	—	59	1st/Canadian	0	3	Semifinals	Cecil Hart
1929-30	21	14	9	—	51	2nd/Canadian	*5	0	Stanley Cup champ	Cecil Hart
1930-31	26	10	8	—	60	1st/Canadian	6	4	Stanley Cup champ	Cecil Hart
1931-32	25	16	7	—	57	1st/Canadian	1	3	Semifinals	Cecil Hart
1932-33	18	25	5	—	41	3rd/Canadian	*0	1	Quarterfinals	Newsy Lalonde
1933-34	22	20	6	—	50	2nd/Canadian	*0	1	Quarterfinals	Newsy Lalonde
1934-35	19	23	6	—	44	3rd/Canadian	*0	1	Quarterfinals	Newsy Lalonde, Leo Dandurand
1935-36	11	26	11	—	33	4th/Canadian	—	—		Sylvio Mantha
1936-37	24	18	6	—	54	1st/Canadian	2	3	Semifinals	Cecil Hart
1937-38	18	17	13	—	49	3rd/Canadian	1	2	Quarterfinals	Cecil Hart
1938-39	15	24	9	—	39	6th	1	2	Quarterfinals	Cecil Hart, Jules Dugal
1939-40	10	33	5	—	25	7th	—	—		Pit Lepine
1940-41	16	26	6	—	38	6th	1	2	Quarterfinals	Dick Irvin
1941-42	18	27	3	—	39	6th	1	2	Quarterfinals	Dick Irvin
1942-43	19	19	12	—	50	4th	1	4	League semifinals	Dick Irvin
1943-44	38	5	7	—	83	1st	8	1	Stanley Cup champ	Dick Irvin
1944-45	38	8	4	—	80	1st	2	4	League semifinals	Dick Irvin
1945-46	28	17	5	—	61	1st	8	1	Stanley Cup champ	Dick Irvin
1946-47	34	16	10	—	78	1st	6	5	Stanley Cup finals	Dick Irvin
1947-48	20	29	11	—	51	5th	—	—		Dick Irvin
1948-49	28	23	9	—	65	3rd	3	4	League semifinals	Dick Irvin
1949-50	29	22	19	—	77	2nd	1	4	League semifinals	Dick Irvin
1950-51	25	30	15	—	65	3rd	5	6	Stanley Cup finals	Dick Irvin
1951-52	34	26	10	—	78	2nd	4	7	Stanley Cup finals	Dick Irvin
1952-53	28	23	19	—	75	2nd	8	4	Stanley Cup champ	Dick Irvin
1953-54	35	24	11	—	81	2nd	7	4	Stanley Cup finals	Dick Irvin
1954-55	41	18	11	—	93	2nd	7	5	Stanley Cup finals	Dick Irvin
1955-56	45	15	10	—	100	1st	8	2	Stanley Cup champ	Toe Blake
1956-57	35	23	12	—	82	2nd	8	2	Stanley Cup champ	Toe Blake
1957-58	43	17	10	—	96	1st	8	2	Stanley Cup champ	Toe Blake

		REGULAR SEASON					PLAYOFFS		
Season	W	L	T	RT	Pts.	Finish	W	L	Highest round	Coach
1958-59	39	18	13	—	91	1st	8	3	Stanley Cup champ	Toe Blake
1959-60	40	18	12	—	92	1st	8	0	Stanley Cup champ	Toe Blake
1960-61	41	19	10	—	92	1st	2	4	League semifinals	Toe Blake
1961-62	42	14	14	—	98	1st	2	4	League semifinals	Toe Blake
1962-63	28	19	23	—	79	3rd	1	4	League semifinals	Toe Blake
1963-64	36	21	13	—	85	1st	3	4	League semifinals	Toe Blake
1964-65	36	23	11	—	83	2nd	8	5	Stanley Cup champ	Toe Blake
1965-66	41	21	8	—	90	1st	8	2	Stanley Cup champ	Toe Blake
1966-67	32	25	13	—	77	2nd	6	4	Stanley Cup finals	Toe Blake
1967-68	42	22	10	—	94	1st/East	12	1	Stanley Cup champ	Toe Blake
1968-69	46	19	11	—	103	1st/East	12	2	Stanley Cup champ	Claude Ruel
1969-70	38	22	16	—	92	5th/East	—	—		Claude Ruel
1970-71	42	23	13	—	97	3rd/East	12	8	Stanley Cup champ	Claude Ruel, Al MacNeil
1971-72	46	16	16	—	108	3rd/East	2	4	Division semifinals	Scotty Bowman
1972-73	52	10	16	—	120	1st/East	12	5	Stanley Cup champ	Scotty Bowman
1973-74	45	42	9	—	99	2nd/East	2	4	Division semifinals	Scotty Bowman
1974-75	47	14	19	—	113	1st/Norris	6	5	Semifinals	Scotty Bowman
1975-76	58	11	11	—	127	1st/Norris	12	1	Stanley Cup champ	Scotty Bowman
1976-77	60	8	12	—	132	1st/Norris	12	2	Stanley Cup champ	Scotty Bowman
1977-78	59	10	11	—	129	1st/Norris	12	3	Stanley Cup champ	Scotty Bowman
1978-79	52	17	11	—	115	1st/Norris	12	4	Stanley Cup champ	Scotty Bowman
1979-80	47	20	13	—	107	1st/Norris	6	4	Quarterfinals	Bernie Geoffrion, Claude Ruel
1980-81	45	22	13	—	103	1st/Norris	0	3	Preliminaries	Claude Ruel
1981-82	46	17	17	—	109	1st/Adams	2	3	Division semifinals	Bob Berry
1982-83	42	24	14	—	98	2nd/Adams	0	3	Division semifinals	Bob Berry
1983-84	35	40	5	—	75	4th/Adams	9	6	Conference finals	Bob Berry, Jacques Lemaire
1984-85	41	27	12	—	94	1st/Adams	6	6	Division finals	Jacques Lemaire
1985-86	40	33	7	—	87	2nd/Adams	15	5	Stanley Cup champ	Jean Perron
1986-87	41	29	10	—	92	2nd/Adams	10	7	Conference finals	Jean Perron
1987-88	45	22	13	—	103	1st/Adams	5	6	Division finals	Jean Perron
1988-89	53	18	9	—	115	1st/Adams	14	7	Stanley Cup finals	Pat Burns
1989-90	41	28	11	—	93	3rd/Adams	5	6	Division finals	Pat Burns
1990-91	39	30	11	—	89	2nd/Adams	7	6	Division finals	Pat Burns
1991-92	41	28	11	—	93	1st/Adams	4	7	Division finals	Pat Burns
1992-93	48	30	6	—	102	3rd/Adams	16	4	Stanley Cup champ	Jacques Demers
1993-94	41	29	14	—	96	3rd/Northeast	3	4	Conference quarterfinals	Jacques Demers
1994-95	18	23	7	—	43	6th/Northeast	—	—		Jacques Demers
1995-96	40	32	10	—	90	3rd/Northeast	2	4	Conference quarterfinals	Jacques Demers, Mario Tremblay
1996-97	31	36	15	—	77	T3rd/Northeast	1	4	Conference quarterfinals	Mario Tremblay
1997-98	37	32	13	—	87	4th/Northeast	4	6	Conference semifinals	Alain Vigneault
1998-99	32	39	11	—	75	5th/Northeast	—	—		Alain Vigneault
1999-00	35	38	9	4	83	4th/Northeast	—	—		Alain Vigneault

*Won-lost record does not indicate tie(s) resulting from two-game, total-goals series that year (two-game, total-goals series were played from 1917-18 through 1935-36).

†1918-19 series abandoned with no Cup holder due to influenza epidemic.

FIRST-ROUND ENTRY DRAFT CHOICES

Year   Player, Overall, Last amateur team (league)

1969—Rejean Houle, 1, Montreal (OHL)*
      Marc Tardif, 2, Montreal (OHL)
1970—Ray Martiniuk, 5, Flin Flon (WCHL)
      Chuck Lefley, 6, Canadian Nationals
1971—Guy Lafleur, 1, Quebec (QMJHL)*
      Chuck Arnason, 7, Flin Flon (WCHL)
      Murray Wilson, 11, Ottawa (OHL)
1972—Steve Shutt, 4, Toronto (OHL)
      Michel Larocque, 6, Ottawa (OHL)
      Dave Gardner, 8, Toronto (OHL)
      John Van Boxmeer, 14, Guelph (SOJHL)
1973—Bob Gainey, 8, Peterborough (OHL)
1974—Cam Connor, 5, Flin Flon (WCHL)
      Doug Risebrough, 7, Kitchener (OHL)
      Rick Chartraw, 10, Kitchener (OHL)
      Mario Tremblay, 12, Montreal (OHL)
      Gord McTavish, 15, Sudbury (OHL)
1975—Robin Sadler, 9, Edmonton (WCHL)
      Pierre Mondou, 15, Montreal (QMJHL)
1976—Peter Lee, 12, Ottawa (OHL)
      Rod Schutt, 13, Sudbury (OHL)
      Bruce Baker, 18, Ottawa (OHL)

1977—Mark Napier, 10, Birmingham (WHA)
      Normand Dupont, 18, Montreal (QMJHL)
1978—Danny Geoffrion, 8, Cornwall (QMJHL)
      Dave Hunter, 17, Sudbury (OHL)
1979—No first-round selection
1980—Doug Wickenheiser, 1, Regina (WHL)*
1981—Mark Hunter, 7, Brantford (OHL)
      Gilbert Delorme, 18, Chicoutimi (QMJHL)
      Jan Ingman, 19, Farjestads (Sweden)
1982—Alain Heroux, 19, Chicoutimi (QMJHL)
1983—Alfie Turcotte, 17, Portland (WHL)
1984—Petr Svoboda, 5, Czechoslovakia
      Shayne Corson, 8, Brantford (OHL)
1985—Jose Charbonneau, 12, Drummondville (QMJHL)
      Tom Chorske, 16, Minneapolis SW H.S. (Minn.)
1986—Mark Pederson, 15, Medicine Hat (WHL)
1987—Andrew Cassels, 17, Ottawa (OHL)
1988—Eric Charron, 20, Trois-Rivieres (QMJHL)
1989—Lindsay Vallis, 13, Seattle (WHL)
1990—Turner Stevenson, 12, Seattle (WHL)
1991—Brent Bilodeau, 17, Seattle (WHL)
1992—David Wilkie, 20, Kamloops (WHL)

NHL HISTORY *Team by team*

Year	Player, Overall, Last amateur team (league)
1993—Saku Koivu, 21, TPS Turku (Finland)
1994—Brad Brown, 18, North Bay (OHL)
1995—Terry Ryan, 8, Tri-City (WHL)
1996—Matt Higgins, 18, Moose Jaw (WHL)
1997—Jason Ward, 11, Erie (OHL)

Year	Player, Overall, Last amateur team (league)
1998—Eric Chouinard, 16, Quebec (QMJHL)
1999—No first-round selection
2000—Ron Hainsey, 13, Univ. of Mass.-Lowell
Marcel Hossa, 16, Portland (WHL)
*Designates first player chosen in draft.

SINGLE-SEASON INDIVIDUAL RECORDS

FORWARDS/DEFENSEMEN

Most goals
60—Steve Shutt, 1976-77
Guy Lafleur, 1977-78

Most assists
82—Pete Mahovlich, 1974-75

Most points
136—Guy Lafleur, 1976-77

Most penalty minutes
358—Chris Nilan, 1984-85

Most power play goals
20—Yvan Cournoyer, 1966-67

Most shorthanded goals
8—Guy Carbonneau, 1983-84

Most games with three or more goals
7—Joe Malone, 1917-18

GOALTENDERS

Most games
70—Gerry McNeil, 1950-51
Gerry McNeil, 1951-52
Jacques Plante, 1961-62

Most minutes
4,200—Gerry McNeil, 1950-51
Gerry McNeil, 1951-52
Jacques Plante, 1961-62

Lowest goals-against average
0.92—George Hainsworth, 1928-29

Most shutouts
22—George Hainsworth, 1928-29

Most wins
42—Jacques Plante, 1955-56
Jacques Plante, 1961-62
Ken Dryden, 1975-76

FRANCHISE LEADERS

Players in boldface played for club in 1999-2000

FORWARDS/DEFENSEMEN

Games
Henri Richard 1256
Larry Robinson 1202
Bob Gainey 1160
Jean Beliveau 1125
Claude Provost 1005

Goals
Maurice Richard 544
Guy Lafleur.............................518
Jean Beliveau 507
Yvan Cournoyer......................428
Steve Shutt............................408

Assists
Guy Lafleur.............................728
Jean Beliveau 712
Henri Richard 688
Larry Robinson 686
Jacques Lemaire 469

Points
Guy Lafleur............................1246
Jean Beliveau 1219
Henri Richard 1046
Maurice Richard 965
Larry Robinson 883

Penalty minutes
Chris Nilan.............................2248
Lyle Odelein...........................1367
Shayne Corson 1341
Maurice Richard 1285
John Ferguson 1214

GOALTENDERS

Games
Jacques Plante 556
Patrick Roy.............................551
Ken Dryden 397
Bill Durnan 383
George Hainsworth 318

Shutouts
George Hainsworth 75
Jacques Plante 58
Ken Dryden 46
Bill Durnan 34
Patrick Roy............................29

Wins
Jacques Plante 314
Patrick Roy............................289
Ken Dryden 258
Bill Durnan 208
George Hainsworth 167

MONTREAL MAROONS (DEFUNCT)
YEAR-BY-YEAR RECORDS

	REGULAR SEASON					PLAYOFFS			
Season	W	L	T	Pts.	Finish	W	L	Highest round	Coach
1924-25	9	19	2	20	5th	—	—		Eddie Gerard
1925-26	20	11	5	45	2nd	3	1	Stanley Cup champ	Eddie Gerard
1926-27	20	20	4	44	3rd/Canadian	*0	1	Quarterfinals	Eddie Gerard
1927-28	24	14	6	54	2nd/Canadian	*5	3	Stanley Cup finals	Eddie Gerard
1928-29	15	20	9	39	5th/Canadian	—	—		Eddie Gerard
1929-30	23	16	5	51	1st/Canadian	1	3	Semifinals	Dunc Munro
1930-31	20	18	6	46	3rd/Canadian	*0	2	Quarterfinals	Dunc Munro, George Boucher
1931-32	19	22	7	45	3rd/Canadian	*1	1	Semifinals	Sprague Cleghorn
1932-33	22	20	6	50	2nd/Canadian	0	2	Quarterfinals	Eddie Gerard
1933-34	19	18	11	49	3rd/Canadian	*1	2	Semifinals	Eddie Gerard
1934-35	24	19	5	53	2nd/Canadian	*5	0	Stanley Cup champ	Tommy Gorman
1935-36	22	16	10	54	1st/Canadian	0	3	Semifinals	Tommy Gorman
1936-37	22	17	9	53	2nd/Canadian	2	3	Semifinals	Tommy Gorman
1937-38	12	30	6	30	4th/Canadian	—	—		King Clancy, Tommy Gorman

NHL HISTORY Team by team

MONTREAL WANDERERS (DEFUNCT)
YEAR-BY-YEAR RECORDS

			REGULAR SEASON				PLAYOFFS			
Season	W	L	T	Pts.	Finish	W	L	Highest round		Coach
1917-18*	1	5	0	2	4th					Art Ross

*Franchise disbanded after Montreal Arena burned down. Montreal Canadiens and Toronto each counted one win for defaulted games with Wanderers.

NASHVILLE PREDATORS
YEAR-BY-YEAR RECORDS

				REGULAR SEASON			PLAYOFFS			
Season	W	L	T	RT	Pts.	Finish	W	L	Highest round	Coach
1998-99	28	47	7	—	63	4th/Central	—	—		Barry Trotz
1999-00	28	47	7	7	70	4th/Central	—	—		Barry Trotz

FIRST-ROUND ENTRY DRAFT CHOICES

Year Player, Overall, Last amateur team (league)
1998—David Legwand, 2, Plymouth (OHL)
1999—Brian Finley, 6, Barrie (OHL)

Year Player, Overall, Last amateur team (league)
2000—Scott Hartnell, 6, Prince Albert (WHL)

SINGLE-SEASON INDIVIDUAL RECORDS

FORWARDS/DEFENSEMEN

Most goals
26—Cliff Ronning, 1999-2000

Most assists
36—Cliff Ronning, 1999-2000

Most points
62—Cliff Ronning, 1999-2000

Most penalty minutes
242—Patrick Cote, 1998-99

Most power play goals
10—Sergei Krivokrasov, 1998-99

Most shorthanded goals
3—Greg Johnson, 1998-99
    Tom Fitzgerald, 1999-2000

Most games with three or more goals
1—Robert Valicevic, 1999-2000

Most shots
248—Cliff Ronning, 1999-2000

GOALTENDERS

Most games
52—Mike Dunham, 1999-2000

Most minutes
3,077—Mike Dunham, 1999-2000

Most goals allowed
146—Mike Dunham, 1999-2000

Lowest goals-against average
2.78—Tomas Vokoun, 1999-2000

Most shutouts
1—Mike Dunham, 1998-99
    Tomas Vokoun, 1998-99
    Tomas Vokoun, 1999-2000

Most wins
19—Mike Dunham, 1999-2000

Most losses
27—Mike Dunham, 1999-2000

Most ties
6—Mike Dunham, 1999-2000

FRANCHISE LEADERS

Players in boldface played for club in 1999-2000

FORWARDS/DEFENSEMEN

Games
Tom Fitzgerald 162
Cliff Ronning 154
Drake Berehowsky 153
Patric Kjellberg 153
Greg Johnson 150

Goals
Cliff Ronning 44
Patric Kjellberg 34
Sergei Krivokrasov 34
Greg Johnson 27
Sebastien Bordeleau 26
Tom Fitzgerald 26

Assists
Cliff Ronning 71
Greg Johnson 67

Scott Walker 46
Patric Kjellberg 43
Sergei Krivokrasov 40

Points
Cliff Ronning 115
Greg Johnson 94
Patric Kjellberg 77
Sergei Krivokrasov 74
Scott Walker 68

Penalty minutes
Patrick Cote 312
Bob Boughner 234
Drake Berehowsky 227
Denny Lambert 218
Scott Walker 193

GOALTENDERS

Games
Mike Dunham 96
Tomas Vokoun 70
Eric Fichaud 9
Chris Mason 3

Shutouts
Tomas Vokoun 2
Mike Dunham 1

Goals-against average
(2400 minutes minimum)
Tomas Vokoun 2.86
Mike Dunham 2.95

Wins
Mike Dunham 35
Tomas Vokoun 21

NHL HISTORY *Team by team*

NEW JERSEY DEVILS
YEAR-BY-YEAR RECORDS

	REGULAR SEASON						PLAYOFFS			
Season	W	L	T	RT	Pts.	Finish	W	L	Highest round	Coach
1982-83	17	49	14	—	48	5th/Patrick	—	—		Billy MacMillan
1983-84	17	56	7	—	41	5th/Patrick	—	—		Billy MacMillan, Tom McVie
1984-85	22	48	10	—	54	5th/Patrick	—	—		Doug Carpenter
1985-86	28	49	3	—	59	5th/Patrick	—	—		Doug Carpenter
1986-87	29	45	6	—	64	6th/Patrick	—	—		Doug Carpenter
1987-88	38	36	6	—	82	4th/Patrick	11	9	Conference finals	Doug Carpenter, Jim Schoenfeld
1988-89	27	41	12	—	66	5th/Patrick	—	—		Jim Schoenfeld
1989-90	37	34	9	—	83	2nd/Patrick	2	4	Division semifinals	Jim Schoenfeld, John Cunniff
1990-91	32	33	15	—	79	4th/Patrick	3	4	Division semifinals	John Cunniff, Tom McVie
1991-92	38	31	11	—	87	4th/Patrick	3	4	Division semifinals	Tom McVie
1992-93	40	37	7	—	87	4th/Patrick	1	4	Division semifinals	Herb Brooks
1993-94	47	25	12	—	106	2nd/Atlantic	11	9	Conference finals	Jacques Lemaire
1994-95	22	18	8	—	52	2nd/Atlantic	16	4	Stanley Cup champ	Jacques Lemaire
1995-96	37	33	12	—	86	6th/Atlantic	—	—		Jacques Lemaire
1996-97	45	23	14	—	104	1st/Atlantic	5	5	Conference semifinals	Jacques Lemaire
1997-98	48	23	11	—	107	1st/Atlantic	2	4	Conference quarterfinals	Jacques Lemaire
1998-99	47	24	11	—	105	1st/Atlantic	3	4	Conference quarterfinals	Robbie Ftorek
1999-00	45	29	8	5	103	2nd/Atlantic	16	7	Stanley Cup champ	Robbie Ftorek, Larry Robinson

Franchise was originally known as Kansas City Scouts and relocated to become Colorado Rockies following 1975-76 season; franchise relocated and became New Jersey Devils following 1981-82 season.

FIRST-ROUND ENTRY DRAFT CHOICES

Year Player, Overall, Last amateur team (league)
1982—Rocky Trottier, 8, Billings (WHL)
       Ken Daneyko, 18, Seattle (WHL)
1983—John MacLean, 6, Oshawa (OHL)
1984—Kirk Muller, 2, Guelph (OHL)
1985—Craig Wolanin, 3, Kitchener (OHL)
1986—Neil Brady, 3, Medicine Hat (WHL)
1987—Brendan Shanahan, 2, London (OHL)
1988—Corey Foster, 12, Peterborough (OHL)
1989—Bill Guerin, 5, Springfield (Mass.) Jr.
       Jason Miller, 18, Medicine Hat (WHL)
1990—Martin Brodeur, 20, St. Hyacinthe (QMJHL)
1991—Scott Niedermayer, 3, Kamloops (WHL)
       Brian Rolston, 11, Detroit Compuware Jr.

Year Player, Overall, Last amateur team (league)
1992—Jason Smith, 18, Regina (WHL)
1993—Denis Pederson, 13, Prince Albert (WHL)
1994—Vadim Sharifjanov, 25, Salavat (Russia)
1995—Petr Sykora, 18, Detroit (IHL)
1996—Lance Ward, 10, Red Deer (WHL)
1997—Jean-Francois Damphousse, 24, Moncton (QMJHL)
1998—Mike Van Ryn, 26, Michigan
       Scott Gomez, 27, Tri-City (WHL)
1999—Ari Ahonen, 27, Jyvaskyla, Finland
2000—David Hale, 22, Sioux City (USHL)

SINGLE-SEASON INDIVIDUAL RECORDS

FORWARDS/DEFENSEMEN

Most goals
46—Pat Verbeek, 1987-88

Most assists
60—Scott Stevens, 1993-94

Most points
94—Kirk Muller, 1987-88

Most penalty minutes
295—Krzysztof Oliwa, 1997-98

Most power play goals
19—John MacLean, 1990-91

Most shorthanded goals
6—John Madden, 1999-2000

Most games with three or more goals
3—Kirk Muller, 1987-88
    John MacLean, 1988-89

Most shots
322—John MacLean, 1989-90

GOALTENDERS

Most games
77—Martin Brodeur, 1995-96

Most minutes
4,433—Martin Brodeur, 1995-96

Most goals allowed
242—Chico Resch, 1982-83

Lowest goals-against average
1.88—Martin Brodeur, 1996-97

Most shutouts
10—Martin Brodeur, 1996-97
    Martin Brodeur, 1997-98

Most wins
43—Martin Brodeur, 1997-98
    Martin Brodeur, 1999-2000

Most losses
35—Chico Resch, 1982-83

Most ties
13—Martin Brodeur, 1996-97

NHL HISTORY *Team by team*

FRANCHISE LEADERS

Players in boldface played for club in 1999-2000

FORWARDS/DEFENSEMEN

Games
Ken Daneyko	**1070**
John MacLean	934
Bruce Driver	702
Scott Stevens	**674**
Randy McKay	**628**

Goals
John MacLean	347
Kirk Muller	185
Pat Verbeek	170
Bobby Holik	**158**
Aaron Broten	147

Assists
John MacLean	354
Kirk Muller	335
Bruce Driver	316
Aaron Broten	283
Scott Stevens	**274**

Points
John MacLean	701
Kirk Muller	520
Aaron Broten	430
Bruce Driver	399
Bobby Holik	**359**

Penalty minutes
Ken Daneyko	2339
Randy McKay	**1303**
John MacLean	1168
Pat Verbeek	943
Joe Cirella	886

GOALTENDERS

Games
Martin Brodeur	**447**
Chris Terreri	**292**
Chico Resch	198
Sean Burke	162
Alain Chevrier	140

Shutouts
Martin Brodeur	**42**
Chris Terreri	**7**
Craig Billington	4
Sean Burke	4
Mike Dunham	3

Goals-against average
(2400 minutes minimum)
Martin Brodeur	**2.20**
Chris Terreri	**3.08**
Sean Burke	3.66
Bob Sauve	3.87
Craig Billington	3.98

Wins
Martin Brodeur	**244**
Chris Terreri	**116**
Sean Burke	62
Alain Chevrier	53
Chico Resch	49

NEW YORK AMERICANS (DEFUNCT)
YEAR-BY-YEAR RECORDS

	REGULAR SEASON					PLAYOFFS			
Season	W	L	T	Pts.	Finish	W	L	Highest round	Coach
1925-26	12	20	4	28	5th	—	—		Tommy Gorman
1926-27	17	25	2	36	4th/Canadian	—	—		Newsy Lalonde
1927-28	11	27	6	28	5th/Canadian	—	—		Wilf Green
1928-29	19	13	12	50	2nd/Canadian	*0	1	Semifinals	Tommy Gorman
1929-30	14	25	5	33	5th/Canadian	—	—		Lionel Conacher
1930-31	18	16	10	46	4th/Canadian	—	—		Eddie Gerard
1931-32	16	24	8	40	4th/Canadian	—	—		Eddie Gerard
1932-33	15	22	11	41	4th/Canadian	—	—		Joe Simpson
1933-34	15	23	10	40	4th/Canadian	—	—		Joe Simpson
1934-35	12	27	9	33	4th/Canadian	—	—		Joe Simpson
1935-36	16	25	7	39	3rd/Canadian	2	3	Semifinals	Red Dutton
1936-37	15	29	4	34	4th/Canadian	—	—		Red Dutton
1937-38	19	18	11	49	2nd/Canadian	3	3	Semifinals	Red Dutton
1938-39	17	21	10	44	4th	0	2	Quarterfinals	Red Dutton
1939-40	15	29	4	34	6th	1	2	Quarterfinals	Red Dutton
1940-41	8	29	11	27	7th	—	—		Red Dutton
1941-42†	16	29	3	35	7th	—	—		Red Dutton

Franchise was originally known as Quebec Bulldogs and relocated to become Hamilton Tigers following 1919-20 season; franchise relocated and became New York Americans following 1924-25 season.

*Won-lost record does not indicate tie(s) resulting from two-game, total goals series that year (two-game, total-goals series were played from 1917-18 through 1935-36).

†Brooklyn Americans.

NEW YORK ISLANDERS
YEAR-BY-YEAR RECORDS

	REGULAR SEASON						PLAYOFFS			
Season	W	L	T	RT	Pts.	Finish	W	L	Highest round	Coach
1972-73	12	60	6	—	30	8th/East	—	—		Phil Goyette, Earl Ingarfield
1973-74	19	41	18	—	56	8th/East	—	—		Al Arbour
1974-75	33	25	22	—	88	3rd/Patrick	9	8	Semifinals	Al Arbour
1975-76	42	21	17	—	101	2nd/Patrick	7	6	Semifinals	Al Arbour
1976-77	47	21	12	—	106	2nd/Patrick	8	4	Semifinals	Al Arbour
1977-78	48	17	15	—	111	1st/Patrick	3	4	Quarterfinals	Al Arbour
1978-79	51	15	14	—	116	1st/Patrick	6	4	Semifinals	Al Arbour
1979-80	39	28	13	—	91	2nd/Patrick	15	6	Stanley Cup champ	Al Arbour
1980-81	48	18	14	—	110	1st/Patrick	15	3	Stanley Cup champ	Al Arbour
1981-82	54	16	10	—	118	1st/Patrick	15	4	Stanley Cup champ	Al Arbour

Season	W	L	T	RT	Pts.	Finish	W	L	Highest round	Coach
REGULAR SEASON									**PLAYOFFS**	
1982-83	42	26	12	—	96	2nd/Patrick	15	5	Stanley Cup champ	Al Arbour
1983-84	50	26	4	—	104	1st/Patrick	12	9	Stanley Cup finals	Al Arbour
1984-85	40	34	6	—	86	3rd/Patrick	4	6	Division finals	Al Arbour
1985-86	39	29	12	—	90	3rd/Patrick	0	3	Division semifinals	Al Arbour
1986-87	35	33	12	—	82	3rd/Patrick	7	7	Division finals	Terry Simpson
1987-88	39	31	10	—	88	1st/Patrick	2	4	Division semifinals	Terry Simpson
1988-89	28	47	5	—	61	6th/Patrick	—	—		Terry Simpson, Al Arbour
1989-90	31	38	11	—	73	4th/Patrick	1	4	Division semifinals	Al Arbour
1990-91	25	45	10	—	60	6th/Patrick	—	—		Al Arbour
1991-92	34	35	11	—	79	5th/Patrick	—	—		Al Arbour
1992-93	40	37	7	—	87	3rd/Patrick	9	9	Conference finals	Al Arbour
1993-94	36	36	12	—	84	4th/Atlantic	0	4	Conference quarterfinals	Al Arbour, Lorne Henning
1994-95	15	28	5	—	35	7th/Atlantic	—	—		Lorne Henning
1995-96	22	50	10	—	54	7th/Atlantic	—	—		Mike Milbury
1996-97	29	41	12	—	70	7th/Atlantic	—	—		Mike Milbury, Rick Bowness
1997-98	30	41	11	—	71	4th/Atlantic	—	—		Rick Bowness, Mike Milbury
1998-99	24	48	10	—	58	5th/Atlantic	—	—		Mike Milbury, Bill Stewart
1999-00	24	49	9	1	58	5th/Atlantic	—	—		Butch Goring

FIRST-ROUND ENTRY DRAFT CHOICES

Year Player, Overall, Last amateur team (league)

1972—Billy Harris, 1, Toronto (OHL)*
1973—Denis Potvin, 1, Ottawa (OHL)*
1974—Clark Gillies, 4, Regina (WCHL)
1975—Pat Price, 11, Vancouver (WHA)
1976—Alex McKendry, 14, Sudbury (OHL)
1977—Mike Bossy, 15, Laval (QMJHL)
1978—Steve Tambellini, 15, Lethbridge (WCHL)
1979—Duane Sutter, 17, Lethbridge (WHL)
1980—Brent Sutter, 17, Red Deer (AJHL)
1981—Paul Boutilier, 21, Sherbrooke (QMJHL)
1982—Pat Flatley, 21, University of Wisconsin
1983—Pat LaFontaine, 3, Verdun (QMJHL)
      Gerald Diduck, 16, Lethbridge (WHL)
1984—Duncan MacPherson, 20, Saskatoon (WHL)
1985—Brad Dalgarno, 6, Hamilton (OHL)
      Derek King, 13, Sault Ste. Marie (OHL)
1986—Tom Fitzgerald, 17, Austin Prep (Mass.)
1987—Dean Chynoweth, 13, Medicine Hat (WHL)
1988—Kevin Cheveldayoff, 16, Brandon (WHL)

Year Player, Overall, Last amateur team (league)

1989—Dave Chyzowski, 2, Kamloops (WHL)
1990—Scott Scissons, 6, Saskatoon (WHL)
1991—Scott Lachance, 4, Boston University
1992—Darius Kasparaitis, 5, Dynamo Moscow (CIS)
1993—Todd Bertuzzi, 23, Guelph (OHL)
1994—Brett Lindros, 9, Kingston (OHL)
1995—Wade Redden, 2, Brandon (WHL)
1996—Jean-Pierre Dumont, 3, Val-d'Or (QMJHL)
1997—Roberto Luongo, 4, Val d'Or (QMJHL)
      Eric Brewer, 5, Prince George (WHL)
1998—Michael Rupp, 9, Erie (OHL)
1999—Tim Connolly, 5, Erie (OHL)
      Taylor Pyatt, 8, Sudbury (OHL)
      Branislav Mezei, 10, Belleville (OHL)
      Kristian Kudroc, 28, Michalovce, Slovakia
2000—Rick DiPietro, 1, Boston University*
      Raffi Torres, 5, Brampton (OHL)

*Designates first player chosen in draft.

SINGLE-SEASON INDIVIDUAL RECORDS

FORWARDS/DEFENSEMEN

Most goals
69—Mike Bossy, 1978-79

Most assists
87—Bryan Trottier, 1978-79

Most points
147—Mike Bossy, 1981-82

Most penalty minutes
356—Brian Curran, 1986-87

Most power play goals
28—Mike Bossy, 1980-81

Most shorthanded goals
7—Bob Bourne, 1980-81

Most games with three or more goals
9—Mike Bossy, 1980-81

GOALTENDERS

Most games
65—Ron Hextall, 1993-94

Most minutes
3,581—Ron Hextall, 1993-94

Most goals allowed
195—Gerry Desjardins, 1972-73

Lowest goals-against average
2.07—Chico Resch, 1975-76

Most shutouts
7—Chico Resch, 1975-76

Most wins
32—Billy Smith, 1981-82

Most losses
35—Gerry Desjardins, 1972-73

Most ties
17—Billy Smith, 1974-75

FRANCHISE LEADERS

Players in boldface played for club in 1999-2000

FORWARDS/DEFENSEMEN

Games

Bryan Trottier	1123
Denis Potvin	1060
Bob Nystrom	900

Clark Gillies	872
Bob Bourne	814

Goals

Mike Bossy	573
Bryan Trottier	500
Denis Potvin	310

Clark Gillies	304
Pat LaFontaine	287
Brent Sutter	287

Assists

Bryan Trottier	853
Denis Potvin	742

Mike Bossy 553
Clark Gillies 359
John Tonelli 338

Points

Bryan Trottier 1353
Mike Bossy 1126
Denis Potvin 1052
Clark Gillies 663
Brent Sutter 610

Penalty minutes

Mick Vukota 1879
Rich Pilon 1525
Garry Howatt 1466
Denis Potvin 1354
Bob Nystrom 1248

GOALTENDERS
Games
Billy Smith 675
Chico Resch 282
Kelly Hrudey 241
Tommy Salo 187
Glenn Healy 176

Shutouts
Chico Resch 25
Billy Smith 22
Tommy Salo 14
Kelly Hrudey 6
Wade Flaherty 3

Goals-against average
(2400 minutes minimum)
Chico Resch 2.56
Tommy Salo 2.77
Ron Hextall 3.08
Eric Fichaud 3.14
Roland Melanson 3.14

Wins
Billy Smith 304
Chico Resch 157
Kelly Hrudey 106
Roland Melanson 77
Glenn Healy 66

NEW YORK RANGERS
YEAR-BY-YEAR RECORDS

	REGULAR SEASON						PLAYOFFS			
Season	W	L	T	RT	Pts.	Finish	W	L	Highest round	Coach
1926-27	25	13	6	—	56	1st/American	*0	1	Semifinals	Lester Patrick
1927-28	19	16	9	—	47	2nd/American	*5	3	Stanley Cup champ	Lester Patrick
1928-29	21	13	10	—	52	2nd/American	*3	2	Stanley Cup finals	Lester Patrick
1929-30	17	17	10	—	44	3rd/American	*1	2	Semifinals	Lester Patrick
1930-31	19	16	9	—	47	3rd/American	2	2	Semifinals	Lester Patrick
1931-32	23	17	8	—	54	1st/American	3	4	Stanley Cup finals	Lester Patrick
1932-33	23	17	8	—	54	3rd/American	*6	1	Stanley Cup champ	Lester Patrick
1933-34	21	19	8	—	50	3rd/American	*0	1	Quarterfinals	Lester Patrick
1934-35	22	20	6	—	50	3rd/American	*1	1	Semifinals	Lester Patrick
1935-36	19	17	12	—	50	4th/American	—	—		Lester Patrick
1936-37	19	20	9	—	47	3rd/American	6	3	Stanley Cup finals	Lester Patrick
1937-38	27	15	6	—	60	2nd/American	1	2	Quarterfinals	Lester Patrick
1938-39	26	16	6	—	58	2nd	3	4	Semifinals	Lester Patrick
1939-40	27	11	10	—	64	2nd	8	4	Stanley Cup champ	Frank Boucher
1940-41	21	19	8	—	50	4th	1	2	Quarterfinals	Frank Boucher
1941-42	29	17	2	—	60	1st	2	4	Semifinals	Frank Boucher
1942-43	11	31	8	—	30	6th	—	—		Frank Boucher
1943-44	6	39	5	—	17	6th	—	—		Frank Boucher
1944-45	11	29	10	—	32	6th	—	—		Frank Boucher
1945-46	13	28	9	—	35	6th	—	—		Frank Boucher
1946-47	22	32	6	—	50	5th	—	—		Frank Boucher
1947-48	21	26	13	—	55	4th	2	4	League semifinals	Frank Boucher
1948-49	18	31	11	—	47	6th	—	—		Frank Boucher, Lynn Patrick
1949-50	28	31	11	—	67	4th	7	5	Stanley Cup finals	Lynn Patrick
1950-51	20	29	21	—	61	5th	—	—		Neil Colville
1951-52	23	34	13	—	59	5th	—	—		Neil Colville, Bill Cook
1952-53	17	37	16	—	50	6th	—	—		Bill Cook
1953-54	29	31	10	—	68	5th	—	—		Frank Boucher, Muzz Patrick
1954-55	17	35	18	—	52	5th	—	—		Muzz Patrick
1955-56	32	28	10	—	74	3rd	1	4	League semifinals	Phil Watson
1956-57	26	30	14	—	66	4th	1	4	League semifinals	Phil Watson
1957-58	32	25	13	—	77	2nd	2	4	League semifinals	Phil Watson
1958-59	26	32	12	—	64	5th	—	—		Phil Watson
1959-60	17	38	15	—	49	6th	—	—		Phil Watson, Alf Pike
1960-61	22	38	10	—	54	5th	—	—		Alf Pike
1961-62	26	32	12	—	64	4th	2	4	League semifinals	Doug Harvey
1962-63	22	36	12	—	56	5th	—	—		Muzz Patrick, Red Sullivan
1963-64	22	38	10	—	54	5th	—	—		Red Sullivan
1964-65	20	38	12	—	52	5th	—	—		Red Sullivan
1965-66	18	41	11	—	47	6th	—	—		Red Sullivan, Emile Francis
1966-67	30	28	12	—	72	4th	0	4	League semifinals	Emile Francis
1967-68	39	23	12	—	90	2nd/East	2	4	Division semifinals	Emile Francis
1968-69	41	26	9	—	91	3rd/East	0	4	Division semifinals	Bernie Geoffrion, Emile Francis
1969-70	38	22	16	—	92	4th/East	2	4	Division semifinals	Emile Francis
1970-71	49	18	11	—	109	2nd/East	7	6	Division finals	Emile Francis
1971-72	48	17	13	—	109	2nd/East	10	6	Stanley Cup finals	Emile Francis
1972-73	47	23	8	—	102	3rd/East	5	5	Division finals	Emile Francis
1973-74	40	24	14	—	94	3rd/East	7	6	Division finals	Larry Popein, Emile Francis

			REGULAR SEASON					PLAYOFFS		
Season	W	L	T	RT	Pts.	Finish	W	L	Highest round	Coach
1974-75	37	29	14	—	88	2nd/Patrick	1	2	Preliminaries	Emile Francis
1975-76	29	42	9	—	67	4th/Patrick	—	—		Ron Stewart, John Ferguson
1976-77	29	37	14	—	72	4th/Patrick	—	—		John Ferguson
1977-78	30	37	13	—	73	4th/Patrick	1	2	Preliminaries	Jean-Guy Talbot
1978-79	40	29	11	—	91	3rd/Patrick	11	7	Stanley Cup finals	Fred Shero
1979-80	38	32	10	—	86	3rd/Patrick	4	5	Quarterfinals	Fred Shero
1980-81	30	36	14	—	74	4th/Patrick	7	7	Semifinals	Fred Shero, Craig Patrick
1981-82	39	27	14	—	92	2nd/Patrick	5	5	Division finals	Herb Brooks
1982-83	35	35	10	—	80	4th/Patrick	5	4	Division finals	Herb Brooks
1983-84	42	29	9	—	93	4th/Patrick	2	3	Division semifinals	Herb Brooks
1984-85	26	44	10	—	62	4th/Patrick	0	3	Division semifinals	Herb Brooks, Craig Patrick
1985-86	36	38	6	—	78	4th/Patrick	8	8	Conference finals	Ted Sator
1986-87	34	38	8	—	76	4th/Patrick	2	4	Division semifinals	Ted Sator, Tom Webster, Phil Esposito
1987-88	36	34	10	—	82	4th/Patrick	—	—		Michel Bergeron
1988-89	37	35	8	—	82	3rd/Patrick	0	4	Division semifinals	Michel Bergeron, Phil Esposito
1989-90	36	31	13	—	85	1st/Patrick	5	5	Division finals	Roger Neilson
1990-91	36	31	13	—	85	2nd/Patrick	2	4	Division semifinals	Roger Neilson
1991-92	50	25	5	—	105	1st/Patrick	6	7	Division finals	Roger Neilson
1992-93	34	39	11	—	79	6th/Patrick	—	—		Roger Neilson, Ron Smith
1993-94	52	24	8	—	112	1st/Atlantic	16	7	Stanley Cup champ	Mike Keenan
1994-95	22	23	3	—	47	4th/Atlantic	4	6	Conference semifinals	Colin Campbell
1995-96	41	27	14	—	96	2nd/Atlantic	5	6	Conference semifinals	Colin Campbell
1996-97	38	34	10	—	86	4th/Atlantic	9	6	Conference finals	Colin Campbell
1997-98	25	39	18	—	68	5th/Atlantic	—	—		Colin Campbell, John Muckler
1998-99	33	38	11	—	77	4th/Atlantic	—	—		John Muckler
1999-00	29	41	12	3	73	4th/Atlantic	—	—		John Muckler, John Tortorella

*Won-lost record does not indicate tie(s) resulting from two-game, total goals series that year (two-game, total-goals series were played from 1917-18 through 1935-36).

FIRST-ROUND ENTRY DRAFT CHOICES

Year Player, Overall, Last amateur team (league)
1969—Andre Dupont, 8, Montreal (OHL)
    Pierre Jarry, 12, Ottawa (OHL)
1970—Normand Gratton, 11, Montreal (OHL)
1971—Steve Vickers, 10, Toronto (OHL)
    Steve Durbano, 13, Toronto (OHL)
1972—Albert Blanchard, 10, Kitchener (OHL)
    Bobby MacMillan, 15, St. Catharines (OHL)
1973—Rick Middleton, 14, Oshawa (OHL)
1974—Dave Maloney, 14, Kitchener (OHL)
1975—Wayne Dillon, 12, Toronto (WHA)
1976—Don Murdoch, 6, Medicine Hat (WCHL)
1977—Lucien DeBlois, 8, Sorel (QMJHL)
    Ron Duguay, 13, Sudbury (OHL)
1978—No first-round selection
1979—Doug Sulliman, 13, Kitchener (OHL)
1980—Jim Malone, 14, Toronto (OHL)
1981—James Patrick, 9, Prince Albert (AJHL)
1982—Chris Kontos, 15, Toronto (OHL)
1983—Dave Gagner, 12, Brantford (OHL)

Year Player, Overall, Last amateur team (league)
1984—Terry Carkner, 14, Peterborough (OHL)
1985—Ulf Dahlen, 7, Ostersund (Sweden)
1986—Brian Leetch, 9, Avon Old Farms Prep (Ct.)
1987—Jayson More, 10, New Westminster (WCHL)
1988—No first-round selection
1989—Steven Rice, 20, Kitchener (OHL)
1990—Michael Stewart, 13, Michigan State University
1991—Alexei Kovalev, 15, Dynamo Moscow (USSR)
1992—Peter Ferraro, 24, Waterloo (USHL)
1993—Niklas Sundstrom, 8, Ornskoldsvik (Sweden)
1994—Dan Cloutier, 26, Sault Ste. Marie (OHL)
1995—No first-round selection
1996—Jeff Brown, 22, Sarnia (OHL)
1997—Stefan Cherneski, 19, Brandon (WHL)
1998—Manny Malhotra, 7, Guelph (OHL)
1999—Pavel Brendl, 4, Calgary (WHL)
    Jamie Lundmark, 9, Moose Jaw (WHL)
2000—No first-round selection

SINGLE-SEASON INDIVIDUAL RECORDS

FORWARDS/DEFENSEMEN

Most goals
52—Adam Graves, 1993-94

Most assists
88—Brian Leetch, 1991-92

Most points
109—Jean Ratelle, 1971-72

Most penalty minutes
305—Troy Mallette, 1989-90

Most power play goals
23—Vic Hadfield, 1971-72

Most shorthanded goals
5—Don Maloney, 1980-81
   Mike Rogers, 1982-83
   Mike Gartner, 1993-94
   Mark Messier, 1996-97

Most games with three or more goals
4—Tomas Sandstrom, 1986-87

Most shots
344—Phil Esposito, 1976-77

GOALTENDERS

Most games
72—Mike Richter, 1997-98

Most minutes
4,143—Mike Richter, 1997-98

Lowest goals-against average
1.48—John Ross Roach, 1928-29

Most shutouts
13—John Ross Roach, 1928-29

Most wins
42—Mike Richter, 1993-94

FRANCHISE LEADERS

Players in boldface played for club in 1999-2000

FORWARDS/DEFENSEMEN

Games

Harry Howell	1160
Rod Gilbert	1065
Ron Greschner	982
Walt Tkaczuk	945
Jean Ratelle	862

Goals

Rod Gilbert	406
Jean Ratelle	336
Andy Bathgate	272
Adam Graves	**270**
Vic Hadfield	262

Assists

Rod Gilbert	615
Brian Leetch	**597**
Jean Ratelle	481
Andy Bathgate	457
Walt Tkaczuk	451

Points

Rod Gilbert	1021
Jean Ratelle	817
Brian Leetch	**781**
Andy Bathgate	729
Walt Tkaczuk	678

Penalty minutes

Ron Greschner	1226
Jeff Beukeboom	1157
Harry Howell	1147
Don Maloney	1113
Vic Hadfield	1036

GOALTENDERS

Games

Gump Worsley	583
Mike Richter	**553**
Ed Giacomin	539
John Vanbiesbrouck	449
Chuck Rayner	377

Shutouts

Ed Giacomin	49
Dave Kerr	40
John Ross Roach	30
Chuck Rayner	24
Gump Worsley	24

Goals-against average (2400 minutes minimum)

Lorne Chabot	1.61
Dave Kerr	2.07
John Ross Roach	2.16
Andy Aitkenhead	2.42
Johnny Bower	2.62
Gilles Villemure	2.62

Wins

Ed Giacomin	266
Mike Richter	**252**
Gump Worsley	204
John Vanbiesbrouck	200
Dave Kerr	157

OTTAWA SENATORS (FIRST CLUB—DEFUNCT)
YEAR-BY-YEAR RECORDS

Season	W	L	T	Pts.	Finish	W	L	Highest round	Coach
1917-18	9	13	0	18	3rd	—	—		Eddie Gerard
1918-19	12	6	0	24	1st	1	4	Semifinals	Alf Smith
1919-20	19	5	0	38	1st	3	2	Stanley Cup champ	Pete Green
1920-21	14	10	0	28	2nd	*4	2	Stanley Cup champ	Pete Green
1921-22	14	8	2	30	1st	*0	1	Semifinals	Pete Green
1922-23	14	9	1	29	1st	6	2	Stanley Cup champ	Pete Green
1923-24	16	8	0	32	1st	0	2	Semifinals	Pete Green
1924-25	17	12	1	35	4th	—	—		Pete Green
1925-26	24	8	4	52	1st	*0	1	Semifinals	Pete Green
1926-27	30	10	4	64	1st/Canadian	*3	0	Stanley Cup champ	Dave Gill
1927-28	20	14	10	50	3rd/Canadian	0	2	Quarterfinals	Dave Gill
1928-29	14	17	13	41	4th/Canadian	—	—		Dave Gill
1929-30	21	15	8	50	3rd/Canadian	*0	1	Semifinals	Newsy Lalonde
1930-31	10	30	4	24	5th/Canadian	—	—		Newsy Lalonde
1931-32					Club suspended operations for one season.				
1932-33	11	27	10	32	5th/Canadian	—	—		Cy Denneny
1933-34	13	29	6	32	5th/Canadian	—	—		George Boucher

*Won-lost record does not indicate tie(s) resulting from two-game, total goals series that year (two-game, total-goals series were played from 1917-18 through 1935-36).

Franchise relocated and became St. Louis Eagles following 1933-34 season.

OTTAWA SENATORS (SECOND CLUB)
YEAR-BY-YEAR RECORDS

Season	W	L	T	RT	Pts.	Finish	W	L	Highest round	Coach
1992-93	10	70	4	—	24	6th/Adams	—	—		Rick Bowness
1993-94	14	61	9	—	37	7th/Northeast	—	—		Rick Bowness
1994-95	9	34	5	—	23	7th/Northeast	—	—		Rick Bowness
1995-96	18	59	5	—	41	6th/Northeast	—	—		Rick Bowness, Dave Allison, Jacques Martin
1996-97	31	36	15	—	77	T3rd/Northeast	3	4	Conference quarterfinals	Jacques Martin
1997-98	34	33	15	—	83	5th/Northeast	5	6	Conference semifinals	Jacques Martin
1998-99	44	23	15	—	103	1st/Northeast	0	4	Conference quarterfinals	Jacques Martin
1999-00	41	30	11	2	95	2nd/Northeast	2	4	Conference quarterfinals	Jacques Martin

FIRST-ROUND ENTRY DRAFT CHOICES

Year	Player, Overall, Last amateur team (league)
1992	Alexei Yashin, 2, Dynamo Moscow (CIS)
1993	Alexandre Daigle, 1, Victoriaville (QMJHL)*
1994	Radek Bonk, 3, Las Vegas (IHL)
1995	Bryan Berard, 1, Detroit (OHL)*
1996	Chris Phillips, 1, Prince Albert (WHL)*

Year	Player, Overall, Last amateur team (league)
1997	Marian Hossa, 12, Dukla Trencin, Czechoslovakia
1998	Mathieu Chouinard, 15, Shawinigan (QMJHL)
1999	Martin Havlat, 26, Trinec, Czech Republic
2000	Anton Volchenkov, 21, CSKA, Russia

*Designates first player chosen in draft.

SINGLE-SEASON INDIVIDUAL RECORDS

FORWARDS/DEFENSEMEN

Most goals
44—Alexei Yashin, 1998-99

Most assists
50—Alexei Yashin, 1998-99

Most points
94—Alexei Yashin, 1998-99

Most penalty minutes
318—Mike Peluso, 1992-93

Most power play goals
19—Alexei Yashin, 1998-99

Most shorthanded goals
4—Magnus Arvedson, 1998-99

Most games with three or more goals
1—Held by many players

Most shots
337—Alexei Yashin, 1998-99

GOALTENDERS

Most games
64—Peter Sidorkiewicz, 1992-93

Most minutes
3,388—Peter Sidorkiewicz, 1992-93

Most shots against
1,801—Craig Billington, 1993-94

Most goals allowed
254—Craig Billington, 1993-94

Lowest goals-against average
1.79—Ron Tugnutt, 1998-99

Most shutouts
5—Damian Rhodes, 1997-98

Most wins
22—Damian Rhodes, 1998-99
    Ron Tugnutt, 1998-99

Most losses
46—Peter Sidorkiewicz, 1992-93

Most ties
14—Damian Rhodes, 1996-97

FRANCHISE LEADERS

Players in boldface played for club in 1999-2000

FORWARDS/DEFENSEMEN

Games
Alexei Yashin	422
Radek Bonk	**397**
Daniel Alfredsson	**328**
Andreas Dackell	320
Wade Redden	**315**

Goals
Alexei Yashin	178
Daniel Alfredsson	**99**
Shawn McEachern	**95**
Alexandre Daigle	74
Radek Bonk	**70**

Assists
Alexei Yashin	225
Daniel Alfredsson	**170**
Radek Bonk	**102**
Alexandre Daigle	98
Andreas Dackell	**97**

Points
Alexei Yashin	403
Daniel Alfredsson	**269**
Shawn McEachern	**186**
Radek Bonk	**172**
Alexandre Daigle	172

Penalty minutes
Dennis Vial	625
Denny Lambert	467
Troy Mallette	372
Randy Cunneyworth	360
Mike Peluso	318

GOALTENDERS

Games
Damian Rhodes	181
Ron Tugnutt	**166**
Craig Billington	72
Don Beaupre	71
Peter Sidorkiewicz	64

Shutouts
Ron Tugnutt	**13**
Damian Rhodes	11
Patrick Lalime	**3**
Don Beaupre	2

Goals-against average
(2400 minutes minimum)
Ron Tugnutt	**2.32**
Damian Rhodes	2.56
Don Beaupre	3.53
Peter Sidorkiewicz	4.43
Craig Billington	4.53

Wins
Ron Tugnutt	**72**
Damian Rhodes	65
Patrick Lalime	**19**
Don Beaupre	14
Craig Billington	11

PHILADELPHIA FLYERS
YEAR-BY-YEAR RECORDS

	REGULAR SEASON						PLAYOFFS			
Season	W	L	T	RT	Pts.	Finish	W	L	Highest round	Coach
1967-68	31	32	11	—	73	1st/West	3	4	Division semifinals	Keith Allen
1968-69	20	35	21	—	61	3rd/West	0	4	Division semifinals	Keith Allen
1969-70	17	35	24	—	58	5th/West	—	—		Vic Stasiuk
1970-71	28	33	17	—	73	3rd/West	0	4	Division semifinals	Vic Stasiuk
1971-72	26	38	14	—	66	5th/West	—	—		Fred Shero
1972-73	37	30	11	—	85	2nd/West	5	6	Division finals	Fred Shero
1973-74	50	16	12	—	112	1st/West	12	5	Stanley Cup champ	Fred Shero
1974-75	51	18	11	—	113	1st/Patrick	12	5	Stanley Cup champ	Fred Shero
1975-76	51	13	16	—	118	1st/Patrick	8	8	Stanley Cup finals	Fred Shero
1976-77	48	16	16	—	112	1st/Patrick	4	6	Semifinals	Fred Shero

Season	W	L	T	RT	Pts.	Finish	W	L	Highest round	Coach
						REGULAR SEASON			PLAYOFFS	
1977-78	45	20	15	—	105	2nd/Patrick	7	5	Semifinals	Fred Shero
1978-79	40	25	15	—	95	2nd/Patrick	3	5	Quarterfinals	Bob McCammon, Pat Quinn
1979-80	48	12	20	—	116	1st/Patrick	13	6	Stanley Cup finals	Pat Quinn
1980-81	41	24	15	—	97	2nd/Patrick	6	6	Quarterfinals	Pat Quinn
1981-82	38	31	11	—	87	3rd/Patrick	1	3	Division semifinals	Pat Quinn, Bob McCammon
1982-83	49	23	8	—	106	1st/Patrick	0	3	Division semifinals	Bob McCammon
1983-84	44	26	10	—	98	3rd/Patrick	0	3	Division semifinals	Bob McCammon
1984-85	53	20	7	—	113	1st/Patrick	12	7	Stanley Cup finals	Mike Keenan
1985-86	53	23	4	—	110	1st/Patrick	2	3	Division semifinals	Mike Keenan
1986-87	46	26	8	—	100	1st/Patrick	15	11	Stanley Cup finals	Mike Keenan
1987-88	38	33	9	—	85	2nd/Patrick	3	4	Division semifinals	Mike Keenan
1988-89	36	36	8	—	80	4th/Patrick	10	9	Conference finals	Paul Holmgren
1989-90	30	39	11	—	71	6th/Patrick	—	—		Paul Holmgren
1990-91	33	37	10	—	76	6th/Patrick	—	—		Paul Holmgren
1991-92	32	37	11	—	75	6th/Patrick	—	—		Paul Holmgren, Bill Dineen
1992-93	36	37	11	—	83	5th/Patrick	—	—		Bill Dineen
1993-94	35	39	10	—	80	6th/Atlantic	—	—		Terry Simpson
1994-95	28	16	4	—	60	1st/Atlantic	10	5	Conference finals	Terry Murray
1995-96	45	24	13	—	103	1st/Atlantic	6	6	Conference semifinals	Terry Murray
1996-97	45	24	13	—	103	2nd/Atlantic	12	7	Stanley Cup finals	Terry Murray
1997-98	42	29	11	—	95	2nd/Atlantic	1	4	Conference quarterfinals	Wayne Cashman, Roger Neilson
1998-99	37	26	19	—	93	2nd/Atlantic	2	4	Conference quarterfinals	Roger Neilson
1999-00	45	25	12	3	105	1st/Atlantic	11	7	Conference finals	Roger Neilson, Craig Ramsay

FIRST-ROUND ENTRY DRAFT CHOICES

Year   Player, Overall, Last amateur team (league)
1969—Bob Currier, 6, Cornwall (QMJHL)
1970—No first-round selection
1971—Larry Wright, 8, Regina (WCHL)
    Pierre Plante, 9, Drummondville (QMJHL)
1972—Bill Barber, 7, Kitchener (OHL)
1973—No first-round selection
1974—No first-round selection
1975—Mel Bridgeman, 1, Victoria (WCHL)*
1976—Mark Suzor, 17, Kingston (OHL)
1977—Kevin McCarthy, 17, Winnipeg (WCHL)
1978—Behn Wilson, 6, Kingston (OHL)
    Ken Linseman, 7, Birmingham (WHA)
    Dan Lucas, 14, Sault Ste. Marie (OHL)
1979—Brian Propp, 14, Brandon (WHL)
1980—Mike Stothers, 21, Kingston (OHL)
1981—Steve Smith, 16, Sault Ste. Marie (OHL)
1982—Ron Sutter, 4, Lethbridge (WHL)
1983—No first-round selection
1984—No first-round selection

Year   Player, Overall, Last amateur team (league)
1985—Glen Seabrooke, 21, Peterborough (OHL)
1986—Kerry Huffman, 20, Guelph (OHL)
1987—Darren Rumble, 20, Kitchener (OHL)
1988—Claude Boivin, 14, Drummondville (QMJHL)
1989—No first-round selection
→ 1990—Mike Ricci, 4, Peterborough (OHL)
1991—Peter Forsberg, 6, Modo, Sweden
1992—Ryan Sittler, 7, Nichols H.S. (N.Y.)
    Jason Bowen, 15, Tri-City (WHL)
1993—No first-round selection
1994—No first-round selection
1995—Brian Boucher, 22, Tri-City (WHL)
1996—Dainius Zubrus, 15, Pembroke, Tier II
1997—No first-round selection
1998—Simon Gagne, 22, Quebec (QMJHL)
1999—Maxime Ouellet, 22, Quebec (QMJHL)
2000—Justin Williams, 28, Plymouth (OHL)
*Designates first player chosen in draft.

SINGLE-SEASON INDIVIDUAL RECORDS

FORWARDS/DEFENSEMEN

Most goals
61—Reggie Leach, 1975-76

Most assists
89—Bobby Clarke, 1974-75
    Bobby Clarke, 1975-76

Most points
123—Mark Recchi, 1992-93

Most penalty minutes
472—Dave Schultz, 1974-75

Most power play goals
34—Tim Kerr, 1985-86

Most shorthanded goals
7—Brian Propp, 1984-85
    Mark Howe, 1985-86

Most games with three or more goals
5—Tim Kerr, 1984-85

Most shots
380—Bill Barber, 1975-76

GOALTENDERS

Most games
73—Bernie Parent, 1973-74

Most minutes
4,314—Bernie Parent, 1973-74

Most goals allowed
208—Ron Hextall, 1987-88

Lowest goals-against average
1.89—Bernie Parent, 1973-74

Most shutouts
12—Bernie Parent, 1973-74
    Bernie Parent, 1974-75

Most wins
47—Bernie Parent, 1973-74

Most losses
29—Bernie Parent, 1969-70

Most ties
20—Bernie Parent, 1969-70

FRANCHISE LEADERS

Players in boldface played for club in 1999-2000

FORWARDS/DEFENSEMEN

Games

Bobby Clarke	1144
Bill Barber	903
Brian Propp	790
Joe Watson	746
Bob Kelly	741
Rick MacLeish	741

Goals

Bill Barber	420
Brian Propp	369
Tim Kerr	363
Bobby Clarke	358
Rick MacLeish	328

Assists

Bobby Clarke	852
Brian Propp	480
Bill Barber	463
Rick MacLeish	369
Rod Brind'Amour	**366**

Points

Bobby Clarke	1210
Bill Barber	883
Brian Propp	849
Rick MacLeish	697
Eric Lindros	**659**

Penalty minutes

Rick Tocchet	1683
Paul Holmgren	1600
Andre Dupont	1505
Bobby Clarke	1453
Dave Schultz	1386

GOALTENDERS

Games

Ron Hextall	**489**
Bernie Parent	486
Doug Favell	215
Pete Peeters	179
Wayne Stephenson	165

Shutouts

Bernie Parent	50
Ron Hextall	18
Doug Favell	16
Bob Froese	12
Wayne Stephenson	10

Goals-against average (2400 minutes minimum)

John Vanbiesbrouck	**2.19**
Bernie Parent	2.42
Garth Snow	2.59
Bob Froese	2.74
Wayne Stephenson	2.77

Wins

Ron Hextall	240
Bernie Parent	232
Wayne Stephenson	93
Bob Froese	92
Pelle Lindbergh	87

PHOENIX COYOTES

YEAR-BY-YEAR RECORDS

	REGULAR SEASON						PLAYOFFS			
Season	W	L	T	RT	Pts.	Finish	W	L	Highest round	Coach
1996-97	38	37	7	—	83	T3rd/Central	3	4	Conference quarterfinals	Don Hay
1997-98	35	35	12	—	82	4th/Central	2	4	Conference quarterfinals	Jim Schoenfeld
1998-99	39	31	12	—	90	2nd/Pacific	3	4	Conference quarterfinals	Jim Schoenfeld
1999-00	39	35	8	4	90	3rd/Pacific	1	4	Conference quarterfinals	Bob Francis

Franchise was formerly known as Winnipeg Jets and relocated to Phoenix following 1995-96 season.

FIRST-ROUND ENTRY DRAFT CHOICES

Year Player, Overall, Last amateur team (league)
1997—No first-round selection
1998—Patrick DesRochers, 14, Sarnia (OHL)

Year Player, Overall, Last amateur team (league)
1999—Scott Kelman, 15, Seattle (WHL)
      Kirill Safronov, 19, SKA St. Petersburg, Russia
2000—Krystofer Kolanos, 19, Boston College

SINGLE-SEASON INDIVIDUAL RECORDS

FORWARDS/DEFENSEMEN

Most goals
52—Keith Tkachuk, 1996-97

Most assists
48—Jeremy Roenick, 1998-99

Most points
86—Keith Tkachuk, 1996-97

Most penalty minutes
228—Keith Tkachuk, 1996-97

Most power play goals
13—Mike Gartner, 1996-97

Most shorthanded goals
5—Bob Corkum, 1997-98

Most games with three or more goals
3—Keith Tkachuk, 1996-97
    Keith Tkachuk, 1997-98

Most shots
296—Keith Tkachuk, 1996-97

GOALTENDERS

Most games
72—Nikolai Khabibulin, 1996-97

Most minutes
4,091—Nikolai Khabibulin, 1996-97

Most shots against
2,094—Nikolai Khabibulin, 1996-97

Most goals allowed
193—Nikolai Khabibulin, 1996-97

Lowest goals-against average
2.55—Sean Burke, 1999-2000

Most shutouts
8—Nikolai Khabibulin, 1998-99

Most wins
32—Nikolai Khabibulin, 1998-99

Most losses
33—Nikolai Khabibulin, 1996-97

Most ties
10—Nikolai Khabibulin, 1997-98

FRANCHISE LEADERS

Players in boldface played for club in 1999-2000

FORWARDS/DEFENSEMEN

Games

Teppo Numminen	325
Jeremy Roenick	304
Keith Tkachuk	268
Shane Doan	256
Dallas Drake	255

Goals

Keith Tkachuk	150
Jeremy Roenick	111
Rick Tocchet	64
Dallas Drake	52
Mike Gartner	44

Assists

Jeremy Roenick	164
Teppo Numminen	129
Keith Tkachuk	113
Dallas Drake	100
Craig Janney	81

Points

Jeremy Roenick	275
Keith Tkachuk	263
Teppo Numminen	160
Dallas Drake	152
Rick Tocchet	130

Penalty minutes

Keith Tkachuk	608
Jeremy Roenick	450
Rick Tocchet	371
Jim McKenzie	346
Dallas Drake	250

GOALTENDERS

Games

Nikolai Khabibulin	205
Sean Burke	35
Jim Waite	33
Bob Essensa	30
Mikhail Shtalenkov	19

Shutouts

Nikolai Khabibulin	19
Sean Burke	3
Mikhail Shtalenkov	2
Jim Waite	2
Bob Essensa	1
Darcy Wakaluk	1

Goals-against average
(2400 minutes minimum)

Nikolai Khabibulin	2.58

Wins

Nikolai Khabibulin	92
Sean Burke	17
Bob Essensa	13
Jim Waite	11
Mikhail Shtalenkov	8
Darcy Wakaluk	8

PITTSBURGH PENGUINS
YEAR-BY-YEAR RECORDS

		REGULAR SEASON					PLAYOFFS			
Season	W	L	T	RT	Pts.	Finish	W	L	Highest round	Coach
1967-68	27	34	13	—	67	5th/West	—	—		Red Sullivan
1968-69	20	45	11	—	51	5th/West	—	—		Red Sullivan
1969-70	26	38	12	—	64	2nd/West	6	4	Division finals	Red Kelly
1970-71	21	37	20	—	62	6th/West	—	—		Red Kelly
1971-72	26	38	14	—	66	4th/West	0	4	Division semifinals	Red Kelly
1972-73	32	37	9	—	73	5th/West	—	—		Red Kelly, Ken Schinkel
1973-74	28	41	9	—	65	5th/West	—	—		Ken Schinkel, Marc Boileau
1974-75	37	28	15	—	89	3rd/Norris	5	4	Quarterfinals	Marc Boileau
1975-76	35	33	12	—	82	3rd/Norris	1	2	Preliminaries	Marc Boileau, Ken Schinkel
1976-77	34	33	13	—	81	3rd/Norris	1	2	Preliminaries	Ken Schinkel
1977-78	25	37	18	—	68	4th/Norris	—	—		Johnny Wilson
1978-79	36	31	13	—	85	2nd/Norris	2	5	Quarterfinals	Johnny Wilson
1979-80	30	37	13	—	73	3rd/Norris	2	3	Preliminaries	Johnny Wilson
1980-81	30	37	13	—	73	3rd/Norris	2	3	Preliminaries	Eddie Johnston
1981-82	31	36	13	—	75	4th/Patrick	2	3	Division semifinals	Eddie Johnston
1982-83	18	53	9	—	45	6th/Patrick	—	—		Eddie Johnston
1983-84	16	58	6	—	38	6th/Patrick	—	—		Lou Angotti
1984-85	24	51	5	—	53	5th/Patrick	—	—		Bob Berry
1985-86	34	38	8	—	76	5th/Patrick	—	—		Bob Berry
1986-87	30	38	12	—	72	5th/Patrick	—	—		Bob Berry
1987-88	36	35	9	—	81	6th/Patrick	—	—		Pierre Creamer
1988-89	40	33	7	—	87	2nd/Patrick	7	4	Division finals	Gene Ubriaco
1989-90	32	40	8	—	72	5th/Patrick	—	—		Gene Ubriaco, Craig Patrick
1990-91	41	33	6	—	88	1st/Patrick	16	8	Stanley Cup champ	Bob Johnson
1991-92	39	32	9	—	87	3rd/Patrick	16	5	Stanley Cup champ	Scotty Bowman
1992-93	56	21	7	—	119	1st/Patrick	7	5	Division finals	Scotty Bowman
1993-94	44	27	13	—	101	1st/Northeast	2	4	Conference quarterfinals	Eddie Johnston
1994-95	29	16	3	—	61	2nd/Northeast	5	7	Conference semifinals	Eddie Johnston
1995-96	49	29	4	—	102	1st/Northeast	11	7	Conference finals	Eddie Johnston
1996-97	38	36	8	—	84	2nd/Northeast	1	4	Conference quarterfinals	Eddie Johnston, Craig Patrick
1997-98	40	24	18	—	98	1st/Northeast	2	4	Conference quarterfinals	Kevin Constantine
1998-99	38	30	14	—	90	3rd/Atlantic	6	7	Conference semifinals	Kevin Constantine
1999-00	37	37	8	6	88	3rd/Atlantic	6	5	Conference semifinals	Kevin Constantine, Herb Brooks

FIRST-ROUND ENTRY DRAFT CHOICES

Year   Player, Overall, Last amateur team (league)
1969—No first-round selection
1970—Greg Polis, 7, Estevan (WCHL)

Year   Player, Overall, Last amateur team (league)
1971—No first-round selection
1972—No first-round selection

Year	Player, Overall, Last amateur team (league)
1973	Blaine Stoughton, 7, Flin Flon (WCHL)
1974	Pierre Larouche, 8, Sorel (QMJHL)
1975	Gord Laxton, 13, New Westminster (WCHL)
1976	Blair Chapman, 2, Saskatoon (WCHL)
1977	No first-round selection
1978	No first-round selection
1979	No first-round selection
1980	Mike Bullard, 9, Brantford (OHL)
1981	No first-round selection
1982	Rich Sutter, 10, Lethbridge (WHL)
1983	Bob Errey, 15, Peterborough (OHL)
1984	Mario Lemieux, 1, Laval (QMJHL)*
	Doug Bodger, 9, Kamloops (WHL)
	Roger Belanger, 16, Kingston (OHL)
1985	Craig Simpson, 2, Michigan State University
1986	Zarley Zalapski, 4, Team Canada

Year	Player, Overall, Last amateur team (league)
1987	Chris Joseph, 5, Seattle (WHL)
1988	Darrin Shannon, 4, Windsor (OHL)
1989	Jamie Heward, 16, Regina (WHL)
1990	Jaromir Jagr, 5, Poldi Kladno, Czech. Republic
1991	Markus Naslund, 16, MoDo, Sweden
1992	Martin Straka, 19, Skoda Plzen, Czech. Republic
1993	Stefan Bergqvist, 26, Leksand, Sweden
1994	Chris Wells, 24, Seattle (WHL)
1995	Alexei Morozov, 24, Krylja Sovetov, CIS
1996	Craig Hillier, 23, Ottawa (OHL)
1997	Robert Dome, 17, Las Vegas (IHL)
1998	Milan Kraft, 23, Plzen (Czech.)
1999	Konstantin Koltsov, 18, Cherepovec, Russia
2000	Brooks Orpik, 18, Boston College

*Designates first player chosen in draft.

SINGLE-SEASON INDIVIDUAL RECORDS

FORWARDS/DEFENSEMEN

Most goals
85—Mario Lemieux, 1988-89

Most assists
114—Mario Lemieux, 1988-89

Most points
199—Mario Lemieux, 1988-89

Most penalty minutes
409—Paul Baxter, 1981-82

Most power play goals
31—Mario Lemieux, 1988-89
Mario Lemieux, 1995-96

Most shorthanded goals
13—Mario Lemieux, 1988-89

Most games with three or more goals
9—Mario Lemieux, 1988-89

Most shots
403—Jaromir Jagr, 1995-96

GOALTENDERS

Most games
63—Greg Millen, 1980-81
Tom Barrasso, 1992-93
Tom Barrasso, 1997-98

Most minutes
3,721—Greg Millen, 1980-81

Most goals allowed
258—Greg Millen, 1980-81

Lowest goals-against average
2.07—Tom Barrasso, 1997-98

Most shutouts
7—Tom Barrasso, 1997-98

Most wins
43—Tom Barrasso, 1992-93

Most losses
31—Les Binkley, 1968-69

Most ties
15—Denis Herron, 1977-78

FRANCHISE LEADERS

Players in boldface played for club in 1999-2000

FORWARDS/DEFENSEMEN

Games

Jean Pronovost	753
Mario Lemieux	745
Jaromir Jagr	**725**
Rick Kehoe	722
Ron Stackhouse	621

Goals

Mario Lemieux	613
Jaromir Jagr	**387**
Jean Pronovost	316
Rick Kehoe	312
Kevin Stevens	251

Assists

Mario Lemieux	867
Jaromir Jagr	**571**
Ron Francis	449
Syl Apps	349
Paul Coffey	332

Points

Mario Lemieux	1494
Jaromir Jagr	**958**
Rick Kehoe	636
Ron Francis	613
Jean Pronovost	603

Penalty minutes

Troy Loney	980
Kevin Stevens	968
Rod Buskas	959
Bryan Watson	871
Paul Baxter	851

GOALTENDERS

Games

Tom Barrasso	**458**
Denis Herron	290
Ken Wregget	212
Les Binkley	196
Michel Dion	151

Shutouts

Tom Barrasso	**22**
Les Binkley	11
Denis Herron	6
Ken Wregget	6
Dunc Wilson	5

**Goals-against average
(2400 minutes minimum)**

Peter Skudra	**2.65**
Al Smith	3.07
Les Binkley	3.12
Jim Rutherford	3.14
Tom Barrasso	**3.27**

Wins

Tom Barrasso	**226**
Ken Wregget	104
Denis Herron	88
Les Binkley	58
Greg Millen	57

NHL HISTORY *Team by team*

PITTSBURGH PIRATES (DEFUNCT)
YEAR-BY-YEAR RECORDS

Season	W	L	T	Pts.	REGULAR SEASON Finish	PLAYOFFS W	L	Highest round	Coach
1925-26	19	16	1	39	3rd	—	—		Odie Cleghorn
1926-27	15	26	3	33	4th/American	—	—		Odie Cleghorn
1927-28	19	17	8	46	3rd/American	1	1	Quarterfinals	Odie Cleghorn
1928-29	9	27	8	26	4th/American	—	—		Odie Cleghorn
1929-30	5	36	3	13	5th/American	—	—		Frank Frederickson
1930-31*	4	36	4	12	5th/American	—	—		Cooper Smeaton

*Philadelphia Quakers.

QUEBEC BULLDOGS (DEFUNCT)
YEAR-BY-YEAR RECORDS

Season	W	L	T	Pts.	REGULAR SEASON Finish	PLAYOFFS W	L	Highest round	Coach
1919-20	4	20	0	8	4th	—	—		Mike Quinn

Franchise relocated and became Hamilton Tigers following 1919-20 season; franchise later relocated and became New York Americans after 1924-25 season.

QUEBEC NORDIQUES (DEFUNCT)
YEAR-BY-YEAR RECORDS

Season	W	L	T	Pts.	REGULAR SEASON Finish	PLAYOFFS W	L	Highest round	Coach
1972-73*	33	40	5	71	5th	—	—		Maurice Richard, Maurice Filion
1973-74*	38	36	4	80	5th	—	—		Jacques Plante
1974-75*	46	32	0	92	1st	8	7	Avco World Cup finals	Jean-Guy Gendron
1975-76*	50	27	4	104	2nd	1	4	League quarterfinals	Jean-Guy Gendron
1976-77*	47	31	3	97	1st	12	5	Avco World Cup champ	Marc Boileau
1977-78*	40	37	3	83	4th	5	6	League semifinals	Marc Boileau
1978-79*	41	34	5	87	2nd	0	4	League semifinals	Jacques Demers
1979-80	25	44	11	61	5th/Adams	—	—		Jacques Demers
1980-81	30	32	18	78	4th/Adams	2	3	Preliminaries	Maurice Filion, Michel Bergeron
1981-82	33	31	16	82	4th/Adams	7	9	Conference finals	Michel Bergeron
1982-83	34	34	12	80	4th/Adams	1	3	Division semifinals	Michel Bergeron
1983-84	42	28	10	94	3rd/Adams	5	4	Division finals	Michel Bergeron
1984-85	41	30	9	91	2nd/Adams	9	9	Conference finals	Michel Bergeron
1985-86	43	31	6	92	1st/Adams	0	3	Division semifinals	Michel Bergeron
1986-87	31	39	10	72	4th/Adams	7	6	Division finals	Michel Bergeron
1987-88	32	43	5	69	5th/Adams	—	—		Andre Savard, Ron Lapointe
1988-89	27	46	7	61	5th/Adams	—	—		Ron Lapointe, Jean Perron
1989-90	12	61	7	31	5th/Adams	—	—		Michel Bergeron
1990-91	16	50	14	46	5th/Adams	—	—		Dave Chambers
1991-92	20	48	12	52	5th/Adams	—	—		Dave Chambers, Pierre Page
1992-93	47	27	10	104	2nd/Adams	2	4	Division semifinals	Pierre Page
1993-94	34	42	8	76	5th/Northeast	—	—		Pierre Page
1994-95	30	13	5	65	1st/Northeast	2	4	Conference quarterfinals	Marc Crawford

*Members of World Hockey Association.
Franchise relocated and became Colorado Avalanche following 1994-95 season.

FIRST-ROUND ENTRY DRAFT CHOICES

Year	Player, Overall, Last amateur team (league)
1979	Michel Goulet, 20, Birmingham (WHA)
1980	No first-round selection
1981	Randy Moller, 11, Lethbridge (WHL)
1982	David Shaw, 13, Kitchener (OHL)
1983	No first-round selection
1984	Trevor Steinburg, 15, Guelph (OHL)
1985	Dave Latta, 15, Kitchener (OHL)
1986	Ken McRae, 18, Sudbury (OHL)
1987	Bryan Fogarty, 9, Kingston (OHL)
	Joe Sakic, 15, Swift Current (WHL)
1988	Curtis Leschyshyn, 3, Saskatoon (WHL)
	Daniel Dore, 5, Drummondville (QMJHL)

Year	Player, Overall, Last amateur team (league)
1989	Mats Sundin, 1, Nacka (Sweden)*
1990	Owen Nolan, 1, Cornwall (OHL)*
1991	Eric Lindros, 1, Oshawa (OHL)*
1992	Todd Warriner, 4, Windsor (OHL)
1993	Jocelyn Thibault, 10, Sherbrooke (QMJHL)
	Adam Deadmarsh, 14, Portland (WHL)
1994	Wade Belak, 12, Saskatoon (WHL)
	Jeffrey Kealty, 22, Catholic Memorial H.S.
1995	Marc Denis, 25, Chicoutimi (QMJHL)

*Designates first player chosen in draft.
NOTE: Quebec chose Paul Baxter, Richard Brodeur and Garry Larivierre as priority selections before the 1979 expansion draft.

FORWARDS/DEFENSEMEN

Most goals
57—Michel Goulet, 1982-83

Most assists
93—Peter Stastny, 1981-82

Most points
139—Peter Stastny, 1981-82

Most penalty minutes
301—Gord Donnelly, 1987-88

Most power play goals
29—Michel Goulet, 1987-88

Most shorthanded goals
6—Michel Goulet, 1981-82
Scott Young, 1992-93

Most games with three or more goals
4—Miroslav Frycer, 1981-82
Peter Stastny, 1982-83

GOALTENDERS

Most games
60—Dan Bouchard, 1981-82

Most minutes
3,572—Dan Bouchard, 1981-82

Most goals allowed
230—Dan Bouchard, 1981-82

Lowest goals-against average
2.78—Stephane Fiset, 1994-95

Most shutouts
4—Clint Malarchuk, 1985-86

Most wins
29—Dan Bouchard, 1983-84
Ron Hextall, 1992-93

Most losses
29—Ron Tugnutt, 1990-91

Most ties
11—Dan Bouchard, 1981-82

FRANCHISE LEADERS

FORWARDS/DEFENSEMEN

Games

Michel Goulet	813
Peter Stastny	737
Alain Cote	696
Anton Stastny	650
Steven Finn	606

Goals

Michel Goulet	456
Peter Stastny	380
Anton Stastny	252
Joe Sakic	235
Dale Hunter	140

Assists

Peter Stastny	668
Michel Goulet	489
Joe Sakic	391
Anton Stastny	384
Dale Hunter	318

Points

Peter Stastny	1048
Michel Goulet	945
Anton Stastny	636
Joe Sakic	626
Dale Hunter	458

Penalty minutes

Dale Hunter	1545
Steven Finn	1511
Paul Gillis	1351
Randy Moller	1002
Mario Marois	778

GOALTENDERS

Games

Dan Bouchard	225
Mario Gosselin	192
Ron Tugnutt	153
Stephane Fiset	152
Clint Malarchuk	140

Shutouts

Mario Gosselin	6
Dan Bouchard	5
Stephane Fiset	5
Clint Malarchuk	5
Michel Dion	2

Goals-against average
(2400 minutes minimum)

Jocelyn Thibault	2.95
Ron Hextall	3.45
Dan Bouchard	3.59
Clint Malarchuk	3.63
Maril Gosselin	3.67

Wins

Dan Bouchard	107
Mario Gosselin	79
Stephane Fiset	62
Clint Malarchuk	62
Ron Tugnutt	35

ST. LOUIS BLUES
YEAR-BY-YEAR RECORDS

	REGULAR SEASON					PLAYOFFS			
Season	W	L	T	RT	Pts.	Finish	W	L	Highest round	Coach
1967-68	27	31	16	—	70	3rd/West	8	10	Stanley Cup finals	Lynn Patrick, Scotty Bowman
1968-69	37	25	14	—	88	1st/West	8	4	Stanley Cup finals	Scotty Bowman
1969-70	37	27	12	—	86	1st/West	8	8	Stanley Cup finals	Scotty Bowman
1970-71	34	25	19	—	87	2nd/West	2	4	Division semifinals	Al Arbour, Scotty Bowman
1971-72	28	39	11	—	67	3rd/West	4	7	Division finals	Sid Abel, Bill McCreary, Al Arbour
1972-73	32	34	12	—	76	4th/West	1	4	Division semifinals	Al Arbour, Jean-Guy Talbot
1973-74	26	40	12	—	64	6th/West	—	—		Jean-Guy Talbot, Lou Angotti
1974-75	35	31	14	—	84	2nd/Smythe	0	2	Preliminaries	Lou Angotti, Lynn Patrick, Garry Young
1975-76	29	37	14	—	72	3rd/Smythe	1	2	Preliminaries	Garry Young, Lynn Patrick, Leo Boivin
1976-77	32	39	9	—	73	1st/Smythe	0	4	Quarterfinals	Emile Francis
1977-78	20	47	13	—	53	4th/Smythe	—	—		Leo Boivin, Barclay Plager
1978-79	18	50	12	—	48	3rd/Smythe	—	—		Barclay Plager
1979-80	34	34	12	—	80	2nd/Smythe	0	3	Preliminaries	Barclay Plager, Red Berenson
1980-81	45	18	17	—	107	1st/Smythe	5	6	Quarterfinals	Red Berenson
1981-82	32	40	8	—	72	3rd/Norris	5	5	Division finals	Red Berenson, Emile Francis
1982-83	25	40	15	—	65	4th/Norris	1	3	Division semifinals	Emile Francis, Barclay Plager
1983-84	32	41	7	—	71	2nd/Norris	6	5	Division finals	Jacques Demers
1984-85	37	31	12	—	86	1st/Norris	0	3	Division semifinals	Jacques Demers

NHL HISTORY *Team by team*

Season	W	L	T	RT	Pts.	Finish	W	L	Highest round	Coach
1985-86	37	34	9	—	83	3rd/Norris	10	9	Conference finals	Jacques Demers
1986-87	32	33	15	—	79	1st/Norris	2	4	Division semifinals	Jacques Martin
1987-88	34	38	8	—	76	2nd/Norris	5	5	Division finals	Jacques Martin
1988-89	33	35	12	—	78	2nd/Norris	5	5	Division finals	Brian Sutter
1989-90	37	34	9	—	83	2nd/Norris	7	5	Division finals	Brian Sutter
1990-91	47	22	11	—	105	2nd/Norris	6	7	Division finals	Brian Sutter
1991-92	36	33	11	—	83	3rd/Norris	2	4	Division semifinals	Brian Sutter
1992-93	37	36	11	—	85	4th/Norris	7	4	Division finals	Bob Plager, Bob Berry
1993-94	40	33	11	—	91	4th/Central	0	4	Conference quarterfinals	Bob Berry
1994-95	28	15	5	—	61	2nd/Central	3	4	Conference quarterfinals	Mike Keenan
1995-96	32	34	16	—	80	T3rd/Central	7	6	Conference semifinals	Mike Keenan
1996-97	36	35	11	—	83	T3rd/Central	2	4	Conference quarterfinals	Mike Keenan, Jimmy Roberts, Joel Quenneville
1997-98	45	29	8	—	98	3rd/Central	6	4	Conference semifinals	Joel Quenneville
1998-99	37	32	13	—	87	2nd/Central	6	7	Conference semifinals	Joel Quenneville
1999-00	51	20	11	1	114	1st/Central	3	4	Conference quarterfinals	Joel Quenneville

FIRST-ROUND ENTRY DRAFT CHOICES

Year   Player, Overall, Last amateur team (league)

1969—No first-round selection
1970—No first-round selection
1971—Gene Carr, 4, Flin Flon (WCHL)
1972—Wayne Merrick, 9, Ottawa (OHL)
1973—John Davidson, 5, Calgary (WCHL)
1974—No first-round selection
1975—No first-round selection
1976—Bernie Federko, 7, Saskatoon (WCHL)
1977—Scott Campbell, 9, London (OHL)
1978—Wayne Babych, 3, Portland (WCHL)
1979—Perry Turnbull, 2, Portland (WHL)
1980—Rik Wilson, 12, Kingston (OHL)
1981—Marty Ruff, 20, Lethbridge (WHL)
1982—No first-round selection
1983—No first-round selection
1984—No first-round selection

Year   Player, Overall, Last amateur team (league)

1985—No first-round selection
1986—Jocelyn Lemieux, 10, Laval (QMJHL)
1987—Keith Osborne, 12, North Bay (OHL)
1988—Rod Brind'Amour, 9, Notre Dame Academy (Sask.)
1989—Jason Marshall, 9, Vernon (B.C.) Tier II
1990—No first-round selection
1991—No first-round selection
1992—No first-round selection
1993—No first-round selection
1994—No first-round selection
1995—No first-round selection
1996—Marty Reasoner, 14, Boston College
1997—No first-round selection
1998—Christian Backman, 24, Frolunda HC Goteborg (Sweden)
1999—Barret Jackman, 17, Regina (WHL)
2000—Jeff Taffe, 30, University of Minnesota

SINGLE-SEASON INDIVIDUAL RECORDS

FORWARDS/DEFENSEMEN

Most goals
86—Brett Hull, 1990-91

Most assists
90—Adam Oates, 1990-91

Most points
131—Brett Hull, 1990-91

Most penalty minutes
306—Bob Gassoff, 1975-76

Most power play goals
29—Brett Hull, 1990-91
    Brett Hull, 1992-93

Most shorthanded goals
8—Chuck Lefley, 1975-76
   Larry Patey, 1980-81

Most games with three or more goals
8—Brett Hull, 1991-92

Most shots
408—Brett Hull, 1991-92

GOALTENDERS

Most games
79—Grant Fuhr, 1995-96

Most minutes
4,365—Grant Fuhr, 1995-96

Most shots against
2,382—Curtis Joseph, 1993-94

Most goals allowed
250—Mike Liut, 1991-92

Lowest goals-against average
1.95—Roman Turek, 1999-2000

Most shutouts
8—Glenn Hall, 1968-69

Most wins
42—Roman Turek, 1999-2000

Most losses
29—Mike Liut, 1983-84

Most ties
16—Grant Fuhr, 1995-96

FRANCHISE LEADERS

Players in boldface played for club in 1999-2000

FORWARDS/DEFENSEMEN

Games
Bernie Federko 927
Brian Sutter 779
Brett Hull 744
Garry Unger 662
Bob Plager 615

Goals
Brett Hull 527
Bernie Federko 352
Brian Sutter 303
Garry Unger 292
Red Berenson 172

Assists
Bernie Federko 721
Brett Hull 409
Brian Sutter 334
Garry Unger 283
Red Berenson 240

NHL HISTORY Team by team

Points		
Bernie Federko	1073
Brett Hull	936
Brian Sutter	636
Garry Unger	575
Red Berenson	412

Penalty minutes

Brian Sutter	1786
Kelly Chase	**1497**
Barclay Plager	1115
Rob Ramage	998
Bob Gassoff	866

GOALTENDERS

Games

Mike Liut	347
Curtis Joseph	280
Grant Fuhr	249
Greg Millen	209
Rick Wamsley	154

Shutouts

Glenn Hall	16
Grant Fuhr	11
Mike Liut	10
Jacques Plante	10
Greg Millen	9

Goals-against average (2400 minutes minimum)

Jacques Plante	2.07
Glenn Hall	2.43
Grant Fuhr	2.68
Ernie Wakely	2.77
Jacques Caron	3.02

Wins

Mike Liut	151
Curtis Joseph	137
Grant Fuhr	108
Greg Millen	85
Rick Wamsley	75

ST. LOUIS EAGLES (DEFUNCT)
YEAR-BY-YEAR RECORDS

	REGULAR SEASON					PLAYOFFS			
Season	W	L	T	Pts.	Finish	W	L	Highest round	Coach
1934-35	11	31	6	28	5th/Canadian	—	—		Eddie Gerard, George Boucher

Franchise was formerly known as Ottawa Senators and relocated to St. Louis following 1933-34 season.

SAN JOSE SHARKS
YEAR-BY-YEAR RECORDS

	REGULAR SEASON						PLAYOFFS			
Season	W	L	T	RT	Pts.	Finish	W	L	Highest round	Coach
1991-92	17	58	5	—	39	6th/Smythe	—	—		George Kingston
1992-93	11	71	2	—	24	6th/Smythe	—	—		George Kingston
1993-94	33	35	16	—	82	3rd/Pacific	7	7	Conference semifinals	Kevin Constantine
1994-95	19	25	4	—	42	3rd/Pacific	4	7	Conference semifinals	Kevin Constantine
1995-96	20	55	7	—	47	7th/Pacific	—	—		Kevin Constantine, Jim Wiley
1996-97	27	47	8	—	62	7th/Pacific	—	—		Al Sims
1997-98	34	38	10	—	78	4th/Pacific	2	4	Conference quarterfinals	Darryl Sutter
1998-89	31	33	18	—	80	4th/Pacific	2	4	Conference quarterfinals	Darryl Sutter
1999-00	35	37	10	7	87	4th/Pacific	5	7	Conference semifinals	Darryl Sutter

OFIRST-ROUND ENTRY DRAFT CHOICES

Year Player, Overall, Last amateur team (league)
1991—Pat Falloon, 2, Spokane (WHL)
1992—Mike Rathje, 3, Medicine Hat (WHL)
    Andrei Nazarov, 10, Dynamo Moscow, CIS
1993—Viktor Kozlov, 6, Moscow, CIS
1994—Jeff Friesen, 11, Regina (WHL)
1995—Teemu Riihijarvi, 12, Espoo Jrs., Finland
1996—Andrei Zyuzin, 2, Salavat Yulayev UFA, CIS
   Marco Sturm, 21, Landshut, Germany

Year Player, Overall, Last amateur team (league)
1997—Patrick Marleau, 2, Seattle (WHL)
   Scott Hannan, 23, Kelowna (WHL)
1998—Brad Stuart, 3, Regina (WHL)
1999—Jeff Jillson, 14, University of Michigan
2000—No first-round selection

SINGLE-SEASON INDIVIDUAL RECORDS

FORWARDS/DEFENSEMEN

Most goals
44—Owen Nolan, 1999-2000

Most assists
52—Kelly Kisio, 1992-93

Most points
84—Owen Nolan, 1999-2000

Most penalty minutes
326—Link Gaetz, 1991-92

Most power play goals
18—Owen Nolan, 1999-2000

Most shorthanded goals
6—Jamie Baker, 1995-96

Most games with three or more goals
2—Rob Gaudreau, 1992-93
    Igor Larionov, 1993-94
    Tony Granato, 1996-97

Most shots
261—Tony Granato, 1996-97

GOALTENDERS

Most games
74—Arturs Irbe, 1993-94

Most minutes
4,412—Arturs Irbe, 1993-94

Most shots against
2,064—Arturs Irbe, 1993-94

Most goals allowed
209—Arturs Irbe, 1993-94

Lowest goals-against average
2.46—Mike Vernon, 1997-98

Most shutouts
5—Mike Vernon, 1997-98

Most wins
30—Arturs Irbe, 1993-94
    Mike Vernon, 1997-98

Most losses
30—Jeff Hackett, 1992-93

Most ties
16—Arturs Irbe, 1993-94

NHL HISTORY Team by team

FRANCHISE LEADERS

Players in boldface played for club in 1999-2000

FORWARDS/DEFENSEMEN

Games

Jeff Friesen.............................448
Mike Rathje 376
Owen Nolan 375
Marcus Ragnarsson...................356
Jeff Odgers...................................334

Goals

Jeff Friesen.............................137
Owen Nolan 137
Pat Falloon 76
Tony Granato 53
Patrick Marleau 51

Assists

Jeff Friesen.............................177
Owen Nolan 157
Marcus Ragnarsson 91
Pat Falloon 86
Johan Garpenlov 86

Points

Jeff Friesen.............................314
Owen Nolan 294
Pat Falloon 162
Johan Garpenlov 132
Ray Whitney..................................121

Penalty minutes

Jeff Odgers....................................1001
Owen Nolan 675
Jay More 545
Andrei Nazarov.............................490
Dody Wood 471

GOALTENDERS

Games

Arturs Irbe...................................183
Mike Vernon...........................126
Steve Shields 104
Jeff Hackett 78
Kelly Hrudey 76

Shutouts

Mike Vernon..............................9
Arturs Irbe..8
Steve Shields 8
Ed Belfour 1
Wade Flaherty..................................1
Kelly Hrudey......................................1

Goals-against average
(2400 minutes minimum)

Mike Vernon...........................2.39
Steve Shields 2.44
Kelly Hrudey.................................3.04
Chris Terreri 3.39
Arturs Irbe......................................3.47

Wins

Arturs Irbe.....................................57
Mike Vernon 52
Steve Shields...........................42
Kelly Hrudey.................................20
Chris Terreri 19

TAMPA BAY LIGHTNING
YEAR-BY-YEAR RECORDS

		REGULAR SEASON					PLAYOFFS			
Season	W	L	T	RT	Pts.	Finish	W	L	Highest round	Coach
1992-93	23	54	7	—	53	6th/Norris	—	—		Terry Crisp
1993-94	30	43	11	—	71	7th/Atlantic	—	—		Terry Crisp
1994-95	17	28	3	—	37	6th/Atlantic	—	—		Terry Crisp
1995-96	38	32	12	—	88	5th/Atlantic	2	4	Conference quarterfinals	Terry Crisp
1996-97	32	40	10	—	74	6th/Atlantic	—	—		Terry Crisp
1997-98	17	55	10	—	44	7th/Atlantic	—	—		Terry Crisp, Rick Paterson, Jacques Demers
1998-99	19	54	9	—	47	4th/Southeast	—	—		Jacques Demers
1999-00	19	54	9	7	54	4th/Southeast	—	—		Steve Ludzik

FIRST-ROUND ENTRY DRAFT CHOICES

Year   Player, Overall, Last amateur team (league)
1992—Roman Hamrlik, 1, Zlin (Czech.)*
1993—Chris Gratton, 3, Kingston (OHL)
1994—Jason Weimer, 8, Portland (WHL)
1995—Daymond Langkow, 5, Tri-City (WHL)
1996—Mario Larocque, 16, Hull (QMJHL)

Year   Player, Overall, Last amateur team (league)
1997—Paul Mara, 7, Sudbury (OHL)
1998—Vincent Lecavalier, 1, Rimouski (QMJHL)*
1999—No first-round selection
2000—Nikita Alexeev, 8, Erie (OHL)
*Designates first player chosen in draft.

SINGLE-SEASON INDIVIDUAL RECORDS

FORWARDS/DEFENSEMEN

Most goals
42—Brian Bradley, 1992-93

Most assists
56—Brian Bradley, 1995-96

Most points
86—Brian Bradley, 1992-93

Most penalty minutes
258—Enrico Ciccone, 1995-96

Most power play goals
16—Brian Bradley, 1992-93

Most shorthanded goals
4—Rob Zamuner, 1994-95
    Rob Zamuner, 1995-96

Most games with three or more goals
3—Wendel Clark, 1998-99

Most shots
281—Roman Hamrlik, 1995-96

GOALTENDERS

Most games
63—Daren Puppa, 1993-94

Most minutes
3,653—Daren Puppa, 1993-94

Most shots against
1,637—Daren Puppa, 1993-94

Most goals allowed
165—Daren Puppa, 1993-94

Lowest goals-against average
2.46—Daren Puppa, 1995-96

Most shutouts
5—Daren Puppa, 1995-96

Most wins
29—Daren Puppa, 1995-96

Most losses
33—Daren Puppa, 1993-94

Most ties
9—Daren Puppa, 1995-96

NHL HISTORY Team by team

FRANCHISE LEADERS

Players in boldface played for club in 1999-2000

FORWARDS/DEFENSEMEN

Games
Rob Zamuner	475
Mikael Andersson	435
Chris Gratton	**404**
Roman Hamrlik	377
Cory Cross	336

Goals
Brian Bradley	111
Chris Gratton	**88**
Rob Zamuner	84
Alexander Selivanov	78
Petr Klima	63

Assists
Brian Bradley	189
Chris Gratton	**148**
Roman Hamrlik	133
Rob Zamuner	116
John Tucker	82

Points
Brian Bradley	300
Chris Gratton	**236**
Rob Zamuner	200
Roman Hamrlik	185
Alexander Selivanov	155

Penalty minutes
Chris Gratton	**741**
Enrico Ciccone	604
Roman Hamrlik	472
Rudy Poeschek	418
Jason Wiemer	391

GOALTENDERS

Games
Daren Puppa	**206**
Corey Schwab	87
Pat Jablonski	58
Rick Tabaracci	55
J.C. Bergeron	53

Shutouts
Daren Puppa	12
Rick Tabaracci	4
Corey Schwab	3
J.C. Bergeron	1
Mark Fitzpatrick	1
Pat Jablonski	1
Bill Ranford	1
Wendell Young	1

Goals-against average
(2400 minutes minimum)
Daren Puppa	**2.68**
Rick Tabaracci	2.75
Corey Schwab	3.25
Dan Cloutier	**3.49**
J.C. Bergeron	3.65

Wins
Daren Puppa	**77**
Corey Schwab	21
Rick Tabaracci	20
J.C. Bergeron	14
Pat Jablonski	13

TORONTO MAPLE LEAFS
YEAR-BY-YEAR RECORDS

		REGULAR SEASON					PLAYOFFS			
Season	W	L	T	RT	Pts.	Finish	W	L	Highest round	Coach
1917-18‡	13	9	0	—	26	2nd	4	3	Stanley Cup champ	Dick Carroll
1918-19‡	5	13	0	—	10	3rd	—	—		Dick Carroll
1919-20§	12	12	0	—	24	3rd	—	—		Frank Heffernan, Harry Sproule
1920-21§	15	9	0	—	30	1st	0	2	Semifinals	Dick Carroll
1921-22§	13	10	1	—	27	2nd	*4	2	Stanley Cup champ	Eddie Powers
1922-23§	13	10	1	—	27	3rd	—	—		Charlie Querrie, Jack Adams
1923-24§	10	14	0	—	20	3rd	—	—		Eddie Powers
1924-25§	19	11	0	—	38	2nd	0	2	Semifinals	Eddie Powers
1925-26§	12	21	3	—	27	6th	—	—		Eddie Powers
1926-27§	15	24	5	—	35	5th/Canadian	—	—		Conn Smythe
1927-28	18	18	8	—	44	4th/Canadian	—	—		Alex Roveril, Conn Smythe
1928-29	21	18	5	—	47	3rd/Canadian	2	2	Semifinals	Alex Roveril, Conn Smythe
1929-30	17	21	6	—	40	4th/Canadian	—	—		Alex Roveril, Conn Smythe
1930-31	22	13	9	—	53	2nd/Canadian	*0	1	Quarterfinals	Conn Smythe, Art Duncan
1931-32	23	18	7	—	53	2nd/Canadian	5	2	Stanley Cup champ	Art Duncan, Dick Irvin
1932-33	24	18	6	—	54	1st/Canadian	4	5	Stanley Cup finals	Dick Irvin
1933-34	26	13	9	—	61	1st/Canadian	2	3	Semifinals	Dick Irvin
1934-35	30	14	4	—	64	1st/Canadian	3	4	Stanley Cup finals	Dick Irvin
1935-36	23	19	6	—	52	2nd/Canadian	4	5	Stanley Cup finals	Dick Irvin
1936-37	22	21	5	—	49	3rd/Canadian	0	2	Quarterfinals	Dick Irvin
1937-38	24	15	9	—	57	1st/Canadian			Stanley Cup finals	Dick Irvin
1938-39	19	20	9	—	47	3rd	5	5	Stanley Cup finals	Dick Irvin
1939-40	25	17	6	—	56	3rd	6	4	Stanley Cup finals	Dick Irvin
1940-41	28	14	6	—	62	2nd	3	4	Semifinals	Hap Day
1941-42	27	18	3	—	57	2nd	8	5	Stanley Cup champ	Hap Day
1942-43	22	19	9	—	53	3rd	2	4	League semifinals	Hap Day
1943-44	23	23	4	—	50	3rd	1	4	League semifinals	Hap Day
1944-45	24	22	4	—	52	3rd	8	5	Stanley Cup champ	Hap Day
1945-46	19	24	7	—	45	5th	—	—		Hap Day
1946-47	31	19	10	—	72	2nd	8	3	Stanley Cup champ	Hap Day
1947-48	32	15	13	—	77	1st	8	1	Stanley Cup champ	Hap Day
1948-49	22	25	13	—	57	4th	8	1	Stanley Cup champ	Hap Day
1949-50	31	27	12	—	74	3rd	3	4	League semifinals	Hap Day
1950-51	41	16	13	—	95	2nd	†8	2	Stanley Cup champ	Joe Primeau
1951-52	29	25	16	—	74	3rd	0	4	League semifinals	Joe Primeau
1952-53	27	30	13	—	67	5th	—	—		Joe Primeau
1953-54	32	24	14	—	78	3rd	1	4	League semifinals	King Clancy
1954-55	24	24	22	—	70	3rd	0	4	League semifinals	King Clancy

NHL HISTORY *Team by team*

Season	W	L	T	RT	Pts.	Finish	W	L	Highest round	Coach
					REGULAR SEASON				**PLAYOFFS**	
1955-56	24	33	13	—	61	4th	1	4	League semifinals	King Clancy
1956-57	21	34	15	—	57	5th	—	—		Howie Meeker
1957-58	21	38	11	—	53	6th	—	—		Billy Reay
1958-59	27	32	11	—	65	4th	5	7	Stanley Cup finals	Billy Reay, Punch Imlach
1959-60	35	26	9	—	79	2nd	4	6	Stanley Cup finals	Punch Imlach
1960-61	39	19	12	—	90	2nd	1	4	League semifinals	Punch Imlach
1961-62	37	22	11	—	85	2nd	8	4	Stanley Cup champ	Punch Imlach
1962-63	35	23	12	—	82	1st	8	2	Stanley Cup champ	Punch Imlach
1963-64	33	25	12	—	78	3rd	8	6	Stanley Cup champ	Punch Imlach
1964-65	30	26	14	—	74	4th	2	4	League semifinals	Punch Imlach
1965-66	34	25	11	—	79	3rd	0	4	League semifinals	Punch Imlach
1966-67	32	27	11	—	75	3rd	8	4	Stanley Cup champ	Punch Imlach
1967-68	33	31	10	—	76	5th/East	—	—		Punch Imlach
1968-69	35	26	15	—	85	4th/East	0	4	Division semifinals	Punch Imlach
1969-70	29	34	13	—	71	6th/East	—	—		John McLellan
1970-71	37	33	8	—	82	4th/East	2	4	Division semifinals	John McLellan
1971-72	33	31	14	—	80	4th/East	1	4	Division semifinals	John McLellan
1972-73	27	41	10	—	64	6th/East	—	—		John McLellan
1973-74	35	27	16	—	86	4th/East	0	4	Division semifinals	Red Kelly
1974-75	31	33	16	—	78	3rd/Adams	2	5	Quarterfinals	Red Kelly
1975-76	34	31	15	—	83	3rd/Adams	5	5	Quarterfinals	Red Kelly
1976-77	33	32	15	—	81	3rd/Adams	4	5	Quarterfinals	Red Kelly
1977-78	41	29	10	—	92	3rd/Adams	4	2	Quarterfinals	Roger Neilson
1978-79	34	33	13	—	81	3rd/Adams	4	7	Quarterfinals	Roger Neilson
1979-80	35	40	5	—	75	4th/Adams	0	3	Preliminaries	Floyd Smith
1980-81	28	37	15	—	71	5th/Adams	0	3	Preliminaries	Punch Imlach, Joe Crozier
1981-82	20	44	16	—	56	5th/Norris	—	—		Mike Nykoluk
1982-83	28	40	12	—	68	3rd/Norris	1	3	Division semifinals	Mike Nykoluk
1983-84	26	45	9	—	61	5th/Norris	—	—		Mike Nykoluk
1984-85	20	52	8	—	48	5th/Norris	—	—		Dan Maloney
1985-86	25	48	7	—	57	4th/Norris	6	4	Division finals	Dan Maloney
1986-87	32	42	6	—	70	4th/Norris	7	6	Division finals	John Brophy
1987-88	21	49	10	—	52	4th/Norris	2	4	Division semifinals	John Brophy
1988-89	28	46	6	—	62	5th/Norris	—	—		John Brophy, George Armstrong
1989-90	38	38	4	—	80	3rd/Norris	1	4	Division semifinals	Doug Carpenter
1990-91	23	46	11	—	57	5th/Norris	—	—		Doug Carpenter, Tom Watt
1991-92	30	43	7	—	67	5th/Norris	—	—		Tom Watt
1992-93	44	29	11	—	99	3rd/Norris	11	10	Conference finals	Pat Burns
1993-94	43	29	12	—	98	2nd/Central	9	9	Conference finals	Pat Burns
1994-95	21	19	8	—	50	4th/Central	3	4	Conference quarterfinals	Pat Burns
1995-96	34	36	12	—	80	T3rd/Central	2	4	Conference quarterfinals	Pat Burns, Nick Beverley
1996-97	30	44	8	—	68	6th/Central	—	—		Mike Murphy
1997-98	30	43	9	—	69	6th/Central	—	—		Mike Murphy
1998-99	45	30	7	—	97	2nd/Northeast	9	8	Conference finals	Pat Quinn
1999-00	45	30	7	3	100	1st/Northeast	6	6	Conference semifinals	Pat Quinn

*Won-lost record does not indicate tie(s) resulting from two-game, total-goals series that year (two-game, total-goals series were played from 1917-18 through 1935-36).
†Tied after one overtime (curfew law).
‡Toronto Arenas.
§Toronto St. Patricks (until April 14, 1927).

FIRST-ROUND ENTRY DRAFT CHOICES

Year   Player, Overall, Last amateur team (league)
1969—Ernie Moser, 9, Esteven (WCHL)
1970—Darryl Sittler, 8, London (OHL)
1971—No first-round selection
1972—George Ferguson, 11, Toronto (OHL)
1973—Lanny McDonald, 4, Medicine Hat (WCHL)
    Bob Neely, 10, Peterborough (OHL)
    Ian Turnbull, 15, Ottawa (OHL)
1974—Jack Valiquette, 13, Sault Ste. Marie (OHL)
1975—Don Ashby, 6, Calgary (WCHL)
1976—No first-round selection
1977—John Anderson, 11, Toronto (OHA)
    Trevor Johansen, 12, Toronto (OHA)
1978—No first-round selection
1979—Laurie Boschman, 9, Brandon (WHL)
1980—No first-round selection
1981—Jim Benning, 6, Portland (WHL)

Year   Player, Overall, Last amateur team (league)
1982—Gary Nylund, 3, Portland (WHL)
1983—Russ Courtnall, 7, Victoria (WHL)
1984—Al Iafrate, 4, U.S. Olympics/Belleville (OHL)
1985—*Wendel Clark, 1, Saskatoon (WHL)
1986—Vincent Damphousse, 6, Laval (QMJHL)
1987—Luke Richardson, 7, Peterborough (OHL)
1988—Scott Pearson, 6, Kingston (OHL)
1989—Scott Thornton, 3, Belleville (OHL)
    Rob Pearson, 12, Belleville (OHL)
    Steve Bancroft, 21, Belleville (OHL)
1990—Drake Berehowsky, 10, Kingston (OHL)
1991—No first-round selection
1992—Brandon Convery, 8, Sudbury (OHL)
    Grant Marshall, 23, Ottawa (OHL)
1993—Kenny Jonsson, 12, Rogle, Sweden
    Landon Wilson, 19, Dubuque (USHL)

SINGLE-SEASON INDIVIDUAL RECORDS

FORWARDS/DEFENSEMEN

Most goals
54—Rick Vaive, 1981-82

Most assists
95—Doug Gilmour, 1992-93

Most points
127—Doug Gilmour, 1992-93

Most penalty minutes
351—Tiger Williams, 1977-78

Most shorthanded goals
8—Dave Keon, 1970-71
Dave Reid, 1990-91

Most games with three or more goals
5—Darryl Sittler, 1980-81

GOALTENDERS

Most games
74—Felix Potvin, 1996-97

Most minutes
4,271—Felix Potvin, 1996-97

Lowest goals-against average
1.56—Lorne Chabot, 1928-29

Most shutouts
13—Harry Lumley, 1953-54

Most wins
36—Curtis Joseph, 1999-2000

Most losses
38—Ed Chadwick, 1957-58

Most ties
22—Harry Lumley, 1954-55

FRANCHISE LEADERS

Players in boldface played for club in 1999-2000

FORWARDS/DEFENSEMEN

Games
George Armstrong	1187
Tim Horton	1185
Borje Salming	1099
Dave Keon	1062
Ron Ellis	1034

Goals
Darryl Sittler	389
Dave Keon	365
Ron Ellis	332
Rick Vaive	299
Frank Mahovlich	296
George Armstrong	296

Assists
Borje Salming	620
Darryl Sittler	527
Dave Keon	493
George Armstrong	417
Tim Horton	349

Points
Darryl Sittler	916
Dave Keon	858
Borje Salming	768
George Armstrong	713
Ron Ellis	640

Penalty minutes
Dave Williams	1670
Wendel Clark	**1535**
Tim Horton	1389
Borje Salming	1292
Red Horner	1264

GOALTENDERS

Games
Turk Broda	629
Johnny Bower	472
Felix Potvin	369
Mike Palmateer	296
Harry Lumley	267

Shutouts
Turk Broda	62
Harry Lumley	34
Lorne Chabot	33
Johnny Bower	32
George Hainsworth	19

**Goals-against average
(2400 minutes minimum)**
John Ross Roach	2.00
Al Rollins	2.05
Lorne Chabot	2.20
Harry Lumley	2.21
George Hainsworth	2.26

Wins
Turk Broda	302
Johnny Bower	220
Felix Potvin	160
Mike Palmateer	129
Lorne Chabot	108

VANCOUVER CANUCKS
YEAR-BY-YEAR RECORDS

	REGULAR SEASON						PLAYOFFS			
Season	W	L	T	RT	Pts.	Finish	W	L	Highest round	Coach
1970-71	24	46	8	—	56	6th/East	—	—		Hal Laycoe
1971-72	20	50	8	—	48	7th/East	—	—		Hal Laycoe
1972-73	22	47	9	—	53	7th/East	—	—		Vic Stasiuk
1973-74	24	43	11	—	59	7th/East	—	—		Bill McCreary, Phil Maloney
1974-75	38	32	10	—	86	1st/Smythe	1	4	Quarterfinals	Phil Maloney
1975-76	33	32	15	—	81	2nd/Smythe	0	2	Preliminaries	Phil Maloney
1976-77	25	42	13	—	63	4th/Smythe	—	—		Phil Maloney, Orland Kurtenbach
1977-78	20	43	17	—	57	3rd/Smythe	—	—		Orland Kurtenbach
1978-79	25	42	13	—	63	2nd/Smythe	1	2	Preliminaries	Harry Neale
1979-80	27	37	16	—	70	3rd/Smythe	1	3	Preliminaries	Harry Neale
1980-81	28	32	20	—	76	3rd/Smythe	0	3	Preliminaries	Harry Neale
1981-82	30	33	17	—	77	2nd/Smythe	11	6	Stanley Cup finals	Harry Neale, Roger Neilson
1982-83	30	35	15	—	75	3rd/Smythe	1	3	Division semifinals	Roger Neilson
1983-84	32	39	9	—	73	3rd/Smythe	1	3	Division semifinals	Roger Neilson, Harry Neale
1984-85	25	46	9	—	59	5th/Smythe	—	—		Bill Laforge, Harry Neale

NHL HISTORY Team by team

Season	W	L	T	RT	Pts.	Finish	W	L	Highest round	Coach
1985-86	23	44	13	—	59	4th/Smythe	0	3	Division semifinals	Tom Watt
1986-87	29	43	8	—	66	5th/Smythe	—	—		Tom Watt
1987-88	25	46	9	—	59	5th/Smythe	—	—		Bob McCammon
1988-89	33	39	8	—	74	4th/Smythe	3	4	Division semifinals	Bob McCammon
1989-90	25	41	14	—	64	5th/Smythe	—	—		Bob McCammon
1990-91	28	43	9	—	65	4th/Smythe	2	4	Division semifinals	Bob McCammon, Pat Quinn
1991-92	42	26	12	—	96	1st/Smythe	6	7	Division finals	Pat Quinn
1992-93	46	29	9	—	101	1st/Smythe	6	6	Division finals	Pat Quinn
1993-94	41	40	3	—	85	2nd/Pacific	15	9	Stanley Cup finals	Pat Quinn
1994-95	18	18	12	—	48	2nd/Pacific	4	7	Conference semifinals	Rick Ley
1995-96	32	35	15	—	79	T2nd/Pacific	2	4	Conference quarterfinals	Rick Ley, Pat Quinn
1996-97	35	40	7	—	77	4th/Pacific	—	—		Tom Renney
1997-98	25	43	14	—	64	7th/Pacific	—	—		Tom Renney, Mike Keenan
1998-99	23	47	12	—	58	4th/Northwest	—	—		Mike Keenan, Marc Crawford
1999-00	30	37	15	8	83	3rd/Northwest	—	—		Marc Crawford

Column group headers: REGULAR SEASON (W L T RT Pts. Finish), PLAYOFFS (W L Highest round), Coach

FIRST-ROUND ENTRY DRAFT CHOICES

Year   Player, Overall, Last amateur team (league)

1970—Dale Tallon, 2, Toronto (OHL)
1971—Jocelyn Guevremont, 3, Montreal (OHL)
1972—Don Lever, 3, Niagara Falls (OHL)
1973—Dennis Ververgaert, 3, London (OHL)
        Bob Dailey, 9, Toronto (OHL)
1974—No first-round selection
1975—Rick Blight, 10, Brandon (WCHL)
1976—No first-round selection
1977—Jere Gillis, 4, Sherbrooke (QMJHL)
1978—Bill Derlago, 4, Brandon (WCHL)
1979—Rick Vaive, 5, Birmingham (WHA)
1980—Rick Lanz, 7, Oshawa (OHL)
1981—Garth Butcher, 10, Regina (WHL)
1982—Michel Petit, 11, Sherbrooke (QMJHL)
1983—Cam Neely, 9, Portland (WHL)
1984—J.J. Daigneault, 10, Can. Ol./Longueuil (QMJHL)
1985—Jim Sandlak, 4, London (OHL)

Year   Player, Overall, Last amateur team (league)

1986—Dan Woodley, 7, Portland (WHL)
1987—No first-round selection
1988—Trevor Linden, 2, Medicine Hat (WHL)
1989—Jason Herter, 8, University of North Dakota
1990—Petr Nedved, 2, Seattle (WHL)
        Shawn Antoski, 18, North Bay (OHL)
1991—Alex Stojanov, 7, Hamilton (OHL)
1992—Libor Polasek, 21, TJ Vikovice (Czech.)
1993—Mike Wilson, 20, Sudbury (OHL)
1994—Mattias Ohlund, 13, Pitea Div. I (Sweden)
1995—No first-round selection
1996—Josh Holden, 12, Regina (WHL)
1997—Brad Ference, 10, Spokane (WHL)
1998—Bryan Allen, 4, Oshawa (OHL)
1999—Daniel Sedin, 2, Modo Ornskoldsvik, Sweden
        Henrik Sedin, 3, Modo Ornskoldsvik, Sweden
2000—Nathan Smith, 23, Swift Current (WHL)

SINGLE-SEASON INDIVIDUAL RECORDS

FORWARDS/DEFENSEMEN

Most goals
60—Pavel Bure, 1992-93
      Pavel Bure, 1993-94

Most assists
62—Andre Boudrias, 1974-75

Most points
110—Pavel Bure, 1992-93

Most penalty minutes
372—Donald Brashear, 1997-98

Most power play goals
25—Pavel Bure, 1993-94

Most shorthanded goals
7—Pavel Bure, 1992-93

Most games with three or more goals
4—Petri Skriko, 1986-87

Most shots
407—Pavel Bure, 1992-93

GOALTENDERS

Most games
72—Gary Smith, 1974-75

Most minutes
3,852—Kirk McLean, 1991-92

Most goals allowed
240—Richard Brodeur, 1985-86

Lowest goals-against average
2.59—Felix Potvin, 1999-2000

Most shutouts
6—Gary Smith, 1974-75
      Garth Snow, 1998-99

Most wins
38—Kirk McLean, 1991-92

Most losses
33—Gary Smith, 1973-74

Most ties
16—Richard Brodeur, 1980-81

FRANCHISE LEADERS

Players in boldface played for club in 1999-2000

FORWARDS/DEFENSEMEN

Games

Stan Smyl	896
Harold Snepsts	781
Trevor Linden	702
Dennis Kearns	677
Doug Lidster	666

Goals

Stan Smyl	262
Pavel Bure	254
Tony Tanti	250
Trevor Linden	247
Thomas Gradin	197

Assists

Stan Smyl	411
Thomas Gradin	353
Trevor Linden	322
Dennis Kearns	290
Andre Boudrias	267

WASHINGTON CAPITALS
YEAR-BY-YEAR RECORDS

Season	W	L	T	RT	Pts.	Finish	W	L	Highest round	Coach
1974-75	8	67	5	—	21	5th/Norris	—	—		Jim Anderson, Red Sullivan, Milt Schmidt
1975-76	11	59	10	—	32	5th/Norris	—	—		Milt Schmidt, Tom McVie
1976-77	24	42	14	—	62	4th/Norris	—	—		Tom McVie
1977-78	17	49	14	—	48	5th/Norris	—	—		Tom McVie
1978-79	24	41	15	—	63	4th/Norris	—	—		Dan Belisle
1979-80	27	40	13	—	67	5th/Patrick	—	—		Dan Belisle, Gary Green
1980-81	26	36	18	—	70	5th/Patrick	—	—		Gary Green
1981-82	26	41	13	—	65	5th/Patrick	—	—		Gary Green, Roger Crozier, Bryan Murray
1982-83	39	25	16	—	94	3rd/Patrick	1	3	Division semifinals	Bryan Murray
1983-84	48	27	5	—	101	2nd/Patrick	4	4	Division finals	Bryan Murray
1984-85	46	25	9	—	101	2nd/Patrick	2	3	Division semifinals	Bryan Murray
1985-86	50	23	7	—	107	2nd/Patrick	5	4	Division finals	Bryan Murray
1986-87	38	32	10	—	86	2nd/Patrick	3	4	Division semifinals	Bryan Murray
1987-88	38	33	9	—	85	2nd/Patrick	7	7	Division finals	Bryan Murray
1988-89	41	29	10	—	92	1st/Patrick	2	4	Division semifinals	Bryan Murray
1989-90	36	38	6	—	78	3rd/Patrick	8	7	Conference finals	Bryan Murray, Terry Murray
1990-91	37	36	7	—	81	3rd/Patrick	5	6	Division finals	Terry Murray
1991-92	45	27	8	—	98	2nd/Patrick	3	4	Division semifinals	Terry Murray
1992-93	43	34	7	—	93	2nd/Patrick	2	4	Division semifinals	Terry Murray
1993-94	39	35	10	—	88	3rd/Atlantic	5	6	Conference semifinals	Terry Murray, Jim Schoenfeld
1994-95	22	18	8	—	52	3rd/Atlantic	4	3	Conference quarterfinals	Jim Schoenfeld
1995-96	39	32	11	—	89	4th/Atlantic	2	4	Conference quarterfinals	Jim Schoenfeld
1996-97	33	40	9	—	75	5th/Atlantic	—	—		Jim Schoenfeld
1997-98	40	30	12	—	92	3rd/Atlantic	12	9	Stanley Cup finals	Ron Wilson
1998-99	31	45	6	—	68	3rd/Southeast	—	—		Ron Wilson
1999-00	44	26	12	2	102	1st/Southeast	1	4	Conference quarterfinals	Ron Wilson

FIRST-ROUND ENTRY DRAFT CHOICES

Year   Player, Overall, Last amateur team (league)

1974—Greg Joly, 1, Regina (WCHL)*
1975—Alex Forsyth, 18, Kingston (OHA)
1976—Rick Green, 1, London (OHL)*
        Greg Carroll, 15, Medicine Hat (WCHL)
1977—Robert Picard, 3, Montreal (QMJHL)
1978—Ryan Walter, 2, Seattle (WCHL)
        Tim Coulis, 18, Hamilton (OHL)
1979—Mike Gartner, 4, Cincinnati (WHA)
1980—Darren Veitch, 5, Regina (WHL)
1981—Bobby Carpenter, 3, St. John's H.S. (Mass.)
1982—Scott Stevens, 5, Kitchener (OHL)
1983—No first-round selection
1984—Kevin Hatcher, 17, North Bay (OHL)
1985—Yvon Corriveau, 19, Toronto (OHL)
1986—Jeff Greenlaw, 19, Team Canada
1987—No first-round selection
1988—Reggie Savage, 15, Victoriaville (QMJHL)
1989—Olaf Kolzig, 19, Tri-City (WHL)

Year   Player, Overall, Last amateur team (league)

1990—John Slaney, 9, Cornwall (OHL)
1991—Pat Peake, 14, Detroit (OHL)
        Trevor Halverson, 21, North Bay (OHL)
1992—Sergei Gonchar, 14, Dynamo Moscow, CIS
1993—Brendan Witt, 11, Seattle (WHL)
        Jason Allison, 17, London (OHL)
1994—Nolan Baumgartner, 10, Kamloops (WHL)
        Alexander Kharlamov, 15, CSKA Moscow, CIS
1995—Brad Church, 17, Prince Albert (WHL)
        Miikka Elomo, 23, Kiekko-67, Finland
1996—Alexander Volchkov, 4, Barrie (OHL)
1997—Nick Boynton, 9, Ottawa (OHL)
        Jaroslav Svejkovsky, 17, Tri-City (WHL)
1998—No first-round selection
1999—Kris Beech, 7, Calgary (WHL)
2000—Brian Sutherby, 26, Moose Jaw (WHL)
*Designates first player chosen in draft.

NHL HISTORY *Team by team*

SINGLE-SEASON INDIVIDUAL RECORDS

FORWARDS/DEFENSEMEN

Most goals
60—Dennis Maruk, 1981-82

Most assists
76—Dennis Maruk, 1981-82

Most points
136—Dennis Maruk, 1981-82

Most penalty minutes
339—Alan May, 1989-90

Most power play goals
20—Dennis Maruk, 1981-82

Most shorthanded goals
6—Mike Gartner, 1986-87
　　Peter Bondra, 1994-95

Most games with three or more goals
4—Dennis Maruk, 1980-81
　　Dennis Maruk, 1981-82
　　Peter Bondra, 1995-96

Most shots
330—Mike Gartner, 1984-85

GOALTENDERS

Most games
73—Olaf Kolzig, 1999-2000

Most minutes
4,371—Olaf Kolzig, 1999-2000

Most shots against
1,957—Olaf Kolzig, 1999-2000

Most goals allowed
235—Ron Low, 1974-75

Lowest goals-against average
2.13—Jim Carey, 1994-95

Most shutouts
9—Jim Carey, 1995-96

Most wins
41—Olaf Kolzig, 1999-2000

Most losses
36—Ron Low, 1974-75

Most ties
11—Olaf Kolzig, 1999-2000

FRANCHISE LEADERS

Players in boldface played for club in 1999-2000

FORWARDS/DEFENSEMEN

Games
Kelly Miller	940
Dale Hunter	872
Michal Pivonka	825
Calle Johansson	**814**
Mike Gartner	758

Goals
Mike Gartner	397
Peter Bondra	**337**
Mike Ridley	218
Bengt Gustafsson	196
Dave Christian	193

Assists
Michal Pivonka	418
Mike Gartner	392
Dale Hunter	375
Bengt Gustafsson	359
Scott Stevens	331

Points
Mike Gartner	789
Michal Pivonka	599
Peter Bondra	**583**
Dale Hunter	556
Bengt Gustafsson	555

Penalty minutes
Dale Hunter	2003
Scott Stevens	1630
Craig Berube	1202
Alan May	1189
Kevin Hatcher	998

GOALTENDERS

Games
Olaf Kolzig	**272**
Don Beaupre	269
Al Jensen	173
Ron Low	145
Pat Riggin	143

Goals-against average
(2400 minutes minimum)
Jim Carey	2.37
Olaf Kolzig	**2.49**
Rick Tabaracci	2.71
Pat Riggin	3.02
Don Beaupre	3.05

Wins
Don Beaupre	128
Olaf Kolzig	**114**
Al Jensen	94
Jim Carey	70
Pete Peeters	70

Shutouts
Olaf Kolzig	**16**
Jim Carey	14
Don Beaupre	12
Al Jensen	8
Pete Peeters	7

WINNIPEG JETS (DEFUNCT)
YEAR-BY-YEAR RECORDS

	REGULAR SEASON					PLAYOFFS			
Season	W	L	T	Pts.	Finish	W	L	Highest round	Coach
1972-73*	43	31	4	90	1st	9	5	Avco World Cup finals	Nick Mickoski, Bobby Hull
1973-74*	34	39	5	73	4th	0	4	League quarterfinals	Nick Mickoski, Bobby Hull
1974-75*	38	35	5	81	3rd	—	—		Rudy Pilous
1975-76*	52	27	2	106	1st	12	1	Avco World Cup champ	Bobby Kromm
1976-77*	46	32	2	94	2nd	11	9	Avco World Cup finals	Bobby Kromm
1977-78*	50	28	2	102	1st	8	1	Avco World Cup champ	Larry Hillman
1978-79*	39	35	6	84	3rd	8	2	Avco World Cup champ	Larry Hillman, Tom McVie
1979-80	20	49	11	51	5th/Smythe	—	—		Tom McVie
1980-81	9	57	14	32	6th/Smythe	—	—		Tom McVie, Bill Sutherland, Mike Smith
1981-82	33	33	14	80	2nd/Norris	1	3	Division semifinals	Tom Watt
1982-83	33	39	8	74	4th/Smythe	0	3	Division semifinals	Tom Watt
1983-84	31	38	11	73	3rd/Smythe	0	3	Division semifinals	Tom Watt, Barry Long
1984-85	43	27	10	96	2nd/Smythe	3	5	Division finals	Barry Long
1985-86	26	47	7	59	3rd/Smythe	0	3	Division semifinals	Barry Long, John Ferguson
1986-87	40	32	8	88	3rd/Smythe	4	6	Division finals	Dan Maloney
1987-88	33	36	11	77	3rd/Smythe	1	4	Division semifinals	Dan Maloney
1988-89	26	42	12	64	5th/Smythe	—	—		Dan Maloney, Rick Bowness
1989-90	37	32	11	85	3rd/Smythe	3	4	Division semifinals	Bob Murdoch

Season	REGULAR SEASON					PLAYOFFS			
	W	L	T	Pts.	Finish	W	L	Highest round	Coach
1990-91	26	43	11	63	5th/Smythe	—	—		Bob Murdoch
1991-92	33	32	15	81	4th/Smythe	3	4	Division semifinals	John Paddock
1992-93	40	37	7	87	4th/Smythe	2	4	Division semifinals	John Paddock
1993-94	24	51	9	57	6th/Central	—	—		John Paddock
1994-95	16	25	7	39	6th/Central	—	—		John Paddock, Terry Simpson
1995-96	36	40	6	78	5th/Central	—	—		Terry Simpson

*Members of World Hockey Association.
Franchise relocated and became Phoenix Coyotes following 1995-96 season.

FIRST-ROUND ENTRY DRAFT CHOICES

Year Player, Overall, Last amateur team (league)
1979—Jimmy Mann, 19, Sherbrooke (QMJHL)
1980—David Babych, 2, Portland (WHL)
1981—Dale Hawerchuk, 1, Cornwall (QMJHL)*
1982—Jim Kyte, 12, Cornwall (OHL)
1983—Andrew McBain, 8, North Bay (OHL)
      Bobby Dollas, 14, Laval (QMJHL)
1984—No first-round selection
1985—Ryan Stewart, 18, Kamloops (WHL)
1986—Pat Elynuik, 8, Prince Albert (WHL)
1987—Bryan Marchment, 16, Belleville (OHL)
1988—Teemu Selanne, 10, Jokerit (Finland)
1989—Stu Barnes, 4, Tri-City (WHL)

Year Player, Overall, Last amateur team (league)
1990—Keith Tkachuk, 19, Malden Cath. H.S. (Mass.)
1991—Aaron Ward, 5, University of Michigan
1992—Sergei Bautin, 17, Dynamo Moscow (CIS)
1993—Mats Lindgren, 15, Skelleftea (Sweden)
1994—No first-round selection
1995—Shane Doan, 7, Kamloops (WHL)
1996—Dan Focht, 11, Tri-City (WHL)
      Daniel Briere, 24, Drummondville (QMJHL)
*Designates first player chosen in draft.
NOTE: Winnipeg chose Scott Campbell, Morris Lukowich and Markus Mattsson as priority selections before the 1979 expansion draft.

SINGLE-SEASON INDIVIDUAL RECORDS

FORWARDS/DEFENSEMEN

Most goals
76—Teemu Selanne, 1992-93

Most assists
79—Phil Housley, 1992-93

Most points
132—Teemu Selanne, 1992-93

Most penalty minutes
347—Tie Domi, 1993-94

Most power play goals
24—Teemu Selanne, 1992-93

Most shorthanded goals
7—Dave McLlwain, 1989-90

Most games with three or more goals
5—Teemu Selanne, 1992-93

Most shots
387—Teemu Selanne, 1992-93

GOALTENDERS

Most games
67—Bob Essensa, 1992-93

Most minutes
3,855—Bob Essensa, 1992-93

Most goals allowed
227—Bob Essensa, 1992-93

Lowest goals-against average
2.88—Bob Essensa, 1991-92

Most shutouts
5—Bob Essensa, 1991-92

Most wins
33—Brian Hayward, 1984-85
     Bob Essensa, 1992-93

Most losses
30—Bob Essensa, 1993-94

Most ties
8—Doug Soetaert, 1981-82

FRANCHISE LEADERS

FORWARDS/DEFENSEMEN

Games

Thomas Steen	950
Dale Hawerchuk	713
Doug Smail	691
Randy Carlyle	564
Teppo Numminen	547

Goals

Dale Hawerchuk	379
Thomas Steen	264
Paul MacLean	248
Doug Smail	189
Morris Lukowich	168

Assists

Thomas Steen	553
Dale Hawerchuk	550
Paul MacLean	270
Fredrik Olausson	249
Dave Babych	248

Points

Dale Hawerchuk	929
Thomas Steen	817
Paul MacLean	518
Doug Smail	397
Laurie Boschman	379

Penalty minutes

Laurie Boschman	1338
Keith Tkachuk	792
Jim Kyte	772
Tim Watters	760
Thomas Steen	753

GOALTENDERS

Games

Bob Essensa	281
Brian Hayward	165
Doug Soetaert	130
Daniel Berthiaume	120
Pokey Reddick	117

Shutouts

Bob Essensa	14
Daniel Berthiaume	4
Markus Mattsson	3
Stephane Beauregard	2
Dan Bouchard	2
Doug Soetaert	2
Ed Staniowski	2

Goals-against average (2400 minutes minimum)

Nikolai Khabibulin	3.22
Bob Essensa	3.38
Stephane Beauregard	3.48
Daniel Berthiaume	3.63
Pokey Reddick	3.73

Wins

Bob Essensa	116
Brian Hayward	63
Daniel Berthiaume	50
Doug Soetaert	50
Pokey Reddick	41

MINOR LEAGUES

American Hockey League

International Hockey League

East Coast Hockey League

Central Hockey League

United Hockey League

AMERICAN HOCKEY LEAGUE

LEAGUE OFFICE

Chairman of the board
Jack A. Butterfield
President/CEO and treasurer
David A. Andrews
General counsel
Joe Rodio
Director, finance and administration
Drew Griffin
Director of hockey operations
Jim Mill

Dir. of corporate sales & bus. dev.
Ross Yanco
Exec. assistant to the president
Liz Sylvia
Coordinator of event mgmt. & licensing
Sean Lavoine
Coordinator of marketing services
Megan Rowe
Dir. of communications & media rel.
Bret Stothart

Address
1 Monarch Place
Springfield, MA 01144
Phone
413-781-2030
Fax
413-733-4767

TEAMS

ALBANY RIVER RATS

Chief executive officer
Garen Szableski
Head coach
John Cunniff
Home ice
Pepsi Arena
Address
51 South Pearl St.
Albany, NY 12207
Seating capacity
6,500
Phone
518-487-2244
FAX
518-487-2248

HARTFORD WOLFPACK

Senior vice president
Don Maloney
Head coach
John Paddock
Home ice
Hartford Civic Center
Address
196 Trumbull Street
Hartford, CT 06103
Seating capacity
15,635
Phone
860-246-7825
FAX
860-240-7618

LOUISVILLE PANTHERS

President & governor
Tamer Afr
Head coach
Joe Paterson
Home ice
Freedom Hall
Address
1701 UPS Drive
Louisville, KY 40223
Seating capacity
17,200
Phone
502-992-7825
FAX
502-992-7834

CINCINNATI MIGHTY DUCKS

General manager
David McNab
Head coach
Mike Babcock
Home ice
Cincinnati Gardens
Address
2250 Seymour Ave.
Cincinnati, OH 45212
Seating capacity
10,326
Phone
513-351-3999
FAX
513-351-5898

HERSHEY BEARS

General manager
Doug Yingst
Head coach
Mike Foligno
Home ice
Hersheypark Arena
Address
P.O. Box 866
Hershey, PA 17033
Seating capacity
7,225
Phone
717-534-3380
FAX
717-534-3383

LOWELL LOCK MONSTERS

Executive v.p./general manager
Tom Rowe
Head coach
Bruce Boudreau
Home ice
Tsongas Arena
Address
300 Arcand Dr.
Lowell, MA 01852
Seating capacity
6,400
Phone
978-458-7825
FAX
978-453-8452

HAMILTON BULLDOGS

President
Cary Kaplan
Head coach
Walt Kyle
Home ice
Copps Coliseum
Address
85 York Blvd.
Hamilton, Ont. L8R 3L4
Seating capacity
8,919
Phone
905-529-8500
FAX
905-529-1188

KENTUCKY THOROUGHBLADES

President/chief executive officer
Ron DeGregorio
Head coach
Roy Sommer
Home ice
Rupp Arena
Address
410 West Vine St.
Lexington, KY 40507
Seating capacity
21,000
Phone
859-259-1996
FAX
859-252-3684

NORFOLK ADMIRALS

General manager
Al MacIsaac
Head coach
Trent Yawney
Home ice
Norfolk Scope
Address
2181 Landstown Road
Virginia Beach, VA 23456
Seating capacity
8,974
Phone
757-430-8873
FAX
757-430-8803

PHILADELPHIA PHANTOMS
Chief operating officer
Frank Miceli
Head coach
Bill Barber
Home ice
First Union Spectrum
Address
3601 S. Broad Street
Philadelphia, PA 19148
Seating capacity
17,380
Phone
215-465-4522
FAX
215-952-5245

PORTLAND PIRATES
President
Jeff Eisenberg
Head coach
Glen Hanlon
Home ice
Cumberland County Civic Center
Address
85 Free St.
Portland, ME 04101
Seating capacity
6,746
Phone
207-828-4665
FAX
207-773-3278

PROVIDENCE BRUINS
Chief executive officer
Ed Anderson
Head coach
Bill Armstrong
Home ice
Providence Civic Center
Address
1 LaSalle Square
Providence, RI 02903
Seating capacity
11,605
Phone
401-273-5000
FAX
401-273-5004

QUEBEC CITADELLES
General manager
Raymond Bolduc
Head coach
Michel Therrien
Home ice
Colisee de Quebec
Address
250 Hamel Blvd.
Quebec City, Que. G1L 5A7
Seating capacity
15,399

Phone
418-525-5333
FAX
418-525-5057

ROCHESTER AMERICANS
General manager
Jody Gage
Head coach
Brian McCutcheon
Home ice
Blue Cross Arena
Address
One War Memorial Square
Rochester, NY 14614
Seating capacity
11,200
Phone
716-454-5335
FAX
716-454-3954

SAINT JOHN FLAMES
General manager
To be announced
Head coach
Rick Vaive
Home ice
Harbour Station
Address
P.O. Box 4040, Station B
Saint John, NB E2M 5E6
Seating capacity
6,153
Phone
506-635-2637
FAX
506-633-4625

ST. JOHN'S MAPLE LEAFS
Director of operations
Glenn Stanford
Head coach
To be announced
Home ice
St. John's Memorial Stadium
Address
49 Elizabeth Ave., Suite 302
St. John's, Newfoundland A1A 1W9
Seating capacity
3,765
Phone
709-726-1010
FAX
709-726-1511

SPRINGFIELD FALCONS
President
Bruce Landon
Head coach
Marc Potvin
Home ice
Springfield Civic Center

Address
P.O. Box 3190
Springfield, MA 01101
Seating capacity
7,452
Phone
413-739-3344
FAX
413-739-3389

SYRACUSE CRUNCH
General manager/chief financial officer
Vance Lederman
Head coach
Gary Agnew
Home ice
Onondaga County War Memorial
Address
800 South State St.
Syracuse, NY 13202
Seating capacity
6,230
Phone
315-473-4444
FAX
315-473-4449

WILKES-BARRE/SCRANTON PENGUINS
President
Jeff Barrett
Head coach
Glenn Patrick
Home ice
First Union Arena at Casey Plaza
Address
60 Public Square, Suite 150
Wilkes-Barre, PA 18701
Seating capacity
8,457
Phone
570-208-7367
FAX
570-208-5432

WORCESTER ICECATS
Executive vice president
Peter Ricciardi
Head coach
Greg Gilbert
Home ice
Worcester's Centrum Centre
Address
303 Main St.
Worcester, MA 01608
Seating capacity
12,316
Phone
508-798-5400
FAX
508-799-5267

MINOR LEAGUES *AHL*

1999-2000 REGULAR SEASON
FINAL STANDINGS

EASTERN CONFERENCE

ATLANTIC DIVISION

Team	G	W	L	T	RT	Pts.	GF	GA
Quebec	80	37	34	5	4	83	227	238
Saint John	80	32	32	11	5	80	267	283
Lowell	80	33	36	7	4	77	228	240
St. John's	80	23	45	8	4	58	202	277

NEW ENGLAND DIVISION

Team	G	W	L	T	RT	Pts.	GF	GA
Hartford	80	49	22	7	2	107	249	198
Portland	80	46	23	10	1	103	256	202
Worcester	80	34	31	11	4	83	249	250
Springfield	80	33	35	11	1	78	272	252
Providence	80	33	38	6	3	75	231	269

WESTERN CONFERENCE

EMPIRE DIVISION

Team	G	W	L	T	RT	Pts.	GF	GA
Rochester	80	46	22	9	3	104	247	201
Syracuse	80	35	35	9	1	80	290	294
Hamilton	80	27	34	13	6	73	225	262
Albany	80	30	40	7	3	70	225	250
Wilkes-Barre	80	23	43	9	5	60	236	306

MID-ATLANTIC DIVISION

Team	G	W	L	T	RT	Pts.	GF	GA
Kentucky	80	42	25	9	4	97	250	211
Hershey	80	43	29	5	3	94	297	267
Philadelphia	80	44	31	3	2	93	281	239
Louisville	80	42	30	7	1	92	278	254
Cincinnati	80	30	37	9	4	73	227	244

INDIVIDUAL LEADERS

Goals: Mike Maneluk, Philadelphia (47)
Assists: Christian Matte, Hershey (61)
Points: Christian Matte, Hershey (104)
Penalty minutes: Garrett Burnett, Kentucky (506)
Goaltending average: Milan Hnilicka, Hartford (2.15)
Shutouts: Mika Noronen, Rochester (6)

	Games	G	A	Pts.
Steve Brule, Albany	75	30	46	76
Eric Bogusniecki, Louisville	57	33	42	75
Daniel Cleary, Hamilton	58	22	52	74
Jean-Guy Trudel, Springfield	72	34	39	73
Daniel Briere, Springfield	58	29	42	71
Steve Washburn, Philadelphia	61	19	52	71
Reggie Savage, Syracuse	78	36	34	70
Mike Gaul, Hershey	65	12	57	69
Eric Houde, Ham.-Spr.	75	31	38	69
Brad Tiley, Springfield	80	14	54	68
Pierre Sevigny, Quebec	78	24	43	67
Rob Shearer, Hershey	70	21	46	67
Eric Landry, Kentucky	79	35	31	66
Daniel Tkaczuk, Saint John	80	25	41	66
Mark Smith, Kentucky	79	21	45	66
Benoit Gratton, Saint John	65	17	49	66

TOP SCORERS

	Games	G	A	Pts.
Christian Matte, Hershey	73	43	61	104
Mike Maneluk, Philadelphia	73	47	40	87
Mark Greig, Philadelphia	68	34	48	82
Derek Armstrong, Hartford	77	28	54	82
Serge Aubin, Hershey	58	42	38	80
Mike Craig, Kentucky	76	39	39	78
Brad Smyth, Hartford	80	39	37	76

INDIVIDUAL STATISTICS

ALBANY RIVER RATS
SCORING

	Games	G	A	Pts.	PIM
Steve Brule	75	30	46	76	18
Pierre Dagenais	80	35	30	65	47
Steve Kelly	76	21	36	57	131
Jeff Williams	71	29	20	49	24
Sylvain Cloutier	66	15	28	43	127
Jiri Bicek	80	7	36	43	51
Sascha Goc	64	9	22	31	35
Stanislav Gron	65	19	10	29	17
Sasha Lakovic	51	10	16	26	144
Colin White	52	5	21	26	176
Richard Rochefort	55	12	12	24	22
Ken Sutton	57	5	16	21	129
Willie Mitchell	63	5	14	19	71
George Awada	63	8	8	16	29
David Maley	60	5	10	15	52
Josh DeWolf	58	3	11	14	38
David Cunniff	68	3	11	14	88
Andre Lakos	65	1	7	8	41
Carlyle Lewis	69	1	2	3	181
Daryl Andrews	9	0	2	2	9
Vlastimil Kroupa	1	1	0	1	0
Scott Cameron	3	1	0	1	0
Mathieu Benoit	1	0	0	0	0
Josh MacNevin	10	0	0	0	4
Alex Johnstone	13	0	0	0	22

	Games	G	A	Pts.	PIM
Mike Buzak (goalie)	14	0	0	0	0
Lucas Nehrling	18	0	0	0	27
J.-Francois Damphousse (g)	26	0	0	0	0
Rob Skrlac	37	0	0	0	115
Frederic Henry (goalie)	53	0	0	0	6

GOALTENDING

	Gms.	Min.	W	L	T	G	SO	Avg.
J.-F. Damphousse	26	1326	9	11	2	62	0	2.81
Frederic Henry	53	2732	18	23	3	138	1	3.03
Mike Buzak	14	776	3	9	2	41	1	3.17

CINCINNATI MIGHTY DUCKS
SCORING

	Games	G	A	Pts.	PIM
Bob Wren	57	24	38	62	61
B.J. Young	71	25	26	51	147
Philippe Audet	62	19	22	41	115
Frank Banham	72	19	22	41	58
Johan Davidsson	56	9	31	40	24
Torrey DiRoberto	73	18	16	34	41
Jay Legault	70	15	19	34	75
Marc Chouinard	70	17	16	33	29
Scott Ferguson	77	7	25	32	166
Shane Hnidy	68	9	19	28	153
Dan Trebil	52	7	21	28	48
Joel Kwiatkowski	70	4	22	26	28

	Games	G	A	Pts.	PIM
Jeremy Stevenson	41	11	14	25	100
Alexandre Jacques	59	9	14	23	22
Darryl Laplante	35	13	9	22	47
Maxim Balmochnykh	40	9	12	21	82
Jesse Wallin	75	3	14	17	61
Maxim Kuznetsov	47	2	9	11	36
Rastisl Pavlikovsky	17	3	5	8	10
Lloyd Shaw	57	1	6	7	155
Vitaly Vishnevski	35	1	3	4	45
Gregg Naumenko (goalie)	50	0	4	4	10
Peter LeBoutillier	19	2	1	3	69
Tony Tuzzolino	15	0	3	3	8
Jeff Mitchell	20	0	3	3	16
Jiri Fischer	7	0	2	2	10
Dwayne Zinger	14	0	2	2	33
Ryan Hoople (goalie)	15	0	2	2	0
Aren Miller (goalie)	18	0	2	2	0
Doug Nolan	2	0	1	1	0
Mike Isherwood	3	0	1	1	2
Jerry Keefe	7	0	1	1	2
Yuri Butsayev	9	0	1	1	0
Jason Payne	27	0	1	1	51
Chad Wagner	1	0	0	0	4
Julian Dal Cin	2	0	0	0	0
Ryan Gaucher	2	0	0	0	0
Niclas Havelid	2	0	0	0	0
Blaine Russell (goalie)	2	0	0	0	0
Hugues Gervais	3	0	0	0	0
Jean-Francois Houle	3	0	0	0	2
Brendan Buckley	4	0	0	0	6

GOALTENDING

	Gms.	Min.	W	L	T	G	SO	Avg.
Ryan Hoople	15	903	9	5	1	34	0	2.26
Gregg Naumenko	50	2877	17	25	7	143	2	2.98
Aren Miller	18	1010	4	10	1	56	1	3.33
Blaine Russell	2	53	0	1	0	3	0	3.40

HAMILTON BULLDOGS
SCORING

	Games	G	A	Pts.	PIM
Daniel Cleary	58	22	52	74	108
Michel Riesen	73	29	31	60	20
Kevin Brown	54	21	38	59	53
Brian Swanson	69	19	40	59	18
Peter Sarno	67	10	36	46	31
Dan LaCouture	70	23	17	40	85
Rob Murray	55	11	20	31	100
Sergei Yerkovich	72	2	28	30	64
Jason Chimera	78	15	13	28	77
Sean Selmser	72	14	12	26	151
Vladimir Vorobiev	37	9	9	18	16
Alexander Zhurik	54	2	16	18	54
Brad Norton	40	5	12	17	104
Ryan Risidore	45	3	13	16	61
Mathieu Descoteaux	49	5	7	12	29
Martin Laitre	56	5	7	12	208
Alexandre Volchkov	25	2	6	8	11
Chris Hajt	54	0	8	8	30
Maxim Spiridonov	10	5	2	7	2
Eric Houde	18	3	4	7	10
Chad Kilger	7	4	2	6	4
Brent Cullaton	3	3	3	6	0
Trevor Roenick	11	3	3	6	9
Paul Comrie	12	3	3	6	6
Chad Hinz	18	1	4	5	2
Kevin Bolibruck	54	1	4	5	67
Elias Abrahamsson	56	1	3	4	90
Brian Urick	14	2	1	3	2
Bert Robertsson	6	0	3	3	12
Adam Copeland	15	1	0	1	10
Alex Henry	60	1	0	1	69
Joaquin Gage (goalie)	1	0	1	1	0
Jonathan Fauteux	2	0	0	0	0

	Games	G	A	Pts.	PIM
Todd Kidd	2	0	0	0	4
Ian Perkins (goalie)	4	0	0	0	0
Andy Silverman	10	0	0	0	2
Alain Nasreddine	11	0	0	0	12
Mike Minard (goalie)	38	0	0	0	6
Eric Heffler (goalie)	47	0	0	0	8

GOALTENDING

	Gms.	Min.	W	L	T	G	SO	Avg.
Joaquin Gage	1	59	0	1	0	3	0	3.03
Mike Minard	38	1987	16	12	5	102	0	3.08
Eric Heffler	47	2643	11	25	7	138	5	3.13
Ian Perkins	4	158	0	2	1	10	0	3.79

HARTFORD WOLFPACK
SCORING

	Games	G	A	Pts.	PIM
Derek Armstrong	77	28	54	82	101
Brad Smyth	80	39	37	76	62
Ken Gernander	79	28	29	57	24
Todd Hall	74	11	34	45	14
Johan Witehall	73	17	24	41	65
Mike Harder	56	18	21	39	33
Alexei Vasiliev	75	10	28	38	20
P.J. Stock	64	13	23	36	290
Daniel Goneau	51	15	17	32	48
Chris Kenady	71	15	16	31	196
Terry Virtue	67	5	22	27	166
Drew Bannister	44	6	14	20	121
Alexander Daigle	16	6	13	19	4
Jason Dawe	27	9	9	18	24
Francois Fortier	63	6	9	15	14
Burke Henry	64	3	12	15	47
Jason Doig	27	3	11	14	70
Tony Tuzzolino	32	3	8	11	41
Tomas Kloucek	73	2	8	10	113
John Namestnikov	33	1	9	10	14
Dale Purinton	62	4	4	8	415
Manny Malhotra	12	1	5	6	2
Chris Wells	14	2	2	4	6
Benjamin Carpentier	54	1	1	2	89
David Wilkie	1	0	2	2	0
Milan Hnilicka (goalie)	36	0	2	2	0
Jan Hlavac	3	1	0	1	0
Alexander Korobolin	22	1	0	1	22
Jean-Francois Labbe (goalie)	49	1	0	1	12
Stefan Cherneski	1	0	0	0	0
Rumun Ndur	2	0	0	0	0
Kevin Colley	5	0	0	0	2
Jeff Brown	6	0	0	0	2
Boyd Kane	8	0	0	0	9
David Oliver	9	0	0	0	19

GOALTENDING

	Gms.	Min.	W	L	T	G	SO	Avg.
Milan Hnilicka	36	1979	22	11	0	71	5	2.15
J.-Francois Labbe	49	2853	27	13	7	120	1	2.52

HERSHEY BEARS
SCORING

	Games	G	A	Pts.	PIM
Christian Matte	73	43	61	104	85
Serge Aubin	58	42	38	80	56
Mike Gaul	65	12	57	69	52
Rob Shearer	70	21	46	67	55
Dan Hinote	55	28	31	59	96
Brian Willsie	78	20	39	59	44
Ville Nieminen	74	21	30	51	54
Yuri Babenko	75	20	25	45	53
Brad Larsen	52	13	26	39	66
Steffon Walby	49	19	13	32	50
Rick Berry	64	9	16	25	148
Ben Storey	65	6	18	24	69
Dan Smith	49	7	15	22	56

MINOR LEAGUES *AHL*

	Games	G	A	Pts.	PIM
Brian White	79	3	19	22	78
Scott Parker	68	12	7	19	206
Nick Bootland	59	5	13	18	108
Evgeny Lazarev	46	2	11	13	44
Guy Dupuis	43	2	8	10	43
Jason Bowen	54	2	8	10	152
Frank Bialowas	40	4	3	7	65
Paul Vincent	5	3	2	5	0
Bruce Richardson	17	2	2	4	61
Sanny Lindstrom	42	1	2	3	57
Kelly Perrault	5	0	3	3	4
Lorne Toews	6	0	3	3	6
Frederic Cassivi (goalie)	31	0	2	2	2
Alexander Ryazantsev	2	0	1	1	2
Sami Helenius	12	0	1	1	31
David Aebischer (goalie)	58	0	1	1	7
Chris Aldous	1	0	0	0	0
Peter Cermak	1	0	0	0	0
Marc Dupuis	1	0	0	0	0
Scott Kirton	1	0	0	0	0
Eric Normandin	1	0	0	0	0
K.C. Timmons	1	0	0	0	2
Sean Venedam	1	0	0	0	0
Hugues Gervais	2	0	0	0	0
Harold Hersh	3	0	0	0	2
Darryl LaFrance	3	0	0	0	2
Jeff Ruzinski	5	0	0	0	8

GOALTENDING

	Gms.	Min.	W	L	T	G	SO	Avg.
Frederic Cassivi	31	1554	14	9	3	78	1	3.01
David Aebischer	58	3259	29	23	2	180	1	3.31

KENTUCKY THOROUGHBLADES
SCORING

	Games	G	A	Pts.	PIM
Mike Craig	76	39	39	78	116
Eric Landry	79	35	31	66	170
Mark Smith	79	21	45	66	153
Shawn Heins	69	11	52	63	238
Chris Armstrong	78	9	48	57	77
Chris Lipsett	70	25	23	48	38
Jarrett Deuling	75	17	25	42	83
Matt Bradley	80	22	19	41	81
Doug Friedman	73	13	23	36	237
Peter Roed	75	13	19	32	54
Larry Courville	61	11	12	23	107
Robert Jindrich	78	2	21	23	51
Rejean Stringer	40	6	13	19	12
Scott Hannan	41	5	12	17	40
Jon Coleman	66	1	14	15	43
Ryan Kraft	15	7	6	13	2
Adam Colagiacomo	42	5	8	13	27
Garrett Burnett	58	3	3	6	506
Adam Nittel	29	2	4	6	116
Brantt Myhres	10	1	5	6	18
Johan Hedberg (goalie)	33	0	4	4	6
Christian Gosselin	68	0	4	4	266
Andy Lundbohm	22	2	1	3	8
Kris Porter	3	0	1	1	0
Andy Sutton	3	0	1	1	0
Eric Brule	5	0	1	1	4
Chad Dameworth	13	0	1	1	6
Miikka Kiprusoff (goalie)	47	0	1	1	10
Joe Vandermeer	1	0	0	0	0
Matt Eldred	2	0	0	0	0
John Nabokov (goalie)	2	0	0	0	2
Jason Lawmaster	3	0	0	0	22
Robert Mulick	52	0	0	0	52

GOALTENDING

	Gms.	Min.	W	L	T	G	SO	Avg.
John Nabokov	2	120	1	1	0	3	1	1.50
Miikka Kiprusoff	47	2759	23	19	4	114	3	2.48
Johan Hedberg	33	1973	18	9	5	88	3	2.68

LOUISVILLE PANTHERS
SCORING

	Games	G	A	Pts.	PIM
Eric Boguniecki	57	33	42	75	148
David Duerden	74	25	38	63	6
Craig Reichert	72	16	42	58	41
Craig Ferguson	61	29	27	56	28
Kirby Law	66	31	21	52	173
Dan Boyle	58	14	38	52	75
Paul Brousseau	36	19	24	43	10
Ivan Novoseltsev	47	14	21	35	22
Marcus Nilson	64	9	23	32	52
Dwayne Hay	41	11	20	31	18
Chad Cabana	65	10	17	27	173
Peter Ratchuk	76	9	17	26	64
Brent Thompson	67	4	22	26	311
Lance Ward	80	4	16	20	190
Chris Wells	31	8	10	18	20
Joey Tetarenko	57	3	11	14	136
Nick Smith	53	8	4	12	8
Alex Hicks	17	6	5	11	23
Chris Allen	36	5	6	11	12
John Jakopin	23	4	6	10	47
Jeff Ware	51	0	10	10	128
Curtis Doell	33	2	7	9	85
Paul Harvey	34	2	7	9	50
Brad Ference	58	2	7	9	231
Andrew Long	29	3	2	5	14
Jay Neal	6	1	4	5	0
Chris Winnes	12	1	3	4	6
Ryan Burgoyne	16	2	1	3	17
Wes Mason	8	1	2	3	2
Sean Gauthier (goalie)	39	0	3	3	6
David Mayes	1	1	0	1	0
Jason Simon	11	1	0	1	28
Rocky Thompson	3	0	1	1	54
Eric Godard	4	0	1	1	16
Jon Hillebrandt (goalie)	7	0	1	1	0
Kevin Brown	1	0	0	0	2
Scott Fankhouser (goalie)	1	0	0	0	0
Jason Gladney	1	0	0	0	0
Trevor Kidd (goalie)	1	0	0	0	0
Lee Cole	2	0	0	0	0
Ryan Bach (goalie)	11	0	0	0	0
Richard Shulmistra (goalie)	27	0	0	0	2

GOALTENDING

	Gms.	Min.	W	L	T	G	SO	Avg.
Sean Gauthier	39	2259	24	12	2	102	3	2.71
Scott Fankhouser	1	59	0	1	0	3	0	3.05
Ryan Bach	11	603	4	4	1	33	0	3.28
Richard Shulmistra	27	1447	12	11	2	80	2	3.32
Jon Hillebrandt	7	413	2	2	2	25	0	3.63
Trevor Kidd	1	60	0	1	0	5	0	5.04

LOWELL LOCK MONSTERS
SCORING

	Games	G	A	Pts.	PIM
Jason Podollan	71	29	26	55	91
Rich Brennan	67	15	30	45	110
Eric Belanger	65	15	25	40	20
Dave Hymovitz	67	19	17	36	30
Dmitri Nabokov	51	8	26	34	42
Ray Giroux	49	12	21	33	34
Greg Phillips	62	20	10	30	140
Donald MacLean	40	11	17	28	18
Jason Krog	45	6	21	27	22
Cody Bowtell	61	13	13	26	24
Dave MacIsaac	77	1	25	26	179
Nathan LaFayette	42	7	15	22	33
Craig Charron	22	8	13	21	14
Vladimir Orszagh	55	8	12	20	22
Chris Schmidt	38	8	10	18	38
Petr Mika	50	8	9	17	20

	Games	G	A	Pts.	PIM
Mike Watt	16	6	11	17	6
Brad Chartrand	16	5	10	15	8
Greg Bullock	14	3	10	13	4
Evgeny Korolev	57	1	10	11	61
Vladimir Chebaturkin	63	1	8	9	118
Josh Green	17	6	2	8	19
Mark Lawrence	18	4	4	8	8
Richard Seeley	36	5	1	6	37
Sean Blanchard	54	1	5	6	28
Steve Cheredaryk	16	1	4	5	22
Peter Hogan	23	1	4	5	16
Jeff Daw	10	0	5	5	4
Bill Huard	13	2	2	4	65
Eric Brewer	25	2	2	4	26
Travis Scott (goalie)	46	0	3	3	10
Dan Bylsma	2	1	1	2	2
Frantisek Kaberle	4	0	2	2	0
Vaclav Nedomansky	2	1	0	1	4
Calvin Elfring	4	0	1	1	2
Hugues Gervais	5	0	1	1	4
Cail MacLean	5	0	1	1	0
Mark Cornforth	1	0	0	0	2
Bryan Fitzgerald	1	0	0	0	0
Bret Meyers	1	0	0	0	2
Vince Williams	1	0	0	0	0
D.J. Mando	2	0	0	0	0
Steve Sabo	2	0	0	0	4
Scott Bertoli	3	0	0	0	0
Mike Mader	5	0	0	0	13
Scott Ricci	5	0	0	0	2
Trevor Gillies	8	0	0	0	38
Steve Valiquette (goalie)	14	0	0	0	0
Martin Laitre	16	0	0	0	73
Roberto Luongo (goalie)	26	0	0	0	0
Roger Maxwell	26	0	0	0	137

GOALTENDING

	Gms.	Min.	W	L	T	G	SO	Avg.
Travis Scott	46	2595	15	23	3	126	3	2.91
Roberto Luongo	26	1517	10	12	4	74	1	2.93
Steve Valiquette	14	727	8	5	0	36	0	2.97

PHILADELPHIA PHANTOMS

SCORING

	Games	G	A	Pts.	PIM
Mike Maneluk	73	47	40	87	158
Mark Greig	68	34	48	82	116
Steve Washburn	61	19	52	71	93
Peter White	62	20	41	61	38
Jeff Tory	76	17	41	58	44
Ruslan Fedotenko	67	16	34	50	42
Tomas Divisek	59	18	31	49	30
Todd White	32	19	24	43	12
Dean Melanson	58	11	25	36	178
Andy Delmore	39	12	14	26	31
Mark Eaton	47	9	17	26	6
Sean O'Brien	61	6	11	17	139
Mikhail Chernov	67	10	6	16	54
Chris Albert	57	6	10	16	240
Matt Henderson	51	4	8	12	37
Francis Lessard	78	4	8	12	416
Jim Montgomery	13	3	9	12	22
Francis Belanger	35	5	6	11	112
Rastisl Pavlikovsky	12	4	7	11	8
Ryan Bast	71	1	9	10	198
Eric Bertrand	15	3	6	9	67
Brian Wesenberg	22	3	5	8	44
Jesse Boulerice	40	3	4	7	85
Kirby Law	12	1	4	5	6
Jeff Lank	26	1	4	5	16
Travis Brigley	15	2	2	4	15
Todd Fedoruk	19	1	2	3	40
Steve McLaren	64	1	2	3	247
Neil Little (goalie)	51	0	2	2	21

	Games	G	A	Pts.	PIM
Roman Vopat	12	1	0	1	12
Bruno St. Jacques	3	0	1	1	0
Brian Boucher (goalie)	1	0	0	0	0
Kam White	1	0	0	0	0
Cail MacLean	3	0	0	0	0
Dan Murphy (goalie)	5	0	0	0	0
Sergei Skrobot	5	0	0	0	2
Bujar Amidovski (goalie)	6	0	0	0	0
Jason Zent	11	0	0	0	22
Jean-Marc Pelletier (goalie)	24	0	0	0	0

GOALTENDING

	Gms.	Min.	W	L	T	G	SO	Avg.
Bujar Amidovski	6	250	3	1	0	8	0	1.92
Jean-Marc Pelletier	24	1405	14	10	0	58	3	2.48
Brian Boucher	1	65	0	0	1	3	0	2.77
Neil Little	51	2830	26	18	2	143	1	3.03
Dan Murphy	5	258	1	4	0	17	0	3.95

PORTLAND PIRATES

SCORING

	Games	G	A	Pts.	PIM
Glen Metropolit	48	18	42	60	73
Mike Peluso	71	25	29	54	86
Jeff Nelson	73	24	30	54	38
Trent Whitfield	79	18	35	53	52
Barrie Moore	80	18	33	51	50
Matt Herr	77	22	21	43	51
Kent Hulst	53	13	26	39	24
Jeff Toms	33	16	21	37	16
Ryan Mulhern	73	20	16	36	61
Miika Elomo	59	21	14	35	50
Alexandre Volchkov	35	11	15	26	47
Brad Church	56	9	17	26	52
Nolan Baumgartner	71	5	18	23	56
Jakub Ficenec	58	11	9	20	32
Patrick Boileau	63	2	15	17	61
Alexei Tezikov	53	6	9	15	70
Steve Poapst	58	0	14	14	20
Jamie Huscroft	56	0	12	12	154
Jean-Francois Fortin	43	3	5	8	44
Steve Shirreffs	44	3	5	8	14
Jason Shmyr	53	3	4	7	170
Richard Pitirri	9	2	4	6	4
Rob Zettler	23	2	2	4	27
Mike Omicioli	6	1	3	4	4
Duane Harmer	7	1	3	4	2
Martin Brochu (goalie)	54	0	3	3	6
Michael Farrell	7	2	0	2	0
Louis Bedard	3	0	1	1	14
Dwight Parrish	7	0	1	1	7
Curtis Cruickshank (goalie)	10	0	1	1	0
Dean Stork	3	0	0	0	2
Rob DeCiantis	4	0	0	0	2
Gerad Adams	8	0	0	0	10
Mike Siklenka	9	0	0	0	14
Etienne Drapeau	10	0	0	0	45
Sebastien Charpentier (goalie)	18	0	0	0	0

GOALTENDING

	Gms.	Min.	W	L	T	G	SO	Avg.
Martin Brochu	54	3192	32	15	6	116	4	2.18
S. Charpentier	18	1041	10	4	3	48	0	2.77
Curtis Cruickshank	10	605	4	5	1	30	0	2.98

PROVIDENCE BRUINS

SCORING

	Games	G	A	Pts.	PIM
Peter Ferraro	48	21	25	46	98
Jay Henderson	60	18	27	45	200
Brandon Smith	55	8	30	38	20
Jeremy Brown	80	11	25	36	49
Eric Manlow	46	17	16	33	14

	Games	G	A	Pts.	PIM
Andre Savage	30	15	17	32	22
Jeff Wells	74	9	23	32	51
Sean Pronger	51	11	18	29	26
Joel Prpic	70	9	20	29	143
Tim Lovell	40	13	14	27	32
Antti Laaksonen	40	10	12	22	57
Cameron Mann	29	7	12	19	45
Nick Boynton	53	5	14	19	66
Chris Ferraro	21	9	9	18	32
Jason Krog	11	9	8	17	4
Jassen Cullimore	16	5	10	15	31
Johnathan Aitken	70	2	12	14	121
Shane Belter	51	4	9	13	77
Eric Nickulas	40	6	6	12	37
Neil Fewster	33	3	9	12	27
Aaron Downey	47	6	4	10	221
Landon Wilson	17	5	5	10	45
Dany Bousquet	14	5	4	9	6
Joe Hulbig	15	4	5	9	17
Jeff Zehr	12	3	3	6	37
Marquis Mathieu	18	3	3	6	45
Martin Masa	11	2	2	4	6
John Spoltore	5	1	3	4	2
Duane Harmer	16	1	3	4	10
Konstantin Shafranov	8	0	4	4	0
Bob Beers	13	0	4	4	14
Mark DeSantis	6	1	2	3	17
Terry Hollinger	4	0	3	3	2
Chris Winnes	2	1	1	2	0
Eric Cairns	4	1	1	2	14
Jason Ialongo	8	1	1	2	2
Roger Maxwell	14	1	1	2	85
Elias Abrahamsson	19	1	1	2	45
Kevin Kaminski	5	0	2	2	17
Aris Brimanis	7	0	2	2	2
Kay Whitmore (goalie)	43	0	2	2	12
Keith McCambridge	47	0	2	2	135
Mike Sylvia	2	1	0	1	0
Kevin Paden	3	1	0	1	0
Ken Tasker	6	1	0	1	15
Andy Brickley	3	0	1	1	0
Vratislav Cech	3	0	1	1	0
Steve O'Brien	3	0	1	1	2
Justin Cardwell	5	0	1	1	0
Jonathan Girard	5	0	1	1	0
Stefan Rivard	6	0	1	1	4
Joel Trottier	6	0	1	1	2
Matt Van Horlick	6	0	1	1	8
Maxime Gingras (goalie)	15	0	1	1	2
Denis Timofeev	16	0	1	1	14
Eric Brule	1	0	0	0	0
David Brumby (goalie)	1	0	0	0	0
Dion Delmonte	1	0	0	0	2
Steve Valiquette (goalie)	1	0	0	0	0
Todd Barclay	2	0	0	0	0
Scott Kirton	2	0	0	0	2
Mark Krys	2	0	0	0	2
Jon Sorg	2	0	0	0	2
Keith O'Connell	3	0	0	0	4
Curtis Wilgosh	3	0	0	0	0
Alexander Yudin	3	0	0	0	28
Dave Jesiolowski	4	0	0	0	5
Eric Van Acker	4	0	0	0	2
Mike Peron	6	0	0	0	20
John Grahame (goalie)	27	0	0	0	6

GOALTENDING

	Gms.	Min.	W	L	T	G	SO	Avg.
David Brumby	1	61	1	0	0	1	0	0.98
Steve Valiquette	1	60	1	0	0	3	0	3.00
Maxime Gingras	15	780	3	9	1	40	0	3.08
Kay Whitmore	43	2393	17	19	3	127	1	3.18
John Grahame	27	1528	11	13	2	86	1	3.38

QUEBEC CITADELLES
SCORING

	Games	G	A	Pts.	PIM
Pierre Sevigny	78	24	43	67	154
Andrei Bashkirov	78	28	33	61	17
Xavier Delisle	42	17	28	45	8
Stephane Robidas	76	14	31	45	36
Stephane Roy	73	13	28	41	43
Marc Beaucage	63	20	13	33	54
Jesse Belanger	36	15	18	33	20
Francois Groleau	63	7	24	31	48
Jason Ward	40	14	12	26	30
Jonathan Delisle	62	7	19	26	142
Jason McBain	51	8	16	24	29
Patrice Tardif	18	9	10	19	23
Miloslav Guren	29	5	12	17	16
Trent McCleary	27	7	9	16	56
Matt Higgins	29	1	15	16	21
Oleg Petrov	16	7	7	14	4
Mike McBain	53	5	7	12	34
Gennady Razin	66	2	9	11	29
Kimbi Daniels	25	6	4	10	4
Arron Asham	13	4	5	9	32
Chris Albert	15	4	4	8	51
Boyd Olson	33	3	5	8	24
Alain Nasreddine	59	1	6	7	178
Dave Morissette	47	2	4	6	231
Mathieu Descoteaux	12	0	6	6	6
Simon Tremblay	46	1	3	4	34
Christian Caron	27	1	2	3	11
Byron Briske	26	0	3	3	47
Eric Brule	4	0	2	2	6
Jeff Shevalier	5	0	2	2	2
Olivier Morin	10	1	0	1	5
Josh DeWolf	15	1	0	1	17
Sergei Zholtok	1	0	1	1	2
Jeff McLean	2	0	1	1	0
Darcy Harris	36	0	1	1	94
Joel Theriault	36	0	1	1	170
Mathieu Garon (goalie)	53	0	1	1	6
Carl Fleury	2	0	0	0	0
Barry Richter	2	0	0	0	0
Justin Kearns	3	0	0	0	2
Mike Ribeiro	3	0	0	0	2
Konstantin Sidulov	5	0	0	0	2
Eric Fichaud (goalie)	6	0	0	0	0
Gordie Dwyer	7	0	0	0	37
Dan Murphy (goalie)	33	0	0	0	0

GOALTENDING

	Gms.	Min.	W	L	T	G	SO	Avg.
Dan Murphy	33	1573	16	9	1	62	3	2.37
Eric Fichaud	6	368	4	1	1	17	0	2.77
Mathieu Garon	53	2884	17	28	3	149	2	3.10

ROCHESTER AMERICANS
SCORING

	Games	G	A	Pts.	PIM
Domenic Pittis	53	17	48	65	85
Denis Hamel	76	34	24	58	122
Jason Cipolla	73	23	34	57	77
Chris Taylor	49	21	28	49	21
Jeremy Adduono	51	23	22	45	20
Mike Hurlbut	74	10	29	39	83
Darren VanOene	80	20	18	38	153
Francois Methot	80	14	18	32	20
Matt Davidson	80	12	20	32	30
Brian Campbell	67	2	24	26	22
Randy Cunneyworth	52	8	16	24	81
Doug Houda	79	7	17	24	175
Craig Fisher	17	15	8	23	8
Dmitri Kalinin	75	2	19	21	52
Scott Nichol	37	7	11	18	141
Maxim Afinogenov	15	6	12	18	8

	Games	G	A	Pts.	PIM
Jason Holland	54	3	15	18	24
Jean-Pierre Dumont	13	7	10	17	18
Dane Jackson	21	6	9	15	8
Jean-Luc Grand-Pierre	62	5	8	13	124
Cory Sarich	15	0	6	6	44
Joe Murphy	32	0	6	6	8
Eric Boulton	76	2	2	4	276
Mika Noronen (goalie)	54	0	3	3	8
Paul Traynor	41	0	2	2	34
Chris Palmer	3	1	0	1	4
Chris Aldous	4	1	0	1	0
Ryan Mougenel	20	1	0	1	2
Marc Dupuis	5	0	1	1	12
Kirk Daubenspeck (goalie)	22	0	1	1	2
Dion Delmonte	1	0	0	0	0
Mark Dutiaume	1	0	0	0	0
Andrew Luciuk	1	0	0	0	0
Dustin Whitecotton	1	0	0	0	0
Scott Kirton	2	0	0	0	0
Andre Payette	2	0	0	0	0
Khalil Thomas	2	0	0	0	0
Tom Buckley	3	0	0	0	0
Adam Calder	3	0	0	0	2
Chris Grenville	3	0	0	0	2
Mike Nicholishen	3	0	0	0	4
Danny Lorenz (goalie)	4	0	0	0	0
Scott Ricci	4	0	0	0	0
Kelly Perrault	5	0	0	0	2
Martin Biron (goalie)	6	0	0	0	8

GOALTENDING

	Gms.	Min.	W	L	T	G	SO	Avg.
Martin Biron	6	344	6	0	0	12	1	2.09
Mika Noronen	54	3089	33	13	4	112	6	2.18
Kirk Daubenspeck	22	1235	7	10	4	53	1	2.57
Danny Lorenz	4	168	0	2	1	15	0	5.36

SAINT JOHN FLAMES

SCORING

	Games	G	A	Pts.	PIM
Daniel Tkaczuk	80	25	41	66	56
Benoit Gratton	65	17	49	66	137
Rico Fata	76	29	29	58	65
Ronald Petrovicky	67	23	33	56	131
Dave Roche	67	22	21	43	130
Sergei Varlamov	68	20	21	41	88
Lee Sorochan	60	4	37	41	124
Brett McLean	72	15	23	38	115
Darrel Scoville	64	11	25	36	99
Chris Clark	48	16	17	33	134
Martin St. Louis	17	15	11	26	14
Jeff Cowan	47	15	10	25	77
Steve Begin	47	13	12	25	99
Chris St. Croix	75	5	16	21	51
Eric Charron	37	2	15	17	82
Jeff Staples	72	2	14	16	89
John Tripp	29	8	7	15	38
Hnat Domenichelli	12	6	7	13	8
Curtis Sheptak	21	2	8	10	27
Rocky Thompson	53	2	8	10	125
Jason Botterill	21	3	4	7	39
Allan Egeland	11	1	5	6	42
Derrick Walser	14	2	3	5	10
Jody Shelley	22	1	4	5	93
Matt O'Dette	69	1	4	5	177
Travis Brigley	9	3	1	4	4
Rob Concannon	5	2	2	4	2
Joel Irving	7	1	2	3	5
Jeff Sullivan	9	0	3	3	16
Jean-Sebastien Giguere (g)	41	0	2	2	39
Lee Jinman	3	1	0	1	0
Jason Bowen	11	0	1	1	28
Sean Matile (goalie)	14	0	1	1	2
John Jarvis	1	0	0	0	0

	Games	G	A	Pts.	PIM
Rick Poirier (goalie)	1	0	0	0	0
Fred Brathwaite (goalie)	2	0	0	0	0
Andrew Dale	2	0	0	0	0
Grant Fuhr (goalie)	2	0	0	0	0
Brent Gauvreau	2	0	0	0	0
Pavel Nestak (goalie)	2	0	0	0	0
Mike Vellinga	2	0	0	0	0
Luc Roy	3	0	0	0	0
Marc Tropper	3	0	0	0	0
Scott Bailey (goalie)	4	0	0	0	0
Michel Larocque (goalie)	4	0	0	0	0
Frederic Deschenes (goalie)	5	0	0	0	0
Robyn Regehr	5	0	0	0	0
Jeremy Mylymok	7	0	0	0	7
Fredrik Oduya	10	0	0	0	42
Tyrone Garner (goalie)	19	0	0	0	2

GOALTENDING

	Gms.	Min.	W	L	T	G	SO	Avg.
Michel Larocque	4	243	2	1	1	8	0	1.98
Fred Brathwaite	2	120	2	0	0	4	0	2.00
Sean Matile	14	709	6	3	3	35	1	2.96
J.-S. Giguere	41	2243	17	17	3	114	0	3.05
Pavel Nestak	2	108	0	2	0	6	0	3.35
Frederic Deschenes	5	259	1	3	0	19	1	4.40
Tyrone Garner	19	940	4	8	4	70	0	4.47
Scott Bailey	4	135	0	1	0	11	0	4.90
Grant Fuhr	2	99	0	2	0	10	0	6.05
Rick Poirier	1	9	0	0	0	2	0	12.70

ST. JOHN'S MAPLE LEAFS

SCORING

	Games	G	A	Pts.	PIM
Bobby House	68	24	29	53	46
Adam Mair	66	22	27	49	124
David Nemirovsky	57	18	25	43	69
Aaron Brand	80	12	25	37	68
Craig Charron	32	11	18	29	14
Konstantin Kalmikov	76	8	20	28	21
D.J. Smith	74	6	22	28	197
Nathan Dempsey	44	15	12	27	40
Donald MacLean	21	14	12	26	8
Terry Ryan	50	7	17	24	176
Jason Sessa	30	7	14	21	54
Jason Bonsignore	29	6	13	19	30
Dennis Maxwell	36	5	14	19	171
Ryan Pepperall	77	11	7	18	83
Kevyn Adams	23	6	11	17	24
Shawn Thornton	60	4	12	16	316
Dimitri Yakushin	64	1	13	14	106
Vladimir Antipov	45	6	7	13	14
Justin Hocking	68	4	9	13	175
Syl Apps	58	5	7	12	87
Terran Sandwith	78	1	10	11	155
Tyler Harlton	56	2	6	8	62
Marek Posymk	38	1	6	7	57
Forbes MacPherson	10	1	3	4	8
Rob Sinclair	7	1	2	3	0
Darrin Shannon	8	2	0	2	2
Alyn McCauley	5	1	1	2	0
Dan Preston	10	0	2	2	8
Keith Delaney	5	1	0	1	0
Matt Hogan	3	0	1	1	4
Jimmy Waite (goalie)	62	0	1	1	10
Blair Scott	1	0	0	0	0
Nikolai Antropov	2	0	0	0	4
Bryan Fogarty	3	0	0	0	0
Hugo Marchand	7	0	0	0	23
Chris Bogas	8	0	0	0	6
Marc Robitaille (goalie)	27	0	0	0	2

GOALTENDING

	Gms.	Min.	W	L	T	G	SO	Avg.
Jimmy Waite	62	3461	20	37	4	176	6	3.05
Marc Robitaille	27	1369	3	12	4	93	0	4.08

MINOR LEAGUES AHL

SPRINGFIELD FALCONS
SCORING

	Games	G	A	Pts.	PIM
Jean-Guy Trudel	72	34	39	73	80
Daniel Briere	58	29	42	71	56
Brad Tiley	80	14	54	68	51
Eric Houde	57	28	34	62	43
Shayne Toporowski	80	27	28	55	191
Tavis Hansen	59	21	27	48	164
Sean McCann	62	5	38	43	77
Wyatt Smith	60	14	26	40	26
David Cullen	78	10	21	31	57
Eric Healey	32	14	15	29	51
Craig Mills	78	10	13	23	151
Chris Winnes	38	6	17	23	4
Ryan Huska	61	12	9	21	77
Steven King	23	10	6	16	20
Martin Gendron	14	6	10	16	6
Mark Streit	43	3	12	15	18
Jeremiah McCarthy	43	5	9	14	16
Kevin Sawyer	56	4	8	12	321
Dan Focht	44	2	9	11	86
Philippe Audet	14	3	7	10	6
Robert Schnabel	40	2	8	10	133
Francois Leroux	64	3	6	9	162
John Kosobud	27	4	3	7	18
Scott King	12	2	4	6	8
Rob Murray	22	1	3	4	70
Robert Francz	36	0	3	3	89
David Bell	48	1	1	2	174
Sean Berens	6	0	2	2	4
Trent Cull	28	0	2	2	74
Dave Paradise	1	1	0	1	0
Nic Beaudoin	2	1	0	1	0
Radoslav Suchy	2	0	1	1	0
Patrick DesRochers (goalie)	52	0	1	1	36
Mark Cornforth	1	0	0	0	2
Justin Plamondon	1	0	0	0	2
Ryan Van Buskirk	1	0	0	0	0
Dieter Kochan (goalie)	2	0	0	0	0
Andrew Proskurnicki	2	0	0	0	0
Erasmo Saltarelli (goalie)	2	0	0	0	0
Jon Sturgis	3	0	0	0	0
Pierre-Luc Therrien (goalie)	4	0	0	0	2
Sylvain Daigle (goalie)	11	0	0	0	0
Robert Esche (goalie)	21	0	0	0	2

GOALTENDING

	Gms.	Min.	W	L	T	G	SO	Avg.
Erasmo Saltarelli	2	88	0	1	0	3	0	2.06
Dieter Kochan	2	120	1	1	0	5	1	2.50
Pierre-Luc Therrien	4	204	1	2	0	10	0	2.94
Patrick DesRochers	52	2710	21	17	7	137	1	3.03
Robert Esche	21	1207	9	9	2	61	2	3.03
Sylvain Daigle	11	509	1	6	2	29	0	3.42

SYRACUSE CRUNCH
SCORING

	Games	G	A	Pts.	PIM
Reggie Savage	78	36	34	70	135
Chris O'Sullivan	59	18	47	65	24
Jarkko Ruutu	65	26	32	58	164
Josh Holden	45	19	32	51	113
Brian Bonin	67	19	28	47	20
Harold Druken	47	20	25	45	32
Lubomir Vaic	63	13	29	42	42
Steve Kariya	29	18	23	41	22
Brad Leeb	61	19	18	37	50
Martin Gendron	64	19	17	36	16
Mike Brown	71	13	18	31	284
Brent Sopel	50	6	25	31	67
Trent Klatt	24	13	10	23	6
Chad Allan	76	3	18	21	100

	Games	G	A	Pts.	PIM
Pat Kavanagh	68	12	8	20	56
Ryan Bonni	71	5	13	18	125
Zenith Komarniski	42	4	12	16	130
Ryan Ready	70	4	12	16	59
Artem Chubarov	14	7	6	13	4
Matt Cooke	18	5	8	13	27
Darby Hendrickson	20	5	8	13	16
Ryan Shannon	52	1	11	12	68
Sean McCann	11	0	9	9	12
Trevor Doyle	77	2	6	8	235
Christian Bronsard (goalie)	37	1	5	6	10
Chris Aldous	12	0	5	5	2
Paul Ferone	21	1	2	3	69
Stewart Bodtker	10	0	3	3	0
Clint Cabana	15	0	3	3	79
Bryan Allen	9	1	1	2	11
Rick Mrozik	1	0	0	0	0
Mike Valley (goalie)	1	0	0	0	0
Harry York	1	0	0	0	15
Peter Schaefer	2	0	0	0	2
Jonas Soling	4	0	0	0	0
Brad Dexter	5	0	0	0	0
Corey Schwab (goalie)	12	0	0	0	31
Alfie Michaud (goalie)	38	0	0	0	0

GOALTENDING

	Gms.	Min.	W	L	T	G	SO	Avg.
Christian Bronsard	37	2069	18	14	4	113	1	3.28
Corey Schwab	12	720	7	5	0	42	0	3.50
Alfie Michaud	38	2052	10	17	5	132	0	3.86
Mike Valley	1	4	0	0	0	1	0	14.23

WILKES-BARRE/SCRANTON PENGUINS
SCORING

	Games	G	A	Pts.	PIM
John Slaney	49	30	30	60	25
Tom Kostopoulos	76	26	32	58	121
Martin Sonnenberg	62	20	33	53	109
Greg Crozier	71	22	22	44	33
Sven Butenschon	75	19	21	40	101
Valentin Morozov	59	14	25	39	4
Robert Dome	51	12	26	38	83
Alexei Kolkunov	75	12	25	37	33
Boris Protsenko	64	15	21	36	41
Mark Murphy	38	11	22	33	35
Dennis Bonvie	42	5	26	31	243
Andrew Ference	44	8	20	28	58
Pavel Skrbek	51	7	16	23	50
Tyler Wright	25	5	15	20	86
Casey Harris	74	6	6	12	149
Josef Melichar	80	3	9	12	126
Chris Kelleher	67	0	12	12	40
Dacry Verot	23	5	5	10	96
Jean-Paul Tessier	77	3	6	9	106
Alexandre Mathieu	52	4	4	8	18
Kurtis Drummond	66	3	3	6	28
Steve Leach	4	2	3	5	4
Dylan Gyori	36	2	2	4	23
Mike Yeo	19	1	3	4	4
Mike Pomichter	16	1	2	3	11
Tom O'Connor	17	0	1	1	4
David Weninger (goalie)	25	0	1	1	0
Tyler Moss (goalie)	4	0	0	0	0
Peter Vandermeer	4	0	0	0	7
Louis Bedard	5	0	0	0	12
Jean-Sebastien Aubin (goalie)	11	0	0	0	0
Craig Hillier (goalie)	11	0	0	0	0
Michel Larocque (goalie)	13	0	0	0	0
Ryan Bach (goalie)	28	0	0	0	20

GOALTENDING

	Gms.	Min.	W	L	T	G	SO	Avg.
Michel Larocque	13	727	5	6	1	34	0	2.81
Tyler Moss	4	188	1	1	1	11	0	3.52

	Gms.	Min.	W	L	T	G	SO	Avg.
David Weninger	25	1277	6	9	3	76	0	3.57
Ryan Bach	28	1590	8	18	2	100	0	3.77
Craig Hillier	11	520	1	6	2	36	0	4.15
J.-Sebastien Aubin	11	538	2	8	0	39	0	4.35

WORCESTER ICECATS
SCORING

	Games	G	A	Pts.	PIM
Jim Campbell	66	31	34	65	88
Daniel Corso	71	21	34	55	19
Marty Reasoner	44	23	28	51	39
Ladislav Nagy	69	23	28	51	67
Andrej Podkonicky	77	16	25	41	68
Derek Bekar	71	21	19	40	26
Bryan Helmer	54	10	25	35	124
Sylvain Blouin	70	16	18	34	337
Jamie Thompson	64	17	13	30	31
Reed Low	80	12	16	28	203
Tyler Rennette	55	8	17	25	16
Marc Brown	72	13	11	24	17
Jame Pollock	56	12	12	24	50
Peter Smrek	64	5	19	24	26
Darren Rumble	39	0	17	17	31
Trevor Wasyluk	47	6	7	13	14
Tyler Willis	32	3	10	13	98
Bryce Salvador	55	0	13	13	53
Lubos Bartecko	12	4	7	11	4
Dan Keczmer	25	1	9	10	12
Jan Horacek	68	1	8	9	145
Libor Prochazka	36	2	6	8	32
Didier Tremblay	27	1	6	7	8
Chris McAlpine	10	1	4	5	4
Jason Widmer	12	0	5	5	23
Rory Fitzpatrick	28	0	5	5	48
Brent Johnson (goalie)	58	0	3	3	25
Pascal Rheaume	7	1	1	2	4
Josh Harrold	4	0	2	2	0
Jaroslav Obsut	7	0	2	2	4
James Desmarais	8	0	2	2	0
Jamey Hicks	8	1	0	1	2
Ricard Persson	2	0	1	1	0
Cody Rudkowsky (goalie)	28	0	1	1	8
Shawn Mamane	1	0	0	0	0
Tomaz Razingar	1	0	0	0	0
Maxim Linnik	2	0	0	0	2
Tyler Harlton	3	0	0	0	4
Rick Mrozik	3	0	0	0	0
Kenric Exner (goalie)	4	0	0	0	0
Rudy Poeschek	5	0	0	0	4
Matt Smith	6	0	0	0	6

GOALTENDING

	Gms.	Min.	W	L	T	G	SO	Avg.
Brent Johnson	58	3319	24	27	5	161	3	2.91
Cody Rudkowsky	28	1405	9	7	6	75	0	3.20
Kenric Exner	4	121	1	1	0	8	0	3.95

PLAYERS WITH TWO OR MORE TEAMS

SCORING

	Games	G	A	Pts.	PIM
Elias Abrahamsson, Providence	19	1	1	2	45
Elias Abrahamsson, Hamilton	56	1	3	4	90
Totals	75	2	4	6	135
Chris Albert, Philadelphia	57	6	10	16	240
Chris Albert, Quebec	15	4	4	8	51
Totals	72	10	14	24	291
Chris Aldous, Hershey	1	0	0	0	0
Chris Aldous, Syracuse	12	0	5	5	2
Chris Aldous, Rochester	4	1	0	1	0
Totals	17	1	5	6	2
Philippe Audet, Cincinnati	62	19	22	41	115

	Games	G	A	Pts.	PIM
Philippe Audet, Springfield	14	3	7	10	6
Totals	76	22	29	51	121
Ryan Bach, Louisville (g)	11	0	0	0	0
Ryan Bach, W.-B./Scran. (g)	28	0	0	0	20
Totals	39	0	0	0	20
Louis Bedard, W.-B./Scran.	5	0	0	0	12
Louis Bedard, Portland	3	0	1	1	14
Totals	8	0	1	1	26
Jason Bowen, Hershey	54	2	8	10	152
Jason Bowen, Saint John	11	0	1	1	28
Totals	65	2	9	11	180
Travis Brigley, Saint John	9	3	1	4	4
Travis Brigley, Philadelphia	15	2	2	4	15
Totals	24	5	3	8	19
Eric Brule, Providence	1	0	0	0	0
Eric Brule, Quebec	4	0	2	2	6
Eric Brule, Kentucky	5	0	1	1	4
Totals	10	0	3	3	10
Craig Charron, St. John's	32	11	18	29	14
Craig Charron, Lowell	22	8	13	21	14
Totals	54	19	31	50	28
Mark Cornforth, Lowell	1	0	0	0	2
Mark Cornforth, Springfield	1	0	0	0	2
Totals	2	0	0	0	4
Josh DeWolf, Albany	58	3	11	14	38
Josh DeWolf, Quebec	15	1	0	1	17
Totals	73	4	11	15	55
Dion Delmonte, Rochester	1	0	0	0	0
Dion Delmonte, Providence	1	0	0	0	2
Totals	2	0	0	0	2
Mathieu Descoteaux, Hamilton	49	5	7	12	29
Mathieu Descoteaux, Quebec	12	0	6	6	6
Totals	61	5	13	18	35
Marc Dupuis, Rochester	5	0	1	1	12
Marc Dupuis, Hershey	1	0	0	0	0
Totals	6	0	1	1	12
Martin Gendron, Syracuse	64	19	17	36	16
Martin Gendron, Springfield	14	6	10	16	6
Totals	78	25	27	52	22
Hugues Gervais, Hershey	2	0	0	0	0
Hugues Gervais, Lowell	5	0	1	1	4
Hugues Gervais, Cincinnati	3	0	0	0	0
Totals	10	0	1	1	4
Tyler Harlton, Worcester	3	0	0	0	4
Tyler Harlton, St. John's	56	2	6	8	62
Totals	59	2	6	8	66
Duane Harmer, Portland	7	1	3	4	2
Duane Harmer, Providence	16	1	3	4	10
Totals	23	2	6	8	12
Eric Houde, Hamilton	18	3	4	7	10
Eric Houde, Springfield	57	28	34	62	43
Totals	75	31	38	69	53
Scott Kirton, Providence	2	0	0	0	2
Scott Kirton, Hershey	1	0	0	0	0
Scott Kirton, Rochester	2	0	0	0	0
Totals	5	0	0	0	2
Jason Krog, Lowell	45	6	21	27	22
Jason Krog, Providence	11	9	8	17	4
Totals	56	15	29	44	26
Martin Laitre, Lowell	16	0	0	0	73
Martin Laitre, Hamilton	56	5	7	12	208
Totals	72	5	7	12	281
Michel Larocque, S.J. (g)	4	0	0	0	0
Michel Larocque, W.-B./S. (g)	13	0	0	0	0
Totals	17	0	0	0	0
Kirby Law, Louisville	66	31	21	52	173
Kirby Law, Philadelphia	12	1	4	5	6
Totals	78	32	25	57	179
Cail MacLean, Lowell	5	0	1	1	0
Cail MacLean, Philadelphia	3	0	0	0	0
Totals	8	0	1	1	0
Donald MacLean, Lowell	40	11	17	28	18
Donald MacLean, St. John's	21	14	12	26	8
Totals	61	25	29	54	26

	Games	G	A	Pts.	PIM
Roger Maxwell, Providence	14	1	1	2	85
Roger Maxwell, Lowell	26	0	0	0	137
Totals	40	1	1	2	222
Sean McCann, Springfield	62	5	38	43	77
Sean McCann, Syracuse	11	0	9	9	12
Totals	73	5	47	52	89
Rick Mrozik, Worcester	3	0	0	0	0
Rick Mrozik, Syracuse	1	0	0	0	0
Totals	4	0	0	0	0
Dan Murphy, Quebec (g)	33	0	0	0	0
Dan Murphy, Philadelphia (g)	5	0	0	0	0
Totals	38	0	0	0	0
Rob Murray, Springfield	22	1	3	4	70
Rob Murray, Hamilton	55	11	20	31	100
Totals	77	12	23	35	170
Alain Nasreddine, Quebec	59	1	6	7	178
Alain Nasreddine, Hamilton	11	0	0	0	12
Totals	70	1	6	7	190
Rastisl Pavlikovsky, Phil.	12	4	7	11	8
Rastisl Pavlikovsky, Cincinnati	17	3	5	8	10
Totals	29	7	12	19	18
Kelly Perrault, Hershey	5	0	3	3	4
Kelly Perrault, Rochester	5	0	0	0	2
Totals	10	0	3	3	6
Scott Ricci, Rochester	4	0	0	0	0
Scott Ricci, Lowell	5	0	0	0	2
Totals	9	0	0	0	2
Rocky Thompson, Saint John	53	2	8	10	125
Rocky Thompson, Louisville	3	0	1	1	54
Totals	56	2	9	11	179
Tony Tuzzolino, Cincinnati	15	0	3	3	8

	Games	G	A	Pts.	PIM
Tony Tuzzolino, Hartford	32	3	8	11	41
Totals	47	3	11	14	49
Steve Valiquette, Prov. (g)	1	0	0	0	0
Steve Valiquette, Lowell (g)	14	0	0	0	0
Totals	15	0	0	0	0
Alexandre Volchkov, Portland	35	11	15	26	47
Alexandre Volchkov, Hamilton	25	2	6	8	11
Totals	60	13	21	34	58
Chris Wells, Louisville	31	8	10	18	20
Chris Wells, Hartford	14	2	2	4	6
Totals	45	10	12	22	26
Chris Winnes, Louisville	12	1	3	4	6
Chris Winnes, Providence	2	1	1	2	0
Chris Winnes, Springfield	38	6	17	23	4
Totals	52	8	21	29	10

GOALTENDING

	Gms.	Min.	W	L	T	G	SO	Avg.
Ryan Bach, Lou.	11	603	4	4	1	33	0	3.28
R. Bach, W.-B./S.	28	1590	8	18	2	100	0	3.77
Totals	39	2193	12	22	3	133	0	3.64
M. Larocque, S.J.	4	243	2	1	1	8	0	1.98
Larocque, W.B./S.	13	727	5	6	1	34	0	2.81
Totals	17	969	7	7	2	42	0	2.60
Dan Murphy, Que.	33	1573	16	9	1	62	3	2.37
Dan Murphy, Phil.	5	258	1	4	0	17	0	3.95
Totals	38	1831	17	13	1	79	3	2.59
S. Valiquette, Prov.	1	60	1	0	0	3	0	3.00
S. Valiquette, Low.	14	727	8	5	0	36	0	2.97
Totals	15	787	9	5	0	39	0	2.97

2000 CALDER CUP PLAYOFFS
RESULTS

CONFERENCE QUARTERFINALS

	W	L	Pts.	GF	GA
Providence	3	0	6	14	9
Quebec	0	3	0	9	14

(Providence won series, 3-0)

	W	L	Pts.	GF	GA
Lowell	3	0	6	10	5
Saint John	0	3	0	5	10

(Lowell won series, 3-0)

	W	L	Pts.	GF	GA
Hartford	3	2	6	20	15
Springfield	2	3	4	15	20

(Hartford won series, 3-2)

	W	L	Pts.	GF	GA
Worcester	3	1	6	17	9
Portland	1	3	2	9	17

(Worcester won series, 3-1)

	W	L	Pts.	GF	GA
Rochester	3	2	6	11	7
Albany	2	3	4	7	11

(Rochester won series, 3-2)

	W	L	Pts.	GF	GA
Hamilton	3	1	6	11	9
Syracuse	1	3	2	9	11

(Hamilton won series, 3-1)

	W	L	Pts.	GF	GA
Kentucky	3	1	6	16	8
Louisville	1	3	2	8	16

(Kentucky won series, 3-1)

	W	L	Pts.	GF	GA
Hershey	3	2	6	15	13
Philadelphia	2	3	4	13	15

(Hershey won series, 3-2)

CONFERENCE SEMIFINALS

	W	L	Pts.	GF	GA
Providence	4	0	8	17	9
Lowell	0	4	0	9	17

(Providence won series, 4-0)

	W	L	Pts.	GF	GA
Hartford	4	1	8	14	10
Worcester	1	4	2	10	14

(Hartford won series, 4-1)

	W	L	Pts.	GF	GA
Rochester	4	2	8	20	12
Hamilton	2	4	4	12	20

(Rochester won series, 4-2)

	W	L	Pts.	GF	GA
Hershey	4	1	8	16	14
Kentucky	1	4	2	14	16

(Hershey won series, 4-1)

CONFERENCE FINALS

	W	L	Pts.	GF	GA
Hartford	4	3	8	20	20
Providence	3	4	6	20	20

(Hartford won series, 4-3)

	W	L	Pts.	GF	GA
Rochester	4	0	8	19	8
Hershey	0	4	0	8	19

(Rochester won series, 4-0)

CALDER CUP FINALS

	W	L	Pts.	GF	GA
Hartford	4	2	8	14	10
Rochester	2	4	4	10	14

(Hartford won series, 4-2)

Goals: Brad Smyth, Hartford (13)
Assists: Domenic Pittis, Rochester (26)
Points: Domenic Pittis, Rochester (30)
Penalty minutes: Dale Purinton, Hartford (87)
Goaltending average: Mika Noronen, Rochester (1.80)
Shutouts: Mika Noronen, Rochester (6)

TOP SCORERS

	Games	G	A	Pts.
Domenic Pittis, Rochester	21	4	26	30
Brad Smyth, Hartford	23	13	10	23
Derek Armstrong, Hartford	23	7	16	23
Jean-Pierre Dumont, Rochester	21	14	7	21
Jason Dawe, Hartford	21	10	7	17
Jeremy Adduono, Rochester	21	6	11	17
Christian Matte, Hershey	14	8	6	14
Eric Manlow, Providence	14	6	8	14
Cameron Mann, Providence	11	6	7	13
Andre Savage, Providence	14	6	7	13
Johan Witehall, Hartford	17	6	7	13
Denis Hamel, Rochester	21	6	7	13

MINOR LEAGUES AHL

INDIVIDUAL STATISTICS

ALBANY RIVER RATS
(Lost conference quarterfinals to Rochester, 3-2)

SCORING

	Games	G	A	Pts.	PIM
Steve Brule	5	1	2	3	0
Willie Mitchell	5	1	2	3	4
Sascha Goc	5	2	0	2	6
Steve Kelly	3	1	1	2	2
Stanislav Gron	5	1	1	2	2
Jiri Bicek	4	0	2	2	0
Andre Lakos	5	0	2	2	4
Pierre Dagenais	5	1	0	1	14
David Maley	5	0	1	1	4
Scott Cameron	1	0	0	0	0
Jean-Francois Damphousse (g)	2	0	0	0	0
George Awada	4	0	0	0	0
Frederic Henry (goalie)	4	0	0	0	0
Carlyle Lewis	4	0	0	0	0
Lucas Nehrling	4	0	0	0	0
Daryl Andrews	5	0	0	0	0
Sylvain Cloutier	5	0	0	0	6
David Cunniff	5	0	0	0	4
Sasha Lakovic	5	0	0	0	14
Richard Rochefort	5	0	0	0	0
Jeff Williams	5	0	0	0	2

GOALTENDING

	Gms.	Min.	W	L	T	G	SO	Avg.
Frederic Henry	4	236	2	2	0	6	1	1.52
J.F. Damphousse	2	62	0	1	0	4	0	3.86

HAMILTON BULLDOGS
(Lost conference semifinals to Rochester, 4-2)

SCORING

	Games	G	A	Pts.	PIM
Michel Riesen	10	3	5	8	4
Sean Selmser	10	3	4	7	10
Brian Swanson	10	2	5	7	6
Daniel Cleary	5	2	3	5	18
Rob Murray	10	2	3	5	4
Brad Norton	10	1	4	5	26
Kevin Brown	4	2	2	4	8
Sergei Yerkovich	10	1	3	4	16
Dan LaCouture	6	2	1	3	0
Alexander Zhurik	10	0	3	3	10
Maxim Spiridonov	4	1	1	2	0
Alain Nasreddine	10	1	1	2	14
Jason Chimera	10	0	2	2	12
Chris Hajt	10	0	2	2	0
Chad Hinz	5	1	0	1	0
Brian Urick	6	1	0	1	0
Ryan Risidore	10	1	0	1	17
Elias Abrahamsson	10	0	1	1	4

	Games	G	A	Pts.	PIM
Kevin Bolibruck	10	0	1	1	4
Joaquin Gage (goalie)	10	0	1	1	2
Mike Minard (goalie)	1	0	0	0	0
Adam Copeland	2	0	0	0	0
Alexei Semenov	3	0	0	0	0
Martin Laitre	5	0	0	0	6

GOALTENDING

	Gms.	Min.	W	L	T	G	SO	Avg.
Mike Minard	1	23	0	0	0	0	0	0.00
Joaquin Gage	10	580	5	5	0	28	0	2.89

HARTFORD WOLFPACK
(Winner of 2000 Calder Cup playoffs)

SCORING

	Games	G	A	Pts.	PIM
Brad Smyth	23	13	10	23	8
Derek Armstrong	23	7	16	23	24
Jason Dawe	21	10	7	17	37
Johan Witehall	17	6	7	13	10
P.J. Stock	23	1	11	12	69
Chris Kenady	21	8	3	11	40
Drew Bannister	18	2	9	11	53
Ken Gernander	23	5	5	10	0
Terry Virtue	23	3	7	10	51
Todd Hall	23	2	6	8	8
Chris Wells	20	3	4	7	38
Jason Doig	21	1	5	6	20
Alexei Vasiliev	15	3	1	4	2
Tony Tuzzolino	19	2	2	4	16
Mike Harder	12	0	4	4	4
Tomas Kloucek	23	0	4	4	18
Daniel Goneau	22	1	2	3	6
Manny Malhotra	23	1	2	3	10
Dale Purinton	23	0	3	3	87
Jean-Francois Labbe (goalie)	22	0	2	2	14
Pavel Brendl	2	0	0	0	0
Benjamin Carpentier	3	0	0	0	2
Milan Hnilicka (goalie)	3	0	0	0	0
Burke Henry	5	0	0	0	2

GOALTENDING

	Gms.	Min.	W	L	T	G	SO	Avg.
J.F. Labbe	22	1320	15	7	0	48	3	2.18
Milan Hnilicka	3	99	0	1	0	6	0	3.64

HERSHEY BEARS
(Lost conference finals to Rochester, 4-0)

SCORING

	Games	G	A	Pts.	PIM
Christian Matte	14	8	6	14	10
Steffon Walby	14	3	9	12	11
Dan Hinote	14	4	5	9	19

	Games	G	A	Pts.	PIM
Rob Shearer	14	1	8	9	10
Brian Willsie	12	2	6	8	8
Mike Gaul	12	0	8	8	6
Brad Larsen	14	5	2	7	29
Yuri Babenko	14	4	3	7	37
Ville Nieminen	9	2	5	7	6
Rick Berry	13	2	3	5	39
Nick Bootland	14	2	2	4	26
Ben Storey	14	2	2	4	8
Brian White	14	0	3	3	21
Alexander Ryazantsev	6	1	1	2	0
Scott Parker	11	1	1	2	56
Guy Dupuis	14	1	1	2	12
Frank Bialowas	8	1	0	1	32
Kelly Perrault	5	0	1	1	4
Evgeny Lazarev	8	0	1	1	2
Jordan Krestanovich	1	0	0	0	0
Frederic Cassivi (goalie)	2	0	0	0	0
K.C. Timmons	4	0	0	0	15
Sami Helenius	9	0	0	0	40
David Aebischer (goalie)	14	0	0	0	6

GOALTENDING

	Gms.	Min.	W	L	T	G	SO	Avg.
David Aebischer	14	788	7	6	0	40	2	3.05
Frederic Cassivi	2	63	0	1	0	5	0	4.75

KENTUCKY THOROUGHBLADES
(Lost conference semifinals to Hershey, 4-1)

SCORING

	Games	G	A	Pts.	PIM
Mike Craig	9	5	5	10	14
Matt Bradley	9	6	3	9	9
Eric Landry	9	3	6	9	2
Chris Lipsett	9	0	7	7	8
Shawn Heins	9	3	3	6	44
Jon Coleman	9	2	4	6	2
Chris Armstrong	9	1	5	6	4
Larry Courville	9	1	5	6	16
Peter Roed	9	3	2	5	2
Mark Smith	9	0	5	5	22
Ryan Kraft	5	3	1	4	0
Doug Friedman	9	1	3	4	45
Robert Jindrich	9	0	4	4	6
Jarrett Deuling	8	1	1	2	6
Adam Colagiacomo	1	1	0	1	0
Brantt Myhres	7	0	1	1	21
Andy Lundbohm	2	0	0	0	5
Rejean Stringer	2	0	0	0	0
Garrett Burnett	4	0	0	0	31
Johan Hedberg (goalie)	5	0	0	0	2
Miikka Kiprusoff (goalie)	5	0	0	0	2
Christian Gosselin	9	0	0	0	34
Robert Mulick	9	0	0	0	10

GOALTENDING

	Gms.	Min.	W	L	T	G	SO	Avg.
Johan Hedberg	5	311	3	2	0	10	1	1.93
Miikka Kiprusoff	5	239	1	3	0	13	0	3.27

LOUISVILLE PANTHERS
(Lost conference quarterfinals to Kentucky, 3-1)

SCORING

	Games	G	A	Pts.	PIM
Eric Boguniecki	4	3	2	5	20
Craig Ferguson	4	1	3	4	2
Peter Ratchuk	4	1	2	3	0
Paul Brousseau	4	1	1	2	12
Craig Reichert	4	1	1	2	2
Dan Boyle	4	0	2	2	8
Ivan Novoseltsev	4	1	0	1	6
David Duerden	4	0	1	1	0

	Games	G	A	Pts.	PIM
Brad Fenence	2	0	0	0	2
Paul Harvey	2	0	0	0	0
Wes Mason	3	0	0	0	0
Brent Thompson	3	0	0	0	11
Chad Cabana	4	0	0	0	26
Sean Gauthier (goalie)	4	0	0	0	0
Marcus Nilson	4	0	0	0	2
Nick Smith	4	0	0	0	0
Joey Tetarenko	4	0	0	0	2
Rocky Thompson	4	0	0	0	4
Lance Ward	4	0	0	0	6
Jeff Ware	4	0	0	0	4

GOALTENDING

	Gms.	Min.	W	L	T	G	SO	Avg.
Sean Gauthier	4	239	1	3	0	14	0	3.52

LOWELL LOCK MONSTERS
(Lost conference semifinals to Providence, 4-0)

SCORING

	Games	G	A	Pts.	PIM
Eric Belanger	7	3	3	6	2
Vladimir Orszagh	7	3	3	6	2
Rich Brennan	7	1	5	6	0
Craig Charron	7	2	3	5	4
Mark Lawrence	7	2	2	4	10
Vladimir Chebaturkin	7	0	4	4	11
Greg Phillips	7	3	0	3	10
Chris Schmidt	7	2	1	3	8
Dmitri Nabokov	6	1	2	3	2
Jeff Daw	7	1	2	3	6
Mike Watt	7	1	1	2	4
Roberto Luongo	6	0	1	1	0
Cody Bowtell	7	0	1	1	2
Dave MacIsaac	7	0	1	1	4
Travis Scott (goalie)	1	0	0	0	2
Sean Blanchard	3	0	0	0	2
Jason Podollan	4	0	0	0	4
Evgeny Korolev	6	0	0	0	4
Petr Mika	6	0	0	0	0
Eric Brewer	7	0	0	0	0
Ray Giroux	7	0	0	0	2

GOALTENDING

	Gms.	Min.	W	L	T	G	SO	Avg.
Travis Scott	1	60	0	1	0	2	0	2.01
Roberto Luongo	6	359	3	3	0	18	0	3.01

PHILADELPHIA PHANTOMS
(Lost conference quarterfinals to Hershey, 3-2)

SCORING

	Games	G	A	Pts.	PIM
Mark Greig	5	3	2	5	6
Dean Melanson	4	2	3	5	10
Jeff Tory	5	1	3	4	4
Todd White	5	2	1	3	8
Mike Maneluk	4	1	2	3	4
Mikhail Chernov	5	1	2	3	22
Tomas Divisek	5	0	3	3	2
Kirby Law	5	2	0	2	2
Jesse Boulerice	4	0	2	2	4
Steve Washburn	5	0	2	2	8
Travis Brigley	5	1	0	1	4
Todd Fedoruk	5	0	1	1	2
Francis Lessard	5	0	1	1	7
Bruno St. Jacques	1	0	0	0	0
Ruslan Fedotenko	2	0	0	0	0
Mark Murphy	2	0	0	0	0
Jeff Lank	3	0	0	0	2
Ryan Bast	5	0	0	0	0
Matt Henderson	5	0	0	0	4
Neil Little (goalie)	5	0	0	0	0
Sean O'Brien	5	0	0	0	2

GOALTENDING

	Gms.	Min.	W	L	T	G	SO	Avg.
Neil Little	5	298	2	3	0	15	0	3.02

PORTLAND PIRATES

(Lost conference quarterfinals to Worcester, 3-1)

SCORING

	Games	G	A	Pts.	PIM
Nolan Baumgartner	4	1	2	3	10
Mike Peluso	4	2	0	2	0
Trent Whitfield	3	1	1	2	2
Brad Church	4	1	1	2	4
Matt Herr	4	1	1	2	4
Jeff Toms	4	1	1	2	2
Krys Barch	4	0	2	2	2
Darren McAusland	4	0	2	2	2
Glen Metropolit	1	1	0	1	0
Steve Poapst	3	1	0	1	2
Mike Farrell	4	0	1	1	0
Jeff Nelson	1	0	0	0	0
Richard Pitirri	1	0	0	0	0
Martin Brochu (goalie)	2	0	0	0	0
Jason Shmyr	2	0	0	0	2
Jean-Francois Fortin	2	0	0	0	0
Sebastien Charpentier (goalie)	3	0	0	0	0
Ryan Mulhern	3	0	0	0	6
Patrick Boileau	4	0	0	0	4
Jakub Ficenec	4	0	0	0	4
Kent Hulst	4	0	0	0	0
Jamie Huscroft	4	0	0	0	14
Barrie Moore	4	0	0	0	6

GOALTENDING

	Gms.	Min.	W	L	T	G	SO	Avg.
S. Charpentier	3	183	1	1	0	9	0	2.96
Martin Brochu	2	80	0	2	0	7	0	5.27

PROVIDENCE BRUINS

(Lost conference finals to Hartford, 4-3)

SCORING

	Games	G	A	Pts.	PIM
Eric Manlow	14	6	8	14	8
Cameron Mann	11	6	7	13	0
Andre Savage	14	6	7	13	22
Peter Ferraro	13	5	7	12	14
Brandon Smith	14	1	11	12	2
Antti Laaksonen	14	5	4	9	4
Aris Brimanis	14	3	4	7	10
Joel Prpic	14	3	4	7	58
Bob Beers	14	1	5	6	9
Landon Wilson	9	2	3	5	38
Eric Nickulas	12	2	3	5	20
Duane Harmer	10	1	4	5	4
Terry Hollinger	10	1	4	5	6
Jason Krog	6	2	2	4	0
Jay Henderson	14	1	2	3	16
Peter Vandermeer	9	0	3	3	2
Jeff Wells	6	2	0	2	0
Johnathan Aitken	11	1	0	1	26
Nick Boynton	12	1	0	1	6
Jeremy Brown	14	1	0	1	6
Aaron Downey	14	1	0	1	37
Kay Whitmore (goalie)	1	0	0	0	0
John Grahame (goalie)	13	0	0	0	4

GOALTENDING

	Gms.	Min.	W	L	T	G	SO	Avg.
Kay Whitmore	1	59	0	1	0	2	0	2.04
John Grahame	13	839	10	3	0	35	0	2.50

QUEBEC CITADELLES

(Lost conference quarterfinals to Providence, 3-0)

SCORING

	Games	G	A	Pts.	PIM
Pierre Sevigny	3	3	0	3	17
Jason Ward	3	2	1	3	4
Xavier Delisle	3	1	2	3	0
Andrei Bashkirov	3	0	3	3	0
Jesse Belanger	3	0	3	3	4
Stephane Roy	3	1	1	2	0
Patrice Tardif	3	1	1	2	8
Francois Groleau	3	0	2	2	0
Marc Beaucage	3	1	0	1	4
Mathieu Descoteaux	2	0	1	1	0
Josh DeWolf	3	0	1	1	0
Stephane Robidas	3	0	1	1	0
Mathieu Garon (goalie)	1	0	0	0	0
Arron Asham	2	0	0	0	2
Dave Morissette	2	0	0	0	0
Chris Albert	3	0	0	0	0
Jonathan Delisle	3	0	0	0	4
Eric Fichaud (goalie)	3	0	0	0	10
Miloslav Guren	3	0	0	0	2
Mike McBain	3	0	0	0	2
Gennady Razin	3	0	0	0	0

GOALTENDING

	Gms.	Min.	W	L	T	G	SO	Avg.
Eric Fichaud	3	177	0	3	0	10	0	3.39
Mathieu Garon	1	20	0	0	0	3	0	8.82

ROCHESTER AMERICANS

(Lost league finals to Hartford, 4-2)

SCORING

	Games	G	A	Pts.	PIM
Domenic Pittis	21	4	26	30	28
Jean-Pierre Dumont	21	14	7	21	32
Jeremy Adduono	21	6	11	17	2
Denis Hamel	21	6	7	13	49
Mike Hurlbut	21	5	6	11	14
Dmitri Kalinin	21	2	9	11	8
Doug Houda	21	1	8	9	39
Jason Cipolla	21	4	4	8	27
Matt Davidson	19	4	2	6	8
Joe Murphy	21	4	2	6	27
Francois Methot	21	2	4	6	16
Maxim Afinogenov	8	3	1	4	4
Darren VanOene	21	1	3	4	24
Eric Boulton	18	2	1	3	53
Brian Campbell	21	0	3	3	0
Tom Buckley	6	1	0	1	0
Jason Holland	12	1	0	1	2
Chris Aldous	4	0	1	1	0
Jean-Luc Grand-Pierre	17	0	1	1	40
Jared Bednar	1	0	0	0	0
Joe Bianchi	1	0	0	0	0
Kirk Daubenspeck (goalie)	1	0	0	0	0
Ryan Mougenel	1	0	0	0	0
Curtis Stanford	1	0	0	0	0
Ben Schust	2	0	0	0	0
Paul Traynor	9	0	0	0	6
Mika Noronen (goalie)	21	0	0	0	6

GOALTENDING

	Gms.	Min.	W	L	T	G	SO	Avg.
Mika Noronen	21	1235	13	8	0	37	6	1.80
Curtis Stanford	1	14	0	0	0	1	0	4.25
Kirk Daubenspeck	1	4	0	0	0	1	0	14.06

SAINT JOHN FLAMES
(Lost conference quarterfinals to Lowell, 3-0)

SCORING

	Games	G	A	Pts.	PIM
Lee Sorochan	3	2	1	3	12
Darrel Scoville	3	1	2	3	0
Lee Jinman	3	1	1	2	0
Ronald Petrovicky	3	1	1	2	6
Benoit Gratton	3	0	1	1	4
Brett McLean	3	0	1	1	2
Dave Roche	3	0	1	1	8
Chris St. Croix	3	0	1	1	2
Curtis Sheptak	1	0	0	0	2
Jason Bowen	2	0	0	0	4
Steve Montador	2	0	0	0	0
Jeff Staples	2	0	0	0	0
Jason Botterill	3	0	0	0	19
Rico Fata	3	0	0	0	4
Jean-Sebastien Giguere (goalie)	3	0	0	0	0
Matt O'Dette	3	0	0	0	0
Jody Shelley	3	0	0	0	2
Daniel Tkaczuk	3	0	0	0	0
John Tripp	3	0	0	0	2
Sergei Varlamov	3	0	0	0	24

GOALTENDING

	Gms.	Min.	W	L	T	G	SO	Avg.
J.-S. Giguere	3	178	0	3	0	9	0	3.03

SYRACUSE CRUNCH
(Lost conference quarterfinals to Hamilton, 3-1)

SCORING

	Games	G	A	Pts.	PIM
Jarkko Ruutu	4	3	1	4	8
Steve Kariya	4	2	1	3	0
Harold Druken	4	1	2	3	6
Lubomir Vaic	4	0	3	3	8
Zenith Komarniski	4	2	0	2	6
Sean McCann	4	0	2	2	0
Brent Sopel	4	0	2	2	8
Josh Holden	4	1	0	1	10
Ryan Bonni	2	0	1	1	2
Brian Bonin	4	0	1	1	0
Chris O'Sullivan	4	0	1	1	0
Artem Chubarov	1	0	0	0	0
Bryan Allen	2	0	0	0	2
Ryan Ready	2	0	0	0	0
Chad Allan	4	0	0	0	0
Mike Brown	4	0	0	0	0
Pat Kavanagh	4	0	0	0	0
Brad Leeb	4	0	0	0	6
Reggie Savage	4	0	0	0	8
Corey Schwab (goalie)	4	0	0	0	0

GOALTENDING

	Gms.	Min.	W	L	T	G	SO	Avg.
Corey Schwab	4	246	1	3	0	11	1	2.69

SPRINGFIELD FALCONS
(Lost conference quarterfinals to Hartford, 3-2)

SCORING

	Games	G	A	Pts.	PIM
Wyatt Smith	5	2	3	5	13
Philippe Audet	5	3	1	4	14
Eric Houde	5	2	2	4	2
Chris Winnes	5	2	2	4	0
Brad Tiley	5	0	4	4	2
Tavis Hansen	5	2	1	3	4
Craig Mills	5	2	1	3	6
Jeremiah McCarthy	5	1	1	2	0
Martin Gendron	4	0	2	2	4
David Bell	5	1	0	1	2
Jean-Guy Trudel	3	0	1	1	4
Ryan Huska	4	0	1	1	0
Dan Focht	5	0	1	1	2
Shayne Toporowski	5	0	1	1	10
Eric Healey	1	0	0	0	2
David Cullen	2	0	0	0	2
Patrick DesRochers (goalie)	2	0	0	0	0
Robert Francz	2	0	0	0	0
Robert Esche (goalie)	3	0	0	0	0
Kevin Sawyer	4	0	0	0	6
Francois Leroux	5	0	0	0	2
Robert Schnabel	5	0	0	0	4
Mark Streit	5	0	0	0	2

GOALTENDING

	Gms.	Min.	W	L	T	G	SO	Avg.
Patrick DesRochers	2	120	1	1	0	7	1	3.50
Robert Esche	3	180	1	2	0	12	0	4.01

WORCESTER ICECATS
(Lost conference semifinals to Hartford, 4-1)

SCORING

	Games	G	A	Pts.	PIM
Jame Pollock	9	5	3	8	6
Jamie Thompson	7	3	5	8	6
Sylvain Blouin	8	3	5	8	30
Andrej Podkonicky	9	2	5	7	6
Tyler Rennette	7	2	3	5	4
Daniel Corso	9	2	3	5	10
Bryan Helmer	9	1	4	5	10
Marc Brown	9	3	1	4	0
Reed Low	9	1	3	4	16
Jim Campbell	9	1	2	3	6
Tyler Willis	9	1	2	3	8
Derek Bekar	7	0	3	3	2
Shawn Mamane	3	1	1	2	0
Darren Rumble	9	0	2	2	6
Ladislav Nagy	2	1	0	1	0
Trevor Wasyluk	4	1	0	1	0
Brent Johnson (goalie)	9	0	1	1	0
Dan Keczmer	9	0	1	1	10
Bryce Salvador	9	0	1	1	2
Dale Clarke	2	0	0	0	0
Barret Jackman	2	0	0	0	13
Peter Smrek	2	0	0	0	4
Libor Prochazka	3	0	0	0	2
Jan Horacek	9	0	0	0	2

GOALTENDING

	Gms.	Min.	W	L	T	G	SO	Avg.
Brent Johnson	9	561	4	5	0	23	1	2.46

1999-2000 AWARD WINNERS

ALL-STAR TEAMS

First team	Pos.	Second team
Martin Brochu, Portland	G	Mika Noronen, Rochester
Brad Tiley, Springfield	D	Mike Gaul, Hershey
Shawn Heins, Kentucky	D	Dan Boyle, Louisville
Mike Maneluk, Philadelphia	LW	Jean-Guy Trudel, Springfield
Serge Aubin, Hershey	C	Derek Armstrong, Hartford
Christian Matte, Hershey	RW	Daniel Cleary, Hamilton

TROPHY WINNERS

John B. Sollenberger Trophy: Christian Matte, Hershey
Les Cunningham Award: Martin Brochu, Portland
Harry (Hap) Holmes Memorial Trophy:
   Milan Hnilicka, Hartford
   Jean-Francois Labbe, Hartford
Dudley (Red) Garrett Memorial Trophy: Mika Noronen, Rochester
Eddie Shore Award: Brad Tiley, Springfield

Fred Hunt Memorial Award: Randy Cunneyworth, Rochester
Louis A.R. Pieri Memorial Award: Glen Hanlon, Portland

Baz Bastien Trophy: Martin Biron, Rochester
Jack Butterfield Trophy: Peter Ferraro, Providence

ALL-TIME AWARD WINNERS

JOHN B. SOLLENBERGER TROPHY
(Leading scorer)

Season	Player, Team
1936-37	Jack Markle, Syracuse
1937-38	Jack Markle, Syracuse
1938-39	Don Deacon, Pittsburgh
1939-40	Norm Locking, Syracuse
1940-41	Les Cunningham, Cleveland
1941-42	Pete Kelly, Springfield
1942-43	Wally Kilrea, Hershy
1943-44	Tommy Burlington, Cleveland
1944-45	Bob Gracie, Pittsburgh
	Bob Walton, Pittsburgh
1945-46	Les Douglas, Indianapolis
1946-47	Phil Hergesheimer, Philadelphia
1947-48	Carl Liscombe, Providence
1948-49	Sid Smith, Pittsburgh
1949-50	Les Douglas, Cleveland
1950-51	Ab DeMarco, Buffalo
1951-52	Ray Powell, Providence
1952-53	Eddie Olson, Cleveland
1953-54	George Sullivan, Hershey
1954-55	Eddie Olson, Cleveland
1955-56	Zellio Toppazzini, Providence
1956-57	Fred Glover, Cleveland
1957-58	Willie Marshall, Hershey
1958-59	Bill Hicke, Rochester
1959-60	Fred Glover, Cleveland
1960-61	Bill Sweeney, Springfield
1961-62	Bill Sweeney, Springfield
1962-63	Bill Sweeney, Springfield
1963-64	Gerry Ehman, Rochester
1964-65	Art Stratton, Buffalo
1965-66	Dick Gamble, Rochester
1966-67	Gordon Labossiere, Quebec
1967-68	Simon Nolet, Quebec
1968-69	Jeannot Gilbert, Hershey
1969-70	Jude Drouin, Montreal
1970-71	Fred Speck, Baltimore
1971-72	Don Blackburn, Providence
1972-73	Yvon Lambert, Nova Scotia
1973-74	Steve West, New Haven
1974-75	Doug Gibson, Rochester
1975-76	Jean-Guy Gratton, Hershey
1976-77	Andre Peloffy, Springfield
1977-78	Gord Brooks, Philadelphia
	Rick Adduono, Rochester
1978-79	Bernie Johnston, Maine
1979-80	Norm Dube, Nova Scotia
1980-81	Mark Lofthouse, Hershey
1981-82	Mike Kasczyki, New Brunswick
1982-83	Ross Yates, Binghamton
1983-84	Claude Larose, Sherbrooke
1984-85	Paul Gardner, Binghamton
1985-86	Paul Gardner, Rochester
1986-87	Tim Tookey, Hershey
1987-88	Bruce Boudreau, Springfield
1988-89	Stephan Lebeau, Sherbrooke
1989-90	Paul Ysebaert, Utica
1990-91	Kevin Todd, Utica
1991-92	Shaun Van Allen, Cape Breton
1992-93	Don Biggs, Binghamton
1993-94	Tim Taylor, Adirondack
1994-95	Peter White, Cape Breton
1995-96	Brad Smyth, Carolina
1996-97	Peter White, Philadelphia
1997-98	Peter White, Philadelphia
1998-99	Domenic Pittis, Rochester
1999-00	Christian Matte, Hershey

LES CUNNINGHAM AWARD
(Most Valuable Player)

Season	Player, Team
1947-48	Carl Liscombe, Providence
1948-49	Carl Liscombe, Providence
1949-50	Les Douglas, Cleveland
1950-51	Ab DeMarco, Buffalo
1951-52	Ray Powell, Providence
1952-53	Eddie Olson, Cleveland
1953-54	George "Red" Sullivan, Hershey
1954-55	Ross Lowe, Springfield
1955-56	Johnny Bower, Providence
1956-57	Johnny Bower, Providence
1957-58	Johnny Bower, Cleveland
1958-59	Bill Hicke, Rochester
	Rudy Migay, Rochester
1959-60	Fred Glover, Cleveland
1960-61	Phil Maloney, Buffalo
1961-62	Fred Glover, Cleveland
1962-63	Denis DeJordy, Buffalo
1963-64	Fred Glover, Cleveland
1964-65	Art Stratton, Buffalo
1965-66	Dick Gamble, Rochester
1966-67	Mike Nykoluk, Hershey
1967-68	Dave Creighton, Providence
1968-69	Gilles Villemure, Buffalo
1969-70	Gilles Villemure, Buffalo
1970-71	Fred Speck, Baltimore
1971-72	Garry Peters, Boston
1972-73	Billy Inglis, Cincinnati
1973-74	Art Stratton, Rochester
1974-75	Doug Gibson, Rochester
1975-76	Ron Andruff, Nova Scotia
1976-77	Doug Gibson, Rochester
1977-78	Blake Dunlop, Maine
1978-79	Rocky Saganiuk, New Brunswick
1979-80	Norm Dube, Nova Scotia
1980-81	Pelle Lindbergh, Maine
1981-82	Mike Kasczyki, New Brunswick
1982-83	Ross Yates, Binghamton
1983-84	Mal Davis, Rochester
	Garry Lariviere, St. Catharines
1984-85	Paul Gardner, Binghamton
1985-86	Paul Gardner, Rochester
1986-87	Tim Tookey, Hershey
1987-88	Jody Gage, Rochester
1988-89	Stephan Lebeau, Sherbrooke
1989-90	Paul Ysebaert, Utica
1990-91	Kevin Todd, Utica
1991-92	John Anderson, Hew Haven
1992-93	Don Biggs, Binghamton
1993-94	Rich Chernomaz, St. John's
1994-95	Steve Larouche, Prince Edward Island
1995-96	Brad Smyth, Carolina
1996-97	Jean-Francois Labbe, Hershey
1997-98	Steve Guolla, Kentucky
1998-99	Randy Robitaille, Providence
1999-00	Martin Brochu, Portland

HARRY (HAP) HOLMES MEMORIAL TROPHY
(Outstanding goaltender)

Season	Player, Team
1936-37	Bert Gardiner, Philadelphia
1937-38	Frank Brimsek, Providence
1938-39	Alfie Moore, Hershey
1939-40	Moe Roberts, Cleveland
1940-41	Chuck Rayner, Springfield
1941-42	Bill Beveridge, Cleveland
1942-43	Gordie Bell, Buffalo

Season	Player, Team
1943-44	Nick Damore, Hershey
1944-45	Yves Nadon, Buffalo
1945-46	Connie Dion, St. Louis-Buffalo
1946-47	Baz Bastien, Pittsburgh
1947-48	Baz Bastien, Pittsburgh
1948-49	Baz Bastien, Pittsburgh
1949-50	Gil Mayer, Pittsburgh
1950-51	Gil Mayer, Pittsburgh
1951-52	Johnny Bower, Cleveland
1952-53	Gil Mayer, Pittsburgh
1953-54	Jacques Plante, Buffalo
1954-55	Gil Mayer, Pittsburgh
1955-56	Gil Mayer, Pittsburgh
1956-57	Johnny Bower, Providence
1957-58	Johnny Bower, Cleveland
1958-59	Bob Perreault, Hershey
1959-60	Ed Chadwick, Rochester
1960-61	Marcel Paille, Springfield
1961-62	Marcel Paille, Springfield
1962-63	Denis DeJordy, Buffalo
1963-64	Roger Crozier, Pittsburgh
1964-65	Gerry Cheevers, Rochester
1965-66	Les Binkley, Cleveland
1966-67	Andre Gill, Hershey
1967-68	Bob Perreault, Rochester
1968-69	Gilles Villemure, Buffalo
1969-70	Gilles Villemure, Buffalo
1970-71	Gary Kurt, Cleveland
1971-72	Dan Bouchard, Boston
	Ross Brooks, Boston
1972-73	Michel Larocque, Nova Scotia
1973-74	Jim Shaw, Nova Scotia
	Dave Elenbaas, Nova Scotia
1974-75	Ed Walsh, Nova Scotia
	Dave Elenbaas, Nova Scotia
1975-76	Dave Elenbaas, Nova Scotia
	Ed Walsh, Nova Scotia
1976-77	Ed Walsh, Nova Scotia
	Dave Elenbaas, Nova Scotia
1977-78	Bob Holland, Nova Scotia
	Maurice Barrette, Nova Scotia
1978-79	Pete Peeters, Maine
	Robbie Moore, Maine
1979-80	Rick St. Croix, Maine
	Robbie Moore, Maine
1980-81	Pelle Lindbergh, Maine
	Robbie Moore, Maine
1981-82	Bob Janecyk, New Brunswick
	Warren Skorodenski, New Brunswick
1982-83	Brian Ford, Fredericton
	Clint Malarchuk, Fredericton
1983-84	Brian Ford, Fredericton
1984-85	Jon Casey, Baltimore
1985-86	Sam St. Laurent, Maine
	Karl Friesen, Maine
1986-87	Vincent Riendeau, Sherbrooke
1987-88	Vincent Riendeau, Sherbrooke
	Jocelyn Perreault, Sherbrooke
1988-89	Randy Exelby, Sherbrooke
	Francois Gravel, Sherbrooke
1989-90	Jean Claude Bergeron, Sherbrooke
	Andre Racicot, Sherbrooke
1990-91	David Littman, Rochester
	Darcy Wakaluk, Rochester
1991-92	David Littman, Rochester
1992-93	Corey Hirsch, Binghamton
	Boris Rousson, Binghamton
1993-94	Byron Dafoe, Portland
	Olaf Kolzig, Portland
1994-95	Mike Dunham, Albany
	Corey Schwab, Albany
1995-96	Scott Langkow, Springfield
	Manny Legace, Springfield
1996-97	Jean-Francois Labbe, Hershey

Season	Player, Team
1997-98	Jean-Sebastien Giguere, Saint John
	Tyler Moss, Saint John
1998-99	Martin Biron, Rochester
	Tom Draper, Rochester
1999-00	Milan Hnilicka, Hartford
	Jean-Francois Labbe, Hartford

Beginning with the 1983-84 season, the award goes to the top goaltending team with each goaltender having played a minimum of 25 games for the team with the fewest goals against.

DUDLEY (RED) GARRETT MEMORIAL TROPHY
(Top rookie)

Season	Player, Team
1947-48	Bob Solinger, Cleveland
1948-49	Terry Sawchuk, Indianapolis
1949-50	Paul Meger, Buffalo
1950-51	Wally Hergesheimer, Cleveland
1951-52	Earl "Dutch" Reibel, Indianapolis
1952-53	Guyle Fielder, St. Louis
1953-54	Don Marshall, Buffalo
1954-55	Jimmy Anderson, Springfield
1955-56	Bruce Cline, Providence
1956-57	Boris "Bo" Elik, Cleveland
1957-58	Bill Sweeney, Providence
1958-59	Bill Hicke, Rochester
1959-60	Stan Baluik, Providence
1960-61	Ronald "Chico" Maki, Buffalo
1961-62	Les Binkley, Cleveland
1962-63	Doug Robinson, Buffalo
1963-64	Roger Crozier, Pittsburgh
1964-65	Ray Cullen, Buffalo
1965-66	Mike Walton, Rochester
1966-67	Bob Rivard, Quebec
1967-68	Gerry Desjardins, Cleveland
1968-69	Ron Ward, Rochester
1969-70	Jude Drouin, Montreal
1970-71	Fred Speck, Baltimore
1971-72	Terry Caffery, Cleveland
1972-73	Ron Anderson, Boston
1973-74	Rick Middleton, Providence
1974-75	Jerry Holland, Providence
1975-76	Greg Holst, Providence
	Pierre Mondou, Nova Scotia
1976-77	Rod Schutt, Nova Scotia
1977-78	Norm Dupont, Nova Scotia
1978-79	Mike Meeker, Binghamton
1979-80	Darryl Sutter, New Brunswick
1980-81	Pelle Lindbergh, Maine
1981-82	Bob Sullivan, Binghamton
1982-83	Mitch Lamoureux, Baltimore
1983-84	Claude Verret, Rochester
1984-85	Steve Thomas, St. Catharines
1985-86	Ron Hextall, Hershey
1986-87	Brett Hull, Moncton
1987-88	Mike Richard, Binghamton
1988-89	Stephan Lebeau, Sherbrooke
1989-90	Donald Audette, Rochester
1990-91	Patrick Lebeau, Fredericton
1991-92	Felix Potvin, St. John's
1992-93	Corey Hirsch, Binghamton
1993-94	Rene Corbet, Cornwall
1994-95	Jim Carey, Portland
1995-96	Darcy Tucker, Fredericton
1996-97	Jaroslav Svejkovsky, Portland
1997-98	Daniel Briere, Springfield
1998-99	Shane Willis, New Haven
1999-00	Mika Noronen, Rochester

EDDIE SHORE PLAQUE
(Outstanding defenseman)

Season	Player, Team
1958-59	Steve Kraftcheck, Rochester
1959-60	Larry Hillman, Providence
1960-61	Bob McCord, Springfield

Season	Player, Team
1961-62	Kent Douglas, Springfield
1962-63	Marc Reaume, Hershey
1963-64	Ted Harris, Cleveland
1964-65	Al Arbour, Rochester
1965-66	Jim Morrison, Quebec
1966-67	Bob McCord, Pittsburgh
1967-68	Bill Needham, Cleveland
1968-69	Bob Blackburn, Buffalo
1969-70	Noel Price, Springfield
1970-71	Marshall Johnston, Cleveland
1971-72	Noel Price, Nova Scotia
1972-73	Ray McKay, Cincinnati
1973-74	Gordon Smith, Springfield
1974-75	Joe Zanussi, Providence
1975-76	Noel Price, Nova Scotia
1976-77	Brian Engblom, Nova Scotia
1977-78	Terry Murray, Maine
1978-79	Terry Murray, Maine
1979-80	Rick Vasko, Adirondack
1980-81	Craig Levie, Nova Scotia
1981-82	Dave Farrish, New Brunswick
1982-83	Greg Tebbutt, Baltimore
1983-84	Garry Lariviere, St. Catharines
1984-85	Richie Dunn, Binghamton
1985-86	Jim Wiemer, New Haven
1986-87	Brad Shaw, Binghamton
1987-88	Dave Fenyves, Hershey
1988-89	Dave Fenyves, Hershey
1989-90	Eric Weinrich, Utica
1990-91	Norm Maciver, Cape Breton
1991-92	Greg Hawgood, Cape Breton
1992-93	Bobby Dollas, Adirondack
1993-94	Chris Snell, St. John's
1994-95	Jeff Serowik, Providence
1995-96	Barry Richter, Binghamton
1996-97	Darren Rumble, Philadelphia
1997-98	Jamie Heward, Philadelphia
1998-99	Ken Sutton, Albany
1999-00	Brad Tiley, Springfield

FRED HUNT MEMORIAL AWARD
(Sportsmanship, determination and dedication)

Season	Player, Team
1977-78	Blake Dunlop, Maine
1978-79	Bernie Johnston, Maine
1979-80	Norm Dube, Nova Scotia
1980-81	Tony Cassolato, Hershey
1981-82	Mike Kasczyki, New Brunswick
1982-83	Ross Yates, Binghamton
1983-84	Claude Larose, Sherbrooke
1984-85	Paul Gardner, Binghamton
1985-86	Steve Tsujiura, Maine
1986-87	Glenn Merkosky, Adirondack
1987-88	Bruce Boudreau, Springfield
1988-89	Murray Eaves, Adirondack
1989-90	Murray Eaves, Adirondack
1990-91	Glenn Merkosky, Adirondack
1991-92	John Anderson, New Haven
1992-93	Tim Tookey, Hershey
1993-94	Jim Nesich, Cape Breton
1994-95	Steve Larouche, Prince Edward Island
1995-96	Ken Gernander, Binghamton
1996-97	Steve Passmore, Hamilton
1997-98	Craig Charron, Rochester
1998-99	Mitch Lamoureux, Hershey
1999-00	Randy Cunneyworth, Rochester

LOUIS A.R. PIERI MEMORIAL AWARD
(Top coach)

Season	Coach, Team
1967-68	Vic Stasiuk, Quebec
1968-69	Frank Mathers, Hershey
1969-70	Fred Shero, Buffalo
1970-71	Terry Reardon, Baltimore

Season	Coach, Team
1971-72	Al MacNeil, Nova Scotia
1972-73	Floyd Smith, Cincinnati
1973-74	Don Cherry, Rochester
1974-75	John Muckler, Providence
1975-76	Chuck Hamilton, Hershey
1976-77	Al MacNeil, Nova Scotia
1977-78	Bob McCammon, Maine
1978-79	Parker MacDonald, New Haven
1979-80	Doug Gibson, Hershey
1980-81	Bob McCammon, Maine
1981-82	Orval Tessier, New Brunswick
1982-83	Jacques Demers, Fredericton
1983-84	Gene Ubriaco, Baltimore
1984-85	Bill Dineen, Adirondack
1985-86	Bill Dineen, Adirondack
1986-87	Larry Pleau, Binghamton
1987-88	John Paddock, Hershey
	Mike Milbury, Maine
1988-89	Tom McVie, Utica
1989-90	Jimmy Roberts, Springfield
1990-91	Don Lever, Rochester
1991-92	Doug Carpenter, New Haven
1992-93	Marc Crawford, St. John's
1993-94	Barry Trotz, Portland
1994-95	Robbie Ftorek, Albany
1995-96	Robbie Ftorek, Albany
1996-97	Greg Gilbert, Worcester
1997-98	Bill Stewart, Saint John
1998-99	Peter Laviolette, Providence
1999-00	Glen Hanlon, Portland

BAZ BASTIEN TROPHY
(Coaches pick as top goaltender)

Season	Player, Team
1983-84	Brian Ford, Fredericton
1984-85	Jon Casey, Baltimore
1985-86	Sam St. Laurent, Maine
1986-87	Mark Laforest, Adirondack
1987-88	Wendell Young, Hershey
1988-89	Randy Exelby, Sherbrooke
1989-90	Jean Claude Bergeron, Sherbrooke
1990-91	Mark Laforest, Binghamton
1991-92	Felix Potvin, St. John's
1992-93	Corey Hirsch, Binghamton
1993-94	Frederic Chabot, Hershey
1994-95	Jim Carey, Portland
1995-96	Manny Legace, Springfield
1996-97	Jean-Francois Labbe, Hershey
1997-98	Scott Langkow, Springfield
1998-99	Martin Biron, Rochester
1999-00	Martin Brochu, Portland

JACK BUTTERFIELD TROPHY
(Calder Cup playoff MVP)

Season	Player, Team
1983-84	Bud Stefanski, Maine
1984-85	Brian Skrudland, Sherbrooke
1985-86	Tim Tookey, Hershey
1986-87	Dave Fenyves, Rochester
1987-88	Wendell Young, Hershey
1988-89	Sam St. Laurent, Adirondack
1989-90	Jeff Hackett, Springfield
1990-91	Kay Whitmore, Springfield
1991-92	Allan Bester, Adirondack
1992-93	Bill McDougall, Cape Breton
1993-94	Olaf Kolzig, Portland
1994-95	Mike Dunham, Albany
	Corey Schwab, Albany
1995-96	Dixon Ward, Rochester
1996-97	Mike McHugh, Hershey
1997-98	Mike Maneluk, Philadelphia
1998-99	Peter Ferraro, Providence
1999-00	Derek Armstrong, Hartford

ALL-TIME LEAGUE CHAMPIONS

	REGULAR-SEASON CHAMPION		PLAYOFF CHAMPION	
Season	Team	Coach	Team	Coach
1936-37—	Philadelphia (E)	Herb Gardiner	Syracuse	Eddie Powers
	Syracuse (W)	Eddie Powers		
1937-38—	Providence (E)	Bun Cook	Providence	Bun Cook
	Cleveland (W)	Bill Cook		
1938-39—	Philadelphia (E)	Herb Gardiner	Cleveland	Bill Cook
	Hershey (W)	Herb Mitchell		
1939-40—	Providence (E)	Bun Cook	Providence	Bun Cook
	Indianapolis (W)	Herb Lewis		
1940-41—	Providence (E)	Bun Cook	Cleveland	Bill Cook
	Cleveland (W)	Bill Cook		
1941-42—	Springfield (E)	Johnny Mitchell	Indianapolis	Herb Lewis
	Indianapolis (W)	Herb Lewis		
1942-43—	Hershey	Cooney Weiland	Buffalo	Art Chapman
1943-44—	Hershey (E)	Cooney Weiland	Buffalo	Art Chapman
	Cleveland (W)	Bun Cook		
1944-45—	Buffalo (E)	Art Chapman	Cleveland	Bun Cook
	Cleveland (W)	Bun Cook		
1945-46—	Buffalo (E)	Frank Beisler	Buffalo	Frank Beisler
	Indianapolis (W)	Earl Seibert		
1946-47—	Hershey (E)	Don Penniston	Hershey	Don Penniston
	Cleveland (W)	Bun Cook		
1947-48—	Providence (E)	Terry Reardon	Cleveland	Bun Cook
	Cleveland (W)	Bun Cook		
1948-49—	Providence (E)	Terry Reardon	Providence	Terry Reardon
	St. Louis (W)	Ebbie Goodfellow		
1949-50—	Buffalo (E)	Roy Goldsworthy	Indianapolis	Ott Heller
	Cleveland (W)	Bun Cook		
1950-51—	Buffalo (E)	Roy Goldsworthy	Cleveland	Bun Cook
	Cleveland (W)	Bun Cook		
1951-52—	Hershey (E)	John Crawford	Pittsburgh	King Clancy
	Pittsburgh (W)	King Clancy		
1952-53—	Cleveland	Bun Cook	Cleveland	Bun Cook
1953-54—	Buffalo	Frank Eddolls	Cleveland	Bun Cook
1954-55—	Pittsburgh	Howie Meeker	Pittsburgh	Howie Meeker
1955-56—	Providence	John Crawford	Providence	John Crawford
1956-57—	Providence	John Crawford	Cleveland	Jack Gordon
1957-58—	Hershey	Frank Mathers	Hershey	Frank Mathers
1958-59—	Buffalo	Bobby Kirk	Hershey	Frank Mathers
1959-60—	Springfield	Pat Egan	Springfield	Pat Egan
1960-61—	Springfield	Pat Egan	Springfield	Pat Egan
1961-62—	Springfield (E)	Pat Egan	Springfield	Pat Egan
	Cleveland (W)	Jack Gordon		
1962-63—	Providence (E)	Fern Flaman	Buffalo	Billy Reay
	Buffalo (W)	Billy Reay		
1963-64—	Quebec (E)	Floyd Curry	Cleveland	Fred Glover
	Pittsburgh (W)	Vic Stasiuk		
1964-65—	Quebec (E)	Bernie Geoffrion	Rochester	Joe Crozier
	Rochester (W)	Joe Crozier		
1965-66—	Quebec (E)	Bernie Geoffrion	Rochester	Joe Crozier
	Rochester (W)	Joe Crozier		
1966-67—	Hershey (E)	Frank Mathers	Pittsburgh	Baz Bastien
	Pittsburgh (W)	Baz Bastien		
1967-68—	Hershey (E)	Frank Mathers	Rochester	Joe Crozier
	Rochester (W)	Joe Crozier		
1968-69—	Hershey (E)	Frank Mathers	Hershey	Frank Mathers
	Buffalo (W)	Fred Shero		
1969-70—	Montreal (E)	Al MacNeil	Buffalo	Fred Shero
	Buffalo (W)	Fred Shero		
1970-71—	Providence (E)	Larry Wilson	Springfield	John Wilson
	Baltimore (W)	Terry Reardon		
1971-72—	Boston (E)	Bep Guidolin	Nova Scotia	Al MacNeil
	Baltimore (W)	Terry Reardon		
1972-73—	Nova Scotia (E)	Al MacNeil	Cincinnati	Floyd Smith
	Cincinnati (W)	Floyd Smith		
1973-74—	Rochester (N)	Don Cherry	Hershey	Chuck Hamilton
	Baltimore (S)	Terry Reardon		
1974-75—	Providence (N)	John Muckler	Springfield	Ron Stewart
	Virginia (S)	Doug Barkley		
1975-76—	Nova Scotia (N)	Al MacNeil	Nova Scotia	Al MacNeil
	Hershey (S)	Chuck Hamilton		

REGULAR-SEASON CHAMPION   PLAYOFF CHAMPION

Season	Team	Coach	Team	Coach
1976-77—	Nova Scotia	Al MacNeil	Nova Scotia	Al MacNeil
1977-78—	Maine (N)	Bob McCammon	Maine	Bob McCammon
	Rochester (S)	Duane Rupp		
1978-79—	Maine (N)	Bob McCammon	Maine	Bob McCammon
	New Haven (S)	Parker MacDonald		
1979-80—	New Brunswick (N)	Joe Crozier-Lou Angotti	Hershey	Doug Gibson
	New Haven (S)	Parker MacDonald		
1980-81—	Maine (N)	Bob McCammon	Adirondack	Tom Webster-J.P. LeBlanc
	Hershey (S)	Bryan Murray		
1981-82—	New Brunswick (N)	Orval Tessier	New Brunswick	Orval Tessier
	Binghamton (S)	Larry Kish		
1982-83—	Fredericton (N)	Jacques Demers	Rochester	Mike Keenan
	Rochester (S)	Mike Keenan		
1983-84—	Fredericton (N)	Earl Jessiman	Maine	John Paddock
	Baltimore (S)	Gene Ubriaco		
1984-85—	Maine (N)	Tom McVie-John Paddock	Sherbrooke	Pierre Creamer
	Binghamton (S)	Larry Pleau		
1985-86—	Adirondack (N)	Bill Dineen	Adirondack	Bill Dineen
	Hershey (S)	John Paddock		
1986-87—	Sherbrooke (N)	Pierre Creamer	Rochester	John Van Boxmeer
	Rochester (S)	John Van Boxmeer*		
1987-88—	Maine (N)	Mike Milbury	Hershey	John Paddock
	Hershey (S)	John Paddock		
1988-89—	Sherbrooke (N)	Jean Hamel	Adirondack	Bill Dineen
	Adirondack (S)	Bill Dineen		
1989-90—	Sherbrooke (N)	Jean Hamel	Springfield	Jimmy Roberts
	Rochester (S)	John Van Boxmeer		
1990-91—	Springfield (N)	Jimmy Roberts	Springfield	Jimmy Roberts
	Rochester (S)	Don Lever		
1991-92—	Springfield (N)	Jay Leach	Adirondack	Barry Melrose
	Binghamton (S)	Ron Smith		
	Fredericton (A)	Paulin Bordeleau		
1992-93—	Providence (N)	Mike O'Connell	Cape Breton	George Burnett
	Binghamton (S)	Ron Smith-Colin Campbell		
	St. John's (A)	Marc Crawford		
1993-94—	Adirondack (N)	Newell Brown	Portland	Barry Trotz
	Hershey (S)	Jay Leach		
	St. John's (A)	Marc Crawford		
1994-95—	Albany (N)	Robbie Ftorek	Albany	Robbie Ftorek
	Binghamton (S)	Al Hill		
	Prince Edward Island (A)	Dave Allison		
1995-96—	Albany (N)	Robbie Ftorek	Rochester	John Tortorella
1996-97—	Philadelphia (MA)	Bill Barber	Hershey	Bob Hartley
1997-98—	Philadelphia (MA)	Bill Barber	Philadelphia	Bill Barber
1998-99—	Providence (NE)	Peter Laviolette	Providence	Peter Laviolette
1999-00—	Hartford (NE)	John Paddock	Hartford	John Paddock

*Rochester awarded division championship based on season-series record.

MINOR LEAGUES *AHL*

— 271 —

INTERNATIONAL HOCKEY LEAGUE

LEAGUE OFFICE

President and chief executive officer
Douglas G. Moss
Vice president of business operations
Mike McEvoy
Vice president of hockey operations
Bob McCammon

Communications managers
Sean Krabach
Nicole Norris

Address
1395 East Twelve Mile Road
Madison Heights, MI 48071
Phone
248-546-3230
FAX
248-546-1811

TEAMS

CHICAGO WOLVES

General manager
Kevin Cheveldayoff
Head coach
John Anderson
Home ice
Allstate Arena
Address
2301 Ravine Way
Glenview, IL 60025
Seating capacity
16,682
Phone
847-724-4625
FAX
847-724-1652

CINCINNATI CYCLONES

General manager and head coach
Ron Smith
Home ice
Firstar Center
Address
100 Broadway
Cincinnati, OH 45202
Seating capacity
10,326
Phone
513-421-7825
FAX
513-421-1210

CLEVELAND LUMBERJACKS

General manager
Larry Gordon
Co-coaches
Perry Ganchar
Blair MacDonald
Phil Russell
Home ice
Gund Arena
Address
One Center Ice
200 Huron Road
Cleveland, OH 44115
Seating capacity
19,941
Phone
216-420-0000
FAX
216-420-2500

DETROIT VIPERS

General manager
Grant Sonier

Head coach
Paulin Bordeleau
Home ice
Palace of Auburn Hills
Address
Two Championship Drive
Auburn Hills, MI 48326
Seating capacity
20,804
Phone
248-377-8613
FAX
248-377-2695

GRAND RAPIDS GRIFFINS

General manager
Bob McNamara
Head coach
Guy Charron
Home ice
Van Andel Arena
Address
130 W. Fulton
Grand Rapids, MI 49503
Seating capacity
10,834
Phone
616-774-4585
FAX
616-336-5464

HOUSTON AEROS

General manager/head coach
Dave Barr
Home ice
Compaq Center
Address
3100 Wilcrest Drive
Houston, TX 77042
Seating capacity
11,207
Phone
713-974-7825
FAX
713-361-7900

KANSAS CITY BLADES

Vice president and general manager
Doug Soetaert
Head coach
Paul MacLean
Home ice
Kemper Arena
Address
1800 Genesee
Kansas City, MO 64102

Seating capacity
17,753
Phone
816-842-5233
FAX
816-842-5610

MANITOBA MOOSE

General manager and head coach
Randy Carlyle
Home ice
Winnipeg Arena
Address
1430 Maroons Road
Winnipeg, Manitoba, Canada R3G 0L5
Seating capacity
10,842
Phone
204-987-7825
FAX
204-896-6673

MILWAUKEE ADMIRALS

General manager and executive v.p.
Phil Wittliff
Head coach
Al Sims
Home ice
Bradley Center
Address
1001 North Fourth St.
Milwaukee, WI 53203
Seating capacity
18,394
Phone
414-227-0550
FAX
414-227-0568

ORLANDO SOLAR BEARS

General manager
John Weisbrod
Head coach
Peter Horachek
Home ice
TD Waterhouse Centre
Address
Two Magic Place
8701 Maitland Summit Blvd.
Orlando, FL 32810
Seating capacity
10,660
Phone
407-916-2400
FAX
407-916-2830

UTAH GRIZZLIES
General manager and head coach
Bob Bourne
Home ice
The "E" Center

Address
3200 S. Decker Lake Dr.
West Valley City, UT 84119
Seating capacity
10,207

Phone
801-988-8000
FAX
801-988-8001

1999-2000 REGULAR SEASON
FINAL STANDINGS

EAST DIVISION

Team	G	W	L	SOP	Pts.	GF	GA
Grand Rapids	82	51	22	9	111	254	200
Orlando	82	47	23	12	106	250	202
Cincinnati	82	44	30	8	96	244	246
Cleveland	82	40	30	12	92	225	238
Milwaukee	82	37	36	9	83	222	246
Michigan	82	33	37	12	78	178	223
Detroit	82	22	52	8	52	163	277

WEST DIVISION

Team	G	W	L	SOP	Pts.	GF	GA
Chicago	82	53	21	8	114	270	228
Utah	82	45	25	12	102	265	220
Houston	82	44	29	9	97	219	197
Long Beach	82	44	31	7	95	234	216
Manitoba	82	37	31	14	88	227	237
Kansas City	82	36	37	9	81	249	270

Note: SOP denotes shootout point. Teams earn one point when game is tied at the end of regulation and enters a shootout. The team that wins the shootout earns an additional point and is credited with a win in the standings.

INDIVIDUAL LEADERS

Goals: Steve Maltais, Chicago (44)
Assists: Steve Larouche, Chicago (57)
Points: Steve Maltais, Chicago (90)
Penalty minutes: Dody Wood, Kansas City (341)
Goaltending average: Nikolai Khabibulin, Long Beach (1.83)
Shutouts: Marty Turco, Michigan (7)

	Games	G	A	Pts.
Brett Harkins, Cleveland	76	20	50	70
Michel Picard, Grand Rapids	65	33	35	68
Todd Simon, Cincinnati	71	19	48	67
Sean Tallaire, Utah	82	31	34	65
Chris Marinucci, Chicago	80	31	33	64
Jeff Christian, Cleveland	77	29	35	64
John Purves, Utah	78	36	27	63
Slava Butsayev, Grand Rapids	68	28	35	63
Brian Noonan, Chicago	80	30	32	62
Kelly Fairchild, Michigan	78	21	41	62
Bill Bowler, Manitoba	75	20	42	62
Mark Lamb, Houston	79	15	46	61
Shane Willis, Cincinnati	80	35	25	60
Richard Park, Utah	82	28	32	60
Sean Haggerty, Kansas City	76	27	33	60
Herbert Vasiljevs, Orlando	73	25	35	60
Brett Hauer, Manitoba	77	13	47	60

TOP SCORERS

	Games	G	A	Pts.
Steve Maltais, Chicago	82	44	46	90
Steve Larouche, Chicago	82	31	57	88
David Ling, Kansas City	82	35	48	83
Gilbert Dionne, Cincinnati	81	34	49	83
Jarrod Skalde, Utah	77	25	54	79
Mark Beaufait, Orlando	78	28	50	78
Dave Chyzowski, Kansas City	81	37	33	70

INDIVIDUAL STATISTICS

CHICAGO WOLVES
SCORING

	Games	G	A	Pts.	PIM
Steve Maltais	82	44	46	90	78
Steve Larouche	82	31	57	88	52
Chris Marinucci	80	31	33	64	18
Brian Noonan	80	30	32	62	80
Bob Nardella	77	10	36	46	26
Nick Andersson	52	20	21	41	59
Tom Tilley	75	2	34	36	42
Scott Pearson	77	19	14	33	124
Guy Larose	79	9	24	33	100
Dallas Eakins	68	5	26	31	99
Chris Ferraro	25	7	18	25	40
Greg Andrusak	54	2	23	25	50
Dan Plante	79	11	11	22	71
Glen Featherstone	62	7	12	19	109
Sean Berens	31	4	9	13	34
Daniel Lacroix	61	3	10	13	194
Mark Lawrence	16	4	6	10	32
Dean Malkoc	62	2	8	10	130
Dave Mackey	45	5	2	7	54
Kris King	15	2	4	6	19
Darrin Shannon	9	1	3	4	6
Chris LiPuma	42	0	4	4	98

	Games	G	A	Pts.	PIM
Derek Plante	4	2	1	3	2
Gord Dineen	17	1	2	3	14
Kevin Dahl	27	1	2	3	44
Andrei Trefilov (goalie)	37	0	1	1	6
Wendell Young (goalie)	48	0	1	1	66
Martin Hlinka	1	0	0	0	0
Brett Lievers	1	0	0	0	0
Lonnie Loach	1	0	0	0	0
Derek Wilkinson (goalie)	1	0	0	0	0
Brent Gretsky	2	0	0	0	0
Jeremy Mylymok	3	0	0	0	6
Guy Dupuis	4	0	0	0	6

GOALTENDING

	Gms.	Min.	W	L	SP	G	SO	Avg.
Andrei Trefilov	37	2060	21	9	3	81	3	2.36
Wendell Young	48	2781	32	12	4	128	6	2.76
Derek Wilkinson	1	60	0	0	1	5	0	5.00

CINCINNATI CYCLONES
SCORING

	Games	G	A	Pts.	PIM
Gilbert Dionne	81	34	49	83	88
Todd Simon	71	19	48	67	58

	Games	G	A	Pts.	PIM
Shane Willis	80	35	25	60	64
Stefan Ustorf	79	20	34	54	53
Ian MacNeil	81	19	18	37	100
Craig MacDonald	78	12	24	36	76
Brian Felsner	38	15	17	32	18
Todd Hawkins	61	14	17	31	98
Greg Koehler	74	12	13	25	157
Len Esau	78	8	17	25	64
Craig Adams	73	12	12	24	124
Nikos Tselios	80	3	19	22	75
Byron Ritchie	34	8	13	21	81
Steve Bancroft	39	6	14	20	37
Pat MacLeod	62	1	18	19	29
Mike Rucinski	66	3	10	13	34
Dave Tanabe	32	0	13	13	14
Eric Dandenault	62	4	5	9	201
Dave Karpa	39	1	8	9	147
Erik Cole	9	4	3	7	2
Jason Morgan	15	1	3	4	14
Matt Demarski	3	1	2	3	0
Tom Nemeth	2	0	3	3	2
Greg Kuznik	46	0	3	3	53
Brad Williamson	5	0	2	2	4
Fred Knipscheer	8	1	0	1	2
Doug MacDonald	7	0	1	1	2
Marc Magliarditi (goalie)	14	0	1	1	2
Jean-Marc Pelletier (goalie)	22	0	1	1	6
Mark McMahon	1	0	0	0	4
Jeff Mitchell	1	0	0	0	0
Alex Westlund (goalie)	1	0	0	0	0
Jamie Ling	2	0	0	0	2
Mark Fitzpatrick (goalie)	24	0	0	0	61
Randy Petruk (goalie)	26	0	0	0	4

GOALTENDING

	Gms.	Min.	W	L	SP	G	SO	Avg.
Jean-Marc Pelletier	22	1278	14	4	2	52	2	2.44
Mark Fitzpatrick	24	1379	11	11	1	59	4	2.57
Marc Magliarditi	14	752	5	6	2	35	1	2.79
Randy Petruk	26	1436	13	9	3	84	2	3.51
Alex Westlund	1	60	1	0	0	4	0	4.01

CLEVELAND LUMBERJACKS

SCORING

	Games	G	A	Pts.	PIM
Brett Harkins	76	20	50	70	79
Jeff Christian	77	29	35	64	202
Todd White	42	21	30	51	32
Chris Herperger	73	22	26	48	122
Jock Callander	64	16	27	43	83
Chris Longo	75	16	20	36	75
Kyle Calder	74	14	22	36	43
Radim Bicanek	70	5	27	32	125
Ted Crowley	61	9	20	29	94
Casey Hankinson	82	7	22	29	140
Jim Paek	69	2	20	22	27
Nathan Perrott	65	12	9	21	248
Remi Royer	57	3	13	16	204
Dmitri Tolkunov	65	3	12	15	54
Geoff Peters	68	10	4	14	87
Todd Rohloff	77	1	13	14	88
Jeff Paul	69	6	6	12	210
Jean-Pierre Dumont	7	5	2	7	8
Jeff Daw	9	4	1	5	2
Joe Frederick	9	3	2	5	6
Marc Lamothe (goalie)	44	0	5	5	8
Sean Berens	11	3	1	4	12
Reid Simpson	12	2	2	4	56
Marty Wilford	7	0	3	3	24
Ty Jones	10	1	1	2	34
Eric Lavigne	11	0	2	2	21
Colin Pepperall	22	0	2	2	16

	Games	G	A	Pts.	PIM
Ryan Kraft	1	0	1	1	0
Brian McCullough	6	0	1	1	0
Tomas Kapusta	1	0	0	0	0
Michel Larocque (goalie)	1	0	0	0	0
Don Parsons	1	0	0	0	2
Mike Tamburro (goalie)	1	0	0	0	0
Kam White	1	0	0	0	2
Shawn McNeil	2	0	0	0	0
Steve Passmore (goalie)	2	0	0	0	0
Chris Feil	3	0	0	0	2
J.P. O'Connor	5	0	0	0	0
Ian Gordon (goalie)	9	0	0	0	0
Rick Tabaracci (goalie)	10	0	0	0	15
Yevgeni Nabokov (goalie)	20	0	0	0	4
Ryan Gillis	23	0	0	0	17

GOALTENDING

	Gms.	Min.	W	L	SP	G	SO	Avg.
Steve Passmore	2	120	1	0	1	3	1	1.50
Michel Larocque	1	60	0	0	1	2	0	2.00
Yevgeni Nabokov	20	1164	12	4	3	52	0	2.68
Marc Lamothe	44	2455	19	18	4	112	2	2.74
Ian Gordon	9	480	2	3	3	22	2	2.75
Rick Tabaracci	10	568	5	5	0	28	0	2.96
Mike Tamburro	1	60	1	0	0	4	0	4.00

DETROIT VIPERS

SCORING

	Games	G	A	Pts.	PIM
Steve Walker	76	15	31	46	67
Jeff Shevalier	46	11	25	36	42
Eduard Pershin	65	14	15	29	75
Dale Rominski	78	14	15	29	68
Peter Ciavaglia	41	5	22	27	14
Dave Baseggio	48	5	21	26	28
Andrei Skopintsev	51	4	15	19	44
Matt Elich	48	12	4	16	12
Shawn Maltby	42	11	5	16	55
Travis Brigley	29	6	10	16	24
Samuel St. Pierre	47	11	4	15	25
Alek Stojanov	43	4	10	14	135
Kaspars Astashenko	51	1	10	11	86
Ben Clymer	19	1	9	10	30
Nils Ekman	10	7	2	9	8
Corey Spring	22	5	4	9	48
Paul Mara	15	3	5	8	22
Xavier Delisle	20	2	6	8	18
Tim Lovell	16	2	5	7	19
Shawn Burr	10	2	4	6	10
Ian Herbers	13	1	4	5	22
Mario Larocque	60	0	5	5	234
Byron Briske	28	1	3	4	56
Matt Sanders	27	0	4	4	10
Dan Kesa	5	3	0	3	2
Jonathan Weaver	7	2	1	3	2
Andy Bezeau	19	2	1	3	148
Joel Dezainde	14	1	2	3	20
Kyle Kos	44	1	2	3	77
Chris Gignac	11	0	3	3	2
Mike McBain	16	0	3	3	4
Jan Sulc	21	0	3	3	15
Shannon Finn	28	2	0	2	48
Jeff Blanchard	13	0	2	2	2
Doug Doull	17	0	2	2	69
Gordie Dwyer	27	0	2	2	147
Tim Thomas (goalie)	36	0	2	2	22
Erich Goldmann	11	1	0	1	8
Justin Clark	13	1	0	1	8
Paul Lawson	14	1	0	1	11
Mark Thompson	19	1	0	1	14
Andrew Luciuk	1	0	1	1	0
Marek Posmyk	1	0	1	1	0

	Games	G	A	Pts.	PIM
Tim Findlay	4	0	1	1	2
Zac Bierk (goalie)	15	0	1	1	4
Trevor Koenig (goalie)	21	0	1	1	6
Kyle Freadrich	45	0	1	1	203
Joe Cardarelli	1	0	0	0	0
Steve Kelly	1	0	0	0	4
Lorne Knauft	1	0	0	0	4
Vlad Serov	1	0	0	0	2
Dariusz Zabawa	1	0	0	0	0
James Patterson	2	0	0	0	0
Stephane G. Richer	2	0	0	0	0
Manny LaBranche	4	0	0	0	5
Mikko Kuparinen	5	0	0	0	2
Kurt Seher	7	0	0	0	0
Chris McAlpine	8	0	0	0	6
Kevin Hodson (goalie)	9	0	0	0	13
Dmitri Rodine	9	0	0	0	6
Rich Parent (goalie)	10	0	0	0	0
Jason Robinson	14	0	0	0	51
Karel Betik	17	0	0	0	22

GOALTENDING

	Gms.	Min.	W	L	SP	G	SO	Avg.
Rich Parent	10	539	3	5	1	23	1	2.56
Kevin Hodson	9	505	2	6	0	22	0	2.61
Trevor Koenig	21	988	3	12	2	47	1	2.85
Zac Bierk	15	846	4	8	2	46	1	3.26
Tim Thomas	36	2020	10	21	3	120	1	3.56

GRAND RAPIDS GRIFFINS

SCORING

	Games	G	A	Pts.	PIM
Michel Picard	65	33	35	68	50
Slava Butsayev	68	28	35	63	85
Kevin Miller	63	20	34	54	51
Derek King	52	19	30	49	25
Yves Sarault	62	17	26	43	77
Ed Patterson	74	20	21	41	141
Petr Schastlivy	46	16	12	28	10
Travis Richards	71	5	23	28	47
John Emmons	64	10	16	26	78
Karel Rachunek	62	6	20	26	64
Ivan Ciernik	66	13	12	25	64
Konstantin Gorovikov	57	9	14	23	30
John Gruden	50	5	17	22	24
Chris Neil	51	9	10	19	301
Todd Nelson	73	2	15	17	47
Philippe Plante	63	3	11	14	24
Darren Rumble	29	3	10	13	20
Konstantin Shafranov	24	3	8	11	15
Kory Karlander	22	5	5	10	31
Chris Szysky	32	5	4	9	44
Robert Petrovicky	7	5	3	8	4
Kelly Miller	26	4	4	8	8
Jason McBain	16	1	6	7	23
Dave Baseggio	15	0	7	7	6
Dave Van Drunen	36	0	6	6	76
Rastislav Pavlikovsky	15	0	5	5	24
Mike Maurice	6	1	2	3	5
Shane Kenny	24	1	1	2	38
Erich Goldmann	26	1	1	2	15
Dieter Kochan (goalie)	2	0	1	1	0
Buddy Wallace	4	0	1	1	4
Andrei Sryubko	28	0	1	1	109
Mike Fountain (goalie)	36	0	1	1	4
Jani Hurme (goalie)	52	0	1	1	30
Frederick Beaubien (goalie)	1	0	0	0	0
Dennis Pinfold	1	0	0	0	7
Danton Cole	2	0	0	0	0
Jason Metcalfe	2	0	0	0	9
Jeff Shevalier	2	0	0	0	0
Warren Norris	3	0	0	0	0
Kevin Grimes	4	0	0	0	13

GOALTENDING

	Gms.	Min.	W	L	SP	G	SO	Avg.
Dieter Kochan	2	93	1	0	1	1	0	0.64
Jani Hurme	52	2948	29	15	4	107	4	2.18
Mike Fountain	36	1851	21	7	4	77	3	2.50
Frederick Beaubien	1	15	0	0	0	1	0	4.07

HOUSTON AEROS

SCORING

	Games	G	A	Pts.	PIM
Mark Lamb	79	15	46	61	58
Mark Freer	75	20	35	55	55
Brian Wiseman	72	15	38	53	52
Greg Pankewicz	62	22	19	41	134
Bobby Reynolds	51	13	21	34	21
Lane Lambert	77	21	9	30	88
David Wilkie	57	4	24	28	71
David Oliver	45	16	11	27	40
Terry Marchant	66	11	13	24	41
Sandy Moger	45	13	10	23	43
Brian Felsner	28	7	16	23	20
Steve Bancroft	37	2	18	20	47
Jeff Daw	44	9	8	17	12
Brad Williamson	65	2	12	14	40
Dave Hymovitz	18	10	3	13	16
Scott Swanson	67	6	7	13	38
Greg Walters	63	4	7	11	192
Filip Kuba	27	3	6	9	13
Trent Cull	35	2	7	9	133
Paul Dyck	76	2	7	9	58
Marty Wilford	45	0	9	9	30
Mark Ferner	25	2	6	8	20
Rudy Poeschek	32	2	6	8	51
Lee Jinman	5	1	2	3	7
David Brosseau	13	1	2	3	8
Dan Price	10	0	3	3	2
Kelly Smart	19	1	1	2	8
Ryan Brindley	9	0	2	2	10
Jeff Ulmer	5	1	0	1	0
Mark Major	20	1	0	1	81
Simon Olivier	19	0	1	1	45
Frederic Chabot (goalie)	62	0	1	1	24
Yvan Corbin	1	0	0	0	2
Maxime Gingras (goalie)	1	0	0	0	0
Todd Kidd	1	0	0	0	0
Mike Johnson	2	0	0	0	2
Jeremy Mylymok	2	0	0	0	2
Jim Shepherd	4	0	0	0	2
Robert Esche (goalie)	7	0	0	0	0
Shannon Finn	8	0	0	0	6
Tom Askey (goalie)	13	0	0	0	0

GOALTENDING

	Gms.	Min.	W	L	SP	G	SO	Avg.
Maxime Gingras	1	59	0	1	0	2	0	2.04
Frederic Chabot	62	3695	36	19	7	131	4	2.13
Robert Esche	7	419	4	2	1	16	2	2.29
Tom Askey	13	727	4	7	1	33	0	2.72

KANSAS CITY BLADES

SCORING

	Games	G	A	Pts.	PIM
David Ling	82	35	48	83	210
Dave Chyzowski	81	37	33	70	138
Sean Haggerty	76	27	33	60	94
Michal Pivonka	52	16	34	50	38
Jason Cirone	71	19	24	43	133
Dody Wood	77	13	28	41	341
Nick Naumenko	54	9	27	36	79
Brendan Yarema	61	13	19	32	139
Pat Ferschweiler	82	8	21	29	66
David Vallieres	70	16	12	28	57
Steve Lingren	75	10	15	25	54

	Games	G	A	Pts.	PIM
Jon Rohloff	44	5	18	23	38
Aris Brimanis	46	5	17	22	28
Eric Perrin	21	3	15	18	16
Grant Richison	58	4	13	17	89
Jamie Ling	18	3	10	13	10
Joe Blaznek	38	4	8	12	2
Shane Kenny	26	3	8	11	47
Ray Schultz	65	5	5	10	208
Jan Vodrazka	66	2	8	10	280
Greg Bullock	15	1	6	7	6
Brad Mehalko	11	1	3	4	2
Rhett Gordon	12	1	3	4	0
Forrest Gore	27	1	3	4	16
Marty Standish	9	2	1	3	8
Dan Harrison	5	0	2	2	2
Eric Schneider	11	0	2	2	4
Wade Simpson	19	0	2	2	13
Michal Stastny	4	1	0	1	0
Paul Vincent	5	0	1	1	0
Ryan Bach (goalie)	6	0	1	1	0
Jeremy Rebek	6	0	1	1	4
Trevor Sherban	12	0	1	1	10
Greg Labenski	1	0	0	0	0
Steve Moore	1	0	0	0	2
Colin Chaulk	2	0	0	0	0
Perry Johnson	2	0	0	0	0
Brad Dexter	3	0	0	0	2
Brian Stacey	3	0	0	0	2
Tom Askey (goalie)	13	0	0	0	0
Bruce Racine (goalie)	33	0	0	0	4
Tyler Moss (goalie)	36	0	0	0	24

GOALTENDING

	Gms.	Min.	W	L	SP	G	SO	Avg.
Bruce Racine	33	1765	12	17	1	84	1	2.86
Tyler Moss	36	2116	18	12	5	105	3	2.98
Ryan Bach	6	358	3	3	0	19	0	3.18
Tom Askey	13	658	3	5	3	43	0	3.92

LONG BEACH ICE DOGS
SCORING

	Games	G	A	Pts.	PIM
Pavel Rosa	74	22	31	53	76
Doug Ast	79	22	26	48	84
Mike Crowley	67	9	39	48	35
Rob Pearson	60	17	23	40	145
Dmitri Leonov	82	17	21	38	165
Alex Vasilevski	51	8	25	33	109
Scott Thomas	52	15	16	31	18
Dieter Kalt	54	11	14	25	20
Jan Nemecek	71	9	15	24	22
Nils Ekman	27	11	12	23	26
Len Barrie	17	10	10	20	16
Robb Gordon	50	7	11	18	54
Pavel Torgaev	36	8	9	17	47
Allan Egeland	47	4	12	16	104
Philippe Boucher	14	4	11	15	8
Rod Aldoff	42	7	6	13	35
Vladimir Vorobiev	23	6	7	13	0
Alexei Yegorov	20	4	9	13	8
Claude Jutras	36	5	7	12	130
Frantisek Kaberle	18	2	8	10	8
Jason Blake	7	3	6	9	2
Scott Malone	13	5	8	8	17
Claude Boivin	42	2	6	8	147
Wes Walz	6	4	3	7	8
Rene Chapdelaine	59	1	6	7	116
Vladimir Antipov	16	3	3	6	18
Jaroslav Modry	11	2	4	6	8
Bobby Dollas	13	2	4	6	8
Luke Curtin	11	4	1	5	8
Zarley Zalapski	7	0	5	5	6
Mike Matteucci	64	0	4	4	170

	Games	G	A	Pts.	PIM
Olaf Kjenstad	6	1	2	3	2
Shane Kenny	11	1	2	3	19
Dan Bylsma	6	0	3	3	2
Jere Karalahti	10	0	3	3	4
Kaspars Astashenko	14	0	3	3	10
Dion Darling	43	0	3	3	108
Frederick Jobin	10	1	0	1	7
Petr Marek	2	0	1	1	2
Jeff Helperl	5	0	1	1	0
Gavin Morgan	7	0	1	1	10
Kelly Perrault	8	0	1	1	14
Mike O'Neill (goalie)	25	0	1	1	0
Nikolai Khabibulin (goalie)	33	0	1	1	2
Brad Chartrand	1	0	0	0	0
Micki DuPont	1	0	0	0	0
Brett Larson	1	0	0	0	0
Brian Leitza (goalie)	1	0	0	0	0
Steven Low	1	0	0	0	0
Barry Potomski	1	0	0	0	0
Paul Rosebush	1	0	0	0	0
Terry Ryan	1	0	0	0	4
Christian Skoryna	1	0	0	0	0
Byron Briske	2	0	0	0	9
Mike Nicholishen	2	0	0	0	8
Dennis Purdie	2	0	0	0	0
Bob Quinnell	2	0	0	0	5
Mikko Kuparinen	4	0	0	0	4
Steve Vezina (goalie)	4	0	0	0	0
Marcel Cousineau (goalie)	23	0	0	0	2

GOALTENDING

	Gms.	Min.	W	L	SP	G	SO	Avg.
Nikolai Khabibulin	33	1936	21	11	1	59	5	1.83
Marcel Cousineau	23	1328	15	6	1	62	0	2.80
Mike O'Neill	25	1423	7	12	5	71	0	2.99
Brian Leitza	1	60	0	1	0	3	0	3.00
Steve Vezina	4	160	1	1	0	10	0	3.75

MANITOBA MOOSE
SCORING

	Games	G	A	Pts.	PIM
Bill Bowler	75	20	42	62	59
Brett Hauer	77	13	47	60	92
Lonny Bohonos	63	18	33	51	45
Jim Montgomery	67	18	28	46	111
Mike Prokopec	68	23	21	44	100
Brian Chapman	80	7	30	37	153
Rusty Fitzgerald	53	18	15	33	31
Patrice Tardif	50	12	18	30	70
Eric Veilleux	73	14	13	27	102
Jimmy Roy	74	12	9	21	187
Vlad Serov	51	11	9	20	16
Marc Rodgers	34	8	10	18	77
Justin Kurtz	66	3	15	18	94
Michael Stewart	76	6	11	17	156
Jason MacDonald	30	5	10	15	77
Cory Cyrenne	30	5	9	14	13
Terry Hollinger	18	3	10	13	4
Mike Ruark	75	5	7	12	261
Barry Richter	19	5	4	9	6
Doug Doull	45	4	4	8	184
Sean Pronger	14	3	5	8	21
Quinn Hancock	22	2	6	8	6
Jeff Parrott	68	1	5	6	48
Shawn Burr	18	3	2	5	6
Corey Spring	8	2	2	4	8
Jim Campbell	10	1	3	4	10
Patrick Rochon	1	0	1	1	0
Andy MacIntyre	2	0	1	1	0
Keith McCambridge	3	0	1	1	4
Buddy Wallace	8	0	1	1	2
Shane Calder	1	0	0	0	0
Dan Kesa	1	0	0	0	0

	Games	G	A	Pts.	PIM
Jessie Rezansoff	1	0	0	0	0
Jeff Salajko (goalie)	3	0	0	0	0
Derek Landmesser	10	0	0	0	4
Larry Shapley	18	0	0	0	83
Manny Legace (goalie)	42	0	0	0	6
Jason Elliott (goalie)	43	0	0	0	8

GOALTENDING

	Gms.	Min.	W	L	SP	G	SO	Avg.
Jeff Salajko	3	139	1	1	0	5	0	2.16
Manny Legace	42	2409	17	18	5	104	2	2.59
Jason Elliott	43	2349	19	12	9	108	1	2.76

MICHIGAN K-WINGS

SCORING

	Games	G	A	Pts.	PIM
Kelly Fairchild	78	21	41	62	89
Ryan Christie	76	24	25	49	140
Jon Sim	35	14	16	30	65
Aaron Gavey	28	14	15	29	73
Greg Leeb	73	9	17	26	76
Mike Martin	74	8	15	23	99
Kelly Hurd	38	12	7	19	25
Richard Jackman	50	3	16	19	51
Steve Gainey	58	8	10	18	41
Greg Bullock	25	5	12	17	18
Jamie Wright	49	12	4	16	64
Gregor Baumgartner	59	6	9	15	11
Alan Letang	51	1	12	13	30
Keith Aldridge	55	2	10	12	55
Matt Martin	76	0	11	11	66
Kory Karlander	39	4	6	10	32
Mark Wotton	70	3	7	10	72
Gaetan Royer	20	6	2	8	64
Chris Murray	31	5	2	7	78
Richard Keyes	19	4	3	7	7
Mel Angelstad	33	3	4	7	144
Roman Lyashenko	9	3	2	5	8
Derek Plante	13	0	4	4	2
Warren Norris	8	1	2	3	0
Cail MacLean	14	0	3	3	4
Jeff MacMillan	53	0	3	3	54
Brenden Morrow	9	2	0	2	18
Warren Luhning	3	1	1	2	4
Bobby Stewart	2	0	2	2	0
Shawn Anderson	6	0	2	2	2
Mike McCourt	9	0	2	2	4
Eric Lavigne	22	0	2	2	70
Jim Logan	34	0	2	2	68
Evgueni Tsybouk	50	0	2	2	82
Michael Kiesman	9	0	1	1	10
Marty Turco (goalie)	60	0	1	1	44
Frederic Bouchard	1	0	0	0	0
Sacha Molin	2	0	0	0	0
Jay Neal	2	0	0	0	0
Bruce Ramsay	3	0	0	0	7
Jason Goulet	4	0	0	0	0
Ryan Lindsay	4	0	0	0	4
Mike O'Neill (goalie)	4	0	0	0	0
Guy Dupuis	6	0	0	0	12
Milt Mastad	12	0	0	0	20
Mike Bales (goalie)	25	0	0	0	0

GOALTENDING

	Gms.	Min.	W	L	SP	G	SO	Avg.
Mike O'Neill	4	155	1	1	0	6	1	2.33
Marty Turco	60	3399	23	27	7	139	7	2.45
Mike Bales	25	1341	9	9	5	56	0	2.50

MILWAUKEE ADMIRALS

SCORING

	Games	G	A	Pts.	PIM
Marian Cisar	78	20	32	52	82
Ryan Tobler	78	19	28	47	293

	Games	G	A	Pts.	PIM
David Gosselin	70	21	20	41	118
Paul Healey	76	21	18	39	28
Jayme Filipowicz	76	9	23	32	120
Brent Peterson	66	8	24	32	62
Fred Knipscheer	40	8	23	31	26
Rob Bonneau	33	7	20	27	10
Andrew Berenzweig	79	4	23	27	48
Mark Mowers	23	11	15	26	34
Jason Dawe	41	11	13	24	24
Richard Lintner	31	13	8	21	37
Dan Riva	67	8	12	20	18
Eric Fenton	72	7	12	19	256
Eric Bertrand	27	7	9	16	56
Matt Loen	45	7	9	16	4
Karlis Skrastins	19	3	8	11	10
Matt Eldred	64	3	8	11	140
Marc Moro	64	5	5	10	203
Alexandre Boikov	58	1	6	7	120
Craig Millar	8	1	5	6	6
John Namestnikov	12	2	3	5	17
Trevor Baker	9	3	1	4	29
Phil Crowe	20	3	1	4	31
Dan Keczmer	18	1	3	4	10
Steve Washburn	12	0	4	4	16
Rory Fitzpatrick	27	2	1	3	27
Scott King	12	1	2	3	0
Jonas Andersson	2	1	0	1	0
Jan Vopat	2	1	0	1	2
Vadim Podrezov	8	1	0	1	2
Greg Classen	11	1	0	1	2
Daniel Hodge	1	0	1	1	0
Randy Holmes	1	0	1	1	0
Justin Kearns	1	0	1	1	0
Aaron Fox	2	0	1	1	0
Steve Parsons	2	0	1	1	2
Petr Sykora	3	0	1	1	2
Chris Mason (goalie)	53	0	1	1	12
Josh Boni	1	0	0	0	0
Peter Cermak	1	0	0	0	0
Jason Christie	1	0	0	0	0
Luke Curtin	1	0	0	0	0
Mike Dunham (goalie)	1	0	0	0	0
Jeff Kealty	1	0	0	0	2
Jamie Ling	1	0	0	0	0
Derek Paget	1	0	0	0	0
Jason Reesor	1	0	0	0	0
Jeff Scharf	1	0	0	0	0
B.J. Adams	4	0	0	0	2
Adam Calder	4	0	0	0	0
Chad Dameworth	4	0	0	0	5
Samy Nasreddine	6	0	0	0	6
Kent Sauer	6	0	0	0	0
Pavel Skrbek	6	0	0	0	0
Tomas Vokoun (goalie)	7	0	0	0	0
Mike Buzak (goalie)	8	0	0	0	0
Joe Rybar	9	0	0	0	2
Corey Hirsch (goalie)	19	0	0	0	0

GOALTENDING

	Gms.	Min.	W	L	SP	G	SO	Avg.
Mike Dunham	1	60	1	0	0	1	0	1.00
Corey Hirsch	19	1098	9	8	1	49	0	2.68
Chris Mason	53	2952	20	21	8	137	2	2.78
Tomas Vokoun	7	364	5	2	0	17	0	2.80
Mike Buzak	8	426	2	5	0	24	0	3.38

ORLANDO SOLAR BEARS

SCORING

	Games	G	A	Pts.	PIM
Mark Beaufait	78	28	50	78	87
Herbert Vasiljevs	73	25	35	60	60
Bob Lachance	76	13	38	51	112
Curtis Murphy	81	8	43	51	59
Shawn Carter	81	20	30	50	120

	Games	G	A	Pts.	PIM
Gary Shuchuk	71	16	33	49	94
Bryan Adams	64	16	18	34	27
Sergei Vyshedkevich	69	11	23	34	32
Wes Mason	33	11	15	26	30
Brett Clark	63	9	17	26	31
Dan Snyder	71	12	13	25	123
Todd Richards	43	7	18	25	26
Todd Krygier	28	7	13	20	12
Jason Botterill	17	7	8	15	27
Jason MacDonald	29	7	7	14	113
Barry Dreger	75	3	11	14	263
Brian Wesenberg	31	9	3	12	50
Andreas Karlsson	18	5	5	10	6
Per Svartvadet	27	4	6	10	10
Ed Campbell	81	2	8	10	217
Terry Hollinger	20	4	4	8	13
Dean Sylvester	16	4	3	7	43
Bill Huard	19	4	2	6	85
Jeff Williams	6	2	4	6	0
Geordie Kinnear	69	1	5	6	231
Sylvain Cloutier	9	1	1	2	25
Carlin Nordstrom	6	0	2	2	24
Scott Langkow (goalie)	27	0	2	2	35
Kirby Law	1	1	0	1	0
J.P. Vigier	3	1	0	1	0
Martin Masa	5	0	1	1	2
Jeff Bes	1	0	0	0	0
Jody Hull	1	0	0	0	0
Reggie Berg	2	0	0	0	0
Joel Irving	2	0	0	0	2
Judd Lambert (goalie)	2	0	0	0	0
David Littman (goalie)	2	0	0	0	0
Dieter Kochan (goalie)	4	0	0	0	2
Mike Nicholishen	4	0	0	0	0
Kevin Kaminski	5	0	0	0	9
Jeff Rucinski	5	0	0	0	2
Scott Fankhouser (goalie)	6	0	0	0	0
Scott Ricci	6	0	0	0	4
Richard Shulmistra (goalie)	9	0	0	0	0
Corey Schwab (goalie)	16	0	0	0	16
Sean Ritchlin	19	0	0	0	6
Rick Tabaracci (goalie)	21	0	0	0	6

GOALTENDING

	Gms.	Min.	W	L	SP	G	SO	Avg.
Dieter Kochan	4	240	4	0	0	4	1	1.00
Richard Shulmistra	9	520	5	1	3	16	1	1.85
Corey Schwab	16	868	9	4	2	31	1	2.14
Scott Langkow	27	1487	14	8	2	57	4	2.30
Rick Tabaracci	21	1231	11	6	4	53	1	2.58
Scott Fankhouser	6	320	2	2	1	14	0	2.63
Judd Lambert	2	119	1	1	0	6	0	3.02
David Littman	2	119	1	1	0	7	0	3.52

UTAH GRIZZLIES

SCORING

	Games	G	A	Pts.	PIM
Jarrod Skalde	77	25	54	79	98
Sean Tallaire	82	31	34	65	85
John Purves	78	36	27	63	40
Richard Park	82	28	32	60	36
Neil Brady	82	14	36	50	129
Brad Lauer	71	26	22	48	73
Micah Aivazoff	80	15	31	46	81
Darcy Werenka	82	15	24	39	34
Zarley Zalapski	56	4	24	28	69
Rob Bonneau	37	11	16	27	14
Patrick Neaton	80	5	21	26	80
Paul Kruse	44	10	13	23	71
Mick Vukota	71	6	15	21	249
Gord Dineen	50	0	18	18	26
Joe Frederick	31	8	7	15	36
Taj Melson	43	4	10	14	18

	Games	G	A	Pts.	PIM
Stewart Malgunas	34	4	9	13	55
Dave Archibald	27	7	4	11	10
Jeff Sharples	33	2	9	11	49
Ted Crowley	16	3	2	5	16
Shawn Penn	35	2	2	4	157
Brad Miller	49	0	4	4	118
Terry Ryan	6	0	3	3	24
Rich Parent (goalie)	27	0	3	3	2
Andrei Sryubko	5	1	1	2	32
Paul Traynor	9	1	1	2	4
Calvin Elfring	3	0	2	2	0
Gavin Morgan	10	0	2	2	4
Corey Hirsch (goalie)	17	0	2	2	6
Chris Newans	2	1	0	1	7
Mark Streit	1	0	1	1	2
John Shockey	4	0	1	1	5
Brian Goudie	7	0	1	1	6
Eric Rud	7	0	1	1	2
Rick Tabaracci (goalie)	11	0	1	1	8
Kyle Kos	12	0	1	1	24
Chad Alban (goalie)	1	0	0	0	0
Andrei Lupandin	1	0	0	0	0
Bob Quinnell	1	0	0	0	0
Ben Schust	1	0	0	0	0
Peter Zurba	1	0	0	0	0
Mike Buzak (goalie)	4	0	0	0	0
Ian Gordon (goalie)	29	0	0	0	0

GOALTENDING

	Gms.	Min.	W	L	SP	G	SO	Avg.
Rich Parent	27	1571	17	7	3	58	1	2.21
Rick Tabaracci	11	626	4	4	3	24	1	2.30
Mike Buzak	4	168	0	1	1	7	0	2.50
Ian Gordon	29	1568	15	7	4	70	2	2.68
Corey Hirsch	17	937	9	5	1	42	3	2.69
Chad Alban	1	35	0	1	0	3	0	5.16

PLAYERS WITH TWO OR MORE TEAMS

SCORING

	Games	G	A	Pts.	PIM
Tom Askey, Kansas City (g)	13	0	0	0	0
Tom Askey, Houston (goalie)	13	0	0	0	0
Totals	26	0	0	0	0
Steve Bancroft, Cincinnati	39	6	14	20	37
Steve Bancroft, Houston	37	2	18	20	47
Totals	76	8	32	40	84
Dave Baseggio, Detroit	48	5	21	26	28
Dave Baseggio, Grand Rapids	15	0	7	7	6
Totals	63	5	28	33	34
Rob Bonneau, Utah	37	11	16	27	14
Rob Bonneau, Milwaukee	33	7	20	27	10
Totals	70	18	36	54	24
Byron Briske, Detroit	28	1	3	4	56
Byron Briske, Long Beach	2	0	0	0	9
Totals	30	1	3	4	65
Greg Bullock, Kansas City	15	1	6	7	6
Greg Bullock, Michigan	25	5	12	17	18
Totals	40	6	18	24	24
Shawn Burr, Detroit	10	2	4	6	10
Shawn Burr, Manitoba	18	3	2	5	6
Totals	28	5	6	11	16
Mike Buzak, Utah (goalie)	4	0	0	0	0
Mike Buzak, Milwaukee (goalie)	8	0	0	0	0
Totals	12	0	0	0	0
Ted Crowley, Cleveland	61	9	20	29	94
Ted Crowley, Utah	16	3	2	5	16
Totals	77	12	22	34	110
Luke Curtin, Long Beach	11	4	1	5	8
Luke Curtin, Milwaukee	1	0	0	0	0
Totals	12	4	1	5	8
Jeff Daw, Cleveland	9	4	1	5	2

	Games	G	A	Pts.	PIM
Jeff Daw, Houston	44	9	8	17	12
Totals	53	13	9	22	14
Gord Dineen, Utah	50	0	18	18	26
Gord Dineen, Chicago	17	1	2	3	14
Totals	67	1	20	21	40
Doug Doull, Detroit	17	0	2	2	69
Doug Doull, Manitoba	45	4	4	8	184
Totals	62	4	6	10	253
Guy Dupuis, Chicago	4	0	0	0	6
Guy Dupuis, Michigan	6	0	0	0	12
Totals	10	0	0	0	18
Nils Ekman, Detroit	10	7	2	9	8
Nils Ekman, Long Beach	27	11	12	23	26
Totals	37	18	14	32	34
Brian Felsner, Houston	28	7	16	23	20
Brian Felsner, Cincinnati	38	15	17	32	18
Totals	66	22	33	55	38
Shannon Finn, Houston	8	0	0	0	6
Shannon Finn, Detroit	28	2	0	2	48
Totals	36	2	0	2	54
Joe Frederick, Utah	31	8	7	15	36
Joe Frederick, Cleveland	9	3	2	5	6
Totals	40	11	9	20	42
Erich Goldmann, Grand Rapids	26	1	1	2	15
Erich Goldmann, Detroit	11	1	0	1	13
Totals	37	2	1	3	28
Ian Gordon, Utah (goalie)	29	0	0	0	0
Ian Gordon, Cleveland (goalie)	9	0	0	0	0
Totals	38	0	0	0	0
Corey Hirsch, Milwaukee (g)	19	0	0	0	6
Corey Hirsch, Utah (goalie)	17	0	2	2	6
Totals	36	0	2	2	6
Terry Hollinger, Orlando	20	4	4	8	14
Terry Hollinger, Manitoba	18	3	10	13	4
Totals	38	7	14	21	17
Kory Karlander, Grand Rapids	22	5	5	10	31
Kory Karlander, Michigan	39	4	6	10	32
Totals	61	9	11	20	63
Shane Kenny, Grand Rapids	24	1	1	2	38
Shane Kenny, Long Beach	11	1	2	3	19
Shane Kenny, Kansas City	26	3	8	11	47
Totals	61	5	11	16	104
Dan Kesa, Detroit	5	3	0	3	2
Dan Kesa, Manitoba	1	0	0	0	0
Totals	6	3	0	3	2
Fred Knipscheer, Cincinnati	8	1	0	1	2
Fred Knipscheer, Milwaukee	40	8	23	31	26
Totals	48	9	23	32	28
Dieter Kochan, Orl. (goalie)	4	0	0	0	2
Dieter Kochan, G.R. (goalie)	2	0	1	1	0
Totals	6	0	1	1	2
Kyle Kos, Detroit	44	1	2	3	77
Kyle Kos, Utah	12	0	1	1	24
Totals	56	1	3	4	101
Mikko Kuparinen, Detroit	5	0	0	0	2
Mikko Kuparinen, Long Beach	4	0	0	0	4
Totals	9	0	0	0	6
Eric Lavigne, Cleveland	11	0	2	2	21
Eric Lavigne, Michigan	22	0	2	2	70
Totals	33	0	4	4	91
Jamie Ling, Milwaukee	1	0	0	0	0
Jamie Ling, Cincinnati	2	0	0	0	2
Jamie Ling, Kansas City	18	3	10	13	10
Totals	21	3	10	13	12
Jason MacDonald, Manitoba	30	5	10	15	77
Jason MacDonald, Orlando	29	7	7	14	113
Totals	59	12	17	29	190
Gavin Morgan, Long Beach	7	0	1	1	10
Gavin Morgan, Utah	10	0	2	2	4
Totals	17	0	3	3	14
Jeremy Mylymok, Chicago	3	0	0	0	6
Jeremy Mylymok, Houston	2	0	0	0	2
Totals	5	0	0	0	8
Mike Nicholishen, Long Beach	2	0	0	0	8
Mike Nicholishen, Orlando	4	0	0	0	0

	Games	G	A	Pts.	PIM
Totals	6	0	0	0	8
Warren Norris, Grand Rapids	3	0	0	0	0
Warren Norris, Michigan	8	1	2	3	0
Totals	11	1	2	3	0
Mike O'Neill, Long Beach (g)	25	0	1	1	0
Mike O'Neill, Michigan (goalie)	4	0	0	0	0
Totals	29	0	1	1	0
Rich Parent, Utah (goalie)	27	0	3	3	2
Rich Parent, Detroit (goalie)	10	0	0	0	0
Totals	37	0	3	3	2
Derek Plante, Michigan	13	0	4	4	2
Derek Plante, Chicago	4	2	1	3	2
Totals	17	2	5	7	4
Bob Quinnell, Long Beach	2	0	0	0	5
Bob Quinnell, Utah	1	0	0	0	2
Totals	3	0	0	0	7
Terry Ryan, Long Beach	1	0	0	0	4
Terry Ryan, Utah	6	0	3	3	24
Totals	7	0	3	3	28
Vlad Serov, Manitoba	51	11	9	20	16
Vlad Serov, Detroit	1	0	0	0	2
Totals	52	11	9	20	18
Jeff Shevalier, Detroit	46	11	25	36	42
Jeff Shevalier, Grand Rapids	2	0	0	0	0
Totals	48	11	25	36	42
Corey Spring, Manitoba	8	2	2	4	8
Corey Spring, Detroit	22	5	4	9	48
Totals	30	7	6	13	56
Andrei Sryubko, Utah	5	1	1	2	32
Andrei Sryubko, Grand Rapids	28	0	1	1	109
Totals	33	1	2	3	141
Rick Tabaracci, Orlando (goalie)	21	0	0	0	6
Rick Tabaracci, Cleveland (g)	10	0	0	0	15
Rick Tabaracci, Utah (goalie)	11	0	1	1	8
Totals	42	0	1	1	29
Buddy Wallace, Grand Rapids	4	0	1	1	4
Buddy Wallace, Manitoba	8	0	1	1	2
Totals	12	0	2	2	6
Marty Wilford, Cleveland	7	0	3	3	24
Marty Wilford, Houston	45	0	9	9	30
Totals	52	0	12	12	54
Brad Williamson, Cincinnati	5	0	2	2	4
Brad Williamson, Houston	65	2	12	14	40
Totals	70	2	14	16	44
Zarley Zalapski, Long Beach	7	0	5	5	6
Zarley Zalapski, Utah	56	4	24	28	69
Totals	63	4	29	33	75

GOALTENDING

	Gms.	Min.	W	L	SP	G	SO	Avg.
Tom Askey, K.C.	13	658	3	5	3	43	0	3.92
Tom Askey, Hou.	13	727	4	7	1	33	0	2.72
Totals	26	1386	7	12	4	76	0	3.29
Mike Buzak, Utah	4	168	0	1	1	7	0	2.50
Mike Buzak, Mil.	8	426	2	5	0	24	0	3.38
Totals	12	593	2	6	1	31	0	3.13
Ian Gordon, Utah	29	1568	15	7	4	70	2	2.68
Ian Gordon, Cle.	9	480	2	3	3	22	2	2.75
Totals	38	2048	17	10	7	92	4	2.70
Corey Hirsch, Mil.	19	1098	9	8	1	49	0	2.68
Corey Hirsch, Utah	17	937	9	5	1	42	3	2.69
Totals	36	2036	18	13	2	91	3	2.68
Dieter Kochan, Orl.	4	240	4	0	1	4	1	1.00
D. Kochan, G.R.	2	93	1	0	1	1	0	0.64
Totals	6	333	5	0	1	5	1	0.90
Mike O'Neill, L.B.	25	1423	7	12	5	71	0	2.99
Mike O'Neill, Mich.	4	155	1	1	0	6	1	2.33
Totals	29	1578	8	13	5	77	1	2.93
Rich Parent, Utah	27	1571	17	7	3	58	1	2.21
Rich Parent, Det.	10	539	3	5	1	23	1	2.56
Totals	37	2111	20	12	4	81	2	2.30
R. Tabaracci, Orl.	21	1231	11	6	4	53	1	2.58
R. Tabaracci, Clev.	10	568	5	5	0	28	0	2.96
R. Tabaracci, Utah	11	626	4	4	3	24	1	2.30
Totals	42	2425	20	15	7	105	2	2.60

2000 TURNER CUP PLAYOFFS
RESULTS

PRELIMINARY ROUND

	W	L	Pts.	GF	GA
Cleveland	2	1	4	11	8
Milwaukee	1	2	2	8	11

(Cleveland won series, 2-1)

	W	L	Pts.	GF	GA
Long Beach	2	0	4	8	4
Manitoba	0	2	0	4	8

(Long Beach won series, 2-0)

CONFERENCE SEMIFINALS

	W	L	Pts.	GF	GA
Grand Rapids	4	2	8	16	10
Cleveland	2	4	4	10	16

(Grand Rapids won series, 4-2)

	W	L	Pts.	GF	GA
Cincinnati	4	2	8	19	11
Orlando	2	4	4	11	19

(Cincinnati won series, 4-2)

	W	L	Pts.	GF	GA
Chicago	4	0	8	16	4
Long Beach	0	4	0	4	16

(Chicago won series, 4-0)

	W	L	Pts.	GF	GA
Houston	4	1	8	11	5
Utah	1	4	2	5	11

(Houston won series, 4-1)

CONFERENCE FINALS

	W	L	Pts.	GF	GA
Grand Rapids	4	1	8	25	8
Cincinnati	1	4	2	8	25

(Grand Rapids won series, 4-1)

	W	L	Pts.	GF	GA
Chicago	4	2	8	16	17
Houston	2	4	4	17	16

(Chicago won series, 4-2)

TURNER CUP FINALS

	W	L	Pts.	GF	GA
Chicago	4	2	8	23	18
Grand Rapids	2	4	4	18	23

(Chicago won series, 4-2)

INDIVIDUAL LEADERS

Goals: Kevin Miller, Grand Rapids (11)
Assists: Slava Butsayev, Grand Rapids (12)
Points: Kevin Miller, Grand Rapids (18)
  Michel Picard, Grand Rapids (18)
Penalty minutes: Chris Szysky, Grand Rapids (45)
Goaltending average: Andre Trefilov, Chicago (1.35)
Shutouts: Frederic Chabot, Houston (3)

TOP SCORERS

	Games	G	A	Pts.
Kevin Miller, Grand Rapids	17	11	7	18
Michel Picard, Grand Rapids	17	8	10	18
Slava Butsayev, Grand Rapids	17	4	12	16
Petr Schastlivy, Grand Rapids	17	8	7	15
Derek King, Grand Rapids	17	7	8	15
Steve Larouche, Chicago	16	6	8	14
Steve Maltais, Chicago	16	9	4	13
Chris Ferraro, Chicago	16	5	8	13
Bob Nardella, Chicago	16	2	11	13
Yves Sarault, Grand Rapids	17	7	4	11
Brian Noonan, Chicago	16	4	7	11

INDIVIDUAL STATISTICS

CHICAGO WOLVES
(Winner of 2000 Turner Cup playoffs)

SCORING

	Games	G	A	Pts.	PIM
Steve Larouche	16	6	8	14	22
Steve Maltais	16	9	4	13	14
Chris Ferraro	16	5	8	13	14
Bob Nardella	16	2	11	13	10
Brian Noonan	16	4	7	11	10
Scott Pearson	16	5	5	10	28
Chris Marinucci	16	5	4	9	10
Glen Featherstone	16	3	5	8	38
Dan Plante	16	3	5	8	14
Nick Andersson	9	6	1	7	4
Tom Tilley	12	1	6	7	6
Greg Andrusak	11	1	5	6	20
Dallas Eakins	16	1	4	5	16
Guy Larose	16	1	4	5	14
Gord Dineen	16	0	5	5	12
Derek Plante	8	3	1	4	6
Lonnie Loach	8	0	3	3	0
Kevin Dahl	3	0	1	1	2
Wendell Young (goalie)	9	0	1	1	0
Dean Malkoc	1	0	0	0	0
Chris LiPuma	5	0	0	0	8
Daniel Lacroix	7	0	0	0	28
Andrei Trefilov (goalie)	9	0	0	0	14

GOALTENDING

	Gms.	Min.	W	L	SP	G	SO	Avg.
Andrei Trefilov	9	489	7	1	0	11	1	1.35
Wendell Young	9	488	5	3	0	27	0	3.32

CINCINNATI CYCLONES
(Lost division finals to Grand Rapids, 4-1)

SCORING

	Games	G	A	Pts.	PIM
Brian Felsner	11	4	5	9	20
Shane Willis	11	5	3	8	8
Todd Simon	11	2	6	8	23
Gilbert Dionne	11	4	3	7	8
Byron Ritchie	10	1	6	7	32
Craig MacDonald	11	4	1	5	8
Ian MacNeil	11	3	2	5	25
Dave Tanabe	11	1	4	5	6
Stefan Ustorf	11	1	4	5	10
Greg Koehler	8	0	3	3	14
Tom Nemeth	9	0	3	3	0
Erik Cole	7	1	1	2	2

	Games	G	A	Pts.	PIM
Len Esau	10	0	2	2	14
Nikos Tselios	10	0	2	2	4
Todd Hawkins	1	1	0	1	0
Pat MacLeod	7	0	1	1	0
Craig Adams	8	0	1	1	14
Randy Petruk (goalie)	9	0	1	1	12
Eric Dandenault	3	0	0	0	29
Jean-Marc Pelletier (goalie)	3	0	0	0	0
Greg Kuznik	4	0	0	0	4
Mike Rucinski	11	0	0	0	28

GOALTENDING

	Gms.	Min.	W	L	SP	G	SO	Avg.
Randy Petruk	9	551	4	4	1	27	1	2.94
Jean-Marc Pelletier	3	160	1	1	0	8	1	3.00

CLEVELAND LUMBERJACKS
(Lost division semifinals to Grand Rapids, 4-2)

SCORING

	Games	G	A	Pts.	PIM
Brett Harkins	9	2	8	10	6
Joe Frederick	9	3	3	6	6
Chris Herperger	9	3	3	6	8
Jock Callander	9	1	5	6	6
Sean Berens	9	3	2	5	8
Jeff Christian	9	1	4	5	20
Radim Bicanek	9	2	2	4	8
Kyle Calder	9	2	2	4	14
Nathan Perrott	9	2	1	3	19
Geoff Peters	7	0	3	3	4
Remi Royer	8	1	1	2	12
Jim Paek	9	0	2	2	2
Jeff Paul	9	1	0	1	12
Casey Hankinson	2	0	0	0	2
Ryan Gillis	3	0	0	0	0
Marc Lamothe (goalie)	4	0	0	0	0
Ian Gordon (goalie)	5	0	0	0	0
Chris Longo	5	0	0	0	0
Dmitri Tolkunov	8	0	0	0	2
Todd Rohloff	9	0	0	0	6

GOALTENDING

	Gms.	Min.	W	L	SP	G	SO	Avg.
Ian Gordon	5	301	2	3	0	11	1	2.20
Marc Lamothe	4	325	2	0	2	12	0	2.21

GRAND RAPIDS GRIFFINS
(Lost league finals to Chicago, 4-2)

SCORING

	Games	G	A	Pts.	PIM
Kevin Miller	17	11	7	18	30
Michel Picard	17	8	10	18	4
Slava Butsayev	17	4	12	16	24
Petr Schastlivy	17	8	7	15	6
Derek King	17	7	8	15	8
Yves Sarault	17	7	4	11	32
Travis Richards	17	1	7	8	18
Jason McBain	15	2	5	7	12
Ivan Ciernik	6	0	6	6	2
Dave Baseggio	15	0	6	6	6
Chris Szysky	15	2	3	5	45
John Gruden	12	1	4	5	8
John Emmons	16	1	4	5	28
Karel Rachunek	9	0	5	5	6
Ed Patterson	5	4	0	4	2
Philippe Plante	14	2	0	2	4
Mike Maurice	3	0	2	2	0
Chris Neil	8	0	2	2	24
Jani Hurme (goalie)	17	0	2	2	4
Todd Nelson	17	0	2	2	10
Konstantin Gorovikov	8	1	0	1	4

	Games	G	A	Pts.	PIM
Kelly Miller	7	0	1	1	2
Mike Fountain (goalie)	1	0	0	0	0
Dave Van Drunen	1	0	0	0	2
Andrei Sryubko	2	0	0	0	9

GOALTENDING

	Gms.	Min.	W	L	SP	G	SO	Avg.
Jani Hurme	17	1028	10	5	2	37	1	2.16
Mike Fountain	1	20	0	0	0	4	0	12.00

HOUSTON AEROS
(Lost division finals to Chicago, 4-2)

SCORING

	Games	G	A	Pts.	PIM
Mark Lamb	11	2	7	9	6
David Wilkie	11	1	8	9	10
Steve Bancroft	10	2	6	8	40
Dave Hymovitz	11	3	4	7	8
David Oliver	11	3	4	7	8
Terry Marchant	11	4	2	6	4
Jeff Ulmer	11	2	4	6	6
Marty Wilford	11	2	2	4	18
Mark Freer	11	0	4	4	4
Bobby Reynolds	11	3	0	3	10
Greg Pankewicz	5	2	1	3	18
Lane Lambert	7	2	1	3	10
Filip Kuba	11	1	2	3	4
Sandy Moger	2	1	1	2	4
Brad Williamson	11	0	2	2	4
Brian Wiseman	3	0	1	1	6
Greg Walters	5	0	1	1	4
Scott Swanson	6	0	1	1	6
Simon Olivier	1	0	0	0	0
Trent Cull	5	0	0	0	24
Frederic Chabot (goalie)	11	0	0	0	2
Paul Dyck	11	0	0	0	12

GOALTENDING

	Gms.	Min.	W	L	SP	G	SO	Avg.
Frederic Chabot	11	658	6	5	0	20	3	1.82

LONG BEACH ICE DOGS
(Lost division semifinals to Chicago, 4-0)

SCORING

	Games	G	A	Pts.	PIM
Philippe Boucher	6	0	9	9	8
Nils Ekman	5	3	3	6	4
Pavel Rosa	6	2	2	4	4
Mike Crowley	4	2	1	3	6
Scott Thomas	6	2	1	3	6
Alex Vasilevski	5	0	3	3	4
Doug Ast	6	1	1	2	4
Jan Nemecek	6	1	0	1	4
Alexei Yegorov	6	1	0	1	2
Vladimir Antipov	1	0	0	0	0
Mike O'Neill (goalie)	1	0	0	0	0
Vladimir Vorobiev	1	0	0	0	2
Rod Aldoff	2	0	0	0	0
Claude Boivin	4	0	0	0	12
Brad Chartrand	4	0	0	0	0
Rob Pearson	4	0	0	0	8
Nikolai Khabibulin (goalie)	5	0	0	0	0
Rene Chapdelaine	6	0	0	0	4
Dion Darling	6	0	0	0	14
Allan Egeland	6	0	0	0	19
Dmitri Leonov	6	0	0	0	6
Mike Matteucci	6	0	0	0	16

GOALTENDING

	Gms.	Min.	W	L	SP	G	SO	Avg.
Nikolai Khabibulin	5	321	2	3	0	15	0	2.81
Mike O'Neill	1	60	0	1	0	3	0	3.01

MINOR LEAGUES *IHL*

MANITOBA MOOSE

(Lost preliminary round to Long Beach, 2-0)

SCORING

	Games	G	A	Pts.	PIM
Bill Bowler	2	1	2	3	6
Barry Richter	2	1	1	2	0
Shawn Burr	2	1	0	1	6
Marc Rodgers	2	1	0	1	6
Brett Hauer	2	0	1	1	2
Sean Pronger	2	0	1	1	2
Mike Ruark	2	0	1	1	4
Troy Stonier	2	0	1	1	0
Eric Veilleux	2	0	1	1	2
Rusty Fitzgerald	1	0	0	0	2
Jimmy Roy	1	0	0	0	16
Lonny Bohonos	2	0	0	0	2
Brian Chapman	2	0	0	0	2
Cory Cyrenne	2	0	0	0	0
Doug Doull	2	0	0	0	2
Justin Kurtz	2	0	0	0	0
Manny Legace (goalie)	2	0	0	0	0
Michael Stewart	2	0	0	0	0

GOALTENDING

	Gms.	Min.	W	L	SP	G	SO	Avg.
Manny Legace	2	141	0	1	1	7	0	2.97

MILWAUKEE ADMIRALS

(Lost preliminary round to Cleveland, 2-1)

SCORING

	Games	G	A	Pts.	PIM
Brent Peterson	3	3	2	5	4
Fred Knipscheer	3	2	2	4	0
Andrew Berenzweig	3	1	2	3	0
Paul Healey	3	1	2	3	0
Matt Loen	3	1	2	3	2
Rory Fitzpatrick	3	0	2	2	2
Jayme Filipowicz	3	0	1	1	0
Chris Mason (goalie)	3	0	1	1	0
Rob Bonneau	1	0	0	0	2
Marian Cisar	1	0	0	0	0
Luke Curtin	1	0	0	0	0
Samy Nasreddine	1	0	0	0	0
Jonas Andersson	2	0	0	0	2
Greg Classen	2	0	0	0	2
Aaron Kriss	2	0	0	0	6
Ryan Tobler	2	0	0	0	0
Eric Bertrand	3	0	0	0	2
Matt Eldred	3	0	0	0	4
David Gosselin	3	0	0	0	10
John Namestnikov	3	0	0	0	0
Dan Riva	3	0	0	0	2

GOALTENDING

	Gms.	Min.	W	L	SP	G	SO	Avg.
Chris Mason	3	252	1	1	1	11	0	2.62

ORLANDO SOLAR BEARS

(Lost division semifinals to Cincinnati, 4-2)

SCORING

	Games	G	A	Pts.	PIM
Sergei Vyshedkevich	6	3	3	6	8
Todd Richards	6	0	5	5	4
Herbert Vasiljevs	6	2	2	4	6
Todd Krygier	6	2	1	3	2
Dan Snyder	6	1	2	3	4
Mark Beaufait	6	2	0	2	4
Gary Shuchuk	6	1	1	2	12
Shawn Carter	6	0	2	2	4
Curtis Murphy	6	0	2	2	6
Bryan Adams	4	0	1	1	6
Bob Lachance	4	0	1	1	16
Per Svartvadet	5	0	1	1	0
Brett Clark	6	0	1	1	0
Richard Shulmistra (goalie)	1	0	0	0	0
Ed Campbell	3	0	0	0	6
Barry Dreger	3	0	0	0	18
Bill Huard	3	0	0	0	10
Jason MacDonald	4	0	0	0	19
Brian Wesenberg	4	0	0	0	9
Geordie Kinnear	6	0	0	0	9
Scott Langkow (goalie)	6	0	0	0	4

GOALTENDING

	Gms.	Min.	W	L	SP	G	SO	Avg.
Scott Langkow	6	381	2	2	1	16	0	2.52
Richard Shulmistra	1	30	0	1	0	3	0	5.90

UTAH GRIZZLIES

(Lost division semifinals to Houston, 4-1)

SCORING

	Games	G	A	Pts.	PIM
Paul Kruse	5	0	3	3	28
Ted Crowley	5	1	1	2	12
Zarley Zalapski	5	1	1	2	4
Gavin Morgan	2	1	0	1	2
Richard Park	5	1	0	1	0
John Purves	5	1	0	1	2
Kyle Kos	2	0	1	1	0
Brad Lauer	5	0	1	1	2
Patrick Neaton	5	0	1	1	6
Jarrod Skalde	5	0	1	1	10
Brad Miller	1	0	0	0	4
Jeff Petruic	1	0	0	0	0
Brian Goudie	2	0	0	0	4
Corey Hirsch (goalie)	2	0	0	0	2
Neil Brady	3	0	0	0	2
Rick Tabaracci (goalie)	3	0	0	0	2
Mick Vukota	4	0	0	0	2
Micah Aivazoff	5	0	0	0	4
Dave Archibald	5	0	0	0	0
Taj Melson	5	0	0	0	6
Sean Tallaire	5	0	0	0	10
Darcy Werenka	5	0	0	0	0

GOALTENDING

	Gms.	Min.	W	L	SP	G	SO	Avg.
Corey Hirsch	2	121	0	1	1	4	0	1.99
Rick Tabaracci	3	179	1	2	0	7	0	2.34

ALL-STAR TEAMS

First team	Pos.	Second team
Frederic Chabot, Houston	G	Jani Hurme, Grand Rapids
Brett Hauer, Manitoba	D	Dallas Eakins, Chicago
Mike Crowley, Long Beach	D	Robert Nardella, Chicago
Steve Maltais, Chicago	LW	Gilbert Dionne, Cincinnati
Jarrod Skalde, Utah	C	Steve Larouche, Chicago
David Ling, Kansas City	RW	Niklas Andersson, Chicago

TROPHY WINNERS

James Gatschene Memorial Trophy: Frederic Chabot, Houston
Nikolai Khabibulin, L.B.
Leo P. Lamoureux Memorial Trophy: Steve Maltais, Chicago
James Norris Memorial Trophy: Frederic Chabot, Houston
Larry D. Gordon Trophy: Brett Hauer, Manitoba
Garry F. Longman Memorial Trophy: Nils Ekman, Long Beach
Ken McKenzie Trophy: Andrew Berenzweig, Milwaukee
Commissioner's Trophy: Guy Charron, Grand Rapids
N.R. (Bud) Poile Trophy: Andrei Trefilov, Chicago

ALL-TIME AWARD WINNERS

JAMES GATSCHENE MEMORIAL TROPHY
(Most Valuable Player)

Season   Player, Team
1946-47—Herb Jones, Detroit Auto Club
1947-48—Lyle Dowell, Det. Bright's Goodyears
1948-49—Bob McFadden, Det. Jerry Lynch
1949-50—Dick Kowcinak, Sarnia
1950-51—John McGrath, Toledo
1951-52—Ernie Dick, Chatham
1952-53—Donnie Marshall, Cincinnati
1953-54—No award given
1954-55—Phil Goyette, Cincinnati
1955-56—George Hayes, Grand Rapids
1956-57—Pierre Brillant, Indianapolis
1957-58—Pierre Brillant, Indianapolis
1958-59—Len Thornson, Fort Wayne
1959-60—Billy Reichart, Minneapolis
1960-61—Len Thornson, Fort Wayne
1961-62—Len Thornson, Fort Wayne
1962-63—Len Thornson, Fort Wayne
        Eddie Lang, Fort Wayne
1963-64—Len Thornson, Fort Wayne
1964-65—Chick Chalmers, Toledo
1965-66—Gary Schall, Muskegon
1966-67—Len Thornson, Fort Wayne
1967-68—Len Thornson, Fort Wayne
        Don Westbrooke, Dayton
1968-69—Don Westbrooke, Dayton
1969-70—Cliff Pennington, Des Moines
1970-71—Lyle Carter, Muskegon
1971-72—Len Fontaine, Port Huron
1972-73—Gary Ford, Muskegon
1973-74—Pete Mara, Des Moines
1974-75—Gary Ford, Muskegon
1975-76—Len Fontaine, Port Huron
1976-77—Tom Mellor, Toledo
1977-78—Dan Bonar, Fort Wayne
1978-79—Terry McDougall, Fort Wayne
1979-80—Al Dumba, Fort Wayne
1980-81—Marcel Comeau, Saginaw
1981-82—Brent Jarrett, Kalamazoo
1982-83—Claude Noel, Toledo
1983-84—Darren Jensen, Fort Wayne
1984-85—Scott Gruhl, Muskegon
1985-86—Darrell May, Peoria
1986-87—Jeff Pyle, Saginaw
        Jock Callander, Muskegon
1987-88—John Cullen, Flint
1988-89—Dave Michayluk, Muskegon
1989-90—Michel Mongeau, Peoria
1990-91—David Bruce, Peoria
1991-92—Dmitri Kvartalnov, San Diego
1992-93—Tony Hrkac, Indianapolis
1993-94—Rob Brown, Kalamazoo
1994-95—Tommy Salo, Denver
1995-96—Stephane Beauregard, San Francisco

Season   Player, Team
1996-97—Frederic Chabot, Houston
1997-98—Patrice Lefebvre, Las Vegas
1998-99—Brian Wiseman, Houston
1999-00—Frederic Chabot, Houston
        Nikolai Khabibulin, Long Beach

LEO P. LAMOUREUX MEMORIAL TROPHY
(Leading scorer)

Season   Player, Team
1946-47—Harry Marchand, Windsor
1947-48—Dick Kowcinak, Det. Auto Club
1948-49—Leo Richard, Toledo
1949-50—Dick Kowcinak, Sarnia
1950-51—Herve Parent, Grand Rapids
1951-52—George Parker, Grand Rapids
1952-53—Alex Irving, Milwaukee
1953-54—Don Hall, Johnstown
1954-55—Phil Goyette, Cincinnati
1955-56—Max Mekilok, Cincinnati
1956-57—Pierre Brillant, Indianapolis
1957-58—Warren Hynes, Cincinnati
1958-59—George Ranieri, Louisville
1959-60—Chick Chalmers, Louisville
1960-61—Ken Yackel, Minneapolis
1961-62—Len Thornson, Fort Wayne
1962-63—Moe Bartoli, Minneapolis
1963-64—Len Thornson, Fort Wayne
1964-65—Lloyd Maxfield, Port Huron
1965-66—Bob Rivard, Fort Wayne
1966-67—Len Thornson, Fort Wayne
1967-68—Gary Ford, Muskegon
1968-69—Don Westbrooke, Dayton
1969-70—Don Westbrooke, Dayton
1970-71—Darrel Knibbs, Muskegon
1971-72—Gary Ford, Muskegon
1972-73—Gary Ford, Muskegon
1973-74—Pete Mara, Des Moines
1974-75—Rick Bragnalo, Dayton
1975-76—Len Fontaine, Port Huron
1976-77—Jim Koleff, Flint
1977-78—Jim Johnston, Flint
1978-79—Terry McDougall, Fort Wayne
1979-80—Al Dumba, Fort Wayne
1980-81—Marcel Comeau, Saginaw
1981-82—Brent Jarrett, Kalamazoo
1982-83—Dale Yakiwchuk, Milwaukee
1983-84—Wally Schreiber, Fort Wayne
1984-85—Scott MacLeod, Salt Lake
1985-86—Scott MacLeod, Salt Lake
1986-87—Jock Callander, Muskegon
        Jeff Pyle, Saginaw
1987-88—John Cullen, Flint
1988-89—Dave Michayluk, Muskegon
1989-90—Michel Mongeau, Peoria
1990-91—Lonnie Loach, Fort Wayne
1991-92—Dmitri Kvartalnov, San Diego

Season   Player, Team
1992-93—Tony Hrkac, Indianapolis
1993-94—Rob Brown, Kalamazoo
1994-95—Stephane Morin, Minnesota
1995-96—Rob Brown, Chicago
1996-97—Rob Brown, Chicago
1997-98—Patrice Lefebvre, Las Vegas
1998-99—Brian Wiseman, Houston
1999-00—Steve Maltais, Chicago
The award was originally known as the George H. Wilkinson Trophy from 1946-47 through 1959-60.

JAMES NORRIS MEMORIAL TROPHY
(Outstanding goaltenders)

Season   Player, Team
1955-56—Bill Tibbs,Troy
1956-57—Glenn Ramsey, Cincinnati
1957-58—Glenn Ramsey, Cincinnati
1958-59—Don Rigazio, Louisville
1959-60—Rene Zanier, Fort Wayne
1960-61—Ray Mikulan, Minneapolis
1961-62—Glenn Ramsey, Omaha
1962-63—Glenn Ramsey, Omaha
1963-64—Glenn Ramsey, Toledo
1964-65—Chuck Adamson, Fort Wayne
1965-66—Bob Sneddon, Port Huron
1966-67—Glenn Ramsey, Toledo
1967-68—Tim Tabor, Muskegon
        Bob Perani, Muskegon
1968-69—Pat Rupp, Dayton
        John Adams, Dayton
1969-70—Gaye Cooley, Des Moines
        Bob Perreault, Des Moines
1970-71—Lyle Carter, Muskegon
1971-72—Glenn Resch, Muskegon
1972-73—Robbie Irons, Fort Wayne
        Don Atchison, Fort Wayne
1973-74—Bill Hughes, Muskegon
1974-75—Bob Volpe, Flint
        Merlin Jenner, Flint
1975-76—Don Cutts, Muskegon
1976-77—Terry Richardson, Kalamazoo
1977-78—Lorne Molleken, Saginaw
        Pierre Chagnon, Saginaw
1978-79—Gord Laxton, Grand Rapids
1979-80—Larry Lozinski, Kalamazoo
1980-81—Claude Legris, Kalamazoo
        Georges Gagnon, Kalamazoo
1981-82—Lorne Molleken, Toledo
        Dave Tardich, Toledo
1982-83—Lorne Molleken, Toledo
1983-84—Darren Jensen, Fort Wayne
1984-85—Rick Heinz, Peoria
1985-86—Rick St. Croix, Fort Wayne
        Pokey Reddick, Fort Wayne
1986-87—Alain Raymond, Fort Wayne
        Michel Dufour, Fort Wayne
1987-88—Steve Guenette, Muskegon
1988-89—Rick Knickle, Fort Wayne
1989-90—Jimmy Waite, Indianapolis
1990-91—Guy Hebert, Peoria
        Pat Jablonski, Peoria
1991-92—Arturs Irbe, Kansas City
        Wade Flaherty, Kansas City
1992-93—Rick Knickle, San Diego
        Clint Malarchuk, San Diego
1993-94—J.C. Bergeron, Atlanta
        Mike Greenlay, Atlanta
1994-95—Tommy Salo, Denver
1995-96—Mark McArthur, Utah
        Tommy Salo, Utah
1996-97—Rich Parent, Detroit
        Jeff Reese, Detroit
1997-98—Mike Buzak, Long Beach
        Kay Whitmore, Long Beach

Season   Player, Team
1998-99—Andrei Trefilov, Detroit
        Steve Weekes, Detroit
1999-00—Frederic Chabot, Houston

LARRY D. GORDON TROPHY
(Outstanding defenseman)

Season   Player, Team
1964-65—Lionel Repka, Fort Wayne
1965-66—Bob Lemieux, Muskegon
1966-67—Larry Mavety, Port Huron
1967-68—Carl Brewer, Muskegon
1968-69—Al Breaule, Dayton
        Moe Benoit, Dayton
1969-70—John Gravel, Toledo
1970-71—Bob LaPage, Des Moines
1971-72—Rick Pagnutti, Fort Wayne
1972-73—Bob McCammon, Port Huron
1973-74—Dave Simpson, Dayton
1974-75—Murry Flegel, Muskegon
1975-76—Murry Flegel, Muskegon
1976-77—Tom Mellor, Toledo
1977-78—Michel LaChance, Milwaukee
1978-79—Guido Tenesi, Grand Rapids
1979-80—John Gibson, Saginaw
1980-81—Larry Goodenough, Saginaw
1981-82—Don Waddell, Saginaw
1982-83—Jim Burton, Fort Wayne
        Kevin Willison, Milwaukee
1983-84—Kevin Willison, Milwaukee
1984-85—Lee Norwood, Peoria
1985-86—Jim Burton, Fort Wayne
1986-87—Jim Burton, Fort Wayne
1987-88—Phil Bourque, Muskegon
1988-89—Randy Boyd, Milwaukee
1989-90—Brian Glynn, Salt Lake
1990-91—Brian McKee, Fort Wayne
1991-92—Jean-Marc Richard, Fort Wayne
1992-93—Bill Houlder, San Diego
1993-94—Darren Veitch, Peoria
1994-95—Todd Richards, Las Vegas
1995-96—Greg Hawgood, Las Vegas
1996-97—Brad Werenka, Indianapolis
1997-98—Dan Lambert, Long Beach
1998-99—Greg Hawgood, Houston
1999-00—Brett Hauer, Manitoba
The award was originally known as the Governors Trophy from 1964-65 through 1998-99.

GARRY F. LONGMAN MEMORIAL TROPHY
(Outstanding rookie)

Season   Player, Team
1961-62—Dave Richardson, Fort Wayne
1962-63—John Gravel, Omaha
1963-64—Don Westbrooke, Toledo
1964-65—Bob Thomas, Toledo
1965-66—Frank Golembrowsky, Port Huron
1966-67—Kerry Bond, Columbus
1967-68—Gary Ford, Muskegon
1968-69—Doug Volmar, Columbus
1969-70—Wayne Zuk, Toledo
1970-71—Corky Agar, Flint
        Herb Howdle, Dayton
1971-72—Glenn Resch, Muskegon
1972-73—Danny Gloor, Des Moines
1973-74—Frank DeMarco, Des Moines
1974-75—Rick Bragnalo, Dayton
1975-76—Sid Veysey, Fort Wayne
1976-77—Ron Zanussi, Fort Wayne
        Garth MacGuigan, Muskegon
1977-78—Dan Bonar, Fort Wayne
1978-79—Wes Jarvis, Port Huron
1979-80—Doug Robb, Milwaukee
1980-81—Scott Vanderburgh, Kalamazoo
1981-82—Scott Howson, Toledo

– 284 –

Season	Player, Team
1982-83	Tony Fiore, Flint
1983-84	Darren Jensen, Fort Wayne
1984-85	Gilles Thibaudeau, Flint
1965-66	Guy Benoit, Muskegon
1986-87	Michel Mongeau, Saginaw
1987-88	Ed Belfour, Saginaw
	John Cullen, Flint
1988-89	Paul Ranheim, Salt Lake
1989-90	Rob Murphy, Milwaukee
1990-91	Nelson Emerson, Peoria
1991-92	Dmitri Kvartalnov, Kansas City
1992-93	Mikhail Shtalenkov, Milwaukee
1993-94	Radek Bonk, Las Vegas
1994-95	Tommy Salo, Denver
1995-96	Konstantin Shafranov, Fort Wayne
1996-97	Sergei Samsonov, Detroit
1997-98	Todd White, Indianapolis
1998-99	Marty Turco, Michigan
1999-00	Nils Ekman, Long Beach

KEN MC KENZIE TROPHY
(Outstanding American-born rookie)

Season	Player, Team
1977-78	Mike Eruzione, Toledo
1978-79	Jon Fontas, Saginaw
1979-80	Bob Janecyk, Fort Wayne
1980-81	Mike Labianca, Toledo
	Steve Janaszak, Fort Wayne
1981-82	Steve Salvucci, Saginaw
1982-83	Paul Fenton, Peoria
1983-84	Mike Krensing, Muskegon
1984-85	Bill Schafhauser, Kalamazoo
1985-86	Brian Noonan, Saginaw
1986-87	Ray LeBlanc, Flint
1987-88	Dan Woodley, Flint
1988-89	Paul Ranheim, Salt Lake
1989-90	Tim Sweeney, Salt Lake
1990-91	C.J. Young, Salt Lake
1991-92	Kevin Wortman, Salt Lake
1992-93	Mark Beaufait, Kansas City
1993-94	Chris Rogles, Indianapolis
1994-95	Chris Marinucci, Denver
1995-96	Brett Lievers, Utah
1996-97	Brian Felsner, Orlando
1997-98	Eric Nickulas, Orlando
1998-99	Mark Mowers, Milwaukee
1999-00	Andrew Berenzweig, Milwaukee

COMMISSIONER'S TROPHY
(Coach of the year)

Season	Coach, Team
1984-85	Rick Ley, Muskegon
	Pat Kelly, Peoria
1985-86	Rob Laird, Fort Wayne
1986-87	Wayne Thomas, Salt Lake
1987-88	Rick Dudley, Flint
1988-89	B. J. MacDonald, Muskegon
	Phil Russell, Muskegon
1989-90	Darryl Sutter, Indianapolis
1990-91	Bob Plager, Peoria
1991-92	Kevin Constantine, Kansas City
1992-93	Al Sims, Fort Wayne
1993-94	Bruce Boudreau, Fort Wayne
1994-95	Butch Goring, Denver
1995-96	Butch Goring, Utah
1996-97	John Van Boxmeer, Long Beach
1997-98	John Torchetti, Fort Wayne
1998-99	Dave Tippett, Houston
1999-00	Guy Charron, Grand Rapids

N.R. (BUD) POILE TROPHY
(Playoff MVP)

Season	Player, Team
1984-85	Denis Cyr, Peoria
1985-86	Jock Callander, Muskegon
1986-87	Rick Heinz, Salt Lake
1987-88	Peter Lappin, Salt Lake
1988-89	Dave Michayluk, Muskegon
1989-90	Mike McNeill, Indianapolis
1990-91	Michel Mongeau, Peoria
1991-92	Ron Handy, Kansas City
1992-93	Pokey Reddick, Fort Wayne
1993-94	Stan Drulia, Atlanta
1994-95	Kip Miller, Denver
1995-96	Tommy Salo, Utah
1996-97	Peter Ciavaglia, Detroit
1997-98	Alexander Semak, Chicago
1998-99	Mark Freer, Houston
1999-00	Andre Trefilov, Chicago

The award was originally known as the Turner Cup Playoff MVP from 1984-85 through 1988-89.

ALL-TIME LEAGUE CHAMPIONS

	REGULAR-SEASON CHAMPION		PLAYOFF CHAMPION	
Season	Team	Coach	Team	Coach
1945-46	No trophy awarded		Detroit Auto Club	Jack Ward
1946-47	Windsor Staffords	Jack Ward	Windsor Spitfires	Ebbie Goodfellow
1947-48	Windsor Hettche Spitfires	Dent-Goodfellow	Toledo Mercurys	Andy Mulligan
1948-49	Toledo Mercurys	Andy Mulligan	Windsor Hettche Spitfires	Jimmy Skinner
1949-50	Sarnia Sailors	Dick Kowcinak	Catham Maroons	Bob Stoddart
1950-51	Grand Rapids Rockets	Lou Trudell	Toledo Mercurys	Alex Wood
1951-52	Grand Rapids Rockets	Lou Trudell	Toledo Mercurys	Alex Wood
1952-53	Cincinnati Mohawks	Buddy O'Conner	Cincinnati Mohawks	Buddy O'Conner
1953-54	Cincinnati Mohawks	Roly McLenahan	Cincinnati Mohawks	Roly McLenahan
1954-55	Cincinnati Mohawks	Roly McLenahan	Cincinnati Mohawks	Roly McLenahan
1955-56	Cincinnati Mohawks	Roly McLenahan	Cincinnati Mohawks	Roly McLenahan
1956-57	Cincinnati Mohawks	Roly McLenahan	Cincinnati Mohawks	Roly McLenahan
1957-58	Cincinnati Mohawks	Bill Gould	Indiana. Chiefs	Leo Lamoureux
1958-59	Louisville Rebels	Leo Gasparini	Louisville Rebels	Leo Gasparini
1959-60	Fort Wayne Komets	Ken Ullyot	St. Paul Saints	Fred Shero
1960-61	Minneapolis Millers	Ken Yachel	St. Paul Saints	Fred Shero
1961-62	Muskegon Zephrys	Moose Lallo	Muskegon Zephrys	Moose Lallo
1962-63	Fort Wayne Komets	Ken Ullyot	Fort Wayne Komets	Ken Ullyot
1963-64	Toledo Blades	Moe Benoit	Toledo Blades	Moe Benoit
1964-65	Port Huron Flags	Lloyd Maxfield	Fort Wayne Komets	Eddie Long

	REGULAR-SEASON CHAMPION		PLAYOFF CHAMPION	
Season	Team	Coach	Team	Coach
1965-66—	Muskegon Mohawks	Moose Lallo	Port Huron Flags	Lloyd Maxfield
1966-67—	Dayton Gems	Warren Back	Toledo Blades	Terry Slater
1967-68—	Muskegon Mohawks	Moose Lallo	Muskegon Mohawks	Moose Lallo
1968-69—	Dayton Gems	Larry Wilson	Dayton Gems	Larry Wilson
1969-70—	Muskegon Mohawks	Moose Lallo	Dayton Gems	Larry Wilson
1970-71—	Muskegon Mohawks	Moose Lallo	Port Huron Flags	Ted Garvin
1971-72—	Muskegon Mohawks	Moose Lallo	Port Huron Flags	Ted Garvin
1972-73—	Fort Wayne Komets	Marc Boileau	Fort Wayne Komets	Marc Boileau
1973-74—	Des Moines Capitals	Dan Belisle	Des Moines Capitals	Dan Belisle
1974-75—	Muskegon Mohawks	Moose Lallo	Toledo Goaldiggers	Ted Garvin
1975-76—	Dayton Gems	Ivan Prediger	Dayton Gems	Ivan Prediger
1976-77—	Saginaw Gears	Don Perry	Saginaw Gears	Don Perry
1977-78—	Fort Wayne Komets	Gregg Pilling	Toledo Goaldiggers	Ted Garvin
1978-79—	Grand Rapids Owls	Moe Bartoli	Kalamazoo Wings	Bill Purcell
1979-80—	Kalamazoo Wings	Doug McKay	Kalamazoo Wings	Doug McKay
1980-81—	Kalamazoo Wings	Doug McKay	Saginaw Gears	Don Perry
1981-82—	Toledo Goaldiggers	Bill Inglis	Toledo Goaldiggers	Bill Inglis
1982-83—	Toledo Goaldiggers	Bill Inglis	Toledo Goaldiggers	Bill Inglis
1983-84—	Fort Wayne Komets	Ron Ullyot	Flint Generals	Dennis Desrosiers
1984-85—	Peoria Rivermen	Pat Kelly	Peoria Rivermen	Pat Kelly
1985-86—	Fort Wayne Komets	Rob Laird	Muskegon Lumberjacks	Rick Ley
1986-87—	Fort Wayne Komets	Rob Laird	Salt Lake Golden Eagles	Wayne Thomas
1987-88—	Muskegon Lumberjacks	Rick Ley	Salt Lake Golden Eagles	Paul Baxter
1988-89—	Muskegon Lumberjacks	B.J. MacDonald	Muskegon Lumberjacks	B.J. MacDonald
1989-90—	Muskegon Lumberjacks	B.J. MacDonald	Indianapolis Ice	Darryl Sutter
1990-91—	Peoria Rivermen	Bob Plager	Peoria Rivermen	Bob Plager
1991-92—	Kansas City Blades	Kevin Constantine	Kansas City Blades	Kevin Constantine
1992-93—	San Diego Gulls	Rick Dudley	Fort Wayne Komets	Al Sims
1993-94—	Las Vegas Thunder	Butch Goring	Atlanta Knights	Gene Ubriaco
1994-95—	Denver Grizzlies	Butch Goring	Denver Grizzlies	Butch Goring
1995-96—	Las Vegas Thunder	Chris McSorley	Utah Grizzlies	Butch Goring
1996-97—	Detroit Vipers	Steve Ludzik	Detroit Vipers	Steve Ludzik
1997-98—	Long Beach Ice Dogs	John Van Boxmeer	Chicago Wolves	John Anderson
1998-99—	Houston Aeros	Dave Tippett	Houston Aeros	Dave Tippett
1999-00—	Chicago Wolves	John Anderson	Chicago Wolves	John Anderson

The IHL regular-season champion is awarded the Fred A. Huber Trophy and the playoff champion is awarded the Joseph Turner Memorial Cup.

The regular-season championship award was originally called the J.P. McGuire Trophy from 1946-47 through 1953-54.

EAST COAST HOCKEY LEAGUE

LEAGUE OFFICE

President/chief executive officer
Richard W. Adams
Commissioner emeritus
Patrick J. Kelly
Sr. v.p. of business operations
Scott Sabatino
V.p of marketing and sales
Jason Siegel
Vice president of hockey administration
Doug Price

Director of communications
Jason Rothwell
Director of finance
Anthony King
Director of special projects
Melissa Adams
Assistant director of sales/marketing
Kelly Jutras

Address
103 Main Street, Suite 300
Princeton, NJ 08540
Phone
609-452-0770
FAX
609-452-7147

TEAMS

ARKANSAS RIVERBLADES
President and chief executive officer
Dave Berryman
Head coach
To be announced
Home ice
Alltel Arena
Address
425 W. Broadway, Suite A
North Little Rock, AR 72114
Seating capacity
16,377
Phone
501-975-2327
FAX
501-907-2327

AUGUSTA LYNX
General manager
Paul Gamsby
Head coach
Dan MacPherson
Home ice
Richmond County Civic Center
Address
712 Telfair St.
Augusta, GA 30901
Seating capacity
6,604
Phone
706-724-4423
FAX
706-724-2423

BATON ROUGE KINGFISH
General manager
To be announced
Head coach
Dave Lohrei
Home ice
Centroplex
Address
P.O. Box 2142
Baton Rouge, LA 70821
Seating capacity
8,600
Phone
225-336-4625
FAX
225-336-4011

BIRMINGHAM BULLS
President
Charles Felix

Head coach
Mike Zruna
Home ice
Jefferson County Civic Center
Address
P.O. Box 1506
Birmingham, AL 35201
Seating capacity
16,850
Phone
205-458-8833
FAX
205-458-8489

CHARLOTTE CHECKERS
General manager
Sam Russo
Head coach
Don MacAdam
Home ice
Independence Arena
Address
2700 E. Independence Blvd.
Charlotte, NC 28205
Seating capacity
9,570
Phone
704-342-4423
FAX
704-377-4595

DAYTON BOMBERS
General manager
Ed Gingher
Head coach
Greg Ireland
Home ice
Nutter Center
Address
3640 Colonel Glenn Highway, Suite 417
Dayton, OH 45435
Seating capacity
9,950
Phone
937-775-4747
FAX
937-775-4749

FLORIDA EVERBLADES
President
Craig Brush
Head coach
Bob Ferguson
Home ice
TECO Arena

Address
11000 Everblades Parkway
Estero, FL 33928
Seating capacity
7,181
Phone
941-948-7825
FAX
941-948-2248

GREENSBORO HOCKEY CLUB
President
Art Donaldson
Head coach
Jeff Brubaker
Home ice
Greensboro Coliseum
Address
P.O. Box 3387
Greensboro, NC 27402
Seating capacity
20,800
Phone
336-218-5428
FAX
336-218-5498

GREENVILLE GRRROWL
President
Carl Scheer
Head coach
John Marks
Home ice
BI-LO Center
Address
P.O. Box 10348
Greenville, SC 29603
Seating capacity
14,108
Phone
864-467-4777
FAX
864-241-3872

JACKSON BANDITS
General manager
Brad Ewing
Head coach
Derek Clancey
Home ice
Mississippi Coliseum
Address
P.O. Box 517
Jackson, MS 39205

Seating capacity
6,200
Phone
601-352-7825
FAX
601-352-2715

JOHNSTOWN CHIEFS

General manager
Toby O'Brien
Head coach
Scott Allen
Home ice
Cambria County War Memorial
Address
326 Napoleon Street
Johnstown, PA 15901
Seating capacity
4,050
Phone
814-539-1799
FAX
814-536-1316

LOUISIANA ICEGATORS

General manager
Jady Regard
Head coach
To be announced
Home ice
Cajundome
Address
444 Cajundome Blvd.
Lafayette, LA 70506
Seating capacity
11,700
Phone
337-234-4423
FAX
337-232-1254

MISSISSIPPI SEA WOLVES

General manager
Jean Gagnon
Head coach
To be announced
Home ice
Mississippi Coast Coliseum
Address
2350 Beach Blvd.
Biloxi, MS 39531
Seating capacity
9,150
Phone
228-388-6151
FAX
228-388-5848

MOBILE MYSTICKS

General manager
Steve Chapman
Head coach
Jeff Pyle
Home ice
Mobile Civic Center
Address
P.O. Box 263
Mobile, AL 36601-0263
Seating capacity
8,033
Phone
334-208-7825
FAX
334-434-7931

NEW ORLEANS BRASS

General manager
Dan Belisle
Head coach
Ted Sator
Home ice
New Orleans Arena
Address
1660 Girod Street
New Orleans, LA 70113
Seating capacity
17,000
Phone
504-522-7825
FAX
504-523-7295

PEE DEE PRIDE

Senior vice president
Jack Capuano
Head coach
Frank Anzalone
Home ice
Florence City-County Civic Center
Address
One Civic Center Plaza
3300 West Radio Drive
Florence, SC 29501
Seating capacity
7,426
Phone
843-669-7825
FAX
843-669-7149

PENSACOLA ICE PILOTS

Director of hockey operations
Joe Bucchino
Head coach
Wayne Cashman
Home ice
Pensacola Civic Center
Address
201 East Gregory St.-Rear
Pensacola, FL 32501-4956
Seating capacity
8,150
Phone
850-432-7825
FAX
850-432-1929

PEORIA RIVERMEN

President
John Butler
Head coach
Don Granato
Home ice
Peoria Civic Center
Address
201 SW Jefferson
Peoria, IL 61602
Seating capacity
9,470
Phone
309-676-1040
FAX
309-676-2488

RICHMOND RENEGADES

President/hockey operations
Bill Stewart
Head coach
Mark Kaufman

Home ice
Richmond Coliseum
Address
601 East Leigh St.
Richmond, VA 23219
Seating capacity
11,088
Phone
804-643-7865
FAX
804-649-0651

ROANOKE EXPRESS

General manager
Tony Benizio
Head coach
Perry Florie
Home ice
Roanoke Civic Center
Address
4504 Starkey Road S.W., Suite 208
Roanoke, VA 24014
Seating capacity
8,706
Phone
540-989-4625
FAX
540-989-8681

SOUTH CAROLINA STINGRAYS

President
Gary Grondines
Head coach
Rick Adduono
Home ice
North Charleston Coliseum
Address
3107 Firestone Road
N. Charleston, SC 29418
Seating capacity
10,529
Phone
843-744-2248
FAX
843-744-2898

TALLAHASSEE TIGER SHARKS

General manager
Larry Kish
Head coach
Gerry Fleming
Home ice
Leon County Civic Center
Address
505 W. Pensacola St., Suite B
Tallahassee, FL 32301
Seating capacity
11,048
Phone
850-224-4625
FAX
850-224-6300

TOLEDO STORM

General manager
Pat Pylypuik
Head coach
Dennis Holland
Home ice
Toledo Sports Arena
Address
One Main Street
Toledo, OH 43605
Seating capacity
5,160

Phone
419-691-0200
FAX
419-698-8998

TRENTON TITANS
President and general manager
Brian McKenna
Head coach
To be announced
Home ice
Sovereign Bank Arena
Address
650 S. Broad Street
Trenton, NJ 08611

Seating capacity
7,850
Phone
609-599-9500
FAX
609-599-3600

WHEELING NAILERS
General manager
Fred Traynor
Head coach
Alain Lemieux
Home ice
Wheeling Civic Center

Address
1144 Market Street, Suite 202
Wheeling, WV 26003
Seating capacity
5,406
Phone
304-234-4625
FAX
304-233-4846

1999-2000 REGULAR SEASON
FINAL STANDINGS

NORTHERN CONFERENCE

NORTHEAST DIVISION

Team	G	W	L	T	Pts.	GF	GA
Roanoke	70	44	20	6	94	221	181
Richmond	70	44	21	5	93	258	205
Hampton Roads	70	44	22	4	92	241	198
Trenton	70	37	29	4	78	233	199
Charlotte	70	25	38	7	57	186	254
Greensboro	70	20	43	7	47	229	337

NORTHWEST DIVISION

Team	G	W	L	T	Pts.	GF	GA
Peoria	70	45	20	5	95	273	216
Huntington	70	35	25	10	80	230	238
Johnstown	70	33	28	9	75	235	234
Dayton	70	32	28	10	74	230	226
Wheeling	70	25	40	5	55	202	246
Toledo	70	22	41	7	51	214	306

SOUTHERN CONFERENCE

SOUTHEAST DIVISION

Team	G	W	L	T	Pts.	GF	GA
Florida	70	53	15	2	108	277	181
Pee Dee	70	47	18	5	99	233	175
Greenville	70	46	18	6	98	277	198
South Carolina	70	35	25	10	80	253	242
Augusta	70	34	31	5	73	243	248
Tallahassee	70	31	33	6	68	256	261
Jacksonville	70	27	34	9	63	246	291

SOUTHWEST DIVISION

Team	G	W	L	T	Pts.	GF	GA
Louisiana	70	43	18	9	95	281	241
Mobile	70	40	28	2	82	275	230
New Orleans	70	36	27	7	79	230	219
Mississippi	70	35	27	8	78	241	221
Pensacola	70	35	29	6	76	215	216
Baton Rouge	70	33	32	5	71	253	277
Jackson	70	32	32	6	70	201	227
Birmingham	70	29	37	4	62	255	297
Arkansas	70	18	49	3	39	192	316

INDIVIDUAL LEADERS

Goals: Andrew Williamson, Toledo (63)
Assists: John Spoltore, Louisiana (92)
Points: John Spoltore, Louisiana (119)
Penalty minutes: Peter Vandermeer, Richmond (457)
Goaltending average: Sandy Allan, Pee Dee (2.26)
Shutouts: David Brumby, Jackson (7)

TOP SCORERS

	Games	G	A	Pts.
John Spoltore, Louisiana	66	27	92	119
Andrew Williamson, Toledo	63	63	39	102
Sean Venedam, Greenville	68	33	60	93
Lars Pettersen, Augusta	70	31	62	93
Chris Gignac, Toledo	59	33	56	89
Jason Elders, Mobile	67	37	51	88

	Games	G	A	Pts.
Jamey Hicks, Birmingham	62	33	55	88
Tom Buckley, Florida	69	28	59	87
Jamie Ling, Dayton	63	29	57	86
Andrew Shier, Richmond	68	22	62	84
Jay Murphy, Louisiana	69	55	28	83
Mark Turner, Mobile	61	45	37	82
Jeff Lazaro, New Orleans	70	24	56	80
Jon Sturgis, Baton Rouge	69	32	47	79
Joe Bianchi, Richmond	64	41	36	77
Dany Bousquet, Pee Dee	56	38	39	77
Bobby Stewart, Mobile	65	31	46	77
Dan Shermerhorn, Baton Rouge	68	27	50	77
Tom Nemeth, Dayton	66	21	56	77
Luke Curtin, Baton Rouge	61	32	43	75
Scott Kirton, Greenville	59	25	50	75

INDIVIDUAL STATISTICS

ARKANSAS RIVERBLADES

SCORING

	Games	G	A	Pts.	PIM
Trevor Gallant	68	28	38	66	33
Mark Cadotte	49	20	32	52	92
Jarret Whidden	48	17	24	41	38
Steve O'Brien	70	6	28	34	63
Mark Edmundson	37	12	18	30	19
Steve Zoryk	49	15	14	29	66
Rob Weingartner	41	12	16	28	114
Mikhail Kravets	30	10	17	27	64
Tyler McMillan	37	9	18	27	4
Vince Malts	38	14	11	25	116
Peter Rozic	45	10	11	21	25
John Varga	21	5	13	18	8
Kris Bragnalo	70	4	11	15	24
Aaron Boh	20	3	12	15	90
Mark McMahon	35	4	10	14	149
Peter Cava	32	4	7	11	31
Jason Johnson	60	0	11	11	53
Ryan Pawluk	20	3	5	8	4
Todd Markus	32	2	5	7	67
Alex Radzinsky	49	2	4	6	34
Don MacPherson	24	1	5	6	34
Justin Clark	12	3	1	4	12
Ryan Lee	22	0	4	4	116
David Haynes	26	2	1	3	15
Brad Gratton	4	1	2	3	2
Ron Handy	9	1	1	2	8
Kenzie Homer	13	1	1	2	16
Dereck Gosselin	8	0	2	2	18
Iuori Krivokhija	15	0	2	2	29
Jeff Salajko (goalie)	48	0	2	2	20
Jeremy Vokes	2	1	0	1	2
Matt Golden	4	1	0	1	11
Brad Goulet	5	1	0	1	2
Dan Back	2	0	1	1	4
Mike Coveny	2	0	1	1	9
Sergei Tkachenko (goalie)	2	0	1	1	2
Tim Hill	4	0	1	1	21
Nicholas Ouimet	10	0	1	1	4
Yauheni Kurylin	11	0	1	1	4
Mark Scott	15	0	1	1	50
Lucas Nehrling	16	0	1	1	51
Blaz Emersic	1	0	0	0	0
Nick Hriczov	1	0	0	0	0
Chad Nelson	1	0	0	0	2
Andrei Sharkevich	1	0	0	0	0
Roland Grelle	2	0	0	0	0
Mike Olaski	2	0	0	0	6
Jure Penko (goalie)	2	0	0	0	0
Henrik Smangs (goalie)	2	0	0	0	0
Jackson Hegland	3	0	0	0	0
Kevin Westlake	4	0	0	0	2
Jeff Heil (goalie)	25	0	0	0	30

GOALTENDING

	Gms.	Min.	W	L	T	G	SO	Avg.
Sergei Tkachenko	2	120	0	0	2	7	0	3.51
Jeff Salajko	48	2679	14	30	1	186	1	4.17
Jeff Heil	25	1221	4	17	0	97	0	4.77
Jure Penko	2	95	0	1	0	8	0	5.05
Henrik Smangs	2	70	0	1	0	8	0	6.83

AUGUSTA LYNX

SCORING

	Games	G	A	Pts.	PIM
Lars Pettersen	70	31	62	93	70
Louis Dumont	44	26	37	63	38
Dean Tiltgen	69	31	27	58	60
Chris Thompson	65	23	30	53	184
Jonas Soling	66	22	31	53	49
Wes Mason	28	18	20	38	41
Andrei Chouroupov	52	16	20	36	34
Sandy Lamarre	69	18	17	35	184
Ken Ruddick	64	3	22	25	62
Stacey Rayan	55	15	8	23	24
John Whitwell	67	5	16	21	105
Stewart Bodtker	29	6	14	20	57
Corey Smith	60	3	16	19	26
Dan Kopec	67	2	17	19	267
Bryan Duce	50	3	15	18	26
Wes Swinson	35	0	15	15	71
Sam Ftorek	29	6	7	13	49
Mike Piersol	20	1	10	11	23
Paul Ferone	20	3	5	8	14
Clint Cabana	31	2	5	7	124
Jessie Rezansoff	10	3	3	6	57
Mark DeSantis	16	1	5	6	31
Likit Andersson	12	0	4	4	8
Mike Schultz	14	1	2	3	15
Jon Coe	9	1	1	2	2
Henry Kuster	9	1	1	2	6
Alex Johnstone	21	0	2	2	88
Peter Constantine	7	1	0	1	33
Lucas Nehrling	9	1	0	1	12
Jason Gudmundson	4	0	1	1	0
Judd Lambert (goalie)	54	0	1	1	4
Dan Ronan	2	0	0	0	5
Mike Buzak (goalie)	3	0	0	0	0
Mike Valley (goalie)	3	0	0	0	0
Leorr Shtrom (goalie)	4	0	0	0	0
Adam Lewis	6	0	0	0	4
J.F. Damphousse (goalie)	14	0	0	0	0

GOALTENDING

	Gms.	Min.	W	L	T	G	SO	Avg.
Leorr Shtrom	4	121	0	0	1	3	0	1.49
Judd Lambert	54	3086	27	23	4	159	3	3.09
J.-F. Damphousse	14	676	4	7	0	49	0	4.35
Mike Buzak	3	150	2	0	0	11	0	4.40
Mike Valley	3	150	0	2	0	11	0	4.40

BATON ROUGE KINGFISH

SCORING

	Games	G	A	Pts.	PIM
Jon Sturgis	69	32	47	79	37
Dan Shermerhorn	68	27	50	77	106
Luke Curtin	61	32	43	75	36
Bryan Richardson	55	29	34	63	30
Cam Brown	70	23	38	61	194
Joe Seroski	66	17	35	52	15
Eric Normandin	51	24	26	50	111
Paul Croteau	66	11	35	46	10
Ted Laviolette	63	8	21	29	75
Mike Lankshear	62	5	22	27	42
Chris Aldous	43	8	17	25	14
Sylvain Dufresne	66	8	12	20	53
Brett Abrahamson	69	3	12	15	72
Casey Wolak	40	4	8	12	120
Todd Miller	20	4	6	10	17
Mike Pozzo	14	6	3	9	0
Samy Nasreddine	16	4	4	8	30
Jeremy Vokes	12	2	3	5	21
Sanny Lindstrom	11	1	2	3	16
Jason Hamilton	46	1	2	3	291
Mike Lenarduzzi (goalie)	54	0	3	3	2
Jeremy Kyte	8	2	0	2	0
Jared Reigstad	5	1	1	2	4
Keith Bland	28	0	2	2	165
Anders Sorensen	8	1	0	1	6
Todd Markus	12	0	1	1	21

	Games	G	A	Pts.	PIM
Tim Keyes (goalie)	15	0	1	1	4
Pavel Nestak (goalie)	15	0	1	1	14
Danny Bujold	3	0	0	0	0

GOALTENDING

	Gms.	Min.	W	L	T	G	SO	Avg.
Mike Lenarduzzi	54	2749	25	20	2	167	0	3.64
Pavel Nestak	15	785	4	7	3	52	0	3.97
Tim Keyes	15	657	2	6	1	46	0	4.20

BIRMINGHAM BULLS
SCORING

	Games	G	A	Pts.	PIM
Jamey Hicks	62	33	55	88	71
Hugo Belanger	68	34	40	74	44
Jeff Scharf	70	30	39	69	67
Denis Smakovsky	70	27	26	53	82
Kelly Perrault	51	12	36	48	71
Tyler Johnston	67	6	41	47	80
Craig Lutes	66	21	25	46	61
Stefan Rivard	58	18	28	46	156
Kory Mullin	70	2	29	31	77
Eon Macfarlane	70	8	22	30	91
Rick Smith	69	13	14	27	117
Ian Hebert	24	12	12	24	6
Michael Ford	57	9	10	19	22
Scott Wray	67	9	9	18	85
Tyler Prosofsky	31	3	11	14	127
Mike Bodnarchuk	13	7	4	11	17
Kenny Corupe	6	4	1	5	2
Oak Hewer	31	2	3	5	46
Kurt Mallett	7	0	5	5	2
Rob Stanfield	50	1	3	4	135
Dereck Gosselin	3	1	1	2	6
Jeremy Kyle	3	1	0	1	0
Paul Bailley	4	1	0	1	0
Kevin Popp	37	1	0	1	166
Shane Stewart	9	0	1	1	33
Avi Karunakar (goalie)	26	0	1	1	0
Everett Caldwell	1	0	0	0	0
Toby Carlow	2	0	0	0	0
Mark Spence	2	0	0	0	5
Mike Herrera	9	0	0	0	0
Mike Torchia (goalie)	14	0	0	0	4
Scott Roche (goalie)	39	0	0	0	2

GOALTENDING

	Gms.	Min.	W	L	T	G	SO	Avg.
Scott Roche	39	2199	16	19	2	147	1	4.01
Avi Karunakar	26	1281	12	5	2	88	0	4.12
Mike Torchia	14	705	4	10	0	52	0	4.43

CHARLOTTE CHECKERS
SCORING

	Games	G	A	Pts.	PIM
Kevin Hilton	67	17	31	48	54
Marc Tropper	53	18	25	43	64
David-Al Beauregard	53	20	20	40	22
Darryl Noren	66	11	26	37	54
Mike Rucinski	70	15	19	34	69
Tyler Deis	56	15	15	30	145
Boyd Kane	47	10	19	29	110
Jason Dailey	68	10	17	27	52
Jeff Brown	51	7	18	25	107
Kurt Seher	70	8	15	23	60
Martin Cerven	33	7	14	21	22
Kurt Mallett	32	8	10	18	6
Van Burgess	17	6	12	18	0
Dave Risk	36	4	8	12	21
D.J. Mando	29	5	6	11	56
Tracy Egeland	12	3	8	11	13
Kevin Pozzo	23	0	11	11	34
Lee Hamilton	51	2	8	10	122
Anthony Terzo	11	6	2	8	6

	Games	G	A	Pts.	PIM
Mike Jaros	42	3	4	7	85
Frank Littlejohn	14	2	4	6	31
Rocky Welsing	64	2	4	6	63
Richard Scott	55	1	5	6	317
Kevin Colley	5	2	1	3	10
Brooke Chateau	21	1	2	3	8
Scott Bailey (goalie)	31	0	3	3	14
Deny Gaudet	4	1	1	2	0
Ivan Loginov	7	1	1	2	2
Shannon Basaraba	6	0	2	2	0
Reggie Brezeault	12	1	0	1	33
Bob MacIssac	7	0	1	1	15
Derek Wilkinson (goalie)	31	0	1	1	2
Tom Noble (goalie)	2	0	0	0	2
Craig Hillier (goalie)	3	0	0	0	0
Brent Belecki (goalie)	4	0	0	0	0
Alexandre Yudin	8	0	0	0	47
Taras Lendzyk (goalie)	12	0	0	0	10

GOALTENDING

	Gms.	Min.	W	L	T	G	SO	Avg.
Scott Bailey	31	1735	10	16	4	93	2	3.22
Derek Wilkinson	31	1435	11	13	2	83	0	3.47
Taras Lendzyk	12	636	4	4	1	38	0	3.58
Tom Noble	2	119	0	2	0	8	0	4.05
Brent Belecki	4	141	0	1	0	11	0	4.68
Craig Hillier	3	121	0	2	0	10	0	4.95

DAYTON BOMBERS
SCORING

	Games	G	A	Pts.	PIM
Jamie Ling	63	29	57	86	63
Tom Nemeth	66	21	56	77	79
Forbes MacPherson	57	23	49	72	109
Brad Holzinger	58	10	34	44	86
Jeff Mitchell	36	23	17	40	186
Jim Baxter	58	10	26	36	35
Brian Ridolfi	57	18	16	34	68
Travis Dillabough	36	10	14	24	78
Aaron Kriss	45	6	14	20	139
Earl Cronan	26	11	7	18	57
Trent Walford	28	6	12	18	18
Justin Krall	62	4	13	17	38
Andy Powers	41	11	5	16	30
Julian Dal Cin	66	0	15	15	103
Kevin Colley	24	8	6	14	111
Doug Nolan	52	6	8	14	64
Dan Lupo	12	4	10	14	13
Matt Oates	12	3	7	10	8
Cody Leibel	36	3	6	9	118
Ryan Cirillo	39	5	3	8	116
Jon Sorg	12	4	4	8	39
Stacy Prevost	45	3	4	7	18
Jason Payne	26	2	4	6	211
Mark McMahon	21	2	3	5	71
Chad Wagner	22	3	1	4	216
Dennis Mullen	20	1	3	4	94
Jason Saal (goalie)	29	0	3	3	2
Alex Westlund (goalie)	40	0	3	3	6
Pavol Pekarik	12	2	0	2	34
Glenn Crawford	4	1	0	1	4
Greg Kuznik	7	1	0	1	16
Torrey DiRoberto	1	0	1	1	0
Brandon Sugden	13	0	1	1	110
Jeremy Bautch	1	0	0	0	0
Josh Mizerek	1	0	0	0	0
Adam DeLeeuw	2	0	0	0	2
Jay Legault	2	0	0	0	2
Chris Wismer	2	0	0	0	16
Jamie Fawcett	3	0	0	0	5
Tyrone Garner (goalie)	3	0	0	0	0
David Weninger (goalie)	5	0	0	0	0
Jackson Hegland	10	0	0	0	4
Peter Constantine	22	0	0	0	75

GOALTENDING

	Gms.	Min.	W	L	T	G	SO	Avg.
Alex Westlund	40	2316	18	15	7	99	3	2.56
Jason Saal	29	1650	14	10	3	88	1	3.20
David Weninger	5	104	0	1	0	8	0	4.62
Tyrone Garner	3	113	0	2	0	11	0	5.86

FLORIDA EVERBLADES

SCORING

	Games	G	A	Pts.	PIM
Tom Buckley	69	28	59	87	70
Andy MacIntyre	68	36	38	74	64
Joe Cardarelli	69	30	40	70	25
Reg Berg	52	27	26	53	64
Matt Demarski	50	28	16	44	24
Steve Tardif	70	16	23	39	136
Jason Morgan	48	14	25	39	79
Eric Manlow	26	14	24	38	24
Ty Jones	48	11	26	37	81
Harlan Pratt	68	4	29	33	38
Hugh Hamilton	68	7	24	31	53
Dane Litke	62	6	25	31	12
Brent Cullaton	32	20	10	30	16
Eric Rud	59	8	19	27	47
Tim Ferguson	42	9	17	26	18
Terry Lindgren	70	5	17	22	118
Steve Moffat	41	3	10	13	19
John Varga	20	5	7	12	28
Peter Kasper	63	1	10	11	22
Todd Kidd	31	1	9	10	96
Greg Kuznik	9	1	4	5	6
Jeff Maund (goalie)	37	0	5	5	2
Jamie Coady	11	3	1	4	2
Pat MacLeod	3	0	2	2	4
Randy Petruk (goalie)	6	0	2	2	2
Jason Prokopetz	2	0	1	1	4
Marc Magliarditi (goalie)	33	0	0	0	10

GOALTENDING

	Gms.	Min.	W	L	T	G	SO	Avg.
Marc Magliarditi	33	1794	22	9	0	69	3	2.31
Jeff Maund	37	2055	26	6	1	89	3	2.60
Randy Petruk	6	339	0	1	0	19	0	3.36

GREENSBORO GENERALS

SCORING

	Games	G	A	Pts.	PIM
Sal Manganaro	67	31	34	65	178
David Whitworth	61	17	42	59	109
Alexei Krovopuskov	62	25	29	54	134
Joel Irwin	69	22	24	46	77
Oleg Timchenko	56	20	21	41	51
Justin Cardwell	37	16	22	38	53
Aniket Dhadphale	51	18	17	35	50
Tracy Egeland	38	15	18	33	108
Martin Galik	58	11	18	29	20
Van Burgess	37	9	13	22	9
Mike Sylvia	15	6	12	18	8
David-Al Beauregard	17	9	7	16	26
Igor Boiko	57	1	15	16	103
Clay Awe	52	1	14	15	154
Marc Tropper	17	6	8	14	42
Keith O'Connell	69	2	11	13	225
Wes Swinson	21	2	9	11	60
Ian Walterson	28	2	8	10	32
T.J. Tanberg	32	2	6	8	34
Juraj Slovak	52	1	7	8	77
Ryan Faubert	24	4	3	7	8
Chad Woollard	15	3	4	7	8
Dean Shmyr	50	2	5	7	298
Mike Piersol	21	0	7	7	14
Mike Bayrack	15	1	5	6	4
Dean Zayonce	28	2	2	4	87
Kevin Diachina	14	0	3	3	28
Greg Willers	6	1	1	2	4

	Games	G	A	Pts.	PIM
Francis Larivee (goalie)	31	0	2	2	49
John McCabe	10	0	1	1	7
Matt Eisler (goalie)	36	0	1	1	16
Jason Carriere	1	0	0	0	0
Sergei Exseev	2	0	0	0	0
Roger Larche	2	0	0	0	0
Oleg Romashko (goalie)	2	0	0	0	0
Mike Varhaug	3	0	0	0	7
Michel Larocque (goalie)	4	0	0	0	7
Rob Schweyer	4	0	0	0	10
Phil Berger	5	0	0	0	10
Brent Belecki (goalie)	9	0	0	0	0

GOALTENDING

	Gms.	Min.	W	L	T	G	SO	Avg.
Oleg Romashko	2	30	0	0	0	1	0	2.02
Matt Eisler	36	1852	10	16	5	128	0	4.15
Francis Larivee	31	1626	7	17	2	128	0	4.72
Michel Larocque	4	229	1	3	0	20	0	5.24
Brent Belecki	9	443	2	7	0	42	0	5.69

GREENVILLE GRRROWL

SCORING

	Games	G	A	Pts.	PIM
Sean Venedam	68	33	60	93	70
Scott Kirton	59	25	50	75	135
Martin Masa	57	21	41	62	75
Ajay Baines	67	24	31	55	102
Davis Payne	48	22	25	47	104
Dana Mulvihill	46	16	26	42	68
Ryan Stewart	65	15	21	36	118
Jay Panzer	45	11	23	34	10
Charles Paquette	70	14	19	33	186
Mike Sylvia	42	11	20	31	51
Joel Trottier	49	10	20	30	53
Neil Fewster	37	11	18	29	20
Sean Ritchlin	39	13	13	26	19
Bill McCauley	43	12	13	25	39
Vratislav Cech	55	7	15	22	51
Justin Cardwell	15	8	12	20	8
Jason Kelly	40	5	13	18	66
Yanick Jean	67	4	14	18	103
Dennis Maxwell	12	5	8	13	29
Eric Lundin	19	3	7	10	11
Eric Van Acker	46	0	8	8	112
Denis Timofeev	24	2	3	5	30
David Bell	21	2	2	4	70
Kevin Diachina	36	1	3	4	50
Nick Vitucci (goalie)	34	0	3	3	6
Todd Markus	8	1	1	2	9
Omar Ennaffati	3	1	0	1	0
Scott Fankhouser (goalie)	7	0	1	1	2
Mike Tamburro (goalie)	20	0	1	1	8
Sergei Tkachenko (goalie)	13	0	0	0	12

GOALTENDING

	Gms.	Min.	W	L	T	G	SO	Avg.
Nick Vitucci	34	1916	21	9	2	79	1	2.47
Scott Fankhouser	7	419	6	1	0	18	0	2.58
Sergei Tkachenko	13	708	6	3	2	34	1	2.88
Mike Tamburro	20	1142	13	5	2	57	1	3.00

HAMPTON ROADS ADMIRALS

SCORING

	Games	G	A	Pts.	PIM
Rick Kowalsky	67	23	47	70	109
Rod Taylor	60	36	33	69	89
Dominic Maltais	66	36	31	67	199
Mike Omicioli	47	19	41	60	100
John Parco	52	19	33	52	34
Bobby Russell	60	15	27	42	18
Marty Clapton	64	17	23	40	49
Chad Ackerman	69	4	36	40	32

	Games	G	A	Pts.	PIM
Colin Pepperall	45	14	22	36	157
Richard Pitirri	58	8	17	25	29
Etienne Drapeau	46	10	12	22	167
Louis Bedard	60	5	17	22	307
Dean Stork	52	5	13	18	69
Ryan Gillis	47	4	13	17	54
Dwight Parrish	62	5	9	14	199
Gerad Adams	58	3	11	14	165
Trevor Johnson	55	3	10	13	140
Mike Siklenka	58	7	4	11	62
Brad Church	11	4	3	7	31
Steve Sherriffs	14	3	3	6	8
Jan Lasak (goalie)	59	0	5	5	23
Derek Ernest	40	1	2	3	91
Jean-Francois Fortin	7	0	2	2	0
Jason Hamilton	2	0	1	1	20
Jamie Coady	3	0	0	0	5
Curtis Cruickshank (goalie)	7	0	0	0	0
Brent Belecki (goalie)	9	0	0	0	0

GOALTENDING

	Gms.	Min.	W	L	T	G	SO	Avg.
Jan Lasak	59	3409	36	17	4	145	0	2.55
Curtis Cruickshank	7	375	4	3	0	22	0	3.52
Brent Belecki	9	378	4	2	0	23	0	3.65

HUNTINGTON BLIZZARD

SCORING

	Games	G	A	Pts.	PIM
Kelly Harper	65	20	44	64	34
Jim Bermingham	60	23	36	59	95
Jamie Sokolsky	70	19	39	58	87
Butch Kaebel	70	22	31	53	47
Pete Brearley	55	23	23	46	59
Jamie Pegg	59	5	39	44	96
Jason Bermingham	63	19	20	39	44
Anthony Terzo	51	19	16	35	24
Curtis Bois	64	12	22	34	136
Mark Spence	41	13	15	28	39
Bill Baaki	58	12	9	21	118
Tony Tuzzolino	20	6	13	19	43
Keith Cassidy	66	4	14	18	121
Mike Perna	56	4	12	16	154
David Oliver	26	6	9	15	151
Jim Moss	66	1	14	15	158
Sean Robertson	29	5	9	14	11
Van Burgess	16	4	10	14	10
Anthony Cappelletti	52	5	7	12	72
Mark Edmundson	18	4	0	4	26
Mike Mulligan	17	2	2	4	33
Andrew Pearsall	44	1	3	4	33
Torrey DiRoberto	3	1	1	2	6
Frank Littlejohn	5	0	1	1	6
Brodie Coffin	6	0	1	1	17
Donnie Kinney	6	0	1	1	15
Mike Jaros	10	0	1	1	0
Blaine Russell (goalie)	41	0	1	1	21
Brent Belecki (goalie)	1	0	0	0	0
Owen Lessard	1	0	0	0	0
Lance Perschau (goalie)	1	0	0	0	0
Jordan Flodell	2	0	0	0	2
Rob Stanfield	3	0	0	0	4
Pierre-Luc Therrien (goalie)	3	0	0	0	0
Rob Murdoch (goalie)	4	0	0	0	4
Ryan Hoople (goalie)	31	0	0	0	2

GOALTENDING

	Gms.	Min.	W	L	T	G	SO	Avg.
Pierre-Luc Therrien	3	160	2	1	0	6	0	2.25
Rob Murdoch	4	104	0	1	0	5	0	2.88
Brent Belecki	1	60	1	0	0	3	0	3.00
Blaine Russell	41	2200	20	10	7	119	1	3.24
Ryan Hoople	31	1652	12	13	3	92	0	3.34
Lance Perschau	1	12	0	0	0	1	0	5.00

JACKSON BANDITS

SCORING

	Games	G	A	Pts.	PIM
Glenn Crawford	59	14	39	53	36
Lee Jinman	44	19	32	51	30
Brian Callahan	70	28	18	46	168
Brandon Lafrance	52	20	14	34	23
J.P. O'Connor	62	14	19	33	84
Jamie O'Leary	61	12	18	30	112
Mike Bayrack	50	16	13	29	20
Adam Borzecki	65	7	21	28	153
Jim Brown	30	11	15	26	36
Brad Peddle	48	6	15	21	51
Denny Felsner	28	10	10	20	6
Jason Knox	52	2	16	18	38
Troy Mann	30	9	8	17	6
Matt Mulhern	58	7	9	16	26
Jeremy Mylymok	43	1	15	16	79
Dave Stewart	65	5	8	13	307
Tim Green	51	0	13	13	32
Dan Carney	36	5	7	12	16
Chris Wismer	64	1	8	9	147
Chad Woollard	17	3	4	7	17
Brad Holzinger	10	2	3	5	16
Mike Piersol	13	2	3	5	10
Scott Malone	10	0	5	5	29
Dennis Mullen	10	0	5	5	37
Brodie Coffin	11	2	2	4	16
Tracy Egeland	16	1	3	4	64
Mark Loeding	9	3	0	3	2
Bob Thornton	8	0	3	3	18
Jay Woodcroft	1	1	0	1	0
Ryan Hacker	6	0	1	1	13
Greg Callahan	10	0	1	1	30
Drew Kehler	19	0	1	1	9
David Brumby (goalie)	60	0	1	1	16
Ryan Christie	1	0	0	0	0
Dan Ronan	2	0	0	0	0
Chris Peyton	3	0	0	0	0
Marco Emond (goalie)	18	0	0	0	2

GOALTENDING

	Gms.	Min.	W	L	T	G	SO	Avg.
David Brumby	59	3368	28	25	4	167	7	2.97
Marco Emond	18	827	4	7	2	49	0	3.55

JACKSONVILLE LIZARD KINGS

SCORING

	Games	G	A	Pts.	PIM
Brad Federenko	70	25	41	66	22
Mike Hurley	56	38	27	65	28
Bryan Forslund	70	22	43	65	73
Ritchie Bronilla	70	12	39	51	42
Alexei Podalinski	57	15	33	48	55
Patrick Gingras	70	18	26	44	189
Mark Giannetti	64	15	27	42	64
Mario Therrien	47	18	20	38	64
Derek Eberle	47	17	21	38	28
Jeff Bes	28	12	24	36	27
Eric Naud	51	16	18	34	242
Vitali Kozel	44	9	25	34	40
Danny Reja	21	8	9	17	29
Jean-Philippe Soucy	59	2	13	15	124
Matt Golden	46	4	7	11	41
Joel Theriault	17	4	6	10	47
Bob Thornton	12	2	7	9	16
Brooke Chateau	31	4	3	7	20
Sergei Fedotov	19	3	3	6	14
Mario Cormier	46	0	4	4	34
Ray LeBlanc (goalie)	56	0	4	4	2
Ryan Cirillo	11	0	3	3	8
Todd Markus	7	1	1	2	16
Dereck Gosselin	20	1	1	2	18
Dennis Mullen	3	0	2	2	5
Dan Back	15	0	2	2	8

	Games	G	A	Pts.	PIM
Domenic Perna	3	0	1	1	2
Chris Bonvie	7	0	1	1	0
Jan Jas	1	0	0	0	0
Dennis Rybin	1	0	0	0	0
Sean Brouns	2	0	0	0	0
Dan Ronan	2	0	0	0	2
Brad Gratton	3	0	0	0	0
Pat Mazzoli (goalie)	3	0	0	0	0
Wil Tormey	3	0	0	0	2
Jarret Whidden	3	0	0	0	0
Henry Kuster	4	0	0	0	0
Mike Pietrangelo	4	0	0	0	2
Phillippe Lakos	5	0	0	0	2
Mark McMahon	5	0	0	0	2
Forest Karr (goalie)	10	0	0	0	0
Jeff Levy (goalie)	12	0	0	0	0

GOALTENDING

	Gms.	Min.	W	L	T	G	SO	Avg.
Ray LeBlanc	56	3030	22	25	8	183	0	3.62
Forest Karr	10	480	2	3	1	35	0	4.37
Pat Mazzoli	3	164	1	1	0	12	0	4.38
Jeff Levy	12	507	2	5	0	43	0	5.09

JOHNSTOWN CHIEFS

SCORING

	Games	G	A	Pts.	PIM
Andrew Dale	64	26	42	68	73
Carl Fleury	55	18	38	56	93
Joel Irving	61	25	26	51	152
Andrew Clark	65	26	21	47	41
Derrick Walser	54	17	26	43	104
Brent Bilodeau	70	8	26	34	94
Shawn Frappier	58	8	25	33	51
Mike Thompson	37	14	16	30	55
Ryan Chaytors	54	13	16	29	45
Kris Porter	30	13	13	26	16
Jody Shelley	36	9	17	26	256
John Tripp	38	13	11	24	64
Bryan McKinney	57	5	16	21	140
Dmitri Tarabrin	67	5	14	19	95
Mike Vellinga	69	2	17	19	144
E.J. Bradley	35	5	13	18	14
Chuck Mindell	41	9	8	17	18
Brett McLean	8	4	7	11	6
Jeff Sullivan	58	2	8	10	181
Bruce Coles	8	3	5	8	8
Ryan Tocher	11	2	4	6	23
Kevin Kellet	37	1	3	4	53
Jason Spence	36	2	1	3	106
Brett Gibson	6	1	2	3	0
Brent Dodginghorse	17	1	2	3	62
Matt Eldred	11	0	3	3	33
Frederic Deschenes	49	0	3	3	2
Frank Littlejohn	1	2	0	2	4
Tyrone Garner (goalie)	17	0	2	2	2
Yauheni Kurylin	5	1	0	1	0
Mikko Sivonen	3	0	0	0	0
Craig Hillier (goalie)	5	0	0	0	2
Pavel Nestak (goalie)	5	0	0	0	0
Tom Field	8	0	0	0	0

GOALTENDING

	Gms.	Min.	W	L	T	G	SO	Avg.
Pavel Nestak	5	210	1	1	0	10	0	2.85
Tyrone Garner	17	971	8	6	3	48	0	2.97
Frederic Deschenes	49	2786	23	19	6	146	2	3.14
Craig Hillier	5	212	1	2	0	15	0	4.24

LOUISIANA ICEGATORS

SCORING

	Games	G	A	Pts.	PIM
John Spoltore	66	27	92	119	89
Jay Murphy	69	55	28	83	167

	Games	G	A	Pts.	PIM
Chris Valicevic	70	27	45	72	46
Ryan Shanahan	61	28	33	61	172
Shawn McNeil	62	26	28	54	30
John DePourcq	44	19	32	51	2
Vaclav Nedomansky	40	14	35	49	80
Mike Murray	49	14	26	40	92
Corey Neilson	56	10	16	26	127
Matthew Pagnutti	69	6	17	23	109
Mike Oliveira	45	8	13	21	24
Chris Bogas	60	7	12	19	76
Jessie Rezansoff	34	5	11	16	155
Rob Weingartner	26	5	7	12	92
Stan Melanson	68	2	10	12	218
Ryan Pawluk	16	3	8	11	11
Jason McQuat	29	3	8	11	88
Paul Strand	12	5	5	10	25
Ryan Gaucher	16	3	5	8	10
Mark Cadotte	13	5	2	7	22
Mike Kucsulain	42	3	4	7	159
Rob Sinclair	14	3	2	5	12
Jason Sessa	17	1	4	5	14
Mark Loeding	7	1	1	2	0
Cam Severson	7	0	2	2	22
Steve O'Rourke	10	0	2	2	12
Nick Hriczov	24	0	2	2	82
Dave Arsenault (goalie)	26	0	2	2	23
Hugo Marchand	48	1	0	1	149
Sean Gauthier (goalie)	22	0	1	1	6
Mike Valley (goalie)	28	0	1	1	2
Ryan Christie	2	0	0	0	4
Kyle Freadrich	3	0	0	0	17
Sean Basilio (goalie)	5	0	0	0	0
John Wickstrom	10	0	0	0	4

GOALTENDING

	Gms.	Min.	W	L	T	G	SO	Avg.
Sean Gauthier	22	1230	12	6	3	62	0	3.02
Dave Arsenault	26	1375	14	6	1	75	0	3.27
Mike Valley	28	1466	15	6	5	81	1	3.32
Sean Basilio	5	118	2	0	0	8	0	4.06

MISSISSIPPI SEA WOLVES

SCORING

	Games	G	A	Pts.	PIM
J.F. Aube	67	27	41	68	30
Dave Paradise	66	23	35	58	106
Mark Rupnow	70	26	31	57	30
Bob Woods	70	19	35	54	33
Scott King	42	16	35	51	54
Brad Essex	67	17	17	34	231
Ryan Gaucher	50	5	27	32	27
John Evangelista	54	10	21	31	65
Patrick Rochon	68	5	25	30	166
John Kosobud	44	18	11	29	56
Mikhail Kravets	23	7	20	27	27
Steve Duke	70	5	18	23	73
Jonathan Weaver	28	4	17	21	4
Ryan Pawluk	24	11	8	19	23
Sean Gillam	51	4	15	19	63
Cody Bowtell	22	9	7	16	57
Vaclav Nedomansky	14	6	10	16	44
Andrew Proskurnicki	26	6	9	15	146
Brad Goulet	54	6	7	13	29
Mike Martone	62	3	9	12	133
Robert Francz	16	7	4	11	56
Jan Melichercik	13	5	2	7	2
Trevor Gillies	53	0	6	6	202
Alex Andreyev	21	1	2	3	43
Jon Gaskins	7	1	0	1	4
Dan Focht	4	0	1	1	0
Chuck Thuss (goalie)	40	0	1	1	24
Dominic Bergeron (goalie)	1	0	0	0	0
Todd Miller	1	0	0	0	0
Pat Staerker	2	0	0	0	0

	Games	G	A	Pts.	PIM
Wes Blevins	3	0	0	0	2
Scott Page	4	0	0	0	19
Pierre-Luc Therrier (goalie)	10	0	0	0	0
Sylvain Daigle (goalie)	25	0	0	0	4

GOALTENDING

	Gms.	Min.	W	L	T	G	SO	Avg.
Pierre-Luc Therrier	10	596	2	7	1	26	1	2.62
Chuck Thuss	39	2199	20	11	5	106	2	2.89
Sylvain Daigle	25	1333	13	8	2	71	0	3.20
Dominic Bergeron	1	59	0	1	0	4	0	4.07

MOBILE MYSTICKS

SCORING

	Games	G	A	Pts.	PIM
Jason Elders	67	37	51	88	16
Mark Turner	61	45	37	82	54
Bobby Stewart	65	31	46	77	64
Tom Nolan	63	30	31	61	73
Russ Guzior	66	28	31	59	59
Jason Clarke	57	18	38	56	373
Hugues Gervais	65	20	33	53	187
B.J. Kilbourne	63	14	25	39	45
Josh Harrold	64	12	25	37	59
Chad Onufrechuk	46	16	17	33	30
Jeff Kozakowski	59	0	30	30	90
Benoit Cotnoir	66	7	21	28	55
Mitch Vig	69	2	17	19	107
David Craievich	27	1	14	15	20
Scott Cherrey	62	6	8	14	45
Dave Van Drunen	29	1	9	10	78
Chad Alban (goalie)	39	0	7	7	24
John McCabe	25	2	3	5	72
Ian Walterson	35	0	5	5	23
Dennis Mullen	15	2	2	4	68
Jason Metcalfe	13	0	4	4	34
Anders Sorensen	29	2	1	3	8
David Whitworth	3	0	3	3	2
Chris Neil	4	0	2	2	39
Sean Farmer	12	0	2	2	10
Lee Svangstu	23	1	0	1	82
Dereck Gosselin	5	0	1	1	4
Steve DeBus (goalie)	31	0	0	0	2

GOALTENDING

	Gms.	Min.	W	L	T	G	SO	Avg.
Chad Alban	39	2334	25	13	1	114	0	2.93
Steve DeBus	31	1853	15	15	1	107	1	3.46

NEW ORLEANS BRASS

SCORING

	Games	G	A	Pts.	PIM
Jeff Lazaro	70	24	56	80	109
Andrew Taylor	70	26	34	60	93
Mark Polak	70	26	30	56	66
Stephane Soulliere	69	24	28	52	77
Darryl LaFrance	47	23	25	48	29
Janne Salpa	63	20	26	46	27
Darren Sinclair	58	11	32	43	28
Marcus Gustafsson	65	16	17	33	41
Samy Nasreddine	55	8	21	29	104
Steve Cheredaryk	56	8	17	25	192
Rejean Stringer	30	6	13	19	6
Sami Jarvenpaa	50	6	11	17	28
Adam Colagiacomo	18	7	7	14	12
Kris Porter	25	6	7	13	16
Antti Ahokas	61	6	7	13	150
Dean Moore	40	4	8	12	133
Jay McGee	35	2	10	12	39
Chris Aldous	12	2	7	9	6
Chad Dameworth	54	0	6	6	41
Adam Nittel	26	2	3	5	96

	Games	G	A	Pts.	PIM
Mikko Koivisto	16	0	5	5	22
Andy Lundbohm	12	2	2	4	4
Didier Pietropaolo	44	1	3	4	27
Roger Holeczy	6	0	2	2	0
Chris Slater	8	0	1	1	8
Doug Bonner (goalie)	50	0	1	1	8
John Schiller	1	0	0	0	0
Walter Wellenreiter	1	0	0	0	0
Bill Newson	2	0	0	0	2
Mike Morrone	9	0	0	0	42
Terry Friesen (goalie)	26	0	0	0	4

GOALTENDING

	Gms.	Min.	W	L	T	G	SO	Avg.
Doug Bonner	50	2828	25	17	5	130	2	2.76
Terry Friesen	26	1356	11	10	2	76	2	3.36

PEE DEE PRIDE

SCORING

	Games	G	A	Pts.	PIM
Dany Bousquet	56	38	39	77	59
Allan Sirois	69	20	38	58	108
Casey Kesselring	69	23	30	53	35
Buddy Smith	63	16	37	53	37
Ryan Petz	70	23	28	51	77
Peter Geronazzo	70	21	27	48	55
Buddy Wallace	43	19	16	35	98
Kevin Haupt	68	13	21	34	14
Trevor Demmans	70	7	22	29	64
Rick Mrozik	60	9	19	28	44
Brian Goudie	47	7	19	26	116
Kyle Knopp	57	10	14	24	10
Bryan Tapper	67	7	9	16	67
Darcy Dallas	58	4	9	13	82
J.F. Tremblay	17	3	6	9	31
Brodie Coffin	30	1	8	9	72
Dan Fournel	35	1	7	8	93
Rich Metro	29	2	4	6	8
Earl Cronan	25	1	5	6	27
Wes Goldie	7	3	1	4	2
Sandy Cohen	6	2	2	4	0
Bob Prier	3	1	2	3	17
Andy Powers	7	1	2	3	6
Kevin Grimes	41	1	2	3	87
Lee Jinman	12	0	3	3	20
Jeff Burgoyne	9	0	2	2	6
Mike Dombkiewicz	9	0	2	2	4
Nick Hriczov	12	0	1	1	51
Sandy Allan (goalie)	33	0	1	1	10
Jeff Boettger	1	0	0	0	0
Tim Warrilow	4	0	0	0	7
Mike Rodrigues	5	0	0	0	2
Paxton Schafer (goalie)	41	0	0	0	4

GOALTENDING

	Gms.	Min.	W	L	T	G	SO	Avg.
Sandy Allan	33	1856	21	8	3	70	5	2.26
Paxton Schafer	41	2331	26	10	2	94	2	2.42

PENSACOLA ICE PILOTS

SCORING

	Games	G	A	Pts.	PIM
Harold Hersh	65	17	30	47	38
John McNabb	66	17	30	47	34
Paul Strand	57	19	26	45	69
Rob Smillie	70	18	24	42	20
Shane Calder	68	15	26	41	150
Albie O'Connell	67	13	28	41	48
Darcy George	55	20	19	39	38
Lorne Toews	63	22	14	36	111
Nick Checco	57	15	21	36	23
Jeff Trembecky	43	12	16	28	30
Marc Dupuis	57	8	20	28	27

	Games	G	A	Pts.	PIM
Joe Harney	70	3	23	26	93
Bruce Richardson	29	7	13	20	83
Chad Nelson	26	8	7	15	50
Bill Kohn	59	3	12	15	42
Kirk DeWaele	61	3	11	14	59
Alexandre Couture	30	5	7	12	32
Steve Dumonski	17	3	8	11	38
Raitis Ivanans	59	3	7	10	146
Evgeny Lazarev	11	3	5	8	23
Jon Coe	4	1	2	3	0
Jeff Rucinski	23	0	3	3	21
Luc Fournier	14	0	2	2	6
Chris Libett	1	0	1	1	4
Dale Masson (goalie)	19	0	1	1	2
Garth Gartner	3	0	0	0	5
Scott LaGrand (goalie)	51	0	0	0	2

GOALTENDING

	Gms.	Min.	W	L	T	G	SO	Avg.
Scott LaGrand	51	3050	26	20	5	139	0	2.73
Dale Masson	19	1138	9	9	1	66	1	3.48

PEORIA RIVERMEN

SCORING

	Games	G	A	Pts.	PIM
Joe Rybar	58	17	51	68	40
Blaine Fitzpatrick	61	31	32	63	231
James Desmarais	59	26	33	59	51
Darren Clark	69	24	32	56	40
Jason Christie	64	21	35	56	199
J.F. Boutin	42	22	19	41	136
Craig Anderson	55	5	27	32	12
Jason Lawmaster	56	10	20	30	264
Jason Deleurme	47	14	15	29	78
Daniel Hodge	69	8	20	28	30
Cam Severson	56	19	8	27	138
Matt Smith	57	11	15	26	101
Darren Maloney	65	6	20	26	72
Trevor Baker	34	10	11	21	135
Didier Tremblay	36	5	16	21	14
Aaron Boh	15	5	12	17	49
Tomaz Razingar	51	2	13	15	44
Matt Golden	16	6	8	14	6
Luke Gruden	50	1	13	14	104
Trevor Wasyluk	7	8	5	13	6
John Gurskis	20	5	7	12	31
Tyler Willis	19	5	6	11	89
Alexandre Couture	25	5	6	11	35
Tyler McMillan	19	4	5	9	4
Bret Meyers	3	1	2	3	4
Duane Derksen (goalie)	43	0	3	3	15
Peter Smrek	4	1	1	2	2
Kenzie Homer	24	1	1	2	51
Chris Bonvie	2	0	1	1	0
Blaz Emersic	12	0	1	1	0
Kenric Exner (goalie)	22	0	1	1	15
Sami Mettovaara	1	0	0	0	0
Sean Farmer	2	0	0	0	2
Darin Kimble	10	0	0	0	21
Cody Rudkowsky (goalie)	10	0	0	0	0

GOALTENDING

	Gms.	Min.	W	L	T	G	SO	Avg.
Duane Derksen	43	2487	30	9	3	122	1	2.94
Kenric Exner	22	1102	9	7	2	54	0	2.94
Cody Rudkowsky	10	599	6	4	0	32	0	3.20

RICHMOND RENEGADES

SCORING

	Games	G	A	Pts.	PIM
Andrew Shier	68	22	62	84	106
Joe Bianchi	64	41	36	77	152

	Games	G	A	Pts.	PIM
Ryan Kraft	44	32	35	67	32
Peter Vandermeer	58	31	25	56	457
Frank Novock	70	23	28	51	26
Kevin Knopp	70	12	35	47	134
Matt Noga	47	13	32	45	40
Joe Vandermeer	70	8	32	40	122
Steve Dumonski	49	12	26	38	169
Neal Rech	66	21	15	36	100
Dylan Gyori	29	11	20	31	50
Marc Bouchard	69	6	23	29	33
Trevor Senn	43	7	13	20	269
Dan Vandermeer	68	2	16	18	165
Craig Paterson	62	6	9	15	144
David Lambeth	47	2	12	14	59
Clayton Read	37	2	9	11	16
Darren Wetherill	41	1	7	8	86
David Hoogsteen	14	5	2	7	0
Jesse Bull	32	1	4	5	10
Jeff Rucinski	16	0	2	2	12
Dennis Bassett (goalie)	21	0	2	2	2
Kris Cumming	3	0	1	1	0
Maxime Gingras (goalie)	7	0	1	1	0
Tom Noble (goalie)	20	0	1	1	4
Brad Frattaroli	1	0	0	0	0
Rick Nichol (goalie)	1	0	0	0	0
Greg Callahan	2	0	0	0	2
John Lovell	2	0	0	0	0
Scott Prekaski (goalie)	3	0	0	0	0
Sean Matile (goalie)	30	0	0	0	6

GOALTENDING

	Gms.	Min.	W	L	T	G	SO	Avg.
Scott Prekaski	3	1	0	0	0	0	0	0.00
Rick Nichol	1	60	1	0	0	2	0	2.00
Maxime Gingras	7	379	5	1	1	14	1	2.22
Sean Matile	30	1690	18	10	1	74	1	2.63
Tom Noble	20	1074	10	5	2	54	0	3.02
Dennis Bassett	21	982	10	5	1	51	2	3.12

ROANOKE EXPRESS

SCORING

	Games	G	A	Pts.	PIM
Dion Delmonte	67	19	39	58	105
Ben Schust	66	27	25	52	28
Paul Di Francesco	64	24	26	50	49
Duane Harmer	47	10	37	47	59
Calvin Elfring	63	6	40	46	92
Mike Peron	46	12	28	40	122
Troy Lake	70	18	16	34	87
Joe Murphy	34	12	19	31	34
Kris Cantu	34	19	11	30	35
Todd Compeau	57	14	14	28	46
Brent Ozarowski	65	9	17	26	33
Rob Schweyer	54	10	12	22	91
John Poapst	30	8	8	16	21
Aniket Dhadphale	15	9	5	14	8
Travis Smith	69	4	10	14	133
David Froh	28	1	13	14	12
Tim Christian	32	5	7	12	14
Steve Sabo	61	4	7	11	145
Aaron Gates	65	2	9	11	84
John Evangelista	12	4	4	8	14
J.F. Tremblay	42	4	4	8	131
Ryan Faubert	35	0	4	4	19
Dave Gagnon (goalie)	37	0	2	2	0
Gerald Moriarity	25	0	1	1	68
Nate Handrahan	3	0	0	0	2
Daniel Berthiaume (goalie)	37	0	0	0	0

GOALTENDING

	Gms.	Min.	W	L	T	G	SO	Avg.
Daniel Berthiaume	37	2103	21	12	4	87	2	2.48
Dave Gagnon	37	2085	23	8	2	87	0	2.50

SOUTH CAROLINA STINGRAYS
SCORING

	Games	G	A	Pts.	PIM
Dave Seitz	68	25	48	73	60
Brad Dexter	63	7	59	66	44
Greg Schmidt	69	30	27	57	114
Brett Marietti	69	27	28	55	172
Brendan Concannon	43	19	36	55	20
Adam Calder	41	22	22	44	84
Rob Concannon	59	23	20	43	202
Damian Prescott	54	17	19	36	35
Mike Nicholishen	61	11	24	35	79
Jason Wright	69	5	26	31	80
Joe Ciccarello	55	12	18	30	45
Jeff Romfo	59	10	14	24	71
Luc Theoret	48	9	10	19	74
Jason Sessa	15	10	8	18	30
Marc Tardif	50	4	14	18	196
Jared Bednar	61	4	13	17	214
Shaun Peet	66	1	11	12	194
Joe Van Volsen	21	4	5	9	27
Chris Wheaton	47	6	1	7	118
Doug Schmidt	41	2	5	7	50
Vladimir Antipov	4	0	4	4	2
Gino Pulente	13	1	2	3	10
Chad Remackel	5	2	0	2	0
Shannon Briske	3	1	1	2	2
Jody Lehman (goalie)	57	0	2	2	26
John Maksymiu	3	1	0	1	0
Todd Barclay	1	0	1	1	0
Kirk Daubenspeck (goalie)	6	0	1	1	6
Tom Noble (goalie)	1	0	0	0	0
Forest Karr (goalie)	2	0	0	0	0
Eric Linkowski	2	0	0	0	0
Nolan McDonald (goalie)	2	0	0	0	0
Jason Saal (goalie)	8	0	0	0	6

GOALTENDING

	Gms.	Min.	W	L	T	G	SO	Avg.
Kirk Daubenspeck	6	360	4	2	0	17	0	2.83
Forest Karr	2	78	0	2	0	4	0	3.06
Jody Lehman	57	3284	28	18	8	169	2	3.09
Tom Noble	1	60	0	1	0	4	0	4.03
Jason Saal	8	355	3	1	2	29	0	4.90
Nolan McDonald	2	54	0	1	0	6	0	6.72

TALLAHASSEE TIGER SHARKS
SCORING

	Games	G	A	Pts.	PIM
Paul Buczkowski	69	25	44	69	28
Olivier Morin	53	29	26	55	113
Maxim Spiridonov	57	22	30	52	67
Matt Oates	53	28	21	49	51
J.F. Houle	55	18	30	48	71
David Thibeault	68	17	30	47	108
Adam Copeland	53	21	23	44	32
Brian Urick	45	21	20	41	14
Chad Hinz	49	15	25	40	35
Derek Paget	63	11	28	39	59
Darren McAusland	63	6	25	31	34
Brent Cullaton	31	10	14	24	19
Kimbi Daniels	34	11	12	23	38
Jeff McLean	16	3	15	18	2
Jason Kelly	18	1	11	12	44
Simon Tremblay	16	4	7	11	17
Mike Thompson	24	8	2	10	24
Alexandre LaPorte	60	3	7	10	47
Todd Kidd	38	1	8	9	105
Marc Gaudet	49	0	9	9	28
Jim Baxter	12	2	5	7	4
Christian Caron	8	0	5	5	2
Mark Streit	14	0	5	5	16
Kevin Kellet	32	0	4	4	44
Jason Reid	57	0	4	4	32

	Games	G	A	Pts.	PIM
T.J. Tanberg	8	0	3	3	4
Andy Silverman	11	0	3	3	23
Pavel Smirnov	3	0	2	2	2
Wes Swinson	4	0	2	2	2
Gino Pulente	5	0	1	1	0
Jason Weinrich	12	0	1	1	11
Ryan Hartung	1	0	0	0	0
Konstantin Sidulov	1	0	0	0	0
Atrars Tribuncovs	4	0	0	0	0
Larry Shapley	11	0	0	0	48
Ian Perkins (goalie)	14	0	0	0	0
Danny Lorenz (goalie)	33	0	0	0	0
Chris Wickenheiser (goalie)	36	0	0	0	14

GOALTENDING

	Gms.	Min.	W	L	T	G	SO	Avg.
Chris Wickenheiser	36	1715	11	17	2	101	0	3.53
Danny Lorenz	33	1749	15	12	2	105	0	3.60
Ian Perkins	14	727	5	4	2	44	0	3.63

TOLEDO STORM
SCORING

	Games	G	A	Pts.	PIM
Andrew Williamson	63	63	39	102	114
Chris Gignac	59	33	56	89	36
Rob Thorpe	66	34	31	65	104
Tim Christian	39	9	25	34	24
Mark DeSantis	44	4	28	32	235
Jason Robinson	65	3	23	26	185
Jan Sulc	51	10	11	21	40
Tyler Prosofsky	28	8	12	20	118
Andrei Chouroupov	15	6	7	13	14
Eduard Pershin	12	3	10	13	29
Shawn Maltby	16	8	3	11	51
Jeff White	38	2	9	11	30
Jarno Mensonen	32	4	4	8	4
Jarret Whidden	13	3	5	8	4
Aaron Boh	10	0	8	8	94
Todd Steinmetz	30	4	3	7	72
Justin Clark	38	1	6	7	25
Karel Betik	22	0	7	7	42
Walker McDonald	38	3	3	6	45
Mike Mulligan	35	2	4	6	30
Igor Malykhin	15	4	0	4	10
Brad Cruikshank	13	2	2	4	16
Alex Radzinsky	27	1	3	4	14
Gerald Moriarity	41	1	3	4	239
Ryan Hartung	21	0	4	4	10
Mark Thompson	53	1	2	3	122
Mike Jaros	3	0	3	3	2
Jason Ricci	3	0	3	3	2
Donnie Kinney	10	0	3	3	0
Sergei Olympiev	8	2	0	2	2
Mike Morrone	26	2	0	2	112
Rob Millar	8	0	2	2	4
Trevor Koenig	30	0	2	2	12
Ken Tasker	42	1	0	1	438
Xavier Delisle	2	0	1	1	0
Dave Zunic	2	0	1	1	2
Seabrook Satterlund	6	0	1	1	6
Kevin St. Pierre (goalie)	35	0	1	1	27
Jason Carriere	1	0	0	0	9
Peter Constantine	1	0	0	0	10
Ladislav Hampeis	1	0	0	0	0
Mike Herrera	1	0	0	0	0
Danny Prudhomme	1	0	0	0	0
Jason Johnson	2	0	0	0	0
Mark Loeding	2	0	0	0	2
Brett Severson	2	0	0	0	0
Leorr Shtrom (goalie)	3	0	0	0	0
Mark Deazeley	4	0	0	0	17
Greg Tsouklas	4	0	0	0	0
Brian Hamilton (goalie)	6	0	0	0	0

	Games	G	A	Pts.	PIM
Daniel Kletke	6	0	0	0	2
Craig Hillier (goalie)	9	0	0	0	2
Qamil Elezi	14	0	0	0	31

GOALTENDING

	Gms.	Min.	W	L	T	G	SO	Avg.
Leorr Shtrom	3	83	0	1	0	5	0	3.62
Kevin St. Pierre	35	1895	11	15	6	116	0	3.67
Trevor Koenig	30	1669	10	17	1	108	1	3.88
Craig Hillier	9	375	1	6	0	41	0	6.56
Brian Hamilton	6	165	0	2	0	24	0	8.74

TRENTON TITANS

SCORING

	Games	G	A	Pts.	PIM
Scott Bertoli	65	21	44	65	46
Cail MacLean	50	34	25	59	24
Jed Whitchurch	65	22	37	59	10
Mike Hall	45	14	32	46	16
Mike Mader	53	17	27	44	138
Mark Murphy	37	21	18	39	60
Eric Brule	47	5	34	39	78
Jerry Keefe	26	7	15	22	14
David Hoogsteen	15	9	12	21	0
Sergei Skrobot	58	4	17	21	24
D.J. Mando	36	4	13	17	73
Jesse Boulerice	25	8	8	16	90
Jeff Trembecky	27	4	11	15	33
Vince Williams	64	4	11	15	91
Dave Risk	31	9	5	14	31
Likit Andersson	45	5	8	13	33
Chris Masters	40	6	6	12	31
Kam White	55	0	12	12	159
Matt Hogan	30	5	6	11	20
Ruslan Fedotenko	8	5	3	8	9
Kurt Mallett	13	4	4	8	6
Sasha Cucuz	9	3	5	8	0
Bob Thornton	24	3	5	8	36
Martin Cerven	28	1	7	8	6
Stewart Bodtker	9	2	5	7	21
Todd Fedoruk	18	2	5	7	118
Benoit Morin	7	2	4	6	9
Matt Henderson	16	2	4	6	47
Ryan Brown	30	1	5	6	59
Adam Edinger	3	3	1	4	0
Chris Feil	43	2	2	4	70
Keith Dupee	4	1	3	4	0
Eric Weichselbaumer	18	1	3	4	10
Scott Kelsey	20	0	3	3	21
Francis Belanger	9	1	1	2	29
Bujar Amidovski (goalie)	34	0	2	2	0
Anthony Cappelletti	8	1	0	1	4
Mike Tamburro (goalie)	5	0	1	1	4
Taras Lendzyk (goalie)	19	0	1	1	2
Sean Blanchard	2	0	0	0	0
Jeff Mercer	2	0	0	0	19
Marty Phillips (goalie)	2	0	0	0	0
Eon Macfarlane	3	0	0	0	2
Michael Morostega	3	0	0	0	0
Steve Valiquette (goalie)	12	0	0	0	0

GOALTENDING

	Gms.	Min.	W	L	T	G	SO	Avg.
Taras Lendzyk	19	1136	11	8	0	44	1	2.32
Bujar Amidovski	34	1979	19	11	3	82	2	2.49
Steve Valiquette	12	692	5	6	1	36	1	3.12
Mike Tamburro	5	298	2	3	0	19	0	3.83
Marty Phillips	2	79	0	1	0	9	0	6.84

WHEELING NAILERS

SCORING

	Games	G	A	Pts.	PIM
Derek Smith	66	18	29	47	139
Curtis Wilgosh	69	20	26	46	80
Rob Millar	55	13	31	44	20
Vladimir Gratchev	49	15	25	40	27
Kevin Paden	62	16	20	36	77
Dimitri Sergeev	57	9	26	35	20
Shannon Basaraba	49	11	18	29	11
Jeff Burgoyne	60	11	17	28	35
Rob Sinclair	45	9	18	27	6
Brandon Bagnell	68	9	16	25	26
Jon Sorg	54	7	18	25	102
Scott Burt	43	10	14	24	65
Darcy Verot	44	7	12	19	240
Matt Van Horlick	62	8	10	18	233
Doug Schmidt	14	5	8	13	46
Chris Slater	48	4	8	12	96
Tom O'Connor	32	4	7	11	15
Vadim Slivchenko	9	2	7	9	6
Joe Ciccarello	5	4	4	8	0
Ivan Loginov	19	4	4	8	12
John Wickstrom	48	4	4	8	23
Shawn Allard	12	5	1	6	4
Doug Battaglia	16	1	3	4	29
Frank Littlejohn	5	2	1	3	11
Duane Vandale	10	2	1	3	16
Brandon Christian	7	1	1	2	97
Wally Wuttunee	10	0	2	2	29
Trevor Prior (goalie)	37	0	2	2	12
Pascal Gasse (goalie)	41	0	2	2	8
Keith Bland	29	1	0	1	190
Ladislav Hampeis	7	0	1	1	14
Alexandre Yudin	11	0	1	1	94
Dominic Bergeron (goalie)	1	0	0	0	0
Josh Ray	1	0	0	0	0
Grant Van Laar (goalie)	1	0	0	0	0
David Weninger (goalie)	1	0	0	0	0
Randy Best	3	0	0	0	2
Chris Rowland	6	0	0	0	15
Leon Delorme	13	0	0	0	100

GOALTENDING

	Gms.	Min.	W	L	T	G	SO	Avg.
Grant Van Laar	1	18	0	0	0	0	0	0.00
Trevor Prior	37	2052	12	21	2	112	2	3.27
Pascal Gasse	41	1966	13	17	3	109	1	3.33
David Weninger	1	60	0	1	0	4	0	4.00
Dominic Bergeron	1	59	0	1	0	6	0	6.10

PLAYERS WITH TWO OR MORE TEAMS

SCORING

	Games	G	A	Pts.	PIM
Chris Aldous, Baton Rouge	43	8	17	25	14
Chris Aldous, New Orleans	12	2	7	9	6
Totals	55	10	24	34	20
Likit Andersson, Trenton	45	5	8	13	33
Likit Andersson, Augusta	12	0	4	4	8
Totals	57	5	12	17	41
Dan Back, Arkansas	2	0	1	1	4
Dan Back, Jacksonville	15	0	2	2	8
Totals	17	0	3	3	12
Shannon Basaraba, Charlotte	6	0	2	2	0
Shannon Basaraba, Wheeling	49	11	18	29	11
Totals	55	11	20	31	11
Jim Baxter, Dayton	58	10	26	36	35
Jim Baxter, Tallahassee	12	2	5	7	4
Totals	70	12	31	43	39
Mike Bayrack, Jackson	50	16	13	29	20
Mike Bayrack, Greensboro	15	1	5	6	4
Totals	65	17	18	35	24
David-Al Beauregard, Greens.	17	9	7	16	26
David-Al Beauregard, Charlotte	53	20	20	40	22
Totals	70	29	27	56	48
Brent Belecki, Greensboro (g)	9	0	0	0	0
Brent Belecki, Charlotte (g)	4	0	0	0	0

Name	Games	G	A	Pts.	PIM
Brent Belecki, Huntington (g)	1	0	0	0	0
Brent Belecki, H. Roads (g)	9	0	0	0	0
Totals	23	0	0	0	0
Dominic Bergeron, Miss. (g)	1	0	0	0	0
Dominic Bergeron, Wheel. (g)...	1	0	0	0	0
Totals	2	0	0	0	0
Keith Bland, Baton Rouge.........	28	0	2	2	165
Keith Bland, Wheeling............	29	1	0	1	190
Totals	57	1	2	3	355
Stewart Bodtker, Augusta	29	6	14	20	57
Stewart Bodtker, Trenton	9	2	5	7	21
Totals	38	8	19	27	78
Aaron Boh, Toledo	10	0	8	8	94
Aaron Boh, Arkansas	20	3	12	15	90
Aaron Boh, Peoria.....................	15	5	12	17	49
Totals	45	8	32	40	233
Chris Bonvie, Peoria.................	2	0	1	1	0
Chris Bonvie, Jacksonville.........	7	0	1	1	0
Totals	9	0	2	2	0
Van Burgess, Charlotte.............	17	6	12	18	0
Van Burgess, Greensboro..........	37	9	13	22	9
Van Burgess, Huntington...........	16	4	10	14	10
Totals	70	19	35	54	19
Jeff Burgoyne, Pee Dee	9	0	2	2	6
Jeff Burgoyne, Wheeling	60	11	17	28	35
Totals	69	11	19	30	41
Mark Cadotte, Louisiana...........	13	5	2	7	22
Mark Cadotte, Arkansas............	49	20	32	52	92
Totals	62	25	34	59	114
Greg Callahan, Jackson	10	0	1	1	30
Greg Callahan, Richmond	2	0	0	0	2
Totals	12	0	1	1	32
Anthony Cappelletti, Trenton	8	1	0	1	4
Anthony Cappelletti, Hunt.	52	5	7	12	72
Totals	60	6	7	13	76
Justin Cardwell, Greensboro	37	16	22	38	53
Justin Cardwell, Greenville	15	8	12	20	8
Totals	52	24	34	58	61
Jason Carriere, Toledo	1	0	0	0	9
Jason Carriere, Greensboro.......	1	0	0	0	0
Totals	2	0	0	0	9
Martin Cerven, Trenton..............	28	1	7	8	6
Martin Cerven, Charlotte............	33	7	14	21	22
Totals	61	8	21	29	28
Brooke Chateau, Charlotte.........	21	1	2	3	8
Brooke Chateau, Jacksonville	31	4	3	7	20
Totals	52	5	5	10	28
Andrei Chouroupov, Toledo	15	6	7	13	14
Andrei Chouroupov, Augusta.....	52	16	20	36	34
Totals	67	22	27	49	48
Tim Christian, Roanoke	32	5	7	12	14
Tim Christian, Toledo................	39	9	25	34	24
Totals	71	14	32	46	38
Ryan Christie, Louisiana	2	0	0	0	4
Ryan Christie, Jackson	1	0	0	0	0
Totals	3	0	0	0	4
Joe Ciccarello, South Carolina...	55	12	18	30	45
Joe Ciccarello, Wheeling	5	4	4	8	0
Totals	60	16	22	38	45
Ryan Cirillo, Jacksonville	11	0	3	3	8
Ryan Cirillo, Dayton	39	5	3	8	116
Totals	50	5	6	11	124
Justin Clark, Toledo	38	1	6	7	25
Justin Clark, Arkansas	12	3	1	4	12
Totals	50	4	7	11	37
Jamie Coady, Florida................	11	3	1	4	2
Jamie Coady, Hampton Roads ..	3	0	0	0	5
Totals	14	3	1	4	7
Jon Coe, Augusta	9	1	1	2	2
Jon Coe, Pensacola	4	1	2	3	0
Totals	13	2	3	5	2
Brodie Coffin, Huntington..........	6	0	1	1	17
Brodie Coffin, Jackson..............	11	2	2	4	16
Brodie Coffin, Pee Dee.............	30	1	8	9	72

Name	Games	G	A	Pts.	PIM
Totals	47	3	11	14	105
Kevin Colley, Charlotte.............	5	2	1	3	10
Kevin Colley, Dayton	24	8	6	14	111
Totals	29	10	7	17	121
Peter Constantine, Augusta	7	1	0	1	33
Peter Constantine, Dayton	22	0	0	0	75
Peter Constantine, Toledo.........	1	0	0	0	10
Totals	30	1	0	1	118
Alexandre Couture, Peoria.........	25	5	6	11	35
Alexandre Couture, Pensacola..	30	5	7	12	32
Totals	55	10	13	23	67
Glenn Crawford, Dayton	4	1	0	1	4
Glenn Crawford, Jackson...........	59	14	39	53	36
Totals	63	15	39	54	40
Earl Cronan, Pee Dee	25	1	5	6	27
Earl Cronan, Dayton	26	11	7	18	57
Totals	51	12	12	24	84
Brent Cullaton, Tallahassee	31	10	14	24	19
Brent Cullaton, Florida..............	32	20	10	30	16
Totals	63	30	24	54	35
Mark DeSantis, Augusta	16	1	5	6	31
Mark DeSantis, Toledo.............	44	4	28	32	235
Totals	60	5	33	38	266
Aniket Dhadphale, Greensboro..	51	18	17	35	50
Aniket Dhadphale, Roanoke......	15	9	5	14	8
Totals	66	27	22	49	58
Torrey DiRoberto, Huntington ...	3	1	1	2	6
Torrey DiRoberto, Dayton	1	0	1	1	0
Totals	4	1	2	3	6
Kevin Diachina, Greenville	36	1	3	4	50
Kevin Diachina, Greensboro......	14	0	3	3	28
Totals	50	1	6	7	78
Steve Dumonski, Richmond.......	49	12	26	38	169
Steve Dumonski, Pensacola	17	3	8	11	38
Totals	66	15	34	49	207
Mark Edmundson, Huntington ...	18	4	0	4	26
Mark Edmundson, Arkansas	37	12	18	30	19
Totals	55	16	18	34	45
Tracy Egeland, Charlotte...........	12	3	8	11	13
Tracy Egeland, Greensboro........	38	15	18	33	108
Tracy Egeland, Jackson............	16	1	3	4	64
Totals	66	19	29	48	185
Blaz Emersic, Arkansas	1	0	0	0	0
Blaz Emersic, Peoria................	12	0	1	1	0
Totals	13	0	1	1	0
John Evangelista, Roanoke........	12	4	4	8	14
John Evangelista, Mississippi.....	54	10	21	31	65
Totals	66	14	25	39	79
Sean Farmer, Peoria.................	2	0	0	0	2
Sean Farmer, Mobile................	12	0	2	2	10
Totals	14	0	2	2	12
Ryan Faubert, Roanoke	35	0	4	4	19
Ryan Faubert, Greensboro.........	24	4	3	7	8
Totals	59	4	7	11	27
Tyrone Garner, Dayton (g)	3	0	0	0	0
Tyrone Garner, Johnstown (g)...	17	0	2	2	2
Totals	20	0	2	2	2
Ryan Gaucher, Louisiana	16	3	5	8	10
Ryan Gaucher, Mississippi........	50	5	27	32	27
Totals	66	8	32	40	37
Matt Golden, Arkansas	4	1	0	1	11
Matt Golden, Jacksonville.........	46	4	7	11	41
Matt Golden, Peoria.................	16	6	8	14	6
Totals	66	11	15	26	58
Dereck Gosselin, Jacksonville ...	20	1	1	2	18
Dereck Gosselin, Mobile............	5	0	1	1	4
Dereck Gosselin, Birmingham....	3	1	1	2	6
Dereck Gosselin, Arkansas	8	0	2	2	18
Totals	36	2	5	7	46
Brad Goulet, Arkansas	5	1	0	1	2
Brad Goulet, Mississippi............	54	6	7	13	29
Totals	59	7	7	14	31
Brad Gratton, Arkansas	4	1	2	3	2
Brad Gratton, Jacksonville.........	3	0	0	0	0

MINOR LEAGUES *ECHL*

	Games	G	A	Pts.	PIM
Tom Noble, Charlotte (g)	2	0	0	0	2
Tom Noble, South Carolina (g)	1	0	0	0	0
Tom Noble, Richmond (g)	20	0	1	1	4
Totals	23	0	1	1	6
Matt Oates, Tallahassee	53	28	21	49	51
Matt Oates, Dayton	12	3	7	10	8
Totals	65	31	28	59	59
Ryan Pawluk, Louisiana	16	3	8	11	11
Ryan Pawluk, Mississippi	24	11	8	19	23
Ryan Pawluk, Arkansas	20	3	5	8	4
Totals	60	17	21	38	38
Mike Piersol, Augusta	20	1	10	11	23
Mike Piersol, Greensboro	21	0	7	7	14
Mike Piersol, Jackson	13	2	3	5	10
Totals	54	3	20	23	47
Kris Porter, New Orleans	25	6	7	13	16
Kris Porter, Johnstown	30	13	13	26	16
Totals	55	19	20	39	32
Andy Powers, Dayton	41	11	5	16	30
Andy Powers, Pee Dee	7	1	2	3	6
Totals	48	12	7	19	36
Tyler Prosofsky, Birmingham	31	3	11	14	127
Tyler Prosofsky, Toledo	28	8	12	20	118
Totals	59	11	23	34	245
Gino Pulente, Tallahassee	5	0	1	1	0
Gino Pulente, South Carolina	13	1	2	3	10
Totals	18	1	3	4	10
Alex Radzinsky, Arkansas	49	2	4	6	34
Alex Radzinsky, Toledo	27	1	3	4	14
Totals	76	3	7	10	48
Jessie Rezansoff, Augusta	10	3	3	6	57
Jessie Rezansoff, Louisiana	34	5	11	16	155
Totals	44	8	14	22	212
Dave Risk, Charlotte	36	4	8	12	21
Dave Risk, Trenton	31	9	5	14	31
Totals	67	13	13	26	52
Dan Ronan, Augusta	2	0	0	0	5
Dan Ronan, Jackson	2	0	0	0	0
Dan Ronan, Jacksonville	2	0	0	0	2
Totals	6	0	0	0	7
Jeff Rucinski, Pensacola	23	0	3	3	21
Jeff Rucinski, Richmond	16	0	2	2	12
Totals	39	0	5	5	33
Jason Saal, Dayton (g)	29	0	3	3	2
Jason Saal, South Carolina (g)	8	0	0	0	6
Totals	37	0	3	3	8
Doug Schmidt, South Carolina	41	2	5	7	50
Doug Schmidt, Wheeling	14	5	8	13	46
Totals	55	7	13	20	96
Rob Schweyer, Greensboro	4	0	0	0	10
Rob Schweyer, Roanoke	54	10	12	22	91
Totals	58	10	12	22	101
Jason Sessa, Louisiana	17	1	4	5	14
Jason Sessa, South Carolina	15	10	8	18	30
Totals	32	11	12	23	44
Cam Severson, Louisiana	7	0	2	2	22
Cam Severson, Peoria	56	19	8	27	138
Totals	63	19	10	29	160
Leorr Shtrom, Toledo (g)	3	0	0	0	0
Leorr Shtrom, Augusta (g)	4	0	0	0	0
Totals	7	0	0	0	0
Rob Sinclair, Louisiana	14	3	2	5	12
Rob Sinclair, Wheeling	45	9	18	27	6
Totals	59	12	20	32	18
Chris Slater, Wheeling	48	4	8	12	96
Chris Slater, New Orleans	8	0	1	1	8
Totals	56	4	9	13	104
Anders Sorensen, Mobile	29	2	1	3	8
Anders Sorensen, B. Rouge	8	1	0	1	6
Totals	37	3	1	4	14
Jon Sorg, Wheeling	54	7	18	25	102
Jon Sorg, Dayton	12	4	4	8	39
Totals	66	11	22	33	141
Mark Spence, Birmingham	2	0	0	0	5
Mark Spence, Huntington	41	13	15	28	39
Totals	43	13	15	28	44
Rob Stanfield, Huntington	3	0	0	0	4
Rob Stanfield, Birmingham	50	1	3	4	135
Totals	53	1	3	4	139
Paul Strand, Louisiana	12	5	5	10	25
Paul Strand, Pensacola	57	19	26	45	69
Totals	69	24	31	55	94
Wes Swinson, Tallahassee	4	0	2	2	2
Wes Swinson, Greensboro	21	2	9	11	60
Wes Swinson, Augusta	35	0	15	15	71
Totals	60	2	26	28	133
Mike Sylvia, Greenville	42	11	20	31	51
Mike Sylvia, Greensboro	15	6	12	18	8
Totals	57	17	32	49	59
Mike Tamburro, Greenville (g)	20	0	1	1	8
Mike Tamburro, Trenton (g)	5	0	1	1	4
Totals	25	0	2	2	12
T.J. Tanberg, Tallahassee	8	0	3	3	4
T.J. Tanberg, Greensboro	32	2	6	8	34
Totals	40	2	9	11	38
Anthony Terzo, Charlotte	11	6	2	8	6
Anthony Terzo, Huntington	51	19	16	35	24
Totals	62	25	18	43	30
Mike Thompson, Tallahassee	24	8	2	10	24
Mike Thompson, Johnstown	37	14	16	30	55
Totals	61	22	18	40	79
Bob Thornton, Jackson	8	0	3	3	18
Bob Thornton, Jacksonville	12	2	7	9	16
Bob Thornton, Trenton	24	3	5	8	36
Totals	44	5	15	20	70
Sergei Tkachenko, Ark. (g)	2	0	1	1	2
Sergei Tkachenko, Green. (g)	13	0	0	0	12
Totals	15	0	1	1	14
Jeff Trembecky, Pensacola	43	12	16	28	30
Jeff Trembecky, Trenton	27	4	11	15	33
Totals	70	16	27	43	63
J.F. Tremblay, Roanoke	42	4	4	8	131
J.F. Tremblay, Pee Dee	17	3	6	9	31
Totals	59	7	10	17	162
Marc Tropper, Greensboro	17	6	8	14	42
Marc Tropper, Charlotte	53	18	25	43	64
Totals	70	24	33	57	106
Mike Valley, Augusta (g)	3	0	0	0	0
Mike Valley, Louisiana (g)	28	0	1	1	2
Totals	31	0	1	1	2
John Varga, Arkansas	21	5	13	18	8
John Varga, Florida	20	5	7	12	28
Totals	41	10	20	30	36
Jeremy Vokes, Arkansas	2	1	0	1	2
Jeremy Vokes, Baton Rouge	12	2	3	5	21
Totals	14	3	3	6	23
Ian Walterson, Greensboro	28	2	8	10	32
Ian Walterson, Mobile	35	0	5	5	23
Totals	63	2	13	15	55
Rob Weingartner, Arkansas	41	12	16	28	114
Rob Weingartner, Louisiana	26	5	7	12	92
Totals	67	17	23	40	206
David Weninger, Wheeling (g)	1	0	0	0	0
David Weninger, Dayton (g)	5	0	0	0	0
Totals	6	0	0	0	0
Jarret Whidden, Jacksonville	3	0	0	0	0
Jarret Whidden, Toledo	13	3	5	8	4
Jarret Whidden, Arkansas	48	17	24	41	38
Totals	64	20	29	49	42
David Whitworth, Mobile	3	0	3	3	2
David Whitworth, Greensboro	61	17	42	59	109
Totals	64	17	45	62	111
John Wickstrom, Louisiana	10	0	0	0	4
John Wickstrom, Wheeling	48	4	4	8	23
Totals	58	4	4	8	27
Chris Wismer, Dayton	2	0	0	0	16
Chris Wismer, Jackson	64	1	8	9	147
Totals	66	1	8	9	163

	Games	G	A	Pts	PIM
Chad Woollard, Jackson............	17	3	4	7	17
Chad Woollard, Greensboro	15	3	4	7	8
Totals......................................	32	6	8	14	25
Alexandre Yudin, Charlotte	8	0	0	0	47
Alexandre Yudin, Wheeling.......	11	0	1	1	94
Totals......................................	19	0	1	1	141

GOALTENDING

	Gms.	Min.	W	L	T	G	SO	Avg.
B. Belecki, G'boro ...	9	443	2	7	0	42	0	5.69
B. Belecki, Char.	4	141	0	1	0	11	0	4.68
B. Belecki, Hunt.	1	60	1	0	0	3	0	3.00
B. Belecki, H.R.	9	378	4	2	0	23	0	3.65
Totals	23	1021	7	10	0	79	0	4.64
D. Bergeron, Miss. .	1	59	0	1	0	4	0	4.07
D. Bergeron, Whe. .	1	59	0	1	0	6	0	6.10
Totals	2	118	0	2	0	10	0	5.08
T. Garner, Day.	3	113	0	2	0	11	0	5.86
T. Garner, John.	17	971	8	6	3	48	0	2.97
Totals	20	1084	8	8	3	59	0	3.27
Craig Hillier, John. .	5	212	1	2	0	15	0	4.24
Craig Hillier, Char. ..	3	121	0	2	0	10	0	4.95
Craig Hillier, Toledo. .	9	375	1	6	0	41	0	6.56
Totals	17	708	2	10	0	66	0	5.59
Forest Karr, J'ville ...	10	480	2	3	1	35	0	4.37
Forest Karr, S.C.......	2	78	0	2	0	4	0	3.06
Totals	12	558	2	5	1	39	0	4.19
T. Lendzyk, Char.	12	636	4	4	1	38	0	3.58

	Gms.	Min.	W	L	T	G	SO	Avg.
T. Lendzyk, Tren.	19	1136	11	8	0	44	1	2.32
Totals	31	1773	15	12	1	82	1	2.78
P. Nestak, John. ...	5	210	1	1	0	10	0	2.85
Pavel Nestak, B.R....	15	785	4	7	3	52	0	3.97
Totals	20	995	5	8	3	62	0	3.74
Tom Noble, Char. ...	2	119	0	2	0	8	0	4.05
Tom Noble, S.C. ...	1	60	0	1	0	4	0	4.03
Tom Noble, Rich. ...	20	1074	10	5	2	54	0	3.02
Totals	23	1252	10	8	2	66	0	3.16
Jason Saal, Day. ...	29	1650	14	10	3	88	1	3.20
Jason Saal, S.C.......	8	355	3	1	2	29	0	4.90
Totals	37	2005	17	11	5	117	1	3.50
Leorr Shtrom, Tol. .	3	83	0	1	0	5	0	3.62
Leorr Shtrom, Aug. .	4	121	0	0	1	3	0	1.49
Totals	7	204	0	1	1	8	0	2.36
M. Tamburro, G'ville.	20	1142	13	5	2	57	1	3.00
M. Tamburro, Tren..	5	298	2	3	0	19	0	3.83
Totals	25	1440	15	8	2	76	1	3.17
S. Tkachenko, Ark. .	2	120	0	0	2	7	0	3.51
S. Tkachenko, G'ville.	13	708	6	3	2	34	1	2.88
Totals	15	827	6	3	4	41	1	2.97
Mike Valley, Aug. ...	3	150	0	2	0	11	0	4.40
Mike Valley, Lou. ...	28	1466	15	6	5	81	1	3.32
Totals	31	1616	15	8	5	92	1	3.42
D. Weninger, Whe. .	1	60	0	1	0	4	0	4.00
D. Weninger, Day. ..	5	104	0	1	0	8	0	4.62
Totals	6	164	0	2	0	12	0	4.39

2000 KELLY CUP PLAYOFFS

RESULTS

WILD-CARD ROUND

	W	L	Pts.	GF	GA
South Carolina..............................	2	0	4	11	6
Baton Rouge.................................	0	2	0	6	11

(South Carolina won series, 2-0)

	W	L	Pts.	GF	GA
Augusta..	2	1	4	8	5
New Orleans	1	2	2	5	8

(Augusta won series, 2-1)

	W	L	Pts.	GF	GA
Mississippi...................................	2	1	4	9	4
Pensacola....................................	1	2	2	4	9

(Mississippi won series, 2-1)

CONFERENCE QUARTERFINALS

	W	L	Pts.	GF	GA
Peoria..	3	0	6	13	7
Dayton...	0	3	0	7	13

(Peoria won series, 3-0)

	W	L	Pts.	GF	GA
Johnstown....................................	3	1	6	14	5
Roanoke	1	3	2	5	14

(Johnstown won series, 3-1)

	W	L	Pts.	GF	GA
Trenton	3	0	6	9	2
Richmond.....................................	0	3	0	2	9

(Trenton won series, 3-0)

	W	L	Pts.	GF	GA
Hampton Roads	3	2	6	16	14
Huntington	2	3	4	14	16

(Hampton Roads won series, 3-2)

	W	L	Pts.	GF	GA
Augusta..	3	2	6	17	14
Florida	2	3	4	14	17

(Augusta won series, 3-2)

	W	L	Pts.	GF	GA
Louisiana......................................	3	1	6	16	10
Mississippi...................................	1	3	2	10	16

(Louisiana won series, 3-1)

	W	L	Pts.	GF	GA
South Carolina.............................	3	2	6	18	14
Pee Dee	2	3	4	14	18

(South Carolina won series, 3-2)

	W	L	Pts.	GF	GA
Greenville	3	2	6	21	15
Mobile	2	3	4	15	21

(Greenville won series, 3-2)

CONFERENCE SEMIFINALS

	W	L	Pts.	GF	GA
Peoria..	3	0	6	13	8
Johnstown....................................	0	3	0	8	13

(Peoria won series, 3-0)

	W	L	Pts.	GF	GA
Trenton	3	2	6	16	12
Hampton Roads	2	3	4	12	16

(Trenton won series, 3-2)

	W	L	Pts.	GF	GA
Greenville	3	1	6	13	7
Augusta..	1	3	2	7	13

(Greenville won series, 3-1)

	W	L	Pts.	GF	GA
Louisiana......................................	3	0	6	18	8
South Carolina.............................	0	3	0	8	18

(Louisiana won series, 3-0)

CONFERENCE FINALS

	W	L	Pts.	GF	GA
Peoria..	4	2	8	26	17
Trenton	2	4	2	17	26

(Peoria won series, 4-2)

	W	L	Pts.	GF	GA
Louisiana......................................	4	2	8	28	20
Greenville	2	4	4	20	28

(Louisiana won series, 4-2)

LEAGUE FINALS

	W	L	Pts.	GF	GA
Peoria..	4	2	8	24	23
Louisiana......................................	2	4	4	23	24

(Peoria won series, 4-2)

GOALTENDING

	Gms.	Min.	W	L	T	G	SO	Avg.
Jeff Maund	2	89	1	1	0	4	0	2.69
Marc Magliarditi	4	209	1	2	0	12	0	3.44

GREENVILLE GRRROWL
(Lost conference finals to Louisiana, 4-2)

SCORING

	Games	G	A	Pts.	PIM
Martin Masa	13	8	8	16	23
Jason Kelly	15	4	11	15	36
Niel Fewster	15	5	8	13	6
Sean Ritchlin	15	8	4	12	18
Sean Venedam	15	7	5	12	14
Justin Cardwell	15	3	7	10	30
Bill McCauley	13	2	8	10	32
Scott Kirton	14	2	7	9	45
Ajay Baines	15	2	5	7	13
Yanick Jean	15	1	6	7	26
Charles Paquette	15	4	2	6	30
Dana Mulvihill	14	1	5	6	12
Ryan Stewart	15	4	1	5	26
Vratislav Cech	15	0	5	5	16
Dennis Maxwell	4	2	0	2	34
Eric Van Acker	13	1	0	1	37
Denis Timofeev	10	0	1	1	24
Nick Vitucci (goalie)	15	0	1	1	12
Davis Payne	5	0	0	0	6

GOALTENDING

	Gms.	Min.	W	L	T	G	SO	Avg.
Nick Vitucci	15	966	8	5	2	49	1	3.04

HAMPTON ROADS ADMIRALS
(Lost conference semifinals to Trenton, 3-2)

SCORING

	Games	G	A	Pts.	PIM
Mike Omicioli	10	1	10	11	2
Dominic Maltais	10	8	2	10	18
Rick Kowalsky	10	7	1	8	20
Bobby Russell	10	3	4	7	19
Colin Pepperall	9	1	5	6	43
Rod Taylor	10	0	6	6	42
Marty Clapton	10	2	3	5	6
Etienne Drapeau	10	2	3	5	14
John Parco	3	1	3	4	2
Louis Bedard	9	2	1	3	14
Dean Stork	8	0	3	3	2
Chad Ackerman	10	0	3	3	4
Gerad Adams	10	0	2	2	35
Dwight Parrish	10	0	2	2	17
Mike Siklenka	8	1	0	1	15
Jan Lasak (goalie)	10	0	1	1	4
Steve Sherriffs	10	0	1	1	25
Curtis Cruickshank (goalie)	1	0	0	0	0
Richard Pitirri	3	0	0	0	0
Trevor Johnson	10	0	0	0	9

GOALTENDING

	Gms.	Min.	W	L	T	G	SO	Avg.
Jan Lasak	10	610	5	4	1	28	1	2.75
Curtis Cruickshank	1	12	0	0	0	2	0	10.23

HUNTINGTON BLIZZARD
(Lost conference quarterfinals to Hampton Roads, 3-2)

SCORING

	Games	G	A	Pts.	PIM
Van Burgess	5	3	4	7	2
Jim Bermingham	5	2	4	6	9
Pete Brearley	5	3	2	5	6
Kelly Harper	5	2	2	4	0
Jamie Pegg	5	0	3	3	14
Jamie Sokolsky	5	2	0	2	12

	Games	G	A	Pts.	PIM
Mike Perna	5	1	1	2	27
Jason Bermingham	5	1	0	1	11
Curtis Bois	5	0	1	1	23
Anthony Cappelletti	5	0	1	1	17
Butch Kaebel	5	0	1	1	0
David Oliver	5	0	1	1	17
Anthony Terzo	1	0	0	0	0
Blaine Russell (goalie)	3	0	0	0	0
Ryan Hoople (goalie)	4	0	0	0	0
Mark Spence	4	0	0	0	2
Bill Baaki	5	0	0	0	17
Keith Cassidy	5	0	0	0	10
Jim Moss	5	0	0	0	6

GOALTENDING

	Gms.	Min.	W	L	T	G	SO	Avg.
Blaine Russell	3	131	1	1	0	5	1	2.30
Ryan Hoople	4	168	1	2	0	10	1	3.56

JOHNSTOWN CHIEFS
(Lost conference semifinals to Peoria, 3-0)

SCORING

	Games	G	A	Pts.	PIM
Carl Fleury	7	3	4	7	12
Derrick Walser	7	3	3	6	8
Kris Porter	7	4	1	5	8
Andrew Dale	7	3	2	5	8
Dmitri Tarabrin	7	3	1	4	21
Andrew Clark	5	2	2	4	13
Joel Irving	7	2	2	4	20
Brent Bilodeau	7	0	4	4	8
Kevin Kellet	7	0	4	4	14
Ryan Chaytors	4	1	2	3	0
Mike Thompson	7	1	2	3	6
Mikko Sivonen	6	0	3	3	2
Shawn Frappier	7	0	3	3	8
Jeff Sullivan	7	0	2	2	32
Chuck Mindel	4	0	1	1	12
Mike Vellinga	7	0	1	1	18
E.J. Bradley	1	0	0	0	0
Tyrone Garner (goalie)	1	0	0	0	0
Ryan Tocher	2	0	0	0	2
Frederic Deschenes (goalie)	6	0	0	0	2
Brett Gibson	6	0	0	0	12

GOALTENDING

	Gms.	Min.	W	L	T	G	SO	Avg.
Tyrone Garner	1	59	0	1	0	2	0	2.03
Frederic Deschenes	6	369	3	2	1	15	2	2.44

LOUISIANA ICEGATORS
(Lost finals to Peoria, 4-2)

SCORING

	Games	G	A	Pts.	PIM
John Spoltore	17	8	26	34	14
Vaclav Nedomansky	19	11	14	25	30
Chris Valicevic	19	5	18	23	30
Shawn McNeil	19	11	11	22	2
Mike Murray	19	11	9	20	18
Jay Murphy	19	12	7	19	46
Ryan Shanahan	18	5	7	12	66
Mike Kucsulain	19	4	7	11	42
Rob Weingartner	11	1	9	10	16
Matthew Pagnutti	19	6	2	8	34
Corey Neilson	19	0	7	7	36
Mike Oliveira	13	3	3	6	4
John DePourq	16	3	3	6	4
Chris Bogas	18	2	4	6	42
Stan Melanson	19	1	5	6	31
Steve O'Rourke	13	1	2	3	10
Jessie Rezansoff	18	1	1	2	26
Dave Arsenault (goalie)	3	0	1	1	0
Mike Valley (goalie)	17	0	1	1	6
Jason McQuat	9	0	0	0	6

GOALTENDING

	Gms.	Min.	W	L	T	G	SO	Avg.
Mike Valley	17	1049	12	1	3	48	1	2.75
Dave Arsenault	3	208	0	1	2	13	0	3.75

MISSISSIPPI SEA WOLVES

(Lost conference quarterfinals to Louisiana, 3-1)

SCORING

	Games	G	A	Pts.	PIM
Bob Woods	7	3	4	7	6
Mikhail Kravets	7	1	6	7	8
Brad Essex	7	4	2	6	11
Mark Rupnow	7	0	6	6	4
John Evangelista	7	2	2	4	4
Jonathan Weaver	6	1	3	4	0
Ryan Gaucher	7	2	1	3	8
Patrick Rochon	7	2	1	3	26
John Kosobud	7	1	1	2	13
Mike Martone	7	1	1	2	23
Jan Melichercik	7	1	1	2	6
Sean Gillam	7	0	2	2	8
Scott King	7	0	2	2	10
Dave Paradise	6	1	0	1	0
J.F. Aube	1	0	0	0	0
Sylvain Daigle (goalie)	1	0	0	0	0
Steve Duke	7	0	0	0	6
Scott Page	7	0	0	0	9
Chuck Thuss (goalie)	7	0	0	0	4

GOALTENDING

	Gms.	Min.	W	L	T	G	SO	Avg.
Chuck Thuss	7	405	3	4	0	16	1	2.37
Sylvain Daigle	1	23	0	0	0	3	0	7.95

MOBILE MYSTICS

(Lost conference quarterfinals to Greenville, 3-2)

SCORING

	Games	G	A	Pts.	PIM
Jason Elders	5	3	3	6	2
Bobby Stewart	5	3	3	6	0
Mark Turner	5	1	5	6	8
Hugues Gervais	5	2	3	5	16
Tom Nolan	3	1	2	3	4
Josh Harrold	5	1	2	3	4
Benoit Cotnoir	5	0	3	3	8
B.J. Kilbourne	5	2	0	2	6
Jason Clarke	5	1	1	2	27
Dave Van Drunen	5	1	1	2	14
Jason Metcalfe	5	0	1	1	6
Chad Onufrechuk	5	0	1	1	2
Mitch Vig	5	0	1	1	10
Dennis Mullen	1	0	0	0	2
Lee Svangstu	2	0	0	0	2
Russ Guzoir	4	0	0	0	4
Chad Alban (goalie)	5	0	0	0	2
Scott Cherrey	5	0	0	0	0
Jeff Kozakowski	5	0	0	0	0

GOALTENDING

	Gms.	Min.	W	L	T	G	SO	Avg.
Chad Alban	5	299	2	3	0	20	0	4.01

NEW ORLEANS BRASS

(Lost wild-card round to Augusta, 2-1)

SCORING

	Games	G	A	Pts.	PIM
Chad Dameworth	3	1	1	2	0
Chris Slater	3	1	1	2	6
Stephane Soulliere	3	1	1	2	9
Adam Colagiacomo	3	0	2	2	2
Jeff Lazaro	3	1	0	1	4
Jay McGee	3	1	0	1	4
Sami Jarvenpaa	2	0	1	1	0

	Games	G	A	Pts.	PIM
Adam Nittel	3	0	1	1	28
Mark Polak	3	0	1	1	4
Janne Salpa	3	0	1	1	0
Terry Friesen (goalie)	1	0	0	0	0
Antti Ahokas	2	0	0	0	0
Mikko Koivisto	2	0	0	0	0
Chris Aldous	3	0	0	0	0
Doug Bonner (goalie)	3	0	0	0	0
Steve Cheredaryk	3	0	0	0	23
Marcus Gustafsson	3	0	0	0	0
Rejean Stringer	3	0	0	0	0
Andrew Taylor	3	0	0	0	0

GOALTENDING

	Gms.	Min.	W	L	T	G	SO	Avg.
Doug Bonner	3	169	1	1	1	7	0	2.48
Terry Friesen	1	16	0	0	0	1	0	3.86

PEE DEE PRIDE

(Lost conference quarterfinals to South Carolina, 3-2)

SCORING

	Games	G	A	Pts.	PIM
Buddy Smith	5	0	5	5	2
Dany Bousquet	5	1	3	4	20
Allan Sirois	5	1	3	4	2
Peter Geronazzo	5	3	0	3	4
Darcy Dallas	5	2	1	3	8
Trevor Demmans	5	1	2	3	12
Kevin Haupt	5	0	3	3	2
Casey Kesselring	5	2	0	2	6
Rick Mrozik	5	2	0	2	6
Wes Goldie	4	1	0	1	0
J.F. Tremblay	5	1	0	1	8
Dan Fournel	1	0	1	1	7
Kyle Knopp	5	0	1	1	2
Ryan Petz	5	0	1	1	5
Bryan Tapper	5	0	1	1	14
Tim Warrilow	1	0	0	0	0
Paxton Schafer (goalie)	2	0	0	0	0
B. Wallace	3	0	0	0	8
Sandy Allan (goalie)	4	0	0	0	0
Mike Dombkiewicz	5	0	0	0	4

GOALTENDING

	Gms.	Min.	W	L	T	G	SO	Avg.
Sandy Allan	4	203	2	1	1	10	0	2.95
Paxton Schafer	2	98	0	1	0	8	0	4.91

PENSACOLA ICE PILOTS

(Lost wild-card round to Mississippi, 2-1)

SCORING

	Games	G	A	Pts.	PIM
Lorne Toews	3	2	0	2	6
Paul Strand	3	1	1	2	6
Bruce Richardson	3	0	2	2	8
Albie O'Connell	3	1	0	1	2
Alexandre Couture	2	0	1	1	0
Shane Calder	3	0	1	1	0
Marc Dupuis	3	0	1	1	4
Rob Smillie	3	0	1	1	0
John McNabb	1	0	0	0	2
Raitis Ivanans	2	0	0	0	0
Nick Checco	3	0	0	0	0
Kirk DeWaele	3	0	0	0	8
Steve Dumonski	3	0	0	0	24
Darcy George	3	0	0	0	0
Joe Harney	3	0	0	0	4
Harold Hersh	3	0	0	0	0
Bill Kohn	3	0	0	0	4
Scott LaGrand (goalie)	3	0	0	0	0

GOALTENDING

	Gms.	Min.	W	L	T	G	SO	Avg.
Scott LaGrand	3	177	1	2	0	8	0	2.70

PEORIA RIVERMEN
(Winner of 2000 Kelly Cup playoffs)

SCORING

	Games	G	A	Pts.	PIM
J.F. Boutin	18	17	15	32	26
Joe Rybar	18	6	17	23	14
Jason Deleurme	18	8	12	20	10
Didier Tremblay	18	6	7	13	18
Jason Christie	17	3	10	13	14
Matt Golden	18	4	8	12	10
Blaine Fitzpatrick	18	5	6	11	47
Aaron Boh	15	2	9	11	57
Darren Clark	18	4	6	10	30
Trevor Wasyluk	9	3	6	9	6
Trevor Baker	18	4	4	8	41
Daniel Hodge	18	2	6	8	4
Cam Severson	18	3	4	7	41
Jason Lawmaster	18	3	3	6	60
Matt Smith	13	2	3	5	11
Darren Maloney	17	2	3	5	12
Craig Anderson	8	2	1	3	0
Tomaz Razingar	11	0	1	1	4
Duane Derksen (goalie)	16	0	1	1	2
Cody Rudkowsky (goalie)	2	0	0	0	0

GOALTENDING

	Gms.	Min.	W	L	T	G	SO	Avg.
Duane Derksen	16	1036	13	2	1	47	0	2.72
Cody Rudkowsky	2	119	1	1	0	6	0	3.02

RICHMOND RENEGADES
(Lost conference quarterfinals to Trenton, 3-0)

SCORING

	Games	G	A	Pts.	PIM
Dylan Gyori	3	1	0	1	6
Frank Novock	3	1	0	1	4
Kevin Knopp	3	0	1	1	6
Matt Noga	3	0	1	1	0
Andrew Shier	3	0	1	1	8
Peter Vandermeer	3	0	1	1	20
Jeff Rucinski	2	0	0	0	2
Joe Bianchi	3	0	0	0	2
Marc Bouchard	3	0	0	0	2
Maxime Gingras (goalie)	3	0	0	0	2
David Lambeth	3	0	0	0	2
Craig Paterson	3	0	0	0	2
Neal Rech	3	0	0	0	0
Trevor Senn	3	0	0	0	10
Dan Vandermeer	3	0	0	0	6
Joe Vandermeer	3	0	0	0	10
Darren Wetherill	3	0	0	0	11

GOALTENDING

	Gms.	Min.	W	L	T	G	SO	Avg.
Maxime Gingras	3	177	0	3	0	8	0	2.72

ROANOKE EXPRESS
(Lost conference quarterfinals to Johnstown, 3-1)

SCORING

	Games	G	A	Pts.	PIM
Mike Peron	4	0	3	3	28
Duane Harmer	4	1	1	2	24
Kris Cantu	4	0	2	2	2
Dion Delmonte	4	0	2	2	6
Calvin Elfring	4	1	0	1	6
Troy Lake	4	1	0	1	2
Brent Ozarowski	4	1	0	1	0
Rob Schweyer	4	1	0	1	6
Paul Di Francesco	4	0	1	1	2
John Poapst	1	0	0	0	2
Daniel Berthiaume (goalie)	2	0	0	0	0
Dave Gagnon (goalie)	2	0	0	0	2

	Games	G	A	Pts.	PIM
Todd Compeau	3	0	0	0	4
Aniket Dhadphale	4	0	0	0	6
Aaron Gates	4	0	0	0	16
Nate Handrahan	4	0	0	0	0
Steve Sabo	4	0	0	0	12
Ben Schust	4	0	0	0	4
Travis Smith	4	0	0	0	21

GOALTENDING

	Gms.	Min.	W	L	T	G	SO	Avg.
Daniel Berthiaume	2	118	0	2	0	6	0	3.04
Dave Gagnon	2	120	1	1	0	7	0	3.50

SOUTH CAROLINA STINGRAYS
(Lost conference semifinals to Louisiana, 3-0)

SCORING

	Games	G	A	Pts.	PIM
Adam Calder	10	4	8	12	12
Brendan Concannon	10	6	4	10	0
Dave Seitz	10	4	6	10	29
Damian Prescott	10	6	3	9	18
Rob Conncannon	10	4	5	9	38
Greg Schmidt	10	3	6	9	28
Brad Dexter	10	1	7	8	2
Jason Sessa	7	4	1	5	2
Brett Marietti	10	0	5	5	10
Luc Theoret	10	2	2	4	10
Mike Nicholishen	8	2	1	3	4
Shannon Briske	8	0	3	3	6
Jason Wright	10	0	3	3	2
Chad Remackel	3	1	1	2	2
Jared Bednar	10	0	2	2	25
Jody Lehman (goalie)	6	0	1	1	6
Marc Tardif	10	0	1	1	21
Shaun Peet	1	0	0	0	12
Jason Saal (goalie)	7	0	0	0	0
Jeff Romfo	10	0	0	0	6

GOALTENDING

	Gms.	Min.	W	L	T	G	SO	Avg.
Jason Saal	7	349	3	3	0	20	0	3.44
Jody Lehman	6	266	2	2	0	18	0	4.06

TRENTON TITANS
(Lost conference finals to Peoria, 4-2)

SCORING

	Games	G	A	Pts.	PIM
Cail MacLean	14	10	5	15	6
Jerry Keefe	10	7	5	12	4
Dave Risk	14	4	8	12	12
Mark Murphy	12	2	8	10	17
Eric Brule	14	0	10	10	22
Scott Bertoli	14	1	8	9	12
Mike Hall	13	3	5	8	10
Sergei Skrobot	14	3	5	8	6
Jed Whitchurch	13	5	1	6	0
Stewart Bodtker	13	3	2	5	36
Mike Mader	14	2	3	5	73
David Hoogsteen	12	0	5	5	0
Vince Williams	14	1	3	4	16
Benoit Morin	8	0	3	3	29
Kam White	14	1	1	2	62
Taras Lendzyk (goalie)	11	0	1	1	2
Kurt Mallett	13	0	1	1	4
Keith Dupee	1	0	0	0	0
Bujar Amidovski (goalie)	5	0	0	0	0
Ryan Brown	12	0	0	0	29

GOALTENDING

	Gms.	Min.	W	L	T	G	SO	Avg.
Taras Lendzyk	11	606	6	3	0	25	1	2.48
Bujar Amidovski	5	254	2	3	0	13	1	3.07

MINOR LEAGUES *ECHL*

ALL-STAR TEAMS

First team	Pos.	Second team
Jan Lasak, Hampton Roads	G	Daniel Berthiaume, Roanoke
Chris Valicevic, Louisiana	D	Duane Harmer, Roanoke
Tom Nemeth, Dayton	D	Brad Dexter, South Carolina
Andy MacIntyre, Florida	LW	Jason Elders, Mobile
John Spoltore, Louisiana	C	Jamie Ling, Dayton
Andrew Williamson, Toledo	RW	Jay Murphy, Louisiana

TROPHY WINNERS

Most Valuable Player: Andrew Williamson, Toledo
Scoring leader: John Spoltore, Louisiana
Outstanding defenseman: Tom Nemeth, Dayton
Outstanding goaltender: Jan Lasak, Hampton Roads
Rookie of the Year: Jan Lasak, Hampton Roads
Playoff MVP: J.F. Boutin, Peoria
       Jason Christie, Peoria
Coach of the Year: Bob Ferguson, Florida

ALL-TIME AWARD WINNERS

MOST VALUABLE PLAYER

Season	Player, Team
1988-89	Daryl Harpe, Erie
1989-90	Bill McDougall, Erie
1990-91	Stan Drulia, Knoxville
1991-92	Phil Berger, Greensboro
1992-93	Trevor Jobe, Nashville
1993-94	Joe Flanagan, Birmingham
1994-95	Vadim Slivchenko, Wheeling
1995-96	Hugo Belanger, Nashville
1996-97	Mike Ross, South Carolina
1997-98	Jamey Hicks, Birmingham
1998-99	Chris Valicevic, Louisiana
1999-00	Andrew Williamson, Toledo

TOP SCORER

Season	Player, Team
1988-89	Daryl Harpe, Erie
1989-90	Bill McDougall, Erie
1990-91	Stan Drulia, Knoxville
1991-92	Phil Berger, Greensboro
1992-93	Trevor Jobe, Nashville
1993-94	Phil Berger, Greensboro
1994-95	Scott Burfoot, Erie
1995-96	Hugo Belanger, Nashville
1996-97	Ed Courtenay, South Carolina
	Mike Ross, South Carolina
1997-98	Jamey Hicks, Birmingham
1998-99	John Spoltore, Louisiana
1999-00	John Spoltore, Louisiana

ROOKIE OF THE YEAR

Season	Player, Team
1988-89	Tom Sasso, Johnstown
1989-90	Bill McDougall, Erie
1990-91	Dan Gauthier, Knoxville
1991-92	Darren Colbourne, Dayton
1992-93	Joe Flanagan, Birmingham
1993-94	Dan Gravelle, Greensboro
1994-95	Kevin McKinnon, Erie
1995-96	Keli Corpse, Wheeling
1996-97	Dany Bousquet, Birmingham
1997-98	Sean Venedam, Toledo
1998-99	Maxime Gingras, Richmond
1999-00	Jan Lasak, Hampton Roads

TOP GOALTENDER

Season	Player, Team
1988-89	Scott Gordon, Johnstown
1989-90	Alain Raymond, Hampton Roads
1990-91	Dean Anderson, Knoxville
1991-92	Frederic Chabot, Winston-Salem
1992-93	Nick Vitucci, Hampton Roads
1993-94	Cory Cadden, Knoxville
1994-95	Chris Gordon, Huntington
1995-96	Alain Morissette, Louisville
1996-97	Marc Delorme, Louisiana
1997-98	Nick Vitucci, Toledo
1998-99	Maxime Gingras, Richmond
1999-00	Jan Lasak, Hampton Roads

PLAYOFF MVP

Season	Player, Team
1988-89	Nick Vitucci, Carolina
1989-90	Wade Flaherty, Greensboro
1990-91	Dave Gagnon, Hampton Rds.
	Flanagan, Hampton Roads
1991-92	Mark Bernard, Hampton Roads
1992-93	Rick Judson, Toledo
1993-94	Dave Gagnon, Toledo
1994-95	Blaine Moore, Richmond
1995-96	Nick Vitucci, Charlotte
1996-97	Jason Fitzsimmons, South Carolina
1997-98	Sebastian Charpentier, Hampton Roads
1998-99	Travis Scott, Mississippi
1999-00	J.F. Boutin, Peoria
	Jason Christie, Peoria

COACH OF THE YEAR

Season	Coach, Team
1988-89	Ron Hansis, Erie
1989-90	Dave Allison, Virginia
1990-91	Don Jackson, Knoxville
1991-92	Doug Sauter, Winston-Salem
1992-93	Kurt Kleinendorst, Raleigh
1993-94	Barry Smith, Knoxville
1994-95	Jim Playfair, Dayton
1995-96	Roy Sommer, Richmond
1996-97	Brian McCutcheon, Columbus
1997-98	Chris Nilan, Chesapeake
1998-99	Bob Ferguson, Florida
1999-00	Bob Ferguson, Florida

TOP DEFENSEMAN

Season	Player, Team
1988-89	Kelly Szautner, Erie
1989-90	Bill Whitfield, Virginia
1990-91	Brett McDonald, Nashville
1991-92	Scott White, Greensboro
1992-93	Derek Booth, Toledo
1993-94	Tom Nemeth, Dayton
1994-95	Brandon Smith, Dayton
1995-96	Chris Valicevic, Louisiana
1996-97	Chris Valicevic, Louisiana
1997-98	Chris Valicevic, Louisiana
1998-99	Chris Valicevic, Louisiana
1999-00	Tom Nemeth, Dayton

ALL-TIME LEAGUE CHAMPIONS

REGULAR-SEASON CHAMPION

Season	Team	Coach
1988-89	Erie Panthers	Ron Hansis
1989-90	Winston-Salem Thunderbirds	C. McSorley, J. Fraser
1990-91	Knoxville Cherokees	Don Jackson
1991-92	Toledo Storm	Chris McSorley
1992-93	Wheeling Thunderbirds	Doug Sauter
1993-94	Knoxville Cherokees	Barry Smith
1994-95	Wheeling Thunderbirds	Doug Sauter
1995-96	Richmond Renegades	Roy Sommer
1996-97	South Carolina Stingrays	Rick Vaive
1997-98	Louisiana Icegators	Doug Shedden
1998-99	Pee Dee Pride	Jack Capuano
1999-00	Florida Everblades	Bob Ferguson

PLAYOFF CHAMPION

Team	Coach
Carolina Thunderbirds	Brendon Watson
Greensboro Monarchs	Jeff Brubaker
Hampton Roads Admirals	John Brophy
Hampton Roads Admirals	John Brophy
Toledo Storm	Chris McSorley
Toledo Storm	Chris McSorley
Richmond Renegades	Roy Sommer
Charlotte Checkers	John Marks
South Carolina Stingrays	Rick Vaive
Hampton Roads Admirals	John Brophy
Mississippi Sea Wolves	Bruce Boudreau
Peoria Rivermen	Don Granato

The ECHL regular season champion is awarded the Brabham Cup. The playoff champion was awarded the Riley Cup through the 1995-96 season. Playoff champions are now awarded the Patrick J. Kelly Cup.

CENTRAL HOCKEY LEAGUE

LEAGUE OFFICE

Commissioner
N. Thomas Berry Jr.
Special assignments
Michael A. Meyers
Director of finance
Charlene Smoll

Director of marketing
Brad Johnson
Director of communications
Amy Pickett
Address
5501 East 71st Street, Suite 1A
Indianapolis, IN 46220

Phone
317-257-2455
FAX
317-916-0563

TEAMS

BORDER CITY BANDITS

General manager
Derek Prue
Head coach
Peter South
Home ice
Four States Fair Entertainment Center
Address
601 Pine Street
Texarkana, TX 75503
Seating capacity
5,600
Phone
903-794-4625
FAX
903-793-4793

COLUMBUS COTTONMOUTHS

General manager
Phil Roberto
Head coach
Bruce Garber
Home ice
Columbus Civic Center
Address
P.O. Box 1886
400 Fourth Street
Columbus, GA 31902-1886
Seating capacity
7,509
Phone
706-571-0086
FAX
706-571-0080

FAYETTEVILLE FORCE

Chief operating officer
Norm Eberle
Head coach
To be announced
Home ice
Crown Coliseum
Address
1960 Coliseum Drive
Fayetteville, NC 28306
Seating Capacity
9,715
Phone
910-438-9000
FAX
910-438-9004

HUNTSVILLE TORNADO

General manager
John Cherney
Head coach
Craig Coxe
Home ice
Von Braun Center

Address
700 Monroe Street
Huntsville, AL 35801
Seating capacity
6,552
Phone
256-564-8500
FAX
256-564-8498

INDIANAPOLIS ICE

General manager
Brad Beery
Coach
Rod Davidson
Home ice
Pepsi Coliseum/Conseco Fieldhouse
Address
1202 East 38th Street
Indianapolis, IN 46205
Seating capacity
8,200/13,000
Phone
317-925-4423
FAX
317-931-4511

MACON WHOOPEE

General manager and head coach
Graeme Townshend
Home ice
Macon Centreplex
Address
200 Coliseum St.
Macon, GA 31217
Seating capacity
7,100
Phone
912-741-1000
FAX
912-464-0655

MEMPHIS RIVERKINGS

General manager
Jim Riggs
Head coach
Doug Shedden
Home ice
DeSoto County Civic Center
Address
315 S. Hollywood, Bldg. E
Memphis, TN 38104
Seating capacity
8,100
Phone
901-278-9009
FAX
901-323-3262

OKLAHOMA CITY BLAZERS

General manager
Brad Lund
Head coach
Doug Sauter
Home ice
Myriad Convention Center
Address
119 N. Robinson, Suite 630
Oklahoma City, OK 73102
Seating capacity
13,479
Phone
405-235-7825
FAX
405-272-9875

SAN ANTONIO IGUANAS

General manager
David Oldham
Head coach
Chris Stewart
Home ice
Freeman Coliseum
Address
8546 Broadway, Suite 165
San Antonio, TX 78217
Seating Capacity
9,500
Phone
210-227-4449
FAX
210-821-4592

TOPEKA SCARECROWS

General manager
Doug Miller
Head coach
Paul Kelly
Home ice
Landon Arena
Address
1800 Exduster Blvd.
Topeka, KS 66612-1442
Seating Capacity
7,777
Phone
785-232-7697
FAX
785-232-7423

TULSA OILERS

General manager
Jeff Lund
Head coach
Shaun Clouston
Home ice
Tulsa Convention Center

Address	WICHITA THUNDER	Address
9128 E. 46th Street		505 W. Maple, Suite 100
Tulsa, OK 74145	**General manager**	Wichita, KS 67213
Seating Capacity	Bill Shuck	**Seating Capacity**
7,111	**Head coach**	9,686
Phone	Bryan Wells	**Phone**
918-632-7825	**Home ice**	316-264-4625
FAX	Kansas Coliseum	**FAX**
918-632-0006		316-264-3037

1999-2000 REGULAR SEASON
FINAL STANDINGS

EASTERN DIVISION

Team	G	W	L	SOL	Pts.	GF	GA
Fayetteville	70	45	22	3	93	255	202
Columbus	70	39	20	11	89	233	203
Huntsville	70	37	27	6	80	242	244
Macon	70	34	26	10	78	259	237
Memphis	70	9	57	4	22	175	341

WESTERN DIVISION

Team	G	W	L	SOL	Pts.	GF	GA
Oklahoma City	70	39	24	7	85	248	220
Indianapolis	70	39	28	3	81	290	244
Tulsa	70	38	27	5	81	251	244
Wichita	70	37	26	7	81	245	231
Topeka	70	35	27	8	78	245	243
San Antonio	70	33	32	5	71	229	263

INDIVIDUAL LEADERS

Goals: Yvan Corbin, Indianapolis (62)
Assists: Chris MacKenzie, Indianapolis (80)
Points: Yvan Corbin, Indianapolis (127)
Chris MacKenzie, Indianapolis (127)
Penalty minutes: Curtis Voth, Tulsa (466)
Goaltending average: Frankie Ouellette, Columbus (2.43)
Shutouts: Brent Belecki, Huntsville (3)
Brian Elder, Macon (3)
Lance Leslie, Wichita (3)
Benoit Thibert, Indianapolis (3)

	Games	G	A	Pts.
Doug Lawrence, Tulsa	65	29	71	100
Brett Seguin, Topeka	70	22	75	97
Chris George, Huntsville	70	50	36	86
Travis Clayton, Wichita	66	42	43	85
Johnny Brdarovic, San Antonio	68	34	49	83
Jonathan DuBois, Huntsville	59	22	61	83
Brett Colborne, Fayetteville	70	21	60	81
Luc Beausoleil, Tulsa	68	25	55	80
Scott Green, San Antonio	65	41	38	79
Steve Moore, Topeka	67	36	40	76
Michael Martens, Columbus	62	30	46	76
John Vary, Topeka	69	20	56	76
Chris Brassard, Macon	70	31	43	74
Alexsander Chunchukov, Fayetteville.	69	25	49	74
Bernie John, Indianapolis	61	21	52	73
Justin Tomberlin, Fayetteville	68	43	28	71
Joe Burton, Oklahoma City	67	40	31	71

TOP SCORERS

	Games	G	A	Pts.
Yvan Corbin, Indianapolis	66	62	65	127
Chris MacKenzie, Indianapolis	67	47	80	127
Brian Shantz, San Antonio	70	30	79	109

INDIVIDUAL STATISTICS

COLUMBUS COTTONMOUTHS
SCORING

	Games	G	A	Pts.	PIM
Michael Martens	62	30	46	76	58
Marcel Richard	50	28	34	62	20
Per Fernhall	66	26	33	59	74
Ryan Aikia	68	23	34	57	133
Mick Kempffer	69	6	47	53	78
Jason Given	65	21	19	40	20
Derek Crimin	56	18	22	40	39
Kevin Plager	58	16	15	31	145
Jerome Bechard	62	12	16	28	341
Andy Powers	15	9	12	21	12
Donnie Margettie	34	8	13	21	104
Rob Frid	47	8	8	16	297
Olaf Kjenstad	14	6	7	13	32
Jackson Hegland	53	2	8	10	42
Brodie Coffin	12	1	9	10	61
Doug Mann	51	3	5	8	204
Jaroslav Kerestes	63	2	6	8	191
Kamil Kuriplach	52	4	3	7	167
Jon Cameron	18	2	4	6	28
Roman Marakhovski	36	2	4	6	37
Jomi Santala	11	2	2	4	0
Kelly Von Hiltgen	15	0	4	4	65
Mark Scott	9	0	3	3	19
Sebastien Parent	10	0	2	2	26

	Games	G	A	Pts.	PIM
Aaron Vickar (goalie)	33	0	2	2	0
Grady Manson	3	1	0	1	2
Markus Kolomainen	13	1	0	1	31
Vlad Klochkov	3	0	1	1	2
Kevin Fricke	11	0	1	1	8
Stewart Nowosad	15	0	1	1	10
Jula Linnonmaa	1	0	0	0	0
Mark Robinson	1	0	0	0	2
Todd Miller	2	0	0	0	0
Chris Ross	2	0	0	0	0
Derek Gosselin	8	0	0	0	8
Frankie Ouellette (goalie)	42	0	0	0	20

GOALTENDING

	Games	Min.	W	L	SOL	G	SO	Avg.
Frankie Ouellette	42	2344	22	10	7	95	1	2.43
Aaron Vickar	33	1855	17	10	4	92	1	2.98

FAYETTEVILLE FORCE
SCORING

	Games	G	A	Pts.	PIM
Brett Colborne	70	21	60	81	176
Alexsander Chunchukov	69	25	49	74	48
Justin Tomberlin	68	43	28	71	26
Matt Erredge	63	31	34	65	42
Chris Ford	69	29	36	65	65
C.J. Buzzell	70	28	33	61	78

	Games	G	A	Pts.	PIM
Roddy MacCormick	65	15	34	49	94
Jasen Rintala	70	7	21	28	113
Brad Frattaroli	61	10	16	26	16
Thom Cullen	67	13	9	22	69
Rob White	67	5	17	22	72
Ryan Schmidt	70	5	12	17	204
Jeff Antonovich	11	6	6	12	6
Colin Muldoon	70	0	9	9	63
Ronalds Ozolinsh	70	2	4	6	69
Kelly Leroux	69	0	6	6	152
Lance Robson	11	1	2	3	7
Brian Rasmussen	21	2	0	2	53
Bob Westerby	4	0	2	2	5
Stacy Prevost	4	0	1	1	0
Joe Wassilyn	6	0	1	1	5
Ken Shepard (goalie)	36	0	1	1	23
Nathan Grobins (goalie)	42	0	1	1	39
Spencer Ward	1	0	0	0	0
Greg Wilkinson	6	0	0	0	5
Doug Pirnak	7	0	0	0	7

GOALTENDING

	Games	Min.	W	L	SOL	G	SO	Avg.
Nathan Grobins	42	2239	24	11	1	96	2	2.57
Ken Shepard	36	1946	21	11	2	97	0	2.99

INDIANAPOLIS ICE

SCORING

	Games	G	A	Pts.	PIM
Yvan Corbin	66	62	65	127	60
Chris MacKenzie	67	47	80	127	83
Bernie John	61	21	52	73	28
Jan Jas	45	26	21	47	18
Lubos Krajcovic	70	19	24	43	44
Blaz Emersic	38	20	18	38	36
Mike Berger	67	10	26	36	72
Sebastian Pajerski	65	16	19	35	31
Peter Jas	42	10	25	35	18
Eric Landry	66	9	23	32	132
Mike Torkoff	44	8	16	24	47
Ken Boone	70	10	13	23	346
Dan Cousineau	68	3	17	20	38
Jason Mansoff	24	1	12	13	14
Thomas Stewart	24	5	7	12	8
Jay Hern	45	5	6	11	77
Steven Toll	26	4	5	9	18
Taj Schaffnit	38	4	4	8	51
Robert Davidson	39	1	6	7	112
Daniel Villeneuve	35	0	7	7	146
Jamie Morris (goalie)	21	0	3	3	2
Benoit Cassan	8	2	0	2	0
Benoit Thibert (goalie)	55	0	2	2	2
Cheyne Lazar	4	0	1	1	0
Chris Droeske	6	0	1	1	36
Jason Carriere	18	0	1	1	36
Jeff Schmidt	1	0	0	0	0
Eric Soltys (goalie)	1	0	0	0	0
Doug Altschul	2	0	0	0	0
Paul McInnis	5	0	0	0	2

GOALTENDING

	Games	Min.	W	L	SOL	G	SO	Avg.
Jamie Morris	21	1008	12	5	1	56	1	3.33
Benoit Thibert	55	3152	27	23	2	178	3	3.39
Eric Soltys	1	27	0	0	0	3	0	6.66

HUNTSVILLE CHANNEL CATS

SCORING

	Games	G	A	Pts.	PIM
Chris George	70	50	36	86	27
Jonathan DuBois	59	22	61	83	272
James Patterson	61	34	25	59	42
Mario Dumoulin	68	6	41	47	263
Tyler Quiring	45	13	23	36	42
Mike DeGurse	51	16	18	34	241

	Games	G	A	Pts.	PIM
Ken Richardson	46	12	21	33	201
Greg Lakovic	57	12	19	31	203
John Gibson	55	8	22	30	80
Aigars Mironovics	65	10	19	29	36
Andy Doktorchik	65	12	16	28	105
Alex Dumas	46	6	13	19	73
Jeff Antonovich	21	8	6	14	6
Tom Moulton	53	4	10	14	99
Garth Gartner	53	9	4	13	178
Steve Herniman	55	1	9	10	129
Joe Coombs	9	5	4	9	6
Ryan Wood	19	0	8	8	24
Brent Scott	8	3	2	5	54
Todd Dougherty	35	1	4	5	99
Brendan Flynn	9	0	5	5	6
Jason MacIntyre	7	1	2	3	17
Mitch Shawara	9	0	3	3	15
Roman Marakhovski	9	2	0	2	4
Derek Reynolds	5	1	1	2	13
Tim Lozinik	2	0	2	2	0
Terry Snyder (goalie)	28	0	2	2	0
Matt Gorman	3	1	0	1	2
Sean Basilio (goalie)	14	0	1	1	15
Josh Erdman	14	0	1	1	40
Mike Zeller (goalie)	1	0	0	0	0
Brent Belecki (goalie)	9	0	0	0	0
Matt Carmichael (goalie)	28	0	0	0	14

GOALTENDING

	Games	Min.	W	L	SOL	G	SO	Avg.
Mike Zeller	1	29	0	0	0	0	0	0.00
Brent Belecki	9	515	6	2	0	20	3	2.33
Sean Basilio	14	757	7	5	2	41	2	3.25
Matt Carmichael	28	1373	14	8	2	78	1	3.41
Terry Snyder	28	1518	10	12	2	93	1	3.68

MACON WHOOPEE

SCORING

	Games	G	A	Pts.	PIM
Chris Brassard	70	31	43	74	227
Steve Suk	64	17	48	65	69
Todd MacIsaac	60	27	22	49	127
Jocelyn Langlois	28	13	28	41	22
Bob Berg	31	12	28	40	33
Jeff Antonovich	38	18	21	39	51
Bob Rapoza	53	15	22	37	70
Vitali Andreev	63	19	17	36	20
Samuel Paquet	57	15	19	34	118
Phil Valk	65	6	25	31	456
Jason Gudmundson	24	14	16	30	14
Rob Phillips	56	9	15	24	31
Mike Ross	52	6	18	24	60
Thomas Stewart	32	12	10	22	63
Peter Robertson	70	8	11	19	56
Eric Linkowski	50	8	10	18	32
Jason Ricci	37	0	17	17	22
Todd Newton	29	4	12	16	58
Jarno Mensonen	19	2	8	10	14
Ryan Campbell	7	4	4	8	0
Todd Steinmetz	23	3	5	8	49
Mark McFarlane	10	4	3	7	59
Cosmo Clarke	12	2	3	5	4
Jan Jas	12	1	3	4	4
Andrew Rodgers	28	0	3	3	248
Craig Perrett	7	1	1	2	10
Matt Carey	14	0	2	2	0
Eric Brown	17	0	2	2	6
Benoit Cassan	6	1	0	1	4
Don Clipperton	11	1	0	1	5
Marijan Ivanusec	5	0	1	1	11
Erik Zachrisson	1	0	0	0	0
Martin Fillion (goalie)	2	0	0	0	2
Scott Galt (goalie)	2	0	0	0	0
Rick Nichol (goalie)	2	0	0	0	0

MINOR LEAGUES *Central*

	Games	G	A	Pts.	PIM
Marco Panzeri (goalie)	5	0	0	0	0
Trevor Anderson (goalie)	12	0	0	0	7
Scott Barber (goalie)	15	0	0	0	26
Brian Elder (goalie)	39	0	0	0	12

GOALTENDING

	Games	Min.	W	L	SOL	G	SO	Avg.
Martin Fillion	2	120	1	0	1	5	0	2.50
Brian Elder	39	2209	19	13	5	94	3	2.55
Trevor Anderson	12	672	7	3	1	38	0	3.39
Scott Galt	2	80	1	1	0	5	0	3.75
Rick Nichol	2	62	0	1	0	4	0	3.89
Scott Barber	15	817	6	6	1	56	0	4.11
Marco Panzeri	5	245	0	2	2	23	0	5.64

MEMPHIS RIVERKINGS
SCORING

	Games	G	A	Pts.	PIM
Derek Grant	63	33	35	68	73
Jason Sangiuliano	68	16	28	44	56
Leonard Bonanno	53	19	21	40	184
Grady Manson	39	18	15	33	52
Thomas Migdal	59	13	10	23	46
Greg Wilkinson	57	10	13	23	29
Josh Erdman	36	8	13	21	58
Dan Brown	57	3	18	21	114
Travis Tipler	31	3	14	17	18
Rostyslav Saglo	38	3	9	12	6
Stas Tkatch	20	5	6	11	8
Tom Gordon	70	1	10	11	62
Oleg Tsirkounov	18	4	6	10	32
Stewart Nowosad	35	3	7	10	24
Bob Westerby	9	3	6	9	96
Kelly Von Hiltgen	16	2	7	9	42
Mike Wolf	27	3	5	8	68
Stephane Desjardins	39	2	6	8	38
Rob Szatmary	28	6	1	7	106
Chris Dashney	17	2	5	7	12
Brian Rasmussen	26	2	5	7	106
Rich Navin	8	1	6	7	0
Tony Columbo	8	1	4	5	0
Scot Bell	11	1	4	5	11
Kevin Evans	7	0	5	5	64
Greg Ambrose	23	3	1	4	26
Cosmo Clarke	8	2	2	4	2
Benoit Cassan	16	2	2	4	14
Jay Pylypuik	34	0	4	4	26
Mike Varhaug	14	0	3	3	159
Ken Corp	6	1	1	2	4
Derrek Harper	11	1	1	2	61
Ryan Howell	5	0	2	2	0
Cory Holland	16	0	2	2	85
Ryan Tempel (goalie)	34	0	2	2	2
Brian Hickey	8	1	0	1	0
Kurt Walsten	1	0	1	1	0
Nolan Weir	1	0	0	0	0
Kevin Fricke	2	0	0	0	0
Ryan Hall	2	0	0	0	2
Sean McEachran	2	0	0	0	17
Trevor Tokarczyk	2	0	0	0	0
Vlad Klochkov	3	0	0	0	6
Josh McCready	4	0	0	0	0
Rick Nichol (goalie)	4	0	0	0	0
Dave Lyons (goalie)	5	0	0	0	0
Todd Steinmetz	6	0	0	0	13
Steve Briere (goalie)	7	0	0	0	2
Mark Falkowski	7	0	0	0	0
Gregg Lalonde	13	0	0	0	12
Rob Friesen (goalie)	30	0	0	0	8

GOALTENDING

	Games	Min.	W	L	SOL	G	SO	Avg.
Steve Briere	7	386	2	4	0	21	1	3.27
Rob Friesen	30	1677	6	19	2	116	0	4.15
Ryan Tempel	34	1741	1	28	2	152	0	5.24

	Games	Min.	W	L	SOL	G	SO	Avg.
Rick Nichol	4	168	0	3	0	15	0	5.34
Dave Lyons	5	226	0	3	0	29	0	7.70

OKLAHOMA CITY BLAZERS
SCORING

	Games	G	A	Pts.	PIM
Joe Burton	67	40	31	71	54
Hardy Sauter	70	13	56	69	38
Sean Brady	70	23	35	58	96
Corey MacIntyre	58	17	37	54	61
Rod Butler	69	30	17	47	164
Simon Olivier	50	15	26	41	150
Mark O'Donnell	62	14	25	39	41
Mike Tobin	68	3	31	34	124
Scott Davies	51	20	9	29	49
Peter Arvanitis	47	17	10	27	114
Sam Katsuras	40	11	11	22	31
Wade Brookbank	68	3	9	12	354
Jim Jensen	19	8	3	11	31
Ricky Jacob	15	4	6	10	2
Mike Pozzo	24	4	6	10	18
Chris Dashney	40	2	8	10	35
Donnie Margettie	19	5	4	9	42
Charlie Elezi	48	2	7	9	160
Paul Johnson	63	1	8	9	98
Marco Cefalo	50	3	5	8	221
Jared Dumba	9	3	3	6	4
Stewart Nowosad	8	1	3	4	13
Kent Silbernagel	6	1	2	3	0
Shane Bowler	2	1	0	1	2
Richard Peacock	6	1	0	1	21
Chris Morseth	4	0	1	1	2
Tyler Fleck	6	0	1	1	14
Rob Galatiuk (goalie)	30	0	1	1	6
Jean-Ian Filiatrault (goalie)	45	0	1	1	4
Mike Wolf	2	0	0	0	0
Pierre Gendron	3	0	0	0	13
Michael Henderson	3	0	0	0	6
Mark Scott	3	0	0	0	7
Travis Tipler	3	0	0	0	5
Troy Yarosh	4	0	0	0	4
Scott Buhler (goalie)	5	0	0	0	0

GOALTENDING

	Games	Min.	W	L	SOL	G	SO	Avg.
Scott Buhler	5	300	4	1	0	11	1	2.20
Jean-Ian Filiatrault	45	2358	21	17	3	116	1	2.95
Rob Galatiuk	30	1530	14	6	4	82	1	3.22

SAN ANTONIO IGUANAS
SCORING

	Games	G	A	Pts.	PIM
Brian Shantz	70	30	79	109	97
Johnny Brdarovic	68	34	49	83	24
Scott Green	65	41	38	79	62
Ricky Jacob	51	18	20	38	34
Henry Kuster	42	15	18	33	31
Blair Rota	60	11	17	28	92
Wade Gibson	30	6	18	24	40
Jarret Zukiwsky	28	7	12	19	112
Jason MacIntyre	56	2	16	18	171
Marc Laforge	61	2	15	17	243
Mitch Shawara	60	4	11	15	185
Jason Pain	28	7	7	14	6
Garnet Jacobson	62	8	5	13	213
Rhett Dudley	21	4	9	13	18
Gatis Tseplis	17	2	10	12	16
Troy Caley	13	5	6	11	23
Jeff Boettger	56	4	7	11	51
Bob Westerby	36	3	8	11	218
Trevor Matschke	46	1	10	11	39
Tyler Quiring	8	5	4	9	0
Andrei Lupandin	10	3	4	7	0
Craig Coxe	20	1	5	6	33

	Games	G	A	Pts.	PIM
Serge Bourgeois	22	3	2	5	16
Mike Pozzo	13	2	3	5	2
Shawn Penn	12	1	4	5	29
Sam Fields	52	2	2	4	199
Dmitri Pigolitsyn	3	3	0	3	0
Tom MacDonald	16	1	1	2	31
Scott Usmail	2	0	1	1	2
Greg Ambrose	7	0	1	1	2
Ryan Edwards	7	0	1	1	0
Ian Perkins (goalie)	12	0	1	1	0
Corwin Saurdiff (goalie)	45	0	1	1	0
Martin Fillion (goalie)	2	0	0	0	0
Ryan Pisiak	2	0	0	0	29
Fred Goltz	3	0	0	0	2
Dave Lylyk	3	0	0	0	0
Ryan Hartung	4	0	0	0	2
Trevor Anderson (goalie)	17	0	0	0	0

GOALTENDING

	Games	Min.	W	L	SOL	G	SO	Avg.
Ian Perkins	12	687	6	4	2	37	0	3.23
Corwin Saurdiff	45	2575	22	19	1	149	0	3.47
Trevor Anderson	17	852	5	8	2	55	0	3.87
Martin Fillion	2	74	0	1	0	6	0	4.87

TOPEKA SCARECROWS

SCORING

	Games	G	A	Pts.	PIM
Brett Seguin	70	22	75	97	34
Steve Moore	67	36	40	76	99
John Vary	69	20	56	76	89
Blair Manning	70	17	42	59	79
Bill Monkman	65	38	15	53	151
Joe Coombs	59	26	22	48	67
Tom Gomes	29	21	14	35	86
Mike Rusk	67	2	26	28	40
Trevor Hanas	70	11	16	27	107
Oleg Tsirkounov	48	14	10	24	70
Kirk Llano	67	4	15	19	83
David Bouskill	65	5	9	14	49
Grady Manson	23	2	8	10	31
Scot Bell	26	3	6	9	8
Gary Coupal	20	5	3	8	60
Kevin Fricke	25	3	2	5	10
Alex Mukhanov	24	0	5	5	16
Jason Lafreniere	3	3	1	4	2
Dale LaFrance	13	1	3	4	7
Mike DeGurse	9	2	1	3	15
Sergei Olympiev	10	1	2	3	14
Randy Best	15	1	2	3	12
Mike Hiebert	18	0	3	3	93
Joe Beaudry	21	1	1	2	40
John Gibson	9	0	2	2	13
Sergei Deschevy	43	0	2	2	161
Yuri Moscevsky	4	1	0	1	7
Sylvain Thibault	8	1	0	1	10
Zybnek Neckar	3	0	1	1	2
Rod Branch (goalie)	56	0	1	1	18
Jan Melichar	1	0	0	0	0
Jason Girodat	3	0	0	0	0
Andre Quesnel	3	0	0	0	17
Kyle Haviland	15	0	0	0	35
Michal Podolka (goalie)	17	0	0	0	0

GOALTENDING

	Games	Min.	W	L	SOL	G	SO	Avg.
Rod Branch	56	3250	25	22	6	168	2	3.10
Michal Podolka	17	940	10	5	2	63	0	4.02

TULSA OILERS

SCORING

	Games	G	A	Pts.	PIM
Doug Lawrence	65	29	71	100	212
Luc Beausoleil	68	25	55	80	72
Craig Hamelin	68	25	42	67	50

	Games	G	A	Pts.	PIM
Sylvain Naud	70	26	25	51	132
Marty Diamond	65	22	26	48	88
Jean-Francois Gregoire	41	25	17	42	28
Chris Smith	70	13	25	38	131
Brad Cook	67	4	33	37	90
Jorin Welsh	70	9	21	30	103
Jon Cameron	44	17	11	28	99
Troy Caley	32	10	12	22	59
Mike Mohr	68	5	17	22	73
Daniel Chaput	70	4	17	21	86
Curtis Voth	66	13	4	17	466
Todd Newton	43	5	7	12	40
Doug Pirnak	51	1	9	10	151
Jason Abel	29	3	3	6	69
Bobby Clouston	11	1	4	5	20
Ryan Reid	48	1	3	4	274
Carl Paradis	11	2	1	3	10
Mark Scott	7	0	2	2	22
Jim Cashman	3	1	0	1	0
James Ronayne (goalie)	30	0	1	1	2
Rob Szatmary	3	0	0	0	17
Chad Erickson (goalie)	45	0	0	0	23

GOALTENDING

	Games	Min.	W	L	SOL	G	SO	Avg.
James Ronayne	30	1642	13	11	3	88	0	3.22
Chad Erickson	45	2541	25	16	2	145	1	3.42

WICHITA THUNDER

SCORING

	Games	G	A	Pts.	PIM
Travis Clayton	66	42	43	85	155
Jason Duda	55	27	41	68	60
Mark Karpen	49	27	23	50	26
Mark Strohack	70	14	29	43	78
Bob Berg	36	9	34	43	61
Sean O'Reilly	58	4	33	37	104
Kevin Powell	69	17	18	35	98
Kris Schultz	68	13	22	35	389
Trevor Folk	58	7	26	33	130
Mike Donaghue	68	5	22	27	37
Jerod Bina	58	10	16	26	58
Jim McGeough	37	12	13	25	30
Rhett Dudley	42	1	19	20	79
Aaron Novak	54	6	13	19	54
Trevor Converse	51	7	8	15	119
Troy Caley	15	9	4	13	8
Rocky Florio	31	6	7	13	91
Mike Hiebert	41	5	6	11	191
Kevin Tucker	26	4	4	8	8
Walker McDonald	18	5	1	6	44
Chris Dashney	9	2	4	6	16
Lance Leslie (goalie)	49	0	5	5	4
Dwayne Gylywoychuk	30	1	3	4	48
Jeff Leiter	2	1	1	2	0
Sheldon Moser	4	1	1	2	0
Greg Smith (goalie)	25	0	2	2	52
Chris O'Rourke	7	1	0	1	44
Thomas Migdal	4	0	1	1	4
Derrek Harper	28	0	0	0	47

GOALTENDING

	Games	Min.	W	L	SOL	G	SO	Avg.
Lance Leslie	49	2794	24	15	7	141	3	3.03
Greg Smith	25	1401	13	11	0	76	1	3.26

PLAYERS WITH TWO OR MORE TEAMS

SCORING

	Games	G	A	Pts.	PIM
Greg Ambrose, San Antonio	7	0	1	1	2
Greg Ambrose, Memphis	23	3	1	4	26
Totals	30	3	2	5	28
Trevor Anderson, S.A. (goalie)	17	0	0	0	0
Trevor Anderson, Mac. (goalie)	12	0	0	0	7

MINOR LEAGUES *Central*

	Games	G	A	Pts.	PIM
Totals	29	0	0	0	7
Jeff Antonovich, Macon	38	18	21	39	51
Jeff Antonovich, Huntsville	21	8	6	14	6
Jeff Antonovich, Fayetteville	11	6	6	12	6
Totals	70	32	33	65	63
Scot Bell, Memphis	11	1	4	5	11
Scot Bell, Topeka	26	3	6	9	8
Totals	37	4	10	14	19
Bob Berg, Wichita	36	9	34	43	61
Bob Berg, Macon	31	12	28	40	33
Totals	67	21	62	83	94
Troy Caley, Tulsa	32	10	12	22	59
Troy Caley, Wichita	15	9	4	13	8
Troy Caley, San Antonio	13	5	6	11	23
Totals	60	24	22	46	90
Jon Cameron, Columbus	18	2	4	6	28
Jon Cameron, Tulsa	44	17	11	28	99
Totals	62	19	15	34	127
Benoit Cassan, Indianapolis	8	2	0	2	0
Benoit Cassan, Macon	6	1	0	1	4
Benoit Cassan, Memphis	16	2	2	4	14
Totals	30	5	2	7	18
Cosmo Clarke, Memphis	8	2	2	4	2
Cosmo Clarke, Macon	12	2	3	5	4
Totals	20	4	5	9	6
Joe Coombs, Topeka	59	26	22	48	67
Joe Coombs, Huntsville	9	5	4	9	6
Totals	68	31	26	57	73
Chris Dashney, Wichita	9	2	4	6	16
Chris Dashney, Memphis	17	2	5	7	12
Chris Dashney, Oklahoma City	40	2	8	10	35
Totals	66	6	17	23	63
Mike DeGurse, Huntsville	51	16	18	34	241
Mike DeGurse, Topeka	9	2	1	3	15
Totals	60	18	19	37	256
Rhett Dudley, Wichita	42	1	19	20	79
Rhett Dudley, San Antonio	21	4	9	13	18
Totals	63	5	28	33	97
Josh Erdman, Huntsville	14	0	1	1	40
Josh Erdman, Memphis	36	8	13	21	58
Totals	50	8	14	22	98
Martin Fillion, Macon (goalie)	2	0	0	0	2
Martin Fillion, S.A. (goalie)	2	0	0	0	0
Totals	4	0	0	0	2
Kevin Fricke, Columbus	11	0	1	1	8
Kevin Fricke, Topeka	25	3	2	5	10
Kevin Fricke, Memphis	2	0	0	0	0
Totals	38	3	3	6	18
John Gibson, Huntsville	55	8	22	30	80
John Gibson, Topeka	9	0	2	2	13
Totals	64	8	24	32	93
Derrek Harper, Memphis	11	1	1	2	61
Derrek Harper, Wichita	28	0	0	0	47
Totals	39	1	1	2	108
Mike Hiebert, Topeka	18	0	3	3	93
Mike Hiebert, Wichita	41	5	6	11	191
Totals	59	5	9	14	284
Ricky Jacob, San Antonio	51	18	20	38	34
Ricky Jacob, Oklahoma City	15	4	6	10	2
Totals	66	22	26	48	36
Jan Jas, Macon	12	1	3	4	4
Jan Jas, Indianapolis	45	26	21	47	18
Totals	57	27	24	51	22
Vlad Klochkov, Columbus	3	0	1	1	2
Vlad Klochkov, Memphis	3	0	0	0	6
Totals	6	0	1	1	8
Jason MacIntyre, San Antonio	56	2	16	18	171
Jason MacIntyre, Huntsville	7	1	2	3	17
Totals	63	3	18	21	188
Grady Manson, Columbus	3	1	0	1	2
Grady Manson, Memphis	39	18	15	33	52
Grady Manson, Topeka	23	2	8	10	31
Totals	65	21	23	44	85
Roman Marakhovski, Col.	36	2	4	6	37
Roman Marakhovski, Hunts.	9	2	0	2	4
Totals	45	4	4	8	41

	Games	G	A	Pts.	PIM
Donnie Margettie, Columbus	34	8	13	21	104
Donnie Margettie, Okla. City	19	5	4	9	42
Totals	53	13	17	30	146
Thomas Migdal, Wichita	4	0	1	1	4
Thomas Migdal, Memphis	59	13	10	23	46
Totals	63	13	11	24	50
Todd Newton, Tulsa	43	5	7	12	40
Todd Newton, Macon	29	4	12	16	58
Totals	72	9	19	28	98
Rick Nichol, Macon (goalie)	2	0	0	0	0
Rick Nichol, Memphis (goalie)	4	0	0	0	0
Totals	6	0	0	0	0
Stewart Nowosad, Columbus	15	0	1	1	10
Stewart Nowosad, Okla. City	8	1	3	4	13
Stewart Nowosad, Memphis	35	3	7	10	24
Totals	58	4	11	15	47
Doug Pirnak, Tulsa	51	1	9	10	151
Doug Pirnak, Fayetteville	7	0	0	0	7
Totals	58	1	9	10	158
Mike Pozzo, Oklahoma City	24	4	6	10	18
Mike Pozzo, San Antonio	13	2	3	5	2
Totals	37	6	9	15	20
Tyler Quiring, Huntsville	45	13	23	36	42
Tyler Quiring, San Antonio	8	5	4	9	0
Totals	53	18	27	45	42
Brian Rasmussen, Fayetteville	21	2	0	2	53
Brian Rasmussen, Memphis	26	2	5	7	106
Totals	47	4	5	9	159
Mark Scott, Oklahoma City	3	0	0	0	7
Mark Scott, Columbus	9	0	3	3	19
Mark Scott, Tulsa	7	0	2	2	22
Totals	19	0	5	5	48
Mitch Shawara, San Antonio	60	4	11	15	185
Mitch Shawara, Huntsville	9	0	3	3	15
Totals	69	4	14	18	200
Todd Steinmetz, Macon	23	3	5	8	49
Todd Steinmetz, Memphis	6	0	0	0	13
Totals	29	3	5	8	62
Thomas Stewart, Indianapolis	24	5	7	12	8
Thomas Stewart, Macon	32	12	10	22	63
Totals	56	17	17	34	71
Rob Szatmary, Tulsa	3	0	0	0	17
Rob Szatmary, Memphis	28	6	1	7	106
Totals	31	6	1	7	123
Travis Tipler, Memphis	31	3	14	17	18
Travis Tipler, Oklahoma City	3	0	0	0	5
Totals	34	3	14	17	23
Oleg Tsirkounov, Topeka	48	14	10	24	70
Oleg Tsirkounov, Memphis	18	4	6	10	32
Totals	66	18	16	34	102
Kelly Von Hiltgen, Memphis	16	2	7	9	42
Kelly Von Hiltgen, Columbus	15	0	4	4	65
Totals	31	2	11	13	107
Bob Westerby, Memphis	9	3	6	9	96
Bob Westerby, Fayetteville	4	0	2	2	5
Bob Westerby, San Antonio	36	3	8	11	218
Totals	49	6	16	22	319
Greg Wilkinson, Fayetteville	6	0	0	0	5
Greg Wilkinson, Memphis	57	10	13	23	29
Totals	63	10	13	23	34
Mike Wolf, Oklahoma City	2	0	0	0	0
Mike Wolf, Memphis	27	3	5	8	68
Totals	29	3	5	8	68

GOALTENDING

	Gms.	Min.	W	L	SOL	G	SO	Avg.
T. Anderson, S.A.	17	852	5	8	2	55	0	3.87
T. Anderson, Mac.	12	672	7	3	1	38	0	3.39
Totals	29	1524	12	11	3	93	0	3.66
M. Fillion, Mac.	2	120	1	0	1	5	0	2.50
M. Fillion, S.A.	2	74	0	1	0	6	0	4.87
Totals	4	194	1	1	1	11	0	3.40
R. Nichol, Mac.	2	62	0	1	0	4	0	3.89
R. Nichol, Mem.	4	168	0	3	0	15	0	5.34
Totals	6	230	0	4	0	19	0	4.96

QUARTERFINALS

	W	L	Pts.	GF	GA
Macon	3	1	6	14	5
Fayetteville	1	3	2	5	14

(Macon won series, 3-1)

	W	L	Pts.	GF	GA
Columbus	3	2	6	13	14
Huntsville	2	3	4	14	13

(Columbus won series, 3-2)

	W	L	Pts.	GF	GA
Oklahoma City	3	2	6	19	15
Wichita	2	3	4	15	19

(Oklahoma City won series, 3-2)

	W	L	Pts.	GF	GA
Indianapolis	3	2	6	15	11
Tulsa	2	3	4	11	25

(Indianapolis won series, 3-2)

SEMIFINALS

	W	L	Pts.	GF	GA
Columbus	3	1	6	16	11
Macon	1	3	2	11	16

(Columbus won series, 3-1)

	W	L	Pts.	GF	GA
Indianapolis	3	0	6	8	4
Oklahoma City	0	3	0	4	8

(Indianapolis won series, 3-0)

FINALS

	W	L	Pts.	GF	GA
Indianapolis	4	3	8	16	14
Columbus	3	4	6	14	16

(Indianapolis won series, 4-3)

INDIVIDUAL LEADERS

Goals: Michael Martens, Columbus (16)
Assists: Marcel Richard, Columbus (16)
Points: Marcel Richard, Columbus (22)
Penalty minutes: Ken Boone, Indianapolis (82)
Goaltending average: Jamie Morris, Indianapolis (1.63)
Shutouts: Frankie Ouellette, Columbus (3)

TOP SCORERS

	Games	G	A	Pts.
Marcel Richard, Columbus	16	6	16	22
Michael Martens, Columbus	16	12	9	21
Chris MacKenzie, Indianapolis	15	7	14	21
Yvan Corbin, Indianapolis	15	7	8	15
Peter Jas, Indianapolis	15	7	5	12
Derek Crimin, Columbus	16	6	4	10
Mick Kempffer, Columbus	13	3	7	10
Jan Jas, Indianapolis	15	3	7	10
Andy Powers, Columbus	16	3	7	10
Joe Burton, Oklahoma City	8	5	4	9
Jason Duda, Wichita	5	3	6	9
Bernie John, Indianapolis	15	3	6	9

INDIVIDUAL STATISTICS

COLUMBUS COTTONMOUTHS
(Lost finals to Indianapolis, 4-3)

SCORING

	Games	G	A	Pts.	PIM
Marcel Richard	16	6	16	22	10
Michael Martens	16	12	9	21	6
Derek Crimin	16	6	4	10	10
Mick Kempffer	13	3	7	10	6
Andy Powers	16	3	7	10	8
Jerome Bechard	16	2	5	7	68
Doug Mann	16	4	2	6	31
Ryan Aikia	16	1	5	6	33
Per Fernhall	15	4	1	5	10
Kevin Plager	16	2	2	4	11
Brodie Coffin	14	0	4	4	28
Scott Schoneck	14	0	3	3	10
Kamil Kuriplach	14	0	2	2	12
Jackson Hegland	16	0	2	2	6
Jaroslav Kerestes	16	0	2	2	24
Jason Given	16	0	1	1	2
Aaron Vickar (goalie)	2	0	0	0	0
Kelly Von Hiltgen	4	0	0	0	7
Jeff Cheeseman	5	0	0	0	12
Frankie Ouellette (goalie)	16	0	0	0	2

GOALTENDING

	Games	Min.	W	L	T	G	SO	Avg.
Aaron Vickar	2	40	0	0	0	1	0	1.50
Frankie Ouellette	16	944	9	6	1	38	3	2.41

FAYETTEVILLE FORCE
(Lost quarterfinals to Macon, 3-1)

SCORING

	Games	G	A	Pts.	PIM
Jeff Antonovich	4	2	1	3	2
Brett Colborne	4	2	0	2	0
Ryan Schmidt	4	0	2	2	4
Justin Tomberlin	4	0	2	2	0
Rob White	4	1	0	1	0
Matt Erredge	4	0	1	1	0
Brad Frattaroli	4	0	1	1	2
Roddy MacCormick	4	0	1	1	4
Nathan Grobins (goalie)	2	0	0	0	0
Ken Shepard (goalie)	2	0	0	0	2
C.J. Buzzell	4	0	0	0	0
Alexsand Chunchukov	4	0	0	0	4
Thom Cullen	4	0	0	0	2
Chris Ford	4	0	0	0	2
Kelly Leroux	4	0	0	0	2
Colin Muldoon	4	0	0	0	2
Ronalds Ozolinsh	4	0	0	0	2
Jasen Rintala	4	0	0	0	8

GOALTENDING

	Games	Min.	W	L	T	G	SO	Avg.
Nathan Grobins	2	185	1	1	0	4	0	1.30
Ken Shepard	2	120	0	2	0	10	0	5.00

HUNTSVILLE CHANNEL CATS
(Lost quarterfinals to Columbus, 3-2)

SCORING

	Games	G	A	Pts.	PIM
Chris George	5	2	3	5	4
Brendan Flynn	5	1	4	5	4
James Patterson	5	2	2	4	2
Jonathan DuBois	5	0	4	4	15
Alex Dumas	5	2	1	3	2
Andy Doktorchik	5	1	2	3	20
Greg Lakovic	5	1	2	3	0
Derek Reynolds	5	2	0	2	9
Mario Dumoulin	3	1	1	2	17
Joe Coombs	5	1	0	1	2
Roman Marakhovski	5	1	0	1	2
Garth Gartner	3	0	0	0	2
Steve Herniman	3	0	0	0	2
Mitch Shawara	4	0	0	0	0
Brent Belecki (goalie)	5	0	0	0	2
Jason MacIntyre	5	0	0	0	2
Aigars Mironovics	5	0	0	0	4
Ken Richardson	5	0	0	0	34

GOALTENDING

	Games	Min.	W	L	T	G	SO	Avg.
Brent Belecki	5	304	2	2	1	13	0	2.56

INDIANAPOLIS ICE
(Winner of 2000 playoffs)

SCORING

	Games	G	A	Pts.	PIM
Chris MacKenzie	15	7	14	21	43
Yvan Corbin	15	7	8	15	27
Peter Jas	15	7	5	12	4
Jan Jas	15	3	7	10	10
Bernie John	15	3	6	9	6
Lubos Krajcovic	15	2	6	8	14
Dan Cousineau	15	1	5	6	55
Blaz Emersic	12	2	2	4	0
Mike Torkoff	15	1	3	4	37
Daniel Villeneuve	15	1	2	3	39
Jamie Morris (goalie)	12	0	3	3	2
Mike Berger	9	2	0	2	38
Ken Boone	15	1	1	2	82
Sebastian Pajerski	14	1	0	1	19
Robert Davidson	15	1	0	1	26
Arvid Rekis	4	0	0	0	0
Benoit Thibert (goalie)	4	0	0	0	0
Corey Waring	6	0	0	0	0
Eric Landry	15	0	0	0	17
Taj Schaffnit	15	0	0	0	37

GOALTENDING

	Games	Min.	W	L	T	G	SO	Avg.
Jamie Morris	12	737	8	2	1	20	2	1.63
Benoit Thibert	4	202	2	2	0	9	0	2.67

MACON WHOOPEE
(Lost semifinals to Columbus, 3-1)

SCORING

	Games	G	A	Pts.	PIM
Todd Newton	7	4	3	7	8
Ryan Campbell	8	3	4	7	4
Bob Berg	8	2	5	7	15
Chris Brassard	8	4	2	6	32
Todd MacIsaac	8	4	2	6	4
Jocelyn Langlois	8	2	3	5	2
Steve Suk	8	1	4	5	2
Jason Gudmundson	8	2	1	3	0
Vitali Andreev	8	1	2	3	0
Eric Linkowski	8	0	3	3	2
Thomas Stewart	8	1	1	2	10
Phil Valk	8	1	1	2	55
Bob Rapoza	8	0	2	2	8
Mike Ross	8	0	2	2	0
Peter Robertson	4	0	1	1	0

	Games	G	A	Pts.	PIM
Eric Pinoul	4	0	0	0	4
Brian Elder (goalie)	8	0	0	0	2
Samuel Paquet	8	0	0	0	23

GOALTENDING

	Games	Min.	W	L	T	G	SO	Avg.
Brian Elder	8	546	4	3	1	21	1	2.31

OKLAHOMA CITY BLAZERS
(Lost semifinals to Indianapolis, 3-0)

SCORING

	Games	G	A	Pts.	PIM
Joe Burton	8	5	4	9	4
Peter Arvanitis	8	4	3	7	2
Hardy Sauter	8	1	6	7	2
Sean Brady	8	2	4	6	22
Chris Dashney	8	2	4	6	12
Corey MacIntyre	8	1	4	5	10
Rod Butler	8	3	0	3	24
Ricky Jacob	7	2	1	3	2
Michael Henderson	8	2	1	3	16
Wade Brookbank	7	1	1	2	29
Paul Johnson	8	0	2	2	8
Scott Davies	7	0	1	1	18
Mark O'Donnell	8	0	1	1	2
Jared Dumba	3	0	0	0	0
Jean-Ian Filiatrault (goalie)	3	0	0	0	0
Scott Buhler (goalie)	5	0	0	0	0
Tyler Fleck	8	0	0	0	4
Pierre Gendron	8	0	0	0	4
Mike Tobin	8	0	0	0	11

GOALTENDING

	Games	Min.	W	L	T	G	SO	Avg.
Scott Buhler	5	299	3	2	0	12	1	2.41
Jean-Ian Filiatrault	3	211	0	1	2	11	0	3.12

TULSA OILERS
(Lost quarterfinals to Indianapolis, 3-2)

SCORING

	Games	G	A	Pts.	PIM
Doug Lawrence	5	2	3	5	31
Jean-Francois Gregoire	5	3	1	4	17
Luc Beausoleil	5	2	2	4	6
Craig Hamelin	5	1	3	4	8
Curtis Voth	5	2	1	3	35
Chris Smith	2	0	2	2	0
Daniel Chaput	5	1	0	1	16
Chad Erickson (goalie)	3	0	1	1	0
Brad Cook	5	0	1	1	19
Marty Diamond	5	0	1	1	4
Mike Mohr	5	0	1	1	25
Sylvain Naud	5	0	1	1	14
Carl Paradis	5	0	1	1	17
Ryan Reid	5	0	1	1	18
Jorin Welsh	5	0	1	1	31
James Ronayne (goalie)	3	0	0	0	0
Jon Cameron	5	0	0	0	0
Mark Scott	5	0	0	0	20

GOALTENDING

	Games	Min.	W	L	T	G	SO	Avg.
James Ronayne	3	140	2	1	0	5	1	2.14
Chad Erickson	3	164	0	1	1	10	0	3.67

WICHITA THUNDER
(Lost quarterfinals to Oklahoma City, 3-2)

SCORING

	Games	G	A	Pts.	PIM
Jason Duda	5	3	6	9	2
Travis Clayton	5	5	3	8	6
Mark Strohack	5	0	4	4	10
Kris Schultz	5	2	1	3	2
Sheldon Moser	5	1	2	3	0
Sean O'Reilly	5	0	3	3	14
Jim McGeough	5	1	1	2	4

	Games	G	A	Pts.	PIM
Jeff Leiter	3	1	0	1	6
Trevor Converse	5	1	0	1	6
Mike Hiebert	5	1	0	1	15
Trevor Folk	2	0	1	1	0
Walker McDonald	3	0	1	1	0
Mike Donaghue	5	0	1	1	0
Derek Harper	5	0	1	1	12
Mark Karpen	5	0	1	1	2
Kevin Powell	5	0	1	1	11

	Games	G	A	Pts.	PIM
Greg Smith (goalie)	1	0	0	0	0
Jerod Bina	2	0	0	0	2
Lance Leslie (goalie)	4	0	0	0	0
Dwayne Gylywoychuk	5	0	0	0	14

GOALTENDING

	Games	Min.	W	L	T	G	SO	Avg.
Lance Leslie	4	255	2	2	0	13	0	3.06
Greg Smith	1	59	0	1	0	3	0	3.06

1999-2000 AWARD WINNERS

ALL-STAR TEAMS

The Central Hockey League did not name an
All-Star team for the 1999-2000 season.

TROPHY WINNERS

Most Valuable Player: Yvan Corbin, Indianapolis
Chris MacKenzie, Indianapolis
Ken McKenzie Trophy: Yvan Corbin, Indianapolis
Chris MacKenzie, Indianapolis
Goaltender of the Year: Frankie Ouellette, Columbus
Defenseman of the Year: Brett Colborne, Fayetteville
Rookie of the Year: James Patterson, Huntsville
President's Trophy: Jamie Morris, Indianapolis
Commissioner's Trophy: David Lohrie, Fayetteville

ALL-TIME AWARD WINNERS

MOST VALUABLE PLAYER

Season   Player, Team
1992-93—Sylvain Fleury, Oklahoma City
1993-94—Robert Desjardins, Wichita
1994-95—Paul Jackson, San Antonio
1995-96—Brian Shantz, San Antonio
1996-97—Trevor Jobe, Columbus-Wichita
1997-98—Joe Burton, Oklahoma City
1998-99—Derek Puppa, Huntsville
1999-00—Yvan Corbin, Indianapolis
Chris MacKenzie, Indianapolis

Season   Player, Team
1995-96—Dan Brown, Memphis
1996-97—Hardy Sauter, Oklahoma City
1997-98—Hardy Sauter, Oklahoma City
1998-99—Igor Bondarev, Huntsville
1999-00—Brett Colborne, Fayetteville

KEN MCKENZIE TROPHY
(Leading Scorer)

Season   Player, Team
1992-93—Sylvain Fleury, Oklahoma City
1993-94—Paul Jackson, Wichita
1994-95—Brian Shantz, San Antonio
1995-96—Brian Shantz, San Antonio
1996-97—Trevor Jobe, Columbus-Wichita
1997-98—Luc Beausoleil, Tulsa
1998-99—Derek Grant, Memphis
1999-00—Yvan Corbin, Indianapolis
Chris MacKenzie, Indianapolis

ROOKIE OF THE YEAR

Season   Player, Team
1992-93—Robert Desjardins, Wichita
1993-94—Chad Seibel, Memphis
1994-95—Michel St. Jacques, Oklahoma City
1995-96—Derek Grant, Memphis
1996-97—Cory Dosdall, Wichita
1997-98—David Beauregard, Wichita
1998-99—Johnny Brdarovic, San Antonio
1999-00—James Patterson, Huntsville

GOALTENDER OF THE YEAR

Season   Player, Team
1992-93—Tony Martino, Tulsa
1993-94—Alan Perry, Oklahoma City
1994-95—Alan Perry, Oklahoma City
1995-96—Jean-ian Filiatrault, Oklahoma City
1996-97—Jean-ian Filiatrault, Oklahoma City
1997-98—Brian Elder, Oklahoma City
1998-99—Jean-Ian Filiatrault, Oklahoma City
1999-00—Frankie Ouellette, Columbus

PRESIDENT'S TROPHY
(Playoff MVP)

Season   Player, Team
1992-93—Tony Fiore, Tulsa
1993-94—Ron Handy, Wichita
1994-95—Ron Handy, Wichita
1995-96—Jean-ian Filiatrault, Oklahoma City
1996-97—Steve Plouffe, Fort Worth
1997-98—Mike Martens, Columbus
1998-99—Derek Puppa, Huntsville
1999-00—Jamie Morris, Indianapolis

COMMISSIONER'S TROPHY
(Coach of the year)

Season   Coach, Team
1992-93—Garry Unger, Tulsa
1993-94—Doug Shedden, Wichita
1994-95—John Torchetti, San Antonio
1995-96—Doug Sauter, Oklahoma City
1996-97—Bill McDonald, Fort Worth
1997-98—David Lohrei, Nashville
1998-99—Chris Stewart, Huntsville
1999-00—David Lohrie, Fayetteville

DEFENSEMAN OF THE YEAR

Season   Player, Team
1992-93—Dave Doucette, Dallas
1993-94—Guy Girouard, Oklahoma City
1994-95—Eric Ricard, Fort Worth

MINOR LEAGUES Central

ALL-TIME LEAGUE CHAMPIONS

	REGULAR-SEASON CHAMPION		PLAYOFF CHAMPION	
Season	Team	Coach	Team	Coach
1992-93—	Oklahoma City Blazers	Michael McEwen	Tulsa Oilers	Garry Unger
1993-94—	Wichita Thunder	Doug Shedden	Wichita Thunder	Doug Shedden
1994-95—	Wichita Thunder	Doug Shedden	Wichita Thunder	Doug Shedden
1995-96—	Oklahoma City Blazers	Doug Sauter	Oklahoma City Blazers	Doug Sauter
1996-97—	Oklahoma City Blazers	Doug Sauter	Fort Worth Fire	Bill McDonald
1997-98—	Columbus Cottonmouths	Bruce Garber	Columbus Cottonmouths	Bruce Garber
1998-99—	Oklahoma City Blazers	Doug Sauter	Huntsville Channel Cats	Chris Stewart
1999-00—	Fayetteville Force	David Lohrie	Indianapolis Ice	Rod Davidson

The Central League regular season champion is awarded the Adams Cup. The playoff champion is awarded the Ray Miron Cup. Prior to the 1999-2000 season, the playoff champion was awarded the William "Bill" Levins Cup.

UNITED HOCKEY LEAGUE

(NOTE: The United Hockey League operated under the name Colonial Hockey League through the 1996-97 season.)

LEAGUE OFFICE

Commissioner/chief executive officer
Richard Brosal
Vice president of hockey operations
Mitch Lamoureux
Director of business operations
Ron Caron
Director of hockey administration
Lori Kessel

Director of media relations
Will Wolper
Address
1831 Lake St. Louis Blvd.
Lake St. Louis, MO 63367

Phone
636-625-6011
FAX
636-625-2009

TEAMS

ADIRONDACK ICEHAWKS
President
Art Shaver
Head coach
Gates Orlando
Home ice
Glens Falls Civic Center
Address
1 Civic Center Plaza
Glens Falls, NY 12801
Seating capacity
4,806
Phone
518-926-7825
FAX
518-761-9112

ASHEVILLE SMOKE
President and general manager
Dan Wilhelm
Head coach
Pat Bingham
Home ice
Asheville Civic Center
Address
87 Haywood Street
Asheville, NC 28801
Seating capacity
5,522
Phone
828-252-7825
FAX
828-252-8756

B.C. ICEMEN
General manager
Patrick Snyder
Head coach
Brad Jones
Home ice
Broome County Veterans Mem. Arena
Address
One Stuart Street
Binghamton, NY 13901
Seating capacity
4,680
Phone
607-772-9300
FAX
607-772-0707

ELMIRA JACKALS
President
Tamer Afr

Head coach
Todd Brost
Home ice
Coach USA Center
Address
P.O. Box 669
Elmira, NY 14902
Seating capacity
4,700
Phone
607-734-7825
FAX
607-733-2237

FLINT GENERALS
General manager
Dan Heisserer
Head coach
Bill Thurlow
Home ice
IMA Sports Arena
Address
3501 Lapeer Road
Flint, MI 48503
Seating capacity
4,021
Phone
810-742-9422
FAX
810-742-5892

FORT WAYNE KOMETS
General manager
David Franke
Head coach
Dave Allison
Home ice
Allen County War Mem. Coliseum
Address
1010 Memorial Way, Suite 100
Fort Wayne, IN 46805
Seating capacity
8,003
Phone
219-483-0011
FAX
219-483-3899

KNOXVILLE SPEED
President
Andy Wilhelm
General manager/head coach
Terry Ruskowski
Home ice
Knoxville Civic Coliseum

Address
500 East Church Street
Knoxville, TN 37915
Seating capacity
4,900
Phone
865-521-9991
FAX
865-524-2639

LEHIGH VALLEY XTREME
Vice president
Mark Mead
General manager/head coach
Dave Schultz
Home ice
Allentown Sports and Entertainment
Center
Address
P.O. Box 4441
Allentown, PA 18105-4441
Seating capacity
5,600
Phone
610-439-3400
FAX
610-439-7330

MADISON KODIAKS
General manager
Bill Benish
Head coach
Kent Hawley
Home ice
Dane County Memorial Coliseum
Address
1881 Expo Mall East
Madison, WI 53713
Seating capacity
8,500
Phone
608-250-2611
FAX
608-250-2614

MISSOURI RIVER OTTERS
General manager
Matt McSparin
Head coach
Mark Reeds
Home ice
Family Arena
Address
324 Main Street
St. Charles, MO 63301

Seating capacity
10,000
Phone
636-946-0003
FAX
636-946-3844

MOHAWK VALLEY PROWLERS
President
Jacques Tompkins
Head coach
Shawn Evans
Home ice
Utica Memorial Auditorium
Address
400 Oriskany Street West
Utica, NY 13502
Seating capacity
3,992
Phone
315-733-0100
FAX
315-733-8154

MUSKEGON FURY
General manager
Tony Lisman
Head coach
Rich Kromm
Home ice
L.C. Walker Arena
Address
470 West Western Avenue
Muskegon, MI 49440
Seating capacity
5,000

Phone
231-726-3879
FAX
231-728-0428

NEW HAVEN KNIGHTS
General manager
Chris Presson
Head coach
To be announced
Home ice
New Haven Veterans Mem. Coliseum
Address
275 South Orange St.
New Haven, CT 06510
Seating capacity
8,829
Phone
203-503-6090
FAX
203-503-6092

PORT HURON BORDER CATS
General manager and head coach
Greg Puhalski
Home ice
Kimball Entertainment and Sports
Center
Address
1661 Range Road, Ste. B-130
Kimball, MI 48074
Seating capacity
7,000
Phone
810-388-2287
FAX
810-388-9365

QUAD CITY MALLARDS
General manager
Howard Cornfield
Head coach
Matt Shaw
Home ice
The MARK of the Quad Cities
Address
1509 Third Avenue A
Moline, IL 61265
Seating capacity
9,175
Phone
309-764-7825
FAX
309-764-7858

ROCKFORD ICEHOGS
General manager
Kevin Cummings
Head coach
Dale DeGray
Home ice
Rockford MetroCentre
Address
P.O. Box 5984
Rockford, IL 61125-0984
Seating capacity
7,000
Phone
815-986-6465
FAX
815-963-0974

1999-2000 REGULAR SEASON
FINAL STANDINGS

CENTRAL DIVISION
Team	G	W	L	SOL	Pts.	GF	GA
Flint	74	51	14	9	111	379	250
Port Huron	74	47	21	6	100	269	202
Muskegon	74	43	26	5	91	266	250
Fort Wayne	74	40	27	7	87	281	251
Ohio	74	12	57	5	29	198	370

EASTERN DIVISION
Team	G	W	L	SOL	Pts.	GF	GA
Binghamton	74	47	20	7	101	279	222
Mohawk Valley	74	28	31	15	71	254	295
Asheville	74	34	38	2	70	279	315
Adirondack	74	28	34	12	68	260	308
Knoxville	74	29	41	4	62	236	314

WESTERN DIVISION
Team	G	W	L	SOL	Pts.	GF	GA
Quad City	74	53	16	5	111	369	264
Missouri	74	39	29	6	84	275	252
Madison	74	35	33	6	76	254	276
Rockford	74	32	34	8	72	238	268

NOTE: Ohio Gears of Central Division known as Saginaw Gears through Dec. 20, 1999.

INDIVIDUAL LEADERS

Goals: Trevor Jobe, Adirondack (61)
Assists: Brent Gretzky, Asheville (92)
Points: Brent Gretzky, Asheville (128)
Penalty minutes: Garry Gulash, Quad City (358)
Goaltending average: Matt Mullin, Port Huron (2.33)
Shutouts: Brian Regan, Missouri (7)

TOP SCORERS
	Games	G	A	Pts.
Brent Gretzky, Asheville	74	36	92	128
Trevor Jobe, Knox.-Adi.	74	61	61	122
Glenn Stewart, Quad City	71	56	55	111
Jason Firth, Rockford	73	37	73	110
Don Parsons, Flint	60	46	57	103
Ross Wilson, Flint	68	42	59	101
Hugo Proulx, Quad City	70	40	60	100
Josh Boni, Madison	73	25	74	99
Kevin Kerr, Quad City	68	49	49	98
Keli Corpse, Fort Wayne	69	27	67	94
Chris Palmer, Mohawk Valley	70	40	52	92
Patrice Robitaille, Binghamton	72	30	59	89
John Vecchiarelli, Mohawk Valley	70	38	50	88
Alexei Deev, Adirondack	69	31	54	85

	Games	G	A	Pts.
Lonnie Loach, Missouri	58	29	56	85
Mike Figliomeni, Rockford	74	33	49	82
Shawn Ulrich, Asheville	73	39	42	81
Gary Roach, Flint	69	20	60	80

	Games	G	A	Pts.
Jim Duhart, Madison	71	43	36	79
Randy Holmes, Madison	70	30	48	78
Jeremy Rebek, Missouri	69	20	58	78

INDIVIDUAL STATISTICS

MINOR LEAGUES UHL

ADIRONDACK ICEHAWKS
SCORING

	Games	G	A	Pts.	PIM
Alexei Deev	69	31	54	85	27
Trevor Jobe	43	37	42	79	42
Francois Sasseville	70	32	23	55	38
Shawn Yakimishyn	65	18	25	43	156
Alexei Yegorov	41	16	26	42	35
Guillaume Rodrigue	71	14	28	42	69
Stephan Brochu	55	8	34	42	41
Bob Cunningham	42	20	20	40	27
John Batten	33	10	29	39	38
Francois Sasseville	50	22	14	36	20
Tony Cimellaro	46	11	24	35	46
Wade Welte	50	16	11	27	141
Trent Schachle	64	7	19	26	89
Sergei Petrov	26	6	16	22	75
Steve Sangermano	20	10	10	20	55
David Dartsch	70	4	15	19	227
Larry Empey	56	2	10	12	62
Chris Ross	40	8	2	10	45
Justin Morrison	18	3	7	10	52
Alexandre Alepin	27	2	7	9	150
Matt Garver	15	4	3	7	6
Mikhail Nemirovsky	9	3	2	5	6
Nolan Weir	14	3	1	4	12
Randy Hankinson	30	0	3	3	10
Eric Boyte	45	0	3	3	18
David Kontzie	8	1	0	1	4
Dan McGuire	4	0	1	1	0
Craig Martin	7	0	1	1	26
Dieter Bloem	10	0	1	1	16
Chris Morseth	12	0	1	1	13
Steve Schick	20	0	1	1	53
Chad Ford (goalie)	36	0	1	1	48
Branislav Beliar	1	0	0	0	0
C.J. Carlson	1	0	0	0	0
Sean Kelly	1	0	0	0	0
Dan Kletke	1	0	0	0	0
Mike Masini	1	0	0	0	0
Nick Ross	1	0	0	0	0
Marty Wells	3	0	0	0	0
Mickey Gebo	7	0	0	0	10
Frederick Beaubien (goalie)	8	0	0	0	0
Trevor Bremner	8	0	0	0	43
Mathieu Normandin	8	0	0	0	4
Mark Robinson	8	0	0	0	40
Jan Klimes	9	0	0	0	2
Ben Metzger	10	0	0	0	2
Jack Greig	11	0	0	0	44
Mathieu Melancon	11	0	0	0	19
Cameron MacDonald (goalie)	13	0	0	0	8
Mike Varhaug	15	0	0	0	51
Todd MacDonald (goalie)	24	0	0	0	2

GOALTENDING

	Gms.	Min.	W	L	SOL	G	SO	Avg.
Chad Ford	36	2017	17	12	6	116	1	3.45
Todd MacDonald	24	1308	6	14	3	91	0	4.17
Cam. MacDonald	13	489	4	2	1	34	0	4.17
Dan McGuire	4	156	0	1	1	12	0	4.61
Frederick Beaubien	8	459	1	5	1	38	0	4.97

ASHEVILLE SMOKE
SCORING

	Games	G	A	Pts.	PIM
Brent Gretzky	74	36	92	128	68
Shawn Ulrich	73	39	42	81	64
Lindsay Vallis	69	24	52	76	54
Peter Cermak	42	31	33	64	16
Paul Giblin	74	27	31	58	25
Frank DeFrenza	51	29	19	48	107
Francois Leroux	61	23	25	48	77
Bruce Watson	60	12	17	29	229
Hayden O'Rear	64	2	20	22	71
Jon Pirrong	65	6	15	21	81
Cory Peterson	52	4	15	19	39
Dean Roach	18	4	12	16	18
Rob Milliken	36	2	13	15	36
Richie Walcott	37	9	4	13	93
Josh Tymchak	44	5	6	11	185
Vaclav Pazourek	61	3	7	10	133
Ken Plaquin	45	1	9	10	48
Jonas Eden	20	6	3	9	6
Ben White	14	1	7	8	21
Francois Bourdeau	22	1	6	7	14
Dale Greenwood	5	0	3	3	8
Eric Kelly	7	1	1	2	8
Paul Bailley	8	1	1	2	12
Wade Welte	8	1	1	2	29
Ryan Prentice	20	0	2	2	32
Dan Brenzavich (goalie)	23	0	2	2	6
Dan Davies	4	1	0	1	13
Fredrik Svensson	14	1	0	1	15
Kelly Hrycun	2	0	1	1	0
Petr Sachl	3	0	1	1	4
Rick MacDonald	6	0	1	1	6
Sean Honeysett	9	0	1	1	6
Sergei Tkachenko (goalie)	12	0	1	1	0
David Bourque	19	0	1	1	19
Dan McIntyre (goalie)	40	0	1	1	4
Jeff Azar	1	0	0	0	2
Jan Klimes	1	0	0	0	0
Charlie Lawson	1	0	0	0	0
John Rae	1	0	0	0	5
Joni Ahmavuo	2	0	0	0	0
Adam Lord (goalie)	2	0	0	0	0
Jason Lehman	3	0	0	0	2
Mike Williams	4	0	0	0	18
Marek Babic	5	0	0	0	0
Danny Laviolette (goalie)	5	0	0	0	2
Jayme Adduono	7	0	0	0	14
Jack Greig	11	0	0	0	28

GOALTENDING

	Gms.	Min.	W	L	SOL	G	SO	Avg.
Dan McIntyre	40	2124	17	14	2	137	0	3.87
Sergei Tkachenko	12	602	6	6	0	41	1	4.09
Dan Brenzavich	23	1329	9	14	0	92	0	4.15
Danny Laviolette	5	251	2	2	0	20	0	4.79
Adam Lord	2	119	0	2	0	12	0	6.07

B.C. ICEMEN
SCORING

	Games	G	A	Pts.	PIM
Patrice Robitaille	72	30	59	89	30
Derek Wood	72	30	45	75	103
Yevgeny Shaldybin	71	16	52	68	36

	Games	G	A	Pts.	PIM
Chris Grenville	67	38	29	67	88
Mark Dutiaume	58	20	46	66	48
Derek Knorr	67	26	32	58	141
Justin Plamondon	71	15	34	49	57
Matt Ruchty	64	23	20	43	321
Jason Norrie	72	20	22	42	172
Greg Pajor	41	8	17	25	30
Jamie Bird	69	5	16	21	37
Scott Ricci	57	4	17	21	53
Matt Garver	26	10	4	14	13
Chris Winnes	14	7	7	14	0
Rob Voltera	54	7	5	12	115
Ales Dvorak	69	3	5	8	47
Jack Greig	14	3	1	4	29
Alex Andreyev	21	1	3	4	80
Jarno Mensonen	7	0	4	4	0
Blair Sherrit	10	2	1	3	4
Randy Hankinson	13	0	3	3	12
Nick Lent	7	2	0	2	8
Boyd Kane	3	0	2	2	4
Martin Cote	48	0	2	2	77
Anthony Belza	71	0	2	2	156
Jeff Schmidt	14	1	0	1	4
Erasmo Saltarelli (goalie)	29	0	1	1	16
Dieter Kochan (goalie)	43	0	1	1	2
Sean Cowan	1	0	0	0	0
Ben White	2	0	0	0	0
David Bell	4	0	0	0	0
Pat Stachniak	4	0	0	0	0
Jim Dinneen (goalie)	9	0	0	0	2

GOALTENDING

	Gms.	Min.	W	L	SOL	G	SO	Avg.
Jim Dinneen	9	189	2	0	0	7	0	2.23
Dieter Kochan	43	2544	29	11	3	110	4	2.59
Erasmo Saltarelli	29	1700	16	9	4	90	1	3.18

FLINT GENERALS

SCORING

	Games	G	A	Pts.	PIM
Don Parsons	60	46	57	103	104
Ross Wilson	68	42	59	101	44
Gary Roach	69	20	60	80	72
Nick Stajduhar	67	22	49	71	106
Chad Grills	70	28	40	68	160
Khalil Thomas	53	24	41	65	35
Bobby Reynolds	32	22	37	59	18
Frank LaScala	50	27	22	49	43
Dmitri Rodine	60	11	36	47	63
Dale Greenwood	57	14	28	42	54
Mark Major	36	23	18	41	135
Ian Hebert	32	10	27	37	22
Cory Cyrenne	19	12	22	34	10
Luch Nasato	63	10	23	33	246
Dean Roach	38	14	14	28	43
Vlad Serov	17	15	11	26	23
Dariusz Zabawa	54	12	13	25	18
Lorne Knauft	34	5	20	25	70
Slav Krzak	67	5	14	19	56
Emmanuel LaBranche	57	1	11	12	186
Jason Modopoulos	56	2	5	7	304
B.J. Johnston	15	2	4	6	17
Jonas Eden	39	1	5	6	16
Travis Riggin	8	1	4	5	0
Francois Leroux	5	2	1	3	10
Mark Richards (goalie)	48	0	3	3	43
Jake Ream	12	0	1	1	0
Mark Fox	14	0	1	1	6
Todd Chinnick	1	0	0	0	0
Richard Irwin	3	0	0	0	10
Jeff Kugel	4	0	0	0	0
Martin Bradette (goalie)	6	0	0	0	0
Wayne Cowley (goalie)	7	0	0	0	2
Alan Hitchen (goalie)	24	0	0	0	4

GOALTENDING

	Gms.	Min.	W	L	SOL	G	SO	Avg.
Mark Richards	48	2641	32	7	5	128	3	2.91
Wayne Cowley	7	419	6	1	0	21	0	3.01
Alan Hitchen	23	1131	12	5	2	72	0	3.82
Martin Bradette	6	241	1	1	2	19	0	4.73

FORT WAYNE KOMETS

SCORING

	Games	G	A	Pts.	PIM
Keli Corpse	69	27	67	94	26
Frederic Bouchard	71	33	41	74	78
Jason Goulet	71	28	43	71	50
Petr Sachl	55	30	24	54	28
Konstanti Shafranov	20	15	15	30	6
Jon Austin	53	11	18	29	8
John Gurskis	42	14	14	28	23
Richard Keyes	26	15	12	27	26
Bruce Ramsay	65	6	21	27	241
Kelly Hurd	31	14	12	26	26
Ryan Black	35	10	15	25	16
Dave Lemay	56	6	19	25	119
Justin Kearns	35	10	9	19	34
Mike Burman	29	6	13	19	25
Igor Malykhin	39	5	14	19	37
Sacha Molin	39	4	13	17	33
Charlie Lawson	61	5	11	16	42
Vadim Sharapov	14	9	5	14	16
Jim Logan	18	7	7	14	46
Daniel Ronan	59	2	10	12	59
Milt Mastad	46	2	7	9	126
Jeff McKercher	72	2	7	9	55
Kevin Slota	34	4	2	6	62
Dan Tompkins	9	3	3	6	8
Doug Teskey (goalie)	48	0	5	5	8
Peter Cermak	7	0	4	4	0
Randy Hankinson	8	1	2	3	4
Dennis Pinfold	16	0	3	3	52
Steve Parsons	17	0	3	3	108
Derek Campbell	3	2	0	2	5
Jeff MacMillan	7	1	1	2	25
Francis Boulay	2	0	2	2	0
Aaron MacDonald (goalie)	9	0	2	2	0
Ben Metzger	22	0	2	2	41
Taj Melson	3	0	1	1	2
Patrick Labrecque (goalie)	7	0	1	1	0
Steve Gainey	1	0	0	0	0
Mike Williams	1	0	0	0	2
Ryan Caley (goalie)	2	0	0	0	0
Paul McInnis	2	0	0	0	0
Alex Mukhanov	2	0	0	0	2
Evgeny Tsybouk	2	0	0	0	0
Jason Lehman	3	0	0	0	4
Parris Duffus (goalie)	4	0	0	0	2
Todd MacDonald (goalie)	4	0	0	0	0
Anton Pavlychev	4	0	0	0	0
Nolan Weir	6	0	0	0	7
Jas Hueppelsheuser	7	0	0	0	8
Trevor Matter (goalie)	8	0	0	0	8
Jan Melicher	11	0	0	0	10

GOALTENDING

	Gms.	Min.	W	L	SOL	G	SO	Avg.
Patrick Labrecque	7	337	4	1	0	11	1	1.96
Doug Teskey	48	2680	24	16	6	128	3	2.87
Todd MacDonald	4	238	2	2	0	12	0	3.02
Parris Duffus	3	180	3	0	0	10	0	3.33
Trevor Matter	8	423	4	3	0	30	0	4.26
Aaron MacDonald	9	479	3	4	1	36	0	4.51
Ryan Caley	2	89	0	1	0	8	0	5.37

KNOXVILLE SPEED

SCORING

	Games	G	A	Pts.	PIM
Eric Schneider	36	19	32	51	15
Eric Montreuil	74	27	23	50	60

	Games	G	A	Pts.	PIM
Dan Myre	59	22	26	48	26
Trevor Jobe	31	24	19	43	52
Mike Schultz	47	24	17	41	25
Dmitry Ustyuzhanin	70	8	33	41	46
Doug Searle	71	7	34	41	77
Jeremy Thompson	47	8	17	25	148
Jeff Suggitt	50	8	14	22	17
Andrew Tortorella	37	8	12	20	33
Rusty McKie	43	4	14	18	312
Sergei Petrov	19	11	6	17	27
Bryan Fogarty	16	5	12	17	29
Bradley Denis	73	1	13	14	141
Janis Tomans	22	8	5	13	14
Jordan Shaw	63	6	7	13	171
Alexandre Alepin	33	4	9	13	110
Dominic Chiasson	12	8	3	11	4
Mike T. Murray	22	6	4	10	6
Sergei Radchenko	56	2	8	10	145
Corey Ignas	30	1	8	9	27
Cam Law	50	1	8	9	95
Chris Bonvie	19	3	5	8	8
Mike Moran	12	1	6	7	13
Iannique Renaud	8	3	3	6	37
Mark Scott	22	1	5	6	62
Konstantine Simchuk (goalie)	64	0	6	6	30
Jan Beran	9	3	2	5	2
Jon Marshall	3	1	4	5	2
Jeff Azar	4	1	3	4	10
Marc Lirette	16	1	3	4	4
Rick Scott	8	1	2	3	2
Vladislav Kouroedov	9	1	2	3	4
Chad Brandimore	14	2	0	2	4
Andrew Rodgers	6	0	2	2	52
Bill Russell (goalie)	6	0	2	2	0
Mark Fox	10	0	2	2	4
J.F. Levesque	17	0	2	2	8
Trevor Tokarczyk	12	1	0	1	19
Joey Spencer	13	1	0	1	0
Andrei Rundso	4	0	1	1	10
Jake Soper (goalie)	8	0	1	1	0
Jon Sikkema (goalie)	1	0	0	0	0
Andrei Vasin	1	0	0	0	0
Anders Akerberg	2	0	0	0	2
Randy Hankinson	3	0	0	0	0
Marty Phillips (goalie)	3	0	0	0	0
Anton Pavlychev	4	0	0	0	2
Dmitri Kluchko	5	0	0	0	2

GOALTENDING

	Gms.	Min.	W	L	SOL	G	SO	Avg.
Kon. Simchuk	64	3580	24	35	3	233	2	3.90
Bill Russell	6	309	3	0	1	23	0	4.47
Jake Soper	8	328	1	4	0	27	0	4.94
Marty Phillips	3	180	1	2	0	16	0	5.33
Jon Sikkema	1	40	0	0	0	6	0	9.00

MADISON KODIAKS
SCORING

	Games	G	A	Pts.	PIM
Josh Boni	73	25	74	99	103
Jim Duhart	71	43	36	79	127
Randy Holmes	70	30	48	78	66
Brad Englehart	74	20	38	58	68
Matt Loen	35	19	27	46	30
Dave MacIntyre	42	21	20	41	63
Andy Faulkner	74	13	22	35	32
Mikhail Nemirovsky	31	16	17	33	40
Jeff Winter	65	3	25	28	57
Brian Wilson	74	12	14	26	16
Eric Brown	51	2	13	15	22
Dave Jesiolowski	26	6	8	14	156
Brian Tucker	40	7	6	13	103
Jason Hughes	57	2	11	13	141
Dennis Pinfold	18	4	7	11	74

	Games	G	A	Pts.	PIM
Dominic Chiasson	17	4	6	10	10
Jeff Foster	41	1	9	10	33
Don Martin	17	6	3	9	28
Janis Tomans	11	3	6	9	2
Steve Parsons	39	3	6	9	241
Luke Strand	57	3	6	9	101
Derek Beuselinck	66	2	6	8	95
Todd Passini	21	0	5	5	20
Mike Williams	17	0	3	3	25
Eoin McInerney (goalie)	35	0	3	3	6
Jamie Dabanovich	3	0	2	2	0
Jake Ream	27	0	2	2	12
Mathias Frelin	1	0	0	0	0
Paul Mathesen	1	0	0	0	0
Daniel Ruoho	1	0	0	0	0
Derek Toninato	7	0	0	0	2
David Fletcher (goalie)	46	0	0	0	0

GOALTENDING

	Gms.	Min.	W	L	SOL	G	SO	Avg.
Eoin McInerney	35	1916	18	11	3	115	0	3.60
David Fletcher	46	2510	17	22	3	153	2	3.66

MISSOURI RIVER OTTERS
SCORING

	Games	G	A	Pts.	PIM
Lonnie Loach	58	29	56	85	20
Jeremy Rebek	69	20	58	78	89
Colin Chaulk	50	19	47	66	88
Alain St. Hilaire	53	19	40	59	38
Michal Statsny	69	20	23	43	99
Jay Hebert	62	22	20	42	41
Tomas Baluch	65	12	24	36	51
Jeremiah McCarthy	33	10	25	35	45
Kiley Hill	28	20	12	32	94
Forrest Gore	25	13	19	32	111
Ben Gorewich	69	16	15	31	63
Marty Standish	46	14	14	28	143
Darin Kimble	24	10	13	23	49
Randy Gallatin	68	9	12	21	62
Charlie Blyth	57	5	15	20	55
Chris Tok	57	3	17	20	96
Dan Tompkins	48	10	8	18	48
Allan Roulette	44	5	10	15	43
Trevor Sherban	36	2	11	13	88
Curtis Sayler	64	6	4	10	237
Ryan Hartung	28	0	9	9	14
Jan Kobezda	43	2	5	7	48
Kevin Adams	5	4	2	6	4
Scott Bell	4	1	1	2	10
Jay Pylypuik	16	0	2	2	20
Randy Best	23	0	2	2	18
Brian Regan (goalie)	49	0	2	2	4
Troy Michalski	7	0	1	1	8
David Mitchell (goalie)	7	0	1	1	0
Chris Bernard (goalie)	15	0	1	1	2
Jason Stewart	1	0	0	0	0
Darcy Anderson	2	0	0	0	0
Scott Bokal (goalie)	2	0	0	0	0
Yuri Gerasimov (goalie)	2	0	0	0	0
Mark Fox	6	0	0	0	0
Bob Murdoch (goalie)	6	0	0	0	2
Curtis Sanford (goalie)	6	0	0	0	4
Adam Campbell	7	0	0	0	8

GOALTENDING

	Gms.	Min.	W	L	SOL	G	SO	Avg.
Curtis Sanford	6	237	3	1	0	6	0	1.52
Brian Regan	49	2745	29	12	4	115	7	2.51
David Mitchell	7	409	4	2	1	24	1	3.52
Yuri Gerasimov	2	79	0	1	0	5	0	3.78
Scott Bokal	2	76	0	2	0	5	0	3.96
Chris Bernard	15	732	3	9	1	66	0	5.41
Bob Murdoch	6	140	0	2	0	17	0	7.28

MOHAWK VALLEY PROWLERS

SCORING

	Games	G	A	Pts.	PIM
Chris Palmer	70	40	52	92	49
John Vecchiarelli	70	38	50	88	137
Nic Beaudoin	61	33	39	72	64
Mark Kotary	72	22	25	47	23
Tim Harris	68	12	21	33	74
Andre Payette	58	9	23	32	160
Bob Ferrais	74	4	28	32	77
Don Martin	51	13	17	30	121
Frederik Last	71	12	18	30	27
Christian Lariviere	74	2	26	28	93
Mario Roberge	36	7	14	21	100
Dave Jesiolowski	31	10	10	20	159
Dominic Chiasson	31	9	10	19	12
Roman Mucha	28	6	12	18	14
John Batten	17	6	10	16	81
Serge Roberge	54	3	7	10	207
Mark Yannetti	41	3	5	8	43
Kevin Tucker	63	2	6	8	58
Francis Boulay	9	2	5	7	0
Francois Hardy	24	1	5	6	33
Libor Svindl	45	1	3	4	39
Ben White	8	0	4	4	6
Corey Payment	45	2	1	3	22
Patrick Charbonneau (goalie)	50	0	3	3	14
Mike Torchia	23	1	1	2	0
Todd Barclay	1	1	0	1	0
Denis Lamoureux	4	0	1	1	0
Chad Ford (goalie)	1	0	0	0	0
Sandy MacKenzie	1	0	0	0	2
Jeff Ozmankowksi (goalie)	1	0	0	0	0
Eric Belanger	3	0	0	0	0
Dale Gignac	3	0	0	0	0
Jyrki Koskinen	4	0	0	0	0
Jonathan Forest (goalie)	6	0	0	0	0
Jim Sheehan	6	0	0	0	8

GOALTENDING

	Gms.	Min.	W	L	SOL	G	SO	Avg.
Pat. Charbonneau	50	2851	20	20	7	164	0	3.45
Mike Torchia	23	1248	8	9	4	80	0	3.85
Chad Ford	1	59	0	0	1	4	0	4.04
Jonathan Forest	6	242	0	2	3	21	0	5.20
Jeff Ozmankowksi	1	19	0	0	0	2	0	6.47

MUSKEGON FURY

SCORING

	Games	G	A	Pts.	PIM
Andrew Luciuk	70	34	38	72	40
Tomas Kapusta	73	33	37	70	80
Robin Bouchard	58	33	34	67	125
Quinn Hancock	49	32	34	66	27
Sergei Kharin	59	11	50	61	13
Mike McCourt	64	14	42	56	44
Scott Feasby	64	7	32	39	100
Vadim Podrezov	42	9	21	30	41
Francis Nault	74	8	22	30	86
Mikhail Nemirovsky	29	11	14	25	44
Dalen Hrooshkin	42	9	16	25	23
Aaron Porter	67	13	9	22	21
Mark Vilneff	65	3	18	21	64
Alexei Vasilevski	19	10	8	18	22
Jason Rose	63	5	11	16	71
Rob Melanson	62	2	10	12	168
Bob Cunningham	9	5	6	11	4
Brian Tucker	31	3	8	11	101
Rob Hutson	10	4	4	8	19
Scott Hlady	10	2	5	7	6
Alain LaPlante	52	2	4	6	101
Joel Gardner	12	1	4	5	2
Chris Maillet	20	2	2	4	65
Don McSween	6	1	3	4	5

	Games	G	A	Pts.	PIM
Andrei Petrunin	9	1	3	4	10
Jeff Kostuch	7	2	1	3	6
Dave Butler	11	2	1	3	4
Lucas Nehrling	22	1	2	3	86
Joe Dimaline (goalie)	53	0	2	2	8
Mike Kolenda	2	0	1	1	4
Virgil Rutili	2	0	1	1	2
Ben Metzger	7	0	1	1	12
Mike Feasby	24	0	1	1	37
Bob Janosz (goalie)	28	0	1	1	4
David Graham	2	0	0	0	0

GOALTENDING

	Gms.	Min.	W	L	SOL	G	SO	Avg.
Bob Janosz	28	1411	13	7	2	71	1	3.02
Joe Dimaline	53	3020	30	19	3	167	2	3.32

OHIO GEARS

SCORING

	Games	G	A	Pts.	PIM
Keith Osborne	70	15	55	70	71
Jeff Loder	69	32	37	69	107
Steve Richards	56	12	29	41	22
Steve Lowe	63	12	26	38	73
Troy Mann	31	11	20	31	14
Justin Kearns	35	14	15	29	12
Phil Miaskowski	31	12	16	28	30
J.D. Eaton	47	12	12	24	95
Patrick Charbonneau	69	10	13	23	80
Francois Sasseville	20	10	9	19	18
Phil Husak	54	8	9	17	36
Bob Cunningham	18	7	10	17	38
Caleb Wyse	41	7	6	13	28
Brian Mueller	26	3	10	13	36
Ben White	39	1	10	11	52
Justin Morrison	8	3	6	9	13
Tony Prpic	13	2	7	9	14
Mike Torkoff	19	2	7	9	47
Don Coyne	41	2	7	9	33
John Nelson	9	3	5	8	82
Ryan Prentice	31	3	5	8	28
Jamie Leinhos	44	6	1	7	85
Ralphael Protopapas	5	2	3	5	2
Jason Lehman	62	1	4	5	55
Sean McEachran	31	2	2	4	37
Corey Bricknell	11	1	2	3	30
Richie Walcott	12	1	2	3	58
Zdenek Sikl	11	0	3	3	2
Shawn Randall	18	1	1	2	67
Francis Boulay	3	0	2	2	0
Trevor Bremner	7	0	2	2	39
Dennis Pinfold	16	0	2	2	92
Taner Gorica	16	1	0	1	79
Paul Van De Perre	2	0	1	1	7
Pete Mehalic	4	0	1	1	9
Chris Morseth	5	0	1	1	7
Mike Tamburro (goalie)	8	0	1	1	2
Jamie Hayden	10	0	1	1	4
Bryan McMullen (goalie)	11	0	1	1	15
Shawn Flynn	1	0	0	0	0
Trent Mann (goalie)	1	0	0	0	0
Travis Meguinis	2	0	0	0	2
Jeff Ricci	2	0	0	0	0
Francois Bourbeau (goalie)	3	0	0	0	0
Stu Monan (goalie)	3	0	0	0	10
Greg Bailey	5	0	0	0	36
Justin Leinhos	6	0	0	0	16
Brady Alstead (goalie)	7	0	0	0	71
Todd MacDonald (goalie)	8	0	0	0	0
Joe Cipriani	9	0	0	0	0
Jack Greig	11	0	0	0	74
Jonathan Forest (goalie)	22	0	0	0	4
Mike Brusseau (goalie)	24	0	0	0	0

GOALTENDING

	Gms.	Min.	W	L	SOL	G	SO	Avg.
Trent Mann	1	20	0	0	0	1	0	3.00
Todd MacDonald	8	438	2	5	0	28	0	3.84
Mike Brusseau	24	1317	3	17	2	95	0	4.33
Bryan McMullen	11	610	2	6	2	46	0	4.52
Stu Monan	2	80	0	1	0	6	0	4.52
Jonathan Forest	22	1085	4	14	1	92	0	5.09
Francois Bourbeau	3	160	1	2	0	15	0	5.63
Brady Alstead	7	290	0	4	0	31	0	6.41
Mike Tamburro	8	429	0	8	0	46	0	6.43

NOTE: Team known as Saginaw Gears through Dec. 20, 1999.

PORT HURON BORDER CATS
SCORING

	Games	G	A	Pts.	PIM
Jay Neal	65	33	43	76	55
Rick Judson	67	32	30	62	18
Mike Maurice	48	24	38	62	40
Kevin Brown	54	22	33	55	30
Jason Simon	45	21	22	43	118
Mike Bondy	70	14	27	41	87
David Mayes	73	11	28	39	64
Jason Gladney	61	8	30	38	40
Kraig Nienhuis	37	13	22	35	33
Ryan Burgoyne	59	12	18	30	24
Paul Fioroni	66	11	18	29	214
Jamie Dabanovich	64	9	20	29	43
Luke Murphy	69	9	19	28	31
Adam Robbins	55	9	12	21	39
Lee Cole	62	4	13	17	133
Dalen Hrooshkin	26	2	11	13	12
Chris Bergeron	13	6	6	12	14
Dave Butler	31	2	10	12	20
Shayne Tomlinson	69	1	11	12	64
Darren Banks	17	3	5	8	12
Andrew Long	5	4	3	7	2
Steve Barnes	19	3	4	7	14
Paul Harvey	16	1	5	6	22
Craig Miller	12	3	0	3	8
Chris Allen	6	2	1	3	4
Nick Smith	2	1	1	2	0
Jeff Blum	3	0	1	1	0
Kevin Schmidt	6	0	1	1	4
Kevin Stone (goalie)	9	0	1	1	0
Jon Hillebrandt (goalie)	31	0	1	1	2
Matt Mullin (goalie)	31	0	1	1	8
Kelly Selix	1	0	0	0	0
Andrei Sryubko	2	0	0	0	7
Chad Ford (goalie)	14	0	0	0	6
Jeff Stahlbrand	15	0	0	0	2

GOALTENDING

	Gms.	Min.	W	L	SOL	G	SO	Avg.
Matt Mullin	31	1623	14	10	3	63	2	2.33
Chad Ford	14	735	10	2	0	31	0	2.53
Jon Hillebrandt	31	1617	19	6	2	78	1	2.89
Kevin Stone	9	453	4	3	1	22	0	2.92

QUAD CITY MALLARDS
SCORING

	Games	G	A	Pts.	PIM
Glenn Stewart	71	56	55	111	34
Hugo Proulx	70	40	60	100	91
Kevin Kerr	68	49	49	98	162
Patrick Nadeau	65	31	39	70	59
Ryan Lindsay	49	24	46	70	79
Martin Hlinka	71	21	46	67	74
Rob DeCiantis	54	25	36	61	62
Mike Melas	56	21	38	59	94
Brendan Brooks	73	26	26	52	102
Garry Gulash	64	9	37	46	358
Mark McFarlane	56	15	27	42	162
Rick Emmett	56	8	33	41	67
Brian LaFleur	70	9	29	38	30

	Games	G	A	Pts.	PIM
Kelly Hultgren	69	7	27	34	56
Rusty Fitzgerald	18	8	9	17	13
Paul Johnson	71	3	12	15	63
Brendan Buckley	61	1	10	11	73
Kerry Toporowski	21	0	11	11	118
Scott Levins	11	4	4	8	46
Yannick Latour	42	0	7	7	41
Anton Pavlychev	18	3	1	4	2
Steve Gibson	10	1	1	2	6
Dan Brenzavich (goalie)	17	0	1	1	2
Iannique Renaud	31	0	1	1	182
Martin Villeneuve (goalie)	31	0	1	1	10
Miroslav Lazo	1	0	0	0	2
Martin Fillion	7	0	0	0	8
Scott Buhler (goalie)	23	0	0	0	0

GOALTENDING

	Gms.	Min.	W	L	SOL	G	SO	Avg.
Martin Villeneuve	31	1854	26	4	1	92	1	2.98
Dan Brenzavich	17	938	12	3	1	54	0	3.46
Scott Buhler	23	1337	12	7	3	85	0	3.81
Martin Fillion	7	299	3	2	0	20	0	4.01

ROCKFORD ICEHOGS
SCORING

	Games	G	A	Pts.	PIM
Jason Firth	73	37	73	110	66
Mike Figliomeni	74	33	49	82	26
Brant Blackned	62	36	29	65	65
Wayne Strachan	41	18	27	45	32
Sheldon Gorski	67	14	24	38	67
Derek Landmesser	55	10	27	37	95
Curtis Tipler	67	16	18	34	46
Barry McKinlay	37	11	23	34	26
Norm Paquet	72	20	9	29	30
Evgeny Krivomaz	69	5	19	24	100
Peter Cava	36	7	14	21	35
Jesse Welling	63	4	10	14	87
Shawn Smith	43	3	8	11	86
Raymond Delarosbil	36	0	7	7	42
Carlos Soke	66	4	2	6	220
Rob Milliken	29	3	3	6	44
Scott Burfoot	11	1	5	6	18
Thero Koskela	11	1	5	6	10
Dan Davies	52	2	2	4	72
Jim Alauria	24	1	3	4	71
Patrice Charbonneau	43	1	2	3	37
Alexandre Makombo	35	1	1	2	137
Fredrik Lindh	5	0	1	1	2
Bruce Watson	8	0	1	1	15
Jeff Kostuch	12	0	1	1	10
Adam Lewis	16	0	1	1	41
Kevin Holliday	20	0	1	1	169
J.F. Rivard (goalie)	63	0	1	1	2
Mark Sinerchia (goalie)	2	0	0	0	0
Troy Giesegh	3	0	0	0	0
Scott Cullain	4	0	0	0	0
Jaso Hueppelsheuser	5	0	0	0	2
Cory Peterson	7	0	0	0	4
Mike Correia (goalie)	17	0	0	0	0
Sean McEachran	20	0	0	0	21

GOALTENDING

	Gms.	Min.	W	L	SOL	G	SO	Avg.
J.F. Rivard	63	3602	26	30	6	193	2	3.21
Mike Correia	17	782	6	4	2	54	1	4.14
Mark Sinerchia	2	42	0	0	0	5	0	7.09

PLAYERS WITH TWO OR MORE TEAMS

SCORING

	Games	G	A	Pts.	PIM
Alexandre Alepin, Adirondack	27	2	7	9	150
Alexandre Alepin, Knoxville	33	4	9	13	110
Totals	60	6	16	22	260

	Games	G	A	Pts.	PIM
John Batten, Mohawk Valley	17	6	10	16	81
John Batten, Adirondack	33	10	29	39	38
Totals	50	16	39	55	119
Francis Boulay, Mohawk Valley .	9	2	5	7	0
Francis Boulay, Ohio	3	0	2	2	0
Francis Boulay, Ft. Wayne.........	2	0	2	2	0
Totals	14	2	9	11	0
Trevor Bremner, Adirondack......	8	0	0	0	43
Trevor Bremner, Ohio	7	0	2	2	39
Totals	15	0	2	2	82
Dan Brenzavich, Quad City (g) ..	17	0	1	1	2
Dan Brenzavich, Asheville (g)....	23	0	2	2	6
Totals	40	0	3	3	8
Dave Butler, Muskegon..............	11	2	1	3	4
Dave Butler, Port Huron	31	2	10	12	20
Totals	42	4	11	15	24
Peter Cermak, Ft. Wayne	7	0	4	4	0
Peter Cermak, Asheville............	42	31	33	64	16
Totals	49	31	37	68	16
Dominic Chiasson, M.V.	31	9	10	19	12
Dominic Chiasson, Madison......	17	4	6	10	10
Dominic Chiasson, Knoxville	12	8	3	11	4
Totals	60	21	19	40	26
Bob Cunningham, Ohio	18	7	10	17	38
Bob Cunningham, Adirondack...	42	20	20	40	27
Bob Cunningham, Muskegon	9	5	6	11	4
Totals	69	32	36	68	69
Jamie Dabanovich, Madison......	3	0	2	2	0
Jamie Dabanovich, Port Huron .	64	9	20	29	43
Totals	67	9	22	31	43
Dan Davies, Asheville	4	1	0	1	13
Dan Davies, Rockford	52	2	2	4	72
Totals	56	3	2	5	85
Jonas Eden, Flint	39	1	5	6	16
Jonas Eden, Asheville	20	6	3	9	6
Totals	59	7	8	15	22
Chad Ford, Mohawk Valley (g) ..	1	0	0	0	0
Chad Ford, Port Huron (g).........	14	0	0	0	6
Chad Ford, Adirondack (g)	36	0	1	1	48
Totals	51	0	1	1	54
Jonathan Forest, Ohio (g)..........	22	0	0	0	4
Jonathan Forest, M.V. (g)	6	0	0	0	0
Totals	28	0	0	0	4
Mark Fox, Knoxville	10	0	2	2	4
Mark Fox, Flint	14	0	1	1	6
Mark Fox, Missouri....................	6	0	0	0	0
Totals	30	0	3	3	10
Dale Greenwood, Asheville	5	0	3	3	8
Dale Greenwood, Flint..............	57	14	28	42	54
Totals	62	14	31	45	62
Jack Greig, Ohio	11	0	0	0	74
Jack Greig, Adirondack.............	11	0	0	0	44
Jack Greig, Binghamton	14	3	1	4	29
Jack Greig, Asheville................	11	0	0	0	28
Totals	47	3	1	4	175
Randy Hankinson, Adirondack ..	30	0	3	3	10
Randy Hankinson, Ft. Wayne.....	8	1	2	3	4
Randy Hankinson, Knoxville	3	0	0	0	0
Randy Hankinson, Binghamton .	13	0	3	3	12
Totals	54	1	8	9	26
Dalen Hrooshkin, Port Huron	26	2	11	13	12
Dalen Hrooshkin, Muskegon	42	9	16	25	23
Totals	68	11	27	38	35
Dave Jesiolowski, Madison	26	6	8	14	156
Dave Jesiolowski, M.V.	31	10	10	20	159
Totals	57	16	18	34	315
Trevor Jobe, Knoxville	31	24	19	43	52
Trevor Jobe, Adirondack	43	37	42	79	42
Totals	74	61	61	122	94
Justin Kearns, Ft. Wayne	35	10	9	19	34
Justin Kearns, Ohio	35	14	15	29	12
Totals	70	24	24	48	46
Jeff Kostuch, Rockford..............	12	0	1	1	10
Jeff Kostuch, Muskegon............	7	2	1	3	6

	Games	G	A	Pts.	PIM
Totals	19	2	2	4	16
Charlie Lawson, Asheville..........	1	0	0	0	0
Charlie Lawson, Ft. Wayne	61	5	11	16	42
Totals	62	5	11	16	42
Jason Lehman, Asheville............	3	0	0	0	2
Jason Lehman, Ft. Wayne	3	0	0	0	4
Jason Lehman, Ohio..................	62	1	4	5	55
Totals	68	1	4	5	61
Francois Leroux, Flint	5	2	1	3	10
Francois Leroux, Asheville........	61	23	25	48	77
Totals	66	25	26	51	87
Todd MacDonald, Adi. (g)	24	0	0	0	2
Todd MacDonald, Ohio (g)	8	0	0	0	0
Todd MacDonald, Ft.W. (g)........	4	0	0	0	0
Totals	36	0	0	0	2
Don Martin, Mohawk Valley.......	51	13	17	30	121
Don Martin, Madison.................	17	6	3	9	28
Totals	68	19	20	39	149
Sean McEachran, Rockford........	20	0	0	0	21
Sean McEachran, Ohio	31	2	2	4	37
Totals	51	2	2	4	58
Ben Metzger, Adirondack..........	10	0	0	0	2
Ben Metzger, Ft. Wayne	22	0	2	2	41
Ben Metzger, Muskegon............	7	0	1	1	12
Totals	39	0	3	3	55
Rob Milliken, Rockford..............	29	3	3	6	44
Rob Milliken, Asheville..............	36	2	13	15	36
Totals	65	5	16	21	80
Justin Morrison, Adirondack	18	3	7	10	52
Justin Morrison, Ohio	8	3	6	9	13
Totals	26	6	13	19	65
Chris Morseth, Adirondack	12	0	1	1	13
Chris Morseth, Ohio	5	0	1	1	7
Totals	17	0	2	2	20
Mikhail Nemirovsky, Madison....	31	16	17	33	40
Mikhail Nemirovsky, Muskegon.	29	11	14	25	44
Mikhail Nemirovsky, Adi.	9	3	2	5	6
Totals	69	30	33	63	90
Steve Parsons, Madison............	39	3	6	9	241
Steve Parsons, Ft. Wayne	17	0	3	3	108
Totals	56	3	9	12	349
Anton Pavlychev, Quad City......	18	3	1	4	2
Anton Pavlychev, Knoxville	4	0	0	0	2
Anton Pavlychev, Ft. Wayne	4	0	0	0	0
Totals	26	3	1	4	4
Cory Peterson, Rockford	7	0	0	0	4
Cory Peterson, Asheville...........	52	4	15	19	39
Totals	59	4	15	19	43
Sergei Petrov, Adirondack	26	6	16	22	75
Sergei Petrov, Knoxville............	19	11	6	17	27
Totals	45	17	22	39	102
Dennis Pinfold, Ohio.................	16	0	2	2	92
Dennis Pinfold, Ft. Wayne	16	0	3	3	52
Dennis Pinfold, Madison...........	18	4	7	11	74
Totals	50	4	12	16	218
Ryan Prentice, Ohio	31	3	5	8	28
Ryan Prentice, Asheville............	20	0	2	2	32
Totals	51	3	7	10	60
Jake Ream, Madison	27	0	2	2	12
Jake Ream, Flint	12	0	1	1	0
Totals	39	0	3	3	12
Iannique Renaud, Quad City	31	0	1	1	182
Iannique Renaud, Knoxville	8	3	3	6	37
Totals	39	3	4	7	219
Dean Roach, Flint......................	38	14	14	28	43
Dean Roach, Asheville	18	4	12	16	18
Totals	56	18	26	44	61
Petr Sachl, Asheville	3	0	1	1	4
Petr Sachl, Ft. Wayne	55	30	24	54	28
Totals	58	30	25	55	32
Francois Sasseville, Ohio..........	20	10	9	19	18
Francois Sasseville, Adirondack	50	22	14	36	20
Totals	70	32	23	55	38
Janis Tomans, Knoxville	22	8	5	13	14

	Games	G	A	Pts.	PIM
Janis Tomans, Madison	11	3	6	9	2
Totals	33	11	11	22	16
Dan Tompkins, Missouri	48	10	8	18	48
Dan Tompkins, Ft. Wayne	9	3	3	6	8
Totals	57	13	11	24	56
Brian Tucker, Muskegon	31	3	8	11	101
Brian Tucker, Madison	40	7	6	13	103
Totals	71	10	14	24	204
Richie Walcott, Ohio	12	1	2	3	58
Richie Walcott, Asheville	37	9	4	13	93
Totals	49	10	6	16	151
Bruce Watson, Rockford	8	0	1	1	15
Bruce Watson, Asheville	60	12	17	29	229
Totals	68	12	18	30	244
Nolan Weir, Adirondack	14	3	1	4	12
Nolan Weir, Ft. Wayne	6	0	0	0	7
Totals	20	3	1	4	19
Wade Welte, Asheville	8	1	1	2	29
Wade Welte, Adirondack	50	16	11	27	141
Totals	58	17	12	29	170
Ben White, Binghamton	2	0	0	0	0
Ben White, Asheville	14	1	7	8	21
Ben White, Ohio	39	1	10	11	52

	Games	G	A	Pts.	PIM
Ben White, Mohawk Valley	8	0	4	4	6
Totals	63	2	21	23	79
Mike Williams, Madison	17	0	3	3	25
Mike Williams, Ft. Wayne	1	0	0	0	2
Mike Williams, Asheville	4	0	0	0	18
Totals	22	0	3	3	45

GOALTENDING

	Gms.	Min.	W	L	SOL	G	SO	Avg.
D. Brenzavich, Q.C.	17	938	12	3	1	54	0	3.46
D. Brenzavich, Ash..	23	1329	9	14	0	92	0	4.15
Totals	40	2267	21	17	1	146	0	3.86
Chad Ford, M.V.	1	59	0	0	1	4	0	4.04
Chad Ford, P.H.	14	735	10	2	0	31	0	2.53
Chad Ford, Adi.	36	2017	17	12	6	116	1	3.45
Totals	51	2812	27	14	7	151	1	3.22
Jonathan Forest, O.	22	1085	4	14	1	92	0	5.09
J. Forest, M.V.	6	242	0	2	3	21	0	5.20
Totals	28	1327	4	16	4	113	0	5.11
T. MacDonald, Adi. .	24	1308	6	14	3	91	0	4.17
T. MacDonald, O..	8	438	2	5	0	28	0	3.84
T. MacDonald, F.W.	4	238	2	2	0	12	0	3.02
Totals	36	1984	10	21	3	131	0	3.96

2000 COLONIAL CUP PLAYOFFS

RESULTS

FIRST ROUND

	W	L	Pts.	GF	GA
Muskegon	2	0	4	11	2
Adirondack	0	2	0	2	11

(Muskegon won series, 2-0)

	W	L	Pts.	GF	GA
Fort Wayne	2	0	4	7	4
Asheville	0	2	0	4	7

(Fort Wayne won series, 2-0)

	W	L	Pts.	GF	GA
Mohawk Valley	2	1	4	12	10
Missouri	1	2	2	10	12

(Mohawk Valley won series, 2-1)

	W	L	Pts.	GF	GA
Madison	2	1	4	13	10
Rockford	1	2	2	10	13

(Madison won series, 2-1)

QUARTERFINALS

	W	L	Pts.	GF	GA
Quad City	4	1	8	26	16
Mohawk Valley	1	4	2	16	26

(Quad City won series, 4-1)

	W	L	Pts.	GF	GA
Flint	4	2	8	24	20
Madison	2	4	4	20	24

(Flint won series, 4-2)

	W	L	Pts.	GF	GA
Fort Wayne	4	2	8	21	16
B.C.	2	4	4	16	21

(Fort Wayne won series, 4-2)

	W	L	Pts.	GF	GA
Muskegon	4	2	8	18	15
Port Huron	2	4	4	15	18

(Muskegon won series, 4-2)

SEMIFINALS

	W	L	Pts.	GF	GA
Quad City	4	1	8	22	16
Fort Wayne	1	4	2	16	22

(Quad City won series, 4-1)

	W	L	Pts.	GF	GA
Flint	4	1	8	24	15
Muskegon	1	4	2	15	24

(Flint won series, 4-1)

FINALS

	W	L	Pts.	GF	GA
Flint	4	0	8	19	10
Quad City	0	4	0	10	19

(Flint won series, 4-0)

INDIVIDUAL LEADERS

Goals: Jim Duhart, Madison (10)
Mark Major, Flint (10)
Don Parsons, Flint (10)
Assists: Nick Stajduhar, Flint (21)
Points: Nick Stajduhar, Flint (26)
Penalty minutes: Garry Gulash, Quad City (86)
Goaltending average: Joe Dimaline, Muskegon (2.98)
Shutouts: Joe Dimaline, Muskegon (1)
Jon Hillebrandt, Port Huron (1)

TOP SCORERS

	Games	G	A	Pts.
Nick Stajduhar, Flint	15	5	21	26
Jim Duhart, Madison	9	10	10	20
Ross Wilson, Flint	15	6	11	17
Hugo Proulx, Quad City	13	5	12	17
Don Parsons, Flint	15	10	6	16
Vlad Serov, Flint	15	9	7	16
Robin Bouchard, Muskegon	13	7	9	16
Tomas Kapusta, Muskegon	13	4	12	16
Cory Cyrenne, Flint	11	3	13	16
Keli Corpse, Fort Wayne	13	6	9	15

ADIRONDACK ICEHAWKS
(Lost first round to Muskegon, 2-0)
SCORING

	Games	G	A	Pts.	PIM
Alexei Deev	2	1	0	1	0
Shawn Yakimishyn	2	1	0	1	2
Trevor Jobe	2	0	1	1	0
Trent Schachle	2	0	1	1	4
John Batten	1	0	0	0	2
Eric Boyte	1	0	0	0	0
David Kontzie	1	0	0	0	0
Chris Ross	1	0	0	0	2
Stephan Brochu	2	0	0	0	4
Tony Cimellaro	2	0	0	0	0
David Dartsch	2	0	0	0	7
Larry Empey	2	0	0	0	0
Chad Ford (goalie)	2	0	0	0	0
Matt Garver	2	0	0	0	0
Mikhail Nemirovsky	2	0	0	0	0
Guillaume Rodrigue	2	0	0	0	0
Francois Sasseville	2	0	0	0	4
Mike Varhaug	2	0	0	0	2
Wade Welte	2	0	0	0	9

GOALTENDING

	Gms.	Min.	W	L	T	G	SO	Avg.
Chad Ford	2	120	0	2	0	11	0	5.50

ASHEVILLE SMOKE
(Lost first round to Fort Wayne, 2-0)
SCORING

	Games	G	A	Pts.	PIM
Brent Gretzky	2	1	2	3	0
Bruce Watson	2	2	0	2	4
Dean Roach	1	1	0	1	0
Jack Greig	1	0	1	1	0
Rob Milliken	2	0	1	1	2
Lindsay Vallis	2	0	1	1	2
Peter Cermak	1	0	0	0	0
Shawn Ulrich	1	0	0	0	2
David Bourque	2	0	0	0	4
Jonas Eden	2	0	0	0	0
Paul Giblin	2	0	0	0	0
Sean Honeysett	2	0	0	0	0
Francois Leroux	2	0	0	0	4
Dan McIntyre (goalie)	2	0	0	0	0
Hayden O'Rear	2	0	0	0	0
Vaclav Pazourek	2	0	0	0	4
Cory Peterson	2	0	0	0	2
Jon Pirrong	2	0	0	0	0
Richie Walcott	2	0	0	0	0

GOALTENDING

	Gms.	Min.	W	L	T	G	SO	Avg.
Dan McIntyre	2	117	0	2	0	7	0	3.58

B.C. ICEMEN

(Lost quarterfinals to Fort Wayne, 4-2)
SCORING

	Games	G	A	Pts.	PIM
Chris Grenville	6	5	1	6	7
Mark Dutiaume	6	0	6	6	11
Greg Pajor	6	4	1	5	0
Yevgeny Shaldybin	6	1	4	5	8
Jason Norrie	6	1	3	4	6
Chris Winnes	3	0	4	4	0
Justin Plamondon	6	1	2	3	6
Matt Ruchty	6	1	2	3	12
Derek Knorr	6	0	3	3	19
Patrice Robitaille	6	2	0	2	2
Derek Wood	6	1	1	2	8
Jamie Bird	6	0	2	2	6

	Games	G	A	Pts.	PIM
Jim Dinneen (goalie)	1	0	0	0	0
Boyd Kane	1	0	0	0	0
Ales Dvorak	2	0	0	0	2
Blair Sherrit	2	0	0	0	0
Randy Hankinson	4	0	0	0	2
Alex Andreyev	6	0	0	0	4
Scott Ricci	6	0	0	0	0
Erasmo Saltarelli (goalie)	6	0	0	0	16
Pat Stachniak	6	0	0	0	4

GOALTENDING

	Gms.	Min.	W	L	T	G	SO	Avg.
Erasmo Saltarelli	6	380	2	4	0	19	0	3.00
Jim Dinneen	1	2	0	0	0	1	0	34.62

FLINT GENERALS
(Winner of 2000 United Hockey League playoffs)
SCORING

	Games	G	A	Pts.	PIM
Nick Stajduhar	15	5	21	26	24
Ross Wilson	15	6	11	17	6
Don Parsons	15	10	6	16	18
Vlad Serov	15	9	7	16	17
Cory Cyrenne	11	3	13	16	6
Mark Major	15	10	3	13	67
Luch Nasato	14	4	9	13	34
Gary Roach	15	3	8	11	20
Ian Hebert	10	4	4	8	18
Khalil Thomas	13	3	5	8	2
Chad Grills	14	4	3	7	49
Frank LaScala	12	3	4	7	21
Dariusz Zabawa	15	1	5	6	12
Dale Greenwood	15	1	4	5	12
Lorne Knauft	12	0	5	5	36
Emmanuel LaBranche	12	1	2	3	28
Dmitri Rodine	7	0	1	1	6
Alan Hitchen (goalie)	1	0	0	0	0
Jake Ream	9	0	0	0	14
Mark Richards (goalie)	15	0	0	0	16

GOALTENDING

	Gms.	Min.	W	L	T	G	SO	Avg.
Alan Hitchen	1	19	0	0	0	0	0	0.00
Mark Richards	15	884	12	3	0	45	0	3.06

FORT WAYNE KOMETS
(Lost semifinals to Quad City, 4-1)
SCORING

	Games	G	A	Pts.	PIM
Keli Corpse	13	6	9	15	4
Konstanti Shafranov	13	6	8	14	8
Jason Goulet	13	7	4	11	12
Petr Sachl	10	4	7	11	8
Kelly Hurd	9	6	3	9	12
Frederic Bouchard	13	5	3	8	18
Igor Malykhin	10	2	6	8	6
Derek Campbell	7	1	5	6	29
Richard Keyes	12	4	1	5	8
John Gurskis	12	2	2	4	2
Bruce Ramsay	13	1	3	4	67
Jeff McKercher	11	0	4	4	4
Jon Austin	8	0	3	3	4
Dave Lemay	13	0	3	3	23
Jeff MacMillan	9	0	2	2	10
Dan Tompkins	4	0	1	1	2
Todd MacDonald (goalie)	12	0	1	1	14
Milt Mastad	13	0	1	1	28
Daniel Ronan	13	0	1	1	16
Patrick Labrecque (goalie)	1	0	0	0	0
Charlie Lawson	1	0	0	0	2
Doug Teskey (goalie)	2	0	0	0	0
Steve Parsons	11	0	0	0	29

GOALTENDING

	Gms.	Min.	W	L	T	G	SO	Avg.
Doug Teskey	2	63	1	0	0	1	0	0.95
Pat Labrecque	1	59	0	1	0	3	0	3.07
Todd MacDonald	12	704	6	2	3	37	0	3.16

MADISON KODIAKS
(Lost quarterfinals to Flint, 4-2)

SCORING

	Games	G	A	Pts.	PIM
Jim Duhart	9	10	10	20	23
Randy Holmes	9	5	6	11	10
Dave MacIntyre	9	4	4	8	18
Don Martin	9	1	6	7	39
Janis Tomans	8	0	7	7	16
Josh Boni	5	2	3	5	20
Brian Tucker	6	2	3	5	21
Brad Englehart	7	1	4	5	18
Jeff Winter	8	0	4	4	4
Brian Wilson	9	3	0	3	2
Andy Faulkner	9	2	1	3	8
Derek Toninato	5	1	1	2	0
Luke Strand	9	1	1	2	19
Todd Passini	9	0	2	2	8
Dennis Pinfold	1	1	0	1	7
Jason Hughes	7	0	1	1	4
Eric Brown	9	0	1	1	6
Eoin McInerney (goalie)	4	0	0	0	2
David Fletcher (goalie)	6	0	0	0	0
Derek Beuselink	8	0	0	0	10

GOALTENDING

	Gms.	Min.	W	L	T	G	SO	Avg.
David Fletcher	6	325	2	2	1	19	0	3.50
Eoin McInerney	4	220	2	2	0	14	0	3.82

MISSOURI RIVER OTTERS
(Lost first round to Mohawk Valley, 2-1)

SCORING

	Games	G	A	Pts.	PIM
Lonnie Loach	3	3	2	5	2
Jeremy Rebek	3	1	4	5	14
Alain St. Hilaire	3	1	4	5	4
Kiley Hill	3	2	1	3	6
Jay Hebert	3	1	1	2	6
Forrest Gore	3	0	2	2	4
Darin Kimble	3	1	0	1	4
Allan Roulette	3	1	0	1	4
Adam Campbell	2	0	1	1	0
Brian Regan (goalie)	3	0	1	1	2
Marty Standish	3	0	1	1	4
Michal Statsny	3	0	1	1	6
Troy Michalski	1	0	0	0	0
Charlie Blyth	2	0	0	0	0
Randy Gallatin	3	0	0	0	2
Ben Gorewich	3	0	0	0	2
Trevor Sherban	3	0	0	0	8
Chris Tok	3	0	0	0	10

GOALTENDING

	Gms.	Min.	W	L	T	G	SO	Avg.
Brian Regan	3	186	1	1	1	11	0	3.55

MOHAWK VALLEY PROWLERS
(Lost quarterfinals to Quad City, 4-1)

SCORING

	Games	G	A	Pts.	PIM
John Vecchiarelli	8	5	8	13	16
Chris Palmer	8	5	4	9	21
Mark Kotary	8	1	5	6	12
Bob Ferrais	8	0	6	6	12
Andre Payette	7	4	1	5	33
Christian Lariviere	8	0	5	5	23
Todd Barclay	8	3	1	4	2
Serge Roberge	7	2	2	4	34
Francois Hardy	7	1	3	4	8

	Games	G	A	Pts.	PIM
Nic Beaudoin	3	3	0	3	0
Tim Harris	8	2	1	3	12
Mario Roberge	7	0	3	3	27
Frederik Last	8	0	3	3	0
Dave Jesiolowski	3	1	1	2	24
Ben White	8	1	1	2	23
Ryan Hartung	7	0	1	1	0
Ben Metzger	5	0	0	0	2
Patrick Charbonneau (goalie)	8	0	0	0	0
Kevin Tucker	8	0	0	0	12

GOALTENDING

	Gms.	Min.	W	L	T	G	SO	Avg.
P. Charbonneau	8	484	3	5	0	35	0	4.34

MUSKEGON FURY
(Lost semifinals to Flint, 4-1)

SCORING

	Games	G	A	Pts.	PIM
Robin Bouchard	13	7	9	16	38
Tomas Kapusta	13	4	12	16	10
Andrew Luciuk	13	7	7	14	18
Quinn Hancock	13	6	8	14	4
Bob Cunningham	12	4	9	13	4
Vadim Podrezov	13	2	5	7	10
Curtis Huppe	11	3	3	6	6
Mike McCourt	13	2	4	6	8
Scott Feasby	13	1	4	5	51
Scott Hlady	10	0	5	5	4
Rob Hutson	10	2	2	4	17
Jeff Kostuch	12	2	2	4	4
Francis Nault	13	1	2	3	4
Joel Gardner	3	1	1	2	0
Michael Kiesman	7	1	0	1	19
Jason Rose	8	1	0	1	9
Rob Melanson	12	0	1	1	19
Joe Dimaline (goalie)	13	0	1	1	0
Mark Vilneff	13	0	1	1	10
Dalen Hrooshkin	1	0	0	0	0
Bob Janosz (goalie)	2	0	0	0	16
Lucas Nehrling	2	0	0	0	2

GOALTENDING

	Gms.	Min.	W	L	T	G	SO	Avg.
Bob Janosz	2	53	0	0	0	2	0	2.27
Joe Dimaline	13	786	7	6	0	39	1	2.98

PORT HURON BORDER CATS
(Lost quarterfinals to Muskegon, 4-2)

SCORING

	Games	G	A	Pts.	PIM
Mike Maurice	6	3	4	7	10
Chris Bergeron	6	2	4	6	2
Rick Judson	6	2	4	6	2
Jason Gladney	6	0	5	5	6
Kevin Brown	6	3	1	4	17
Jay Neal	6	3	1	4	8
David Mayes	6	0	3	3	0
Jamie Dabanovich	6	0	2	2	4
Paul Harvey	3	1	0	1	2
Shayne Tomlinson	6	1	0	1	4
Mike Bondy	5	0	1	1	6
Kevin Schmidt	5	0	1	1	0
Jon Hillebrandt (goalie)	3	0	0	0	0
Matt Mullin (goalie)	3	0	0	0	0
Luke Murphy	4	0	0	0	0
Ryan Burgoyne	6	0	0	0	0
Lee Cole	6	0	0	0	13
Paul Fioroni	6	0	0	0	2
Adam Robbins	6	0	0	0	8

GOALTENDING

	Gms.	Min.	W	L	T	G	SO	Avg.
Jon Hillebrandt	3	194	1	1	1	7	1	2.16
Matt Mullin	3	225	1	1	1	10	0	2.67

MINOR LEAGUES *UHL*

QUAD CITY MALLARDS
(Lost finals to Flint, 4-0)
SCORING

	Games	G	A	Pts.	PIM
Hugo Proulx	13	5	12	17	18
Glenn Stewart	14	7	7	14	0
Patrick Nadeau	13	6	8	14	4
Rick Emmett	14	2	12	14	16
Ryan Lindsay	14	2	11	13	16
Rob DeCiantis	13	8	2	10	24
Brendan Brooks	14	6	3	9	35
Kevin Kerr	10	2	5	7	24
Martin Hlinka	14	0	7	7	24
Garry Gulash	14	5	1	6	86
Kelly Hultgren	13	2	4	6	10
Brian LaFleur	14	1	5	6	6
Steve Gibson	9	4	1	5	4
Mike Melas	7	2	3	5	8
Mark McFarlane	11	2	3	5	36
Paul Johnson	14	2	2	4	4
Kerry Toporowski	12	1	2	3	75
Brendan Buckley	9	1	0	1	10
Bob Crummer	1	0	1	1	2
Martin Fillion (goalie)	3	0	1	1	2
Martin Villeneuve (goalie)	12	0	0	0	4

GOALTENDING

	Gms.	Min.	W	L	T	G	SO	Avg.
Martin Fillion	3	168	1	2	0	9	0	3.21
Martin Villeneuve	12	690	7	3	1	39	0	3.39

ROCKFORD ICEHOGS
(Lost first round to Madison, 2-1)
SCORING

	Games	G	A	Pts.	PIM
Jason Firth	3	3	2	5	2
Derek Landmesser	3	1	4	5	4
Peter Cava	3	1	2	3	4
Mike Figliomeni	3	1	1	2	0
Wayne Strachan	3	1	1	2	8
Curtis Tipler	3	1	1	2	0
Scott Burfoot	3	0	2	2	4
Evgeny Krivomaz	3	0	2	2	6
Carlos Soke	2	1	0	1	9
Brant Blackned	3	1	0	1	2
Norm Paquet	3	0	1	1	17
Mike Correia (goalie)	1	0	0	0	0
Kevin Holliday	2	0	0	0	19
Alexandre Makombo	2	0	0	0	18
Patrice Charbonneau	3	0	0	0	4
Raymond Delarosbil	3	0	0	0	8
Sheldon Gorski	3	0	0	0	4
J.F. Rivard (goalie)	3	0	0	0	0
Jesse Welling	3	0	0	0	0

GOALTENDING

	Gms.	Min.	W	L	T	G	SO	Avg.
Mike Correia	1	34	0	0	0	1	0	1.75
J.F. Rivard	3	146	1	2	0	12	0	4.94

1999-2000 AWARD WINNERS

ALL-STAR TEAMS

First team	Pos.	Second team
Brian Regan, Missouri	G	Dieter Kochan, B.C.
Jeremy Rebek, Missouri	D	Frederic Bouchard, Ft. Wayne
Gary Roach, Flint	D	Nick Stajduhar, Flint
Brent Gretzky, Asheville	C	Jason Firth, Rockford
Glenn Stewart, Quad City	LW	Don Parsons, Flint
Kevin Kerr, Quad City	RW	Mike Figliomeni, Rockford

TROPHY WINNERS

Most Valuable Player: Brian Regan, Missouri
Scoring leader: Brent Gretzky, Asheville
Outstanding defenseman: Gary Roach, Flint
Outstanding defensive forward: Jay Neal, Port Huron
Outstanding goaltender: Brian Regan, Missouri
Rookie of the Year: Jason Goulet, Fort Wayne
Most sportsmanlike player: Keli Corpse, Fort Wayne
Playoff MVP: Nick Stajduhar, Flint
Coach of the Year: Brad Jones, B.C.

ALL-TIME AWARD WINNERS

MOST VALUABLE PLAYER

Season	Player, Team
1991-92	Terry McCutcheon, Brantford
1992-93	Jason Firth, Thunder Bay
1993-94	Kevin Kerr, Flint
1994-95	Mark Green, Utica
	Paul Polillo, Brantford
1995-96	Paul Polillo, Brantford
1996-97	Paul Polillo, Brantford
1997-98	Jason Firth, Thunder Bay
1998-99	Jason Firth, Thunder Bay
1999-00	Brian Regan, Missouri

SCORING LEADER

Season	Player, Team
1991-92	Tom Sasso, Flint
1992-93	Len Soccio, St. Thomas
1993-94	Paul Polillo, Brantford
1994-95	Paul Polillo, Brantford
1995-96	Paul Polillo, Brantford
1996-97	Paul Polillo, Brantford
1997-98	Paul Polillo, Brantford
1998-99	Jason Firth, Thunder Bay
1999-00	Brent Gretzky, Asheville

ROOKIE OF THE YEAR

Season	Player, Team
1991-92	Kevin Butt, St. Thomas
1992-93	Jason Firth, Thunder Bay
1993-94	Jean-Francois Labbe, Thunder Bay
1994-95	Lance Leslie, Thunder Bay
1995-96	Matt Loen, Madison
1996-97	Forbes MacPherson, Thunder Bay
1997-98	Jason Weaver, Muskegon
1998-99	Mike Melas, Quad City
1999-00	Jason Goulet, Fort Wayne

DEFENSEMAN OF THE YEAR

Season	Player, Team
1991-92	Tom Searle, Brantford
1992-93	Tom Searle, Brantford
1993-94	Barry McKinlay, Thunder Bay
1994-95	Barry McKinlay, Thunder Bay
1995-96	Chris Hynnes, Thunder Bay
1996-97	Barry McKinlay, Thunder Bay
1997-98	John Vary, Muskegon
1998-99	Stephan Brochu, Flint
1999-00	Gary Roach, Flint

BEST DEFENSIVE FORWARD

Season	Player, Team
1991-92	Tim Bean, St. Thomas
1992-93	Todd Howarth, Thunder Bay
1993-94	Jamie Hicks, Brantford
1994-95	Terry Menard, Thunder Bay
1995-96	Brian Downey, Madison
1996-97	Brian Downey, Madison
1997-98	Brad Jones, B.C.
1998-99	Paul Willett, Muskegon
1999-00	Jay Neal, Port Huron

BEST GOALTENDER

Season	Player, Team
1991-92	Jamie Stewart, Detroit
1992-93	Jamie Stewart, Detroit
1993-94	J.F. Labbe, Thunder Bay
1994-95	Maxim Machialovsky, Detroit
1995-96	Rich Parent, Muskegon
1996-97	Sergei Zvyagin, Quad City
1997-98	Darryl Gilmour, Madison
1998-99	Joe Dimaline, Muskegon
1999-00	Brian Regan, Missouri

MOST SPORTSMANLIKE PLAYER

Season	Player, Team
1991-92	Tom Sasso, Flint
1992-93	Paul Polillo, Brantford
1993-94	Paul Polillo, Brantford
1994-95	Paul Polillo, Brantford

Season	Player, Team
1995-96	Scott Burfoot, Flint
1996-97	Kent Hawley, Madison
1997-98	Brian Sakic, Flint
1998-99	Brian Sakic, Flint
1999-00	Keli Corpse, Fort Wayne

PLAYOFF MVP

Season	Player, Team
1991-92	Gary Callaghan, Thunder Bay
1992-93	Roland Melanson, Brantford
1993-94	Jean-Francois Labbe, Thunder Bay
1994-95	Lance Leslie, Thunder Bay
1995-96	Scott Burfoot, Flint
1996-97	Sergei Zvyagin, Quad City
1997-98	Jim Brown, Quad City
1998-99	Sergei Kharin, Muskegon
1999-00	Nick Stajduhar, Flint

COACH OF THE YEAR

Season	Coach, Team
1991-92	Peter Horachek, St. Thomas
1992-93	Bill McDonald, Thunder Bay
1993-94	Tom Barrett, Chatham
1994-95	Steve Ludzik, Muskegon
1995-96	Mark Johnson, Madison
1996-97	Robbie Nichols, Flint
1997-98	Robert Dirk, Winston-Salem
1998-99	Rich Kromm, Muskegon
1999-00	Brad Jones, B.C.

ALL-TIME LEAGUE CHAMPIONS

REGULAR-SEASON CHAMPION

Season	Team	Coach
1991-92	Michigan Falcons	Terry Christensen
1992-93	Brantford Smoke	Ken Mann & Ken Gratton
1993-94	Thunder Bay Senators	Bill MacDonald
1994-95	Thunder Bay Senators	Bill MacDonald
1995-96	Flint Generals	Robbie Nichols
1996-97	Flint Generals	Robbie Nichols
1997-98	Quad City Mallards	Paul Gillis
1998-99	Muskegon Fury	Rich Kromm
1999-00	Flint Generals	Doug Shedden

PLAYOFF CHAMPION

Team	Coach
Thunder Bay Thunder Hawks	Bill MacDonald
Brantford Smoke	Ken Gratton
Thunder Bay Senators	Bill MacDonald
Thunder Bay Senators	Bill MacDonald
Flint Generals	Robbie Nichols
Quad City Mallards	John Anderson
Quad City Mallards	Paul Gillis
Muskegon Fury	Rich Kromm
Flint Generals	Doug Shedden

MAJOR JUNIOR LEAGUES

Canadian Hockey League

Ontario Hockey League

Quebec Major Junior Hockey League

Western Hockey League

CANADIAN HOCKEY LEAGUE

GENERAL INFORMATION

The Canadian Hockey League is an alliance of the three Major Junior leagues—Ontario Hockey League, Quebec Major Junior Hockey League and Western Hockey League. After the regular season, the three leagues compete in a round-robin tournament to decide the Memorial Cup championship. Originally awarded to the national Junior champion, the Memorial Cup later signified Junior A supremacy (after Junior hockey in Canada was divided into ``A'' and ``B'' classes). Beginning in 1971, when Junior A hockey was split into Major Junior and Tier II Junior A, the Memorial Cup was awarded to the Major Junior champion.

LEAGUE OFFICE

Member leagues
Ontario Hockey League
Quebec Major Junior Hockey League
Western Hockey League
President
David E. Branch
Vice president
Gilles Courteau
V.p., marketing and corp. development
John Hudson

Directors
Bruce Hamilton
Charles Henry
Jim Rooney
Secretary treasurer
John Horman
Director of marketing
Colin Campbell
Director of information
Dave Lord

Director of officiating
Richard Doerksen
Address
305 Milner Ave., Suite 201
Scarborough, Ont. M1B 3V4
Phone
416-332-9711
FAX
416-332-1477

2000 MEMORIAL CUP

FINAL STANDINGS

Team (League)	W	L	Pts.	GF	GA
Rimouski (QMJHL)	4	0	8	21	8
Halifax (QMJHL)	2	2	4	18	14
Barrie (OHL)	2	3	4	15	23
Kootenay (WHL)	0	3	0	4	13

RESULTS

SATURDAY, MAY 20
Halifax 5, Barrie 2

SUNDAY, MAY 21
Rimouski 3, Kootenay 1

MONDAY, MAY 22
Halifax 7, Kootenay 1

TUESDAY, MAY 23
Rimouski 7, Barrie 2

WEDNESDAY, MAY 24
Barrie 3, Kootenay 2 (2OT)

THURSDAY, MAY 25
Rimouski 5, Halifax 3

SATURDAY, MAY 27
Barrie 6, Halifax 3

SUNDAY, MAY 28
Rimouski 6, Barrie 2

TOP TOURNAMENT SCORERS

	Games	G	A	Pts.
Ramzi Abid, Halifax	4	*6	4	*10
Juraj Kolnik, Rimouski	4	5	5	*10
Brad Richards, Rimouski	4	4	*6	*10
Jasmin Gelinas, Halifax	4	3	5	8
Michel Periard, Rimouski	4	2	*6	8
Brandon Reid, Halifax	4	1	*6	7
Jonathan Beaulieu, Rimouski	4	4	2	6
Benoit Dusablon, Halifax	4	3	3	6
Benoit Martin, Rimouski	4	3	2	5
Sheldon Keefe, Barrie	5	2	3	5

*Indicates tournament leader.

1999-2000 AWARD WINNERS

ALL-STAR TEAMS

First team	Pos.	Second team
Andrew Raycroft, Kingston	G	Bryce Wandler, Swift Current
Michel Periard, Rimouski	D	John Erskine, London
Micki Dupont, Kamloops	D	Lawrence Nycholat, S.C.
Ramzi Abid, Halifax	LW	Simon Gamache, Val-d'Or
Brad Richards, Rimouski	C	Brad Moran, Calgary
Norm Milley, Sudbury	RW	Sheldon Keefe, Barrie

TROPHY WINNERS

Player of the year: Brad Richards, Rimouski
Top scorer award: Brad Richards, Rimouski
Plus/minus award: Brad Richards, Rimouski
Face-off award: Dan Tessier, Ottawa
Rookie of the year: Dan Blackburn, Kootenay
Defenseman of the year: Micki Dupont, Kamloops
Goaltender of the year: Andrew Raycroft, Kingston
Scholastic player of the year: Brad Boyes, Erie
Coach of the year: Peter DeBoer, Plymouth
Executive of the year: Maurice Tanguay, Rimouski
Most sportsmanlike player of the year: Jonathan Roy, Moncton
Top draft prospect award: Rostislav Klesla, Brampton
Humanitarian award: Simon Gamache, Val-d'Or

MAJOR JUNIOR LEAGUES CHL

HISTORY

ALL-TIME MEMORIAL CUP WINNERS

Season	Team
1918-19	Univ. of Toronto Schools
1919-20	Toronto Canoe Club
1920-21	Winnipeg Falcons
1921-22	Fort William War Veterans
1922-23	Univ. of Manitoba-Winnipeg
1923-24	Owen Sound Greys
1924-25	Regina Pats
1925-26	Calgary Canadians
1926-27	Owen Sound Greys
1927-28	Regina Monarchs
1928-29	Toronto Marlboros
1929-30	Regina Pats
1930-31	Winnipeg Elmwoods
1931-32	Sudbury Wolves
1932-33	Newmarket
1933-34	Toronto St. Michael's
1934-35	Winnipeg Monarchs
1935-36	West Toronto Redmen
1936-37	Winnipeg Monarchs
1937-38	St. Boniface Seals
1938-39	Oshawa Generals
1939-40	Oshawa Generals
1940-41	Winnipeg Rangers
1941-42	Portage la Prairie
1942-43	Winnipeg Rangers
1943-44	Oshawa Generals
1944-45	Toronto St. Michael's
1945-46	Winnipeg Monarchs

Season	Team
1946-47	Toronto St. Michael's
1947-48	Port Arthur W. End Bruins
1948-49	Montreal Royals
1949-50	Montreal Jr. Canadiens
1950-51	Barrie Flyers
1951-52	Guelph Biltmores
1952-53	Barrie Flyers
1953-54	St. Catharines Tee Pees
1954-55	Toronto Marlboros
1955-56	Toronto Marlboros
1956-57	Flin Flon Bombers
1957-58	Ottawa-Hull Jr. Canadiens
1958-59	Winnipeg Braves
1959-60	St. Catharines Tee Pees
1960-61	Tor. St. Michael's Majors
1961-62	Hamilton Red Wings
1962-63	Edmonton Oil Kings
1963-64	Toronto Marlboros
1964-65	Niagara Falls Flyers
1965-66	Edmonton Oil Kings
1966-67	Toronto Marlboros
1967-68	Niagara Falls Flyers
1968-69	Montreal Jr. Canadiens
1969-70	Montreal Jr. Canadiens
1970-71	Quebec Remparts
1971-72	Cornwall Royals
1972-73	Toronto Marlboros
1973-74	Regina Pats

Season	Team
1974-75	Toronto Marlboros
1975-76	Hamilton Fincups
1976-77	New Westminster Bruins
1977-78	New Westminster Bruins
1978-79	Peterborough Petes
1979-80	Cornwall Royals
1980-81	Cornwall Royals
1981-82	Kitchener Rangers
1982-83	Portland Winter Hawks
1983-84	Ottawa 67's
1984-85	Prince Albert Raiders
1985-86	Guelph Platers
1986-87	Medicine Hat Tigers
1987-88	Medicine Hat Tigers
1988-89	Swift Current Broncos
1989-90	Oshawa Generals
1990-91	Spokane Chiefs
1991-92	Kamloops Blazers
1992-93	Sault Ste. Marie Greyhounds
1993-94	Kamloops Blazers
1994-95	Kamloops Blazers
1995-96	Granby Predateurs
1996-97	Hull Olympics
1997-98	Portland Winter Hawks
1998-99	Ottawa 67's
1999-00	Rimouski Oceanic

ALL-TIME AWARD WINNERS

PLAYER OF THE YEAR AWARD

Season	Player, Team
1974-75	Ed Staniowski, Regina
1975-76	Peter Lee, Ottawa
1976-77	Dale McCourt, Ste. Catharines
1977-78	Bobby Smith, Ottawa
1978-79	Pierre LaCroix, Trois-Rivieres
1979-80	Doug Wickenheiser, Regina
1980-81	Dale Hawerchuk, Cornwall
1981-82	Dave Simpson, London
1982-83	Pat LaFontaine, Verdun
1983-84	Mario Lemieux, Laval
1984-85	Dan Hodgson, Prince Albert
1985-86	Luc Robitaille, Hull
1986-87	Rob Brown, Kamloops
1987-88	Joe Sakic, Swift Current
1988-89	Bryan Fogarty, Niagara Falls
1989-90	Mike Ricci, Peterborough
1990-91	Eric Lindros, Oshawa
1991-92	Charles Poulin, St. Hyacinthe
1992-93	Pat Peake, Detroit
1993-94	Jason Allison, London
1994-95	David Ling, Kingston
1995-96	Christian Dube, Sherbrooke
1996-97	Alyn McCauley, Ottawa
1997-98	Sergei Varlamov, Swift Current
1998-99	Brian Campbell, Ottawa
1999-00	Brad Richards, Rimouski

TOP SCORER AWARD

Season	Player, Team
1993-94	Jason Allison, London
1994-95	Marc Savard, Oshawa
1995-96	Daniel Briere, Drummondville
1996-97	Pavel Rosa, Hull
1997-98	Ramzi Abid, Chicoutimi
1998-99	Mike Ribeiro, Rouyn-Noranda
1999-00	Brad Richards, Rimouski

PLUS/MINUS AWARD

Season	Player, Team
1986-87	Rob Brown, Kamloops
1987-88	Marc Saumier, Hull
1988-89	Bryan Fogarty, Niagara Falls
1989-90	Len Barrie, Kamloops
1990-91	Eric Lindros, Oshawa
1991-92	Dean McAmmond, Prince Albert
1992-93	Chris Pronger, Peterborough
1993-94	Mark Wotton, Saskatoon
1994-95	Darren Ritchie, Brandon
1995-96	Daniel Goneau, Granby
1996-97	Nick Boynton, Ottawa
1997-98	Andrew Ference, Portland
1998-99	Simon Tremblay, Quebec
1999-00	Brad Richards, Rimouski

FACE-OFF AWARD

Season	Player, Team
1997-98	Mark Smith, Lethbridge
1998-99	Dan Tessier, Ottawa
1999-00	Dan Tessier, Ottawa

ROOKIE AWARD

Season	Player, Team
1987-88	Martin Gelinas, Hull
1988-89	Yanic Perreault, Trois-Rivieres
1989-90	Petr Nedved, Seattle
1990-91	Philippe Boucher, Granby
1991-92	Alexandre Daigle, Victoriaville
1992-93	Jeff Freisen, Regina
1993-94	Vitali Yachmenev, North Bay
1994-95	Bryan Berard, Detroit
1995-96	Joe Thornton, Sault Ste. Marie
1996-97	Vincent Lecavalier, Rimouski
1997-98	David Legwand, Plymouth
1998-99	Pavel Brendl, Calgary
1999-00	Dan Blackburn, Kootenay

MAJOR JUNIOR LEAGUES CHL

DEFENSEMAN OF THE YEAR AWARD

Season   Player, Team
1987-88—Greg Hawgood, Kamloops
1988-89—Bryan Fogarty, Niagara Falls
1989-90—John Slaney, Cornwall
1990-91—Patrice Brisebois, Drummondville
1991-92—Drake Berehowsky, North Bay
1992-93—Chris Pronger, Peterborough
1993-94—Steve Gosselin, Chicoutimi
1994-95—Nolan Baumgartner, Kamloops
1995-96—Bryan Berard, Detroit
1996-97—Sean Blanchard, Ottawa
1997-98—Derrick Walser, Rimouski
1998-99—Brad Stuart, Calgary
1999-00—Micki Dupont, Kootenay

GOALTENDER OF THE YEAR AWARD

Season   Player, Team
1987-88—Stephane Beauregard, St. Jean
1988-89—Stephane Fiset, Victoriaville
1989-90—Trevor Kidd, Brandon
1990-91—Felix Potvin, Chicoutimi
1991-92—Corey Hirsch, Kamloops
1992-93—Jocelyn Thibault, Sherbrooke
1993-94—Norm Maracle, Saskatoon
1994-95—Martin Biron, Beauport
1995-96—Frederic Deschenes, Granby
1996-97—Marc Denis, Chicoutimi
1997-98—Mathieu Garon, Victoriaville
1998-99—Cody Rudkowsky, Seattle
1999-00—Andrew Raycroft, Kingston

SCHOLASTIC PLAYER OF THE YEAR AWARD

Season   Player, Team
1987-88—Darrin Shannon, Windsor
1988-89—Jeff Nelson, Prince Albert
1989-90—Jeff Nelson, Prince Albert
1990-91—Scott Niedermayer, Kamloops
1991-92—Nathan LaFayette, Cornwall
1992-93—David Trofimenkoff, Lethbridge
1993-94—Patrick Boileau, Laval
1994-95—Perry Johnson, Regina
1995-96—Boyd Devereaux, Kitchener
1996-97—Stefan Cherneski, Brandon
1997-98—Kyle Rossiter, Spokane
1998-99—Rob Zepp, Plymouth
1999-00—Brad Boyes, Erie

COACH OF THE YEAR AWARD

Season   Coach, Team
1987-88—Alain Vigneault, Hull
1988-89—Joe McDonnell, Kitchener
1989-90—Ken Hitchcock, Kamloops
1990-91—Joe Canale, Chicoutimi
1991-92—Bryan Maxwell, Spokane
1992-93—Marcel Comeau, Tacoma
1993-94—Bert Templeton, North Bay
1994-95—Craig Hartsburg, Guelph
1995-96—Bob Lowes, Brandon
1996-97—Brian Kilrea, Ottawa
1997-98—Dean Clark, Calgary
1998-99—Guy Chouinard, Quebec
1999-00—Peter DeBoer, Plymouth

EXECUTIVE OF THE YEAR AWARD

Season   Executive, Team or League
1988-89—John Horman, QMJHL
1989-90—Russ Farwell, Seattle
1990-91—Sherwood Bassin, Sault Ste. Marie
1991-92—Bert Templeton, North Bay
1992-93—Jim Rutherford, Detroit
1993-94—Bob Brown, Kamloops
1994-95—Kelly McCrimmon, Brandon
1995-96—Tim Speltz, Spokane
1996-97—Harold MacKay, Halifax
1997-98—Paul McIntosh, London
1998-99—Jeff Hunt, Ottawa
1999-00—Maurice Tanguay, Rimouski

MOST SPORTSMANLIKE PLAYER OF THE YEAR AWARD

Season   Player, Team
1989-90—Andrew McKim, Hull
1990-91—Pat Falloon, Spokane
1991-92—Martin Gendron, St. Hyacinthe
1992-93—Rick Girard, Swift Current
1993-94—Yanick Dube, Laval
1994-95—Eric Daze, Beauport
1995-96—Hnat Domenichelli, Kamloops
1996-97—Kelly Smart, Brandon
1997-98—Cory Cyrenne, Brandon
1998-99—Matt Kinch, Calgary
1999-00—Jonathan Roy, Moncton

TOP DRAFT PROSPECT AWARD

Season   Player, Team
1990-91—Eric Lindros, Oshawa
1991-92—Todd Warriner, Windsor
1992-93—Alexandre Daigle, Victoriaville
1993-94—Jeff O'Neill, Guelph
1994-95—Bryan Berard, Detroit
1995-96—Chris Phillips, Prince Albert
1996-97—Joe Thornton, Sault Ste. Marie
1997-98—Vincent Lecavalier, Rimouski
1998-99—Pavel Brendl, Calgary
1999-00—Rostislav Klesla, Brampton

HUMANITARIAN AWARD

Season   Player, Team
1992-93—Keli Corpse, Kingston
1993-94—Stephane Roy, Val d'Or
1994-95—David-Alexandre Beauregard, St. Hyacinthe
1995-96—Craig Mills, Belleville
1996-97—Jesse Wallin, Red Deer
1997-98—Jason Metcalfe, London
1998-99—Philippe Sauve, Rimouski
1999-00—Simon Gamache, Val-d'Or

ONTARIO HOCKEY LEAGUE

LEAGUE OFFICE

Commissioner
David E. Branch
Chairman of the board
Jim Rooney
Director of administration
Herb Morell
Dir. of hockey op./referee in chief
Ted Baker

Director of information & special events
Aaron Bell
Director of central scouting
Bill Neeham
Address
305 Milner Avenue
Suite 200
Scarborough, Ontario M1B 3V4

Phone
416-299-8700
FAX
416-299-8787

1999-2000 REGULAR SEASON
FINAL STANDINGS

EAST DIVISION

Team	G	W	L	T	RT	Pts.	GF	GA
Ottawa	68	43	21	4	1	91	269	189
Belleville	68	44	22	2	0	90	319	227
Kingston	68	38	25	5	3	84	258	245
Peterborough	68	34	27	7	1	76	242	219
Oshawa	68	32	32	4	2	70	227	224

CENTRAL DIVISION

Team	G	W	L	T	RT	Pts.	GF	GA
Barrie	68	43	19	6	1	93	306	212
Sudbury	68	39	24	5	1	84	262	221
North Bay	68	24	38	6	3	57	214	253
Toronto	68	18	48	2	4	42	203	281
Mississauga	68	9	58	1	2	21	160	346

MIDWEST DIVISION

Team	G	W	L	T	RT	Pts.	GF	GA
Erie	68	33	31	4	3	73	224	229
Kitchener	68	28	34	6	4	66	229	256
Brampton	68	25	32	11	4	65	213	226
Guelph	68	29	35	4	1	63	250	256
Owen Sound	68	21	41	6	6	54	237	292

WEST DIVISION

Team	G	W	L	T	RT	Pts.	GF	GA
Plymouth	68	45	19	4	1	95	256	172
Sault Ste. Marie	68	37	25	6	5	85	270	217
Sarnia	68	33	27	8	0	74	211	189
Windsor	68	35	31	2	1	73	213	231
London	68	22	39	7	3	54	186	250

INDIVIDUAL LEADERS

Goals: Norm Milley, Sudbury (52)
Assists: Sheldon Keefe, Barrie (73)
Points: Sheldon Keefe, Barrie (121)
Penalty minutes: Brett Clouthier, Kingston (266)
Goaltending average: Rob Zepp, Plymouth (2.38)
Shutouts: J.F. Perras, Erie (6)

	Games	G	A	Pts.
Taylor Pyatt, Sudbury	68	40	49	89
Jonathan Schill, Kingston	65	39	48	87
Mike Jefferson, Barrie	58	34	53	87
Brent Gauvreau, Oshawa	59	34	53	87
Derek Roy, Kitchener	66	34	53	87
Michael Henrich, Barrie	66	38	48	86
Dan Tessier, Ottawa	55	39	45	84
Sean Avery, Kingston	55	28	56	84
Justin Williams, Plymouth	68	37	46	83
Brad Boyes, Erie	68	36	46	82
Damian Surma, Plymouth	66	34	44	78
Vladimir Repnev, Oshawa	62	30	48	78
Ryan Jardine, Sault Ste. Marie	65	43	34	77
Jeff Heerema, Sarnia	67	36	41	77
Kevin Mitchell, Guelph	68	19	58	77

TOP SCORERS

	Games	G	A	Pts.
Sheldon Keefe, Barrie	66	48	73	121
Norm Milley, Sudbury	68	52	60	112
Jason Jaspers, Sudbury	68	46	61	107
Denis Shvidki, Barrie	61	41	65	106
Michael Zigomanis, Kingston	59	40	54	94
Jonathan Cheechoo, Belleville	66	45	46	91
Raffi Torres, Brampton	68	43	48	91

INDIVIDUAL STATISTICS

BARRIE COLTS

SCORING

	Games	G	A	Pts.	PIM
Sheldon Keefe	66	48	73	121	95
Denis Shvidki	61	41	65	106	55
Mike Jefferson	58	34	53	87	203
Michael Henrich	66	38	48	86	69
Matthew Dziedusycki	46	22	26	48	23
Mike Christian	61	19	22	41	107
Blaine Down	43	17	22	39	49
Mike Henderson	43	18	19	37	23
Tim Verbeek	67	21	15	36	107
Ryan O'Keefe	67	7	28	35	112

	Games	G	A	Pts.	PIM
Shawn Cation	53	4	27	31	103
Ryan Barnes	31	17	12	29	98
Nick Robinson	65	6	22	28	69
Tim Branham	38	3	16	19	46
Ed Hill	66	1	18	19	63
Aaron Power	64	2	15	17	70
Eric Reitz	63	2	10	12	85
Scott Cameron	21	2	4	6	19
Kyle Wailes	58	2	3	5	34
Matt Passfield	47	1	3	4	19
Jerry Connell	20	0	4	4	26
Rick Hwodeky	51	1	2	3	43
Jordan Brenner	40	0	3	3	13

	Games	G	A	Pts.	PIM
Brian Finley (goalie)	47	0	3	3	0
Devon Francon	4	0	1	1	4
Matt Nichol	2	0	0	0	0
Dana Bannerman (goalie)	3	0	0	0	4
Ben Vanderklok (goalie)	15	0	0	0	6
Mike D'Alessandro (goalie)	16	0	0	0	0
Vladimir Chernenko	19	0	0	0	4

GOALTENDING

	Gms.	Min.	W	L	T	G	SO	Avg.
Dana Bannerman	3	111	2	0	0	3	0	1.62
Mike D'Alessandro	16	787	11	3	0	35	1	2.67
Brian Finley	47	2540	24	12	6	130	2	3.07
Ben Vanderklok	15	683	6	4	0	42	0	3.69

BELLEVILLE BULLS

SCORING

	Games	G	A	Pts.	PIM
Jonathan Cheechoo	66	45	46	91	102
Justin Papineau	60	40	36	76	52
Branko Radivojevic	59	23	49	72	86
Randy Rowe	67	25	39	64	24
Chris Stanley	68	25	39	64	14
Kevin Baker	60	28	31	59	90
Kyle Wellwood	65	14	37	51	14
Michael Jacobsen	68	9	40	49	18
Mark Chaplin	51	18	28	46	24
Mike Renzi	60	19	21	40	58
Nathan Robinson	61	19	18	37	45
Branislav Mezei	58	7	21	28	99
Kris Newbury	34	6	18	24	72
David Cornacchia	34	3	20	23	45
Josh Sands	52	11	8	19	23
Malcolm Hutt	68	2	13	15	48
Adam Paiement	48	6	8	14	28
Rick Bertran	62	1	13	14	91
Nick Policelli	64	5	8	13	198
Peter Campbell	9	4	4	8	4
Kelly Paddon	34	4	4	8	28
Cody McCormick	45	3	4	7	42
Tyler Longo	2	1	1	2	0
Jamie Lovell	22	1	1	2	19
Luc Bergeron (goalie)	1	0	0	0	0
David Silverstone	1	0	0	0	0
Justin Grady	5	0	0	0	6
Corey Batten (goalie)	30	0	0	0	4
Cory Campbell (goalie)	43	0	0	0	12

GOALTENDING

	Gms.	Min.	W	L	T	G	SO	Avg.
Corey Batten	30	1615	20	8	0	81	2	3.01
Cory Campbell	43	2458	24	14	2	138	0	3.37
Luc Bergeron	1	22	0	0	0	3	0	8.18

BRAMPTON BATTALION

SCORING

	Games	G	A	Pts.	PIM
Raffi Torres	68	43	48	91	40
Jeff Bateman	64	23	41	64	62
Lukas Havel	55	21	29	50	26
Rostislav Klesla	67	16	29	45	174
Aaron VanLeusen	57	17	20	37	24
Kurt MacSweyn	51	18	15	33	27
Scott Thompson	57	15	17	32	16
Jason Maleyko	63	5	27	32	108
Jay McClement	63	13	16	29	34
Richard Kearns	56	12	11	23	27
Chris Rowan	64	4	16	20	60
Jay Harrison	68	2	18	20	139
Brad Woods	68	5	11	16	30
Mike Rice	52	5	9	14	51
Matt Grennier	58	7	3	10	23

	Games	G	A	Pts.	PIM
Tyler Hanchuck	58	0	8	8	81
Matt Reynolds	52	1	6	7	43
Nathan Herrington	28	1	4	5	11
Chris Cook	30	3	1	4	15
Blair McLaughlin	28	1	2	3	9
Paul Flache	54	1	0	1	59
Tyler Dukelow	30	0	1	1	2
Cam McLaughlin	32	0	1	1	36
David Chant (goalie)	51	0	1	1	2
Todd Meehan	1	0	0	0	0
Scott Della Vedova (goalie)	27	0	0	0	0

GOALTENDING

	Gms.	Min.	W	L	T	G	SO	Avg.
David Chant	51	2791	19	17	7	140	1	3.01
Scott Della Vedova	27	1353	6	15	4	80	2	3.55

ERIE OTTERS

SCORING

	Games	G	A	Pts.	PIM
Brad Boyes	68	36	46	82	38
Shane Nash	63	29	43	72	33
Jason Baird	53	26	31	57	103
Michael Rupp	58	32	21	53	134
Nikita Alexeev	64	24	29	53	42
Peter Campbell	55	17	31	48	54
Arvid Rekis	57	6	29	35	93
Brad Yeo	65	12	16	28	162
Darren McMillan	66	5	22	27	41
Carlo Colaiacovo	52	4	18	22	12
Jourdan Lagace	66	4	13	17	80
Sean Dixon	68	5	11	16	56
Troy Ilijow	59	5	8	13	45
Scott Rozendal	60	5	6	11	75
Scott Neil	53	3	7	10	22
Mike Nelson	27	4	5	9	18
Riley Moher	67	4	4	8	104
Jarret Richburg	63	1	5	6	13
Derek McNamara	6	2	3	5	6
J.F. Perras (goalie)	53	0	5	5	8
Kenny Jung	52	0	2	2	12
Julius Halfkenny	12	0	1	1	9
Ryan Lee	1	0	0	0	0
Steve Nobili	1	0	0	0	2
Wade Clubb	3	0	0	0	4
Corey Batten (goalie)	6	0	0	0	4
Jim McGillivray	6	0	0	0	2
John Cilladi	12	0	0	0	17
Adam Munroe (goalie)	22	0	0	0	0
Marc Higgenbotham	47	0	0	0	20

GOALTENDING

	Gms.	Min.	W	L	T	G	SO	Avg.
Adam Munroe	22	948	8	7	1	48	1	3.04
J.F. Perras	53	2860	22	22	3	152	6	3.19
Corey Batten	6	299	3	2	0	22	0	4.41

GUELPH STORM

SCORING

	Games	G	A	Pts.	PIM
Kevin Mitchell	68	19	58	77	94
Joe Gerbe	68	28	45	73	25
Eric Beaudoin	68	38	34	72	126
Kent McDonell	56	35	35	70	100
Lindsay Plunkett	66	32	34	66	68
Brent Kelly	68	23	42	65	22
Kevin Dallman	67	13	46	59	38
Charlie Stephens	56	16	34	50	87
Morgan McCormick	59	8	21	29	105
Matthew House	48	8	12	20	33
Bohuslav Subr	64	4	10	14	77
Jon Hedberg	68	3	11	14	68

	Games	G	A	Pts.	PIM
Aran Myers	45	3	6	9	19
Peter Flache	56	3	6	9	40
Ian Forbes	62	2	7	9	143
Andrew Brown	59	5	3	8	17
Radek Matalik	57	1	4	5	44
Manny Malhotra	5	2	2	4	4
Colt King	53	2	2	4	41
Chris Madden (goalie)	40	0	4	4	2
Derek Hennessey	26	3	0	3	11
Nick Jones	20	1	2	3	75
Nathan Herrington	6	1	1	2	4
Bob Crummer	1	0	1	1	4
Matt Rock	23	0	1	1	14
Craig Andersson (goalie)	38	0	1	1	6
Francois Jolette	4	0	0	0	12
Jon Peters	39	0	0	0	26

GOALTENDING

	Gms.	Min.	W	L	T	G	SO	Avg.
Craig Andersson	38	1955	12	17	2	117	0	3.59
Chris Madden	40	2146	17	18	2	130	2	3.63

KINGSTON FRONTENACS

SCORING

	Games	G	A	Pts.	PIM
Michael Zigomanis	59	40	54	94	49
Jonathan Schill	65	39	48	87	79
Sean Avery	55	28	56	84	215
Andrew Ianiero	67	23	33	56	42
Jason Polera	49	31	23	54	51
Tomas Skvaridlo	66	19	25	44	14
Travis Lisabeth	62	20	23	43	40
Brett Clouthier	65	13	26	39	266
Nathan Tennant	68	5	23	28	113
Cory Stillman	61	13	10	23	27
Darryl Knight	33	5	13	18	6
Jean-Francois Seguin	58	4	14	18	36
Doug MacIver	60	3	10	13	132
Eric Braff	66	1	10	11	38
Sean Griffin	40	0	11	11	93
Brad Horan	55	3	7	10	22
Shaun Peet	36	1	9	10	16
Darryl Thomson	45	5	3	8	42
Nathan Herrington	31	2	5	7	16
Matt Junkins	61	1	5	6	12
Chris Cook	27	1	2	3	13
Andrew Raycroft (goalie)	61	0	3	3	12
Ian Turner	18	0	2	2	8
Morgan McCormick	8	1	0	1	13
Ryan Rivard	8	0	1	1	9
Mike Smith (goalie)	15	0	1	1	2
Mike Konieczny	34	0	1	1	6
Jamie Young	1	0	0	0	0
Chad Lynch (goalie)	2	0	0	0	0
Colin Scotland	6	0	0	0	5

GOALTENDING

	Gms.	Min.	W	L	T	G	SO	Avg.
Andrew Raycroft	61	3340	33	20	5	191	0	3.43
Mike Smith	15	666	4	5	0	42	0	3.78
Chad Lynch	2	95	1	0	0	6	0	3.79

KITCHENER RANGERS

SCORING

	Games	G	A	Pts.	PIM
Derek Roy	66	34	53	87	44
Ryan Held	64	31	43	74	62
Allan Rourke	67	31	43	74	57
Mike Wehrstedt	66	14	30	44	29
Serge Payer	44	10	26	36	53
John Dunphy	46	18	13	31	10
Brandon Merli	38	15	10	25	51

	Games	G	A	Pts.	PIM
Matt Armstrong	67	11	14	25	71
Ruslan Akhmadulin	58	12	12	24	33
Chris Brannen	30	5	15	20	21
Andrew Peters	42	6	13	19	95
Jimmy Gagnon	66	10	7	17	155
Ryan Milanovic	32	9	8	17	90
Steve Eminger	50	2	14	16	74
Maxim Sharifijanov	53	2	11	13	6
Mike Mazzuca	60	6	3	9	134
Andrew Yardy	38	2	6	8	41
Sal Lettieri	31	0	8	8	28
Bobby Naylor	47	3	2	5	48
Mike Amodeo	46	2	3	5	84
Travis Lisabeth	5	2	2	4	17
Bill Browne	30	1	3	4	48
John Eminger	46	0	4	4	30
Brent Labre	31	1	2	3	39
Mike Vaillaincourt	5	2	0	2	2
Chad Staats	28	0	2	2	22
Reg Bourcier (goalie)	59	0	2	2	18
Barry Graham	8	0	1	1	33
Sean McMorrow	31	0	1	1	67
Trevor Hitchings	8	0	0	0	4
Wyatt McTavish	9	0	0	0	0
Scott Dickie (goalie)	16	0	0	0	6

GOALTENDING

	Gms.	Min.	W	L	T	G	SO	Avg.
Reg Bourcier	59	3400	24	27	6	202	3	3.56
Scott Dickie	16	726	4	7	0	48	0	3.97

LONDON KNIGHTS

SCORING

	Games	G	A	Pts.	PIM
Chris Kelly	63	29	43	72	57
Brett Gibson	66	31	38	69	103
Joel Scherban	68	16	38	54	6
Krys Barch	56	23	26	49	78
John Erskine	58	12	31	43	177
Adam Saffer	66	18	15	33	18
Mike Stathopulos	65	11	15	26	6
Dan Jancevski	59	8	15	23	138
Dan Sullivan	53	9	7	16	139
D.J. Maracle	47	3	12	15	124
Justin Olden	40	4	7	11	31
Matthew Albiani	63	3	8	11	12
Aaron Lobb	58	2	9	11	23
Max Linnik	55	0	10	10	65
Tim Zafiris	24	5	4	9	38
Tomas Gron	20	3	6	9	0
Brett Angel	62	3	5	8	119
Bobby Turner	68	1	6	7	126
Chris Osborne	57	2	4	6	22
Tyler Durham	29	1	4	5	31
Jason Harshaw	51	1	2	3	18
Ian Turner	21	1	1	2	6
Steven Rawski	7	0	2	2	0
Aaron Molnar (goalie)	28	0	1	1	0
Bill Byers	2	0	0	0	0
Ivan Curic	2	0	0	0	0
Jeff Kaufman	2	0	0	0	0
Cody Spicer (goalie)	2	0	0	0	0
Bill Ruggiero (goalie)	3	0	0	0	4
Trevor Luck	31	0	0	0	6
Gene Chiarello (goalie)	50	0	0	0	8

GOALTENDING

	Gms.	Min.	W	L	T	G	SO	Avg.
Gene Chiarello	50	2990	17	26	6	157	2	3.15
Aaron Molnar	17	888	4	10	1	61	0	4.12
Cody Spicer	2	67	1	0	0	6	0	5.37
Bill Ruggiero	3	180	0	3	0	21	0	7.00

MAJOR JUNIOR LEAGUES   OHL

MISSISSAUGA ICEDOGS

SCORING

	Games	G	A	Pts.	PIM
Chad Wiseman	68	23	45	68	53
Jason Spezza	52	24	37	61	33
Lou Dickenson	66	21	25	46	46
Julian Smith	46	14	16	30	6
Jason Goldenberg	50	12	13	25	25
Scott Page	47	15	9	24	166
Brian McGrattan	42	9	13	22	166
Chris Thaler	63	10	10	20	32
Omar Ennaffati	52	3	16	19	109
Fraser Clair	64	3	10	13	39
Darryl Knight	13	2	9	11	2
Brett Ormond	39	3	7	10	24
B.J. Ketcheson	62	3	7	10	84
Darrell Cowen	46	6	3	9	8
Matt Coughlin	67	1	8	9	163
Phil Knapp	41	1	7	8	26
Andrew Yardy	24	1	6	7	17
Adam Solnik	54	1	6	7	19
Andrew Davis	51	2	4	6	50
Nathan Kalverda	36	1	4	5	41
Sebastien Savage	8	0	5	5	8
Greg McCauley	19	2	2	4	4
Marcus Smith	15	1	2	3	0
John Jarram	56	1	2	3	70
Michael Mole (goalie)	37	0	3	3	2
David Dalliday	51	0	3	3	21
Blake Orr	28	1	1	2	14
Nick Foley (goalie)	39	0	2	2	4
Nick Jones	3	0	1	1	15
Ivan Curic	2	0	0	0	0
Sebastian Harts	3	0	0	0	0
Mark Jerant	3	0	0	0	0
Jesse MacLeish	8	0	0	0	0
Marc Davison	9	0	0	0	0

GOALTENDING

	Gms.	Min.	W	L	T	G	SO	Avg.
Nick Foley	39	2085	4	30	1	169	0	4.86
Michael Mole	37	2007	5	28	0	173	0	5.17

NORTH BAY CENTENNIALS

SCORING

	Games	G	A	Pts.	PIM
Jonas Andersson	67	31	36	67	27
Scott Cameron	49	26	28	54	13
Mike Cirillo	64	25	28	53	206
Konrad McKay	58	20	33	53	179
Samu Isosalo	48	17	25	42	26
Derrell Upton	46	13	27	40	12
Kyle Werner	63	20	16	36	75
Peter Reynolds	61	3	29	32	53
Chris Eade	58	5	25	30	64
Chris Thorburn	56	12	8	20	33
Ryan Armstrong	68	9	11	20	51
John Dean	55	8	8	16	61
Steve Chabbert	65	5	7	12	103
Rob Davison	67	4	6	10	194
Lorne Misita	19	2	6	8	16
Robert Hillier	10	3	4	7	2
Oak Hewer	17	2	4	6	11
Dave Csumrik	17	2	3	5	4
Peter Veltman	64	2	3	5	56
George Halkidis	66	2	3	5	15
Brad Walford	42	1	3	4	17
Josh Legge	28	0	4	4	29
Matt Bacon	64	2	1	3	51
Brad Pierce	29	0	2	2	22
David Culham	1	0	0	0	0
Nevin Hamilton	1	0	0	0	0

	Games	G	A	Pts.	PIM
Mathieu Shank	1	0	0	0	0
Matt Sikora	1	0	0	0	0
Scott Wray	1	0	0	0	0
Brett Angel	2	0	0	0	4
Andrew Penner (goalie)	22	0	0	0	0
Alex Auld (goalie)	55	0	0	0	0

GOALTENDING

	Gms.	Min.	W	L	T	G	SO	Avg.
Alex Auld	55	3047	21	26	6	167	2	3.29
Andrew Penner	22	1070	3	12	0	79	0	4.43

OSHAWA GENERALS

SCORING

	Games	G	A	Pts.	PIM
Brent Gauvreau	59	34	53	87	74
Vladimir Repnev	62	30	48	78	20
Brad Ralph	56	28	35	63	68
Brian Passmore	58	22	36	58	98
John Kozoriz	64	23	33	56	57
Ilja Demidov	62	11	37	48	105
Greg Willers	43	10	26	36	36
Brandon Cullen	52	13	18	31	125
Stacey Britstone	55	11	12	23	74
Shane Fryia	35	12	10	22	71
Jonah Leroux	66	4	11	15	51
Nick Lees	61	8	6	14	18
Derrell Upton	16	5	8	13	0
Pat Montgomery	62	5	5	10	90
Richard Spence	57	2	7	9	132
T.J. Reynolds	59	1	6	7	115
Ian Courville	14	3	3	6	13
Ryan Fraser	52	2	2	4	77
Adam Walsh	11	1	3	4	4
Neill Posillico	51	2	0	2	116
Bryan Allen	3	0	2	2	12
Mike Rusenstrom	60	0	2	2	87
Scott Ransom	1	0	1	1	0
Tyler Durham	15	0	1	1	16
Derek Dolson (goalie)	40	0	1	1	0
Andrew Archer	47	0	1	1	24
Alain Chevrier	51	0	1	1	28
Kevin Rainey (goalie)	1	0	0	0	0
Aaron Bailie	2	0	0	0	2
Rob Howes	2	0	0	0	0
Chris Alarie	4	0	0	0	0
Chris Moher	4	0	0	0	0
Jens Dubreuil	7	0	0	0	12
Barry Graham	14	0	0	0	32
T.J. Aceti (goalie)	36	0	0	0	17

GOALTENDING

	Gms.	Min.	W	L	T	G	SO	Avg.
Derek Dolson	40	2259	19	18	2	111	2	2.95
T.J. Aceti	36	1823	13	14	2	106	2	3.49
Kevin Rainey	1	30	0	0	3	0	0	6.00

OTTAWA 67'S

SCORING

	Games	G	A	Pts.	PIM
Dan Tessier	55	39	45	84	66
Mark Bell	48	34	38	72	95
Joe Talbot	68	36	33	69	37
Jonathan Zion	66	7	52	59	16
Lance Galbraith	62	25	25	50	193
Miguel Delisle	54	20	29	49	73
Luke Sellars	56	8	34	42	147
Kevin Malcolm	54	18	22	40	120
Ian Jacobs	59	13	26	39	56
Randy Davidson	58	15	19	34	8
Brendan Bell	48	1	32	33	34
Josh Tataryn	65	12	8	20	10

	Games	G	A	Pts.	PIM
Adam Chapman	61	10	9	19	12
Zenon Konopka	59	8	11	19	107
Vince Grant	18	5	14	19	4
Jeremy Van Hoof	66	4	14	18	71
Matt Zultek	28	9	6	15	34
Russ Moyer	65	3	10	13	59
Marc Lefebvre	61	1	7	8	21
Chris Cava	36	0	8	8	100
Kevin Holdridge	30	0	7	7	34
Seamus Kotyk (goalie)	26	0	4	4	2
Mike Gresdal	26	1	2	3	9
Franz Fritzmeier	8	0	2	2	2
Mark Boisvert	3	0	1	1	0
Cody Glasper	7	0	0	0	6
Mike James	10	0	0	0	11
Corey Sabourin	23	0	0	0	23
Levente Szuper (goalie)	53	0	0	0	0

GOALTENDING

	Gms.	Min.	W	L	T	G	SO	Avg.
Levente Szuper	53	2862	31	15	2	122	5	2.56
Seamus Kotyk	26	1241	12	6	2	65	1	3.14

OWEN SOUND PLATERS

SCORING

	Games	G	A	Pts.	PIM
Wes Goldie	68	40	35	75	49
Bryan Kazarian	68	22	38	60	87
Derek Campbell	59	18	35	53	122
Kyle McAllister	48	24	28	52	28
Joel Ward	63	23	20	43	51
Greg Jacina	66	12	29	41	62
Daniel Sisca	68	22	18	40	36
Agris Saviels	65	7	25	32	56
Mike Dombkiewicz	41	7	20	27	32
Chris Minard	38	12	14	26	39
Nick Vukovic	67	5	18	23	71
Kenny Corupe	24	9	13	22	30
Brent Sullivan	64	9	12	21	79
Adam Campbell	53	1	16	17	207
Shawn Snider	45	8	7	15	46
Bill Zalba	51	4	8	12	46
Alexei Salashenko	28	6	5	11	8
Mike Barrett	60	1	9	10	101
Kris Fraser	43	2	5	7	2
Trevor Blanchard	61	2	5	7	78
Dave Stephenson	28	2	4	6	32
Chris Hopiavuori	28	0	3	3	16
Matt Rock	35	0	3	3	29
Curtis Sanford (goalie)	53	0	3	3	6
D.J. Maracle	13	1	1	2	35
Juri Golicic	2	0	1	1	2
Randy Davidson	6	0	1	1	0
Michael Lymer	11	0	1	1	10
Vladimir Chernenko	1	0	0	0	9
Tim Hamel	2	0	0	0	0
Jason Kowalski	10	0	0	0	5
Corey Roberts (goalie)	20	0	0	0	7

GOALTENDING

	Gms.	Min.	W	L	T	G	SO	Avg.
Curtis Sanford	53	3124	18	28	6	198	1	3.80
Corey Roberts	20	1000	3	13	0	88	0	5.28

PETERBOROUGH PETES

SCORING

	Games	G	A	Pts.	PIM
Jason Williams	66	36	37	73	64
Sergei Kuznetzov	68	33	32	65	54
Preston Mizzi	67	27	35	62	80
Steve Montador	64	14	42	56	97
Jamie Chamberlain	65	12	29	41	53
Adam Dewan	56	17	20	37	152
Marcel Rodman	61	17	20	37	16

	Games	G	A	Pts.	PIM
John Brioux	64	14	22	36	16
Brad Self	68	18	16	34	18
Brandon Verner	57	4	28	32	40
Bob Crummer	50	16	13	29	134
Kurtis Foster	68	6	18	24	116
Ryan Ramsay	63	8	13	21	65
Matt Carkner	62	3	13	16	177
Dustin Wood	66	2	13	15	29
Jon Howse	50	5	7	12	21
Matt Herneisen	21	4	4	8	21
Darcy Morris	34	3	5	8	46
Josh Chambers	42	1	6	7	20
T.J. Eason	60	1	2	3	66
Jesse MacLeish	10	1	1	2	9
Mark Phibbs	6	0	2	2	13
Stephen Hoar	37	0	2	2	41
Joey MacDonald (goalie)	48	0	2	2	4
Mike Pickard (goalie)	28	0	1	1	4
David Currie (goalie)	2	0	0	0	0
A.J. Howe	2	0	0	0	0
Mike Clarke	14	0	0	0	2

GOALTENDING

	Gms.	Min.	W	L	T	G	SO	Avg.
Joey MacDonald	48	2641	20	15	6	125	2	2.84
Mike Pickard	28	1452	14	10	1	83	0	3.43
David Currie	2	23	0	2	0	5	0	13.04

PLYMOUTH WHALERS

SCORING

	Games	G	A	Pts.	PIM
Justin Williams	68	37	46	83	46
Damian Surma	66	34	44	78	114
Stephen Weiss	64	24	42	66	35
Shaun Fisher	59	17	49	66	57
Tomas Kurka	64	36	28	64	37
Randy Fitzgerald	50	18	24	42	89
Eric Gooldy	53	14	28	42	128
Kristopher Vernarsky	64	16	22	38	63
Steven Morris	65	13	18	31	16
Jamie Lalonde	35	10	11	21	115
Rob McBride	58	8	12	20	31
Kevin Holdridge	31	4	12	16	36
Jared Newman	50	1	15	16	123
Libor Ustrnul	68	0	15	15	208
George Nistas	26	5	9	14	18
Cole Jarrett	57	3	7	10	47
Jon Billy	33	4	5	9	5
Andre Robichaud	58	2	7	9	48
Nate Kiser	63	3	5	8	102
Julian Smith	8	4	2	6	4
Bryan Thompson	29	1	5	6	28
James Ramsay	53	2	3	5	164
Scott Wray	8	0	5	5	11
Chris Cava	29	0	3	3	71
Danny Armstrong	4	0	1	1	4
Rob Zepp (goalie)	53	0	1	1	0
Kristopher Purdy	7	0	0	0	6
Bill Ruggiero (goalie)	10	0	0	0	0
Aaron Molnar (goalie)	11	0	0	0	0
Pete Barker	20	0	0	0	9

GOALTENDING

	Gms.	Min.	W	L	T	G	SO	Avg.
Bill Ruggiero	10	524	6	2	0	17	2	1.95
Rob Zepp	53	3005	36	11	3	119	3	2.38
Aaron Molnar	11	576	3	6	1	31	0	3.23

SARNIA STING

SCORING

	Games	G	A	Pts.	PIM
Jeff Heerema	67	36	41	77	62
Maxim Rybin	66	29	27	56	47

	Games	G	A	Pts.	PIM
Alexander Buturlin	57	20	27	47	46
Eric Himelfarb	62	14	33	47	26
Mike Van Ryn	61	6	35	41	34
Robb Palahnuk	55	16	16	32	65
Dusty Jamieson	50	15	17	32	15
Ryan Hare	68	12	20	32	28
Ryan VanBuskirk	45	8	20	28	62
Andy Burnham	57	11	11	22	148
Jamie Johnson	61	6	14	20	24
Chris Berti	62	8	11	19	131
Dan Watson	68	1	15	16	40
Scott Heffernan	55	5	10	15	24
Kris Newbury	27	6	8	14	44
David Cornacchia	35	1	11	12	33
Tyler Coleman	59	4	5	9	24
Luc Chaisson	36	3	6	9	14
Corey Brekelmans	65	3	4	7	42
Kelly Paddon	25	2	5	7	24
Jason Penner	56	1	4	5	33
Sal Lettieri	21	2	2	4	10
Greg Hewitt (goalie)	52	0	4	4	2
Travis Albers	11	1	2	3	18
Ryan Chapman	7	1	0	1	2
Sean McMorrow	31	0	1	1	75
Doug MacIver	2	0	0	0	5
Steve Kennedy	5	0	0	0	0
Tim Sinasac	5	0	0	0	20
Andrew Sim (goalie)	22	0	0	0	4

GOALTENDING

	Gms.	Min.	W	L	T	G	SO	Avg.
Greg Hewitt	52	3062	24	20	7	129	3	2.53
Andrew Sim	22	1064	9	7	1	52	0	2.93

SAULT STE. MARIE GREYHOUNDS

SCORING

	Games	G	A	Pts.	PIM
Ryan Jardine	65	43	34	77	58
Josef Vasicek	54	26	46	72	49
Cory Pecker	65	33	36	69	38
Chad Spurr	61	18	39	57	97
John Osborne	49	19	32	51	41
Trevor Daley	54	16	30	46	77
Cleon Smith	62	14	27	41	30
Daniel Passero	52	13	25	38	58
Ryan Healy	49	19	12	31	56
Jeff Richards	49	11	20	31	38
Malcolm McMillan	61	4	22	26	181
Paul Ballantyne	58	4	15	19	60
Tim Zafiris	23	8	9	17	46
Brent Theobald	64	6	11	17	41
Rob Chapman	60	7	8	15	61
Vaclav Zavoral	57	3	11	14	89
Derek Fox	58	3	10	13	64
Josh Bennett	31	5	7	12	72
Nick Jones	27	6	3	9	115
Mike Nelson	30	5	4	9	17
Ryan Milanovic	23	4	5	9	29
Jake Gibson	64	2	7	9	111
Bill Browne	36	1	4	5	67
Shawn Snider	14	0	4	4	6
Darren Strilchuk	47	0	3	3	93
Jason Flick (goalie)	54	0	2	2	6
Ben Brown	1	0	0	0	0
Chris McLean	1	0	0	0	0
Jeff Kugel	2	0	0	0	0
Jeremy Elliott (goalie)	3	0	0	0	0
Jeremy Day (goalie)	4	0	0	0	0
Scott Hazen	4	0	0	0	0
Ray Emery (goalie)	16	0	0	0	0

GOALTENDING

	Gms.	Min.	W	L	T	G	SO	Avg.
Jeremy Elliott	3	153	1	0	1	5	0	1.96
Jeremy Day	4	138	1	0	1	5	0	2.17
Ray Emery	16	716	9	3	0	36	1	3.02
Jason Flick	54	3118	26	22	4	171	0	3.29

SUDBURY WOLVES

SCORING

	Games	G	A	Pts.	PIM
Norm Milley	68	52	60	112	47
Jason Jaspers	68	46	61	107	107
Taylor Pyatt	68	40	49	89	98
Brad Morgan	65	9	50	59	53
Derek MacKenzie	68	24	33	57	110
Alexei Semenov	65	9	35	44	135
Dennis Wideman	63	10	26	36	64
Kip Brennan	55	16	16	32	228
Warren Hefford	65	9	20	29	44
Tom Kotsopoulos	59	12	16	28	94
Sebastien Savage	39	7	14	21	55
Mike Vaillaincourt	58	7	12	19	46
Abe Herbst	45	1	18	19	24
Steven Ellis	62	6	6	12	13
Kyle Dafoe	64	1	11	12	201
Jerry Connell	38	5	5	10	58
Brian McGrattan	25	2	8	10	79
Drew Kivell	64	1	7	8	29
Alexei Salashenko	31	2	4	6	29
R.A. Mobile	45	1	2	3	17
Scott Smith	17	1	0	1	2
Ryan Philips	34	1	0	1	43
Corey Sabourin	28	0	1	1	17
Mike Gorman (goalie)	49	0	1	1	0
Kevin Beaumont	1	0	0	0	0
Sebastien Leplante (goalie)	2	0	0	0	0
Victor Spadafora	2	0	0	0	0
Matt Best	3	0	0	0	0
Troy Kahler	4	0	0	0	12
Kevin Mota	7	0	0	0	10
Vladimir Chernenko	12	0	0	0	4
Miguel Beaudry (goalie)	25	0	0	0	2

GOALTENDING

	Gms.	Min.	W	L	T	G	SO	Avg.
Mike Gorman	49	2755	27	16	4	137	2	2.98
Miguel Beaudry	25	1272	12	7	1	74	1	3.49
Sebastien Leplante	2	80	0	1	0	5	0	3.75

TORONTO ST. MICHAEL'S MAJORS

SCORING

	Games	G	A	Pts.	PIM
Keith Delaney	67	24	38	62	60
Ryan Walsh	68	21	34	55	66
Darryl Bootland	65	24	30	54	166
Kenny Corupe	40	22	24	46	47
Mark Popovic	68	11	29	40	68
Matt Ellis	59	15	20	35	20
Adam DeLeeuw	45	11	19	30	107
Matt Bannan	66	7	20	27	71
Jeffrey Doyle	65	8	18	26	89
Chad Woollard	26	13	10	23	31
Chris Minard	28	5	14	19	6
Chris Boucher	67	3	14	17	154
Dave Csumrik	31	7	6	13	42
Michael Gough	63	7	5	12	95
Greg Mizzi	49	5	7	12	128
Lorne Misita	21	6	4	10	33
Brian Simpson	44	3	6	9	131
George Nistas	22	1	8	9	8
Tyler Cook	48	1	8	9	58

MAJOR JUNIOR LEAGUES OHL

	Games	G	A	Pts.	PIM
Brad Pierce	40	3	5	8	47
Philippe Lakos	56	1	7	8	107
Mike Sellan	64	2	2	4	55
Steve Farquharson	59	2	1	3	163
Michal Kolarik	45	1	1	2	46
Kyle McAllister	3	0	2	2	4
Peter Budaj (goalie)	34	0	2	2	6
Dwayne Bateman (goalie)	47	0	1	1	10
Ryan Delaney	1	0	0	0	0
Ryan Rasmussen	1	0	0	0	0
Brent Mulder	2	0	0	0	7
Rory Glaves	6	0	0	0	0

GOALTENDING

	Gms.	Min.	W	L	T	G	SO	Avg.
Dwayne Bateman	47	2425	12	30	1	160	0	3.96
Peter Budaj	34	1676	6	18	1	112	1	4.01

WINDSOR SPITFIRES

SCORING

	Games	G	A	Pts.	PIM
Steve Ott	66	23	39	62	131
Shawn Mather	64	24	31	55	24
Robin Boucher	68	16	29	45	32
Pavel Shtefan	54	17	23	40	10
Ryan Courtney	65	10	22	32	44
Joey Sewell	63	13	18	31	137

	Games	G	A	Pts.	PIM
Luc Rioux	64	12	19	31	30
Jeff Martin	38	15	15	30	23
Patrick Finnegan	54	8	21	29	74
Craig Kennedy	45	10	14	24	27
Vince Grant	30	10	12	22	10
Mark Ridout	57	7	15	22	101
Kyle Chapman	68	7	13	20	144
Blair Stayzer	44	14	5	19	100
Tim Gleason	55	5	13	18	101
Fedor Fedorov	60	7	10	17	115
Craig Mahon	64	1	10	11	145
Curtis Watson	60	3	7	10	69
Jason Polera	16	3	3	6	10
Frank Sinacori	32	2	4	6	17
Dan Growden	61	2	4	6	41
Steven Rawski	49	0	6	6	18
Ivan Rachunek	15	2	2	4	21
Jason Goldenberg	5	1	2	3	2
Max Linnik	6	1	0	1	21
Mike Leighton	42	0	1	1	6
Matt Livingston	4	0	0	0	0
Mike James	5	0	0	0	5
Ryan Aschaber	36	0	0	0	6

GOALTENDING

	Gms.	Min.	W	L	T	G	SO	Avg.
Mike Leighton	42	2272	17	17	2	118	1	3.12
Ryan Aschaber	36	1826	18	14	0	104	1	3.42

PLAYERS WITH TWO OR MORE TEAMS

SCORING

	Games	G	A	Pts.	PIM
Brett Angel, North Bay	2	0	0	0	4
Brett Angel, London	62	3	5	8	119
Totals	64	3	5	8	123
Corey Batten, Erie (g)	6	0	0	0	4
Corey Batten, Belleville (g)	30	0	0	0	4
Totals	36	0	0	0	8
Bill Browne, Sault Ste. Marie	36	1	4	5	67
Bill Browne, Kitchener	30	1	3	4	48
Totals	66	2	7	9	115
Scott Cameron, Barrie	21	2	4	6	19
Scott Cameron, North Bay	49	26	28	54	13
Totals	70	28	32	60	32
Peter Campbell, Belleville	9	4	4	8	4
Peter Campbell, Erie	55	17	31	48	54
Totals	64	21	35	56	58
Chris Cava, Ottawa	36	0	8	8	100
Chris Cava, Plymouth	29	0	3	3	71
Totals	65	0	11	11	171
Vladimir Chernenko, Barrie	19	0	0	0	4
Vladimir Chernenko, O. Sound	1	0	0	0	9
Vladimir Chernenko, Sudbury	12	0	0	0	4
Totals	32	0	0	0	17
Jerry Connell, Barrie	20	0	4	4	26
Jerry Connell, Sudbury	38	5	5	10	58
Totals	58	5	9	14	84
Chris Cook, Brampton	30	3	1	4	15
Chris Cook, Kingston	27	1	2	3	13
Totals	57	4	3	7	28
David Cornacchia, Sarnia	35	1	11	12	33
David Cornacchia, Belleville	34	3	20	23	45
Totals	69	4	31	35	78
Kenny Corupe, Toronto	40	22	24	46	47
Kenny Corupe, Owen Sound	24	9	13	22	30
Totals	64	31	37	68	77
Bob Crummer, Guelph	1	0	1	1	4
Bob Crummer, Peterborough	50	16	13	29	134
Totals	51	16	14	30	138
Dave Csumrik, North Bay	17	2	3	5	4
Dave Csumrik, Toronto	31	7	6	13	42
Totals	48	9	9	18	46

	Games	G	A	Pts.	PIM
Ivan Curic, Mississauga	2	0	0	0	0
Ivan Curic, London	2	0	0	0	0
Totals	4	0	0	0	0
Randy Davidson, Owen Sound	6	0	1	1	0
Randy Davidson, Ottawa	58	15	19	34	8
Totals	64	15	20	35	8
Tyler Durham, London	29	1	4	5	31
Tyler Durham, Oshawa	15	0	1	1	16
Totals	44	1	5	6	47
Jason Goldenberg, Windsor	5	1	2	3	2
Jason Goldenberg, Mississauga	50	12	13	25	25
Totals	55	13	15	28	27
Barry Graham, Kitchener	8	0	1	1	33
Barry Graham, Oshawa	14	0	0	0	32
Totals	22	0	1	1	65
Vince Grant, Ottawa	18	5	14	19	4
Vince Grant, Windsor	30	10	12	22	10
Totals	48	15	26	41	14
Nathan Herrington, Guelph	6	1	1	2	4
Nathan Herrington, Kingston	31	2	5	7	16
Nathan Herrington, Brampton	28	1	4	5	11
Totals	65	4	10	14	31
Kevin Holdridge, Plymouth	31	4	12	16	36
Kevin Holdridge, Ottawa	30	0	7	7	34
Totals	61	4	19	23	70
Mike James, Ottawa	10	0	0	0	11
Mike James, Windsor	5	0	0	0	5
Totals	15	0	0	0	16
Nick Jones, Mississauga	3	0	1	1	15
Nick Jones, Guelph	20	1	2	3	75
Nick Jones, Sault Ste. Marie	27	6	3	9	115
Totals	50	7	6	13	205
Darryl Knight, Mississauga	13	2	9	11	2
Darryl Knight, Kingston	33	5	13	18	6
Totals	46	7	22	29	8
Sal Lettieri, Kitchener	31	0	8	8	28
Sal Lettieri, Sarnia	21	2	2	4	10
Totals	52	2	10	12	38
Max Linnik, Windsor	6	1	0	1	21
Max Linnik, London	55	0	10	10	65
Totals	61	1	10	11	86

MAJOR JUNIOR LEAGUES OHL

	Games	G	A	Pts.	PIM
Travis Lisabeth, Kitchener.........	5	2	2	4	17
Travis Lisabeth, Kingston	62	20	23	43	40
Totals	67	22	25	47	57
Doug MacIver, Sarnia	2	0	0	0	5
Doug MacIver, Kingston	60	3	10	13	132
Totals	62	3	10	13	137
Jesse MacLeish, Peterborough .	10	1	1	2	9
Jesse MacLeish, Mississauga ...	8	0	0	0	0
Totals	18	1	1	2	9
D.J. Maracle, Owen Sound	13	1	1	2	35
D.J. Maracle, London	47	3	12	15	124
Totals	60	4	13	17	159
Kyle McAllister, Toronto............	3	0	2	2	4
Kyle McAllister, Owen Sound.....	48	24	28	52	28
Totals	51	24	30	54	32
Morgan McCormick, Kingston.....	8	1	0	1	13
Morgan McCormick, Guelph	59	8	21	29	105
Totals	67	9	21	30	118
Brian McGrattan, Sudbury.........	25	2	8	10	79
Brian McGrattan, Mississauga...	42	9	13	22	166
Totals	67	11	21	32	245
Sean McMorrow, Sarnia	31	0	1	1	75
Sean McMorrow, Kitchener	31	0	1	1	67
Totals	62	0	2	2	142
Ryan Milanovic, Kitchener	32	9	8	17	90
Ryan Milanovic, S. Ste. Marie ...	23	4	5	9	29
Totals	55	13	13	26	119
Chris Minard, Owen Sound	38	12	14	26	39
Chris Minard, Toronto...............	28	5	14	19	6
Totals	66	17	28	45	45
Lorne Misita, North Bay............	19	2	6	8	16
Lorne Misita, Toronto...............	21	6	4	10	33
Totals	40	8	10	18	49
Aaron Molnar, Plymouth (g)......	11	0	0	0	0
Aaron Molnar, London (g)........	17	0	1	1	0
Totals	28	0	1	1	0
Mike Nelson, Sault Ste. Marie ...	30	5	4	9	17
Mike Nelson, Erie	27	4	5	9	18
Totals	57	9	9	18	35
Kris Newbury, Belleville	34	6	18	24	72
Kris Newbury, Sarnia................	27	6	8	14	44
Totals	61	12	26	38	116
George Nistas, Toronto.............	22	1	8	9	8
George Nistas, Plymouth...........	26	5	9	14	18
Totals	48	6	17	23	26
Kelly Paddon, Belleville	34	4	4	8	28
Kelly Paddon, Sarnia................	25	2	5	7	24
Totals	59	6	9	15	52
Brad Pierce, Toronto................	40	3	5	8	47
Brad Pierce, North Bay	29	0	2	2	22
Totals	69	3	7	10	69
Jason Polera, Windsor	16	3	3	6	10
Jason Polera, Kingston.............	49	31	23	54	51
Totals	65	34	26	60	61

	Games	G	A	Pts.	PIM
Steven Rawski, London	7	0	2	2	0
Steven Rawski, Windsor............	49	0	6	6	18
Totals	56	0	8	8	18
Matt Rock, Guelph...................	23	0	1	1	14
Matt Rock, Owen Sound...........	35	0	3	3	29
Totals	58	0	4	4	43
Bill Ruggiero, London (g).........	3	0	0	0	4
Bill Ruggiero, Plymouth (g).......	10	0	0	0	0
Totals	13	0	0	0	4
Corey Sabourin, Sudbury	28	0	1	1	17
Corey Sabourin, Ottawa............	23	0	0	0	23
Totals	51	0	1	1	40
Alexei Salashenko, Sudbury	31	2	4	6	29
Alexei Salashenko, O. Sound.....	28	6	5	11	8
Totals	59	8	9	17	37
Sebastien Savage, Mississauga.	8	0	5	5	8
Sebastien Savage, Sudbury	39	7	14	21	55
Totals	47	7	19	26	63
Julian Smith, Plymouth	8	4	2	6	4
Julian Smith, Mississauga.........	46	14	16	30	6
Totals	54	18	18	36	10
Shawn Snider, Sault Ste. Marie .	14	0	4	4	6
Shawn Snider, Owen Sound	45	8	7	15	46
Totals	59	8	11	19	52
Ian Turner, Kingston	18	0	2	2	8
Ian Turner, London	21	1	1	2	6
Totals	39	1	3	4	14
Derrell Upton, Oshawa.............	16	5	8	13	0
Derrell Upton, North Bay	46	13	27	40	12
Totals	62	18	35	53	12
Mike Vaillancourt, Kitchener	5	2	0	2	2
Mike Vaillancourt, Sudbury........	58	7	12	19	46
Totals	63	9	12	21	48
Scott Wray, North Bay	1	0	0	0	0
Scott Wray, Plymouth...............	8	0	5	5	11
Totals	9	0	5	5	11
Andrew Yardy, Kitchener	38	2	6	8	41
Andrew Yardy, Mississauga.......	24	1	6	7	17
Totals	62	3	12	15	58
Tim Zafiris, Sault Ste. Marie	23	8	9	17	46
Tim Zafiris, London	24	5	4	9	38
Totals	47	13	13	26	84

GOALTENDING

	Games	Min.	W	L	T	G	SO	Avg.
Corey Batten, Erie ...	6	299	3	2	0	22	0	4.41
Corey Batten, Bel. ..	30	1615	20	8	0	81	2	3.01
Totals	36	1914	23	10	0	103	2	3.23
Aaron Molnar, Ply. ..	11	576	3	6	1	31	0	3.23
Aaron Molnar, Lon..	17	888	4	10	1	61	0	4.12
Totals	28	1464	7	16	2	92	0	3.77
Bill Ruggiero, Lon. .	3	180	0	3	0	21	0	7.00
Bill Ruggiero, Ply. ..	10	524	6	2	0	17	2	1.95
Totals	13	704	6	5	0	38	2	3.24

2000 J. ROSS ROBERTSON CUP PLAYOFFS
RESULTS

FIRST ROUND

	W	L	Pts.	GF	GA
Barrie............................	4	2	8	12	12
North Bay	2	4	4	12	12

(Barrie won series, 4-2)

	W	L	Pts.	GF	GA
Ottawa...........................	4	1	8	17	12
Oshawa..........................	1	4	2	12	17

(Ottawa won series, 4-1)

	W	L	Pts.	GF	GA
Belleville	4	1	8	22	12
Peterborough	1	4	2	12	22

(Belleville won series, 4-1)

	W	L	Pts.	GF	GA
Sudbury..........................	4	1	8	21	13
Kingston.........................	1	4	2	13	21

(Sudbury won series, 4-1)

	W	L	Pts.	GF	GA
Plymouth.........................	4	2	8	24	15
Guelph...........................	2	4	4	15	24

(Plymouth won series, 4-2)

	W	L	Pts.	GF	GA
Erie................................	4	2	8	19	15
Brampton	2	4	4	15	19

(Erie won series, 4-2)

	W	L	Pts.	GF	GA
Sault Ste. Marie	4	1	8	23	18
Kitchener	1	4	2	18	23

(Sault Ste. Marie won series, 4-1)

	W	L	Pts.	GF	GA
Windsor	4	3	8	20	22
Sarnia	3	4	6	22	20

(Windsor won series, 4-3)

QUARTERFINALS

	W	L	Pts.	GF	GA
Barrie	4	3	8	18	18
Sudbury	3	4	6	18	18

(Barrie won series, 4-3)

	W	L	Pts.	GF	GA
Belleville	4	2	8	24	16
Ottawa	2	4	4	16	24

(Belleville won series, 4-2)

	W	L	Pts.	GF	GA
Plymouth	4	1	8	21	7
Windsor	1	4	2	7	21

(Plymouth won series, 4-1)

	W	L	Pts.	GF	GA
Sault Ste. Marie	4	3	8	25	17
Erie	3	4	6	17	25

(Sault Ste. Marie won series, 4-3)

SEMIFINALS

	W	L	Pts.	GF	GA
Barrie	4	1	8	26	13
Belleville	1	4	2	13	26

(Barrie won series, 4-1)

	W	L	Pts.	GF	GA
Plymouth	4	1	8	13	8
Sault Ste. Marie	1	4	2	8	13

(Plymouth won series, 4-1)

J. ROSS ROBERTSON CUP FINALS

	W	L	Pts.	GF	GA
Barrie	4	3	8	25	21
Plymouth	3	4	6	21	25

(Barrie won series, 4-3)

INDIVIDUAL LEADERS

Goals: Justin Williams, Plymouth (14)
Assists: Shaun Fisher, Plymouth (21)
Points: Justin Williams, Plymouth (30)
Penalty minutes: Mike Jefferson, Barrie (107)
Goaltending average: Ray Emery, Sault Ste. Marie (2.24)
Shutouts: Ray Emery, Sault Ste. Marie (3)

TOP SCORERS

	Games	G	A	Pts.
Justin Williams, Plymouth	23	14	16	30
Michael Henrich, Barrie	25	10	18	28
Stephen Weiss, Plymouth	23	8	18	26
Shaun Fisher, Plymouth	23	4	21	25
Randy Fitzgerald, Plymouth	23	13	10	23
Sheldon Keefe, Barrie	25	10	13	23
Mike Jefferson, Barrie	25	7	16	23
Mike Christian, Barrie	25	6	15	21
Randy Rowe, Belleville	16	7	13	20
Josef Vasicek, Sault Ste. Marie	17	5	15	20

INDIVIDUAL STATISTICS

BARRIE COLTS
(Winner of 2000 J. Ross Robertson Cup)

SCORING

	Games	G	A	Pts.	PIM
Michael Henrich	25	10	18	28	30
Sheldon Keefe	25	10	13	23	41
Mike Jefferson	25	7	16	23	107
Mike Christian	25	6	15	21	37
Blaine Down	22	10	6	16	18
Ryan Barnes	25	7	7	14	49
Shawn Cation	25	6	8	14	20
Mike Henderson	25	5	8	13	8
Matthew Dziedusycki	25	5	7	12	16
Tim Branham	25	4	7	11	17
Tim Verbeek	25	5	5	10	23
Nick Robinson	25	1	5	6	8
Eric Reitz	25	0	5	5	44
Denis Shvidki	9	3	1	4	2
Ed Hill	25	1	3	4	14
Brian Finley (goalie)	23	0	2	2	2
Rick Hwodeky	22	1	0	1	11
Kyle Wailes	21	0	1	1	0
Aaron Power	25	0	1	1	27
Ryan O'Keefe	1	0	0	0	0
Mike D'Alessandro (goalie)	4	0	0	0	2
Matt Passfield	25	0	0	0	5

GOALTENDING

	Gms.	Min.	W	L	T	G	SO	Avg.
Mike D'Alessandro	4	166	2	1	0	3	0	1.08
Brian Finley	23	1353	14	8	0	58	1	2.57

BELLEVILLE BULLS
(Lost semifinals to Barrie, 4-1)

SCORING

	Games	G	A	Pts.	PIM
Randy Rowe	16	7	13	20	6
Jonathan Cheechoo	16	5	12	17	16
Kevin Baker	16	11	5	16	22
Justin Papineau	16	4	12	16	16
Branko Radivojevic	16	5	8	13	32
David Cornacchia	16	1	11	12	32
Chris Stanley	16	4	7	11	2
Kyle Wellwood	16	3	7	10	6
Mark Chaplin	15	6	3	9	15
Mike Renzi	16	4	3	7	18
Nathan Robinson	15	3	4	7	10
Michael Jacobsen	16	2	5	7	7
Adam Paiement	16	1	2	3	20
Branislav Mezei	6	0	3	3	10
Malcolm Hutt	16	2	0	2	10
Rick Bertran	16	0	2	2	30
Nick Policelli	16	1	0	1	33
Cody McCormick	9	0	1	1	10
Josh Sands	9	0	1	1	2
Corey Batten (goalie)	7	0	0	0	2
Jamie Lovell	10	0	0	0	2
Cory Campbell (goalie)	13	0	0	0	4

GOALTENDING

	Gms.	Min.	W	L	T	G	SO	Avg.
Cory Campbell	13	685	7	5	0	36	0	3.15
Corey Batten	7	278	2	2	0	18	0	3.88

BRAMPTON BATTALION
(Lost first round to Erie, 4-2)

SCORING

	Games	G	A	Pts.	PIM
Raffi Torres	6	5	2	7	23
Lukas Havel	6	3	2	5	12
Jason Maleyko	6	0	4	4	8
Jay McClement	6	0	4	4	8
Jeff Bateman	6	2	1	3	4
Aaron VanLeusen	6	2	1	3	6
Rostislav Klesla	6	1	1	2	21
Jay Harrison	6	0	2	2	15
Nathan Herrington	6	1	0	1	2
Chris Rowan	6	1	0	1	4
Kurt MacSweyn	6	0	1	1	8
Mike Rice	6	0	1	1	14
Scott Della Vedova (goalie)	1	0	0	0	0
Scott Thompson	2	0	0	0	0
Matt Reynolds	4	0	0	0	7
David Chant (goalie)	5	0	0	0	0
Paul Flache	6	0	0	0	8
Matt Grennier	6	0	0	0	0
Tyler Hanchuck	6	0	0	0	8
Richard Kearns	6	0	0	0	0
Brad Woods	6	0	0	0	8

GOALTENDING

	Gms.	Min.	W	L	T	G	SO	Avg.
David Chant	5	300	2	3	0	14	1	2.80
Scott Della Vedova	1	60	0	1	0	4	0	4.00

ERIE OTTERS
(Lost quarterfinals to Sault Ste. Marie, 4-3)

SCORING

	Games	G	A	Pts.	PIM
Brad Boyes	13	6	8	14	10
Jason Baird	13	7	4	11	34
Michael Rupp	13	5	5	10	22
Nikita Alexeev	13	4	3	7	6
Peter Campbell	13	1	6	7	8
Shane Nash	10	2	4	6	6
Carlo Colaiacovo	13	2	4	6	9
Mike Nelson	13	3	2	5	15
Troy Ilijow	13	1	4	5	32
Arvid Rekis	13	1	4	5	17
Darren McMillan	13	0	4	4	10
Brad Yeo	13	2	0	2	49
Sean Dixon	13	0	2	2	10
Kenny Jung	13	0	2	2	4
Riley Moher	13	1	0	1	12
Scott Rozendal	13	1	0	1	11
Jourdan Lagace	13	0	1	1	5
Adam Munroe (goalie)	1	0	0	0	0
Jarret Richburg	3	0	0	0	2
Scott Neil	13	0	0	0	4
J.F. Perras (goalie)	13	0	0	0	2

GOALTENDING

	Gms.	Min.	W	L	T	G	SO	Avg.
J.F. Perras	13	801	7	6	0	36	1	2.70
Adam Munroe	1	5	0	0	0	1	0	12.00

GUELPH STORM
(Lost first round to Plymouth, 4-2)

SCORING

	Games	G	A	Pts.	PIM
Brent Kelly	6	4	1	5	0
Lindsay Plunkett	6	2	3	5	8
Kent McDonell	6	1	4	5	6
Joe Gerbe	6	1	3	4	6
Charlie Stephens	6	1	3	4	15
Eric Beaudoin	6	3	0	3	2

	Games	G	A	Pts.	PIM
Kevin Mitchell	6	1	2	3	10
Matthew House	6	1	1	2	2
Bohuslav Subr	6	1	1	2	4
Kevin Dallman	6	0	2	2	11
Manny Malhotra	6	0	2	2	4
Radek Matalik	6	0	1	1	4
Morgan McCormick	6	0	1	1	7
Craig Andersson (goalie)	3	0	0	0	0
Andrew Brown	6	0	0	0	0
Ian Forbes	6	0	0	0	11
Jon Hedberg	6	0	0	0	2
Derek Hennessey	6	0	0	0	0
Colt King	6	0	0	0	5
Chris Madden (goalie)	6	0	0	0	4

GOALTENDING

	Gms.	Min.	W	L	T	G	SO	Avg.
Craig Andersson	3	110	0	1	0	5	0	2.73
Chris Madden	6	249	2	3	0	18	0	4.34

KINGSTON FRONTENACS
(Lost first round to Sudbury, 4-1)

SCORING

	Games	G	A	Pts.	PIM
Andrew Ianiero	5	5	0	5	4
Travis Lisabeth	5	2	3	5	6
Sean Avery	5	2	2	4	26
Michael Zigomanis	5	0	4	4	0
Nathan Tennant	5	0	3	3	8
Brett Clouthier	5	2	0	2	17
Jonathan Schill	3	1	1	2	6
Jason Polera	5	0	2	2	6
Darryl Knight	5	1	0	1	0
Sean Griffin	5	0	1	1	15
Darryl Thomson	1	0	0	0	4
Shaun Peet	2	0	0	0	0
Matt Junkins	4	0	0	0	2
Eric Braff	5	0	0	0	2
Chris Cook	5	0	0	0	2
Brad Horan	5	0	0	0	0
Doug MacIver	5	0	0	0	8
Andrew Raycroft (goalie)	5	0	0	0	0
Jean-Francois Seguin	5	0	0	0	0
Tomas Skvaridlo	5	0	0	0	2
Cory Stillman	5	0	0	0	0

GOALTENDING

	Gms.	Min.	W	L	T	G	SO	Avg.
Andrew Raycroft	5	300	1	4	0	21	0	4.20

KITCHENER RANGERS
(Lost first round to Sault Ste. Marie, 4-1)

SCORING

	Games	G	A	Pts.	PIM
Ryan Held	5	4	3	7	4
Brandon Merli	5	4	3	7	10
Allan Rourke	5	0	6	6	13
Derek Roy	5	4	1	5	6
Matt Armstrong	5	2	2	4	10
Mike Wehrstedt	5	2	2	4	5
Chris Brannen	5	0	4	4	6
Serge Payer	5	0	3	3	6
Jimmy Gagnon	5	0	2	2	8
Bobby Naylor	3	1	0	1	15
John Eminger	5	1	0	1	4
Andrew Peters	4	0	1	1	14
Mike Amodeo	5	0	1	1	12
Mike Mazzuca	5	0	1	1	16
Scott Dickie (goalie)	1	0	0	0	0
Brent Labre	6	0	0	0	0
Maxim Sharifijanov	3	0	0	0	0
Sean McMorrow	4	0	0	0	12

	Games	G	A	Pts.	PIM
Ruslan Akhmadulin	5	0	0	0	0
Reg Bourcier (goalie)	5	0	0	0	4
Bill Browne	5	0	0	0	14
Steve Eminger	5	0	0	0	0

GOALTENDING

	Gms.	Min.	W	L	T	G	SO	Avg.
Scott Dickie	1	40	0	1	0	2	0	3.00
Reg Bourcier	5	275	1	3	0	20	0	4.36

NORTH BAY CENTENNIALS
(Lost first round to Barrie, 4-2)

SCORING

	Games	G	A	Pts.	PIM
Mike Cirillo	6	6	3	9	20
Jonas Andersson	6	2	2	4	2
Peter Reynolds	6	1	3	4	10
Konrad McKay	6	0	4	4	8
Scott Cameron	6	3	0	3	4
Ryan Armstrong	6	0	2	2	4
Chris Thorburn	6	0	2	2	0
Kyle Werner	6	0	2	2	6
Josh Legge	4	0	1	1	0
Rob Davison	6	0	1	1	8
John Dean	6	0	1	1	2
David Culham	1	0	0	0	0
Tylor Dunford	1	0	0	0	0
Derrell Upton	1	0	0	0	0
Chris Eade	3	0	0	0	4
Samu Isosalo	3	0	0	0	0
Brad Walford	3	0	0	0	0
Alex Auld (goalie)	6	0	0	0	0
Matt Bacon	6	0	0	0	4
Steve Chabbert	6	0	0	0	10
George Halkidis	6	0	0	0	0
Brad Pierce	6	0	0	0	0
Peter Veltman	6	0	0	0	2

GOALTENDING

	Gms.	Min.	W	L	T	G	SO	Avg.
Alex Auld	6	374	2	4	0	12	0	1.93

OSHAWA GENERALS
(Lost first round to Ottawa, 4-1)

SCORING

	Games	G	A	Pts.	PIM
Brian Passmore	5	0	5	5	10
Greg Willers	5	2	2	4	8
Vladimir Repnev	5	3	0	3	0
Brandon Cullen	5	1	2	3	13
Brent Gauvreau	5	1	2	3	4
Nick Lees	4	2	0	2	2
John Kozoriz	5	1	1	2	2
Brad Ralph	5	1	1	2	4
Stacey Britstone	5	0	2	2	6
Ilja Demidov	5	0	2	2	24
Shane Fryia	5	0	2	2	6
Richard Spence	5	1	0	1	12
Andrew Archer	3	0	1	1	2
T.J. Reynolds	5	0	1	1	16
Tyler Durham	1	0	0	0	0
T.J. Aceti (goalie)	2	0	0	0	2
Neill Posillico	2	0	0	0	2
Bryan Allen	3	0	0	0	13
Derek Dolson (goalie)	4	0	0	0	0
Ryan Fraser	4	0	0	0	2
Jonah Leroux	4	0	0	0	0
Pat Montgomery	4	0	0	0	2
Alain Chevrier	5	0	0	0	2

GOALTENDING

	Gms.	Min.	W	L	T	G	SO	Avg.
Derek Dolson	4	256	0	3	0	9	0	2.11
T.J. Aceti	2	75	1	1	0	8	0	6.40

OTTAWA 67'S
(Lost quarterfinals to Belleville, 4-2)

SCORING

	Games	G	A	Pts.	PIM
Jonathan Zion	11	3	10	13	8
Joe Talbot	11	3	9	12	16
Luke Sellars	11	4	6	10	28
Lance Galbraith	11	4	5	9	41
Matt Zultek	11	3	5	8	12
Miguel Delisle	11	4	1	5	28
Dan Tessier	6	2	2	4	14
Adam Chapman	11	2	2	4	8
Randy Davidson	11	2	2	4	2
Ian Jacobs	11	1	3	4	11
Russ Moyer	11	1	3	4	4
Josh Tataryn	11	0	4	4	2
Zenon Konopka	11	1	2	3	8
Kevin Holdridge	11	1	1	2	20
Kevin Malcolm	3	1	0	1	4
Jeremy Van Hoof	11	1	0	1	12
Mark Bell	2	0	1	1	0
Brendan Bell	5	0	1	1	4
Marc Lefebvre	11	0	1	1	2
Paul Schonfelder (goalie)	1	0	0	0	0
Cody Glasper	7	0	0	0	0
Corey Sabourin	9	0	0	0	2
Levente Szuper (goalie)	11	0	0	0	0

GOALTENDING

	Gms.	Min.	W	L	T	G	SO	Avg.
Paul Schonfelder	1	11	0	0	0	0	0	0.00
Levente Szuper	11	680	6	5	0	35	1	3.09

PETERBOROUGH PETES
(Lost first round to Belleville, 4-1)

SCORING

	Games	G	A	Pts.	PIM
Sergei Kuznetzov	5	0	4	4	2
Jason Williams	5	2	1	3	2
Kurtis Foster	5	1	2	3	4
Marcel Rodman	5	1	2	3	0
Brandon Verner	5	0	3	3	10
Jamie Chamberlain	5	2	0	2	6
Brad Self	5	2	0	2	0
Bob Crummer	5	1	1	2	6
Preston Mizzi	5	1	1	2	6
John Brioux	5	0	2	2	2
Steve Montador	5	0	2	2	4
Adam Dewan	4	1	0	1	22
T.J. Eason	5	1	0	1	0
Matt Carkner	5	0	1	1	6
Matt Herneisen	5	0	1	1	9
Ryan Ramsay	5	0	1	1	16
Dustin Wood	5	0	1	1	0
Mike Pickard (goalie)	1	0	0	0	0
Stephen Hoar	2	0	0	0	2
Jon Howse	4	0	0	0	0
Joey MacDonald (goalie)	5	0	0	0	0

GOALTENDING

	Gms.	Min.	W	L	T	G	SO	Avg.
Joey MacDonald	5	280	1	4	0	16	1	3.43
Mike Pickard	1	20	0	0	0	4	0	12.00

PLYMOUTH WHALERS
(Lost finals to Barrie, 4-3)

SCORING

	Games	G	A	Pts.	PIM
Justin Williams	23	14	16	30	10
Stephen Weiss	23	8	18	26	18
Shaun Fisher	23	4	21	25	24
Randy Fitzgerald	23	13	10	23	47

MAJOR JUNIOR LEAGUES OHL

	Games	G	A	Pts.	PIM
Damian Surma	20	9	8	17	10
Eric Gooldy	23	7	8	15	41
Tomas Kurka	17	7	6	13	6
George Nistas	21	6	6	12	2
Cole Jarrett	23	3	7	10	19
Kristopher Vernarsky	19	3	6	9	24
Jared Newman	23	0	5	5	34
Chris Cava	23	0	4	4	26
Steven Morris	23	2	1	3	8
Andre Robichaud	17	1	2	3	2
Libor Ustrnul	23	0	3	3	29
Nate Kiser	23	1	1	2	18
Rob McBride	23	0	2	2	4
Jamie Lalonde	17	1	0	1	17
James Ramsay	12	0	1	1	20
Jon Billy	14	0	1	1	0
Rob Zepp (goalie)	23	0	1	1	2
Bill Ruggiero (goalie)	1	0	0	0	0

GOALTENDING

	Gms.	Min.	W	L	T	G	SO	Avg.
Rob Zepp	23	1374	15	8	0	52	2	2.27
Bill Ruggiero	1	20	0	0	0	1	0	3.00

SARNIA STING
(Lost first round to Windsor, 4-3)

SCORING

	Games	G	A	Pts.	PIM
Alexander Buturlin	7	4	2	6	12
Jeff Heerema	7	4	2	6	10
Maxim Rybin	7	4	1	5	2
Dusty Jamieson	7	3	2	5	0
Eric Himelfarb	7	1	4	5	4
Mike Van Ryn	7	0	5	5	4
Robb Palahnuk	7	2	1	3	15
Ryan VanBuskirk	7	1	2	3	16
Kris Newbury	7	0	3	3	16
Kelly Paddon	7	0	3	3	9
Ryan Hare	7	0	2	2	4
Jamie Johnson	7	0	2	2	2
Jason Penner	3	1	0	1	2
Chris Berti	7	1	0	1	13
Andy Burnham	7	1	0	1	15
Tyler Coleman	4	0	1	1	0
Scott Heffernan	7	0	1	1	4
Andrew Sim (goalie)	1	0	0	0	0
Sal Lettieri	2	0	0	0	0
Corey Brekelmans	5	0	0	0	2
Greg Hewitt (goalie)	7	0	0	0	2
Dan Watson	7	0	0	0	4

GOALTENDING

	Gms.	Min.	W	L	T	G	SO	Avg.
Andrew Sim	1	20	0	0	0	0	0	0.00
Greg Hewitt	7	420	3	4	0	20	0	2.86

SAULT STE. MARIE GREYHOUNDS
(Lost semifinals to Plymouth, 4-1)

SCORING

	Games	G	A	Pts.	PIM
Josef Vasicek	17	5	15	20	8
Ryan Jardine	17	11	8	19	16
Chad Spurr	17	7	12	19	16
Cory Pecker	12	6	8	14	8
Ryan Milanovic	15	4	8	12	22
Trevor Daley	15	3	7	10	12
Daniel Passero	17	3	7	10	24
John Osborne	17	6	3	9	26
Paul Ballantyne	17	2	3	5	17
Ryan Healy	13	3	1	4	27
Cleon Smith	15	2	2	4	4
Malcolm McMillan	17	0	4	4	49

	Games	G	A	Pts.	PIM
Rob Chapman	12	2	1	3	11
Josh Bennett	17	1	2	3	44
Derek Fox	16	0	3	3	29
Jake Gibson	14	0	2	2	8
Vaclav Zavoral	14	0	2	2	28
Jeff Richards	13	1	0	1	16
Darren Strilchuk	6	0	1	1	2
Brent Theobald	13	0	1	1	2
Ray Emery (goalie)	15	0	1	1	2
Jeremy Day (goalie)	1	0	0	0	0
Jason Flick (goalie)	4	0	0	0	0
Nick Jones	12	0	0	0	42

GOALTENDING

	Gms.	Min.	W	L	T	G	SO	Avg.
Ray Emery	15	883	8	7	0	33	3	2.24
Jason Flick	4	165	1	1	0	11	0	4.00
Jeremy Day	1	26	0	0	0	4	0	9.23

SUDBURY WOLVES
(Lost quarterfinals to Barrie, 4-3)

SCORING

	Games	G	A	Pts.	PIM
Norm Milley	12	8	11	19	6
Taylor Pyatt	12	8	7	15	25
Derek MacKenzie	12	5	9	14	16
Brad Morgan	12	2	12	14	15
Jason Jaspers	12	4	6	10	27
Kip Brennan	12	3	3	6	67
Sebastien Savage	12	2	4	6	13
Tom Kotsopoulos	12	1	4	5	28
Jerry Connell	12	2	2	4	13
Alexei Semenov	12	1	3	4	23
Abe Herbst	12	0	4	4	6
Dennis Wideman	12	1	2	3	22
Kyle Dafoe	12	1	1	2	18
Warren Hefford	12	0	2	2	12
Steven Ellis	12	1	0	1	2
Mike Gorman (goalie)	12	0	1	1	2
Vladimir Chernenko	3	0	0	0	0
Drew Kivell	9	0	0	0	7
Ryan Philips	12	0	0	0	0
Mike Vaillaincourt	12	0	0	0	2

GOALTENDING

	Gms.	Min.	W	L	T	G	SO	Avg.
Mike Gorman	12	720	7	5	0	29	1	2.42

WINDSOR SPITFIRES
(Lost quarterfinals to Plymouth, 4-1)

SCORING

	Games	G	A	Pts.	PIM
Vince Grant	12	5	5	10	2
Robin Boucher	12	5	3	8	6
Steve Ott	12	3	5	8	21
Tim Gleason	12	2	4	6	14
Mark Ridout	12	4	1	5	10
Shawn Mather	11	2	3	5	2
Patrick Finnegan	10	1	4	5	8
Craig Kennedy	12	1	4	5	6
Blair Stayzer	11	1	3	4	14
Luc Rioux	12	0	4	4	6
Curtis Watson	11	1	2	3	14
Joey Sewell	7	0	3	3	7
Jeff Martin	4	1	1	2	2
Fedor Fedorov	12	1	0	1	4
Pavel Shtefan	6	0	1	1	0
Dan Growden	10	0	1	1	6
Craig Mahon	11	0	1	1	14
Ryan Courtney	12	0	1	1	9
Mike Leighton (goalie)	12	0	1	1	2
Ryan Aschaber (goalie)	3	0	0	0	2

	Games	G	A	Pts.	PIM
Frank Sinacori	5	0	0	0	9
Kyle Chapman	11	0	0	0	18
Steven Rawski	11	0	0	0	2

GOALTENDING

	Gms.	Min.	W	L	T	G	SO	Avg.
Mike Leighton	12	616	5	6	0	32	0	3.12
Ryan Aschaber	3	123	0	1	0	9	0	4.39

1999-2000 AWARD WINNERS

ALL-STAR TEAMS

First team	Pos.	Second team
Andrew Raycroft, Kingston	G	Rob Zepp, Plymouth
John Erskine, London	D	Allan Rourke, Kitchener
Branislav Mezei, Belleville	D	Kevin Mitchell, Guelph
Taylor Pyatt, Sudbury	LW	Raffi Torres, Brampton
Dan Tessier, Ottawa	C	Jason Jaspers, Sudbury
Norm Milley, Sudbury	RW	Sheldon Keefe, Barrie

TROPHY WINNERS

Red Tilson Trophy: Andrew Raycroft, Kingston
Eddie Powers Memorial Trophy: Sheldon Keefe, Barrie
Dave Pinkney Trophy: Bill Ruggiero, Plymouth
Rob Zepp, Plymouth
Max Kaminsky Trophy: John Erskine, London
William Hanley Trophy: Mike Zigomanis, Kingston
Emms Family Award: Derek Roy, Kitchener
Matt Leyden Trophy: Peter DeBoer, Plymouth
Jim Mahon Memorial Trophy: Sheldon Keefe, Barrie
F.W. Dinty Moore Trophy: Andrew Sim, Sarnia
Leo Lalonde Memorial Trophy: Dan Tessier, Ottawa
Hamilton Spectator Trophy: Plymouth Whalers
J. Ross Robertson Cup: Barrie Colts

ALL-TIME AWARD WINNERS

RED TILSON TROPHY
(Outstanding player)

Season	Player, Team
1944-45	Doug McMurdy, St. Catharines
1945-46	Tod Sloan, St. Michael's
1946-47	Ed Sanford, St. Michael's
1947-48	George Armstrong, Stratford
1948-49	Gil Mayer, Barrie
1949-50	George Armstrong, Marlboros
1950-51	Glenn Hall, Windsor
1951-52	Bill Harrington, Kitchener
1952-53	Bob Attersley, Oshawa
1953-54	Brian Cullen, St. Catharines
1954-55	Hank Ciesla, St. Catharines
1955-56	Ron Howell, Guelph
1956-57	Frank Mahovlich, St. Michael's
1957-58	Murray Oliver, Hamilton
1958-59	Stan Mikita, St. Catharines
1959-60	Wayne Connelly, Peterborough
1960-61	Rod Gilbert, Guelph
1961-62	Pit Martin, Hamilton
1962-63	Wayne Maxner, Niagara Falls
1963-64	Yvan Cournoyer, Montreal
1964-65	Andre Lacroix, Peterborough
1965-66	Andre Lacroix, Peterborough
1966-67	Mickey Redmond, Peterborough
1967-68	Walt Tkaczuk, Kitchener
1968-69	Rejean Houle, Montreal
1969-70	Gilbert Perreault, Montreal
1970-71	Dave Gardner, Marlboros
1971-72	Don Lever, Niagara Falls
1972-73	Rick Middleton, Oshawa
1973-74	Jack Valiquette, Sault Ste. Marie
1974-75	Dennis Maruk, London
1975-76	Peter Lee, Ottawa
1976-77	Dale McCourt, St. Catharines
1977-78	Bobby Smith, Ottawa
1978-79	Mike Foligno, Sudbury
1979-80	Jim Fox, Ottawa
1980-81	Ernie Godden, Windsor
1981-82	Dave Simpson, London
1982-83	Doug Gilmour, Cornwall
1983-84	John Tucker, Kitchener
1984-85	Wayne Groulx, Sault Ste. Marie
1985-86	Ray Sheppard, Cornwall
1986-87	Scott McCrory, Oshawa

Season	Player, Team
1987-88	Andrew Cassels, Ottawa
1988-89	Bryan Fogarty, Niagara Falls
1989-90	Mike Ricci, Peterborough
1990-91	Eric Lindros, Oshawa
1991-92	Todd Simon, Niagara Falls
1992-93	Pat Peake, Detroit
1993-94	Jason Allison, London
1994-95	David Ling, Kingston
1995-96	Alyn McCauley, Ottawa
1996-97	Alyn McCauley, Ottawa
1997-98	David Legwand, Plymouth
1998-99	Brian Campbell, Ottawa
1999-00	Andrew Raycroft, Kingston

EDDIE POWERS MEMORIAL TROPHY
(Scoring champion)

Season	Player, Team
1933-34	J. Groboski, Oshawa
1934-35	J. Good, Toronto Lions
1935-36	John O'Flaherty, West Toronto
1936-37	Billy Taylor, Oshawa
1937-38	Hank Goldup, Tor. Marlboros
1938-39	Billy Taylor, Oshawa
1939-40	Jud McAtee, Oshawa
1940-41	Gaye Stewart, Tor. Marlboros
1941-42	Bob Wiest, Brantford
1942-43	Norman ``Red'' Tilson, Oshawa
1943-44	Ken Smith, Oshawa
1944-45	Leo Gravelle, St. Michael's
1945-46	Tod Sloan, St. Michael's
1946-47	Fleming Mackell, St. Michael's
1947-48	George Armstrong, Stratford
1948-49	Bert Giesebrecht, Windsor
1949-50	Earl Reibel, Windsor
1950-51	Lou Jankowski, Oshawa
1951-52	Ken Laufman, Guelph
1952-53	Jim McBurney, Galt
1953-54	Brian Cullen, St. Catharines
1954-55	Hank Ciesla, St. Catharines
1955-56	Stan Baliuk, Kitchener
1956-57	Bill Sweeney, Guelph
1957-58	John McKenzie, St. Catharines
1958-59	Stan Mikita, St. Catharines
1959-60	Chico Maki, St. Catharines
1960-61	Rod Gilbert, Guelph
1961-62	Andre Boudrias, Montreal

Season	Player, Team
1962-63	Wayne Maxner, Niagara Falls
1963-64	Andre Boudrias, Montreal
1964-65	Ken Hodge, St. Catharines
1965-66	Andre Lacroix, Peterborough
1966-67	Derek Sanderson, Niagara Falls
1967-68	Tom Webster, Niagara Falls
1968-69	Rejean Houle, Montreal
1969-70	Marcel Dionne, St. Catharines
1970-71	Marcel Dionne, St. Catharines
1971-72	Bill Harris, Toronto
1972-73	Blake Dunlop, Ottawa
1973-74	Jack Valiquette, Sault Ste. Marie
	Rick Adduono, St. Catharines
1974-75	Bruce Boudreau, Toronto
1975-76	Mike Kaszycki, Sault Ste. Marie
1976-77	Dwight Foster, Kitchener
1977-78	Bobby Smith, Ottawa
1978-79	Mike Foligno, Sudbury
1979-80	Jim Fox, Ottawa
1980-81	John Goodwin, Sault Ste. Marie
1981-82	Dave Simpson, London
1982-83	Doug Gilmour, Cornwall
1983-84	Tim Salmon, Kingston
1984-85	Dave MacLean, Belleville
1985-86	Ray Sheppard, Cornwall
1986-87	Scott McCrory, Oshawa
1987-88	Andrew Cassels, Ottawa
1988-89	Bryan Fogarty, Niagara Falls
1989-90	Keith Primeau, Niagara Falls
1990-91	Eric Lindros, Oshawa
1991-92	Todd Simon, Niagara Falls
1992-93	Andrew Brunette, Owen Sound
1993-94	Jason Allison, London
1994-95	Marc Savard, Oshawa
1995-96	Aaron Brand, Sarnia
1996-97	Marc Savard, Oshawa
1997-98	Peter Sarno, Windsor
1998-99	Peter Sarno, Sarnia
1999-00	Sheldon Keefe, Barrie

DAVE PINKNEY TROPHY
(Top team goaltending)

Season	Player, Team
1948-49	Gil Mayer, Barrie
1949-50	Don Lockhart, Marlboros
1950-51	Don Lockhart, Marlboros
	Lorne Howes, Barrie
1951-52	Don Head, Marlboros
1952-53	John Henderson, Marlboros
1953-54	Dennis Riggin, Hamilton
1954-55	John Albani, Marlboros
1955-56	Jim Crockett, Marlboros
1956-57	Len Broderick, Marlboros
1957-58	Len Broderick, Marlboros
1958-59	Jacques Caron, Peterborough
1959-60	Gerry Cheevers, St. Michael's
1960-61	Bud Blom, Hamilton
1961-62	George Holmes, Montreal
1962-63	Chuck Goddard, Peterborough
1963-64	Bernie Parent, Niagara Falls
1964-65	Bernie Parent, Niagara Falls
1965-66	Ted Quimet, Montreal
1966-67	Peter MacDuffe, St. Catharines
1967-68	Bruce Mullet, Montreal
1968-69	Wayne Wood, Montreal
1969-70	John Garrett, Peterborough
1970-71	John Garrett, Peterborough
1971-72	Michel Larocque, Ottawa
1972-73	Mike Palmateer, Toronto
1973-74	Don Edwards, Kitchener
1974-75	Greg Millen, Peterborough
1975-76	Jim Bedard, Sudbury

Season	Player, Team
1976-77	Pat Riggin, London
1977-78	Al Jensen, Hamilton
1978-79	Nick Ricci, Niagara Falls
1979-80	Rick LaFerriere, Peterborough
1980-81	Jim Ralph, Ottawa
1981-82	Marc D'Amour, Sault Ste. Marie
1982-83	Peter Sidorkiewicz, Oshawa
	Jeff Hogg, Oshawa
1983-84	Darren Pang, Ottawa
	Greg Coram, Ottawa
1984-85	Scott Mosey, Sault Ste. Marie
	Marty Abrams, Sault Ste. Marie
1985-86	Kay Whitmore, Peterborough
	Ron Tugnutt, Peterborough
1986-87	Sean Evoy, Oshawa
	Jeff Hackett, Oshawa
1987-88	Todd Bojcun, Peterborough
	John Tanner, Peterborough
1988-89	Todd Bojcun, Peterborough
	John Tanner, Peterborough
1989-90	Jeff Wilson, Peterborough
	Sean Gauthier, Kingston
1990-91	Kevin Hodson, Sault Ste. Marie
	Mike Lenarduzzi, Sault Ste. Marie
1991-92	Kevin Hodson, Sault Ste. Marie
1992-93	Chad Lang, Peterborough
	Ryan Douglas, Peterborough
1993-94	Sandy Allan, North Bay
	Scott Roche, North Bay
1994-95	Andy Adams, Guelph
	Mark McArthur, Guelph
1995-96	Dan Cloutier, Guelph
	Brett Thompson, Guelph
1996-97	Craig Hillier, Ottawa
	Tim Keyes, Ottawa
1997-98	Craig Hillier, Ottawa
	Seamus Kotyk, Ottawa
1998-99	Robert Holsinger, Plymouth
	Rob Zepp, Plymouth
1999-00	Bill Ruggiero, Plymouth
	Rob Zepp, Plymouth

MAX KAMINSKY TROPHY
(Outstanding defenseman)

Season	Player, Team
1969-70	Ron Plumb, Peterborough
1970-71	Jocelyn Guevremont, Montreal
1971-72	Denis Potvin, Ottawa
1972-73	Denis Potvin, Ottawa
1973-74	Jim Turkiewicz, Peterborough
1974-75	Mike O'Connell, Kingston
1975-76	Rick Green, London
1976-77	Craig Hartsburg, S. Ste. Marie
1977-78	Brad Marsh, London
	Rob Ramage, London
1978-79	Greg Theberge, Peterborough
1979-80	Larry Murphy, Peterborough
1980-81	Steve Smith, Sault Ste. Marie
1981-82	Ron Meighan, Niagara Falls
1982-83	Allan MacInnis, Kitchener
1983-84	Brad Shaw, Ottawa
1984-85	Bob Halkidis, London
1985-86	Terry Carkner, Peterborough
	Jeff Brown, Sudbury
1986-87	Kerry Huffman, Guelph
1987-88	Darryl Shannon, Windsor
1988-89	Bryan Fogarty, Niagara Falls
1989-90	John Slaney, Cornwall
1990-91	Chris Snell, Ottawa
1991-92	Drake Berehowsky, North Bay
1992-93	Chris Pronger, Peterborough
1993-94	Jamie Rivers, Sudbury

Season	Player, Team
1994-95	Bryan Berard, Detroit
1995-96	Bryan Berard, Detroit
1996-97	Sean Blanchard, Ottawa
1997-98	Chris Allen, Kingston
1998-99	Brian Campbell, Ottawa
1999-00	John Erskine, London

WILLIAM HANLEY TROPHY
(Most gentlemanly)

Season	Player, Team
1960-61	Bruce Draper, St. Michael's
1961-62	Lowell MacDonald, Hamilton
1962-63	Paul Henderson, Hamilton
1963-64	Fred Stanfield, St. Catharines
1964-65	Jimmy Peters, Hamilton
1965-66	Andre Lacroix, Peterborough
1966-67	Mickey Redmond, Peterborough
1967-68	Tom Webster, Niagara Falls
1968-69	Rejean Houle, Montreal
1969-74	No award presented
1974-75	Doug Jarvis, Peterborough
1975-76	Dale McCourt, Hamilton
1976-77	Dale McCourt, St. Catharines
1977-78	Wayne Gretzky, S.S. Marie
1978-79	Sean Simpson, Ottawa
1979-80	Sean Simpson, Ottawa
1980-81	John Goodwin, Sault Ste. Marie
1981-82	Dave Simpson, London
1982-83	Kirk Muller, Guelph
1983-84	Kevin Conway, Kingston
1984-85	Scott Tottle, Peterborough
1985-86	Jason Lafreniere, Belleville
1986-87	Scott McCrory, Oshawa
	Keith Gretzky, Hamilton
1987-88	Andrew Cassels, Ottawa
1988-89	Kevin Miehm, Oshawa
1989-90	Mike Ricci, Peterborough
1990-91	Dale Craigwell, Oshawa
1991-92	John Spoltore, North Bay
1992-93	Pat Peake, Detroit
1993-94	Jason Allison, London
1994-95	Vitali Yachmenev, North Bay
1995-96	Jeff Williams, Guelph
1996-97	Alyn McCauley, Ottawa
1997-98	Matt Bradley, Kingston
1998-99	Brian Campbell, Ottawa
1999-00	Mike Zigomanis, Kingston

EMMS FAMILY AWARD
(Rookie of the year)

Season	Player, Team
1972-73	Dennis Maruk, London
1973-74	Jack Valiquette, Sault Ste. Marie
1974-75	Danny Shearer, Hamilton
1975-76	John Travella, Sault Ste. Marie
1976-77	Yvan Joly, Ottawa
1977-78	Wayne Gretzky, S.S. Marie
1978-79	John Goodwin, Sault Ste. Marie
1979-80	Bruce Dowie, Toronto
1980-81	Tony Tanti, Oshawa
1981-82	Pat Verbeek, Sudbury
1982-83	Bruce Cassidy, Ottawa
1983-84	Shawn Burr, Kitchener
1984-85	Derek King, Sault Ste. Marie
1985-86	Lonnie Loach, Guelph
1986-87	Andrew Cassels, Ottawa
1987-88	Rick Corriveau, London
1988-89	Owen Nolan, Cornwall
1989-90	Chris Longo, Peterborough
1990-91	Cory Stillman, Windsor
1991-92	Chris Gratton, Kingston
1992-93	Jeff O'Neill, Guelph

Season	Player, Team
1993-94	Vitali Yachmenev, North Bay
1994-95	Bryan Berard, Detroit
1995-96	Joe Thornton, Sault Ste. Marie
1996-97	Peter Sarno, Windsor
1997-98	David Legwand, Plymouth
1998-99	Sheldon Keefe, Barrie
1999-00	Derek Roy, Kitchener

MATT LEYDEN TROPHY
(Coach of the year)

Season	Coach, Team
1971-72	Gus Bodnar, Oshawa
1972-73	George Armstrong, Toronto
1973-74	Jack Bownass, Kingston
1974-75	Bert Templeton, Hamilton
1975-76	Jerry Toppazzini, Sudbury
1976-77	Bill Long, London
1977-78	Bill White, Oshawa
1978-79	Gary Green, Peterborough
1979-80	Dave Chambers, Toronto
1980-81	Brian Kilrea, Ottawa
1981-82	Brian Kilrea, Ottawa
1982-83	Terry Crisp, Sault Ste. Marie
1983-84	Tom Barrett, Kitchener
1984-85	Terry Crisp, Sault Ste. Marie
1985-86	Jacques Martin, Guelph
1986-87	Paul Theriault, Oshawa
1987-88	Dick Todd, Peterborough
1988-89	Joe McDonnell, Kitchener
1989-90	Larry Mavety, Kingston
1990-91	George Burnett, Niagara Falls
1991-92	George Burnett, Niagara Falls
1992-93	Gary Agnew, London
1993-94	Bert Templeton, North Bay
1994-95	Craig Hartsburg, Guelph
1995-96	Brian Kilrea, Ottawa
1996-97	Brian Kilrea, Ottawa
1997-98	Gary Agnew, London
1998-99	Peter DeBoer, Plymouth
1999-00	Peter DeBoer, Plymouth

JIM MAHON MEMORIAL TROPHY
(Top scoring right wing)

Season	Player, Team
1971-72	Bill Harris, Toronto
1972-73	Dennis Ververgaert, London
1973-74	Dave Gorman, St. Catharines
1974-75	Mark Napier, Toronto
1975-76	Peter Lee, Ottawa
1976-77	John Anderson, Toronto
1977-78	Dino Ciccarelli, London
1978-79	Mike Foligno, Sudbury
1979-80	Jim Fox, Ottawa
1980-81	Tony Tanti, Oshawa
1981-82	Tony Tanti, Oshawa
1982-83	Ian MacInnis, Cornwall
1983-84	Wayne Presley, Kitchener
1984-85	Dave MacLean, Belleville
1985-86	Ray Sheppard, Cornwall
1986-87	Ron Goodall, Kitchener
1987-88	Sean Williams, Oshawa
1988-89	Stan Drulia, Niagara Falls
1989-90	Owen Nolan, Cornwall
1990-91	Rob Pearson, Oshawa
1991-92	Darren McCarty, Belleville
1992-93	Kevin J. Brown, Detroit
1993-94	Kevin J. Brown, Detroit
1994-95	David Ling, Kingston
1995-96	Cameron Mann, Peterborough
1996-97	Joe Seroski, Sault Ste. Marie
1997-98	Maxim Spiridonov, London
1998-99	Norm Milley, Sudbury
1999-00	Sheldon Keefe, Barrie

MAJOR JUNIOR LEAGUES OHL

F.W. DINTY MOORE TROPHY
(Lowest average by a rookie goalie)

Season	Player, Team
1975-76	Mark Locken, Hamilton
1976-77	Barry Heard, London
1977-78	Ken Ellacott, Peterborough
1978-79	Nick Ricci, Niagara Falls
1979-80	Mike Vezina, Ottawa
1980-81	John Vanbiesbrouck, Sault Ste. Marie
1981-82	Shawn Kilroy, Peterborough
1982-83	Dan Burrows, Belleville
1983-84	Jerry Iuliano, Sault Ste. Marie
1984-85	Ron Tugnutt, Peterborough
1985-86	Paul Henriques, Belleville
1986-87	Jeff Hackett, Oshawa
1987-88	Todd Bojcun, Peterborough
1988-89	Jeff Wilson, Kingston
1989-90	Sean Basilio, London
1990-91	Kevin Hodson, Sault Ste. Marie
1991-92	Sandy Allan, North Bay
1992-93	Ken Shepard, Oshawa
1993-94	Scott Roche, North Bay
1994-95	David MacDonald, Sudbury
1995-96	Brett Thompson, Guelph
1996-97	Shawn Degane, Kitchener
1997-98	Seamus Kotyk, Ottawa
1998-99	Lavente Szuper, Ottawa
1999-00	Andrew Sim, Sarnia

LEO LALONDE MEMORIAL TROPHY
(Overage player of the year)

Season	Player, Team
1983-84	Don McLaren, Ottawa
1984-85	Dunc MacIntyre, Belleville
1985-86	Steve Guenette, Guelph
1986-87	Mike Richard, Toronto
1987-88	Len Soccio, North Bay
1988-89	Stan Drulia, Niagara Falls
1989-90	Iain Fraser, Oshawa
1990-91	Joey St. Aubin, Kitchener
1991-92	John Spoltore, North Bay
1992-93	Scott Hollis, Oshawa
1993-94	B.J. MacPherson, North Bay
1994-95	Bill Bowler, Windsor
1995-96	Aaron Brand, Sarnia
1996-97	Zac Bierk, Peterborough
1997-98	Bujar Amidovski, Toronto
1998-99	Ryan Ready, Belleville
1999-00	Dan Tessier, Ottawa

ALL-TIME LEAGUE CHAMPIONS

Season	REGULAR-SEASON CHAMPION Team	PLAYOFF CHAMPION Team
1933-34	No trophy awarded	St. Michael's College
1934-35	No trophy awarded	Kitchener
1935-36	No trophy awarded	West Toronto Redmen
1936-37	No trophy awarded	St. Michael's College
1937-38	No trophy awarded	Oshawa Generals
1938-39	No trophy awarded	Oshawa Generals
1939-40	No trophy awarded	Oshawa Generals
1940-41	No trophy awarded	Oshawa Generals
1941-42	No trophy awarded	Oshawa Generals
1942-43	No trophy awarded	Oshawa Generals
1943-44	No trophy awarded	Oshawa Generals
1944-45	No trophy awarded	St. Michael's College
1945-46	No trophy awarded	St. Michael's College
1946-47	No trophy awarded	St. Michael's College
1947-48	No trophy awarded	Barrie Flyers
1948-49	No trophy awarded	Barrie Flyers
1949-50	No trophy awarded	Guelph Biltmores
1950-51	No trophy awarded	Barrie Flyers
1951-52	No trophy awarded	Guelph Biltmores
1952-53	No trophy awarded	Barrie Flyers
1953-54	No trophy awarded	St. Catharines Tee Pees
1954-55	No trophy awarded	Toronto Marlboros
1955-56	No trophy awarded	Toronto Marlboros
1956-57	No trophy awarded	Guelph Biltmores
1957-58	St. Catharines Tee Pees	Toronto Marlboros
1958-59	St. Catharines Tee Pees	Peterborough TPTs
1959-60	Toronto Marlboros	St. Catharines Tee Pees
1960-61	Guelph Royals	St. Michael's College
1961-62	Montreal Jr. Canadiens	Hamilton Red Wings
1962-63	Niagara Falls Flyers	Niagara Falls Flyers
1963-64	Toronto Marlboros	Toronto Marlboros
1964-65	Niagara Falls Flyers	Niagara Falls Flyers
1965-66	Peterborough Petes	Oshawa Generals
1966-67	Kitchener Rangers	Toronto Marlboros
1967-68	Kitchener Rangers	Niagara Falls Flyers
1968-69	Montreal Jr. Canadiens	Montreal Jr. Canadiens
1969-70	Montreal Jr. Canadiens	Montreal Jr. Canadiens
1970-71	Peterborough Petes	St. Catharines Black Hawks
1971-72	Toronto Marlboros	Peterborough Petes

REGULAR-SEASON CHAMPION

Season	Team
1972-73—	Toronto Marlboros
1973-74—	Kitchener Rangers
1974-75—	Toronto Marlboros
1975-76—	Sudbury Wolves
1976-77—	St. Catharines Fincups
1977-78—	Ottawa 67's
1978-79—	Peterborough Petes
1979-80—	Peterborough Petes
1980-81—	Sault St. Marie Greyhounds
1981-82—	Ottawa 67's
1982-83—	Sault Ste. Marie Greyhounds
1983-84—	Kitchener Rangers
1984-85—	Sault Ste. Marie Greyhounds
1985-86—	Peterborough Petes
1986-87—	Oshawa Generals
1987-88—	Windsor Compuware Spitfires
1988-89—	Kitchener Rangers
1989-90—	Oshawa Generals
1990-91—	Oshawa Generals
1991-92—	Peterborough Petes
1992-93—	Peterborough Petes
1993-94—	North Bay Centennials
1994-95—	Guelph Storm
1995-96—	Guelph Storm
1996-97—	Ottawa 67's
1997-98—	Guelph Storm
1998-99—	Plymouth Whalers
1999-00—	Plymouth Whalers

PLAYOFF CHAMPION

Team
Toronto Marlboros
St. Catharines Black Hawks
Toronto Marlboros
Hamilton Steelhawks
Ottawa 67's
Peterborough Petes
Peterborough Petes
Peterborough Petes
Kitchener Rangers
Kitchener Rangers
Oshawa Generals
Ottawa 67's
Sault Ste. Marie Greyhounds
Guelph Platers
Oshawa Generals
Windsor Compuware Spitfires
Peterborough Petes
Oshawa Generals
Sault Ste. Marie Greyhounds
Sault Ste. Marie Greyhounds
Peterborough Petes
North Bay Centennials
Detroit Jr. Red Wings
Peterborough Petes
Oshawa Generals
Guelph Storm
Belleville Bulls
Barrie Colts

The OHL regular-season champion is awarded the Hamilton Spectator Trophy and the playoff champion is awarded the J. Ross Robertson Cup.

QUEBEC MAJOR JUNIOR HOCKEY LEAGUE

LEAGUE OFFICE

President
Gilles Courteau
Chairman of the board
Conrad Chapdelaine
Vice president
Maurice Filion
Statistician
Denis Demers
Director of public relations
Manon Gagnon-Leroux

Referee in chief
Doug Hayward
Director of hockey operations
Marcel Patenaude
Marketing director
Paul Girard
Address
255 Roland-Therien Blvd.
Suite 101
Longueuil, Quebec J4H 4A6

Phone
450-442-3590
FAX
450-442-3593

1999-2000 REGULAR SEASON
FINAL STANDINGS

ROBERT LE BEL CONFERENCE

West Division

Team	G	W	L	T	RT	Pts.	GF	GA
Hull	72	42	24	6	0	90	339	256
Rouyn-Noranda	72	33	35	4	2	72	272	288
Montreal	72	29	37	6	5	69	276	313
Val-d'Or	72	19	46	7	5	50	244	367

Central Division

Team	G	W	L	T	RT	Pts.	GF	GA
Shawinigan	72	37	30	5	5	84	295	257
Drummondville	72	38	30	4	1	81	307	280
Sherbrooke	72	35	30	7	2	79	267	255
Victoriaville	72	27	42	3	6	63	286	316

FRANK DILIO CONFERENCE

East Division

Team	G	W	L	T	RT	Pts.	GF	GA
Rimouski	72	48	20	4	2	102	370	274
Quebec	72	44	24	4	4	96	289	213
Baie-Comeau	72	31	36	5	5	72	257	285
Chicoutimi	72	22	47	3	3	50	226	320

Maritime Division

Team	G	W	L	T	RT	Pts.	GF	GA
Moncton	72	44	23	5	3	96	292	211
Halifax	72	41	25	6	5	93	316	259
Cape Breton	72	24	45	3	6	57	230	302
Acadie-Bathurst	72	20	44	8	4	52	227	311

INDIVIDUAL LEADERS

Goals: Brad Richards, Rimouski (71)
Assists: Brad Richards, Rimouski (115)
Points: Brad Richards, Rimouski (186)
Penalty minutes: Guy Turmel, Baie-Comeau (574)
Goaltending average: Simon Lajeunesse, Moncton (2.61)
Shutouts: Simon Lajeunesse, Moncton (6)

	Games	G	A	Pts.
Jonathan Roy, Drum.-Monc.	73	64	61	125
Carl Mallette, Victoriaville	69	49	76	125
Brandon Reid, Halifax	62	44	80	124
Jerome Tremblay, Rouyn-Noranda	71	46	70	116
Dominic Forget, Shawinigan	67	38	78	116
Marco Charpentier, Baie-Comeau	72	51	62	113
Miroslav Zalesak, Drummondville	60	50	61	111
Jan-Philippe Cadieux, Rimouski	71	44	66	110
Michael Ryder, Hull	63	50	58	108
Juraj Kolnik, Rimouski	47	53	53	106
Patrick Grandmaitre, Quebec	70	38	68	106
Wesley Scanzano, Quebec	71	31	75	106
Pascal Dupuis, Shawinigan	61	50	55	105
Eric Chouinard, Quebec	50	57	47	104
Mathieu Benoit, A. Bath.-Monc.	53	57	44	101

TOP SCORERS

	Games	G	A	Pts.
Brad Richards, Rimouski	63	71	115	186
Ramzi Abid, A. Bath.-Hal.	72	67	91	158
Simon Gamache, Val-d'Or	72	64	79	143
Benoit Dusablon, V.d'O.-Hal.	72	47	88	135
Marc-Andre Thinel, Victoriaville	71	59	73	132

INDIVIDUAL STATISTICS

BAIE-COMEAU DRAKKAR
SCORING

	Games	G	A	Pts.	PIM
Marco Charpentier	72	51	62	113	39
Sylvain Deschatelets	68	41	59	100	157
Yanick Lehoux	67	31	61	92	14
Jerome Bergeron	58	17	31	48	143
Evgeny Gusakov	61	25	22	47	135
Bruno St. Jacques	60	8	28	36	120
Charles Linglet	64	14	20	34	13

	Games	G	A	Pts.	PIM
Andre Mercure	66	9	18	27	12
Eric Tremblay	47	6	21	27	296
Christopher Page	41	1	26	27	42
Duilio Grande	49	13	12	25	155
Dominic Periard	61	4	20	24	191
Maxime Fortunus	68	6	15	21	36
Robin Leblanc	51	6	11	17	40
Jonathan Gautier	29	3	14	17	19
Danny Roussy	29	6	8	14	21
Jerome Petit	21	7	6	13	39

	Games	G	A	Pts.	PIM
Kevin Deslauriers	58	2	7	9	30
Daniel Bergeron	49	3	3	6	104
Serge Crochetiere	31	1	3	4	176
Paul Lavoie	63	2	1	3	71
Ghyslain Rousseau (goalie)	46	0	2	2	2
Olivier Maltais	12	1	0	1	4
David St. Germain (goalie)	23	0	1	1	10
Steve Vallee	1	0	0	0	0
Darryl Baker	3	0	0	0	0
Jonathan Walsh	4	0	0	0	0
Philippe Germain	7	0	0	0	19
Jean-Sebastien Larocque	7	0	0	0	5
Chris Pryputniewitz	7	0	0	0	2
Mitchel Zappitelli	8	0	0	0	17
Jean-Philippe Chartier (goalie)	16	0	0	0	0
Keven Poulin	21	0	0	0	98
Eric Bleau	26	0	0	0	91
Mathieu Desjardins	26	0	0	0	17
Guy Turmel	55	0	0	0	574

GOALTENDING

	Games	Min.	W	L	T	G	SO	Avg.
David St. Germain	23	1287	10	11	2	77	2	3.59
Ghyslain Rousseau	46	2301	19	15	1	147	0	3.83
Jean-Philippe Chartier	16	774	3	9	2	59	1	4.57

ACADIE-BATHURST TITANS
SCORING

	Games	G	A	Pts.	PIM
Alex Matieroukhine	57	21	28	49	47
Francois Beauchemin	38	11	36	47	64
Samuel Seguin	50	16	28	44	57
Olivier Fillion	71	10	33	43	34
Mathieu Benoit	20	29	10	39	38
David Comeau	20	10	24	34	42
Jules-Edy Laraque	43	13	20	33	39
Martin Autotte	54	11	20	31	191
Karl Fournier	60	5	24	29	39
Frederic Girard	72	8	15	23	114
Francois Fortin	27	7	16	23	29
Ramzi Abid	13	10	11	21	61
Yannick Guay	23	10	9	19	2
Daniel MacLeod	33	8	11	19	71
Hugo Levesque	72	3	13	16	97
Martin Lavergne	32	7	8	15	65
Grant Donovan	54	7	8	15	167
Luc Ratelle	53	5	9	14	176
Ondrej Latal	39	7	6	13	10
Jean-Sebastien Trudelle	44	3	10	13	149
Yannick Lachance	29	4	8	12	42
Jean-Philippe Cote	27	2	10	12	6
Louis Deault	54	6	4	10	40
Patrick Mbaraga	67	3	7	10	83
Alain Charbonneau	17	2	4	6	16
Daniel Robert	34	0	6	6	11
Steve North	34	3	2	5	16
Tyler Reid	24	1	3	4	24
Tim Sinasac	26	1	3	4	178
Louis Alfred	31	1	3	4	75
Frederic Cloutier (goalie)	58	0	3	3	10
Jonathan Lomax	43	1	1	2	15
Jonathan Frenette	5	1	0	1	0
Shane Lomax	16	1	0	1	65
Eric Litalien	1	0	0	0	0
Mariano D'Agostino	2	0	0	0	0
Charles Faber (goalie)	2	0	0	0	0
William Brown	3	0	0	0	0
Ian Harvey	4	0	0	0	12
Charline Labonte (goalie)	26	0	0	0	0

GOALTENDING

	Games	Min.	W	L	T	G	SO	Avg.
Frederic Cloutier	58	3262	16	34	6	208	1	3.83
Charline Labonte	26	1046	4	9	2	91	0	5.22
Charles Faber	2	48	0	1	0	10	0	12.63

CAPE BRETON SCREAMING EAGLES
SCORING

	Games	G	A	Pts.	PIM
Olivier Proulx	63	30	49	79	128
Artem Rybin	71	37	40	77	74
Jerome Marois	66	28	34	62	95
Guillaume Lefebvre	44	26	28	54	82
Chris Lyness	43	15	29	44	114
Pierre-Luc Laprise	70	11	33	44	89
Dominic Noel	43	12	24	36	40
Frederic Belanger	43	9	20	29	48
Josh Dill	29	9	17	26	47
Stuart MacRae	28	11	9	20	23
Jonathan Gagnon	26	8	12	20	25
Yannick Searles	63	4	10	14	33
P.J. Lynch	24	3	9	12	22
Charles Gauthier	63	7	4	11	25
Sandro Sbrocca	35	3	8	11	205
Jonathan Andrews	40	3	8	11	78
Trevor Ettinger	44	1	8	9	328
Rodrigue Boucher	71	1	8	9	45
Mathieu Dumas	65	3	5	8	35
Robert Horak	22	1	7	8	20
Maxime Lessard	29	2	4	6	26
Kris Barnett	11	1	5	6	4
Kevin Bergin	35	1	5	6	25
Pascal Morency	37	2	3	5	35
Jean-Philippe Cote	28	0	4	4	21
Donald Johnstone	39	1	2	3	45
Robbie Sutherland	7	0	3	3	4
Hunter Lahache	59	0	3	3	317
Jean-Francois Demers	19	1	1	2	29
Dallas Ashford	23	1	1	2	59
Tim Sinasac	24	0	2	2	97
Michael McIntyre	12	0	1	1	26
Daniel Boisclair (goalie)	29	0	1	1	4
Justin Hawco	2	0	0	0	0
Richard Tubrett	2	0	0	0	0
Norman Doucette	3	0	0	0	0
Aaron Rice	3	0	0	0	0
Sebastien Gagnon	9	0	0	0	46
Dany Dallaire (goalie)	18	0	0	0	19
David St. Germain (goalie)	36	0	0	0	0

GOALTENDING

	Games	Min.	W	L	T	G	SO	Avg.
Dany Dallaire	18	934	7	8	0	54	1	3.47
Daniel Boisclair	29	1421	7	14	1	95	0	4.01
David St. Germain	36	1986	10	23	2	147	0	4.44

CHICOUTIMI SAGUENEENS
SCORING

	Games	G	A	Pts.	PIM
Yannick Carpentier	65	25	40	65	59
Jonathan Francoeur	50	24	28	52	34
Roustam Bakhriddinov	63	11	40	51	55
Alex Turcotte	72	19	28	47	35
Eric Betournay	72	13	33	46	40
Simon Tremblay	57	21	24	45	102
Sebastien Lucier	72	23	15	38	27
Gilbert Lefrançois	45	19	16	35	68
Francois Fortin	45	10	23	33	37
David Girard	42	15	17	32	50
Guillaume Karrer	66	6	24	30	139
Sylvain Watt	72	5	22	27	22
Christian Larrivee	69	8	15	23	18
Dominic Desbiens	63	3	17	20	94
Karl St. Pierre	62	5	13	18	88
Yannick Guay	35	7	8	15	8
Joey D'Amico	29	2	11	13	68
Sebastien Laprise	26	3	7	10	2
David McCutcheon	65	2	5	7	314
Simon Lagace-Daigle	27	1	5	6	18
Jean-Francois Talbot	28	2	3	5	2

	Games	G	A	Pts.	PIM
Jean-Michel Martin	17	1	4	5	21
Jean-Francois Demers	38	1	2	3	93
Remi Bergeron (goalie)	58	0	3	3	58
Pascal Morency	12	0	1	1	9
Alain Chenard	47	0	1	1	18
Olivier Spenard	50	0	1	1	66
Enock Cormier (goalie)	1	0	0	0	0
Patrick Provencal (goalie)	1	0	0	0	2
Dave Belanger	2	0	0	0	7
Olivier Dannel (goalie)	28	0	0	0	4

GOALTENDING

	Games	Min.	W	L	T	G	SO	Avg.
Remi Bergeron	58	3031	17	34	1	186	2	3.68
Patrick Provencal	1	54	0	1	0	4	0	4.43
Olivier Dannel	28	1228	5	12	2	119	0	5.81
Enock Cormier	1	20	0	0	0	4	0	12.00

DRUMMONDVILLE VOLTIGEURS

SCORING

	Games	G	A	Pts.	PIM
Miroslav Zalesak	60	50	61	111	40
Zoltan Batovsky	63	27	60	87	151
Julien Desrosiers	68	28	57	85	38
Jonathan Roy	42	39	33	72	30
Frederic Faucher	68	23	36	59	47
Jean-Philippe Glaude	71	4	52	56	134
Nicholas Bilotto	58	13	37	50	195
Jonathan St. Louis	40	17	28	45	137
Jonathan Gagnon	27	16	21	37	38
Eric Dubois	25	11	14	25	34
David Girard	26	9	16	25	13
Vincent Tougas	72	16	6	22	104
Jean-Philippe Morin	66	1	21	22	147
Simon Lagace-Daigle	40	11	9	20	50
Pierre-Luc Emond	58	8	11	19	74
David Jacob-Tancrede	45	5	13	18	18
Simon Poirier	71	2	16	18	119
Alexandre Couture	18	3	14	17	47
Eric Jean	72	6	9	15	183
Louis-Philippe Lessard	30	8	6	14	31
Justin Mongeon	34	1	11	12	52
Daniel Hudgin	15	4	6	10	35
Joey D'Amico	26	2	4	6	83
Stephane Labrie	49	1	2	3	272
Eric Bleau	15	1	1	2	39
David Lessard	59	1	1	2	31
Thierry Kaszap	24	0	2	2	27
Frederick Malette (goalie)	10	0	1	1	2
Guillaume Beaudry	1	0	0	0	0
Charles-Philippe Barbe	2	0	0	0	2
Dwight Wolfe	2	0	0	0	2
Jean-Charles Parenteau	3	0	0	0	0
Andre Corbeil Jr.	4	0	0	0	39
Jean-Francois Gouin	7	0	0	0	64
Pascal Poirier (goalie)	1	0	0	0	0
Didier Bochatay	17	0	0	0	48
Jean-Francois Racine (goalie)	20	0	0	0	0
Dany Dallaire (goalie)	24	0	0	0	0
Philippe Sauve (goalie)	28	0	0	0	0

GOALTENDING

	Games	Min.	W	L	T	G	SO	Avg.
Pascal Poirier	1	25	0	0	0	0	0	0.00
Frederick Malette	10	507	5	2	1	25	0	2.96
Jean-Francois Racine	20	1152	14	6	0	63	1	3.28
Philippe Sauve	28	1526	12	12	2	106	0	4.17
Dany Dallaire	24	1126	7	10	1	80	0	4.26

HALIFAX MOOSEHEADS

SCORING

	Games	G	A	Pts.	PIM
Ramzi Abid	59	57	80	137	148
Brandon Reid	62	44	80	124	10

	Games	G	A	Pts.	PIM
Jasmin Gelinas	72	17	70	87	64
Andrei Shefer	72	34	42	76	30
Joey DiPenta	63	13	43	56	83
Benoit Dusablon	31	18	35	53	18
Brandon Benedict	69	19	30	49	46
Ryan Flinn	67	14	19	33	365
Jonathan St. Louis	31	16	15	31	72
Ali MacEachern	65	5	22	27	127
Jules-Edy Laraque	28	8	9	17	6
Jason Troini	20	7	9	16	33
Gary Zinck	67	4	12	16	195
Jonathan Gagnon	19	11	4	15	37
Frederic Belanger	21	5	10	15	30
Marc-Andre Binette	11	9	5	14	2
Darrell Jerrett	66	9	4	13	242
Robbie Sutherland	42	4	9	13	59
Eric Dubois	19	4	7	11	15
Samuel Séguin	11	5	5	10	20
Jason King	53	3	7	10	8
P.J. Lynch	35	2	5	7	42
Nick Greenough	31	3	3	6	147
Tyler Reid	43	2	2	4	38
Hugo Lehoux	25	1	2	3	110
Bruce Gillis	38	1	2	3	20
Jonathan Boone	56	1	2	3	81
Jonathan Andrews	22	0	2	2	105
Joe Groleau	34	0	2	2	47
Shawn Lewis	5	0	1	1	2
Mathieu Paul	19	0	1	1	8
Jonathan Jolette	28	0	1	1	23
Pascal Leclaire (goalie)	31	0	1	1	4
Nathan States	1	0	0	0	0
David Leddicote	2	0	0	0	0
Pierre-Luc Bacon	3	0	0	0	0
Carlos Sayde (goalie)	3	0	0	0	0
Sacha Boyer	4	0	0	0	0
David Hemsworth	6	0	0	0	10
Vincent Laroche (goalie)	6	0	0	0	0
Alexei Volkov (goalie)	40	0	0	0	2

GOALTENDING

	Games	Min.	W	L	T	G	SO	Avg.
Carlos Sayde	3	51	0	0	0	2	0	2.37
Alexei Volkov	40	2222	23	13	2	124	1	3.35
Pascal Leclaire	31	1729	16	8	4	103	1	3.57
Vincent Laroche	6	358	2	4	0	22	0	3.69

HULL OLYMPIQUES

SCORING

	Games	G	A	Pts.	PIM
Michael Ryder	63	50	58	108	50
Alexandre Giroux	72	52	47	99	117
Radim Vrbata	58	29	45	74	26
Paul Spadafora	41	23	49	72	119
Ryan Lauzon	49	24	35	59	37
Brock Boucher	50	24	34	58	32
Philippe Lacasse	61	16	41	57	29
Adam Rivet	68	10	45	55	71
Bruno Lemire	56	17	36	53	54
Dustin Russell	71	20	23	43	35
Michal Pinc	31	11	27	38	67
Daniel Clermont	64	15	15	30	75
Mario Joly	63	8	19	27	247
Roberto Bissonnette	60	5	15	20	318
Andrew Carver	61	1	18	19	88
Jason Lehoux	29	11	7	18	109
Daniel Hudgin	26	6	9	15	28
Derick Martin	70	4	11	15	92
Erich Paroshy	43	0	15	15	119
Sebastien Strozynski	28	3	8	11	20
Patrick Lafreniere	41	4	3	7	104
Bobby Clarke	52	1	6	7	32
Benoit Beaudoin	17	2	4	6	0

	Games	G	A	Pts.	PIM
Simon Nadeau	23	2	2	4	7
Michael Parent	33	0	4	4	53
Donald Johnstone	17	1	2	3	33
Ryan Lee	24	0	3	3	118
Robert Horak	4	0	1	1	4
Eric Lafrance (goalie)	40	0	1	1	2
Daniel Dupuis	2	0	0	0	0
Yannick Lavigne	3	0	0	0	0
Luc Bergeron (goalie)	6	0	0	0	0
Philippe Sauve (goalie)	17	0	0	0	23
Frederick Malette (goalie)	19	0	0	0	0

GOALTENDING

	Games	Min.	W	L	T	G	SO	Avg.
Eric Lafrance	40	2024	21	11	3	114	0	3.38
Philippe Sauve	17	992	9	7	1	57	0	3.45
Frederick Malette	19	1061	11	5	0	63	1	3.56
Luc Bergeron	6	274	1	1	2	20	0	4.38

MONCTON WILDCATS

SCORING

	Games	G	A	Pts.	PIM
Martin Bartek	69	32	44	76	36
Simon Laliberte	65	39	36	75	66
Mirko Murovic	72	19	51	70	113
Morgan Warren	65	29	36	65	53
Mathieu Benoit	33	28	34	62	21
Jonathan Roy	31	25	28	53	20
Patrick Yetman	65	18	34	52	33
Alexandre Vigneault	62	12	34	46	70
Francois Beauchemin	33	8	31	39	35
Jonathan Girard	26	10	25	35	36
Kory Baker	65	10	25	35	115
Jonathan Desroches	60	3	28	31	43
Olivier Dubuc	70	7	23	30	91
David Comeau	40	13	16	29	112
Bobby Reed	67	10	20	20	197
Sergei Kaltygen	60	8	7	15	172
Louis-Philippe Lessard	38	3	9	12	50
Jonathan Ferland	52	3	6	9	21
Dominic Noel	24	5	3	8	37
Steeve Vandal	20	2	4	6	27
Martin Lavergne	33	4	1	5	16
Daniel MacLeod	26	1	4	5	93
Patrice Thériault	36	1	3	4	26
Thierry Kaszap	35	1	2	3	36
Ian Seguin	28	1	1	2	28
Trevor Ettinger	24	0	2	2	153
Simon Lajeunesse (goalie)	55	0	2	2	27
Martin Dube	2	0	1	1	0
Leon Martin	16	0	1	1	2
Carl McLean	46	0	1	1	29
James Kinsman	1	0	0	0	0
Jordan Udle	1	0	0	0	0
Tyson Maloney	5	0	0	0	62
David Philpott	6	0	0	0	0
Matt Belanger	7	0	0	0	13
Jean-Francois Racine (goalie)	10	0	0	0	0
David Walker	10	0	0	0	89
Danny Bowie (goalie)	22	0	0	0	17

GOALTENDING

	Games	Min.	W	L	T	G	SO	Avg.
Simon Lajeunesse	55	2922	31	15	1	127	6	2.61
Danny Bowie	22	1023	9	5	3	53	1	3.11
Jean-Francois Racine	10	410	3	3	1	28	0	4.10

MONTREAL ROCKETS

SCORING

	Games	G	A	Pts.	PIM
Alain O'Driscoll	62	34	55	89	83
Randy Copley	54	34	47	81	70
Yann Joseph	58	20	57	77	83

	Games	G	A	Pts.	PIM
Edo Terglav	62	35	38	73	37
Chris Montgomery	59	23	46	69	28
Jean-Michel Boisvert	67	23	39	62	32
Nicolas Pelletier	68	18	23	41	35
Lauri Kinos	69	12	17	29	80
Marc Villeneuve	70	16	10	26	83
Louis Robitaille	71	3	21	24	266
Francis Emery	71	7	16	23	271
Philippe Forest	65	7	12	19	22
Eric Dubois	20	9	9	18	24
Casey Burnette	72	4	14	18	170
Guillaume Lamoureux	26	6	9	15	2
Olivier Maltais	28	5	10	15	14
Jerome Petit	12	7	5	12	21
Maxime Pelletier	38	5	5	10	92
Mathieu Paul	46	0	10	10	53
David Cloutier	33	2	7	9	36
Michael Lanthier	35	0	8	8	111
Marc-Andre Beaulieu	64	0	8	8	36
Benoit Beausoleil	57	2	3	5	259
Jordan Trew	40	0	5	5	145
Jonathan Pilotte	21	2	2	4	57
Brett Lutes	4	2	1	3	0
Steve Castonguay	18	0	3	3	4
Marc-Andre Leclerc (goalie)	1	0	0	0	0
Maxime Nadeau	2	0	0	0	2
Jonathan Wilhelmy (goalie)	2	0	0	0	0
Alexandre Simoneau	3	0	0	0	0
Jonathan Cayer (goalie)	27	0	0	0	0
Frederik Brindamour (goalie)	59	0	0	0	16

GOALTENDING

	Games	Min.	W	L	T	G	SO	Avg.
Frederik Brindamour	59	3087	23	25	5	211	3	4.10
Jonathan Cayer	27	1141	5	11	1	88	0	4.63
Jonathan Wilhelmy	2	120	1	1	0	10	0	5.00
Marc-Andre Leclerc	1	20	0	0	0	3	0	9.00

QUEBEC REMPARTS

SCORING

	Games	G	A	Pts.	PIM
Patrick Grandmaitre	70	38	68	106	84
Wesley Scanzano	71	31	75	106	107
Eric Chouinard	50	57	47	104	105
Eric Laplante	47	24	35	59	234
Martin Moise	56	21	29	50	42
Martin Grenier	67	11	35	46	302
Mike Ribeiro	21	17	28	45	30
Andre Martineau	69	15	28	43	33
Kirill Safronov	55	11	32	43	95
Khristian Kudroc	57	9	22	31	172
Shawn Collymore	64	8	16	24	22
Stuart MacRae	41	6	13	19	6
Philippe Paris	50	4	15	19	12
Chris Lyness	26	5	13	18	30
Sylvain Plamondon	49	7	7	14	263
Eric Cloutier	62	4	6	10	17
Nicholas Bilotto	12	3	7	10	22
Jean-Philippe Cote	34	0	10	10	15
Alexandre Morel	22	2	6	8	31
Jean Mallette	68	2	6	8	47
Ken Elliott	41	3	3	6	26
Tommy Bolduc	56	3	2	5	352
Guillaume Lefebvre	2	3	1	4	0
Casey Leggett	22	1	3	4	21
Remi Bergeron	7	1	2	3	13
Joey Fetta	6	0	3	3	47
Karl Morin	32	0	3	3	16
Tyler Noye	35	0	3	3	8
Patrick Chouinard	37	0	3	3	14
Jean-Francois Touchette	14	1	1	2	4
Justin Stewart	4	1	0	1	0

	Games	G	A	Pts.	PIM
Mathieu Sioui	5	1	0	1	0
Jonathan Charron (goalie)	10	0	1	1	0
Maxime Ouellet (goalie)	53	0	1	1	4
Billy Rochefort	2	0	0	0	0
Chris Fougere	3	0	0	0	0
Jean-Francois Gagne	3	0	0	0	2
Alan Horic	3	0	0	0	0
Kevin Lachance	3	0	0	0	0
Yann Collin (goalie)	4	0	0	0	2
Dustin Traylen	6	0	0	0	0
Andre Hart	10	0	0	0	23
Martin Pare (goalie)	15	0	0	0	2

GOALTENDING

	Games	Min.	W	L	T	G	SO	Avg.
Maxime Ouellet	53	2984	31	16	4	133	2	2.67
Martin Pare	15	669	8	2	0	31	0	2.78
Jonathan Charron	10	513	3	6	0	32	0	3.75
Yann Collin	4	181	2	0	0	13	0	4.32

RIMOUSKI OCEANIC

SCORING

	Games	G	A	Pts.	PIM
Brad Richards	63	71	115	186	69
Jan-Philippe Cadieux	71	44	66	110	16
Juraj Kolnik	47	53	53	106	53
Michel Periard	70	25	75	100	58
Michel Ouellet	72	36	53	89	38
Thatcher Bell	53	26	43	69	61
Jonathan Beaulieu	71	25	39	64	149
Jean-Philippe Briere	70	13	34	47	40
Benoit Martin	70	19	23	42	48
Jacques Lariviere	61	12	24	36	309
Joe Rullier	49	3	32	35	161
Rene Vydareny	51	7	23	30	41
Alexandre Tremblay	17	12	10	22	30
Casey Leggett	30	6	14	20	35
Philippe Grondin	30	6	9	15	22
Brent MacLellan	69	2	13	15	98
Aaron Johnson	63	1	14	15	57
Nicolas Poirier	64	5	8	13	103
Shawn Scanzano	20	0	9	9	207
Alex Castonguay	62	1	3	4	351
Denis Desmarais	33	0	4	4	70
Nicolas Pilote	24	0	3	3	14
Jean-Francois Babin	48	2	0	2	192
Sebastien Caron (goalie)	54	0	2	2	4
Mathieu Simard	1	0	1	1	0
Mathieu Pigeon	4	0	1	1	2
David Boilard	29	0	1	1	14
Ronnie Decontie	40	0	1	1	20
Mathieu Bernatchez (goalie)	2	0	0	0	0
Kris MacPhee	2	0	0	0	0
Philippe Lauze	3	0	0	0	0
Eric Salvail (goalie)	28	0	0	0	0

GOALTENDING

	Games	Min.	W	L	T	G	SO	Avg.
Mathieu Bernatchez	2	50	0	0	0	1	0	1.21
Sebastien Caron	54	3040	38	11	3	179	1	3.53
Eric Salvail	28	1263	10	9	1	92	0	4.37

ROUYN-NORANDA HUSKIES

SCORING

	Games	G	A	Pts.	PIM
Jerome Tremblay	71	46	70	116	83
Kevin Cloutier	72	34	57	91	54
Jonathan Gauthier	70	32	49	81	104
Marc-Andre Binette	48	26	49	75	25
Maxime Bouchard	71	29	39	68	171
Steeve Vandal	44	17	30	47	88
Alain Turcotte	63	13	21	34	240
Matthew Quinn	72	15	16	31	26

	Games	G	A	Pts.	PIM
Kyrill Alexeyev	67	5	26	31	175
Jason Tessier	60	8	21	29	72
Michal Pinc	27	8	16	24	64
Louis Mandeville	50	5	11	16	31
Shawn Scanzano	42	3	13	16	336
Sebastien Strozynski	27	7	8	15	14
Guillaume Lefebvre	25	4	11	15	39
Steve Waters	35	6	5	11	25
Jason Lehoux	14	4	7	11	54
Robert Horak	44	1	8	9	95
Patrick Gilbert	72	1	8	9	128
Bertrand-Pierre Plouffe	61	2	6	8	124
Alexandre Morel	15	1	7	8	66
Mathieu Leclerc	57	2	5	7	26
Steve Fillion	12	2	3	5	4
Mike Ribeiro	2	1	3	4	0
Jonathan Pelletier (goalie)	32	0	4	4	6
Eric L'Italien	41	0	2	2	8
Bruno Cadieux	50	0	2	2	47
Jonathan Gagnon	10	0	1	1	14
Francis Claude	17	0	1	1	0
Sebastien Centomo (goalie)	50	0	1	1	18
Michael Parent	21	0	0	0	12
Andre Hart	36	0	0	0	28

GOALTENDING

	Games	Min.	W	L	T	G	SO	Avg.
Sebastien Centomo	50	2758	24	17	3	160	1	3.48
Jonathan Pelletier	32	1580	9	18	1	120	0	4.56

SHAWINIGAN CATARACTES

SCORING

	Games	G	A	Pts.	PIM
Dominic Forget	67	38	78	116	28
Pascal Dupuis	61	50	55	105	164
Jean-Philippe Pare	72	32	60	92	99
Marc-Andre Bergeron	70	24	50	74	173
Alexandre Tremblay	47	31	31	62	63
Jean-Francois Dufort	70	14	34	48	218
Philippe Deblois	68	12	26	38	108
Yannick Noiseux	71	16	21	37	74
Francis Deslauriers	63	13	22	35	47
Jonathan Bellemarre	63	11	19	30	26
Gilbert Lefrançois	24	12	11	23	18
Anthony Quessy	24	7	14	21	119
Jason Pominville	60	4	17	21	12
Jean-Francois David	71	7	11	18	90
Philippe Gelinas	48	8	9	17	83
Jean-Francois Pilon	31	3	6	9	55
Jonathan Lessard	68	1	8	9	124
Denis Desmarais	25	4	4	8	59
Alexandre Blackburn	64	1	7	8	253
Jean-Sebastien Trudelle	22	2	4	6	71
David Chicoine	65	2	3	5	84
Connor McGuire	23	1	3	4	4
Mathieu Chouinard (goalie)	59	0	3	3	10
Francis Mongrain	20	2	0	2	6
Miroslav Talarovic	25	0	2	2	46
Andre Landry	30	0	2	2	17
Samuel Duplain	42	0	2	2	338
Francis Charlebois (goalie)	1	0	0	0	0
François Gagnon	1	0	0	0	0
Olivier Michaud (goalie)	1	0	0	0	0
Sebastien Buisson	3	0	0	0	0
Martin Briere	6	0	0	0	0
Dave Verville (goalie)	6	0	0	0	4
Jean-Francois Laniel (goalie)	14	0	0	0	0

GOALTENDING

	Games	Min.	W	L	T	G	SO	Avg.
Olivier Michaud	1	49	0	1	0	2	0	2.44
Mathieu Chouinard	59	3339	32	20	5	186	4	3.34
Jean-Francois Laniel	14	630	2	7	0	40	0	3.81

MAJOR JUNIOR LEAGUES QMJHL

	Games	Min.	W	L	T	G	SO	Avg.
Dave Verville	6	335	3	2	0	22	0	3.94
Francis Charlebois	1	10	0	0	0	3	0	17.58

SHERBROOKE FAUCONS

SCORING

	Games	G	A	Pts.	PIM
Dmitri Afanassenkov	60	56	43	99	70
Eric Pinoul	63	25	52	77	55
Maxim Potapov	51	30	46	76	42
Eric Lavigne	65	12	49	61	68
Pierre-Luc Courchesne	72	13	38	51	73
Michel Beausoleil	58	21	27	48	48
Francois Belanger	59	20	25	45	66
Jean Morin Jr.	59	12	30	42	76
Steve Morency	72	22	17	39	48
Patrick Vincent	55	11	28	39	198
Benoit Genesse	70	11	24	35	40
Bryan Lachance	57	1	23	24	263
Nicolas Corbeil	64	9	12	21	28
Martin Beauchesne	66	3	15	18	138
Jonathan Robert	72	4	9	13	72
Joey Neale	57	7	5	12	16
Alexandre Page	29	3	8	11	20
Patrice Tassy	58	3	6	9	8
Philippe Parent	22	2	5	7	23
Colin Keith	62	0	6	6	173
Jean-Philippe Paradis	17	0	5	5	8
Eric Dagenais	33	2	2	4	23
Dany Sabourin (goalie)	55	0	2	2	14
Jeremy Knight	5	0	1	1	0
Olivier Bourdon-Landry	1	0	0	0	0
Sebastien Crete (goalie)	1	0	0	0	0
Jocelyn Guimond (goalie)	1	0	0	0	0
Aaron Fraser	3	0	0	0	0
Louis-Philippe Lemay	4	0	0	0	0
Paul Matthews	4	0	0	0	0
Samuel Bessette	19	0	0	0	17
Drew MacIntyre (goalie)	24	0	0	0	0

GOALTENDING

	Games	Min.	W	L	T	G	SO	Avg.
Sebastien Crete	1	32	0	1	0	1	0	1.87
Drew MacIntyre	24	1254	10	7	2	67	0	3.21
Dany Sabourin	55	3067	25	22	5	181	1	3.54
Jocelyn Guimond	1	6	0	0	0	1	0	11.13

VAL D'OR FOREURS

SCORING

	Games	G	A	Pts.	PIM
Simon Gamache	72	64	79	143	74
Benoit Dusablon	41	29	53	82	45
Eric Fortier	72	7	47	54	49
Mathieu Lendick	62	20	30	50	52
Seneque Hyacinthe	49	15	30	45	43
Stephane Veilleux	50	14	28	42	100
Jason Troini	30	12	17	29	12
Jan Choteborsky	40	4	25	29	70
Guillaume Lamoureux	41	10	15	25	33
Sebastien Laprise	45	10	13	23	34
Anthony Quessy	45	9	13	22	219
Denis Boily	27	8	13	21	38
Luc Girard	72	3	13	16	27
Alexandre Page	26	3	11	14	32
Jonathan Fauteux	19	6	7	13	34
David Cloutier	30	5	8	13	24
Sebastien Gagnon	44	6	6	12	214
Nick Greenough	41	4	5	9	220
Alexandre Rouleau	41	3	3	6	39
Mathieu Bastien	41	2	4	6	131
Philippe Ouellette	15	0	6	6	41
Mathieu Roy	48	1	4	5	66
Jean-Francois Soucy	55	1	4	5	9

	Games	G	A	Pts.	PIM
Antoine Bergeron	8	3	1	4	10
Thomas Psenka	61	0	3	3	112
Eric Labelle	21	2	0	2	160
Frederick Bedard	28	1	1	2	19
Gabriel Proulx	4	1	0	1	0
Patrick Morneau	21	1	0	1	27
Christopher Page	2	0	1	1	0
Eric Frechette	19	0	1	1	10
Samuel Duplain	26	0	1	1	99
Daniel Cloutier	1	0	0	0	0
Ian Gravel (goalie)	2	0	0	0	0
Rene Nadeau	2	0	0	0	0
Jocelyn Potvin	2	0	0	0	0
Eric Malenfant	5	0	0	0	0
Jerome Morin	6	0	0	0	2
Jean-Francois Payant (goalie)	7	0	0	0	0
Jonathan Charron (goalie)	8	0	0	0	0
Andre Corbeil Jr.	11	0	0	0	61
Jean-Francois Laniel (goalie)	11	0	0	0	2
Adam Morneau (goalie)	25	0	0	0	31
Dave Verville (goalie)	36	0	0	0	0
Hugo Lehoux	41	0	0	0	115

GOALTENDING

	Games	Min.	W	L	T	G	SO	Avg.
Ian Gravel	2	7	0	0	0	0	0	0.00
Dave Verville	36	2069	11	19	5	145	1	4.20
Jonathan Charron	8	391	2	4	0	34	0	5.22
Jean-Francois Laniel	11	479	1	6	0	46	0	5.76
Adam Morneau	25	1165	4	15	2	112	0	5.77
Jean-Francois Payant	7	246	0	3	0	26	0	6.34

VICTORIAVILLE TIGRES

SCORING

	Games	G	A	Pts.	PIM
Marc-Andre Thinel	71	59	73	132	55
Carl Mallette	69	49	76	125	97
Sebastien Thinel	70	34	61	95	94
Antoine Vermette	71	30	41	71	87
Danny Groulx	66	12	55	67	131
Alexander Riazantsev	48	17	45	62	45
Eric Cote	70	18	29	47	30
Matthew Lombardi	65	18	26	44	28
Kristian Kovac	65	11	18	29	50
Teddy Kyres	60	8	16	24	33
Pierre-Luc Sleigher	70	9	4	13	287
Antoine Bergeron	24	2	8	10	30
Carl Gagnon	38	3	4	7	4
Joey Fetta	33	2	4	6	173
Eric Labelle	39	2	4	6	175
Pierre-Luc Daneau	61	2	4	6	66
Jonathan Fauteux	18	4	1	5	36
Stephane Veilleux	22	1	4	5	17
Sandro Sbrocca	21	1	2	3	178
Mathieu Wathier	42	1	2	3	31
Luc Levesque	30	0	3	3	75
Michael McIntyre	38	2	0	2	155
Bramwell Beck	5	0	2	2	27
Guillaume Beaudoin	32	0	2	2	82
Billy Rochefort	43	0	2	2	27
Richard Paul	21	1	0	1	147
Simon St. Pierre	10	0	1	1	0
Patrick Chouinard	20	0	1	1	51
Guillaume Lavoie	44	0	1	1	76
David Masse	2	0	0	0	0
Patrice Poissant	3	0	0	0	0
Marc St. Louis	10	0	0	0	2
Jean-Francois Nogues (goalie)	39	0	0	0	0
Philippe Ozga (goalie)	46	0	0	0	46

GOALTENDING

	Games	Min.	W	L	T	G	SO	Avg.
Jean-Francois Nogues	39	1898	14	17	0	134	0	4.24
Philippe Ozga	46	2444	13	25	3	174	4	4.27

PLAYERS WITH TWO OR MORE TEAMS

MAJOR JUNIOR LEAGUES QMJHL

SCORING

	Games	G	A	Pts.	PIM
Ramzi Abid, A.-Bathurst	13	10	11	21	61
Ramzi Abid, Halifax	59	57	80	137	148
Totals	72	67	91	158	209
Jonathan Andrews, Halifax	22	0	2	2	105
Jonathan Andrews, C. Breton	40	3	8	11	78
Totals	62	3	10	13	183
Francois Beauchemin, A.-Bath.	38	11	36	47	64
Francois Beauchemin, Monc. ...	33	8	31	39	35
Totals	71	19	67	86	99
Frederic Belanger, Halifax	21	5	10	15	30
Frederic Belanger, Cape Breton	43	9	20	29	48
Totals	64	14	30	44	78
Mathieu Benoit, A.-Bathurst	20	29	10	39	38
Mathieu Benoit, Moncton	33	28	34	62	21
Totals	53	57	44	101	59
Antoine Bergeron, Victoriaville	24	2	8	10	30
Antoine Bergeron, Val-d'Or	8	3	1	4	10
Totals	32	5	9	14	40
Nicholas Bilotto, Quebec	12	3	7	10	22
Nicholas Bilotto, Drum.	58	13	37	50	195
Totals	70	16	44	60	217
Marc-Andre Binette, Halifax	11	9	5	14	2
Marc-Andre Binette, R.-Nor.	48	26	49	75	25
Totals	59	35	54	89	27
Eric Bleau, Baie-Comeau	26	0	0	0	91
Eric Bleau, Drummondville	15	1	1	2	39
Totals	41	1	1	2	130
Jonathan Charron, Val-d'Or (g) .	8	0	0	0	0
Jonathan Charron, Quebec (g) ..	10	0	1	1	0
Totals	18	0	1	1	0
Patrick Chouinard, Victoriaville..	20	0	1	1	51
Patrick Chouinard, Quebec	37	0	3	3	14
Totals	57	0	4	4	65
David Cloutier, Montreal	33	2	7	9	36
David Cloutier, Val-d'Or	30	5	8	13	24
Totals	63	7	15	22	60
David Comeau, Moncton	40	13	16	29	112
David Comeau, A.-Bathurst	20	10	24	34	42
Totals	60	23	40	63	154
Andre Corbeil Jr., Val-d'Or	11	0	0	0	61
Andre Corbeil Jr., Drum.	4	0	0	0	39
Totals	15	0	0	0	100
Jean-Philippe Cote, Quebec	34	0	10	10	15
Jean-Philippe Cote, C. Breton	28	0	4	4	21
Totals	62	0	14	14	36
Dany Dallaire, Drum. (g)	24	0	0	0	0
Dany Dallaire, Cape Breton (g) .	18	0	0	0	19
Totals	42	0	0	0	19
Joey D'Amico, Chicoutimi	29	2	11	13	68
Joey D'Amico, Drummondville..	26	2	4	6	83
Totals	55	4	15	19	151
Jean-Francois Demers, C.B.	19	1	1	2	29
Jean-Francois Demers, Chi.	38	1	2	3	93
Totals	57	2	3	5	122
Denis Desmarais, Rimouski	33	0	4	4	70
Denis Desmarais, Shawinigan	25	4	4	8	59
Totals	58	4	8	12	129
Eric Dubois, Montreal	20	9	9	18	24
Eric Dubois, Halifax	19	4	7	11	15
Eric Dubois, Drummondville	25	11	14	25	34
Totals	64	24	30	54	73
Samuel Duplain, Shawinigan	42	0	2	2	338
Samuel Duplain, Val-d'Or	26	0	1	1	99
Totals	68	0	3	3	437
Benoit Dusablon, Val-d'Or	41	29	53	82	45
Benoit Dusablon, Halifax	31	18	35	53	18
Totals	72	47	88	135	63
Trevor Ettinger, Cape Breton	44	1	8	9	328
Trevor Ettinger, Moncton	24	0	2	2	153

	Games	G	A	Pts.	PIM
Totals	68	1	10	11	481
Jonathan Fauteux, Val-d'Or	19	6	7	13	34
Jonathan Fauteux, Victoriaville ..	18	4	1	5	36
Totals	37	10	8	18	70
Joey Fetta, Quebec	6	0	3	3	47
Joey Fetta, Victoriaville	33	2	4	6	173
Totals	39	2	7	9	220
Francois Fortin, Chicoutimi	45	10	23	33	37
Francois Fortin, A.-Bathurst	27	7	16	23	29
Totals	72	17	39	56	66
Jonathan Gagnon, Cape Breton	26	8	12	20	25
Jonathan Gagnon, Halifax	19	11	4	15	37
Jonathan Gagnon, Drum.	27	16	21	37	38
Totals	72	35	37	72	100
Sebastien Gagnon, C. Breton	9	0	0	0	46
Sebastien Gagnon, Val-d'Or	44	6	6	12	214
Totals	53	6	6	12	260
David Girard, Chicoutimi	42	15	17	32	50
David Girard, Drummondville	26	9	16	25	13
Totals	68	24	33	57	63
Nick Greenough, Val-d'Or	41	4	5	9	220
Nick Greenough, Halifax	31	3	3	6	147
Totals	72	7	8	15	367
Yannick Guay, Chicoutimi	35	7	8	15	8
Yannick Guay, A.-Bathurst	23	10	9	19	2
Totals	58	17	17	34	10
Andre Hart, Rouyn-Noranda	36	0	0	0	28
Andre Hart, Quebec	10	0	0	0	23
Totals	46	0	0	0	51
Robert Horak, Rouyn-Noranda..	44	1	8	9	95
Robert Horak, Hull	4	0	1	1	4
Robert Horak, Cape Breton	22	1	7	8	20
Totals	70	2	16	18	119
Daniel Hudgin, Drummondville .	15	4	6	10	35
Daniel Hudgin, Hull	26	6	9	15	28
Totals	41	10	15	25	63
Donald Johnstone, C. Breton	39	1	2	3	45
Donald Johnstone, Hull	17	1	2	3	33
Totals	56	2	4	6	78
Thierry Kaszap, Moncton	35	1	2	3	36
Thierry Kaszap, Drum.	24	0	2	2	27
Totals	59	1	4	5	63
Eric Labelle, Victoriaville	39	2	4	6	175
Eric Labelle, Val-d'Or	21	2	0	2	160
Totals	60	4	4	8	335
Simon Lagace-Daigle, Drum.	40	11	9	20	50
Simon Lagace-Daigle, Chi.	27	1	5	6	18
Totals	67	12	14	26	68
Guillaume Lamoureux, V.-d'Or	41	10	15	25	33
Guillaume Lamoureux, Mont. ...	26	6	9	15	2
Totals	67	16	24	40	35
Jean-Francois Laniel, Shaw. (g)	14	0	0	0	0
Jean-Francois Laniel, Val. (g)	11	0	0	0	2
Totals	25	0	0	0	2
Sebastien Laprise, Val-d'Or	45	10	13	23	34
Sebastien Laprise, Chicoutimi	26	3	7	10	2
Totals	71	13	20	33	36
Jules-Edy Laraque, A.-Bathurst.	43	13	20	33	39
Jules-Edy Laraque, Halifax	28	8	9	17	6
Totals	71	21	29	50	45
Martin Lavergne, A.-Bathurst	32	7	8	15	65
Martin Lavergne, Moncton	33	4	1	5	16
Totals	65	11	9	20	81
Guillaume Lefebvre, C. Breton	44	26	28	54	82
Guillaume Lefebvre, Quebec	2	3	1	4	0
Guillaume Lefebvre, R.-Nor.	25	4	11	15	39
Totals	71	33	40	73	121
Gilbert Lefrancois, Chicoutimi	45	19	16	35	68
Gilbert Lefrancois, Shawinigan..	24	12	11	23	18
Totals	69	31	27	58	86

	Games	G	A	Pts.	PIM
Casey Leggett, Rimouski	30	6	14	20	35
Casey Leggett, Quebec	22	1	3	4	21
Totals	52	7	17	24	56
Hugo Lehoux, Val-d'Or	41	0	0	0	115
Hugo Lehoux, Halifax	25	1	2	3	110
Totals	66	1	2	3	225
Jason Lehoux, Rouyn-Noranda	14	4	7	11	54
Jason Lehoux, Hull	29	11	7	18	109
Totals	43	15	14	29	163
Louis-Philippe Lessard, Monc.	38	3	9	12	50
Louis-Philippe Lessard, Drum.	30	8	6	14	31
Totals	68	11	15	26	81
P.J. Lynch, Halifax	35	2	5	7	42
P.J. Lynch, Cape Breton	24	3	9	12	22
Totals	59	5	14	19	64
Chris Lyness, Cape Breton	43	15	29	44	114
Chris Lyness, Quebec	26	5	13	18	30
Totals	69	20	42	62	144
Daniel MacLeod, Moncton	26	1	4	5	93
Daniel MacLeod, A.-Bathurst	33	8	11	19	71
Totals	59	9	15	24	164
Stuart MacRae, Quebec	41	6	13	19	6
Stuart MacRae, Cape Breton	28	11	9	20	23
Totals	69	17	22	39	29
Frederick Malette, Hull (g)	19	0	0	0	0
Frederick Malette, Drum. (g)	10	0	1	1	2
Totals	29	0	1	1	2
Olivier Maltais, Baie-Comeau	12	1	0	1	4
Olivier Maltais, Montreal	28	5	10	15	14
Totals	40	6	10	16	18
Michael McIntyre, Victoriaville	38	2	0	2	155
Michael McIntyre, Cape Breton	12	0	1	1	26
Totals	50	2	1	3	181
Alexandre Morel, Quebec	22	2	6	8	31
Alexandre Morel, R.-Noranda	15	1	7	8	66
Totals	37	3	13	16	97
Pascal Morency, Chicoutimi	12	0	1	1	9
Pascal Morency, Cape Breton	37	2	3	5	35
Totals	49	2	4	6	44
Dominic Noel, Moncton	24	5	3	8	37
Dominic Noel, Cape Breton	43	12	24	36	40
Totals	67	17	27	44	77
Alexandre Page, Val-d'Or	26	3	11	14	32
Alexandre Page, Sherbrooke	29	3	8	11	20
Totals	55	6	19	25	52
Christopher Page, B.-Comeau	41	1	26	27	42
Christopher Page, Val-d'Or	2	0	1	1	0
Totals	43	1	27	28	42
Michael Parent, Hull	33	0	4	4	53
Michael Parent, R.-Noranda	21	0	0	0	12
Totals	54	0	4	4	65
Mathieu Paul, Halifax	19	0	1	1	8
Mathieu Paul, Montreal	46	0	10	10	53
Totals	65	0	11	11	61
Jerome Petit, Montreal	12	7	5	12	21
Jerome Petit, Baie-Comeau	21	7	6	13	39
Totals	33	14	11	25	60
Michal Pinc, Hull	31	11	27	38	67
Michal Pinc, Rouyn-Noranda	27	8	16	24	64
Totals	58	19	43	62	131
Anthony Quessy, Val-d'Or	45	9	13	22	219
Anthony Quessy, Shawinigan	24	7	14	21	119
Totals	69	16	27	43	338
J.-Francois Racine, Monc. (g)	10	0	0	0	0
J.-Francois Racine, Drum. (g)	20	0	0	0	0
Totals	30	0	0	0	0
Tyler Reid, Halifax	43	2	2	4	38
Tyler Reid, A.-Bathurst	24	1	3	4	24
Totals	67	3	5	8	62
Mike Ribeiro, Rouyn-Noranda	2	1	3	4	0
Mike Ribeiro, Quebec	21	17	28	45	30
Totals	23	18	31	49	30

	Games	G	A	Pts.	PIM
Billy Rochefort, Quebec	2	0	0	0	0
Billy Rochefort, Victoriaville	43	0	2	2	27
Totals	45	0	2	2	27
Jonathan Roy, Drummondville	42	39	33	72	30
Jonathan Roy, Moncton	31	25	28	53	20
Totals	73	64	61	125	50
David St. Germain, C.B. (g)	36	0	0	0	0
David St. Germain, Baie-C. (g)	23	0	1	1	10
Totals	59	0	1	1	10
Philippe Sauve, Drum. (g)	28	0	0	0	0
Philippe Sauve, Hull (g)	17	0	0	0	23
Totals	45	0	0	0	23
Sandro Sbrocca, Cape Breton	35	3	8	11	205
Sandro Sbrocca, Victoriaville	21	1	2	3	178
Totals	56	4	10	14	383
Shawn Scanzano, R.-Noranda	42	3	13	16	336
Shawn Scanzano, Rimouski	20	0	9	9	207
Totals	62	3	22	25	543
Samuel Seguin, Halifax	11	5	5	10	20
Samuel Seguin, A.-Bathurst	50	16	28	44	57
Totals	61	21	33	54	77
Tim Sinasac, Cape Breton	24	0	2	2	97
Tim Sinasac, A.-Bathurst	26	1	3	4	178
Totals	50	1	5	6	275
Jonathan St. Louis, Drum.	40	17	28	45	137
Jonathan St. Louis, Halifax	31	16	15	31	72
Totals	71	33	43	76	209
Sebastien Strozynski, Hull	28	3	8	11	20
Sebastien Strozynski, R.-Nor.	27	7	8	15	14
Totals	55	10	16	26	34
Robbie Sutherland, C. Breton	7	0	3	3	4
Robbie Sutherland, Halifax	42	4	9	13	59
Totals	49	4	12	16	63
Alexandre Tremblay, Shaw.	47	31	31	62	63
Alexandre Tremblay, Rimouski	17	12	10	22	30
Totals	64	43	41	84	93
Jason Troini, Halifax	20	7	9	16	33
Jason Troini, Val-d'Or	30	12	17	29	12
Totals	50	19	26	45	45
J.-Sebastien Trudelle, A.-Bath.	44	3	10	13	149
J.-Sebastien Trudelle, Shaw.	22	2	4	6	71
Totals	66	5	14	19	220
Steeve Vandal, Rouyn-Noranda	44	17	30	47	88
Steeve Vandal, Moncton	20	2	4	6	27
Totals	64	19	34	53	115
Stephane Veilleux, Victoriaville	22	1	4	5	17
Stephane Veilleux, Val-d'Or	50	14	28	42	100
Totals	72	15	32	47	117
Dave Verville, Val-d'Or (g)	36	0	0	0	0
Dave Verville, Shawinigan (g)	6	0	0	0	4
Totals	42	0	0	0	4

GOALTENDING

	Games	Min.	W	L	T	G	SO	Avg.
Jonathan Charron, Val.	8	391	2	4	0	34	0	5.22
Jonathan Charron, Que.	10	513	3	6	0	32	0	3.75
Totals	18	904	5	10	0	70	0	4.65
Dany Dallaire, Drum.	24	1126	7	10	1	80	0	4.26
Dany Dallaire, C.B.	18	934	7	8	0	54	1	3.47
Totals	42	2060	14	18	1	134	1	3.90
J.-F. Laniel, Shaw.	14	630	2	7	0	40	0	3.81
J.-Francois Laniel, Val.	11	479	1	6	0	46	0	5.76
Totals	25	1109	3	13	0	86	0	4.65
Frederick Malette, Hull	19	1061	11	5	0	63	1	3.56
F. Malette, Drum.	10	507	5	2	1	25	0	2.96
Totals	29	1568	16	7	1	88	1	3.37
J.-F. Racine, Monc.	10	410	3	3	1	28	0	4.10
J.-F. Racine, Drum.	20	1152	14	6	0	63	1	3.28
Totals	30	1562	17	9	1	91	1	3.50
Philippe Sauve, Drum.	28	1526	12	12	2	106	0	4.17
Philippe Sauve, Hull	17	992	9	7	1	57	0	3.45
Totals	45	2518	21	19	3	163	0	3.88

MAJOR JUNIOR LEAGUES QMJHL

	Games	Min.	W	L	T	G	SO	Avg.
D. St. Germain, C.B.	36	1986	10	23	2	147	0	4.44
D. St. Germain, B.-C.	23	1287	10	11	2	77	2	3.59
Totals	59	3273	20	34	4	224	2	4.11

	Games	Min.	W	L	T	G	SO	Avg.
Dave Verville, Val-d'Or	36	2069	11	19	5	145	1	4.20
Dave Verville, Shaw.	6	335	3	2	0	22	0	3.94
Totals	42	2404	14	21	5	167	1	4.17

2000 PRESIDENT CUP PLAYOFFS
RESULTS

DIVISION QUARTERFINALS

	W	L	Pts.	GF	GA
Halifax	4	2	8	22	17
Baie-Comeau	2	4	4	17	22

(Halifax won series, 4-2)

	W	L	Pts.	GF	GA
Moncton	4	0	8	22	7
Acadie Bathurst	0	4	0	7	22

(Moncton won series, 4-0)

	W	L	Pts.	GF	GA
Quebec	4	2	8	24	6
Cape Breton	2	4	4	6	24

(Quebec won series, 4-2)

	W	L	Pts.	GF	GA
Drummondville	4	1	8	23	11
Montreal	1	4	2	11	23

(Drummondville won series, 4-2)

	W	L	Pts.	GF	GA
Rouyn-Noranda	4	1	8	19	16
Sherbrooke	1	4	2	16	19

(Rouyn-Noranda won series, 4-1)

	W	L	Pts.	GF	GA
Shawinigan	4	2	8	29	18
Victoriaville	2	4	4	18	29

(Shawinigan won series, 4-2)

DIVISION SEMIFINALS

	W	L	Pts.	GF	GA
Rimouski	4	0	8	28	16
Halifax	0	4	0	16	28

(Rimouski won series, 4-0)

	W	L	Pts.	GF	GA
Moncton	4	3	8	23	26
Quebec	3	4	6	26	23

(Moncton won series, 4-3)

	W	L	Pts.	GF	GA
Hull	4	2	8	27	18
Rouyn-Noranda	2	4	4	18	27

(Hull won series, 4-2)

	W	L	Pts.	GF	GA
Drummondville	4	3	8	26	26
Shawinigan	3	4	6	26	26

(Drummondville won series, 4-3)

DIVISION FINALS

	W	L	Pts.	GF	GA
Hull	4	0	8	17	11
Drummondville	0	4	0	11	17

(Hull won series, 4-0)

	W	L	Pts.	GF	GA
Rimouski	4	1	8	21	23
Moncton	1	4	2	23	21

(Rimouski won series, 4-1)

LEAGUE FINALS

	W	L	Pts.	GF	GA
Rimouski	4	1	8	26	18
Hull	1	4	2	18	26

(Rimouski won series, 4-1)

INDIVIDUAL LEADERS

Goals: Mathieu Benoit, Moncton (15)
Pascal Dupuis, Shawinigan (15)
Assists: Brad Richards, Rimouski (24)
Points: Brad Richards, Rimouski (37)
Penalty minutes: Eric Laplante, Quebec (83)
Goaltending average: Maxime Ouellet, Quebec (2.63)
Shutouts: Maxime Ouellet, Quebec (2)

TOP SCORERS

	Games	G	A	Pts.
Brad Richards, Rimouski	12	13	24	37
Mathieu Benoit, Moncton	16	15	15	30
Zoltan Batovsky, Drummondville	16	10	19	29
Michael Ryder, Hull	15	11	17	28
Juraj Kolnik, Rimouski	14	10	17	27
Jonathan Beaulieu, Rimouski	14	14	12	26
Paul Spadafora, Hull	15	7	18	25
Ramzi Abid, Halifax	10	10	13	23
Martin Bartek, Moncton	16	10	13	23
Mike Ribeiro, Quebec	11	3	20	23

INDIVIDUAL STATISTICS

BAIE-COMEAU DRAKKAR
(Lost division quarterfinals to Halifax, 4-2)
SCORING

	Games	G	A	Pts.	PIM
Evgeny Gusakov	6	5	1	6	10
Charles Linglet	6	3	3	6	4
Sylvain Deschatelets	6	2	4	6	6
Marco Charpentier	6	3	2	5	16
Jonathan Gautier	6	1	3	4	2
Robin Leblanc	5	2	1	3	8
Yanick Lehoux	6	1	2	3	2
Jerome Bergeron	6	0	2	2	8
Bruno St. Jacques	6	0	2	2	10
Danny Roussy	4	0	1	1	0
Kevin Deslauriers	6	0	1	1	2
Dominic Periard	6	0	1	1	16
Eric Tremblay	6	0	1	1	2
Paul Lavoie	1	0	0	0	0
Ghyslain Rousseau (goalie)	1	0	0	0	0
Andre Mercure	3	0	0	0	0
Daniel Bergeron	5	0	0	0	4
Maxime Fortunus	6	0	0	0	2

	Games	G	A	Pts.	PIM
Duilio Grande	6	0	0	0	2
Keven Poulin	6	0	0	0	4
David St. Germain (goalie)	6	0	0	0	0
Guy Turmel	6	0	0	0	2

GOALTENDING

	Games	Min.	W	L	T	G	SO	Avg.
Ghyslain Rousseau	1	1	0	0	0	0	0	0.00
David St. Germain	6	361	2	4	0	21	0	3.49

ACADIE-BATHURST TITANS
(Lost division quarterfinals to Moncton, 4-0)
SCORING

	Games	G	A	Pts.	PIM
Samuel Seguin	4	3	2	5	0
David Comeau	4	2	2	4	6
Francois Fortin	4	1	3	4	4
Daniel MacLeod	4	1	3	4	12
Frederic Girard	4	2	0	2	4
Yannick Guay	4	0	2	2	2
Olivier Fillion	4	1	0	1	6
Karl Fournier	4	1	0	1	6
Hugo Levesque	4	0	1	1	6
Alex Matieroukhine	4	0	1	1	21
Patrick Mbaraga	4	0	1	1	4
Tim Sinasac	4	0	1	1	21
Frederic Cloutier (goalie)	1	0	0	0	0
Grant Donovan	1	0	0	0	2
Daniel Robert	1	0	0	0	0
Charline Labonte	2	0	0	0	0
Jonathan Lomax	2	0	0	0	0
Charles Faber (goalie)	3	0	0	0	0
Louis Alfred	4	0	0	0	0
Jean-Philippe Cote	4	0	0	0	2
Louis Deault	4	0	0	0	6
Luc Ratelle	4	0	0	0	2
Tyler Reid	4	0	0	0	8

GOALTENDING

	Games	Min.	W	L	T	G	SO	Avg.
Charles Faber	3	200	0	3	0	16	0	4.82
Frederic Cloutier	1	60	0	1	0	5	0	5.00

CAPE BRETON SCREAMING EAGLES
(Lost division quarterfinals to Quebec, 4-0)
SCORING

	Games	G	A	Pts.	PIM
Jerome Marois	4	2	1	3	14
Olivier Proulx	4	1	2	3	2
Frederic Belanger	4	1	1	2	4
Jonathan Andrews	4	1	0	1	18
Artem Rybin	4	1	0	1	4
Rodrigue Boucher	4	0	1	1	12
Jean-Philippe Cote	4	0	1	1	4
Josh Dill	4	0	1	1	10
Mathieu Dumas	4	0	1	1	0
Pierre-Luc Laprise	4	0	1	1	4
Dominic Noel	4	0	1	1	0
Michael McIntyre	1	0	0	0	0
Pascal Morency	1	0	0	0	0
Dallas Ashford	3	0	0	0	2
Daniel Boisclair (goalie)	3	0	0	0	0
Dany Dallaire (goalie)	3	0	0	0	0
P.J. Lynch	3	0	0	0	2
Charles Gauthier	4	0	0	0	2
Robert Horak	4	0	0	0	2
Hunter Lahache	4	0	0	0	23
Stuart MacRae	4	0	0	0	4
Yannick Searles	4	0	0	0	0

GOALTENDING

	Games	Min.	W	L	T	G	SO	Avg.
Daniel Boisclair	3	86	0	1	0	6	0	4.21
Dany Dallaire	3	154	0	3	0	18	0	7.01

DRUMMONDVILLE VOLTIGEURS
(Lost division finals to Hull, 4-0)
SCORING

	Games	G	A	Pts.	PIM
Zoltan Batovsky	16	10	19	29	12
Miroslav Zalesak	16	7	11	18	4
Julien Desrosiers	16	7	10	17	12
Jonathan Gagnon	14	4	12	16	8
Nicholas Bilotto	16	2	12	14	38
Eric Dubois	16	7	6	13	16
Pierre-Luc Emond	16	6	3	9	10
Frederic Faucher	15	5	3	8	20
Jean-Philippe Morin	16	3	5	8	24
David Girard	16	4	3	7	19
Vincent Tougas	15	1	5	6	8
Joey D'Amico	15	2	3	5	38
Jean-Philippe Glaude	16	1	3	4	12
Thierry Kaszap	16	1	2	3	17
Louis-Philippe Lessard	16	0	3	3	16
Eric Jean	15	0	2	2	26
Simon Poirier	16	0	2	2	35
Frederick Malette (goalie)	16	0	1	1	6
Eric Bleau	3	0	0	0	2
Jean-Francois Racine (goalie)	3	0	0	0	7
David Lessard	5	0	0	0	0
Stephane Labrie	13	0	0	0	23

GOALTENDING

	Games	Min.	W	L	T	G	SO	Avg.
Frederick Malette	16	952	8	8	0	47	0	2.96
Jean-Francois Racine	3	65	0	0	0	5	0	4.60

HALIFAX MOOSEHEADS
(Lost division semifinals to Rimouski, 4-0)
SCORING

	Games	G	A	Pts.	PIM
Ramzi Abid	10	10	13	23	18
Brandon Reid	10	7	11	18	4
Benoit Dusablon	10	6	7	13	12
Jasmin Gelinas	10	3	5	8	12
Brandon Benedict	10	3	4	7	10
Joey DiPenta	10	3	4	7	26
Jules-Edy Laraque	10	2	4	6	6
Jonathan St. Louis	10	2	4	6	21
Andrei Shefer	10	0	5	5	4
Robbie Sutherland	10	2	1	3	16
Ali MacEachern	10	0	3	3	12
Darrell Jerrett	9	0	1	1	11
Nick Greenough	10	0	1	1	31
Gary Zinck	10	0	1	1	8
Bruce Gillis	1	0	0	0	0
Shawn Lewis	1	0	0	0	0
Pierre-Luc Bacon	3	0	0	0	2
Pascal Leclaire (goalie)	5	0	0	0	0
Hugo Lehoux	6	0	0	0	13
Alexei Volkov (goalie)	8	0	0	0	0
Jonathan Boone	10	0	0	0	14
Joe Groleau	10	0	0	0	2
Jason King	10	0	0	0	2

GOALTENDING

	Games	Min.	W	L	T	G	SO	Avg.
Pascal Leclaire	5	198	1	2	0	12	0	3.65
Alexei Volkov	8	417	3	4	0	29	0	4.18

HULL OLYMPIQUES
(Lost league finals to Rimouski, 4-1)
SCORING

	Games	G	A	Pts.	PIM
Michael Ryder	15	11	17	28	28
Paul Spadafora	15	7	18	25	25
Alexandre Giroux	15	12	6	18	30
Ryan Lauzon	15	6	8	14	8

	Games	G	A	Pts.	PIM
Radim Vrbata	15	3	9	12	8
Jason Lehoux	15	6	4	10	14
Brock Boucher	15	3	6	9	20
Mario Joly	15	1	8	9	38
Adam Rivet	15	1	7	8	8
Dustin Russell	15	4	3	7	6
Philippe Lacasse	15	3	4	7	0
Bruno Lemire	15	2	5	7	14
Erich Paroshy	15	0	4	4	19
Daniel Hudgin	15	2	1	3	8
Andrew Carver	15	0	3	3	22
Derick Martin	15	0	3	3	15
Roberto Bissonnette	15	1	1	2	22
Eric Lafrance (goalie)	3	0	1	1	0
Philippe Sauve (goalie)	12	0	0	0	0
Bobby Clarke	15	0	0	0	4

GOALTENDING

	Games	Min.	W	L	T	G	SO	Avg.
Eric Lafrance	3	180	3	0	0	7	0	2.33
Philippe Sauve	12	735	6	6	0	47	0	3.84

MONCTON WILDCATS
(Lost division finals to Rimouski, 4-1)
SCORING

	Games	G	A	Pts.	PIM
Mathieu Benoit	16	15	15	30	6
Martin Bartek	16	10	13	23	24
Jonathan Girard	16	3	15	18	36
Patrick Yetman	16	7	9	16	27
Simon Laliberte	13	6	10	16	10
Alexandre Vigneault	16	3	11	14	6
François Beauchemin	16	2	11	13	14
Morgan Warren	16	7	5	12	4
Steeve Vandal	15	4	6	10	45
Jonathan Desroches	14	2	8	10	22
Jonathan Roy	8	1	6	7	10
Mirko Murovic	7	2	4	6	2
Kory Baker	15	2	4	6	28
Olivier Dubuc	16	3	1	4	14
Bobby Reed	16	0	3	3	35
Martin Lavergne	16	1	0	1	12
Jonathan Ferland	11	0	1	1	0
Patrice Theriault	15	0	1	1	10
Danny Bowie (goalie)	3	0	0	0	0
Ian Seguin	4	0	0	0	15
Sergei Kaltygen	10	0	0	0	4
Trevor Ettinger	15	0	0	0	40
Simon Lajeunesse (goalie)	16	0	0	0	2

GOALTENDING

	Games	Min.	W	L	T	G	SO	Avg.
Danny Bowie	3	68	0	1	0	2	0	1.78
Simon Lajeunesse	16	910	9	6	0	56	1	3.69

MONTREAL ROCKETS
(Lost division quarterfinals to Drummondville, 4-1)
SCORING

	Games	G	A	Pts.	PIM
Alain O'Driscoll	5	3	2	5	12
Casey Burnette	5	0	3	3	23
Nicolas Pelletier	5	2	0	2	2
Randy Copley	5	1	1	2	20
Lauri Kinos	5	1	1	2	6
Louis Robitaille	5	1	1	2	18
Yann Joseph	5	1	0	1	16
Guillaume Lamoureux	5	1	0	1	2
Marc Villeneuve	5	1	0	1	6
Olivier Maltais	2	0	1	1	2
Francis Emery	4	0	1	1	26
Maxime Pelletier	4	0	1	1	2
Chris Montgomery	5	0	1	1	8
Edo Terglav	5	0	1	1	4

	Games	G	A	Pts.	PIM
Jonathan Cayer (goalie)	1	0	0	0	2
Benoit Beausoleil	2	0	0	0	2
Michael Lanthier	4	0	0	0	19
Jordan Trew	4	0	0	0	34
Marc-Andre Beaulieu	5	0	0	0	2
Jean-Michel Boisvert	5	0	0	0	0
Frederik Brindamour (goalie)	5	0	0	0	0
Mathieu Paul	5	0	0	0	8

GOALTENDING

	Games	Min.	W	L	T	G	SO	Avg.
Frederik Brindamour	5	329	1	4	0	20	0	3.65
Jonathan Cayer	1	20	0	0	0	3	0	9.19

QUEBEC REMPARTS
(Lost division semifinals to Moncton, 4-3)
SCORING

	Games	G	A	Pts.	PIM
Mike Ribeiro	11	3	20	23	38
Patrick Grandmaitre	11	10	11	21	8
Wesley Scanzano	11	6	13	19	0
Eric Chouinard	11	14	4	18	8
Eric Laplante	10	3	5	8	83
Khristian Kudroc	11	2	5	7	29
Chris Lyness	11	1	6	7	4
Kirill Safronov	11	2	4	6	14
Martin Moise	11	3	2	5	0
Andre Martineau	11	2	3	5	8
Martin Grenier	7	1	4	5	27
Philippe Paris	11	3	1	4	19
Shawn Collymore	11	0	2	2	0
Casey Leggett	11	0	1	1	27
Jean Mallette	11	0	1	1	16
Karl Morin	11	0	1	1	29
Sylvain Plamondon	11	0	1	1	8
Eric Cloutier	1	0	0	0	0
Martin Pare (goalie)	1	0	0	0	0
Patrick Chouinard	4	0	0	0	2
Tommy Bolduc	11	0	0	0	35
Maxime Ouellet (goalie)	11	0	0	0	2

GOALTENDING

	Games	Min.	W	L	T	G	SO	Avg.
Maxime Ouellet	11	638	7	4	0	28	2	2.63
Martin Pare	1	20	0	0	0	1	0	3.00

RIMOUSKI OCEANIC
(Winner of 2000 President Cup playoffs)
SCORING

	Games	G	A	Pts.	PIM
Brad Richards	12	13	24	37	16
Juraj Kolnik	14	10	17	27	16
Jonathan Beaulieu	14	14	12	26	16
Michel Periard	14	5	17	22	16
Alexandre Tremblay	14	9	10	19	32
Jan-Philippe Cadieux	14	5	6	11	8
Benoit Martin	14	2	8	10	10
Michel Ouellet	14	4	5	9	14
Joe Rullier	14	1	8	9	34
Jacques Lariviere	14	4	3	7	50
Jean-Philippe Briere	14	2	3	5	18
Rene Vydareny	14	2	2	4	20
Shawn Scanzano	14	1	3	4	52
Brent MacLellan	14	2	1	3	4
Nicolas Poirier	12	1	2	3	12
Sebastien Caron (goalie)	14	0	2	2	2
Ronnie Decontie	1	0	0	0	0
Eric Salvail (goalie)	1	0	0	0	0
Nicolas Pilote	4	0	0	0	0
Thatcher Bell	5	0	0	0	15
Aaron Johnson	8	0	0	0	0
Jean-Francois Babin	14	0	0	0	21
Alex Castonguay	14	0	0	0	46

GOALTENDING

	Games	Min.	W	L	T	G	SO	Avg.
Sebastien Caron............	14	828	12	2	0	50	0	3.62
Eric Salvail....................	1	28	0	0	0	7	0	14.98

ROUYN-NORANDA HUSKIES
(Lost division semifinals to Hull, 4-2)

SCORING

	Games	G	A	Pts.	PIM
Marc-Andre Binette..................	11	5	6	11	2
Maxime Bouchard....................	11	5	6	11	10
Jonathan Gauthier...................	11	3	7	10	18
Steve Waters..........................	11	2	5	7	15
Kevin Cloutier........................	9	3	3	6	8
Mathieu Leclerc......................	11	2	4	6	8
Sebastien Strozynski	10	1	5	6	10
Matthew Quinn	11	1	5	6	12
Jerome Tremblay	5	4	1	5	6
Alexandre Morel	11	2	3	5	6
Michal Pinc	11	0	5	5	18
Guillaume Lefebvre	11	4	0	4	25
Patrick Gilbert	11	2	2	4	14
Alain Turcotte	10	1	3	4	6
Jason Tessier	11	0	4	4	16
Louis Mandeville	11	2	1	3	4
Bertrand-Pierre Plouffe.............	11	0	1	1	6
Kyrill Alexeyev	1	0	0	0	2
Bruno Cadieux	7	0	0	0	4
Sebastien Centomo (goalie)	11	0	0	0	0
Michael Parent.......................	11	0	0	0	20
Jonathan Pelletier	11	0	0	0	0

GOALTENDING

	Games	Min.	W	L	T	G	SO	Avg.
Sebastien Centomo...	11	695	6	5	0	41	0	3.54

SHAWINIGAN CATARACTES
(Lost division semifinals to Drummondville, 4-3)

SCORING

	Games	G	A	Pts.	PIM
Pascal Dupuis.........................	13	15	7	22	4
Dominic Forget	13	2	18	20	8
Jean-Philippe Pare	13	6	13	19	8
Anthony Quessy	13	7	7	14	26
Yannick Noiseux	13	2	11	13	13
Marc-Andre Bergeron	13	4	7	11	45
Francis Deslauriers	13	2	9	11	10
Philippe Deblois	13	0	8	8	23
Jean-Francois David	13	5	2	7	10
Jean-Francois Dufort	6	2	4	6	2
Jonathan Bellemarre	13	2	4	6	8
Denis Desmarais	13	1	5	6	28
Jason Pominville	13	2	3	5	0
Gilbert Lefrancois	13	2	1	3	12
David Chicoine........................	13	1	2	3	22
Philippe Gelinas	7	1	1	2	2
Jean-Sebastien Trudelle	13	1	1	2	28
Dave Verville (goalie)	2	0	0	0	0
Alexandre Blackburn	13	0	0	0	11
Mathieu Chouinard (goalie)	13	0	0	0	0
Jonathan Lessard	13	0	0	0	34

GOALTENDING

	Games	Min.	W	L	T	G	SO	Avg.
Mathieu Chouinard...	13	770	7	6	0	41	0	3.20
Dave Verville	2	22	0	0	0	2	0	5.41

SHERBROOKE FAUCONS
(Lost division quarterfinals to Rouyn-Noranda, 4-1)

SCORING

	Games	G	A	Pts.	PIM
Maxim Potapov........................	5	3	4	7	2
Dmitri Afanassenkov................	5	3	2	5	4
Eric Lavigne	5	2	3	5	10
Francois Belanger	5	0	5	5	6
Michel Beausoleil.....................	5	2	2	4	12
Patrick Vincent........................	5	2	1	3	37
Steve Morency	5	1	2	3	2
Jean Morin Jr..........................	5	1	2	3	6
Eric Pinoul	5	1	2	3	4
Bryan Lachance	4	0	2	2	2
Nicolas Corbeil........................	5	1	0	1	0
Eric Dagenais	4	0	1	1	2
Alexandre Page	5	0	1	1	4
Philippe Parent	5	0	1	1	8
Pierre-Luc Courchesne	1	0	0	0	0
Colin Keith	2	0	0	0	0
Martin Beauchesne	4	0	0	0	13
Benoit Genesse	5	0	0	0	2
Drew MacIntyre	5	0	0	0	0
Jonathan Robert	5	0	0	0	6
Dany Sabourin (goalie)	5	0	0	0	0
Patrice Tassy	5	0	0	0	0

GOALTENDING

	Games	Min.	W	L	T	G	SO	Avg.
Dany Sabourin	5	324	1	4	0	18	0	3.33

VICTORIAVILLE TIGRES
(Lost division quarterfinals to Shawinigan, 4-2)

SCORING

	Games	G	A	Pts.	PIM
Marc-Andre Thinel	6	5	6	11	18
Carl Mallette..........................	6	6	3	9	28
Alexander Riazantsev...............	6	2	5	7	20
Sebastien Thinel......................	6	1	5	6	8
Jonathan Fauteux.....................	6	2	2	4	12
Danny Groulx	6	0	4	4	14
Eric Cote................................	6	1	1	2	4
Carl Gagnon	6	1	1	2	0
Joey Fetta..............................	6	0	1	1	31
Pierre-Luc Sleigher	6	0	1	1	28
Antoine Vermette	6	0	1	1	6
Patrice Cadieux.......................	1	0	0	0	0
Billy Rochefort	1	0	0	0	0
Philippe Ozga (goalie)...............	3	0	0	0	0
Sandro Sbrocca	4	0	0	0	44
Mathieu Wathier	4	0	0	0	0
Kristian Kovac	5	0	0	0	4
Guillaume Lavoie	5	0	0	0	5
Luc Levesque..........................	5	0	0	0	6
Jean-Francois Nogues (goalie)..	5	0	0	0	0
Pierre-Luc Daneau	6	0	0	0	4
Teddy Kyres	6	0	0	0	0
Matthew Lombardi	6	0	0	0	6

GOALTENDING

	Games	Min.	W	L	T	G	SO	Avg.
Jean-Francois Nogues....	5	259	2	3	0	19	0	4.41
Philippe Ozga	3	100	0	1	0	10	0	6.00

ALL-STAR TEAMS

First team	Pos.	Second team
Simon Lajeunesse, Moncton	G	Maxime Ouellet, Quebec
Jonathan Girard, Moncton	D	Jonathan Gauthier, R.-Nor.
Michel Periard, Rimouski	D	Francois Beauchemin, Monc.
Ramzi Abid, Halifax	LW	Simon Gamache, Val-d'Or
Brad Richards, Rimouski	C	Brandon Reid, Halifax
Marc-Andre Thinel, Vic.	RW	Mathieu Benoit, Moncton

TROPHY WINNERS

Frank Selke Trophy: Jonathan Roy, Moncton
Michel Bergeron Trophy: Chris Montgomery, Montreal
Raymond Lagace Trophy: Kirill Safronov, Quebec
Jean Beliveau Trophy: Brad Richards, Rimouski
Michel Briere Trophy: Brad Richards, Rimouski
Marcel Robert Trophy: Yanick Lehoux, Baie-Comeau
Mike Bossy Trophy: Antoine Vermette, Victoriaville
Emile "Butch" Bouchard Trophy: Michel Periard, Rimouski
Jacques Plante Trophy: Simon Lajeunesse, Moncton
Guy Lafleur Trophy: Brad Richards, Rimouski
Robert LeBel Trophy: Moncton Wildcats
John Rougeau Trophy: Rimouski Oceanic
President Cup: Rimouski Oceanic

ALL-TIME AWARD WINNERS

FRANK SELKE TROPHY
(Most gentlemanly player)

Season	Player, Team
1970-71	Norm Dube, Sherbrooke
1971-72	Gerry Teeple, Cornwall
1972-73	Claude Larose, Drummondville
1973-74	Gary MacGregor, Cornwall
1974-75	Jean-Luc Phaneuf, Montreal
1975-76	Norm Dupont, Montreal
1976-77	Mike Bossy, Laval
1977-78	Kevin Reeves, Montreal
1978-79	Ray Bourque, Verdun
	Jean-Francois Sauve, Trois-Rivieres
1979-80	Jean-Francois Sauve, Trois-Rivieres
1980-81	Claude Verret, Trois-Rivieres
1981-82	Claude Verret, Trois-Rivieres
1982-83	Pat LaFontaine, Verdun
1983-84	Jerome Carrier, Verdun
1984-85	Patrick Emond, Chicoutimi
1985-86	Jimmy Carson, Verdun
1986-87	Luc Beausoleil, Laval
1987-88	Stephan Lebeau, Shawinigan
1988-89	Steve Cadieux, Shawinigan
1989-90	Andrew McKim, Hull
1990-91	Yanic Perreault, Trois-Rivieres
1991-92	Martin Gendron, St. Hyacinthe
1992-93	Martin Gendron, St. Hyacinthe
1993-94	Yanick Dube, Laval
1994-95	Eric Daze, Beauport
1995-96	Christian Dube, Sherbrooke
1996-97	Daniel Briere, Drummondville
1997-98	Simon Laliberte, Moncton
1998-99	Eric Chouinard, Quebec
1999-00	Jonathan Roy, Moncton

MICHEL BERGERON TROPHY
(Top rookie forward)

Season	Player, Team
1969-70	Serge Martel, Verdun
1970-71	Bob Murphy, Cornwall
1971-72	Bob Murray, Cornwall
1972-73	Pierre Larouche, Sorel
1973-74	Mike Bossy, Laval
1974-75	Dennis Pomerleau, Hull
1975-76	Jean-Marc Bonamie, Shawinigan
1976-77	Rick Vaive, Sherbrooke
1977-78	Norm Rochefort, Trois-Rivieres
	Denis Savard, Montreal
1978-79	Alan Grenier, Laval
1979-80	Dale Hawerchuk, Cornwall
1980-81	Claude Verret, Trois-Rivieres
1981-82	Sylvain Turgeon, Hull
1982-83	Pat LaFontaine, Verdun
1983-84	Stephane Richer, Granby
1984-85	Jimmy Carson, Verdun
1985-86	Pierre Turgeon, Granby

Season	Player, Team
1986-87	Rob Murphy, Laval
1987-88	Martin Gelinas, Hull
1988-89	Yanic Perreault, Trois-Rivieres
1989-90	Martin Lapointe, Laval
1990-91	Rene Corbet, Drummondville
1991-92	Alexandre Daigle, Victoriaville
1992-93	Steve Brule, St. Jean
1993-94	Christian Dube, Sherbrooke
1994-95	Daniel Briere, Drummondville
1995-96	Pavel Rosa, Hull
1996-97	Vincent Lecavalier, Rimouski
1997-98	Mike Ribeiro, Rouyn-Noranda
1998-99	Ladislav Nagy, Halifax
1999-00	Chris Montgomery, Montreal

Prior to 1980-81 season, award was given to QMJHL rookie of the year.

RAYMOND LAGACE TROPHY
(Top rookie defenseman or goaltender)

Season	Player, Team
1980-81	Billy Campbell, Montreal
1981-82	Michel Petit, Sherbrooke
1982-83	Bobby Dollas, Laval
1983-84	James Gasseau, Drummondville
1984-85	Robert Desjardins, Shawinigan
1985-86	Stephane Guerard, Shawinigan
1986-87	Jimmy Waite, Chicoutimi
1987-88	Stephane Beauregard, St. Jean
1988-89	Karl Dykhuis, Hull
1989-90	Francois Groleau, Shawinigan
1990-91	Philippe Boucher, Granby
1991-92	Philippe DeRouville, Longueuil
1992-93	Stephane Routhier, Drummondville
1993-94	Jimmy Drolet, St. Hyacinthe
1994-95	Martin Biron, Beauport
1995-96	Mathieu Garon, Victoriaville
1996-97	Christian Bronsard, Hull
1997-98	Alexei Tezikov, Moncton
1998-99	Alexei Volkov, Halifax
1999-00	Kirill Safronov, Quebec

JEAN BELIVEAU TROPHY
(Scoring leader)

Season	Player, Team
1969-70	Luc Simard, Trois-Rivieres
1970-71	Guy Lafleur, Quebec
1971-72	Jacques Richard, Quebec
1972-73	Andre Savard, Quebec
1973-74	Pierre Larouche, Sorel
1974-75	Norm Dupont, Montreal
1975-76	Richard Dalpe, Trois-Rivieres
	Sylvain Locas, Chicoutimi
1976-77	Jean Savard, Quebec
1977-78	Ron Carter, Sherbooke
1978-79	Jean-Francois Sauve, Trois-Rivieres

MAJOR JUNIOR LEAGUES QMJHL

Season	Player, Team
1979-80—Jean-Francois Sauve, Trois-Rivieres
1980-81—Dale Hawerchuk, Cornwall
1981-82—Claude Verret, Trois-Rivieres
1982-83—Pat LaFontaine, Verdun
1983-84—Mario Lemieux, Laval
1984-85—Guy Rouleau, Longueuil
1985-86—Guy Rouleau, Hull
1986-87—Marc Fortier, Chicoutimi
1987-88—Patrice Lefebvre, Shawinigan
1988-89—Stephane Morin, Chicoutimi
1989-90—Patrick Lebeau, Victoriaville
1990-91—Yanic Perreault, Trois-Rivieres
1991-92—Patrick Poulin, St. Hyacinthe
1992-93—Rene Corbet, Drummondville
1993-94—Yanick Dube, Laval
1994-95—Patrick Carignan, Shawinigan
1995-96—Daniel Briere, Drummondville
1996-97—Pavel Rosa, Hull
1997-98—Ramzi Abid, Chicoutimi
1998-99—Mike Ribeiro, Rouyn-Noranda
1999-00—Brad Richards, Rimouski

MICHEL BRIERE TROPHY
(Most Valuable Player)

Season	Player, Team
1972-73—Andre Savard, Quebec
1973-74—Gary MacGregor, Cornwall
1974-75—Mario Viens, Cornwall
1975-76—Peter Marsh, Sherbrooke
1976-77—Lucien DeBlois, Sorel
1977-78—Kevin Reeves, Montreal
1978-79—Pierre Lacroix, Trois-Rivieres
1979-80—Denis Savard, Montreal
1980-81—Dale Hawerchuk, Cornwall
1981-82—John Chabot, Sherbrooke
1982-83—Pat LaFontaine, Verdun
1983-84—Mario Lemieux, Laval
1984-85—Daniel Berthiaune, Chicoutimi
1985-86—Guy Rouleau, Hull
1986-87—Robert Desjardins, Longueuil
1987-88—Marc Saumier, Hull
1988-89—Stephane Morin, Chicoutimi
1989-90—Andrew McKim, Hull
1990-91—Yanic Perreault, Trois-Rivieres
1991-92—Charles Poulin, St. Hyacinthe
1992-93—Jocelyn Thibault, Sherbrooke
1993-94—Emmanuel Fernandez, Laval
1994-95—Frederic Chartier, Laval
1995-96—Christian Dube, Sherbrooke
1996-97—Daniel Corso, Victoriaville
1997-98—Ramzi Abid, Chicoutimi
1998-99—Mathieu Chouinard, Shawinigan
1999-00—Brad Richards, Rimouski

MARCEL ROBERT TROPHY
(Top scholastic/athletic performer)

Season	Player, Team
1981-82—Jacques Sylvestre, Granby
1982-83—Claude Gosselin, Quebec
1983-84—Gilbert Paiement, Chicoutimi
1984-85—Claude Gosselin, Longueuil
1985-86—Bernard Morin, Laval
1986-87—Patrice Tremblay, Chicoutimi
1987-88—Stephane Beauregard, St. Jean
1988-89—Daniel Lacroix, Granby
1989-90—Yanic Perreault, Trois-Rivieres
1990-91—Benoit Larose, Laval
1991-92—Simon Toupin, Beauport
1992-93—Jocelyn Thibault, Sherbrooke
1993-94—Patrick Boileau, Laval
1994-95—Daniel Briere, Drummondville
1995-96—Marc Denis, Chicoutimi
1996-97—Luc Vaillancourt, Beauport
1997-98—Michel Tremblay, Shawinigan
1998-99—Christian Robichaud, Victoriaville
1999-00—Yanick Lehoux, Baie-Comeau

MIKE BOSSY TROPHY
(Top pro prospect)

Season	Player, Team
1980-81—Dale Hawerchuk, Cornwall
1981-82—Michel Petit, Sherbrooke
1982-83—Pat LaFontaine, Verdun
Sylvain Turgeon, Hull
1983-84—Mario Lemieux, Laval
1984-85—Jose Charbonneau, Drummondville
1985-86—Jimmy Carson, Verdun
1986-87—Pierre Turgeon, Granby
1987-88—Daniel Dore, Drummondville
1988-89—Patrice Brisebois, Laval
1989-90—Karl Dykhuis, Hull
1990-91—Philippe Boucher, Granby
1991-92—Paul Brousseau, Hull
1992-93—Alexandre Daigle, Victoriaville
1993-94—Eric Fichaud, Chicoutimi
1994-95—Martin Biron, Beauport
1995-96—Jean-Pierre Dumont, Val d'Or
1996-97—Roberto Luongo, Val d'Or
1997-98—Vincent Lecavalier, Rimouski
1998-99—Maxime Ouellet, Quebec
1999-00—Antoine Vermette, Victoriaville

Originally known as Association of Journalism of Hockey Trophy from 1980-81 through 1982-83.

EMILE "BUTCH" BOUCHARD TROPHY
(Top defenseman)

Season	Player, Team
1975-76—Jean Gagnon, Quebec
1976-77—Robert Picard, Montreal
1977-78—Mark Hardy, Montreal
1978-79—Ray Bourque, Verdun
1979-80—Gaston Therrien, Quebec
1980-81—Fred Boimistruck, Cornwall
1981-82—Paul Andre Boutilier, Sherbrooke
1982-83—J.J. Daigneault, Longueuil
1983-84—Billy Campbell, Verdun
1984-85—Yves Beaudoin, Shawinigan
1985-86—Sylvain Cote, Hull
1986-87—Jean Marc Richard, Chicoutimi
1987-88—Eric Desjardins, Granby
1988-89—Yves Racine, Victoriaville
1989-90—Claude Barthe, Victoriaville
1990-91—Patrice Brisebois, Drummondville
1991-92—Francois Groleau, Shawinigan
1992-93—Benoit Larose, Laval
1993-94—Steve Gosselin, Chicoutimi
1994-95—Stephane Julien, Sherbrooke
1995-96—Denis Gauthier, Drummondville
1996-97—Stephane Robidas, Shawinigan
1997-98—Derrick Walser, Rimouski
1998-99—Jiri Fischer, Hull
1999-00—Michel Periard, Rimouski

JACQUES PLANTE TROPHY
(Top goaltender)

Season	Player, Team
1969-70—Michael Deguise, Sorel
1970-71—Reynald Fortier, Quebec
1971-72—Richard Brodeur, Cornwall
1972-73—Pierre Perusee, Quebec
1973-74—Claude Legris, Sorel
1974-75—Nick Sanza, Sherbrooke
1975-76—Tim Bernhardt, Cornwall
1976-77—Tim Bernhardt, Cornwall
1977-78—Tim Bernhardt, Cornwall
1978-79—Jacques Cloutier, Trois-Rivieres
1979-80—Corrado Micalef, Sherbrooke
1980-81—Michel Dufour, Sorel
1981-82—Jeff Barratt, Montreal
1982-83—Tony Haladuick, Laval
1983-84—Tony Haladuick, Laval
1984-85—Daniel Berthiaume, Chicoutimi

Season	Player, Team
1985-86	Robert Desjardins, Hull
1986-87	Robert Desjardins, Longueuil
1987-88	Stephane Beauregard, St. Jean
1988-89	Stephane Fiset, Victoriaville
1989-90	Pierre Gagnon, Victoriaville
1990-91	Felix Potvin, Chicoutimi
1991-92	Jean-Francois Labbe, Trois-Rivieres
1992-93	Jocelyn Thibault, Sherbrooke
1993-94	Philippe DeRouville, Verdun
1994-95	Martin Biron, Beauport
1995-96	Frederic Deschenes, Granby
1996-97	Marc Denis, Chicoutimi
1997-98	Mathieu Garon, Victoriaville
1998-99	Maxime Ouellet, Quebec
1999-00	Simon Lajeunesse, Moncton

GUY LAFLEUR TROPHY
(Playoff MVP)

Season	Player, Team
1977-78	Richard David, Trois-Rivieres
1978-79	Jean-Francois Sauve, Trois-Rivieres
1979-80	Dale Hawerchuk, Cornwall
1980-81	Alain Lemieux, Trois-Rivieres
1981-82	Michel Morissette, Sherbrooke
1982-83	Pat LaFontaine, Verdun
1983-84	Mario Lemieux, Laval
1984-85	Claude Lemieux, Verdun
1985-86	Sylvain Cote, Hull
	Luc Robitaille, Hull
1986-87	Marc Saumier, Longueuil
1987-88	Marc Saumier, Hull
1988-89	Donald Audette, Laval
1989-90	Denis Chalifoux, Laval
1990-91	Felix Potvin, Chicoutimi
1991-92	Robert Guillet, Longueuil

Season	Player, Team
1992-93	Emmanuel Fernandez, Laval
1993-94	Eric Fichaud, Chicoutimi
1994-95	Jose Theodore, Hull
1995-96	Jason Doig, Granby
1996-97	Christian Bronsard, Hull
1997-98	Jean-Pierre Dumont, Val d'Or
1998-99	Mathieu Benoit, Acadie-Bathurst
1999-00	Brad Richards, Rimouski

ROBERT LEBEL TROPHY
(Best team defensive average)

Season	Team
1977-78	Trois-Rivieres Draveurs
1978-79	Trois-Rivieres Draveurs
1979-80	Sherbrooke Beavers
1980-81	Sorel Black Hawks
1981-82	Montreal Juniors
1982-83	Shawinigan Cataracts
1983-84	Shawinigan Cataracts
1984-85	Shawinigan Cataracts
1985-86	Hull Olympiques
1986-78	Longueuil Chevaliers
1987-88	St. Jean Castors
1988-89	Hull Olympiques
1989-90	Victoriaville Tigres
1990-91	Chicoutimi Sagueneens
1991-92	Trois-Rivieres Draveurs
1992-93	Sherbrooke Faucons
1993-94	College Francais de Verdun
1994-95	Beauport Harfangs
1995-96	Granby Predateurs
1996-97	Hull Olympics
1997-98	Quebec Remparts
1998-99	Halifax Mooseheads
1999-00	Moncton Wildcats

ALL-TIME LEAGUE CHAMPIONS

REGULAR-SEASON CHAMPION / PLAYOFF CHAMPION

Season	Team (Regular-Season)	Team (Playoff)
1969-70	Quebec Remparts	Quebec Remparts
1970-71	Quebec Remparts	Quebec Remparts
1971-72	Cornwall Royals	Cornwall Royals
1972-73	Quebec Remparts	Quebec Remparts
1973-74	Sorel Black Hawks	Quebec Remparts
1974-75	Sherbrooke Beavers	Sherbrooke Beavers
1975-76	Sherbrooke Beavers	Quebec Remparts
1976-77	Quebec Remparts	Sherbrooke Beavers
1977-78	Trois-Rivieres Draveurs	Trois-Rivieres Draveurs
1978-79	Trois-Rivieres Draveurs	Trois-Rivieres Draveurs
1979-80	Sherbrooke Beavers	Cornwall Royals
1980-81	Cornwall Royals	Cornwall Royals
1981-82	Sherbrooke Beavers	Sherbrooke Beavers
1982-83	Laval Voisins	Verdun Juniors
1983-84	Laval Voisins	Laval Voisins
1984-85	Shawinigan Cataracts	Verdun Junior Canadiens
1985-86	Hull Olympiques	Hull Olympiques
1986-87	Granby Bisons	Longueuil Chevaliers
1987-88	Hull Olympiques	Hull Olympiques
1988-89	Trois-Rivieres Draveurs	Laval Titans
1989-90	Victoriaville Tigres	Laval Titans
1990-91	Chicoutimi Sagueneens	Chicoutimi Sagueneens
1991-92	Longueuil College Francais	Longueuil College Francais
1992-93	Sherbrooke Faucons	Laval Titans
1993-94	Laval Titans	Chicoutimi Sagueneens
1994-95	Laval Titans	Hull Olympiques
1995-96	Granby Predateurs	Granby Predateurs
1996-97	Hull Olympics	Hull Olympics
1997-98	Quebec Remparts	Val d'Or Foreurs
1998-99	Quebec Remparts	Acadie-Bathurst Titans
1999-00	Rimouski Oceanic	Rimouski Oceanic

The QMJHL regular-season champion is awarded the John Rougeau Trophy and the playoff champion is awarded the Presidents Cup. The John Rougeau Trophy was originally called the Governors Trophy from 1969-70 through 1982-83.

WESTERN HOCKEY LEAGUE

LEAGUE OFFICE

Note: League was known as Canadian Major Junior Hockey League in 1966-67 and Western Canadian Hockey League from 1967-68 through 1977-78.

Commissioner
To be announced
Vice president
Richard Doerksen
Dir. of marketing and public relations
Lloyd Hamshaw
Director of information
Leroy McKinnon

Education consultant
Jim Donlevy
Secretary
Connie Watson
Address
Suite 308, 8989 Macleod Trail S.
Calgary, Alberta T2H 0M2

Phone
403-253-8113
FAX
403-258-1455

1999-2000 REGULAR SEASON
FINAL STANDINGS

EAST DIVISION

Team	G	W	L	T	RT	Pts.	GF	GA
Swift Current	72	47	21	4	3	101	257	170
Saskatoon	72	34	30	8	3	79	216	223
Regina	72	32	34	6	5	75	234	255
Prince Albert	72	26	40	6	7	65	221	257
Moose Jaw	72	25	38	9	4	63	221	259
Brandon	72	25	43	4	5	59	212	260

CENTRAL DIVISION

Team	G	W	L	T	RT	Pts.	GF	GA
Calgary	72	58	12	2	2	120	313	182
Kootenay	72	44	17	11	3	102	275	200
Red Deer	72	32	31	9	0	73	227	229
Lethbridge	72	25	43	4	6	60	220	250
Medicine Hat	72	21	45	6	6	54	222	295

WEST DIVISION

Team	G	W	L	T	RT	Pts.	GF	GA
Spokane	72	47	21	4	2	100	272	191
Prince George	72	43	25	4	5	95	279	228
Seattle	72	34	30	8	4	80	250	221
Kamloops	72	36	31	5	1	78	244	228
Kelowna	72	25	43	4	3	57	193	228
Tri-City	72	24	41	7	2	57	231	288
Portland	72	16	49	7	0	39	173	296

INDIVIDUAL LEADERS

Goals: Pavel Brendl, Calgary (59)
Assists: Brad Moran, Calgary (72)
Points: Brad Moran, Calgary (120)
Penalty minutes: Eric Godard, Lethbridge (310)
Goaltending average: Bryce Wandler, Swift Current (2.06)
Shutouts: Kevin Swanson, Kelowna (7)

TOP SCORERS

	Games	G	A	Pts.
Brad Moran, Calgary	72	48	72	120
Pavel Brendl, Calgary	61	59	52	111
Radek Duda, Lethbridge	69	42	64	106
Layne Ulmer, Swift Current	71	50	54	104
Justin Mapletoft, Red Deer	72	39	57	96
Tim Smith, Spokane	71	26	70	96

	Games	G	A	Pts.
Trent Hunter, Prince George	67	46	49	95
Mike Green, Kootenay	69	43	49	92
Zdenek Blatny, Sea.-Koot.	68	47	44	91
Jeremy Reich, Swift Current	72	33	58	91
Micki DuPont, Kamloops	70	26	62	88
Kris Beech, Calgary	66	32	54	86
Nathan Barrett, Lethbridge	72	44	38	82
Alan Manness, Reg.-Sea.	76	29	53	82
Scott Hartnell, Prince Albert	62	27	55	82
Jason Hegberg, Lethbridge	72	35	46	81
Lawrence Nycholat, Swift Current	70	22	58	80
Brett Lysak, Regina	70	38	40	78
Derek Schutz, Spokane	65	32	44	76
Jarret Stoll, Kootenay	71	37	38	75
Matt Kinch, Calgary	62	14	61	75

INDIVIDUAL STATISTICS

BRANDON WHEAT KINGS
SCORING

	Games	G	A	Pts.	PIM
Brad Twordik	72	24	45	69	57
Jan Fadrny	55	26	25	51	56
Aaron Goldade	56	14	28	42	33
Milan Bartovic	38	18	22	40	28
Kevin Harris	72	9	31	40	34
Brett Girard	54	13	26	39	27
Ryan Craig	65	17	19	36	40

	Games	G	A	Pts.	PIM
Randy Ponte	66	14	13	27	306
Mike Wirll	37	9	18	27	16
Colin McRae	68	12	13	25	15
Bart Rushmer	43	6	15	21	122
Mark Ardelan	63	4	16	20	60
Jordin Tootoo	45	6	10	16	214
Les Borsheim	31	5	9	14	105
Dan Tetrault	31	4	10	14	43
Petr Kudrna	19	4	7	11	9
Cory Unser	63	3	7	10	61

	Games	G	A	Pts.	PIM
J.D. Kehler	24	6	3	9	7
Brett Thurston	43	3	6	9	61
James Marquis	15	2	4	6	8
Ryan Diduck	23	3	2	5	13
Richard Mueller	7	2	3	5	4
Tim Konsorada	5	1	2	3	0
James Ardelan	9	1	1	2	2
Brett Dickie	67	1	1	2	41
Wade Skolney	13	0	2	2	23
Robert McVicar (goalie)	14	0	1	1	0
Jomar Cruz (goalie)	21	0	1	1	2
Jamie Hodson (goalie)	39	0	1	1	8
Bill Gerry (goalie)	1	0	0	0	0
Ray Fraser (goalie)	3	0	0	0	0
Lance Monych	3	0	0	0	0

GOALTENDING

	Games	Min.	W	L	T	G	SO	Avg.
Bill Gerry	1	20	0	0	0	0	0	0.00
Ray Fraser	3	156	0	1	0	7	0	2.69
Jamie Hodson	39	2321	13	21	3	129	2	3.33
Jomar Cruz	21	1151	7	13	1	73	1	3.81
Robert McVicar	14	687	5	7	0	44	0	3.84

CALGARY HITMEN
SCORING

	Games	G	A	Pts.	PIM
Brad Moran	72	48	72	120	84
Pavel Brendl	61	59	52	111	94
Kris Beech	66	32	54	86	99
Matt Kinch	62	14	61	75	24
Chris Nielsen	62	38	31	69	86
Kenton Smith	71	7	46	53	128
Jordan Krestanovich	72	19	24	43	22
Jerred Smithson	66	14	25	39	111
Sean McAslan	72	18	16	34	117
Shaun Norrie	67	12	13	25	94
Matt Pettinger	27	14	6	20	41
Wade Davis	61	3	15	18	59
Michael Bubnick	69	7	8	15	36
Anders Lovdahl	36	5	9	14	28
Rod Sarich	70	3	11	14	76
Owen Fussey	51	7	6	13	35
Robin Gomez	56	5	5	10	170
Jared Carli	64	3	6	9	61
Brandon Segal	44	2	6	8	76
Stephen Peat	23	0	8	8	100
Eric Clark	26	2	4	6	29
Jeff Feniak	29	0	6	6	106
Toni Bader	33	0	3	3	50
Curtis Rich	3	0	2	2	27
Rastislav Stana (goalie)	16	0	2	2	2
Chad Wolkowski	3	1	0	1	2
Alexandre Fomitchev (goalie)	1	0	1	1	0
Brent Williams (goalie)	5	0	0	0	0
Shaun Sutter	6	0	1	1	8
Brent Krahn (goalie)	39	0	1	1	4
Chris Beston	6	0	0	0	4
Sean Connors (goalie)	14	0	0	0	0

GOALTENDING

	Games	Min.	W	L	T	G	SO	Avg.
Rastislav Stana	16	971	13	2	1	37	1	2.29
Brent Krahn	39	2315	33	6	0	92	4	2.38
Sean Connors	14	744	9	1	1	32	1	2.58
Brent Williams	5	250	2	3	0	14	0	3.36
Alexandre Fomitchev	1	60	1	0	0	5	0	5.00

KAMLOOPS BLAZERS
SCORING

	Games	G	A	Pts.	PIM
Micki DuPont	70	26	62	88	156
Konstantin Panov	64	43	30	73	47

	Games	G	A	Pts.	PIM
Jonathan Hobson	71	22	36	58	61
Jared Aulin	57	17	38	55	70
Jordan Walker	61	15	39	54	30
Steve Shrum	54	22	26	48	28
Brett Draney	62	18	27	45	63
Gable Gross	71	25	19	44	93
Paul Deniset	70	14	27	41	74
Anton Borodkin	55	6	19	25	77
Kevin Mackie	72	6	18	24	144
Erik Christensen	66	9	5	14	41
Aaron Gionet	68	5	6	11	243
Chad Starling	51	4	7	11	87
Mark Rooneem	50	3	8	11	39
Kyle Ladobruk	58	4	5	9	13
Shaonne Morrison	57	1	6	7	80
Chad Schockenmaier	46	2	4	6	68
Jason Bone	58	1	5	6	197
Blaine Depper	54	1	3	4	78
Mike Munro	46	0	2	2	92
Kyle Bruce	1	0	0	0	2
Derek Krestanovich	4	0	0	0	7
David Klatt (goalie)	8	0	0	0	0
Curtis Austring	11	0	0	0	4
Davis Parley (goalie)	26	0	0	0	2
Grant McCune (goalie)	41	0	0	0	2

GOALTENDING

	Games	Min.	W	L	T	G	SO	Avg.
Grant McCune	41	2390	25	11	3	104	2	2.61
Davis Parley	26	1497	8	15	2	80	2	3.21
David Klatt	8	450	3	4	0	34	0	4.53

KELOWNA ROCKETS
SCORING

	Games	G	A	Pts.	PIM
Quintin Laing	68	22	30	52	61
J.J. Hunter	66	22	26	48	61
Vernon Fiddler	64	20	28	48	60
Carsen Germyn	71	16	29	45	111
Kiel McLeod	59	17	13	30	100
Gavin McLeod	71	3	25	28	129
David Johansson	62	3	24	27	36
David Selthun	54	8	17	25	38
Ryan Cuthbert	65	8	15	23	48
Dallas Flaman	50	9	10	19	41
Kevin Korol	39	8	9	17	36
Diarmuid Kelly	50	6	10	16	33
Travis Moen	66	9	6	15	96
Richie Regehr	50	6	8	14	22
Nolan Yonkman	71	5	7	12	153
Curtis Rich	58	1	11	12	135
Lubomir Pistek	28	7	4	11	30
Seth Leonard	40	7	4	11	16
Cam Paddock	46	5	5	10	42
Chris Di Ubaldo	49	4	6	10	45
Bruce Harrison	27	2	5	7	80
Mitch Fritz	58	4	2	6	204
B. J. Fehr	23	0	4	4	16
Joe Suderman	52	1	0	1	138
Rory McDade	2	0	0	0	2
Vaughan Watson (goalie)	9	0	0	0	0
Kevin Swanson (goalie)	68	0	0	0	2

GOALTENDING

	Games	Min.	W	L	T	G	SO	Avg.
Kevin Swanson	68	3951	25	40	3	195	7	2.96
Vaughan Watson	9	373	0	3	1	26	0	4.18

KOOTENAY ICE
SCORING

	Games	G	A	Pts.	PIM
Mike Green	69	43	49	92	63
Zdenek Blatny	61	43	39	82	119

MAJOR JUNIOR LEAGUES WHL

	Games	G	A	Pts.	PIM
Jarret Stoll	71	37	38	75	64
Jaroslav Svoboda	56	23	43	66	97
Jason Jaffray	71	24	28	52	104
Tyler Beechey	58	12	28	40	23
Wade Burt	68	20	17	37	65
Steve McCarthy	37	13	23	36	36
Brad Tutschek	59	17	16	33	90
Trevor Johnson	65	5	26	31	100
Matt Walker	31	4	19	23	53
Colin Sinclair	66	6	15	21	101
Dion Lassu	70	5	14	19	219
Cole Fischer	56	3	13	16	91
Graham Belak	49	4	9	13	197
Richard Hamula	49	3	9	12	6
Dean Arsene	66	4	7	11	150
Jesse Ferguson	37	1	9	10	49
Pat Iannone	58	1	5	6	65
Scott Roles	7	0	6	6	4
Kyle Wanvig	6	2	2	4	12
Nick Marach	20	2	1	3	14
Tyler Dyck	40	1	1	2	12
Stacey Bublitz	12	0	2	2	26
B.J. Boxma (goalie)	25	0	2	2	0
Chris Chubb	64	0	2	2	94
Kevin Livingston	1	1	0	1	5
Kyle Sheen	3	1	0	1	0
Jordan Wallin	39	0	1	1	8
Dan Blackburn (goalie)	51	0	1	1	10
Andy Thompson	2	0	0	0	0

GOALTENDING

	Games	Min.	W	L	T	G	SO	Avg.
Dan Blackburn	51	3004	34	8	7	126	3	2.52
B.J. Boxma	24	1314	9	9	4	72	0	3.29

LETHBRIDGE HURRICANES

SCORING

	Games	G	A	Pts.	PIM
Radek Duda	69	42	64	106	193
Nathan Barrett	72	44	38	82	38
Jason Hegberg	72	35	46	81	114
Brian Ballman	69	17	27	44	100
Scott Borders	64	15	29	44	72
Brandon Janes	54	6	33	39	57
Derek Ruck	71	10	23	33	46
Angel Krstev	31	5	11	16	66
Derek Atkinson	58	6	7	13	57
Thomas Scantlebury	57	3	9	12	111
Bart Rushmer	28	2	8	10	40
Darren Lynch	50	3	5	8	19
Eric Godard	60	3	5	8	310
Petr Kudrna	32	5	2	7	8
Phil Cole	51	1	6	7	112
Simon Ferguson	51	1	6	7	100
Ryan Jorde	54	1	6	7	112
Justin Ossachuk	27	4	2	6	96
Jordon Flodell	38	3	3	6	79
Warren McCutheon	62	2	4	6	39
Dustin Kazak	57	1	5	6	23
Derek Parker	43	3	2	5	266
Brian Patterson	55	3	1	4	37
Eric Sonnenberg	36	1	0	1	22
Brady Block (goalie)	55	0	1	1	19
Tyler Howe (goalie)	1	0	0	0	0
Logan Koopmans (goalie)	5	0	0	0	0
Marcus Wright (goalie)	10	0	0	0	0
Chad Yaremko (goalie)	16	0	0	0	2

GOALTENDING

	Games	Min.	W	L	T	G	SO	Avg.
Brady Block	55	3014	19	29	3	160	4	3.19
Chad Yaremko	16	727	4	6	1	45	1	3.71
Marcus Wright	10	304	1	4	0	19	0	3.75

	Games	Min.	W	L	T	G	SO	Avg.
Logan Koopmans	5	285	1	2	0	18	0	3.79
Tyler Howe	1	15	0	1	0	2	0	8.00

MEDICINE HAT TIGERS

SCORING

	Games	G	A	Pts.	PIM
Ben Thomson	69	23	40	63	45
Ryan Hollweg	54	19	27	46	107
Martin Cibak	58	16	29	45	77
Berkeley Buchko	71	19	25	44	55
Paul Elliott	66	15	28	43	91
Chris St. Jacques	61	21	18	39	65
Jay Bouwmeester	64	13	21	34	26
Vladimir Sicak	72	7	27	34	73
Ken Davis	61	23	10	33	86
Denny Johnston	62	7	21	28	62
Kevin Labbe	62	13	14	27	20
Tyson Mulock	59	11	15	26	14
Cody Jensen	34	7	16	23	46
Brad Voth	58	9	7	16	222
Ryan Kinasewich	47	3	10	13	19
Konrad Brand	62	2	11	13	107
Josh Maser	68	5	7	12	233
Brett Scheffelmaier	71	1	9	10	281
Josh Morrow	49	1	8	9	57
Shaun Sutter	29	1	7	8	43
Justin Taylor	39	1	5	6	11
Ben McMullin (goalie)	19	0	1	1	6
B. J. Fehr	26	0	1	1	22
Justin Yeoman	1	0	0	0	0
Cam Ondrik (goalie)	3	0	0	0	2
Kyle Kettles (goalie)	57	0	0	0	10

GOALTENDING

	Games	Min.	W	L	T	G	SO	Avg.
Cam Ondrik	3	180	1	2	0	8	1	2.67
Kyle Kettles	57	3265	16	33	5	215	1	3.95
Ben McMullin	18	856	4	9	1	64	0	4.49

MOOSE JAW WARRIORS

SCORING

	Games	G	A	Pts.	PIM
Jason Weitzel	72	25	39	64	126
Ben Knopp	72	30	30	60	101
Scott Schoneck	72	13	44	57	90
Shawn Limpright	72	22	32	54	146
Jamie Lundmark	37	21	27	48	33
Jarrett Thompson	53	17	27	44	127
Nathan Paetsch	68	9	35	44	49
Steven Crampton	69	22	20	42	91
Brian Sutherby	47	18	17	35	102
Shawn Skolney	61	8	19	27	113
Bobby Chad Mitchell	65	6	10	16	157
Sean O'Connor	51	5	8	13	166
Cory Hintz	27	4	6	10	23
Kris Mallette	61	3	6	9	213
Martin Beck	69	7	1	8	39
Dustin Bru	46	5	3	8	32
Dayle Wilcox	35	1	6	7	32
Harlan Anderson	50	0	7	7	23
Conor MacKenzie	60	1	4	5	32
Deryk Engelland	55	0	5	5	62
Anders Lovdahl	31	3	0	3	8
David Bararuk	21	0	2	2	0
Brent Hobday	6	1	0	1	23
Sean Connors (goalie)	10	0	0	0	2
Rastislav Stana (goalie)	14	0	0	0	13
Tim Barlow (goalie)	53	0	0	0	11

GOALTENDING

	Games	Min.	W	L	T	G	SO	Avg.
Tim Barlow	53	3098	21	22	8	166	4	3.21
Rastislav Stana	14	730	4	9	0	48	0	3.95
Sean Connors	10	539	0	7	1	41	0	4.56

PORTLAND WINTER HAWKS

SCORING

	Games	G	A	Pts.	PIM
Marcel Hossa	60	24	29	53	58
Blake Robson	70	20	27	47	96
Josef Balej	65	22	23	45	33
Dean Beuker	64	16	26	42	67
Michael Kiesman	61	22	17	39	118
Kent Sauer	65	12	13	25	116
Kevin Young	51	4	21	25	60
Shawn Roed	25	7	15	22	43
Nick Marach	48	12	8	20	66
Ryan Kehrig	69	6	14	20	55
Jesse Ferguson	28	1	14	15	38
Paul Gaustad	56	6	8	14	110
Chad Grisdale	67	3	9	12	168
Daniel McIvor	58	3	7	10	15
James DeMone	56	2	8	10	181
Matt Walker	38	2	7	9	97
Christian Bolding	44	2	7	9	72
Eric Bowen	69	2	5	7	184
Ken Davis	6	1	2	3	18
Tyler Cronk	56	1	2	3	14
Luke Molotowsky	3	1	0	1	0
Kris Callaway	21	1	0	1	46
Ryan Thrussell	9	0	1	1	4
Brant Middelton	49	0	1	1	38
Jesse Ferguson	1	0	0	0	0
Patrick Wellar	1	0	0	0	0
Shaun Lee (goalie)	16	0	0	0	0
Lanny Ramage (goalie)	25	0	0	0	0
Jason LaBarbera (goalie)	34	0	0	0	6
Jonathan Lupul	46	0	0	0	28
Dustin Bauer	49	0	0	0	58

GOALTENDING

	Games	Min.	W	L	T	G	SO	Avg.
Jason LaBarbera	34	2005	8	24	2	123	1	3.68
Shaun Lee	16	955	3	13	0	66	0	4.15
Lanny Ramage	25	1386	5	12	5	101	0	4.37

PRINCE ALBERT RAIDERS

SCORING

	Games	G	A	Pts.	PIM
Scott Hartnell	62	27	55	82	124
Milan Kraft	56	34	35	69	42
Garrett Prosofsky	70	26	38	64	58
Michal Sivek	53	23	37	60	65
Jarrett Smith	72	27	32	59	53
Nick Schultz	72	11	33	44	38
Brent Hobday	49	10	19	29	93
Blaine Stowards	72	11	12	23	48
Jeremy Goetzinger	71	3	17	20	74
Clayton Chartrand	43	1	18	19	44
Ross Lupaschuk	22	8	8	16	42
Chris Harper	51	7	9	16	30
Greg Watson	67	10	5	15	63
Riley Cote	67	6	7	13	71
Ryan Thrussell	42	1	9	10	38
Regan Darby	44	1	9	10	143
Cody Jensen	10	4	4	8	11
Dallas Flaman	9	3	3	6	22
Kyle Bruce	8	2	1	3	13
Evan Lindsay (goalie)	54	0	3	3	10
Steven MacIntyre	47	1	1	2	100
Grant McNeil	58	1	1	2	43
Craig Brunel	17	0	2	2	59
Ryan Haggerty	32	0	2	2	12
Jon Kress	34	1	0	1	18
Scott C. McQueen	46	1	0	1	14
Jordan Clarke	66	1	0	1	154
Shaun Hill	0	0	0	0	0
Jeff Schmidt	2	0	0	0	0

	Games	G	A	Pts.	PIM
Grant McCune (goalie)	13	0	0	0	2
Duane Perillat (goalie)	15	0	0	0	2

GOALTENDING

	Games	Min.	W	L	T	G	SO	Avg.
Evan Lindsay	54	3081	17	30	5	175	1	3.41
Grant McCune	13	723	7	5	0	44	0	3.65
Duane Perillat	15	543	2	5	1	36	0	3.98

PRINCE GEORGE COUGARS

SCORING

	Games	G	A	Pts.	PIM
Trent Hunter	67	46	49	95	47
Justin Cox	71	33	38	71	74
Tyler Bouck	57	30	33	63	183
Blair Betts	44	24	35	59	38
Garry Toor	45	16	36	52	20
Christian Chartier	57	16	36	52	60
Jon Barkman	51	16	29	45	24
Jozef Mrena	58	17	27	44	28
Dan Hamhuis	70	10	23	33	140
Tim Wedderburn	70	8	20	28	93
Travis Eagles	59	8	15	23	81
Aaron Foster	72	9	13	22	90
Justin Hansen	45	7	12	19	75
Chris Falloon	60	11	5	16	15
Dan Baum	55	6	10	16	82
Roman Takac	56	5	11	16	16
Jeff Zorn	14	6	8	14	19
Shon Jones-Parry	67	3	6	9	237
Willy Glover	27	2	3	5	15
Justin Yeoman	54	2	3	5	40
Brent McDonald	7	1	3	4	6
Devin Wilson	49	1	3	4	17
Scott Myers (goalie)	49	0	3	3	4
Jonathan Parker	5	1	1	2	5
Ryan Chieduch	58	1	1	2	135
Marty Maurice (goalie)	29	0	1	1	4
Kevin Seibel	1	0	0	0	0
Billy Thompson (goalie)	1	0	0	0	0
Paul Valaitis (goalie)	1	0	0	0	0
John Filewich	3	0	0	0	2
Derek Boogaard	33	0	0	0	149

GOALTENDING

	Games	Min.	W	L	T	G	SO	Avg.
Scott Myers	49	2693	30	15	3	128	1	2.85
Marty Maurice	29	1535	12	9	1	86	2	3.36
Paul Valaitis	1	60	1	0	0	4	0	4.00
Billy Thompson	1	60	0	1	0	5	0	5.00

RED DEER REBELS

SCORING

	Games	G	A	Pts.	PIM
Justin Mapletoft	72	39	57	96	135
Dustin Paul	72	37	29	66	54
Ross Lupaschuk	46	13	27	40	116
Kyle Wanvig	58	21	18	39	123
Colby Armstrong	68	13	25	38	122
Jim Vandermeer	71	8	30	38	221
Boyd Gordon	66	10	26	36	24
Lyle Steenbergen	63	16	15	31	107
Joel Stepp	65	11	13	24	59
Justin Wallin	58	7	12	19	26
Andrew Bergen	61	8	9	17	43
Bryce Thoma	69	4	13	17	36
Jeff Woywitka	67	4	12	16	40
Jeff Smith	63	9	6	15	74
Doug Lynch	65	9	5	14	57
Regan Darby	18	3	6	9	79
Devin Francon	26	3	4	7	35
Jordan Walker	10	2	5	7	6
Jarrett Thompson	10	2	4	6	19

	Games	G	A	Pts.	PIM
Colin Johnson	61	0	6	6	16
Craig Brunel	35	3	2	5	140
Adam Dombrowski	46	1	4	5	54
Brent Hobday	11	1	3	4	17
Jearum Kurtz	33	1	3	4	10
Alexei Zhurba	29	1	1	2	0
Scott C. McQueen	16	0	2	2	14
Shane Bendera (goalie)	69	0	1	1	6
Rhett Nevill	0	0	0	0	0
Michael Garnett (goalie)	1	0	0	0	0
Dustin Schwartz (goalie)	4	0	0	0	0
Aaron Sproule (goalie)	5	0	0	0	0
Steven MacIntyre	20	0	0	0	65

GOALTENDING

	Games	Min.	W	L	T	G	SO	Avg.
Michael Garnett	1	14	0	0	0	0	0	0.00
Shane Bendera	69	4006	31	27	9	202	0	3.03
Dustin Schwartz	4	174	1	2	0	11	0	3.79
Aaron Sproule	5	165	0	2	0	13	0	4.73

REGINA PATS

SCORING

	Games	G	A	Pts.	PIM
Brett Lysak	70	38	40	78	24
Joey Bastien	69	37	36	73	72
Karel Mosovsky	56	24	34	58	80
Barret Jackman	53	9	37	46	175
Alan Manness	42	17	26	43	21
Garth Murray	68	14	26	40	155
Ryan Annesley	69	10	30	40	52
Filip Novak	47	7	32	39	70
Matt Hubbauer	71	16	18	34	113
Andrew Kaminsky	48	5	15	20	31
Ryan Thomas	64	7	12	19	226
Chris Anderson	67	3	15	18	74
Travis Churchman	63	10	7	17	238
Grant Jacobsen	56	7	7	14	20
Kevin Korol	29	5	9	14	20
Scott Balan	67	3	11	14	157
Landon Boyko	42	3	9	12	62
Curtis Austring	34	4	6	10	19
David McDonald	55	5	3	8	17
Jonathan Parker	47	4	4	8	19
Justin Lucyshyn	43	1	4	5	34
Brett Bartell	41	2	1	3	19
Zack Roe	2	1	0	1	0
Donald Choukalos (goalie)	58	0	1	1	12
Travis Swyripa	1	0	0	0	0
Paul Brown	3	0	0	0	0
Derek Boogaard	5	0	0	0	17
Shaun Fleming (goalie)	22	0	0	0	2

GOALTENDING

	Games	Min.	W	L	T	G	SO	Avg.
Shaun Fleming	22	1107	6	10	2	58	0	3.14
Donald Choukalos	58	3259	26	24	4	194	2	3.57

SASKATOON BLADES

SCORING

	Games	G	A	Pts.	PIM
Mathieu Cusson	72	33	34	67	69
Garrett Bembridge	72	27	31	58	41
Tyler Shybunka	68	25	33	58	42
David Cameron	72	19	37	56	46
Martin Erat	66	27	26	53	82
Bobby Almeida	66	14	28	42	57
Jeff Zorn	60	12	30	42	53
Warren Peters	70	11	17	28	97
Chris Ovington	68	2	19	21	59
Derek Halldorson	48	6	13	19	106
Justin Kelly	54	6	11	17	36

	Games	G	A	Pts.	PIM
Lubomir Pistek	28	4	11	15	20
Darcy Hordichuk	63	6	8	14	269
Darcy Robinson	59	5	9	14	91
Jon Barkman	11	7	4	11	4
Garnet Exelby	63	1	8	9	79
Chris Manchakowski	55	1	7	8	68
Aaron Rome	47	0	6	6	22
Davin Heintz	28	3	1	4	4
Christian Chartier	11	2	2	4	4
Craig Valette	47	2	1	3	25
Adrian Foster	7	1	2	3	6
Jeff Coulter	43	1	2	3	50
Mark Forth	45	1	2	3	92
Kane Ludwar	23	0	2	2	12
Ryan Stempfle	0	0	0	0	0
Aaron Sproule (goalie)	2	0	0	0	0
Tyler MacKay (goalie)	5	0	0	0	4
Tony Kolewaski (goalie)	18	0	0	0	2
Cam Ondrik (goalie)	55	0	0	0	8

GOALTENDING

	Games	Min.	W	L	T	G	SO	Avg.
Cam Ondrik	55	3198	29	22	4	151	4	2.83
Aaron Sproule	2	98	1	0	0	5	0	3.06
Tony Kolewaski	18	804	2	5	4	42	1	3.13
Tyler MacKay	5	273	2	3	0	21	0	4.62

SEATTLE THUNDERBIRDS

SCORING

	Games	G	A	Pts.	PIM
Oleg Saprykin	48	30	36	66	91
Jason McKee	69	23	39	62	47
David Morisset	60	23	34	57	69
Bret DeCecco	51	29	26	55	56
Shane Endicott	70	23	32	55	62
Scott Kelman	64	13	42	55	104
Alan Manness	34	12	27	39	12
Nathan Forster	51	9	28	37	104
Gerard DiCaire	68	11	25	36	38
Tim Preston	68	16	17	33	62
Keegan McAvoy	57	12	11	23	77
Paul Hurd	67	7	16	23	117
David Ullmann	64	14	7	21	46
Jason Beckett	70	3	15	18	183
Greg Black	63	8	7	15	114
Matthew Spiller	60	1	10	11	108
Craig Olynick	65	1	9	10	120
Zdenek Blatny	7	4	5	9	12
Darren McLachlan	54	5	1	6	175
David Kaczowka	63	3	3	6	211
Brennan Evans	52	1	2	3	40
Jeffrey Beatch	39	0	3	3	24
Mark Kelts	2	1	0	1	0
Chris Manchakowski	6	1	0	1	10
Tyler Metcalfe	4	0	1	1	2
Dustin Johner	6	0	1	1	0
Thomas Vicars (goalie)	30	0	1	1	15
Ray Fraser (goalie)	1	0	0	0	0
Tyler Metcalfe	3	0	0	0	0
Igor Agarunov	5	0	0	0	0
Alexandre Fomitchev (goalie)	46	0	0	0	4

GOALTENDING

	Games	Min.	W	L	T	G	SO	Avg.
Alexandre Fomitchev	46	2685	20	21	4	126	3	2.82
Thomas Vicars	30	1654	14	8	4	85	2	3.08
Ray Fraser	1	28	0	1	0	2	0	4.29

SPOKANE CHIEFS

SCORING

	Games	G	A	Pts.	PIM
Tim Smith	71	26	70	96	65
Derek Schutz	65	32	44	76	122

	Games	G	A	Pts.	PIM
Daniel Bohac	70	39	33	72	40
Roman Tvrdon	69	26	44	70	40
Brent McDonald	61	28	30	58	77
Brandin Cote	71	19	32	51	66
Scott Roles	61	14	37	51	50
Lynn Loyns	71	20	29	49	47
Tim Krymusa	69	20	15	35	44
Kyle Rossiter	63	11	22	33	155
Mason Wallin	61	10	8	18	26
Jeff Lucky	57	8	10	18	12
Shawn Thompson	59	4	14	18	81
Kurt Sauer	71	3	12	15	48
David Boychuk	72	4	8	12	226
Ryan Thorpe	51	3	9	12	31
Kris Callaway	32	0	9	9	55
Chris Heid	44	1	7	8	25
Jeremy Farr	49	1	7	8	77
Steven Mann	7	0	5	5	4
Matthew Keith	39	1	3	4	37
Mark Forth	5	0	2	2	16
Joff Kehler	18	0	2	2	2
Chris Barr	29	1	0	1	47
Jared Smyth	11	0	1	1	16
Jason LaBarbera (goalie)	21	0	1	1	0
Tyler MacKay (goalie)	37	0	1	1	23
Brad Schell	1	0	0	0	0
Cole Fischer	2	0	0	0	4
Shane Gris (goalie)	3	0	0	0	0
Chris Harper	7	0	0	0	28
Mike Lencucha (goalie)	17	0	0	0	0

GOALTENDING

	Games	Min.	W	L	T	G	SO	Avg.
Shane Gris	3	143	2	0	0	6	0	2.52
Tyler MacKay	37	2083	23	8	2	88	2	2.53
Jason LaBarbera	21	1146	12	6	2	50	0	2.62
Mike Lencucha	17	973	10	7	0	47	0	2.90

SWIFT CURRENT BRONCOS
SCORING

	Games	G	A	Pts.	PIM
Layne Ulmer	71	50	54	104	66
Jeremy Reich	72	33	58	91	167
Lawrence Nycholat	70	22	58	80	92
Brett Allan	70	26	25	51	48
Jay Langager	71	14	36	50	65
Nathan Smith	70	21	28	49	72
Brent Twordik	72	15	32	47	75
Scott Henkelman	70	17	29	46	63
Duncan Milroy	68	15	15	30	20
Ben Ondrus	67	14	15	29	138
James Hiebert	52	8	11	19	114
Jakub Cutta	71	2	12	14	114
Igor Valeev	36	7	5	12	78
Clay Thoring	64	1	7	8	36
Dean Serdachny	64	1	6	7	196
Dan Hulak	46	2	4	6	42
Todd Hornung	22	3	2	5	28
Colton Orr	61	3	2	5	130
Jay Batchelor	45	0	5	5	20
Craig Priestlay	33	1	3	4	20
Matt Sommerfeld	67	1	3	4	215
Houston Hair	14	1	0	1	12
Bryce Wandler (goalie)	56	0	1	1	2
Kevin Seibel	2	0	0	0	2
Brendan Vanthuyne	14	0	0	0	4
Tyson Motz (goalie)	20	0	0	0	6

GOALTENDING

	Games	Min.	W	L	T	G	SO	Avg.
Bryce Wandler	56	3255	37	15	2	112	6	2.06
Tyson Motz	20	1084	10	6	2	55	1	3.04

TRI-CITY AMERICANS
SCORING

	Games	G	A	Pts.	PIM
Blake Evans	72	27	43	70	110
Eric Johannson	72	24	36	60	38
Jaroslav Kristek	45	26	25	51	16
Darrell Hay	64	15	36	51	85
K.C. Timmons	69	24	24	48	193
Tim Green	67	16	24	40	37
Jeff Katcher	58	6	28	34	134
Ryley Layden	71	8	23	31	105
Jared Smyth	50	11	17	28	74
Ben Kilgour	64	11	10	21	86
Eric Clark	43	8	13	21	21
Curtis Huppe	17	7	12	19	23
Andrew Downing	34	2	17	19	28
Mike Lee	46	11	6	17	115
Milan Bartovic	18	8	9	17	12
Jesse Schultz	62	10	6	16	34
Dustin Barker	49	3	13	16	8
Andrew Davidson	63	7	2	9	50
Jeff Feniak	45	1	7	8	106
Toni Bader	22	2	3	5	54
Brad Zanon	53	2	2	4	38
Andrew DeSousa	59	1	3	4	90
Adam Johnson	52	0	3	3	90
Aaron Winterholt	17	1	1	2	6
Stephen Peat	12	0	2	2	48
Jomar Cruz (goalie)	35	0	1	1	4
Thomas Huling	1	0	0	0	0
Chris Houle (goalie)	2	0	0	0	0
Clint Chalmers (goalie)	9	0	0	0	0
Blake Ward (goalie)	37	0	0	0	19

GOALTENDING

	Games	Min.	W	L	T	G	SO	Avg.
Blake Ward	37	1853	14	12	2	111	1	3.59
Jomar Cruz	35	1968	8	22	4	126	0	3.84
Chris Houle	2	118	1	1	0	9	0	4.58
Clint Chalmers	9	404	1	6	1	37	0	5.50

PLAYERS WITH TWO OR MORE TEAMS

SCORING

	Games	G	A	Pts.	PIM
Curtis Austring, Kamloops	11	0	0	0	4
Curtis Austring, Regina	34	4	6	10	19
Totals	45	4	6	10	23
Toni Bader, Tri-City	22	2	3	5	54
Toni Bader, Calgary	33	0	3	3	50
Totals	55	2	6	8	104
Jon Barkman, Saskatoon	11	7	4	11	4
Jon Barkman, Prince George	51	16	29	45	24
Totals	62	23	33	56	28
Milan Bartovic, Tri-City	18	8	9	17	12
Milan Bartovic, Brandon	38	18	22	40	28
Totals	56	26	31	57	40
Zdenek Blatny, Seattle	7	4	5	9	12
Zdenek Blatny, Kootenay	61	43	39	82	119
Totals	68	47	44	91	131
Derek Boogaard, Regina	5	0	0	0	17
Derek Boogaard, Prince George	33	0	0	0	149
Totals	38	0	0	0	166
Kyle Bruce, Kamloops	1	0	0	0	2
Kyle Bruce, Prince Albert	8	2	1	3	13
Totals	9	2	1	3	15
Craig Brunel, Prince Albert	17	0	2	2	59
Craig Brunel, Red Deer	35	3	2	5	140
Totals	52	3	4	7	199
Kris Callaway, Spokane	32	0	9	9	55
Kris Callaway, Portland	21	1	0	1	46
Totals	53	1	9	10	101
Christian Chartier, Saskatoon	11	2	2	4	4

	Games	G	A	Pts.	PIM
Christian Chartier, P.G.	57	16	36	52	60
Totals	68	18	38	56	64
Eric Clark, Calgary	26	2	4	6	29
Eric Clark, Tri-City	43	8	13	21	21
Totals	69	10	17	27	50
Sean Connors, Calgary (g)	14	0	0	0	0
Sean Connors, Moose Jaw (g)	10	0	0	0	2
Totals	24	0	0	0	2
Jomar Cruz, Brandon (g)	21	0	1	1	2
Jomar Cruz, Tri-City (g)	35	0	1	1	4
Totals	56	0	2	2	6
Regan Darby, Red Deer	18	3	6	9	79
Regan Darby, Prince Albert	44	1	9	10	143
Totals	62	4	15	19	222
Ken Davis, Portland	6	1	2	3	18
Ken Davis, Medicine Hat	61	23	10	33	86
Totals	67	24	12	36	104
B. J. Fehr, Kelowna	23	0	4	4	16
B. J. Fehr, Medicine Hat	26	0	1	1	22
Totals	49	0	5	5	38
Jeff Feniak, Calgary	29	0	6	6	106
Jeff Feniak, Tri-City	45	1	7	8	106
Totals	74	1	13	14	212
Jesse Ferguson, Kootenay	37	1	9	10	49
Jesse Ferguson, Portland	29	1	14	15	38
Totals	66	2	23	25	87
Cole Fischer, Spokane	2	0	0	0	4
Cole Fischer, Kootenay	56	3	13	16	91
Totals	58	3	13	16	95
Dallas Flaman, Prince Albert	9	3	3	6	22
Dallas Flaman, Kelowna	50	9	10	19	41
Totals	59	12	13	25	63
Alexandre Fomitchev, Cal. (g)	1	0	1	1	0
Alexandre Fomitchev, Sea. (g)	46	0	0	0	4
Totals	47	0	1	1	4
Ray Fraser, Seattle (g)	1	0	0	0	0
Ray Fraser, Brandon (g)	3	0	0	0	0
Totals	4	0	0	0	0
Mark Forth, Spokane	5	0	2	2	16
Mark Forth, Saskatoon	45	1	2	3	92
Totals	50	1	4	5	108
Chris Harper, Spokane	7	0	0	0	28
Chris Harper, Prince Albert	51	7	9	16	30
Totals	58	7	9	16	58
Brent Hobday, Moose Jaw	6	1	0	1	23
Brent Hobday, Red Deer	11	1	3	4	17
Brent Hobday, Prince Albert	49	10	19	29	93
Totals	66	12	22	34	133
Cody Jensen, Prince Albert	10	4	4	8	11
Cody Jensen, Medicine Hat	34	7	16	23	46
Totals	44	11	20	31	57
Kevin Korol, Kelowna	39	8	9	17	36
Kevin Korol, Regina	29	5	9	14	20
Totals	68	13	18	31	56
Petr Kudrna, Brandon	19	4	7	11	9
Petr Kudrna, Lethbridge	32	5	2	7	8
Totals	51	9	9	18	17
Jason LaBarbera, Portland (g)	34	0	0	0	6
Jason LaBarbera, Spokane (g)	21	0	1	1	0
Totals	55	0	1	1	6
Anders Lovdahl, Calgary	36	5	9	14	28
Anders Lovdahl, Moose Jaw	31	3	0	3	8
Totals	67	8	9	17	36
Ross Lupaschuk, Prince Albert	22	8	8	16	42
Ross Lupaschuk, Red Deer	46	13	27	40	116
Totals	68	21	35	56	158
Steven MacIntyre, Red Deer	20	0	0	0	65
Steven MacIntyre, Prince Albert	47	1	1	2	100
Totals	67	1	1	2	165
Tyler MacKay, Saskatoon (g)	5	0	0	0	4
Tyler MacKay, Spokane (g)	37	0	1	1	23
Totals	42	0	1	1	27
Chris Manchakowski, Seattle	6	1	0	1	10
Chris Manchakowski, Sask.	55	1	7	8	68
Totals	61	2	7	9	78
Alan Manness, Regina	42	17	26	43	21
Alan Manness, Seattle	34	12	27	39	12
Totals	76	29	53	82	33
Nick Marach, Kootenay	20	2	1	3	14
Nick Marach, Portland	48	12	8	20	66
Totals	68	14	9	23	80
Grant McCune, P.A. (g)	13	0	0	0	2
Grant McCune, Kamloops (g)	41	0	0	0	2
Totals	54	0	0	0	4
Brent McDonald, Prince George	7	1	3	4	6
Brent McDonald, Spokane	61	28	30	58	77
Totals	68	29	33	62	83
Scott C. McQueen, Red Deer	16	0	2	2	14
Scott C. McQueen, P. Albert	46	1	0	1	14
Totals	62	1	2	3	28
Tyler Metcalfe, Seattle	3	0	0	0	0
Tyler Metcalfe, Seattle	4	0	1	1	2
Totals	7	0	1	1	2
Cam Ondrik, Medicine Hat (g)	3	0	0	0	2
Cam Ondrik, Saskatoon (g)	55	0	0	0	8
Totals	58	0	0	0	10
Jonathan Parker, Prince George	5	1	1	2	5
Jonathan Parker, Regina	47	4	4	8	19
Totals	52	5	5	10	24
Stephen Peat, Tri-City	12	0	2	2	48
Stephen Peat, Calgary	23	0	8	8	100
Totals	35	0	10	10	148
Lubomir Pistek, Kelowna	28	7	4	11	30
Lubomir Pistek, Saskatoon	28	4	11	15	20
Totals	56	11	15	26	50
Curtis Rich, Calgary	3	0	2	2	27
Curtis Rich, Kelowna	58	1	11	12	135
Totals	61	1	13	14	162
Scott Roles, Kootenay	7	0	6	6	4
Scott Roles, Spokane	61	14	37	51	50
Totals	68	14	43	57	54
Bart Rushmer, Lethbridge	28	2	8	10	40
Bart Rushmer, Brandon	43	6	15	21	122
Totals	71	8	23	31	162
Kevin Seibel, Prince George	1	0	0	0	0
Kevin Seibel, Swift Current	2	0	0	0	2
Totals	3	0	0	0	2
Jared Smyth, Spokane	11	0	1	1	16
Jared Smyth, Tri-City	50	11	17	28	74
Totals	61	11	18	29	90
Aaron Sproule, Saskatoon (g)	2	0	0	0	0
Aaron Sproule, Red Deer (g)	5	0	0	0	0
Totals	7	0	0	0	0
Rastislav Stana, M.J. (g)	14	0	0	0	13
Rastislav Stana, Calgary (g)	16	0	2	2	2
Totals	30	0	2	2	15
Shaun Sutter, Medicine Hat	29	1	7	8	43
Shaun Sutter, Calgary	6	0	1	1	8
Totals	35	1	8	9	51
Jarrett Thompson, Red Deer	10	2	4	6	19
Jarrett Thompson, Moose Jaw	53	17	27	44	127
Totals	63	19	31	50	146
Ryan Thrussell, Portland	9	0	1	1	4
Ryan Thrussell, Prince Albert	42	1	9	10	38
Totals	51	1	10	11	42
Jordan Walker, Red Deer	10	2	5	7	6
Jordan Walker, Kamloops	61	15	39	54	30
Totals	71	17	44	61	36
Matt Walker, Portland	38	2	7	9	97
Matt Walker, Kootenay	31	4	19	23	53
Totals	69	6	26	32	150
Kyle Wanvig, Kootenay	6	2	2	4	12
Kyle Wanvig, Red Deer	58	21	18	39	123
Totals	64	23	20	43	135

	Games	G	A	Pts.	PIM
Justin Yeoman, Medicine Hat....	1	0	0	0	0
Justin Yeoman, Prince George..	54	2	3	5	40
Totals	55	2	3	5	40
Jeff Zorn, Prince George	14	6	8	14	19
Jeff Zorn, Saskatoon................	60	12	30	42	53
Totals	74	18	38	56	72

GOALTENDING

	Games	Min.	W	L	T	G	SO	Avg.
Sean Connors, Cal. .	14	744	9	1	1	32	1	2.58
Sean Connors, M.J. .	10	539	0	7	1	41	0	4.56
Totals	24	1283	9	8	2	73	1	3.41
Jomar Cruz, Bran. ..	21	1151	7	13	1	73	1	3.81
Jomar Cruz, Tri-City.	35	1968	8	22	4	126	0	3.84
Totals	56	3119	15	35	5	199	1	3.83
A. Fomitchev, Cal. ..	1	60	1	0	0	5	0	5.00
A. Fomitchev, Sea. .	46	2685	20	21	4	126	3	2.82
Totals	47	2745	21	21	4	131	3	2.86
Ray Fraser, Sea.	1	28	0	1	0	2	0	4.29
Ray Fraser, Bran. ...	3	156	0	1	0	7	0	2.69

	Games	Min.	W	L	T	G	SO	Avg.
Totals	4	184	0	2	0	9	0	2.93
J. LaBarbera, Port. .	34	2005	8	24	2	123	1	3.68
J. LaBarbera, Spo. .	21	1146	12	6	2	50	0	2.62
Totals	55	3151	20	30	4	173	1	3.29
T. MacKay, Sask.	5	273	2	3	0	21	0	4.62
T. MacKay, Spo.	37	2083	23	8	2	88	2	2.53
Totals	42	2356	25	11	2	109	2	2.78
G. McCune, Kam. ...	41	2390	25	11	3	104	2	2.61
G. McCune, P.A.	13	723	7	5	0	44	0	3.65
Totals	54	3113	32	16	3	148	2	2.85
Cam Ondrik, M.H. ..	3	180	1	2	0	8	1	2.67
Cam Ondrik, Sask. .	55	3198	29	22	4	151	4	2.83
Totals	58	3378	30	24	4	159	5	2.82
A. Sproule, R.D.	5	165	0	2	0	13	0	4.73
A. Sproule, Sask. ...	2	98	1	0	0	5	0	3.06
Totals	7	263	1	2	0	18	0	4.11
R. Stana, Cal.	16	971	13	2	1	37	1	2.29
R. Stana, M.J.	14	730	4	9	0	48	0	3.95
Totals	30	1701	17	11	1	85	1	3.00

2000 PLAYOFFS
RESULTS

FIRST ROUND

	W	L	Pts.	GF	GA
Calgary	4	0	8	23	11
Moose Jaw	0	4	0	11	23

(Calgary won series, 4-0)

	W	L	Pts.	GF	GA
Swift Current	4	2	8	24	17
Prince Albert....................	2	4	4	17	24

(Swift Current won series, 4-2)

	W	L	Pts.	GF	GA
Kootenay	4	0	8	24	9
Red Deer	0	4	0	9	24

(Kootenay won series, 4-0)

	W	L	Pts.	GF	GA
Saskatoon.......................	4	3	8	25	23
Regina	3	4	6	23	25

(Saskatoon won series, 4-3)

	W	L	Pts.	GF	GA
Spokane	4	0	8	19	5
Tri-City...........................	0	4	0	5	19

(Spokane won series, 4-0)

	W	L	Pts.	GF	GA
Prince George..................	4	1	8	18	10
Kelowna..........................	1	4	2	10	18

(Prince George won series, 4-1)

	W	L	Pts.	GF	GA
Seattle	4	0	8	20	8
Kamloops	0	4	0	8	20

(Seattle won series, 4-0)

SECOND ROUND

	W	L	Pts.	GF	GA
Calgary	4	0	8	23	6
Saskatoon.......................	0	4	0	6	23

(Calgary won series, 4-0)

	W	L	Pts.	GF	GA
Kootenay	4	2	8	21	10
Swift Current	2	4	4	10	21

(Kootenay won series, 4-2)

	W	L	Pts.	GF	GA
Prince George..................	3	0	6	16	4
Seattle	0	3	0	4	16

(Prince George won series, 3-0)

THIRD ROUND

	W	L	Pts.	GF	GA
Kootenay	4	1	8	17	14
Calgary	1	4	2	14	17

(Kootenay won series, 4-1)

	W	L	Pts.	GF	GA
Spokane	4	1	8	17	15
Prince George..................	1	4	2	15	17

(Spokane won series, 4-1)

WHL FINALS

	W	L	Pts.	GF	GA
Kootenay	4	2	8	14	10
Spokane	2	4	4	10	14

(Kootenay won series, 4-2)

INDIVIDUAL LEADERS

Goals: Jaroslav Svoboda, Kootenay (15)
Assists: Zdenek Blatny, Kootenay (17)
Points: Jaroslav Svoboda, Kootenay (28)
Penalty minutes: Graham Belak, Kootenay (61)
Goaltending average: Tyler MacKay, Spokane (1.87)
Shutouts: Scott Myers, Prince George (3)

TOP SCORERS

	Games	G	A	Pts.
Jaroslav Svoboda, Kootenay	21	15	13	28
Zdenek Blatny, Kootenay	21	10	17	27
Mike Green, Kootenay	21	9	16	25
Chris Nielsen, Calgary	13	14	9	23
Blair Betts, Prince George	13	11	11	22
Trent Hunter, Prince George	13	7	15	22
Brad Moran, Calgary........................	13	7	15	22
Jason Jaffray, Kootenay	21	10	9	19
Pavel Brendl, Calgary.......................	10	7	12	19
Tyler Bouck, Prince George	13	6	13	19

CALGARY HITMEN
(Lost third round to Kootenay, 4-1)

SCORING

	Games	G	A	Pts.	PIM
Chris Nielsen	13	14	9	23	20
Brad Moran	13	7	15	22	18
Pavel Brendl	10	7	12	19	8
Jordan Krestanovich	13	7	7	14	4
Matt Kinch	13	2	12	14	8
Kenton Smith	13	3	8	11	25
Kris Beech	5	3	5	8	16
Matt Pettinger	11	2	6	8	30
Owen Fussey	12	3	4	7	2
Sean McAslan	13	4	2	6	49
Shaun Norrie	13	3	2	5	8
Michael Bubnick	13	1	3	4	6
Robin Gomez	12	2	1	3	30
Jerred Smithson	10	1	1	2	16
Brandon Segal	13	1	1	2	13
Wade Davis	13	0	2	2	15
Rod Sarich	13	0	2	2	8
Toni Bader	11	0	1	1	30
Stephen Peat	13	0	1	1	33
Chad Wolkowski	1	0	0	0	0
Chris Beston	3	0	0	0	0
Jared Carli	3	0	0	0	0
Brent Krahn (goalie)	5	0	0	0	0
Rastislav Stana (goalie)	9	0	0	0	2

GOALTENDING

	Games	Min.	W	L	T	G	SO	Avg.
Rastislav Stana	9	526	7	2	0	21	1	2.40
Brent Krahn	5	266	2	2	0	13	0	2.93

KAMLOOPS BLAZERS
(Lost first round to Seattle, 4-0)

SCORING

	Games	G	A	Pts.	PIM
Jonathan Hobson	4	1	3	4	8
Steve Shrum	3	1	2	3	6
Gable Gross	3	2	0	2	6
Jordan Walker	4	2	0	2	0
Anton Borodkin	4	1	1	2	6
Brett Draney	4	1	1	2	11
Micki DuPont	4	0	2	2	17
Kevin Mackie	4	0	2	2	2
Jared Aulin	4	0	1	1	6
Jason Bone	4	0	1	1	5
Paul Deniset	4	0	1	1	4
Davis Parley (goalie)	1	0	0	0	0
Kyle Ladobruk	2	0	0	0	0
Blaine Depper	3	0	0	0	2
Erik Christensen	4	0	0	0	2
Aaron Gionet	4	0	0	0	8
Grant McCune (goalie)	4	0	0	0	0
Shaonne Morrison	4	0	0	0	6
Mike Munro	4	0	0	0	0
Mark Rooneem	4	0	0	0	4
Chad Starling	4	0	0	0	6

GOALTENDING

	Games	Min.	W	L	T	G	SO	Avg.
Grant McCune	4	199	0	4	0	15	0	4.52
Davis Parley	1	37	0	0	0	3	0	4.86

KELOWNA ROCKETS
(Lost first round to Prince George, 4-1)

SCORING

	Games	G	A	Pts.	PIM
Carsen Germyn	5	3	3	6	4
Vernon Fiddler	5	1	3	4	4
David Selthun	5	1	3	4	2

	Games	G	A	Pts.	PIM
Kiel McLeod	5	2	1	3	2
Quintin Laing	5	1	1	2	8
Travis Moen	5	1	1	2	2
J.J. Hunter	5	1	0	1	2
Richie Regehr	5	0	1	1	0
Curtis Rich	5	0	1	1	10
Ryan Cuthbert	1	0	0	0	0
Vaughan Watson (goalie)	1	0	0	0	0
David Johansson	2	0	0	0	0
Diarmuid Kelly	2	0	0	0	5
Seth Leonard	2	0	0	0	0
Chris Di Ubaldo	3	0	0	0	2
Dallas Flaman	5	0	0	0	2
Mitch Fritz	5	0	0	0	0
Bruce Harrison	5	0	0	0	7
Gavin McLeod	5	0	0	0	8
Cam Paddock	5	0	0	0	0
Joe Suderman	5	0	0	0	2
Kevin Swanson (goalie)	5	0	0	0	0
Nolan Yonkman	5	0	0	0	8

GOALTENDING

	Games	Min.	W	L	T	G	SO	Avg.
Vaughan Watson	1	1	0	0	0	0	0	0.00
Kevin Swanson	5	297	1	4	0	16	0	3.23

KOOTENAY ICE
(Winner of 2000 WHL playoffs)

SCORING

	Games	G	A	Pts.	PIM
Jaroslav Svoboda	21	15	13	28	51
Zdenek Blatny	21	10	17	27	46
Mike Green	21	9	16	25	20
Jason Jaffray	21	10	9	19	17
Matt Walker	21	5	13	18	24
Jarret Stoll	20	7	9	16	24
Tyler Beechey	21	5	9	14	10
Wade Burt	21	4	7	11	25
Brad Tutschek	21	4	5	9	25
Trevor Johnson	21	2	7	9	35
Cole Fischer	21	0	8	8	14
Dion Lassu	21	0	8	8	53
Graham Belak	21	2	3	5	61
Colin Sinclair	21	0	4	4	41
Dean Arsene	21	1	2	3	59
Richard Hamula	21	2	0	2	2
Chris Chubb	21	0	1	1	25
Jordan Wallin	1	0	0	0	0
Stacey Bublitz	8	0	0	0	7
Pat Iannone	13	0	0	0	2
Dan Blackburn (goalie)	21	0	0	0	2

GOALTENDING

	Games	Min.	W	L	T	G	SO	Avg.
Dan Blackburn	21	1272	16	5	0	43	2	2.03

MOOSE JAW WARRIORS
(Lost first round to Calgary, 4-0)

SCORING

	Games	G	A	Pts.	PIM
Jason Weitzel	4	2	3	5	8
Ben Knopp	4	2	2	4	4
Scott Schoneck	4	2	2	4	2
Jarrett Thompson	4	1	3	4	18
Steven Crampton	4	0	3	3	9
Harlan Anderson	4	1	1	2	5
Martin Beck	4	1	1	2	2
Shawn Limpright	4	1	1	2	12
Brian Sutherby	4	1	1	2	12
Conor MacKenzie	4	0	1	1	6
Nathan Paetsch	4	0	1	1	0

WHL

MAJOR JUNIOR LEAGUES

	Games	G	A	Pts.	PIM
David Bararuk	2	0	0	0	0
Sean O'Connor	2	0	0	0	2
Tim Barlow (goalie)	4	0	0	0	0
Dustin Bru	4	0	0	0	0
Deryk Engelland	4	0	0	0	0
Anders Lovdahl	4	0	0	0	2
Kris Mallette	4	0	0	0	19
Bobby Chad Mitchell	4	0	0	0	18
Shawn Skolney	4	0	0	0	9

GOALTENDING

	Games	Min.	W	L	T	G	SO	Avg.
Tim Barlow	4	242	0	4	0	22	0	5.45

PRINCE ALBERT RAIDERS
(Lost first round to Swift Current, 4-2)

SCORING

	Games	G	A	Pts.	PIM
Jarrett Smith	6	2	4	6	20
Milan Kraft	6	4	1	5	4
Scott Hartnell	6	3	2	5	6
Michal Sivek	6	1	4	5	10
Brent Hobday	6	1	3	4	6
Ryan Thrussell	6	0	4	4	2
Jeremy Goetzinger	6	2	1	3	4
Garrett Prosofsky	6	1	2	3	10
Nick Schultz	6	0	3	3	2
Scott C. McQueen	6	1	1	2	7
Greg Watson	6	0	2	2	2
Riley Cote	3	1	0	1	2
Chris Harper	6	1	0	1	8
Regan Darby	6	0	1	1	23
Grant McNeil	6	0	1	1	0
Kyle Bruce	2	0	0	0	2
Jon Kress	3	0	0	0	5
Steven MacIntyre	4	0	0	0	22
Jordan Clarke	6	0	0	0	15
Evan Lindsay (goalie)	6	0	0	0	2
Blaine Stowards	6	0	0	0	2

GOALTENDING

	Games	Min.	W	L	T	G	SO	Avg.
Evan Lindsay	6	359	2	4	0	24	0	4.01

PRINCE GEORGE COUGARS
(Lost third round to Spokane, 4-1)

SCORING

	Games	G	A	Pts.	PIM
Blair Betts	13	11	11	22	6
Trent Hunter	13	7	15	22	6
Tyler Bouck	13	6	13	19	36
Garry Toor	13	4	10	14	6
Christian Chartier	13	4	9	13	12
Jon Barkman	8	4	2	6	0
Justin Cox	13	2	4	6	16
Dan Hamhuis	13	2	3	5	35
Tim Wedderburn	13	2	3	5	9
Travis Eagles	13	4	0	4	17
Aaron Foster	10	0	4	4	27
Jozef Mrena	10	1	1	2	6
Justin Hansen	13	1	1	2	4
Shon Jones-Parry	13	0	2	2	25
Dan Baum	12	1	0	1	19
Chris Falloon	13	0	1	1	2
Devin Wilson	3	0	0	0	0
Justin Yeoman	9	0	0	0	2
Ryan Chieduch	13	0	0	0	2
Willy Glover	13	0	0	0	0
Scott Myers (goalie)	13	0	0	0	0

GOALTENDING

	Games	Min.	W	L	T	G	SO	Avg.
Scott Myers	13	796	8	5	0	28	3	2.11

RED DEER REBELS
(Lost first round to Kootenay, 4-0)

SCORING

	Games	G	A	Pts.	PIM
Dustin Paul	4	3	0	3	8
Justin Mapletoft	4	2	1	3	28
Jeff Woywitka	4	0	3	3	2
Andrew Bergen	4	1	1	2	7
Lyle Steenbergen	4	0	2	2	2
Bryce Thoma	4	0	2	2	0
Devin Francon	4	1	0	1	8
Joel Stepp	4	1	0	1	8
Kyle Wanvig	4	1	0	1	4
Colby Armstrong	2	0	1	1	11
Craig Brunel	4	0	1	1	22
Boyd Gordon	4	0	1	1	2
Ross Lupaschuk	4	0	1	1	10
Jim Vandermeer	4	0	1	1	16
Justin Wallin	4	0	1	1	0
Michael Garnett (goalie)	1	0	0	0	0
Colin Johnson	2	0	0	0	4
Alexei Zhurba	2	0	0	0	0
Shane Bendera (goalie)	3	0	0	0	0
Adam Dombrowski	3	0	0	0	0
Jearum Kurtz	3	0	0	0	2
Aaron Sproule (goalie)	3	0	0	0	2
Doug Lynch	4	0	0	0	5

GOALTENDING

	Games	Min.	W	L	T	G	SO	Avg.
Michael Garnett	1	65	0	1	0	2	0	1.85
Aaron Sproule	3	102	0	1	0	6	0	3.53
Shane Bendera	3	76	0	2	0	15	0	11.84

REGINA PATS
(Lost first round to Saskatoon, 4-3)

SCORING

	Games	G	A	Pts.	PIM
Brett Lysak	7	5	4	9	2
Joey Bastien	7	3	6	9	12
Kevin Korol	7	1	5	6	10
Matt Hubbauer	7	3	2	5	12
Filip Novak	7	1	4	5	5
Karel Mosovsky	7	3	1	4	12
Ryan Thomas	7	1	3	4	21
Travis Churchman	7	0	3	3	21
Chris Anderson	4	1	1	2	2
Barret Jackman	6	1	1	2	19
Ryan Annesley	7	1	1	2	2
Garth Murray	7	1	1	2	7
Grant Jacobsen	7	0	2	2	0
Andrew Kaminsky	7	0	2	2	2
Justin Lucyshyn	4	1	0	1	0
Landon Boyko	7	1	0	1	14
Scott Balan	7	0	1	1	17
Shaun Fleming (goalie)	1	0	0	0	0
Brett Bartell	2	0	0	0	0
Jonathan Parker	5	0	0	0	0
Donald Choukalos (goalie)	7	0	0	0	4
David McDonald	7	0	0	0	5

GOALTENDING

	Games	Min.	W	L	T	G	SO	Avg.
Shaun Fleming	1	34	0	0	0	0	0	0.00
Donald Choukalos	7	385	3	4	0	24	0	3.74

SASKATOON BLADES
(Lost second round to Calgary, 4-0)

SCORING

	Games	G	A	Pts.	PIM
Martin Erat	11	4	8	12	16
Garrett Bembridge	11	5	5	10	2
Mathieu Cusson	11	3	7	10	6

	Games	G	A	Pts.	PIM
David Cameron	11	4	5	9	4
Tyler Shybunka	11	3	6	9	10
Darcy Hordichuk	11	4	2	6	43
Bobby Almeida	11	3	2	5	13
Jeff Zorn	10	1	4	5	10
Darcy Robinson	10	1	3	4	13
Derek Halldorson	8	1	2	3	16
Warren Peters	10	1	2	3	13
Davin Heintz	11	0	3	3	5
Lubomir Pistek	11	1	1	2	4
Garnet Exelby	11	0	2	2	21
Chris Ovington	11	0	2	2	13
Justin Kelly	11	0	1	1	9
Aaron Rome	1	0	0	0	0
Jeff Coulter	2	0	0	0	0
Craig Valette	3	0	0	0	0
Tony Kolewaski (goalie)	4	0	0	0	0
Cam Ondrik (goalie)	10	0	0	0	2
Kane Ludwar	11	0	0	0	6
Chris Manchakowski	11	0	0	0	14

GOALTENDING

	Games	Min.	W	L	T	G	SO	Avg.
Cam Ondrik	10	500	4	6	0	34	2	4.08
Tony Kolewaski	4	159	0	1	0	12	0	4.53

SEATTLE THUNDERBIRDS
(Lost second round to Prince George, 3-0)
SCORING

	Games	G	A	Pts.	PIM
Alan Manness	7	5	6	11	4
David Morisset	7	3	4	7	12
Shane Endicott	7	1	6	7	6
Bret DeCecco	4	4	2	6	4
Oleg Saprykin	6	3	3	6	37
Jason McKee	7	1	5	6	13
Nathan Forster	7	1	4	5	30
Tim Preston	7	2	2	4	4
Keegan McAvoy	7	0	3	3	15
Jason Beckett	7	1	1	2	12
Paul Hurd	7	1	1	2	13
Craig Olynick	7	1	0	1	17
David Ullmann	7	1	0	1	4
Greg Black	7	0	1	1	14
Gerard DiCaire	7	0	1	1	6
Brennan Evans	1	0	0	0	0
David Kaczowka	1	0	0	0	0
Scott Kelman	2	0	0	0	2
Jeffrey Beatch	7	0	0	0	0
Alexandre Fomitchev (goalie)	7	0	0	0	0
Darren McLachlan	7	0	0	0	9
Matthew Spiller	7	0	0	0	25

GOALTENDING

	Games	Min.	W	L	T	G	SO	Avg.
Alex. Fomitchev	7	420	4	3	0	24	0	3.43

SPOKANE CHIEFS
(Lost WHA finals to Kootenay)
SCORING

	Games	G	A	Pts.	PIM
Scott Roles	15	4	11	15	6
Tim Smith	15	7	7	14	32
Brent McDonald	15	5	8	13	42
Daniel Bohac	15	5	7	12	6
Roman Tvrdon	15	4	7	11	16
Derek Schutz	15	4	6	10	18
Tim Krymusa	10	5	1	6	4
Brandin Cote	15	0	6	6	14
Lynn Loyns	14	3	2	5	12
Kyle Rossiter	15	1	4	5	25
Shawn Thompson	15	2	2	4	20

	Games	G	A	Pts.	PIM
Kurt Sauer	15	2	1	3	8
Matthew Keith	15	1	2	3	11
Mason Wallin	15	1	2	3	4
Steven Mann	10	0	2	2	0
Jeff Lucky	13	1	0	1	2
Jeremy Farr	15	1	0	1	15
David Boychuk	15	0	1	1	21
Joff Kehler	1	0	0	0	0
Chris Heid	6	0	0	0	4
Ryan Thorpe	6	0	0	0	4
Tyler MacKay (goalie)	8	0	0	0	0
Jason LaBarbera (goalie)	9	0	0	0	0

GOALTENDING

	Games	Min.	W	L	T	G	SO	Avg.
Tyler MacKay	8	481	4	4	0	15	0	1.87
Jason LaBarbera	9	435	6	1	0	18	1	2.48

SWIFT CURRENT BRONCOS
(Lost second round to Kootenay, 4-2)
SCORING

	Games	G	A	Pts.	PIM
Layne Ulmer	12	12	6	18	16
Jeremy Reich	12	2	10	12	19
Duncan Milroy	12	3	5	8	12
Jay Langager	12	2	6	8	8
Brett Allan	12	4	3	7	20
Nathan Smith	12	1	6	7	4
Scott Henkelman	12	3	3	6	8
Brent Twordik	12	2	3	5	32
Todd Hornung	11	2	1	3	11
Dan Hulak	12	1	1	2	21
Jakub Cutta	12	0	2	2	24
Dean Serdachny	12	0	2	2	25
Ben Ondrus	12	1	0	1	22
Colton Orr	12	1	0	1	25
Clay Thoring	10	0	1	1	6
Craig Priestlay	12	0	1	1	10
Tyson Motz (goalie)	2	0	0	0	0
Lawrence Nycholat	2	0	0	0	0
James Hiebert	3	0	0	0	4
Jay Batchelor	4	0	0	0	0
Matt Sommerfeld	5	0	0	0	15
Igor Valeev	6	0	0	0	19
Kevin Seibel	7	0	0	0	0
Bryce Wandler (goalie)	10	0	0	0	0

GOALTENDING

	Games	Min.	W	L	T	G	SO	Avg.
Bryce Wandler	10	597	5	5	0	29	0	2.91
Tyson Motz	2	120	1	1	0	7	0	3.50

TRI-CITY AMERICANS
(Lost first round to Spokane, 4-0)
SCORING

	Games	G	A	Pts.	PIM
Tim Green	4	2	1	3	2
Jesse Schultz	4	1	1	2	2
Andrew Davidson	4	0	2	2	2
Dustin Barker	4	1	0	1	0
Blake Evans	4	1	0	1	6
Eric Clark	3	0	1	1	0
Darrell Hay	4	0	1	1	8
Curtis Huppe	4	0	1	1	2
Adam Johnson	4	0	1	1	4
Ryley Layden	4	0	1	1	2
Jaroslav Kristek	2	0	0	0	0
Brad Zanon	2	0	0	0	0
Jomar Cruz (goalie)	3	0	0	0	0
Andrew DeSousa	4	0	0	0	8
Jeff Feniak	4	0	0	0	12
Eric Johannson	4	0	0	0	2

MAJOR JUNIOR LEAGUES WHL

	Games	G	A	Pts.	PIM
Jeff Katcher	4	0	0	0	6
Ben Kilgour	4	0	0	0	8
Mike Lee	4	0	0	0	8
K.C. Timmons	4	0	0	0	4
Blake Ward (goalie)	4	0	0	0	0

GOALTENDING

	Games	Min.	W	L	T	G	SO	Avg.
Blake Ward	4	187	0	3	0	12	0	3.85
Jomar Cruz	3	51	0	1	0	7	0	8.24

1999-2000 AWARD WINNERS

ALL-STAR TEAMS

EASTERN CONFERENCE

First team	Pos.	Second team
Bryce Wandler, S. Current	G	Dan Blackburn, Kootenay
Lawrence Nycholat, S. Cur.	D	Matt Kinch, Calgary
Steve McCarthy, Kootenay	D	Barret Jackman, Regina
Brad Moran, Calgary	F	Pavel Brendl, Calgary
Layne Ulmer, Swift Current	F	Mike Green, Kootenay
Justin Mapletoft, Red Deer	F	Zdenek Blatny, Kootenay

WESTERN CONFERENCE

First team	Pos.	Second team
Kevin Swanson, Kelowna	G	Grant McCune, Kamloops
Micki Dupont, Kamloops	D	Darrell Hay, Tri-City
Garry Toor, Prince George	D	Christian Chartier, P. George
Trent Hunter, Prince George	F	Derek Schutz, Spokane
Tyler Bouck, Prince George	F	Konstantin Panov, Kamloops
Tim Smith, Spokane	F	Oleg Saprykin, Seattle

TROPHY WINNERS

Four Broncos Memorial Trophy: Brad Moran, Calgary
Bob Clarke Trophy: Brad Moran, Calgary
Jim Piggott Memorial Trophy: Dan Blackburn, Kootenay
Brad Hornung Trophy: Trent Hunter, Prince George
Bill Hunter Trophy: Micki Dupont, Kamloops
Del Wilson Trophy: Bryce Wandler, Swift Current
Dunc McCallum Memorial Trophy: Todd McLellan, S. Current
Scott Munro Memorial Trophy: Calgary Hitmen
President's Cup: Kootenay Ice
Playoff MVP: Dan Blackburn, Kootenay

ALL-TIME AWARD WINNERS

FOUR BRONCOS MEMORIAL TROPHY
(Player of the year—selected by coaches)

Season	Player, Team
1966-67	Gerry Pinder, Saskatoon
1967-68	Jim Harrison, Estevan
1968-69	Bobby Clarke, Flin Flon
1969-70	Reggie Leach, Flin Flon
1970-71	Ed Dyck, Calgary
1971-72	John Davidson, Calgary
1972-73	Dennis Sobchuk, Regina
1973-74	Ron Chipperfield, Brandon
1974-75	Bryan Trottier, Lethbridge
1975-76	Bernie Federko, Saskatoon
1976-77	Barry Beck, New Westminster
1977-78	Ryan Walter, Seattle
1978-79	Perry Turnbull, Portland
1979-80	Doug Wickenheiser, Regina
1980-81	Steve Tsujiura, Medicine Hat
1981-82	Mike Vernon, Calgary
1982-83	Mike Vernon, Calgary
1983-84	Ray Ferraro, Brandon
1984-85	Cliff Ronning, New Westminster
1985-86	Emanuel Viveiros, Prince Albert (East Div.)
	Rob Brown, Kamloops (West Div.)
1986-87	Joe Sakic, Swift Current (East Div.)
	Rob Brown, Kamloops (West Div.)
1987-88	Joe Sakic, Swift Current
1988-89	Stu Barnes, Tri-City
1989-90	Glen Goodall, Seattle
1990-91	Ray Whitney, Spokane
1991-92	Steve Konowalchuk, Portland
1992-93	Jason Krywulak, Swift Current
1993-94	Sonny Mignacca, Medicine Hat
1994-95	Marty Murray, Brandon
1995-96	Jarome Iginla, Kamloops
1996-97	Peter Schaefer, Brandon
1997-98	Sergei Varlamov, Swift Current
1998-99	Cody Rudkowsky, Seattle
1999-00	Brad Moran, Calgary

The trophy was awarded to the most valuable player prior to the 1994-95 season.

BOB CLARKE TROPHY
(Top scorer)

Season	Player, Team
1966-67	Gerry Pinder, Saskatoon
1967-68	Bobby Clarke, Flin Flon
1968-69	Bobby Clarke, Flin Flon
1969-70	Reggie Leach, Flin Flon
1970-71	Chuck Arnason, Flin Flon
1971-72	Tom Lysiak, Medicine Hat
1972-73	Tom Lysiak, Medicine Hat
1973-74	Ron Chipperfield, Brandon
1974-75	Mel Bridgman, Victoria
1975-76	Bernie Federko, Saskatoon
1976-77	Bill Derlago, Brandon
1977-78	Brian Propp, Brandon
1978-79	Brian Propp, Brandon
1979-80	Doug Wickenheiser, Regina
1980-81	Brian Varga, Regina
1981-82	Jack Callander, Regina
1982-83	Dale Derkatch, Regina
1983-84	Ray Ferraro, Brandon
1984-85	Cliff Ronning, New Westminster
1985-86	Rob Brown, Kamloops
1986-87	Rob Brown, Kamloops
1987-88	Joe Sakic, Swift Current
	Theo Fleury, Moose Jaw
1988-89	Dennis Holland, Portland
1989-90	Len Barrie, Kamloops
1990-91	Ray Whitney, Spokane
1991-92	Kevin St. Jacques, Lethbridge
1992-93	Jason Krywulak, Swift Current
1993-94	Lonny Bohonos, Portland
1994-95	Daymond Langkow, Tri-City
1995-96	Mark Deyell, Saskatoon
1996-97	Todd Robinson, Portland
1997-98	Sergei Varlamov, Swift Current
1998-99	Pavel Brendl, Calgary
1999-00	Brad Moran, Calgary

The award was originally known as the Bob Brownridge Memorial Trophy.

JIM PIGGOTT MEMORIAL TROPHY
(Rookie of the year)

Season   Player, Team
1966-67—Ron Garwasiuk, Regina
1967-68—Ron Fairbrother, Saskatoon
1968-69—Ron Williams, Edmonton
1969-70—Gene Carr, Flin Flon
1970-71—Stan Weir, Medicine Hat
1971-72—Dennis Sobchuk, Regina
1972-73—Rick Blight, Brandon
1973-74—Cam Connor, Flin Flon
1974-75—Don Murdoch, Medicine Hat
1975-76—Steve Tambellini, Lethbridge
1976-77—Brian Propp, Brandon
1977-78—John Orgrodnick, New Westminster
         Keith Brown, Portland
1978-79—Kelly Kisio, Calgary
1979-80—Grant Fuhr, Victoria
1980-81—Dave Michayluk, Regina
1981-82—Dale Derkatch, Regina
1982-83—Dan Hodgson, Prince Albert
1983-84—Cliff Ronning, New Westminster
1984-85—Mark Mackay, Moose Jaw
1985-86—Neil Brady, Medicine Hat (East Div.)
         Ron Shudra, Kamloops, (West Div.)
         Dave Waldie, Portland (West Div.)
1986-87—Joe Sakic, Swift Current (East Div.)
         Dennis Holland, Portland (West Div.)
1987-88—Stu Barnes, New Westminster
1988-89—Wes Walz, Lethbridge
1989-90—Petr Nedved, Seattle
1990-91—Donevan Hextall, Prince Albert
1991-92—Ashley Buckberger, Swift Current
1992-93—Jeff Friesen, Regina
1993-94—Wade Redden, Brandon
1994-95—Todd Robinson, Portland
1995-96—Chris Phillips, Prince Albert
1996-97—Donovan Nunweiler, Moose Jaw
1997-98—Marian Hossa, Portland
1998-99—Pavel Brendl, Calgary
1999-00—Dan Blackburn, Kootenay
   The award was originally known as the Stewart "Butch" Paul Memorial Trophy.

BRAD HORNUNG TROPHY
(Most sportsmanlike player)

Season   Player, Team
1966-67—Morris Stefaniw, Estevan
1967-68—Bernie Blanchette, Saskatoon
1968-69—Bob Liddington, Calgary
1969-70—Randy Rota, Calgary
1970-71—Lorne Henning, Estevan
1971-72—Ron Chipperfield, Brandon
1972-73—Ron Chipperfield, Brandon
1973-74—Mike Rogers, Calgary
1974-75—Danny Arndt, Saskatoon
1975-76—Blair Chapman, Saskatoon
1976-77—Steve Tambellini, Lethbridge
1977-78—Steve Tambellini, Lethbridge
1978-79—Errol Rausse, Seattle
1979-80—Steve Tsujiura, Medicine Hat
1980-81—Steve Tsujiura, Medicine Hat
1981-82—Mike Moller, Lethbridge
1982-83—Darren Boyko, Winnipeg
1983-84—Mark Lamb, Medicine Hat
1984-85—Cliff Ronning, New Westminster
1985-86—Randy Smith, Saskatoon (East Division)
         Ken Morrison, Kamloops (West Division)
1986-87—Len Nielsen, Regina (East Division)
         Dave Archibald, Portland (West Division)
1987-88—Craig Endean, Regina
1988-89—Blair Atcheynum, Moose Jaw
1989-90—Bryan Bosch, Lethbridge
1990-91—Pat Falloon, Spokane

Season   Player, Team
1991-92—Steve Junker, Spokane
1992-93—Rick Girard, Swift Current
1993-94—Lonny Bohonos, Portland
1994-95—Darren Ritchie, Brandon
1995-96—Hnat Domenichelli, Kamloops
1996-97—Kelly Smart, Brandon
1997-98—Cory Cyrenne, Brandon
1998-99—Matt Kinch, Calgary
1999-00—Trent Hunter, Prince George
   The award was originally known as the Frank Boucher Memorial Trophy for most gentlemanly player.

BILL HUNTER TROPHY
(Top defenseman)

Season   Player, Team
1966-67—Barry Gibbs, Estevan
1967-68—Gerry Hart, Flin Flon
1968-69—Dale Hoganson, Estevan
1969-70—Jim Hargreaves, Winnipeg
1970-71—Ron Jones, Edmonton
1971-72—Jim Watson, Calgary
1972-73—George Pesut, Saskatoon
1973-74—Pat Price, Saskatoon
1974-75—Rick LaPointe, Victoria
1975-76—Kevin McCarthy, Winnipeg
1976-77—Barry Beck, New Westminster
1977-78—Brad McCrimmon, Brandon
1978-79—Keith Brown, Portland
1979-80—David Babych, Portland
1980-81—Jim Benning, Portland
1981-82—Gary Nylund, Portland
1982-83—Gary Leeman, Regina
1983-84—Bob Rouse, Lethbridge
1984-85—Wendel Clark, Saskatoon
1985-86—Emanuel Viveiros, Prince Albert (East Division)
         Glen Wesley, Portland (West Division)
1986-87—Wayne McBean, Medicine Hat (East Division)
         Glen Wesley, Portland (West Division)
1987-88—Greg Hawgood, Kamloops
1988-89—Dan Lambert, Swift Current
1989-90—Kevin Haller, Regina
1990-91—Darryl Sydor, Kamloops
1991-92—Richard Matvichuk, Saskatoon
1992-93—Jason Smith, Regina
1993-94—Brendan Witt, Seattle
1994-95—Nolan Baumgartner, Kamloops
1995-96—Nolan Baumgartner, Kamloops
1996-97—Chris Phillips, Lethbridge
1997-98—Michal Rozsival, Swift Current
1998-99—Brad Stuart, Calgary
1999-00—Micki Dupont, Kamloops

DEL WILSON TROPHY
(Top goaltender)

Season   Player, Team
1966-67—Ken Brown, Moose Jaw
1967-68—Chris Worthy, Flin Flon
1968-69—Ray Martyniuk, Flin Flon
1969-70—Ray Martyniuk, Flin Flon
1970-71—Ed Dyck, Calgary
1971-72—John Davidson, Calgary
1972-73—Ed Humphreys, Saskatoon
1973-74—Garth Malarchuk, Calgary
1974-75—Bill Oleschuk, Saskatoon
1975-76—Carey Walker, New Westminster
1976-77—Glen Hanlon, Brandon
1977-78—Bart Hunter, Portland
1978-79—Rick Knickle, Brandon
1979-80—Kevin Eastman, Victoria
1980-81—Grant Fuhr, Victoria
1981-82—Mike Vernon, Calgary
1982-83—Mike Vernon, Calgary
1983-84—Ken Wregget, Lethbridge
1984-85—Troy Gamble, Medicine Hat

PLAYER OF THE YEAR
(Selected by fans and media)

The award merged with the Four Broncos Memorial Trophy after the 1993-94 season.

DUNC MC CALLUM MEMORIAL TROPHY
(Coach of the year)

PLAYOFF MVP

ALL-TIME LEAGUE CHAMPIONS

MAJOR JUNIOR LEAGUES *WHL*

REGULAR-SEASON CHAMPION	PLAYOFF CHAMPION
Season **Team**	**Team**
1988-89— Swift Current Broncos	Swift Current Broncos
1989-90— Kamloops Blazers	Kamloops Blazers
1990-91— Kamloops Blazers	Spokane Chiefs
1991-92— Kamloops Blazers	Kamloops Blazers
1992-93— Swift Current Broncos	Swift Current Broncos
1993-94— Kamloops Blazers	Kamloops Blazers
1994-95— Kamloops Blazers	Kamloops Blazers
1995-96— Brandon Wheat Kings	Brandon Wheat Kings
1996-97— Lethbridge Hurricanes	Lethbridge Hurricanes
1997-98— Portland Winter Hawks	Portland Winter Hawks
1998-99— Calgary Hitmen	Calgary Hitmen
1999-00— Calgary Hitmen	Kootenay Ice

The WHL regular-season champion is awarded the Scott Munro Memorial Trophy and the playoff champion is awarded the President's Cup.

MAJOR JUNIOR LEAGUES *WHL*

COLLEGE HOCKEY

NCAA Division I

Central Collegiate Hockey Association

Eastern College Athletic Conference

Hockey East

Western Collegiate Hockey Association

Independents

Canadian Interuniversity Athletic Union

Canadian colleges

NCAA DIVISION I

NCAA TOURNAMENT

EAST REGIONAL
(Albany, N.Y.)
FIRST ROUND
Boston University 5, St. Cloud State 3
Michigan 4, Colgate 3 (OT)
QUARTERFINALS
St. Lawrence 3, Boston University 2 (4OT)
Maine 5, Michigan 2

WEST REGIONAL
(Minneapolis, Minn.)
FIRST ROUND
Boston College 6, Michigan State 5 (OT)
Niagara 4, New Hampshire 1
QUARTERFINALS
Boston College 4, Wisconsin 1
North Dakota 4, Niagara 1

NCAA FINALS
(Providence, R.I.)
North Dakota 2, Maine 0
Boston College 4, St. Lawrence 2

CHAMPIONSHIP GAME
(Providence, R.I.)
North Dakota 4, Boston College 2

ALL-TOURNAMENT TEAM

Player	Pos.	College
Karl Goehring	G	North Dakota
Mike Commodore	D	North Dakota
Mike Mottau	D	Boston College
Jeff Farkas	F	Boston College
Lee Goren	F	North Dakota
Bryan Lundbohm	F	North Dakota

ALL-AMERICA TEAMS

EAST

First team	Pos.	Second team
Joel Laing, Rensselaer	G	Ty Conklin, New Hampshire
Justin Harney, St. Lawrence	D	Chris Dyment, Boston Univ.
Mike Mottau, Boston College	D	Brian Pothier, Rensselaer
Andy McDonald, Colgate	F	Brad Tapper, Rensselaer
Jeff Farkas, Boston College	F	Cory Larose, Maine
Brian Gionta, Boston College	F	Brandon Dietrich, St. Law.

WEST

First team	Pos.	Second team
Karl Goehring, North Dakota	G	Jayme Platt, L. Superior St.
Jeff Dessner, Wisconsin	D	Mike Pudlick, St. Cloud State
Jeff Jillson, Michigan	D	Mike Weaver, Michigan State
Steve Reinprecht, Wisconsin	F	Mike Comrie, Michigan
Jeff Panzer, North Dakota	F	Dany Heatley, Wisconsin
Shawn Horcoff, Michigan St.	F	Lee Goren, North Dakota

HISTORY

TOURNAMENT CHAMPIONS

Year	Champion	Coach	Score	Runner-up	Most outstanding player
1948	Michigan	Vic Heyliger	8-4	Dartmouth	Joe Riley, F, Dartmouth
1949	Boston College	John Kelley	4-3	Dartmouth	Dick Desmond, G, Dartmouth
1950	Colorado College	Cheddy Thompson	13-4	Boston University	Ralph Bevins, G, Boston University
1951	Michigan	Vic Heyliger	7-1	Brown	Ed Whiston, G, Brown
1952	Michigan	Vic Heyliger	4-1	Colorado College	Kenneth Kinsley, G, Colorado College
1953	Michigan	Vic Heyliger	7-3	Minnesota	John Matchefts, F, Michigan
1954	Rensselaer	Ned Harkness	*5-4	Minnesota	Abbie Moore, F, Rensselaer
1955	Michigan	Vic Heyliger	5-3	Colorado College	Philip Hilton, D, Colorado College
1956	Michigan	Vic Heyliger	7-5	Michigan Tech	Lorne Howes, G, Michigan
1957	Colorado College	Thomas Bedecki	13-6	Michigan	Bob McCusker, F, Colorado College
1958	Denver	Murray Armstrong	6-2	North Dakota	Murray Massier, F, Denver
1959	North Dakota	Bob May	*4-3	Michigan State	Reg Morelli, F, North Dakota
1960	Denver	Murray Armstrong	5-3	Michigan Tech	Bob Marquis, F, Boston University
					Barry Urbanski, G, Boston University
					Louis Angotti, F, Michigan Tech
1961	Denver	Murray Armstrong	12-2	St. Lawrence	Bill Masterton, F, Denver
1962	Michigan Tech	John MacInnes	7-1	Clarkson	Louis Angotti, F, Michigan Tech
1963	North Dakota	Barney Thorndycraft	6-5	Denver	Al McLean, F, North Dakota
1964	Michigan	Allen Renfrew	6-3	Denver	Bob Gray, G, Michigan
1965	Michigan Tech	John MacInnes	8-2	Boston College	Gary Milroy, F, Michigan Tech
1966	Michigan State	Amo Bessone	6-1	Clarkson	Gaye Cooley, G, Michigan State
1967	Cornell	Ned Harkness	4-1	Boston University	Walt Stanowski, D, Cornell
1968	Denver	Murray Armstrong	4-0	North Dakota	Gerry Powers, G, Denver
1969	Denver	Murray Armstrong	4-3	Cornell	Keith Magnuson, D, Denver
1970	Cornell	Ned Harkness	6-4	Clarkson	Daniel Lodboa, D, Cornell
1971	Boston University	Jack Kelley	4-2	Minnesota	Dan Brady, G, Boston University
1972	Boston University	Jack Kelley	4-0	Cornell	Tim Regan, G, Boston University
1973	Wisconsin	Bob Johnson	4-2	Vacated	Dean Talafous, F, Wisconsin
1974	Minnesota	Herb Brooks	4-2	Michigan Tech	Brad Shelstad, G, Minnesota
1975	Michigan Tech	John MacInnes	6-1	Minnesota	Jim Warden, G, Michigan Tech
1976	Minnesota	Herb Brooks	6-4	Michigan Tech	Tom Vanelli, F, Minnesota

Year	Champion	Coach	Score	Runner-up	Most outstanding player
1977	Wisconsin	Bob Johnson	*6-5	Michigan	Julian Baretta, G, Wisconsin
1978	Boston University	Jack Parker	5-3	Boston College	Jack O'Callahan, D, Boston University
1979	Minnesota	Herb Brooks	4-3	North Dakota	Steve Janaszak, G, Minnesota
1980	North Dakota	John Gasparini	5-2	Northern Michigan	Doug Smail, F, North Dakota
1981	Wisconsin	Bob Johnson	6-3	Minnesota	Marc Behrend, G, Wisconsin
1982	North Dakota	John Gasparini	5-2	Wisconsin	Phil Sykes, F, North Dakota
1983	Wisconsin	Jeff Sauer	6-2	Harvard	Marc Behrend, G, Wisconsin
1984	Bowling Green State	Jerry York	*5-4	Minnesota-Duluth	Gary Kruzich, G, Bowling Green State
1985	Rensselaer	Mike Addesa	2-1	Providence	Chris Terreri, G, Providence
1986	Michigan State	Ron Mason	6-5	Harvard	Mike Donnelly, F, Michigan State
1987	North Dakota	John Gasparini	5-3	Michigan State	Tony Hrkac, F, North Dakota
1988	Lake Superior State	Frank Anzalone	*4-3	St. Lawrence	Bruce Hoffort, G, Lake Superior State
1989	Harvard	Bill Cleary	*4-3	Minnesota	Ted Donato, F, Harvard
1990	Wisconsin	Jeff Sauer	7-3	Colgate	Chris Tancill, F, Wisconsin
1991	Northern Michigan	Rick Comley	*8-7	Boston University	Scott Beattie, F, Northern Michigan
1992	Lake Superior State	Jeff Jackson	5-3	Wisconsin	Paul Constantin, F, Lake Superior State
1993	Maine	Shawn Walsh	5-4	Lake Superior State	Jim Montgomery, F, Maine
1994	Lake Superior State	Jeff Jackson	9-1	Boston University	Sean Tallaire, F, Lake Superior State
1995	Boston University	Jack Parker	6-2	Maine	Chris O'Sullivan, F, Boston University
1996	Michigan	Red Berenson	*3-2	Colorado College	Brendan Morrison, F, Michigan
1997	North Dakota	Dean Blais	6-4	Boston University	Matt Henderson, F, North Dakota
1998	Michigan	Red Berenson	*3-2	Boston College	Marty Turco, G, Michigan
1999	Maine	Shawn Walsh	*3-2	New Hampshire	Alfie Michaud, G, Maine
2000	North Dakota	Dean Blais	4-2	Boston College	Lee Goren, F, North Dakota

*Overtime.

ALL-TIME TOURNAMENT RECORDS

	Visits	W	L	GF	GA	Pct.	Finished 1st	Finished 2nd
Michigan	23	36	16	266	175	.692	9	2
North Dakota	17	28	13	164	120	.683	7	3
‡Lake Superior State	10	20	11	143	105	.645	3	1
§Wisconsin	18	29	16	184	142	.644	5	2
Maine	9	19	11	120	108	.633	2	1
Denver	14	19	12	144	91	.613	5	2
Colgate	2	3	2	13	15	.600	0	1
Michigan Tech	10	13	9	118	85	.591	3	4
Minnesota	22	28	24	259	234	.538	3	6
Boston University	25	33	29	252	250	.532	4	5
†Michigan State	19	23	23	188	179	.500	2	2
Northern Michigan	7	8	8	66	67	.500	1	1
‡Rensselaer Polytechnic Institute	8	8	8	52	55	.500	2	0
Northeastern	3	3	3	30	30	.500	0	0
Merrimack	1	2	2	14	16	.500	0	0
Niagara	1	1	1	5	5	.500	0	0
Ohio State	2	2	2	12	12	.500	0	0
Cornell	11	10	12	76	84	.455	2	2
Minnesota-Duluth	4	5	6	43	41	.455	0	1
Colorado College	14	12	15	111	123	.444	2	3
Dartmouth	5	4	5	38	37	.444	0	2
Providence	7	9	12	72	78	.429	0	1
Boston College	21	20	30	176	127	.400	1	4
*Bowling Green State	9	8	12	66	88	.400	1	0
§Lowell	3	2	3	19	23	.400	0	0
Clarkson	17	12	20	103	135	.375	0	3
†Harvard	16	14	24	143	166	.368	1	2
Yale	2	1	2	7	9	.333	0	0
New Hampshire	11	7	15	65	101	.318	0	1
Alaska-Anchorage	3	2	5	22	39	.286	0	0
Brown	4	2	5	31	45	.286	0	1
St. Lawrence	14	6	23	83	134	.207	0	2
Vermont	3	1	4	10	21	.200	0	0
Princeton	1	0	1	1	2	.000	0	0
St. Cloud State	2	0	3	8	15	.000	0	0
Miami of Ohio	2	0	2	3	7	.000	0	0
Western Michigan	3	0	4	8	23	.000	0	0

(Denver also participated in 1973 tournament but its record was voided by the NCAA in 1977 upon discovery of violations by the University. The team had finished second in '73.)

*Bowling Green State and Northeastern played to a 2-2 tie in 1981-82.

†Harvard and Michigan State played to a 3-3 tie in 1982-83.

‡Lake Superior State and RPI played to a 3-3 tie in 1984-85.

§Wisconsin and Lowell played to a 4-4 tie in 1987-88.

HOBEY BAKER AWARD WINNERS

(Top college hockey player in United States)

Year—Player, College
1981—Neal Broten, Minnesota
1982—George McPhee, Bowling Green St.
1983—Mark Fusco, Harvard
1984—Tom Kurvers, Minnesota-Duluth
1985—Bill Watson, Minnesota-Duluth
1986—Scott Fusco, Harvard
1987—Tony Hrkac, North Dakota

Year—Player, College
1988—Robb Stauber, Minnesota
1989—Lane MacDonald, Harvard
1990—Kip Miller, Michigan State
1991—David Emma, Boston College
1992—Scott Pellerin, Maine
1993—Paul Kariya, Maine
1994—Chris Marinucci, Min.-Duluth

Year—Player, College
1995—Brian Holzinger, Bowling Green St.
1996—Brian Bonin, Minnesota
1997—Brendan Morrison, Michigan
1998—Chris Drury, Boston University
1999—Jason Krog, New Hampshire
2000—Mike Mottau, Boston College

COLLEGE HOCKEY *NCAA Division I*

CENTRAL COLLEGIATE HOCKEY ASSOCIATION

1999-2000 SEASON

FINAL STANDINGS

Team	G	W	L	T	Pts.	GF	GA
Michigan (27-10-4)......	28	19	6	3	41	112	65
Michigan St. (27-11-4)	28	18	8	2	38	84	46
Lake Sup. St. (18-16-2).	28	17	9	2	36	76	66
N. Michigan (22-13-4) .	28	16	8	4	36	93	64
Notre Dame (16-18-8) .	28	11	10	7	29	65	76
Ferris St. (21-16-2)......	28	13	13	2	28	85	79
Neb.-Omaha (16-19-7)	28	10	12	6	26	83	95
Bowl. Green (17-19-1).	28	12	15	1	25	90	88
Mia. of Ohio (13-20-3).	28	10	15	3	23	75	89
W. Michigan (12-21-3).	28	10	15	3	23	83	109
Ohio State (13-19-4)....	28	9	16	3	21	56	90
A. Fairbanks (6-25-3)...	28	4	22	2	10	65	100

Overall record in parentheses.

PLAYOFF RESULTS

FIRST ROUND

Michigan 4, Western Michigan 2
Michigan 6, Western Michigan 2
(Michigan won series, 2-0)

Michigan State 6, Miami of Ohio 2
Michigan State 5, Miami of Ohio 1
(Michigan State won series, 2-0)

Bowling Green State 2, Lake Superior State 1 (OT)
Bowling Green State 3, Lake Superior State 2
(Bowling Green State won series, 2-0)

Nebraska-Omaha 4, Northern Michigan 2
Northern Michigan 5, Nebraska-Omaha 1
Nebraska-Omaha 2, Northern Michigan 1
(Nebraska-Omaha won series, 2-1)

Notre Dame 4, Ferris State 3
Ferris State 6, Notre Dame 1
Notre Dame 4, Ferris State 2
(Notre Dame won series, 2-1)

PLAY-IN GAME

Nebraska-Omaha 3, Bowling Green State 1

SEMIFINALS

Michigan State 4, Notre Dame 0
Nebraska-Omaha 7, Michigan 4

FINALS

Michigan State 6, Nebraska-Omaha 0

ALL-STAR TEAMS

First team	Pos.	Second team
Jayme Platt, Lake Sup. St.	G	Ryan Miller, Mich. State
Jeff Jillson, Michigan	D	Dave Huntzicker, Michigan
Mike Weaver, Mich. State	D	Kevin Schmidt, N. Michigan
Mike Comrie, Michigan	F	Brian McCullough, Ferris St.
Shawn Horcoff, Mich. State	F	Adam Hall, Michigan State
Roger Trudeau, N. Michigan	F	David Gove, Western Mich.

AWARD WINNERS

Player of the year: Shawn Horcoff, Michigan State
Rookie of the year: Chris Gobert, Northern Michigan
Coach of the year: Scott Borek, Lake Superior State
Leading scorer: Shawn Horcoff, Michigan State
Playoff MVP: Ryan Miller, Michigan State

INDIVIDUAL LEADERS

Goals: Adam Hall, Michigan State (25)
Assists: Shawn Horcoff, Michigan State (48)
Points: Shawn Horcoff, Michigan State (62)
Penalty minutes: Eric Meloche, Ohio State (136)
Goaltending average: Ryan Miller, Michigan State (1.36)

TOP SCORERS

	Games	G	A	Pts.
Shawn Horcoff, Michigan State.........	41	14	48	62
Mike Comrie, Michigan....................	38	21	34	55
Brian McCullough, Ferris State........	39	24	24	48
David Gove, Western Michigan	36	18	28	46
Adam Hall, Michigan State	39	25	13	38
Pat Leahy, Miami of Ohio	36	16	22	38
Dustin Whitecotton, Miami of Ohio...	36	12	26	38
Michael Bishai, Western Michigan	35	18	19	37
Rustyn Dolyny, Michigan State	40	17	19	36
Kevin Swider, Ferris State................	39	15	21	36
Roger Trudeau, Northern Michigan...	39	21	15	36

INDIVIDUAL STATISTICS

ALASKA-FAIRBANKS NANOOKS

SCORING

	Pos.	Class	Games	G	A	Pts.	PIM
Bobby Andrews........	F	So.	34	13	12	25	72
Nathan Rocheleau....	F	Sr.	34	9	13	22	65
Daniel Carriere	D	So.	34	8	12	20	34
Dwayne Zinger	D	Sr.	34	10	4	14	36
Ryan Reinheller........	F	Jr.	34	3	11	14	34
Blaine Bablitz	F	Fr.	34	4	9	13	10
Sjon Wynia	F	Sr.	34	7	4	11	63
Aaron Grosul............	D	So.	34	3	8	11	28
Pat Hallett	F	Jr.	32	4	6	10	32
Jim Lawrence...........	F	Jr.	28	3	7	10	14
Casey Bartzen	F	Fr.	33	3	7	10	18
Kevin McNeill..........	F	Sr.	34	4	5	9	32
Scott McIlroy	F	Jr.	26	4	2	6	16
Scott Farrell	D	Fr.	33	0	6	6	20
Chad Hamilton	D	Jr.	33	1	4	5	83
Darren Tiemstra	D	Jr.	34	1	4	5	38
Jacob Flora	F	So.	25	0	2	2	10
Efren Larranaga	F	Fr.	33	1	0	1	41
Joe Borro.................	D	So.	2	0	0	0	4
Brandon Wheeler	G	Fr.	2	0	0	0	0
Nathan Wheeler	G	Fr.	3	0	0	0	0
Dirk Menard	G	Fr.	6	0	0	0	0
Mike Barren	F	Jr.	7	0	0	0	0

	Pos.	Class	Games	G	A	Pts.	PIM
Kerry Hafele	F	Sr.	10	0	0	0	6
Lance Mayes	G	Fr.	29	0	0	0	0

GOALTENDING

	Games	Min.	W	L	T	Goals	SO	Avg.
Lance Mayes	29	1686	5	20	2	87	0	3.10
Nathan Wheeler	3	178	0	3	0	11	0	3.70
Dirk Menard	6	181	0	2	1	13	0	4.32

BOWLING GREEN STATE FALCONS

SCORING

	Pos.	Class	Games	G	A	Pts.	PIM
Adam Edinger	F	Sr.	36	14	18	32	34
Greg Day	F	So.	37	13	16	29	20
Ryan Fultz	F	Fr.	36	17	10	27	12
Grady Moore	D	So.	37	7	19	26	38
Austin de Luis	F	So.	35	7	14	21	58
Tyler Knight	F	Fr.	37	7	13	20	40
Craig Desjarlais	F	Sr.	36	5	15	20	44
Ryan Murphy	F	Jr.	36	9	10	19	63
Michael Jones	D	Sr.	34	6	13	19	71
Marc Barlow	D	So.	31	5	12	17	10
Scott Hewson	F	So.	30	7	6	13	48
Curtis Valentine	F	Jr.	37	5	7	12	24
Doug Schueller	D	Jr.	32	2	5	7	85
B.J. Adams	D	Sr.	35	2	5	7	82
Zach Ham	F	Sr.	37	2	5	7	52
Ryan Wetterberg	F	So.	37	2	4	6	48
Dennis Williams	F	Jr.	30	3	1	4	48
Louis Mass	D	Jr.	35	1	2	3	46
Chris Bonvie	F	Jr.	5	1	0	1	6
Tyler Masters	G	Fr.	30	0	1	1	0
Tom Lawson	G	Fr.	3	0	0	0	0
Brad Newman	F	Sr.	5	0	0	0	6
Shawn Timm	G	Jr.	11	0	0	0	2
Joe Statkus	D	So.	23	0	0	0	14

GOALTENDING

	Games	Min.	W	L	T	Goals	SO	Avg.
Shawn Timm	11	469	4	2	1	19	0	2.43
Tyler Masters	30	1579	13	14	0	75	2	2.85
Tom Lawson	3	173	0	3	0	14	0	4.86

FERRIS STATE BULLDOGS

SCORING

	Pos.	Class	Games	G	A	Pts.	PIM
Brian McCullough	F	Sr.	39	24	24	48	52
Kevin Swider	F	Jr.	39	15	21	36	22
Rob Collins	F	So.	38	11	20	31	39
Chris Kunitz	F	Fr.	38	20	9	29	68
Phil Lewandowski	F	Fr.	37	9	13	22	64
Rob Kozak	F	Sr.	39	6	14	20	12
Jim Dube	D	Jr.	39	4	16	20	30
Troy Milam	D	Fr.	39	6	13	19	62
Rob Lightfoot	F	So.	39	5	14	19	22
Jason Basile	D	So.	37	7	11	18	36
Brent Wishart	F	Sr.	39	4	10	14	40
Scott Lewis	D	Jr.	39	4	8	12	38
Christian Schroder	D	So.	36	3	6	9	24
Chad McIver	D	So.	38	1	5	6	66
Jon Rogger	F	Jr.	32	2	2	4	8
Eric Evans	F	Sr.	36	1	3	4	28
Scott Markowsky	F	Fr.	26	2	1	3	6
Josh Bowers	D	Fr.	21	1	2	3	6
Nick Field	F	Fr.	8	2	0	2	2
Vince Owen	G	Jr.	18	0	2	2	0
Phil Osaer	G	So.	25	0	1	1	0
Kevin Caudill	F	Fr.	5	0	0	0	0
Gary Ricciardi	D	Sr.	37	0	0	0	41

GOALTENDING

	Games	Min.	W	L	T	Goals	SO	Avg.
Phil Osaer	25	1350	13	8	2	49	2	2.18
Vince Owen	18	995	8	8	0	49	1	2.95

LAKE SUPERIOR STATE LAKERS

SCORING

	Pos.	Class	Games	G	A	Pts.	PIM
Ryan Vince	F	Jr.	34	6	17	23	70
Ryan Knox	D	Jr.	32	4	17	21	50
Jeremy Bachusz	F	So.	35	10	9	19	18
Jason Nightingale	F	So.	36	9	10	19	40
Ben Keup	F	Sr.	36	13	5	18	64
Mike Vigilante	F	Jr.	36	6	12	18	22
Chris McNamara	F	So.	33	8	9	17	50
Aaron Davis	F	Fr.	34	7	10	17	49
Fred Slukynsky	F	Sr.	33	5	11	16	34
Blaine McCauley	D	Sr.	33	2	11	13	57
Trent Walford	F	Sr.	18	7	5	12	22
Jeff Cheeseman	F	Sr.	29	7	3	10	36
Tyson Turgeon	D	So.	29	1	7	8	16
Yevgeniy Dubravin	F	So.	27	3	4	7	10
Bart Redden	F	Jr.	29	3	3	6	20
Trevor Weisgerber	F	Fr.	21	1	3	4	2
Tyler Palmer	D	Sr.	22	0	3	3	30
Mike Henderson	F	So.	6	1	1	2	0
Matt Frick	D	Jr.	19	1	1	2	8
Aaron Phillips	F	Fr.	19	1	1	2	12
Will Magnuson	D	So.	27	0	2	2	38
Chris Thompson	D	So.	26	1	0	1	79
Klemen Kelgar	D	Jr.	17	0	1	1	14
Jayme Platt	G	Jr.	35	0	1	1	2
Scott Murray	G	Fr.	4	0	0	0	0
Cory Bast	F	So.	5	0	0	0	8
Kevin Wilson	D	Fr.	11	0	0	0	20

GOALTENDING

	Games	Min.	W	L	T	Goals	SO	Avg.
Jayme Platt	35	2025	18	13	2	81	2	2.40
Scott Murray	4	152	0	3	0	12	0	4.73

MIAMI OF OHIO REDSKINS

SCORING

	Pos.	Class	Games	G	A	Pts.	PIM
Pat Leahy	F	Jr.	36	16	22	38	89
Dustin Whitecotton	F	Sr.	36	12	26	38	14
Nick Jardine	F	Fr.	32	12	10	22	14
Evan Cheverie	F	So.	31	8	12	20	30
Ernie Hartlieb	F	Jr.	36	3	15	18	30
Josh Mizerek	D	Sr.	36	3	11	14	34
Mike Glumac	F	So.	36	8	5	13	52
Mark Shalawylo	F	Sr.	25	3	9	12	6
Jeremy Bautch	F	Sr.	35	6	3	9	46
Ken Marsch	D	So.	34	4	5	9	24
Danny Stewart	F	Fr.	34	2	7	9	34
Matt Chandler	F	So.	34	4	4	8	45
Matt Medvecz	D	Fr.	31	3	5	8	30
Gregor Krajnc	F	Sr.	9	6	1	7	2
Jake Ortmeyer	F	So.	32	3	4	7	34
Chris Knupp	F	Sr.	28	3	1	4	22
Clarke Walford	F	Jr.	33	1	3	4	30
Steve Hildenbrand	F	Fr.	35	0	4	4	56
Anthony Donskov	F	Jr.	16	2	1	3	10
Mike Tedesco	D	Fr.	5	0	1	1	4
David Burleigh	G	Fr.	25	0	1	1	2
Bart Stevens	D	So.	26	0	1	1	30
Pavel Nejezchleb	D	So.	30	0	1	1	28
Jason Deskins	F	Jr.	1	0	0	0	0
Ian Olsen	G	Sr.	5	0	0	0	0
Andy Marsch	G	Sr.	15	0	0	0	0

GOALTENDING

	Games	Min.	W	L	T	Goals	SO	Avg.
Andy Marsch	15	643	1	6	2	32	0	2.99
David Burleigh	25	1368	11	13	0	76	3	3.33
Ian Olsen	5	157	1	1	1	11	0	4.19

MICHIGAN WOLVERINES

SCORING

	Pos.	Class	Games	G	A	Pts.	PIM
Mike Comrie	F	So.	38	21	34	55	93
Jeff Jillson	D	So.	36	8	26	34	111
Mark Kosick	F	Jr.	35	18	15	33	16
Andy Hilbert	F	Fr.	36	17	16	33	41
Scott Matzka	F	Jr.	38	15	15	30	46
Josh Langfeld	F	Jr.	37	9	20	29	56
Geoff Koch	F	Jr.	34	11	16	27	52
Mike Cammalleri	F	Fr.	37	13	10	23	32
John Shouneyia	F	Fr.	35	5	18	23	24
Jed Ortmeyer	F	Fr.	39	8	14	22	36
Mark Mink	F	Fr.	39	7	12	19	38
Sean Peach	D	Sr.	37	7	11	18	72
Dave Huntzicker	D	Jr.	38	2	11	13	32
Jay Vancik	D	So.	38	3	5	8	38
Andrew Merrick	F	Sr.	17	2	3	5	36
J.J. Swistak	F	Fr.	34	3	1	4	43
Bill Trainor	F	Jr.	25	2	2	4	4
Craig Murray	F	So.	22	2	1	3	12
Bob Gassoff	D	Jr.	27	1	2	3	69
Mike Roemensky	D	Fr.	17	0	3	3	16
Josh Blackburn	G	So.	20	0	2	2	6
Krikor Arman	F	Jr.	11	1	0	1	8
Kevin O'Malley	G	So.	13	0	1	1	2
Brad Fraser	D	Fr.	18	0	1	1	8
L.J. Scarpace	G	Jr.	12	0	0	0	0
Kevin Magnuson	D	Sr.	18	0	0	0	46

GOALTENDING

	Games	Min.	W	L	T	Goals	SO	Avg.
L.J. Scarpace	12	552	5	2	0	17	0	1.85
Josh Blackburn	20	1205	13	3	4	46	1	2.29
Kevin O'Malley	13	612	8	4	0	27	0	2.65

MICHIGAN STATE SPARTANS

SCORING

	Pos.	Class	Games	G	A	Pts.	PIM
Shawn Horcoff	F	Sr.	41	14	48	62	46
Adam Hall	F	So.	39	25	13	38	36
Rustyn Dolyny	F	Jr.	40	17	19	36	58
Brian Maloney	F	Fr.	41	12	18	30	87
John-Michael Liles	D	Fr.	39	7	19	26	26
Damon Whitten	F	Jr.	38	10	14	24	74
Sean Patchell	F	Jr.	41	9	10	19	68
Brad Hodgins	D	Sr.	40	7	10	17	79
Andrew Hutchinson	D	So.	41	4	11	15	62
Brad Fast	D	Fr.	41	5	9	14	20
John Nail	F	Jr.	41	4	9	13	26
Troy Ferguson	F	Fr.	41	5	7	12	10
Andrew Bogle	F	Jr.	41	5	3	8	26
Mike Weaver	D	Sr.	37	0	8	8	34
Joe Goodenow	F	So.	15	2	5	7	14
Jon Insana	D	So.	41	3	3	6	44
Steve Clark	F	Fr.	33	2	3	5	6
Brody Brandstatter	D	Jr.	25	2	2	4	16
Kris Koski	F	Jr.	34	2	1	3	18
Steve Jackson	D	Fr.	17	1	1	2	8
Ryan Miller	G	Fr.	25	0	1	1	0
Mike Gresl	G	Sr.	1	0	0	0	0
Joe Blackburn	G	Jr.	18	0	0	0	0

GOALTENDING

	Games	Min.	W	L	T	Goals	SO	Avg.
Mike Gresl	1	9	0	0	0	0	0	0.00
Ryan Miller	25	1453	16	4	3	33	7	1.36
Joe Blackburn	18	1025	11	6	1	37	1	2.17

NEBRASKA-OMAHA MAVERICKS

SCORING

	Pos.	Class	Games	G	A	Pts.	PIM
David Brisson	F	Fr.	42	17	15	32	48
Allan Carr	F	Jr.	42	11	20	31	20
Greg Zanon	D	Fr.	42	3	26	29	56
Jason Cupp	F	Jr.	37	5	22	27	22
Jeff Hoggan	F	So.	34	16	9	25	82
Derek Reynolds	F	Sr.	40	8	15	23	63
Jason White	F	Jr.	39	7	13	20	32
Zach Scribner	D	So.	32	7	7	14	30
Dave Noel-Bernier	F	Jr.	40	9	4	13	28
James Chalmers	F	Jr.	37	5	8	13	72
Nick Fohr	F	So.	35	9	3	12	18
Jeff Edwards	F	Sr.	42	5	6	11	18
Mike Skogland	F	Sr.	37	3	8	11	22
Ed Cassin	D	Jr.	40	2	9	11	75
Billy Pugliese	F	Jr.	37	7	3	10	47
Ryan Bencurik	D	Sr.	27	2	7	9	38
Joe Pereira	F	Fr.	14	4	1	5	22
Shane Glover	F	So.	26	0	4	4	6
John Rosso	D	Jr.	38	1	2	3	18
Dan Zaluski	D	Jr.	10	0	2	2	8
Joe Yurecko	F	Jr.	20	0	2	2	6
Kendall Sidoruk	G	Sr.	33	0	2	2	4
Daniel Samuelsson	D	So.	42	0	2	2	32
Josh Lampman	D	Sr.	2	0	0	0	13
Rodney McLeod	G	So.	15	0	0	0	0

GOALTENDING

	Games	Min.	W	L	T	Goals	SO	Avg.
Rodney McLeod	15	691	3	8	0	39	0	3.39
Kendall Sidoruk	33	1858	13	11	7	105	0	3.39

NORTHERN MICHIGAN WILDCATS

SCORING

	Pos.	Class	Games	G	A	Pts.	PIM
Roger Trudeau	F	Sr.	39	21	15	36	48
J.P. Vigier	F	Sr.	39	18	17	35	72
Chris Gobert	F	Fr.	37	18	15	33	32
Chad Theuer	F	So.	38	11	16	27	36
Bryan Phillips	F	Sr.	39	7	19	26	30
Tyson Holly	F	Sr.	39	5	14	19	34
Jimmy Jackson	D	Fr.	38	8	10	18	85
Sean Connolly	D	So.	35	2	14	16	64
Kevin Schmidt	D	Sr.	38	1	14	15	30
Mike Sandbeck	D	Jr.	34	4	10	14	44
Ryan Riipi	F	Jr.	32	3	9	12	18
Lee Ruff	F/D	Sr.	29	7	4	11	26
Fred Mattersdorfer	F	Jr.	29	5	5	10	44
Bryce Cockburn	F	Fr.	32	5	5	10	40
Mike Stutzel	F	Fr.	29	3	6	9	44
Peter Michelutti	F	Fr.	26	2	7	9	0
Sean Owens	D	So.	32	1	8	9	64
Terry Harrison	F	Fr.	17	3	4	7	8
Dan Donnette	F	Fr.	27	2	5	7	4
Tyler Barabanoff	D	Sr.	25	2	2	4	30
Tim Lindberg	D	Fr.	17	0	4	4	10
Colin Young	D	Jr.	25	1	1	2	28
Dan Ragusett	G	Jr.	29	0	1	1	0
Dan Donette	F	Fr.	1	0	0	0	0
Jeff White	D	Jr.	1	0	0	0	2
Willy Todd	F	Fr.	3	0	0	0	6
Duane Hoey	G	Sr.	12	0	0	0	0

GOALTENDING

	Games	Min.	W	L	T	Goals	SO	Avg.
Dan Ragusett	29	1701	16	9	3	61	5	2.15
Duane Hoey	12	658	6	4	1	25	3	2.28

COLLEGE HOCKEY CCHA

NOTRE DAME FIGHTING IRISH
SCORING

	Pos.	Class	Games	G	A	Pts.	PIM
Dan Carlson	F	Jr.	42	17	18	35	36
Ben Simon	F	Sr.	40	13	19	32	53
Joe Dusbabek	F	Sr.	37	8	19	27	30
Ryan Dolder	F	Jr.	42	10	14	24	36
David Inman	F	So.	32	13	7	20	12
Connor Dunlop	F	Fr.	35	3	13	16	34
Evan Nielsen	D	Fr.	41	4	10	14	54
Tyson Fraser	D	Sr.	41	3	11	14	56
Michael Chin	F	Fr.	37	6	7	13	36
Andy Jurkowski	D	Sr.	38	5	8	13	10
Jay Kopischke	F	Jr.	33	6	5	11	34
Brett Henning	F	So.	36	3	7	10	16
Sean Molina	D	Sr.	40	1	8	9	28
Sean Seyferth	D	Sr.	33	2	4	6	26
Matt Van Arkel	F	Jr.	26	4	1	5	20
Troy Bagne	F	Sr.	27	2	3	5	10
Ryan Clark	D	Jr.	36	1	3	4	60
Nathan Borega	D	Sr.	41	1	3	4	70
John Wroblewski	F	Fr.	30	0	4	4	8
Jake Wiegand	F	Fr.	26	1	0	1	16
Sam Cornelius	D	So.	16	0	1	1	10
Kyle Kolquist	G	Jr.	2	0	0	0	0
Paul Harris	D	Fr.	9	0	0	0	4
Chad Chipchase	F	Jr.	15	0	0	0	18
Jeremiah Kimento	G	So.	16	0	0	0	0
Tony Zasowski	G	Fr.	31	0	0	0	0

GOALTENDING

	Games	Min.	W	L	T	Goals	SO	Avg.
Tony Zasowski	31	1737	13	9	6	74	2	2.56
J. Kimento	16	759	3	8	2	37	1	2.92
Kyle Kolquist	2	60	0	1	0	4	0	4.00

OHIO STATE BUCKEYES
SCORING

	Pos.	Class	Games	G	A	Pts.	PIM
J.-Francois Dufour	F	Jr.	35	13	22	35	47
Eric Meloche	F	Sr.	35	20	11	31	136
Luke Pavlas	F	Fr.	32	7	11	18	34
Nick Ganga	F	So.	34	4	10	14	112
Ryan Jestadt	D	Sr.	29	2	11	13	70
Andre Signoretti	D	Jr.	34	2	11	13	42
Louie Colsant	F	Sr.	29	4	8	12	32
Jason Crain	D	So.	35	2	9	11	32
Mike McCormick	F	So.	35	5	5	10	20
Jaisen Freeman	D	Jr.	24	1	8	9	26
Miguel Lafleche	F	Fr.	36	4	3	7	24
Yan Des Gagne	F	So.	27	2	4	6	26
Rob Gubala	F	Jr.	13	1	5	6	8
Benji Wolke	F	Jr.	25	3	2	5	10

	Pos.	Class	Games	G	A	Pts.	PIM
Nic Boileau	F	Fr.	29	3	2	5	18
Ryan Smith	F	Fr.	32	3	2	5	24
Jason Selleke	F	Sr.	36	1	4	5	69
Vinnie Grant	F	Jr.	12	2	2	4	8
Ray Aho	G	Sr.	35	0	3	3	4
Pete Broccoli	D	Fr.	36	0	3	3	30
T.J. Latorre	F	Fr.	14	1	1	2	8
Scott Titus	D	So.	36	0	2	2	52
Jeff Marshall	D	So.	2	0	1	1	0
Peter Wishloff	G	Fr.	6	0	0	0	2
Ryan Skaleski	D	Sr.	23	0	0	0	48

GOALTENDING

	Games	Min.	W	L	T	Goals	SO	Avg.
Ray Aho	35	1994	13	17	4	94	0	2.83
Peter Wishloff	6	150	0	2	0	11	0	4.40

WESTERN MICHIGAN BRONCOS
SCORING

	Pos.	Class	Games	G	A	Pts.	PIM
David Gove	F	Jr.	36	18	28	46	22
Michael Bishai	F	So.	35	18	19	37	52
Corey Waring	F	Sr.	36	10	16	26	20
David Cousineau	D	Fr.	36	8	17	25	44
Steve Rymsha	F	Jr.	34	13	11	24	76
Ben Gagnon	F	Fr.	34	9	12	21	36
Daryl Andrews	D	Sr.	36	3	16	19	52
Ryan Crane	D	So.	25	3	12	15	31
Brent Rumble	F	Fr.	34	8	5	13	30
Anthony Battaglia	F	So.	36	4	8	12	22
Brett Mills	F	Jr.	34	3	7	10	42
Jeff Lukasak	D	Sr.	33	1	6	7	73
Bryan Farquhar	F	So.	31	4	1	5	14
Jason Redenius	F	Sr.	36	3	1	4	34
Austin Miller	D	So.	35	0	3	3	42
Matt Addesa	F	Sr.	12	0	2	2	26
Andy Townsend	D	Fr.	19	0	2	2	18
Shaun Rose	F	Fr.	23	0	2	2	0
Caley Jones	F	Sr.	33	0	2	2	28
Rob Yamashita	D	Fr.	29	0	1	1	24
Jeff Reynaert	G	So.	35	0	1	1	6
Josh Akright	D	Fr.	1	0	0	0	0
Greg Mitchell	F	Sr.	1	0	0	0	0
J.J. Weaks	G	Fr.	1	0	0	0	0
Chris Peck	G	Jr.	2	0	0	0	0
Mark Wilkinson	F	Jr.	17	0	0	0	18

GOALTENDING

	Games	Min.	W	L	T	Goals	SO	Avg.
Chris Peck	2	68	0	1	0	4	0	3.55
Jeff Reynaert	35	2196	12	19	3	128	0	3.66
J.J. Weaks	1	4	0	1	0	2	0	26.97

EASTERN COLLEGE
ATHLETIC CONFERENCE

FINAL STANDINGS

Team	G	W	L	T	Pct.	GF	GA
St. Lawrence (27-8-2)..	20	16	3	1	.825	76	47
Colgate (24-9-2)	20	14	4	2	.750	85	61
Rensselaer (22-13-2)...	21	11	9	1	.548	61	49
Cornell (16-14-2)	20	10	9	1	.525	70	54
Clarkson (17-15-3)	20	9	8	3	.525	69	71
Princeton (10-16-4)	21	8	9	4	.476	66	66
Harvard (11-17-2)........	21	9	10	2	.476	65	63
Dartmouth (9-17-4)	21	8	10	3	.452	54	63
Yale (9-16-5)................	21	6	11	4	.381	45	63
Union (8-24-1)	21	6	14	1	.310	48	75
Brown (6-19-3)............	21	4	15	2	.238	52	78
Vermont (5-9-3)...........	7	3	2	2	.571	25	26

Overall record in parentheses.

Note: Vermont cancelled its final 15 games of the season, due to allegations of a hazing incident. For this reason, the league decided to base its standings on winning percentage, rather than points.

PLAYOFF RESULTS

FIRST ROUND

St. Lawrence 8, Union 4
St. Lawrence 4, Union 3 (OT)
(St. Lawrence won series, 2-0)

Colgate 5, Yale 4 (OT)
Colgate 4, Yale 2
(Colgate won series, 2-0)

Clarkson 3, Princeton 2
Clarkson 2, Princeton 1
(Clarkson won series, 2-0)

Cornell 4, Harvard 3
Cornell 4, Harvard 3
(Cornell won series, 2-0)

Rensselaer 7, Dartmouth 2
Rensselaer 3, Dartmouth 2 (OT)
(Rensselaer won series, 2-0)

PLAY-IN GAME

Cornell 4, Clarkson 2

SEMIFINALS

Rensselaer 3, Colgate 1
St. Lawrence 3, Cornell 2 (OT)

CONSOLATION GAME

Colgate 4, Cornell 0

CHAMPIONSHIP GAME

St. Lawrence 2, Rensselaer 0

ALL-STAR TEAMS

First team	Pos.	Second team
Joel Laing, Rensselaer	G	Derek Gustafson, St. Law.
Kent Huskins, Clarkson	D	Justin Harney, St. Lawrence
Cory Murphy, Colgate	D	Brian Pothier, Rensselaer
Andy McDonald, Colgate	F	Kirk Lamb, Princeton
Brad Tapper, Rensselaer	F	Erik Cole, Clarkson
Brandon Dietrich, St. Law.	F	Erik Anderson, St. Lawrence

AWARD WINNERS

Player of the year: Andy McDonald, Colgate
Rookies of the year: Derek Gustafson, St. Lawrence
Coach of the year: Don Vaughan, Colgate
Leading scorer: Andy McDonald, Colgate
Playoff MVP: Derek Gustafson, St. Lawrence

INDIVIDUAL LEADERS

Goals: Brad Tapper, Rensselaer (31)
Assists: Andy McDonald, Colgate (33)
Points: Andy McDonald, Colgate (58)
Penalty minutes: Benoit Morin, Princeton (107)
Goaltending average: Joel Laing, Rensselaer (1.82)

TOP SCORERS

	Games	G	A	Pts.
Andy McDonald, Colgate	34	25	33	58
Brad Tapper, Rensselaer	37	31	20	51
Darryl Campbell, Colgate..................	35	20	25	45
Brandon Dietrich, St. Lawrence........	36	15	26	41
Erik Anderson, St. Lawrence	36	14	25	39
Matt Murley, Rensselaer...................	35	9	29	38
Sean Nolan, Colgate	32	19	18	37
Mike Gellard, St. Lawrence..............	36	14	22	36
Alan Fyfe, St. Lawrence	36	17	18	35
Brian Pothier, Rensselaer	36	9	24	33

INDIVIDUAL STATISTICS

BROWN BEARS

SCORING

	Pos.	Class	Games	G	A	Pts.	PIM
Matt Kohansky.........	F	Jr.	27	9	8	17	23
James Duval	F	Sr.	28	4	11	15	12
Tyler Garrow	F	Sr.	27	7	7	14	40
Keith Kirley	F	Fr.	25	4	10	14	16
Michael Bent...........	F	Sr.	24	6	6	12	2
John Petricig...........	F	Jr.	26	6	5	11	12
Jon Zielinski............	F	Jr.	27	5	4	9	29
Paul Esdale	D	Fr.	27	5	4	9	26
Josh Barker.............	D	So.	27	3	6	9	28

	Pos.	Class	Games	G	A	Pts.	PIM
Jeff Lawler	F	Sr.	11	3	4	7	6
Jason Wilson	F	Fr.	28	3	4	7	18
Gianni Cantini	F	So.	27	0	7	7	18
Doug Janjevich	F	Jr.	20	3	3	6	4
Owen Walter	D	Fr.	27	2	4	6	22
Chris Legg	F	Fr.	23	2	3	5	4
Mike Pratt	D	Jr.	22	0	4	4	22
Chris Dirkes	D	So.	23	2	0	2	12
J-F Labarre..............	F	So.	11	0	2	2	4
Tye Korbl................	F	Fr.	27	0	2	2	18
Greg Hayes	D	Sr.	9	1	0	1	4
Christian Warrington.	D	Jr.	24	1	0	1	28

	Pos.	Class	Games	G	A	Pts.	PIM
Graham McNally	G	So.	4	0	0	0	0
Brian Eklund	G	So.	12	0	0	0	0
Ryan Longfield	D	Sr.	14	0	0	0	14
Scott Stirling	G	Sr.	17	0	0	0	4

GOALTENDING

	Games	Min.	W	L	T	Goals	SO	Avg.
Brian Eklund	12	569	1	6	2	28	1	2.95
Scott Stirling	17	935	5	11	1	52	0	3.34
Graham McNally	4	191	0	2	0	13	0	4.08

CLARKSON GOLDEN KNIGHTS

SCORING

	Pos.	Class	Games	G	A	Pts.	PIM
Erik Cole	F	Jr.	33	19	11	30	46
David Evans	F	So.	34	11	17	28	16
Matt Poapst	F	So.	32	14	13	27	36
Murray Kuntz	F	Jr.	33	11	10	21	34
K. Ellis-Toddington	D	So.	34	3	17	20	44
Carl Drakensjo	F	Sr.	35	6	13	19	24
Chris Bahen	D	Fr.	34	8	10	18	54
Kent Huskins	D	Jr.	28	2	16	18	30
Philippe Roy	D	Sr.	33	3	14	17	28
Don Smith	F	Jr.	35	7	9	16	20
Ian Manzano	D	So.	25	3	9	12	26
Yan Turgeon	F	Sr.	35	2	10	12	22
Mikko Ruutu	F	Fr.	33	5	5	10	26
Kevin O'Flaherty	F	Fr.	35	5	3	8	24
Jim Sheehan	F	Sr.	34	2	6	8	14
Matt Saper	F	Sr.	24	1	6	7	16
Chris Line	F	So.	28	3	2	5	10
Marc Garceau	F	So.	9	1	4	5	2
Dave Reid	D	Fr.	26	1	4	5	6
Adam Campana	F	Fr.	15	2	2	4	8
Joe Carosa	D	Fr.	22	2	2	4	4
Andy Kostka	G	So.	1	0	0	0	0
Nate Strong	D	Sr.	1	0	0	0	2
Mike Walsh	G	Fr.	6	0	0	0	0
Gasper Sekelj	D	Jr.	12	0	0	0	12
Karl Mattson	G	Fr.	17	0	0	0	0
Shawn Grant	G	So.	24	0	0	0	2

GOALTENDING

	Games	Min.	W	L	T	Goals	SO	Avg.
Karl Mattson	17	856	10	5	0	39	2	2.73
Shawn Grant	24	1106	6	7	3	56	0	3.04
Mike Walsh	6	130	1	3	0	12	0	5.55
Andy Kostka	1	1	0	0	0	1	0	48.60

COLGATE RED RAIDERS

SCORING

	Pos.	Class	Games	G	A	Pts.	PIM
Andy McDonald	F	Sr.	34	25	33	58	49
Darryl Campbell	F	Sr.	35	20	25	45	28
Sean Nolan	F	Jr.	32	19	18	37	40
Kevin Johns	F	Jr.	32	10	20	30	28
Cory Murphy	D	Jr.	35	10	19	29	26
Mike Marostega	D	Sr.	35	8	17	25	14
Chad MacDonald	F	Jr.	34	9	13	22	76
Etienne Morin	F	So.	35	7	10	17	32
Mike O'Malley	F	Jr.	28	2	12	14	26
Bryan Long	D	Jr.	34	4	9	13	33
P.J. Yedon	F	Fr.	22	5	6	11	12
Scooter Smith	F	Fr.	23	2	7	9	8
Erkki Rajamaki	F	Fr.	31	1	6	7	20
Pat Varecka	F	Jr.	30	4	2	6	31
Sam Sturgis	F	Jr.	26	2	4	6	8
Ben Bryce	D	So.	29	2	4	6	24
Brad D'Arco	F	Fr.	19	1	3	4	4
Jeff Potter	D	Sr.	29	1	3	4	26

	Pos.	Class	Games	G	A	Pts.	PIM
Steve Silversides	D	Fr.	14	0	3	3	14
Dan Stay	F	Jr.	25	0	3	3	16
Bob Vandersluis	F	So.	17	0	1	1	8
Byron Pool	D	Sr.	31	0	1	1	26
Jason Lefevre	G	So.	10	0	0	0	0
Shep Harder	G	Sr.	31	0	0	0	15

GOALTENDING

	Games	Min.	W	L	T	Goals	SO	Avg.
Shep Harder	31	1776	21	7	2	72	5	2.43
Jason Lefevre	10	343	3	2	0	20	0	3.50

CORNELL BIG RED

SCORING

	Pos.	Class	Games	G	A	Pts.	PIM
Doug Stienstra	F	Sr.	28	15	17	32	44
Mike Rutter	F	Sr.	32	11	17	28	46
Ryan Moynihan	F	Sr.	32	11	15	26	24
Denis Ladouceur	F	So.	31	10	15	25	30
Matt McRae	F	Fr.	31	8	16	24	22
Mark McRae	D	Fr.	27	5	16	21	10
Stephen Båby	F	Fr.	31	4	10	14	52
Larry Pierce	D	Jr.	30	6	6	12	26
Krzysztof Wieckowski	F	So.	32	5	6	11	22
David Hovey	F	Jr.	18	0	11	11	12
Andrew McNiven	F	Jr.	24	6	4	10	27
Doug Murray	D	Fr.	32	3	6	9	38
Danny Powell	D	Jr.	32	2	7	9	24
Shane Palahicky	F	Fr.	27	0	9	9	16
Frank Kovac	F	Sr.	24	3	5	8	22
Dan Svoboda	F	Jr.	24	5	2	7	10
David Adler	D	Sr.	25	4	3	7	10
David Francis	F	So.	18	2	3	5	8
Sam Paolini	F	Fr.	12	1	4	5	0
Rick Sacchetti	D	Sr.	25	2	2	4	35
David Kozier	F	So.	13	1	2	3	6
Brian McMeekin	D	So.	11	0	1	1	8
Travis Bell	D	Fr.	12	0	1	1	27
Ian Burt	G	Jr.	15	0	1	1	0
Matt Underhill	G	So.	17	0	1	1	12
Alex Gregory	D	So.	3	0	0	0	0
Chris Gartman	G	Fr.	3	0	0	0	0

GOALTENDING

	Games	Min.	W	L	T	Goals	SO	Avg.
Ian Burt	15	918	8	6	1	36	0	2.35
Chris Gartman	3	123	0	1	0	5	0	2.44
Matt Underhill	17	911	8	7	1	44	1	2.90

DARTMOUTH BIG GREEN

SCORING

	Pos.	Class	Games	G	A	Pts.	PIM
Frank Nardella	F	So.	30	8	12	20	18
Mike Maturo	F	So.	30	8	8	16	22
Pete Summerfelt	D	Fr.	30	5	11	16	38
Ryan Sinclair	F	So.	28	5	10	15	15
Jamie Herrington	F	So.	30	4	9	13	14
Trevor Byrne	D	Fr.	30	3	9	12	40
Michael Byrne	F	Jr.	25	2	9	11	20
Ryan Poulton	D	Sr.	30	5	5	10	18
Dan Casella	F	So.	28	4	6	10	32
Chris Taliercio	F	So.	22	4	4	8	22
Dory Tisdale	D	Jr.	29	1	7	8	10
Chris Baldwin	D	So.	23	4	3	7	18
Peter Mahler	F	Jr.	28	5	1	6	29
P.J. Martin	D	Fr.	24	2	4	6	19
Ryan Burkart	D	Sr.	30	2	4	6	26
Chris Hontvet	F	Fr.	14	1	5	6	14
Craig Lund	F	So.	25	2	3	5	4
Gary Hunter	F	So.	11	0	5	5	4

	Pos.	Class	Games	G	A	Pts.	PIM
Mike Murray	F	Fr.	29	2	2	4	44
Halsey Coughlin	F	Fr.	15	2	1	3	8
Kent Gillings	F	Fr.	22	0	2	2	2
Rob Delwo	G	So.	1	0	0	0	0
Pascal Lalonde	D	So.	3	0	0	0	0
Carl Desjardins	D	So.	4	0	0	0	8
Eric Almon	G	Sr.	10	0	0	0	0
Nick Boucher	G	Fr.	24	0	0	0	2

GOALTENDING

	Games	Min.	W	L	T	Goals	SO	Avg.
Nick Boucher	24	1378	8	12	3	66	1	2.87
Eric Almon	10	434	1	5	1	29	0	4.01
Rob Delwo	1	20	0	0	0	2	0	6.00

HARVARD CRIMSON

SCORING

	Pos.	Class	Games	G	A	Pts.	PIM
Steve Moore	F	Jr.	27	10	16	26	53
Dominic Moore	F	Fr.	30	12	12	24	28
Chris Bala	F	Jr.	30	10	14	24	18
Scott Turco	F	Sr.	30	9	10	19	10
Brett Nowak	F	Fr.	26	6	11	17	20
Peter Capouch	D	So.	30	5	10	15	10
Trevor Allman	F	Sr.	30	7	7	14	22
Brett Chodorow	F	Jr.	28	5	8	13	40
Matt Scorsune	D	Sr.	30	5	8	13	38
Harry Schwefel	F	Jr.	30	5	6	11	10
Matt Macleod	F	Sr.	29	5	5	10	18
Jeff Stonehouse	F	So.	30	4	4	8	36
Aaron Kim	D	Fr.	25	1	3	4	14
Jamin Kerner	F	Sr.	11	1	2	3	0
Jared Cantanucci	F	So.	15	0	3	3	2
Tim Stay	D	Jr.	22	0	3	3	10
Kyle Clark	F	So.	22	0	3	3	30
Derek Nowak	F	So.	23	0	3	3	6
Mark Moore	D	Sr.	28	0	2	2	48
Liam McCarthy	D	Jr.	26	0	1	1	24
Oliver Jonas	G	Jr.	6	0	0	0	0
Leif Ericson	D	So.	18	0	0	0	14
J.R. Prestifilippo	G	Sr.	25	0	0	0	2

GOALTENDING

	Games	Min.	W	L	T	Goals	SO	Avg.
J.R. Prestifilippo	25	1468	8	15	2	71	1	2.90
Oliver Jonas	6	328	3	2	0	20	0	3.65

PRINCETON TIGERS

SCORING

	Pos.	Class	Games	G	A	Pts.	PIM
Kirk Lamb	F	Jr.	30	8	20	28	20
Benoit Morin	F	Sr.	30	9	18	27	107
Chris Corrinet	F	Jr.	30	10	14	24	41
Brad Parsons	F	So.	28	11	10	21	24
Shane Campbell	F	Jr.	30	9	10	19	26
David Schneider	D	So.	30	5	11	16	22
Ethan Doyle	F	Jr.	29	5	7	12	24
Dave Bennett	D	So.	30	4	7	11	28
Darren Yopyk	D	Sr.	25	5	5	10	32
David Del Monte	F	So.	30	4	5	9	40
Josh Roberts	F	So.	30	5	2	7	16
Brad Meredith	F	Sr.	29	2	5	7	6
George Parros	F	Fr.	27	4	2	6	14
Chris Barber	D	Sr.	27	1	4	5	2
Ryan Kraliz	F	So.	11	2	1	3	6
Scott Prime	F	Fr.	14	0	3	3	4
Trevor Beaney	D	Fr.	24	0	3	3	12
Rob Chisholm	F	So.	24	0	3	3	12
Neil McCann	D	Fr.	23	0	2	2	10
Craig Bradley	G	Sr.	6	0	0	0	0

	Pos.	Class	Games	G	A	Pts.	PIM
Nate Nomeland	G	Fr.	6	0	0	0	0
Jason Dillow	D	Jr.	11	0	0	0	0
Dave Stathos	G	So.	25	0	0	0	2
Peter Zavodny	D	Jr.	28	0	0	0	32

GOALTENDING

	Games	Min.	W	L	T	Goals	SO	Avg.
Dave Stathos	25	1340	9	11	1	63	0	2.82
Nate Nomeland	6	168	1	2	0	8	0	2.86
Craig Bradley	6	301	0	3	3	23	0	4.59

RENSSELAER POLYTECHNIC INSTITUTE ENGINEERS

SCORING

	Pos.	Class	Games	G	A	Pts.	PIM
Brad Tapper	F	Jr.	37	31	20	51	81
Matt Murley	F	So.	35	9	29	38	42
Brian Pothier	D	Sr.	36	9	24	33	44
Marc Cavosie	F	Fr.	33	12	18	30	26
Pete Gardiner	F	Sr.	36	11	13	24	62
Doug Shepherd	F	Sr.	37	8	14	22	22
Steve Caley	F	Sr.	32	5	16	21	12
Andrew McPherson	F	So.	37	10	6	16	22
Jared Reigstad	D	Sr.	36	5	11	16	62
Keith Dupee	F	Sr.	36	8	7	15	22
Glenn Coupal	D	Jr.	35	3	6	9	30
Carson Butterwick	F	Fr.	35	5	3	8	47
Nolan Graham	F	Fr.	35	2	6	8	38
Danny Eberly	D	Fr.	21	2	5	7	8
Jim Henkel	F	So.	34	2	5	7	28
Steve Munn	D	So.	34	0	7	7	65
Francois Senez	D	Fr.	27	1	4	5	12
Eric Cavosie	F	Fr.	21	0	3	3	10
Jim Vickers	D	So.	22	0	3	3	18
Hamish Cunning	D	So.	11	0	2	2	2
Scott Prekaski	G	Sr.	11	0	1	1	0
Chris Migliore	F	So.	17	0	1	1	12
Joel Laing	G	Sr.	27	0	1	1	0
Jim Palmer	G	So.	1	0	0	0	0
Michael Duffy	F	Fr.	9	0	0	0	2
Wally Siggins	F	Fr.	10	0	0	0	0

GOALTENDING

	Games	Min.	W	L	T	Goals	SO	Avg.
Joel Laing	27	1613	17	7	2	49	6	1.82
Scott Prekaski	11	621	5	6	0	34	0	3.28
Jim Palmer	1	4	0	0	0	1	0	14.10

ST. LAWRENCE SAINTS

SCORING

	Pos.	Class	Games	G	A	Pts.	PIM
Brandon Dietrich	F	So.	36	15	26	41	20
Erik Anderson	F	Jr.	36	14	25	39	20
Mike Gellard	F	So.	36	14	22	36	36
Alan Fyfe	F	Jr.	36	17	18	35	32
Matt Desrosiers	D	So.	36	8	15	23	35
Dale Clarke	D	Sr.	36	6	17	23	24
Justin Harney	D	Sr.	37	4	18	22	73
Jason Windle	F	Sr.	37	13	3	16	10
Jim Lorentz	F	Fr.	35	6	8	14	20
Charlie Daniels	F	So.	33	5	9	14	18
Andy Marchetti	F	Jr.	25	4	10	14	12
Josh LeRoy	D	Sr.	37	1	13	14	34
Robin Carruthers	F	So.	37	5	8	13	16
Kevin Veneruzzo	D	Jr.	33	4	8	12	28
Ray DiLauro	D	So.	37	3	9	12	42
Jack O'Brien	F	So.	23	7	2	9	18
Sean Muir	F	So.	31	3	1	4	12
Blair Clarance	F	Fr.	21	1	2	3	20
Mike Muir	F	So.	33	0	3	3	6
Ryan Ward	F	Sr.	5	0	1	1	4

	Pos.	Class	Games	G	A	Pts.	PIM
Kris Margherio.........	F	Sr.	12	0	1	1	6
Jake Harney	D	Sr.	13	0	1	1	8
Derek Gustafson	G	Fr.	24	0	1	1	0
Sean Coakley	G	Jr.	7	0	0	0	0
Jeremy Symington...	G	Jr.	9	0	0	0	0

GOALTENDING

	Games	Min.	W	L	T	Goals	SO	Avg.
D. Gustafson......	24	1475	17	4	2	51	2	2.07
Sean Coakley	7	397	4	3	0	17	0	2.57
J. Symington	9	490	6	1	0	25	0	3.06

UNION SKATING DUTCHMEN

SCORING

	Pos.	Class	Games	G	A	Pts.	PIM
Jeff Sproat	D	Sr.	33	8	17	25	10
Jason Ralph	F	Jr.	33	9	12	21	40
Ryan Campbell.........	F	Sr.	33	11	8	19	22
Jeff Hutchins...........	F	So.	28	4	14	18	22
Charles Simard	D	So.	29	1	17	18	50
Clark Jones	F	Jr.	33	8	9	17	32
Jeff Wilson..............	F	So.	32	8	8	16	14
Drew Taylor.............	F	So.	32	5	11	16	2
Kris Goodjohn	F	Fr.	33	4	8	12	14
Alex Todd	F	Jr.	31	5	3	8	68
Nathan Gillies..........	F	Fr.	27	1	6	7	12
Doug Christiansen ...	D	So.	25	4	2	6	24
Bryan Yackel	F	Jr.	31	4	2	6	20
Jay Varady	F	Jr.	24	1	3	4	57
Jason Kean	F	Fr.	23	3	0	3	14
Steve Levac.............	F	Fr.	18	1	2	3	2
Frederic Cyr	D	So.	24	1	2	3	6
Mason Anderson......	F	Jr.	14	0	3	3	28
Randy Dagenais	D	Fr.	25	0	3	3	24
Bryant Westerman ...	F	Jr.	26	1	0	1	34
Jordy Federko	F	Fr.	1	0	0	0	0
Marc Wise...............	G	Fr.	7	0	0	0	0
Seamus Galligan	D	So.	8	0	0	0	2
Paul Kilfoy..............	D	Jr.	30	0	0	0	30
Brandon Snee	G	So.	31	0	0	0	4

GOALTENDING

	Games	Min.	W	L	T	Goals	SO	Avg.
Marc Wise	7	214	0	2	0	9	0	2.52
Brandon Snee	31	1775	8	22	1	113	0	3.82

VERMONT CATAMOUNTS

SCORING

	Pos.	Class	Games	G	A	Pts.	PIM
J.F. Caudron	F	Jr.	15	10	12	22	14
Kevin Karlander.......	F	Sr.	16	7	13	20	18
Jerry Gernander.......	F	Jr.	16	6	11	17	10
Andreas Moborg	D	Jr.	17	1	13	14	12
Graham Mink	F	So.	17	7	4	11	18
Ryan Cox	F	So.	16	8	2	10	12
Bryson Busniuk.......	F	Fr.	16	6	2	8	6
Benoit Lampron	F	Sr.	16	3	3	6	0
Mike Torney	F	Jr.	14	1	5	6	16
Mark Gouett............	D	So.	14	0	6	6	18

	Pos.	Class	Games	G	A	Pts.	PIM
Martin Wilde	D	Jr.	11	1	3	4	12
Matt Sanders	F	Sr.	12	0	4	4	18
Jim Gernander	D	Jr.	16	1	2	3	6
Thomas Hajek	D	Fr.	12	0	3	3	10
John Longo.............	F	Fr.	17	0	3	3	12
Ian Morse	F	Fr.	13	1	1	2	4
Chris Hills	F	So.	17	1	0	1	4
Ryan Miller	F	Fr.	14	0	1	1	4
Shawn Conschafter..	G	Fr.	5	0	0	0	2
Tim Peters	G	So.	8	0	0	0	0
David Noble	D	Fr.	11	0	0	0	6
Andrew Allen...........	G	Jr.	11	0	0	0	0
Joe Flammia	D	So.	13	0	0	0	12
J.F. Gamelin	F	Fr.	13	0	0	0	14

GOALTENDING

	Games	Min.	W	L	T	Goals	SO	Avg.
S. Conschafter ...	5	218	1	1	1	13	0	3.57
Tim Peters	8	258	1	3	1	18	0	4.18
Andrew Allen	11	558	3	5	1	41	0	4.41

YALE BULLDOGS

SCORING

	Pos.	Class	Games	G	A	Pts.	PIM
Ben Stafford............	F	Jr.	30	10	20	30	16
Jeff Brow	F	Sr.	28	11	14	25	26
Nick Deschenes	F	Fr.	29	6	9	15	15
Jay Quenville	F	Sr.	30	7	7	14	28
Paul Lawson	F	Sr.	25	5	6	11	50
Keith Fitzpatrick	D	Sr.	28	1	8	9	10
Cory Shea	F	Sr.	28	4	4	8	42
Bryan Freeman.........	D	Fr.	25	3	5	8	8
Spencer Rodgers	F	So.	30	3	5	8	26
Luke Earl................	F	So.	27	3	4	7	6
John Gauger	D	Jr.	26	2	3	5	67
Stacey Bauman	D	Fr.	27	1	4	5	14
Joe Dart	D	Jr.	30	1	4	5	12
Gabe Polsky	F	So.	8	3	1	4	4
Adam Sauve	F	Jr.	11	1	3	4	0
Jason Noe...............	F	So.	18	3	0	3	4
Mark Sproule	F	Sr.	20	0	3	3	10
John Chyz	F	Sr.	27	0	3	3	18
James Chyz.............	D	Sr.	30	0	3	3	51
Lee Jelenic	F	Jr.	22	2	0	2	20
Evan Wax	F	Fr.	10	1	1	2	0
Peter Toomey	F	Jr.	7	0	2	2	2
Robert Mutter	D	So.	7	0	2	2	4
David Sproule	D	So.	4	1	0	1	0
Jeff Hamilton	F	Sr.	2	0	1	1	0
Greg Boucher..........	D	Fr.	3	0	1	1	0
Matt Zamec.............	G	Sr.	1	0	0	0	0
Denis Nam	F	Fr.	8	0	0	0	0
Trevor Hanger	G	Sr.	14	0	0	0	0
Dan Lombard	G	So.	16	0	0	0	0

GOALTENDING

	Games	Min.	W	L	T	Goals	SO	Avg.
Matt Zamec.........	1	60	1	0	0	1	0	1.00
Dan Lombard.....	16	921	2	10	3	43	1	2.80
Trevor Hanger....	14	835	6	6	2	39	1	2.80

HOCKEY EAST

1999-2000 SEASON

FINAL STANDINGS

Team	G	W	L	T	Pts.	GF	GA
Boston U. (25-10-7)	24	15	3	6	36	85	69
New Hamp. (23-9-6)....	24	13	5	6	32	75	68
Boston Col. (29-12-1)..	24	15	8	1	31	91	50
Maine (27-8-5).............	24	13	7	4	30	88	67
Providence (18-18-2)...	24	10	13	1	21	65	79
Northeastern (12-19-5).	24	8	11	5	21	67	76
Merrimack (11-19-6)	24	6	12	6	18	58	81
Mass. (11-20-5)...........	24	5	15	4	14	50	71
Lowell (9-22-3).............	24	5	16	3	13	60	78

Overall record in parentheses.

PLAYOFF RESULTS

QUARTERFINALS

Maine 5, Providence 3
Maine 5, Providence 4 (OT)
    (Maine won series, 2-0)

Boston College 8, Northeastern 4
Boston College 3, Northeastern 2
    (Boston College won series, 2-0)

New Hampshire 5, Merrimack 2
New Hampshire 3, Merrimack 2 (OT)
    (New Hampshire won series, 2-0)

Boston University 4, Massachusetts 2
Boston University 5, Massachusetts 2
    (Boston University won series, 2-0)

SEMIFINALS

Maine 4, Boston University 2
Boston College 2, New Hampshire 1

CHAMPIONSHIP GAME

Maine 2, Boston College 1 (OT)

ALL-STAR TEAM

First team	Pos.	Second team
Ty Conklin, N. Hampshire	G	Ricky DiPietro, Boston Univ.
Chris Dyment, Boston Univ.	D	Bobby Allen, Boston College
Mike Mottau, Boston College	D	Pat Aufiero, Boston Univ.
Jeff Farkas, Boston College	F	Blake Bellefeuille, B.C.
Brian Gionta, Boston College	F	Mike Souza, New Hampshire
Cory Larose, Maine	F	Darren Haydar, N. Hampshire

AWARD WINNERS

Player of the year: Ty Conklin, New Hampshire
    Mike Mottau, Boston College
Rookie of the year: Ricky DiPietro, Boston University
Coach of the year: Jack Parker, Boston University
Leading scorer: Jeff Farkas, Boston College
Playoff MVP: Niko Dimitrakos, Maine

INDIVIDUAL LEADERS

Goals: Brian Gionta, Boston College (33)
Assists: Mike Mottau, Boston College (37)
Points: Jeff Farkas, Boston College (58)
Penalty minutes: Brendan Walsh, Maine (106)
Goaltending average: Tim Kelleher, Boston College (2.02)

TOP SCORERS

	Games	G	A	Pts.
Jeff Farkas, Boston College	41	32	26	58
Brian Gionta, Boston College............	42	33	23	56
Blake Bellefeuille, Boston College......	41	19	32	51
Cory Larose, Maine	39	15	36	51
Doug Sheppard, Providence................	38	18	26	44
Tommi Degerman, Boston Univ.	42	19	24	43
Chris Heron, Boston University	42	18	25	43
Mike Mottau, Boston College	42	6	37	43
Carl Corazzini, Boston University	42	22	20	42
Darren Haydar, New Hampshire	38	22	19	41

INDIVIDUAL STATISTICS

BOSTON COLLEGE EAGLES

SCORING

	Pos.	Class	Games	G	A	Pts.	PIM
Jeff Farkas	F	Sr.	41	32	26	58	59
Brian Gionta	F	Jr.	42	33	23	56	66
Blake Bellefeuille	F	Sr.	41	19	32	51	30
Mike Mottau	D	Sr.	42	6	37	43	57
Mike Lephart	F	Jr.	42	14	19	33	64
Krys Kolanos	F	Fr.	42	16	16	32	50
Bobby Allen	D	Jr.	42	4	23	27	40
Jeff Giuliano	F	So.	42	10	13	23	16
Marty Hughes	D	Jr.	42	5	17	22	28
Ales Dolinar	F	So.	42	9	10	19	18
Kevin Caulfield	F	Sr.	42	5	14	19	88
Rob Scuderi	D	Jr.	42	1	13	14	24
Brooks Orpik............	D	So.	38	1	9	10	104
Bill Cass	D	Fr.	41	1	9	10	26
Mark McLennan	F	Jr.	37	4	2	6	14
Paul Kelly	F	Fr.	40	3	2	5	8
Tony Hutchins	F	Sr.	20	2	2	4	8
Jeremy Wilson	F	Fr.	34	0	3	3	20
Scott Clemmensen...	G	Jr.	29	0	1	1	2
Tom Egan.................	G	Fr.	4	0	0	0	0

	Pos.	Class	Games	G	A	Pts.	PIM
A.J. Walker...............	F	Fr.	8	0	0	0	0
Dan Sullivan.............	D	Jr.	9	0	0	0	0
Tim Kelleher.............	G	Fr.	18	0	0	0	2
Anthony D'Arpino	D	Fr.	24	0	0	0	4

GOALTENDING

	Games	Min.	W	L	T	Goals	SO	Avg.
Tom Egan..........	4	3	0	0	0	0	0	0.00
Tim Kelleher.......	18	919	10	5	1	31	2	2.02
S. Clemmensen..	29	1610	19	7	0	59	3	2.20

BOSTON UNIVERSITY TERRIERS

SCORING

	Pos.	Class	Games	G	A	Pts.	PIM
Tommi Degerman	F	Sr.	42	19	24	43	18
Chris Heron.............	F	Sr.	42	18	25	43	38
Carl Corazzini.........	F	Jr.	42	22	20	42	44
Dan Cavanaugh........	F	So.	40	9	25	34	62
Jack Baker	F	So.	41	13	19	32	38
Chris Dyment	D	So.	42	11	20	31	42
Nick Gillis	F	Jr.	42	8	18	26	26
Brian Collins	F	Fr.	42	13	11	24	52
Mike Pandolfo	F	So.	41	13	10	23	37

COLLEGE HOCKEY *Hockey East*

	Pos.	Class	Games	G	A	Pts.	PIM
Pat Aufiero	D	So.	38	3	20	23	37
John Sabo	F	Fr.	39	8	10	18	89
Freddy Meyer	D	Fr.	25	1	11	12	52
John Cronin	D	Fr.	28	3	5	8	26
Mike Bussoli	D	Fr.	42	1	6	7	56
Keith Emery	D	Jr.	41	1	5	6	43
Bobby Hanson	F	Sr.	32	3	2	5	30
Greg Quebec	F	Sr.	29	3	0	3	12
Juha Vuori	F/D	Jr.	17	0	3	3	18
Ricky DiPietro	G	Fr.	30	0	3	3	6
Scott Perry	F	Jr.	40	0	3	3	18
Colin Sheen	D	Jr.	9	1	0	1	8
Mike DiMella	F	So.	18	0	1	1	12
Ryan Priem	F	Fr.	22	0	1	1	24
Jason Tapp	G	Fr.	16	0	0	0	14

GOALTENDING

	Games	Min.	W	L	T	Goals	SO	Avg.
Ricky DiPietro	30	1791	18	5	5	73	1	2.45
Jason Tapp	16	826	5	2	44		0	3.20

LOWELL RIVER HAWKS

SCORING

	Pos.	Class	Games	G	A	Pts.	PIM
Chris Bell	F	Sr.	34	9	21	30	20
Ed McGrane	F	Fr.	33	10	12	22	14
Yorick Treille	F	So.	33	10	12	22	34
Dan Fontas	F	So.	29	2	18	20	16
Kevin Bertram	D	Sr.	32	10	8	18	72
Brad Rooney	F	Jr.	32	7	11	18	43
John Campbell	F	Sr.	32	4	13	17	26
Tom Rouleau	F	So.	30	8	8	16	14
Jeff Boulanger	F	Jr.	29	3	12	15	51
Josh Reed	D	Fr.	30	2	10	12	24
Kyle Kidney	F	Jr.	28	4	7	11	26
Ron Hainsey	D	Fr.	30	3	8	11	20
Craig Brown	F	Sr.	23	4	5	9	43
Kevin Kotyluk	D	So.	20	3	5	8	30
Nicholas Carso	F	Jr.	21	1	7	8	6
Mark Concannon	F	Fr.	23	4	3	7	8
Stephen Slonina	F	Fr.	24	3	4	7	41
Chris Gustafson	D	So.	33	4	1	5	20
Josh Allison	D	So.	33	3	2	5	20
Jeremy Kyte	F	Jr.	9	2	2	4	2
Geoff Schomogyi	F	Fr.	11	2	0	2	4
Andy Wozniewski	D	Fr.	17	1	1	2	8
Dan Weinrieb	G	Fr.	5	0	0	0	0
Mark Fontas	D	Jr.	6	0	2	2	6
Ken Farrell	D	Fr.	4	0	1	1	2
Mike Sgroi	F	Fr.	6	0	0	0	4
R.J. Tolan	D	So.	7	0	0	0	6
Jimi St. John	G	So.	11	0	0	0	2
Cam McCormick	G	Fr.	25	0	0	0	4

GOALTENDING

	Games	Min.	W	L	T	Goals	SO	Avg.
Jimi St. John	11	606	2	7	1	31	0	3.07
C. McCormick	25	1350	7	13	2	72	0	3.20
Dan Weinrieb	5	92	0	2	0	6	0	3.91

MAINE BLACK BEARS

SCORING

	Pos.	Class	Games	G	A	Pts.	PIM
Cory Larose	F	Sr.	39	15	36	51	45
Barrett Heisten	F	So.	37	13	24	37	86
Ben Guite	F	Sr.	40	22	14	36	36
Brendan Walsh	F	Sr.	39	9	21	30	106
Niko Dimitrakos	F	So.	32	11	16	27	14
Dan Kerluke	F	Jr.	39	12	14	26	22
Martin Kariya	F	Fr.	35	8	17	25	6
Peter Metcalf	D	So.	40	4	17	21	56
Chris Heisten	F	Fr.	30	12	7	19	18

	Pos.	Class	Games	G	A	Pts.	PIM
Matthias Trattnig	F	Jr.	39	8	11	19	26
Doug Janik	D	So.	36	6	13	19	54
Jim Leger	F	Sr.	40	9	9	18	20
Robert Liscak	F	Fr.	27	6	7	13	30
Tom Reimann	F	Fr.	21	2	11	13	8
Anders Lundback	D	Jr.	40	2	10	12	40
Robert Ek	D	Sr.	38	4	7	11	42
Michael Schutte	D	Fr.	23	2	7	9	14
Lucas Lawson	F	Fr.	23	2	3	5	12
A.J. Begg	D	So.	38	2	3	5	34
Cliff Loya	D	Fr.	29	0	5	5	22
Gray Shaneberger	F	Fr.	14	2	1	3	8
Matt Yeats	G	Fr.	32	0	2	2	0
Magnus Lundback	F	Jr.	2	0	1	1	0
Eric Turgeon	D	So.	2	0	1	1	2
Ed Boudreau	F	Fr.	4	0	1	1	0
Mike Morrison	G	So.	13	0	1	1	0
Ryan Baker	F	Fr.	1	0	0	0	0
Trapper Clark	G	Fr.	1	0	0	0	0
Michael Koch	D	Fr.	1	0	0	0	0
Kevin Clauson	D	Jr.	7	0	0	0	2

GOALTENDING

	Games	Min.	W	L	T	Goals	SO	Avg.
Matt Yeats	32	1821	20	6	4	79	0	2.60
Mike Morrison	13	613	7	2	1	27	0	2.64

MASSACHUSETTS MINUTEMEN

SCORING

	Pos.	Class	Games	G	A	Pts.	PIM
Jeff Turner	F	Jr.	35	15	19	34	32
Jeff Blanchard	F	Sr.	36	10	17	27	36
Tim Turner	F	Fr.	34	5	21	26	20
Jedd Crumb	F	So.	30	8	10	18	12
Toni Soderholm	D	So.	34	3	12	15	32
Kris Wallis	F	Jr.	36	6	8	14	6
Nathan Sell	F	Sr.	35	7	6	13	30
Darcy King	F	So.	36	7	6	13	2
Ray Geever	F	Jr.	33	3	7	10	28
Jay Shaw	F	Jr.	33	3	7	10	68
R.J. Gates	F	Jr.	28	2	7	9	32
Joe Culgin	D	Jr.	33	3	5	8	38
Martin Miljko	F	So.	11	5	2	7	10
Samuli Jalkanen	D	Fr.	30	1	5	6	18
Luke DuPlessis	D	Fr.	32	3	2	5	54
Randy Drohan	D	So.	34	2	3	5	72
Kevin Poulin	F	Sr.	18	1	3	4	6
Nick Stephens	F	Jr.	32	1	2	3	45
Brad Nizwantowski	F	Fr.	16	1	1	2	8
Justin Shaw	D	So.	12	0	1	1	14
Kelly Sickavish	D	Fr.	31	0	1	1	22
Chris Thornton	F	Fr.	2	0	0	0	0
Anthony Scaparotti	F	Fr.	3	0	0	0	0
J.R. Zavisza	F	Fr.	6	0	0	0	0
Dmitri Vasiliev	F	Sr.	7	0	0	0	0
Chris Brannen	D	So.	12	0	0	0	21
Mike Johnson	G	So.	9	0	0	0	0
Markus Helanen	G	Jr.	31	0	0	0	4

GOALTENDING

	Games	Min.	W	L	T	Goals	SO	Avg.
Markus Helanen	31	1788	10	16	3	84	0	2.82
Mike Johnson	9	403	1	4	2	20	1	2.98

MERRIMACK WARRIORS

SCORING

	Pos.	Class	Games	G	A	Pts.	PIM
Greg Classen	F	So.	36	14	16	30	16
Anthony Aquino	F	Fr.	36	15	14	29	12
John Pyliotis	F	Jr.	36	6	20	26	60
Sandy Cohen	F	Sr.	36	14	11	25	30
Vincent Clevenger	F	Jr.	35	10	14	24	36

	Pos.	Class	Games	G	A	Pts.	PIM
Chris Halecki	F	Sr.	33	6	14	20	71
Tony White	D	Sr.	33	5	8	13	10
Ryan Kiley	F	Fr.	34	5	6	11	28
Nick Cammarata	F	Fr.	30	2	7	9	14
Nick Parillo	F	So.	34	2	7	9	26
Drew Hale	D	Sr.	28	1	8	9	42
Joey Gray	F	Jr.	36	2	6	8	60
Stephen Moon	D	Jr.	30	2	3	5	16
Mike Rodrigues	D	Sr.	34	2	3	5	47
Ron Mongeau	F	Jr.	36	1	4	5	8
Brad Mills	D	So.	20	0	3	3	10
Andrew Fox	D	Sr.	35	0	3	3	22
Alex Sikatchev	D	Fr.	6	0	1	1	0
Luke Smith	F	Fr.	16	0	1	1	0
Tim Foster	D	So.	25	0	1	1	14
Nick Torretti	F	So.	32	0	1	1	2
Lucas Smith	F	Fr.	2	0	0	0	0
Jason Wolfe	G	So.	4	0	0	0	0
Peter Catalano	D	Fr.	5	0	0	0	4
Tom Welby	G	Jr.	19	0	0	0	8
Chris Classen	G	Sr.	20	0	0	0	0

GOALTENDING

	Games	Min.	W	L	T	Goals	SO	Avg.
Jason Wolfe	4	47	0	0	0	2	0	2.54
Cris Classen	20	1097	7	8	4	51	3	2.79
Tom Welby	19	1058	4	11	2	61	1	3.46

NEW HAMPSHIRE WILDCATS

SCORING

	Pos.	Class	Games	G	A	Pts.	PIM
Darren Haydar	F	So.	38	22	19	41	42
Mike Souza	F	Sr.	38	15	25	40	58
John Sadowski	F	Sr.	38	9	19	28	38
Matt Swain	F	Jr.	29	8	16	24	14
Lanny Gare	F	Fr.	32	6	14	20	16
Jason Shipulski	F	Sr.	38	9	10	19	12
Corey-Joe Ficek	F	Jr.	31	10	6	16	16
Mark White	D	Jr.	37	4	10	14	24
Jim Abbott	F	Fr.	28	7	6	13	22
Sean Austin	D	Jr.	38	2	11	13	25
Johnny Rogers	F	Jr.	34	1	12	13	12
Tim Walsh	F	Sr.	36	3	9	12	20
Garrett Stafford	D	Fr.	38	3	9	12	28
David Busch	F	So.	30	8	2	10	4
Patrick Foley	F	Fr.	30	3	7	10	61
Dan Enders	D	Sr.	38	2	8	10	36
Colin Hemingway	F	Fr.	22	3	5	8	6
Joshua Prudden	F	Fr.	16	2	3	5	12
Ryan Cordeiro	F	So.	12	3	1	4	6
Eric Lind	D	Jr.	38	1	3	4	18
Matt Dzieduszycki	F	So.	5	1	2	3	12
Ty Conklin	G	Jr.	37	0	3	3	8
Kevin Truelson	D	Fr.	28	0	2	2	16
Chris Dube	F	Fr.	1	0	0	0	0
Matt Carney	G	So.	4	0	0	0	0
Brendon McEniry	D	Sr.	11	0	0	0	10

GOALTENDING

	Games	Min.	W	L	T	Goals	SO	Avg.
Ty Conklin	37	2194	22	8	6	91	1	2.49
Matt Carney	4	123	1	1	0	10	0	4.87

NORTHEASTERN HUSKIES

SCORING

	Pos.	Class	Games	G	A	Pts.	PIM
Graig Mischler	F	Jr.	34	9	14	23	22
Willie Levesque	F	So.	33	9	13	22	45
Roger Holeczy	F	Sr.	36	5	17	22	26
Matt Keating	F	Jr.	32	10	10	20	44

	Pos.	Class	Games	G	A	Pts.	PIM
Jim Fahey	D	So.	36	3	17	20	62
Chris Lynch	F	So.	35	5	14	19	49
Billy Newson	F	Sr.	35	8	9	17	28
Todd Barclay	F	Sr.	21	10	3	13	14
Bobby Davis	F	Sr.	26	9	4	13	6
Mike Ryan	F	Fr.	32	4	9	13	47
Mike Jozefowicz	D	Jr.	36	4	9	13	16
Brian Cummings	F	Jr.	36	4	7	11	51
Arik Engbrecht	D	So.	36	1	9	10	30
Rich Spiller	F	So.	35	1	7	8	46
Ryan Zoller	F	So.	27	4	3	7	10
Leon Hayward	F	So.	35	5	1	6	22
John Peterman	D	Jr.	14	1	5	6	27
Joe Mastronardi	F	Fr.	27	2	1	3	22
Kevin Welch	F	Jr.	18	1	1	2	20
Joe Mancuso	D	So.	18	0	2	2	8
Sean MacDonald	F	Jr.	21	0	1	1	4
Brian Sullivan	D	Fr.	23	0	1	1	8
Matt Brown	D	Jr.	1	0	0	0	2
Bob Haglund	F	Jr.	1	0	0	0	0
Doug Carlson	D	Jr.	2	0	0	0	0
Matt Coates	G	Fr.	3	0	0	0	0
Jason Braun	G	So.	16	0	0	0	0
Mike Gilhooly	G	Fr.	27	0	0	0	0

GOALTENDING

	Games	Min.	W	L	T	Goals	SO	Avg.
Jason Braun	16	781	4	8	2	40	0	3.07
Mike Gilhooly	27	1396	8	11	3	73	0	3.14
Matt Coates	3	10	0	0	0	1	0	5.90

PROVIDENCE FRIARS

SCORING

	Pos.	Class	Games	G	A	Pts.	PIM
Doug Sheppard	F	Sr.	38	18	26	44	26
Fernando Pisani	F	Sr.	38	14	24	38	56
Peter Fregoe	F	So.	34	14	15	29	28
Jon DiSalvatore	F	Fr.	38	15	12	27	12
Drew Omicioli	F	So.	36	11	12	23	76
Devin Rask	F	Fr.	38	7	14	21	18
Jason Ialongo	D	Sr.	38	1	20	21	24
Josh MacNevin	D	Sr.	38	4	14	18	54
Adam Lee	F	Jr.	29	3	9	12	20
Michael Lucci	F	Fr.	37	4	6	10	40
Jay Leach	D	Jr.	37	1	9	10	101
Nick Lent	F	Sr.	37	6	3	9	63
Michael Farrell	D	Jr.	36	3	6	9	71
Jerry Keefe	F	So.	17	0	9	9	6
Matt Libby	D	Jr.	38	4	4	8	22
Doug Wright	F	Fr.	32	2	6	8	32
Heath Gordon	F	Jr.	29	4	3	7	26
Shawn Weiman	D	Fr.	28	2	2	4	30
Cole Gendreau	F	Jr.	23	0	2	2	18
Marc Suderman	F	So.	22	1	0	1	2
J.J. Picinic	F	Jr.	7	0	1	1	2
Boyd Ballard	G	Jr.	27	0	1	1	0
Richard Miller	D	Sr.	7	0	0	0	12
Dave Gunderson	D	Sr.	10	0	0	0	20
Nolan Schaefer	G	Fr.	14	0	0	0	0
Jamie Vanek	G	Fr.	2	0	0	0	0

GOALTENDING

	Games	Min.	W	L	T	Goals	SO	Avg.
Boyd Ballard	27	1511	12	13	1	76	0	3.02
Nolan Schaefer	14	778	6	5	1	42	0	3.24
Jamie Vanek	2	31	0	0	0	2	0	3.85

COLLEGE HOCKEY Hockey East

WESTERN COLLEGIATE HOCKEY ASSOCIATION

FINAL STANDINGS

Team	G	W	L	T	Pts.	GF	GA
Wisconsin (31-9-1)......	28	23	5	0	46	112	70
N. Dakota (31-8-5)......	28	17	6	5	39	113	61
St. Cloud St. (23-14-3)	28	16	9	3	35	105	66
Mankato St. (21-14-4).	28	15	10	3	33	90	82
Colorado C. (18-18-3)..	28	14	11	3	31	88	69
Minnesota (20-19-2)...	28	13	13	2	28	95	84
A'ka-Anch. (15-18-3) ...	28	11	14	3	25	65	87
M.-Duluth (15-22-0)	28	10	18	0	20	59	114
Denver (16-23-2)	28	9	18	1	19	92	97
Mich. Tech (4-34-0).....	28	2	26	0	4	47	136

Overall record in parentheses.

PLAYOFF RESULTS

FIRST ROUND

Wisconsin 4, Michigan Tech 0
Wisconsin 4, Michigan Tech 0
    (Wisconsin won series, 2-0)
Mankato State 2, Alaska-Anchorage 1 (OT)
Mankato State 3, Alaska-Anchorage 2
    (Mankato State won series, 2-0)
Minnesota-Duluth 5, St. Cloud State 4
St. Cloud State 3, Minnesota-Duluth 0
St. Cloud State 7, Minnesota-Duluth 3
    (St. Cloud State won series, 2-1)
Minnesota 4, Colorado College 2
Minnesota 3, Colorado College 2 (OT)
    (Minnesota won series, 2-0)
North Dakota 4, Denver 0
Denver 2, North Dakota 1
North Dakota 9, Denver 4
    (North Dakota won series, 2-1)

SUDDEN-DEATH QUARTERFINAL

Minnesota 6, Mankato State 4

SEMIFINALS

North Dakota 7, St. Cloud State 3
Wisconsin 5, Minnesota 3

CONSOLATION GAME

St. Cloud State 6, Minnesota 4

FINALS

North Dakota 5, Wisconsin 3

ALL-STAR TEAMS

First team	Pos.	Second team
Karl Goehring, North Dakota	D	Scott Meyer, St. Cloud State
Jeff Dessner, Wisconsin	D	Dylan Mills, Minnesota
Mike Pudlick, St. Cloud St.	D	Jordan Leopold, Minnesota
Steve Reinprecht, Wisconsin	F	Lee Goren, North Dakota
Jeff Panzer, North Dakota	F	John Pohl, Minnesota
Dany Heatley, Wisconsin	F	Tyler Arnason, St. Cloud St.

AWARD WINNERS

Player of the year: Steve Reinprecht, Wisconsin
Rookie of the year: Dany Heatley, Wisconsin
Coach of the year: Don Brose, Mankato State
Leading scorer: Steve Reinprecht, Wisconsin
Playoff MVP: Lee Goren, North Dakota

INDIVIDUAL LEADERS

Goals: Lee Goren, North Dakota (34)
Assists: Jeff Panzer, North Dakota (44)
Points: Steve Reinprecht, Wisconsin (66)
Penalty minutes: Mike Commodore, North Dakota (154)
Goaltending average: Karl Goehring, North Dakota (1.89)

TOP SCORERS

	Games	G	A	Pts.
Steve Reinprecht, Wisconsin............	37	26	40	66
Lee Goren, North Dakota.................	44	34	29	63
Jeff Panzer, North Dakota................	44	19	44	63
John Pohl, Minnesota......................	41	18	41	59
Jason Ulmer, North Dakota	44	18	39	57
Dany Heatley, Wisconsin	38	28	28	56
Erik Westrum, Minnesota	39	27	26	53
Aaron Fox, Mankato State	39	12	38	50
Tyler Arnason, St. Cloud State	39	19	30	49
Bryan Lundbohm, North Dakota	44	22	22	44

INDIVIDUAL STATISTICS

ALASKA-ANCHORAGE SEAWOLVES

SCORING

	Pos.	Class	Games	G	A	Pts.	PIM
Steve Cygan	F	So.	35	14	13	27	29
Mike Scott.................	F	So.	35	8	15	23	34
Gregg Zaporzan	F	So.	33	8	12	20	22
Reggie Simon	F	Jr.	36	5	10	15	8
Klage Kaebel	F	Sr.	27	7	7	14	2
Chris Pont	F	Sr.	33	9	4	13	14
Matt Williams............	D	Sr.	31	6	5	11	10
Petr Chytka	F	Fr.	36	5	6	11	18
Corey Hessler...........	D	So.	35	2	7	9	18
Matt Shasby.............	D	Fr.	32	1	8	9	36
Rob Douglas	F	So.	11	3	5	8	12
Chris Sikich..............	F	Jr.	31	4	3	7	19
Steve Suihkonen	D	Fr.	28	1	5	6	4
Dan Gilkerson	F	Fr.	35	3	2	5	4
Joe Garvin................	F	Fr.	36	3	2	5	12
Morgan Roach	F	Fr.	25	3	1	4	6
Wade Chiodo	F	Fr.	11	2	1	3	0
Jesse Unklesbay	F	Fr.	30	0	3	3	4
Eric Lawson	D	So.	34	0	3	3	10
Ted Suihkonen	F	Jr.	13	1	1	2	8
Steve Ludwig	D	Jr.	9	0	2	2	0
Jonas Hedberg	F	Fr.	3	0	1	1	2
Mark Filipenko	D	Sr.	23	0	1	1	4
Mark Leitner.............	D	Jr.	26	0	1	1	12
Cory McEachran	G	Fr.	16	0	0	0	0
Corey Strachan	G	Fr.	21	0	0	0	0

GOALTENDING

	Games	Min.	W	L	T	Goals	SO	Avg.
C. McEachran	16	928	6	8	2	42	1	2.72
Corey Strachan..	21	1247	9	10	1	60	1	2.89

COLORADO COLLEGE TIGERS
SCORING

	Pos.	Class	Games	G	A	Pts.	PIM
Noah Clarke	F	Fr.	39	17	20	37	30
Toby Petersen	F	Sr.	37	14	19	33	8
Mark Cullen.............	F	So.	37	11	20	31	22
Jesse Heerema........	F	So.	39	12	14	26	23
Justin Morrison	F	Jr.	38	7	19	26	28
K.J. Voorhees..........	F	Sr.	36	16	8	24	18
Paul Manning..........	D	Jr.	39	6	17	23	26
Mike Colgan	D	Jr.	39	4	16	20	12
Tom Preissing.........	D	Fr.	36	4	14	18	20
Cam Kryway.........	F	Sr.	34	9	7	16	46
Trent Clark	F	So.	38	4	7	11	36
Joe Cullen	F	Fr.	29	4	6	10	30
Dan Peters	D	Sr.	27	2	8	10	58
Ian Petersen...........	F	Sr.	35	5	4	9	12
Mike Stuart	D	So.	32	2	5	7	26
Brent Voorhees	D	Jr.	28	1	6	7	18
Aaron Karpan	F	Sr.	26	3	3	6	12
Chris Hartsburg	F	So.	33	3	2	5	50
Jason Jozsa	D	Fr.	31	0	5	5	16
Shaun Winkler	F	So.	29	1	2	3	14
Colin Zulianello.......	G	Jr.	12	0	2	2	0
Joe Heinbecker	D	Sr.	6	1	0	1	0
Berk Nelson	F	Sr.	13	0	0	0	8
Jeff Sanger	G	So.	29	0	0	0	0

GOALTENDING

	Games	Min.	W	L	T	Goals	SO	Avg.
Jeff Sanger	29	1701	14	14	1	70	3	2.47
Colin Zulianello..	12	656	4	4	2	28	1	2.56

DENVER PIONEERS
SCORING

	Pos.	Class	Games	G	A	Pts.	PIM
Kelly Popadynetz......	F	Jr.	41	15	25	40	56
Jon Nerman	F	Sr.	41	14	23	37	28
Joe Ritson..............	F	Sr.	40	20	14	34	34
Mark Rycroft...........	F	Jr.	41	17	17	34	87
Bjorn Engstrom........	F	Jr.	41	12	18	30	12
Kevin Doell.............	F	Fr.	40	8	15	23	18
Chris Paradise.........	D	So.	40	4	19	23	46
Joe Casey...............	F	Sr.	38	12	8	20	8
Greg Barber	F	Fr.	40	7	8	15	24
Jesse Cook	D	So.	41	2	12	14	40
J.J. Hartmann	F	Fr.	35	6	7	13	18
Judd Stauss............	D	Jr.	37	4	7	11	38
Aaron MacKenzie	D	Fr.	40	1	9	10	56
Bryce Wallnutt	F	Sr.	32	5	4	9	32
David Neale	F	So.	31	3	6	9	34
Matt Pettinger.........	F	So.	19	2	6	8	49
Jordan Bianchin.......	F	Fr.	32	0	8	8	18
Bryan Vines............	D	Jr.	41	0	7	7	22
Erik Adams	D	So.	40	0	4	4	26
Paul Cox	F	So.	10	0	1	1	10
Stephen Wagner	G	Sr.	33	0	1	1	4
Neil Phippen	F	Jr.	2	0	0	0	0
Justin Flaishans	F	Fr.	2	0	0	0	0
James Armstrong	D	Jr.	7	0	0	0	10
Jason Grahame........	D	Fr.	7	0	0	0	4
Wade Dubielewicz....	G	Fr.	13	0	0	0	0

GOALTENDING

	Games	Min.	W	L	T	Goals	SO	Avg.
W. Dubielewicz ..	13	596	3	5	1	27	1	2.72
S. Wagner..........	33	1870	13	18	1	102	2	3.27

MANKATO STATE MAVERICKS
SCORING

	Pos.	Class	Games	G	A	Pts.	PIM
Aaron Fox	F	Sr.	39	12	38	50	6
T.J. Guidarelli...........	F	Jr.	39	11	16	27	36
Tim Wolfe	F	Sr.	39	20	6	26	74
Jesse Rooney..........	F	Jr.	37	19	6	25	28
Peter Holoien	F	Jr.	37	2	23	25	36
Ryan Schrick...........	F	Sr.	39	8	16	24	36
Todd George	D	Sr.	39	6	16	22	73
B.J. Abel	F	Fr.	38	5	17	22	35
Tyler Baines	F	Jr.	39	5	14	19	6
Jerry Cunningham ...	F	Fr.	30	6	9	15	22
Ben Christopherson .	D	Jr.	39	3	12	15	36
Josh Kern	F	So.	21	7	5	12	43
Ryan Severson........	F	Jr.	37	7	1	8	16
Andy Hedlund	D	So.	36	4	2	6	58
Justin Martin...........	F	So.	30	3	3	6	12
Peter Runkel	D	Fr.	26	2	4	6	22
Andy Fermoyle	F	Sr.	39	1	5	6	24
B.J. Anderson..........	F	So.	22	0	5	5	5
Joe Bourne	D	Fr.	24	2	2	4	20
Jon Bushy...............	D	Jr.	26	1	3	4	18
David Graham	D	So.	4	1	2	3	0
Eric Pateman	G	So.	38	0	3	3	2
Nate Mauer	F	So.	16	1	1	2	18
Brian Nelson	G	Sr.	1	0	0	0	0
Todd Kelzenberg	G	So.	2	0	0	0	0
Shane Joseph	F	Fr.	5	0	0	0	0

GOALTENDING

	Games	Min.	W	L	T	Goals	SO	Avg.
Eric Pateman	38	2283	21	13	4	104	4	2.73
Brian Nelson	1	20	0	0	0	2	0	6.00
T. Kelzenberg	2	53	0	1	0	7	0	7.86

MICHIGAN TECH HUSKIES
SCORING

	Pos.	Class	Games	G	A	Pts.	PIM
Jarrett Weinberger ...	F	Jr.	37	10	9	19	92
Matt Ulwelling..........	F	Jr.	38	6	12	18	46
Paul Cabana............	F	So.	37	10	5	15	89
Brad Mueller............	F	Sr.	38	9	5	14	64
Clint Way	D	Jr.	36	1	12	13	44
Tab Lardner.............	F	Jr.	34	7	5	12	51
Devin Hartnell	F	Sr.	28	6	4	10	34
Mat Snesrud	D	Jr.	38	3	7	10	44
Riley Nelson............	F	Sr.	36	2	8	10	8
Brad Patterson	F	So.	33	1	9	10	28
Jeff Keiver..............	F	Fr.	37	4	5	9	20
Jaron Doetzel..........	F	So.	27	2	3	5	16
Chuck Fabry............	F	Fr.	32	2	3	5	12
Tim Laurila..............	F	So.	27	1	4	5	34
Tom Kaiman............	D	So.	36	2	2	4	34
Quinton Krueger	D	Jr.	25	1	3	4	10
Adrian Fure	D	Jr.	35	0	4	4	20
Chris Durno	F	Fr.	24	1	1	2	30
A.J. Aitken..............	F	Sr.	30	0	1	1	37
O.J. Bottoms...........	F	Fr.	2	0	0	0	0
Brian Eovaldi...........	F	So.	3	0	0	0	0
Landon Boyko..........	D	So.	4	0	0	0	8
Brian Rogers...........	G	Fr.	8	0	0	0	0
Matt Lewis	D	So.	9	0	0	0	4
Todd Weninger	G	Jr.	12	0	0	0	2
Jason Moilanen........	G	Jr.	22	0	0	0	2
Greg Amadio	D	Fr.	37	0	0	0	106

GOALTENDING

	Games	Min.	W	L	T	Goals	SO	Avg.
Jason Moilanen ..	22	1211	2	19	0	87	1	4.31
Todd Weninger ..	12	631	2	8	0	54	0	5.13
Brian Rogers......	8	436	0	7	0	38	0	5.23

MINNESOTA GOLDEN GOPHERS

SCORING

	Pos.	Class	Games	G	A	Pts.	PIM
John Pohl	F	So.	41	18	41	59	26
Erik Westrum	F	Jr.	39	27	26	53	99
Nate Miller	F	Sr.	41	16	19	35	38
Aaron Miskovich	F	Jr.	41	16	16	32	24
Dylan Mills	D	Jr.	40	8	21	29	50
Jordan Leopold	D	So.	39	6	18	24	20
Jeff Taffe	F	Fr.	39	10	10	20	22
Dave Spehar	F	Sr.	39	9	10	19	24
Dan Welch	F	Fr.	36	6	8	14	31
Stuart Senden	F	Jr.	40	7	5	12	28
Ben Tharp	D	Fr.	32	0	12	12	16
Shawn Roed	F	Fr.	12	3	6	9	10
Nick Angell	D	So.	37	3	6	9	42
Nick Anthony	F	Fr.	34	4	4	8	16
Pat O'Leary	F	So.	25	6	1	7	8
Matt DeMarchi	D	Fr.	39	1	6	7	82
Erik Wendell	F	So.	32	4	2	6	26
Matt Leimbek	F	Jr.	23	1	4	5	2
Mark Nenovich	D	So.	29	2	2	4	22
Doug Meyer	F	So.	26	1	3	4	18
Rico Pagel	F	Sr.	17	0	2	2	6
Mike Lyons	D	Sr.	25	0	2	2	28
Ryan Trebil	D	Sr.	11	0	1	1	24
Erik Young	G	Fr.	3	0	0	0	0
Pete Samargia	G	Fr.	6	0	0	0	0
Adam Hauser	G	So.	36	0	0	0	2

GOALTENDING

	Games	Min.	W	L	T	Goals	SO	Avg.
Adam Hauser	36	2114	20	14	2	104	1	2.95
Pete Samargia	6	238	0	2	0	13	0	3.28
Erik Young	3	139	0	3	0	11	0	4.76

MINNESOTA-DULUTH BULLDOGS

SCORING

	Pos.	Class	Games	G	A	Pts.	PIM
Colin Anderson	F	Sr.	37	18	22	40	44
Jeff Scissons	F	Sr.	37	14	19	33	32
Derek Derow	F	Jr.	37	10	17	27	8
Mark Carlson	D	So.	37	7	19	26	14
Drew Otten	F	Fr.	36	9	10	19	53
Tom Nelson	F	So.	33	4	11	15	24
Andy Reierson	D	So.	37	4	11	15	32
Jon Francisco	F	Fr.	35	4	7	11	28
Jesse Fibiger	D	Jr.	37	4	6	10	83
Mark Gunderson	F	Jr.	32	3	5	8	18
Judd Medak	F	So.	37	2	6	8	73
Shawn Pogreba	F	Sr.	35	3	4	7	46
Ryan Homstol	F	Jr.	37	3	4	7	26
Richie Anderson	F	Sr.	33	4	1	5	14
Ryan Nosan	F	Sr.	24	2	1	3	6
Pasi Korhonen	F	Fr.	8	1	2	3	0
Ryan Coole	D	Jr.	34	1	2	3	56
Nate Anderson	F	So.	23	0	3	3	5
Craig Pierce	D	Jr.	30	0	3	3	19
John Conboy	D	Fr.	27	0	2	2	20
Brant Nicklin	G	Sr.	29	0	2	2	0
Rob Anderson	G	Fr.	15	0	1	1	2
Jason Gregoire	G	Fr.	1	0	0	0	0
Tim Schneider	D	Fr.	4	0	0	0	0
Steve Rodberg	D	Fr.	5	0	0	0	8
Michael Miskovich	F	Fr.	11	0	0	0	8

GOALTENDING

	Games	Min.	W	L	T	Goals	SO	Avg.
Brant Nicklin	29	1584	10	16	0	100	1	3.79
Rob Anderson	15	629	5	6	0	41	0	3.91
Jason Gregoire	1	7	0	0	0	2	0	16.90

NORTH DAKOTA FIGHTING SIOUX

SCORING

	Pos.	Class	Games	G	A	Pts.	PIM
Lee Goren	F	Sr.	44	34	29	63	42
Jeff Panzer	F	Jr.	44	19	44	63	16
Jason Ulmer	F	Sr.	44	18	39	57	33
Bryan Lundbohm	F	So.	44	22	22	44	14
Ryan Bayda	F	Fr.	44	17	23	40	30
Wes Dorey	F	Jr.	39	15	13	28	16
Travis Roche	D	Fr.	42	6	22	28	60
Brad DeFauw	F	Sr.	43	13	9	22	52
Tim Skarperud	F	Fr.	37	11	10	21	16
Aaron Schneekloth	D	So.	34	3	14	17	24
Kevin Spiewak	F	Fr.	38	8	8	16	26
Jason Noterman	F	Fr.	39	7	9	16	33
Chad Mazurak	D	So.	25	5	10	15	22
Ryan Hale	F	Fr.	40	4	11	15	20
Mike Commodore	D	Jr.	38	5	7	12	154
Trevor Hammer	D	Jr.	32	2	10	12	14
Peter Armbrust	F	Sr.	43	1	10	11	33
Tim O'Connell	D	Sr.	38	0	9	9	52
Chris Lienweber	D	Fr.	36	0	8	8	16
Paul Murphy	D	So.	15	0	7	7	4
Jeff Yurecko	F	Fr.	14	2	1	3	8
Adrian Hasbargen	D	So.	7	0	2	2	4
Karl Goehring	G	Jr.	30	0	2	2	2
Andy Kollar	G	So.	15	0	1	1	4
Jason Endres	G	Fr.	2	0	0	0	0
Pat Kenny	F	So.	4	0	0	0	0
Mike Possin	F	So.	7	0	0	0	8

GOALTENDING

	Games	Min.	W	L	T	Goals	SO	Avg.
Jason Endres	2	69	1	0	0	2	0	1.73
Karl Goehring	30	1747	19	6	4	55	8	1.89
Andy Kollar	15	856	11	2	1	38	1	2.66

ST. CLOUD STATE HUSKIES

SCORING

	Pos.	Class	Games	G	A	Pts.	PIM
Tyler Arnason	F	So.	39	19	30	49	18
Nate DiCasmirro	F	So.	40	19	24	43	26
Mark Hartigan	F	So.	37	22	20	42	24
Brandon Sampair	F	Jr.	40	18	24	42	20
Ryan Malone	F	Fr.	38	9	21	30	68
Mike Pudlick	D	So.	40	8	22	30	65
Joe Motzko	F	Fr.	36	9	15	24	52
Keith Anderson	F	Jr.	40	12	7	19	14
Duvie Westcott	D	So.	36	1	18	19	67
Jon Cullen	F	Fr.	29	5	11	16	10
Geno Parrish	D	Sr.	40	3	13	16	32
Lee Brooks	F	So.	39	8	7	15	24
Ritchie Larson	D	So.	35	4	8	12	24
Chris Purslow	F	Fr.	14	7	4	11	6
Matt Noga	F	Sr.	14	3	5	8	12
Mike Walsh	F	Fr.	32	4	3	7	28
Peter Torsson	F	Jr.	20	1	6	7	12
Matt Bailey	F	Sr.	14	2	3	5	2
Brian Gaffaney	D	Jr.	38	1	4	5	51
Tom Lund	D	Sr.	39	0	4	4	44
Bryce Macken	D	Sr.	28	1	2	3	26
Archie Bifulk	F	So.	4	0	1	1	0
Aaqron Dwyer	D	So.	13	0	1	1	4
Derek Eastman	D	So.	17	0	1	1	16
Scott Meyer	G	Jr.	32	0	1	1	2
Jake Moreland	G	Fr.	3	0	0	0	0
Dean Weasler	G	So.	7	0	0	0	0

GOALTENDING

	Games	Min.	W	L	T	Goals	SO	Avg.
Scott Meyer	32	1922	20	8	3	76	7	2.37
Jake Moreland	3	179	1	2	0	8	0	2.68
Dean Weasler	7	331	2	4	0	19	0	3.44

WISCONSIN BADGERS

SCORING

	Pos.	Class	Games	G	A	Pts.	PIM
Steve Reinprecht......	F	Sr.	37	26	40	66	14
Dany Heatley............	F	Fr.	38	28	28	56	32
Dustin Kuk	F	Sr.	39	17	22	39	63
David Hukalo...........	F	So.	41	15	24	39	44
Kevin Granato	F	Jr.	41	10	19	29	24
Jeff Dessner............	D	Jr.	40	11	16	27	61
Dan Bjornlie	D	Sr.	40	7	12	19	26
Brad Winchester	F	Fr.	33	9	9	18	48
Brian Fahey	D	Fr.	41	6	11	17	40
Matt Hussey............	F	So.	35	5	11	16	8
Alex Brooks..............	D	Jr.	41	4	10	14	78
Andy Wheeler..........	F	So.	40	4	9	13	26
Matt Doman	F	So.	22	1	12	13	53
Matt Murray	F	So.	36	5	7	12	66
Dave Hergert............	F	So.	36	5	7	12	2
Kent Davyduke.........	F	So.	30	4	7	11	21
Niki Siren	F	Sr.	40	4	6	10	18
Erik Jensen	F	Fr.	20	3	3	6	30
Rob Vega	D	So.	35	0	4	4	16
Jason Reimers	D	Fr.	9	1	0	1	16
Mark Jackson...........	D	Fr.	26	1	0	1	18
Rick Spooner	D	Jr.	12	0	1	1	8
Graham Melanson....	G	Jr.	41	0	1	1	2
Mark Baranczyk	G	So.	1	0	0	0	0
Chad Stauffacher	F	Jr.	2	0	0	0	0
Scott Kabotoff..........	G	Fr.	3	0	0	0	2
Mike Cerniglia	F	Jr.	3	0	0	0	2

GOALTENDING

	Games	Min.	W	L	T	Goals	SO	Avg.
G. Melanson	41	2416	31	9	1	101	4	2.51
Scott Kabotoff....	3	66	0	0	0	5	0	4.56
Mark Baranczyk .	1	4	0	0	0	1	0	16.22

INDEScription...

INDEPENDENTS

1999-2000 SEASON

FINAL STANDINGS

Team	G	W	L	T	Pct.	GF	GA
Niagara	42	30	8	4	.762	165	65
Air Force	39	19	18	2	.513	131	125
Army	32	13	17	2	.438	102	95

INDIVIDUAL STATISTICS

AIR FORCE FALCONS

SCORING

	Pos.	Class	Games	G	A	Pts.	PIM
Brian Gornick	F	So.	39	13	25	38	26
Scott Bradley	F	Jr.	39	13	25	38	26
Derek Olson	F	So.	39	15	20	35	16
Andy Berg	F	Fr.	35	11	22	33	30
Brian Rodgers	F	So.	39	13	17	30	49
Scott Zwiers	F	Fr.	39	14	12	26	50
Brendan Connelly	F	So.	37	11	15	26	31
Nels Grafstrom	F	Sr.	39	12	13	25	12
Jace Anders	D	So.	39	7	14	21	8
Billy O'Reilly	F	Jr.	39	9	8	17	26
Brian Reaney	D	Fr.	37	4	13	17	66
Mike Keough	D	Sr.	34	1	5	6	56
Kyle Fransdal	F	Fr.	21	3	2	5	4
Jeff Zurick	D	So.	25	1	3	4	14
James Ord	F	Jr.	10	2	1	3	0
Kirk Zerkel	F	Sr.	29	1	2	3	36
Justin Hamilton	F	Fr.	19	0	3	3	6
Matt Zitzlsperger	F	Sr.	33	0	3	3	16
Marc Kielkucki	G	Jr.	37	0	3	3	14
Jake Tesar	D	Fr.	38	1	1	2	30
Marcus Peters	F	Jr.	10	0	2	2	2
Bobby Pate	D	Fr.	30	0	2	2	26
Ryan Smith	D	So.	21	0	1	1	12
Jeremy High	G	Fr.	1	0	0	0	0
Neil Barner	F	So.	3	0	0	0	2
Pete Johnston	F	Fr.	4	0	0	0	0
Sean Broderick	G	Jr.	10	0	0	0	0

GOALTENDING

	Games	Min.	W	L	T	Goals	SO	Avg.
Jeremy High	1	20	0	0	0	1	0	3.00
Marc Kielkucki	37	2009	18	1	2	102	3	3.05
Sean Broderick	10	323	1	2	0	21	0	3.91

ARMY CADETS

SCORING

	Pos.	Class	Games	G	A	Pts.	PIM
Mike Fairman	F	Jr.	29	19	10	29	4
Tim Fisher	F	So.	31	14	14	28	30
Nathan Mayfield	F	So.	23	3	16	19	27
Joe Carpenter	D	So.	32	6	12	18	18
Joe Dudek	F	Fr.	30	7	9	16	40
Paul Gonzalez	F	Sr.	32	4	12	16	10
John Williams	D	Sr.	29	3	13	16	24
T.J. McMeniman	D	Sr.	32	2	14	16	16
Josh Morino	D	So.	32	4	11	15	42
Garrett Brougham	F	Jr.	29	6	8	14	12
Nic Serre	F	Fr.	14	2	10	12	8
K.C. Finnegan	F	Jr.	27	6	4	10	32
Brian Sarner	F	Fr.	20	6	3	9	4
Bill Griffith	F	Sr.	25	5	2	7	42
Jeff Gallo	F	Jr.	22	2	5	7	26

	Pos.	Class	Games	G	A	Pts.	PIM
Tim Murphy	F	So.	22	3	3	6	8
Jon Toftey	F	So.	17	2	3	5	8
Scott Lensky	D	So.	26	0	5	5	14
Dave Keiser	F	Jr.	24	4	0	4	6
Eric Joyce	D	So.	27	2	2	4	47
Andy Haskell	D	Jr.	9	0	3	3	6
Derek Hines	F	Fr.	24	2	0	2	8
Sean Donahue	D	Fr.	4	0	2	2	4
Kevin Emore	F	Fr.	3	0	1	1	0
Corey Winer	G	Sr.	21	0	1	1	0
Jed Richard	F	Fr.	1	0	0	0	0
Ford Lannan	G	Jr.	1	0	0	0	0
Justin Nash	D	Jr.	5	0	0	0	6
Joe Kocer	F	Fr.	7	0	0	0	0
Scott Hamilton	G	So.	11	0	0	0	2

GOALTENDING

	Games	Min.	W	L	T	Goals	SO	Avg.
Ford Lannan	1	60	1	0	0	1	0	1.00
Scott Hamilton	11	606	4	5	1	29	1	2.87
Corey Winer	21	1259	8	12	1	61	1	2.91

NIAGARA PURPLE EAGLES

SCORING

	Pos.	Class	Games	G	A	Pts.	PIM
Mikko Sivonen	F	Sr.	42	24	26	50	16
Mike Isherwood	F	Sr.	42	16	33	49	32
Kyle Martin	F	Sr.	42	26	22	48	10
Peter DeSantis	F	Sr.	42	20	24	44	24
Jay Kasperek	F	Sr.	42	16	19	35	16
Chris MacKenzie	D	Sr.	38	5	27	32	20
John Heffernan	F	So.	42	16	13	29	10
Timo Makela	D	Jr.	42	0	27	27	46
Nate Handrahan	D	Sr.	42	4	21	25	28
Randy Harris	F	Fr.	41	12	9	21	16
Chris Sebastian	F	Fr.	41	7	6	13	10
Scott McDonald	F	Sr.	32	5	7	12	19
Thomas Clayton	F	So.	32	1	10	11	6
John Maksymiu	F	Sr.	30	2	8	10	6
Colin Rows	D	Sr.	31	2	8	10	76
Jon Marshall	F	Sr.	36	2	7	9	24
Adam Morris	F	Sr.	22	2	4	6	24
Richard DeCaprio	F	Sr.	19	3	2	5	4
Darwin Murray	D	Jr.	38	2	3	5	8
Greg Gardner	G	Sr.	41	0	5	5	10
Mike Bozoian	D	Fr.	33	0	2	2	4
Peter Ricketts	D	Sr.	17	0	1	1	8
Jim Whalen	G	So.	1	0	0	0	0
Todd Elliott	F	Jr.	10	0	0	0	2

GOALTENDING

	Games	Min.	W	L	T	Goals	SO	Avg.
Jim Whalen	1	60	1	0	0	1	0	1.00
Greg Gardner	41	2503	29	8	4	64	12	1.53

COLLEGE HOCKEY *Independents*

CANADIAN INTERUNIVERSITY ATHLETIC UNION

GENERAL INFORMATION

The Canadian Interuniversity Athletic Union is an alliance of three Canadian college leagues—the Atlantic Universities Athletic Association, Canada West University Athletic Association and Ontario Universities Athletic Association. After the regular season, the three leagues compete in an elimination tournament to decide the CIAU national champion. The award and trophy winners are based on regular-season play.

2000 NATIONAL CHAMPIONSHIPS

PLAYOFF STANDINGS

POOL A

Team (League)	W	L	Pts.	GF	GA
New Brunswick (AUS)	2	1	4	12	11
Saskatchewan (CWUAA)	1	1	2	7	7
Western Ontario (OUA)	0	2	0	4	6

POOL B

Team (League)	W	L	Pts.	GF	GA
Alberta (CWUAA)	3	0	6	12	7
Trois-Rivieres (OUA)	1	1	2	4	5
Calgary (CWUAA)	0	2	0	4	7

RESULTS

ROUND-ROBIN POOL PLAY

THURSDAY, MARCH 23

Trois-Rivieres 3, Calgary 2
New Brunswick 3, Western Ontario 2 (OT)

FRIDAY, MARCH 24

Alberta 4, Calgary 2
Saskatchewan 3, Western Ontario 2 (OT)

SATURDAY, MARCH 25

Alberta 3, Trois-Rivieres 1
New Brunswick 4, Saskatchewan 4 (2OT)

FINAL

SUNDAY, MARCH 26

Alberta 5, New Brunswick 4 (2OT)

ALL-TOURNAMENT TEAM

Player	Pos.	College
Carlton (C.J.) Denomme	G	Western Ontario
Mike Garrow	D	Alberta
Jeff Shakotko	D	New Brunswick
Colin Beardsmore	F	New Brunswick
Kevin Marsh	F	Alberta
Ryan Wade	F	Alberta

Tournament Most Valuable Player: Kevin Marsh, Alberta

1999-2000 AWARD WINNERS

CIAU ALL-CANADIAN TEAM

Pos.	Player
G	Luc Belanger, Trois-Rivieres
	Clayton Pool, Alberta
D	David Bahl, McGill
	Mike Garrow, Alberta
	Dan Preston, St. Thomas
	Dion Zukiwsky, Alberta
F	Mathieu Darche, McGill
	Yanick Evola, St. Francis Xavier
	Russ Hewson, Alberta
	Jim Midgley, St. Mary's
	Sheldon Moser, Saskatchewan
	Jeff Petrie, Western Ontario

TROPHY WINNERS

Player of the year: Russ Hewson, Alberta
Rookie of the year: Clayton Pool, Alberta
Most sportsmanlike player: Sheldon Moser, Saskatchewan
Scholastic player of the year: Mathieu Darche, McGill
Coach of the year: Trevor Steinburg, St. Mary's

TOP SCORERS

	Games	G	A	Pts.
Mathieu Darche, McGill	26	27	35	62
Russ Hewson, Alberta	28	22	32	54
Dave Gourde, McGill	21	21	26	47
Jean-Francois Brunelle, T.-Rivieres	26	19	28	47
Yanick Evola, St. Francis Xavier	26	22	24	46
Jim Midgley, St. Mary's	26	15	30	45
Philippe Tremblay, Trois-Rivieres	26	17	27	44
Sheldon Moser, Saskatchewan	26	13	31	44
Guy Loranger, St. Francis Xavier	25	16	26	42
Ryan Davis, St. Mary's	26	19	21	40
Daniel Payette, Trois-Rivieres	25	10	30	40

TOP GOALTENDERS

	Games	Min.	GA	Avg.
Luc Belanger, Trois-Rivieres	22	1316	39	1.78
Clayton Pool, Alberta	23	1382	46	2.00
Denver England, Western Ontario	12	692	28	2.43
C.J. Denomme, Western Ontario	15	883	36	2.45
Jason Wright, Saskatchewan	18	1050	45	2.57

COLLEGE HOCKEY CIAU

CANADIAN COLLEGES

ATLANTIC UNIVERSITIES SPORTS, 1999-2000 SEASON

FINAL STANDINGS

KELLY DIVISION

Team (Overall)	G	W	L	T	Pts.	GF	GA
St. Mary's (25-12-0)	26	18	8	0	36	118	82
St. F'cis Xavier (18-16-0)	26	15	11	0	30	103	85
Acadia (21-20-0)	26	13	13	0	26	80	82
Dalhousie (7-25-0)	26	5	21	0	10	71	114

MAC ADAM DIVISION

Team (Overall)	G	W	L	T	Pts.	GF	GA
St. Thomas (26-10-0)	26	18	8	0	36	128	94
New Brunswick (27-17-0)	26	15	11	0	30	99	93
Moncton (14-16-0)	26	14	12	0	28	115	110
P. Edward Island (6-25-0)	26	6	20	0	12	72	126

PLAYOFF RESULTS

KELLY DIVISION
SEMIFINALS

St. Mary's 4, Dalhousie 1
Dalhousie 5, St. Mary's 4
St. Mary's 6, Dalhousie 3

Acadia 2, St. F. Xavier 1
Acadia 4, St. F. Xavier 2

KELLY DIVISION
FINALS

St. Mary's 6, Acadia 2
Acadia 4, St. Mary's 1
Acadia 2, St. Mary's 1 (OT)

MAC ADAM DIVISION
SEMIFINALS

St. Thomas 9, P.E.I. 1
St. Thomas 5, P.E.I. 2

N. Bruns.6, Moncton 5 (OT)
N. Bruns. 3, Moncton 0

MAC ADAM DIVISION
FINALS

St. Thomas 6, N. Bruns. 2
N. Bruns. 2, St. Thomas 1 (OT)
N. Bruns. 7, St. Thomas 0

LEAGUE FINALS

Acadia 4, New Brunswick 2
New Brunswick 5, Acadia 4
New Brunswick 3, Acadia 2 (2OT)
New Brunswick 4, Acadia 3 (2OT)

ALL-STAR TEAMS

KELLY DIVISION Player, team	Pos.	MAC ADAM DIVISION Player, team
Mike Weatherbie, St. Mary's	G	David Mitchell, P.E.I.
Dominique Auger, St.F.X.	D	J.-Benoit Deschamps, Monc.
Steven Gallace, St. Mary's	D	Dan Preston, St. Thomas
Yanick Evola, St.F.X.	F	Deny Gaudet, Moncton
Jim Midgley, St. Mary's	F	Peter MacKellar, N. Bruns.
Josh St. Louis, Acadia	F	Jason Sands, St. Thomas

AWARD WINNERS

Most Valuable Player: Yanick Evola, St. Francis Xavier
Rookie of the year: Mike Hanson, St. Thomas
Most sportsmanlike player: Peter MacKellar, New Brunswick
Coach of the year: Trevor Stienburg, St. Mary's
Leading scorer: Yanick Evola, St. Francis Xavier

INDIVIDUAL LEADERS

Goals: Yanick Evola, St. Francis Xavier (22)
Assists: Jim Midgley, St. Mary's (30)
Points: Yanick Evola, St. Francis Xavier (46)
Penalty minutes: Mike Hanson, St. Thomas (108)
Goaltending average: Mike Weatherbie, St. Mary's (2.60)

TOP SCORERS

	Games	G	A	Pts.
Yanick Evola, St. Francis Xavier	26	22	24	46
Jim Midgley, St. Mary's	26	15	30	45
Guy Loranger, St. Francis Xavier	25	16	26	42
Ryan Davis, St. Mary's	26	19	21	40
Mike Hanson, St. Thomas	26	20	19	39
Jason Sands, St. Thomas	26	10	28	38
Deny Gaudet, Moncton	25	11	27	38
Carl Prudhomme, Moncton	25	18	15	33
Travis Kennedy, St. Mary's	26	11	21	32
Dan Preston, St. Thomas	25	8	23	31

CANADA WEST UNIVERSITY ATHLETIC ASSOCIATION, 1999-2000 SEASON

FINAL STANDINGS

EAST DIVISION

Team (Overall)	G	W	L	T	Pts.	GF	GA
Sask. (32-7-3)	28	22	3	3	47	143	81
Manitoba (17-22-2)	28	11	15	2	24	105	109
Brandon (17-25-1)	28	11	17	0	22	101	129
Regina (6-27-4)	28	4	21	3	11	88	178

WEST DIVISION

Team (Overall)	G	W	L	T	Pts.	GF	GA
Alberta (33-8-7)	28	20	3	5	45	141	60
Calgary (25-17-3)	28	16	9	3	35	110	86
Lethbridge (20-16-3)	28	12	14	2	26	103	95
Brit. Columbia (8-26-5)	28	5	19	4	14	69	122

PLAYOFF RESULTS

EAST DIVISION
SEMIFINALS

Brandon 6, Manitoba 2
Brandon 4, Manitoba 2

WEST DIVISION
SEMIFINALS

Calgary 5, Lethbridge 4
Calgary 5, Lethbridge 3

EAST DIVISION FINALS

Saskatchewan 6, Brandon 5
Saskatchewan 5, Brandon 0

WEST DIVISION FINALS

Alberta 9, Calgary 3
Alberta 3, Calgary 2

CONFERENCE FINALS

Saskatchewan 7, Alberta 6 (OT)
Alberta 5, Saskatchewan 1
Saskatchewan 7, Alberta 3

CONFERENCE WILD CARD FINALS (CONSOLATION)

Calgary 4, Brandon 2
Calgary 7, Brandon 3

ALL-STAR TEAMS

First team	Pos.	Second team
Clayton Pool, Alberta	G	Colin Ryder, Brandon
Dion Zukiwsky, Alberta	D	Shannon Briske, Sask.
Mike Garrow, Alberta	D	Jeff Henkelman, Sask.
Russ Hewson, Alberta	F	Kevin Marsh, Alberta
Sheldon Moser, Sask.	F	Dan Heilman, Lethbridge
Jeremy Stasiuk, Sask.	F	Ron Grimard, Calgary
		Kris Knoblauch, Alberta

AWARD WINNERS

Most Valuable Player: Russ Hewson, Alberta
Rookie of the year: Clayton Pool, Alberta
Most sportsmanlike player: Sheldon Moser, Saskatchewan
Coach of the year: Dave Adolph, Saskatchewan
Leading scorer: Russ Hewson, Alberta

INDIVIDUAL LEADERS

Goals: Russ Hewson, Alberta (22)
Assists: Russ Hewson, Alberta (32)
Points: Russ Hewson, Alberta (54)
Penalty minutes: Jeremy Stasiuk, Saskatchewan (96)
Goaltending average: Jeff Calvert, Saskatchewan (2.00)

TOP SCORERS

	Games	G	A	Pts.
Russ Hewson, Alberta	28	22	32	54
Sheldon Moser, Saskatchewan	28	13	31	44
Ron Grimard, Calgary	25	10	27	37
Jeremy Stasiuk, Saskatchewan	27	21	15	36
Trevor Ethier, Saskatchwan	26	16	20	36
Marc Gaudet, Manitoba	28	12	23	35
Ryan Wade, Alberta	28	15	19	34
Matt Holmes, Calgary	28	12	22	34
Marlin Murray, Brandon	27	11	23	34
Trevor Winkler, Saskatchewan	26	19	14	33

ONTARIO UNIVERSITY ATHLETICS, 1999-2000 SEASON

FINAL STANDINGS

FAR EAST DIVISION

Team	G	W	L	T	Pts.	GF	GA
Trois-Rivieres (26-6-5)	26	20	2	4	44	125	48
McGill (27-9-1)	26	21	5	0	42	146	75
Concordia (16-14-3)	26	14	9	3	31	107	88
Ottawa (13-16-4)	26	8	14	4	20	77	102

MID EAST DIVISION

Team	G	W	L	T	Pts.	GF	GA
Guelph (15-20-3)	26	10	12	4	24	76	86
Toronto (13-21-3)	26	10	13	3	23	77	104
Queen's (16-22-2)	26	9	15	2	20	90	108
Royal Military (5-27-0)	26	3	23	0	6	45	134

MID WEST DIVISION

Team	G	W	L	T	Pts.	GF	GA
Brock (16-17-4)	26	13	10	3	29	113	104
Laurentian (11-18-3)	26	9	14	3	21	73	111
York (18-18-3)	26	9	14	3	21	101	92
Ryerson (11-21-1)	26	9	16	1	19	91	117

FAR WEST DIVISION

Team	G	W	L	T	Pts.	GF	GA
W. Ontario (31-7-4)	26	19	3	4	42	127	64
Windsor (12-17-6)	26	11	9	6	28	81	80
W. Laurier (16-19-5)	26	11	10	5	27	101	98
Waterloo (14-21-1)	26	9	16	1	19	81	101

PLAYOFF RESULTS

DIVISION SEMIFINALS
McGill 6, Concordia 4
McGill 4, Concordia 2

Toronto 5, Queen's 4
Queen's 4, Toronto 2
Queen's 6, Toronto 4

York 4, Laurentian 2
York 7, Laurentian 4

Wilfrid Laurier 5, Windsor 3
Wilfrid Laurier 3, Windsor 2

DIVISION FINALS
McGill 4, Trois-Rivieres 2
Trois-Rivieres 6, McGill 0
Trois-Rivieres 5, McGill 2

Queen's 4, Guelph 3
Queen's 3, Guelph 2 (OT)

Brock 5, York 2
York 4, Brock 2
York 8, Brock 7 (OT)

W. Ont. 1, W. Laurier 0
W. Ont. 3, W. Laurier 2 (OT)

LEAGUE SEMIFINALS
Trois-Rivieres 3, Queen's 1
Western Ontario 5, York 1

LEAGUE FINALS
Trois-Rivieres 3, W. Ontario 2

ALL-STAR TEAMS

EAST DIVISION

First team	Pos.	Second team
Luc Belanger, T.-R.	G	Marc-Andre Blondeau, Con.
Mike Van Volsen, Guelph	D	Sebastian Bety, T.-R.
David Bahl, McGill	D	Karl Castonguay, Concordia
Mathieu Darche, McGill	F	Rob Mailloux, Queen's
Philippe Tremblay, T.-R.	F	David Gourde, McGill
George Trifon, Toronto	F	Jean-Francois Brunelle, T.-R.

WEST DIVISION

First team	Pos.	Second team
Ryan Gelinas, Windsor	G	Jarrett Rose, Laurentian
Ryan McKie, W. Ontario	D	Matt Osborne, Brock
Rob Maric, Waterloo	D	Matt Monro, W. Ontario
Jeff Petrie, W. Ontario	F	Blair Sherrit, Laurentian
Jeff Ambrosio, W. Laurier	F	Damon Hardy, W. Ontario
Sasha Cucuz, York	F	Jamie Carr, Windsor

AWARD WINNERS

East Division Most Valuable Player: Mathieu Darche, McGill
West Division Most Valuable Player: Ryan Gelinas, Windsor
East Division rookie of the year: George Trifon, Toronto
West Division rookie of the year: Darren Mortier, W. Ontario
East Division most sportsmanlike player: David Burgess, McGill
West Division most sportsmanlike player: Rob Maric, Waterloo
East Division coach of the year: Martin Raymond, McGill
West Division coach of the year: Clarke Singer, W. Ontario
Leading scorer: Mathieu Darche, McGill

INDIVIDUAL LEADERS

Goals: Mathieu Darche, McGill (27)
Assists: Mathieu Darche, McGill (35)
Points: Mathieu Darche, McGill (62)
Goaltending average: Luc Belanger, Trois-Rivieres (1.78)

TOP SCORERS

	Games	G	A	Pts.
Mathieu Darche, McGill	26	27	35	62
Dave Gourde, McGill	21	21	26	47
Jean-Francois Brunelle, T.-Rivieres	26	19	28	47
Philippe Tremblay, Trois-Rivieres	26	17	27	44
Daniel Payette Trois-Rivieres	25	10	30	40
David Burgess, McGill	26	11	28	39
Jeff Petrie, Western Ontario	26	13	25	38
Sasha Cucuz, York	26	9	28	37
Rob Frost, Western Ontario	23	18	18	36
Darren Mortier, Western Ontario	24	13	22	35
David Bahl, McGill	26	10	25	35

COLLEGE HOCKEY *Canadian Colleges*

INDEX OF TEAMS